Central Europe

a Lonely Planet shoestring guide

Steve Fallon
Mark Honan
Clem Lindenmayer
David Stanley
Greg Videon

Central Europe

1st edition

Published by

Lonely Planet Publications

Head Office: PO Box 617, Hawthorn, Vic 3122, Australia
Branches: 155 Filbert St, Suite 251, Oakland, CA 94607, USA
10 Barley Mow Passage, Chiswick, London W4 4PH, UK
71 bis rue du Cardinal Lemoine, 75005 Paris, France

Printed by

SNP Printing Pte Ltd., Singapore

Photographs by

Krzysztof Dydyński (KD)
Mark Honan (MH)
Richard Nebeský (RN)
Tony Wheeler (TW)
Hungarian Tourist Board (HTB)
Vaudois Tourist Office (VTO)
Front cover: Gruyères, Fribourg, Switzerland from International Photographic Library (Edmond Noegele)

First Published

January 1995

Although the authors and publisher have tried to make the information as accurate as possible, they accept no responsibility for any loss, injury or inconvenience sustained by any person using this book.

National Library of Australia Cataloguing in Publication Data

Fallon, Steve
Central Europe on a shoestring

1st ed.
Includes index.
ISBN 0 86442 244 X.

1. Central Europe – Guidebooks. 2. Europe, Eastern – Guidebooks. I. Title. (Series: Lonely Planet on a shoestring).

914.045

Steve Fallon

Born in Boston, Steve Fallon says he can't remember a time when he was not obsessed with travel, other cultures and foreign languages. As a teenager he worked an assortment of jobs to finance trips to Europe and South America, and he graduated from Georgetown University in 1975 with a Bachelor of Science in modern languages. The following year he taught English at the University of Silesia near Katowice, Poland. After he had worked for several years for a Gannett newspaper and obtained a master's degree in journalism, his fascination with the 'new' Asia took him to Hong Kong, where he lived and worked for 13 years for a variety of publications and was editor of *Business Traveller* magazine. In 1987 he put journalism on hold when he opened Wanderlust Books, Asia's only travel bookshop. Steve lived in Budapest for two years until 1994, when he moved to London.

Mark Honan

After a university degree in Philosophy opened up a glittering career as an office clerk, Mark decided 'the meaning of life' lay elsewhere and set off on a two-year trip around the world. As a freelance travel writer, he then went campervanning around Europe to write a series of articles for a London magazine. When the magazine went bust, Mark joined a travel agent, from which he was rescued by Lonely Planet. Mark wrote *Switzerland – a travel survival kit* and is currently working on *Austria – a travel survival kit* and the *Vienna city guide*.

Clem Lindenmayer

Clem has variously worked as a dishwasher, telex operator, translator and assembler of exhibition stands. With a keen interest in languages and mountain sports, he remains a proud undergraduate despite years of scattered studies. Clem researched and authored Lonely Planet's *Trekking in the Patagonian Andes* and helped update *China – a travel survival kit*; his current pet project is a hiking guide to Switzerland.

David Stanley

A quarter century ago David's right thumb carried him out of Toronto, Canada, and on to a journey which has so far wound through 169 countries, including a three-year trip from Tokyo to Kabul. His travel guidebooks for the South Pacific, Micronesia and Eastern Europe opened those areas to budget travellers for the first time. During the late 1960s David got involved in Mexican culture by spending a year in several small towns near Guanajuato. Later he studied at the universities of Barcelona and Florence, before settling down to get an honours degree (with distinction) in Spanish literature from the University of Guelph, Canada. This landed him a job as a tour guide in Fidel Castro's Cuba and there he developed an interest in 'socialist tourism'. Since then he's visited all the Eastern Europe countries covered in this book many times. Having had the rare opportunity to spend long periods in Eastern Europe researching *Eastern Europe on a shoestring* in the years immediately before and after 1989, David is a keen observer of the changes presently taking place. From his base in Amsterdam he makes frequent trips to Eastern Europe (jammed between journeys to the 85 countries worldwide he still hasn't visited). In travel writing David has found a perfect outlet for his restless wanderlust. His zodiac sign is Virgo.

Greg Videon

Greg Videon practised journalism and studied Swedish and German before spending time in Sweden as a student and travelling in Europe. Unemployment, cricket and travelling for Lonely Planet fill in the time.

From the Authors

Steve Fallon Special thanks to Michael Rothschild for his support and assistance. Thanks also to Caddie Grenier in Budapest and, from London, Margaret Leung who helped with updates for which I am very grateful.

Mark Honan Thanks to the following for suggestions and support: Reinhart and Ewa in Austria; Jim, Sue, Imre, Berta, Beat and Ruth in Switzerland. SNTO in London and Zürich and ANTO in London were also very helpful.

Clem Lindenmayer Thanks to Fritz and Frieda Arm (Switzerland), Till Oswald (Mainz), Willy Schuster (Frankfurt/Main), 'Monty' (Dresden), Ester Wolf (Leipzig), Simon Upton (UK), Erich Latz (Stuttgart), and the helpful staff at every tourist office I visited in Germany.

David Stanley Special thanks to Sheldon Zelsman (C) for his thought-provoking observations about Auschwitz, to Kristin Lister (D) and Jürgen Grotz (D) for a 25-page letter detailing their 80-day odyssey around the region, to Shirley Hudson (USA), Martin Fedorski (UK) and Chris & Kay Nellins (UK) for their extensive cycling notes, to Michael van Verk (Nl) for six pages of precise information on Romania, to Mirjana Žilić (Cr) of the Croatian National Tourism Office for convincing me to go back to Dubrovnik, to Tomaž Lovrenčič (Slo) for carefully checking all the Slovene spellings in that chapter, to Iztok Altbauer (Slo), Adrian Grigorescu (Ro), Sandi Jejčič (Slo), Maria Krajnak/Legulky (Sk), Igor Nikolovski (USA), Lise Noemi (Cr), Andrej Oštrbenk (Slo) and Nives Posavec (Cr) for help in translating the vocabularies, to Jos Poelman of the Dutch STD Foundation, Box 9074, 3506 UK Utrecht (Nl), for information on AIDS, to Musiques du Monde, Singel 281, Amsterdam (Nl), for providing the dozens of CDs used to prepare the music sections and to Ria de Vos (Nl) for her criticism, suggestions and support.

While out doing my field research I keep my identity to myself and of the dozens of shoestring travellers I bumped into during my last six-month trip, the only one who connected me with Lonely Planet was Russell Gripper of Concord West, Australia. For the record, no 'freebies' from hotels, restaurants, tour operators, airlines etc were solicited or received during the field research involved in the preparation of this book.

The following government officials and tourism workers took the trouble to reply to written enquiries:

Fiona Anelay (UK), Lisa Arlt (USA), Gordon Bastin (UK), J H Beran (CZ), Mike Bugsgang (UK), Bonnie Jo Campbell (USA), N Dandolova (Bg), Walter Danner (C), Gilbert Dingle (Aus), Alexander Duma (UK), Jana Erzetič (Slo), Jon Harbour (D), Attila Hetey (UK), Svilen Iliev (Bg), George Janaček (CZ), Desanka Kocic (Yu), Nena Komarica (Cr), Rolf Kunze (D), Kathryn Kutrubes (USA), Silvija Letica (Cr), John Lewis (C), Valerie Nagy (H), Rüdiger Pier (D), László Pordány (H), Prof Stjepan Puljiz (Cr), Pavli Qesku (Al), Pavel Řehák (CZ), Alexandra Ruppeldtová (Sk), Miroslav Sekel (Sk), Jack Shulman (USA), Dan Sitaru (Ro), Jože Stare (Slo), Tomas Stockel (Sk), Robert Strauss (UK), András Szarvas (H), András Szilágyi (H), Vlado Tance (Slo), Hugo Verweij (Nl), Jaroslava Votavová (CZ), Manuela Vulpe (Ro), Bee Whilems (UK), Frank & Doreen Whitebrook (Aus), Ralph Wilczkowski (USA), Maria A Williamson (UK) and Callon Zukowski (CZ).

A – Austria, Al – Albania, Aus – Australia, B – Belgium, Bg – Bulgaria, C – Canada, Cr – Croatia, CZ – Czech Republic, D – Germany, Dk – Denmark, Fin – Finland, H – Hungary, I – Italy, Ire – Ireland, Isr – Israel, J – Japan, Nl – Netherlands, NZ – New Zealand, Pl – Poland, Ro – Romania, S – Sweden, SA – South Africa, Sk – Slovakia, Slo – Slovenia, Sp – Spain, UK – United Kingdom, USA – United States of America, Yu – Yugoslavia

Greg Videon Warm thank-yous to Thomas Diester of Olfen; David Holmes of Berlin; Sandy Moritz of the Australian Consulate-General, Berlin; Christine Bichlmaier of Hanover Tourist Information; Amrum Tourist Information; Clem, Romy and the Arm family for their kindness; Andreas Kadowski, Christoph Hesse, Roman Kalden and Marcel Leutemann of Plau, and most importantly, to Karen for love, support, assistance and sundry research, without which this work would not have appeared.

This Book

Central Europe on a shoestring is Lonely Planet's latest title in its *Europe on a shoestring* series which includes Eastern Europe, Western Europe, Mediterranean Europe and Scandinavian & Baltic Europe. Each guide is complemented by a phrasebook covering the languages of that region – more details can be found in the back of this book.

Material for this book has been adapted from the *Western Europe* and *Eastern Europe* shoestring guides. The Austria, Liechtenstein and Switzerland chapters were written and updated by Mark Honan, who also wrote this book's Getting Around chapter. Clem Lindenmayer and Greg Videon updated the Germany chapter while David Stanley wrote and updated the Czech Republic, Slovakia, Poland and Hungary chapters. The introductory chapters were updated by Steve Fallon.

From the Publisher

This first edition of *Central Europe* was edited at the Lonely Planet office in Australia by Miriam Cannell and Frith Pike, assisted by David Collins, Ian Folletta, Sally Green, Sue Harvey, Lyn McGaur, Katie Purvis, Debbie Rossdale and Steve Womersley. Miriam Cannell, David Collins, Adrienne Costanzo, Rob Flynn, Sue Harvey, Kristin Odijk, Frith Pike, Paul Smitz and Ian Ward proofed the text. Samantha Carew took the book through production.

The maps were drawn or updated by Marcel Gaston and Michelle Stamp, assisted by Jane Hart, Louise Keppie, Matt King, Chris Klep, Maliza Kruh, Adam McCrow, Jacqui Saunders, Andrew Tudor and Sally Woodward. Jane Hart designed the cover, and Matt King was responsible for the illustrations and layout.

Thanks to Rob van Driesum for his invaluable help and research with the introductory chapters and the Germany chapter; to Dan Levin for creating the accented fonts; to Chris Lee Ack for his work with the fonts for the cartography; to Richard Nebeský who helped proof the Czech Republic and Slovakia chapters; and to Sharon Wertheim for indexing.

Thanks also to the many readers who wrote in with their suggestions and comments on the last editions of *Western Europe on a shoestring* and *Eastern Europe on a shoestring*. We have had the benefit of using feedback from these travellers in producing this first edition. They are listed at the end of the book.

Warning & Request

Things change – prices go up, schedules change, good places go bad and bad places go bankrupt – nothing stays the same. So if you find things better or worse, recently opened or long since closed, please write and tell us and help make the next edition better.

Your letters will be used to help update future editions and, where possible, important changes will also be included in a Stop Press section in reprints.

We greatly appreciate all information that is sent to us by travellers. Back at Lonely Planet we employ a hard-working readers' letters team to sort through the many letters we receive. The best ones will be rewarded with a free copy of the next edition or another Lonely Planet guide if you prefer. We give away lots of books, but, unfortunately, not every letter/postcard receives one.

Contents

Map Legend

BOUNDARIES

- International Boundary
- Provincial Boundary
- Marine Park Boundary

ROUTES

- Motorway
- Highway
- Major Road
- Unsealed Road or Track
- City Road, City Street
- Railway
- Underground Railway
- Tram
- Walking Track
- Walking Tour
- Ferry Route
- Cable Car or Chairlift

AREA FEATURES

- Park, Gardens
- National Park
- Forest
- Built-Up Area
- Pedestrian Mall
- Market
- Christian Cemetery
- Non-Christian Cemetery
- Rocks

HYDROGRAPHIC FEATURES

- Coastline
- River, Creek
- Intermittent River or Creek
- Lake, Intermittent Lake
- Canal
- Swamp

SYMBOLS

- CAPITAL .... National Capital
- Capital .... Provincial Capital
- CITY .... Major City
- City .... City
- TOWN .... Town
- Village .... Village
- Place to Stay
- Place to Eat
- Pub, Bar
- Hostel, Cafe
- Post Office, Telephone
- Tourist Information, Bank
- Transport, Parking
- Caravan Park, Camping Ground
- Church, Cathedral
- Mosque, Synagogue
- Temple, Museum
- Hospital, Police Station
- Airport, Airfield
- Swimming Pool, Gardens
- Shopping Centre, Petrol Station
- N25 One Way Street, Route Number
- Winery or Vineyard, Picnic Site
- Archaeological Site, Zoo
- Stately Home, Monument
- Castle, Tomb
- Cave, Pass
- Mountain or Hill, Lookout
- Lighthouse, Ski Field
- Ancient or City Wall
- Rapids, Waterfalls
- Cliff or Escarpment, Tunnel
- Railway Station
- U M Underground or Metro Station

Note: not all symbols displayed above appear in this book

Introduction

Central Europe encompasses the nations of Austria, the Czech Republic, Germany, Hungary, Liechtenstein, Poland, Slovakia and Switzerland. Its boundaries reach from the Baltic Sea in the north, southward to the Dráva River and from the Rhine-Ruhr industrial area in the west to the vast plains of Belorussia and the Carpathian Mountains in the east and south-east. It is the very heart of the continent of Europe.

In 1989, Lonely Planet first published *Eastern Europe on a shoestring*, followed four years later by shoestring guides to *Western, Mediterranean* and *Scandinavian & Baltic Europe*. These titles reflected the way most of us have seen Europe all our lives, now *Central Europe on a shoestring* fills a gap that is partly geographical, political and historical.

During previous centuries Europe was viewed differently; until 1945 there was the predominantly industrialised West at one end of the spectrum and an undeveloped, almost medieval Balkan region at the other. In the middle sat a third region, comprising the *Mitteleuropa* of Prussian rule and the Habsburg dynasty's Austro-Hungarian Empire. Some parts of this area may have had more in common with the West and others with the Balkans, but all together they formed a single, unique region: Central Europe.

Since the 'changes of 1989' – the democratisation of Eastern Europe, the fall of the Berlin Wall, the dissolution of the Soviet Union – history has come full circle and a more forward-thinking Central Europe has emerged. The Czech Republic, Hungary, Poland and Slovakia once again stand alongside their erstwhile Central European neighbours of Austria, Germany, Liechtenstein and Switzerland – but this time with full independence and a lot more confidence.

Central Europe has been the source of much of what we know as Western culture, not just in music and literature (Mozart, Beethoven, Dvořák, Liszt, Chopin, Goethe, Kafka etc) but in so many other disciplines: just think of the works of Freud and Jung, Marx and Engels. The region's cities – Prague, Vienna, Berlin – have, at various times, been the centres of European culture, and their museums, theatres, concert halls and historical sites continue to beckon.

But Central Europe boasts more than cultural wealth and history. It is also a region of startling beauty, from the soaring Alps and the High Tatra Mountains to the rugged Baltic coastline and the mighty Danube, offering some of the best hiking, skiing and water sports in all of Europe. And there are places here where it's simply fun to be: try bopping in post-modern discos after dark in Berlin, crawling through the beer halls of Prague or watching the world go by from the terrace of a Budapest *cukrászda* (cake shop/café).

This book covers this diverse collection of countries, offering an insight into their history, people and culture as well as providing the practical information to help you make the most of your time and money. It takes you through Central Europe from predeparture preparations to packing your bag for the return home. There's information on how to get to Central Europe and how to get around once you're here. There are extensive details on what to see, when to see it and how much it all costs. The thousands of recommendations on places to stay range from Swiss camping sites, German hostels and Polish mountain refuges to Hungary's wonderful *fizetővendég szolgálat* ('paying guest' accommodation service) and cheap hotels in Prague. Cafés, restaurants and bars are covered in equally exhaustive detail, with suggestions from the cheapest of cheap eats to the ideal place for that long-awaited splurge. There are even recommendations on what to buy and where (and when) to buy it.

Central Europe is the very essence of the continent – there's lot's there waiting to be enjoyed. All you have to do is go.

Facts for the Visitor

There are those who say that Central Europe is so well developed you don't have to plan a thing before your trip since anything can be arranged on the spot. As any experienced traveller knows, the problems you thought about at home often turn out to be irrelevant or will sort themselves out once you start moving.

This theory is fine if you've decided to blow the massive inheritance sitting in your bank account, but if your financial status is more modest, some prior knowledge and a bit of careful planning can make your hard-earned travel budget stretch further than you thought it would. You'll also want to make sure that the things you plan to see and do will be possible at the particular time of year when you'll be travelling.

PLANNING

Maps

Good maps are easy to come by once you're in Europe, but you might want to buy a few beforehand. The maps in this book will help you get an idea of where you might want to go and will be a useful first reference when you arrive in a city. Proper road maps are essential if you're driving or cycling.

You can't go wrong with Michelin maps and, because of their soft covers, they fold up easily so you can stick them in your pocket. Some people prefer the meticulously produced Freytag & Berndt, Kümmerly & Frey or Hallwag maps. The British AA maps are also good – as a rule, maps published by European automobile associations are excellent, and they're sometimes free if membership of your local association gives you reciprocal rights. Tourist offices are another good source of maps.

When to Go

Any time can be the best time to visit Central Europe, depending on what you want to do. Summer lasts roughly from June to September, but it can begin earlier and stretch well into October; Hungary's indian summers, for example, are legendary. Unfortunately, you won't be the only tourist in Central Europe during summer – most Europeans take their holidays in August. Prices can be high, accommodation fully booked and the sights packed. You'll find much better deals and fewer people in the shoulder seasons either side of summer. In April and May, for instance, flowers are in bloom and the weather can be surprisingly mild. September and even October can be summer- like in parts of Central Europe.

On the other hand, if you're keen on winter sports, resorts in the Alps and the High Tatra Mountains generally begin operating in early December and move into full swing after the New Year, closing down

Countries & Populations

Country	*Area (sq km)*	*Country Population*	*Capital*	*Capital Population*
Austria	83,855	7,834,000	Vienna	1,500,000
Czech Republic	78,864	10,464,000	Prague	1,212,000
Germany	356,866	79,360,000	Berlin	3,400,000
Hungary	93,030	10,479,000	Budapest	2,018,035
Liechtenstein	160	28,074	Vaduz	4920
Poland	312,680	38,621,000	Warsaw	1,655,700
Slovakia	49,035	5,354,000	Bratislava	440,000
Switzerland	41,295	6,910,800	Bern	150,000

again when the snows begin to melt in March or April.

The Climate & When to Go sections in the individual country chapters explain what to expect and when, and the Climate Charts appendix in the back of the book will help you compare different destinations. As a rule, spring and autumn tend to be wetter and windier than summer and winter in Central Europe, and the extremes between summer and winter can be great.

The climate will have a bearing on the clothes you bring along. Don't pack too much – you can buy almost anything you need along the way. Insulation works on the principle of trapped air; several layers of thin clothing are warmer than just one thick layer (and will be easier to dry, too). You'll also be much more flexible if the weather suddenly turns warm. Be prepared for rain at any time of year but absolutely expect it in April and November.

How Long?

The amount of time you spend in Central Europe is entirely up to you, your interests and your bank account. The more time you spend in one place, the lower your daily expenses are likely to be as you get to know your way around. See the following Money section for an indication of expenses.

If you have a rail pass, you'll have to stay on the move to make the best use of it. Even so, you should be able to save money by timing your arrivals and departures so that you sleep on the train from time to time. See Move or Stay? in the following section.

What Kind of Trip?

Travelling Companions Travelling alone is not a problem in Central Europe. The region is well developed and overall very safe.

If you decide to travel with others, keep in mind that travel can put relationships to the test like few other experiences. You won't find out until you try, but make sure you agree on itineraries and routines beforehand and remain flexible about everything.

If travel is a good way of testing a friendship, it's also a great way of meeting new people. Hostels and camping grounds are good places to meet other travellers with whom to team up or simply share experiences. Even if travelling alone, you need never be lonely while on the road.

The Getting Around chapter has information on organised tours with groups. The young, the elderly and the inexperienced tend to appreciate such tours because they take the daily hassles and uncertainties out of travel. Longer tours, however, can become experiments in social cohesion and friction can develop.

Move or Stay? 'If this is Thursday, it must be Zürich.' Though often ridiculed, the mad dash that crams all eight countries into a month of travel does have its merits. If you've never visited Central Europe, you won't know which areas you'll like, and a quick 'scouting tour' can give an overview of your options. A rail pass that offers unlimited travel within all or most Central European countries in a set period of time is a good way to do this.

But if you know where you want to go, or you find a place you like, you might like to stay for a while. Discover some of the lesser known sights, make a few local friends and settle in.

With your own transport or by buying train and bus tickets as you go along, you can stay in a place long enough to get a bit of a feel for it and then move on.

Working Holiday Central European countries aren't keen to hand out jobs to foreigners. Officially, a citizen of the European Union (EU) is allowed to work in other EU countries, which at present in Central Europe include only Germany and Austria. The paperwork isn't always straightforward for longer term employment, however. Other country/nationality combinations require special work permits that can be almost impossible to arrange, especially for temporary work. That doesn't prevent enterprising travellers from topping up their funds occasionally, and they don't always have to do this illegally either.

Switzerland, for example, has a system of work permits allocated by employers. Your national student-exchange organisation may be able to arrange temporary work permits to several countries through special programmes. For more details on working as a foreigner, see Work in the Facts for the Visitor sections of the individual country chapters. Remember that some Central European countries (among them, Hungary) require an AIDS test as a condition for issuing a work permit.

If you have a parent or grandparent who was born in an EU country, you may have certain rights you never knew about. Get in touch with that country's embassy and ask about dual citizenship and work permits – if you are eligible for citizenship, also ask about any obligations, such as military service, taxation and having to relinquish your first passport. Not all countries allow dual citizenship, so a work permit may be all you can get. Ireland is particularly easy-going about granting citizenship to people with Irish ancestry, and with an Irish passport, the EU is your oyster.

If you do find a temporary job, the pay is likely to be less than that offered to local people. The only exceptions appear to be jobs teaching English – a growth industry in parts of eastern Central Europe and the easiest way to make some extra cash.

Other typical tourist jobs like washing dishes or snow clearing at Alpine resorts often come with board and lodging. The salary is little more than pocket money, but you'll have a good time partying with other travellers.

Work Your Way Around the World by Susan Griffith (paperback) gives good, practical advice on a wide range of issues. The same publisher, Vacation Work, has many other useful titles, including *The Au Pair and Nanny's Guide to Working Abroad* by Susan Griffith & Sharon Legg (paperback).

If you play an instrument or have other artistic talents, you could try working the streets; it's fairly common in certain cities like Prague and Berlin. But beware: busking is illegal in Switzerland and Austria and only tolerated in Germany. Talk to other street artists before you start.

Selling goods on the street in some countries is generally frowned upon and can be tantamount to vagrancy apart from at flea markets. It's also a hard way to make money if you're not selling something special. Austria requires permits for this sort of thing and it's fairly common, though officially illegal, in Germany. You can try your luck at the markets in some towns of Hungary, Poland and the Czech Republic but you'll be competing with illegal immigrants from the east who know the game a lot better than you.

What to Bring

Bringing as little as possible is the best policy. It's very easy to find almost anything you need along the way, and since you'll probably buy things as you go, it's better to start with too little rather than too much.

A backpack is still the most popular method of carrying gear as it is convenient, especially for walking. On the debit side, a backpack doesn't offer too much protection for your valuables, the straps tend to get caught on things and some airlines may refuse to accept responsibility if the pack is damaged or broken into.

Travelpacks, a combination of backpack and shoulder bag, are very popular. The backpack straps zip away inside the pack when they are not needed so you almost have the best of both worlds. Some packs have sophisticated shoulder-strap adjustment systems and can be used comfortably even on long hikes. Packs are always much easier to carry than a bag. Another alternative is a large, soft zip-bag with a wide shoulder strap so it can be carried with relative ease if necessary. Backpacks or travelpacks can be made reasonably theft-proof with small padlocks. Forget suitcases unless you're travelling in style.

As for clothing, begin light and buy local clothes that take your fancy as you go along. See the following Appearances & Conduct section for a rundown on dress standards in Central Europe. A minimum packing list could include:

- underwear, socks and swimming gear
- a pair of jeans and maybe a pair of shorts
- a few T-shirts and shirts
- a warm sweater
- a solid pair of walking shoes
- sandals or thongs for showers
- a coat or jacket
- a raincoat, waterproof jacket or umbrella
- a medical kit and sewing kit
- a padlock
- a Swiss Army knife
- soap and towel
- toothpaste, toothbrush and other toiletries

A padlock is useful to lock your bag to a luggage rack in a bus or train; it may also be needed to secure your hostel locker. A Swiss Army knife comes in handy for all sorts of things. (*Any* pocket knife is fine but make sure it includes such essentials as a bottle opener and strong corkscrew!) Soap, toothpaste and toilet paper are readily obtainable almost anywhere, but you'll need your own supply of paper in many public toilets and those at camping grounds. In some countries, using toilets in public areas costs a nominal sum, so have coins handy. Tampons are available at pharmacies and supermarkets in all but the most remote places. Condoms, both locally made and imported, are widely available in Central Europe.

A tent and sleeping bag are vital if you want to save money by camping. Even if you're not camping, a sleeping bag is still very useful. Get one that can be used as a quilt. A sleeping sheet with pillow cover (case) is necessary if you plan to stay in hostels – you'll have to hire or purchase one if you don't bring your own. In any case, a sheet that fits into your sleeping bag is easier to wash than the bag itself. Make one yourself out of old sheets (include a built-in pillow cover), or buy one from your hostel association.

Other optional items include a compass, a torch (flashlight), an alarm clock, an adapter plug for electrical appliances (such as a cup or coil water heater to save on expensive tea and coffee), a universal bath/sink plug (a film canister sometimes works, too), sunglasses, a few clothes pegs and pre-moistened towelettes or a large cotton handkerchief that you can soak in fountains and use to cool off while touring cities in the hot summer months. During city sightseeing, a small daypack is better than a shoulder bag at deterring snatch thieves (see Theft & Rip-offs in the later Dangers & Annoyances section).

Finally, consider using plastic carry bags or garbage bags inside your backpack to keep things separate but also dry if the pack gets soaked. Airlines do lose luggage from time to time, but you have a much better chance of it not being yours if it is tagged with your name and address *inside* the bag as well as outside; outside tags can always fall off or be removed.

Appearances & Conduct

Central Europeans are tolerant of eccentric fashions and behaviour especially in big cities like Berlin. But although dress standards are fairly informal in Austria, Switzerland and Germany, your clothes may well have some bearing on how you're treated in Poland, Slovakia and Hungary.

By all means dress casually, but keep your clothes clean, and ensure sufficient body cover (trousers or knee-length dress) if your sightseeing includes churches, synagogues or mosques. Apart from the lederhosen (leather shorts with H-shaped braces/suspenders) seen at cultural events and beer festivals, wearing shorts away from the beach or camping ground is not very common among men in Central Europe. Some nightclubs and fancy restaurants may refuse entry to people wearing jeans or a tracksuit; if you are male, consider packing a tie as well, just in case. For more information on dress codes, see the Women Travellers section.

Most border guards and immigration officials are too professional to judge people entirely by their appearance, but first impressions do count, and you'll find life easier if you're well presented when dealing with officialdom.

While nude bathing is usually limited to certain beaches, topless sunbathing is very common throughout Central Europe – even in city parks. Nevertheless, women should be wary of taking their tops off as a matter of course. The rule is, if nobody else seems to be doing it, don't.

You'll soon notice that Central Europeans are very heavily into shaking hands when they greet one another. At least get into the habit of doing so with virtually everyone you meet. It's an important ritual. In Central Europe the male tradition of kissing a woman's hand has gone the way of the dodo, though it can still be seen in Poland. *Csókolom* – 'I kiss it' (your hand) – is a common male-to-female greeting in Hungarian though the actual kissing doesn't usually take place.

It's also customary to greet the proprietor when entering a small shop, café or quiet bar, and to say goodbye when you leave. This is particularly true in Germany, Austria and Hungary.

The Top 10

There is so much to see in Central Europe that compiling a list of top 10 highlights is almost impossible. But we asked the authors of this book to list their personal favourites and here they are:

1. Prague
2. The Alps
3. Budapest
4. Czech beer
5. Berlin
6. The High Tatra Mountains, Poland/Slovakia
7. Zamość, Poland
8. Rynek Główny, Kraków
9. Munich
10. Vienna's Naschmarkt (outdoor market)

The Bottom 10

The writers were also asked to list the 10 worst 'attractions' of the region. The results:

1. Frankfurt Airport
2. The *Sound of Music* tour in Salzburg
3. Siófok on Balaton Lake, Hungary
4. Wine taverns in Vienna's Grinzing suburb
5. McDonald's Restaurant, Warsaw
6. U Fleků Beer Hall, Prague
7. The Romantic Road in Bavaria
8. Prague's Charles Bridge in summer
9. The Munich Oktoberfest (beer festival)
10. Nowa Huta industrial complex near Kraków

PASSPORT & VISAS

Passport

Your most important travel document is a passport, which should remain valid until well after your trip. If it's just about to expire, renew it before you go – having this done by your embassy in Vienna or Warsaw can be inconvenient. Some countries insist that your passport remain valid for a specified minimum period (usually three months but sometimes up to six months) after your visit. Even if they don't insist on this, expect questions from immigration officials if your passport is due to expire in a short time.

If you don't have a passport, you'll have to apply for one, which can be an involved process. A renewal or application can take anything from a few days to several months, depending on many factors, so don't leave it till the last minute (it can sometimes be speeded up with a good excuse, though this may attract a higher fee). Bureaucracy usually grinds faster if you do everything in person at the actual passport issuing office rather than relying on the mail or agents. Check first what you need to bring: photos of a certain size, birth certificate, population register extract, signed statements, exact payment in cash etc.

Australian citizens can apply at a post office or the passport office in their state capital; Britons can get application forms from major post offices, and the passport is issued by the regional passport office; Canadians can apply at regional passport offices; New Zealanders can apply at any district office of the Department of Internal Affairs; US citizens must apply in person (but may usually renew by mail) at a US Passport Agency office or some courthouses and post offices.

Once you start travelling, carry your pass-

A: Czech Republic (RN)
B: Czech Republic (RN)
C: Czech Republic (RN)
D: Czech Republic (RN)
E: Germany (TW)
F: Germany (TW)
G: Hungary (HTB)
H: Hungary (HTB)

Central Europe
0
300
600 km
Approximate North Only
BRITAIN
Glasgow
Edinburgh
Newcastle-upon-Tyne
Liverpool
Leeds
Manchester
Sheffield
Birmingham
Thames
Cambridge
London
NORTH
SEA
English Channel
DENMARK
Göteb
Viborg
Vejle
Copenha
Kolding
Odense
Schleswig
Kiel
Rostock
Lübeck
Hamburg
Wismar
Groningen
Bremen
Oldenberg
Elbe River
Amsterdam
Enschede
The Hague
Osnabrück
River
Hanover
NETHERLANDS
Rotterdam
Brandenburg
Dortmund
Magdeburg
Essen
Weser
Bruges
Antwerp
Göttingen
BELGIUM
Düsseldorf
Halle
Kassel
Lille
Cologne
Brussels
Leipzig
Rhine
Erfurt
Marburg
Weimar
Bonn
Le Havre
Amiens
Rouen
GERMANY
Wiesbaden
Seine
Frankfurt
Main
River
LUXEMBOURG
Reims
Luxembourg
Paris
Bamburg
Saarbrücken
Nuremburg
Le Mans
River
Nancy
Karlsruhe
Stuttgart
Regensbur
Angers
Orléans
Troyes
Strasbourg
Baden-Baden
Danube
Tours
Ulm
Augsburg
Freiburg
Bourges
Dachau
Belfort
Lake Constance
Munich
Dijon
LIECHTEN-
STEIN
Salzbu
Basel
Zürich
Constance
Zugspitze
(2966 m)
FRANCE
Kufstein
Jura Mountains
Lucerne
Innsbruck
Arlberg
Grossglock
(3797 m)
Bern
Mt Titlis
(3239 m)
Vaduz
THE ALPS
Limoges
Lausanne
Lienz
Lake Geneva
SWITZERLAND
Chur
Geneva
Lyon
Matterhorn
(4478 m)
Mt Rosa
(4554 m)
Bolzano
Mont Blanc
(4807 m)
St Étienne
Trento
Como
Bergamo
THE ALPS
Milan
Verona
Venice
Padova
Rhône River
Turin
Alessandria
ITALY
Orange
Toulouse
Genoa
Bologna
Montpellier
Arles
La Spezia
Nice
MONACO
SAN
MARINO
Marseille
Pisa
Florence
ANDORRA
SPAIN

RUSSIA
Gamleby
SWEDEN
Varberg
Alvesta
Halmstad
Nybro
Karlskrona
Malmö
Simrishamn
BALTIC SEA
Riga
LATVIA
LITHUANIA
Kaunas
RUSSIA
Vilnius
Smarhon'
Minsk
Kaliningrad
Lebork
Łeba
Gdynia
Gdańsk
Malbork
Elbląg
Olsztyn
Suwałki
Augustów
Koszalin
Stralsund
Szczecinek
Oder
Szczecin
Piła
Toruń
Białystok
Ostrołęka
Biłowieża
BELORUSSIA
Slutsk
Vistula River
Berlin
River
Bereza
Pripyat River
Brest
Poznań
Kutno
Warsaw
Siedlce
Potsdam
Zielona Góra
Leszno
Łowicz
POLAND
Łódź
Kovel'
Radom
Puławy
Lublin
Meissen
Dresden
Zgorzelec
Wrocław
Częstochowa
Kielce
Zamość
Brzeg
Opole
Rivne
Semily
Trutnov
Nysa
Katowice
Ústí Nad Labem
Hradec Králové
Prague
Kutná Hora
Oświęcim
Kraków
Tarnów
Rzeszów
L'vov
UKRAINE
Przemyśl
Svitavy
Ostrava
Sanok
Plzeň
CZECH REPUBLIC
Rabka
Dnestr River
Zakopane
Bardejov
Brno
Žilina
Telč
Levoča
Prešov
Chortkiv
České Budějovice
Humenne
Ružomberok
Trenčín
Passau
Banská Bystrica
Košice
Rožnava
SLOVAKIA
Trebišov
CARPATHIAN MOUNTAINS
Rakhiv
Dorohoi
Krems
Linz
Melk
Vienna
Trnava
Lučenec
Levice
St Pölten
Bratislava
Miskolc
Tisza River
Nagykálló
Bad Ischl
AUSTRIA
Komárno
Eisenstadt
Sopron
Győr
Esztergom
Stainach
Kőszeg
Budapest
Debrecen
Leoben
HUNGARY
Oradea
Graz
Vésztő
Tihany
Balaton Lake
Danube
Gyula
Gheorghieni
Klagenfurt
Paks
Kecskemét
Turda
Lenti
Dombóvár
Szeged
Arad
ROMANIA
Ljubljana
Nagyatád
Decs
Sibiu
Pécs
SLOVENIA
Barcs
Subotica
Trieste
Zagreb
Rijeka
Sisak
CROATIA
Piteşti
Novi Sad
Belgrade
BOSNIA-HERCEGOVINA
Orşova
Bucharest
Tuzla
ADRIATIC SEA
Zadar
YUGOSLAVIA
Sarajevo
Danube
Livno
BULGARIA

A	B	C
D		E
F	G	

A: Poland (KD)
B: Slovakia (RN)
C: Slovakia (RN)
D: Poland (KD)
E: Poland (KD)
F: Switzerland (MH)
G: Switzerland (VTO)

port at all times and guard it carefully. Some countries require residents and aliens alike to carry personal identification. Camping grounds and hotels sometimes insist that you hand over your passport for the duration of your stay, which is very inconvenient since you won't be able to cash travellers' cheques or arrange visas. They tend to be a lot more flexible about this if you pay in advance. A driving licence or Camping Carnet can also solve the problem (see the Documents section).

See Theft & Rip-offs in the later Dangers & Annoyances section for information on photocopying your passport and other important documents.

Europeans Citizens of many European countries don't always need a valid passport to travel within the region. A national identity card may be sufficient (it is for Germans entering Hungary, for example) and usually demands less paperwork and processing time. An expired passport may be all right, too. An EU citizen travelling to another EU country will generally face the least problems. If you want to exercise any of these options, check with your travel agent or the embassies of the countries you plan to visit.

Visas

A visa is a stamp in your passport permitting you to enter the country in question and stay for a specified period of time. The word is Latin for 'seen' and means that a consular official of that country has taken a look at your passport and decided that it's OK for you to visit. In 99.9% of cases, the procedure is a mere formality but one that you must go through if your passport requires a visa for the country in question. Often you can get the visa at the border or at the airport upon arrival but not always and especially not if you're travelling by train or bus and likely to hold up a carload of people. Check first with the embassies or consulates of the countries you plan to visit.

There's a wide variety of visas, including tourist, transit and business ones. Transit visas are usually cheaper than tourist or business visas, but they only allow a very short stay (one or two days) and can be difficult to extend.

British and US readers of this book will have very little to do with visas. With a valid passport they'll be able to visit most Central European countries for up to three (sometimes even six) months, provided they have some sort of onward or return ticket and/or 'sufficient means of support' (money). Except at international airports, it's unlikely that immigration officials will give you and your passport more than a cursory glance if you look OK (see the earlier Appearances & Conduct section).

Border checks are likely to become even more relaxed now that the EU has abolished passport controls within its borders. Border procedures between EU and non-EU countries and nations with less than sterling relations (Hungary and Slovakia, for example) remain a bit more thorough.

There are a few important exceptions to these easy visa rules. Holders of diplomatic or official passports face different requirements from ordinary passport holders, and they should check with the embassies of the countries they wish to visit. South Africans have had little joy in the past travelling on their 'Green Mamba', though this is changing very rapidly now. Citizens of Hong Kong may need visas to several countries depending on the endorsements in their BNO (British National Overseas) passports. Australians and New Zealanders still need visas to visit most of the countries of the former Soviet bloc, including the Central European countries of Poland, the Czech Republic, Slovakia and Hungary.

Although Central European countries are tolerant of the nationalities they allow in, it pays to beware of 'unpopular' passport markings if you do any further travelling. Visa stamps from Cuba or Vietnam could cause delays at some borders while reference lists are consulted (Germany can be very thorough in this sort of thing). 'Unpopular' countries will often provide a loose-leaf visa if you ask for one.

Visa requirements can change, and you

should always check with the individual embassies or a reputable travel agent before setting out. It's generally easier to get your visas as you go along, rather than arranging them all beforehand. Carry plenty of spare passport photos (you may need up to four every time you apply for a visa). The chart below lists visa requirements for some nationalities.

DOCUMENTS

Apart from your passport, there are a number of documents worth considering.

International Health Certificate

You'll need this yellow booklet only if you're coming into the region from areas where diseases like yellow fever are prevalent, such as Africa and South America. See Immunisation in the Health section for more details.

International Driving Permit

If you hold a non-European driving licence and plan to drive in Central Europe, you should obtain an IDP from your local automobile association before you leave – you'll need a passport photo and a valid licence. They are usually inexpensive and are good for one year only. An IDP helps Europeans make sense of your unfamiliar local licence (make sure you take that with you) and can make life much simpler, especially when hiring cars and motorbikes. Even those with European and US driving licenses, which are usually accepted in Central Europe, should consider getting an IDP.

While you're at it, ask your automobile association for a Letter of Introduction. This reciprocal membership card entitles you to services offered by associated organisations in Europe, usually free of charge (touring maps and information, help with breakdowns, technical and legal advice etc). See the Getting Around chapter for more details.

Camping Carnet

Your local automobile association can also issue a Camping Carnet, which is basically a camping ground ID card. Carnets are also issued by your local camping federation and sometimes on the spot at camping grounds. They incorporate third party insurance for damage you may cause, and many camping grounds offer a small discount if you sign in with one. Some hostels and hotels also accept carnets for signing-in purposes but won't give discounts.

Hostelling Card

A hostelling card is useful – if not always mandatory – for those staying at hostels. Some hostels in Central Europe don't require that you be a hostelling association member, but they often charge less if you have a card. Many hostels will issue one on the spot or

Visa Requirements

	Country of Origin							
	Aust	*Can*	*HK*	*Ire*	*NZ*	*Sing*	*UK*	*USA*
Austria	–	–	–	–	–	–	–	–
Czech Republic	✓	✓	✓	–	✓	✓	–	✢
Germany	–	–	❋	–	–	–	–	–
Hungary	✓	–	✓	–	✓	✓	–	–
Poland	✓	✓	❋	–	✓	✦	–	–
Slovakia	✓	✓	✓	–	✓	✓	–	✢
Switzerland/Liech	–	–	–	–	–	–	–	–

✓ Tourist visa required
❋ Depends on endorsements in passport. Check with embassy.
✦ Maximum stay without visa: 14 days
✢ Maximum stay without visa: one month

after a few stays, though this costs a bit more than getting it in your home country. See Hostels in the later Accommodation section.

Student & Youth Cards

The most useful of these is the International Student Identity Card (ISIC), a plastic ID-style card with your photograph. It can perform all sorts of wonders, particularly attracting discounts on many forms of transport (including airlines and local public transport). Even if you have your own transport, the card will soon pay for itself through cheap or free admission to museums and sights, and cheap meals in some student restaurants.

There is a worldwide industry in fake student cards, and many places now stipulate a maximum age for student discounts or, more simply, they've substituted a 'youth discount' for a student one. If you're aged under 26 but not a student, you can apply for a Federation of International Youth Travel Organisations (FIYTO) card or Euro26 card, which give much the same discounts as an ISIC. Your hostelling organisation should be able to help with this.

These types of card are issued by student unions, hostelling organisations or some 'alternative' travel agencies. They do not automatically entitle you to discounts, but you won't find out until you flash the card.

MONEY

Bring as much of this stuff as you can. You will generally find that US dollars and Deutschmarks are the most easily exchanged currencies in Central Europe, followed by pounds sterling and Swiss and French francs. You lose out through commissions and customer exchange rates every time you change money, so if you plan to visit only Austria, for example, you may be better off buying Schillings straight away if your bank at home can provide them. Also, this will eliminate having to pay exchange commissions, which are sky-high (sometimes up to 10%) in Austria.

Of the seven Central European currencies (Liechtenstein uses the Swiss franc) in circulation, only Deutschmarks, Swiss francs and Austrian Schillings are fully convertible and even the Austrian unit can be difficult to unload outside Austria. The export of Polish złoty, Hungarian forint, and Czech and Slovakian crowns is either illegal or stupid: almost nobody outside Poland, Hungary, the Czech Republic or Slovakia will touch them. Remember, too, that the Czech Republic and Slovakia no longer share a single currency; crowns from one may not be accepted in the other.

Banks are closed on public holidays, which are listed in the individual country chapters. If you get caught out, remember that most airports, central train stations, some fancy hotels and many border posts have banking facilities outside normal office hours, sometimes on a 24-hour basis. Post offices in Central Europe often perform banking tasks, tend to be open longer hours and outnumber banks in remote places. In Poland, some of the ubiquitous *kantor* (private exchange offices) can change your money round the clock.

If you visit several countries, the constant currency conversions can drive you up the wall. Buy a cheap pocket calculator, cut out the list of exchange rates from a newspaper before you leave, and stick it to the back of the calculator for easy reference. The best exchange rates are usually offered at banks. *Bureaux de change* usually (but not always) offer worse rates or charge higher commissions. Hotels are almost always the worst places to change money. American Express and Thomas Cook offices usually do not charge commission for changing their own cheques but may offer a less favourable exchange rate than banks. The queues at these places are often intolerably long.

How Much Money?

The answer is simple: take as much as possible. Travelling in the eastern half of Central Europe – Poland, Hungary, the Czech Republic and Slovakia – can be good value but is no longer as cheap as it was before

1989. In Switzerland and Austria, on the other hand, you could easily throw hundreds of dollars down the drain daily. But the region also attracts its fair share of people whose surname isn't Rockefeller or Rothschild, and they manage to travel quite easily without spending a fortune.

The secret is cheap accommodation. Most of Central Europe has a highly developed network of camping grounds (some of them quite luxurious) and they're great places to meet people. The hostel network, too, is well developed in most of the eight countries, but the clientele during the school holidays might make those aged over 30 feel ancient.

Other money-saving strategies include using a student card, which offers worthwhile discounts (see the previous Documents section); using various rail and public transport passes (see the Getting Around chapter); applying for consumer tax rebates on large purchases (see Money in the introductions to the individual countries); and, generally, following the advice in this book on food and accommodation. Preparing your own meals and avoiding alcohol are other good ways of saving money.

Your budget depends on how you live and travel. If you're moving around fast, going to lots of places and spending time in the big cities, then your day-to-day living costs are going to be quite high. If you stay in one place and get to know your way around, costs are likely to come down.

Including transport but not private motorised transport, your daily expenses could work out to around US$25 to US$30 a day in Poland, Hungary, the Czech Republic and Slovakia. This means camping or staying in hostels or private rooms, eating economically and travelling 2nd class by train or bus.

Travelling on a moderate budget – which is the minimum Switzerland, Austria, Liechtenstein and, to a lesser degree, Germany will demand – you should be able to manage on US$50 to US$75 a day. This would allow you to stay at cheap hotels, guesthouses or bed & breakfasts (B&Bs). You could afford meals in economical restaurants and even a few beers. And if you really want to exercise that gold card, you can begin to live well in this part of Central Europe for US$100 a day.

Price Levels

A general warning about all those prices that we list throughout this book: they're likely to change, usually moving upward, but if last season was particularly slow they may remain the same or even come down. Nevertheless, relative price levels should stay fairly constant – if hotel A costs twice as much as hotel B, it's likely to stay that way.

Tipping

In Central Europe tipping is less prevalent than in North America, but much more so than in Australia, New Zealand and parts of Asia. In many countries (Austria and Germany, for instance), it's common for a service charge to be added to restaurant bills, in which case no tipping is necessary. In other countries you simply round up to the next even figure. But there are exceptions. Hungary on the whole is a very tip-conscious place, and you should add on another 10% if you are satisfied with the service, the food, the 'experience' or whatever. See the individual country chapters for more details.

Cash

Nothing beats cash for convenience or risk. If you lose it, it's gone forever, and very few travel insurers will come to your rescue beyond a maximum payout of a few hundred dollars.

But it's still a good idea to bring some local currency in cash, if only to tide you over until you get to an exchange facility. The equivalent of, say, US$50 should be more than enough. Some extra cash in an easily exchanged currency is a good idea, too. Often, it is much easier to change just a few dollars (when leaving a country, for example) in cash rather than cheques – and more economical.

Remember that banks will always accept paper money but very rarely coins. Before you leave one country for the next, spend your last coins on a cup of coffee, fuel if travelling by car or drop them into a church collection box.

Travellers' Cheques

American Express, Visa and Thomas Cook travellers' cheques are the three brands most widely accepted. But Thomas Cook is not all that fast with refunds for lost cheques, and Visa is usually represented by some inefficient state bank. The main point of carrying cheques rather than cash is the protection they offer from theft, but it doesn't do a lot of good if you have to go back home first to get the refund. Ask about representatives in the Central European countries covered here and their telephone hotline numbers when you buy your cheques. To report stolen cheques, ring American Express reverse charges in the UK (☎ 01-273 571 600). For Thomas Cook, ☎ 01-733 502 995 or visit a Hertz Rent-a-Car office.

Keeping a record of the cheque numbers and the initial purchase details is vital when it comes to replacing lost cheques. Without this, you may well find that 'instant' is a very long time indeed. You should also keep a record of which cheques you have cashed. Keep these details separate from the uncashed cheques. If you're going to remote places, it's worth sticking to American Express since small local banks may not always accept other brands. American Express has offices in most major cities in Central Europe.

Travellers' cheques are available in various currencies. Unless you live in the USA, however, there's little point buying US dollar cheques for Central Europe since you'll lose on the exchange rate to dollars when you buy the cheques and again to the local currency each time you cash one in. Choose the currency you're likely to need most – Deutschmarks, say, if you're going to spend a lot of time and money in Germany.

The trick is to ensure that you only convert currencies once, not twice. On the other hand, using a currency you're not familiar with and watching it converted into still another (for example an Australian cashing Deutschmarks into Czech crowns) is confusing and dangerous; you'll never be able to figure out how much you paid for anything!

When you change cheques, don't look at just the exchange rate; ask about fees and commissions as well. Some places charge a per-cheque service fee, so changing US$100 in five US$20 cheques will be more expensive than a single US$100 cheque. Other places charge a flat transaction fee or a percentage of the total amount irrespective of the number of cheques, and you might want to take advantage of this by changing a few small cheques at once. Some banks charge fees to cash some brands of travellers' cheques but not others. In most countries these days, the exchange rate for travellers' cheques is slightly better than the exchange rate for cash, but it's often better to settle for a worse exchange rate if it's balanced by lower fees or commissions.

Take most of the cheques in large denominations, say US$100s or £100s. It's only towards the end of a stay that you may want to change US$20 or US$10 cheques to make sure you don't get left with too much local currency.

International Transfers

If you run out of money or need more, you can instruct your bank back home to send you a draft. Make sure you specify the city, the bank and the branch to which you want your money directed, or ask your home bank to tell you where a suitable one is, and ensure you get the details correct.

The whole procedure will be easier if you've authorised someone back home to access your account. Also, a transfer to a tiny bank in a remote village in the Tirol is obviously going to be more difficult than to the head office in Vienna. If you have the choice, find a large bank and ask for the international division.

Money sent by telegraphic transfer (there will be costs involved, typically US$30 or more, but ask) should reach you within a week; by mail, allow at least two weeks. When it arrives, it will most likely be converted into local currency – you can take it in cash or buy travellers' cheques.

You can transfer money much, much faster by American Express or Thomas Cook. Americans can also use Western Union although it has fewer offices in Central Europe from which to collect. If you have an American Express card, you can cash up to US$1000 worth of personal cheques at American Express offices in any 21-day period.

Credit Cards & ATMs

A credit card can be an ideal travelling companion. If you're not familiar with credit cards, ask your bank to explain the workings and relative merits of credit, credit/debit, debit and charge cards. Make sure you know what to do in case of theft (telephone hotline numbers).

With a credit card you can put big expenses like airline tickets on your account and save carrying so much cash and so many travellers' cheques around with you. Another major advantage is that they allow you to withdraw cash at selected banks or to draw money from automated telling machines (ATMs).

Found throughout Switzerland, Germany, Austria and parts of the Czech Republic but less so in Poland, Hungary and Slovakia, ATMs are often linked up internationally and you can put your credit card in, punch in a personal identification number (PIN) and get instant cash. But ATMs aren't fail-safe, especially if the card was issued outside Europe; it's safer to go to a human teller. If an ATM swallows your card abroad it can be a major headache. You should also ask which ATMs abroad will accept your particular card. Note that many ATMs in Europe won't accept PIN numbers of more than four digits.

Cash cards, which you use at home to withdraw money directly from your bank account, are slowly becoming more widely linked internationally – ask your bank at home for advice. The Cirrus network is fairly widespread in Europe, though it doesn't always work and in some countries (such as Germany) you may have to search a while to find an ATM that's hooked up to it. Withdrawals may incur a small transaction fee.

If you use a credit card to get money from an ATM, you pay interest on the money from the moment you get it. You can get around that by leaving the card in credit when you depart or by having somebody at home pay money into the card account from time to time. On the plus side, you don't pay commission charges or transaction fees, and the exchange rate is at a better interbank rate than that offered for travellers' cheques or cash exchanges. Bear in mind that if you use a credit card for purchases, exchange rates may have changed by the time your bill is processed, which can work out to your advantage or disadvantage.

Charge cards like American Express and Diners Club have offices in most countries, and they can generally replace a lost card within 24 hours. That's because they treat you as a customer of the company rather than of the bank that issued the card. In theory, the credit they offer is unlimited and they don't charge interest on outstanding accounts, but they do charge fees for joining and annual membership, and payment is due in full within a few weeks of the account statement date. Their major drawback is that they're not widely accepted off the beaten track of mainstream travel. Charge cards can also be hooked up to ATM networks on request.

Credit and credit/debit cards like Visa and MasterCard are more widely accepted because they tend to charge merchants lower commissions. Their major drawback is that they have a credit limit based on your regular income, and this limit is often too low to cover major expenses like long-term car rental or long-distance airline tickets. You can get around this by leaving your card in credit when you leave home. Other drawbacks are that interest is charged on outstanding accounts, either immediately or after a set period (always immediately on cash advances) and that the card can be very difficult to replace if lost abroad.

If you choose to rely on plastic, go for two different cards – a Visa or MasterCard, for instance, with an American Express or

Diners Club backup. Better still is a combination of credit card and travellers' cheques so you have something to fall back on if an ATM swallows your card or the banks in the area won't accept it (a not uncommon and always inexplicable occurrence).

It has not been long since Europe in general embraced credit cards in a major way, and quite a few shops, restaurants and service stations may still accept cash only. This is very true in the eastern half of Central Europe. Visa and MasterCard are the most popular brands all-round. MasterCard (also known as Access in the UK) is linked to Europe's extensive Eurocard system, which makes it widely accepted and thus a convenient card to carry.

A final word of warning: fraudulent shopkeepers have been known to quickly make several charge-slip imprints with customers' credit cards when they're not looking; they then simply copy the signature from the authorised slip. Try not to let your card out of your sight, and always check your statements carefully.

Guaranteed Cheques

Guaranteed personal cheques are another way of carrying money or obtaining cash in Central Europe.

The most popular of these is the Eurocheque system. To get Eurocheques, you need a European bank account; depending on the bank, it takes at least two weeks to apply for them, which may be too long for most visitors.

It's a neat system, though. In many countries of Central Europe, when paying for something in a shop or withdrawing cash from a bank or post office, you write out a Eurocheque (up to its maximum limit, otherwise simply write out two or more cheques) and show the accompanying guarantee card with your signature and registration number. You may also have to show your passport. Once the shopkeeper or bank clerk has checked the signature with that on the card and copied your registration number onto the cheque, it's guaranteed by the issuing bank, which will deduct the amount from your account when the paperwork comes through. The card can double as an ATM card and obviously should be kept separate from the cheques for safety.

COMMUNICATIONS & MEDIA

Post

Details of the main post offices are given in the city Information sections. From major cities in Central Europe, airmail typically takes about a week to North America, and a week to 10 days to Australasian destinations. Postage costs do vary from country to country and so does post office efficiency – the Polish post office, while improving from the 'dark ages' of just five years ago, is still not very reliable.

You can collect mail from post office poste-restante sections. Ask people writing to you to write the number '1' after the city name to ensure that the letter goes to the main post office in that city (though poste restante mail will almost always be sent there automatically). You should also have them print your name clearly and underline your surname. When collecting mail, your passport may be required for identification and you may have to pay a small fee. If an expected letter is not waiting for you, ask to check under your given name: letters do get misfiled. Post offices usually hold mail for about a month, but sometimes less (in Germany, for instance, they only hold mail for a fortnight), so plan your mail drops carefully.

You can also have mail (but not parcels) sent to you at American Express offices so long as you have an American Express card or travellers' cheques. When you buy American Express cheques, ask for a booklet listing all its offices worldwide.

Telephone

The quality of the telephone service in Central Europe depends on the country. It's excellent in Germany, Austria, Switzerland and Liechtenstein; good in Hungary; fair in the Czech Republic and Slovakia; poor in Poland. In Germany, Austria, Switzerland, Liechtenstein and Hungary you can ring abroad from phone booths if you have a phonecard or sufficient coins; generally in the other countries you must ring from a booth inside a post office or telephone centre and settle your bill at the counter. If you ring from a hotel room, the bill can be astronomical. Reverse-charge (collect) calls are often possible, but not always – for a start, you'll have to be able to communicate with the local operator, who might not always speak English. From some Central European countries, however, you can dial direct to your home operator ('Home Direct'), which solves that problem. See the Telephones appendix in the back of this book for more details.

To place an international call you must dial the international access code (which varies from country to country but is usually '00' in Central Europe), the country code, the area or city code (usually without the initial zero) and the number. Area and city codes are provided under the Information sections in the individual chapters. The country codes for Central Europe are: Austria 43, Czech Republic 42, Germany 49, Hungary 36, Liechtenstein 41, Poland 48, Slovakia 42, Switzerland 41.

Newspapers & Magazines

If you want to keep up with the news in English, the *International Herald Tribune*, of a much higher journalistic standard than most British or Australian newspapers, is sold in larger Central European cities on the day of publication, as is the colourful but superficial *USA Today*. The *Guardian*, *Financial Times* and other UK papers are often available but usually a day late. The weekly newspaper *The European* can be found everywhere as can the news magazines *Time*, *Newsweek* and *The Economist*. For a local slant to international coverage and to learn lots more about the country you're in, pick up one of the generally excellent English-language weeklies that have sprouted up in the eastern half of Central Europe like mushrooms after rain. These include the *Warsaw Voice* in Poland; the Czech Republic's *Prague Post* and *Prognosis* (the latter also devotes a page to Slovakia); and in Hungary, *Budapest Week* and *Budapest Sun*.

Radio & TV

In Central Europe, the BBC World Service can be found on medium wave at 648 kHz, on short wave at 6195, 9410, 12095 and 15575 kHz, and on long wave at 198 kHz, the appropriate frequency depending on where you are and the time of day. The Voice of America (VOA) can usually be found on short wave at 15205 kHz. There are also numerous English-language broadcasts (and even BBC World Service and VOA re-broadcasts) on local AM and FM radio stations. Among some of the better local English-language radio stations are Austria's Blue Danube (103.8 mHz FM); the US-style 91.9 mHz FM station in Prague; and Hungary's Radio Bridge (102.1 mHz FM).

Cable and satellite TV have also spread across Central Europe. Sky TV can be found in hotels throughout the region, as can CNN and other networks. Even a small *panzió* (pension) in rural Hungary is likely to be equipped with a satellite dish nowadays.

TIME

All eight countries covered in this book are on Central European Time: that is, GMT/UTC plus one hour. When daylight-saving time is in force from the last Sunday in March to the last Sunday in September, Central European Time is GMT/UTC plus two hours.

ELECTRICITY

By all means bring along the electrical appliances that you feel you can't live without. If they're battery operated, so much the better, but hotel rooms almost always have power points, and these are also pretty widespread in hostels and camping grounds. Voltage and plug design will be your main problems.

Voltage & Cycle

All the countries of Central Europe run on 220 V, 50 Hz AC. Check the voltage and cycle (usually 50 Hz) used in your home country. Most appliances that are set up for 220 V will handle 240 V quite happily without modifications (and vice versa); the same goes for 110 V and 125 V combinations. It's always preferable to adjust your appliance to the exact voltage if you can (some modern battery chargers and radios will do this automatically). Just don't mix 110/125 V with 220/240 V without a transformer, which will be built in if the appliance can be adjusted.

Several countries outside Europe (the USA and Canada, for instance) have 60 Hz AC, which will affect the speed of electric motors even after the voltage has been adjusted so CD and tape players (where motor speed is all-important) will be useless. But things like electric razors, hair dryers, irons and radios will work fine.

Plugs & Sockets

Plugs in Central Europe are the standard round two-pin variety, sometimes called the 'europlug'. Many plugs and some sockets don't have provision for earth, since most local home appliances are double insulated. When provided, earth usually consists of two contact points along the edge, although Switzerland, for example, uses a third round pin in such a way that the standard two-pin plug still fits the sockets.

If your plugs are of a different design, you'll need an adapter. They're available in all their many permutations throughout Central Europe.

Video Systems

If you want to record or buy video tapes to play back home, you won't get a picture if the image registration systems are different. Central Europe generally uses PAL, which is incompatible with the North American and Japanese NTSC system. The one exception is Poland, which has traditionally had the SECAM system used in France. In any case, most of the equipment on the market in Central Europe is multi-system.

HEALTH

Central Europe is a healthy place overall. Your main risks are likely to be sunburn (especially in the mountains), foot blisters, insect bites and upset stomachs from overindulging in food and drink. You might experience some gut problems in Poland where rolled and stuffed foods are common; just avoid things like stuffed cabbage and meat *pierogi* (dumplings) in warm weather.

A healthy trip depends on your predeparture preparations and fitness, your day-to-day health care while travelling, and how you handle any medical problem or emergency that does develop. If you're reasonably fit, the only things you should organise before departure are a visit to your dentist to get your teeth in order and travel insurance with good medical cover (see the following section).

Predeparture Preparations

Health Insurance A travel insurance policy to cover theft, loss and medical problems is a must. There is a wide variety of policies and your travel agent will have recommendations. The international student travel policies handled by STA Travel or other student travel organisations are usually good value. Some policies offer lower and higher medical-expense options – go as high as you can afford, especially if you're doing lots of travel in Germany and Switzerland, where medical costs can be astronomical. Check the small print.

- Some policies specifically exclude 'dangerous activities' which can include scuba diving, motorcycling, skiing, mountaineering, and even trekking. If such activities are on your agenda, you don't want that sort of policy.
- You may prefer a policy that pays doctors or hospitals directly rather than you having to pay on the spot and claim later. If you have to do the latter, make sure you keep all documentation, including the company's forms dutifully filled in by the doctor or other medical staff. Some policies ask you to call back (reverse charges) to a centre in your home country where an immediate assessment of your problem is made.
- Check if the policy covers ambulances or helicopter rescue (not uncommon in Austria among

inexperienced or ill-prepared hikers) and an emergency flight home. If you have to stretch out you will need two seats and somebody has to pay for them!

EU citizens are covered for emergency medical treatment throughout the EU on presentation of an E111 form. Enquire about this at your national health service or travel agent well in advance; post offices in some countries also have these forms. Similar reciprocal arrangements exist between individual countries, but these can change without notice and are not always well known outside major centres. Travel insurance is still advisable because of the flexibility it offers in where and how you're treated, as well as covering expenses for ambulance and repatriation.

Medical Kit A small, straightforward medical kit is a wise thing to carry. A possible kit list includes:

- Aspirin or Panadol – for pain or fever
- Antihistamine (such as Benadryl) – useful as a decongestant for colds, allergies, to ease the itch from insect bites or stings or to help prevent motion sickness
- Kaolin preparation (Pepto-Bismol), Imodium or Lomotil – for possible stomach upsets
- Antiseptic, such as Betadine, and antibiotic powder or similar 'dry' spray – for cuts and grazes
- Calamine lotion – to ease irritation from bites or stings
- Bandages and Band-aids – for minor injuries
- Scissors, tweezers and a thermometer (note that mercury thermometers are prohibited on airlines)
- Insect repellent, sunscreen, suntan lotion, chapstick, perhaps water purification tablets

When buying medicines over the counter, especially in Poland, the Czech Republic, Slovakia and Hungary, make sure that correct storage conditions have been followed and that the expiry date has not passed.

Health Preparations If you wear glasses, take a spare pair and your prescription.

If you require a particular medication, take an adequate supply, as it may not always be available in remote places. The same applies for women's specific oral contraceptives. Take the prescription or, better still, part of the packaging showing the generic rather than the brand name (which may not be locally available).

It's a wise idea to have a legible prescription to show that you legally use the medication – it's surprising how often over-the-counter drugs from one place are illegal without a prescription or even banned in another place. Keep the medication in its original container. If you're carrying a syringe for some reason, have a note from your doctor explaining why you're doing so.

A Medic Alert tag is a good idea if your medical condition is not always easily recognisable (heart trouble, diabetes, asthma, allergic reactions to antibiotics etc).

Immunisations No jabs are necessary for Central Europe, but they may be an entry requirement if you're coming from an infected area (yellow fever is the most likely requirement). If you're travelling to Central Europe with stopovers in Asia, Africa or South America, check with your travel agent or with the embassies of the countries you plan to visit.

There are, however, a few routine vaccinations that are recommended whether you're travelling or not, and this Health section assumes that you've had them: polio (usually administered during childhood), tetanus and diphtheria (usually administered together in childhood, with a booster shot every 10 years) and sometimes measles. See your physician or nearest health agency about these.

All vaccinations should be recorded on an International Health Certificate, which is available from your physician or government health department. Don't leave this till the last minute since the vaccinations may have to be spread out over a period of time.

Basic Rules

Care in what you eat and drink is the most important health rule in the more remote parts of eastern Central Europe; stomach upsets are the most likely travel health problem here, but the majority of these upsets will be relatively minor.

Water Tap water is generally safe to drink in Central Europe. Many Czechs prefer to drink reasonably priced bottled water, and water from the tap doesn't always look so good in Hungary.

Always beware of natural water. The water in the burbling Alpine stream may look crystal clear and very inviting, but before drinking it you want to be absolutely sure there are no people or cattle upstream.

Water Purification This section is only relevant if you are planning extended hikes where you have to rely on natural water.

The simplest way of purifying water is to boil it thoroughly. Technically this means boiling for 10 minutes, something which happens very rarely. Remember that at high altitudes water boils at a lower temperature, so germs are less likely to be killed.

Simple filtering will not remove all dangerous organisms, so if you cannot boil water it should be treated chemically. Chlorine tablets (Puritabs, Steritabs or other brand names) will kill many but not all pathogens. Iodine is very effective in purifying water and is available in tablet form (such as Potable Aqua), but follow the directions carefully and remember that too much iodine can be harmful.

If you can't find tablets, tincture of iodine (2%) can be used. Four drops of tincture of iodine per litre or quart of clear water is the recommended dosage; the treated water should be left to stand for 30 minutes before drinking. Iodine crystals can also be used to purify water but this is a more complicated process, as you have to prepare a saturated iodine solution first. Iodine loses its effectiveness if exposed to air or damp so keep it in a tightly sealed container. Flavoured powder will disguise the taste of treated water and is a good idea if you are travelling with children.

Food Salads and fruit should be safe throughout Central Europe. Ice cream is usually OK, but beware if it has melted and been refrozen. Take great care with fish or shellfish (for instance, cooked mussels that haven't opened properly can be dangerous), and avoid undercooked meat.

If a place looks clean and well run and if the vendor also looks clean and healthy, then the food is probably safe. In general, places that are packed with travellers or local people will be fine. Be careful with food that has been cooked and left to go cold as is often the case in old-style self-service restaurants in Poland, the Czech Republic, Slovakia and Hungary.

Mushroom picking is a favourite pastime – some would say a religion – in parts of Central Europe as autumn approaches, but make sure you don't eat any mushrooms that haven't been positively identified as safe. Some countries like Hungary have free inspection booths at markets and in country parks.

Nutrition If you don't vary your diet, if you're travelling hard and fast and therefore missing meals, or if you simply lose your appetite, you can soon start to lose weight and place your health at risk, just as you could at home.

If you rely on fast foods, you'll get plenty of fats and carbohydrates but little else. Remember that overcooked food loses much of its nutritional value. If your diet isn't well balanced, it's a good idea to take vitamin and iron pills (women lose a lot of iron through menstruation). Fruit and vegetables are good sources of vitamins.

In hot weather (and Central Europe can get very warm indeed in summer) make sure you drink enough fluids – don't rely on feeling thirsty to indicate when you should drink. Not needing to urinate or very dark-yellow urine is a danger sign. Carry a water bottle at all times. Excessive sweating can lead to loss of salt and therefore muscle cramping. Salt tablets are not a good idea as a preventative, but in places where salt is not used much, adding salt to food can help.

Everyday Health A normal body temperature is 37°C or 98.6°F; more than 2°C above that is a 'high' fever. A normal adult pulse rate is 60 to 80 beats per minute (children 80 to 100, babies 100 to 140). You should know how to take a temperature and a pulse rate. As a general rule, the pulse increases about 20 beats per minute for each 1°C rise in fever.

Respiration rate is also an indicator of illness. Count the number of breaths per minute: between 12 and 20 is normal for adults and older children (up to 30 for younger children, 40 for babies). People with a high fever or serious respiratory illness (like pneumonia) breathe more quickly than normal. More than 40 shallow breaths a minute can indicate pneumonia.

Many health problems can be avoided by taking care of yourself. Avoid climatic extremes – keep out of the sun when it's hot, dress warmly when it's cold. Minimise insect bites by covering bare skin when insects are around or by using insect repellents or coils.

Medical Problems & Treatment

Local pharmacies or neighbourhood medical centres are good places to visit if you have a small medical problem and can explain what it is. In Hungary, for example, most pharmacies actually offer a sort of consultation service for a nominal fee (less than US$1). Hospital casualty wards will help if it's more serious, and they will tell you if it's not. Major hospitals and emergency numbers are mentioned in the text. Tourist offices and hotels can put you on to a doctor or dentist, and your embassy or consulate will probably know one who speaks your language.

Sunburn You can get sunburnt surprisingly quickly, even through cloud, anywhere on water, ice, snow or sand. Use a sunscreen and take extra care to cover areas that don't normally see sun – eg your feet. A hat provides added protection, and it may be a good idea to use zinc cream or some other barrier cream for your nose and lips. Calamine lotion is good for mild sunburn.

Remember that too much sunlight can damage your eyes, whether it's direct or reflected (glare). If your plans include being near water, ice, snow or sand, then good sunglasses are doubly important. Make sure they're treated to absorb ultraviolet radiation – if not, they'll actually do more harm than good by dilating your pupils and making it easier for ultraviolet light to damage the retina.

Cold Too much cold is dangerous, particularly if it leads to hypothermia. Cold combined with wind and moisture (ie soaking rain) is particularly risky. If you are trekking at high altitudes or in a cool, wet environment, be prepared.

Hypothermia occurs when the body loses heat faster than it can produce it and the core temperature of the body falls. It is surprisingly easy to progress from very cold to dangerously cold due to a combination of wind, altitude, wet clothing, fatigue and hunger, even if the air temperature is above freezing. It is best to dress in layers – silk, wool and some of the new artificial fibres are all good insulating materials. A hat is important, as a lot of heat is lost through the head. A strong, waterproof outer layer is essential; keeping dry is vital. Carry basic supplies, including food that contains simple sugars to generate heat quickly, and lots of fluids.

Symptoms of hypothermia are exhaustion, numb skin (particularly toes and fingers), shivering, slurred speech, irrational or violent behaviour, lethargy, stumbling, dizzy spells, muscle cramps and violent bursts of energy. Irrationality may take the form of sufferers claiming they are warm and trying to take off their clothes.

To treat hypothermia, first get the person out of the wind and/or rain, remove their clothing if it's wet and replace it with dry, warm clothing. Give them hot liquids – not alcohol – and some high-kilojoule (high-calorie), easily digestible food. This should be enough for the early stages of hypothermia, but if it has gone further, it may be necessary to place victims in warm sleeping bags and get in with them. Do not rub patients, place them near a fire or remove their wet clothes in the wind. If possible, place a sufferer in a warm – not hot – bath.

Altitude Sickness Acute Mountain Sickness, or AMS, occurs at high altitude and can be fatal. There is no hard and fast rule as to how high is too high: AMS can strike at altitudes of 3000 metres, although 3500 to 4500 metres is the usual range. Very few treks or ski runs in the Alps and High Tatras reach heights of 3000 metres or more, so it's unlikely to be a major concern.

Headaches, nausea, dizziness, a dry cough, insomnia, breathlessness and loss of appetite are all signs to heed. Mild altitude problems will generally abate after a day or so, but if the symptoms persist or become worse the only treatment is to descend – even 500 metres can help.

Motion Sickness Eating lightly before and during a trip will reduce the chances of motion sickness. If you are prone to motion sickness, try to find a place that minimises disturbance – near the wing on aircraft, close to midships on boats, near the centre on buses. Fresh air and a steady reference point like the horizon usually help; reading or cigarette smoke can exacerbate the problem. Commercial antimotion-sickness preparations, which can cause drowsiness, have to be taken before the trip commences – when you're feeling sick, it's too late. Ginger is a natural preventative and is available in capsule form.

Diarrhoea A change of water, food or climate can all lead to the runs; diarrhoea caused by contaminated food or water is more serious. Despite all your precautions, you may still have a bout of mild travellers' diarrhoea if you travel beyond the relatively safe confines of Central Europe, but a few rushed toilet trips with no other symptoms is not indicative of a serious problem.

Moderate diarrhoea, involving a half-dozen loose movements in a day, is more of a nuisance. Dehydration is the big danger with any diarrhoea, particularly for children, so fluid replenishment is the number one treatment. Weak black tea with a little sugar, soda water or soft drinks allowed to go flat and diluted 50% with water are all good.

With any diarrhoea more severe than this, go straight to the casualty ward of the nearest hospital and have yourself checked. You may need a rehydrating solution to replace minerals and salts. Stick to a bland diet as you recover.

Viral Gastroenteritis This is caused not by bacteria but, as the name suggests, by a virus. It is characterised by stomach cramps, diarrhoea and sometimes by vomiting and/or a slight fever. All you can do is rest and drink lots of fluids.

Rabies Rabies, caused by a bite or scratch by an infected mammal, is found in certain areas of Central Europe, and the risk has increased since the physical and political barriers were removed between the East and West in 1989. Dogs are a noted carrier, but cats, foxes and bats can also be infected. Any bite, scratch or even lick from a warm-blooded, furry animal should be cleaned immediately and thoroughly. Scrub with soap and running water, and then clean with an alcohol solution. If there is any possibility that the animal is infected, particularly if it froths at the mouth and behaves strangely, medical help should be sought immediately. Even if it is not rabid, all bites should be treated seriously as they can become infected or can result in tetanus.

Tuberculosis (TB) Although this disease is widespread in many developing countries and was a scourge in Central Europe decades ago, it is not a serious risk to healthy travellers. Young children are more susceptible than adults, and vaccination is a sensible precaution for children aged under 12 travelling in endemic areas. TB is commonly spread by coughing or by unpasteurised dairy products from infected cows. Milk that has been boiled is safe to drink; the souring of milk to make yoghurt or cheese also kills the bacilli.

Sexually Transmitted Diseases (STDs) Sexual contact with an infected partner spreads these diseases. Abstinence is the only 100% preventative, but using condoms is also effective. Gonorrhoea and syphilis are the most common of these diseases: sores, blisters or rashes around the genitals, discharges or pain when urinating are common symptoms. Symptoms may be less marked or not observed at all in women. Syphilis symptoms eventually disappear completely, but the disease continues and can cause severe problems in later years. Antibiotics are used to treat gonorrhoea and syphilis. STD clinics are widespread in Central Europe. Don't be shy about visiting them if you think you may have contracted something.

There are numerous other STDs; effective treatment is available for most of them, though as yet there is no cure for herpes or HIV/AIDS. The latter has become a considerable problem in parts of Central Europe, particularly in Poland. HIV, the Human Immunodeficiency Virus, may develop into AIDS (Acquired Immune Deficiency Syndrome). Apart from abstinence, the most effective preventative is always to practise safe sex using condoms. It is impossible to detect the HIV-positive status of an otherwise healthy-looking person without a blood test.

HIV can also be spread through infected blood transfusions or by dirty needles – vaccinations, acupuncture, tattooing and ear or nose-piercing can potentially be as dangerous as intravenous drug use if the equipment is not clean.

HIV *cannot* be transmitted by shaking hands, kissing, cuddling, fondling, sneezing, cooking food together or sharing eating or drinking utensils. Toilet seats, swimming pools and mosquito bites cannot spread AIDS. Ostracising an AIDS victim is not only immoral – it is absurd.

Cuts & Scratches Skin punctures can easily become infected in warm weather and may be difficult to heal. Treat any cut with an antiseptic solution such as Betadine. Where possible, avoid adhesive bandages, which can keep wounds wet.

Bites & Stings Bee and wasp stings are usually painful rather than dangerous. Calamine lotion will give relief and ice packs will reduce the pain and swelling. There are very few spiders with dangerous bites in Central Europe, and antivenins are usually available. One health-threatening pest indigenous to western Hungary and eastern Austria is the forest tick *(kullancs* in Hungarian; *Zeck* in German), which burrows under the skin causing inflammation and even encephalitis. If you plan to do a lot of hiking and camping in these areas, you might consider getting a meningo-encephalitis vaccination.

Mosquitoes Mosquitoes can almost drive you insane during the late spring and summer months in Central Europe. They also cause sleepless nights in wet areas like Balaton Lake in Hungary and the Great Mazurian Lakes in Poland without a mosquito net.

Fortunately, mosquito-borne diseases like malaria are unknown in this part of the world. Most people get used to mosquito bites after a few days as their bodies adjust, and the itching and swelling will become less severe. An antihistamine cream may help alleviate the symptoms.

Snakes Snakes tend to keep a very low profile, but to minimise your chances of being bitten, try to wear boots, socks and long trousers when walking through undergrowth and rocky areas where snakes may be present. Tramp heavily and they'll usually slither away before you come near.

Snake bites do not cause instantaneous death and antivenins are usually available. Keep the victim calm and still, wrap the bitten limb tightly, as you would for a sprained ankle, and attach a splint to immobilise it. Then seek medical help, taking along (if possible) the dead snake for identification. Don't attempt to catch the snake if there is even a remote possibility of being bitten again. The use of tourniquets and sucking out the poison have been totally discredited.

Lice All lice cause itching and discomfort. They make themselves at home in your hair (head lice), your clothing (body lice) or in your pubic hair (crabs). You catch lice through direct contact with infected people or by sharing combs, clothing and the like. Powder or shampoo treatment will kill the lice, and infected clothing should then be washed in very hot water to remove eggs.

Women's Health

Some women experience irregular periods when travelling, due to the upset in routine. Don't forget to take time zones into account if you're on the pill. If you run into intestinal problems, the pill may not be absorbed. Ask your physician about these matters. Poor diet, lowered resistance due to the use of antibiotics for stomach upsets and even contraceptive pills, can lead to vaginal infections when travelling in hot climates. Maintaining good personal hygiene and wearing skirts or loose-fitting trousers and cotton underwear will help to prevent infections.

Yeast infections (thrush), characterised by a rash, itch and discharge, can be treated with a vinegar or even lemon-juice douche or with yoghurt. Nystatin suppositories are the usual medical prescription for thrush. Trichomonas is a more serious infection; symptoms are a discharge and a burning sensation when urinating. If a vinegar-water douche is not effective, medical attention should be sought. Metronidazole (Flagyl) is the prescribed drug. With these infections, male sexual partners must also be treated.

DANGERS & ANNOYANCES

Central Europe is as safe – or unsafe – as any other part of the developed world. If you can handle yourself in the big cities of Western Europe, North America or Australasia, you'll have little trouble dealing with the less pleasant sides of Central Europe. But there are specific things to watch out for.

Whatever you do, don't leave friends and relatives back home worrying about how to get in touch with you in case of emergency. Work out a list of places where they can contact you. See the previous Post section for where to collect mail. Best of all is to phone home now and then – see the Telephones appendix for how and where to make phone calls most efficiently and economically.

Theft & Rip-Offs

Theft is definitely a problem in Central Europe – the threat comes both from local thieves and your fellow travellers. The most important things to guard are your passport, other documents, tickets and money – in that order. It's always best to carry these next to your skin or in a sturdy leather pouch on your belt. Train station lockers or luggage storage counters are useful places to store your luggage (but not valuables) while you get your bearings in a new town. Be very suspicious about people who offer to help you operate your locker. Carry your own padlock for hostel lockers.

You can lessen the risks further by being careful of snatch thieves. Cameras or shoulder bags are great for these people, who sometimes operate from motorbikes or scooters and expertly slash the strap before you have a chance to react. A small daypack is better, but watch your rear. Pickpockets are most active in dense crowds, especially in busy train stations and on buses and metros during peak hours. A common ploy in the Budapest and Prague metros is for a group of well-dressed young people to surround you, chattering away while one of the group zips through your pockets or purse (some of these types would make great magicians!).

Be careful even in hotels; don't leave valuables lying around in your room. Also be wary of sudden friendships. Parked cars are prime targets for petty criminals in most cities, and cars with foreign number plates and/or rental agency stickers in particular. Remove the stickers (or cover them with local football club stickers or something similar), leave a local newspaper on the seat and generally try to make it look like a local car – provided the car does not have rental plates giving the entire game away! Never,

ever leave anything you'd mind losing in a parked vehicle. Regardless of how heavy it is, remove all luggage overnight, even (some would say especially) if it's in a parking garage. In some places, freeway service centres have become unsafe territory: in the time it takes to drink a cup of coffee, your car can be broken into and its contents cleared out. Signs on most Central European highways will warn you of this.

In case of theft or loss, always report the incident to the police and ask for a statement, or your travel insurance won't pay out.

There are many other ways of losing things apart from straightforward theft and robbery. Over the years, Lonely Planet has received letters from unfortunate travellers who have been the victims of just about every scam imaginable. Two favourites have been airline-ticket rackets and 'bargain' antiques. Gambling rackets (such as the one where an operator shuffles matchboxes, one of them containing the token, amidst a cheering crowd of helpers), 'losing' travellers' cheques, guaranteeing loans – they're all scams on which unfortunate or foolish travellers have lost their shirts. Keep your wits about you.

About the most common scam in Central Europe involves changing money on the black market. Not every traveller is going to believe this but it just doesn't make sense changing money on the street nowadays. The saving is only a couple of per cent, it's illegal and you are almost sure to be ripped off – especially by anyone offering more than 10% above the current bank rate. Such moneychangers usually work in pairs. One will approach you and then, in the middle of the transaction, a greasy sidekick will distract you and off goes the first person with your money. You're left with nothing, a fraction of what you should have got or a handful of worthless Yugoslav dinars.

Taking taxis in some parts of Central Europe (especially Prague and Budapest) can be a most unpleasant experience, and you should use them only when absolutely necessary. Scams include claiming a 'broken' meter, rigging the meter so it ticks faster than two teenagers' hearts in the back seat of a car, or unfairly charging for extras (night rate, weekend rate, 'excess' luggage). If you think you're being ripped off, don't argue too forcefully with the driver in Prague or Budapest; he may get violent. The only realistic thing you can do is pay the fare, take down the tag number and report the matter to the police.

Photocopies The hassles created by losing your passport can be considerably reduced if you have a record of its number and issue date somewhere else or, even better, photocopies of the relevant data pages. A photocopy of your birth certificate can also be useful.

Also add the serial numbers of your travellers' cheques (cross them off as you cash them) and photocopies of your credit cards, airline ticket and other travel documents. Keep all this emergency material totally separate from your passport, cheques and other cash, and leave extra copies with someone you can rely on back home. Add some emergency money, say US$50 in cash, to this separate stash as well. If you do lose your passport, notify the police immediately to get a statement, and contact your nearest consulate.

Drugs

Always treat drugs with a great deal of caution. There is a fair bit of dope available in the region, sometimes quite openly, but that doesn't mean it's legal. In recent years, the civil war in what was Yugoslavia has forced drug traders to seek alternative routes from Asia to Western Europe, sometimes crossing through Hungary, Slovakia, the Czech Republic and Poland. These countries, desperately seeking integration into the 'new' Europe, do not look lightly upon drug abuse. Even a little hashish can cause a great deal of trouble in certain parts of the region.

Violence

Though it's unlikely that travellers will encounter violence in Central Europe, skinheads and neo-Nazis have singled out resident Blacks and Asians as scapegoats for their own problems; foreigners have been attacked in both Germany and Hungary. Avoid especially rundown areas of east Berlin and Pest and never fight back. These people can be extremely dangerous.

ACTIVITIES

Central Europe offers countless opportunities to indulge in activities other than sightseeing. The varied geography and excellent climate support the full range of outdoor pursuits: windsurfing, skiing, fishing, trekking, cycling, mountaineering. If your interests are more cerebral, you can enlist in courses on anything from language to alternative medicine. For more local information, see the individual country chapters.

Windsurfing

Of the many water sports on offer in Central Europe, windsurfing could well be the most popular after swimming and fishing – especially in Germany. Wetsuits enable the keener windsurfers to continue their sport throughout the colder months. It's easy to rent sailboards in many tourist centres, and courses are usually on offer for beginners.

Skiing

During winter, many Central Europeans flock to hundreds of resorts in the Alps and High Tatra Mountains for downhill skiing, though cross-country has also become very popular.

Skiing can be expensive due to the costs of ski lifts, accommodation and the inevitable après-ski drinking sessions. Equipment hire (or even purchase), on the other hand, can be relatively cheap. The hassle of transporting your own skis may not be worth it. A skiing holiday in Switzerland, Austria or Germany will work out twice as expensive as a summer holiday of the same length. Cross-country skiing costs less than downhill because you don't rely as much on ski lifts.

The skiing season generally lasts from early December to late March, though at higher altitudes it may extend an extra month either way. Snow conditions can vary greatly from one year to another and from region to region, but January and February tend to be the best (and busiest) months.

Ski resorts in the Swiss Alps offer great skiing and facilities but are also the most expensive. Expect high prices, too, in the German Alps, though Germany has cheaper (but far less spectacular) options in the Black Forest and Harz Mountains. Austria is generally slightly cheaper than Switzerland, especially in Carinthia.

By far the cheapest skiing in Central Europe is to be found in the High Tatras of Poland and Slovakia, but the facilities can't compare with those on offer elsewhere in the region. And don't expect empty slopes or trails; Poles, Czechs and Slovaks are avid skiers.

Hiking

Keen hikers can spend a lifetime exploring Central Europe's many exciting trails. Probably the most spectacular ones are to be found in the Alps, which are littered with well-marked trails (some complete with duration indicators), and food and accommodation are available along the way. The equally sensational High Tatras are less developed, which can add to the experience as you often rely on remote mountain villages for rest and sustenance. Hiking areas that are less well known include the Bieszczady in Poland, Germany's Harz Mountains and the Zemplén hills in Hungary.

The European Rambling Association promotes long-distance walking, can help with maps and information and is keen on environmental issues. Contact the Europäische Wandervereinigung eV (☎ 0681-39 00 70), Reichsstrasse 4, 66111 Saarbrücken, Germany. The British-based agency Ramblers Holidays (☎ 01707-33 1133) offers hiking-oriented trips in Central Europe and elsewhere. A good guide for hiking in the Alps is *Walking in the Alps* by Brian Spencer (paperback).

Every country in Central Europe has national parks and other interesting areas that may qualify as a trekker's paradise, depending on your preferences. Guided treks are often available for those who aren't sure about their physical abilities or who simply don't know what to look for. Read the Hiking information in the individual country chapters in this book and take your pick. Also see Walking in the Getting Around chapter.

Cycling

Along with hiking, cycling is the best way to really get close to the scenery and the people, keeping yourself fit in the process. It's also a good way to get around many cities and towns and a way to see remote corners of a country you wouldn't ordinarily get to.

The hills and mountains of Central Europe can make for heavy going, but this is offset by the dense concentration of things to see. Physical fitness is *not* a major prerequisite for cycling on the plains of eastern Hungary – they're flatter than pancakes!

Popular holiday-cycling areas in Central Europe include the upper reaches of the Danube in southern Germany, anywhere in the Alps (for those fit enough), the Danube Bend in Hungary and most of eastern Slovakia.

If you come from outside Central Europe, you can often bring your own bicycle along on the plane for a surprisingly reasonable fee. Alternatively, this book lists many places where you can hire one (make sure it has plenty of gears if you plan anything serious).

See under Bicycle in the Getting Around chapter for more information on bicycle touring, and the individual country chapters and city/town sections for rental agencies and tips on places to go.

Boating

The Baltic Sea and Central Europe's many lakes and rivers offer a variety of boating options unmatched anywhere else on the Continent. You can row on a peaceful Alpine lake, join a luxurious Rhine River cruise, go sailing on the Baltic coast, canoe on the Danube in Hungary, kayak the lakes and rivers of Poland's Mazuria region – the possibilities are endless. The country chapters have more details.

Horse Riding

Though horse riding is available throughout Central Europe, the sport is best organised – and cheapest – in Hungary, whose people, they say, 'were created by God to sit on horseback'. The best centres are on the Great Plain though you'll also find schools in Transdanubia and the Northern Uplands. Horse riding is also popular in Poland.

Thermal Baths

Central Europeans have been 'taking the waters' for both medicinal and recreational purposes since Roman times and the possibilities to soak are endless. Hungary has the largest number of facilities open to the public at very reasonable prices (there are almost a dozen in Budapest alone), but spas can also be found at Bad Ischl in Austria, at Baden-Baden in Germany and, in the Czech Republic, at Mariánské Lázně and Karlovy Vary.

Courses

Apart from learning new physical skills by doing something like a skiing course in Austria or horse riding in Hungary, you can enrich your mind in a variety of structured ways. Language courses are often available to foreigners through universities or private institutions and are justifiably popular since the best place to learn a language is in the country where it's spoken. But you can also take courses in art, literature, architecture, drama, music, cooking, alternative energy, photography, organic farming – you name it, and chances are that there will be a course somewhere that suits you.

The individual country chapters in this book give pointers on where to start looking. In general, the best sources of information are the cultural institutes maintained by many Central European countries around the world. Failing that, try their embassies. Student exchange organisations, student travel agencies, and organisations like the YMCA/YWCA and Hostelling International (HI) can also put you on the right track. Ask about special holiday packages that include a course.

WOMEN TRAVELLERS

Women often travel alone or in pairs around Central Europe. As a rule this is usually quite safe, but women do tend to attract more unwanted attention than men, and common sense is the best guide to dealing with potentially dangerous situations like hitchhiking, walking alone at night etc. Women should refrain from entering working-class bars alone, particularly in the eastern half of Central Europe.

To avoid attracting attention, wear slightly conservative dress; dark sunglasses help to avoid unwanted eye contact. A wedding ring (on the left ring finger) sometimes helps. Recommended reading is the *Handbook for Women Travellers* by M & G Moss, published by Judy Piatkus Publishers (London).

SPECIAL NEEDS

If you're a traveller with special requirements, national tourist offices can often provide information on facilities. There are local organisations that cater for students, women travelling solo, gays and lesbians, disabled travellers and so on. The country chapters in this book list addresses and phone numbers of some of them.

Student Travellers

There are no specific problems facing students travelling in Central Europe, apart from the obvious one of expense. Your local student travel agency is a great source of information on discounts and special deals for students and other young people – make it your first port of call since it might well help determine what you're going to do in the first place.

Travel with Children

Successful travel with young children requires planning and effort. Don't try to overdo things; even for adults, packing too much into the time available can cause problems. And make sure the activities include the kids as well – balance that day at Berlin's Pergamon Museum with a cruise on the Spree River. Include children in the trip planning; if they've helped to work out where you will be going, they will be much more interested when they get there. See Lonely Planet's *Travel with Children* by Maureen Wheeler for more information.

Disabled Travellers

If you have a physical disability, get in touch with your national support organisation (preferably the 'travel officer') and ask about the countries you plan to visit. They often have complete libraries devoted to travel and can put you in touch with travel agents who specialise in tours for the disabled.

The British-based Royal Association for Disability and Rehabilitation (RADAR) publishes a useful guide titled *Holidays and Travel Abroad: A Guide for Disabled People*, which gives a good overview of facilities available in Europe. Contact RADAR (☎ 0171-250 3222) at 12 City Forum, 250 City Rd, London EC1V 8AF.

Gay & Lesbian Travellers

Gays and lesbians should also get in touch with their national organisation. The *Spartacus Guide for Gay Men*, published by Bruno Gmünder Verlag (Berlin), is a good international directory of gay entertainment venues and lists all the countries in Central Europe with the exception of sleepy little Liechtenstein. Of course, it's best used in conjunction with more up-to-date listings in local papers; as elsewhere, gay venues in Central Europe change with the speed of summer lightning. *Places for Women* (Ferrari Publications) is the best international guide for lesbians.

Senior Travellers

Senior citizens are entitled to many discounts in Central Europe on things like public transport, museum admission fees and so on, provided they show proof of their age. In some cases they might need a special pass. The minimum qualifying age is generally 60 to 65 for men, and 55 to 65 for women.

In your home country, a lower age may already entitle you to all sorts of interesting travel packages and discounts (on car rental, for instance) through organisations and travel agents that cater for senior travellers. Start hunting at your local senior citizens advice bureau.

Special Diets

If you have dietary restrictions – you're a vegetarian or you require kosher food, for example – tourist organisations may be able to advise you or provide lists of suitable restaurants. Some vegetarian restaurants are listed in this book.

ACCOMMODATION

As in the rest of Europe, the cheapest places to stay in Central Europe are camping grounds, followed by hostels and student accommodation. Cheap hotels are not so widespread in Switzerland, Germany and Austria, but guesthouses, pensions, private rooms and B&Bs often present good value. Self-catering flats and cottages are worth considering with a group, especially if you plan to stay in one place for a while.

See the Facts for the Visitor sections in the country chapters for an overview of the local accommodation options. During peak holiday periods, accommodation can be hard to find, and unless you're camping, it's advisable to book ahead. Even camp sites can fill up, particularly popular big-city ones.

Reservations

If you arrive in a country by air, there is often a hotel-booking desk at the airport, although it rarely covers the lower strata of hotels. Tourist offices often have extensive lists of accommodation, and the more helpful ones will really go out of their way to find you something suitable. In most Central European countries the fee for this service is very low (if there is one at all) and can save you a lot of running around and phone calls if accommodation is tight. This is also an easy way to get around any language problems. Agencies offering private rooms can be good value if you don't mind staying with a local family.

Sometimes people will come up to you at the train station or on the street offering a private room or a hostel bed. This can be good or bad – there's no hard and fast rule. Just make sure it's not way out in a suburb somewhere and that you negotiate a clear price. As always, be careful when someone offers to carry your luggage: they might just carry it away.

Camping

Camping is immensely popular in Central Europe and provides the cheapest accommodation. There's usually a charge per tent or site, per vehicle and per person. National tourist offices should have booklets or brochures listing camp sites all over their country. See the previous Documents section for information on Camping Carnets.

In most cases camp sites will be some distance out from the centre in big cities. Most are 'autocamps' intended mainly for motorists. For this reason, camping is most popular for people who have their own transport. If you're on foot, the money you save by camping can quickly be outweighed by the money you spend on commuting to and from a town centre. Unless the camping ground rents bungalows or small cabins on site, you'll also need a tent, sleeping bag, cooking equipment and other bits and pieces, all of which are easier to cart around if you have a vehicle.

Camping other than in designated camping grounds is illegal without permission from the local authorities (the police or local council office) or from the owner of the land. However, don't be shy about asking in the latter case – you may be pleasantly surprised by the response.

In some countries, such as Austria and Germany, freelance camping is illegal on all but private land, and in Hungary it's illegal altogether. This doesn't prevent hikers from occasionally pitching their tent for the night, and they usually get away with it if they keep a low profile (don't disturb local people, build a fire or leave rubbish). At worst, they are woken up by the police and asked to move on.

Hostels

Hostels offer the cheapest roof over your head in Central Europe, and you don't have to be a youngster to use them. Most hostels are part of the national YHA (Youth Hostel Association), which is affiliated with the IYHF (International Youth Hostel Federation). The situation is slightly confused at the moment, as the IYHF has changed its name to Hostelling International (HI) in order to attract a wider clientele and move away from the emphasis on 'youth'. Some countries, such as the USA, have adopted the new name, but many Central European countries may take a few years to change their logos. In practice it makes no difference: YHA, IYHF and HI are all the same thing.

Privately run hostels are not uncommon in Hungary and the Czech Republic.

Technically you're supposed to be a YHA/IYHF/HI member to use affiliated hostels, but you can often stay by simply paying an extra charge and this will often be set against future membership. Stay enough nights as a nonmember and you automatically become a member.

Bavaria in Germany is the only place with an age limit for hostelling members. To join the IYHF/HI, ask at any hostel or contact your national or local hostelling office. The offices for each Central European country are covered in this book. Other national offices include:

Australia
: Each state has its own Youth Hostel Association. The National Administration Office is the Australian Youth Hostels Association, Level 3, 10 Mallett St, Camperdown, NSW 2050 (☎ 02-565 1699)

Canada
: Hostelling International – Canada, 1600 James Naismith Drive, suite 608, Gloucester, Ontario K1B 5N4 (☎ 613-748 5638)

England & Wales
: Youth Hostels Association, Trevelyan House, 8 St Stephen's Hill, St Albans, Herts AL1 2DY (☎ 0727-855215)

Ireland
: An Óige, Irish Youth Hostel Association, 61 Mountjoy St, Dublin 7 (☎ 01-304555)

New Zealand
: Youth Hostels Association of New Zealand, PO Box 436, 173 Gloucester St, Christchurch 1 (☎ 03-379 9970)

Northern Ireland
: Youth Hostel Association of Northern Ireland, 56 Bradbury Place, Belfast BT7 1RU (☎ 0232-324733)

Scotland
: Scottish Youth Hostels Association, 7 Glebe Crescent, Stirling FK8 2JA (☎ 0786-451181)

South Africa
: Hostel Association of South Africa, 606 Boston House, Strand St, Cape Town 8001 (☎ 021-419 1853)

USA
: Hostelling International – American Youth Hostels, 733 15th St NW, suite 840, Washington, DC 20005 (☎ 202-783 6161)

At a hostel, you get a bed for the night, plus use of communal facilities which often include a kitchen where you can prepare your own meals. You are usually required to have a sleeping sheet – simply using your sleeping bag is not permitted. If you don't have your own approved sleeping sheet, you can usually hire or buy one.

Hostels vary widely in character, but the growing number of travellers and the increased competition from other forms of accommodation (particularly private 'backpacker hostels') have prompted many hostels to improve their facilities and cut back on rules and regulations. Increasingly, hostels are open all day, curfews are disappearing and 'wardens' with a sergeant-major mentality are an endangered species. In some Central European hostels, you'll even find single and double rooms. Everywhere the trend has been towards smaller dormitory rooms with just four to six beds.

The HI guide *Budget accommodation you*

can Trust (volume 1) details hostels throughout Central Europe. Many hostels accept reservations by phone or fax but usually not during peak periods; they'll often book the next one for you for a small fee. You can also book hostels through national hostel offices. Popular hostels can be heavily booked in summer and sometimes limits are placed on how many nights you can stay.

Student Accommodation

Some universities rent out student accommodation during holiday periods. This is quite popular in Poland, Slovakia, the Czech Republic and Hungary; see those chapters for more details. These will often be single rooms and may have cooking facilities available. Enquire at the college or university, at student information services or at local tourist offices.

Private Rooms, Guesthouses & Hotels

There's a huge range of accommodation above the hostel level. In Hungary and to a lesser degree in the other countries of Central Europe, the real bargain in this field is a room in a private home or flat. In some areas every other house will have a *'szoba kiadó'* or *'Zimmer frei'* ('room(s) for rent') sign out the front. In other countries, similar private accommodation goes under the name of pension, guesthouse, *Gasthaus* and so on. Although the majority are simple affairs, there are more expensive ones where you will find attached bathrooms and other luxuries.

Above this level are hotels, which at the very bottom of the bracket may be no more expensive than private rooms or guesthouses while at the other extreme they extend to luxury five-star hotels with price tags to match. Although categorisation varies from country to country, the hotels recommended in this book will generally range from no stars to one or two stars. You'll often find hotels clustered around the bus and train station areas – always good places to start hunting.

Check your room and the bathroom before you agree to take it, and make sure you know what it's going to cost – discounts are often available off season or for longer stays. Ask about breakfast: sometimes it's included but other times you may be required to have it and to pay extra for it (which can be a real rip-off in countries like Hungary). If the sheets don't look clean, ask to have them changed right away. Check where the fire exits are.

If you think a hotel room is too expensive, ask if they have anything cheaper. In the eastern half of Central Europe, hotel owners may be open to a little bargaining if times are slack, particularly in the autumn and winter. If you're with a group or plan to stay for a reasonable length of time, it's always worth trying to negotiate a special rate.

FOOD

Sampling the local food is one of the most enjoyable aspects of travel. Central European cuisine, though often a heavy and stodgy one of goulash, sausages, dumplings and schnitzel, comes into its own in soups, game, the use of forest products (mushrooms and wild berries for example) and often extravagant pastries.

The Facts for the Visitor sections in the individual country chapters contain details of local cuisine, and there are many suggestions on places to eat in the chapters themselves.

Restaurant prices vary enormously. The cheapest place for a decent meal is the self-service cafeteria – often called *buffet* or some variation of the word – still found in Poland, the Czech Republic, Slovakia and, to a lesser extent, Hungary. Elsewhere, department-store restaurants are a good bet. Official student *mensas* (university restaurants) are dirt cheap, but the food tends to be bland, and it's not always clear whether you'll be allowed in if you're not a local student. Kiosks often sell cheap snacks that can be as much a part of the national cuisine as fancy dishes.

Self-catering – buying your ingredients at a shop or market and preparing them yourself – can be a cheap and wholesome way of eating. Even if you don't have cooking facilities, a lunch on a park bench with some local bread, salami and wine can be a recurring highlight of your trip.

Vegetarians won't starve. Vegetarianism has taken off in Central Europe (a part of the world that has traditionally been very big on meat) though not everywhere to the same extent. Tourist offices can supply lists of vegetarian restaurants, and some are recommended in this book. Many restaurants have one or two vegetarian dishes – deep-fried mushroom caps, pasta dishes with cheese, vegetable dumplings, Greek-style 'peasant' salads. Others might prepare special dishes on request.

Getting There & Away

Step one for visiting Central Europe is to get to the Continent itself, and in these days of severe competition between airlines, there are plenty of opportunities to find cheap tickets to several 'gateway' cities. But in general, airfares to/from Central Europe are not Europe's biggest bargains so your best bet is to buy the cheapest possible ticket (which will probably be to London, Amsterdam, Athens or Luxembourg) and proceed 'by surface' from there.

Forget shipping – unless by 'shipping' you mean the ferry services operating in the Baltic Sea between Central Europe and Scandinavia or those linking southern Europe and North Africa. Only a handful of ships still carry passengers across the Atlantic; they don't sail often and are very expensive even compared with full-fare air tickets. See the Sea section at the end of this chapter for more details.

Some travellers still arrive in or leave from Europe overland – the options being Africa, the Middle East and Asia, and what used to be the Soviet Union. The trans-Siberian and trans-Mongolian express trains could well begin to carry more people to and from Europe as Russia opens up to tourism. See the following Train and Land sections for more details.

Whichever way you're travelling, make sure you take out travel insurance. This not only covers you for medical expenses and luggage theft or loss but also for cancellation or delays in your travel arrangements. (You could fall seriously ill two days before departure, for example.) Cover depends on your insurance and type of ticket, so ask both your insurer and your ticket-issuing agency to explain where you stand. Ticket loss is also covered by travel insurance. Make sure you have a separate record of all your ticket details or, better still, a photocopy (see Photocopies under Dangers & Annoyances in the earlier Facts for the Visitor chapter). Buy travel insurance as early as possible. If you buy it the week before you fly, you may find, for instance, that you're not covered for delays to your flight caused by strikes or other industrial action that may have been in force before you took out the insurance.

Paying for your ticket with a credit card often provides limited travel accident insurance, and you may be able to reclaim the payment if the operator doesn't deliver. In the UK, for instance, institutions issuing credit cards are required by law to reimburse consumers if a company goes into liquidation and the amount in contention is more than £100. Ask your credit card company what it's prepared to cover.

AIR

Remember always to reconfirm your onward or return bookings by the specified time – at least 72 hours before departure on international flights. Otherwise, there's a real risk that you'll turn up at the airport only to find that you've missed your flight because it was rescheduled or that you've been reclassified as a 'no show' and 'bumped' (see the Air Travel Glossary later in this section).

Buying a Plane Ticket

Your plane ticket will probably be the single most expensive item in your budget, so it's always worth putting aside some time to research the current state of the market. Start early: some of the cheapest tickets have to be bought or at least booked well in advance, and some popular flights sell out early.

Talk to other recent travellers, look at the ads in newspapers and magazines (not forgetting the press of the ethnic group whose country you plan to visit – the Hungarian one in Cleveland, say, or the Polish one in Chicago), and watch for special offers.

Discounted tickets are available in two distinct categories: official and unofficial. Official ones include advance-purchase tickets, budget fares, Apex and super-Apex.

Unofficial ones are simply discounted

tickets that the airlines release through selected travel agencies. Don't look for these discounted tickets directly from the airlines: they are only available through travel agents. Airlines can, however, supply information on routes and timetables, and their low-season, student and senior citizens' fares can be very competitive. Also, the normal, full-fare airline tickets sometimes include one or more free side trips in Europe, which can make them good value.

Return (round-trip) tickets usually work out cheaper than two one-way fares – often *much* cheaper. Beware that some immigration officials ask for return or onward tickets; if you can't show either, you'll have to provide proof of 'sufficient means of support' (a lot of money or, in some cases, valid credit cards).

Round-the-World (RTW) tickets are very popular. The airline RTW tickets are often real bargains and can work out to be no more expensive or even cheaper than an ordinary return ticket. Prices start at about £900 or US$1300, depending on the season. The official airline RTW tickets are usually put together by a combination of two airlines and allow you to fly anywhere you want on their route systems so long as you don't backtrack. Other restrictions are that you (usually) must book the first sector in advance and that cancellation penalties then apply. There may be restrictions on how many stops you are permitted and the tickets are usually valid from 90 days up to a year.

An alternative type of RTW ticket is one 'stitched together' by a travel agent using a combination of discounted tickets. These can be still cheaper.

Generally, you can find discounted tickets at prices as low as or lower than the official advance purchase or budget fares. Phone around the travel agencies for bargains.

You may discover that those very cheap flights are 'fully booked, but we have another one that costs a bit more...' Or the flight is on an airline notorious for its poor safety record and leaves you in the world's least favourite airport in mid-journey for 14 hours – where you're confined to the transit lounge because you don't have a visa. Or the agent claims to have the last two seats available for that country for the whole of August, which he will hold for you for a maximum of two hours. Don't panic – keep ringing around.

If you are travelling from the USA or South-East Asia, or you are trying to get out of Europe from the UK, you will probably find that the cheapest flights are being advertised by obscure agencies whose names haven't yet reached the telephone directory. Many such firms are honest and solvent, but there are a few rogues who will take your money and disappear – only to reopen elsewhere a month or two later under a new name.

If you feel suspicious about a firm, don't give them all the money at once – leave a deposit of 20% or so and pay the balance when you have the ticket in hand. If they insist on total payment up front in cash, go somewhere else or be prepared to take a very big risk. And once you have the ticket, ring the airline to confirm that you are actually booked onto the flight.

You may decide to pay more than the rock-bottom fare by opting for the security of a better-known travel agent. Firms such as STA Travel, which has offices worldwide, Council Travel in the USA or Travel CUTS in Canada offer good prices to most destinations and are unlikely to disappear overnight leaving you clutching a receipt for a nonexistent ticket.

Use the fares quoted in this book as a guide only. They are approximate and based on the rates advertised by travel agents at the time of research. Most are likely to have changed by the time you read this.

Travellers with Special Needs

If you have special needs of any sort – you're vegetarian or require a special diet, you're travelling in a wheelchair, taking the baby, terrified of flying, whatever – let the airline people know as soon as possible so that they can make arrangements. Remind them when you reconfirm your booking (at least 72 hours before departure) and again when you check in at the airport. It may also be worth ringing around the airlines before you make your booking to find out how they can handle your particular needs.

Children aged under two travel for 10% of the full fare (or free on some airlines) as long as they don't occupy a seat. They don't get a baggage allowance in this case. 'Skycots', baby food and nappies (diapers) should be provided by the airline if requested in advance. Children aged between two and 12 can usually occupy a seat for half to two-thirds of the full fare. They do get a standard baggage allowance.

To/From the USA

The North Atlantic is the world's busiest

Air Travel Glossary

Apex Apex ('advance purchase excursion') is a discounted ticket which must be paid for in advance. There are penalties if you wish to change it.

Baggage Allowance This will be written on your ticket: usually one 20-kg item to go in the hold, plus one item of hand luggage.

Bucket Shop An unbonded travel agency specialising in discounted airline tickets.

Bumped Just because you have a confirmed seat doesn't mean you're going to get on the plane – see Overbooking.

Cancellation Penalties If you have to cancel or change an Apex ticket there are often heavy penalties involved – insurance can sometimes be taken out against these penalties. Some airlines impose penalties on regular tickets as well, particularly against 'no show' passengers (see No Shows).

Check In Airlines ask you to check in a certain time ahead of the flight departure (usually two hours on international flights). If you fail to check in on time and the flight is overbooked, the airline can cancel your booking and give your seat to somebody else.

Confirmation Having a ticket written out with the flight and date you want doesn't mean you have a seat until the agent has checked with the airline that your status is 'OK' or confirmed. Meanwhile, you could just be 'on request'. It's also wise to reconfirm onward or return bookings directly with the airline 72 hours before departure (see Reconfirmation).

Discounted Tickets There are two types of discounted fares: officially discounted (see Promotional Fares) and unofficially discounted. The lowest prices often impose drawbacks like flying with unpopular airlines, inconvenient schedules, or unpleasant routes and connections. A discounted ticket can save you other things than money – you may be able to pay Apex prices without the associated Apex advance booking and other requirements. Discounted tickets only exist where there is fierce competition.

Full Fares Airlines traditionally offer 1st-class (coded F), business-class (coded J) and economy-class (coded Y) tickets. These days there are so many promotional and discounted fares available from the regular economy class that few passengers pay full economy fare.

Lost Tickets If you lose your airline ticket, an airline will usually treat it like a travellers' cheque and, after enquiries, issue you with another one. Legally, however, an airline is entitled to treat it like cash and if you lose it then it's gone forever. Take good care of your tickets.

No Shows No shows are passengers who fail to show up for their flight, sometimes due to unexpected delays or disasters, sometimes due to simply forgetting, sometimes because they made more than one booking and didn't bother to cancel the one they didn't want. Full fare passengers who fail to turn up are sometimes entitled to travel on a later flight. The rest of us are penalised (see Cancellation Penalties).

On Request An unconfirmed booking for a flight (see Confirmation).

long-haul air corridor, and the flight options are bewildering. The *New York Times*, *LA Times*, *Chicago Tribune*, *San Francisco Chronicle* and the *Boston Globe* all publish weekly travel sections in which you'll find any number of travel agents' ads. Council Travel and STA Travel have offices in major cities nationwide. You should be able to fly New York-London return for US$350 to US$450 in the low season, US$550 to US$650 in the high season.

One-way fares can work out to about half of this on a stand-by basis. Airhitch (☎ 212-864 2000) specialises in this sort of thing and can get you to Europe one way for US$169/269/229 from the East Coast/West Coast/elsewhere in the USA. Airhitch also has offices in Paris (☎ 1-44 75 39 90) and

Open Jaws A return ticket where you fly out to one place but return from another. If available, this can save you backtracking to your arrival point.

Overbooking Airlines hate to fly empty seats, and since every flight has some passengers who fail to show up (see No Shows), airlines often book more passengers than they have seats. Usually the excess passengers balance those who fail to show up but occasionally somebody gets bumped. If this happens, guess who it is most likely to be? The passengers who check in late.

Promotional Fares Officially discounted fares like Apex fares which are available from travel agents or direct from the airline.

Reconfirmation At least 72 hours prior to departure time of an onward or return flight you must contact the airline and 'reconfirm' that you intend to be on the flight. If you don't do this the airline can delete your name from the passenger list and you could lose your seat. You don't have to reconfirm the first flight on your itinerary or if your stopover is less than 72 hours. It doesn't hurt to reconfirm more than once.

Restrictions Discounted tickets often have various restrictions on them – advance purchase is the most usual one (see Apex). Others are restrictions on the minimum and maximum period you must be away, such as a minimum of 14 days or a maximum of one year. See Cancellation Penalties.

Standby A discounted ticket where you only fly if there is a seat free at the last moment. Standby fares are usually only available on domestic routes.

Tickets Out An entry requirement for many countries is that you have an onward or return ticket – in other words, a ticket out of the country. If you're not sure what you intend to do next, the easiest solution is to buy the cheapest onward ticket to a neighbouring country or a ticket from a reliable airline which can later be refunded if you do not use it.

Transferred Tickets Airline tickets cannot be transferred from one person to another. Travellers sometimes try to sell the return half of their ticket, but officials can ask you to prove that you are the person named on the ticket. This is unlikely to happen on domestic flights, but on international flights, tickets may be compared with passports. Also, if you're flying on a transferred ticket and something goes wrong with the flight (hijack, crash), there will be no record of your presence on board.

Travel Agencies Travel agencies vary widely and you should ensure you use one that suits your needs. Some simply handle tours while full-service agencies handle everything from tours and tickets to car rental and hotel bookings. A good one will do all these things and can save you a lot of money, but if all you want is a ticket at the lowest possible price, then you really need an agency specialising in discounted tickets. A discounted ticket agency, however, may not be useful for other things, like hotel bookings.

Travel Periods Some officially discounted fares, Apex fares in particular, vary with the time of year. There is often a low (off-peak) season and a high (peak) season. Sometimes there's an intermediate or shoulder season as well. At peak times, when everyone wants to fly, not only will the officially discounted fares be higher but so will unofficially discounted fares, or there may simply be no discounted tickets available. Usually the fare depends on your outward flight – if you depart in the high season and return in the low season, you pay the high-season fare. ■

Amsterdam (☎ 020-627 24 32), but you have to be a US or Canadian resident to fly one way to North America.

An interesting alternative to the ordinary New York-London flight is offered by Icelandair (☎ 800-223 5500), which has competitive year-round fares from four American cities to Luxembourg (via Reykjavík) with onward bus connections available to the Central European cities of Cologne, Düsseldorf and Stuttgart. TFI Tours (☎ 212-736 1140 or 800-745 8000), 34 West 32nd St, 12th floor, New York, NY 10001-3898, has cheap flights to Budapest, Kraków, Prague and Warsaw from cities across the USA. Tradesco Tours (☎ 310-649 5808), 6033 West Century Blvd, suite 670, Los Angeles, CA 90045, offers good-value discount packages to Budapest and other cities of Central Europe.

Another option is a courier flight, where you accompany a parcel or freight to be picked up at the other end. A New York-London return courier flight can be had for about US$300/375 low/high season or less (about US$100 more from the West Coast). You can also fly one way. The drawbacks are that your stay in Europe may be limited to one or two weeks on a return ticket, that your luggage is usually restricted to hand baggage (the parcel or freight you carry comes out of your luggage allowance) and that you may have to be a resident and apply for an interview before they'll take you on.

Find out more about courier flights from Discount Travel International in New York (☎ 212-362 3636) and Way to Go in Los Angeles (☎ 213-466 1126). Call two or three months in advance and at the start of the calendar month when rosters are being written.

The *Travel Unlimited* newsletter, PO Box 1058, Allston, MA 02134, publishes details of the cheapest airfares and courier possibilities for destinations all over the world from the USA and other countries including the UK. The newsletter is a treasure trove of information. A single monthly issue costs US$5 and a year's subscription US$25 (US$35 abroad).

To/From Canada

Travel CUTS has offices in all major Canadian cities. Scan the budget travel agents' ads in the *Toronto Globe & Mail*, *Toronto Star* and *Vancouver Province*.

See the previous To/From the USA section for general information on courier flights. For those originating in Canada, contact FB On Board Courier Services at ☎ 514-633 0740 in Montreal or ☎ 604-338 1366 in Vancouver. A courier return flight to London or Paris will set you back about C$350 from Toronto or Montreal, C$425 from Vancouver. Airhitch (see To/From the USA) has stand-by fares to/from Toronto, Montreal and Vancouver.

To/From Australia

STA Travel and Flight Centres International are major dealers in cheap airfares. Check the travel agents' ads in the Yellow Pages and ring around.

The Saturday travel sections of the *Sydney Morning Herald* and Melbourne's *The Age* newspapers have many ads offering cheap fares to Europe, but don't be surprised if they happen to be 'sold out' when you contact the agents: they're usually low-season fares on obscure airlines with lots of conditions attached. With Australia's large and well-organised ethnic populations, it pays to check special deals in the ethnic press – Olympic Airways sometimes has good deals to Athens, for example.

Discounted return fares on mainstream airlines through a reputable agent like STA Travel cost between A$1600 (low season) and A$2500 (high season). Flights to/from Perth are a couple of hundred dollars cheaper. Lauda Air flies from Sydney via Singapore to Vienna in the heart of Central Europe. The return fare is about A$1750 (low season).

To/From New Zealand

As in Australia, STA Travel and Flight Centres International are popular travel agents. Not surprisingly, the cheapest fares to Europe are routed through the USA, and an RTW ticket can be cheaper than a return.

To/From Africa

Nairobi is probably the best place in Africa to buy tickets to Europe, thanks to the many bucket shops and the strong competition between them. Several West African countries such as Burkina Faso and the Gambia offer cheap charter flights to France, and charter fares from Morocco can be incredibly cheap if you're lucky enough to get a seat. If you are thinking of flying to Europe from Cairo, it's often cheaper to fly to Athens and to proceed by budget bus from there.

To/From Asia

Hong Kong is still the discount plane-ticket capital of Asia, and its bucket shops offer some great bargains but be careful: not all are reliable. Ask the advice of other travellers before buying tickets. Many of the cheapest fares from South-East Asia to Europe are offered by Eastern European carriers (LOT, Czechoslovak Airlines, Aeroflot), which could take you to the heart of Central Europe. Lauda Air flies direct to Vienna from Hong Kong via Bangkok. STA Travel has branches in Hong Kong, Tokyo, Singapore, Bangkok and Kuala Lumpur.

To/from India, the cheapest flights tend to be with Eastern European carriers or certain Middle Eastern airlines (Syrian Arab Airlines, Iran Air). Bombay is India's air transport hub, with many transit options to/from South-East Asia, but tickets are slightly cheaper in Delhi.

To/From the UK

If you're looking for a cheap way into or out of Central Europe, London is the Continent's major centre for discounted fares. Low season return flights from London to Central Europe include: Berlin £105, Budapest £140, Frankfurt £126, Geneva £133, Munich £120, Prague £120, Vienna £140, Warsaw £149, Zürich £135.

You can sometimes find airfares from London that either match or beat surface alternatives in terms of cost. A restricted return (valid for one month maximum) from London to Zürich, for example, is available through discount travel agents for between £90 and £140. By comparison, a two-month return by rail between the same cities costs £147. Getting between airports and city centres is rarely a problem in Central Europe thanks to ever improving subway and tram networks and good bus services.

If you are travelling alone, it might be worth looking into courier flights from London, though closer European integration means there's increasingly less call for this service. Polo Express (☎ 0181-759 5383) still has some return courier flights within Europe, however.

People taking flights from Britain pay an Air Passenger Duty; those flying to countries in the EU pay £5; those flying beyond it, £10. This is likely to be included in the price of your ticket; check with your travel agent. At present, there is no departure tax if you depart by sea or tunnel.

The Trailfinders head office (☎ 0171-937 5400), 194 Kensington High St W8, is an amazing place complete with travel library, bookshop, visa service and immunisation centre. STA Travel also has branches in the UK; the London office (☎ 0171-937 9921) is at 74 Old Brompton Road SW7. Campus Travel (☎ 0171-730 3402), 52 Grosvenor Gardens, London SW1W OAG, is helpful and has many interesting deals, including open-jaw returns (flying into one city and out of another). Ask them about courier flights organised by Polo Express (☎ 0181-759 5383) or Courier Travel Service (☎ 0171-351 0300). See also the Air section in the following Getting Around chapter.

The entertainment listings magazine *Time Out*, the Sunday papers, the *Evening Standard* and *Exchange & Mart* carry ads for cheap fares. Also look out for the free magazines and newspapers widely available in London, especially *TNT* and *Southern Cross* – you can often pick them up outside the main train and tube stations.

Make sure the agent is a member of some sort of traveller-protection scheme, such as that offered by the Association of British Travel Agents (ABTA). If you have paid for your flight to an ABTA-registered agent who subsequently goes out of business, ABTA will guarantee a refund or an alternative. Unregistered bucket shops are riskier but sometimes cheaper.

To/From Continental Europe

Though London is Europe's discount airfare capital, there are several other cities on the Continent where you'll find a range of good deals. See the country chapters for details.

Many travel agents have ties with STA Travel, where STA tickets can be altered free of charge (first change only). Outlets in important transport hubs include: Voyages et Découvertes (☎ 1-42 61 00 01), 21 Rue Cambon, Paris; Student & Youth Travel Service (☎ 01-323 3767), Nikis 11, Athens; and SRID Reisen (☎ 069-43 01 91), Berger Strasse 118, Frankfurt. For the addresses and phone numbers of travel agents in other Central European countries, see the Information sections under individual cities.

LAND

Train

To/From Africa & the Mediterranean Morocco and most of Turkey lie outside Europe, but the rail systems of both countries are still covered by Inter-Rail (see the Train section in the Getting Around chapter for details), though only the 26+ version is valid in Turkey. If you don't have an Inter-Rail pass, the price of a cheap return train ticket from London to Morocco compares favourably with equivalent bus fares, which is worth keeping in mind.

To/From Asia A train can work out at about the same price as flying or even a little less travelling to/from central and eastern Asia, depending on how much time and money you spend along the way. And it can be a lot more fun. There are three routes to/from Moscow across Siberia: the trans-Siberian to/from Vladivostok, and the trans-Mongolian and trans-Manchurian, both to/from Beijing. There's a fourth route south from Moscow and across Kazakhstan, following part of the old Silk Route to/from Beijing. Prices can vary enormously, depending on where you buy the ticket and what is included. Prices quoted here are for indication only.

The trans-Siberian takes 8½ days from Moscow via Khabarovsk to Vladivostok, from where there is a boat to Japan (Niigata) or Hong Kong. The boats only run from May to September. The complete rail/boat journey from Moscow to Niigata costs upwards of US$600 per person, for a 2nd-class sleeper in a four-berth cabin.

The trans-Mongolian passes through Mongolia to Beijing and takes about 5½ days. A 2nd-class sleeper in a four-berth compartment would cost about US$200 to US$250 if purchased in Moscow or Beijing; Warsaw is another good place to buy these tickets. If you want to stop off along the way or spend some time in Moscow, you'll need 'visa support' – a letter or fax from a hotel or travel agent or a hotel confirming that they're making your travel/accommodation bookings required in Russia or Mongolia. Locally based companies that do all-inclusive packages (with visa support) that can be arranged from abroad include the Travellers Guest House (☎ 0095-971 40 59; fax 280 76 86) in Moscow and Monkey Business (☎ 723 1376; fax 723 6653) in Hong Kong, with an information centre in Beijing. There are a number of other budget operators.

The trans-Manchurian passes through Manchuria to Beijing and takes six days, costing the same as the trans-Mongolian.

The fourth route runs from Moscow via Alma Ata in Kazakhstan, crosses the border on the new line to Ürümqi (north-western China) and follows part of the old Silk Route to Beijing. At present you can't buy 'through' tickets. In Moscow a 2nd-class ticket to Alma Ata costs around US$120; Alma Ata to Ürümqi is US$65.

There are countless travel options between Moscow and Central Europe. The majority of people will opt for a train, usually to/from Berlin, Warsaw, Munich, Vienna or Budapest.

To/From the UK Going by train from London to Central Europe is cheaper than flying but still no great bargain. See the

Getting There & Away sections in the individual country chapters for more information.

A special 'Eastbound Explorer' ticket from London to Prague, Budapest and Kraków and back (and valid for two months) is available for £206 to people aged under 26 from Campus Travel (☎ 0171-730 3402).

Overland Trails

To/From Africa Discounting the complicated Middle East route, going to/from Africa involves a Mediterranean ferry crossing (see the Sea section later on). Due to political problems in Africa (war between Morocco and the Polisario in the west, civil war in Sudan in the east, trouble in Algeria), the most feasible Africa overland routes of the past have all but closed down.

To/From Asia In the early 1980s, the overland trail to/from Asia lost much of its popularity as the Islamic regime in Iran made life difficult for most independent travellers, and the war in Afghanistan closed that country off to all but the foolhardy. Now that Iran is rediscovering the merits of tourism, the Asia route has begun to pick up again, though unsettled conditions in Afghanistan and southern Pakistan could prevent the trickle of travellers turning into a flood for the time being.

A new overland route through what used to be the Soviet Union could become important over the next few years. At this stage the options are more or less confined to the trans-Siberian/trans-Mongolian railway lines to/from Moscow (see the previous Train section), but other modes of transport are likely to become available beyond the Urals as the newly independent states open up to travellers.

To/From the UK & Western Europe International bus travel tends to take second place to going by train for those travelling between Central Europe and the rest of the Continent, including Britain. The bus has the edge in terms of cost, sometimes quite substantially, but is generally slower and less comfortable. Eurolines (☎ 0171-730 0202), 52 Grosvenor Gardens, Victoria, London SW1, is the main international carrier and has representatives across Europe.

Eurolines' European representatives include: Budget Bus (☎ 020-627 51 51), Rokin 10, Amsterdam; Eurolines (☎ 1-43 54 11 99), 55 Rue Saint Jacques, 75005 Paris; Deutsche Touring (☎ 089-59 18 24), Arnulfstrasse 3, Munich; Lazzi Express (☎ 06-88 40 840), via Tagliamento 27R, Rome; Bohemia Tour (☎ 02-231 2589, Zlatická 7, Prague; PKS (☎ 02-621 3469), Żurawia 26, Warsaw; and Volánbusz (☎ 1-118 2122), Erzsébet tér, Budapest. These may also be able to advise you on other bus companies and deals.

Eurolines has 15 circular explorer routes offering stops in various European cities, always starting and ending in London and valid for six months. One taking in Munich, Barcelona, Rome and Paris costs £230, for example. There are no youth reductions. On ordinary return trips, youth (under 26) fares are around 10% less than the adult full fare (eg a London-Munich return ticket costs £99 for adults or £89 for youths).

Europabus is the motor coach system of the European railways and has information offices in Brussels (☎ 02-217 00 25), Frankfurt (☎ 069-790 3234), Paris (☎ 1-40 38 93 93), Rome (☎ (06-481 82 77) and Vienna (☎ 0222-505 04 79).

The cheapest way to get from London to Central Europe is by bus, and with the opening of the Channel Tunnel, bus routes are multiplying. Discounts are available to those aged under 26 or over 59 years. Destinations (and their one-way/return fares) served by regularly scheduled long-distance coaches from London's Victoria Coach Terminal include: Budapest £79/125 and Prague £56/95 with discounts of about 10% for those under 26.

Information is available from National Express (☎ 0171-730 0202) and in the Getting There & Away sections in the individual country chapters.

SEA

Mediterranean Ferries

There are many ferries across the Mediterranean between Africa and southern Europe from where you can take a bus or train north to Central Europe. The ferry you take will depend on your travels in Africa, but in order of cheapness they are: Spain-Morocco, Italy-Tunisia and France-Algeria/Morocco/Tunisia. At the time of writing, the fate of the Greece-Egypt service was uncertain. Ferries are often filled to capacity in summer, especially to/from Tunisia, so book well in advance if you're taking a vehicle across.

Channel Ferries

Several different ferry companies compete on all the main ferry routes between the UK and France, Belgium and the Netherlands. The resulting service is comprehensive but complicated. The same ferry company can have a whole host of different prices for the same route, depending upon the time of day or year, the validity of the ticket or the length of your vehicle. Vehicle tickets usually cover up to five passengers free of charge. It is worth planning (and booking) ahead where possible as there may be special reductions on off-peak crossings. Apart from one-day or short-term excursion returns, there is little price advantage in buying a return ticket as against two singles when crossing the Channel.

The Stena Sealink Line is the largest ferry company in the world and services British, Irish and Scandinavian routes; other big ones include North Sea Ferries and P&O European Ferries. The shortest cross-Channel

Channel Tunnel

After innumerable delays the Channel Tunnel between England and France opened in late 1994. At 50 km it's the longest undersea tunnel in the world and a remarkable engineering feat.

There are two ways of using the tunnel but neither allows you to transport yourself independently: the Eurostar train link and Le Shuttle for cars, buses and (eventually) foot passengers.

Eurostar The Eurostar train link enables passengers to take a direct train from London, Waterloo to Paris Gare du Nord (three hours) or Brussels Midi/Zuid (3¼ hours). These times will come down once the high-speed rail link has been built on the English side but, thanks to governmental dithering, that won't be completed until the year 2002.

Between 6.30 am and 9 pm there's at least one train per hour in each direction between London and Paris, and London and Brussels. Tickets are widely available from travel agencies and major train stations and include a seat reservation on a particular service. For information and credit card bookings, call ☎ (0233) 617 575.

Le Shuttle Le Shuttle, the vehicle-carrying service, which was scheduled to begin operation at the end of 1994, runs only between the two tunnel terminals, Folkestone and Calais. The crossing takes 35 minutes, but actual travel time is closer to an hour. Shuttle trains run 24 hours a day, departing every 15 minutes in each direction at peak times and at least every hour during the quietest periods of the night.

Shuttles are designed to carry up to 180 cars (or 120 cars and 12 coaches). Passengers with a bicycle, motorbike, car, camper van, caravan or trailer can all be carried, though the maximum vehicle length is 6.5 metres. Ferries normally have a limit of five passengers per car, but with Le Shuttle you can take up to eight, if you can cram them all in (hitchers, take note!). Facilities are minimal, and travellers stay in or with their vehicle. Services are also planned for buses (Le Shuttle is expected to start carrying coaches through the tunnel in spring 1995) and foot passengers.

Prices vary according to the time of year and may also fluctuate as the tunnel and the ferry companies compete for market share. You can pre-pay or pay on arrival (by cash or credit card at the toll booth) but you can't reserve a place on a particular shuttle. For further information or credit card bookings, call the customer service centre on ☎ (0303) 271 100. Passport and immigration controls for the UK and France in either direction are passed before boarding Le Shuttle. ■

routes (Dover to Calais or Boulogne, and Folkestone to Boulogne) are also the busiest; expect competition from the Channel Tunnel to shake up these services.

Rail-pass holders are entitled to discounts or free travel on some lines (see the Train section in the Getting Around chapter), and most ferry companies give discounts to disabled drivers. Food and drink on ferries can be relatively expensive, so it is worth bringing your own when possible. It is also worth knowing that if you take your vehicle on board, you are usually denied access to it during the voyage.

Baltic & North Sea Ferries

Central Europe can be reached from the north, west and east by ferry via the North or Baltic seas. There is only one direct link between Germany and the UK – the 21½-hour ferry between Harwich and Hamburg – but a slew of other seacraft convey cars and people between Germany and Scandinavia. Regularly scheduled services include a one-hour crossing between Puttgarten, north-east of Hamburg, and Rødbyhavn, south-west of Copenhagen, and ferries from Kiel to Bagenkop (on the Danish island of Langeland; 2½ hours), to Gothenburg in Sweden (14 hours) and all the way to Oslo (20 hours). There are also ferries to Denmark and/or Sweden from the eastern German ports of Rostock, Warnemünde and, on Rügen Island, Sassnitz.

Poland also has a ferry service – year-round for the most part – to/from Scandinavia. Routings from Gdańsk include ones to Helsinki and the Swedish ports of Oxelösund near Stockholm and Ystad near Copenhagen. Ferries also sail from Świnoujście to Ystad and Copenhagen. There is sporadic boat service between Gdańsk and the Russian port of Kaliningrad.

See Getting There & Away in the Germany and Poland chapters for more details.

Passenger Ships

The days of earning your passage on a freighter to or from Europe have well and truly passed. Even if you have a mariner's ticket, a shipping company is unlikely to want to sign you up for a single trip.

Regular, long-distance passenger ships disappeared with the advent of cheap air travel and were replaced by a small number of luxury cruise ships. Cunard's *Queen Elizabeth 2* sails between New York and Southampton 28 times a year. The trip takes five nights each way and a return ticket can be had from £1025, though there are also one-way and 'fly one-way' deals. Your travel agent will have more details. The standard reference for passenger ships is the *ABC Cruise & Ferry Guide* published by the Reed Travel Group (☎ 01582-60 0111), Church St, Dunstable, Bedfordshire LU5 4HB.

A more adventurous (though not necessarily cheaper) alternative is to travel as a paying passenger on a freighter. Freighters are far more numerous than cruise ships, and there are many more routes from which to choose. With a bit of homework, you'll be able to sail between Europe and just about anywhere else in the world, with stopovers at exotic ports which you may never have heard of. The previously mentioned *ABC Cruise & Ferry Guide* is the most complete source of information. If you read French, you'll find useful advice in *Le Guide des Voyages en Cargo* by Hugo Verlomme (published by JC Lattès).

Passenger freighters typically carry from six to 12 passengers (more than 12 would require a doctor on board) and, though less luxurious than 'real' cruise ships, they give you a real taste of life at sea. Schedules tend to be flexible and costs vary, but seem to hover around US$95 a day; vehicles can often be included for an additional fee.

LEAVING CENTRAL EUROPE

Departure Taxes

Some countries in Central Europe, including Poland and Slovakia, charge you a small fee for the privilege of leaving from their airports. Some also charge port fees when you're leaving by ship. Such fees are often included in the price of your ticket, but it pays to check this when purchasing your ticket. If not, you'll have to have the fee ready when you leave – usually in local currency. Details are given in the relevant country chapters.

WARNING
This chapter is particularly vulnerable to change – prices for international travel are volatile, routes are introduced and cancelled, schedules change, special deals come and go, rules and visa requirements are amended. Airlines and governments seem to take a perverse pleasure in making price structures and regulations as complicated as possible. You should check directly with the airline or travel agent to make sure you understand how a fare (and ticket you may buy) works. In addition, the travel industry is highly competitive, and there are many schemes, deals and bonuses. The upshot of this is that you should get opinions, quotes and advice from as many airlines and travel agents as possible before you part with your hard-earned cash. The details given in this chapter should be regarded as pointers and are not a substitute for careful, up-to-date research.

Getting Around

AIR

In 1997 air travel within the EU should be fully deregulated, a process that began in 1993. In theory this should result in lower fares due to a wider choice of airlines on which to fly. In practice, however, airport congestion and unavailability of flying 'slots' could lessen the impact; the effect might be more noticeable on flights between smaller airports with less traffic. In any case, such deregulation will have little effect for some years to come on the countries of Central Europe, most of which have yet to obtain EU membership. For the foreseeable future, air travel within Western and Central Europe will remain an expensive luxury.

Air travel is best viewed as a means to get you to the starting point of your itinerary rather than as your main means of travel since it lacks the flexibility of ground transport. If you start taking aeroplanes for relatively short hops, you'll spend a fortune in no time at all – special deals are rarely available on internal flights. This is especially true in Central Europe, where distances between cities and areas of interest hardly ever warrant flying.

Refer to the Air Travel Glossary in the previous Getting There & Away chapter for information on types of air tickets. London is a good centre for picking up cheap, restricted-validity tickets through bucket shops, and there are some discounted air tickets that may be useful for regional travel in Central Europe. Amsterdam and Athens are other bargain centres for tickets such as these.

Open-jaw returns, by which you can travel into one city and out of another, could be useful for regional travel (though such fares can sometimes work out more expensive than straightforward returns). In London, Trailfinders, STA Travel and Campus Travel can give you tailor-made versions of these tickets. Your chosen cities needn't even be in the same country.

BUS

Buses provide a viable alternative to the rail network in most Central European countries. Generally they tend to complement the rail system rather than duplicate it, though in some countries – notably Hungary, the Czech Republic and Slovakia – you'll have a choice.

In general, buses are slightly cheaper and slower than trains in western Central Europe and a bit more expensive in Poland, Hungary, the Czech Republic and Slovakia. Buses tend to be best used for shorter hops such as getting around cities and reaching remote rural villages. They are often the only option in mountainous regions (eg in Austria and Slovakia) where rail tracks fear to tread. Advance reservations are rarely necessary. Many city buses operate on a pay-in-advance system (where you punch your own ticket after boarding) and offer some good-value day and weekly passes. See the individual country chapters and city sections for more details.

TRAIN

Trains are a popular way to get around in Central Europe: they are good meeting places, generally comfortable, frequent and run on time. In some countries, such as those in the eastern half of Central Europe, fares are heavily subsidised; in others, some sort of rail pass will make travel more affordable. Supplements and reservation costs are not covered by passes, and pass holders must always carry their passport on the train for identification purposes.

If you plan to travel extensively by train, it might be worth getting hold of the *Thomas Cook European Timetable*, which gives a complete listing of train schedules and indicates where supplements apply or where reservations are necessary. It is updated monthly and is available from Thomas Cook outlets worldwide.

Like Paris, Amsterdam and Milan, the

Central European cities of Munich, Vienna and Berlin are important hubs for international rail connections. See the relevant city sections for details and budget ticket agents.

Express Trains

Fast trains can be identified by the letters EC (EuroCity) or IC (InterCity). The German ICE is an even faster train. Supplements can apply on fast trains, and it is a good idea (sometimes obligatory) to make seat reservations at peak times and on certain lines.

Overnight Trains

Overnight trains will usually offer a choice of couchette or sleeper if you don't fancy sleeping in your seat with somebody else's elbow in your ear. Again, reservations are advisable – often mandatory – as sleeping options are allocated on a first-come, first-served basis. Couchettes are bunks which number either four (in 1st class) or six (in 2nd class) per compartment and are comfortable enough, if lacking a bit in privacy. A couchette costs a fixed price of US$15 to US$18 for most international trains, regardless of the country or length of the journey.

Sleepers are the most comfortable option, offering beds for one or two passengers in 1st class and two or three passengers in 2nd class. Charges vary depending upon the journey, but they tend to be significantly more expensive than couchettes. Most long-distance trains have a dining or buffet car or an attendant who wheels a drink-and-snack-laden trolley through carriages, but prices tend to be steep.

Security

Stories occasionally surface about train passengers being gassed or drugged and then robbed, however, having your shoulder bag snatched while you are busy putting your backpack on the overhead rack is more of a worry. Sensible security measures include not letting your bags out of your sight (or chain them to the luggage rack) and locking compartment doors overnight.

Rail Passes

Eurail These passes can only be bought by residents of non-European countries and are supposed to be purchased before arriving in Europe. Eurail passes *can* be purchased within Europe so long as your passport proves you've been there for less than six months, but the outlets where you can do this are limited, and the passes will be more expensive than getting them outside Europe. The London office of French National Railways (☎ 0171-493 9731) at 179 Piccadilly is one such outlet as is MÁV (☎ 1-122 8275 or 1-122 4052), the Hungarian state railway, at Andrássy utca 35 in Budapest. If you've lived in Europe for more than six months, you are eligible for an Inter-Rail pass, which is a better buy, particularly for Central Europe. See the following section.

Eurail passes are valid for unlimited travel on national railways and *some* private lines in Austria, Belgium, Denmark, Finland, France (including Monaco), Germany, Greece, Hungary, Italy, Luxembourg, the Netherlands, Norway, Portugal, Ireland, Spain, Sweden and Switzerland (including Liechtenstein). The passes do *not* cover Poland, the Czech Republic or Slovakia – a substantial amount of the territory of Central Europe – making them little use for touring around the region.

Eurail is also valid for ferries between Ireland and France (but not between the UK and France), between Italy and Greece, and from Sweden to Finland, Denmark or Germany – useful for getting to Central Europe. In addition, reductions are given on steamer services in various countries.

Eurail passes offer reasonable value to people aged under 26. A Youthpass is valid for unlimited 2nd-class travel for 15 days (US$398), one month (US$578) or two months (US$768). The Youth Flexipass, also valid for 2nd class, can be used for freely chosen days within a two-month period: five days for US$255, 10 days for US$398, 15 days for US$540. A journey commencing after 7 pm counts as the next day's travel, but there is no leeway beyond midnight at the end of a day's travel. The traveller must fill out in ink the relevant box in the calendar before starting a day's travel; not validating the pass in this way can earn you a fine of US$50. Tampering with the pass (eg using an erasable pen and rubbing out earlier days) costs the perpetrator the full fare plus US$100.

The corresponding passes for those aged over 26 are available in 1st class only. The Flexipass costs US$348, US$560 or US$740 for five, 10 or 15 freely chosen days in two months. The standard Eurail pass has five versions, costing from US$498 for 15 days' unlimited travel up to US$1398 for three months. Two or more people travelling together (minimum of three people between 1 April and 30 September) can get good discounts on a Saverpass, which works like the standard Eurail pass. Eurail passes for children are also available.

If you buy a pass, read the small print, as lost or stolen Eurail passes can only be re-issued in certain circumstances and with the correct supporting documents. Note that you'll get nothing for a Flexipass if the number of days since validation is greater than the number of days purchased.

There is at least one Eurail Aid Office (where duplicates are issued for a fee of US$25) in each country participating in the scheme; addresses are listed in the *Eurail Traveller's Guide* that you'll receive with the pass.

Europass A new rail pass for non-Europeans, the Europass, gives between five and 15 freely chosen days' unlimited travel within a two-month period. Youth (for those aged under 26) and adult versions are available and purchasing requirements and sales outlets are the same as for Eurail passes. Europasses are a little cheaper than Eurail passes as they cover fewer countries. You can choose from any three to all five of the following: France, Italy, Spain, Germany and Switzerland. For a small additional charge, Austria, Belgium (including Luxembourg) or Portugal can be added on. The countries you choose must be adjacent.

Inter-Rail Inter-Rail passes are available to residents of European countries. Terms and conditions vary slightly from country to country but in most cases it applies that in the country of origin there is only a discount of around 50% on normal fares. Strictly speaking, you must have been a resident in the country where you're purchasing the pass for at least six months, and passport identification is necessary (though these requirements have been overlooked in the past in some outlets). Inter-Rail cards should be treated like cash, as you can make no claims in the event of loss or theft.

Travellers aged over 26 can get the Inter-Rail 26+, valid for unlimited rail travel in Austria, Bulgaria, Croatia, the Czech Republic, Denmark, Finland, Germany, Greece, Hungary, Luxembourg, the Netherlands, Norway, Poland, Romania, Ireland, Slovakia, Slovenia, Sweden, Switzerland (including Liechtenstein) and Turkey. Thus all the countries of Central Europe are included. The pass also gives free travel (barring port tax) on shipping routes from Brindisi (Italy) to Patras (Greece), as well as 30 to 50% discounts on various other ferry routes (many more than covered by Eurail) and certain river and lake services. A 15-day pass costs £209 and one month costs £269.

The Inter-Rail pass for those under 26 has been split into seven zones. Zone A is Ireland; B is Sweden, Norway and Finland; C is Denmark, Germany, Switzerland and Austria; D is the Czech Republic, Slovakia, Poland, Hungary, Bulgaria and Romania; E is France, Belgium, the Netherlands and Luxembourg; F is Spain, Portugal and Morocco; G is Italy, Greece, Turkey and Slovenia. The price for any one zone is £179 for 15 days. Multi-zone passes are better value and valid for one month: two zones cost £209; three zones £229; all zones is £249. You would need a pass for Zones C and D to cover all of Central Europe.

Euro-Domino There is a Euro-Domino pass (called a Freedom pass in the UK) for each of the countries covered in the zonal Inter-

Rail pass, plus Croatia and 'rump' Yugoslavia (the current federation of Serbia and Montenegro). Adults (travelling 1st or 2nd class) and youths (under 26) can choose from three, five or 10 days' validity. Youth prices for 10 days range from £23 (for Luxembourg) to £205 (France).

European East Something called a European East pass is available from travel agents in North America at US$185 for five days' 1st-class travel within a 15-day period or US$299 for 10 days' travel within one month. It's valid in five Central European countries: Austria, Hungary, Poland, the Czech Republic and Slovakia.

Other Passes If you intend to travel extensively within one country, check which national rail passes are available. These can sometimes save you a lot of money but not always; with the 1st/2nd class passes offered by the Hungarian state railway MÁV and priced at US$60/40 for a week and US$90/60 for 10 days, you would practically have to live on the train to make the pass pay for itself. Some passes can only be purchased prior to arrival in the country concerned (though this is not true for most of Central Europe), so you may need to plan ahead if you intend to take this option. Details can be found in the Getting Around sections in the individual country chapters.

The Rail Europe Senior Card is worth investigating for travellers aged over 60.

Cheap Tickets

European rail passes are only worth buying if you plan to do a reasonable amount of inter-country travelling within a short space of time. Some people tend to overdo it and spend every night they can on the train, and end up too tired to enjoy the sightseeing the next day.

When weighing up options, consider the cost of other cheap ticket deals. Travellers aged under 26 can pick up BIJ (Billet International de Jeunesse) tickets which cut from 30 to 50% off the normal fares. Unfortunately, it's not possible to always bank on a substantial reduction. The £138 return from London to Zürich represents just a £9 saving on the normal fare; in contrast, London to Munich return saves £47 on the full fare of £180. Various agents issue BIJ tickets in the UK, including Campus Travel (☎ 0171-730 3402), British Rail International (☎ 0171-834 2345) and Wasteels (☎ 0171-834 7066). In Poland you'll find them at Almatur offices, at CKM Student Travel offices in the Czech Republic and Slovakia and at Express in Hungary. Eurotrain options include circular Explorer tickets, allowing a different route for the return trip.

Foreign students without a national student ID card usually cannot get discounts on domestic train tickets. But if you have an ISIC student card, you can get a discount of between 30 and 50% on international train tickets *between* the countries of eastern Central Europe – travelling from Warsaw to Prague, say, or Budapest to Kraków. Check with the local student travel office.

A good deal to know about is the Super Sparpreis fare which offers a return trip anywhere in Germany within one month for DM170 (an accompanying person pays just half price). Unlimited stopovers along the direct route are allowed, though the ticket is not valid at weekends and holidays without paying a supplement.

TAXI

Taxis in countries like Germany, Austria, Switzerland and Liechtenstein are an ill-affordable luxury and best avoided. They are metered and rates are high (watch your savings ebb away), plus there are supplements (depending on the country) for things like luggage, the time of day, the day of the week, the location from which you were picked up, extra people in the cab etc. Good bus, rail and metro networks make the taking of taxis all but unnecessary, but if you need one in a hurry they can usually be found idling near train stations.

In Poland, the Czech Republic, Slovakia and Hungary, lower fares make taxis more viable, but scams, rip-offs and violent drivers (both 'pirates' and legal ones) can make taking a cab an unpleasant, expensive and even dangerous experience. See Theft & Rip-offs under Dangers & Annoyances in the Facts for the Visitor chapter for more information.

CAR & MOTORBIKE

Travelling by private transport beyond Europe requires plenty of paperwork and other preparations; a detailed description is beyond the scope of this book. But we can tell you what's required in Western and, more specifically, Central Europe.

Travelling with your own vehicle is the best way to get to remote places, and it gives you the most flexibility. An added bonus is that, compared to North America or Australia, it is usually not necessary to spend very long on the road between places of interest. Unfortunately, the independence you enjoy does tend to isolate you to some extent from local people. At the same time, cars are inconvenient in most Central European city centres where it is generally worth ditching your trusty chariot and relying on public transport. Various car-carrying trains can help you avoid long, tiring drives.

An useful general reference on motoring in Europe is Eric Bredesen's *Moto Europa* (Seren Publishing). It's updated annually and contains information on renting, buying, documentation, taxes and road rules. It can be ordered from US and Canadian bookshops (US$24.95) or directly from Seren Publishing (☎ 1-800-EUROPA-8) at PO Box 1212, Dubuque, IA 52004, USA. You must add US$3 for shipping.

Paperwork & Preparations

Proof of ownership of a private vehicle should always be carried (eg Vehicle Registration Document for British-registered cars or the state Certificate of Title or equivalent for US ones) when touring Europe. British or other European and US driving licences should be acceptable for driving throughout Central Europe. But to be on the safe side – or if you have any other type of licence – you should obtain an International Driving Permit (IDP) from your motoring organisation (see Documents in the earlier Facts for the Visitor chapter).

Third-party motor insurance is a minimum requirement in Europe; it's sometimes possible to buy it at the border. Most UK motor insurance policies automatically provide this for EU countries and some others. Get your insurer to issue a Green Card (which may cost extra) – an internationally recognised proof of insurance – and check that it lists all the countries you intend to visit. You'll need this in the event of an accident outside the country where the vehicle is insured. Also ask your insurer for a European Accident Statement form, which can simplify things if worse comes to worst. Never sign statements you can't read or understand – insist on a translation and sign that only if it's acceptable to you.

If you want to insure a vehicle you've just purchased (see the following Purchase section) and have a good insurance record, you might be eligible for considerable premium discounts if you can show a letter to this effect from your insurance company back home.

Taking out a European breakdown assistance policy is a good investment, such as the AA Five Star Service or the RAC Eurocover Motoring Assistance. Ask your motoring organisation for a Letter of Introduction, which entitles you to free services offered by affiliated organisations around Europe (see Documents in the earlier Facts for the Visitor chapter).

Every vehicle travelling across an international border should display a nationality plate of its country of registration (see the International Country Abbreviations appendix in the back of this book). A warning triangle, to be used in the event of breakdown on a highway, is compulsory almost everywhere. Recommended accessories are a first-aid kit (compulsory in Austria and Hungary), a spare bulb kit and a fire extinguisher. Contact the RAC (☎ 0181-686 0088) or the AA (☎ 01256-20123) in the UK for more information.

Road Rules

Across Central Europe, driving is on the right. Vehicles brought over from either the UK or Ireland should have their headlights adjusted to avoid blinding oncoming traffic at night (a simple solution on older headlight lenses is to cover up the triangular section of the lens with tape). This is particularly necessary in Hungary, where by law headlights must be illuminated at all times outside built-up areas. The RAC annually brings out its *European Motoring Guide*, which gives an excellent summary of regulations in each country, including parking rules. Motoring organisations in other countries have similar publications.

Take care with speed limits, as they vary significantly from country to country. You may be surprised at the apparent disregard of traffic regulations in some places (particularly in Hungary, where driving in general can be a nightmare), but as a visitor it is always best to err on the side of caution. Many driving infringements are subject to an on-the-spot fine in Central Europe and can be quite expensive, especially in Germany. Always ask for a receipt.

Central Europeans are particularly strict with drink-driving laws. In some countries, the blood-alcohol concentration (BAC) limit when driving is between 0.05 and 0.08% as it is throughout most of Europe. In others, including Poland and Hungary, however, the BAC is *zero* per cent. You will be breathalysed and fined heavily if the result is positive. In the event of an accident in some of these countries, the drinking party is automatically regarded as guilty and can face imprisonment. See the introductory Getting Around sections in the country chapters for more details on traffic laws.

Roads

Conditions and types of roads vary considerably across Central Europe, but it is possible to make some generalisations. The fastest routes are four or six-lane dual carriageways, ie two or three lanes either side (motorway, autobahn, autoroute, autópálya etc). These tend to skirt cities and plough though the countryside in straight lines, often avoiding the most scenic bits. Some of these roads incur tolls, often quite hefty (Switzerland has a one-off yearly charge for visitors), but there will always be an alternative route you can take. Motorways and other primary routes are in good to fair condition depending on the country.

Road surfaces on minor routes are not so reliable in some countries (eg the Czech Republic, Slovakia, Poland), although normally they will be more than adequate. These roads are narrow and winding, progress is slow and horse-drawn vehicles, bicycles and pedestrians may be encountered at any time. To compensate, you can expect much better scenery and plenty of interesting villages along the way.

Rental

The variety of special deals and terms and conditions attached to renting a car can be mind-boggling. However, there are a few pointers that can help you through the morass. The multinationals – Hertz, Avis, Budget Car, Eurodollar and Europe's largest rental agency, Europcar – will give you reliable service and a good standard of vehicle. Usually you will have the option of returning the car to a different outlet at the end of the rental period, often without a drop-off charge.

Unfortunately, if you walk into an office and ask for a car on the spot, you will pay over the odds, even allowing for special weekend deals. If you want an on-the-spot deal like this, look to national or local firms, which can often undercut the big firms by up to 40%. Nevertheless, you need to be wary of the neighbourhood cowboy who will take your money and point you towards some clapped-out wreck. Additionally, the rental agreement you sign might be bad news if you have an accident or the car is stolen – a cause for concern if you can't even read what you sign.

If you plan ahead, the multinationals might have the deal for you. Prebooked and prepaid rates are always cheaper, and there are many fly-drive combinations and other programmes that are worth looking into. Holiday Autos has good rates for Europe, for which you need to prebook; it has offices in the UK (☎ 0171-491 1111), the USA (☎ 909-949 1737) and in most European countries.

No matter where you rent, make sure you understand what is included in the price (unlimited km, tax, injury insurance, collision damage waiver etc) and what your liabilities are. Always take the collision damage waiver, though you can probably skip the injury insurance if you and your passengers have decent travel insurance. The minimum rental age is usually 21, and you'll probably need a credit card or will have to leave an enormous deposit. Note that prices at airport rental offices are usually higher than at branches in the city centre.

Motorbike and moped rental is not very common in most of Central Europe but occasionally bicycle shops and service stations may oblige.

Purchase

The purchase of vehicles in some European countries is illegal for nonresidents of that country. The UK is probably the best place to buy: second-hand prices are good and, whether buying privately or from a dealer, the absence of language difficulties will help you establish exactly what you are getting and what guarantees you can expect in the event of a breakdown.

Remember that you will usually be getting a car with left-hand drive (ie steering wheel on the right) in the UK. If you want right-hand drive and can afford a new car, prices are reasonable in Belgium, the Netherlands, Luxembourg and Greece (without tax), and France, Germany, Belgium and Luxembourg (with tax). Paperwork can be tricky wherever you buy, and many countries have compulsory roadworthiness checks on older vehicles.

Do not even consider buying a used car in Poland, Hungary, the Czech Republic or Slovakia, where the paperwork is a nightmare and most used cars seem to be held together 'with string and paper clips'.

Camper Van

A popular way to tour Europe is for three or four people to band together to buy or rent a camper van. London is the usual embarkation point. Look at the advertisements in London's free magazine *TNT* if you wish to form or join a group. *TNT* is also a good source for purchasing a van, as is *Loot* newspaper and the Van Market in Market Rd, London N7, where private vendors congregate on a daily basis. Some second-hand dealers offer a 'buy-back' scheme for when you return from the Continent, but buying and re-selling privately should be more advantageous if you have the time.

Camper vans usually feature a fixed high-top or elevating roof and two to five bunk beds. Apart from the essential camping gas cooker, professional conversions may include a sink, fridge and built-in cupboards. You will need to spend at least £1000 to £1500 (US$1500 to US$2250) for something reliable enough to get you around Europe. An eternal favourite for budget travellers is the VW Kombi; they aren't made any more, but the old ones seem to go on forever and getting spare parts isn't a problem. Once on the road you should be able to keep budgets lower than backpackers using trains, but don't forget to set some money aside for emergency repairs.

The main advantage of going by camper van is flexibility: with transport, eating and sleeping requirements all taken care of in one unit, you are tied to nobody's timetable but your own.

A disadvantage is that you are in a confined space for much of the time. Four adults in a small van can soon get on each other's nerves, particularly if the group has been formed at short notice. Tensions can be minimised if you agree on daily routines and itineraries before setting off, eg travelling 250 km per day as a sensible maximum.

Other disadvantages of camper vans are that they're not very manoeuvrable around town, and you'll often have to leave your bags unattended inside (many people bolt extra locks onto the van). They're also expensive to buy in spring and hard to sell in autumn. As an alternative, consider a car and tent. Remember, too, that by travelling, sleeping and even eating in the self-contained little 'world' of a van, you'll be missing a lot of the outside.

Motorbike Touring

Central Europe is made for motorbike touring, with winding roads of decent quality, stunning scenery to stimulate the senses and an active motorcycling scene. Just make sure your wet-weather gear is up to scratch.

The wearing of crash helmets for riders and passengers is compulsory everywhere in Central Europe. Austria, Germany and Hungary also require that motorcyclists use headlights during the day; in other countries it is recommended.

On ferries, motorcyclists rarely have to book ahead as they can generally be squeezed in. Take note of the local attitude about parking motorbikes on pavements (sidewalks). Though this is illegal in some countries, the police usually turn a blind eye so long as the vehicle doesn't obstruct pedestrians.

Anyone considering a motorbike tour from the UK might benefit from joining the International Motorcyclists Tour Club (£19 per annum plus £3 joining fee). It organises European (and worldwide) biking jaunts, and members regularly meet to swap information. Contact Ken Brady, Membership Secretary, Cornerways, Chapel Rd, Swanmore, Southampton SO3 2QA, UK.

Fuel

Fuel prices can vary enormously from country to country and may bear little relation to the general cost of living there; expensive Switzerland is fairly cheap when it comes to fuel, for example, while the opposite is true in inexpensive Hungary. Savings can therefore be made if you fill up in the right place – in Poland, for example, before heading for Germany. Motoring organisations (such as the RAC, which supplied this data) can give more details.

Unleaded petrol of 95 octane is now widely available throughout Central Europe (though not always at stations on back roads) and is usually slightly cheaper than super (premium grade). Look for the pump with green markings and the word *Bleifrei*, German for unleaded. Diesel is usually significantly cheaper in Central Europe, though the difference is only marginal in Switzerland.

BICYCLE

A tour of Central Europe by bike may seem a daunting prospect, but one organisation that can help is the Cyclists' Touring Club (CTC, ☎ 01483-417 217), Cotterell House, 69 Meadrow, Godalming, Surrey GU7 3HS, UK. It can supply information to members on cycling conditions throughout Europe as well as detailed routes, itineraries and cheap insurance. Membership costs £24 per annum or £12 for those under 18 years of age.

A worthwhile book is *Europe by Bike*, by Karen & Terry Whitehall, a paperback available in the USA or selected outlets in the UK. It has good descriptions of 18 cycling tours of up to 19 days' duration, although city information is often inaccurate.

A primary consideration on a cycling tour is to travel light, but you should take a few tools and spares including a puncture repair kit and a spare inner tube. Panniers are essential to balance your possessions on either side of the bike frame. A bike helmet is also a very good idea. Take a good bike lock and always use it when you leave your bicycle unattended.

Seasoned cyclists can average 80 km a day, but there's no point in overdoing it. The slower you travel, the more local people you're likely to meet. If you get weary of pedalling or simply want to skip a boring section (like Hungary's Great Plain), you can put your feet up on the train. On slower trains, bikes can usually be taken on board as luggage, subject to a small supplementary fee. Fast trains (IC, EC etc) can rarely accommodate bikes: they need to be sent as registered luggage and may end up on a different train from the one you take. British Rail is not part of the European luggage registration scheme, so you would have to get to the Continent before you could send your bike in this way.

For more information on cycling, see the Activities sections in the earlier Facts for the Visitor chapter and in the individual country chapters.

Rental

It is easy to hire bikes in the western half of Central Europe on a half-day, daily or weekly basis, and sometimes it is possible to return the machine at a different outlet so you don't have to double back. It is very difficult to rent bikes (and most anything else) in Hungary, Poland, the Czech Republic and Slovakia; your best bets are camping grounds and resort hotels in season. Many train stations in Central Europe, including some in Hungary, have bike-rental counters, some of which are open 24 hours a day. See the country chapters for more details.

Bringing Your Own

If you want to bring your own bicycle along, you should be able to take it on the plane relatively easily. You can either take it to pieces and pack everything in a bike bag or box or simply wheel it to the check-in desk, where it should be treated as a piece of baggage. You may have to remove the pedals and turn the handlebars sideways so that it takes up less space in the aircraft's hold; check all this with the airline well in advance, preferably before you pay for your ticket. If your bicycle and other luggage exceed the allowable weight limit, ask about alternatives or you may suddenly find yourself being charged a fortune for excess baggage.

HITCHING

Hitching is never entirely safe in any country in the world, and we don't recommend it. Travellers who decide to hitch should understand that they are taking a small but potentially serious risk. People who do choose to hitch will be safer if they travel in pairs and let someone know where they are planning to go.

Hitching can be the most rewarding and frustrating way of getting around. It's rewarding because you get to meet and interact with local people and are forced into unplanned detours that may yield unexpected treasures off the beaten track. But it can also be very frustrating when you may get stuck on the side of the road to nowhere with nowhere (or nowhere cheap) to stay. Then it begins to rain...

That said, hitchers can end up making good time, but obviously you need to make your plans very flexible. A man and woman travelling together is probably the best combination. Two or more men must expect some delays; two women together will make good time and should be relatively safe. A woman hitching on her own is taking a big risk just about anywhere nowadays.

Don't try to hitch from city centres: take public transport to suburban exit routes. Hitching is usually illegal on motorways (freeways); stand on the slip roads or approach drivers at petrol stations and truck stops. Look presentable and cheerful and make a cardboard sign indicating your intended destination in the local language. Never hitch where drivers can't stop in good time or without causing an obstruction. At dusk, give up and think about finding somewhere to stay. If your itinerary includes a ferry crossing, it might be worth trying to score a ride before the ferry rather than after, since vehicle tickets sometimes include a number of passengers free of charge.

Dedicated hitchers may wish to invest in *Europe – a Manual for Hitch-hikers* by Simon Calder (paperback), even though it's getting a bit old now.

Hitching conditions vary from country to country in Central Europe. They are excellent in Germany, good in the Czech Republic and Austria, only so-so in Hungary. You can count on rides in Switzerland but only from foreigners; the Swiss themselves don't like hitching. Hitchhiking is a way of life in Slovakia and Poland so expect competition (and don't be surprised if a Polish driver asks you for payment).

It is sometimes possible to arrange a lift in

advance: scan student notice boards in colleges or contact car-sharing agencies. Such agencies, for whose services you pay a fee, are particularly popular in Germany and Austria (where they're called Mitfahrzentrale) and in Poland (through PTTK tourist offices), and there's a service in Budapest called Kenguru that matches up drivers and riders. See the relevant country chapters.

WALKING

Most city centres in Central Europe are compact enough to allow you to see most things of interest on a walking tour, but walking really comes into its own in rural areas. Hikes are an excellent way to leave behind the wail of car horns, opaque logic of train schedules and air pollution. For more information, see the Activities section in the earlier Facts for the Visitor chapter, as well as the individual country chapters.

BOAT

Though there are plenty of ferries linking Poland and Germany with Scandinavia and even one between Germany and the UK (see Sea in the Getting There & Away chapter), the only inter-country sea crossing in Central Europe is the Weisse Flotte boat in summer between Sassnitz on eastern Germany's Rügen Island and Świnoujście in Poland. From April to October, Weisse Flotte boats also ply the Baltic coastline of eastern Germany. See that chapter for details.

Some of Central Europe's lakes and rivers are serviced by steamers and ferries; not surprisingly, schedules are more extensive in the summer months. Rail-pass holders are entitled to some discounts (see the earlier Train section). In most cases, extended boat trips should be considered as relaxing and scenic excursions; viewed merely as a functional means of transport, they can be grotesquely expensive. The hydrofoil between Vienna and Budapest costs US$65 one way compared with a train or a bus fare of US$25, for example.

It is possible to take a cruise up the Rhine all the way from the Netherlands to Switzerland, but you'll need a boatload of money to do so. The main operator along the Rhine is the German Köln-Düsseldorfer (KD) Line, (☎ 0221-2 08 82 88) based in Cologne. In Hungary, getting out on the water for the day is cheap and easy: local river ferries link Budapest with the picturesque towns of the Danube Bend to the north and ferries serve all of the built-up areas on Balaton Lake. In Poland, some cities on the Vistula offer river trips in their vicinity. See the relevant country chapters for details.

TOURS

A package tour is really worth considering only if your time is very limited or you have a special interest such as canoeing, birdwatching, bicycling, rock climbing etc. Tailor-made tours of Central Europe abound; see your travel agent or look under Special Interests in the small ads in newspaper travel pages. Specialists in Britain include Ramblers Holidays (☎ 01707-331 133) for walkers and Discover the World (☎ 016977-48 361) for wilderness and wildlife holidays.

Young revellers can take bus tours based on hotel or camping accommodation. Operators include Contiki (☎ 0181-290 6422) and Tracks (☎ 0171-937 3028). Top Deck (☎ 0171-370 6487) has the added novelty of tours where you travel and sleep in a converted double-decker bus; its 16-day Highlights of Europe trip costs £379, plus food fund. Student or youth travel agencies in other countries have similar deals. In the UK, New Millennium Holidays (☎ 0121-711 2232), 20 High St, Solihull, West Midlands B91 3TB, runs inexpensive bus tours year-round to several Central European countries, including Poland, Hungary, the Czech Republic and Slovakia. Another British company specialising in travel to some parts of Central Europe is Regent Holidays (☎ 0117-921 1711), 15 John St, Bristol BS1 2HR.

For people over 60 years of age, Saga Holidays (☎ 01800-300 500), Saga Building, Middelburg Square, Folkstone, Kent CT20 1AZ, UK, offers holidays ranging from cheap coach tours to luxury cruises. Saga also operates in the USA as Saga International Holidays (☎ 800-343 0272), 120 Boylston St, Boston, MA 02116. Also in the USA, Goulash Tours (☎ 616-349 8817), PO Box 2972, Kalamazoo, MI 49003, offers several bicycling tours of Central Europe each summer. Participants must bring their own bicycle and equipment.

National tourist offices in most countries offer organised trips to points of interest. These may range from one-hour city tours to several-day circular excursions. They often work out more expensive than going it alone but can be worth it if you are pressed for time. A short city tour will give you a quick overview of the place and can be a good way to begin your visit.

Austria

Austria (Österreich) is situated at the crossroads of Europe. In the heady days of the Habsburgs, its empire encompassed both east and west. This foot-in-both-doors status has served Austria well, enabling it to bring its strong trading links with the East into the European Union, the capitalist club of the West.

The country thrives on tourism, and is one of the most popular destinations in Europe. Its rich cultural heritage, historic cities, winter sports and stunning scenery are a hard combination to beat. Its capital, Vienna, is one of the world's great cities; Salzburg is a living, baroque museum; and Innsbruck is dramatically situated in a perfect panorama of peaks. And everywhere you go, the country moves to the rhythm of its unrivalled musical tradition.

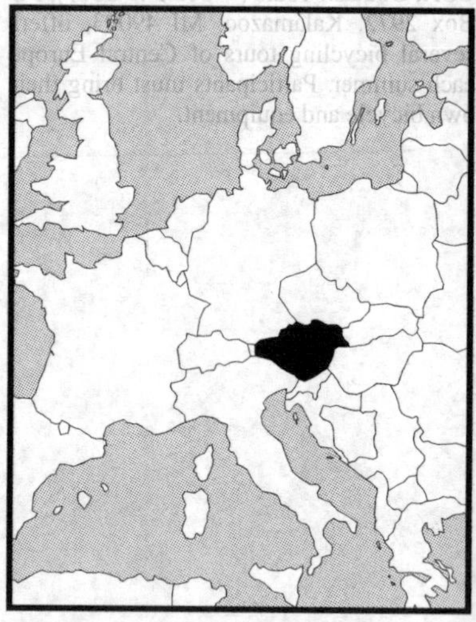

Facts about the Country

HISTORY

In its early years, the land that became Austria was invaded by a succession of tribes and armies using the Danube Valley as a conduit – the Celts, Romans, Vandals, Visigoths, Huns, Avars and Slavs all came and went. Charlemagne established a territory in the Danube Valley known as the Ostmark in 803, and the area became Christianised and predominantly Germanic. Ostmark was undermined by invading Magyars but re-established by Otto I in 955. In 962, Pope John XII crowned Otto as Holy Roman Emperor of the German princes.

A period of growth and prosperity followed under the reign of the House of Babenberg, and the territory acquired the status of a duchy in 1156. Influence in what is now Lower Austria expanded and the duchy of Styria came under central control in 1192. The last Babenberg died in battle in 1246 without an heir. The future of the duchy was uncertain until, in 1278, it fell into the hands of the Habsburgs, who ruled Austria until WW I.

The Habsburg Dynasty

Austrian territory gradually expanded under the rule of the Habsburgs. Carinthia (Kärnten) and Carniola were annexed in 1335, followed by Tirol in 1363. However, the Habsburgs preferred to extend their territory without force. Much of Vorarlberg, for example, was purchased from bankrupt lords and significant gains were achieved by politically motivated marriages. Intermarriage was extremely effective, although it did have a genetic side-effect: a distended lower jaw became an increasingly visible family trait, albeit discreetly ignored in official portraits.

In 1477, Maximilian gained control of Burgundy and the Netherlands by marriage to Maria of Burgundy. His eldest son, Philip, was married to the infanta of Spain in 1496. In 1516, Philip's son became Charles I of

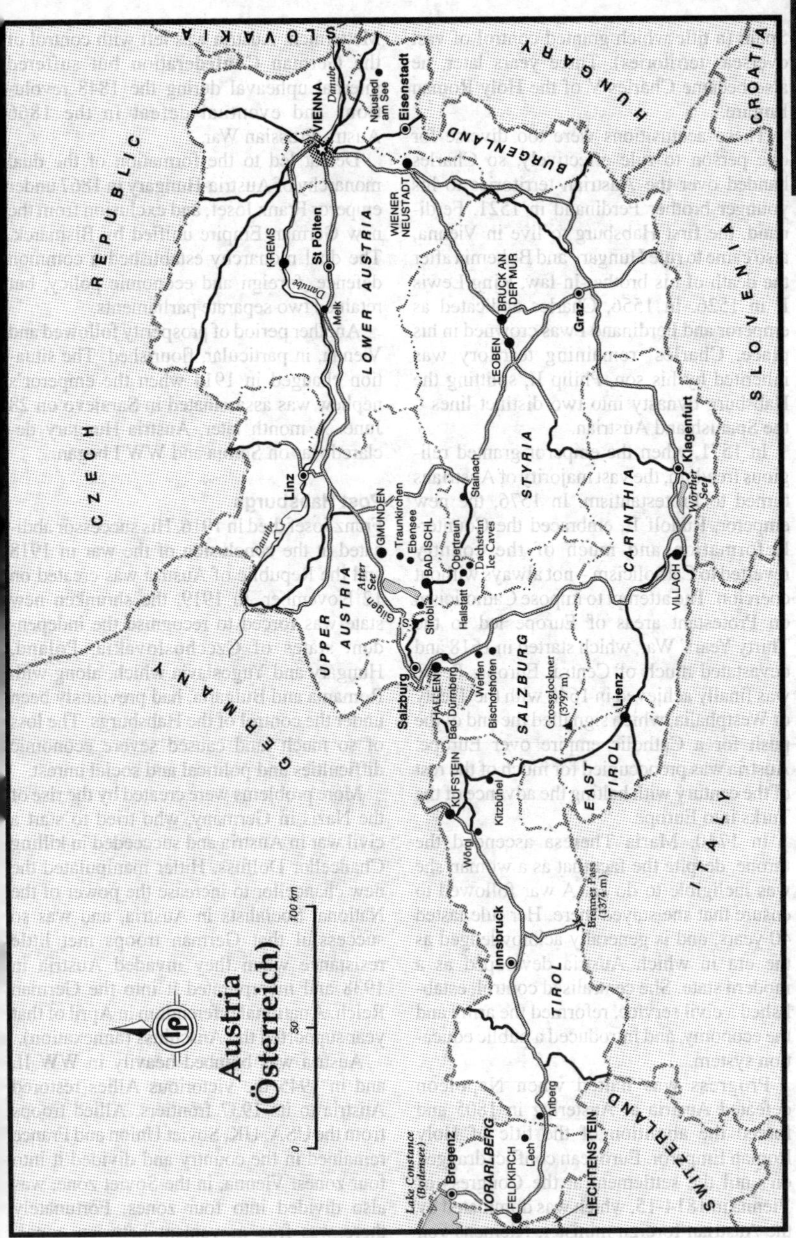
Austria
(Österreich)
0
50
100 km
CZECH
REPUBLIC
SLOVAKIA
GERMANY
HUNGARY
SLOVENIA
CROATIA
ITALY
SWITZERLAND
LIECHTENSTEIN
VORARLBERG
TIROL
EAST TIROL
SALZBURG
UPPER AUSTRIA
LOWER AUSTRIA
BURGENLAND
STYRIA
CARINTHIA
VIENNA
Danube
Neusiedl am See
Eisenstadt
WIENER NEUSTADT
St Pölten
KREMS
Melk
Linz
GMUNDEN
Traunkirchen
Ebensee
BAD ISCHL
Obertraun
Dachstein Ice Caves
Hallstatt
Strobl
St Gilgen
Atter See
Salzburg
HALLEIN
Bad Dürrnberg
Werfen
Bischofshofen
Grossglockner (3797 m)
Stainach
LEOBEN
BRUCK AN DER MUR
Graz
Klagenfurt
Wörther See
VILLACH
Lienz
KUFSTEIN
Kitzbühel
Wörgl
Innsbruck
Brenner Pass (1374 m)
Arlberg
Lech
FELDKIRCH
Bregenz
Lake Constance (Bodensee)

Spain (a title which granted control of vast overseas territories). Three years later, he also became Charles V of the Holy Roman Empire.

These acquisitions were too diverse for one person to rule effectively, so Charles handed over the Austrian territories to his younger brother Ferdinand in 1521. Ferdinand, the first Habsburg to live in Vienna, also came to rule Hungary and Bohemia after the death of his brother-in-law, King Lewis II in 1526. In 1556, Charles abdicated as emperor and Ferdinand I was crowned in his place. Charles' remaining territory was inherited by his son, Philip II, splitting the Habsburg dynasty into two distinct lines – the Spanish and Austrian.

In 1571, when the emperor granted religious freedom, the vast majority of Austrians turned to Protestantism. In 1576, the new emperor, Rudolf II, embraced the Counter-Reformation and much of the country reverted to Catholicism – not always without coercion. The attempt to impose Catholicism on Protestant areas of Europe led to the Thirty Years' War, which started in 1618 and devastated much of Central Europe. Peace was finally achieved in 1648 with the Treaty of Westphalia, which signalled the end of the push for a Catholic empire over Europe. Austria was preoccupied for much of the rest of the century with halting the advance of the Turks into Europe.

In 1740, Maria Theresa ascended the throne, despite the fact that as a woman she was ineligible to do so. A war followed to ensure that she stayed there. Her rule lasted 40 years, and is generally acknowledged as the era in which Austria developed as a modern state. She centralised control, established a civil service, reformed the army and the economy, and introduced a public education system.

Progress was halted when Napoleon defeated Austria at Austerlitz in 1805 and forced the abolition of the title of Holy Roman Emperor. European conflict dragged on until the settlement at the Congress of Vienna in 1814-15, which was dominated by the Austrian foreign minister, Klemens von Metternich. Austria was left with control of the German Confederation but suffered internal upheaval during the 1848 revolutions and eventual defeat in the 1866 Austro-Prussian War.

Defeat led to the formation of the dual monarchy of Austria-Hungary in 1867 under emperor Franz Josef, and exclusion from the new German Empire unified by Bismarck. The dual monarchy established a common defence, foreign and economic policy, but retained two separate parliaments.

Another period of prosperity followed and Vienna, in particular, flourished. The situation changed in 1914 when the emperor's nephew was assassinated in Sarajevo on 28 June. A month later, Austria-Hungary declared war on Serbia and WW I began.

Post Habsburgs

Franz Josef died in 1916. His successor abdicated at the conclusion of the war in 1918 and the Republic of Austria was created on 12 November. In 1919, the shrunken new state was forced to recognise the independent states of Czechoslovakia, Poland, Hungary and Yugoslavia which, along with Romania and Bulgaria, had previously been under the control of the Habsburgs. The loss of so much land caused severe economic difficulties and political and social unrest.

More problems were created by the rise of the Nazis in Germany, who tried to start a civil war in Austria and succeeded in killing Chancellor Dolfuss. Hitler manipulated the new chancellor to increase the power of the National Socialists in Austria, and was so successful that German troops met little resistance when they invaded Austria in 1938 and incorporated it into the German Reich. A national referendum in April of that year supported the Anschluss (annexation).

Austria was bombed heavily in WW II, and in 1945 the victorious Allies restored Austria to its 1937 frontiers. Allied troops from the USA, UK, Soviet Union and France remained in the country and divided it into four zones. Vienna, in the Soviet zone, was also divided into four zones. Fortunately there was free movement between zones, which allowed Vienna to escape the fate that eventually befell Berlin. The ratification of the Austrian State Treaty and the withdrawal of the occupying powers was not completed until 1955, when Austria proclaimed its neutrality and agreed not to confederate with Germany.

Since WW II, Austria has worked hard to overcome economic difficulties. It established a free trade treaty with the European Union (EU; then known as the EC) in 1972, and full membership was applied for in July 1989. Terms of membership were agreed early in 1994, and the Austrian people endorsed Austria's entry in a referendum on 12 June 1994; a resounding 66.4% were in favour. If the timetable is kept to, Austria will be part of the union on 1 January 1995.

GEOGRAPHY

Austria occupies an area of 83,855 sq km, extending for 560 km from west to east, and 280 km from north to south. Two-thirds of the country is mountainous, with three chains running west to east. The Northern Limestone Alps reach nearly 3000 metres. They are separated from the High or Central Alps, which form the highest peaks in Austria, by the valley of the River Inn. Many of the ridges in the Central Alps are topped by glaciers and most of the peaks are above 3000 metres, making north-south travel difficult. The Grossglockner is the highest peak at 3797 metres. The Southern Limestone Alps form a natural barrier along the border with Italy.

The most fertile land is in the Danube Valley, bordered by the Vienna basin, Salzburg and Linz. Cultivation is intensive and 90% of Austria's food is home-grown. North of Linz is an area of forested hills. The only other relatively flat area is south-east of Graz.

GOVERNMENT

The head of state is the president, who is chosen by the electorate for a six-year term. Austria's international image suffered following the election in 1986 of President Kurt Waldheim, who, it was revealed, served in a German Wehrmacht unit that was implicated in WW II war crimes. In 1992, he was succeeded by Thomas Klestil, who, like Waldheim, was a candidate of the right-wing Austrian People's Party (ÖVP).

The country is divided into nine federal provinces (Bundesländer), each with its own head of government (Landeshauptmann) and provincial assembly (Landtag). Each provincial assembly has a degree of autonomy over local issues and elects representatives to the Federal Council (Bundesrat), the upper house of the national legislative body. The lower house, the National Council (Nationalrat), is elected every four years by voters over the age of 18.

The chancellor, appointed by the president, is the head of the federal government and the most influential political figure. Franz Vranitzky has been chancellor since 1986.

The 1970s saw the dominance of the Socialist Party, now called the Social Democrats (SPÖ). In the 1990 election, the SPÖ formed a ruling coalition with the ÖVP. This coalition was expected to retain power in the October 1994 general election.

ECONOMY

Austria is poor in natural resources. Deposits of oil and natural gas are supplemented by hydroelectric power and imported coal. Agriculture employs 10% of the population and forestry 25%. The main exports are machinery, metallurgical products and textiles. Austria generally has a trade deficit in visible earnings, which is offset by income from tourism.

The economy is bolstered by a large contingent of foreign labour, particularly from Eastern Europe. There is a large nationalised sector, though Austria has caught the privatisation bug from its European neighbours. Wide-ranging welfare services include free education and medicine (for locals), good pensions and a benign housing policy. Austria came through the 1990s recession virtually unscathed: estimated figures for 1994 put unemployment under 5% and inflation under 3%.

POPULATION & PEOPLE

Austria has a population of 7,834,000; Vienna accounts for 1.5 million, followed by Graz (238,000), Linz (203,000), Salzburg (144,000), and Innsbruck (118,000). On average, there are 94 inhabitants per sq km. Native Austrians are almost entirely of Germanic origin.

ARTS

Austria is renowned for its musical heritage. Composers throughout Europe were drawn to Austria in the 18th and 19th centuries by the willingness of the Habsburgs to patronise music. The various forms of classical music – symphony, concerto, sonata, opera and operetta – were developed and explored in Austria by the most eminent exponents of the day. The waltz originated in Vienna in the 19th century and was perfected as a musical genre by Johann Strauss senior and junior. The musical tradition continued in the 20th century with the innovative work of Arnold Schönberg. Today, Austrian orchestras have a worldwide reputation, and important annual musical festivals are held in Vienna, Salzburg and Graz.

Architecture is another important part of Austria's cultural heritage. The Gothic style was popular in the 14th, 15th and 16th centuries. The next major stylistic influence was baroque. Learning from the Italian model, Fischer von Erlach developed a national style called Austrian baroque, typified in the National Library and the Church of St Charles in Vienna.

CULTURE

Traditional Lifestyle

Traditional costumes are still worn in rural areas of Tirol, but you're more likely to see local costumes during celebrations and processions. Typical dress for men is shorts with wide braces, and jackets without collars or lapels. The best known form of dress for women is the Dirndl: pleated skirt, apron, and white, pleated corsage with full sleeves.

Many festivals act out ancient traditions, such as welcoming the spring with painted masks and the ringing of bells. The departure of herders and cattle to high alpine pastures in early summer and their return in autumn are the cause of much jollity in village life.

Avoiding Offence

It is customary to greet people, even shop assistants, with the salute *Grüss Gott*. Austrians tend to dress up when going to the opera or theatre, so jeans and trainers may be tolerated, but they won't be appreciated. Attitudes to homosexuality are less tolerant than in most other European countries.

RELIGION

Roman Catholicism is embraced by 90% of the population; most of the rest are Protestants, who are mainly concentrated in Burgenland and Carinthia. Religion plays an important part in the lives of many Austrians. It is not unusual to see small, roadside shrines decorated with fresh flowers.

LANGUAGE

Austrians speak German, although in the eastern province of Burgenland about 25,000 people speak Croatian, and in the southern province of Carinthia about 20,000 people speak Slovene. See the Germany chapter for German words and phrases.

English is widely understood in the main cities and tourist resorts. In smaller towns, hotel and railway staff usually know some English, but don't bank on it. Knowledge of some German phrases would be an asset and would be appreciated by locals.

Facts for the Visitor

VISAS & EMBASSIES

Austria's entry to the EU may alter entry requirements, so double-check before travelling. Visas are not required for EU, US, Canadian, Australian or New Zealand citizens. Visitors may stay a maximum of three months, although passports rarely receive an entry stamp. British and Japanese nationals may stay six months. Some Third World and Arab nationals require a visa.

Austrian Embassies Abroad

Australia
: 12 Talbot St, Forrest, Canberra, ACT 2603 (☎ 06-295 1376)

Canada
: 445 Wilbrod St, Ottawa, Ont KIN 6M7 (☎ 613-789 1444)

New Zealand
: Austrian Consulate, 22-4 Garrett St, Wellington (☎ 04-801 9709) – does not issue visas or passports; contact the Australian office for these services

UK
: 18 Belgrave Mews West, London SW1 8HU (☎ 0171-235 3731)

USA
: 3524 International Court NW, Washington, DC 20008 (☎ 202-895 6700 4474)

Foreign Embassies in Austria

The following is a list of foreign consulates and embassies in Vienna. Note that there are also foreign consulates in Salzburg and Innsbruck; see those sections for details. New Zealand has an embassy in Bonn, Germany, at Bundeskanzlerplatz 2-10, 5300 Bonn 1 (☎ 0228-22 80 70).

Australia
: 4 Mattiellistrasse 2-4 (☎ 0222-512 85 80)

Canada
: 1 Laurenzerberg (☎ 0222-533 36 912

Czech Republic
: 14 Penzingerstrasse 11-13 (☎ 0222-894 37 41)

Hungary
: 1 Bankgasse 4-6 (☎ 0222-533 26 31)

Slovakia
: 19 Armbrustergasse 24 (☎ 0222-37 13 09)

UK
: 3 Jauresgasse 12 (☎ 0222-713 15 75)

USA
: 9 Boltzmanngasse 16 (☎ 0222-313 39)

CUSTOMS

You can bring either 200 cigarettes, 50 cigars or 250 grams of tobacco if you arrive from another European country; the limits are doubled if you arrive from anywhere else. The alcohol allowance is 2.25 litres of wine and one litre of spirits, regardless of where you come from. Tobacco and alcohol may only be imported by those aged 17 or over. However, check these limitations because they are likely to change with Austria's entry into the EU.

MONEY

Currency

The Austrian Schilling (AS, or *ÖS* in German) is divided into 100 Groschen. There are coins to the value of one, five, 10, 25, 50, 100 and 500 Schilling, and for two, five, 10 and 50 Groschen. Banknotes come in denominations of AS20, AS50, AS100, AS500, AS1000 and AS5000. Visa, MasterCard, American Express and Diners Club credit cards are equally acceptable, although a surprising number of shops and restaurants refuse to accept any credit cards at all.

Exchange rates and commission charges can vary between banks, so it pays to shop around. Changing cash attracts a negligible commission, but the exchange rate is between 1% and 4% lower than that offered for travellers' cheques. American Express offices have good rates and the lowest commission charges on their own travellers' cheques (from AS40). The post office charges AS60 commission on up to four cheques, but does not charge commission for cash. Train stations charge AS64 minimum for cheques and about AS20 for cash. Banks charge from AS45 to AS90. Avoid changing a lot of low-value cheques because commission costs will be higher. American Express and Thomas Cook are the best known travellers' cheques. Perhaps the most efficient way to manage your money in Austria is to get cash advances with a Visa card, Eurocard or MasterCard; there are numerous Bankomat machines offering this service.

An international money order is the cheapest way to send money to Austria, although a direct transfer of funds through a bank is possible. There's no charge at the Austrian end to receive an American Express Moneygram.

Exchange Rates

A$1	=	AS8.20
C$1	=	AS8.45
DM1	=	AS6.90

NZ$1	=	AS6.55
Sfr1	=	AS8.10
UK£1	=	AS17.40
US$1	=	AS11.55

Costs
Austria can be reasonably cheap if you keep away from the big cities and main tourist resorts. Budget travellers can get by on AS250 to AS300 a day, after rail card costs; double this if you want to avoid self-catering or staying in hostels. Prices are fixed, so bargaining for goods is not generally an option.

Tipping
It is customary to tip an extra 5% or 10% in restaurants if the service has been good; taxi drivers will expect tips of 10%.

Consumer Taxes
Ice cream, coffee and alcoholic drinks are expensive because they're subject to a refreshment tax on top of the inevitable value-added tax (VAT), called the *Mehrwertsteuer* (MWST). Prices are always displayed inclusive of all taxes.

For purchases over AS1000 in 'Tax Free' shops, the MWST can be reclaimed – either when you leave Austria or afterwards. A U-34 form must be filled out at the time of purchase and presented to customs on departure. The form will be signed and stamped. The airports at Vienna, Salzburg, Innsbruck, Linz and Graz have counters for instant refunds, as do some land crossings, or you can reclaim by post. Austria's entry to the EU will exclude EU citizens from this benefit.

CLIMATE & WHEN TO GO
Austria's temperatures vary according to altitude. Average rainfall is 71 cm per year. Maximum temperatures in Vienna are: January 1°C, April 10°C, July 20°C and October 10°C. Minimum temperatures are lower by about 10°C (summer) to 4°C (winter). Salzburg and Innsbruck match the maximum temperature of Vienna, but average minimum temperatures are a couple of degrees lower. Some people find the *Föhn*, a hot, dry wind which sweeps down from the mountains, rather uncomfortable. Summer sightseeing and winter sports make Austria a year-round destination, but the high season is in July and August and (in ski resorts) Christmas to late February.

WHAT TO BRING
Pack warm clothing for nights at high altitude. Sheets are usually included in hostel prices; occasionally you can save the 'sheet charge' if you have your own.

SUGGESTED ITINERARIES
Depending on the length of your stay, you might want to see and do the following things:

Two days
: Vienna – see the central sights and visit the Opera and a few *Heurigen* (wine taverns).

One week
: Spend four days in Vienna, two days in Salzburg and one day visiting the Salzkammergut lakes.

Two weeks
: Spend five days in Vienna, three days in Salzburg (with a day trip to the Wergen ice caves and fortress), two days at the Salzkammergut lakes, two days in Innsbruck and two days at a ski resort.

One month
: Visit the same places as the two-week scenario at a more leisurely pace, and add a tour of the south, taking in Graz, Klagenfurt and Lienz.

Two months
: Visit all the places mentioned in this chapter.

TOURIST OFFICES
Local tourist offices (called *Verkehrsverein* or *Verkehrsamt*) are efficient and helpful. A centrally situated office can be found in any town or village that tourists are likely to visit, and at least one of the staff will speak English. Most offices have a room-finding service, often without commission. Maps are always available and usually free. Each region has a provincial tourist board.

Tourist Offices Abroad
Austrian National Tourist Office (ANTO) branches abroad include:

MARY BEERS

Australia
1st floor, 36 Carrington St, Sydney, NSW 2000 (☎ 02-299 3621)
Canada
2 Bloor St East, suite 3330, Toronto, Ont M4W 1A8 (☎ 416-9673 381)
UK
30 St George St, London W1R OAL (☎ 0171-629 0461)
USA
500 Fifth Ave, suite 2009-2022, New York, NY 10110 (☎ 212-944 6880)

There are also tourist offices in Los Angeles, Milan, Montreal, Munich, Paris, Rome and Zürich. New Zealanders can get information from the Austrian consulate in Wellington (see the Austrian Embassies Abroad section).

USEFUL ORGANISATIONS

The following organisations might prove useful (the code for Vienna numbers is '1' if calling from outside Austria):

Austrian Youth Hostel Association
(Österreichischer Jugendherbergsverband) – Gonzagagasse 22 or Schottenring 28 (the office is on the corner of the two), A-1010 Vienna (☎ 0222-533 53 53)
Austrian Camping Club
(Österreichischer Camping Club) – An der Au, A-3400 Klosterneuburg (☎ 02243-85 877)
Austrian Automobile Club
(Österreichischer Automobil, Motorrad und Touring Club, ÖAMTC) – Schubertring 1-3, A-1010 Vienna (☎ 0222-71 19 90; dial 120 for emergency assistance)
Austrian Alpine Club
(Österreichischer Alpenverein, ÖAV) – Wilhelm-Greil-Strasse 15, A-6010 Innsbruck (☎ 0512-58 78 28)

BUSINESS HOURS & HOLIDAYS

Shops are open Monday to Friday from 8 am to 6.30 pm, and from 8 am to 1 pm on Saturdays (until 5 pm on the first Saturday in the month). They generally close for up to two hours at noon (except in big cities), and sometimes on Wednesday afternoon too. Banking hours vary but are commonly Monday to Friday from 9 am to 12.30 pm and 1.30 to 3 pm, with late closing on Thursday. Public holidays are 1 and 6 January, Easter Monday, 1 May, Ascension Day, Whit Monday, Corpus Christi, 15 August, 26 October, 1 November, and 8, 25 and 26 December.

CULTURAL EVENTS

Most events are small-scale local affairs, so it's worth checking with local tourist offices. The national tourist office compiles an updated list of annual and one-off events. Vienna has almost continuous music festivals. Salzburg has both an Easter festival and one of Austria's most important music festivals, which lasts from the end of July to the end of August. Linz has the Bruckner Festival in September.

There are fairs in Vienna, Innsbruck and Graz in September. General celebrations take place at New Year and on religious holidays, when you can expect colourful processions. Look out for *Fasching* (Shrovetide carnival) week in early February, maypoles on 1 May, midsummer night's celebrations on 21 June, the autumn cattle roundup at the end of October, much flag-waving on national day on 26 October and also St Nicholas Day parades on 5 and 6 December.

POST

Post office hours vary: typical hours are Monday to Friday from 8 am to noon and 2 to 6 pm (money exchange to 5 pm), and Saturday from 8 to 11 am, but a few main post offices in big cities are open 24 hours. Stamps are also available in tobacco *(Tabak)* shops.

Postcards and letters within Austria cost AS5.50 and AS6 respectively. To other countries in Europe, they cost AS6 and AS7; elsewhere the cost is AS7 and AS10. Sending letters or postcards by airmail *(Flugpost)* incurs a surcharge.

Poste restante is *Postlagernde Briefe* in German. Mail can be sent care of any post office and is held for a month; a passport must be shown to collect mail. American Express will also hold mail for a month for customers who have its card or cheques.

TELEPHONE

Telephone calls are expensive, although just AS1 will get you connected. Calls within Austria are 33% cheaper on weekends and between 6 pm and 8 am on weekdays.

On long-distance calls you're charged at the local rate while you're waiting for the dialled party to pick up the receiver. International direct dialling is nearly always possible, otherwise you can dial ☎ 09 for the operator.

Post offices invariably have telephones. Be wary of using telephones in hotels, because they can cost up to twice as much as public pay phones. You can save money and avoid messing around with change by buying a phonecard *(Telefon-Wertkarte)*. For AS48 you get A50 worth of calls, and for AS95 and AS190 you gain AS5 and AS10 worth of free calls respectively.

Note: The Austrian telephone system is being upgraded; many numbers have already changed, others may change in the near future.

TIME

Austrian time is GMT/UTC plus one hour. If it's noon in Vienna it's 4 am in San Francisco, 7 am in New York and Toronto, 10 pm in Sydney and midnight in Auckland. Clocks go forward one hour on the last Saturday in March, and back an hour on the last Saturday in September.

ELECTRICITY

The current used is 220 V, 50 Hz, and the socket used is the round two-pin variety.

LAUNDRY

Look out for a *Wäscherei* for self-service or service washes. The minimum charge is around AS90 to wash and dry a load. Many hostels have cheaper laundry facilities.

WEIGHTS & MEASURES

The metric system is used. Like other Continental Europeans, Austrians indicate decimals with commas and thousands with points.

BOOKS & MAPS

A useful volume is *Mountain Walking in Austria* by Cecil Davies (paperback). *Off the Beaten Track 'Austria'* (various authors, paperback) concentrates on less well-known regions. The Insight Guides to Austria and Vienna are good for background information. Pocket guides to Vienna include those by Berlitz and AA Publishing. Graham Greene's famous spy story, *The Third Man* (Penguin, paperback), and John Irving's *Setting Free the Bears* (paperback) are both set in Austria.

Freytag & Berndt of Vienna publishes good maps in varying scales. Its 1:100,000 series and 1:50,000 blue series are popular with hikers. Extremely detailed maps are produced by the Austrian Alpine Club.

MEDIA

Austria Radio broadcasts the news in English daily at 8.05 am. The strongest signals are around 90 and 98 FM. Blue Danube Radio (92.9 and 103.8 FM) is a news and music station in English and French (news on the half-hour). English-language newspapers are widely available for AS25 to AS35.

FILM & PHOTOGRAPHY

The Niedermeyer chain store is about the cheapest place to buy film; a 36 exposure roll of film costs AS69 for Kodak Gold 100 and AS129 for Kodachrome 64. Note that slide film usually *excludes* mounting, and sometimes processing too.

HEALTH

No inoculations are required for entry. There is a charge for hospital treatment and consultations with doctors, so private medical insurance is advised. EU nationals can get free emergency treatment; enquire before leaving home about documentation required. Chemist shops *(Apotheken)* operate an out-of-hours service in rotation.

WOMEN TRAVELLERS

Women should experience no special problems. Attacks and verbal harassment are less common than in many countries. Austrian women do not enjoy equal social status to men in conservative areas, but this should not affect travellers.

DANGERS & ANNOYANCES

Dial ☎ 133 for the police, ☎ 144 for an ambulance, or ☎ 122 in the event of a fire. Take care in the mountains: helicopter rescue is expensive unless you are covered by insurance (that's assuming they find you in the first place). Austrian train stations are a habitual haunt of drunks and dropouts. They are sometimes annoying and occasionally intimidating.

WORK

EU nationals can work in Austria without a work permit. Everyone else must obtain a work permit and a residency permit in advance. In ski resorts, where there are often vacancies for jobs with unsociable hours, employers may be prepared to bend the rules. Check with tourist offices, because it might be possible to arrange a Volunteer Work Permit. Otherwise, you may be able to find casual work in return for free board and lodging and pocket money. Likely opportunities are in snow clearing, chalet cleaning, restaurants and ski equipment shops.

ACTIVITIES

Skiing

Skiing in Austria is generally slightly cheaper than in France or Switzerland. Vorarlberg and Tirol are the most popular areas, although there is also skiing in Salzburgerland, Upper Austria and Carinthia, where prices can be lower still. Equipment can always be hired at resorts. You may initially get some strange looks if you ask to buy ex-rental stock, but great bargains can be picked up this way. Also keep your eyes open for discarded equipment that may still be perfectly usable.

Ski coupons for ski lifts can sometimes be bought, but usually there are general passes available for complete or partial days. Count on at least AS240 for a day's ski pass, AS160 for downhill rental and AS90 for cross-country skiing. The skiing season starts in December and lasts well into April in higher resorts. Year-round skiing is possible at the Stubai Glacier near Innsbruck.

Hiking & Mountaineering

Walking and climbing are popular with visitors and locals alike. Mountain paths are marked with direction indicators, and most tourist offices have free maps of hiking routes. Mountaineering is also popular, but should not be undertaken without proper equipment and some previous experience. Tirol province has many mountain guides and mountaineering schools; these are listed in the *Mountains* booklet from the tourist office.

Spa Resorts

There are spa resorts throughout the country. They are identifiable by the prefix *Bad* (Bath); eg Bad Ischl. Leisurely long walks and much wallowing in hot springs are typical ingredients of these salubrious locations.

HIGHLIGHTS

Vienna is the Habsburgs' legacy to the world, offering awe-inspiring public buildings, art treasures culled from the old empire, and music, music, and more music – don't miss a trip to the opera. Salzburg is another shrine to music, and its baroque skyline is a breathtaking sight. A cruise on the not-quite-blue Danube is a must. Visits to the distinctive, provincial capitals of Innsbruck and Graz will be rewarded with interesting sights. Away from the cities, there are endless mountain views and hikes to enjoy. For skiing and glitz, head for Kitzbühel or Lech; for a more laid-back ambience, try St Anton.

ACCOMMODATION

Reservations are recommended in July and August and at the peak times of Christmas and Easter. Reservations are binding on either side and compensation may be claimed if you do not take a reserved room or if a reserved room is unavailable.

Prices are lower out of season. Assume

breakfast is *included* in places listed in this chapter, unless otherwise stated.

A cheap and widely available option is to take a room in a private house (AS120 to AS250 per person). Look out for *Zimmer frei* (room(s) available) signs. Tourist offices can supply listings of all types of accommodation, and often make reservations for little or no commission. Accommodation sometimes costs more for the first night's stay.

In many resorts (rarely in towns) a guest card is issued to people who stay overnight, though entitlement may depend on a minimum stay. The card offers various discounts on useful things such as cable cars. Check with the tourist office if you're not offered one at your resort accommodation.

Camping

There are over 400 camping grounds, but most close in the winter. They charge around AS30 to AS60 per person, plus the same again for a tent and for a car. Sleeping in camper vans is OK, except in urban and protected rural areas, as long as you don't set up camping equipment outside the van.

Alpine Huts

These are maintained by the Austrian Alpine Club. Members of the club take priority and are sometimes entitled to a discount. Huts are rarely full, however, and not too expensive. Most are situated between 900 and 2700 metres in hill-walking regions, and meals or cooking facilities are often available.

Hostels

Austria has an excellent network of private and HI-affiliated hostels. Membership cards are always required, except in a few private hostels. Nonmembers pay a surcharge of AS40 per night for a guest card; after six nights, the guest card counts as a full membership card. Most hostels accept reservations by telephone. Some hostels have a fax reservation service: you pay AS10 for the fax and AS105 deposit, which you get back when you claim your bed at the new hostel. Hostel prices are around AS110 to AS140. Youth hostel in German are *Jugendherberge*.

Hotels & Pensions

With very few exceptions, rooms are clean and adequately appointed. Expect to pay from AS220/380 for a single/double. In low-budget accommodation, a room with a private shower may mean a room with a shower cubicle rather than a proper *en suite* bathroom. Prices in major cities are significantly higher than in rural areas, particularly in Vienna. A small country inn *(Gasthaus)* or a guesthouse *(Pension)* tends to be more intimate than a hotel. Self-catering accommodation is available in ski resorts.

FOOD

The main meal is taken at midday. Most restaurants have a set meal or menu of the day *(Tagesteller* or *Tagesmenu)* which gives the best value for money. The cheapest deal around is in university restaurants *(mensas)*; these are only mentioned in the text if they are open to all. Wine cellars are fairly cheap places to eat, and some food shops have tables for customers to eat on the premises.

Soups are good, often with dumplings *(Knödel)* and pasta added. A great variety of sausages *(Würste)* are available. *Wiener Schnitzel* is a veal (occasionally pork) cutlet coated in breadcrumbs. Paprika is used to flavour several dishes including *Goulasch* (beef stew) and *Paprikahuhn* (paprika chicken). Look out for regional dishes such as *Tiroler Bauernschmaus*, a selection of meats served with sauerkraut, potatoes and dumplings. Austrians eat a lot of meat and vegetarians will have a fairly tough time finding suitable or varied dishes.

Famous desserts include the *Strudel* (baked dough filled with a variety of fruits) and *Salzburger Nockerl* (an egg, flour and sugar pudding); pancakes are also popular.

Hofer is the cheapest of the supermarket chains.

DRINKS

Nonalcoholic Drinks

Tea and coffee are expensive, but bottled

water isn't (tap water is fine to drink anyway). Apple juice (Apfelsaft) is widely available. Coffee houses are an established part of Austrian life, particularly in Vienna. Strong Turkish coffee is popular. Linger over a cup (from AS20) and read the free newspapers.

Alcohol

Eastern Austria specialises in producing white wines. *Österreichisches Weingütesiegel* on the label designates a wine of high quality, *Wein aus Österreich* is standard table wine. Wine bought by the carafe is cheaper. Austria is also famous for its beer, particularly lager. Some well-known brands include Gösser, Schwechater, Stiegl and Zipfer. Beer is usually served as a half litre or a 0.35 litre; in eastern Austria, these are respectively called a *Krügerl* and a *Seidel*.

ENTERTAINMENT

Late opening is common in the cities, and in Vienna you can party all night long. It isn't hard to find bars or taverns featuring traditional or rock music.

Some cinemas show films in their original language (advertising posters will state if the film is dubbed or subtitled).

The main season for opera, theatre and concerts is September to June. Cheap, standing-room tickets are often available shortly before performances begin and they represent excellent value.

Gamblers can indulge at a dozen casinos around the country, including in Vienna, Graz, Linz and Salzburg. The admission fee is AS210, but you are immediately presented with AS250 worth of gambling chips. Smart dress is required; opening hours are typically 3 pm to midnight or later.

THINGS TO BUY

Local crafts such as textiles, pottery, painted glassware, woodcarving and wrought-iron work make popular souvenirs.

Getting There & Away

AIR

The airports at Vienna, Linz, Graz, Salzburg, Innsbruck and Klagenfurt all receive international flights. Vienna is the busiest airport, with several daily, nonstop flights to major transport hubs such as Amsterdam, Berlin, Frankfurt, London, Paris and Zürich. There is no departure tax to pay at the airport when leaving Austria.

LAND

Bus

International bus connections to/from Austria are minimal, although Vienna does have some services to Eastern Europe – see the Vienna Getting There & Away section for details. A bus departs from London's Victoria Station at 8.30 am on Friday and Saturday and arrives in Vienna at 11.30 am the next morning (£99 return).

Train

Austria has excellent rail connections to all important destinations. Vienna is the main hub (see its Getting There & Away section for details). The train departing Vienna's Westbahnhof to Zürich at 9.25 pm is a sleeper service (AS1064; plus AS120 for a fold-down seat, AS280 for couchette). Salzburg has at least hourly trains to Munich (AS272) with onward connections north. Express services to Italy go via Innsbruck or Villach; trains to Slovenia are routed through Graz.

Reserving train seats in 2nd class within Austria (either on national IC or international EC trains) costs AS30; in 1st class, IC costs AS30, and EC AS50. Supplements sometimes apply on international trains.

Car & Motorbike

There are numerous entry points from the Czech Republic, Germany, Hungary, Italy, Slovakia, Slovenia, and Switzerland. Main border crossings are open 24 hours a day.

RIVER
Steamers and hydrofoils operate along the Danube in the summer. See the Vienna and Danube Valley sections for details.

Getting Around

AIR
Vienna has several flights a day to Graz, Klagenfurt and Innsbruck, and at least one a day to Salzburg and Linz. The main national carrier is Austrian Airlines, which has nonstop flights between most domestic airports. Check schedules because they vary according to the season.

BUS
The yellow postbus service backs up the rail network. It's complemented by orange buses run by Austrian Railways, but the distinction is not a significant one for the traveller. The term 'postbus' has been used throughout this chapter for convenience. Some rail routes are duplicated by buses, but buses generally operate in the more inaccessible mountainous regions. Buses are clean, efficient and on time. Advance reservations are possible, but sometimes you can only buy tickets from the drivers. Fares work out at around AS130 per 100 km.

TRAIN
Trains are efficient and frequent. The state network covers the whole country, and is supplemented by a few private lines. Eurail and Inter-Rail passes are valid on the former; enquire before embarking on the latter. Many stations have information centres where the staff speak English. Tickets can be purchased on the train, but they cost around AS10 extra. In this chapter, fares quoted are for 2nd class.

Trains are expensive (eg AS156 for 100 km, AS276 for 200 km) but the cost can be reduced by special passes. The *Bundes-Netzkarte*, a one-month pass valid on all state railways, rack railways and Wolfgangsee ferries, costs AS3600. The *Österreich Puzzle* is not particularly puzzling – it divides the country into four zones – north, south, east and west. You can buy a pass for each zone for AS990 (under 26-year-olds AS600) giving you four days unlimited travel in a 10-day period. Areas overlap, so you can cover the whole country without needing to buy the east zone. The Kilometerbank allows up to six people to travel on journeys over 51 km; the cost is AS2100 for 2000 km, AS3150 for 3000 km, and AS5250 for 5000 km.

The German word for train station is *Bahnhof*, but the main train station is known as the *Hauptbahnhof*. Ordinary return tickets (over 70 km) are valid for two months, and you can break your journey as many times as you like, but you should warn the conductor of your intentions. Return tickets are usually cheaper than two singles. Reduced fares are sometimes available for those aged under 26: wave your passport and ask. In the larger towns, train information can be obtained by dialling ☎ 1717.

CAR & MOTORBIKE
Austrians drive on the right. Roads are generally good, but sufficient respect should be given to difficult mountain routes. There are toll charges for some tunnels through the mountains. The tourist office has details of the few roads and passes which are closed in winter.

On mountain roads, postbuses always have priority, otherwise priority lies with uphill traffic. Drive in low gear on steep downhill stretches. Give priority to vehicles coming from the right. The penalty for drink-driving (over 0.08% BAC) is a hefty on-the-spot fine and confiscation of your driving licence. Speed limits are 50 km/h in towns, 130 km/h on motorways and 100 km/h on other roads. Snow chains are recommended in winter. Cars can be transported by train: Vienna is linked by a daily motorail service to Feldkirch, Innsbruck, Salzburg and Villach. Motorbikes must have their headlights on during the day.

Rental
Hertz, Avis, Eurodollar and Europcar all have offices in main cities. Europcar has the

best unlimited-km rates: from AS708 per day, AS612 per day over seven days or AS1188 for a weekend (noon Friday to 9 am Monday). The reservation office (☎ 0222-505 29 47) is at Kärntner Ring 14, 1010 Vienna. Local rental agencies often have cheaper rates; the local tourist office will be able to supply details.

BICYCLE

Bicycles can be hired from train stations and returned to any other station with a rental office (most of them). The rate is AS90 per day, or AS50 if you can show a train ticket for arrival that day. Cycling is popular even though minor roads can be steep and have sharp bends. There is a fixed fare of AS70 for transporting a bike on a train.

HITCHING

Hitching is patchy, but not too bad. Trucks are often the best bet, and can be enticed to stop at border posts, truck stops or truck parking stops – signposted as *Autohof*. Always carry a sign showing your destination. It is illegal for minors under 16 to hitch in Burgenland, Upper Austria, Styria and Vorarlberg. *Mitfahrzentrale* companies link hitchers with car drivers. Hitchers pay approximately half the equivalent train fare – see the Vienna and Bregenz sections for addresses. See the Hitching section in the introductory Getting Around chapter for general information.

WALKING

There are 10 long-distance, national hiking routes, and three European routes pass through Austria. Options include the northern alpine route from Lake Constance to Vienna, via Dachstein, or the central route from Feldkirch to Hainburger Pforte, via Hohe Tauern. The Austrian Alpine Club (see Useful Organisations) has information, and many bookshops sell detailed hiking maps.

BOAT

Services along the Danube are slow, expensive, scenic excursions rather than functional transport. Nevertheless, a boat ride is definitely worth it if you like lounging on deck and having the scenery come to you rather than the other way round. The larger Salzkammergut lakes have ferry services.

LOCAL TRANSPORT

Buses, trams and underground railways are efficient and reliable. Most towns have an integrated system and offer excellent value one-day or 24-hour tickets (AS20 to AS50), which are available in advance from Tabak shops. Even single tickets can sometimes only be purchased in advance. On-the-spot fines apply to people caught travelling without tickets, though some locals are prepared to take the risk.

Taxis are metered and all but unnecessary given the good public transport. If you need one, look around train stations and large hotels.

For an account of the different modes of mountain transport available, see the introductory Getting Around section in the Switzerland chapter.

TOURS

These vary from two-hour walks in a city centre to all-inclusive packages at ski resorts. Arrangements are made through tourist offices.

Vienna

The character of modern Vienna (Wien) owes much to its colourful political and cultural past. There's so much to see and do that you could still feel pressed for time even if you allowed yourself a week to see the city. It combines impressive architecture and an enviable musical tradition with a busy social scene centred on coffee bars, clubs and taverns.

The Habsburgs settled in Vienna in 1278 and made it the capital of the Austrian Empire. The city flourished under their strong leadership, despite being dragged into various European conflicts and withstanding attacks by the Turks in 1529 and 1683.

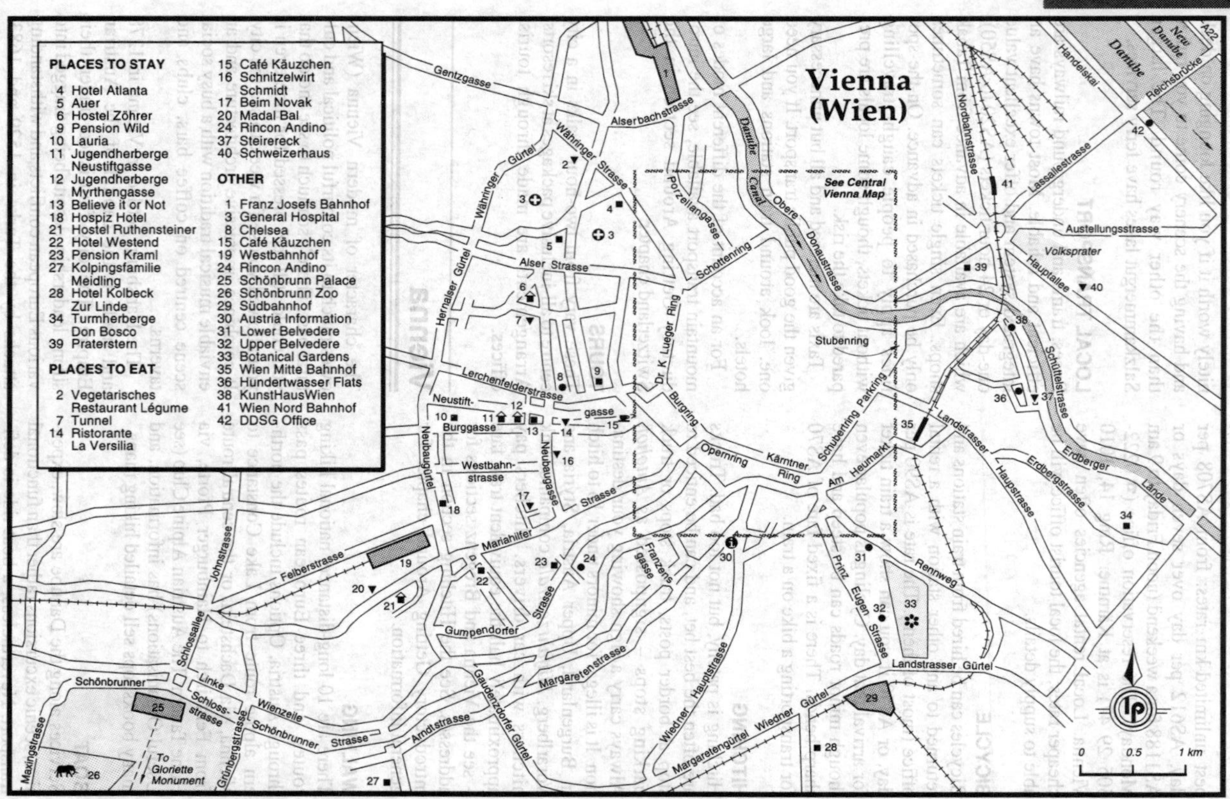
Vienna
(Wien)
See Central
Vienna Map
PLACES TO STAY
4 Hotel Atlanta
5 Auer
6 Hostel Zöhrer
9 Pension Wild
10 Lauria
11 Jugendherberge Neustiftgasse
12 Jugendherberge Myrthengasse
13 Believe it or Not
18 Hospiz Hotel
21 Hostel Ruthensteiner
22 Hotel Westend
23 Pension Kraml
27 Kolpingsfamilie Meidling
28 Hotel Kolbeck Zur Linde
34 Turmherberge Don Bosco
39 Praterstern
15 Café Käuzchen
16 Schnitzelwirt Schmidt
17 Beim Novak
20 Madal Bal
24 Rincon Andino
37 Steirereck
40 Schweizerhaus
PLACES TO EAT
2 Vegetarisches Restaurant Légume
7 Tunnel
14 Ristorante La Versilia
OTHER
1 Franz Josefs Bahnhof
3 General Hospital
8 Chelsea
15 Café Käuzchen
19 Westbahnhof
24 Rincon Andino
25 Schönbrunn Palace
26 Schönbrunn Zoo
29 Südbahnhof
30 Austria Information
31 Lower Belvedere
32 Upper Belvedere
33 Botanical Gardens
35 Wien Mitte Bahnhof
36 Hundertwasser Flats
38 KunstHausWien
41 Wien Nord Bahnhof
42 DDSG Office
Danube
New Danube
A22
Reichsbrücke
Handelskai
Lassallestrasse
Nordbahnstrasse
Austellungsstrasse
Volksprater
Hauptallee
Danube Canal
Obere Donaustrasse
Schüttelstrasse
Erdberger Lände
Erdbergstrasse
Haupstrasse
Landstrasser
Stubenring
Schubertring
Parkring
Kärntner Ring
Opernring
Am Heumarkt
Burgring
Dr K Lueger Ring
Schottenring
Porzellangasse
Alserbachstrasse
Währinger Strasse
Währinger Gürtel
Gentzgasse
Hernalser Gürtel
Alser Strasse
Lerchenfelderstrasse
Neustiftgasse
Burggasse
Westbahnstrasse
Neubaugasse
Neubaugürtel
Mariahilfer Strasse
Felberstrasse
Johnstrasse
Schlossallee
Gumpendorfer Strasse
Franzensgasse
Margaretenstrasse
Wiedner Hauptstrasse
Prinz Eugen Strasse
Rennweg
Landstrasser Gürtel
Wiedner Gürtel
Margaretengürtel
Gaudenzdorfer Gürtel
Arndtstrasse
Schönbrunner Strasse
Linke Wienzeile
Schloss-strasse
Grünbergstrasse
Schönbrunner
Maxingstrasse
To Gloriette Monument
0
0.5
1 km

Vienna's 'golden years' as the cultural centre of Europe were the 18th and 19th centuries. In the 'Who's Who' of classical music during this period, there was only one 'Where'. Strauss, Mozart, Beethoven, Brahms and Schubert are only a few of the great composers who made the city their home. Anybody with an interest in the arts will love Vienna.

Orientation

Many of the historic sights are in the old city, which is encircled by the Danube Canal (to the north-east) and a belt of ring roads known as the Ring. The Ring changes its name along its sections, eg Opern Ring, Kärntner Ring etc. St Stephen's Cathedral is in the heart of the city and is the principal landmark. Most attractions in the centre are within walking distance of each other.

Take care when reading addresses. The number of a building within a street *follows* the street name. Any number *before* the street name denotes the district, of which there are 23. District 1 is the central region, mostly within the Ring, and corresponds to the postal address 1010. Only the middle two digits alter, hence district 23 has the post code 1230. Generally speaking, the higher the district number, the further it is from the city centre.

The main train stations are Franz Josefs Bahnhof to the north, Westbahnhof to the west and Südbahnhof to the south; transferring between them is easy. The majority of hotels and pensions are to the west of the centre, roughly within a triangle bounded by Franz Josefs Bahnhof, Westbahnhof and Karlsplatz. The vicinity of the university, around Universitätsstrasse and Währinger Strasse, just north of Dr K Lueger Ring, is a good area for cheaper restaurants.

Information

Tourist Offices The main tourist office (☎ 0222-513 88 92) is at 1 Kärntner Strasse 38. It is small and hectic, but there is extensive free literature on hand. The city map is excellent, as is the *Youth Scene* magazine, which contains lots of hard information despite the chummy style. The office is open daily from 9 am to 7 pm. There is a tourist office in the arrival hall of the airport, open daily from 8.30 am to 11 pm, except between October and May when it closes at 10 pm.

Information and room reservations are available in Westbahnhof (open daily from 6.15 am to 11 pm); Südbahnhof (open daily from 6.30 am to 10 pm); and the quaintly named Erste Donau Dampfschiffahrts-Gesellschaft (DDSG) boat-landing stage, Reichsbrücke, open April to mid-October from 9 am to 6 pm (8 pm May to September).

Tourist offices are situated at all four corners of the city and are handy for car drivers. In the west, the office is at the A1 autobahn exit Wien-Auhof, open daily from 8 am to 10 pm (Easter to October), from 9 am to 7 pm (November) and from 10 am to 6 pm (December to Easter). The southern office is at the A2 exit Zentrum, Triesterstrasse, open daily from 9 am to 7 pm (Easter to June, and October) and 8 am to 10 pm (July to September). The eastern office is at the A4 exit Simmeringer Haide, Landwehrstrasse 6, open from 9 am to 7 pm (Easter to September). The office in the north is at Floridsdorfer Brücke/Donauinsel, open from 9 am to 7 pm (Easter to September). All of these offices have a room-finding service, which is subject to a AS35 commission.

The Austrian Information Office (☎ 0222-587 20 00), 4 Margaretenstrasse 1, is open Monday to Friday from 10 am to 5 pm (6 pm Thursday). The Lower Austria Information Centre (☎ 0222-533 31 14 28), 1 Heidenschuss 2, is open Monday to Friday from 8.30 am to 5.30 pm. The Youth Information Centre (☎ 0222-526 46 37), 1 Dr Karl Renner Ring, Bellaria Passage, can get tickets for a variety of events at reduced rates for those aged between 14 and 26. It is open from Monday to Friday from noon to 7 pm, and Saturday and school holidays from 10 am to 7 pm.

Money Banks are open Monday to Friday from 8 am to 3 pm, with late opening on Thursday until 5.30 pm; smaller branches close from 12.30 to 1.30 pm. Numerous Bankomat machines allow cash advances with Visa, Eurocard and MasterCard. Train stations have extended hours for exchanging money.

Post & Telephone The main post office is at 1 Fleischmarkt 19. There are also post offices open 24 hours daily at Südbahnhof, Westbahnhof and Franz Josefs Bahnhof. Stamps are sold in Tabak shops. The telephone code for Vienna is 0222, or 1 if you're ringing from outside the country.

Travel Agencies American Express (☎ 515 40), 1 Kärntner Strasse 21-23, is open Monday to Friday from 9 am to 5.30 pm, and Saturday from 9.30 am to noon. The Österreichisches Komitee für Internationalen Studentenaustausch (ÖKISTA) (☎ 401 480), 9 Garnisongasse 7, is a student budget travel agency that nonstudents can use. It's open Monday to Friday from 9.30 am to 5.30 pm. Other offices are at 9 Türkenstrasse 4-6 (☎ 401 48) and 4 Karlsgasse 3 (☎ 505 01 28).

Bookshops Many bookshops stock English-language titles, such as the British Bookshop (☎ 512 19 45), 1 Weihburggasse 24-6, and Shakespeare & Co Booksellers (☎ 535 50 53), 1 Sterngasse 2. Freytag & Berndt (☎ 533 20 94), 1 Kohlmarkt 9, stocks a vast selection of maps. Reiseladen (☎ 513 75 77) is a travel agent and bookshop with many Lonely Planet guides.

Emergency Dial ☎ 144 for an ambulance, ☎ 141 for medical emergencies and ☎ 133 for the police. For out-of-hours dental treatment, call ☎ 512 20 78. The general hospital (☎ 404 00) is at 9 Währinger Gürtel 18-20.

Things to See & Do

Walking is the best way to see the centre. Architectural riches confront you at nearly every corner, testimony to the power and wealth of the Habsburg dynasty. Ostentatious public buildings and statues line both sides of the Ring. Those that stand out include the neo-Gothic **Rathaus** (city hall), the Greek Revival-style Parliament (particularly the Pallas Athene statue), the 19th-century National Theatre and the baroque St Charles' Church. Carefully tended gardens and parks break up the brickwork.

Walking Tour From the tourist office, walk north up the pedestrian-only Kärntner Strasse, a walkway of plush shops, trees, café tables and street entertainers. It leads directly to Stephansplatz and the prime landmark of **St Stephen's Cathedral** (Stephansdom).

The latticework spire of this 13th-century Gothic masterpiece rises high above the city. Interior walls and pillars are decorated with fine statues; the stone pulpit is particularly striking. Take the lift up the north tower (AS40) or the stairs up the higher south tower (AS20) for an impressive view.

The internal organs of the Habsburgs reside in the catacombs (open daily, AS35). One of the privileges of being a Habsburg was to be dismembered and dispersed after death: their hearts are in the Church of the Augustinian Friars, 1 Augustinerstrasse 3; the rest of their bits are in the Imperial Burial Vaults in the Church of the Capuchin Friars, 1 Neuer Markt.

From Stephansplatz, turn west down Graben, which is dominated by the knobbly outline of the Plague Column. Turn left into Kohlmarkt, which leads directly to the St Michael's Gateway of the **Hofburg** (Imperial Palace).

The Hofburg was built in 1530, and has been periodically enlarged since the 13th century, resulting in the current mixture of architectural styles. The Spanish Riding School office is to the left of the entrance (see the Entertainment section). Next to it are the **Imperial Apartments**, which cost AS40 to visit (students aged under 27 AS20). The apartments in Schönbrunn (see the following section) are more impressive. Walk south into the large courtyard, and take a left into a smaller, surprisingly scruffy courtyard. Here you'll find the Royal Chapel, and the **Imperial Treasury** (Schatzkammer), which contains treasures and relics spanning 1000 years, including the crown jewels. Allow up to one hour to get round (entry AS60, students AS30; closed Tuesday).

Schönbrunn Palace The palace can be reached by U-Bahn No 4. Daily guided tours (in English) take in 40 of its 1440 rooms and cost AS95 (daily, open year-round). The interior is suitably majestic, with frescoed ceilings, crystal chandeliers and gilded ornaments. The pinnacle of finery is reached in the Great Gallery. Mozart played his first concert in the Mirror Room at the ripe age of six in the presence of Maria Theresa and the royal family. Extensive formal gardens are enlivened by several fountains. There are excellent views from the **Gloriette monument** on the hill (entry AS20, May to October only). The attractive zoo (Tiergarten) is also worth a look (entry AS80).

Belvedere Palace This baroque palace is within walking distance of the Ring and has good views of the city. It also contains two art collections, located in the two main buildings which flank the spacious gardens. Lower (Untere) Belvedere (entrance Rennweg 6A) contains some interesting baroque pieces, but the more important collection is in Upper (Obere) Belvedere, and includes instantly recognisable works by Gustav Klimt and other Austrian artists from the 19th and 20th centuries (entrance Prinz Eugen Strasse 27). Open Tuesday to Sunday from 10 am to 5 pm, entry for both is AS60, (students AS30).

Museum of Fine Arts This must-see museum, known as the Kunsthistorisches Museum, houses a huge collection of 16th and 17th-century paintings, ornaments and glassware, and Greek, Roman and Egyptian antiquities.

The huge extent of the Habsburg Empire led to many important works of art being funnelled back to Vienna. Rubens was appointed to the service of a Habsburg governor in Brussels, so it's not surprising that the Kunsthistorisches has one of the world's best collections of his works. There is also a great collection of paintings by Peter Brueghel the Elder. Look out for Vermeer's *Allegory of Painting*, Cellini's stunning salt-cellar, and the unbelievably lavish clocks from the 16th and 17th centuries. The composite paintings by Archimboldo in room No 29 predate modern surrealism by nearly 400 years.

The museum is open Tuesday to Sunday from 10 am to 6 pm. Entry is AS45 (students AS30). Guided tours in English at 3 pm cost AS30 extra.

Secession Building This Art-Nouveau 'temple of art', built at 1 Friedrichstrasse 12 in 1898, bears a golden dome that looks like an enormous Ferrero Rocher chocolate wrapper (or a 'golden cabbage', according to some Viennese). The 1902 exhibition here featured the famous 34-metre-long *Beethoven Frieze* by Klimt, which has been restored and can be seen in the basement. The rest of the building is primarily devoted to contemporary art. 'Sometimes people just walk past the art, they think they're in empty rooms', the lady at the desk told me. You have been warned! It's open Tuesday to Friday from 10 am to 6 pm, and Saturday and Sunday to 4 pm; entry costs AS60 (students AS30).

KunstHausWien This gallery at 3 Untere Weissgerberstrasse 13 looks like something out of a toyshop. It was designed by Friedensreich Hundertwasser to house his own works of art. It features coloured ceramics, uneven floors, irregular corners and grass on the roof. His vivid paintings are equally distinctive and there are some interesting models of other building projects. It is open daily from 10 am to 7 pm and costs AS60 to get in (students AS40). When you're in the area, walk down the road to see a block of residential flats built by Hundertwasser on the corner of Löwengasse and Kegelgasse. It is now one of Vienna's most prestigious addresses.

Other Museums Architecturally, the **Museum of Natural History**, at 1 Maria Theresien Platz, is the mirror image of the Art History Museum. It holds temporary

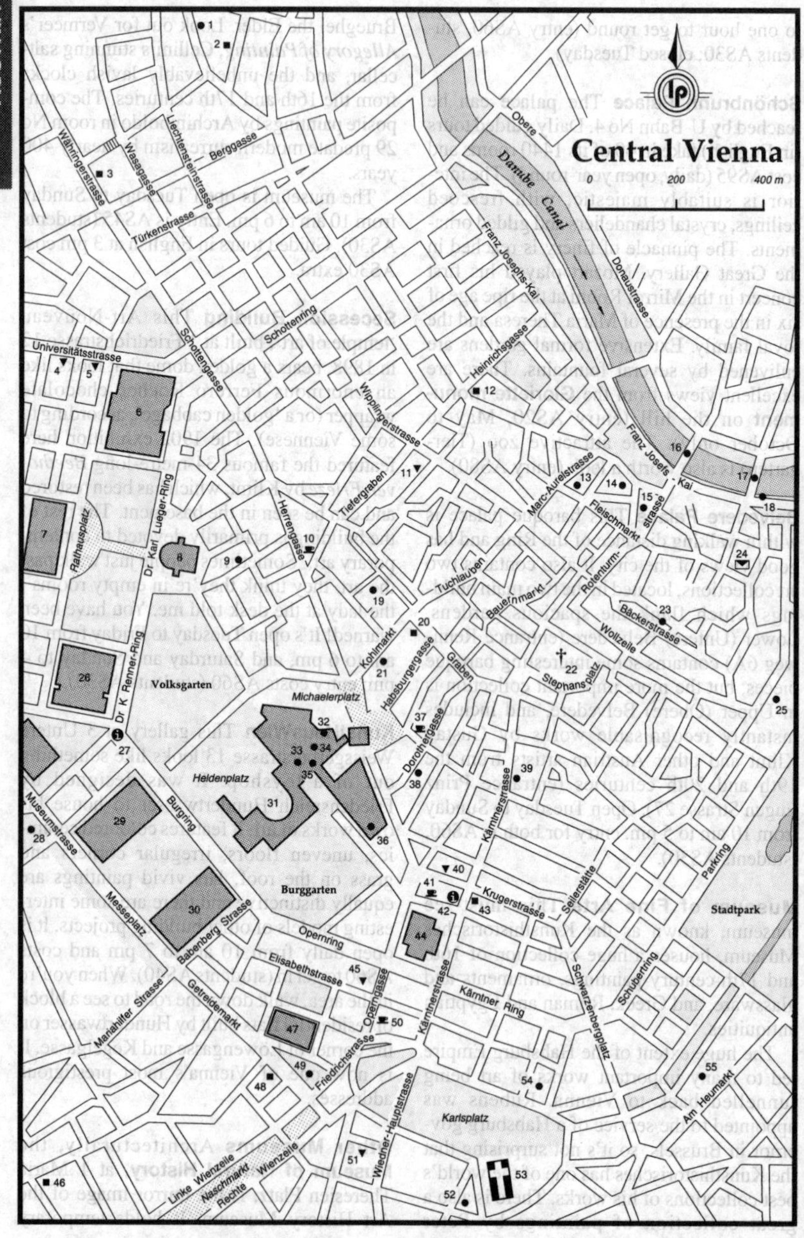
Central Vienna
0
200
400 m
Danube Canal
Obere
Donaustrasse
Franz Josephs-Kai
Franz Josefs - Kai
Heinrichsgasse
Währingerstrasse
Wasagasse
Liechtensteinstrasse
Berggasse
Türkenstrasse
Schottenring
Schottengasse
Universitätsstrasse
Wipplingerstrasse
Dr Karl Lueger-Ring
Rathausplatz
Herrengasse
Tiefergraben
Marc-Aurelstrasse
Fleischmarkt
Rotenturm-strasse
Tuchlauben
Bauernmarkt
Bäckerstrasse
Wollzeile
Stephansplatz
Graben
Kohlmarkt
Habsburgergasse
Dorotheergasse
Dr K Renner-Ring
Volksgarten
Michaelerplatz
Heldenplatz
Burgring
Museumstrasse
Kärntnerstrasse
Seilerstätte
Krugerstrasse
Parkring
Stadtpark
Burggarten
Messeplatz
Babenberg Strasse
Opernring
Elisabethstrasse
Operngasse
Mariahilfer Strasse
Getreidemarkt
Friedrichstrasse
Kärntner Ring
Schwarzenbergplatz
Schubertring
Am Heumarkt
Karlsplatz
Linke Wienzeile
Naschmarkt
Rechte Wienzeile
Wiedner-Hauptstrasse
1
2
3
4
5
6
7
8
9
10
11
12
13
14
15
16
17
18
19
20
21
22
23
24
25
26
27
28
29
30
31
32
33
34
35
36
37
38
39
40
41
42
43
44
45
46
47
48
49
50
51
52
53
54
55

PLACES TO STAY

2 Falstaff
3 Hotel Am Schottenpoint
12 Schweizer Pension Solderer
20 Pension Nossek
43 Pension Am Operneck
46 Kolping-Gästehaus
48 Hotel-Pension Schneider

PLACES TO EAT

4 Mensa
5 Café Bierkeller Zwillings Gewölb
11 China Restaurant Peking
40 Rosenberger Markt
45 Restaurant Smutny
51 Technical University Mensa

OTHER

1 Big Ben Bookshop
6 University
7 City Hall (Rathaus)
8 National Theatre (Burgtheater)
9 Hungarian Embassy
10 Café Central
13 Shakespeare & Co Booksellers
14 Bermuda Triangle area
15 Krah Krah
16 Marienbrücke
17 Schwedenbrücke
18 DDSG Canal Tour Landing Stage
19 Esterházykeller
21 Freytag & Berndt
22 St Stephen's Cathedral (Stephansdom)
23 Alt Wien
24 Main Post Office
25 Reiseladen
26 Parliament
27 Youth Information Centre
28 Volkstheater
29 Natural History Museum
30 Museum of Fine Arts
31 Hofburg
32 Spanish Riding School
33 Royal Chapel
34 Imperial Apartments
35 Imperial Treasury
36 Albertina
37 Café Bräunerhof
38 Dorotheum
39 American Express
41 Hotel Sacher Café
42 Main Tourist Office
44 State Opera (Staatsoper)
47 Academy of Fine Arts
49 Secession Building
50 Café Museum
52 ÖKISTA
53 St Charles' Church
54 Musikverein
55 Konzerthaus

exhibitions and houses a collection of minerals, meteorites and an assortment of animal remains in jars. The museum is open daily except Tuesday; entry costs AS40 (students AS20). If you're going to Salzburg, the equivalent museum there is superior.

You can certainly overdose on art in Vienna. The **Albertina** may be closed until 1999, but other important collections are dotted around the city, notably in the **Museum of Modern Art**, 9 Fürstengasse 1, and the **Academy of Fine Arts**, 1 Schillerplatz 3. The former homes of the great composers are also open to the public; some of these are municipal museums, which are free on Friday morning.

Cemeteries Beethoven, Schubert, Brahms and Schönberg have memorial tombs in the **Central Cemetery**, 11 Simmeringer Hauptstrasse 232-244. Mozart also has a monument here, but he was actually buried in an unmarked grave in the **Cemetery of St Mark**, 3 Leberstrasse 6-8 – nobody quite knows where. It was only many years after the true location had been forgotten that gravediggers cobbled together a poignant memorial from a broken pillar and a discarded stone angel.

Naschmarkt The Naschmarkt is along 6 Linke Wienzeile, and is open Monday to Saturday from 8 am to 6 pm. It consists mainly of fruit, vegetable and meat stalls, but there are a few stalls selling clothing and curios as well. There is also a flea market on Saturday, which is the best day to visit. Snack bars provide cheap, hot food.

Activities

Organised Tours Several companies offer tours of the city and surrounding areas, including walking and cycling tours. An interesting tour is The Third Man Tour, which visits spots featured in the famous film, including the underground sewer. DDSG conducts tours of the Danube Canal, which depart from Schwedenbrücke in the Ring; the tourist office has details. See also under Boat in the following Getting There & Away section.

Volksprater This large amusement park, commonly referred to as the Prater, is dominated by the Giant Wheel, built in 1897, which featured prominently in *The Third Man*. Rides in the park cost AS10 to AS40, but it is also a great place to just have a wander. As you walk, you're liable to bump into one of the colourful metal sculptures depicting humans caught up in strange hallucinogenic happenings. The park adjoins a complex of sports grounds and a large forested area ideal for rambling.

Wienerwald To the west of the city, the rolling hills and marked trails of the Vienna Woods are perfect for walkers; a brochure *(Wandern in der Stadt)* shows trails and how to get there and is available from the information office in the city hall (open Monday to Friday from 8 am to 6 pm).

Watersports In the north-east of the city, the Old Danube and the New Danube provide opportunities for swimming, sailing, boating and windsurfing.

Festivals

The cycle of musical events is unceasing. Mozart features heavily, but all varieties of music get a look-in. The Vienna International Festival (from mid-May to mid-June) has a wide-ranging programme of the arts. Contact Wiener Festwochen (☎ 586 16 76), Lehárgasse 11, A 1060 Vienna, for details. Vienna's Summer of Music (from mid-July to mid-August) fills an otherwise flat spot in the musical calendar. Contact Klangboden (☎ 4000 8400), Laudongasse 29, A 1080 Vienna, before 15 April to reserve tickets in writing. Tickets are available from 1 June at the box office, 1 Friedrich Schmidt Platz 1, open daily from 10 am to 7 pm. Reduced student tickets go on sale 10 minutes before the performance. At the end of June, look out for free rock, jazz and folk concerts in the Donauinselfest.

Vienna's traditional Christmas market takes place in front of the city hall from mid-November to 24 December. Other seasonal events include New Year concerts and gala balls (January and February), the Vienna Spring Marathon (March/April), Vienna trade fairs (March and September), the Spring Festival in the Prater (May), a flower parade in the Prater (June) and the Schubert Festival (November). The tourist office does not sell tickets, but has full details.

Places to Stay

Vienna can be a nightmare for accommodation. Hotels are expensive and often full, especially in the summer. Reserve ahead or at least use the telephone before you trek round everywhere.

Several agencies can help with accommodation, including ÖKISTA (☎ 34 75 26 23), Türkenstrasse 4-6, which concentrates on finding cheaper rooms and charges no commission. The Mitwohnzentrale (☎ 402 60 61), 8 Laudongasse 7, can find private rooms from AS200 and apartments from AS600 (both types of accommodation are for a minimum stay of three days); the office is open Monday to Friday from 10 am to 2 pm and 3 to 6 pm; it charges commission. The tourist office has lists of private rooms as well as the useful *Jugendherbergen* pamphlet which details hostels and camping grounds. Prices for hostels and hotels listed below include breakfast unless stated otherwise. Note that some places mentioned under hostels also have comfortable private rooms.

Camping Vienna has several camping grounds in the outer suburbs. *Wien West II* (☎ 94 23 14), 14 Hüttelbergstrasse 80, is open all year except February. Down the road, at No 40, is *Wien West I* (☎ 94 14 49), which is open in July and August. Both cost AS58 per person and AS53 per tent. To get there, take U4 or S45 to Hütteldorf, then bus No 152. *Camping Neue Donau* (☎ 220 93 10), 22 Am Kleehäufel, is the same price, and is open from the end of April to mid-September. Take the U1 to Kaisermühlen, then the No 91A bus.

Hostels No hostels invade the imperial elegance of the Ring. The nearest are two linked

HI *Jugendherbergen*, at 7 Myrthengasse 7 (☎ 523 63 16) and round the corner at 7 Neustiftgasse 85 (☎ 523 74 62). Both are well run and have new facilities and knowledgeable staff. Enjoy the good showers, lockers and personal bedside light (sheer luxury!). Beds are AS140, lunch or dinner AS60 and laundry AS50 per load. Curfew is at 1 am. You can check in for either hostel any time during the day at Myrthengasse; the Neustiftgasse hostel closes from 11.15 am (10.15 am Sunday) to 3.45 pm. Telephone reservations are accepted and strongly advised.

Believe it or Not (☎ 526 46 58), Apartment 14, 7 Myrthengasse 10, is a small private hostel. There's no clue on the main door that it's anything other than a private house. It has a friendly atmosphere, but one room has triple-level bunks and can get hot in summer. There's no breakfast; use the kitchen facilities instead. Beds are AS160 in summer or AS110 during winter, and you get your own key for late entry. *Lauria* (☎ 52 22 555), Kaiserstrasse 77, is similar – friendly staff, own-key entry, kitchen facilities, no breakfast, no outside advertising. Hostel beds cost AS160, doubles AS530, triples AS700, quads AS850; fully-equipped apartments are also available, but there may be a two-day minimum stay.

Hospiz Hotel (☎ 523 13 04), 7 Kenyongasse 15, is run by the YMCA (CVJM) but anyone can stay here. Simple singles/doubles using hall shower are AS350/620 or AS380/680 with private shower; prices are around AS30 per person lower in winter. In the summer, you can sleep on a mat in the gym for AS150, but you must pack your gear out of the way in the day. Reception is open from 8 am to 10 pm. There's no lift and lots of stairs.

Hostel Zöhrer (☎ 43 07 30), 8 Skodagasse 26, is a private hostel close to the Ring. Four to six-bed dorms are AS160 and doubles (bunk-beds) are AS440 with private shower. There's a kitchen, courtyard and own-key entry; reception is open from 8 am to 10 pm. *Turmherberge Don Bosco* (☎ 713 14 94), 3 Lechnerstrasse 12, south-east of the Ring, has the cheapest beds in town (AS60 without breakfast) and a tendency to attract impoverished locals.

Near Westbahnhof, *Hostel Ruthensteiner* (☎ 893 42 02), 15 Robert Hamerling Gasse 24, is open 24 hours. Dorms are AS129 plus AS20 for sheets (if needed). Basic singles/doubles are AS209 per person. Breakfast costs AS25, but there's a kitchen and also a shady, rear courtyard. Non-HI members pay AS40 extra. *Kolpingsfamilie Meidling* (☎ 813 54 87), 12 Bendlgasse 10-12, is near the U6 stop, Niederhofstrasse, south of Westbahnhof. Beds are AS95 to AS140 in different-sized dorms. Non-HI members pay AS20 extra. Breakfast costs AS42 and sheets are AS65. Curfew is at 1 am, though reception is open 24 hours.

There are two large HI hostels out in the suburbs. *Brigittenau* (☎ 332 82 940), 20 Friedrich Engels Platz 24 (take tram N north), has a 1 am curfew, though reception is open 24 hours. *Hütteldorf-Hacking* (☎ 877 02 63), 13 Schlossberggasse 8 (take the U4 west), has large dorms, locked doors from 9 am to 4 pm and an 11.45 pm curfew. The former costs AS140 per night; the latter is a mighty AS1 cheaper.

Student Rooms These are available to tourists from 1 July to 30 September while students are on holiday. The cheapest is *Porzellaneum* (☎ 34 72 82), 9 Porzellangasse 30, which has singles/doubles for AS160 per person.

Some of the other *Studentenheime* you could try include: 1 Auerspergstrasse 9 (☎ 432 54 90); 8 Pfeilgasse 4-6 (☎ 408 34 45); 9 Bolzmanngasse 10 (☎ 310 31 30); 9 Nussdorfer Strasse 75 (☎ 34 25 85); 9 Alserstrasse 33 (☎ 433 23 17); and 19 Gymnasiumstrasse 85 (☎ 34 76 31).

Hotels & Pensions *Kolping-Gästehaus* (☎ 587 56 31), 6 Gumpendorfer Strasse 39, has singles without shower for just AS230, and doubles with shower for AS800, but it's a newish building with an institutional aura (long-term students stay here). *Auer* (☎ 43 21 21), 9 Lazarettgasse 3, is pleasant and small and feels more Viennese. Singles/doubles start from AS300/430 using hall shower, or doubles with shower cubicle in the room are AS530.

Pension Wild (☎ 43 51 74), 8 Langegasse 10, is quieter than the name suggests and very close to the Ring. Singles/doubles start from AS410/560 and there are some triples/quads from AS810/1000. Make use of the hall shower or indulge in a sauna and steam bath downstairs for AS30. The reception is open 24 hours. Kitchen facilities are a bonus.

Hotel Westend (☎ 597 67 29), at 6 Fügergasse 3, close to Westbahnhof, has reasonable singles/doubles for AS330/590 in a nice building. Reception is open 24 hours. *Pension Kraml* (☎ 587 85 88) is nearby at 6 Brauergasse 5. It's small and friendly, and has singles/doubles for AS260/570 and large doubles with a private shower from AS750.

Pension Falstaff (☎ 34 91 27), 9 Müllnergasse 5, has singles/doubles for AS345/565 (negotiate not to pay AS30 for use of the hall shower) or AS440/680 with private shower. The rooms are long but some lack width; fittings are ageing but adequate. It's convenient for tram D to the Ring and Nussdorf. *Praterstern* (☎ 24 01 23), 2 Mayergasse 6, east of the Ring, has singles/doubles for AS280/530. It's another place that encourages guests to stay dirty, charging AS50 to use the hall shower. Rooms with private shower/WC are AS415/675.

Zum Goldenen Stern Gasthof (☎ 804 13 82), 12 Breitenfurter Strasse 94, has singles/doubles for AS220/400 using a hall shower. To get there, take the train or the S Bahn No 1 or 2 to Hetzendorf. Breitenfurter Strasse is a short walk south. *Hotel Kolbeck Zur Linde* (☎ 604 17 73), 10 Laxenburger Strasse 19, is a 10-minute walk from Südbahnhof. Singles/doubles using hall shower are AS380/660; those with private shower/WC and TV are AS580/980. Reception is open 24 hours.

Inside the Ring, you inevitably pay more for the convenience of a central location. *Schweizer Pension Solderer* (☎ 533 81 56), 1 Heinrichsgasse 2, has singles/doubles from AS380/600 with hall shower. Rooms with private shower/WC are AS680/880, or AS580/750 with shower only. Reception is open from 7 am to 10 pm. *Pension Nossek* (☎ 533 70 41), 1 Graben 17, has good value, clean, comfortable singles from AS480 to AS770 and doubles from AS950 to AS1500. Rooms are priced according to their size, view and private facilities. *Pension Am Operneck* (☎ 512 93 10), 1 Kärntner Strasse 47, opposite the tourist office, has singles/doubles for AS570/840 with private shower and WC.

Mid-Range Hotels The *Hotel Atlanta* (☎ 42 12 30), 9 Währinger Strasse 33, is located in a typically grand Viennese building. It's a good four-star hotel, with spacious, well furnished rooms and elegant touches. Each has a TV and bath or shower. It is especially good value in the low season (November to March) when singles/doubles are AS750/950 and triples are AS1200. The rest of the year, prices go up by around AS250 per person.

Also good is *Hotel Am Schottenpoint* (☎ 310 87 87), Währinger Strasse 22. The entrance is through a small gallery decorated with murals and a stucco ceiling, but the rest of the hotel hasn't got quite the same style. Singles/doubles are AS820/1080, rising to AS890/1320 in the high season.

Hotel-Pension Schneider (☎ 58 83 80), Getreidemarkt 5, is close to the Theater an der Wien, and the theatrical connection is obvious when you enter the lobby and see the signed photos of the actors and opera stars who have stayed here. Singles are AS880 to AS1280, doubles are AS1550, and excellent self-contained two-person apartments are AS1990; prices are lower in winter.

Places to Eat

Supermarkets are shut Saturday afternoon and Sunday, but you can stock up on groceries during these times at the stations. Westbahnhof has a large shop which is open daily from 6 am to 10.50 pm in the main hall; in Franz Josefs Bahnhof there's one open

Monday to Saturday from 6 am to 10 pm, and Sunday from 8 am to noon; Südbahnhof has a few tiny kiosks. Wurst stands are scattered around the city and provide a quick snack of sausage and bread for around AS30.

Vienna's best known dish, the Wiener Schnitzel, is available everywhere; Goulash is also common. Vienna is well known for its excellent pastries and desserts, which are best avoided if your money belt is emptier than your stomach.

Restaurants Inside the Ring These tend to have higher prices, which makes *Rosenberger Markt Restaurant*, Maysedergasse 2, a welcome find. Its downstairs buffet offers a fine array of meats, drinks and desserts, but concentrate on the salad or vegetable buffet (from AS25 or AS27) to really save Schillings. Don't be ashamed to pile a Stephansdom-like spire of food on your plate; everyone else does. It's open daily from 11 am to 11 pm.

China Restaurant Peking, 1 Färbergasse 3, is open Monday to Saturday from 11.30 am to 2.30 pm and 6 to 11.30 pm. Lunchtime specials are AS59, soups start from AS25 and other dishes from AS78. Try the excellent Hunan spicy duck (AS95).

DO & CO (☎ 535 39 69 18), 1 Stephansplatz 12, is situated in the modern and controversial building close to Stephansdom. It has good food to match the view, and specialises in fish and Thai dishes around the AS200 mark. It's open Monday to Saturday from noon to 3 pm and 6 pm to midnight. There's an adjoining café open in the afternoons.

Restaurants Outside the Ring The best deal is in student cafeterias (mensas), which anyone can visit, although they're usually only open for weekday lunches. *Youth Scene* has a full listing of mensas (the Technical University Mensa is at 4 Resselgasse 7-9, not, as quoted, 4 Karlsplatz 13). At the *University Mensa*, 9 Universitätsstrasse 7, dishes start from a mere AS30. Take the lift from the foyer to the top. The adjoining café has the same meals and longer hours (weekdays from 8 am to 7 pm). *Café Bierkeller Zwillings Gewölb* is a popular student haunt close by. It offers daily specials from AS55 served up in its maze of subterranean rooms. It's open Monday to Friday from 8 am to 1 am and Saturday from 9.30 am to 11 pm.

Tunnel (☎ 42 34 65), 8 Floriangasse 39, is another favourite with students. The food is satisfying and easy on the pocket; breakfast costs AS29, lunch specials AS45, spaghetti from AS38, big pizzas from AS60 and salads from AS20. Bottled beer costs from AS24 for half a litre. There is a cellar bar which has live music nightly from 9 pm; entry costs from AS30, though on Monday there's generally free jazz. Tunnel is open daily from 9 am to 2 am.

Schnitzelwirt Schmidt (☎ 93 37 71), 7 Neubaugasse 52, is the best place for schnitzels and prides itself on its enormous portions (from AS57). It's informal and very popular, open Monday to Saturday from 10 am to 10 pm.

Madal Bal, 15 Mariahilfer Strasse 160, is a healthy (no smoking or alcohol) vegetarian restaurant which has background meditative music. Home cooking starts at AS75 and there's a salad buffet for AS35/65. It's open Tuesday to Saturday from 11 am to 10 pm. *Vegetarisches Restaurant Légume* (☎ 425 06 54), Währinger Strasse 57, has a three-course daily menu for AS98, and dishes like cheese schnitzel for AS79. It's open lunchtimes Sunday to Friday, and is run by the owners of the adjoining health food shop, which is open Monday to Friday from 9 am to 6 pm.

For a complete contrast, head down to *Schweizerhaus* in the Prater, 2 Strasse des Ersten Mai 116. It's famous for its roasted pork hocks. A meal consists of a massive chunk of meat on the bone (AS85 for 500 grams, usually 700 to 800 grams minimum), served with mustard and horseradish sauce. Chomping your way through vast slabs of pig smacks of medieval banqueting, but it's very tasty when washed down with draught Czech Budweiser. Schweizerhaus is open daily from 10 am to 11 pm (March to October only) and has many outside tables.

Restaurant Smutny (☎ 587 13 56), 1

Elisabethstrasse 8, serves typical Viennese food in a typical Viennese environment. Dishes are filling and reasonably priced (from AS80), and it's open daily from 10 am to midnight.

Mid-Range Restaurants The attentive *Beim Novak* (☎ 523 32 44), 7 Richtergasse 12, has Austrian food from AS95 to AS265. The house speciality is *Überbackene Fledermaus* (Gratinated Bat) for AS150. The 'bat wings' are actually cuts of beef. It's closed on weekends and holidays. A cut above the usual Italian restaurant is *Ristorante La Versilia* (☎ 526 19 21), 7 Neustiftgasse 47. It's quite elegant and plush, and dishes are AS70 to AS280 (closed Sunday).

The classy *Steirereck* (☎ 713 31 68), 8 Rasumofskygasse 2, is gourmet territory. Different parts of the restaurant have a different ambience, but it's pretty formal throughout. Tempting main courses all top AS300, but you get to choose from lobster, rabbit, pigeon or venison. It's open Monday to Friday; book several days in advance for evening dining.

Coffee Houses The coffee house is an integral part of Viennese life. The tradition supposedly began after retreating Turkish invaders left behind their supplies of coffee beans in the 17th century. Today, Vienna has hundreds (some say thousands) of coffee houses. They're great places for observing the locals in repose and recovering after a hard day's sightseeing. Small coffees cost at least AS20 and the custom is to take your time. Most places have lots of free newspapers (including expensive British titles), which make a coffee an excellent investment.

Coffee houses basically fall into two categories, though the distinction is rather blurred nowadays. A *Kaffeehaus*, traditionally preferred by men, offers games such as chess and billiards and serves wine, beer, spirits and light meals. The *Café Konditorei* attracts more women and typically has a salon look, with rococo mouldings and painted glass. A wide variety of cakes and pastries is usually on offer.

Café Museum, 1 Friedrichstrasse 6, is open daily from 7 am to 11 pm and has chess, billiards, many newspapers and outside tables. *Café Bräunerhof*, 1 Stallburggasse 2, offers free classical music on the weekends from 3 to 6 pm, and British newspapers. It's open weekdays to 7.30 pm (8.30 pm in winter) and weekends to 6 pm.

Café Central, 1 Herrengasse 14, has a fine ceiling and pillars, and piano music from 4 to 6 pm. Trotsky came here to play chess. Opening hours are Monday to Saturday from 8 am to 10 pm. The *Hotel Sacher Café*, 1 Philharmonikerstrasse 4, behind the State Opera, is a picture of opulence, complete with chandeliers, battalions of waiters and rich, red walls and carpets. It's famous for its chocolate apricot cake, *Sachertorte* (AS48 a slice; coffee from AS32).

Heurigen *Heurigen* are wine taverns that only sell 'new' wine produced on the premises, a concession granted by Joseph II. They can be identified by a green wreath or branch hanging over the door. Outside tables are common and you can bring your own food or make a selection from inexpensive hot and cold buffet counters. Heurigen usually have a relaxed atmosphere, which gets more and more lively as the customers get drunk. Many feature traditional live music; these can be a bit touristy but great fun nonetheless. Native Viennese tend to prefer a music-free environment. Opening times are approximately 4 to 11 pm, and wine is around AS100 a litre.

Heurigen are concentrated in the wine-growing suburbs to the north, south and west of the city. Taverns are so close together that it is best to pick a region and just explore. The Heurigen areas of Nussdorf and Heiligenstadt are near each other at the terminus of tram D.

The food and wine are good in *Schübel Auer*, 19 Kahlenberger Strasse 22, Nussdorf. In 1817, Beethoven lived in the *Beethovenhaus*, 19 Pfarrplatz 3, Heiligenstadt, which has a big hall and music. Down the road (bus

No 38A from Heiligenstadt or tram 38 from the Ring) is Grinzing, a large, lively area favoured by tour groups (count the buses lined up outside at closing time). There are several good Heurigen in a row along Cobenzlgasse and Sandgasse. Stammersdorf (tram No 31) and Strebersdorf (tram No 32) are cheaper regions.

Entertainment

See the previous Festivals section for seasonal cultural events. The tourist office has copies of *Vienna Scene* and produces a monthly listing of events. Weekly magazines with extensive listings include *City Tele* (AS3) and *Falter* (AS23).

Nightclubs & Bars Vienna has no shortage of good spots for a night out. The best-known area is around Ruprechtsplatz, Seitenstettengasse and Rabensteig in the Ring, dubbed the 'Bermuda Triangle' because drinkers can disappear into the numerous pubs and clubs and apparently be lost to the outside world. Most places are lively and inexpensive; some have live music, which is either free or subject to a low cover charge. *Krah Krah*, 1 Rabensteig 8, has 50 different brands of beer (from about AS34 a half-litre bottle) and is open daily until 2 am. *Roter Engel* is opposite at 1 Rabensteig 5. It has live music nightly (cover charge between AS20 and AS70) and is open until 2 am (weekdays) or 4 am (weekends).

Alt Wien, 1 Bäckerstrasse 9, is a rather dark coffee house by day and a good drinking hall by night. It's open daily from 10 am to 2 am and is well known for its goulash (AS75 large, AS50 small). *Esterházykeller*, Haarhof 1, off Naglergasse, is a busy wine cellar which has cheap wine (from AS22 for a quarter litre), meals and snacks; it's open daily from 11 am (4 pm weekends) to 10 pm.

Late-night bars are by no means limited to the city centre. *Chelsea*, 8 Piaristengasse 1, is open daily from 7 pm to 4 am. It has a DJ downstairs and live music on Sundays. *Café Käuzchen*, 7 Garde Gasse 8, has interesting décor, including part of an old VW Kombi bursting out of one wall. It's open daily until 2 or 4 am and is good for late-night conversation (and food). *Rincon Andino* (☎ 586 56 71), 6 Münzwardeingasse 2, is a Latin American bar with live rock, soul or funk three times a week (entry averages AS80). It has lively murals, a limited menu and is open daily from 11 am to 2 or 4 am.

One of the most well-known discos in Vienna is *U4* (☎ 85 83 18), 12 Schönbrunner Strasse 222, open daily from 11 pm to 4 or 5 am. Drink prices are reasonable. Each night has a different theme. Sunday (1960s and 1970s music, cover charge AS50) is a popular night; Thursday is gay night.

Performances Classical music is not to everyone's taste, but it is so much a part of Vienna that you really should make an effort to sample some. In fact it's difficult to avoid because so many of the buskers playing along Kärntner Strasse and Graben are classical musicians. Check with the tourist office for free events around town. In summer, there are sometimes free concerts in front of the Rathaus in the afternoon.

Standing-room tickets (AS15 or AS20) for the Staatsoper, Volksoper, Burgtheater and Akademietheater go on sale at around 6 pm on the evening of the performance, but check for starting times because some performances start earlier. You'll need to start queuing around 4 pm to get tickets for major productions; less popular works require only minimal queuing. Don't join the student queue by mistake: same-day student tickets to these places (and some others) cost AS50, if there are seats left (Austrian university ID necessary). The state ticket office, Bundestheaterverkassen (☎ 514 44 2959), 1 Goethegasse 1, does not charge a commission.

Productions in the Staatsoper (state opera) are lavish affairs. Advance tickets for performances are expensive at AS150 to AS600. AS20 standing-room ticket holders get a good position at the back of the stalls; AS15 ticket holders are closer to the roof than the stage. The Viennese take their opera very seriously and dress up accordingly. Wander around the foyer and the refreshment rooms in the interval to fully appreciate the gold and crystal interior. There are no performances in July and August. The Vienna Philharmonic Orchestra performs in the Musikverein.

The Vienna Boy's Choir (Wiener Sängerknaben) sings every Sunday (except during July and August) at 9.15 am in the Royal Chapel in the Hofburg. Tickets are expensive, but standing room is free. Queue by 8.30 am to find a place inside the open doors, but you can get a flavour of what's going on from the TV in the foyer. Just as interesting is the scrum afterwards when everybody struggles to photograph and be photographed with the serenely patient choir. The choir also regularly sings a mixed programme of music in the Konzerthaus.

Spanish Riding School The famous Lipizzaner stallions strut their stuff in the Spanish Riding School behind the Hofburg. Performances are sold out months in advance, so you should write to the Spanische Reitschule, Michaelerplatz 1, A-1010 Wien or ask in the office about cancellations (cancelled tickets are sold two hours before performances). Deal directly with the school to avoid the hefty 22% commission charged by travel agents.

You need to be pretty keen on horses to be happy about paying AS220 to AS800 for seats or AS170 for standing room, although a few of the tricks, such as seeing a stallion bounding along on only its hind legs like a demented kangaroo, do tend to stick in the mind. Tickets to watch them train can be bought the same day (AS80) at gate No 2, Josefsplatz, in the Hofburg. Training is from 10 am to noon, Tuesday to Saturday, from mid-February to the end of October – except in July and August when the stallions go on their summer holidays to Lainzer Tiergarten, west of Vienna. Queues are very long early in the day, but if you try around 11 am you can usually get in fairly quickly.

Cinemas Check local papers for listings. Some cinemas show films in English – *OF (Original Fassung)* means it's shown in the original language, *OmU (Original mit Untertiteln)* means it's shown in the original language with subtitles. All seats are AS60 on Monday. There are performances in English at the English Theatre and the International Theatre.

Things to Buy

Local specialities include porcelain, ceramics, handmade dolls, wrought-iron work and leather goods. Selling works of art is big business; check the art auctions at the state-owned Dorotheum, 1 Dorotheergasse 17. Lots can be inspected in advance with their opening prices marked. Don't forget form U34 if you splash out (see Consumer Taxes in the Facts for the Visitor section).

Getting There & Away

Air Regular scheduled flights link Vienna to Linz, Salzburg, Innsbruck, Klagenfurt and Graz. There are daily nonstop flights to all major European destinations. Austrian Airlines (☎ 505 57 57) has a city office at 1 Kärntner Ring 18.

Bus Bus Tours (☎ 53 41 10) has buses to Prague leaving from 1 Rathausplatz 5 at 7 am daily except Sunday, and at 3 pm daily except Saturday (AS315; five hours). Blaguss Reisen (☎ 501 80) runs daily buses to Budapest at 7 am from the central bus station above Wien Mitte (AS290; 3½ hours).

Train Train schedules are subject to change, and not all destinations are exclusively serviced by one station, so check with train information centres in stations or call ☎ 1717 to confirm details.

Westbahnhof has trains to west and northern Europe and western Austria. Approximately hourly services head to Salzburg, some continue to Munich and terminate in Paris. Four trains a day run to Zürich (AS1064). A direct train goes to Athens at 7.05 pm (via Bucharest), and seven trains a day go to Budapest (AS310; three to four hours).

Südbahnhof has trains to Italy, the Czech Republic, Slovakia, Hungary (two a day to

Budapest) and Poland. Trains depart every two hours to Graz, and four a day go to Rome via Venice and Florence. Four trains a day go to Bratislava (AS120); five (four at weekends) go to Prague (AS412; five hours), some of which continue to Berlin.

Franz Josefs Bahnhof handles local trains. It also has two trains a day to Prague (AS394; 5½ hours). Wien-Mitte has local trains only.

Car & Motorbike The Gürtel is an outer ring road which joins up with the A22 on the north bank of the Danube and the A23 south-east of town. All the main road routes intersect with this system, including the A1 from Linz and Salzburg, and the A2 from Graz.

Hitching Mitfahrzentrale Wien (☎ 715 00 66), 3 Invalidenstrasse 15, links hitchhikers and drivers. It's open Monday to Friday from 9 am to 6 pm and Saturday to 1 pm. Examples of fares are Salzburg AS230, Innsbruck AS280 and Munich AS310. Mitzfahrzentrale Josefstadt (☎ 408 22 10), 8 Daungasse 1A, has similar rates. Telephone to check availability before going to either office. Lifts across Austria are limited, but there are usually many cars going into Germany.

Boat DDSG operates boats along the Danube. Its Vienna office (☎ 727 500) is at Handelskai 265, by the Reichsbrücke bridge. Fast hydrofoils travel eastwards to Bratislava and Budapest. There are two departures a day to Bratislava (AS210/AS330 one way/return; one hour) from mid-April to mid-October. There is one daily departure to Budapest (AS750/AS1100 one way/return; four hours 40 minutes) from 1 April to 31 October (two daily from May to early September).

Steamers ply the Danube from Vienna to Passau, on the German border, every day from May to late September. There are limited services in April and October. See the Danube Valley section for details.

Getting Around

To/From the Airport Wien Schwechat Airport (☎ 711 10) is 19 km from the city centre. There are buses every 30 minutes from 6 am to at least midnight between the airport and the Hotel Hilton. Hourly buses also run from Westbahnhof and Südbahnhof (AS60). It's cheaper (AS34) to take the S-Bahn (S7 line) from Wien Mitte.

If taking a taxi is the only option, negotiate the fare first (it should be under AS400).

Public Transport Vienna has a comprehensive and unified public transport network. Flat-fare tickets are valid for trains, trams, buses, the underground (U lines) and the rapid transport system (S lines). Routes are outlined in the free tourist office map; for a more detailed listing, buy a map from a Vienna Transit window (AS15). Single tickets cost AS20 from ticket machines, or AS17 each in multiples of five from Transit windows or Tabak shops. You may change lines on the same trip.

Daily passes (Stunden-Netzkarte) are a better deal at AS50 (valid 24 hours from first use) or AS130 (valid 72 hours). Validate the ticket in the machine at the beginning of your first journey. An eight-day, multiple-user pass *(Acht-TageStreifenkarte)* costs AS265. The validity depends upon the number of people travelling on the same card – one-person valid eight days; two people valid four days, and so on. Validate the ticket once per day per person. Weekly tickets, valid Monday to Sunday, cost AS142. Ticket inspections are not very frequent, but fare dodgers who are caught pay an on-the-spot fine of AS500, plus the fare. Public transport finishes around midnight.

Taxi Taxis are metered for city journeys (AS24 flagfall, plus AS2 per 200 metres) but the rate for longer trips must be negotiated. There is an AS12 surcharge for phoning a radio taxi.

Car & Motorbike Parking places are very limited in the city centre and there is an irksome system of one-way streets. The tourist office encourages visitors to use public transport for sightseeing and it might be worth heeding their advice. Blue parking zones allow a maximum stop of 30, 60 or 90 minutes. Parking vouchers can be purchased in Tabak shops.

Bicycle Bikes can be hired from the main train stations, open 24 hours daily. Pick up the tourist office's leaflet, *See Vienna by Bike*.

Fiacres The ponies and traps lined up at St Stephen's are strictly for the well-heeled tourist. Commanding prices of AS400 for a 20-minute trot, these ponies must be among Vienna's richest inhabitants.

AROUND VIENNA

Eisenstadt

The provincial capital of Burgenland lies 50 km south of Vienna. The train station is a 10-minute walk from the centre. Walk straight ahead down Bahnstrasse until you get to the pedestrian-only Hauptstrasse. Turn right to get to the tourist office (☎ 02682-67 390) at Schubertplatz 1, which is on the far side of the plush Hotel Burgenland. The office is open daily from 9 am to noon and 2 to 5 pm.

The provincial tourist office (☎ 02682-63 384 16) is the other way down Hauptstrasse in the Esterházy Palace. It's open daily from 9 am to 4 pm (weekdays only from October to May). The post office and postbus ticket office are near the cathedral at Domplatz. The telephone code for Eisenstadt is 02682.

Things to See & Do Joseph Haydn lived and worked in Eisenstadt for 31 years and, although he died in Vienna, his remains were transferred here to the **Bergkirche**, where they now reside in a white, marble tomb. Haydn's skull was stolen from a temporary grave shortly after he died in 1809, and 154 years passed before it was reunited with his body. The church itself is remarkable for the Kalvarienburg, a unique display of life-sized figures depicting the stations of the cross in a series of suitably austere, dungeon-like rooms. It's open daily between 1 April and 31 October from 9 am to noon and 2 to 5 pm; entry is AS20 (students AS10) and includes the mausoleum.

The baroque **Esterházy Palace** features the frescoed Haydn Hall, which is open the same hours as the Burgenland tourist office. Entry costs AS20, (students AS10) for a 40-minute guided tour (sometimes in English, or ask for the English notes). There's a large, relaxing park behind the palace.

Places to Stay & Eat Unfortunately, the nearest HI *Jugendherberge* (☎ 02167-22 52), Herbergsgasse 1, is 30 minutes away by train, on the shores of a lake, in the pleasant town of Neusiedl. Beds are AS135 (AS115 for those aged under 19); sheets are AS15. The hostel is open from March to November.

Gasthof Kutsenits Ludwig (☎ 63511), Mattersburgerstrasse 30, has the cheapest doubles (AS400) in Eisenstadt, excluding rooms in private houses.

For lunch, think Chinese: *Asia*, Hauptstrasse 32, and *Mandarin*, Wienerstrasse 2, both have excellent three-course menus, from AS49 and AS45 respectively (both open daily). *Gasthof Zum Haydnhaus*, Joseph Haydngasse 24, has regional and Austrian dishes for AS55 to AS145 (open daily). There's a *Billa* supermarket near the cathedral.

Getting There & Away Trains depart from Vienna Südbahnhof every two hours from 6.20 am (AS68; 1½ hours – change in Neusiedl). On weekdays, it's quicker to take the direct train from Wien Meidling (1¼ hours). Buses take about 1¼ hours, and depart from Wien Mitte (AS85). Wiener Neustadt is on the Vienna-Graz train route: buses from there take 30 minutes.

The Danube Valley

The strategic importance of the Danube (Donau) Valley as a corridor between the East and Western Europe meant that control of the area was hotly contested. As a result, there are some 550 castles and fortresses in Lower Austria alone. This includes the many monasteries and abbeys which have defences equal to conventional castles. The Wachau section of the Danube, between Krems and Melk, is considered to be the most scenic, with wine-growing villages, forested slopes, vineyards and imposing fortresses at nearly every bend.

DDSG operates steamers along the river west of Vienna from early April to the end of October. It has an office in the German border town of Passau (☎ 0851-330 35), Im Ort 14A, Dreiflusseck; see also the Vienna and Linz Getting There & Away sections. The Danube flows from west to east and you need to be prepared for longer sailing times when travelling upstream. Return fares are approximately 50% more than the one-way fares quoted here.

The route by road is also scenic. Highway 3 links Vienna and Linz and stays close to the north bank of the Danube for much of the way. There is a cycle track along the south bank from Vienna to Krems, and along both sides of the river from Krems to Linz.

St Pölten is the state capital of Lower Austria, and its tourist office (☎ 02749-2747) can supply information on both the town and the region. See also the provincial information office in Vienna.

KREMS

The historic town of Krems reclines on the north bank of the Danube, surrounded by terraced vineyards.

Orientation & Information

The town centre is 300 metres in front of the train station, stretching along Obere and Untere Landstrasse. To the left, it leads to the main city gate, Steinertor, off Südtiroler Platz. The main post office is to the left of the station on Brandströmstrasse 4 (Postamt 3500). Two km west of the station is the suburb of Stein. The tourist office (☎ 02732-82 6 76) is halfway between the two, at Undstrasse 6, in the Kloster Und. It is open Monday to Friday from 8 am to 5 pm. Between mid-April and 31 October it is also open Saturday and Sunday from 10 am to 5 pm and weekdays to 7 pm. There's a AS10.50 daily tax for staying in this resort, with the consequent 'guest card' privileges. The telephone code for Krems is 02732.

Things to See & Do

There's little to do in Krems except relax and enjoy the peaceful ambience. Take your time and wander round the cobbled streets, adjoining courtyards and ancient city walls. The most interesting streets are Landstrasse in Krems and Steiner Landstrasse in Stein. There are several churches worth a look, including the **St Viet**, high on the hill, and the **Dominican Church**, which contains a collection of religious and modern art and wine-making artefacts. There's wine tasting in the Kloster Und (AS100). The street plan available from the tourist office details points of interest.

Places to Stay & Eat

Camping Donau (☎ 84 4 55), Wiedengasse 7, near the boat station, is open from mid-April to 31 October and costs AS35 per person, from AS20 for a tent and AS35 for a car.

The HI *Jugendherberge* (☎ 83 4 52), Ringstrasse 77, has excellent facilities for cyclists, including a garage and on-site repair service. Beds in four or six-bed dorms are AS160.

Many hotels have a 10% surcharge for a single-night stay. The cheapest doubles (AS500 with shower/WC and TV) are at *Aigner* (☎ 84 5 58), Weinzierl 53. In Stein, *Frühstückspension Einzinger* (☎ 82 3 16), Steiner Landstrasse 82, offers similar doubles for AS520, and singles without the private WC for AS300.

Hotel Restaurant Alte Poste (☎ 82 2 76), Obere Landstrasse 32, is a historic 500-year-old house. It has good singles/doubles for AS280/540, or AS400/680 with private shower, and an enchanting rear courtyard. It's a good place to eat too, with daily meals from AS80 and local wine from AS22 per quarter litre.

The restaurant *Zur Wiener Brücke* (☎ 82 1 43), Wienerstrasse 2, has a wide selection of main dishes from AS70 and terrace seating overlooking the canal. It is open daily from 7 am to midnight.

To conserve Schillings, construct a meal in one of several supermarkets (eg the *Spar* opposite Alte Poste or the Konsum by the station) or try the pizza or Wurst snackbars on Landstrasse.

Getting There & Away

The boat station (Schiffsstation) (☎ 82 0 50) is a 20-minute walk from the train station towards Stein on Donaulände. There are up to three departures a day to Melk (AS238; three hours) between 10.30 am and 2.30 pm (Eurail passes are valid, Inter-Rail gets 50% off). Bike rental is AS35 with a boat ticket and these bikes can be taken on board free. Bikes can also be rented at the train and camping ground. Three or four buses a day to Melk (AS64; just over an hour) leave from outside the train station. Trains to Vienna (AS119; one hour) arrive at Franz Josefs Bahnhof.

MELK

Lying in the lee of its imposing monastery-fortress, Melk is an essential stop on the Wachau stretch.

Orientation & Information

The train station is 300 metres from the town centre. Walk straight ahead for 50 metres down Bahnhofstrasse to get to the post office (Postamt 3390), where money exchange is available to 5 pm on weekdays and 10 am on Saturday. Turn right for the HI hostel or carry straight on, taking the Bahngasse path, for the central Rathausplatz. Turn right for the tourist office (☎ 02752-23 07) on Babenbergerstrasse 1, which is open Monday to Friday from 9 am to noon and 3 to 6 pm, and Saturday and Sunday from 10 am to 2 pm; winter hours are shorter. In July and August, hours are daily from 9 am to 7 pm. There's a tax of AS10.50 per night, but the guest card makes up for it with the offer of a free day's bike rental. The telephone code for Melk is 02752.

Things to See & Do

The **Benedictine Monastery** dominates the town from the hill and offers excellent views. Guided tours (up to two a day in English) explain its historical importance and are well worth the extra money.

The huge monastery church is baroque gone mad, with endless prancing angels and gold twirls – but it's very impressive nonetheless. The fine library and the mirror room both have an extra tier painted on the ceiling to give the illusion of greater height. The ceilings are slightly curved to aid the effect.

It is open from the Saturday before Palm Sunday to All Saints' Day from 9 am to 5 pm, except between May and September when it closes at 6 pm. Entry costs AS50 (students aged up to 27 years AS25), and the guided tour is AS10 extra. During winter, the monastery may only be visited by guided tour (☎ 23 12 for information).

There are other interesting buildings around town. Try following the walking route outlined in the tourist office pamphlet. **Schallaburg Castle**, five km south of Melk (AS30 by bus), is a 16th-century Renaissance palace which has marvellous terracotta arches and hosts various exhibitions. It's open from May to October and costs AS60, (students AS20). A combination ticket, which includes the monastery, is available at a reduced price.

Places to Stay & Eat

Camping Melk is on the west bank of the canal which joins the Danube. It's open from April to October and charges AS35 per person, AS35 per tent and AS25 for a car. The reception is in the restaurant *Melker Fährhaus* (☎ 32 91), Kolomaniau 3, open Wednesday to Sunday (daily in summer) from 8 am to midnight. When it's closed, just camp and pay later. The restaurant has good lunchtime fare from AS75.

The HI *Jugendherberge* (☎ 26 81), Abt Karl Strasse 42, is newly painted in pastel pink and green, and has good showers and four-bed dorms. Beds are AS141 (AS120 for those aged under 19), or AS123 (AS102) for stays of three nights or more. The reception and main doors are closed from 10 am to 5 pm, but during the day you can reserve a bed and leave your bags behind the door to the left of the entrance. The hostel is closed from 1 November to 31 March.

Near the station, *Gasthof Baumgartner* (☎ 24 19), Bahnhofstrasse 12, has singles/doubles for AS200/400. Its restaurant is good and cheap and open from 7 am to midnight every day. A large plate of Wiener Schnitzel and chips comes with salad and costs AS70. Beer is AS25 a Krügerl.

The renovated *Gasthof Goldener Hirsch* (☎ 27 52), Rathausplatz 13, in the centre of town, offers singles/doubles with private shower from AS280/480. The restaurant is open daily and has dishes from AS75.

If you want to save Schillings, there is a *Spar* supermarket at Rathausplatz 9.

Getting There & Away

Boats leave from the canal by Pionierstrasse, 400 metres to the rear of the monastery. The 5½-hour boat journey from Melk to Vienna costs AS530; Krems is reached along the way after less than two hours. Bicycle rental is available in the train station and at the boat station. Trains to Vienna Westbahnhof (AS118; one to two hours) travel via St Pölten.

LINZ

Despite the heavy industry based in Linz, the provincial capital of Upper Austria retains a picturesque old-town centre. It's just a pity about the belching smokestacks on the outskirts that smudge your view of the Alps.

Orientation & Information

Most of the town is on the south bank of the Danube. The tourist office (☎ 0732-2393 1777), Hauptplatz 5, is on the main square and has a free room-finding service and an interesting walking tour pamphlet. It is open Monday to Friday from 7 am to 7 pm, and weekends from 8 am to 11.30 am and 12.30 to 7 pm. From 1 November to 30 April, it opens an hour earlier and closes an hour later. To get there from the train station, walk right, then turn left at the far side of the park and continue along Landstrasse for 10 minutes; alternatively, catch tram No 3.

There's also an information office in the station, and 24-hour bike rental. The large post office, opposite the station and to the left, is open 24 hours. The telephone code for Linz is 0732.

American Express (☎ 66 90 13) is at Bürgerstrasse 14. The provincial tourist office (☎ 60 02 210), which has information on Salzkammergut, is at Schillerstrasse 50. Opening hours are Monday to Thursday from 8 am to noon and 1 to 5 pm, and Friday from 8 am to 1 pm.

Things to See & Do

The large, baroque **Hauptplatz** has the Pillar of the Holy Trinity at its centre. The pillar was sculpted in Salzburg marble in 1723. From Hauptplatz, turn into Hofgasse and climb the hill to **Linz Castle**. The castle has been periodically rebuilt since 799 AD and provides a good view of the many church spires in the centre. It also houses the **Schlossmuseum**, open daily except Monday (AS25; temporary exhibitions cost extra).

The neo-Gothic **New Cathedral**, built in 1855, has an incredible array of stained-glass windows, including one depicting the history of the town. Walk, or take the special tram, up **Pöstlingberg**, on the north bank. It's recognisable by the twin-spired church at the summit of the hill. There is a great view from the top. The **Neue Galerie**, Blütenstrasse 15, is also on the north bank. It exhibits modern German and Austrian art. Entry costs from AS30, depending on the exhibitions. It's open daily, except Sunday. The *Posthof* (☎ 77 05 48), Posthofstrasse 43, is a centre for contemporary music, dance and theatre.

Places to Stay

The nearest *camping ground* (☎ 30 53 14) is out of town at Wiener Bundesstrasse 937, Pichlinger See.

There are three HI hostels in Linz. The *Jugendgästehaus* (☎ 66 44 34), Stanglhofweg 3, near Linz Stadium, has two-bed rooms for AS190 per person, and four-bed rooms for AS140. The *Jugendherberge* (☎ 78 27 20), Kapuzinerstrasse 14, is nearer the centre. It has beds, without breakfast, for AS90 to AS130, depending on whether you're under/over 19 or need sheets. It's the smallest hostel, and has no curfew. The *Landesjugendherberge* (☎ 23 70 78), at Blütenstrasse 23, on the north bank, has beds from AS110, also without breakfast. You should be able to check in at all of them during the day, except at Kapuzinerstrasse on weekends, when you'll have to wait till 5 pm.

The cheapest hotel (AS200/370 without breakfast) is *Schiefer Apfelbaum* (☎ 65 31 73), Hanuschstrasse 26, but it's inconveniently south of the station. *Wienerwald* (☎ 77 78 81), Freinbergstrasse 18, is next to the western terminus of bus No 26, 1.5 km from the town centre. It has a restaurant and good rooms from AS270/470. *Goldener Anker* (☎ 77 10 88), Hofgasse 5, off Hauptplatz, has rooms from AS300/560, excluding breakfast.

Places to Eat

There are plenty of cheap Wurst stalls around the park on Landstrasse, and a *Mondo* supermarket at the south-eastern corner of the park in Blumauerplatz. One of the cheapest places to sit down and eat (from AS56) is *Goldenes Kreuz*, Pfarrplatz 11, behind the parish church. It has typical Austrian food plus fish, spaghetti and grilled dishes. It's closed Saturday and Sunday.

Klosterhof, on the corner of Bischofstrasse and Landestrasse, is a large and popular eatery in a 17th-century building. It's open daily from 8 am to midnight, and has midday meals from AS70 and evening dishes between AS90 and AS170.

Café Ex-Blatt, on the corner of Steingasse and Waltherstrasse, is popular with a younger crowd. It has pizza for AS76 and beer for AS36. It's open daily to at least 1 am. Nearby, on the corner of Waltherstrasse and Klammstrasse, are *El Mexicano*, which serves inexpensive Mexican and Italian food, and *Nihonya*, which offers pricey Japanese fare; both are open daily.

Getting There & Away

The DDSG Schiffsstation (☎ 77 10 90) is at Untere Donaulände 1, on the south bank just east of Nibelungen Bridge. Services to Melk (AS328; 5¾ hours) and Passau (AS248; 6½ hours) only operate from mid-May to late September. There is just one departure daily in either direction. Linz is on the main rail and road route between Vienna and Salzburg.

The South

The two principal states in the south, Styria (Steiermark) and Carinthia (Kärnten), are often neglected by visitors, yet they offer mountains and lakes, and interesting influences from the neighbouring countries of Italy, Slovenia and Hungary.

GRAZ

Graz is the capital of Styria, a province characterised by mountains and dense forests. In former times, Graz was an important bulwark against invading Turks; today, it is fast becoming an essential stop on the tourist trail.

Orientation

Graz is dominated by the Schlossberg, the castle hill which rises over the medieval town centre. The river Mur cuts a north-south path west of the hill, dividing the old centre from the main train station. Tram Nos 3 and 6 run from the station to Hauptplatz in the centre. A number of streets radiate from the square, including Sporgasse, an important shopping street, and Herrengasse, the main pedestrian thoroughfare. Jakominiplatz is a major transport hub.

Information

There is an information office (☎ 0316-91 68 37) in the main train station on platform 1.

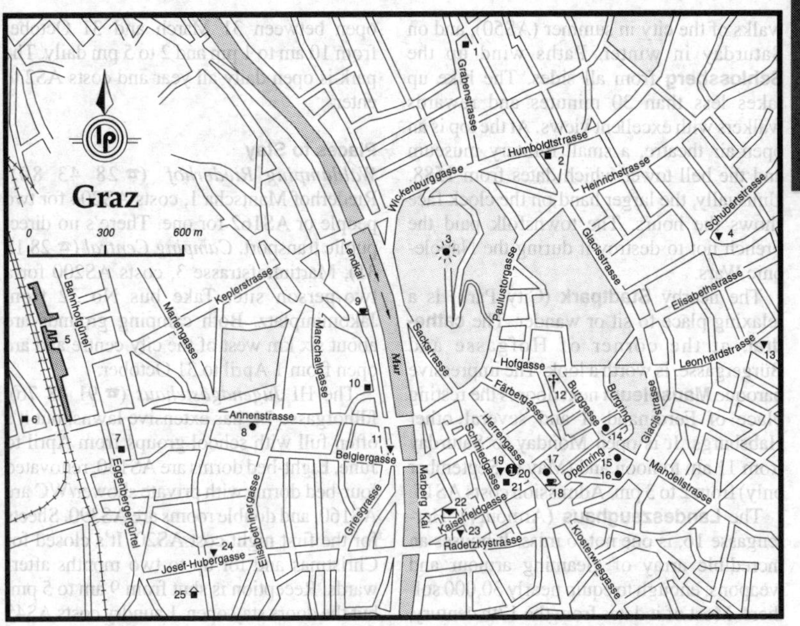

PLACES TO STAY

1 Schmid Greiner
2 Pension Iris
6 Lukas
7 Hotel Strasser
10 Hotel Mariahilf
21 Grazerhof
25 Jugendgästehaus

PLACES TO EAT

4 Mensa
11 Mangolds Vollwert Restaurant
13 Gasthaus Goldene Kugel
19 Landhaus Keller
23 Restaurant Gösser Bräu
24 Restaurant Schweizerhof

OTHER

3 Schlossberg Hill
5 Train Station
8 Billa Supermarket
9 Café art Scherbe
12 Cathedral & Mausoleum
14 Kommod
15 Opera
16 Tageskasse
17 American Express
18 Operncafé
20 Tourist Office & Landeszeughaus
22 Post Office

It's open daily from 9 am to 6 pm (5 pm Saturday, 3 pm Sunday and holidays). The station also has bike rental, a money exchange office and a Bankomat (for credit card cash advances).

The main tourist office (☎ 0316-83 52 41 11), Herrengasse 16, is open Monday to Friday from 9 am to 7 pm, Saturday to 6 pm, and Sunday and holidays from 10 am to 3 pm. The main post office is at Neutorgasse 46 (Hauptpostamt Graz, A-8010), and is open 24 hours for international telephones and for money exchange. American Express (☎ 0316-81 70 10) is at Hamerlingasse 6. The telephone code for Graz is 0316.

Things to See & Do

The tourist office organises daily guided

walks of the city in summer (AS50), and on Saturday in winter. Paths wind up the **Schlossberg** from all sides. The hike up takes less than 30 minutes and rewards walkers with excellent views. At the top is an open-air theatre, a small military museum and the bell tower which dates from 1588. Unusually, the larger hand on the clock face shows the hours. The townsfolk paid the French not to destroy it during the Napoleonic Wars.

The nearby **Stadtpark** (City Park) is a relaxing place to sit or wander. The **cathedral**, at the corner of Hofgasse and Bürgergasse, is worth a look. The impressive baroque **Mausoleum** next door is the resting place of Ferdinand II and several other Habsburgs. It is open Monday to Saturday from 11 am to noon and (May to September only) from 2 to 3 pm. Admission costs AS15.

The **Landeszeughaus** (Armoury), Herrengasse 16, is one not to miss. It houses an incredible array of gleaming armour and weapons, enough to equip nearly 30,000 soldiers. Most of it dates from the 17th century, when the original Armoury was built. Those two-handed swords look too heavy to even lift, let alone wield with any accuracy. The view from the 4th floor to the Landhaus courtyard and the Schlossberg is perfect. The Armoury is open between 1 April and 31 October, Monday to Friday, from 9 am to 5 pm, and on Saturday and Sunday to 1 pm. Entry costs AS25; students free (students get free entry to several other museums in town).

A good activity for those with kids is the **Schlossberg Cave Railway** on Sackstrasse. It's the longest grotto railway in Europe, and winds its way for two km around scenes from fairy tales. It's open daily and admission prices are on a sliding scale: AS30 for one (adults or children), AS55 for two, AS75 for three etc.

Eggenberg Castle, Eggenbergen Allee 90, is four km west of the centre (take tram No 1). The interior of this sumptuous 17th-century residence can be visited by guided tour; it also has three museums and extensive parklands. Entry to the state rooms, the *Prunkräume*, is AS25 (students free); they're open between 31 March and 31 October from 10 am to 1 pm and 2 to 5 pm daily. The park is open daily all year and costs AS2 to enter.

Places to Stay

Waldamping Riederhof (☎ 28 43 80), Riederhof Mantscha 1, costs AS204 for two people or AS162 for one. There's no direct public transport. *Camping Central* (☎ 28 18 31), Martinhofstrasse 3, costs AS200 for a two-person site. Take bus No 32 from Jakominiplatz. Both camping grounds are about six km west of the city centre and are open from 1 April to 31 October.

The HI *Jugendgästehaus* (☎ 91 48 76), Idlhofgasse 74, has extensive lawns, but it's often full with school groups from April to June. Eight-bed dorms are AS130, renovated four-bed dorms with private shower/WC are AS160, and double rooms are AS390. Sheets for the first night cost AS20. It's closed for Christmas and for up to two months afterwards. Reception is shut from 9 am to 5 pm, but the doors stay open. Laundry costs AS45 to wash and dry.

Five minutes from the station is *Hotel Strasser* (☎ 91 39 77), Eggenberger Gürtel 11. It has functional but pleasant singles/doubles for AS380/590 with private shower, or AS290/490 using hall showers. Around the back of the station, *Lukas* (☎ 58 25 90), Waagner Birò Strasse 8, offers a similar standard for AS305/490 single/double with shower, or AS245/440 without. Breakfast isn't included, though its restaurant is inexpensive.

Schmid Greiner (☎ 68 14 82), Grabenstrasse 64, north of Schlossberg, is cosy and old-fashioned, but the traffic outside can be noisy. Singles/doubles are AS340/460, using hall shower. The only place in the old centre is *Grazerhof* (☎ 82 98 24) on Stubenberggasse 10. Smallish, innocuous rooms are AS460/700, or AS520/800 with private shower. The hotel borders two pedestrian streets, but the receptionist can tell you where to park.

The three-star *Hotel Mariahilf* (☎ 91 31 630), Mariahilfer Strasse 9, has singles/

doubles with private shower from AS700/1200. The rooms are very large, but the furnishings in some look like they've been thrown together on a mix-and-mismatch basis – a few of those carpets should have been chucked out with the Third Reich. Three-star comfort is generally a better deal in pensions. *Pension Iris* (☎ 32 20 81), Bergmanngasse 10, has comfortable singles/doubles with shower and WC for AS500/700 (closed July). Double-glazing eliminates traffic noise.

Places to Eat

Supermarkets include the large *Billa* at Annenstrasse 23, but there are lots of cheap restaurants dotted around. The cheapest is the *University Mensa*, downstairs at Schubertstrasse 2-4. Main meals (including a vegetarian choice) are AS34 to AS54, with discounts for students. Food is served Monday to Friday from 11 am to 2 pm. The café on the ground floor is open Monday to Friday from 8 am to 4 pm, and has breakfasts for AS33. There are several other cheap places in the vicinity of the university which are popular with students: wander down Halbärthgasse and Harrachgasse.

Restaurant Schweizerhof, Josef Huber Gasse 24, has terrific three-course lunchtime meals from AS60 and spaghetti from AS45. It's open weekdays from 10 am to 2.30 pm and 5 to 10 pm. *Calafati*, a Chinese restaurant three minutes south of the HI hostel, at Lissagasse 2, has excellent lunch specials from AS42 (not Sunday).

A good place to try local cooking (and about 100 different types of beer!) is *Gasthaus Goldene Kugel*, at Leonhardstrasse 32. It's open Sunday to Friday from 9 am to 1 am. Midday meals cost from AS55; evening dishes are around AS80. *Restaurant Gösser Bräu*, Neutorgasse 48, is a large place which has many different rooms and outside tables. Food is AS60 to AS200, and there's a wide selection of local Gösser beer from AS29. Opening hours are Sunday to Friday from 9 am to midnight.

Cafeteria-style vegetable heaven can be found at *Mangolds Vollwert Restaurant*, Griesgasse 11. Salad is AS13 per 100 grams, daily dishes are AS60 to AS90, and there are various healthy desserts.

For a splurge, head to the 16th-century *Landhaus Keller* (☎ 83 02 76), Schmiedgasse 9. Floral displays, coats of arms, medieval-style murals, and soft background music contribute to the historic ambience. Most dishes, including interesting Styrian specialities, exceed AS175, but the quality is excellent. It's open Monday to Saturday from 11.30 am to midnight.

Entertainment

Graz has several traditional coffee houses, including *Operncafé*, Opernring 22, which is open daily from 7.30 am (9 am Sunday) to midnight. In the centre of town, Mehlplatz and Prokopigasse are full of relatively inexpensive, lively bars, which offer snacks or full meals until late.

Kommod, Burggasse 15, is a bright and busy bar, often packed with students, which serves pizza and pasta from AS64; it's open daily from 5 pm to 2 am. *Café art Scherbe*, Stockergasse 2, off Lendl Platz, is a more relaxed bar, with displays of objets d'art and paintings (which are for sale). It's open Monday to Saturday from 10 am to 3 am, Sunday from 3 pm to midnight.

Graz is an important cultural centre and hosts musical events throughout the year. The Tageskasse (☎ 8000), Kaiser Josef Platz 10, sells tickets without commission for the Schauspielhaus (theatre) and Opernhaus (opera), and also dispenses information. Students aged under 27 pay half price. An hour before performances, students can buy leftover tickets for AS60 at the door, and anybody can buy standing room tickets for AS25 to AS35.

Getting There & Away

Direct IC trains to Vienna's Südbahnhof depart every two hours (AS296; two hours 40 minutes). Trains depart every two hours to Salzburg (AS396), either direct or changing at Bischofshofen. A daily direct train departs for Zagreb (AS208; 3½ hours) at 6.58 pm. The direct service to Budapest leaves at 6.18 am, though two later trains have an onward connection at Szentgottard. Trains to Klagenfurt go via Leoben. The A2 autobahn from Vienna to Klagenfurt passes a few kilometres south of the city.

Getting Around

Public transport tickets cost AS18 each or AS130 for a block of 10 tickets. The Schlossbergbahn (castle hill railway) runs from Sackstrasse up the castle hill; the fare is AS18. The Touristenkarte costs AS42 and is valid for 24 hours, including rides on the Schlossbergbahn.

AROUND GRAZ

The stud farm of the famous Lippizaner stallions who perform in Vienna is about 40 km west of Graz at **Piber**. The farm can be visited from Easter to the end of October; get details from the Graz tourist office or the Köflach tourist office (☎ 03144-25 19 70), which is three km from the farm. Köflach can be reached by train (AS78, private line) or bus from Graz.

KLAGENFURT

The capital of Carinthia since 1518, Klagenfurt may not be prominent as a tourist destination but it is not without its attractions.

Orientation & Information

The main train station is one km south of Neuer Platz, the heart of the city. To get there from the station, walk straight ahead down Bahnhofstrasse and take a left at Paradieser Gasse. The tourist office (☎ 0463-53 72 23) is in the Rathaus on Neuer Platz. Opening hours are Monday to Friday from 8 am to 8 pm, Saturday and Sunday from 10 am to 5 pm; from 1 October to 30 April, hours are reduced to Monday to Friday from 8 am to 6 pm. The staff reserves rooms (no commission), and rents bikes at a low rate of AS30 for three hours or AS70 for the day. The Hauptbahnhof also rents bikes, and is open 24 hours a day. The main post office is on Dr Hermann Gasse (Postamt 9010), one block to the west of Neuer Platz.

The telephone code for Klagenfurt is 0463.

Things to See & Do

The **Neuer Platz** (New Square) is dominated by the Dragon Fountain, the emblem of the city, and also by a statue of Maria Theresa dating from 1765. **Alter Platz** (Old Square) is the oldest part of the city, and an interesting area to explore. The walls of the Hall of Arms (Wappensaal) in the 16th-century **Landhaus** are covered in paintings of 655 coats of arms. The ceiling, which has a gallery painted on it, giving the illusion that it is vaulted, is more impressive than the walls. Stand in the centre of the room for the best effect. The Landhaus is open between 1 April and 31 September, Monday to Friday, from 9 am to noon and 12.30 to 5 pm. Entry costs a nominal AS10 (students AS5).

Lake Wörther, four km west of the city centre, is one of the warmer lakes in the region owing to the presence of subterranean thermal springs. It is ideal for water sports. STW (☎ 21 155), St Veiter Strasse 31, runs steamers on the lake from the end of April to mid-October. A one-day circular tour costs AS170 (AS150 in advance), or AS380 (AS330 in advance). Boats also travel up the canal to the city centre (AS40).

You can swim or go boating in summer at the lakeside **Strandbad** (☎ 26 25 00), near the boat station; there is also tennis and crazy golf nearby. The adjoining **Europa Park** has various attractions, including a reptile zoo and a planetarium. The most touristy offering in the park is **Minimundus**, which displays 150 models of famous international buildings on a 1:25 scale. It is open daily from late April to mid-October and costs AS75 for adults (children AS20). Take bus S or K from Heiligengeistplatz.

Klagenfurt is ringed by castles and stately homes. The tourist office has a free map detailing routes, which is ideal if you have your own transport. It also has a *Radwandern* cycling map listing sights and distances. The longest tour is 34 km.

Places to Stay

Camping Strandbad (☎ 21 1 69) is in a good location by the lake in Europa Park. It costs up to AS92 per person and AS20 to AS100 for a site.

Jugendgästehaus Kolping (☎ 56 9 65), Enzenbergstrasse 26, is a 10-minute walk from Neuer Platz, but it's only open in July and August. The new HI *Jugendherberge Klagenfurt* (☎ 23 00 20), Neckheimgasse 6, near Europa Park, has gleaming facilities and four-bed dorms with private shower/WC for AS160. Dinner is AS50. Reception shuts from 9 am to 5 pm, and the hostel closes from mid-December to 31 January.

Lodging is pretty cheap near the inner ring roads. For B&B, try *Lindenkeller* (☎ 51 32 01), Villacher Ring 9, from AS190 per person. *Liebetegger* (☎ 56 9 35), Völkermarkter Strasse 8, and *Klepp* (☎ 32 2 78), Platzgasse 4, both have beds without breakfast for AS225 per person. For more style and a view of the lake, go to *Hotel Wörther See* (☎ 21 1 58), Villacher Strasse 338. It has well-presented rooms, some with balcony, cable TV and bath or shower. Singles/doubles start at AS590/880, with prices rising around 10% in summer. Extra beds for kids are AS260.

Places to Eat

Eating cheaply in the centre isn't too hard. There are several *Imbiss* (snack) stands dotted around, or you can stock up at the *Spar* supermarket in Adlergasse or Dr Hermann Gasse. *Stefanitsch*, Lidmanskygasse, is a combination deli and snack bar which has weekday lunches under AS60. On the same street, at No 19, is *Zur Chinesischen Mauer*, which has weekday Chinese lunches for AS62. *Capriccio*, a new, cheap, Italian, self-service joint, at No 27, is open daily from 9 am to midnight. *Gasthaus Pirker*, on the corner of Adlergasse and Lidmanskygasse, has typical meat-and-potatoes fare from AS70 to AS120. It's open Monday to Friday from 8 am to midnight.

Getting There & Around

The airport has five flights a day to Vienna and two a day to Zürich and Frankfurt; get there by bus A from the centre, and transfer to bus F at Annabichl. Trains to Graz depart every one to two hours (AS316; three hours). Trains to west Austria, Italy and Germany go via Villach, which is 40 minutes away by train.

City buses cost AS15 for one journey (including changes) or AS36 for a day pass.

Salzburg

The city that delivered Mozart to the world has much to recommend it, despite the fact that in more recent years the nearby hills have been alive to *The Sound of Music*.

The influence of Mozart is everywhere. There is Mozartplatz, the Mozarteum, Mozart House and the Mozart Museum, to name but a few of the attractions that bear his name. He even has chocolate bars and liqueurs named after him.

But even Mozart must take second place to the powerful bishop-princes who shaped the skyline and the destiny of the city after 798 AD.

Orientation

The centre of the city is split by the River Salzach. The old part of town (mostly pedestrian-only) is on the south bank, with the unmistakable Hohensalzburg Fortress dominant on the hill above. Most of the attractions are on this side of the river. The new town and the centre of business activity is on the north bank, along with most of the cheaper hotels.

Information

Tourist Offices The central office (☎ 0662-84 75 68 or 88 98 7 331) is at Mozartplatz 5. It's open daily between April and October from 9 am to 7 pm or later (up to 9 pm in July and August), and from 9 am to 6 pm Monday to Saturday between November and March. The provincial information section in the same building is open Monday to Saturday from 9 am to 6 pm.

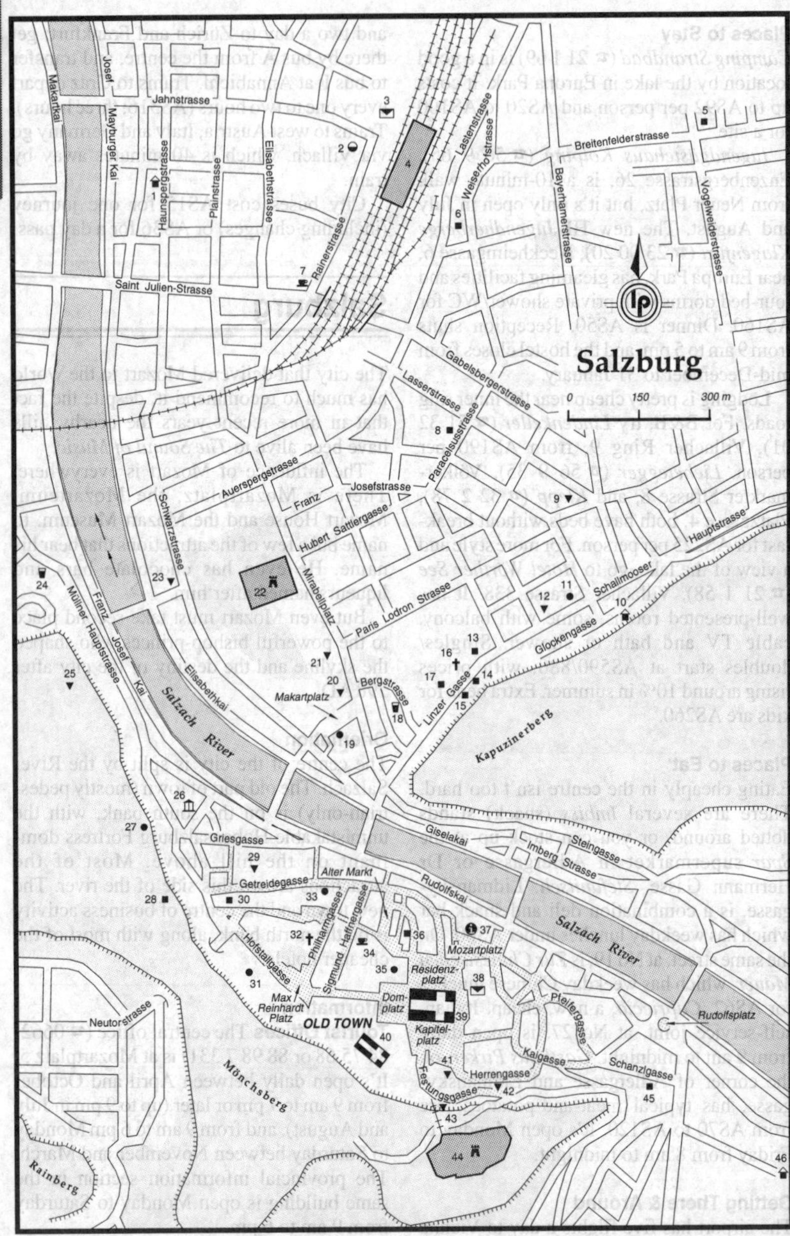
Salzburg
0
150
300 m
Makartkai
Josef
Mayburger Kai
Jahnstrasse
Haunspergstrasse
Plainstrasse
Elisabethstrasse
Rainerstrasse
Lastenstrasse
Weiserhofstrasse
Bayerhamerstrasse
Vogelweiderstrasse
Breitenfelderstrasse
Saint Julien-Strasse
Gabelsbergerstrasse
Lasserstrasse
Paracelsusstrasse
Auerspergstrasse
Josefstrasse
Franz
Hubert Sattlergasse
Schwarzstrasse
Mirabellplatz
Hauptstrasse
Schallmooser
Paris Lodron Strasse
Glockengasse
Linzer Gasse
Bergstrasse
Makartplatz
Elisabethkai
Franz Josef Kai
Müllner Hauptstrasse
Salzach River
Kapuzinerberg
Giselakai
Steingasse
Imberg Strasse
Rudolfskai
Griesgasse
Alter Markt
Getreidegasse
Hofstallgasse
Philharmgasse
Sigmund Haffnergasse
Mozartplatz
Residenzplatz
Domplatz
Kapitelplatz
Max Reinhardt Platz
OLD TOWN
Neutorstrasse
Mönchsberg
Rainberg
Pfeifergasse
Kaigasse
Schanzlgasse
Herrengasse
Festungsgasse
Rudolfsplatz
Salzach River
1
2
3
4
5
6
7
8
9
10
11
12
13
14
15
16
17
18
19
20
21
22
23
24
25
26
27
28
29
30
31
32
33
34
35
36
37
38
39
40
41
42
43
44
45
46

PLACES TO STAY

1 Jugendherberge Haunspergstrasse
5 Elizabeth Pension
6 Sandwirt
8 International Youth Hotel
10 Jugendherberge Glockengasse
13 Amadeus
14 Junger Fuchs
15 Goldene Krone
17 Institut St Sebastian
28 Naturfreundehaus
30 Blaue Gans
36 Zur Goldenen Ente
45 Hinterbrühl
46 Jugendgästehaus

PLACES TO EAT

7 Café-Bistro Tabasco
9 Restaurant Wegscheidstuben
12 Hotel Restaurant Hofwirt
20 Café Gelateria San Marco
21 Michael Haydn Stube
23 Vollwertkost Spezialitäten
25 Schloss Mönchstein
29 Sternbräu
41 Weisses Kreuz
42 St Paul's Stuben
43 Stieglkeller

OTHER

2 Postbus Station
3 Railway Station Post Office
4 Hauptbahnhof
11 Hofer Supermarket
16 St Sebastian Church
18 Schnaitl Musik Pub
19 Mozart's Residence
22 Mirabell Castle & Gardens
24 Augustiner Bräustübl
26 Museum of Natural History
27 Mönchsberg Lift
31 Festival Halls
32 Collegiate Church
33 Mozart's Birthplace
34 Café Tomaselli
35 Residenz Gallery & State Rooms
37 Main Tourist Office & American Express
38 Main Post Office
39 Cathedral
40 St Peter's Abbey & Catacombs
44 Hohensalzburg Castle

Information offices open all year are also in the Hauptbahnhof (☎ 0662-87 17 12) on platform 2A; at Mitte (☎ 0662-43 22 28), Münchner Bundesstrasse 1; and in the south (☎ 0662-62 09 66) at Park & Ride Parkplatz, Alpensiedlung Süd, Alpenstrasse. Other offices are: North (☎ 0662-66 32 20) at Autobahnstation Kasern, open 1 April to 31 October; and West (☎ 0662-85 24 51) at the airport by the BP petrol station, Bundesstrasse 95, open Easter to 31 October.

Money Banks are open Monday to Friday from 8 am to noon, and from 2 to 4.30 pm. Currency exchange at the Hauptbahnhof is available daily from 7 am to 10 pm in the summer, and 7.30 am to 9 pm in the winter. At the airport, money can be exchanged daily between 8 am and 8 pm.

Post & Telephone The post office at the train station (Bahnhofspostamt A-5020) is open 24 hours daily (including money exchange), but poste restante is only open from 7 am to 9.45 pm. In the town centre, the main post office (Postamt A-5010), at Residenzplatz 9, is open Monday to Friday from 7 am to 7 pm, and Saturday from 8 to 10 am.

The telephone code for Salzburg is 0662.

Foreign Consulates The British Consulate (☎ 84 81 33) is right in the centre of the old town at Alter Markt 4. The US Consulate (☎ 84 87 76) is at Herbert von Karaten Platz 1. The German Consulate (☎ 84 15 910) is near the Mönchsberg lift at Bürgerspitalplatz 1-II. The Swiss Consulate (☎ 62 25 30), Alpenstrasse 85, and Italian Consulate (☎ 62 52 33), Alpenstrasse 102-II, are both south of the old town. Foreign embassies are located in Vienna; see the Facts for the Visitor section.

Travel Agents American Express (☎ 84 25 01), Mozartplatz 5, is next to the tourist office. It's open Monday to Friday from 9 am to 5.30 pm, and Saturday to noon. ÖKISTA (☎ 88 32 52), Wolf Dietrich Strasse 31, is open Monday to Friday from 9.30 am to 5.30 pm. Young Austria (☎ 62 57 580), Alpenstrasse 108A, is open Monday to Friday from 9 am until 6 pm, and also on Saturday until noon.

Emergency The hospital, St Johanns-Spital (☎ 44 820), is at Müllner Hauptstrasse 48, just north of the Mönchsberg; ☎ 141 for an ambulance.

Things to See & Do

Walking Tour The old town is a baroque masterpiece set amid the Kapuzinerberg and Mönchsberg mountains, both of which have a good network of footpaths. Take time to wander round the many plazas, courtyards, fountains and churches.

Start at the vast **cathedral** (Dom) on Domplatz, which has three bronze doors symbolising faith, hope and charity. Head west along Franziskanergasse, and turn left into a courtyard for **St Peter's Abbey**, dating from 847 AD. The interesting graveyard contains the catacombs, and there are 20-minute guided tours every hour (AS12; students AS8). The western end of Franziskanergasse opens out into Max Reinhardt Platz, where you'll see the back of Fisher von Erlach's **Collegiate Church** on Universitätsplatz. This is considered an outstanding example of baroque, although the cherubs and clouds above the altar are a bit ridiculous.

Hohensalzburg Castle In many ways this is the high point of a visit to Salzburg. It's a 30-minute walk up the hill to the castle, or you can take the Festungbahn (AS22 up, AS32 return) from Festungsgasse 4. The castle is almost a separate village in its own right. Admission is AS30 (students AS15), but it's worth paying for the guided tour (AS30; students AS20) which allows entrance to the torture chambers, state rooms, the tower and two museums. The view from the castle over the city is stupendous. Look also at the view on the south side: the isolated house in the middle of the big field once belonged to the archbishop's groundkeeper, though tour guides will tell you it was the home of the shunned official executioner.

Museums The stunning **Museum of Natural History** (Haus der Natur) is at Museumsplatz 5. You could spend most of the day wandering round its diverse and well-presented exhibits. In addition to the usual flora, fauna and mineral displays, it has good hands-on exhibits on physics and astronomy, plus bizarre oddities such as the stomach-churning display of deformed human embryos. There are also many tropical fish and an excellent reptile house with lizards, snakes and alligators. It even has an inexpensive terrace café with a lunch menu. The museum is open daily from 9 am to 5 pm, and admission costs AS45 (students AS30).

The other museums don't take too long to get round. In the **Residenz**, Residenzplatz 1, you can visit the baroque state rooms of the archbishop's palace (by guided tour only) and the gallery which houses some good 16th and 17th-century Dutch and Flemish paintings. A combined ticket costs AS60. The **Rupertinium**, Wiener Philharmoniker Gasse 9, has 20th-century works of art and temporary exhibitions. Entry costs AS35 (students AS20).

Mozart's Birthplace (Geburtshaus), at Getreidegasse 9, and **Residence** (Wohnhaus), at Makartplatz 8, are popular but overrated. The former costs AS50 (students AS35); the latter is closed until January 1996. They both contain musical instruments, sheet music and other memorabilia of the great man.

Mirabell Castle The castle was built by the worldy prince-archbishop Wolf Dietrich for his mistress in 1606. Its attractive gardens featured in *The Sound of Music*, and they're a great place to sit down and relax. 'Musical Spring' concerts (among others) are held in the castle. Take a look inside at the marble staircase, which is adorned with baroque sculptures.

Mausoleum of Wolf Dietrich Located in the graveyard of the 16th-century Sebastian Church on Linzer Gasse, this restored mausoleum has some interesting epitaphs. In a wonderful piece of arrogance, the archbishop commands the faithful to 'piously commemorate the founder of this chapel' (ie himself) and 'his close relations', or expect 'God Almighty to be an avenging judge'. Mozart's father and widow are buried in the graveyard.

Organised Tours One-hour walking tours of the old city leave from the main tourist office (AS80). Other tours of the city and environs leave from Mirabellplatz and Residenzplatz, including *The Sound of Music* Tour.

The film was a flop in Austria, but this is the most popular tour with English-speaking visitors. Tours last three to four hours, cost around AS300, take in major city sights featured in the movie and include a visit to Salzkammergut (see the Jugendgästehaus under Places to Stay for a cheaper deal). If you go with a group with the right mix of tongue-in-cheek enthusiasm, it can be brilliant fun. It is hard to forget memories of loutish youths skipping in the summer house, chanting 'I am 16 going on 17', or manic Julie Andrews impersonators flouncing in the fields, screeching 'the hills are alive' in voices to wake the dead. On the other hand, if you go with a serious, earnest group, it can be quite dull.

Festivals

The Summer International Festival takes place from the end of July to the end of August, and includes music ranging from Mozart (of course!) to contemporary music. Several events take place per day in different locations. Prices vary from AS50 to a mere AS3900. Most things sell out months in advance. Write for information as early as September to: Kartenbüro der Salzburger Festspiele, Postfach 140, A-5010 Salzburg. Try checking closer to the event for cancellations. Some venues sell standing-room tickets a day or 45 minutes before performances (AS50 to AS200). Enquire at the ticket office, Hofstallgasse 1. Opening hours during the festival are 10 am to noon and 3 to 5 pm daily. Other important music festivals are at Easter and Whit Sunday.

Places to Stay

Accommodation is at a premium during festivals. Ask for the tourist office's list of private rooms (from AS250) and apartments, and the *Hotelplan* map which lists hotels, pensions, six hostels and six camping grounds.

Camping *Camping Kasern* (☎ 50 576), Kasern 1, just north of the A1 Nord exit, costs AS55 per adult and AS30 each for a car and tent. *Camping Gnigl* (☎ 64 14 44), east of Kapuzinerberg, is only open mid-May to mid-September, but costs less.

Hostels – North Bank If you're travelling for the purpose of partying, head for the *International Youth Hotel* (☎ 87 96 49), Paracelsusstrasse 9. Loud music, cheap beer (AS25 for 0.5 litre), and dancing on the tables add up to a fun time. The staff are almost exclusively young, native English-speakers. Not surprisingly, it is very popular; phone reservations are accepted no earlier than the day before. Beds per person are AS120 (eight-bed dorm), AS140 (four-bed dorm, own key) and AS160 (double room, own key). There is no curfew and it's open all day. Showers cost AS10, lockers AS10 and sheets (if required) are AS20. Breakfasts cost AS15 to AS40, dinners AS60 to AS75. It's not the cleanest place, but most people are too drunk to notice. The hotel also organises outings and shows *The Sound of Music* daily.

The HI *Jugendherberge* (☎ 87 62 41) at Glockengasse 8 is a bit old, and has a tendency to be overrun by noisy school groups, but it's the cheapest hostel in town. Beds in large dorms are AS120 (AS110 after the first night); dinner is AS65. Curfew is at midnight, and the doors are locked from 9 am to 3.30 pm. The hostel is open from 1 April to 30 September, and is conveniently situated for excursions on Kapuzinerberg.

The HI *Jugendherberge* (☎ 87 50 30), Haunspergstrasse 27, near the train station, is only open in July and August, and costs AS135. *Institut St Sebastian* (☎ 87 13 86), Linzer Gasse 41, will re-open around May

1995. It has dorms for AS130 and singles/doubles for AS240/420; breakfast is AS35.

If everywhere is full in town, try the HI *Jugendherberge* (☎ 62 32 48), Aignerstrasse 34, in the southern suburb of Aigen. It's open all year, and dorm beds cost AS135.

Hostels – South Bank The *Naturfreundehaus* (☎ 84 17 29), Mönchsberg 19, is clearly visible high on the hill between the fortress and the casino. Take the footpath up from near Max Reinhardt Platz, or the Mönchsberg lift (AS11 up, AS19 return) from A Neumayr Platz. It offers dorm beds for AS110 (showers AS10) and has marvellous views. It's open all day, but with a 1 am curfew. The café provides breakfast from AS30 and hot meals from AS68 to AS92. It's open from about mid-April to mid-October, but it depends on the weather (phone ahead).

The HI *Jugendgästehaus* (☎ 84 26 700), Josef Preis Allee 18, is large, modern and busy, and probably the most comfortable hostel. Eight-bed dorms are AS135, four-bed rooms are AS185 per person and two-bed rooms are AS235 per person, all with a AS10 surcharge for a single night's stay. Telephone reservations aren't accepted, so turn up at 11 am to be sure of a bed – reception is only open in small shifts during the rest of the day. It has good showers, free lockers and bike rental for AS85 per day. Daily *Sound of Music* tours are the cheapest in town at AS230 for anybody who shows up at 8.45 am or 1.30 pm. The film is also shown daily (AS5). South of town is a year-round HI *Jugendherberge* (☎ 62 59 76), at Eduard Heinrich Strasse 2; beds are AS145.

Hotels & Pensions *Sandwirt* (☎ 87 43 51), Lastenstrasse 6A, is at the back of the station but there is no noise from the trains. Singles/doubles are AS280/420 using hall shower; triples/quads with private shower are AS665/800. The rooms are clean and reasonably large. *Elizabeth Pension* (☎ 87 16 64) is on Vogelweiderstrasse 52. The rooms are smaller and the street is fairly noisy but the building is just around the corner from the Breitenfelderstrasse stop of bus No 15, which heads for the town centre every 15 minutes. Singles/doubles are from AS300/420 using hall shower, or AS300/480 with shower cubicle in the room. The new owners may alter prices.

Junger Fuchs (☎ 87 54 96), Linzer Gasse 54, has singles/doubles/triples for AS250/380/480, without breakfast. The rooms are better than the dingy corridors would suggest and it's in a convenient location. Room rates are the same year-round. More expensive, but merited by its position in the old town, is *Hinterbrühl* (☎ 84 67 98), Schanzlgasse 12. Singles/doubles are AS370/470 using hall shower, and breakfast is AS50. Reception is in the restaurant downstairs, open daily from 10 am to 11 pm.

Mid-Range Hotels *Goldene Krone* (☎ 87 23 001), Linzer Gasse 48, on the north bank, has singles/doubles with private shower for AS550/970; some of the rooms have church-like groined ceilings which add a bit of character. *Amadeus* (☎ 87 14 01) is down the road and opposite, at No 43-45. It has similar facilities but with TV. Prices are AS650/1000 for singles/doubles with private shower; AS450/680 without.

All the rooms in *Zur Goldenen Ente* (☎ 84 56 22), Goldgasse 10, have private bath/shower and TV but prices vary depending upon size and situation – starting at AS720/980 per single/double. The atmospheric restaurant (closed weekends) offers exotic dishes such as fillet of wild boar (AS205). Also in the old town is *Blaue Gans* (☎ 84 13 17), Getreidegasse 43. It has similarly varied prices, starting at AS500/950 with private shower; AS450/750 without.

Places to Eat

North Bank *Michael Haydn Stube*, Aicher Passage, 1 Mirabellplatz, is good value, even if the menu is limited. Lunch specials are AS50 to AS70, and it has snacks and pastries. It's open Monday to Friday from 8.30 am to 6 pm. Just down the passage is the small *Café Gelateria San Marco*, Dreifaltigkeitsgasse 13, which is good for cheap Italian food (from AS50). It's open Monday to Saturday from 9 am to 10 pm. *Restaurant Wegscheidstuben* (☎ 87 46 18), Lasserstrasse 1, has a three-course menu for AS110, available lunchtime and evening. It offers traditional Austrian cooking, which is popular with locals, and it's open Tuesday to Saturday from 8 am to midnight and on Sunday lunchtime.

Hotel Restaurant Hofwirt (☎ 87 21 720), Schallmooser Hauptstrasse 1, is more expensive, but has good lunchtime two-course meals for AS75 (three courses for AS175 on weekends), and there are English menus. One of the few vegetarian places in town is *Vollwertkost Spezialitäten*, Schwartzstrasse 33, also called Fred's Vegy. It's a shop and snack bar with a salad buffet from AS33, and a lunch menu for AS70, including soup. It is open Monday to Friday, 10.30 am to 6 pm.

Café-Bistro Tabasco, Rainerstrasse 25, attracts an older, middle-of-the-road clientele with its tempting array of international and Austrian dishes (AS100 to AS240). The salad buffet is AS62 per bowl, and it's open daily to midnight.

There's a fruit and vegetable market at Mirabellplatz on Thursday mornings, and there's a *Hofer* supermarket at Schallmooser Hauptstrasse 5.

South Bank Between sightseeing, nip into *Eduscho* for a small, strong cup of coffee for just AS7, but be prepared to stand. It's at Getreidegasse 34. The southern end of Kaigasse, near the old town, has a couple of decent and cheapish restaurants. On Universitätsplatz and Kapitelplatz there are market stalls and fast-food stands.

It's almost as if they're trying to keep *St Paul's Stuben*, Herrengasse 16, a secret from the tourists. It's the yellow house, completely anonymous from the outside but for the 1st floor terrace tables. Pasta and tasty wholewheat pizzas (from AS68) are served upstairs until late. It has a good atmosphere for drinking and is a good spot to meet locals. It's open daily from 6 pm to 1 am.

Sternbräu, in a courtyard between Getreidegasse 36 and Griegasse 23, is a bit touristy, but it has a nice garden and many different rooms. It serves good Austrian food and fish specials from AS80 to AS195. Opening hours are 8 am to midnight daily. The adjoining courtyard has a salad buffet eatery and a pizzeria.

Blaue Gans (see Places to Stay) has a good restaurant with three-course meals from AS85, and Mexican specialities from AS80 (closed Wednesday in low season). Its Mexican tavern (open from 8 pm; closed Tuesday and Wednesday) is more atmospheric, and has live music on Friday and Saturday. *Weisses Kreuz* (☎ 84 56 41), Bierjodlgasse 6, has Austrian food from AS70 and some interesting Balkan specialities from AS60 to AS168. It's a small place, so reservations are advised (closed Tuesday in winter).

Right at the top of the range is the restaurant in *Schloss Mönchstein* (☎ 848 55 50), Mönchsberg Park 26. Enjoy lavishly prepared food in an opulent setting, all shining silverware and soft classical music. Inevitably you have to pay for it, with most dishes topping AS300.

Entertainment

The atmospheric *Augustiner Bräustübl*, Augustinergasse 4-6, proves that monks can make beer as well as anybody. The quaffing clerics have been supplying the lubrication for this huge beer hall for years. Cheap beer is served in litre mugs for AS48. Meat, bread and salad ingredients (surprisingly pricey) are available in the delicatessen shops in the foyer. Eat inside or in the large, shady beer garden. It's open daily from 3 pm (2.30 pm weekends) to 11 pm.

Stieglkeller, Festungsgasse 10, is another beer hall. It's rather touristy, as indicated by the live *Sound of Music* show (AS330) in the summer, but there is a good garden overlooking the town. Food in the restaurant costs between AS80 and AS170. Opening hours are 10 am to 10 pm daily. The *Schnaitl Musik Pub*, at Bergstrasse 5, has a young and lively local clientele and live rock or indie music every second Friday from September to June. The cover charge is AS60 to AS80 on music nights. The pub is open daily in the summer from 7.30 pm to 2 am, and in the winter from 6.30 pm to 1 am. Imbergstrasse, Steingasse, and the stretch of road just north of the Mönchsberg lift are good streets to explore for late-night bars.

Coffee houses are a well-established tradition in Salzburg. *Café Tomaselli* and *Café Konditorei Fürst* face each other in an ideal central position overlooking Alter Markt. Both have newspapers, lots of cakes and outside tables.

Things to Buy

Not many people leave without sampling some Mozart confectionery. Chocolate-coated combinations of nougat and marzipan cost AS4 to AS6 per piece and are available individually or in souvenir presentation packs. Getreidegasse is the main shopping street.

Getting There & Away

Air There are regular scheduled flights to Brussels, Frankfurt, London, Paris and Zürich. Austrian Airlines (☎ 87 55 440) has an office at Schrannengasse 5, while British Airways (☎ 84 21 08) has an office at Griesgasse 29.

Bus Postbuses depart from outside the Hauptbahnhof. A timetable is displayed in the ticket office, or ☎ 167 for information. There are at least four departures a day to Kitzbühel (AS110; 2¼ hours), changing at Lofer. Buses to Lienz run only from July to September (AS217, change in Grossglockner). Numerous buses leave for the Salzkammergut region between 6.30 am and 8 pm – destinations include Bad Ischl (AS94), Mondsee (AS52), St Gilgen (AS54) and St Wolfgang (AS88).

Train Fast trains leave for Vienna via Linz every hour. The express service to Klagenfurt goes via Villach. The quickest way to Innsbruck is by the 'corridor' train through Germany via Kufstein (no passport required, no disembarkation possible in Germany). Trains depart every two hours and the fare is AS336. There are trains every 30 to 60 minutes to Munich (AS272; about two hours), some of which continue to Karlsruhe via Stuttgart.

Car & Motorbike Three motorways converge on Salzburg and form a ring road round the city: the A1 from Linz and Vienna and the east, the E11 from Munich and the west, and the A10 from Villach and the south. Heading south, you cross over a series of mountain ranges. The A10 has a long toll section from Altenmarkt to Rennweg. Be aware that the scenic Grossglockner route to Lienz is only open from about mid-May to mid-November.

Getting Around

To/From the Airport Salzburg airport is just four km west of the city centre. Bus No 77 stops near the airport tourist office and terminates at the Hauptbahnhof.

Public Transport Single bus tickets cost AS20 from the bus driver, but it's cheaper to buy a book of tickets from Tabak shops: a book of five costs AS70. The 24-hour pass valid for all city buses (including those to/from Hellbrunn) is excellent value at AS30. Prices are 50% less for children aged six to 15 years; those aged under six travel free.

Car & Motorbike Driving in the city centre is hardly worth the effort. Parking places are limited and much of the old town is pedestrian access only. The largest car park near the centre is the Altstadt Garage under the Mönchsberg. Attended car parks cost around AS25 per hour. Rates are lower on streets with automatic ticket machines, where a 90-minute or three-hour maximum usually applies.

Other Transport Taxis cost AS30, plus AS10 per km inside the city or AS20 per km outside the city. To book a radio taxi, call ☎ 87 44 00. Bike rental in the Hauptbahnhof is open 24 hours; bikes for rent in Residenzplatz are more expensive. Rates for a pony-and-trap (fiacre) for up to four passengers are AS350 for 25 minutes and AS680 for 50 minutes.

AROUND SALZBURG

Hellbrunn

Eight km south of Salzburg's old-town centre is the popular **Hellbrunn Palace**, built in the 17th century by bishop Marcus Sitticus, Wolf Dietrich's nephew. The main attraction is the ingenious trick fountains and water-powered figures installed by the bishop and activated today by the tour guides. Expect to get wet! This section of the gardens is open daily from April to October, with the last tour at 4.30 pm (later in summer). Tickets cost AS48, (students AS24), and include entry to the palace and the small Folklore Museum on the hill (open from 9 am to 5 pm). There is no charge to stroll round the attractive palace gardens, which are open from February to November (until 9 pm in summer).

The **Hellbrunn Zoo** is as naturalistic and as open-plan as possible: unharmful animals are hardly caged at all. It is open daily from 8.30 am to 6 pm (4 pm from October to March). Admission costs AS50 (students AS35).

Getting There & Away Bus No 55 stops directly outside the palace every half-hour. Pick it up from Salzburg's Hauptbahnhof or Rudolfskai in the old town. The last bus back to the city is at 9.10 pm.

Hallein

Hallein is primarily visited for the **salt mine** at Bad Dürrnberg, on the hill above the town. Much of Salzburg's past prosperity was dependent upon salt mines, and this one is the closest to the city and the most convenient to visit. The mine stopped production in 1989, and is now open to guided tours. Some people rave about the experience, others find the one-hour tour disappointing and overpriced (AS160; students AS140). Careering down the wooden slides in the caves is fun, but there's little to see and technical information is limited, especially for English speakers who receive commentary via a tape recorder. It is open daily from mid-April to late October, and the last tour leaves around 5 pm, depending upon demand. Overalls are supplied for the tour.

The tourist office in Hallein (☎ 06245-85 3 94), Unterer Markt 1, is open Monday to Friday from 9 am to 4.30 pm. There's also a summer kiosk at the Stadtsbrücke bridge, open daily from 4 to 9 pm.

Getting There & Away Hallein is an easy half-hour from Salzburg by bus or train. There are several ways to reach Bad Dürrnberg. The easiest option is to take the cable car, which is a signposted 10-minute walk from the train station. The AS230 (students AS200) return fare includes entry to the mines. A cheaper option is the 15-minute bus ride (AS23) from outside the station; departures are synchronised with train arrivals. You could also hike to the mine, but it's a steep 40-minute climb: head straight on from the tourist office, turn left just beyond the church, follow the road round and look for the sign pointing up to the right by the white school building.

Werfen

Werfen is a rewarding day trip from Salzburg. The **Hohenwerfen Fortress** stands on the hill above the village. Originally built in 1077, the present building dates from the 16th century and can be visited daily from Easter to 31 October. Entry costs AS100 (students AS90) and includes an exhibition, a guided tour of the interior and a dramatic falconry show, where birds of prey swoop low over the heads of the crowd. The walk up from the village takes 20 minutes.

The **Eisriesenwelt Höhle** in the mountains are the largest accessible ice caves in the world. Their amazing ice formations make you feel as if you're entering another world. The 70-minute tour (in German) costs AS80. Take warm clothes because it can get cold inside, and you need to be fairly fit. The caves are open from 1 May to early October.

Both attractions can be fitted into the same day if you start early (visit the caves first, and be at the castle by 3 pm for the falconry show). The tourist office (☎ 06468-388) in the village main street is open Monday to Friday from 9 am to 5 pm, except in July and August when it's open Monday to Friday from 9 am to 7 pm and weekends from 5 to 7 pm.

Getting There & Away Werfen (and Hallein) can be reached from Salzburg by Highway 10. By train it takes an hour. The village is a five-minute walk from Werfen station. Getting to the caves is more complicated, though it yields fantastic views. A minibus service (AS65 return) from the station operates along the steep, six-km road to the car park, which is as far as cars can go. A 15-minute walk brings you to the cable car (AS100 return) from which it is a further 15-minute walk to the caves. Allow four hours return from the station, or three hours from the car park (peak-season queues may add an hour). The whole route can be hiked, but it's a hard four-hour ascent, rising 1100 metres above the village.

Salzkammergut

Salzkammergut is a popular year-round holiday region of mountains and lakes to the east of Salzburg. It's an area where you can simply relax and take in the scenery, or get involved in the numerous sports and activities on offer. In summer, hiking and water sports are favoured pursuits; in winter, some hiking paths stay open but downhill and cross-country skiing are more popular.

A winter ski pass is available for the Salzkammergut-Tennengau region, which includes 140 cable cars and ski lifts in 21 ski resorts. It costs AS1325 for five days. Six, seven and 10-day passes are also available.

Orientation

The largest lake is Attersee to the north. West of Attersee is Mondsee, a picturesque warm water lake which is a favoured swimming spot. The village of Mondsee has an attractive church which was used in the wedding scenes in *The Sound of Music*. To the east of Attersee is Traunsee and its three main resorts: Gmunden (famous for twin castles linked by a causeway on the lake), Traunkirchen and Ebensee. South of Traunsee is Bad Ischl, the geographical centre of Salzkammergut. Most of the lakes south of Bad Ischl are much smaller, the largest being Hallstätter See. West of Bad Ischl is the Wolfgangsee.

Information

The Salzburg provincial tourist office has a great deal of information on the area, including bus and train schedules and a list of camping grounds. Most of Salzkammergut is in Upper Austria, so the Linz provincial tourist office is another good source of information. Styria stretches up to claim the area around Bad Aussee, so this is in the jurisdiction of the main Graz tourist office. See the Linz and Graz sections for details of the respective tourist offices.

The area is dotted with hostels and affordable hotels, but the best deal is probably to room in a private home or farmhouse – despite the prevalence of single-night surcharges. Tourist offices can supply lists of private rooms, as well as details of alpine huts at higher elevations. Most resorts offer a holiday/guest card *(Gästekarte)* which offers a variety of discounts. Make sure you ask for a card if it is not offered spontaneously. It must be stamped by the place you're staying (even camping grounds) to be valid.

Getting Around

The main rail routes pass either side of Salzkammergut, but the area can be crossed by regional trains on a north-south route. You can get on this route from Attnang Puchheim on the Salzburg-Linz line. The track from here connects Gmunden, Traunkirchen, Ebensee, Bad Ischl, Hallstatt and Obertraun. After Obertraun, the railway continues east via Bad Aussee before connecting with the main Bischofshofen-Graz line at Stainach Irdning. Attersee can also be reached from the Salzburg-Linz line prior to the Attnang Puchheim stop.

Regular bus services connect all towns and villages in the area. Timetables are displayed at stops, and tickets can be bought from the driver. Enquire about the Salzkammergut ticket, providing four days of specified train and bus travel within a ten-day period (AS220). See the Salzburg Getting There & Away section for more bus information. Passenger boats ply the waters of the Attersee, Traunsee, Mondsee, Hallstätter See and Wolfgangsee.

To reach Salzkammergut from Salzburg by car or motorbike, take the A1 or Highway 158. You can explore Salzkammergut by bicycle, but some of the roads can be steep, and don't expect to find many separate cycling tracks.

BAD ISCHL

This spa town's reputation snowballed after Princess Sophie took a treatment to cure her infertility in 1828. Within two years she had given birth to Franz Josef (the penultimate Habsburg emperor), and two other sons followed.

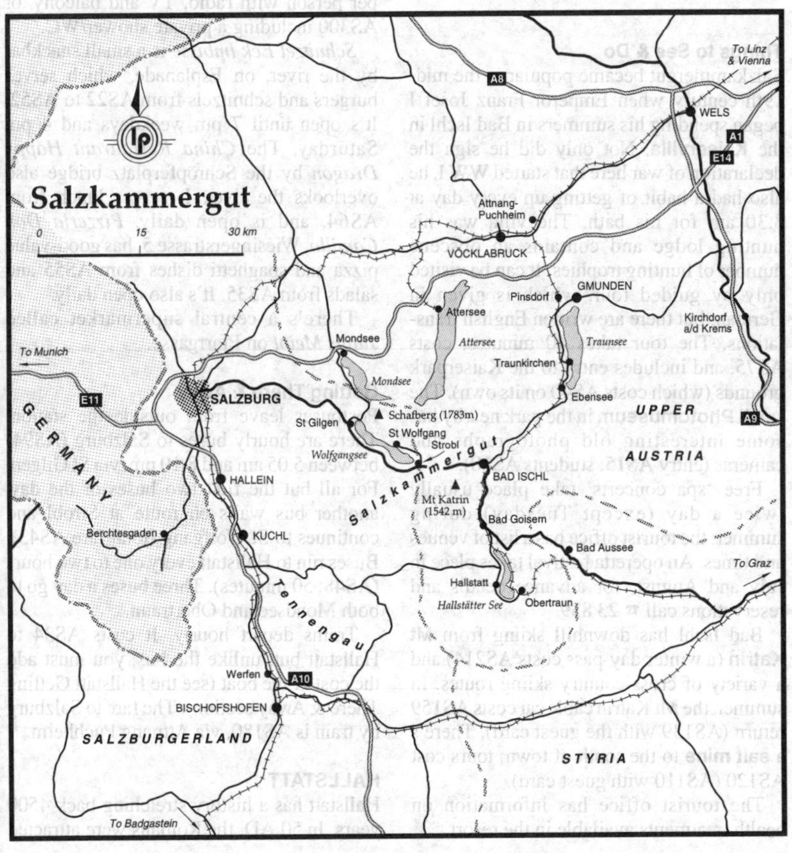

Orientation & Information

The centre of town is compactly contained within a bend of the River Traun.

The tourist office or *Kurdirektion* (☎ 06132-235 200) is close to the train station (straight ahead and bear left) at Bahnhofstrasse 6. It is open Monday to Friday from 8 am to 6 pm, Saturday 9 am to 4 pm and Sunday from 9 am to 11.30 am. The post office (Postamt 4820) is nearby on Bahnhofstrasse. There are money changing facilities at the post office and train station. The station also rents bikes between 5 am and 8.10 pm daily. The telephone code for Bad Ischl is 06132.

Things to See & Do

Salzkammergut became popular in the mid-19th century when Emperor Franz Josef I began spending his summers in Bad Ischl in the **Kaiservilla**. Not only did he sign the declaration of war here that started WW I, he also had a habit of getting up every day at 3.30 am for his bath. The villa was his hunting lodge and contains an obscene number of hunting trophies. It can be visited only by guided tour, which is given in German, but there are written English translations. The tour takes 40 minutes, costs AS75, and includes entry to the Kaiserpark grounds (which costs AS40 on its own). The small **Photomuseum** in the park nearby has some interesting old photographs and cameras (entry AS15; students AS10).

Free 'spa concerts' take place usually twice a day (except Tuesday) during summer; the tourist office has a list of venues and times. An operetta festival takes place in July and August; for advance details and reservations call ☎ 23 839.

Bad Ischl has downhill skiing from **Mt Katrin** (a winter day-pass costs AS214) and a variety of cross-country skiing routes. In summer, the Mt Katrin cable car costs AS159 return (AS139 with the guest card). There's a **salt mine** to the south of town; tours cost AS120 (AS110 with guest card).

The tourist office has information on health treatments available in the resort.

Places to Stay & Eat

The HI *Jugendgätehaus* (☎ 265 77) is at Am Rechensteg 5, in the town centre behind Kreuzplatz. Dorms are AS130 and dinner is AS60. It's closed from 9 am to 5 pm. Frau Unterreiter, at Stiegengasse 1 (☎ 46 072), has four singles and two doubles for around AS140 per person (excellent value). Baths cost AS20 and there are TVs in most rooms.

B&B pensions offer reasonable value. *Stadlmann Josefa* (☎ 23104), west of town at Masteliergasse 21, has basic rooms from AS150 per person. *Haus an der Traun* (☎ 234 72) is just to the right of the station, at Bahnhofstrasse 11. It has rooms at AS270 per person with radio, TV and balcony, or AS300 including a private shower/WC.

Schnitzel Eck Imbisse is a small snackbar by the river, on Esplanade, which serves burgers and schnitzels from AS22 to AS52. It's open until 7 pm weekdays and 4 pm Saturday. The *China Restaurant Happy Dragon* by the Schröpferplatz bridge also overlooks the river. It serves lunch from AS64, and is open daily. *Pizzeria Don Camillo*, Wiesingerstrasse 5, has good-value pizza and spaghetti dishes from AS55 and salads from AS35. It's also open daily.

There's a central supermarket called *Julius Meinl* on Pfarrgasse.

Getting There & Away

Postbuses leave from outside the station. There are hourly buses to Salzburg (AS94) between 5.05 am and 8.10 pm, via St Gilgen. For all but the first two buses of the day, another bus waits en route at Strobl and continues to St Wolfgang (total fare AS43). Buses run to Hallstatt every one to two hours (AS48; 50 minutes). Three buses a day go to both Mondsee and Obertraun.

Trains depart hourly. It costs AS34 to Hallstatt but, unlike the bus, you must add the cost of the boat (see the Hallstatt Getting There & Away section). The fare to Salzburg by train is AS180, via Attnang Puchheim.

HALLSTATT

Hallstatt has a history stretching back 4500 years. In 50 AD, the Romans were attracted by the rich salt deposits. Today, the village is prized mainly for its picturesque location.

Orientation & Information

Seestrasse is the main street. Turn left from the ferry to reach the tourist office (☎ 06134-8208), Seestrasse 169. It is open Monday to Friday from 9 am to 5 pm and weekends from 10 am to 2 pm; from September to May it is closed at weekends and for one hour at noon. The post office (Postamt 4830) is around the corner. It changes money, and also has a Bankomat for credit card cash advances. Get off the 'Lahn' postbus by the stream at the southern end of the road tunnel for the hostel; get off at the 'Parkterrasse' stop for the ferry and the tourist office. The telephone code for Hallstatt is 06134.

Things to See & Do

Hallstatt is set in idyllic, picture-postcard scenery between the mountains and the lake. It is invaded by crowds of day-trippers; fortunately they only stay a few hours and then the village returns to its natural calm.

Above the village are the **Saltworks**, open daily from 9.30 am. In May and October, the last tour is at 3 pm and in summer it's at 4.30 pm (closed winter). Admission costs AS130 (AS115 with guest card). The cable car to the top costs AS95 return (AS80 with guest card), but there are two scenic hiking trails you can take instead. Near the mine, 2000 flat graves were discovered dating from 1000 to 500 BC. Don't miss the macabre **Bone House** near the village parish church; it contains rows of decorated skulls (AS10). Around the lake at Obertraun are the **Dachstein Giant Ice Caves**, open May to mid-October, which cost AS76 (AS70 with guest card) to view – there's also a combined-entry ticket which includes the nearby Mammoth cave. A cable car provides easy access.

Places to Stay & Eat

Some private rooms in the village are only available during the busiest months of July and August; others require a minimum three-night stay. The tourist office can provide details.

Campingplatz Höll (☎ 8329), Lahnstrasse 6, costs AS50 per person, AS35 per tent and AS28 per car. It's open from 1 May to 30 September.

The HI *Jugendherberge* (☎ 8212), Salzbergstrasse 50, is open from around 1 May to 15 October, depending on the weather. Beds cost AS90 and, if required, breakfast and sheets another AS25 each. It has a friendly atmosphere and some newly built rooms. It's closed during the day, but a key is available for late returns beyond the curfew. *TVN Naturfreunde Herberge* (☎ 8318), Kirchenweg 36, is near the ferry, just below the road tunnel. It has dorm beds for AS100, plus AS35 each for sheets and breakfast (if required). It's run by the *Zur Mühle Gasthaus*, which is in the same building. Zur Mühle has pizza and pasta from AS65, and Austrian dishes from AS70 (closed on Wednesday).

Go to *Bräugasthof*, Seestrasse 120, for typical Austrian food in a traditional atmosphere. Lunchtime specials start from AS105, other dishes from AS80. It's open daily, but only from 1 May to 31 October. Double rooms with private WC and shower are available all year for AS760. *Gasthof Hallberg* (☎ 8286), Seestrasse 113, is popular with locals for pizzas and drinking, especially the back room. It also has rooms for AS380 per person with private WC and shower.

Getting There & Away

There are around six buses a day to Obertraun and Bad Ischl, but none after 6 pm. The train station is across the lake. The boat service from there to the village (AS20) coincides with train arrivals (at least nine a day from Bad Ischl; total trip 45 minutes). Parking in the village is free if you have a guest card.

WOLFGANGSEE

This lake can become crowded in summer because of its proximity to Salzburg, but its scenery and lakeside villages make it well worth a visit.

Orientation & Information

The lake is dominated by the Schafberg (1783 metres) on the northern shore. Next to it is the resort of St Wolfgang. The tourist office (☎ 06138-22 390) is on the main street near the bus stop, open Monday to Friday and Saturday morning. St Gilgen, on the western shore, provides easy access to Salzburg, 29 km away. Its tourist office (☎ 06227-348), Mozartplatz 1, in the Rathaus, is open Monday to Friday; daily in July and August.

Things to See & Do

The major sight in St Wolfgang is the **Pilgrimage Church**, built in the 14th and 15th centuries. This incredible church is a museum of altars – nine in all! The best is the winged altarpiece made by Michael Pacher between 1471 and 1481, which has astonishing detail on the carved figures and Gothic designs. The church wardens used to be so protective of this piece that the wings were kept closed except for important festivals. Now, thankfully, they are always open, except for eight weeks before and during Easter. The double altar by Thomas Schwanthaler is also excellent. The church is open daily from 7.30 am to 6 pm.

The **White Horse Inn** in the village centre was the setting for a famous operetta.

Ascend the **Schafberg** for good hikes and views. The Schafberg cog-wheel railway runs from May to early October approximately every 1½ hours during the day, and reaches 1734 metres. The cost is AS130 up and AS110 down; holders of Eurail or Bundes-Netzkarte passes ride free, and an Inter-Rail pass secures a 50% reduction.

St Gilgen has good views of the lake and some swimming spots, but little else of interest – unless you want to see the birthplace of Mozart's mother. In winter, there's downhill and cross-country skiing. Get information from the St Gilgen tourist office or the director of the ski school, Pepi Resch (☎ 06227-275), Liam 136, St Gilgen.

Places to Stay & Eat

Camping Appesbach (☎ 06138-2206), Au 99, is on the lakefront, one km from St Wolfgang in the direction of Strobl. It's open from Easter to 30 September and costs AS60 per person (plus tax), from AS50 for a tent and AS30 for a car.

St Gilgen has a modern HI *Jugendherberge* (☎ 06227-365) at Mondseestrasse 7. Starting prices are singles AS180, doubles AS150, triples AS130 and four-bed dorms AS120. Curfew is at 11 pm and it's closed from noon to 5 pm.

Both St Wolfgang and St Gilgen have a good selection of pensions (from AS170 per person) and private rooms (from AS140 per person). Lists are available from the respective tourist offices. Convenient pensions to try are: *Gästehaus Raudaschl* (☎ 06138-2561), Pilgerstrasse 4, opposite the St Wolfgang tourist office, which has singles/doubles from AS260/340; and *Gasthof Rosam* (☎ 06227-591), Frontfestgasse 2, two minutes from the St Gilgen boat station, which charges from AS300/440. Rosam has decent, hearty meals for about AS80. It's open daily from 8 am to 9 pm (Easter to 31 October only).

There are lots of places to eat in the centre of St Wolfgang, ranging from cheap snack joints to quaint touristy restaurants. *Gasthof Rudolfshöhe* is in the north of the village, up the small hill near the tunnel. It has an excellent menu encompassing Hungarian, Austrian, Indian and vegetarian food from AS65. It sometimes caters for British tour groups, but that doesn't stop the food from being tasty.

Buy picnic materials at the *Konsum* supermarket 100 metres from the Schafberg cog-wheel railway ticket office, towards the village centre.

Getting There & Away

An hourly ferry service operates from Strobl to St Gilgen between May and early October, stopping at various points en route. Services are more frequent during the high season from mid-June to mid-September. The journey from St Wolfgang to St Gilgen takes

40 minutes, boats sail from 8 am to 6 pm (7.30 pm in the high season). The fare is AS48. In the reverse direction, the ferry operates from 9.08 am to 6.10 pm (8.40 pm in the high season). Rail card validity for these services is identical to the Schafberg cog-wheel railway.

Buses from St Wolfgang to Salzburg and to St Gilgen go via Strobl, on the east side of the lake. St Gilgen is 50 minutes from Salzburg by bus, with hourly departures until 7.05 pm. The fare is AS60.

Tirol

The province of Tirol (sometimes spelled Tyrol) has some of the best mountain scenery in Austria. It's an ideal playground for skiers, hikers, mountaineers and anglers, and the tourist offices release plenty of glossy material to promote these pursuits. The province is divided into two parts: East Tirol has been isolated from the main part of the state ever since prosperous South Tirol was ceded to Italy at the end of WW I.

INNSBRUCK

Innsbruck has been an important trading post since the 12th century, thanks in part to the Brenner Pass, the gateway to the south. It wasn't long before the city found favour with the Habsburgs, particularly Maria Theresa and Emperor Maximilian, who built many of the important buildings that still survive in the well-preserved, old town centre. More recently, the capital of Tirol has become an important winter sports centre, and staged the Winter Olympics in 1964 and 1976.

Orientation

Innsbruck is in the valley of the River Inn, scenically squeezed between the northern chain of the Alps and the Tuxer mountain range to the south. Extensive mountain transport facilities surround the city and provide ample hiking and skiing opportunities, particularly to the south and west. The centre of town is very compact, with the main train station (Hauptbahnhof) just a 10-minute walk from the pedestrian-only, old town centre (Altstadt). The main street in the Altstadt is Herzog Friedrich Strasse.

Information

Tourist Offices The main tourist office (☎ 0512-53 56), Burggraben 3, sells ski passes and public transport tickets, and books hotel rooms (AS30 commission). It also gives out free maps like they were going out of fashion. Ask here about 'Club Innsbruck' if you intend to stay at least three nights. Membership is free and provides various discounts; it also allows you to go on free, guided mountain hikes from June to September. Opening hours are 8 am to 7 pm Monday to Saturday, 9am to 6 pm on Sunday.

There are hotel reservation centres in the Hauptbahnhof (open daily from 9 am to 10 pm) and at motorway exits near the city. The youth waiting room *(Jugendwarteraum)* in the Hauptbahnhof also offers useful information.

The Tirol Information office (☎ 0512-53 20), at Wilhelm Greil Strasse 17, is open Monday to Friday from 8.30 am to 6 pm, and Saturday from 9 am to noon.

Money The train station has exchange facilities (compare rates and commission between the ticket counters and the office) and a Bankomat. The tourist office also exchanges money.

Post & Telephone The main post office is at Maximilianstrasse 2 (Hauptpostamt A 6010), and is open daily 24 hours. The train station post office, Brunecker Strasse 1-3, is open Monday to Saturday from 7 am to 9 pm, and Sunday from 9 am to noon. The telephone code for Innsbruck is 0512.

Consulates The British Consulate (☎ 58 83 20) is at Matthias Schmid Strasse 12/I, and the German Consulate (☎ 59 6 65) is at Adamgasse 5. Foreign embassies are in Vienna.

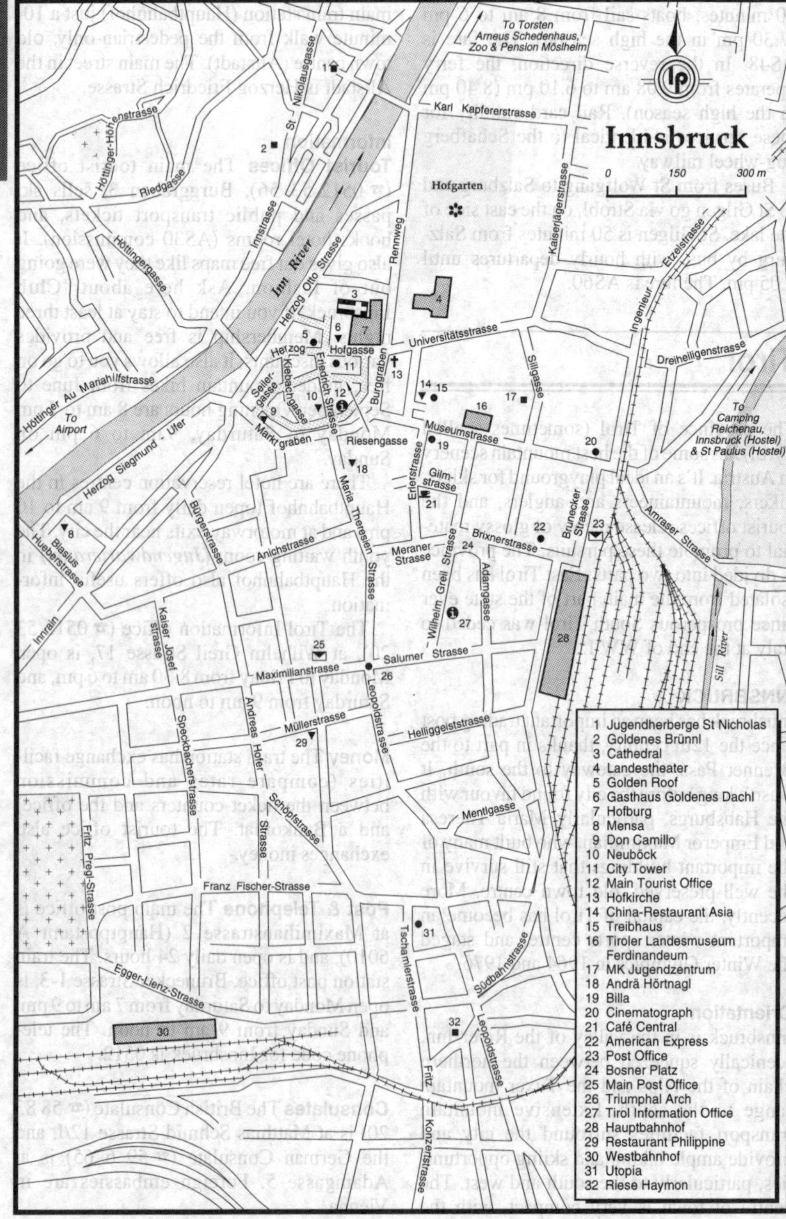
Innsbruck
0 150 300 m
To Torsten Arneus Schedenhaus, Zoo & Pension Möslheim
Hofgarten
To Airport
To Camping Reichenau, Innsbruck (Hostel) & St Paulus (Hostel)
Inn River
Sill River
Karl Kapfererstrasse
Riedgasse
Höttinger-Höhenstrasse
Höttingergasse
Innstrasse
St Nikolausgasse
Herzog Otto Strasse
Rennweg
Kaiserjägerstrasse
Ingenieur Etzelstrasse
Universitätsstrasse
Dreiheiligenstrasse
Höttinger Au Mariahilfstrasse
Herzog Siegmund Ufer
Hofgasse
Herzog Friedrich Strasse
Seilergasse
Kiebachgasse
Marktgraben
Burggraben
Sillgasse
Museumstrasse
Riesengasse
Erlerstrasse
Gilmstrasse
Brunecker Strasse
Brixnerstrasse
Amraser Strasse
Meraner Strasse
Wilhelm Greil Strasse
Adamgasse
Maria Theresien Strasse
Anichstrasse
Bürgerstrasse
Blasius Hueberstrasse
Innrain
Kaiser Josef strasse
Salurner Strasse
Maximilianstrasse
Leopoldstrasse
Müllerstrasse
Heiliggeiststrasse
Andreas Hofer Strasse
Speckbacherstrasse
Schöpfstrasse
Mentlgasse
Franz Fischer-Strasse
Fritz Pregl-Strasse
Tschamlerstrasse
Südbahnstrasse
Egger-Lienz-Strasse
Fritz Konzertstrasse
1 Jugendherberge St Nicholas
2 Goldenes Brünnl
3 Cathedral
4 Landestheater
5 Golden Roof
6 Gasthaus Goldenes Dachl
7 Hofburg
8 Mensa
9 Don Camillo
10 Neuböck
11 City Tower
12 Main Tourist Office
13 Hofkirche
14 China-Restaurant Asia
15 Treibhaus
16 Tiroler Landesmuseum Ferdinandeum
17 MK Jugendzentrum
18 Andrä Hörtnagl
19 Billa
20 Cinematograph
21 Café Central
22 American Express
23 Post Office
24 Bosner Platz
25 Main Post Office
26 Triumphal Arch
27 Tirol Information Office
28 Hauptbahnhof
29 Restaurant Philippine
30 Westbahnhof
31 Utopia
32 Riese Haymon

Travel Agencies American Express (☎ 58 24 91), Brixnerstrasse 3, is open Monday to Friday from 9 am to 5.30 pm and Saturday to noon. Infoeck (☎ 58 55 66), a budget agency, is at Kaiser Josef Strasse 1.

Emergency The University Clinic (☎ 50 40) is at Anichstrasse 35.

Things to See & Do

Consider buying the three-day museum pass for AS150 (students AS90), which entitles you to enter 11 museums.

Walking Tour For an overview of the city, climb the 14th-century **City Tower** (Stadtturm) in Herzog Friedrich Strasse. It's open daily between 1 March and 31 October from 10 am to 5 pm, except in July and August when it closes at 6 pm. Entry costs AS20 (students and children AS10). Combined tickets are available which include the small **Olympic Museum** across the square. The Olympic Museum shows videos of the winter games hosted by the city, but its **Golden Roof** (Goldenes Dachl), is of more interest; it comprises 2657 gilded copper tiles dating from the 16th century. Emperor Maximilian used to observe street performers from the balcony. Behind the Golden Roof is the **cathedral** – its interior is typically over-the-top baroque. Turning back to the south, take note of the elegant 15th and 16th-century buildings on all sides, and stroll down Maria Theresien Strasse to the 1767 **Triumphal Arch**.

Hofburg The Imperial Palace dates from 1397, but has been rebuilt and restyled several times since, particularly by Maria Theresa. The half-hourly 'tour' is a matter of doing it yourself with the aid of a booklet (AS5). The grand rooms are decorated with numerous paintings of Maria Theresa and family; the faces of her 16 children all look identical. The Giant's Hall and the chapel are highlights. The palace is open daily from 9 am to 5 pm (except from mid-October to mid-May when it closes on Sunday and holidays); admission costs AS50 (students AS20).

Hofkirche The Hofkirche (Imperial Church) is opposite the palace. It contains the massive but empty sarcophagus of Maximilian I, which is decorated with scenes of his life. The twin rows of 28 giant bronze figures of the Habsburgs are memorable. The dullness of the bronze has been polished by the sheer number of hands that have touched them; a certain private part of Kaiser Rudolf is very shiny indeed! The church is open daily to 5 pm (5.30 pm in July and August) and it costs AS20 (students AS14) to get in. Combined tickets are available which include the adjoining **Folk Art Museum** (Volkskunst Museum).

Ambras Castle Located east of the centre (take tram No 3 or 6, or bus K), this 16th-century castle features the Renaissance Spanish Hall, fine gardens, exhaustive portraits of Habsburgs and other dignitaries, and collections of weapons and armour. Opening hours from 1 April to 31 October are Wednesday to Monday from 10 am to 5 pm; admission costs AS60 for adults (students and children AS30). From 27 December to 31 March you can only visit the interior by guided tour at 2 pm on weekdays.

Alpine Zoo The zoo is north of the River Inn on Weiherburggasse. It features a comprehensive collection of alpine animals, including amorous bears and combative ibexes. It is open daily from 9 am to 6 pm (5 pm between November and February). Admission costs AS50 for adults (students and children AS25). Walk up the hill to get there or take the Hungerburgbahn, which is free if you buy your zoo ticket at the bottom.

Tiroler Landesmuseum Ferdinandeum This museum, at Museumstrasse 15, houses a good collection of art and artefacts, including Gothic statues and altarpieces. There's a relief map of Tirol in the basement. Opening hours are May to September daily from 10 am to 5 pm (Thursday also from 7 to 9 pm);

October to April, Tuesday to Saturday from 10 am to noon and 2 to 5 pm; and Sunday and holidays from 9 am to noon. Entry costs AS50, (students AS30).

Market There is a large indoor market selling flowers, meat and vegetables by the river in Markthalle, Herzog Siegmund Ufer (closed Sunday).

Skiing Most of the ski runs around Innsbruck are intermediate or easy but there are a few difficult ones as well. Many areas, such as Seefeld, were used in Olympic competitions. A one-day ski pass is around AS280, depending on the area, and there are several versions of multi-day tickets available. Equipment rental starts at AS150.

You can ski all year at the **Stubai Glacier**, which is a popular excursion. The journey there takes 1½ hours by bus No 1 from the train station (tickets from driver; AS137 return). The last bus back is at 5.30 pm. Many places offer complete packages to the glacier, which are only a little more expensive than going it alone. The tourist office has the cheapest deal: AS635 includes transport, passes and equipment rental.

Places to Stay

The tourist office has lists of private rooms in Innsbruck and Igls in the range of AS150 to AS250 per person. Igls is south of town; get there by tram No 6 or bus J.

Camping *Camping Innsbruck Kranebitten* (☎ 28 41 80), Kranebitter Allee 214, is west of the town centre and open from April to October. Prices are AS61 per person, AS35 for a tent and AS35 for a car. There is a restaurant on site.

Hostels A convenient hostel for the centre is *Jugendherberge St Nicholas* (☎ 28 65 15), Innstrasse 95. Reception is also here for the *Glockenhaus* hostel, up the hill at Weiherburggasse 3, which has more secluded singles/doubles for AS300/380 with private shower. The hostel is HI-affiliated but it seems more like an independent backpacker place. Unfortunately, it's not very clean, the shower (AS10 for a token) situation is dire, and the pay-up-or-get-out wake-up call is not particularly friendly. Dorm beds are AS115 for the first night and AS100 for additional nights, including sheets but not breakfast. Reception is closed from 10 am to 5 pm. Get a key for late nights out. The attached restaurant is open to all and is a good place for socialising. The food is so-so, comprising bacon and egg breakfasts (AS55), spaghetti bolognese (AS65) and Wiener Schnitzel (AS85).

Two HI hostels down Reichenauerstrasse are accessible by bus No O from Museumstrasse. *Innsbruck* (☎ 46 1 79), at No 147, costs AS130 the first night, AS100 thereafter (AS6 less if you're aged under 18). Curfew is at 11 pm, and the place is closed from 10 am to 5 pm. It has a kitchen, and a laundry which costs AS45. *St Paulus* hostel (☎ 44 2 91), at No 72, has large dorms for AS90 and sheets for AS20. Breakfast costs AS25, although kitchen facilities are available. Curfew is at 10 pm (but you can get a key) and the doors are locked from 10 am to 5 pm. The hostel is only open from mid-June to mid-August.

Two other hostels to try in the summer are: *MK Jugendzentrum* (☎ 57 13 11), centrally situated at Sillgasse 8A, which has beds for AS140 and sheets for AS10 (open from July to mid-September); and *Torsten Arneus Schwedenhaus* (☎ 58 58 14), at Rennweg 17B, where beds cost AS100, breakfast is AS45 and sheets are AS20 (open July and August).

Hotels & Pensions *Riese Haymon* (☎ 58 98 37), Haymongasse 4, is south of the station. It has long, spacious rooms with a sofa, stucco work on the ceiling and lots of character. The rooms vary in quality, so ask to see a selection. The best rooms are mostly in the older part of the building. Singles/doubles sharing the hall shower cost AS330/550, and doubles with private shower start at AS600. Reception is open between 7 am and 11 pm in the adjoining restaurant. On Saturday, when the restaurant is closed, phone ahead or look for the cleaner on the 1st floor.

Ferrarihof (☎ 58 09 68), Brennerstrasse 8, is south of town, just off the main road. Singles/doubles are AS230/460 with either private or hall shower. Reception is in the bar downstairs from 7 am to midnight. There is plenty of parking space.

Pension Möslheim (☎ 26 71 34), Oberkoflerweg 8, Mühlau, has singles/doubles for AS180/360, using hall showers. It's a quiet, family-run place, just a 10-minute walk from the zoo. Reception is next door at No 4. *Goldenes Brünnl* (☎ 28 35 19), St Nikolaus Gasse 1, is on the other side of the river from the old town. It has reasonable singles/doubles for AS360/650 with hall showers but without breakfast. Reception is in the restaurant, and is open to midnight (closed Tuesday).

The pick of the hotels in the Altstadt is *Weisses Kreuz* (☎ 59 479), Herzog Friedrich Strasse 31, which has singles/doubles for AS410/740 or AS680/1040 with private shower/WC. The 'superior' doubles for AS1120 are worth the extra cost. This 500-year-old inn played host to Mozart when he was 13, and all the rooms are spacious, well presented and comfortable. Prices drop slightly in winter. If it's full, try the *Hotel Happ* (☎ 58 29 80) across the street at No 14. It's slightly more expensive but almost as atmospheric. The reception is closed on Sunday.

Places to Eat

There are various Wurst stands and Imbiss shops for fast, cheap snacks around the city. There are two supermarkets close together on Museumstrasse. *Andrä Hörtnagl*, Maria Theresien Strasse 5, is a supermarket with a café area serving snacks from AS26 and main dishes from AS55. It's open weekdays to 6.30 pm and Saturday morning. The *University Mensa*, Herzog Siegmund Ufer 15, on the 1st floor, serves good lunches between 11 am and 2 pm from Monday to Friday. For AS40 to AS60 you can get a main dish, soup and salad. The mensa closes for holidays from mid-August to mid-September.

Restaurant Philippine (☎ 589 157), Müllerstrasse 9, is a specialist vegetarian restaurant, decked out in cheery colours. It has a wide selection of main dishes in the range of AS75 to AS140, and a fine salad buffet for AS45/82 for a small/big plate. Opening hours are Monday to Saturday from 10 am to midnight (the kitchen closes at 10.30 pm).

Café Central, Gilmstrasse 5, is a typical Austrian coffee house. It has English newspapers, daily menus (with soup) from around AS90, and piano music on Sunday from 8 to 10 pm. It opens daily from 8 am to 11 pm. The *China-Restaurant Asia* is nearby at Angerzellgasse 10. It offers excellent three-course weekday lunch specials; and you get a *lot* of food for just AS59.

Altstadt Area *Neuböck*, a delicatessen on Herzog Friedrich Strasse, is a good place to sit down and chomp cheap, hot or cold snacks. *Don Camillo* is a bar and café, on the corner of Marktgraben and Seilergasse. It has pizza (from AS65), pasta (from AS58), and inexpensive Austrian food. The quality is good and represents the best value in the Altstadt. Opening hours are Monday to Saturday from 11 am to 1 am, and Sunday from 5 to 11 pm.

Most of the other places in the Altstadt are a little pricey, and generally serve a combination of dishes: Tirolean, Austrian and international food. *Gasthaus Goldenes Dachl*, Hofgasse 1, provides soothing background classical music along with specialities such as *Tiroler Herrengröstl*, a beef, potato, egg and cabbage concoction for AS118. It is open daily from 8 am to midnight.

Restaurant Stiftskeller on Burggraben has a big menu, several different rooms, and a beer garden. Dishes start at AS90, and it's open daily to midnight. For more up-market eating, *Restaurant Altstadtstüberl*, Riesengasse 13, is one of the best places to try typical Tirolean food. Main dishes are in the range of AS120 to AS240 (it's closed on Sundays and holidays).

Entertainment

Ask the tourist office about 'Tirolean evenings' (AS200 for brass bands, folk dancing, yodelling and drinks) and summer classical concerts. The Landestheater has year-round performances ranging from opera and ballet to drama and comedy. Get information and tickets from the tourist office.

Utopia (☎ 58 85 87), Tschamlerstrasse 3, stages theatre and live music in the cellar downstairs. It's open Thursday to Saturday; entry costs AS60 to AS140, less for students. There's also a café, open Monday to Saturday from 5 pm to midnight.

Treibhaus (☎ 58 68 74), Angerzellgasse 8, has live music most nights (in a circus-style tent in summer). Entry costs AS150 to AS200, but there is free jazz on Friday nights and Sunday lunch, and a free disco on Saturday night. It's open 11 am to 1 am daily, except Sunday when it opens between 10.30 am and 10 pm.

Cinematograph, Museumstrasse 31, shows independent films in their original language. Tickets are around AS60. Cinemas around town are cheaper on Monday, when all seats are AS50.

Getting There & Away

Air Tyrolean Airlines, the small airport's main carrier, flies daily to Vienna, Amsterdam, Frankfurt, Paris and Zürich.

Bus Postbuses leave from by the Hauptbahnhof. The bus ticket office is near the youth waiting room in the smaller of the station's two halls.

Train Fast trains depart every two hours for Bregenz and Salzburg. Regular express trains head north to Munich (via Kufstein) and south to Verona. Departures are hourly to Kitzbühel (AS156). Three trains a day go to Lienz, passing through Italy. The 7.10 am and 5.04 pm trains (AS264) are 'corridor' trains (no passport necessary; no disembarking in Italy). The 12.43 pm train is an international train, which means you'll need to show your passport. The fare for this train is only AS196, because part of the journey is priced on lower Italian rates. However, if you're travelling on an Austrian Rail Card, you must pay for the Italian section (AS74). For train information, call ☎ 1717.

Car & Motorbike The A12 and the parallel Highway 171 are the main roads to the west and east. Highway 177, to the west of Innsbruck, heads north to Germany and Munich. The A13 motorway is a toll road southwards through the Brenner Pass to Italy; it includes the impressive Europabrücke (Europe Bridge) several km south of the city. Toll-free Highway 182 follows the same route, passing under the bridge.

Getting Around

To/From the Airport The airport is four km to the west of the centre. To get there, take bus F, which leaves every 20 minutes from Maria Theresien Strasse (AS18).

Tickets on buses and trams cost AS18, or AS44 for a block of four. Day passes cost AS23 but are not valid for the Hungerburgbahn. A seven-day pass costs AS105, valid Monday to Sunday.

It's hardly worth using private transport in the compact city centre. You can park without restriction on unmarked streets, but most streets near the centre now have a blue line. This means you can park for a maximum of 1½ hours; the charge is AS10 per half-hour and you get tickets from pavement dispensers. Parking is free on these streets from 6 pm to 8 am, and at weekends and holidays.

Taxis cost AS30, plus AS16 per km. Bike rental in the Hauptbahnhof is open daily from 6.30 am to 11 pm, but only between April and October, depending on the weather.

KITZBÜHEL

Kitzbühel, if you believe the tourist brochures, is 'a sun-kissed, joyful little town, filled with bustle'. It's certainly a fashionable and prosperous winter resort, which offers some excellent skiing and a variety of other sports.

Orientation & Information

The main train station is one km from the town centre. To reach the centre, turn left from Bahnhofstrasse into Josef Pirchl Strasse. Take the right fork (no entry for cars), which is still Josef Pirchl Strasse, and continue past the post office (Postamt 6370). The tourist office (☎ 05356-2155/2272), Hinterstadt 18, is in the centre, open every day (except Sunday in the low season). Ask about the summer guest card, which offers various discounts. The telephone code for Kitzbühel is 05356.

Things to See & Do

In winter, there are good intermediate ski runs on Kitzbüheler Horn to the north and Hahnenkamm to the south. A one-day general ski pass costs AS340; a day's equipment rental is around AS180 for downhill or AS105 for cross-country skiing. The Hahnenkamm professional downhill ski race takes place in January.

Dozens of summer walking trails surround the town and provide a good opportunity to take in the scenery; a free map from the tourist office shows routes. Get a head start to the heights with the three-day cable car pass for AS300. There is an alpine flower garden with free admission on the slopes of the Kitzbüheler Horn.

Places to Stay & Eat

A single-night surcharge (AS20 to AS40) usually applies, but try to negotiate. Many private rooms are available and there is a year-round camping ground (☎ 2806) near Schwarzsee lake. Prices are higher at Christmas and in February, July and August – peaking in the winter high season, which are the prices quoted here.

Centrally located is the *Pension Schmidinger* (☎ 3134), Ehrenbachgasse 13. It has rooms for AS300 per person with shower, or AS240 without. The owner, Barbara, said she would grant a discount to students with this book. *Pension Neuhaus* (☎ 2200), Franz Reisch Strasse 23, is also near the centre of the resort. It has singles/doubles priced from AS430/800 at half-pension (AS230/400 for B&B in summer). This place not only welcomes motorcyclists, it gives them a discount. Both pensions are usually open in the off season.

For more comfort, try *Gasthof Eggerwirt* (☎ 24 55), Untere Gänsbachgasse 12, which has a painted façade and is conveniently located down the steps from the three churches. Singles/doubles with private shower/WC are AS680/1280, and parking is available. This place is also recommended for quality local cuisine from AS100 to AS240.

There is a supermarket behind the tourist office on Franz Reisch Strasse. *Huberbräu Stüberl*, Vorderstadt 18, offers good Austrian food and an AS80 menu. After the kitchens close at 9.30 pm it remains popular with drinkers taking advantage of the low beer prices. It's open daily until midnight. *Adria* is near the post office. It serves Italian food from AS62, and is open daily all year. Next door is *La Cantina*, which offers Mexican food from AS70 (closed Monday).

Getting There & Away

There are approximately hourly train departures from Innsbruck to Kitzbühel (AS156; 1¼ hours) and Salzburg (AS228; 2½ hours). If your train stops at Kitzbühel-Hahnenkamm, get off because it's closer to the centre than the main Kitzbühel stop.

Getting to Lienz is awkward by train: two changes are required and it takes over four hours. The bus is much easier. It leaves from outside the main train station daily at 5 pm (AS139; buy a ticket from the driver), with extra buses at weekends. Heading south to Lienz, you pass through some marvellous scenery. Highway 108 (the Felber Tauern Tunnel) and Highway 107 (the Grossglockner mountain road, closed in winter) both have toll sections.

KUFSTEIN

Tourists are drawn to Kufstein, near the German border, by its lakes and the 13th-century castle.

Orientation & Information

The tourist office (☎ 05372-62207) at Münchner Strasse 2 is near the train station. It's open Monday to Friday from 8.30 am to 12.30 pm and 2 to 5 pm, and Saturday from 9 am to noon. Hours are extended during the peak summer period. It makes room reservations without charge. The main square, Unterer Stadtplatz, is on the other side of the River Inn. The telephone code for Kufstein is 05372.

Things to See & Do

The **fortress** dominates the town from a central hill. There is a lift to the fortress (AS17 return), but the 15-minute walk up is not demanding. The **Heimat Museum** in the castle has a bit of everything but can only be visited by guided tour, which lasts around 1¼ hours. Entry costs AS25 (students AS20), and there are five tours a day. It's open Tuesday to Sunday from late April to October, except in July and August when it's open daily (and tours are more frequent).

The **lakes** around Kufstein are an ideal destination for cyclists; you can rent bikes in the train station. Buses visit only some of the lakes, and then only in summer; they leave from the Bahnhof and from the post office on Unterer Stadtplatz.

Places to Stay & Eat

If you decide to stay overnight, ask for the guest card. There is a *camping ground* by the river (☎ 622 2945), Salurner Strasse 36, which charges AS43 per person, and AS30 each for a tent and a car. *Gasthof Zellerhof* (☎ 62415), Schluiferstrasse 20, behind the station, has rooms from AS220 per person. There are several reasonable restaurants and a supermarket on Unterer Stadtplatz.

Getting There & Away

Kufstein is on the main Innsbruck-Salzburg 'corridor' train route. To reach Kitzbühel (AS78; at least an hour), change at Wörgl; the easiest road route is also via Wörgl.

LIENZ

The capital of East Tirol combines winter sports and summer hiking with a relaxed, small-town ambience. The jagged Dolomite mountain range crowds the southern skyline.

Orientation & Information

The town centre is within the junction of the rivers Isel and Drau. The pivotal Hauptplatz is directly in front of the train station. The post office (Postamt 9900, money exchange available) is located here. The tourist office (☎ 04852-65265) is just off Hauptplatz, at Europaplatz 1. It's open Monday to Friday from 8 am to noon and 2 to 6 pm, and Saturday from 9 am to noon. It opens on Sunday in the summer and winter high seasons. The telephone code for Lienz is 04852.

Things to See & Do

Bruck Castle overlooks the town and contains folklore displays and the work of local, turn-of-the-century artist Albin Egger. Between Palm Sunday and 31 October, it is open Tuesday to Sunday from 10 am to 5 pm, except between mid-June and mid-September when it is open daily from 10 am to 6 pm. Admission costs AS40 (students and guest card-holders AS25). Most of the downhill skiing takes place on the **Zettersfeld** peak north of town (mostly medium to easy runs), and there are several cross-country trails in the valley. **Hockstein** is another skiing area. One-day ski passes are AS290 and the ski lifts are open from November to April. The Hockstein and Zettersfeld cable cars operate in the summer from about June to early October. There are good hikes in the mountains and to surrounding villages.

North of Lienz is the **Grossglockner** (3797 metres), the highest mountain in Austria, which offers excellent hiking. To get there, take the bus to the Franz Josefs Höhe hotel (AS99 plus AS25 toll), which is the closest you can get by road. There are morning departures from mid-June to 1 October. The rest of the year, buses only go as far as Heiligenblut because the road beyond is usually closed. Going it alone, the toll for the north-south Grossglockner

Iochalpenstrasse (Highway 107) is AS280 or cars and AS230 for motorbikes. This egion is part of the National park Höhe Tauern, where flora and fauna are protected. There are places to stay overnight. The elbertaurenstrasse also goes through the ark. If you continue north through the unnel, there's a toll of AS180 for cars and AS100 for motorbikes.

Places to Stay

Camping Falken (☎ 64022), Eichholz 7, is outh of the town, and closed from November to mid-December. Private rooms in and round the town start at AS120 per person. They are excellent value and a single night's tay is often possible. This is the case at *Egger* (☎ 48772), Alleestrasse 33, which osts AS150 per person. The tourist office nakes reservations for all accommodation ree of charge. Lienz no longer has a hostel ut there's a HI *Jugendherberge* (☎ 04824-2 59) on Highway 107 (the Grossglockner road), about 15 km away, at Hof 36, Heiligenblut. It is closed in October and November. *Pension Lugger* (☎ 62104), Andrä Kranz Gasse 7, is plain but it's right in the town centre. Doubles are AS400 with private shower, but without breakfast. There's just one single. *Gästehaus Masnata* (☎ 65536), Drahtzuggasse 4, has a couple of modern, spacious doubles (AS500 or AS520 with private WC/shower), and three excellent apartments with kitchens (sleeping three) for the same price. Unfortunately, the minimum stay for the latter is usually 10 days. The *Hotel Garni Eck* (☎ 64785) has been run by the same family for 500 years. It has large rooms with high ceilings, shower/WC, sofa and comfy chairs, nicely decorated corridors, big breakfasts and an excellent location on Hauptplatz, all for just AS400 to AS500 per person.

Places to Eat

Imbissstube Ortner, Albin Egger Strasse 5,

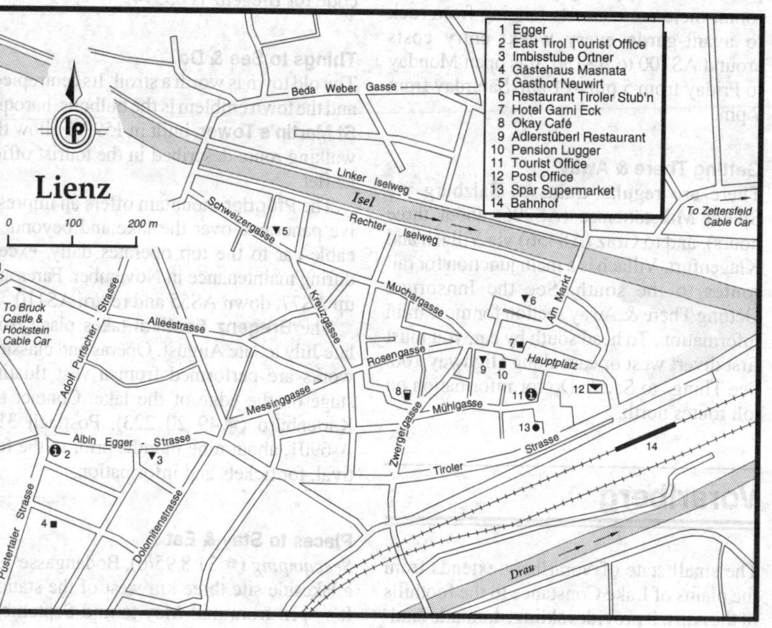

has the best grilled chicken in Austria, which is served with a delicious spicy coating. The smell of the chickens sizzling on the spit outside is enough to make vegetarians join Meat Eaters Anonymous. It's open daily from 10 am to 9 pm; a half chicken *(Hendl)* is just AS32. The *Adlerstüberl Restaurant*, Andrä Kranz Gasse 5, is a good place to try Tirolean specialities, from around AS80. There's also an extensive salad buffet (eat in or takeaway); opening hours are 8.30 am to midnight daily.

Restaurant Tiroler Stub'n, Südtiroler Platz 2, has tasty food from AS100, including the filling *Tiroler Stub'n Platte* (AS440 for two). *Gasthof Neuwirt*, at Schweitzer Gasse 22, offers a good selection of local, Austrian and grilled dishes from AS95, and a daily vegetarian menu.

Entertainment

The *Okay Café* in the Creativ Centre off Zwergergasse is a dark and smoky meeting place for local, young people. In the back room, there are concerts ranging from rock to avant-garde every week; entry costs around AS100 to AS150. It is open Monday to Friday from 5 pm to 1 am, Saturday from 7 pm.

Getting There & Away

There are regular trains to Salzburg via Spittal Millstättersee (AS296; about three hours), and to Graz (AS456) via Villach and Klagenfurt. Villach is a main junction for rail routes to the south. See the Innsbruck Getting There & Away section for more train information. To head south by car, you must first divert west or east along Highway 100. See Things to See & Do for information on toll routes north.

Vorarlberg

The small state of Vorarlberg extends from the plains of Lake Constance to the foothills of the Alps. It provides skiing, dramatic landscapes and access to Liechtenstein, Switzer land and Germany.

BREGENZ

Bregenz, the provincial capital of Vorar berg, offers lake excursions, mountain view and an important annual music festival.

Orientation & Information

The town is on the eastern shore of Lak Constance (Bodensee). As you exit th station, turn left into Bahnhofstrasse t reach the town centre. The tourist offic (☎ 05574-43 39 10), Anton Schneide Strasse 4A, is open Monday to Friday fro 9 am to noon and 1 to 5 pm, and Saturday t noon, except in July and August when hou are extended. The State Tourist Boar Vorarlberg (☎ 05574-42 52 50) is a Römerstrasse 7. The post office is o Seestrasse (Postamt 6900). Bike rental in th station is open daily from 6 am to 9.40 pn postbuses leave from outside. The telephon code for Bregenz is 05574.

Things to See & Do

The old town is worth a stroll. Its centrepie and the town emblem is the bulbous, baroqu **St Martin's Tower**, built in 1599. Follow th walking route described in the tourist offic leaflet.

The **Pfänder** mountain offers an impres ive panorama over the lake and beyond. cable car to the top operates daily, exce during maintenance in November. Fares ar up AS77, down AS55 and return AS110.

The **Bregenz Festival** takes place fro late July to late August. Operas and classic works are performed from a vast floatir stage on the edge of the lake. Contact th Kartenbüro (☎ 49 20 223), Postfach 31 A-6901, about nine months prior to the fe tival, for tickets and information.

Places to Stay & Eat

Seecamping (☎ 31 8 95/6), Bodangasse 7, a lakeside site three km west of the statio It's open from mid-May to mid-Septemb and prices are AS55 each per person, tent and car.

The HI *Jugendherberge* (☎ 22 8 67), Belruptstrasse 16A, is open from April to September. Yes, it is those two sheds that look like army barracks. Beds are AS111, plus AS20 for sheets. Curfew is 10 pm, and it's closed from 9 am to 5 pm.

Lists of private rooms (from AS170 per person), pensions (from AS200 per person) and apartments (from AS500) are supplied by the tourist office. A surcharge normally applies for a single night's stay.

The central but basic *Pension Günz* (☎ 43 6 57), Anton Schneider Strasse 38, has rooms from AS230 per person. It's only open from around Easter to 1 October. *Pension Traube* (☎ 42 4 01), close by at No 34, is a nicer choice, from AS280 per person. It has inexpensive weekday lunches.

Restaurant Charly (☎ 45 9 59), Anton Schneider Strasse 19, serves good pizza and pasta from AS65 (closed Thursday). It gets busy, so you may need to reserve a table. For Austrian food, try *Gasthaus Maurachbund*, Maurachgasse 11, which has main dishes from AS88 to AS190 (closed Thursday), or the similarly priced but more atmospheric *Alte Weinstube Zur Ilge*, Maurachgasse 6 (open daily).

There's a *Familia* supermarket with a cheap self-service restaurant downstairs in the GWL shopping centre on Römerstrasse.

Getting There & Away

Trains to Munich go via Lindau; trains to Constance (AS440) go via the Swiss shore of the lake. There are also regular departures to St Gallen (AS90) and Zürich. Trains to Innsbruck (AS276; three hours) depart every one to two hours. Feldkirch is on the same rail route (AS52).

Boat services operate from late May to late October, with a reduced schedule from late March. For information, call ☎ 428 68. Bregenz to Constance by boat (via Lindau) takes about 3½ hours and there are up to six departures per day.

There is a Mitfahrzentrale (☎ 611 00) for hitchers at Bildsteiner Strasse 7 in nearby Wolfurt.

FELDKIRCH

Feldkirch is the gateway to Liechtenstein, and Vorarlberg's oldest town.

Orientation & Information

The tourist office (☎ 734 67), Herrengasse 12, is open Monday to Friday from 8 am to noon and 2 to 6 pm, and Saturday from 9 am to noon. It reserves rooms free of charge. The telephone code for Feldkirch is 05522.

Things to See & Do

There are good views from the 12th-century **Schattenburg castle**, which houses a museum (AS20, students AS10; closed Monday). There's a free **animal park** *(Wildpark)* with 200 species one km from the centre. Feldkirch recently became host of the important **Schubertiade** summer music festival.

Ski slopes are at Laterns, just 15 minutes away by car. Alternatively, take the ski bus (calling at the town, the station and the hostel) which is free if you buy that day's ski pass (AS280) from the driver.

Places to Stay & Eat

The HI *Jugendherberge* (☎ 731 81), Reichsstrasse 111, is 1.5 km north of the train station in an historic building. It has been completely modernised inside and has good facilities. Beds are AS140, including breakfast. Curfew is at 10 pm; reception is closed and the doors are locked from 9.30 am to 5 pm. The hostel shuts from 1 November to early January and at Easter.

Gasthof Engel (☎ 220 62), on Liechtensteiner Strasse 106, is under two km south-west of the centre in Tisis. It has rooms from AS220 per person.

For cheap eating in town, go to *Löwen City*, Neustadt 17, which has self-service meals from AS50. It's open Monday to Friday from 9 am to 6 pm. There's a *Familia* supermarket next door.

Getting There & Away
Two buses an hour (one at weekends) depart for Liechtenstein from in front of the train station. To reach Liechtenstein's capital, Vaduz (AS30; 40 minutes away), change buses in Schaans. Trains to Buchs on the Swiss border pass through Schaans, but only a few stop there. Buchs has connections to major destinations in Switzerland, including Zürich and Chur.

ARLBERG REGION
The Arlberg region, shared by Vorarlberg and neighbouring Tirol, comprises a number of resorts and is considered to have some of the best skiing in Austria. Summer is less busy, and many of the bars are closed.

St Anton is the largest resort, enjoying an easy-going atmosphere and vigorous nightlife. It has good, medium-to-advanced runs, as well as nursery slopes on Gampen and Kapall. Get full information from the tourist office (☎ 05446-226 90), A-6580 St Anton, Tirol. Accommodation and food prices are reasonable, and the village plays host to a fairly large population of Australasian 'ski bums' who like to crack open the crates of beer outside the tourist office in the early evening.

There are nearly 200 B&B places in and around St Anton; the tourist office brochure has a full listing. Try *Ludwig* (☎ 05446-2610) or *Zentral* (☎ 05446-2509) in the main street. There are good pizzas at *Pomodoro*, otherwise try the takeaway stands which are scattered around town or visit the *IFEA* supermarket. Good après-ski bars include *Krazy Kanguruh*, on the slopes, and *Piccadilly*, in the village.

Lech, a more up-market resort, is a favourite with royalty and film stars. Runs are predominantly medium to advanced. For details, contact the tourist office (☎ 05583-21610), A-6764 Lech, Vorarlberg.

Despite its sophisticated profile, Lech has a *Jugendherberge* (☎ 05583-2419) only two km from the main resort, in the village of Stubenbach. It is closed in May, June, October and November.

A three-day ski pass valid for 88 ski lifts in Lech, Zürs, Stuben, St Anton and St Christoph costs AS445 for one day and AS1200 for four days. Rental starts at AS160 for skis and sticks, and AS80 for boots.

Getting There & Away
St Anton is on the main railway route from Bregenz to Innsbruck. From Bregenz, the train takes 1½ hours and costs AS134. St Anton is close to the eastern entrance of the Arlberg Tunnel, the toll road connecting Vorarlberg and Tirol. The tunnel toll is AS150 for cars and minibuses. You can avoid the toll by taking the B197, but no vehicles with trailers are allowed on this winding road. There are at least three buses a day to Lech (AS36; 40 minutes) from St Anton.

Czech Republic

Bohemia and Moravia together make up the Czech Republic, a Scotland-sized nation on the edge of the Germanic and Slavic worlds. It's one of Europe's most historic countries, full of fairytale castles, chateaux, manors and museums. The medieval cores of several dozen towns have been carefully preserved and there's so much to see that you could make repeated visits.

The Czech Republic is doubly inviting for its cultured, friendly people and excellent facilities. The transportation network is equalled only in Western Europe. Ninety per cent of English-speaking visitors limit themselves to Prague but the clever few who escape the hordes and high prices in the capital soon experience just how helpful the Czech people can be (almost everything outside Prague is still off the beaten tourist track).

Facts about the Country

HISTORY

In antiquity this area was inhabited by the Celts and was never part of the classical Roman Empire. The Celtic Boii tribe which inhabited the Bohemian basin gave the region its present name. Germanic tribes conquered the Celts in the 4th century AD, and between the 5th and 10th centuries the West Slavs settled here. From 830 to 907 the Slavic tribes united in the Great Moravian Empire and adopted Christianity. Cyril and Methodius, two Greek brothers from Thessaloniki, visited Great Moravia personally in 863 and invented the first Slavic alphabet here.

Towards the end of the 9th century, the Czechs seceded from the Great Moravian Empire and formed an independent state. In 995 the Czech lands were united under the native Přemysl dynasty as the principality of Bohemia. The Czech state became a kingdom in the 12th century and reached its peak under Přemysl Otakar II from 1253 to 1278. Many towns were founded at this time.

The Přemysls died out in 1306 and, in 1310, John of Luxembourg gained the Bohemian throne through marriage and annexed the kingdom to the German Empire. His son, Charles IV (depicted on the new 100 Kč banknote), became king of the Germans in 1346 and Holy Roman Emperor in 1355. Inclusion in this medieval empire led to a blossoming of trade and culture. The capital, Prague, was made an archbishopric in 1344 and in 1348 Charles University was founded. These kings were able to keep the feudal nobility in check, but under Wenceslas IV (1378-1419) the strength of the monarchy declined. The church became the largest landowner.

In 1415 the religious reformer Jan Hus, rector of Charles University, was burnt at the stake in Constance. His ideas inspired the nationalistic Hussite movement which swept

Bohemia from 1419 to 1434. After the defeat of the Hussites, the Jagiello dynasty occupied the Bohemian throne. Vladislav Jagiello merged the Bohemian and Hungarian states in 1490.

With the death of Ludovic Jagiello at the Battle of Mohács in 1526, the Austrian Habsburg dynasty ascended to the thrones of Bohemia and Hungary. Thus Bohemia, which was strongly affected by the Protestant Reformation, became subject to the Catholic Counter-Reformation backed by the Habsburgs. The Thirty Years' War, which devastated Europe from 1618 to 1648, began in Prague, and the defeat of the uprising of the Czech Estates at the Battle of White Mountain in 1620 marked the beginning of a long period of forced re-Catholicisation, Germanisation and oppression.

Yet, under the Habsburgs, Czech culture was never as totally suppressed as was Polish culture under the Russian tsars, for example, and during the early 19th century National Revival Movement the Czechs rediscovered their linguistic and cultural roots. Despite the defeat of the democratic revolution of 1848, the industrial revolution took firm hold here as a middle class emerged.

In 1914 Austro-Hungarian expansionism in the Balkans led to war, but no fighting took place in what is now the Czech Republic. Slovakia had been part of Hungary since the 11th century but on 28 October 1918 the Czechoslovak Republic, a common state of the Czechs and Slovaks, was proclaimed. The first president was Tomáš Garrigue Masaryk (who appears on the new 5000 Kč banknote), followed in 1935 by Eduard Beneš, who later headed a government-in-exile in London. Three-quarters of the Austro-Hungarian monarchy's industrial potential fell within Czechoslovakia, as did three million Germans.

After annexing Austria in the Anschluss of March 1938, Hitler turned his attention to Czechoslovakia. By the infamous Munich Pact of September 1938, Britain and France surrendered the border regions of Bohemia – the Sudetenland – to Nazi Germany, and in March 1939 the Germans occupied the rest of the country. The Czech lands were converted into the so-called 'Protectorate of Bohemia and Moravia' while Slovakia became a clero-fascist puppet state.

On 29 May 1942 the acting Nazi Reichs-Protector, Reinhard 'Hangman' Heydrich, was assassinated by two Czechs who had been parachuted in from London for the purpose. As a reprisal, the Nazis surrounded the peaceful village of Lidice, 25 km northwest of Prague, shot all the males and deported all the females to concentration camps. Czechs fought with the Allied forces on all fronts. After the German surrender in May 1945, the Soviet army occupied the country (West Bohemia was liberated by US troops). Unlike Germany and Poland which were devastated during WW II, Czechoslovakia was largely undamaged.

Post WW II

After liberation, a National Front was formed from the parties which had taken part in the antifascist struggle and in April 1945, even before the rest of the country had been freed, a meeting of the Front at Košice (Slovakia) laid down a programme for national reconstruction. A power struggle then developed between the socialists and those who favoured capitalism. After the Munich sellout, resentment against the West was rife and the strength of the Communist Party grew. In the Constituent National Assembly elections of May 1946, the communists won 38% of the votes and the Social Democrats 15.6%, forming a National Front majority. Communist Party chairman Klement Gottwald became prime minister.

In February 1948 the Social Democrats withdrew from the coalition in an attempt to overthrow Gottwald. Demonstrations and a general strike convinced President Beneš to accept the resignations of the 12 government ministers involved and appoint communist replacements. The new communist-led government then revised the constitution and voting system so that in fresh elections in May it received 86% of votes. Beneš resigned in June (and died in August) and, in July, Klement Gottwald became president.

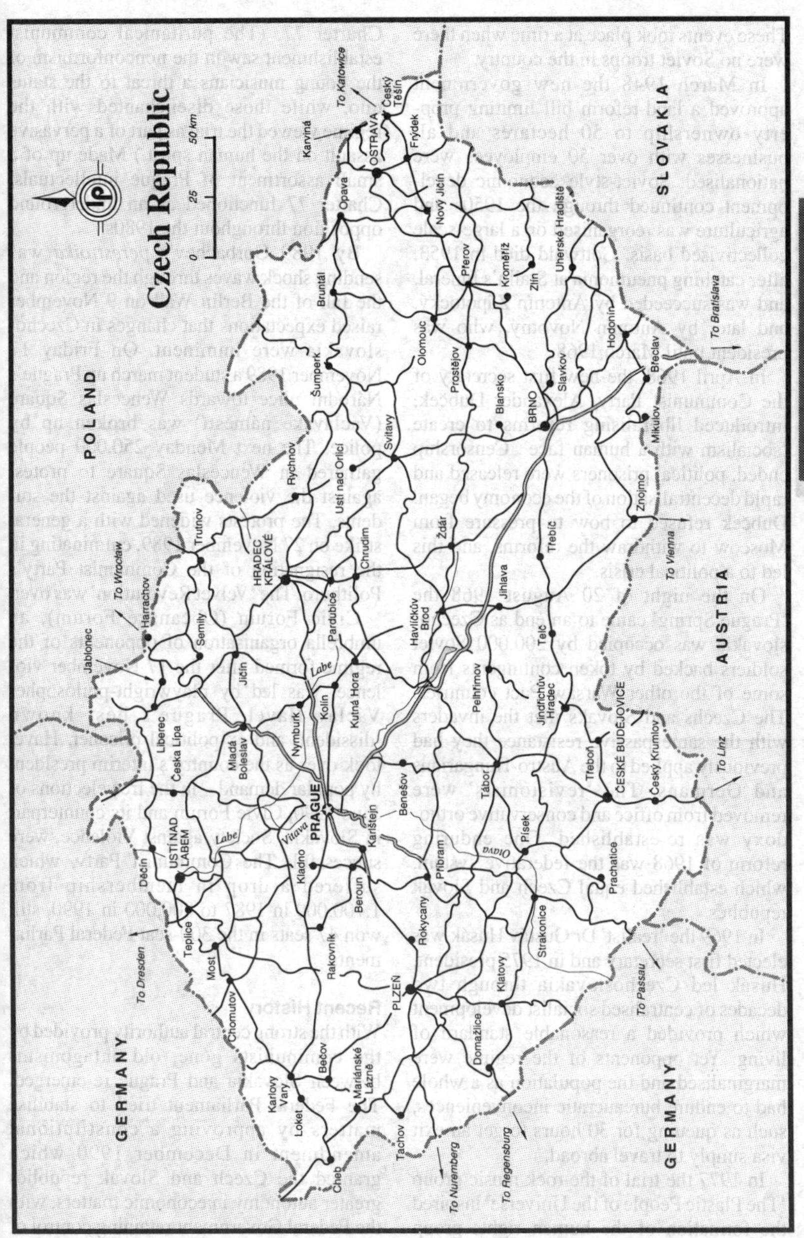
Czech Republic
0 25 50 km
POLAND
GERMANY
SLOVAKIA
AUSTRIA
GERMANY
To Katowice
Český Těšín
Karviná
OSTRAVA
Frýdek
Opava
Nový Jičín
Bruntál
Šumperk
Přerov
Kroměříž
Uherské Hradiště
Zlín
Olomouc
Prostějov
Hodonín
To Bratislava
Břeclav
Slavkov
Blansko
BRNO
Mikulov
Znojmo
To Vienna
Třebíč
Žďár
Svitavy
Rychnov
Ústí nad Orlicí
Chrudim
Trutnov
HRADEC KRÁLOVÉ
To Wrocław
Harrachov
Semily
Jablonec
Liberec
Česká Lípa
Mladá Boleslav
Jičín
Pardubice
Labe
Kolín
Kutná Hora
Nymburk
Havlíčkův Brod
Jihlava
Telč
Pelhřimov
Jindřichův Hradec
ČESKÉ BUDĚJOVICE
Třeboň
Český Krumlov
To Linz
Tábor
Benešov
PRAGUE
Vltava
Karlštejn
Příbram
Písek
Otava
Prachatice
Strakonice
To Passau
Děčín
ÚSTÍ NAD LABEM
Labe
Kladno
Beroun
Teplice
Most
To Dresden
Rakovník
Rokycany
PLZEŇ
Klatovy
Domažlice
Chomutov
Bečov
Karlovy Vary
Loket
Mariánské Lázně
Tachov
Cheb
To Nuremberg
To Regensburg

These events took place at a time when there were no Soviet troops in the country.

In March 1948 the new government approved a land-reform bill limiting property ownership to 50 hectares and all businesses with over 50 employees were nationalised. Soviet-style economic development continued through the 1950s and agriculture was reorganised on a large-scale collectivised basis. Gottwald died in 1953, after catching pneumonia at Stalin's funeral, and was succeeded by Antonín Zápotocký, and later by Antonín Novotný, who was president until March 1968.

In April 1968, the new first secretary of the Communist Party, Alexander Dubček, introduced liberalising reforms to create 'socialism with a human face'. Censorship ended, political prisoners were released and rapid decentralisation of the economy began. Dubček refused to bow to pressure from Moscow to withdraw the reforms, and this led to a political crisis.

On the night of 20 August 1968 the 'Prague Spring' came to an end as Czechoslovakia was occupied by 200,000 Soviet soldiers backed by token contingents from some of the other Warsaw Pact countries. The Czechs and Slovaks met the invaders with the same passive resistance they had previously applied to the Austro-Hungarians and Germans. The 'revisionists' were removed from office and conservative orthodoxy was re-established. One enduring reform of 1968 was the federative system, which established equal Czech and Slovak republics.

In 1969 the 'realist' Dr Gustáv Husák was elected first secretary and in 1975 president. Husák led Czechoslovakia through two decades of centralised socialist development which provided a reasonable standard of living. Yet opponents of the regime were marginalised and the population as a whole had to endure bureaucratic inconveniences, such as queuing for 30 hours to get an exit visa simply to travel abroad.

In 1977 the trial of the rock music group 'The Plastic People of the Universe' inspired the formation of the human rights group Charter 77. (The puritanical communist establishment saw in the nonconformism of the young musicians a threat to the status quo, while those disenchanted with the regime viewed the trial as part of a pervasive assault on the human spirit.) Made up of a small assortment of Prague intellectuals, Charter 77 functioned as an underground opposition throughout the 1980s.

By 1989 Gorbachev's *perestroika* was sending shock waves through the region and the fall of the Berlin Wall on 9 November raised expectations that changes in Czechoslovakia were imminent. On Friday 17 November 1989 a student march up Prague's Národní ulice towards Wenceslas Square (Václavské náměstí) was broken up by police. The next Monday 250,000 people gathered in Wenceslas Square to protest against the violence used against the students. The protests widened with a general strike on 27 November 1989, culminating in the resignation of the Communist Party's Politburo. The 'Velvet Revolution' was over.

Civic Forum (Občanské Forum), an umbrella organisation of opponents of the regime formed after the 17 November violence, was led by playwright-philosopher Václav Havel, Prague's best known 'dissident' and ex-political prisoner. Havel took over as the country's interim president by popular demand – in the free elections of June 1990, Civic Forum and its counterpart in Slovakia, Society against Violence, were successful. The Communist Party, which suffered a drop in membership from 1,700,000 in 1987 to 800,000 in 1990, still won 47 seats in the 300-seat Federal Parliament.

Recent History

With the strong central authority provided by the communists gone, old antagonisms between Slovakia and Prague re-emerged. The Federal Parliament tried to stabilise matters by approving a constitutional amendment in December 1990 which granted the Czech and Slovak republics greater autonomy in economic matters, with the Federal Government retaining control of defence and foreign affairs. Czechoslovakia officially changed its name to the Czech and Slovak Federative Republic (ČSFR), a federation of the Czech Republic (ČR) and the Slovak Republic (SR). Yet these moves failed to satisfy Slovak nationalists.

Meanwhile Civic Forum had split into two factions, the centrist Civic Movement made up of former dissidents such as foreign minister Jiřá Dienstbier and president Václav Havel, and the Civic Democratic Party (ODS) led by right-wing technocrats like finance minister Václav Klaus. In Slovakia several separatist parties emerged.

To weaken the former communists and intimidate other left-wing political opponents, the ODS instigated a purge of former communist officials and alleged secret police informers in 1991, a process known as 'lustrace'. In January 1992 a law was passed banning former high-ranking communists from the public service for five years. Implementation of the law was placed in the hands of bureaucrats and the accused were to be presumed guilty until proven innocent. The 'dissemination of communist ideology' became a crime punishable by up to eight years in prison. These moves attracted the interest of international human rights groups.

The June 1992 elections sealed the fate of Czechoslovakia. Klaus' ODS took 48 seats in 150-seat Federal Parliament while 24 seats went to the Movement for a Democratic Slovakia (HZDS), a left-leaning Slovak nationalist party led by Vladimír Mečiar. The former communists came second in both republics with the Left Bloc (KSCM-LB) taking 19 seats in the Czech Republic and the Party of the Democratic Left (SDL') winning another 10 seats in Slovakia. Dienstbier's Civic Movement was wiped out.

The incompatibility of Klaus and Mečiar soon became apparent with the former pushing for shock-therapy economic reform while the latter wanted state intervention to save key industries in Slovakia. Mečiar's strident demands for Slovak sovereignty convinced Klaus and associates that Slovakia had become an obstacle on the road to fast economic reform. Calls from President Havel for a referendum on national unity were rejected by opportunistic politicians on both sides who only wanted to be masters of their own fiefs.

The defeat in July 1992 of President Havel's re-election bid by Slovak and former communist parliamentary deputies removed the last hope of compromise and Havel decided to step down early rather than preside over the country's dissolution. In August 1992 Klaus and Mečiar agreed that the Czechoslovak federation would cease to exist at the end of the year. In September 1992 Slovakia adopted a new constitution and in November 1992 the Federal Parliament voted itself out of existence. At midnight on 31 December 1992 a peaceful 'velvet divorce' freed both countries from what had become a non-functioning federation.

In January 1993 the Czech parliament elected Václav Havel president of the Czech Republic for a five-year term. Real power lies with parliament which can override the president's veto on most issues by a simple majority and prime minister Klaus has staked his political future on the success of rapid economic reform.

GEOGRAPHY

The Czech Republic is a landlocked country of 78,864 sq km squeezed between Germany, Austria, Slovakia and Poland. The Bohemian Massif is much older than the Carpathian Mountains and the broad, flat mountain ranges of the Czech Republic are quite different from the pronounced valleys, steep slopes, deep canyons and wild rivers of Slovakia. In general the mountains of Slovakia are higher and much more sharply defined than those of the Czech Republic.

Bohemia nestles between the Šumava Mountains along the Bavarian border, the Ore Mountains (Krušné Hory) along the eastern German border and the Giant Mountains (Krkonoše) along the Polish border east of Liberec. The Czech Republic's highest peak, Mt Sněžka (1602 metres), is in the Giant Mountains. The forests of northern

Bohemia have been devastated by acid rain resulting from the burning of poor quality brown coal at thermal power stations and in parts of the eastern Ore Mountains not a single tree has been left standing. Conifers in the Giant Mountains are stricken by airborne pollutants blown in from Polish Silesia.

The Czech Republic has been called 'the roof of Europe' because no rivers or streams flow into the country. The Morava River flows out of Moravia and enters the Danube just west of Bratislava. Bohemia's most famous river is the Vltava (Moldau in German), which originates near the Austrian border and flows north through Český Krumlov, České Budějovice and Prague. At Mělník it joins the Labe, which becomes the Elbe in Germany (where it passes Dresden and Hamburg on its way to the North Sea). The Baltic-bound Odra (Oder) River originates in the Czech Republic near Ostrava but soon enters Poland. Many rivers and streams are highly polluted due to inadequate sewage treatment and chemical fertiliser runoff.

The 120-sq-km Moravian Karst north of Brno features limestone caves, subterranean lakes and the Macocha Abyss, which is 138 metres deep.

ECONOMY

From 1948 to 1989 Czechoslovakia had a centrally planned economy with industry producing 70% of the national income. Cooperatives accounted for about three-quarters of agricultural land and state farms for the rest. The communists left behind a highly developed infrastructure, diversified production and low debt, but the country's industrial equipment was approaching obsolescence and there were many economic inefficiencies. Increased production was sought with scant regard for the environment and in recent years the price has been paid in terms of public health.

The industries and power plants of northern Bohemia and Moravia spew millions of tonnes of sulphur dioxide, nitrogen oxides and carbon monoxide into the atmosphere each year, creating one of Europe's most serious environmental disaster areas. The worst pollutant is sulphur dioxide created by burning lignite, a soft brown coal extracted from huge open-pit mines. In the towns the burning of coal for household heating creates choking smogs in winter and at certain times the sulphur dioxide levels in Prague are 20 times higher than official safety levels. Unfortunately this coal is one of the country's only existing energy sources and most of ex-Czechoslovakia's coal resources were in the Czech Republic. Nuclear generating stations are at Dukovany (between Znojmo and Brno) and Temelín (south-west of Tábor). The Austrian government has expressed fears that the Temelín plant is unsafe.

The largest industrial area is around Ostrava in North Moravia with coal mining, chemicals, a steel mill and car production. About 5000 rugged Tatra trucks a year are built at Kopřivnice near Ostrava. The main Škoda Works are at Plzeň but the Škoda car factory is at Mladá Boleslav, 54 km north-east of Prague, producing about 200,000 vehicles a year. Thanks to a partnership with Volkswagen, the quality of the Škoda automobile has been greatly enhanced in recent years.

In 1894 Tomáš Bat'a founded the Bata shoe factory at Zlín, east of Brno, which today produces over a quarter million pairs of shoes a week. The Bat'a family fled to Canada in 1938 and built a worldwide business and only in 1989 did they return to Czechoslovakia to begin anew. Half of the foreign investment in the Czech Republic has been by German companies. In 1992 the US firm Philip Morris bought a 65% share in the cigarette manufacturer Tabac.

Since 1991 privatisation has taken place in three stages. The first was the restitution to the original owners of some 100,000 small businesses and commercial properties confiscated by the communists. Then about 30,000 small retail outlets or service facilities throughout former Czechoslovakia were auctioned off to owner operators. This stage is now complete and the third and most difficult stage of privatising 1500 medium and large-sized companies in the Czech

Republic is underway. Privatisation in the Czech Republic has been dogged by rumours of widespread corruption, such as former party officials skimming off the assets of firms and free-market advocates grabbing control of choice companies by dubious means.

Due to fears of foreign ownership, the paucity of domestic capital and a desire to involve large numbers of people in the process, the government devised a voucher privatisation scheme in which hundreds of millions of shares in 1200 state corporations arbitrarily valued at US$9 billion would be distributed to Czechs at giveaway prices. Every adult citizen was entitled to purchase 1000 voucher points for 1000 crowns (US$36). The points could be used to bid for shares in companies being privatised and many people assigned their points to investment funds which would act on their behalf.

The vouchers were issued during the winter of 1991-92 but implementation was delayed due to the separation of Slovakia. Finally, in May 1993 the government began distributing shares in 987 formerly state-owned firms purchased by 437 investment funds and millions of Czechs under voucher privatisation. Some 770 remaining companies were covered by a second round of voucher privatisation in late 1993. In April 1993 the Prague stock market opened and trading began in June 1993.

In early 1993 bankruptcy laws came into effect but these were relatively toothless and widespread bankruptcies (and mass unemployment) were postponed by allowing companies to pile up unrepayable debts. Budget deficits and inflation have been kept under control by fiscal restraint. In January 1991 most price controls were removed and prices jumped 49.2% during the first half of 1991 but in the second half of the year prices increased only 5%. Real wages declined 28% in 1991 and the gross domestic product fell 16% that year but unemployment was only 5%.

The Czech Republic is the only country in Eastern Europe with free prices and near one-digit inflation. The average wage is about US$200 a month and the foreign debt stands at US$9 billion.

Tourism is booming with 83 million visitors to former Czechoslovakia in 1992. Germany was the biggest source of visitors, followed by Poland and Austria. Most are low-spending daytrippers: in 1992 the 60 million visitors to France spent US$119 billion while Czechoslovakia's 83 million spent just US$1.4 billion.

Fifty-three per cent of Czechoslovakia's exports went to the Warsaw Pact countries in 1988, but in 1993 that area absorbed only 13% of Czech exports while 55% went west. The same trend appears in import statistics. The Czech Republic's largest trading partners by far in both the import and export categories are Germany, Slovakia, the former USSR and Austria in that order, with most of the trading in both directions in manufactured goods, machinery and transportation equipment. Iron and steel are the Czech Republic's biggest single export item (11% of the total in 1993) yet exports of Czech steel and cement to Western Europe are partly blocked by quotas and tariffs, and trade with Slovakia has dropped 50% since separation (Slovakia bought 20% of Czech exports in 1993).

POPULATION & PEOPLE

The Czech Republic is fairly homogeneous with 94% Czechs and 4% Slovaks. A small Polish minority lives in the borderlands near Ostrava. After WW II three million Sudeten Germans were evicted from Bohemia and only about 60,000 Germans remain today.

A majority of the people are Catholic and there's a saying that it took 40 years of Communism to make good Catholics of the Czechs! Religious tolerance is well established and the church makes little attempt to involve itself in politics. (What intolerance there is falls mainly upon the 115,000 Gypsies.)

There are 10,464,000 inhabitants. The major cities and their populations are Prague (1,212,000), Brno (391,000), Ostrava (331,000), Plzeň (175,000) and Olomouc (107,000).

ARTS

Czech culture has a long and distinguished history. Prague University, the oldest in Central Europe, was founded in 1348, about the time that the Gothic architect Petr Parléř was directing the construction of St Vitus Cathedral, Karlův most (Charles Bridge) and other illustrious works.

In the early 17th century, the region was torn by the Thirty Years' War, and the educational reformer Jan Ámos Comenius (1592-1670) was forced to flee Moravia. In exile Comenius (Komenský in Czech) produced a series of textbooks that were to be used throughout Europe for two centuries. His *The Visible World in Pictures*, featuring woodcuts made at Nuremberg, was the forerunner of today's illustrated schoolbook. (Comenius' portrait appears on the new 200 Kč banknote.)

The National Revival period of the early 19th century saw the re-emergence of the Czech language as a vehicle of culture. Late 19th century romanticism is exemplified in the historical novels of Alois Jirásek (1851-1930), whose works chronicled the entire history of the Czechs. His finest was *Temno* (Darkness) (1915), which dealt with the period of national decline. Karel Čapek, Karel (1890-1938) brought the Czech word *robot* (imitation human being) into international usage through a 1920 play featuring a human-like machine that almost manages to enslave humanity. Čapek's novel *The War with the Newts* (1936) was an allegory of the totalitarianism of the time.

Music

During the 17th century, when Bohemia and Moravia came under Austrian domination and German was the official language, Czech culture survived in folk music. Moravian folk orchestras are built around the *cymbalum*, a copper-stringed dulcimer of Middle Eastern origin which stands on four legs and is played by striking the strings with two mallets.

Bohemia's pre-eminent baroque composer was Jan Dišmaš Zelenka (1679-1745) who spent much of his life in Vienna, Venice and especially Dresden where he was composer to the Saxon court. Though greatly esteemed by his contemporary Bach, Zelenka's works have become widely known only during the past two decades. The symbolism and subtle expression of Zelenka's last masses are unique expressions of his introverted, restrained character.

The works of the Czech Republic's foremost composers, Bedřich Smetana (1824-84) and Antonín Dvořák (1841-1904), express the nostalgia, melancholy and joy – part of the Czech personality. In his operas Smetana used popular songs that display the innate peasant wisdom of the people to capture the nationalist sentiments of his time. Smetana's symphonic cycle *Má Vlast* (My Country) is a musical history of the country. Dvořák attracted world attention to Czech music through his use of native folk materials in works such as *Slavonic Dances* (1878).

The opera composer Leoš Janáček (1854-1928) shared Dvořák's intense interest in folk music and created an original national style by combining the scales and melodies of folk songs with the inflections of the Czech language. His best known works are *Jenufa* (1904) and *Příhody Lišky Bystroušky*, or The Cunning Little Vixen (1924). Janáček's *Christmas Mass* is often sung in Czech churches at Christmas.

Dance

Bohemia's greatest contribution to dance floors is the polka, a lively folk dance in which couples rapidly circle the floor in three-four time with three quick steps and a hop. Since its appearance in Paris in 1843, the form has been popular worldwide. Smetana used the polka in his opera *The Bartered Bride* (1866). In Moravia whirling couples dance the *vrtěná* while the *hošije* and *verbuňk* are vigorous male solo dances.

LANGUAGE

German is widely understood, especially in the western part of the republic. Under the communists everybody learned Russian at school but this now has been replaced by English.

Czech is a strange and convoluted language with a great aversion to the liberal use of vowels. Many words contain nothing that we could identify as a vowel. One famous tongue twister goes *strč prst skrz krk* which means 'stick your finger through your throat' and is pronounced just as it's spelt!

Czech and Slovak are closely related and mutually comprehensible West Slavic languages. In the 19th century Hussite Czech spelling was adopted to render other Slav languages such as Slovene and Croatian in Latin letters.

An English-Czech phrasebook will prove invaluable, but it can be hard to find one in the Czech Republic so consider taking Lonely Planet's *Eastern Europe Phrasebook* along with you. Some useful Czech words that are frequently used in this chapter are: *most* (bridge), *nábřeží* (embankment), *náměstí* (square), *nádraží* (station), *ostrov* (island), *třída* (avenue) and *ulice* (street). Men's toilets may be marked *páni* or *muži*, women's toilets *dámy* or *ženy*.

Pronunciation

Many Czech letters sound about the same as they do in English. An accent lengthens a vowel and the stress is always on the first syllable. It's a phonetic language, so if you follow the guidelines below you'll be understood. When consulting indexes on Czech maps, be aware that 'ch' comes after 'h'.

c	'ts'
č	'ch'
ch	'ch' as in 'loch'
d'	'd' as in 'duty'
ě	'ye'
j	'y' as in 'yet'
ň	'n' as the first 'n' in 'onion'
ř	'rzh'
š	'sh'
t'	't' as the first 't' in 'student'
ž	's' as in 'pleasure'

Greetings & Civilities

hello	*ahoj, dobrý den*
goodbye	*na shledanou*
good morning	*dobré jitro*
good evening	*dobrý večer*
please	*prosím*
thank you	*děkuji*
I am sorry./ Forgive me.	*promiňte*
yes	*ano*
no	*ne*

Small Talk

I don't understand.	*nerozumím*
Could you write it down?	*Můžete to napsat?*
What is it called?	*Jak se to jmenuje?*
Where do you live?	*Kde bydlíte?*
What work do you do?	*Jakou práci děláte?*
I am a student.	*Jsem student.*
I am very happy.	*Jsem velmi šťastný.*

Accommodation

youth hostel	*mládežnická noclehárna*
camping ground	*kemping*
private room	*soukromý pokoj*
How much is it?	*Kolik to je?*
Is that the price per person?	*Je to cena za osobu?*
Is that the total price?	*Je to celková cena?*
Are there any extra charges?	*Jsou tu nějaké zvláštní poplatky?*
Do I pay extra for showers?	*Platí se zvlášť za sprchu?*
Where is there a cheaper hotel?	*Kde je levnější hotel?*
Should I make a reservation?	*Měl bych si zamluvit pokoj?*
single room	*jednolůžkový pokoj*
double room	*dvoulůžkový pokoj*
It is very noisy.	*Je velmi hlučný.*
Where is the toilet?	*Kde je záchod?*

Getting Around

What time does it leave?	*V kolik hodin to odjíždí?*
When is the first bus?	*Kdy jede první autobus?*

CZECH REPUBLIC

When is the last bus?	*Kdy jede poslední autobus?*
When is the next bus?	*Kdy jede příští autobus?*
That's too soon.	*To je příliš brzy.*
When is the next one after that?	*Kdy jede příští potomhle?*
How long does the trip take?	*Jak dlouho trvá cesta?*
arrival	*příjezdy*
departure	*odjezdy*
timetable	*jízdní řád*
Where is the bus stop?	*Kde je autobusová zastávka ?*
Where is the train station?	*Kde je nádraží?*
Where is the left-luggage room?	*Kde je úschovna zavazadel?*

Around Town

Just a minute.	*okamžik*
Where is...?	*Kde je...?*
the bank	*banka*
the post office	*pošta*
the tourist information office	*cestovní kancelář*
the museum	*muzeum*
Where are you going?	*Kam jdete?*
I am going to...	*Já jdu do...*
Where is it?	*Kde je to?*
I can't find it.	*Nemohu to najít.*
Is it far?	*Je to daleko?*
Please show me on the map.	*Prosím, ukažte mi to na mapě.*
left	*vlevo*
right	*vpravo*
straight ahead	*rovně*
I want...	*Já chci...*
Do I need permission?	*Potřebuji povolení?*

Entertainment

Where can I buy a ticket?	*Kde si mohu koupit lístek/vstupenku?*
I want to refund this ticket.	*Chci vrátit tento lístek.*
Is this a good seat?	*Je to dobré místo?*
at the front	*vpředu*

Food

I do not eat meat.	*Nejím maso.*
self-service cafeteria	*samoobslužná restaurace*
grocery store	*obchod potravin*
fish	*ryba*
pork	*vepřové*
soup	*polévka*
salad	*salát*
fresh vegetables	*čerstvá zelenina*
milk	*mléko*
bread	*chléb*
sugar	*cukr*
ice cream	*zmrzlina*
coffee	*káva*
tea	*čaj*
mineral water	*minerální voda*
beer	*pivo*
wine	*víno*
hot/cold	*horké/studené*

Shopping

Where can I buy one?	*Kde si mohu jeden koupit?*
How much does it cost?	*Kolik to stojí?*
That's (much) too expensive.	*To je příliž drahé.*
Is there a cheaper one?	*Je něco levnější?*

Time & Dates

today	*dnes*
tonight	*dnes večer*
tomorrow	*zítra*
the day after tomorrow	*pozítří*
What time does it open?	*Kdy se otevírá?*
What time does it close?	*Kdy se zavírá?*
open	*otevřeno*
closed	*zavřeno*
in the morning	*ráno*
in the evening	*večer*
every day	*každý den*
At what time?	*V kolik hodin?*
when?	*kdy?*

Monday	*pondělí*
Tuesday	*úterý*
Wednesday	*středa*
Thursday	*čtvrtek*
Friday	*pátek*
Saturday	*sobota*
Sunday	*neděle*

January	*leden*
February	*únor*
March	*březen*
April	*duben*
May	*květen*
June	*červen*
July	*červenec*
August	*srpen*
September	*září*
October	*říjen*
November	*listopad*
December	*prosinec*

Numbers

1	*jeden*
2	*dva*
3	*tři*
4	*čtyři*
5	*pět*
6	*šest*
7	*sedm*
8	*osm*
9	*devět*
10	*deset*
11	*jedenáct*
12	*dvanáct*
13	*třináct*
14	*čtrnáct*
15	*patnáct*
16	*šestnáct*
17	*sedmnáct*
18	*osmnáct*
19	*devatenáct*
20	*dvacet*
21	*dvacet jedna*
22	*dvacet dva*
23	*dvacet tři*
30	*třicet*
40	*čtyřicet*
50	*padesát*
60	*šedesát*
70	*sedmdesát*
80	*osmdesát*
90	*devadesát*
100	*sto*
1000	*tisíc*
10,000	*deset tisíc*
1,000,000	*milión*

Facts for the Visitor

VISAS & EMBASSIES

Everyone requires a passport which won't expire within the following eight months. Americans require no visa for a stay of 30 days. Citizens of Austria, Belgium, Denmark, Finland, France, Germany, Greece, Holland, Iceland, Ireland, Italy, Liechtenstein, Luxembourg, Monaco, Norway, Portugal, Spain, Sweden, Switzerland and the UK are allowed three months without a visa. Unfortunately citizens of Australia, Canada, Japan, New Zealand and most other non-European countries still do need a visa which should be obtained in advance at a consulate.

Visas are only available at three highway border crossings, one from Germany (Waidhaus/Rozvadov) and two from Austria (Wullowitz/Dolní Dvořiště and Klein Haugsdorf/Hatě), plus Prague Ruzyně Airport. Elsewhere you'll be refused entry if you need a visa and arrive without one. Visas are never issued on trains.

Czech tourist and transit visas are readily available at consulates throughout Central Europe at a cost of US$25 per entry (Canadians US$50). You will need two photos per entry (maximum two entries per visa). Don't get a transit visa which costs the same and cannot be changed to a tourist visa upon arrival. You'll be asked how many days you wish to stay in the Czech Republic, up to a maximum of 30 days, and this number will be written on your visa. You can use your visa at any time within six months of the date of issue.

There's a space for hotel stamps on the back of the visa form and although the old requirement of police registration is seldom enforced these days a difficult official can bring it up if he or she feels in the mood. Thus it's best to ask official places to stay such as hotels and camping grounds or travel agencies to stamp your visa form as you're checking in. That way you're covered for all eventualities.

Slovakian visas are not accepted at Czech border crossings and vice versa – if you want to visit both countries you must purchase two separate visas.

You can extend your stay at police stations inside the Czech Republic for about US$5. The offices handling these matters open for short hours and have long queues, so don't leave it till the last day. An easier way to solve this problem (provided you don't need a visa) is simply to leave the Czech Republic and return, in which case you'll have to make a point of asking the border guards to stamp your passport as you leave (they often don't bother).

Czech Embassies Abroad

Australia
: 38 Culgoa Circuit, O'Malley, Canberra, ACT 2606 (☎ 062-90 1386)

Canada
: 50 Rideau Terrace, Ottawa, ON K1M 2A1 (☎ 613-749 1566)

Netherlands
: Paleisstr. 4, 2514 JA The Hague (☎ 070-364 7638)

New Zealand
: 12 Anne St, Wadestown, Wellington (☎ 04-472 3142)

UK
: 26 Kensington Palace Gardens, London, W8 4QY (☎ 0171-727 4918)

USA
: 3900 Spring of Freedom St NW, Washington, DC 20008 (☎ 202-363 6315)

MONEY

Changing money in the Czech Republic can be a hassle as many private exchange offices, especially in Prague, deduct exorbitant commissions *(výlohy)* of up to 10%. Some of these advertise higher rates on large boards but don't mention their sky-high commission – if in doubt, ask first.

Hotels charge 5% commission, Čedok travel agencies 3% and the banks take only 2% on better rates. The Komerční Banka is usually efficient about changing travellers' cheques for a standard US$2 commission and we list their branches throughout this chapter but even there you should always ask about the commission as it seems to vary from branch to branch. The American Express and Thomas Cook offices in Prague change their own travellers' cheques without commission but their rates are slightly lower than the banks.

The main drawbacks of the banks are their short opening hours and slowness. You'll sometimes have to spend up to an hour in line. Because of this, it's smart to change enough money to see you through the rest of your stay when you find somewhere offering good rates and charging a low commission. Avoid getting caught without sufficient crowns on a weekend or public holiday when the banks are closed.

Some visitors dabble in the black market but they usually end up a little poorer and a little wiser because most of the people offering to change money on the street are professional thieves with years of experience in cheating tourists. They'll switch the bundle of banknotes after they've been counted for paper or small bills, or use some other trick, such as supplying Polish złoty notes instead of crown bills which are worth 700 times more! It's foolish to risk large amounts of cash with potential criminals, though it's less risky if you are propositioned by someone who can't run away, such as a waiter, taxi driver or hotel receptionist. Czechs are only allowed to legally purchase US$275 in hard currency a year, hence the black market.

However you change your money, once you have Czech currency you'll have to spend it, as it's difficult to change it back into hard currency despite misleading government claims that the crown is now a convertible currency. Most banks will only change crowns back into hard currency if you have a receipt to prove you originally changed with them. If you're going on to Poland and have crowns left over you can asily unload them at any Polish exchange office but you'll lose about 10%. Changing Czech currency in Germany and Hungary is lifficult. The import or export of over 100 Kč is prohibited, so keep any crowns you nay be carrying out of sight at the border.

Currency

On 8 February 1993 the Czech and Slovakian currencies separated and within weeks he Slovakian crown was worth 10% less han the Czech crown. In September 1993 all banknotes issued by the former Czechoslovakian authorities were withdrawn from circulation in the Czech Republic and are iow worthless. Don't accept any notes eading 'Korun Československých'. The old Czechoslovakian coins became invalid in November 1993.

The new banknotes come in denominaions of 50, 100, 200, 500, 1000 and 5000 Czech crowns or 'Korun Českých' (Kč); coins are of 10, 20 and 50 haléřů (cents) and one, two, five, 10, 20 and 50 Kč. Always have a few small coins in your pocket for use n public toilets and for public transport nachines.

Exchange Rates

Compulsory exchange has been abolished in he Czech Republic and everyone now eceives the same standard bank rate. Since early 1991 the exchange rate has been fairly steady with only about 11% annual inflation.

A$1	=	20.74Kč
AS1	=	2.56Kč
DM1	=	18.10Kč
Sk1	=	0.89Kč
UK£1	=	43.40Kč
US$1	=	27.912Kč
¥100	=	0.123Kč

Costs

Food, transportation and admission fees are fairly cheap, and it's mostly accommodation hat makes this one of the most expensive countries in Eastern Europe. If you really want to travel on a low budget you'll have to spend a little more time looking for a cheap place to stay and/or be prepared to rough it. Get out of the capital and your costs will drop dramatically.

A disappointing side of the Czech concept of a 'free market economy' is the two-price system in which foreigners pay double the local price for many things. This may be official as it is at hotels, airline offices and some museums, or unofficial, such as when a waiter or taxi driver tries to pad your bill. A de facto tourist price for theatre tickets exists in Prague as most tickets are cornered by scalpers and travel agencies who resell them to foreigners at several times the original price. Sometimes simply questioning the price difference results in an 'error correction', but if it doesn't, you either pay the higher price or go elsewhere. Whenever you do get something for the local price (as is usually the case when buying beer or domestic train tickets) you'll find it very inexpensive.

There *are* public toilets throughout the Czech Republic and having to pay US$0.10 once or twice a day to use them won't break the budget.

Consumer Taxes

In January 1993 all prices jumped 23% when a value-added tax (VAT) was imposed (it's only 5% on food). This tax is included in the sticker price and not added at the cash register, so you won't feel it directly.

CLIMATE & WHEN TO GO

The climate is temperate with warm summers and cool, humid winters, and clearly defined spring and autumn seasons. Prague has average daily temperatures above 14°C from May to September, above 8°C in April and October, and below freezing in December and January. In winter dense fogs (or smogs) can set in anywhere.

SUGGESTED ITINERARIES

Depending on the length of your stay, you might want to see and do the following things in the Czech Republic:

Two days
   Visit České Budějovice and Český Krumlov.
One week
   Visit České Budějovice, Český Krumlov, Prague and Kutná Hora.
Two weeks
   Visit Prague, Kutná Hora, České Budějovice, Český Krumlov, Telč and Brno.
One month
   Visit all places mentioned in this chapter.

TOURIST OFFICES

There's a municipal information office in Prague called the Prague Information Service and the staff are very knowledgeable about sightseeing, food and entertainment. Receptionists in the expensive hotels are often helpful with information when they're not busy.

The former government tourism monopoly Čedok has numerous branch offices around the country which you can consult if you wish to change money, or want accommodation, travel or sightseeing arrangements made. It is, however, oriented towards the top end of the market. Čedok staff are sometimes willing to answer general questions although this is now a commercial travel agency and they're not paid to provide free information. The American Express office in Prague is in a similar position.

The Czech Republic's youth travel bureau is CKM Student Travel (Cestovní Kancelář Mládeže). Their offices in most cities are a better source of information on money-saving arrangements than Čedok and they also sell student cards.

Čedok Offices Abroad

Čedok offices in countries outside the Czech Republic include:

Netherlands
   Leidsestraat 4, 1017 PA Amsterdam
   (☎ 020-622 0101)

UK
   17-18 Old Bond St, London W1X 3DA
   (☎ 0171-629 6058)

USA
   10 East 40th St, suite 1902, New York,
   NY 10016 (☎ 212-689 9720)

BUSINESS HOURS & HOLIDAYS

On weekdays shops open at around 8.30 am and close at 6 pm although some stay open until 7 pm on Thursday. Bakeries and grocery stores open earlier. Many small shops, particularly in country areas, close for a long lunch, and reopen by 3 pm at the latest. Other shops are closed on Monday mornings. Almost everything closes at around noon on Saturday and is closed all day Sunday but hotel restaurants are open every day. Grocery stores also close at noon on Saturday and often you won't be let in the door after 11.30 am. Large supermarkets in department stores stay open until 2 pm on Saturday but the queues for shopping trolleys double in length. Some private grocery stores open on weekends but may sell out of milk and bread as these are only delivered on weekdays. Towns in the Czech Republic really die on the weekends as the locals retreat to their cottages in the countryside.

Most museums are closed on Monday and the day following a public holiday. Many gardens, castles and historic sites in the Czech Republic are closed from November to March and open on weekends only in April and October. In spring and autumn you may have to wait around for a group to form before being allowed in, so again, it's better to go on weekends. In winter, before making a long trip out to some attraction in the countryside, be sure to check that it's open. Staff at some isolated sights take an hour off for lunch, and ticket offices often close at 4 pm, even if the building itself is open until later. The main town museums stay open all year. Students usually get 50% off the entry price at museums, galleries, theatres, cinemas, fairs etc. Many churches remain closed except for services.

Public holidays include New Year's Day (1 January), Easter Monday (March/April), Labour Day (1 May), Liberation Day (8 May), Cyril and Methodius Day (5 July), Jan Hus Day (6 July), Republic Day (28 October) and Christmas (from 24 to 26 December). Republic Day commemorates 28 October 1918, when the independent Czechoslovak Republic was proclaimed. On

New Year's Eve most restaurants and bars will either be rented out for private parties or closed (a situation repeated throughout much of Eastern Europe).

CULTURAL EVENTS

Since 1946 the Prague Spring International Music Festival has taken place during the second half of May (most performances are sold out well ahead). In June there's a festival of brass band music at Kolín. In August the Frédéric Chopin Music Festival occurs in Mariánské Lázně. Karlovy Vary comes back with the Dvořák Autumn Music Festival in September. Prague's International Jazz Festival is held in October. Brno has a music festival in October.

Moravian folk-art traditions culminate in late June at the Strážnice Folk Festival between Brno and Bratislava. In mid-August the Chod Festival at Domažlice, 57 km south of Plzeň, affords a chance to witness the folk songs and dances of South and West Bohemia.

The Brno International Trade Fair of consumer goods takes place every spring. In August or September an agricultural exhibition is held in České Budějovice.

POST

Postage costs are much lower in the Czech Republic than in Hungary, so catch up on your postcard writing. Poland is also inexpensive but letters posted in Poland tend to move much more slowly than those mailed from the Czech Republic (two weeks to the USA). Always use airmail. Most post offices are open weekdays from 8 am to 7 pm.

To send parcels abroad, you will need to go to a post office with a customs section. Although the main post offices often don't have a customs section, staff there will be able to tell you which post office you should go to. These post offices are usually open from 8 am to 3 pm. Airmail is a little more than double surface mail for parcels. When sending books you'll have to be persistent to get the book rate (which does, in fact, exist).

Don't bother sending a parcel containing textiles. Although the post office may accept it (and your money) it will never leave the Czech Republic due to an archaic law which prohibits the export of textiles (even your own clothes) by post.

General delivery mail should be addressed c/o Poste Restante, Pošta 1, Jindřišská 14, 11000 Praha 1, Czech Republic.

American Express card-holders can receive mail addressed c/o American Express, Václavské náměstí 50, 11000 Praha 1, Czech Republic. American Express holds letters for 30 days, but parcels and registered mail will be returned to sender. This is a reliable place to receive mail.

TELEPHONE

You can make international telephone calls at main post offices and, within Europe, they usually go through right away. Operator-assisted international telephone calls cost US$3 a minute to New Zealand, US$2 a minute to Australia, Canada, the USA and Japan, or US$1 a minute to most of Europe. All calls have a three-minute minimum. Check the rates with the clerk before placing your call and ask for a receipt.

Czech Telecom has installed lots of nice new blue card phones around the country and telephone cards (100-unit card US$4) are easily obtainable at newsstands and post offices. These phones still aren't connected to sufficient international lines so you may have to try a few times to get your call outside the country. Public telephones in post offices are more reliable than those on the street. The international access code is 00.

To call the Czech Republic from abroad, dial your international access code, 42 (the country code for the Czech Republic), the area code and the number. Important area codes include 2 (Prague), 5 (Brno), 17 (Karlovy Vary), 19 (Plzeň), 38 (České Budějovice), 66 (Telč), 165 (Mariánské Lázně), 166 (Cheb), 206 (Mělník), 321 (Kolín), 327 (Kutná Hora), 337 (Český Krumlov), 361 (Tábor), and 659 (Český Těšín). When dialling from within the Czech Republic you must add a 0 before the area code.

TIME

The time in the Czech Republic is GMT/UTC plus one hour. At the end of March the Czech Republic goes on summer time and clocks are set forward an hour. At the end of September they're turned back an hour.

ELECTRICITY

The electric current is 220 V, 50 Hz.

WEIGHTS & MEASURES

The metric system is used in the Czech Republic.

BOOKS

In *The Good Soldier Švejk*, satirist Jaroslav Hašek (1883-1923) pokes fun at the pettiness of the government and military service alike. In this Czech classic, a Prague dog-catcher is drafted into the Austrian army before WW I, and by carrying out stupid orders to the letter he succeeds in completely disrupting military life.

Nightfrost in Prague: the End of Humane Socialism by Zdeněk Mlynář (Karz Publishers, New York, 1980) is an inside political view of the events of 1968 by a former secretary of the Central Committee of the Communist Party of Czechoslovakia. Also interesting is *Hope Dies Last, The Autobiography of Alexander Dubček* (Kodansha America Inc, 114 5th Ave, New York, NY 10011).

Before 1989 the clandestine works of dissident authors were circulated in typewritten 'samizdat' editions of a few dozen carbon copies and the best were smuggled out and published abroad. For an anthology of these underground writings get a copy of *Goodbye samizdat!* edited by M Goetz-Stankiewicz (Northwestern University Press, Illinois, 1993).

Ludvík Vaculík gives an insight into the mood of dissident Prague writers during the 1980s in his collection of chronicles, *A Cup of Coffee with My Interrogator* (Readers International, London, 1987), which has an introduction by Václav Havel.

The collection of papers entitled *Václav Havel or Living in Truth* (Meulenhoff, Amsterdam, 1986), edited by Jan Vladislav, includes Havel's famous 1978 essay 'The power of the powerless'. Havel describes the conformism of those who simply accepted the 'post-totalitarian system' by 'living within the lie'. In contrast, 'dissidents' who dared say, 'The emperor is naked!' endured many difficulties but at least earned respect by 'living within the truth'. Michael Simmons' *The Reluctant President: A Political Life of Václav Havel* portrays this captivating figure well.

After the 1968 Soviet invasion, Czech novelist Milan Kundera saw his early works, *The Joke* and *Laughable Loves*, removed from library shelves; in 1975, he settled in France. In 1979, in response to publication of *The Book of Laughter and Forgetting*, which combines eroticism with political satire, the communist government revoked Kundera's Czech citizenship. His 1984 book, *The Unbearable Lightness of Being*, is about a brain surgeon who is reluctantly cast as a dissident after the 1968 Soviet invasion.

The Czech Republic's foremost resident writer is Ivan Klíma whose works were banned in Czechoslovakia from 1970 to 1989, though he continued to live and write there. Klíma novels such as *Love and Garbage* (1986) and *Waiting for Darkness, Waiting for Light* (1993) tackle the human dimension behind the contradictions of contemporary Czech life. *My Golden Trades* is a collection of stories about six individuals written before 1989 and recently translated into English.

Guidebooks

One of the most substantial guides is *Nagel's Encyclopedia-Guide Czechoslovakia* (Nagel Publishers, Geneva, 1985). Its 480 pages of detailed description and good maps cover the country exhaustively, though the practical information is simply tacked on at the end of the book in the form of lists.

Lonely Planet's *Czech & Slovak Republics – a travel survival kit* by John King and Richard Nebeský is a lot better when it comes to the nuts and bolts of travelling and there's also *Czechoslovakia: The Rough Guide* which fits the area into a different framework.

MEDIA

The first issue of *Prognosis*, a fortnightly English-language newspaper, appeared in March 1991. This high-quality publication carries a wide range of interesting local news and the eight-page 'Visitors' Guide' in every issue is an up-to-date guide to Prague. The restaurant and entertainment listings alone are worth the US$1 newsstand price. To subscribe, send a Visa card authorisation for US$42 (for 12 issues) to *Prognosis*, Africká 17, 160 00 Prague 6.

Also excellent is *The Prague Post*, a weekly business newspaper founded by a group of young US expatriates in October 1991. The *Post's* thick 'Culture' section contains all the practical visitor information you need. A 26-issue subscription costs US$75 inside Europe or US$90 outside Europe from Subscriptions Department, *The Prague Post*, Na poříčí 12, 115 30 Prague 1 (Visa cards accepted).

The *Prague News*, Truhlářská 16, 110 00 Prague 1, is an advertising-oriented tourist paper.

HEALTH

All health care is free to citizens of the Czech Republic. First aid is provided free to visitors in case of an accident. Otherwise, foreigners must pay a fee. British nationals receive free medical attention.

Thermal Baths

There are hundreds of curative mineral springs and dozens of health spas in the Czech Republic which use mineral waters, mud or peat. Most famous are the spas of West Bohemia (Františkovy Lázně, Karlovy Vary and Mariánské Lázně).

Unlike Hungary, where hot-spring waters are open to everyone, in the Czech Republic the spas are reserved for the medical treatment of patients. Yet all the spas have colonnades where you may join in the 'drinking cure', a social ritual that involves imbibing liberal quantities of warm spring water and then parading up and down to stimulate circulation. Admission is free but you need to bring your own cup.

Though the resorts are pleasant to visit, to receive medical treatment at a spa you must book in advance through Balnea (☎ 02-232 3767), Pařížská 11, 110 01 Prague 1. The recommended stay is 21 days though you can book for as few as three days. Daily prices begin at US$45/70 for a single/double in the cheapest category in the winter season, and rise to US$95/160 in the top category during the main summer season. Accompanying persons not taking a spa treatment get about a third off. From October to April prices are reduced. The price includes medical examination and care, spa curative treatment, room and board, and the spa tax. The clientele tends to be elderly. Čedok offices abroad will have full information about spa treatments.

ANNOYANCES

Confusingly, buildings on some streets have two sets of street numbers. In this case, the red number is the actual number while the blue number is the consecutive number though it's sometimes hard to tell which of the two is the one in your address. To make matters worse, the streets themselves are often poorly labelled and the recent name changes haven't helped at all. In case of problems, write the address down on a piece of paper and show it to a local.

Reader Anne Small of Tauranga, New Zealand, sent this:

At Prague Railway Station the need for a lavatory became urgent. A burly woman was sitting with the usual saucer between her huge elbows resting on the table. I was very tired having travelled all night from Poland and was confronted with my tenth new currency since leaving home and no had idea of the value of the money I placed in the saucer. I made only a step or two towards my place of relief when I was grabbed in a deathlock from behind, knocking my bags from my grip, and was frog-marched to the door, my head being belaboured at each step and my bag thrown after me! Two days later I was compelled to use that same place again and, taking no chances, I placed what seemed a huge sum in the saucer. I was able to go unmolested until later, when I tried to clean my teeth at the wash basin and was subjected to the same treatment again. I went to the accommodation office to complain and was told that the police were around the corner, which they weren't. I went down to the ground floor, bought a bottle of water and completed the teeth cleaning in front of the station, affording free amusement to the locals. A frightening experience for a seventy-two year old!

WORK

The Klub mladých cestovatelů or KMC (☎ 02-235 6388), Karolíny Světlé 30, Prague (metro: Národní třída), organises international work camps from June to August renovating historic buildings, doing trail maintenance in national parks, teaching English to children etc. You must sign up for two or three weeks and there's no pay, but room and board are provided. There's a US$10 registration fee. Actually, you're supposed to reserve months ahead through a volunteer organisation in your home country, but KMC often accepts individuals who just show up at their Prague office when they have space available on one of their projects. It's possible the KMC office will have moved by the time you get to Prague but you should be able to track them down with the help of the Prague Information Service. The KMC camps are a great way to do something useful on your trip while making a lot of friends.

It's fairly easy to get jobs teaching English but you'll be paid in crowns and they aren't easily convertible or worth much. It's easier to find a job in provincial centres than it is in Prague and your living costs will be lower. Be aware that companies employing foreigners without working and residence permits face fines of US$8000 for the first offence and US$32,000 for subsequent offences. Obtaining these permits can take up to three months. The laissez faire official attitudes which immediately followed the Velvet Revolution are gradually disappearing.

ACTIVITIES

Hiking

Excellent day hikes are possible in the forests around the West Bohemian spas, Karlovy Vary and Mariánské Lázně. The Moravian Karst area, north of Brno, is another easily accessible hiking area.

Skiing

The Czech Republic's main ski resorts are Špindlerův Mlýn and Pec pod Sněžkou in Krkonoše National Park, north-west of Svoboda nad Upou along the Polish border. The main season here is from January to March.

Cycling

For information on bicycle rentals and suggested trips, see Activities in the Prague and Český Krumlov sections of this chapter.

Canoeing & Yachting

For canoeing and yachting possibilities turn to the Český Krumlov section of this chapter.

Golf

Mariánské Lázně has an 18-hole golf course.

Courses

The Institute of Linguistics & Professional Training of Charles University (fax 42-2-2422 9497), Jindřišká 29, 11000 Praha 1, runs a three-week summer course for foreigners from mid-July to early August. Participants have the choice of studying in Prague (US$756 including accommodation) or at Poděbrady, 50 km east (US$864 including accommodation and all meals). Single rooms are US$60 extra per month and group excursions are additional. Students at Poděbrady are able to use the facilities of the local spa. The application deadline is 15 June. No prior knowledge of the Czech language is required and everyone is welcome.

Charles University also offers regular 10-month winter courses (from September to June) for those interested in further study at Czech universities or specialisation in Slavic studies at a foreign university. (Students wishing to have credits transferred to their home university should obtain written approval from the head of their department before enrolling.) The cost of tuition and materials is US$1910 with 25 hours a week instruction, US$2630 with 35 hours weekly.

One can also opt for one or two four-month semesters at US$980 each (25 hours a week). Special six-week language courses (US$380 tuition) are available from time to time and individual tutors can be hired at US$8 an hour. Participants are eligible for inexpensive accommodation in student dormitories and in addition to Prague, one can study at Dobruška, Mariánské Lázně, Poděbrady, or Teplice.

HIGHLIGHTS

Historic Towns

The Czech Republic is a country of historic towns, and the five most authentic and picturesque are České Budějovice, Český Krumlov, Kutná Hora, Tábor and Telč (see the relevant sections later in this chapter).

Museums & Galleries

The Prague Jewish Museum in the former Prague ghetto is easily the largest and most authentic of its kind in Eastern Europe. Prague's finest art galleries are in the castle area, especially the collections of the National Gallery in the Šternberský Palace and the Basilica of St George. The 'panorama' in Brno's Technological Museum lets you see the world as it was in 1890. The beer museum in Plzeň sums up one of this country's noblest contributions to humanity.

Castles

Holy Roman emperor Charles IV's Karlštejn Castle looks like something out of Disneyland but it's genuine 14th century. Český Krumlov Castle has the same effect. Prague Castle is literally packed with art treasures. Brno's 17th-century Špilberk Castle remains a symbol of Habsburg repression.

ACCOMMODATION

Camping

There are several hundred camping grounds in the Czech Republic, which are usually open from May to September. The camping grounds are primarily intended for motorists so you're often surrounded by noisy caravans and car campers. Those full of German cars with 'D' stickers on the back are invariably more expensive than those with mostly Czech cars, but all are reasonable. They're often accessible on public transport, but there's usually no hot water. Most of these places have a small snack bar where beer is sold and many have small cabins for rent which are cheaper than a hotel room. Pitching your own tent in these camping grounds is definitely the least expensive form of accommodation. Freelance camping is prohibited.

Hostels

The Hostelling International handbook shows an impressive network of hostels in the Czech Republic, but when you actually try to use them, you often find that they're either full, closed or nonexistent. Some of the places listed in the handbook are rather luxurious 'Juniorhotels' with single and double rooms, especially those in Prague (always full), Karlovy Vary (presently closed) and Mariánské Lázně (a good bet).

In July and August many student dormitories become temporary hostels and in recent years a number of such dormitories in Prague have been converted into year-round Western-style hostels.

Hostelling is controlled by the Klub madých cestovatelů (KMC) or Club of Young Travellers (☎ 02-235 6388), Karolíny Světlé 30, Prague (metro: Národní třída), and CKM Student Travel, which has offices in all cities. To get into a hostel, it's sometimes best to go first to the CKM office and ask the staff there to make a reservation for you. These offices keep very short business hours, sometimes only opening on weekday afternoons. If you go directly to the hostel itself, your chances vary. Occasionally CKM offices will agree to make advance bookings for you over the phone at hostels in other cities. A YHA/HI membership card is not usually required to stay at CKM hostels, though it will get you a reduced rate. An ISIC student card may also get you a discount, but only if you book direct (not through a CKM office).

There's another category of hostel not

connected with the CKM. Tourist hostels *(Turistické ubytovny)* are intended for visitors from other Eastern European countries and provide very basic dormitory accommodation without the standards and controls associated with HI hostels (mixed dormitories, smoking in the room, no curfew etc). They're very cheap, but you'll have to be persuasive and persistent to stay in them. Ask about tourist hostels at Čedok offices and watch for the letters 'TU' on accommodation lists published in languages other than English.

Similarly the letters 'UH' refer to an *Ubytovací hostinec*, which is a pub or inn offering basic rooms without private facilities.

Private Rooms & Pensions

Private rooms are usually available, so ask for them at the Čedok offices in Brno, Karlovy Vary, Mariánské Lázně and Plzeň or at Pragotur in Prague. Some have a three-night minimum-stay requirement.

In Prague many private travel agencies now offer private rooms and, though their charges are higher than those of Čedok and Pragotur, the service is also better. This is the easiest way to find accommodation in Prague if you don't mind paying at least US$18/25 for a single/double a night.

Many small pensions (often just glorified private rooms) have appeared in South Bohemia in recent years offering more personalised service than the hotels at lower rates. Look for these and watch out for *privát Zimmer frei* signs, announcing the availability of private rooms.

Hotels

The Czech Republic has a good network of hotels covering the entire country. In Prague the hotels are expensive, whereas hotels in smaller towns are usually cheaper and more likely to have rooms. Between 1990 and 1993 the value of the crown against the dollar remained fairly steady while hotel prices doubled and tripled. Czechs pay less than half as much as foreigners at hotels.

There are five categories of hotels: A* deluxe (five stars), A* (four stars), B* (three stars), B (two stars) and C (one star). The B-category hotels usually offer reasonable comfort for about US$15/25 a single/double with shared bath or US$25/35 with private bath (50% higher in Prague). In small towns and villages, there are sometimes also C-category hotels, but renovations have upgraded most of them to B-category in the cities. In places well off the beaten track, the police may be able to help you find a place where you can stay when all else fails.

Many hotels will not rent rooms till 2 pm, so leave your luggage at the station. If you have a room with shared bath, you may have to pay US$2 extra to use the communal shower and search for the cleaning staff to get the key. Hotel receptionists usually sell soft drinks and beer for just slightly more than shop prices but these drinks are often kept under the counter, so ask.

FOOD

The cheapest places to eat at are the self-service restaurants *(samoobsluha)*. Sometimes these places have really tasty dishes like barbecued chicken or hot German sausage – just right for a quick cooked lunch between sights. Train stations often have good cheap restaurants or buffets but the cheapest meals are to be had in busy beer halls. If the place is crowded with locals, is noisy and looks chaotic, chances are it will have great lunch specials at low prices.

You'll rarely have trouble finding a place to eat, but when you do, try the dining room of any large hotel. Hotel restaurants in the Czech Republic are reasonable in hard-currency terms, though the atmosphere is often stuffy and formal. Check your coat in before entering or the waiter will send you back to do so. Pretentious service aside, these places will usually have menus in English or German with fish dishes available, and even vegetarians should be able to find something suitable. Hotel restaurants stay open later and they don't close on weekends, and there's less likelihood of 'mistakes' on your bill than there might be at an independent tourist restaurant.

Lunches are generally bigger and cheaper than dinners in the less expensive places. Dinner is eaten early and latecomers may have little to choose from. Don't expect to be served at any restaurant if you arrive within half an hour of closing time. It used to be rare for a restaurant to have everything listed on its menu but this has become less common with privatisation. Some waiters will tell tourists that all the cheaper dishes are finished to get them to order something more expensive.

Always check the posted menu before entering a restaurant to get an idea of the price range. If no menu is displayed inside or out, insist on seeing one before ordering. It doesn't matter if it's only in Czech (as is often the case). The main categories are *předkrmy* (hors d'oeuvres), *polévky* (soups), *studené jídlo* (cold dishes), *teplé jídlo* (warm dishes), *masitá jídla* (meat dishes), *ryby* (fish), *zelenina* (vegetables), *saláty* (salads), *ovoce* (fruit), *zákusky* (desserts) and *nápoje* (drinks). Anything that comes with *knedlíky* (dumplings) will be a hearty local meal.

The waiter may be able to translate the names of a few dishes, otherwise just take pot luck. If you simply let the waiter tell you what's available without seeing a price list, you'll be overcharged every time, so if the person serving refuses to show you a written menu, you should just get up and walk out. Some Prague restaurants, especially, are notorious for overcharging foreigners (see Places to Eat in the Prague section). Most beer halls have a system of marking everything you eat or drink on a small piece of paper which is left on your table and in such places you'll seldom have any problems.

Tipping is optional but if you were fairly served you should certainly round up the bill to the next 5 Kč (or to the next 10 Kč if the bill is over 100 Kč) as you're paying. Waiters at Prague restaurants accustomed to serving Americans will expect to be tipped more than this. Never leave coins worth less than 1 Kč as your only tip or you risk having them thrown back at you.

In Bohemia make frequent visits to the great little pastry shops *(kavárna* or *cukrárna)*, which offer cakes, puddings and coffee as good as anything you'll find in neighbouring Austria at a fraction of the price.

Local Specialities

Czech cuisine is strong on sauces and gravies and weak on fresh vegetables. *Pražská šunka* (smoked Prague ham) is often taken as an hors d'oeuvre with Znojmo gherkins, followed by a thick soup, such as *bramborová polévka* (potato soup) and *zeleninová polévka* (vegetable soup). *Dršťková polévka* (tripe soup) is a treat not to be missed. The Czechs love meat dishes with *knedlíky* (flat circular dumplings) and/or sauerkraut. Carp *(kapr)* from the Bohemian fish ponds can be crumbed and fried or baked. Vegetarian dishes include *smažený sýr* (fried cheese) and *knedlíky s vejci* (scrambled eggs with dumplings). Czech fruit dumplings *(ovocné knedlíky)* come with melted butter or curd cheese and a whole fruit inside.

DRINKS

The Czech Republic is a beer drinker's paradise: where else could you get three or four big glasses of top quality Pilsner for under a dollar? You'll pay less than half the price you would in Poland, and Czech beer halls *(pivnice)* put Munich to shame. The Czechs serve their draught beer with a high head of foam which makes for a rather flat brew, so you might want to order bottled beer and pour it yourself. However, the stuff on tap is dirt cheap and you're able to consume large quantities without upsetting your stomach because the gas has been removed.

One of the first words of Czech you'll learn is *pivo* (beer); alcohol-free beer is called *pito*. Bohemian beer is about the best in the world and the most famous brands are Budvar (the original Budweiser) and Plzeňský Prazdroj (the original Pilsner). South Moravia produces excellent wine, either red *(červené víno)* or white *(bílé víno)*. You can be sure of a good feed at a *vinárna* (wine restaurant).

Special things to try include Becherovka (an exquisite bittersweet Czech liqueur made at Karlovy Vary), *zubrovka* (vodka with herb extracts) and *slivovice* (plum brandy). Grog is rum with hot water and sugar – a great pick-me-up. *Limonáda* is a good nonalcoholic drink.

ENTERTAINMENT

Theatres and concert halls were heavily subsidised by the communists so admission prices are still well below those in Western Europe and the programmes are first-rate. In Prague, unfortunately, the best theatre tickets are cornered by scalpers and travel agencies who demand premium prices, but in smaller centres like Karlovy Vary, Plzeň, České Budějovice and Brno you can see top performances at minimal expense. Check the theatres listed early in the day. The Czech Republic is a conservative country when it comes to social customs and you are expected to dress up when going to the theatre. Most theatres are closed in summer.

Outside Prague, the nightlife is rather limited, though after 9 pm there's usually a band playing in the bar of the best hotel in town and on weekends a disco will be pumping up somewhere – ask. You must often contend with overbearing door attendants and contemptuous waiters. Movies are always very cheap and usually shown in the original language with local subtitles.

Spectator Sports

Ice hockey is the national sport, followed by soccer (football) and tennis. Among the best Czech hockey teams are Sparta (the Prague city club), the Dukla (military) club of Jihlava and the Poldi club of Kladno (near Prague), a factory club. Outstanding soccer teams include Sparta and Bohemians (Prague city clubs) and Baník from Ostrava (a factory club). Cross-country ski racing is popular in winter.

THINGS TO BUY

Good buys include china, Bohemian crystal, costume jewellery, garnets, fancy leather goods, special textiles, lace, embroidery, shoes, classical records, colour-photography books and souvenirs. The hardback, blank-page notebooks available at stationery shops in small towns (not Prague) make excellent journals.

Garnet jewellery has been a Bohemian speciality for over a century. The ancient Egyptians used this semiprecious gemstone as a kind of travel insurance that was guaranteed to protect the wearer from accidents.

In most shops and supermarkets the number of people inside is controlled by shopping carts or baskets. You cannot enter without one, so pick one up at the door or stand in line and wait for someone to leave. You must even pick up a shopping basket when you enter a bookshop! Outside Prague the largest department store chain is Prior.

Before making any major purchases, be aware that goods worth over US$50 purchased in the Czech Republic may be subject to export duties as high as 300%. Typical souvenirs are supposed to be exempt but even then Czech customs officers have been known to levy excessive duties. Antiques and valuable-looking artworks are closely scrutinised.

Reader Judith L Nathanson of Andover, Massachusetts, sent us this:

> We had an experience with a Czech border guard when we were taking the train from Prague back to Austria. The guard looked over a large poster, framed and wrapped up with lots of cardboard and bubblewrap, that we had bought in Prague and asked us how much it had cost. He then asked us how much Czech money we had with us, glanced cursorily in some little book and wrote some numbers on a piece of paper telling us that it was our 'duty' (it amounted to US$50). We had been quite deferential up to that point, but when we realised we were in the middle of a shakedown, we went directly into enraged English and told him that there was no way we were paying any duty to take goods *out* of a country. At that point he disappeared with our bill of sale and credit card slip (our only proof of purchase) and said something about talking to his superior, but he left the train and we never saw him (or our bill of sale) again.

Getting There & Away

Air

The national carrier, Czechoslovak Airlines (ČSA), flies to Prague from Abu Dhabi, Bahrain, Bangkok, Beirut, Cairo, Chicago, Damascus, Dubai, Istanbul, Kuwait, Larnaca, Montreal, New York, Sharjah, Singapore, Tel Aviv, Toronto, Tunis, and many European cities. Fare structures are complicated and variable, so in the USA call ☎ 800-223 2365 toll-free for the latest information.

From Western Europe some return excursion flights are cheaper than a one-way ticket but they're nonrefundable once purchased and flight dates cannot be changed. All fares are seasonal, so check with your travel agent.

There's no airport departure tax on international flights leaving the Czech Republic.

Land

Bus

There's a bus several times a day from Vienna (Mitte Busbahnhof) to Brno (129 km, three hours, US$8). Try to buy your ticket the day before.

From London, the Kingscourt Express (☎ 0181-769 9229), 35 Kingscourt Road, London SW16 1JA, and National Express (☎ 0121-456 1122), 4 Vicarde Road, Egbaston, Birmingham B15 3E9, have buses to Prague twice a week year-round (1277 km, 23 hours, £65 one way, £105 return). Youth and senior citizen discounts are available. Returning to Britain, check the Prague departure point carefully.

Compare the price of a bus tour to Prague with New Millennium Holidays (☎ 0121-711 2232), 20 High St, Solihull, West Midlands B91 3TB, England, which will be about double a scheduled coach but bed and breakfast are included. Less expensive New Millennium tours to Brno also include dinner (offered year-round).

A bus operates between Paris and Prague (1066 km, 16½ hours, US$70 one way, US$122 return) five times a week year-round. From April to September this bus is daily. In Paris tickets are available at the Eurolines Paris, Gare Routiere Internationale Galliéni (☎ 4972 5151), Ave du Général de Gaulle (metro: Galliéni). Ask about student discounts. For information on the weekly bus to Prague from Barcelona and Madrid contact Hospitalet de Llobregat (☎ 93-431 9511).

There's a Eurolines bus service twice a week throughout the year from Amsterdam to Prague (1133 km, 19 hours, US$75 one way, US$125 return, with a 10% discount for those aged under 26 or over 59 years). From June to September this bus runs four times a week. This trip is rather tiring because it follows a roundabout route via Rotterdam, Antwerp and Brussels. In mid-1994 Eurolines began offering a special 'Capital Tripper' fare of US$150 for a circular trip from Amsterdam to Budapest, Prague and back to Amsterdam or vice versa (a Slovakian transit visa is required by some nationals). For tickets contact Budget Bus/Eurolines (☎ 020-627 5151), Rokin 10, Amsterdam, or Eurolines (☎ 2-217 0025), Place de Brouckere 50, Brussels.

From Denmark, DSB buses connect Copenhagen and Aalborg to Prague twice a week (13½ hours, US$75). Connections are available to/from Sweden and Norway. Any DSB travel agency in Denmark will have tickets. Numerous buses operate from Germany to Prague and information is easily obtained at German travel agencies and bus stations. Travelling by bus is almost always cheaper than by the train.

Some of the long-distance international buses you see advertised in bus stations around the Czech Republic are only for locals – foreigners are not accepted. Other times foreigners pay a higher fare than Czechs. Bus service to/from Western Europe is still much cheaper than the train. Turn to Travel Agencies in the Prague section for local offices selling tickets for these buses.

Train

The easiest (if not the cheapest) way to get from Western Europe to the Czech Republic is by train. Keep in mind that train fares within the Czech Republic are less expensive than tickets to/from Western Europe. When travelling between Western and Eastern Europe, pay as little of the Czech portion in hard currency as you can and use border towns such as Děčín, Cheb, Plzeň, České Budějovice and Břeclav as entry or exit points. In other words, buy tickets which terminate or begin in these towns.

Sample 2nd-class international train fares from Prague are US$13 to Budapest (616 km, nine hours), US$13 to Kraków, US$17 to Vienna (354 km, six hours), US$18 to Warsaw (740 km, 12 hours), US$27 to Nuremberg (371 km, six hours), US$28 to Berlin (377 km, 5½ hours) and US$37 to Belgrade (986 km, 15½ hours). (These fares are rather low and may soon be sharply increased.) From Amsterdam to Cheb is US$154 one way in 2nd class.

In the Czech Republic you should purchase international train tickets in advance from Čedok, but do this somewhere other than Prague, as the Čedok office there is will most likely be 'mobbed'. All international tickets are valid for two months with unlimited stopovers. Students get a 25% discount on train tickets to other Eastern European countries. Inter-Rail passes (sold to European residents only) are accepted in the Czech Republic but Eurail is not.

Most of the major 'name trains' listed herein travel daily throughout the year and require compulsory seat reservations. First-class sleepers and 2nd-class couchettes are available on almost all of these trains. From mid-June to mid-September additional services are put on.

To/From Western Europe Prague is on the main line used by all direct trains from Berlin to Vienna and Budapest, so access from those cities is easy. The *Balt-Orient, Hungária, Meridian* and *Metropol* express trains all travel daily between Berlin-Lichtenberg and Prague, continuing on to Budapest. The morning *Vindobona* and afternoon *Neptun* also link Berlin to Prague.

The *Sanssouci, Smetana* and *Vindobona* express trains link Vienna to Prague via Tábor. It's also possible to travel north-west from Vienna on local 2nd-class trains by changing at Gmünd and České Velenice, the border points, twice a day. There are six trains from Vienna (Nordbahnhof or Süd) to Břeclav (146 km, 1½ hours, US$13). Twice a day there's a service between Linz, Austria and České Budějovice (125 km, four hours, US$12). Three other connections between Linz and České Budějovice involve a change of trains at Summerau and Horní Dvořiště. A daily train links Vienna (Franz-Josefs-bahnhof) to České Budějovice (219 km, 3½ hours), departing from Vienna in the early morning, České Budějovice in the late afternoon.

From western Germany you'll probably transit Nuremberg and Cheb. The *Západní* express train travels daily between Paris and Prague (1263 km, 18 hours) via Frankfurt/Main, Nuremberg and Cheb. Local railcars shuttle between Cheb and Schirnding, Germany, twice a day (13 km, 15 minutes). Trains from Zürich and Munich go via Furth im Wald and Plzeň. Three times a day there's an unreserved local train from Furth im Wald, Germany, to Domažlice (25 minutes). A lesser known route between eastern Germany and the Czech Republic is Leipzig to Karlovy Vary (the *Karlex* express train, 240 km, five hours). Unreserved local trains from Bad Schandau, Germany, to Děčín (22 km, 30 minutes), and Zittau, Germany, to Liberec (27 km, one hour) operate every couple of hours.

To/From Eastern Europe All express trains running between Budapest and Berlin-Lichtenberg pass through Bratislava, Brno and Prague. Of these, the Eurocity *Hungária* is a day train, and the *Balt-Orient, Metropol* and *Pannónia* are night trains. Going south, the *Balt-Orient* runs during the day, the *Hungária* during the evening and the *Metropol* and *Pannónia* overnight. Southbound, the *Pannónia* express train is convenient as it begins in Prague, but northbound the *Pannónia* and the *Balt-Orient* often run late as they originate in Romania.

Reservations are recommended. Many nationals require a separate Slovak visa to transit Slovakia on their way to Hungary.

Connections between Poland and Prague will go through either Wrocław or Katowice. The *Baltyk* travels to/from Gdynia via Wrocław, and the *Bohemia* runs between Warsaw and Prague via Wrocław, taking 12 hours. Take the *Silesia* if you want to go to/from Warsaw via Katowice to/from Prague (11 hours). All of these trains avoid Slovakia.

Car & Motorbike

Some Czech border crossings may only be used by citizens of the neighbouring countries, but the crossings named below are open to everyone.

To/From Austria There are crossings at Mikulov (24 km west of Břeclav); Hatě, (10 km south of Znojmo); Nová Bystřice (18 km south of Jindřichův Hradec); Halámky (south-east of České Budějovice); České Velenice (opposite Gmünd); Dolní Dvořiště (38 km south of České Budějovice); and Studánky (which is between Český Krumlov and Linz).

To/From Germany You can enter at Strážný (66 km north of Passau); Železná Ruda (81 km south of Plzeň); Folmava (between Regensburg and Plzeň); Rozvadov (between Nuremberg and Plzeň); Pomezí nad Ohří (eight km west of Cheb); Vojtanov (six km north of Františkovy Lázně); and Cinovec (48 km south of Dresden).

To/From Poland You can cross at Harrachov (between Liberec and Jelenia Góra); Náchod (43 km east of Kłodzko); Bohumín (12 km north of Ostrava); and Český Těšín (31 km east of Ostrava).

On Foot

If you want to avoid the hassle or expense of getting an international train ticket, consider walking across the border! To/from Poland, the easiest place to do this is at Český Těšín, which is on the opposite side of the Olše (Olza) River from Cieszyn, Poland. Both towns have good onward train or bus services, making this a viable option for the slightly adventurous traveller. (Turn to the end of this chapter for more information on Český Těšín).

If you want to walk into Austria, a good place to do it is from Mikulov, an unspoiled Moravian town with a large chateau on one hill and a church on another. Mikulov is on the railway line from Břeclav to Znojmo and the station is very close to the Austrian/Czech border point. From Brno, it's much faster to come by bus (50 km). You could easily cross on foot and then hitchhike the 77 km south to Vienna.

For information on crossing into Germany on foot turn to Getting There & Away in the Cheb section.

Getting Around

BUS

Within the Czech Republic, ČAD express buses are often faster and more convenient than the train. Buses are more expensive than trains, but, by European standards, both are cheap. Count on spending about US$1 for every hour of bus travel. You sometimes have to pay a small additional charge for checked luggage.

Because of numerous footnotes, posted bus timetables are almost impossible to read, so patronise information counters. Two crossed hammers as a footnote means the bus only operates on working days Monday to Friday. As more buses leave in the morning, it's better to get an early start. Many bus services don't operate on weekends – trains are more reliable at that time.

Since bus ticketing is computerised at main stations like Prague and Karlovy Vary, you can often book a seat ahead and be sure of a comfortable trip. At large stations, make sure you're in the right ticket line. Way stations are rarely computerised and you must just line up and pay the driver. Reservations can only be made in the originating station of the bus, and at peak periods you may have to stand part of the way if you don't have a reservation.

All over the Czech Republic, if you want to find a bus station or bus stop, write the letters ČAD on a piece of paper and show it to someone. If you want to find a train station, write ČD (which stands for Czech State Railways) on the paper.

Most bus and train stations have a left-luggage room *(úschovna)*. There's a 15-kg maximum-weight limit for left luggage but it's not always enforced. If you lose the receipt, you'll have to pay a fine to recover your bag.

Intercity and municipal bus service could deteriorate over the next few years as there's little new investment to modernise the aging fleets, and private companies will probably stick to the busiest and most profitable routes.

TRAIN

The Czech Railways or České Dráhy (ČD) provides clean, efficient train service to almost every part of the country. Railway lines tend to run south towards Austria, reflecting the region's political alignment in the late 19th century, when the tracks were first laid down. Although a line was built east from Prague to Kiev as early as the 1880s, only in 1955 was this main route to the Soviet border reopened as a modern double-track line – at a cost of a billion crowns.

Using the Czech railway system successfully involves a little ingenuity. Some trains operate only on certain days, but the footnotes on the posted timetables are incomprehensible. The clerks at the information counters seldom speak English (not even in major stations) so, to get a departure time, try writing down your destination and the date you wish to travel, then point to your watch and pray. Some railway information offices in the Czech Republic are computerised and will give you a printout in English with information about your train.

You must tell the ticket seller which type of train you want. On departure *(odjezdy)* notice boards in train stations the *druh vlaku* column indicates the category of each train: Ex (express – these are often international trains and stop at fewer stations than fast trains); R *(rychlík* – fast trains, for which you always pay a surcharge); Sp *(spěšný* – trains to mountain areas); and Os *(osobní* – ordinary trains).

The letter R inside a box or circle means that reservations are mandatory, while an R alone means that it's a fast train. Reservations are not possible on ordinary trains. In major cities, you usually have to make seat reservations *(rezervace míst)* at a different counter, so make sure you're standing in the right queue. A reservation costs only US$0.25, so make one whenever you can.

Express and rychlík trains are usually marked in red, and tickets for these often have a red strip across the middle. If you plan to travel on an express or rychlík train, make sure you get an express ticket, otherwise the conductor will levy a fine. Staff at ticket counters will happily sell you an invalid ticket and you'll have no recourse later. Most train tickets are valid for 48 hours, but check this when you buy your ticket. If you have to purchase a ticket or pay a supplement on the train for any reason, you'll have to pay extra charges to the conductor.

Train tickets are very reasonable at about US$1 for 100 km in 2nd class with a surcharge of US$1 for fast or intercity (IC) trains, US$2 extra for Eurocity (EC) trains. Always check to see if your train is an IC or EC and pay the surcharge in the station when buying your ticket, otherwise the conductor will charge you a supplement three times higher. First-class tickets cost 50% more than 2nd-class ones and nonsmoking compartments are available. Only express trains carry dining cars *(restaurační vůz)*.

In many stations, the complete timetable is posted on notice boards. Look at the map and find the connection you want, then look for the table with the corresponding number. Posted timetables usually give the platform *(nástupiště)* number. If you're going to be in the Czech Republic for any length of time, it's a good idea to purchase the complete railway timetable book, the *Jízdní řád*. It can

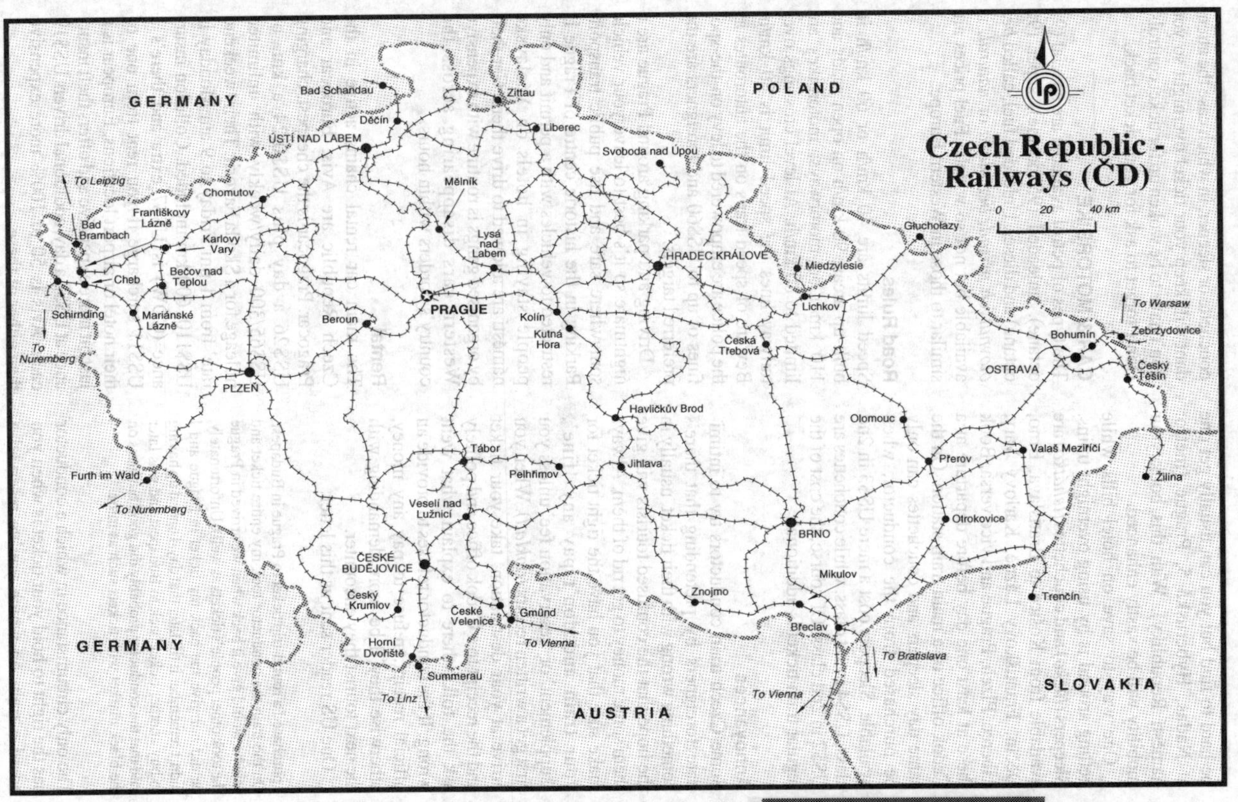

CZECH REPUBLIC

be hard to find but you can usually get one at Nadas, Hybernská 5, Prague (metro: naměstí Republiky). With this book your mobility will be vastly enhanced.

One way to save on hotel bills while getting around is by using overnight trains. Sleepers *(lůžko)* and couchettes *(lehátko)* are available from Košice to Bratislava, Brno, Děčín, Františkovy Lázně, Karlovy Vary, Liberec, Plzeň, Prague and vice versa. Book these at least one day before departure at a Čedok office or a main train station. On the same day sleepers and couchettes can only be purchased from the conductor, when available. Sleepers cost a mere US$3 in 2nd class, US$4 in 1st class, while couchettes are US$2 in 2nd class. Of course, the cost of the regular train ticket is additional.

Annoyances

Some Czech train conductors try to intimidate foreigners by pretending that there's something wrong with their ticket, usually in the hope that the confused tourists will give them some money to get rid of them. Always make sure that you have the right ticket for your train and don't pay any 'fine', 'supplement' or 'reservation fee' unless you first get a written receipt *(doklad)*. When you arrive at your destination, take your ticket and the receipt to a Čedok office and politely ask the folks there to explain what went wrong. If the conductor refuses to provide an official receipt, refuse to pay any money, otherwise they'll be more demanding with the next tourist they encounter.

One US reader sent us this letter:

> I purchased a round-trip ticket to Prague in Budapest. On the train the conductor took my entire ticket and said he would give it back when we arrived in Prague (he took other people's tickets as well). Unfortunately, he did *not* give me back my ticket in Prague and I didn't remember it till later that day. I ended up having to buy another ticket back to Budapest and was later told that the conductor probably did good business on the black market with tickets such as mine.

The only circumstance in which a conductor has the right to hold your ticket is when you board a train on which you've reserved a couchette or sleeper, in which case the attendant will keep your ticket overnight so you don't have to be woken up for ticket controls. Don't forget to ask for your ticket back.

CAR & MOTORBIKE

The types of petrol available are special (91 octane), unleaded (95 octane), super (96 octane) and diesel. Unleaded fuel, called *bez olovnatých přísad*, *bez olova* or *natural*, is available but not so widely. Fuel prices are similar to those in Western Europe.

Road Rules

Speed limits are 40 km/h or 60 km/h in built-up areas, 90 km/h on open roads and 110 km/h on motorways; motorbikes are limited to 80 km/h. At level crossings over railway lines the speed limit is 30 km/h. Beware of speed traps on the autoroutes as the police are empowered to levy on-the-spot fines of up to US$60 and foreigners are the preferred targets.

Driving and parking around Prague are a nightmare so it's best to leave your vehicle somewhere safe and use public transport. Parking in the historic centre of Prague is restricted to vehicles with a permit and only people staying in hotels on Václavské náměstí are allowed to drive there. Car theft by organised gangs is routine with expensive Western cars disappearing across the country's borders within hours.

Rental

The main car rental chains active in the Czech Republic are Avis, Europcar and Pragocar. Pragocar is the cheapest, charging US$26 a day plus US$0.24 a km, or US$65/300 daily/weekly with unlimited mileage for a Škoda Favorit. Their 'weekend rate' from 1 pm Friday to 9 am Monday is US$110, 600 km included. Collision insurance (CDW) is US$7 extra and there's a US$11 surcharge if you rent from one of their hotel or airport locations. Europcar is a just bit more expensive and offers theft insurance at US$8 a day, additional drivers US$19 each. Avis is 50 to 100% more expensive than either of these.

All three companies allow one-way rentals to their other locations in the Czech Republic at no additional charge. When comparing rates, note whether the 23% tax (VAT) is included. You can drive in the Czech Republic using your normal driving licence (international driving licence not required). The police single out foreign cars for traffic fines, so try to get a Škoda when you rent a car.

BICYCLE

After a trip around the Czech Republic by bicycle, Richard Nebeský of Melbourne, Australia, had this to report:

> The Czech Republic is small enough to be traversed on a bicycle. It is fairly safe for cyclists as most drivers will do their utmost to avoid them. Cyclists still should be careful as the roads are very narrow, potholed, and in towns the cobblestones and tram tracks can be a dangerous combination, especially when it has been raining. Theft is a problem especially in Prague, Brno and Plzeň, thus a good long chain and lock are a must.

Many locals use bicycles, so it's fairly easy to transport them on trains. First purchase your train ticket and then take it with your bicycle to the railway luggage office. There you fill out a card which will be attached to your bike; on the card you write your name, address, destination and departing station. You will be given a receipt that should include all the accessories that your bicycle has, such as lights and dynamo. You are not allowed to leave any luggage on the bicycle, and it is advisable to take off the pump and water bottles, as they could disappear along the way. The cost of transporting a bicycle is usually one-tenth of the train ticket. It is best to collect the bicycle from the goods carriage as soon as you arrive at your destination. You can also transport bicycles on most buses if they are not crowded and if the bus driver is willing.

LOCAL TRANSPORT

Buses and trams within cities operate from 4.30 am to 11.30 pm daily. In Prague some main bus and tram routes operate every 40 minutes all night. Tickets sold at newsstands must be validated once you're aboard as there are no conductors. Tickets are hard to find at night, on weekends and out in residential areas, so carry a good supply. Automats at Prague metro stations sell tickets which can be used on all forms of public transport in Prague.

Taxi

Taxis have meters and you pay what they show – just make sure the meter is switched on. Some Prague taxi drivers are highly experienced at overcharging tourists.

Prague

Prague (Praha in Czech) is like a history lesson come true. As you walk among the long stone palaces or across the Karlův most (Charles Bridge), with Smetana's Vltava flowing below and pointed towers all around, you'll feel as if history had stopped somewhere back in the 18th century. Goethe called Prague the prettiest gem in the stone crown of the world. A millennium earlier in 965 the Arab-Jewish merchant Ibrahim Ibn Jacob described Prague as a town of 'stone and lime'.

This story-book city in the centre of Bohemia experienced two architectural golden ages: a Gothic period under Holy Roman emperor Charles IV and then a baroque period during the Habsburg Counter-Reformation. In the 18th century, Czech culture was suppressed, so it's not at all surprising that Prague's two greatest baroque architects, Christopher and Kilian Dientzenhofer, were Germans.

Today Prague is a city of over a million inhabitants, the seat of government and leading centre of much of the country's intellectual and cultural life. Unlike Warsaw, Budapest and Berlin, which were major battlefields during WW II, Prague escaped almost unscathed and after the war, careful planning and preservation prevented haphazard modern development. Since 1989, however, central Prague has been swamped by unfettered capitalism as street vendors, cafés and restaurants take over pavements, streets and parks which were once public.

How you feel about Prague's current tourist glut may depend on where you're coming from. If you're arriving from London, Paris or Rome it may all seem quite normal, but if you've been elsewhere in Eastern Europe for a while, you'll be in for a bit of a shock. As you're being jostled by the hawkers and golden hordes you may begin to feel that Prague has become a tacky tourist trap, but try to overcome those feelings and enjoy this great European art centre for all it's worth. Just take care not to make it your first and last stop in Bohemia.

Orientation

Almost exactly midway between Berlin and Vienna, Prague nestles in a picturesque valley, its high hills topped by castles and its river spanned by 17 bridges. This river, the Vltava (Moldau), swings through the centre of the city like a question mark, separating Malá Strana (Little Quarter), with the baroque homes of the nobility, from Staré Město (Old Town), the early Gothic city centre. North of Malá Strana is Hradčany, the medieval castle district where royalty used to reside, while Nové Město (New Town) is a late Gothic extension of Staré Město to the south, almost as far as the old citadel, Vyšehrad. Only in 1784 did these four royal towns unite within a single system of fortifications.

Unforgettable features include Prague Castle, visible from almost everywhere in the city, and Václavské náměstí (Wenceslas Square), Prague's Champs Elysées, which points north-west to Staroměstské, the old town square. Between these two squares is Na příkopě, a busy pedestrian street where most of the information offices are found. Our maps of Prague are only for initial orientation – buy a detailed city map the first chance you get.

For information on facilities at Prague's various train and bus stations see the Getting There & Away information at the end of this section.

Information

There's a friendly tourist information kiosk in Hlavní nádraží Railway Station, right next to the metro entrance (weekdays 9 am to 7 pm, weekends 9 am to 6 pm).

The best place to pick up brochures and ask questions is at the Prague Information Service (PIS), Na příkopě 20 (metro: náměstí Republiky). Their monthly *Cultural Events* booklet in English is invaluable. They also sell city tours (US$15 for 2½ hours) and concert tickets (US$8 and up). Another PIS information centre is at Staroměstské náměstí 22, right opposite the clock on the old town hall.

Though actually a travel agency, Pragotur, U Obecního domu 2 (metro: náměstí Republiky), is usually helpful in providing general information when they're not too busy. They can also book tours, tickets and rooms for you at competitive rates.

Čedok, Na příkopě 18, also has an information counter.

If you want any information on motoring matters contact the Autoklub České Republiky (☎ 262 651), Opletalova 29, opposite Hlavní nádraží Railway Station. Nearby is Autoturist (☎ 773 455), Opletalova 21 (through the back courtyard).

Most newsstands have the English-language papers *Prognosis* and *The Prague Post* – without doubt, your best sources of the latest information on what's happening in Prague.

Money One of the best places in Prague to change travellers' cheques is the efficient American Express office (☎ 261 747) at Václavské náměstí 50 (weekdays 9 am to 6 pm, Saturday until noon). The three tellers provide fast service and no commission is charged on American Express travellers' cheques. There is a 1% commission on cheques from other companies (US$2 minimum) and 2% commission to change cash. They'll also change their own dollar travellers' cheques into dollars cash for 2%

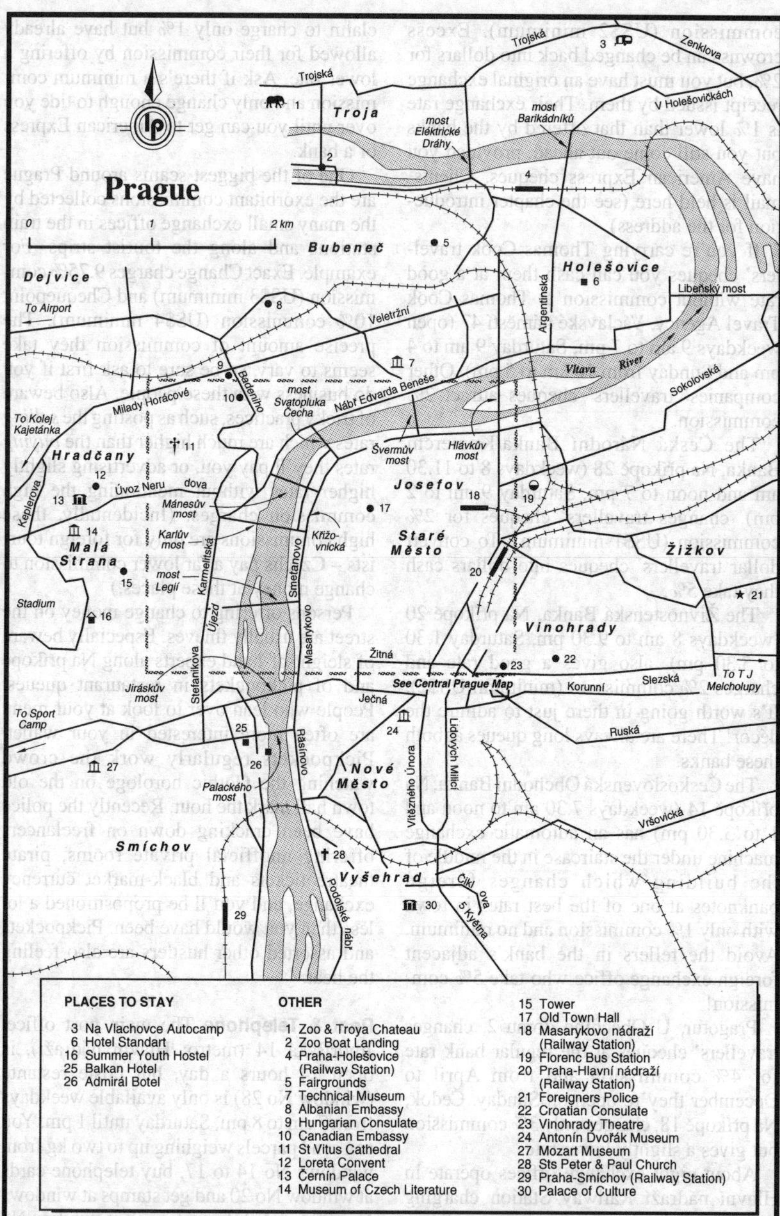
Prague
0
1
2 km
Troja
Trojská
Zenklova
most Barikádníků
V Holešovickách
most Eléktrické Dráhy
Bubeneč
Dejvice
To Airport
Holešovice
Argentinská
Libeňský most
Veletržní
Vltava River
Sokolovská
Milady Horácové
Badeniho
most Svatopluka Čecha
Nábř Edvarda Beneše
To Kolej Kajetánka
Hradčany
Švermův most
Hlávkův most
Úvoz Neru dova
Josefov
Mánesův most
Keplerova
Malá Strana
Karlův most
Křižo-vnická
Staré Město
Žižkov
most Legií
Karmelitská
Smetanovo
Stadium
Újezd
Masarykovo
Vinohrady
Žitná
Stefanikova
Jiráskův most
See Central Prague Map
Korunní
Slezská
To T J Melcholupy
To Sport Camp
Ječná
Rašínovo
Lidových Milicí
Ruská
Nové Město
Vítězného Února
Palackého most
Vršovická
Smíchov
Vyšehrad
Podolské nábř
Čiklova
5 Května
PLACES TO STAY
3 Na Vlachovce Autocamp
6 Hotel Standart
16 Summer Youth Hostel
25 Balkan Hotel
26 Admirál Botel
OTHER
1 Zoo & Troya Chateau
2 Zoo Boat Landing
4 Praha-Holešovice (Railway Station)
5 Fairgrounds
7 Technical Museum
8 Albanian Embassy
9 Hungarian Consulate
10 Canadian Embassy
11 St Vitus Cathedral
12 Loreta Convent
13 Černín Palace
14 Museum of Czech Literature
15 Tower
17 Old Town Hall
18 Masarykovo nádraží (Railway Station)
19 Florenc Bus Station
20 Praha-Hlavní nádraží (Railway Station)
21 Foreigners Police
22 Croatian Consulate
23 Vinohrady Theatre
24 Antonín Dvořák Museum
27 Mozart Museum
28 Sts Peter & Paul Church
29 Praha-Smíchov (Railway Station)
30 Palace of Culture

commission (US$2 minimum). Excess crowns can be changed back into dollars for 2%, but you must have an original exchange receipt issued by them. Their exchange rate is 1% lower than that offered by the banks but you still come out ahead, provided you have American Express cheques. Clients' mail is held here (see the chapter introduction for the address).

If you're carrying Thomas Cook travellers' cheques you can cash them at a good rate without commission at Thomas Cook Travel Agency, Václavské náměstí 47 (open weekdays 9 am to 7 pm, Saturday 9 am to 4 pm and Sunday from 10 am to 5 pm). Other companies' travellers' cheques attract 2% commission.

The Česká Národní Banka/Komerční Banka, Na příkopě 28 (weekdays 8 to 11.30 am and noon to 7 pm, Saturday 9 am to 2 pm), changes travellers' cheques for 2% commission (US$1 minimum). To convert dollar travellers' cheques into dollars cash they take 5%.

The Živnostenská Banka, Na příkopě 20 (weekdays 8 am to 9.30 pm, Saturday 1.30 to 5.30 pm), also gives a good rate and charges 2% commission (minimum US$2). It's worth going in there just to admire the décor! There are always long queues at both these banks.

The Československá Obchodní Banka, Na příkopě 14 (weekdays 7.30 am to noon and 1 to 3.30 pm) has an automatic exchange machine under the staircase in the middle of the building which changes foreign banknotes at one of the best rates in town with only 1% commission and no minimum. Avoid the tellers in the bank's adjacent foreign exchange office who take 5% commission!

Pragotur, U Obecního domu 2, changes travellers' cheques at the regular bank rate for 4% commission and from April to December they're open on Sunday. Čedok, Na příkopě 18, charges only 3% commission but gives a slightly lower rate.

About eight exchange offices operate in Hlavní nádraží Railway Station charging anywhere from 4 to 9% commission. Some claim to charge only 1% but have already allowed for their commission by offering a lower rate. Ask if there's a minimum commission and only change enough to tide you over until you can get to American Express or a bank.

One of the biggest scams around Prague are the exorbitant commissions collected by the many small exchange offices in the train stations and along the tourist strips. For example, Exact Change charges 9.75% commission (US$3 minimum) and Chequepoint 10% commission (US$4 minimum). The precise amount of commission they take seems to vary, so be sure to ask first if you do business with these people. Also beware of tricky practices, such as posting the *selling* rates which are much higher than the *buying* rates they'll pay you, or advertising slightly higher rates without mentioning the high commission charges. (Incidentally, these high commissions are only for foreign tourists – Czechs pay a far lower commission to change money at these places.)

Persons offering to change money on the street are usually thieves. Especially beware of sleight-of-hand experts along Na příkopě and of pickpockets in restaurant queues. People who lean over to look at your menu are often more interested in your wallet. Pickpockets regularly work the crowd watching the Gothic horologe on the old town hall mark the hour. Recently the police have been cracking down on freelancers offering unofficial private rooms, pirate theatre tickets and black-market currency exchange, and you'll be propositioned a lot less than you would have been. Pickpockets and assorted other hustlers are also feeling the heat.

Post & Telephone The main post office, Jindřišská 14 (metro: Hlavní nádraží), is open 24 hours a day, but poste restante (window No 28) is only available weekdays from 7 am to 8 pm, Saturday until 1 pm. You can send parcels weighing up to two kg from windows No 14 to 17, buy telephone cards at window No 20 and get stamps at windows Nos 20 to 24. Information is at window No

30. Philatelic stamps are sold at windows No 38 and 39 (great for dressing up a bland letter or postcard). The telephone centre here is open from 7 am to 11 pm daily.

Parcels weighing over two kg and up to 15 kg maximum must be taken to Pošta 121 Celnice, Plzeňská 139 (metro to Anděl, then three stops west on tram No 4, 7 or 9). The parcel must be open for inspection and there are three forms to fill in. They're open Monday and Wednesday from 8.30 am to 6 pm, Tuesday, Thursday and Friday until 3 pm, and Saturday until 2 pm.

Prague's telephone code is 02.

Western Embassies Several of the foreign embassies are housed in magnificent baroque palaces in Malá Strana, below the castle (metro: Malostranská).

The British Embassy (☎ 533 370), Thunovská 14, also serves New Zealanders.

A block over at Tržiště 15 is the American Embassy (☎ 536 641). This embassy does not hold mail for tourists.

The Canadian Embassy (☎ 312 0251), Mickiewiczova 6 (metro: Hradčanská), provides full consular service to Australians.

Eastern Embassies The Hungarian Embassy, Badeniho 1 (open Monday, Tuesday, Wednesday and Friday from 9 am to noon; visas US$22 per entry), is near Hradčanská Metro Station.

A few blocks from Dejvická Metro Station are the Slovak Embassy, Pod hradbami 1 at Svatovítská (weekdays 8.30 am to noon), and the Embassy of Slovenia, Pod hradbami 15 (weekdays 9 am to noon).

Also accessible from Dejvická Metro Station are the Albanian Embassy, Pod kaštany 22 (Monday, Wednesday, Friday 9 am to noon), and the Russian Federation Embassy, Pod kaštany 16.

From Malostranská Metro Station you can reach the Romanian Embassy, Nerudova 5 (open Monday, Wednesday and Friday from 9 am to noon), and the Embassy of Yugoslavia, Mostecká 15 (open Monday, Wednesday and Friday from 9 am to noon).

On the other side of town near Muzeum Metro Station are the Polish Consulate, Václavské náměstí 49 (open weekdays from 9 am to 1 pm), and the Bulgarian Embassy, Krakovská 6 (open Monday, Tuesday, Thursday and Friday from 9 to 11 am).

The Croatian Embassy, Vinohradská 69 (weekdays 8 am to noon), is accessible from Jiřího z Poděbrad Metro Station.

Travel Agencies The CKM Student Travel Centre, Jindřišská 28 (metro: Hlavní nádraží), is helpful with information, sells ISIC student cards and makes reservations at hostels in Prague.

The travel office of the International Union of Students, Pařížská 25 (weekdays from 1 to 3 pm), also sells ISIC student identification cards (US$3).

Persons aged under 26 years can buy discounted Eurotrain railway tickets to Western Europe at the Wasteels office in Hlavní nádraží Railway Station or from CKM Student Travel, Žitná 11 (metro: Karlovo náměstí). This CKM office also sells bus tickets to Western Europe.

Several offices around Prague sell bus tickets to Western European cities and these usually work out cheaper than the train (though they're less comfortable). The Čedok offices at Na příkopě 18 and Rytířská 16 sell bus tickets to Amsterdam (US$79), Athens (US$90), Brussels (US$58), London (US$83) and Paris (US$79).

Bohemiatour, Zlatnická 7 (weekdays 8 am to 5 pm, Saturday until 4 pm), has international bus tickets to Amsterdam, Athens, Brussels, Cologne, Copenhagen, Frankfurt, Hamburg, London, Madrid, Marseilles, Milan, Munich, Paris, Rome, Sofia, Stockholm, Strasbourg, Vienna, Zagreb, Zürich and many other cities.

The Eurolines representative in Prague, ČAD Klíčov, Štěpánská 63 (top floor), has tickets for international buses to Amsterdam, Bordeaux, Brussels, Budapest, Frankfurt, London, Madrid, Münster, Paris, Stuttgart, Toulouse and Zagreb.

Travel Agency ČD in the arcade at Na příkopě 31 sells bus tickets to points all over Western Europe. The prices posted in the

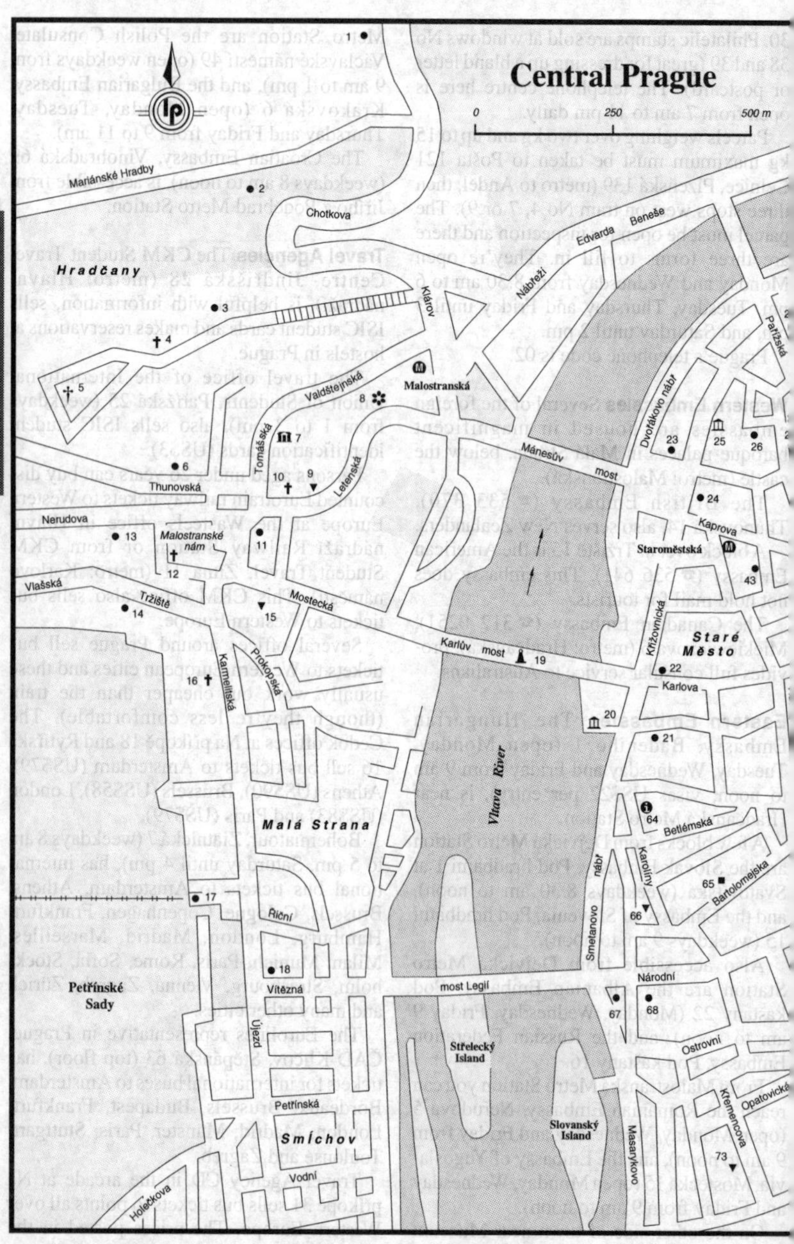
Central Prague
0
250
500 m
Mariánské Hradby
Chotkova
Hradčany
Edvarda Beneše
Nábřeží
Klárov
Pařížská
Valdštejnská
Malostranská
Tomášská
Letenská
Dvořákovo nábř
Mánesův most
Thunovská
Nerudova
Malostranské nám
Kaprova
Staroměstská
Vlašská
Tržiště
Mostecká
Křižovnická
Karlův most
Staré Město
Karmelitská
Prokopská
Karlova
Malá Strana
Vltava River
Betlémská
Karoliny
Bartolomějská
Smetanovo nábř
Říční
Národní
most Legií
Vítězná
Petřínské Sady
Újezd
Střelecký Island
Ostrovní
Petřínská
Slovanský Island
Smíchov
Opatovická
Křemencova
Masarykovo
Vodní
Holečkova

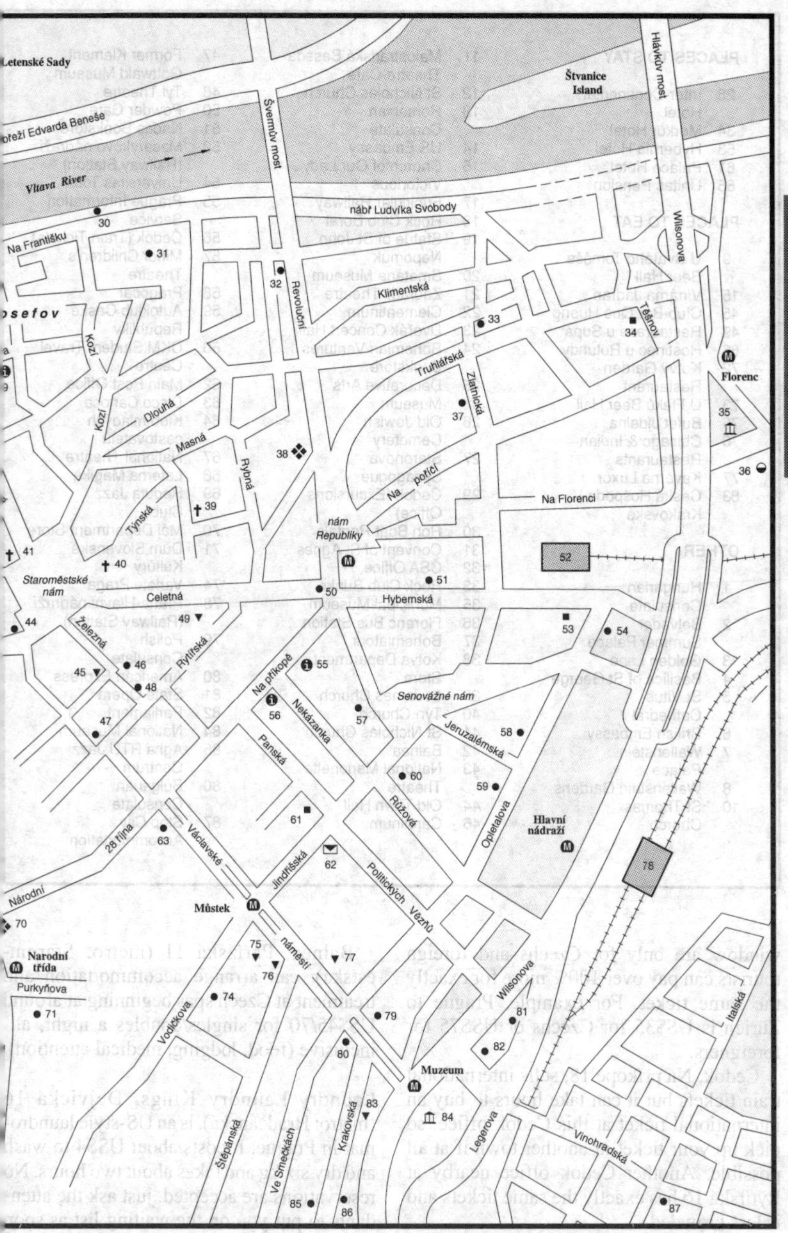

CZECH REPUBLIC

PLACES TO STAY

- 28 Inter-Continental Hotel
- 34 Merkur Hotel
- 53 Hybernia Hotel
- 61 Palace Hotel
- 65 Unitas Pension

PLACES TO EAT

- 9 U Svatého Tomáše Beer Hall
- 15 Vinárna Jadran
- 45 Club-Bar Quě Huong
- 49 Restaurace u Supa
- 66 Hostinec u Rotundy
- 72 Kotvy Garden Restaurant
- 73 U Fleků Beer Hall
- 75 Bufet Jídelna
- 76 Chicago & Indian Restaurants
- 77 Kavárna Luxor
- 83 Česká Hospoda V Krakovské

OTHER

- 1 Hungarian Consulate
- 2 Belveder Summer Palace
- 3 Golden Lane
- 4 Basilica of St George
- 5 St Vitus Cathedral
- 6 British Embassy
- 7 Wallenstein Palace
- 8 Wallenstein Gardens
- 10 St Thomas Church
- 11 Malostranská Beseda Theatre-Café
- 12 St Nicholas Church
- 13 Romanian Consulate
- 14 US Embassy
- 16 Church of Our Lady Victorious
- 17 Funicular Railway
- 18 Rock Club Borat
- 19 Statue of St John Nepomuk
- 20 Smetana Museum
- 21 Zábradlí Theatre
- 22 Clementinum
- 23 Dvořák Concert Hall
- 24 Bohemian Ventures Bookstore
- 25 Decorative Arts Museum
- 26 Old Jewish Cemetery
- 27 Staronová Synagogue
- 29 Čedok (Excursions Office)
- 30 Ron Boat Rentals
- 31 Convent of St Agnes
- 32 ČSA Office
- 33 Rock Club Bunkr
- 35 Municipal Museum
- 36 Florenc Bus Station
- 37 Bohemiatour
- 38 Kotva Department Store
- 39 St James Church
- 40 Týn Church
- 41 St Nicholas Church
- 42 Balnea
- 43 National Marionette Theatre
- 44 Old Town Hall
- 46 Carolinum
- 47 Former Klement Gottwald Museum
- 48 Tyl Theatre
- 50 Powder Gate
- 51 Nadas Bookstore
- 52 Masarykovo nádraží (Railway Station)
- 54 Universitas Tour
- 55 Prague Information Service
- 56 Čedok (Train Tickets)
- 57 Minor Children's Theatre
- 58 Pragocar
- 59 Autoklub České Republiky
- 60 CKM Student Travel Centre
- 62 Main Post Office
- 63 Disco Carioca
- 64 Klub mladých cestovatelů
- 67 National Theatre
- 68 Laterna Magika
- 69 Reduta Jazz Club
- 70 Máj Department Store
- 71 Dům Slovenské Kultůry
- 74 Varieté Praga
- 78 Praha-Hlavní nádraží (Railway Station)
- 79 Polish Consulate
- 80 American Express
- 81 State Opera
- 82 Parliament
- 84 National Museum
- 85 Agha RTU Jazz Centrum
- 86 Bulgarian Consulate
- 87 Stop City Accommodation

window are only for Czechs and foreign tourists can pay over 100% more for exactly the same ticket. For example, Prague to Zürich is US$35 for Czechs or US$75 for foreigners.

Čedok, Na příkopě 18, sells international train tickets but it can take hours to buy an international ticket at this Čedok office, so pick up your ticket in another town if at all possible. Another Čedok office nearby at Rytířská 16 has exactly the same tickets and is less crowded.

Balnea, Pařížská 11 (metro: Staroměstská), can arrange accommodation and treatment at Czech spas beginning at around US$45/70 for singles/doubles a night, all-inclusive (food, lodging, medical attention).

Laundry Laundry Kings, Dejvická 16 (metro: Hradčanská), is an US-style laundromat in Prague. It costs about US$4 to wash and dry six kg and takes about two hours. No reservations are accepted, just ask the attendants to put you on the waiting list as soon as you arrive. Laundry Kings sells detergent or you can bring your own. They also sell drinks and English-language newspapers. While your clothes are washing you can sit around in their lounge – a good place to meet other travellers as most of the clients are foreigners. There's also an interesting notice board here. Opening hours are weekdays from 6 am to 10 pm, weekends 8 am to 10 pm, but you must arrive by 8 pm.

Bookshops Knihy Melantrich, Na příkopě 3 (metro: Můstek), has a good selection of maps and local guidebooks. Prague's international bookshop is at Na příkopě 27. Nadas, Hybernská 5 (metro: náměstí Republiky), sells train timetables *(Jízdní řád)*.

Bohemian Ventures, náměstí Jana Palacha 2 (Faculty of Philosophy building), has an excellent selection of paperbacks in English, including English translations of works by Czech authors (weekdays 9 am to 5 pm).

Československý Spisovatel, Národní 9 (metro: Národní třída), also has many books in English at slightly lower prices.

Vilímkovo Knihkupectví, Spálená 15 (metro: Národní třída), has detailed maps of many parts of the country.

The Ośrodek Kultury Polskiej, Jindřišská 3 (metro: Můstek), sells good maps of Polish cities.

The Geologické Knihy a Mapy, Malostranské náměstí 19 (metro: Malostranská), has geological tomes in English and detailed geological maps of every part of the country. These aren't designed for hiking, but may be useful if you're very interested in a certain area.

Visa Extensions To extend your visa or report a lost passport or visa go to the Foreigners Police, Olšanská 2, about a 10-minute walk from Flora Metro Station (open Monday, Tuesday, Thursday 8 am to 3 pm, Wednesday 9 am to 5 pm, Friday 8 am to 2 pm). Visa extensions cost US$5.

Things to See

Hradčany Prague's finest churches and museums are found in Hradčany, the wonderful castle district stretching along a hilltop west of the river. Be aware that around midday it will be difficult to see many of the marvellous sights up there due to the hundreds of other people trying to do exactly the same thing as you at exactly the same moment. Early morning is the best time to visit and evening is even better (although all the museums will be closed).

The easiest way to organise a visit is to take the metro to Malostranská, then tram No 22 up the hill around to the back of Hradčany as far as the fourth stop, 'Pamatník Písemnictví'. From here Pohořelec and Loretánská streets slope down to the castle gate.

A passage at Pohořelec ulice 8 leads up to the **Museum of Czech Literature** (closed Monday) in the Strahov Monastery, which was founded in 1140 but rebuilt in the 17th century. Before visiting the museum, find the separate entrance to the library (built in 1679) to the right in front of the church, which opens for groups every half-hour. Buy a ticket in the museum, then wait at the library door for a group to form.

The church itself is beautifully decorated, and a lane leading east from the monastery will give you a good view of the city. Return to Pohořelec and go down the hill keeping left.

Nearby on Loretánské náměstí is the baroque **Černín Palace** (1687), now the Ministry of Foreign Affairs. The **Loreta Convent** (closed Monday), opposite the palace, shelters a fabulous treasure of diamonds, pearls and gold, and a replica (1631) of the Santa Casa in the Italian town of Loreto, said to be the Nazareth home of the Virgin Mary carried to Italy by angels in the 13th century. Unfortunately, the tour groups are so thick here that you'll have difficulty getting near the most striking objects in the convent museum. Consider coming back in the afternoon when the multitudes have vanished.

Loretánská soon opens onto Hradčanské náměstí, with the main gate to Prague Castle at its eastern end. At Hradčanské náměstí 2 is the **Military Historical Museum**, which is open from May to October (closed Monday), housed in the Renaissance Schwarzenberg-Lobkowitz Palace (1563).

Just across the square at No 15 is the 18th-century Šternberský Palace which contains the **National Gallery**. This has the country's main collection of European paintings with whole rooms of Cranachs and Picassos. Luckily, the groups never have time to visit, so you can see it in relative peace. This and the many other branches of the National Gallery around Prague open Tuesday to Sunday from 10 am to 6 pm.

Prague Castle Prague Castle was founded in the 9th century, then rebuilt and extended many times. Always the centre of political power, it's still the official residence of the president. As you enter the castle compound under an arch dated 1614, you'll see the **Chapel of the Holy Rood** directly in front. On the north side of this courtyard is the **Castle Picture Gallery** with a good collection of baroque paintings in what was once a stable.

The second courtyard is dominated by **St Vitus Cathedral**, a glorious French Gothic structure begun in 1344 by order of Emperor Charles IV and only completed in 1929. The stained-glass windows, frescos and tombstones (including that of the founder in the crypt) merit careful attention. The 14th-century chapel with the black imperial eagle on the door on the cathedral's south side contains the tomb of St Wenceslas, the 'Good King Wenceslas' of the Christmas carol. Wenceslas' zeal in spreading Christianity and his submission to the German king Henry I led to his murder by his own brother, Boleslav I. Alarmed by reports of miracles at Wenceslas' grave, Boleslav had the remains reinterred in St Vitus Cathedral in 932, and the saint's tomb soon became a great pilgrimage site. The small door beside the chapel windows leads to a chamber where the Bohemian crown jewels are kept; however, entry is not allowed. From Tuesday to Sunday you can climb the 287 steps of the cathedral tower for about a dollar.

On the south side of the cathedral is the entrance to the **Old Royal Palace** (closed Monday) with its huge Vladislav Hall, built between 1486 and 1502. A ramp to one side allowed mounted horsemen to ride into the hall and conduct jousts indoors. On 23 May 1618 two Catholic councillors were thrown from the window of an adjacent chamber by irate Protestant nobles, an act that touched off the Thirty Years' War, which devastated Europe from 1618 to 1648.

As you leave the palace, the **Basilica of St George** (1142), a remarkable Romanesque church, will be directly in front of you. In the Benedictine convent next to the church is the National Gallery's collection of Czech art from the Middle Ages to the 18th century (closed Monday).

Behind this gallery, follow the crowd into **Golden Lane** (Zlatá ulička), a 16th century tradesman's quarter of tiny houses built into the castle walls. The novelist Franz Kafka, who was born in Prague in 1883, lived and wrote in the tiny house at No 22.

On the right, just before the gate leading out of the castle, is **Lobkovický Palace** (closed Monday), Jirská 3, which houses a museum of medieval history containing replicas of the crown jewels. From the eastern end of the castle, a stairway leads back down towards Malostranská Metro Station.

Malá Strana From Malostranská Metro Station, follow Valdštejnská around to Valdštejnskě náměstí, past many impressive palaces, especially the **Wallenstein Palace** (1630), now the Ministry of Culture, which fills the entire east side of the square. A famous figure in the Thirty Years' War, Albrecht Wallenstein started out on the Protestant side then went over to the Catholics and built this palace with the expropriated wealth of his former colleagues. In 1634 the Habsburg emperor Ferdinand II learned that Wallenstein was about to switch sides once again and had him assassinated at Cheb. The palace gardens are accessible from May to September through a gate at Letenská ulice 10, a block away.

Continue south on Tomášská and round the corner to Letenská to reach **St Thomas Church**, a splendid baroque edifice built in

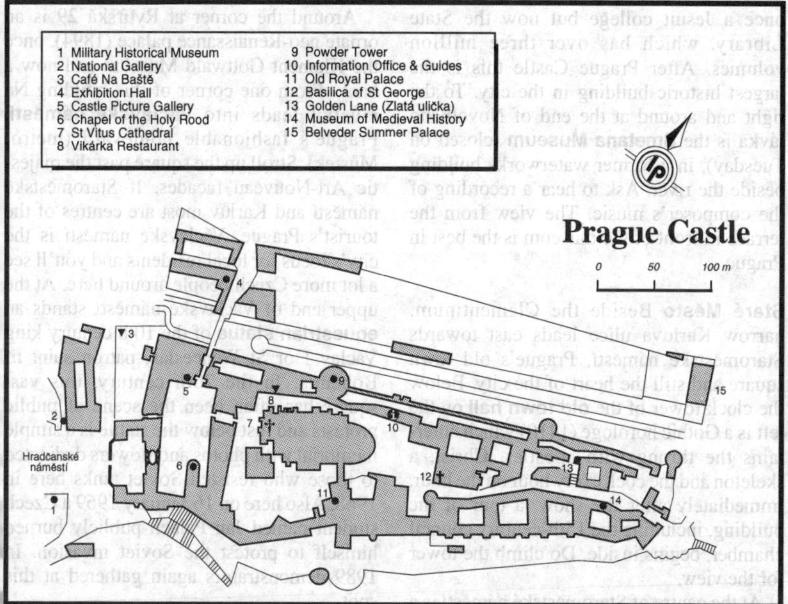

1731. Behind Malostranské náměstí nearby is the formerly Jesuit **St Nicholas Church** (1755), the greatest baroque building in Prague, its dome visible from afar. Malá Strana was built up in the 17th and 18th centuries, below the protective walls of Prague Castle, by the victorious Catholic clerics and nobility on the foundations of the Renaissance palaces of their Protestant predecessors.

After a wander around the square, follow the tram tracks south along Karmelitská. At Karmelitská 9, is the **Church of Our Lady Victorious** (1613) with the venerated wax Holy Infant of Prague (1628). Originally erected by Lutherans, this church was taken over by the Carmelite Order after the Catholic victory at the Battle of White Mountain (1620).

Backtrack a little and take narrow Prokopská ulice towards the river. You'll soon reach a beautiful square surrounded by fine baroque palaces. Continue on the left on Lázeňská towards the massive stone towers of the **Church of Our Lady Below the Chain**.

To the left of the church, Lázeňská leads out to Mostecká with the **Karlův most** to the right. This enchanting bridge, built in 1357 and graced by 30 statues dating from the 18th century, was the only bridge in Prague until 1841. Take a leisurely stroll across it, but first climb the **tower** on the Malá Strana side for a great bird's-eye view. In the middle of the bridge is a bronze statue (1683) of St John Nepomuk who was thrown to his death in the river here in 1393 when he refused to tell King Wenceslas IV what the queen had confided to him at confession. Throughout the day, so many tourists and hawkers squeeze onto the bridge that you can hardly move. To feel the true romance of this bridge consider coming back in the very early morning or after midnight when the moon is full.

Across on the Staré Město side of the bridge is the 17th century **Clementinum**, once a Jesuit college but now the State Library, which has over three million volumes. After Prague Castle this is the largest historic building in the city. To the right and around at the end of Novotného lávka is the **Smetana Museum** (closed on Tuesday), in a former waterworks building beside the river. Ask to hear a recording of the composer's music. The view from the terrace in front of the museum is the best in Prague.

Staré Město Beside the Clementinum, narrow Karlova ulice leads east towards Staroměstské náměstí, Prague's old town square and still the heart of the city. Below the clock tower of the **old town hall** on the left is a Gothic horologe (1410) which entertains the throng with apostles, Christ, a skeleton and the cock every hour on the hour. Immediately after the show, a tour of the building, including the 15th-century council chamber, begins inside. Do climb the tower for the view.

At the centre of Staroměstské náměstí is a **monument** to the religious reformer Jan Hus, erected in 1915 on the 500th anniversary of his death by fire at the stake. Facing one side of the square is the baroque **St Nicholas Church**, designed by Kilian Dientzenhofer. More striking is the Gothic **Týn Church** (1365) with its twin steeples. The tomb of the 16th-century Danish astronomer Tycho Brahe is in front of the main altar and the church is rich in artworks (open afternoons, closed Monday). In the past few years Staroměstské náměstí has been transformed from a quaint Central European town square into a showplace for first world tourism and in summer it's really a circus.

From a corner of Staroměstské náměstí near the horologe, take Železná ulice south-east to the **Carolinum**, Železná 9, the oldest remaining part of Prague University, founded by Charles IV in 1348. Next to this at Železná 11 is the neoclassical **Stavovské Theatre** (1783), where the premiere of Mozart's *Don Giovanni* took place on 29 October 1787 with the composer himself conducting.

Around the corner at Rytířská 29 is an ornate neo-Renaissance palace (1894), once the Klement Gottwald Museum and now a bank. From one corner of this building Na můstku leads into **Václavské náměstí**, Prague's fashionable boulevard (metro: Můstek). Stroll up the square past the majestic Art-Nouveau façades. If Staroměstské náměstí and Karlův most are centres of the tourist's Prague, Václavské náměstí is the city's focus for local residents and you'll see a lot more Czech people around here. At the upper end of Václavské náměstí stands an **equestrian statue** of the 10th century king Václav I or St Wenceslas, patron saint of Bohemia. In the 20th century, this vast square has often been the scene of public protests and just below the statue is a simple memorial with photos and flowers dedicated to those who resisted Soviet tanks here in 1968. Also here on 16 January 1969 a Czech student named Jan Palach publicly burned himself to protest the Soviet invasion. In 1989 demonstrators again gathered at this spot.

Looming above the south-eastern end of Václavské náměstí is the **National Museum** (metro: Muzeum) with ho-hum collections on prehistory, 19th and early 20th century history, mineralogy and a herd of stuffed animals. The captions are only in Czech and the neo-Renaissance museum building (1890) itself is as interesting as what's on display inside (closed Tuesday). The museum café is another saving grace.

Vyšehrad Take the metro to Vyšehrad where the **Palace of Culture** (1981) rises above a deep ravine crossed by the Nuselský Bridge (formerly known as the Klement Gottwald Bridge). During the communist era, unsmiling guards kept the public out of the palace unless they had business inside. Now the doors are wide open and you're free to explore at will.

From here the twin towers of the neo-Gothic **Sts Peter & Paul Church** are visible to the west. Walk towards them along Na Bučance and through the gates of the 17th-century **Vyšehrad Citadel**, seat of the

11th-century Přemysl princes of Bohemia. You pass the Romanesque **Rotunda of St Martin** before reaching **Slavín Cemetery**, right behind the Sts Peter & Paul Church. Many distinguished people are buried here, including the composers Smetana and Dvořák. The view of the Vltava Valley from the citadel battlements along the south side of the Vyšehrad ridge is superb.

Monday Specials In Prague on a Monday? Most museums and galleries will be closed, but the Prague Jewish Ghetto and the Mozart Museum stay open.

The **Prague Ghetto**, Pařížská 19 (metro: Staroměstská), includes a fascinating variety of monuments, now part of the **Prague Jewish Museum** (closed Saturday). The early Gothic Staronová Synagogue (1270) is one of the oldest in Europe. Tickets are sold in the museum across the lane from the synagogue, beside which is the pink Jewish Town Hall with its picturesque clock tower built in the 16th century. Follow the crowd down U Starého Hřbitova to the Klausen Synagogue (1694) and another section of the museum. You must cover your head to enter the synagogues and the staff will try to sell you an expensive cotton cap. If you don't want it, ask for a free paper cap (or bring a cap of your own).

The collections of the Prague Jewish Museum have a remarkable origin. In 1942 the Nazis brought the objects here from 153 Jewish communities in Bohemia and Moravia for a planned 'museum of an extinct people' to be opened once their extermination programme was completed! The interior of one of the buildings bears the names of 77,297 Czech Jews and the names of the camps where they perished. (On the list are the three sisters of Franz Kafka.)

Behind the Klausen Synagogue is the **Old Jewish Cemetery** with 12,000 tombstones – an evocative sight (separate ticket). The oldest grave is dated 1439, and, by 1787, when the cemetery ceased to be used, the area had became so crowded that burials were carried out one on top of the other as many as 12 layers deep!

If you're into music there's the **Mozart Museum** (open daily) in Villa Bertrámka, Mozartova 169 (metro: Anděl, then west on Plzeňská three blocks and left on Mozartova), where Mozart finished composing *Don Giovanni* in 1787. Czech film maker Miloš Forman's Oscar-winning movie *Amadeus* about the life of Mozart was shot mostly in Prague.

Nearby Palaces The early baroque **Troya Chateau** (1685), north of the Vltava River, was recently reopened after many years of restoration work. The 17th-century frescos on the ceilings are now fresh and on the chateau walls hangs a fine collection of 19th-century painting. This impressive red and white building, surrounded by formal gardens and built for Count Václav Vojtěch of Šternberg, is open from May to October only (closed Monday). On a wooded hillside next to the chateau is Prague's **zoo**, which is open daily. Get there on bus No 112 from Nádraží Holešovice Metro Station.

If the crowds in central Prague begin to get to you and you need a little peace, head for the **Hvězda Summer Palace** (closed Monday) which is in a large forest park west of the city. The Habsburgs built this Renaissance chateau in the 16th century as a summer residence and hunting lodge. The bloody final phase of the decisive Battle of White Mountain took place on the chateau grounds on 6 November 1620. The Catholic victory signified the reimposition of Habsburg rule on would-be Protestant Bohemia and the loss of national independence for exactly 300 years.

Today this place of national defeat functions as a **Museum of Czech Culture** especially dedicated to the novelist Alois Jirásek (ground floor) and the painter Mikoláš Aleš (upstairs). In the chateau basement is an exhibit on the battle. The name Hvězda means 'star' and the ground-floor stucco ceiling of this unique six-pointed building is one of the finest Renaissance artworks north of the Alps, yet the tour groups seldom visit. To get there, take the metro to Dejvická, then tram No 2 or 26 west to the end of the line. As you walk south on Libočka, you'll see the chateau's pointed roof rising out of the forest. Go under the train tracks and turn left. A stairway up into the forest is just beyond the large church.

Parks On a hot summer afternoon an easy escape from the throngs at the tourist sites is to take the funicular railway (one transit ticket) from Újezd up to the rose gardens of **Petřínské Sady**. From April to October you can climb an old iron tower (1891) here for one of the best views of Prague (US$1). A stairway behind the tower leads down into a series of picturesque lanes and back to Malostranské náměsti via Vlašská and Tržiště.

One Last Museum On your last afternoon in Prague, set aside a little time for the **Municipal Museum** (closed Monday), the large white neo-Renaissance building above Florenc Metro Station. Here you'll see maps and photos of the numerous monuments you've visited around town, plus interesting artefacts to put them in perspective.

The museum sells a vast selection of postcards made from old photos of Prague. However, the museum's crowning glory is a huge scale model of Prague created in 1834. Don't miss it!

Organised Tours Three times a day from April to October the Pražská Informační Služba, Panská 4 (metro: Můstek), organises 2½-hour bus tours of Prague with commentaries in English and German (US$15). The same office arranges personal guides for three-hour walking tours of the city at US$18 for one person, US$29 for two people or US$11 per person for three or more people (available year-round). Guides fluent in all major European languages are available.

Many private companies operating from kiosks along Na příkopě also offer city bus tours for similar prices. These are okay if your time is very short, though one of our readers, Anne Small of Tauranga, New Zealand, reported the following:

> I took a conducted tour of Prague Castle which turned out to be worse than the Vatican in July/August. It was the very worst tourist crush I have ever had. I saw very little because I had to use all of my energy saving my life. A ghastly experience. The guide was capable but was called upon to give the tour in four languages and only on the bus did I hear any of what she had to say. Your recommendation to visit the National Gallery was taken up and I found it a different world from the crush of the conducted tour spots.

The Čedok offices at Bílkova 6, near the Inter-Continental Hotel, at Na Příkopě 18 and at Rytířská 16 arrange bus excursions to historic sites in the environs, such as Karlštejn/Konopiště (US$49), Kutná Hora (US$41) and Karlovy Vary (US$49). Most, but not all, departures are only during the high season (from 15 May to 15 October). The tours are given in English, French and German only.

The Hotel Meran Tourist Office, Václavské náměstí 27, has a four-hour afternoon bus tour to Karlštejn for US$25 and a three-hour Prague city sightseeing tour from Monday to Saturday at 10 am and 1 pm for US$17.

Places to Stay

Camping The *University Sport Club Caravan Camp* (☎ 524 714) is Prague's easiest camping ground since it's right on Plzeňská, west of the city, next to tram lines Nos 4 and 9 (stop: Hotel Golf). They have four triple bungalows at US$15 for the unit but chances are you'll have to camp at US$4 per person and US$3 per tent.

If this camping ground is full walk three minutes back along Plzeňská towards Prague and you'll see a large sign pointing up the hill to the *Sport Camp* (☎ 520 218). Otherwise take tram No 4 or 9 from Anděl Metro Station to the Poštovka stop, then walk a km up the hill. Night tram No 58 passes hourly throughout the night. This site is less convenient if you're on foot as it's a stiff 10-minute climb from the tram stop but it's much larger, quieter and more likely to have space. It's also set on an incline so you may have to look around for a flat site and the airport flight path passes overhead. Camping is US$4 per person, plus US$3 per tent, and they have 60 small bungalows for US$11 double, US$15 triple or US$18 for four persons. The reception is open from 7 am to 9 pm daily. There's a poor restaurant on the premises. Both camping grounds are under the same management, so you can ask about one at the other, and they're open from April until the end of October.

Hostels The HI handbook lists the *CKM Juniorhotel* (☎ 299 941), at Žitná 12 (metro: Karlovo náměstí), as one of Prague's hostels, but you're invariably told it's full up with groups for the rest of the month. Trying to make an advance booking by mail is a waste of time and even if you do manage to get a room it will be US$47 double with bath and breakfast (no singles). Despite the listing in the HI handbook there are no discounts here for YHA/HI members.

The CKM Accommodation Service (☎ 205 446), Žitná 12 (open daily 9 am to 6 pm), upstairs in the Juniorhotel building (separate entrance), arranges beds in five-bedded rooms for about US$10 per person. Ask about the *Hotel VZ Praha* (☎ 291 118), Sokolská 33 on nearby Náměstí I P Pavlova, where CKM rents beds in triple rooms at US$11 per person with a YHA card, US$13 per person without a card (compared to US$54 double if you go to this hotel direct). This CKM office may agree to make reservations at Juniorhotels in other cities around the Czech Republic if you know your exact itinerary.

Also listed in the HI handbook is the *Hotel Standart* (☎ 806 751), Přístavní 1, a large six-storey hotel on a quiet street north of the centre. Rooms with shared bath are US$21/25/26 double/triple/quad or US$8 per bed in shared rooms if you have a YHA card. This is excellent value and you actually do have a chance of getting in. It's a 10-minute walk from Nádraží Holešovice Railway/Metro Station: walk east on Vrbenského to Ortenovo náměstí, then right and south five short blocks on Osadní to the hotel.

If the Standart is full you could check *Pension Vltava*, Dělnická 35, just around the corner. A cheap stand-up buffet is at Dělnická 39.

The *Hotel Pražská Stavební Obnova* (☎ 427 810), Jemnická 4, a 15-minute walk or a five-minute bus ride from Kačerov Metro Station, offers beds in five-bed apartments at US$11 per person. This eight-storey complex is heavily patronised by groups on cheap bus tours from Germany, but individuals are welcome. The entrance is hard to find, hidden as it is in a corner between two eight-storey buildings, but just ask anyone for the 'PSO'. From Kačerov metro take bus No 106, 139 or 182 north to the second stop ('Na rolích'). There's no curfew.

The *Braník Youth Hostel* (☎ 462 641), Vrbova 1233, is a large 10-storey hostel on the south side of Prague. Bus No 197 from Anděl Metro Station and buses Nos 196, 198 and 199 from Smíchovské Nádraží Metro Station pass the hostel. It's US$10 per person, breakfast included, and a hostel card is not required.

Farther afield is the *TJ Dolní Měcholupy* (☎ 755 748) at the end of Pod Hřištěm, in a suburb about 10 km east of Prague. Take the metro to Skalka, and then bus No 228 or 229 to Dolnoměcholupská. Dorm beds cost US$7, breakfast is available, it's open all year and is often full. It's a good idea to have the CKM Student Travel Centre, Jindřišská 28 (metro: Hlavní nádraží), book a bed for you here before making the long trip out.

If it's getting late and you still don't have a bed, consider spending the night at the *Turistická Ubytovna TJ Sokol Karlín* (☎ 222 009) on Malého ulice, a five-minute walk from Florenc Bus Station (metro: Florenc). To get there, walk east along Křižíkova ulice past the Karlín Theatre and turn right on Pluku ulice just after the railway bridge. The hostel is just before the next railway bridge. The doors don't open until 6 pm and all you'll get is a dorm bed (US$6), but it sure beats the floor at the train station.

Student Dormitories The easiest place to arrange hostel accommodation on the spot is at the Strahov student dormitory complex opposite Spartakiádní Stadión west of the centre. Buses Nos 143, 149 and 217 run directly there from Dejvická Metro Station.

As you get off the bus you'll see 10 huge blocks of flats. All operate as separate hostels competing for your business and if you make the rounds of the various reception desks you should be able to find something. A bed in a double or triple room with shared bath will be around US$8 per person, otherwise it's US$4 per person in a five to 10-person dorm. A hostel or student card is not required (everyone is welcome). Though the capacity is huge, the whole complex does occasionally get booked out by groups.

In July and August every block will be accepting tourists, while in the off season only the *Estec Hostel* (Block No 5), *Juniorhostel* (Block No 7), *Hostel Spus* (block No 4) and the *Strahov Hostel* (block No 11) will be open. Noisy discos operate from 9 pm to 4 am downstairs in blocks Nos 1, 7 and 11, so those should be your last choices. The receptionist at *Hostel Spus* (☎ 557 498) is helpful and can book better rooms in a teachers' hostel elsewhere in the city at US$10 per person. The travel agencies in the train stations will book beds at Strahov, if you want to be sure of a place before coming but this will add a few dollars to your daily costs. There's a midnight curfew at most of the hostels. (We've received a complaint from a reader who had her backpack stolen from a locked room at Hostel Spus. Be suspicious if the desk clerk tells you it's necessary to change rooms at short notice and lock your bag to the furniture if you can.)

A similar place open from July to September only is *Kolej Kajetánka* (☎ 355 557), Radimova 12, Building 1. Take bus No 108 or 174 west from Hradčanská metro to 'Kajetánka' and look for two tall white towers. If the porter doesn't speak English go to the 'Ubytovací Kancelář' office inside the building. Kolej Kajetánka has 150 rooms at US$11/20 single/double.

Room-Finding Services AVE Limited (☎ 236 2560) at Hlavní nádraží and Holešovice train stations and at Ruzyně Airport rents a variety of private rooms, varying between rooms with shared bath in a distant suburb (from US$13/21 single/double) to rooms with bath in the city centre (from US$28/45 single/double). Private apartments in outer suburbs begin around US$32. AVE gives discounts for longer stays. They also know about hostel accommodation (US$16 per person in double rooms, breakfast included). The AVE branch at Hlavní nádraží is open from 6 am to 10 pm daily.

Vesta Tour at Hlavní nádraží Railway Station has private rooms on the metro line for US$15 per person and Agentura B & B at Nádraží Holešovice Railway Station has both hostel and private accommodation beginning at around US$10 per person.

Universitas Tour (☎ 223 550), Opletalova 32 near Hlavní nádraží Railway Station, arranges stays in university dormitories at US$9 per person in double and triple rooms. Pension accommodation is from US$11 per person. From mid-June to mid-September this office is open on weekends (business hours the rest of the year).

A good bet for a private room is Pragotur (☎ 231 7000), U Obecního domu 2 near the Powder Gate (metro: náměstí Republiky). The staff can arrange private rooms at US$18 per person near the centre, US$15 per person in outlying suburbs, plus a one-time US$2 commission. Pragotur also has hotel and dormitory space. They're open daily from April to December, Monday to Saturday in March, and weekdays only in January and February.

Top Tour (☎ 232 1077), Rybná 3, just a block down from Pragotur, is more expensive. First-category rooms (with private bath) are US$39/59 single/double and 2nd-category rooms (with shared bath) are US$24/39. Apartments are also available (US$66 double, US$95 for four people, US$120 for six people). Rooms are available in the city centre for an additional 10%, and the office is open daily all year until 7 pm.

Stop City Accommodation (☎ 257 840), Vinohradská 24, about six blocks from Hlavní nádraží Railway Station, arranges private rooms in the centre or on a metro line for US$13 to US$28 per person. They're open daily year-round from 11 am to 8 pm and the patient staff speaks perfect English.

You can also rent an unofficial private room from householders on the street looking for hard-currency guests. They'll ask about the same (US$18/35 single/double) as the agencies just listed – bargain if you think the price is too high and check the location on a good map before going. Be absolutely certain that you have understood the price correctly.

Libeň District A number of good places to stay exist in the Libeň district north of the centre. One of the strangest (and best) is *Na Vlachovce Autocamp* (☎ 841 290), Zenklova 217. Despite the name, there's no camping ground here. Instead you sleep in a small bungalow shaped like a Budvar beer keg (no joke!) for US$17 double. The kegs are 'uncorked' from April to October only. Get there on tram No 5, 17 or 25 from Nádraží Holešovice Metro Station to 'Ke Stírce' and walk straight through the folk restaurant here to the hotel reception in the back yard (if the restaurant is closed go around the block to the back gate).

A block from the Na Vlachovce is *Hotel Apollo Garni* (☎ 842 108), Kubišova 23, a modern four-storey hotel with rooms with bath at US$34/48 single/double, breakfast included. Across the street from the Apollo is *Pension Louda* (tariff unknown).

A better deal than these is the *Hotelový dům VS* (☎ 843 894), Střelničná 8, one stop further up the hill on the same trams (take tram No 17 or 25 from Nádraží Holešovice Metro Station to 'Střelničná'). The 60 rooms with shared bath in this new six-storey building are US$18/22 single/double, breakfast US$2 per person extra.

There's a year-round hostel in a small sports centre at *TJ Sokol Kobylisy Ubytovna* (☎ 843 531), U školské zahrady 9, two blocks back behind Hotelový dům VS. The hostel reception is open from 5 pm to 9 pm only.

Hotels There are no longer any cheap hotels in Prague – prices at most of the older hotels in the city centre have increased 400% or more in the past few years. This is partly because foreigners are charged prices 50 to 100% higher than Czechs but it's mostly a result of privatisation and the onslaught on Prague by high-spending German and US tourists. Below we list a few survivors but they too could well have been fixed up and pushed out of sight by the time you get there, so you might consider calling ahead.

If you do find a satisfactory room, book for your entire stay in Prague, otherwise you risk having your stay cut short when you learn that your room has been assigned to someone else. Most Prague hotels charge US$2 extra for a shower if there's not one in the room.

Good for the money is the *Hotel Balkán* (☎ 540 777), Třída Svornosti 28, just two blocks from Anděl Metro Station. Rooms in this attractive old four-storey building are US$20/27 single/double without bath, US$32/37 with bath, breakfast included. The hotel also has a good restaurant and is just a block from the Vltava River.

The only budget hotel in the old town is *Unitas Pension* (☎ 232 7700), Bartolomějská 9 (metro: Národní třída). It has 40 dull rooms with shared bath at US$26/31 single/double and a generous breakfast is included. It's a pleasant place to stay but is often fully booked by noisy youth groups.

The five-storey, 65-room *Merkur Hotel* (☎ 231 6951), Těšnov 9, a five-minute walk from Florenc Bus Station, is US$29/47 single/double without bath, US$43/72 with bath, breakfast included. It's usually full of locals and groups who pay a lot less than this, but you can always try for laughs.

The functional, six-storey *Hotel Hybernia* (☎ 220 4312), Hybernská 24 (metro: náměstí Republiky), right next to Masarykova nádraží Railway Station, is US$34/47/63 single/double/triple without bath, US$63 double with bath, breakfast included. It has little to justify these prices other than location. (At last report the building was for sale, so the Hybernia may be gone before you get there.)

The tacky but friendly *Hotel Juventus* (☎ 255 151), Blanická 10 (metro: náměstí Míru), an older four-storey building, has only rooms with shared bath at US$29/47 single/double, breakfast included. Because it's a bit off the beaten track it's more likely to have free rooms.

South of the Centre *Pension Pitaz* (☎ 430 441), Na Pankráci 58, a two-minute walk from Pražského povstání Metro Station, has rooms with bath at US$29/36 single/double. This nondescript, six-storey concrete box is heavily booked by locals who pay much less than this.

Germans on cheap bus tours are the main guests at the *Hotel Zálesí* (☎ 472 1340), Pod višňovkou 21, on the southern side of the city. Get there on bus No 205 from Budějovická Metro Station or on bus No 121 or 196 from Kačerov Metro Station. It's a complex of several six-storey buildings offering rooms with a bath shared between two units at US$20 double, US$29 triple. Travel agencies such as CKM and those at Prague train stations book single beds in the double rooms for US$14 (the hotel reception charges the full double rate to singles who book direct).

Further out on the same metro line is five-room *A V Pension Praha* (☎ 795 2929), Malebná 290, a four-minute walk from Chodov Metro Station. Bed and breakfast is US$42/63 double/triple in winter or US$58/89 in summer (no singles). The quality of the accommodation is high.

If a 20-minute metro ride doesn't deter you, consider the 23-storey *Hotel Kupa* (☎ 791 0323), Anežky Hodinové-Spurné 842, very close to Háje Metro Station. When you come out of the station look for the tallest building around. It's US$28/38/44 single/double/triple, with each two rooms sharing a toilet and shower. The Kupa is another favourite haunt of the cheap bus tour set and it should be treated only as a last resort.

Motel If you're arriving by car from Plzeň or Nuremberg and don't want to drive into town, consider the two-storey *Stop Motel* (☎ 525 648), Jeremiášova 974, near the exit from the motorway in Stodůlky west of the centre (bus No 164 or 184 from Nové Butovice Metro Station). Rooms with shared bath are about US$13 per person and there's a restaurant on the premises.

Up-Market Hotels The *Grand Hotel Europa* (☎ 262 748), Václavské náměstí 25 (metro: Můstek), is an Art-Nouveau extravaganza, brimming with old-world atmosphere for US$41/60 single/double without bath and US$64/85 single/double with bath, breakfast included. Considering the alternatives, this is good value.

Also in the big splurge category is the *Admirál Botel* (☎ 547 445), Hořejší nábřeží, about four blocks from Anděl Metro Station. This gigantic luxury barge permanently moored on the Vltava River has 84 double cabins at US$60/75 single/double including breakfast. The four four-bed cabins go for US$100 triple, US$119 quad. Ask for a room facing the river.

Places to Eat

Tourism has had a heavy impact on the Prague restaurant scene. Cheaper restaurants have been privatised and gone up-market while many low-budget self-services have closed. Almost all the restaurants in the old town, the castle district, and along Václavské náměstí are now highly expensive, and if you're on a low budget it might be worth taking the metro to an outlying station and eating there.

Be aware that the serving staff in some Prague restaurants in the tourist centre shamelessly overcharge foreigners and about the only way to avoid this is to insist on seeing a menu *(jídelní lístek)*, even a menu in Czech, to get an idea of the price range. Menus are often posted somewhere but if they're not, and the waiter refuses to show you one listing specific prices, just get up and walk out. By law, all Prague restaurants are required to have proper menus and a refusal to bring you one is a sure sign that a rip-off is intended.

When checking restaurant menus in Prague always have a glance at the price of the beer *(pivo)* as this varies a lot and can cancel your savings on lower meal prices. If the drink prices aren't listed expect them to be sky high (unless, of course, it's only a beer hall). At lunchtime the waiter may bring you the more expensive dinner menu. Also beware of places with two menus, one for locals and another for tourists. If you don't get the same menu as is posted outside, just leave.

Even if you do check the menu price, the waiter may claim you were served a larger portion and try to charge you more than is listed. If in doubt, you could go to the extreme of writing down the individual price of each dish as you order, in full sight of the waiter. If you order from a Czech menu try to have some idea of what it is you're ordering, otherwise the waiter may bring you a different, cheaper dish but still charge the higher price of whatever it was you asked for (otherwise just order the cheapest dish). Extras like a side salad, bread and butter are charged extra, so if you're served something you didn't order and don't want, send it back. Many restaurants add a US$0.20 cover charge *(couvert)* to the bill and this is usually not mentioned on the menu. Most restaurants are closed by 9 pm and the service is often slow.

In this book we've tried to weed out the bad apples but we can't guarantee that you won't also be cheated at the restaurants listed herein. You take your choice and take your chances. However, if you're sure you were unfairly treated, let us hear about it and we'll consider dropping the offending establishment from the next edition. Several places have been taken out of this edition or had their listings changed solely on the basis of complaints from readers.

Seen from the other side, many Prague locals are pretty pissed off about the way their favourite haunts have been invaded and taken over by high-spending tourists, so if you stray into a place which is obviously a local hangout, be as polite and unobtrusive as possible.

Self-Service About the cheapest self-service in the city centre is *Bufet Jídelna* below the high glass dome at the back of the arcade which you enter from Václavské náměstí 38. Cold beer is on tap (closed Sunday).

At *Bonal*, Václavské náměstí 57, right next to the King Wenceslas statue, you can get good coffee, croissants and sandwiches which you consume standing up.

Imbiss Krone, Václavské náměstí 21, offers tasty grilled chicken which you eat standing up. Study the English translation of the menu before you line up.

A more expensive self-service is on the 4th floor at Máj Department Store, Národní and Spálená (metro: Národní třída).

The *Delicatesse Buffet* at the Palace Hotel, opposite the main post office, near the corner of Jindřišská and Panská, has a self-service salad bar. There are tables to sit at.

Near Staroměstské náměstí, the self-service *Bistro* at Kaprova 14 isn't cheap, but you'll fill your stomach without breaking the bank. As always, the sharp, modern décor has a price.

Off Václavské náměstí The *Češhá Hospoda V Krakovské*, Krakovská 20 (metro: Muzeum), just around the corner from American Express, offers good food, pleasant décor, fast friendly service and reasonable prices. Their menu in English, German and Italian includes a couple of vegetarian items and dark Braník beer is on tap.

If you're dying for a steak, try *Americká Restaurant Chicago* in the basement at Štěpánská 63. This isn't just a crass US transplant but it represents the USA as the Czechs see it, which makes it fun. Next door is *Mayür Indický Snack Bar*, Štěpánská 65, with a dozen tasty choices for vegetarians. Don't confuse the snack bar with the more expensive Indian restaurant adjacent.

The rooftop *Rostov Restaurant*, Václavské náměstí 21 (entry from the side), is much less expensive than other similar places around here. The menu is posted downstairs in Czech. Take the lift up to the 7th floor. After 8 pm this locale becomes a disco.

The *Restaurace Na příkopě*, Na příkopě

17 (metro: Můstek), serves typical Czech and Jewish grilled beef at medium prices.

Bistro Slovanský Dům, Na příkopě 22, has a set three-course lunch *(denní menu)* costing about US$2, as advertised on a blackboard and the menu. You can eat in the dining room or on the terrace.

Off Staroměstské náměstí At Celetná 22 is *Restaurace u Supa*, a rather touristy place with a deep dark beer and meals.

One US reader wrote in recommending *Vinárna U Černého Slunce*, Kamzíková 9, in a tiny alley off Celetná between u Supa and the square, as a cosy, romantic (and very up-market) place to eat.

Also try *U Prince*, Staroměstské náměstí 28, near the old town hall. Beer prices on the terrace outside are higher than those charged inside and the menu is limited out there. Don't expect to find many bargain eateries in a tourist area like this.

The *Club-Bar Quê Huong*, Havelská 29, in the Vietnamese Cultural Centre near the Carolinum, is a good change of pace. It's open Monday to Saturday from 11 am to 8 pm and the menu is in English.

South of Staroměstské náměstí off Karlova is *Pivnice U Vejvodů*, Jilská 4, a tavern which an Austrian reader says is dark and inconspicuous but serves good food.

Off Národní třída For Slovak dishes, try the medium-priced garden restaurant at the *Dům Slovenské Kultůry*, Purkyňova 4, right beside Národní třída Metro Station.

U Fleků, Křemencova 11, is a German-style beer garden where you can sit at long communal tables in the back courtyard or in one of the front halls during bad weather. Waiters circulate periodically with mugs of the excellent dark 13° ale that is brewed in-house. Unfortunately in recent years U Fleků has deteriorated into something of a tourist trap and the food and drink now cost about double what's charged at other beer halls around Prague, so you won't see many Czechs in there. Admission is collected when there's live music. (One reader wrote in to report that the haughty waiters at U Fleků didn't even want to serve him because they figured he wasn't going to spend a lot of money. Another urged us to warn travellers not to go there.)

If you don't like the atmosphere at U Fleků, check *Snack Bar Rytmus*, Křemencova 10, just across the street. Their inexpensive menu in English includes a few Chinese dishes and the waiters are friendly, though of course, there's not the setting of U Fleků.

The *U Kotvy Garden Restaurant*, Spálená 11, is similar to U Fleků but cheaper and thus more local.

Hostinec u Rotundy, Karolíny Světlé 17, is probably the cheapest pub in the old town (no meals are served).

Malá Strana *Grand Restaurant*, Karmelitská 20, has gone up-market and now posts its menu outside in English and German. It's good for grilled meats. Many slightly up-market tourist restaurants are on the side of Malostanské náměstí closest to Karlův most, including *Jo's Bar* at No 7 with Mexican food.

U Svatého Tomáše, Letenská 12 (metro: Malostranská), is a former beer hall which has evolved into a tourist restaurant. During the day the long tables down in the cellar will be full up with groups, so go out onto the back terrace (in summer) or up into the main dining room (in winter). At night head downstairs. The menu lists Bohemian specialties but the 12° Braník beer on tap has a better reputation than the food. (One reader commented: 'Nobody goes to U Svatého Tomáše except busloads of pitiful tourists who are dropped there by their guides and have no choice'.)

Hradčany Big mugs of draught beer and basic meals can be had at *U Černého Vola*, Loretánské náměstí 1, just up from the Loreta Convent.

The up-market *Café Na Baště* (closed Monday), just inside Prague Castle to the left, serves decent meals but terrible coffee. The *Vikárka Restaurant* is right next to St Vitus Cathedral. At *Bonal* in a corner of

Golden Lane you can get self-service coffee and croissants.

You'll see many other touristy restaurants up this way with prices as high as Hradčany itself. If you're on a tight budget have something filling to eat just before heading up this way.

Around Town *U Kalicha Restaurant*, Na bojišti 12 (metro: I P Pavlova), serves traditional Czech meals and big mugs of beer; it's open daily from 11 am to 3 pm and from 5 to 11 pm. Menus in English and German are available. This place featured in the novel *The Good Soldier Švejk* and it's a little expensive but still good for a splurge.

The *Snack Bar* on the ground floor in the Palace of Culture (metro: Vyšehrad) is fine for ice cream, a glass of wine or a pork chop and a beer (menu in English and German).

Restaurace Dejvická Sokolovna, Dejvická 2, just outside Hradčanská Metro Station, serves cheap pub lunches in the rear dining room. Be prepared to choose at random from the Czech menu.

Cafés The café of the *Grand Hotel Europa*, Václavské náměstí 25, is Prague's most elegant (but come before 3 pm when they start collecting a cover charge).

Kavárna Luxor, upstairs at Václavské náměstí 41, is less unpretentious but check the menu before ordering. From 9 pm to 4 am there's a disco here.

The Art-Deco *Kavárna Slávie*, at Národní 1 (metro: Národní třída), right opposite the National Theatre, has been a meeting place of the city's elite for decades.

Entertainment

Unfortunately, you'll only be able to enjoy Prague's many theatrical and musical offerings if you're prepared to spend a considerable amount of money. Official ticket prices are still low but all the best shows are sold out weeks ahead. Large blocks of tickets are reserved months in advance by travel agencies and most of the rest are snapped up by scalpers who resell them to foreigners for hard currency. When making the rounds of theatre box offices, look for the *vyprodáno* (sold out) notices before trying to figure out what's on.

The regular price for the best opera tickets is only about US$10 but you'll be forced to pay at least twice that for seats farther back. You'll probably be approached at the ticket office by a slightly nervous person with just the ticket you want, asking about three times the price printed on it. Sometimes the scalpers end up with more black tickets than they can resell, giving you the opportunity to bargain for a lower price at the door just before the performance. The travel agencies too often send someone to the theatre to sell excess or returned tickets just prior to the performance. Even the theatre ticket clerks themselves sometimes hold back choice tickets which they later sell under the counter at a premium to supplement their incomes.

If this situation annoys you, save your theatre-going until you get to Poland, Slovakia or Hungary where tickets to musical programmes of comparable quality go for about a third the price you'd pay in Prague. In Brno theatre tickets are also much more easily obtained for normal prices and the productions are equally as good.

Another good alternative to the expensive and/or frustrating theatres of Prague is to go to a movie. Cinema tickets are only US$1 and most films are shown in the original language with Czech subtitles. *Prognosis* and *The Prague Post* carry complete listings of what's on with times and cinema addresses.

Lots of organ concerts in old churches and recitals in historic buildings are put on for tourists and you'll see stacks of fliers advertising these in every tourist office or travel agency around Prague. Seats begin around US$8 but the programmes change from week to week so it's hard to give any specific recommendations.

Ticket Agencies A number of travel agencies specialise in selling theatre tickets for about the same price as the scalpers. The largest tourist ticket agency of this kind is the Hotel Meran Tourist Office, Václavské náměstí 27, a good place to begin as what's available is clearly displayed on a board behind the counter and the English-speaking staff is forthcoming with suggestions and advice. They often have tickets for the Laterna Magika (US$19), opera (US$19), National Theatre (US$21) and marionette theatre (US$14). Folklore shows by the Czech Song and Dance Ensemble are US$9. Also known as Bohemia Ticket International or simply BTI, this company has other offices at Na příkopě 16 and Karlova 8.

Even BTI may not have any tickets left for the National Theatre, State Opera, Stavovské Theatre and Laterna Magika, but you can make advance reservations through Bohemia Ticket International (☎ 231 2030; fax 231 2271), Salvátorská 6, Praha 1. Laterna Magika tickets should be ordered at least two months in advance.

Other main tourist ticket agencies include Čedok, Rytířská 16; American Express, Václavské náměstí 50; the Prague Information Service, Na příkopě 20; and Pragotur, Obecního domu 23. Čedok, Na příkopě 18, usually has tickets to the opera (US$14), marionette theatre (US$14), folklore show (US$9) and 'Bohemian Fantasy' (US$34 for the show only or US$50 with dinner). Čedok, Bílkova 6, sometimes has tickets for the State Opera (US$22) and other events, all for hard currency.

A ticket office for Czechs rather than tourists is Melantrich in the arcade at Václavské náměstí 38 and what they offer is advertised on posters. Don't expect them to speak English. Instead, just write down the date for which you need a ticket using a Roman numeral for the month and keep repeating the word 'music'. They often have tickets to rock concerts

Concert tickets are available from the FOK Symfonický Orchestr office on U Prašné brány right between the Powder Gate and Pragotur (metro: náměstí Republiky). They should have something (open weekdays 9 am to 5 pm).

Theatres Opera, ballet and classical drama (in Czech) are performed at the neo-Renaissance *National Theatre* (1883), Národní 2 (metro: Národní třída). Next door is the ultramodern *Laterna Magika* (1983), Národní 4, which offers a widely imitated combination of theatre, dance and film. Regular tickets, however, are usually sold out two months in advance.

Opera and ballet are also presented at the neo-Renaissance *State Opera* on Wilsonova (metro: Muzeum). The State Opera is much smaller than the National Theatre so you get better views from the balconies. Tickets are occasionally available and only opera and ballet are presented, so take anything you can get.

The neoclassical *Stavovské Theatre* (1783), Železná 11 (metro: Můstek), often presents opera, but be prepared to pay US$35 for a seat downstairs, US$15 for a place on an upper balcony. Headphones providing simultaneous translation into English are available for some Czech plays.

The ticket offices for the Laterna Magika and National Theatre (Národní Divadlo) are both just inside the Laterna Magika. The State Opera and Stavovské Theatre have their own ticket offices at the theatres, but all four are usually sold out weeks ahead. Evening performances begin at 7 pm, weekend matinees at 2 pm. Get there half an hour early and stand outside holding a small sign reading *hledám lístek* (I'm looking for a ticket) as someone may have an extra ticket for a companion who didn't show up which they'd be happy to unload at face value.

For operettas and musicals go to the *Karlín Theatre of Music*, Křižíkova 10, near Florenc Bus Station (metro: Florenc). Because it's a little out of the way and not as famous, tickets are often available – highly recommended. The ticket office is open Monday to Saturday from 10 am to 1 pm and 2 to 6 pm.

A take-off of the Laterna Magika is the *Laterna Animata* in the Exhibition Grounds (metro: Holešovice) with a vertical film projected onto a parabolic stage. Tickets (US$22) are available at all the tourist ticket agencies. Several other theatres around town stage similar unspoken 'black theatre' or 'magic theatre' performances combining mime, film, dance, music or whatever. Admission to some is as low as US$8.

Plays in the Czech language by Václav Havel are often put on at the *Zábradlí Theatre*, Amenské náměstí 5 (metro: Staroměstská).

Concert Halls Prague's main concert venue is the neo-Renaissance *Dvořák Hall*, náměstí Jana Palacha (metro: Staroměstská), where the Prague Spring Music Festival is held in late May.

Prague's wonderful Art-Nouveau municipal concert hall, *Smetana Hall* or 'Obecního domu', náměstí Republiky 5, right next to the Powder Gate, is not used that often but when it is, tickets are available from FOK, which is around the corner, or at the box office inside, an hour before the performance.

Also check the *Palace of Culture* (metro: Vyšehrad) for events. Concerts are held there regularly and tickets are usually available at the box office.

Puppet Theatres The *Divadlo Minor*, Senovážné náměstí 28 (metro: náměstí Republiky), offers a mix of puppets and pantomime which is great fun, but sit in the back row if the place is full of school groups. Performances are at 9 am on weekdays and you can usually get a ticket (US$6) at the door just before the show.

A puppet theatre strictly for tourists is the so-called *National Marionette Theatre* or 'Říše loutek', Žatecká 1 (metro: Staroměstská). In midsummer there are evening performances twice daily, while in midwinter they're usually on Tuesday and Thursday. Notices in the entrance hall tell what's on and tickets (US$13) are available at the door.

Jazz Clubs For jazz, try the *Reduta Jazz Club*, Národní 20 (metro: Národní třída). Founded in 1958, this is one of the oldest jazz clubs in Europe. It opens at 9 pm with music from 9.30 pm to midnight (US$3 cover charge). Tickets are sold after 3 pm on weekdays or after 5 pm on Saturday.

There's also the *Press Jazz Club*, upstairs at Pařížská 9 (open from 9 pm to 5 am nightly).

You can see and hear live jazz every night from 9 pm to midnight at the unpretentious *Agha RTA Jazz Centrum*, Krakovská 5 (metro: Muzeum).

Discos & Rock Clubs *Disco Carioca*, downstairs from the passage at Václavské náměstí 4 (metro: Můstek), is open from 9 pm to 5 am. Drinks cost normal prices. Nearby, out the back of the passage and to the left, is *Disco Barbara*, Jungmannovo náměstí 14 (daily 8 pm to 5 am).

Adjacent to the Reduta Jazz Club is the *Rock Cafe*, Národní 20, with a music shop selling punk T-shirts, skull & crossbones necklaces and rings etc. From 8 pm to 3 am there's hard rock music here (US$2 cover, normal drink prices). Wear black clothing if you can. *Club Exodus*, downstairs at Národní 25, offers disco dancing to a different style of music every night from 9 pm to 4 am. If you're looking for reggae or central African pop, try here.

One of Prague's best venues is *Rock Club Borát*, Újezd 18 at Vítězná (open from 8 pm daily except Monday) with a varied clientele. Also recommended is *Rock Club Bunkr*, Lodecká 2 (metro: Florenc), which attracts a younger crowd.

Rock Bar Uzi, Legerova 44, a block and a half south of I P Pavlova Metro Station, has disco dancing from 9 pm to 5 am (US$1 cover).

Malá Strana *Malostranská Beseda*, Malostranské náměstí 21 (metro: Malostranská), presents jazz, folk, country, rock music, rock opera and so on nightly in their theatre-café. Most programmes begin at 8 pm.

Night Clubs The *Revue Alhambra Night Club* (open Tuesday to Sunday from 8.30 pm to 3 am) at the Ambassador Hotel, Václavské náměstí 5 (metro: Můstek), presents a Las Vegas-style floorshow nightly at 10.30 pm (US$18 per person minimum consumption and table charge). You can dance there before and after the show. Reservations should be made at the hotel reception.

A less touristy nightclub is the *Varieté Praha*, Vodičkova 30 just off Václavské náměstí, which has a two-hour floor show daily except Monday at 9.30 pm, then dancing from 11.30 pm to 2 am (US$9 cover charge for the best seats or US$5 near the back).

You'll see ads around town for the 'Bohemian Fantasy' extravaganza at *Palac Lucerna*, Štěpánská 61 off Václavské náměstí. This costs US$50 per person with dinner or US$34 per person for the show only (includes two drinks). It all happens four times a week from May to October and any theatrical ticket agency will have tickets.

Free Entertainment In the evening you can stroll along Na příkopě, where buskers play for the throng, or Václavské náměstí, where fast-food automats, cinemas and night bars stay open till late. Můstek is thick with black-market hustlers after dark. The floodlit Staroměstské náměstí and the Karlův most are other magical attractions of nocturnal Prague.

Things to Buy

You'll find many interesting shops along Celetná, between Staroměstské náměstí and náměstí Republiky. The Kotva Department Store on náměstí Republiky is the largest in the country. There's also the Máj Department Store, Národní and Spálená (metro: Národní třída).

For Bohemian crystal check the two Sklo Glass shops in the Alfa Cinema Arcade, Václavské náměstí 28.

Getting There & Away

Air ČSA Czechoslovak Airlines (☎ 231 7395), Revoluční 25 (metro: náměstí Republiky), books daily flights from Prague to Bratislava (US$66), Poprad-Tatry (US$77) and Košice (US$87).

Bus Buses to Karlovy Vary (122 km), Brno (210 km, 2½ hours) and most other towns in the Czech Republic depart from the Florenc Bus Station, Křižíkova 4 (metro: Florenc). Seven express buses a day cover the 321 km from Florenc to Bratislava in 4½ hours (as compared to 5½ hours on the train). Reservations are recommended on all these services.

Most (but not all) international buses to Western Europe also arrive/depart Florenc Bus Station (for tickets, see Travel Agencies near the beginning of this section).

The left-luggage room at Florenc Bus Station is upstairs above the information office (daily 5 am to 11 pm).

Tickets Reservations at Prague's Florenc Bus Station are computerised. To obtain a ticket, first determine the departure time *(odjezdy)* of your bus by looking at the posted timetable beside platform No 1 or asking at the information counter. Then get in line at any of the ticket counters. Make sure that your bus isn't on the sold-out *(vyprodáno)* list on the TV screens here. If it is, pick another bus. The further ahead you book, the better your chances of getting the bus you want and reservations are possible 10 days in advance. Your bus ticket indicates the platform number *(stání)* and seat number *(sed)*. You may be charged extra for baggage. The coaches are quite comfortable (no standing) and fares are reasonable.

Tickets for private Cebus express buses to Karlovy Vary, Brno and some other points are not sold in the main station but at a kiosk on the pavement between the bus station and Florenc Metro Station.

Train Trains run from Berlin-Lichtenberg to Prague (386 km, seven hours) via Dresden every three or four hours. Several of the trains arriving from Berlin continue on to Vienna. There's a service twice a day from Nuremberg (372 km, 6½ hours) via Cheb and twice daily from Linz, Austria (294 km, 5½ hours) via České Budějovice. Many trains arrive from Budapest (630 km, 10 hours) via Brno and Bratislava. From Poland you have the choice of arriving via Wrocław or Katowice. See Getting There & Away in the chapter introduction for more information.

From Praha-Holešovice and Hlavní nádraží, sleepers and couchettes are available on the nightly *Krušnohor* express train to Bratislava, Žilina, Poprad-Tatry and Košice. This is an excellent way to save one night's accommodation expenses while getting somewhere. A 1st-class sleeper from Prague to Bratislava will be US$11 including the ticket.

Train Stations Prague has four main train stations. International trains between Berlin and Budapest often stop at Praha-Holešovice Railway Station (metro: Nádraží Holešovice) on the north side of the city. Other important trains terminate at Praha-Hlavní nádraží (metro: Hlavní nádraží) or Masarykovo nádraží (metro: náměstí Republiky), both of which are close to the city centre. Some local trains to the south-west depart from Praha-Smíchov Railway Station (metro: Smíchovské nádraží).

Hlavní nádraží handles trains to Benešov (49 km, one hour), České Budějovice (169 km, 2½ hours), Cheb via Plzeň (220 km, four hours), Karlovy Vary via Chomutov (199 km, four hours), Košice (708 km, 10 hours), Mariánské Lázně (190 km, three hours), Plzeň (114 km, two hours) and Tábor (103 km, 1½ hours). Trains to Brno (257 km, 3½ hours) and Bratislava (398 km, 5½ hours) may leave from either Hlavní nádraží, Praha-Holešovice or Masarykovo nádraží.

This is confusing, so carefully study the timetables posted in one of the stations to determine which one you'll be using, then confirm the time and station at the information counter or at Čedok. To go to Kutná Hora (73 km, 1½ hours) you may use Praha-Holešovice or, more frequently, Masarykovo nádraží. Karlštejn trains always depart from Praha-Smíchov.

Hlavní nádraží is Prague's largest train

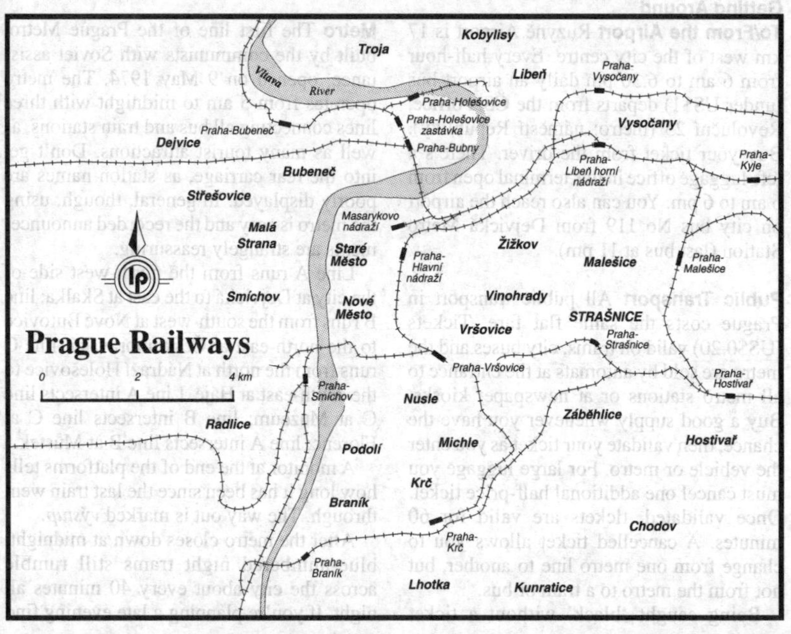

station with several exchange offices and accommodation services upstairs, and a tourist-information booth downstairs. The self-service and full-service restaurants on the top floor are not exciting but they're better than the various fast-food outlets on the main floor.

The 24-hour left-luggage office is in the basement, so drop your bags off upon arrival and stroll into town to look for a room or a meal (you pay the left-luggage fee when you pick the bags up).

International tickets are sold at window No 26 upstairs while international couchettes and seat reservations are purchased at the office with yellow signs downstairs near the metro entrance. Couchettes to Slovakia (Bratislava and Košice) are sold at windows No 16 to 24 downstairs.

At Holešovice Station, window No 1 is for booking couchettes. There are currency exchange facilities in all these stations but high commissions are charged.

Getting Around

To/From the Airport Ruzyně Airport is 17 km west of the city centre. Every half-hour from 6 am to 6.30 pm daily an airport bus (under US$1) departs from the ČSA office, Revoluční 25 (metro: náměstí Republiky). Buy your ticket from the driver. There's a left-luggage office in this terminal open from 6 am to 6 pm. You can also reach the airport on city bus No 119 from Dejvická Metro Station (last bus at 11 pm).

Public Transport All public transport in Prague costs the same flat fare. Tickets (US$0.20) valid on trams, city buses and the metro are sold by automats at the entrance to all metro stations or at newspaper kiosks. Buy a good supply whenever you have the chance, then validate your ticket as you enter the vehicle or metro. For large luggage you must cancel one additional half-price ticket. Once validated, tickets are valid for 60 minutes. A cancelled ticket allows you to change from one metro line to another, but not from the metro to a tram or bus.

Being caught 'black' without a ticket entails a US$8 fine. Inspectors will often demand a higher fine from foreigners and pocket the difference, so insist on a receipt *(potvrzení)* before paying.

Tourist tickets (Turistická Jítová Jízdenka) valid on all forms of public transport are sold for periods of one (US$1), two (US$1.75), three (US$2.50), four (US$3) or five (US$3.50) days. These tickets are usually available at Pragotur, U Obecního domu 2, and Čedok, Na příkopě 18. One place where you can always get these passes is the Centrální Dispečink Městské Dopravy, Na bojišti 5 (metro: I P Pavlova), open weekdays from 6.30 to 6 pm, Saturday 7 am to 1 pm. Compare the price of a monthly pass *(měsíční jízdenka)* if you're staying over a week.

Pragotur, U Obecního domu 2, and Čedok, Na příkopě 18, sell a 'Prague Card' valid for three days use of the public transportation system and admission to 36 museums and sights for US$13. A booklet explaining exactly what you get comes with the card.

Metro The first line of the Prague Metro, built by the communists with Soviet assistance, opened on 9 May 1974. The metro operates from 5 am to midnight with three lines connecting all bus and train stations, as well as many tourist attractions. Don't get into the rear carriage, as station names are poorly displayed. In general, though, using the metro is easy and the recorded announcements are strangely reassuring.

Line A runs from the north-west side of the city at Dejvická to the east at Skalka; line B runs from the south-west at Nové Butovice to the north-east at Českomoravská; line C runs from the north at Nádraží Holešovice to the south-east at Háje. Line A intersects line C at Muzeum; line B intersects line C at Florenc; line A intersects line B at Můstek.

A monitor at the end of the platforms tells how long it has been since the last train went through. The way out is marked *výstup*.

After the metro closes down at midnight, blue-numbered night trams still rumble across the city about every 40 minutes all night. If you're planning a late evening find out if one of these services passes anywhere near where you're staying as taxis can be a rip-off late at night.

Car Rental Pragocar (☎ 222 324), Opletalova 33, is directly across the park in front of Hlavní nádraží Railway Station. Europcar (☎ 231 3405), Pařížská 28, and Avis Rent-a-Car (☎ 231 7865), Elišky Krásnohorské 9, are both near the Inter-Continental Hotel (metro: Staroměstská). Budget has a desk inside the Inter-Continental itself. Most Čedok offices also rent cars at competitive rates. Avis, Budget, Hertz and Europcar all have offices at Ruzyně Airport, however, you'll be charged a US$11 surcharge if you use them.

If you're sure you want a car, you should book well in advance as they're often all taken in summer. Turn to Car Rental in the chapter introduction for sample rates.

Taxi Taxis are reasonable, but only if the meter is turned on. If the driver won't turn on the meter, clearly establish the price before you set out, otherwise you'll end up paying far more than normal. Only four passengers are allowed in a taxi.

Avoid taking taxis from Václavské náměstí or luxury hotels as these are much more expensive. If you feel you're being overcharged ask for a bill *(účet)* which the driver is obliged to provide.

Public transport is so good in Prague that taking a taxi is really a luxury.

Excursion Boats The Prague Passenger Shipping (PPS) riverboat terminal is on the right bank of the Vltava between Jiráskův most and Palackého most (metro: Karlovo náměstí). Thursday to Sunday at 9 am in July and August there are cruises upriver to Štěchovice (28 km, three hours each way). In midsummer this cruise is extended to Slapská Přehrada (37 km, US$3 return). In

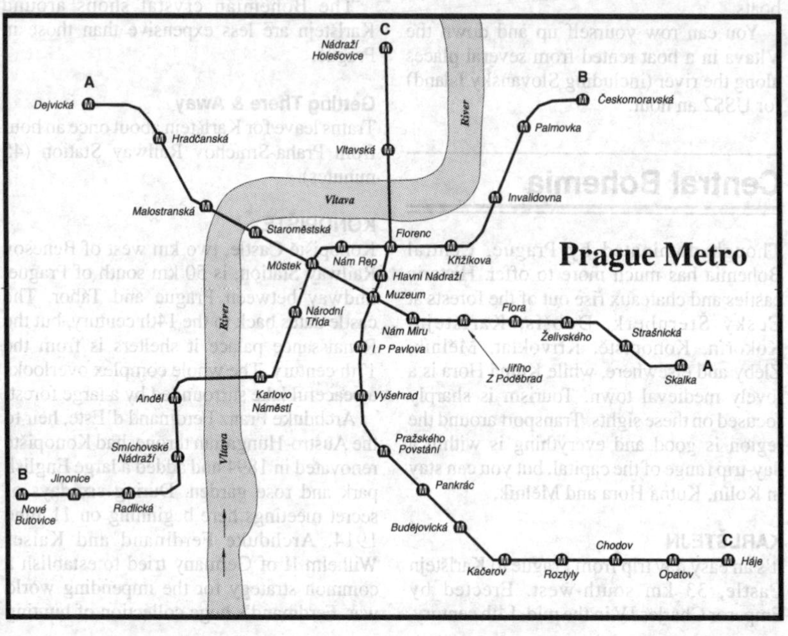

May, June and the first half of September, the boats only run on weekends and holidays.

Shorter trips downriver to the Troja Zoo (10 km, 1¼ hours each way, US$1) depart on the same days as the above at 9.30 am and at 1.30 pm. The morning departures to the zoo are often incredibly crowded with large groups of school children who are allowed to board first, so if you really want to do this trip it's best to take bus No 112 to the zoo (see Things to See earlier in this chapter) and catch the 11 am or the 5 pm boat from the zoo back to Prague. Allow 15 minutes to walk from the zoo to the landing.

Other 90-minute and two-hour lunch or sightseeing cruises run throughout the day and fares are relatively low. This is an excellent alternative to signing up for an expensive bus tour to sights you can easily visit on your own.

The excursion boats of the Evropská Vodní Doprava (EVD) which leave from a landing behind the Inter-Continental Hotel are double or triple the price of the PPS boats.

You can row yourself up and down the Vltava in a boat rented from several places along the river (including Slovanský Island) for US$2 an hour.

Central Bohemia

Though dominated by Prague, Central Bohemia has much more to offer. Historic castles and chateaux rise out of the forests at Český Šternberk, Dobřís, Karlštejn, Kokořín, Konopiště, Křivoklát, Mělník, Žleby and elsewhere, while Kutná Hora is a lovely medieval town. Tourism is sharply focused on these sights. Transport around the region is good and everything is within a day-trip range of the capital, but you can stay in Kolín, Kutná Hora and Mělník.

KARLŠTEJN

It's an easy day trip from Prague to Karlštejn Castle, 33 km south-west. Erected by Emperor Charles IV in the mid-14th century, this towering, fairy-tale castle crowns a ridge above the village, a 20-minute walk from the train station.

A highlight of Karlštejn Castle is the Church of Our Lady (1357) with its medieval frescos. In a corner of this church is the private oratory of the king, the walls of which are covered with precious stones. Even more magnificent is the Chapel of the Holy Rood in the Big Tower, where the coronation jewels were kept until 1420. Some 128 painted panels by Master Theodoric covering the walls make this chapel a veritable gallery of 14th century art.

The castle is open until 5 pm from May to September and until 3 pm the rest of the year (closed Monday). Although the compulsory guided tours (US$4, students US$2) are usually in Czech, there are explanations in English posted in each room. More expensive tours in English are given five times a day. (Unfortunately, the most interesting parts of the castle have been closed for restoration for many years with no end in sight.)

The Bohemian crystal shops around Karlštejn are less expensive than those in Prague.

Getting There & Away

Trains leave for Karlštejn about once an hour from Praha-Smíchov Railway Station (45 minutes).

KONOPIŠTĚ

Konopiště Castle, two km west of Benešov Railway Station, is 50 km south of Prague, midway between Prague and Tábor. The castle dates back to the 14th century, but the Renaissance palace it shelters is from the 17th century. The whole complex overlooks a peaceful lake surrounded by a large forest.

Archduke Franz Ferdinand d'Este, heir to the Austro-Hungarian throne, had Konopiště renovated in 1894 and added a large English park and rose garden. During six days of secret meetings here beginning on 11 June 1914, Archduke Ferdinand and Kaiser Wilhelm II of Germany tried to establish a common strategy for the impending world war. Ferdinand's huge collection of hunting trophies and weapons on display at the castle will shock animal rights activists. On 28 June 1914 the hunter, however, became the hunted and his assassination at Sarajevo touched off the very war the gentlemen had discussed. (In fairness it should be noted that Ferdinand was against military action.)

Konopiště Castle is open from April to October (closed Monday, admission US$2) but you must arrive by 2 pm if you want to see both the state chambers and the palace collections. The castle may only be visited with a boring Czech-speaking guide, so ask for the typed summary in English. Huge tour groups are led through the castle one after another.

Getting There & Away

Local trains leave Prague's Hlavní nádraží for Benešov (49 km, one hour) about once an hour. Most trains to/from Tábor (54 km, one hour) and České Budějovice (120 km, two hours) also stop here. There are occasional buses from Benešov Railway Station to the castle.

KUTNÁ HORA

In the 14th century, Kutná Hora, 66 km east of Prague, was the second-largest town in Bohemia after Prague. This was due to the rich veins of silver below the town itself and the silver *groschen* minted here was the hard currency of Central Europe at the time. During the 16th century, Kutná Hora's boom burst and mining ceased in 1726, so the medieval townscape has come down to us basically unaltered.

If you're planning a day trip from Prague be aware that all of Kutná Hora's museums are closed on Monday and buses are irregular on weekends, so Tuesday to Friday are the best days to come. A better idea, however, is to make Kutná Hora a stopover on your way to/from Slovakia or Brno. There's ample low-budget accommodation and it's always much nicer to see things at a relaxed pace.

Orientation

The main train station is three km east of the centre whereas the bus station is more conveniently located just on the north-eastern edge of the old town.

The easiest way to visit Kutná Hora on a day trip is to arrive on the morning express train from Prague's Masarykovo nádraží, then take a 10-minute walk from Kutná Hora hlavni nadraží Railway Station to Sedlec to visit the ossuary (see Things to See, below). From there it's another 15-minute walk or a five-minute bus ride to old Kutná Hora.

Things to See

At Sedlec, only a km from the train station on the way into town (turn right when you see a huge church), is a cemetery with a Gothic **ossuary** *(kostnice)* decorated with the bones of some 40,000 people. In 1870 František Rint, a local woodcarver, arranged the bones in the form of bells, a chandelier, monstrances and even the Schwarzenberg coat-of-arms – a truly macabre sight (US$1).

Continue two km south-west along Masarykova. As you enter the old town on Na Náměsti you'll see the Gothic **Church of Our Lady** on the left. Keep straight and turn left on Tylova which will take you up into Palackého náměstí, a quaint square created when the Gothic town hall was demolished after a fire in 1770.

From the upper end of Palackého náměstí a lane to the left leads directly to the tall tilting tower of the **St James Church** (1330), just past which is the Gothic Royal Mint, **Vlašský dvůr** or Italian Court, now occupied by city offices but still accessible through an entrance around the corner. Master craftsmen from Florence began stamping silver coins here in 1300.

From the front entrance to St James a series of cobbled, signposted streets slope down and up to the **Hrádek Mining Museum** (closed from November to March). This 15th-century palace contains an exhibit on the mining that made Kutná Hora wealthy. Note especially the huge wooden device used in the Middle Ages to lift up to 1000 kg at a time from shafts that were 200 metres deep. This museum's main attraction, however, is the 45-minute guided tour through 500 metres of **medieval mine**

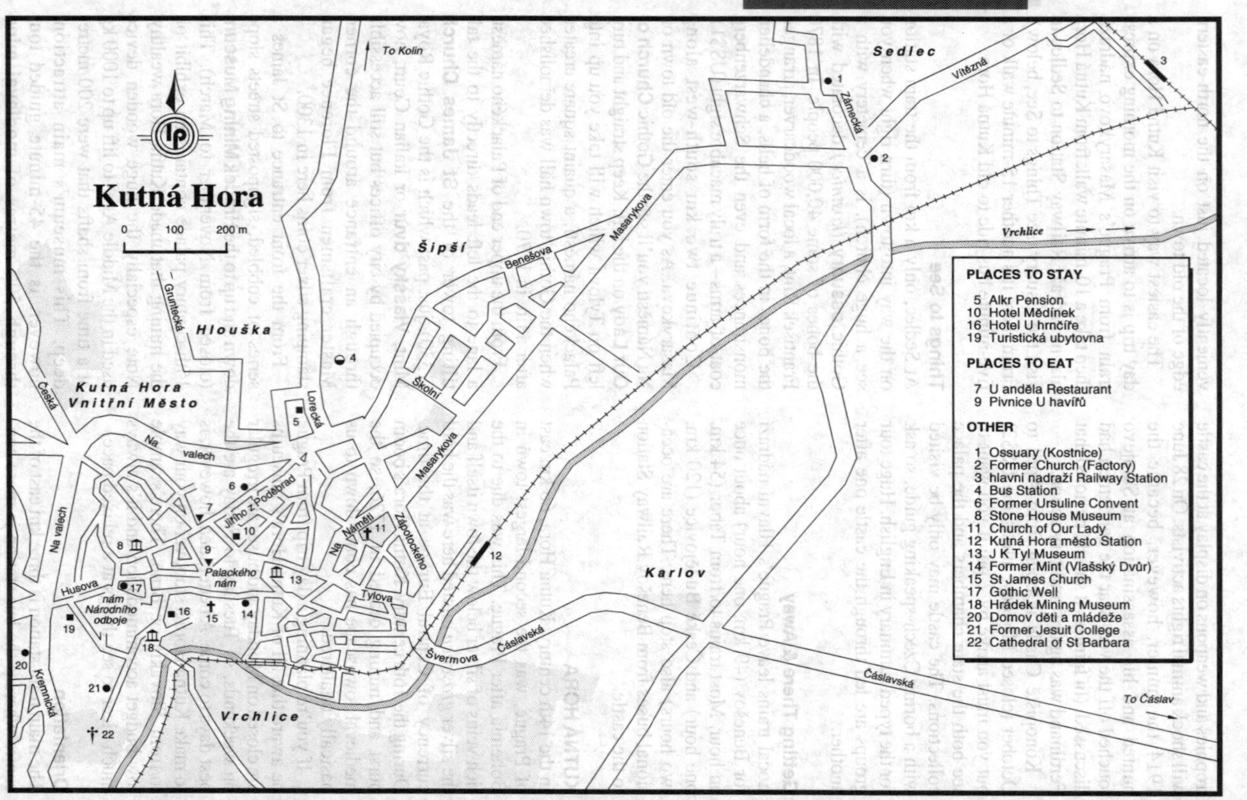
Kutná Hora
0 100 200 m
PLACES TO STAY
5 Alkr Pension
10 Hotel Mědínek
16 Hotel U hrnčíře
19 Turistická ubytovna
PLACES TO EAT
7 U anděla Restaurant
9 Pivnice U havířů
OTHER
1 Ossuary (Kostnice)
2 Former Church (Factory)
3 hlavni nadraží Railway Station
4 Bus Station
6 Former Ursuline Convent
8 Stone House Museum
11 Church of Our Lady
12 Kutná Hora město Station
13 J K Tyl Museum
14 Former Mint (Vlašský Dvůr)
15 St James Church
17 Gothic Well
18 Hrádek Mining Museum
20 Domov děti a mládeže
21 Former Jesuit College
22 Cathedral of St Barbara
To Kolin
Sedlec
Vítězná
Zámecká
Vrchlice
Šipší
Benešova
Masarykova
Hlouška
Gruntecká
Školní
Lorecká
Kutná Hora
Vnitřní Město
Česká
Na valech
Jiřího z Poděbrad
Palackého nám
Na Náměti
Zápotockého
Tylova
Husova
nám Národního odboje
Karlov
Švermova
Čáslavská
To Čáslav
Kremnická
Vrchlice

shafts on one of the 20 levels below Kutná Hora. You don a white coat and helmet, and pick up a miner's lamp, but the tour (US$1.25) only begins when a group of at least five people gathers. This is usually no problem in midsummer or on weekends, but in early spring and late autumn you may have to wait around.

Just beyond the Hrádek is the 17th-century former **Jesuit college** which has baroque sculpture in front of it and a good view of the Vrchlice River Valley from the promenade. Nearby is Kutná Hora's greatest monument, the **Cathedral of St Barbara** (US$1), begun in 1388 by Petr Parléř, the architect of St Vitus Cathedral in Prague, and finished in 1547. The exquisite net vault above the central nave is supported by double flying buttresses in the French high-Gothic style.

From St Barbara retrace your steps past the Jesuit College and the Hrádek and keep straight on Barborská till it ends at Komenského náměstí. Turn left, then right, and right again down Husova two blocks till you see a baroque **plague column** on the left. Walk up the street behind the column till you see an old building with a high triangular gable bearing figures of knights jousting, across the parking lot on the left. This is the **Stone House** (1485), Václavské náměstí 24, now the local historical museum.

Walk north-east down Václavské náměstí, which becomes Jiřího z Poděbrad, to the former **Ursuline convent** (1743) at No 13 on the left, which houses an exhibition of antiques. The bus station is straight ahead and down Lorecká to the left.

Places to Stay

Hostels Kutná Hora has no less than three hostels, all within a few minutes of each other.

A friendly, welcoming place to stay is the *U rytířů Hostel* (☎ 22 56), Rejskovo náměstí 123, just off Husova across the street from the large Gothic well in the middle of the road. The 20 rooms vary in price but average around US$7 per person. Most rooms are doubles with private bath.

Kutná Hora's official HI hostel is the *Domov dětí a mládeže*, conveniently located at Kremnická 8 just west of the old town. If it's closed or full, check out *Prifis Pension*, Kremnická 5, just across the street.

At a pinch you could also try the *Turistická ubytovna* (☎ 34 63), Smíškovo náměstí 56, a basic dormitory with a reception which opens only from 8 to 9 am and 5 to 6 pm.

Hotels The *Hotel Mědínek* (☎ 27 41), a modern four-storey hotel on Palackého náměstí, costs US$18/22 single/double without bath, US$29/43 with bath, breakfast included.

A better choice for a room in Kutná Hora is the *Hotel U hrnčíře* (☎ 21 13), Barborská 24, just down the street from the Hrádek. The five rooms in this quaint privately owned inn go for US$13 per person including breakfast, and they're often fully booked, so be sure to call ahead (the person answering the phone is more likely to speak German than English, an indication of who usually stays here). Even if you don't stay here, the U hrnčíře is an excellent place for a genteel lunch which is served in their garden in summer.

Alkr Pension, Lorecká 7, right near the bus station, has comfortable rooms with private bath and a small kitchenette which cost US$15/18/29 a single/double/triple.

Places to Eat

U anděla, náměstí Václavské 8, is a decent place to eat. In front of the plague column nearby is *Pivnice U havířů* (closed Monday), a local beer hall where inexpensive meals are served, with a more sedate *vinárna* at the back.

Getting There & Away

Kutná Hora is on the main railway line between Prague and Brno via Havlíčkův Brod although many express trains don't stop here (you may have to change at Kolín). Trains arrive from Prague's Masarykovo nádraží (73 km, 1½ hours) via Kolín every couple of hours.

The trains from Prague stop at Kutná Hora

CZECH REPUBLIC

hlavní nádraží, about three km east of the centre. About 10 trains a day (on a branch line to Zruč nad Sázavou) link Kutná Hora hlavní nádraží to Kutná Hora město Station which is adjacent to the old town.

Weekdays there are about six express buses to Prague (70 km) but far fewer buses operate on weekends. If your timing doesn't coincide with a bus direct to Prague, take one to Kolín (12 km) where there are better connections to Prague. At Kutná Hora Bus Station, buses to Prague leave from stand No 6, to Kolín from stands Nos 2 and 10.

KOLÍN

Kolín on the Labe River is a friendly old town seldom visited by tourists. The Kmochův Festival of brass-band music is held here every June. The town centre is next to the river, a 15-minute walk from the adjacent bus and train stations.

It might be worth stopping here for a night if you're passing through on your way to/from Prague and it's a good base from which to visit Kutná Hora and Mělník.

Things to See

Kolín has a picturesque central square with a baroque Marian column (1682) and fountain (1780) in the middle. A block away is the towering Gothic **St Bartholomew Church** begun by Petr Parléř. The **City Museum** (closed Monday) is next to this church.

Places to Stay & Eat

The *Hotel Savoy* (☎ 22 022), Rubešová 61 just off the central square, is US$13/17 single/double without bath, US$21 double with bath.

Two cheaper places are across the river and a couple of blocks to the left (ask). The *Skautská Ubytovna 'Kalcovka'* (Scout's Hostel), off Za Baštou, a block back from Brankovická 25, has beds in double rooms at US$3 per person.

The *Turistická Ubytovna Zimní Stadión* (☎ 20 444), Brankovická 27, has triple rooms at US$13 (bus No 3 from the train station). There's a good restaurant at the Zimní Stadión, open daily until 10 pm.

Getting There & Away

Kolín is a major junction on the Prague-Košice main line, with frequent service to/from Prague (62 km, one hour). All trains to/from Moravia, Slovakia and Poland stop here. Another important line through Kolín is from Havlíčkův Brod to Děčín via Mělník. Buses run regularly from Kolín Bus Station to Kutná Hora, 12 km south by road.

MĚLNÍK

Central Bohemia is drained by the romantic Labe and Vltava rivers, which unite at Mělník, 32 km north of Prague, and flow north towards Germany, where they become the Elbe. It was Emperor Charles IV who introduced Burgundy vines to this fertile area in 1340. The finest Mělník wines are Ludmila, a red wine named after St Wenceslas' pious grandmother, and Chateau Mělník, a sparkling red wine.

On a bluff above the rivers is a Renaissance **chateau** (1554), now an art gallery and museum of viticulture (open from April to October, closed Monday). Both the chateau and the adjacent late Gothic **Sts Peter & Paul Church** are near Mělník's picturesque central square, a 15-minute walk from the bus and train stations.

Places to Stay & Eat

The *Hotel Nádraží* (☎ 624 848), directly across the street from the train station, has large rooms with shared facilities at US$13/20 single/double. Their restaurant serves a tasty pork dish called *Srbské vepřové žebírko*.

The C-category *Hotel Zlatý Beránek* on Mělník's old town square has closed.

Getting There & Away

Direct trains go to Mělník from Kolín (71 km, 1½ hours) and Děčín (89 km, two hours), but services from Vysočany Railway Station in Prague (50 km) involve a change at Všetaty, so you're better off coming by bus from Holešovice Metro Station in Prague (33 km, one hour).

In Prague, Praha-Vysočany Railway Station is a 10-minute walk from Českomoravská Metro Station.

West Bohemia

Cheb and Plzeň are the western gateways to the Czech Republic. All trains from Western Germany pass this way and the stately old Habsburg spas, Karlovy Vary and Mariánské Lázně, are nearby. The proximity to Bavaria helps to explain the famous Pilsner beer which originated in Plzeň. South-west of Plzeň is Domažlice, centre of the Chod people, where folk festivals are held in August. In West Bohemia you can enjoy the charm of southern Germany at a fraction of the price.

KARLOVY VARY

Karlovy Vary (Karlsbad) is the largest and oldest of the Czech Republic's many spas. According to a local tradition, Emperor Charles IV discovered the hot springs by chance while hunting a stag. In 1358 he built a hunting lodge here and gave the town his name. Beginning in the 19th century, famous people such as Beethoven, Bismarck, Brahms, Chopin, Franz Josef I, Goethe, Liszt, Metternich, Paganini, Peter the Great, Schiller and Tolstoy came here to take the waters, and busts of a few of them grace the promenades. Karl Marx came to Karlovy Vary to take the cure in 1874, 1875 and 1876. Ludvík Moser began making glassware at Karlovy Vary in 1857 and today Bohemian crystal is prized around the world.

There are 12 hot springs at Karlovy Vary containing 40 chemical elements that are used in medical treatment of diseases of the digestive tract and metabolic disorders. If you have diarrhoea or constipation, this is the place to come. Mineral deposits from the springs form stone encrustations which are sold as souvenirs. Karlovy Vary's herbal Becherovka liqueur is known as the 13th spring.

Karlovy Vary still bears a definite Victorian air. The elegant colonnades and boulevards complement the many peaceful walks in the surrounding parks. The picturesque river valley winds between wooded hills, yet the spa offers all the facilities of a medium-sized town without the bother. After hustling around Prague this is a nice place to relax amidst charming scenery. It's hard not to like Karlovy Vary.

Orientation

Karlovy Vary has two train stations. Express trains from Prague and Cheb use Karlovy Vary horní nádraží, across the Ohře River, just north of the city. Trains to/from Mariánské Lázně stop at Karlovy Vary dolní nádraží, which is opposite the main ČAD bus station. The city bus station is in front of the market, three blocks east of dolní nádraží. T G Masaryka, the pedestrian mall in Karlovy Vary's city centre, runs east to the Teplá River. Upstream is the heart of the spa.

If you decide to walk from town to horní nádraží, you'll see a huge building labelled 'okresní úřad' directly in front of you as you cross the bridge. Go around behind this building and straight ahead until you see a signposted way on the left which leads through a tunnel and straight up to the station.

There's no left-luggage office at the bus station. Both train stations have left-luggage rooms but left luggage at horní nádraží is larger and more reliably open 24 hours a day.

Information

Čedok has two offices, one on the corner of Bechera and Moskevská, and another at Karla IV 1 closer to the spa.

There's an information office (open weekdays only) in a corner of the Vřídelní Colonnade. This office arranges spa treatment for foreigners beginning at around US$70 per person a day including room and board.

Money Near the bus station, the Komerční

CZECH REPUBLIC

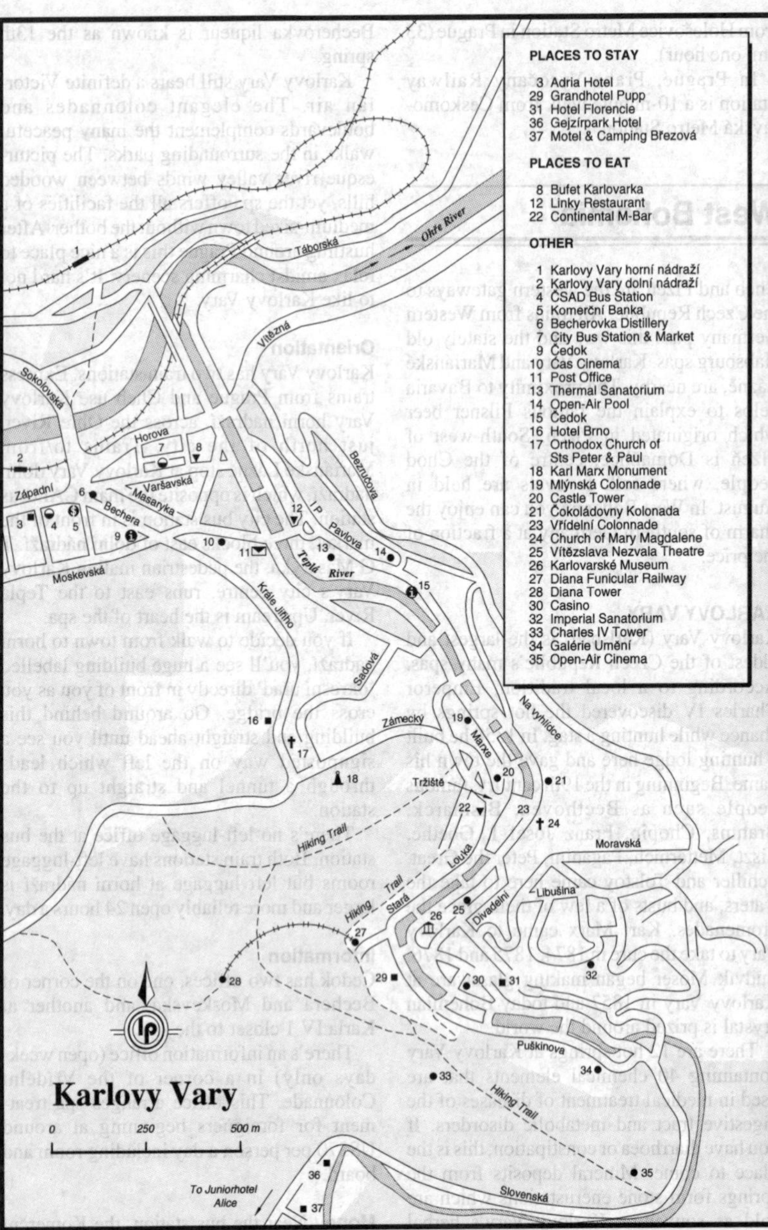
PLACES TO STAY
3 Adria Hotel
29 Grandhotel Pupp
31 Hotel Florencie
36 Gejzírpark Hotel
37 Motel & Camping Březová
PLACES TO EAT
8 Bufet Karlovarka
12 Linky Restaurant
22 Continental M-Bar
OTHER
1 Karlovy Vary horní nádraží
2 Karlovy Vary dolní nádraží
4 ČSAD Bus Station
5 Komerční Banka
6 Becherovka Distillery
7 City Bus Station & Market
9 Čedok
10 Čas Cinema
11 Post Office
13 Thermal Sanatorium
14 Open-Air Pool
15 Čedok
16 Hotel Brno
17 Orthodox Church of Sts Peter & Paul
18 Karl Marx Monument
19 Mlýnská Colonnade
20 Castle Tower
21 Čokoládovny Kolonada
23 Vřídelní Colonnade
24 Church of Mary Magdalene
25 Vítězslava Nezvala Theatre
26 Karlovarské Museum
27 Diana Funicular Railway
28 Diana Tower
30 Casino
32 Imperial Sanatorium
33 Charles IV Tower
34 Galérie Umění
35 Open-Air Cinema
Ohře River
Táborská
Vítězná
Sokolovská
Horova
Varšavská
Západní
Masaryka
Bechera
Moskevská
Bezručova
Pavlova
Teplá River
Krále Jiřího
Sadová
Zámecký
Na vyhlídce
Marxe
Tržiště
Moravská
Louka
Libušina
Divadelní
Stará
Hiking Trail
Puškinova
Slovenská
To Juniorhotel Alice
Karlovy Vary
0
250
500 m

Banka, Bělehradská13, is open weekdays from 7.30 to 11.30 am and 1 to 4.30 pm.

Komerční Banka, Tržiště 11 next to Vřídelní Colonnade, opens weekdays from 9 am to noon and 1 to 4 pm.

Post & Telephone The telephone centre at the main post office, T G Masaryka 1, is open daily from 7.30 am to 8 pm. Karlovy Vary's telephone code is 017.

Things to See

As you follow the riverside promenade south from the stations, you'll pass the modern **Thermal Sanatorium** (1976) and the neoclassical **Mlýnská Colonnade** (1881), designed by Josef Žitek. Temporary exhibitions are held at Lázeňská 3 (once the Karl Marx Museum). On a nearby hill is the **old castle tower** (1608) on the site of Charles IV's 1358 hunting lodge. Today it's a restaurant. Down the hill from the castle is the **House of the Three Moors**, or Dagmar House, Tržiště 25, where Goethe stayed during his many visits to Karlovy Vary.

Opposite this building is a bridge which leads to the pulsing heart of Karlovy Vary, the Vřídlo or Sprundel Spring in the **Vřídelní Colonnade**. Here 2000 litres a minute of 72.2°C water shoot up 12 metres from a depth of 2500 metres. The colonnade, erected in 1975, was formerly named after the world's first astronaut, Yuri Gagarin, who visited the spa in 1961 and 1966. Throngs of Czech tourists, funny little cups in hand, pace up and down the colonnade, taking the drinking cure. Bring a cup of your own for some piping hot liquid refreshment and maybe it'll even do you some good.

Just above the Vřídelní Colonnade is the baroque **Church of Mary Magdalene** (1736) designed by Kilian Dientzenhofer. Follow the Teplá River south-west past the **Vítězslava Nezvala Theatre** (1886) till you reach the **Karlovarské Museum** (closed Monday and Tuesday), Nová Louka 23, which has history and natural history displays on the local area.

Return to the Vřídelní Colonnade, cross the bridge again and follow the promenade west along the river towards the **Grandhotel Pupp**, a former meeting place of the European aristocracy. Just before the hotel you'll see Mariánská, an alley on the right leading to the bottom station of the **Diana Funicular Railway**, which ascends 166 metres to the top every 15 minutes from 10 am to 6 pm. Take a ride up to the **Diana Tower** for great views and pleasant walks through the forest. If the railway is closed, follow the network of footpaths that begins near this station. A café adjoins the Diana Tower.

Loket If you have an afternoon to spare, take a ČAD bus, which passes about every two hours, eight km south-west to Loket, where you'll find an impressive 13th-century **castle** on the hilltop in the centre of town. A museum in the castle is dedicated to the china made in Loket since 1815. On the façade of the Hotel Bílý Kůň, in Loket's picturesque town square, is a plaque commemorating Goethe's seven visits. You might even consider staying at the *Bílý Kůň* (☎ 94 171) which also has a restaurant where you can get lunch.

You can walk back to Karlovy Vary from Loket in about three hours. Follow the blue-and-white trail down the left bank of the Ohře River, which flows between Cheb and Karlovy Vary, to the **Svatošské Rocks**. Here you cross the river on a footbridge and take the road to Doubí (served by Karlovy Vary city bus No 6). This riverside path down the forested valley is lovely.

Activities

Top off your sightseeing with a swim in the large **open-air thermal pool** *(bazén)* on the hill above the Thermal Sanatorium. Karlovy Vary's numerous sanatoriums are reserved for patients undergoing treatment prescribed by physicians – in fact, this is the only place which will let you in.

The bazén is open from 8 am to 9.30 pm daily (from 9 am on Sunday), admission US$1 per hour. The bazén is closed every third Monday. There's also a sauna (reserved for women on Tuesday and Thursday, men on Monday and Wednesday, mixed other

CZECH REPUBLIC

days), a solarium and a fitness club, all open daily. A board at the entrance explains it all in English.

Places to Stay

Private Rooms On weekends Karlovy Vary fills up with Germans on mini holidays and accommodation is tight. Čedok (☎ 22 294), on the corner of Bechera and Moskevská, will place you in a private home, but at US$27 double (no singles) they're greatly overpriced. Even then, the rooms are often full with Czechs who pay much less than you. A second Čedok office with private rooms is at Karla IV 1 and their rooms are sometimes cheaper.

W Private Travel Agency (☎ 27 768), náměstí Republiky 5 next to the bus station, has private rooms at US$10 to US$13 per person and they usually have something available.

Hotels The *Servis Pension Armabeton* (☎ 25 868), Sokolovská 72, is in an untouristed neighbourhood about a km west of horní nádraží Railway Station. It's US$17/23/26 double/triple/quad (no singles) with shared bath in this renovated 1902 building almost opposite the city brewery. There are several cheap bars and restaurants in the vicinity but it's on the opposite side of town from the spa.

If you're only staying for one night, a good bet is the *Adria Hotel* (☎ 23 765), Západní 1, opposite the ČAD bus station (US$18/27 single/double with bath). The C-category *Hotel Turist* (☎ 26 837), Bechera 18 near Čedok, is US$14 per person in double and triple rooms with shared bath (no singles). This place is run-down and not really worth the money.

Closer to the spa is the *Hotel Atlantic* (☎ 24 715), Tržiště 23 next to Vřídelní Colonnade, right in the middle of everything. It has a few bargain singles at US$25 including breakfast. Doubles are more expensive at US$57 without bath, US$69 with bath, breakfast included.

The *Hotel Wolker*, Tržiště 19 next to Hotel Atlantic, is cheap but to get a room you must go first to expensive Hotel Astoria, Vřídelní 23 opposite the Mlýnská Colonnade, where the snotty clerk will tell you the rooms at the Wolker aren't good enough for foreigners and it's full for the rest of the month. This situation could change.

The former state sanatoriums are being privatised and renovated for up-market (mostly German) tourism. For the time being you can get good deals on food and accommodation in these places – ask around. One such is the *Hotel Florencie* (☎ 24 160), Mariánskolázeňská 25, a five-storey Victorian hotel facing the casino. Rooms here are US$20/30 single/double without bath.

Karlovy Vary's premier address is the *Grandhotel Pupp* (☎ 209 111), Mírové náměstí 2, an imposing 358-room hotel founded in 1701 and operated from 1773 to 1945 and 1990 to the present by the Pupp family. A room here with bath and breakfast will set you back US$85 single, US$112 to US$125 double, or you can play the big shot for a lower price by dining at one of the hotel's pretentious restaurants.

Better value if you want to go up-market is the *Hotel Brno* (☎ 25 020), krále Jiřího 1, a four-storey villa on a hill overlooking the Russian Orthodox church and surrounding forests. Rooms without bath aren't cheap at US$25/42 single/double including breakfast, but they're spacious and well appointed. If the price doesn't bother you, it's a good choice.

South of Town There are two places to stay along Slovenská just south of the spa centre, which you can reach from the market on bus No 7 with the sign 'Březová'. The first place you come to is the friendly *Gejzírpark Hotel* (☎ 22 662) beside the public tennis courts, a new building with rooms at US$11 per person with shared bath. The hotel has free hot showers and, unlike those in many other hotels, they're not locked. You can use the 14 adjacent tennis courts at US$5 an hour – ask the hotel receptionist. The hotel restaurant is very slow but the food is good.

Not far from the Gejzírpark Hotel is *Motel Březová* (☎ 25 101), Slovenská 9, where motel rooms are US$25/26 double/triple (no singles) without bath or US$43 double with bath. The rooms are often fully booked by locals who pay much less. The camping ground here charges US$6 for one, US$9 for two. The location in a wooded valley near a stream is nice but it's often crowded with German and Austrian caravans. There's only enough hot water for the first two campers in the morning queue. The motel is open from April to October and camping is from May to September only.

Places to Eat

The *Drůbeží Grill* at Tržiště 31, just up the hill from the Vřídelní Colonnade, has tasty barbecued chicken and cold beer. Order rice (rýže) with your meal as the chips are rather greasy. Another great place for grilled chicken and beer is *Linky*, nábřeží Jana Palacha 2. At Drůbeží you pay a fixed price for a quarter or half chicken, while at Linky you pay by weight.

Restaurant Fortuna, Bechera 16, tries to be an US-style steak house.

Bars & Cafés The best place for coffee, sinfully rich cakes and ice cream is the *Continental M-Bar*, Tržiště 27, near the Vřídelní Colonnade. Entry is through the Bohemia porcelain showroom. Upstairs from the showroom is a more spacious, more expensive café.

Café Elefant, Stará Louka 30, is perhaps Karlovy Vary's most popular non-hotel café.

A self-service beer bar called *Bistro Luisa* is near the lower station of the Diana Funicular Railway.

The *Bufet Karlovarská*, Horova 2, next to the city bus station, has cheap beer on tap.

Local Specialties You can buy a box of the famous Lázeňské oplatky wafers at *Čokoládovny Kolonda*, Vřídelní 57 (next to Pošta No 3 post office).

Lovers of fine liqueurs will wish to stand outside the Becherova distillery at T G Masaryka 57 and look at the displays in the window or drop into the company store at No 53 to buy a bottle at a slightly reduced rate.

Entertainment

Karlovy Vary's main theatre is the *Divadlo Vítězslava Nezvala* on Divadlo náměstí, not far from the Vřídelní Colonnade, but it offers mostly drama in Czech. The main ticket office *(předprodej)* for the theatre is open Monday to Saturday from 1.30 to 6 pm. From mid-May to mid-September concerts are held in the colonnade daily except Monday.

Among the many cultural events are the Jazz Festival in March, the Dvořák Singing Contest in June, the International Magicians Meeting in July, the Dvořák Autumn Festival in September and the International Festival of Touristic Films in September.

Seeing a movie at *Čas Cinema*, T G Masaryka 3, is another option.

Getting There & Away

Bus There are direct trains to Prague, but it's faster and easier to take one of the hourly buses (122 km). Also take a bus between Karlovy Vary and Mariánské Lázně (47 km), as the train takes twice as long. To Cheb, however, the bus takes twice as long as a local train. The only way to go directly to Plzeň (83 km) and České Budějovice (220 km, five hours) is by bus. Seats on express buses can and should be reserved in advance by computer at the ČAD bus station (weekdays 6 am to 6 pm, Saturday until 1 pm).

Train The *Karlex* express train travels daily between Leipzig and Karlovy Vary (240 km, five hours) via Františkovy Lázně (reservations are recommended). To go to Nuremberg or beyond, you'll have to change at Cheb. Cheb (52 km, one hour) and Mariánské Lázně (53 km, two hours) are connected to Karlovy Vary by local trains. Couchettes and sleepers are available to/from Košice (897 km) on the *Krušnohor* express train.

Getting Around

Before boarding a city bus, buy some tickets from an automat (feed it small coins). A good service to know about is bus No 11, which runs hourly from horní nádraží Railway

Station to the city bus station at the market, then on over the hills to Divadlo náměstí and the Vřídelní Colonnade. The more frequent city bus No 13 also runs to the market *tržnice* from horní nádraží.

Bus No 2 runs between the market and the Grandhotel Pupp (Lázně I) every half-hour or better from 6 am to 11 pm daily.

CHEB

This old medieval town on the Ohře River, near the western tip of the Czech Republic, is an easy day trip by train from Karlovy Vary or Mariánské Lázně. You can also visit Cheb as a stopover between Karlovy Vary and Mariánské Lázně as train service to both is good. Only a few km north of the Bavarian border, Cheb (formerly Eger) retains a strong German flavour.

Orientation & Information

The train station at the south-east end of třída Svobody is open all night, so you can wait there if you arrive or depart at an ungodly hour. The left-luggage office at the train station is open 24 hours a day.

Čedok is on the corner of Májová and třída Svobody.

The Cultural Information Office, náměstí krále Jiřího 33, sells theatre and concert tickets.

Money The Komerční Banka has an exchange window in the train station (open daily from 8 am to 1 pm and 2 to 6 pm). They change travellers' cheques for 2% commission (US$1 minimum) and give a good rate.

The main branch of the Komerční Banka is at Obrněné Brigády 20 (weekdays 7.30 to 11.30 am and 1 to 6 pm).

Post & Telephone The main post office is at náměstí krále Jiřího 38.

Cheb's telephone code is 0166.

Things to See

Although the area around the train station is ugly, only a few minutes' away up třída Svobody is the picturesque town square, náměstí krále Jiřího. Burgher houses with sloping red-tile roofs surround the square and in the middle is **Špalíček**, a cluster of 16th-century Gothic houses which were once Jewish shops. Behind these is the **Municipal Museum** (closed Monday) which has an excellent historical exhibition. The Thirty Years' War military commander Duke Albrecht Wallenstein was murdered in the building in 1634 and the museum devotes a room to him. Also on the square is the baroque former new town hall (1728), now the **city art gallery**.

At the back of the Municipal Museum is **St Nicholas Church**, a massive Gothic structure with a sculpture-filled interior. Notice the portal (1270) and the Romanesque features, such as the twin towers. A few blocks away is **Cheb Castle** (open from April to October, closed Monday), erected in the 12th century by Friedrich I Barbarossa, leader of the Eastern crusades. The Black Tower dates from 1222 but the exterior fortifications were built in the 17th century. The 12th-century Romanesque chapel in the castle is a rare sight in the Czech Republic.

Places to Stay

There are a number of small hotels in Cheb. The *Hotel Chebský Dvůr* (☎ 33 400), třída Svobody 93 near the bus station, is US$13 per person. The *Slávie Hotel* (☎ 33 216), třída Svobody 75, is US$14/23 single/double without bath, US$17/26 with bath. The friendly *Hradní Dvůr Hotel* (☎ 22 444), Dlouhá 12, costs US$11/22 single/double without bath, US$25 double with bath.

The *Hvězda Hotel* (☎ 22 549), náměstí krále Jiřího 4, is more expensive at US$18/27 single/double without bath, US$36 to US$58 double with bath, but it's pleasant, with some rooms overlooking the main square.

Private rooms from Čedok are US$15 a double (no singles).

The nearest camping grounds are at Dřenice (☎ 31 591) on Jesenice Lake, five km east of Cheb, and Lake Amerika, two km south-east of Františkovy Lázně. Both are open from mid-May to mid-September.

Places to Eat

Cheb's self-service is the *Restaurant Bohemia* at třída Svobody 18 near Čedok. The *Briga Mléčná Jídelna*, třída Svobody 74 beside the Slávie Hotel, is also fast and easy (both are closed on Sunday).

There are a number of tourist restaurants around náměstí krále Jiřího, for example, the *Fortuna* at No 474 or *Kavarna Špalíček* at No 499.

The restaurant at the *Hradní Dvůr Hotel* is unpretentious and has Chebské pivo on tap. The *Hotel Chebský Dvůr* also has a very good restaurant.

Getting There & Away

Most trains arriving in the Czech Republic from Nuremberg (190 km, three hours) stop here, with express trains to/from Stuttgart (342 km, six hours), Frankfurt/Main (389 km, five hours) and Dortmund (728 km, eight hours) daily. The train from Leipzig stops at nearby Františkovy Lázně, not Cheb. There are trains to Cheb from Prague (220 km, four hours) via Plzeň and Mariánské Lázně.

A railcar covers the 13 km from Cheb to Schirnding, Germany, twice a day. Tickets are available at the station (US$2.50 one

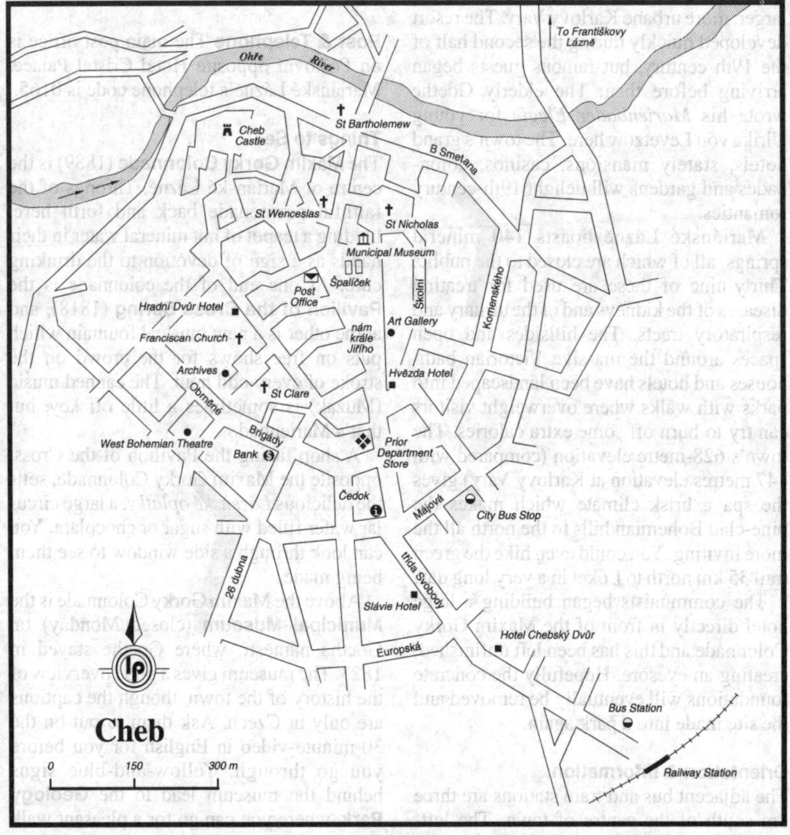

way, US$5 return, valid two months). To board an international train, enter through the door marked *zoll-douane* (customs) to one side of the main station entrance at least an hour before departure. If you miss the train to Schirnding and don't mind hitchhiking, you could take city bus No 5 to Pomezí which is near the border, eight km west of Cheb, and then cross into Germany on foot. The bus to Pomezí leaves from stand No 7 at the train station every hour or so.

MARIÁNSKÉ LÁZNĚ

Small, provincial Mariánské Lázně (Marienbad) is the Czech Republic's most famous spa, but in many ways it ranks second to the larger, more urbane Karlovy Vary. The resort developed quickly during the second half of the 19th century, but famous guests began arriving before then. The elderly Goethe wrote his *Marienbader Elegie* for young Ulrika von Levetzow here. The town's grand hotels, stately mansions, casinos, colonnades and gardens will delight 19th-century romantics.

Mariánské Lázně boasts 140 mineral springs, all of which are closed to the public. Thirty-nine of these are used for treating diseases of the kidneys and of the urinary and respiratory tracts. The hillsides and open spaces around the massive Victorian bathhouses and hotels have been landscaped into parks with walks where overweight visitors can try to burn off some extra calories. The town's 628-metre elevation (compared with 447 metres elevation at Karlovy Vary) gives the spa a brisk climate which makes the pine-clad Bohemian hills to the north all the more inviting. You could even hike the green trail 35 km north to Loket in a very long day.

The communists began building a large hotel directly in front of the Maxim Gorky Colonnade and this has been left unfinished, creating an eyesore. Hopefully the concrete foundations will eventually be removed and the site made into a park again.

Orientation & Information

The adjacent bus and train stations are three km south of the centre of town. The left-luggage office at the train station is open 24 hours. To get to town, head north up Český armády and Hlavní třída. Trolleybus No 5 follows this route from the train station to the centre of town about every 10 minutes and you pay with coins (not a ticket), so have change.

The City Service Tourist Office is on Hlavní třída at the city bus station. Čedok is next to Hotel Europa on Trebizskeho třída.

For information on medical treatment at Mariánské Lázně go to the Spa Information Service, Mírové náměstí 5.

Money The Komerční Banka is inside the town hall building on Ruská.

Post & Telephone The main post office is on Poštovní opposite Hotel Cristal Palace. Mariánské Lázně's telephone code is 0165.

Things to See

The **Maxim Gorky Colonnade** (1889) is the centre of Mariánské Lázně. Throngs of the faithful promenade back and forth here, holding a teapot of hot mineral water in their hands as a sign of devotion to the drinking cure. At one end of the colonnade is the **Pavilion of the Cross Spring** (1818), and at the other is a new musical fountain which puts on free shows for the crowd on the stroke of every odd hour. The canned music (Muzak) is sometimes a little off key, but that's Marienbad.

A shop facing the Pavilion of the Cross, opposite the Maxim Gorky Colonnade, sells the delicious *Lázeňské oplatky*, a large circular wafer filled with sugar or chocolate. You can look through a side window to see them being made.

Above the Maxim Gorky Colonnade is the **Municipal Museum** (closed Monday) on Goetha náměstí, where Goethe stayed in 1823. The museum gives a good overview of the history of the town, though the captions are only in Czech. Ask them to put on the 30-minute video in English for you before you go through. Yellow-and-blue signs behind the museum lead to the **Geology Park**, where you can go for a pleasant walk

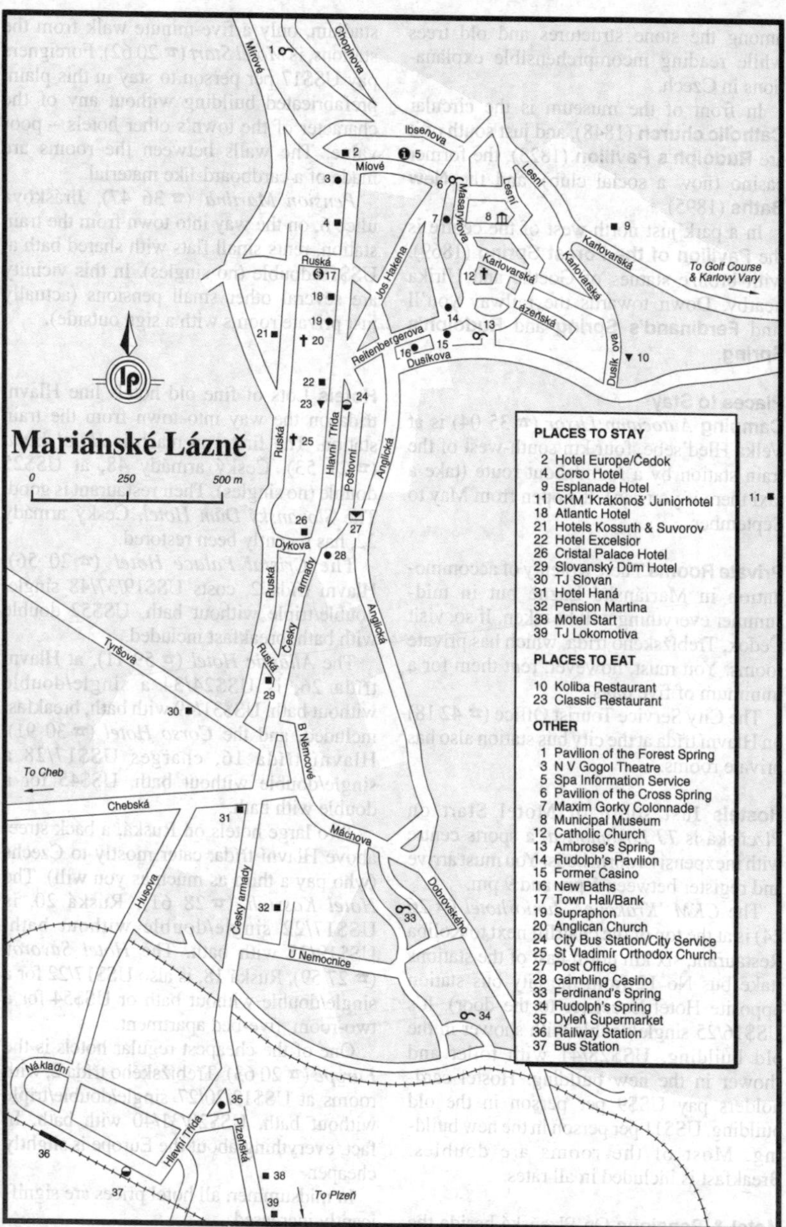

Mariánské Lázně
0
250
500 m
PLACES TO STAY
2 Hotel Europe/Čedok
4 Corso Hotel
9 Esplanade Hotel
11 CKM 'Krakonoš' Juniorhotel
18 Atlantic Hotel
21 Hotels Kossuth & Suvorov
22 Hotel Excelsior
26 Cristal Palace Hotel
29 Slovanský Dům Hotel
30 TJ Slovan
31 Hotel Haná
32 Pension Martina
38 Motel Start
39 TJ Lokomotiva
PLACES TO EAT
10 Koliba Restaurant
23 Classic Restaurant
OTHER
1 Pavilion of the Forest Spring
3 N V Gogol Theatre
5 Spa Information Service
6 Pavilion of the Cross Spring
7 Maxim Gorky Colonnade
8 Municipal Museum
12 Catholic Church
13 Ambrose's Spring
14 Rudolph's Pavilion
15 Former Casino
16 New Baths
17 Town Hall/Bank
19 Supraphon
20 Anglican Church
24 City Bus Station/City Service
25 St Vladimír Orthodox Church
27 Post Office
28 Gambling Casino
33 Ferdinand's Spring
34 Rudolph's Spring
35 Dyleň Supermarket
36 Railway Station
37 Bus Station
To Golf Course & Karlovy Vary
To Cheb
To Plzeň
Mírové
Chopinova
Ibsenova
Mírové
Masarykova
Lesní
Karlovarská
Karlovarská
Karlovarská
Lázeňská
Jos Hakena
Ruská
Reitenbergerova
Dusíkova
Dusíkova
Ruská
Hlavní Třída
Poštovní
Anglická
Dykova
Český armády
Ruská
Anglická
Tyršova
B Němcové
Chebská
Máchova
Dobrovského
Husova
Český armády
U Nemocnice
Nákladní
Hlavní Třída
Plzeňská

among the stone structures and old trees while reading incomprehensible explanations in Czech.

In front of the museum is the circular **Catholic church** (1848), and just south of it are **Rudolph's Pavilion** (1823), the former casino (now a social club), and the **New Baths** (1895).

In a park just north-west of the centre is the **Pavilion of the Forest Spring** (1869), with bronze statues of Goethe and Ulrika nearby. Down towards the railway you'll find **Ferdinand's Spring** and **Rudolph's Spring**.

Places to Stay

Camping *Autocamp Luxor* (☎ 35 04) is at Velká Hled'sebe, four km south-west of the train station by a roundabout route (take a taxi there if you can). It's open from May to September.

Private Rooms There's plenty of accommodation in Mariánské Lázně but in midsummer everything will be taken. If so, visit Čedok, Třebízského třída, which has private rooms. You must, however, rent them for a minimum of five days.

The City Service Tourist Office (☎ 42 18) on Hlavní třída at the city bus station also has private rooms.

Hostels Just south of Motel Start on Plzeňská is *TJ Lokomotiva*, a sports centre with inexpensive dorm beds. You must arrive and register between 5 pm and 9 pm.

The *CKM 'Krakonoš' Juniorhotel* (☎ 26 24) is at the top of the chairlift next to Koliba Restaurant, six km north-east of the stations (take bus No 12 from the city bus station opposite Hotel Excelsior to the door). It's US$16/25 single/double with shower in the old building, US$28/41 with toilet and shower in the new building. Hostel cardholders pay US$9 per person in the old building, US$11 per person in the new building. Most of the rooms are doubles. Breakfast is included in all rates.

Motel & Pensions On Plzeňská beside the stadium, only a five-minute walk from the stations, is *Motel Start* (☎ 20 62). Foreigners pay US$17 per person to stay in this plain, prefabricated building without any of the character of the town's other hotels – poor value. The walls between the rooms are made of a cardboard-like material.

Pension Martina (☎ 36 47), Jiráskova ulice 6, on the way into town from the train station, rents small flats with shared bath at US$18 double (no singles). In this vicinity are several other small pensions (actually just private rooms with a sign outside).

Hotels Lots of fine old hotels line Hlavní třída on the way into town from the train station. The first you reach is *Hotel Haná* (☎ 27 53), Český armády 48, at US$25 double (no singles). Their restaurant is good. The *Slovanský Dům Hotel*, Český armády 22, has recently been restored.

The *Cristal Palace Hotel* (☎ 20 56), Hlavní třída 2, costs US$19/37/48 single/double/triple without bath, US$52 double with bath, breakfast included.

The *Atlantic Hotel* (☎ 59 11), at Hlavní třída 26, is US$24/34 a single/double without bath, US$31/49 with bath, breakfast included, and the *Corso Hotel* (☎ 30 91), Hlavní třída 16, charges US$17/28 a single/double without bath, US$45 for a double with bath.

Two large hotels on Ruská, a back street above Hlavní třída, cater mostly to Czechs (who pay a third as much as you will). The *Hotel Kossuth* (☎ 28 61), Ruská 20, is US$17/22 single/double without bath, US$19/25 with bath. The *Hotel Suvorov* (☎ 27 59), Ruská 18, is also US$17/22 for a single/double without bath or US$54 for a two-room, five-bed apartment.

One of the cheapest regular hotels is the *Europe* (☎ 20 63), Třebízského třída 2, with rooms at US$13/20/27 single/double/triple without bath, US$20/31/40 with bath. In fact, everything about the Europe is slightly cheaper.

In midsummer, all hotel prices are significantly increased.

Places to Eat

The *Jalta Vinárna*, upstairs on Hlavní třída, next to Hotel Corso, serves good food.

The *Classic Restaurant*, Hlavní třída 50 next to the Excelsior Hotel, is good for a filling German-style breakfast of cold meats and cheeses. Their lunch and dinner menus have a special vegetarian section, plus assorted salads and reasonable meat dishes.

The *Zahradní Pivnice* is a German-style beer garden well hidden behind the Atlantic Hotel.

The *Koliba*, on ulice Dušíkova at the north-eastern edge of town, is an up-market, folk-style restaurant.

Entertainment

Check the *N V Gogol Theatre* (1868) for musical programmes. Many events are held at *Chopin Haus*, Hlavní třída 30.

The International Music Festival in May and July and the Chopin Festival in August are special events to ask about at Supraphon, Hlavní třída 30.

Discos The *American Night Club* in the Corso Hotel, Hlavní třída 16, is fine for the over 40s crowd, while the *Havana Club* in the Atlantic Hotel, Hlavní třída 26, is a bit better. The city youth, however, favour the *Cristal Club Disco* in the Cristal Palace Hotel, Hlavní třída 2, which is usually good fun for everyone.

Getting There & Away

There are direct buses between Mariánské Lázně and Karlovy Vary (47 km) which take half the time of the local train. If you'd like to stop off somewhere between the spas, choose Bečov nad Teplou, where you'll find a castle in a wooded valley.

Train services to Cheb (30 km, 30 minutes hours) and Plzeň (76 km, 1¼ hours) are good. Most international express trains between Nuremberg and Prague stop at Mariánské Lázně.

PLZEŇ

The city of Plzeň (Pilsen), midway between Prague and Nuremberg, is the capital of West Bohemia. Located at the confluence of four rivers, this town was once an active medieval trading centre. An ironworks was founded at Plzeň in 1859, which Emil Škoda purchased 10 years later. The Škoda Engineering Works became a producer of high-quality armaments which attracted heavy bombing at the end of WW II. The rebuilt Škoda Works now produces machinery, locomotives and nuclear reactors.

Beer has been brewed at Plzeň for 700 years and the town is famous as the original home of Pilsner. The only genuine Pilsner trademark is Plzeňský Prazdroj, or Pilsner Urquell in its export variety. Although the emphasis is on industry, Plzeň has sights enough to keep you busy for a day. Devoted beer drinkers will not regret the pilgrimage.

Orientation

The main train station, Hlavní nádraží, is on the east side of town. The Central Autobus nádraží is west of the centre on Husova ulice, opposite the Škoda Works. Between these is the old town, which is centred around náměstí Republiky.

Tram No 2 goes from the train station to the centre of town and on to the bus station. The left-luggage office at the bus station is open weekdays from 7.30 am to 6.30 pm, Saturday 5 to 11 am, Sunday 2 to 7 pm. Left luggage at the train station is open 24 hours.

Information

Čedok is at Sedláčkova 12, just off náměstí Republiky.

Motorists in need of assistance can turn to the Autoklub Plzeň (☎ 220 736), Havlíčkova 6, or Autoturist (☎ 220 006), Sady Pětatřicátníků 3.

Money The Komerční Banka, just outside the main entrance to the train station, changes travellers' cheques for 2% commission (weekdays 7 am to 6.30 pm, Saturday until 11.30 am).

Post & Telephone A 24-hour telephone centre is in the main post office at Solní 20. Plzeň's telephone code is 019.

Things to See
The most convenient place to begin sightseeing is on náměstí Republiky, the old town square. Gothic **St Bartholomew Church** in the middle of the square has the highest tower in Bohemia (103 metres); you can climb it daily except Monday. Inside the soaring 13th-century structure are a Gothic Madonna (1390) on the high altar and fine stained-glass windows. On the back of the outer side of the church is an iron grille. Touch the clean angel and make a wish. Outstanding among the many gabled buildings around the square is the Renaissance **town hall** (1558).

An old town house on the east side of the square contains the extensive **Ethnographical Museum** (closed Monday). Just south on Františkanská is the 14th-century **Franciscan church**. Behind this church, around the block, is the **West Bohemian Museum**, with natural history exhibits and paintings (presently closed for renovations).

Beer Lovers Only Plzeň's most interesting sight by far is the **Museum of Beer Brewing** (closed Monday), Veleslavínova ulice 6, north-east of náměstí Republiky. Located in an authentic medieval malt house, the museum displays a fascinating collection of artefacts related to brewing. Ask for the explanatory text in English or German. If all that reading makes you thirsty, visit the *Pivnice na Parkánu*, which is right beside (or behind) the beer museum.

Just around the corner at Perlova 6 is an entrance to one section of the nine km of medieval **underground corridors** below Plzeň. These were originally built as refuges during sieges, hence the numerous wells. Some were later used to store kegs of beer. To enter you must wait for a group of at least five people to gather, then follow them on a boring Czech tour (ask for the text in English). The underground corridors are closed on Monday and Tuesday. The bottle shop at Perova 8 near the entrance to the

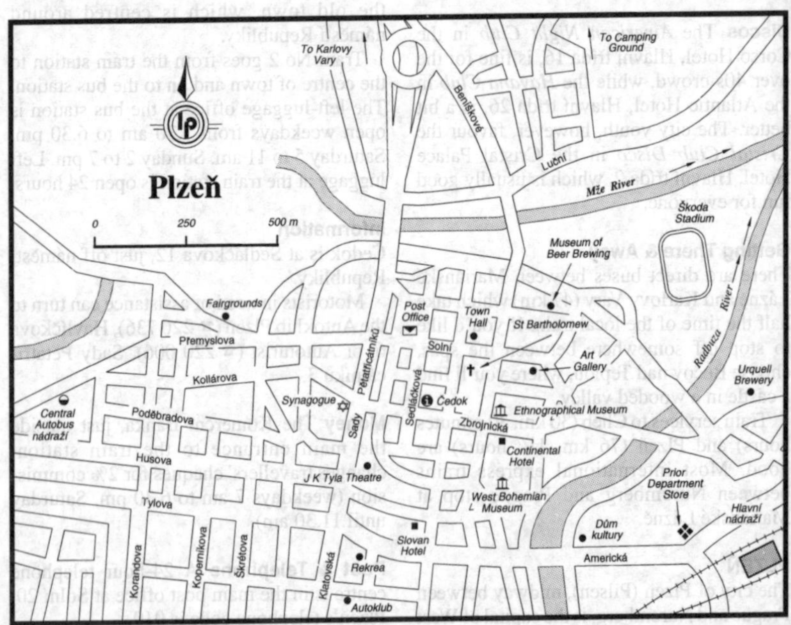

corridors sells takeaway Pilsner Urquell if you get tired of waiting.

The famous **Urquell Brewery** is only a 10-minute walk from here, a little north of Hlavní nádraží. The twin-arched gate dated 1842-92, which appears on every genuine Pilsner label, is here. A tour of the brewing room and fermentation cellar is offered for individuals weekdays at 12.30 (US$1 including a film on the process). Groups are shown through the brewery throughout the day. Near the gate is the *Na spilce Restaurant* with inexpensive meals and brew (Monday to Saturday until 10 pm, Sunday until 9 pm). If you're a vegetarian look for the *sýry* section which lists cheese dishes. This is just the place for a glass of that 12-proof brew.

Places to Stay

Camping The two camping grounds (with bungalows) are at Bílá Hora, five km north of the city (bus No 20). Both are open from May to mid-September.

Hostels The *Sportovní klub učňů* (☎ 282 012) runs a year-round hostel *(ubytovna)* at Vejprnická ulice 56, about three km west of town but easily accessible on tram No 2 (direction Skvrňany) from the train or bus stations. Beds are US$8 per person and everyone is welcome. Ask CKM Student Travel, Dominikánská 1, about this hostel and other accommodation possibilities in student dormitories.

You can also stay at the university residence (☎ 223 049) at Bolevecká 30 just north of town at US$11 per person in double rooms. This 10-storey building can accommodate 500 people. Meals are served and it's open year-round. Get there on tram No 1 from the train station or centre of town. You don't have to be a student to stay there. Čedok, Sedláčkova 12, books beds in this place.

Private Rooms Čedok, Sedláčkova 12, has private rooms for US$6/12 single/double. They don't mind if you only stay a night or two, but the rooms are often full.

Recrea (☎ 35 113), V Špice 6, has private rooms at US$13 per person including breakfast.

Petra Tour (☎ 35 765), Sedláčkova 28 behind the main post office, has private rooms beginning at US$13 per person. Their main advantage is that they're open from 9 am to 7 pm daily and they also change money.

Hotels & Pensions Hotel accommodation in Plzeň is expensive. The B-category *Slovan Hotel* (☎ 227 256), Smetanovy sady 1, a fine old hotel with a magnificent central stairway, is US$30/40/50 single/double/triple, breakfast included.

Also impressive is the *Continental Hotel* (☎ 723 5292), Zbrojnická 8, at US$37/55 single/double with shower, US$54/78 single/double with bathroom, buffet breakfast included. Ask about less expensive rooms without shower. Erected in 1929, the Continental is where you'll find Plzeň's gambling casino. (In 1992 photographer George Janeček from Salt Lake City, Utah, was able to recover the property his family had run until 1945.)

The modern seven-storey *Hotel Central* (☎ 226 757), náměstí Republiky, opposite St Bartholomew Church in the very centre of town, is overpriced at US$37/59 single/double with bath and breakfast.

Better value is *Pension Bárová* (☎ 36 652), Solní 8, in a renovated townhouse just off náměstí Republiky. The three attractive rooms with bath are US$19/32 single/double. *Pension Diaja*, Riegrova ulice 10 right behind Hotel Central, is similar (but with no tram noise).

Places to Eat

Finding a good cheap place to eat in Plzeň is much easier than finding somewhere to sleep.

S & S Grill, Sedláčkova 7, half a block from Čedok, is a private place with attractive décor and great barbecued chicken priced by weight.

Fénix Bistro, náměstí Republiky 18, is an

CZECH REPUBLIC

inexpensive self-service and *Jakko Grill Bar*, náměstí Republiky 14, is also good.

The *Restaurace Na spilce*, at the Urquell Brewery, serves inexpensive meals. The enormous fin-de-siecle restaurant in Hlavní nádraží is another good choice.

Entertainment

For entertainment, try the *J K Tyla Theatre* (1902) or the ultramodern *Dům kultury* beside the river. There's a disco in the basement at the *Continental Hotel*.

Getting There & Away

All international trains from Munich (330 km via Furth im Wald, 5½ hours) and Nuremberg (257 km via Cheb, four hours) stop at Plzeň. There are fast trains to České Budějovice (136 km, two hours), Cheb (106 km, two hours) and Prague (114 km, two hours). Train services to Mariánské Lázně (76 km, 1½ hours) are also good, but if you want to go to Karlovy Vary (83 km), take a bus. Buses also run to Mariánské Lázně, Prague and České Budějovice.

South Bohemia

South Bohemia is the most German-looking part of the Czech Republic. The many quaint little towns have a Bavarian or an Austrian flavour, enhanced by some 5000 medieval carp ponds in the surrounding countryside, many of them dating from the Middle Ages. On the Šumava ridge, south-west of Prachatice, is Mt Boubín (1362 metres) with its primeval forest of spruce, pine and beech trees. The Vltava River originates on this plateau.

After WW I, South Bohemia was given to Czechoslovakia on historical grounds, although over half of its population was German and Hitler's claims to the area nearly touched off war in 1938. After WW II the Germans had to leave and the region became Czech, though Germanic touches linger in the hearty food and drink. Well off the beaten track, South Bohemia is overflowing with history.

ČESKÉ BUDĚJOVICE

České Budějovice (Budweis), the regional capital of South Bohemia, is a charming medieval city halfway between Plzeň and Vienna. Here the Vltava River meets the Malše and flows northwards to Prague. Founded in 1265, České Budějovice controlled the importation of salt and wine from Austria and was a Catholic stronghold in the 15th century. Nearby silver mines made the town rich in the 16th century. After a fire in 1641 much was rebuilt in the baroque style. In 1832 the first horse-drawn railway on the Continent arrived at České Budějovice from Linz, Austria, which is directly south.

High-quality Koh-i-Noor pencils are made here but the city is more famous as the original home of Budweiser beer (Budvar to the Czechs).

České Budějovice is a perfect base for day trips to dozens of nearby attractions, so settle in for a couple of days. Picturesque little Bohemian towns within easy commuting distance include Český Krumlov, Jindřichův Hradec, Písek, Prachatice, Tábor and Třeboň.

Orientation & Information

It's a 10-minute walk west down Lannova třída from the adjacent bus and train stations to náměstí Přemysla Otakara II, the centre of town. There's a left-luggage office is at the bus station (weekdays 6.30 am to 6.30 pm, Saturday until 2 pm, Sunday 2 to 6 pm).

The tourist information office next to the town hall on náměstí Přemysla Otakara II sells maps of towns all around the Czech Republic and is good at answering questions.

The flashy Čedok office at náměstí Přemysla Otakara II 39, upstairs above the casino, is hard to find and the staff is only interested in selling travel services. CKM Student Travel, Karla IV 14, is similar.

Motorists can turn to the Jihočeský Autoklub (☎ 36 177), Žižkova třída 13.

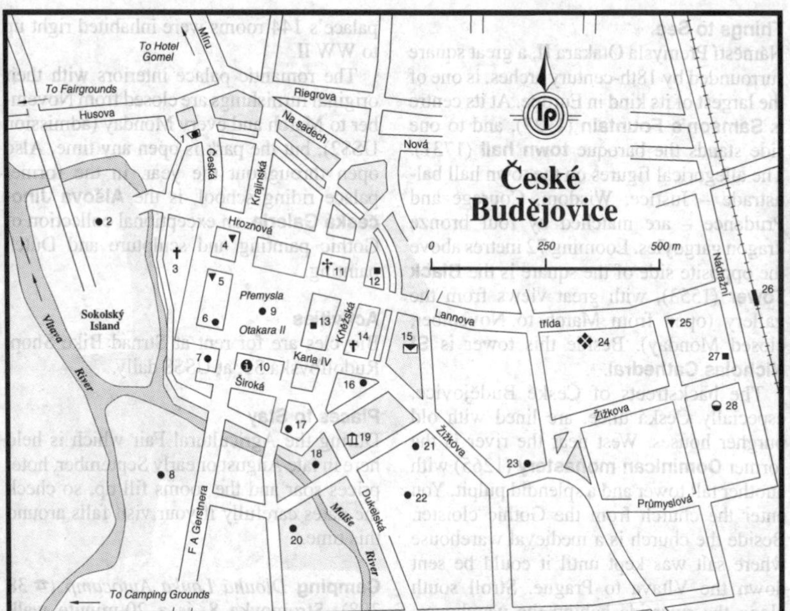

PLACES TO STAY

12 Super Pension
13 Zvon Hotel
27 Grand Hotel

PLACES TO EAT

4 Masné Krámy Beer Hall
5 Cukárna U kláštera
25 Bufet Central

OTHER

1 Rabenstein Tower
2 Sports Stadium
3 Dominican Monastery
6 Town Hall
7 Bishop's Residence
8 Open-Air Theatre
9 Samson's Fountain
10 Čedok
11 St Nicholas Cathedral
14 St Anne's Church & Concert Hall
15 Post Office
16 CKM Student Travel
17 Jihočeské Theatre
18 Městský Dům kultury
19 Museum of South Bohemia
20 State Library
21 Dům kultury
22 Divadelní Sál DK
23 Jihočeský Autoklub
24 Prior Department Store
26 Railway Station
28 Bus Station

Money The Komerční Banka, Krajinská 19, next to Masné Krámy Beer Hall, changes travellers' cheques. It charges 2% commission for the service. Its opening hours are weekdays from 7 am to 5 pm and Saturdays from 9 am until noon.

Post & Telephone The main post office, on Senovážné náměstí, has a telephone centre which is open weekdays from 6 am to 9 pm, Saturday 7 am to 4.30 pm and Sunday noon to 4.30 pm. České Budějovice's telephone code is 038.

Things to See

Náměstí Přemysla Otakara II, a great square surrounded by 18th-century arches, is one of the largest of its kind in Europe. At its centre is **Samson's Fountain** (1727), and to one side stands the baroque **town hall** (1731). The allegorical figures on the town hall balustrade – Justice, Wisdom, Courage and Prudence – are matched by four bronze dragon gargoyles. Looming 72 metres above the opposite side of the square is the **Black Tower** (1553), with great views from the gallery (open from March to November, closed Monday). Beside this tower is **St Nicholas Cathedral**.

The backstreets of České Budějovice, especially Česká ulice, are lined with old burgher houses. West near the river is the former **Dominican monastery** (1265) with another tall tower and a splendid pulpit. You enter the church from the Gothic cloister. Beside the church is a medieval warehouse where salt was kept until it could be sent down the Vltava to Prague. Stroll south along the riverside behind the warehouse, past the remaining sections of the 16th-century walls. The **Museum of South Bohemia** (closed Monday) is just south of the old town.

To visit the **Budvar Brewery** you're supposed to make arrangements in advance by calling ☎ 24 027, extension 338. In fact, this brewery is in an industrial area several km north of the centre (bus No 2 or 6) and lacks the picturesque appearance of the Urquell Brewery in Plzeň. Although it could become easier to visit in future as tourism is developed, it's unlikely to ever become a big attraction.

Hluboká nad Vltavou One side trip not to miss takes in the neo-Gothic Tudor palace at Hluboká nad Vltavou (Frauenberg), 10 km north, which is easily accessible by bus. There used to be a castle here that was built in the 13th century, but between 1841 and 1871 the landowning Schwarzenberg family rebuilt the edifice in the style of Windsor Castle and laid out the extensive park. The palace's 144 rooms were inhabited right up to WW II.

The romantic palace interiors with their original furnishings are closed from November to March and every Monday (admission US$2), but the park is open any time. Also open throughout the year, in the former palace riding school, is the **Alšova Jihočeská Galerie**, an exceptional collection of Gothic painting and sculpture and Dutch painting.

Activities

Bicycles are for rent at Strnad Bike Shop, Rudolfovská 31, at US$8 daily.

Places to Stay

During the Agricultural Fair which is held here in late August or early September, hotel prices soar and the rooms fill up, so check the dates carefully if your visit falls around this time.

Camping *Dlouhá Louka Autocamp* (☎ 38 308), Stromovka 8, is a 20-minute walk south-west of town (bus No 6 from in front of Dům Kultury). Tent space is available here from May to September, and motel rooms (US$36 double with breakfast) are available all year. The showers are clean and the water hot, but beware of bar prices. The restaurant is said to be good.

The *Stromovka Autocamp* (☎ 53 402 or 28 877), just beyond Dlouhá Louka Autocamp, has three-person bungalows for US$12, four-person units for US$16 (open from April to October).

Hostels CKM Student Travel, Karla IV 14, arranges accommodation at the *Škoda Ubytovna*, a high-rise hostel outside town, at US$10 per person in double rooms with bath. You must book and pay at the CKM office (weekdays 9 am to 5 pm). Also ask about the *Branišovská student hostel* (off Husova west of the centre), open in July and August only.

Private Rooms Čedok, náměstí Přemysla Otakara II 39, has private rooms at US$13 per person with breakfast, but not in the centre.

The best place to go for a private room is CTS Travel Service (☎ 25 061), upstairs at Krajinská 1 just off the main square. Rooms begin at US$7 per person, some of them in the old town, and the friendly, helpful staff will show you colour photos of the various possibilities. They can also book rooms in Český Krumlov and elsewhere in South Bohemia. They're open weekdays from 9 am to 6 pm, Saturday until 2 pm year-round, with extended hours from June to September (including Sunday from 9 am to 2 pm). You'd do well to check with them first.

Pensions Small private pensions around České Budějovice are a better deal than the hotels, but the quality varies, so you ought to ask to see the room before accepting it. Often a place will only have one or two rooms and will take in the sign as soon as they're rented, so you just have to walk around the old town looking. An example of this is *Pension Suchánek* (☎ 33 292), Česká 34, behind the Masné Krámy Beer Hall, which charges about US$25 double with bath.

Also check *Super Pension* (☎ 52 030), Mlýnská stoka 6, just off Kanovnická as you enter the old town. The owner doesn't live here, so you'll be lucky to find anyone to let you in.

Hotels The *Hotel Grand* (☎ 56 503), Nádražní 27 opposite the train station, is US$29/36 single/double with bath.

The *Zvon Hotel* (☎ 55 361), náměstí Přemysla Otakara II 28, is good value at US$20/30 single/double without bath, US$35/54 with bath, showers are US$2 extra. The Zvon has been expanded and upgraded in recent years.

Places to Eat

Try the local carp which is on many restaurant menus.

About the best place in town for a colourful meal is the *'Masné Krámy' beer hall* in the old meat market (1560), on the corner of Hroznová and 5 května. It's touristy but good.

A more locally oriented beer hall in this town of beer is *Restaurace Na Dvorku*, Kněžská 11 across from the Concert Hall. If Na Dvorku looks too raucous check out the more up-market *V Loubé*, Kněžská 15.

If Chinese cuisine is your fancy, try the *Čínska Restaurant*, Hroznova 18 near the Black Tower.

Bufet Central, Lannova třída 32, is a good place for a self-service breakfast on the way to the train station as they open at 6 am weekdays and 7 am Saturday (closed Sunday).

Cafés The *Cukrárna U kláštera*, Piaristická 18 just off the main square, is great for coffee and cakes (closed Sunday).

Café filharmonie in the concert hall, Kněžská at Karla IV, is perhaps České Budějovice's most elegant café.

Entertainment

České Budějovice has two cultural centres, both near the Museum of South Bohemia. The old *Městský Dům kultury* is by the river, and another *Dům kultury* is on the square behind the museum. You've a better chance of hearing music at the *Divadelní Sál DK* behind this newer Dům kultury.

The *Jihočeské Theatre*, by the river on ulice Dr Stejskala, presents mostly plays in Czech, but operas, operettas and concerts are also on their calendar, so check. *St Anne's Church*, Kněžská 6, functions as České Budějovice's concert hall.

There's a disco in the *Grand Hotel* across the street from the train station.

Getting There & Away

There are fast trains to Plzeň (136 km, two hours), Tábor (66 km, one hour), Prague (169 km, 2½ hours) and Jihlava (132 km, two hours). For shorter distances you're better off travelling by bus. The bus to Brno (182 km, four hours) travels via Telč (100 km, two hours).

Twice a day there's a train to/from Linz, Austria (125 km, three hours, US$12). On three other occasions you can go to Linz with a change of trains at the border stations (Horní Dvořiště and Summerau). Connections with trains between Prague and Vienna are made at České Velenice, 50 km south-east of České Budějovice. One daily train runs directly to/from Vienna (Franz-Josefsbahnhof).

A bus to Vienna's Mitte Bahnhof (US$7) departs from České Budějovice Bus Station on Friday, and to Linz post office (US$3) via Český Krumlov on Wednesday and Saturday. In July and August this bus operates daily except Sunday and two buses go on to Salzburg. Pay the driver.

ČESKÝ KRUMLOV

Český Krumlov (Krumau), a small medieval town 25 km south of České Budějovice, is one of the most picturesque towns in Europe, its appearance almost unchanged since the 18th century. Built on an S-shaped bend of the Vltava River, the 13th-century castle occupies a ridge along the left bank. The old town centre sits on the high tongue of land on the right bank. South-west are the Šumava Mountains, which separate Bohemia from Austria and Bavaria.

Český Krumlov's Gothic border castle, rebuilt into a huge Renaissance chateau by 16th-century Italian architects, is second only to Prague Castle as a fortified Bohemian palace and citadel. The Renaissance lords of Rožmberk (Rosenberg) seated here possessed the largest landed estate in Bohemia, which passed to the Eggenbergs in 1622 and to the Schwarzenbergs in 1719. Though Český Krumlov is an easy day trip from České Budějovice, there are several places to stay should you care to linger.

Information

The Tourist Service, Zámek 57, sells maps from all over. Ask for local author and staff member Richard Franz who speaks good English and can answer any question about this region. Čedok is at Latrán 75.

Money The Komerční Banka, Latrán 20, changes travellers' cheques for 2% commission (weekdays from 9 am to noon and 1 to 5 pm, Saturday 9 am to noon).

Post & Telephone You can make phone calls from the post office, Latrán 81, weekdays from 7 am to 6.30 pm, Saturday until 1 pm. Český Krumlov's telephone code is 0337.

Things to See

Get off the bus from České Budějovice at Český Krumlov Špičák, the first stop in town. Just above this stop is **Budějovická Gate** (1598), which leads directly into the old town. On the right, two blocks south, is the **castle** entrance. The oldest part of the castle is the lower section with its distinctive round tower, but it's the massive upper castle which contains the palace halls that are open to visitors. It is said that the castle is haunted by a white lady who appears from time to time to forecast doom.

Just across the high bridge behind the palace is the unique rococo **chateau theatre** (1767). Behind this, a ramp to the right leads up to the former **riding school**, now a restaurant. Cherubs above the door offer the head and boots of a vanquished Turk. Above this are the Italian-style castle **gardens**. The **'Bellarie' summer pavilion** and a modern revolving open-air theatre are features of these gardens. The castle interiors are open from April to October only (visits are only conducted when a group forms), but you can walk through the courtyards and gardens almost any time.

On náměstí Svornosti across the river in the old town are the Gothic **town hall** and a baroque plague column (1716). Just above the square is **St Vitus Church** (1439), a striking Gothic hall church. Nearby is the **Regional Museum** (closed Monday) with a surprisingly good collection housed in the old Jesuit seminary (1652). The scale model of Český Krumlov as it was in 1800 is a highlight. Continue in the same direction, turn left and you'll soon find the autobusové nádraží (bus station) and a bus back to České Budějovice. (You might ask directions as this bus station is not visible from the main road and is easy to miss.) There's a great view of town from near the bus station.

Activities

The Tourist Service (☎ 46 05), Zámek 57, knows about yachting possibilities on Upper Lipno Lake, south-west of Český Krumlov (about US$15 a day for three or four people). There are also canoe and rubber raft rentals in Vyšší Brod which allow you to paddle down the Vltava River 32 km to Český Krumlov in one day or all the way to České Budějovice in two days (US$22 a day). Tourist Service just outside the castle gate can arrange all this.

Several places around town rent bicycles and it's a pleasant two-hour ride south-west to Lake Lipno, involving a climb then a drop to the lake and a great downhill on the way back. There's a nice casual café in Horní Planá on the north shore where you can get lunch. If the weather turns bad you can take your bike back to Český Krumlov from Horní Planá by train (six times a day).

Places to Stay

Camping The camping ground is on the

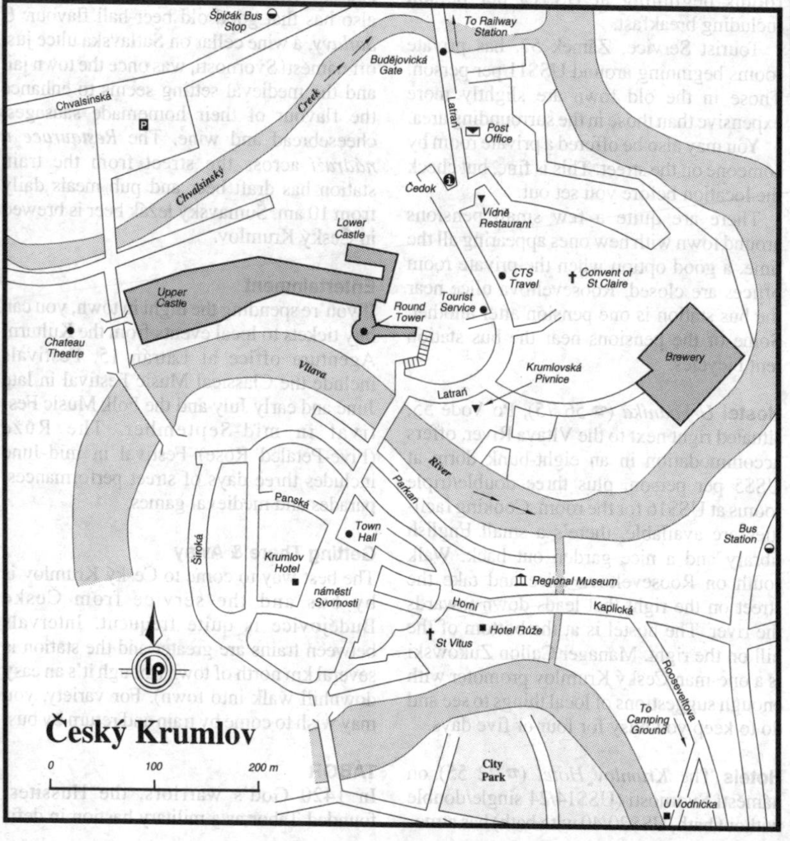

right (east) bank of the Vltava River about two km south of town. The facilities are basic but the management is friendly, the location idyllic and the tariff reasonable. The owners organise one-hour canoe trips down the river through a series of weirs and white-water stretches at US$5 per person (minimum of four).

Private Rooms & Pensions CTS Travel Service (☎ 28 21), Latrán 67, has private rooms from US$9 per person. They also rent bicycles and canoes in summer, and are happy to answer questions anytime.

Čedok (☎ 34 44), Latrán 75, has private rooms beginning at US$13 per person including breakfast.

Tourist Service, Zámek 57, has private rooms beginning around US$11 per person. Those in the old town are slightly more expensive than those in the surrounding area.

You may also be offered a private room by someone on the street. This is fine, but check the location before you set out.

There are quite a few small pensions around town with new ones appearing all the time, a good option when the private room offices are closed. Rooseveltova ulice near the bus station is one pension after another. Some of the pensions near the bus station rent bicycles.

Hostel *U Vodníka* (☎ 56 75), Po Vodě 55, situated right next to the Vltava River, offers accommodation in an eight-bunk dorm at US$5 per person, plus three double/triple rooms at US$16 for the room. Cooking facilities are available, there's a small English library and a nice garden out back. Walk south on Rooseveltova ulice and take the street on the right that leads down towards the river. The hostel is at the bottom of the hill on the right. Manager Callon Zukowski is a one-man Český Krumlov promoter with enough suggestions of local things to see and do to keep you busy for four or five days.

Hotels The *Krumlov Hotel* (☎ 22 55) on náměstí Svornosti (US$14/24 single/double without bath, US$20/40 with bath) has atmosphere, as does the very expensive *Hotel Růže*, a Jesuit college building dating from 1588, which is opposite the Regional Museum.

Hotel Vyšehrad (☎ 53 11), a three-storey hotel on a hill north of town between the train station and the centre, has rooms with shower at US$14/20 single/double. Several pension signs are near the hotel.

Places to Eat

The breakfast served at the Krumlov Hotel's restaurant is good. For lunch try the *Krumlovská Pivnice*, Latrán 13, below the castle. Their English menu includes fried cheese. The *Vídně Restaurant*, Latrán 78, also has that good old beer-hall flavour. *U Šatlavy*, a wine cellar on Šatlavska ulice just off náměstí Svornosti, was once the town jail and the medieval setting seems to enhance the flavour of their homemade sausages, cheesebread and wine. The *Restaurace u nádraží* across the street from the train station has draft beer and pub meals daily from 10 am. Šumavský ležák beer is brewed in Český Krumlov.

Entertainment

If you're spending the night in town, you can buy tickets to local events from the Kulturní Agentura office at Latrán 15. Festivals include the Classical Music Festival in late June and early July and the Folk Music Festival in mid-September. The Růže (Five-Petaled Rose) Festival in mid-June includes three days of street performances, parades and medieval games.

Getting There & Away

The best way to come to Český Krumlov is by bus and the service from České Budějovice is quite frequent. Intervals between trains are greater and the station is several km north of town (though it's an easy downhill walk into town). For variety, you may wish to come by train and return by bus.

TÁBOR

In 1420 God's warriors, the Hussites, founded Tábor as a military bastion in defiance of Catholic Europe. The town was organised according to the biblical precept that 'nothing is mine and nothing is yours, because the community is owned equally by everyone'. New arrivals threw all their worldly possessions into large casks at the marketplace and joined in communal work. This extreme nonconformism helped to give the word Bohemian the connotations we associate with it today.

Planned as a bulwark against Catholic reactionaries in České Budějovice and farther south, Tábor is a warren of narrow broken streets with protruding houses which were intended to weaken and shatter an enemy attack. Below ground, catacombs totalling 14 km provided a refuge for the defenders. This friendly old town, 100 km south of Prague, is well worth a brief stop.

Orientation & Information

From the train station walk west through the park between Hotel Bohemia and the bus station. Continue west down ulice 9 května until you reach a major intersection. Žižkovo náměstí, the old town square, is straight ahead on Palackého třída, a 15-minute walk from the stations. The left-luggage office at the bus station closes at 7 pm, so it's better to use the 24-hour facility at the train station.

Čedok is on třída 9 května next to the Palcát Hotel.

Money The Komerční Banka, on třída 9 května halfway into town from the stations, changes travellers' cheques weekdays from 7.30 am to 11.30 am and 1 pm to 4 pm.

Post & Telephone The post office/telephone centre is in the pink building on the opposite side of Žižkovo náměstí from the museum.

Tábor's telephone code is 0361.

Things to See

A statue of the Hussite commander, Jan Žižka, graces Žižkovo náměstí, Tábor's main square. Žižka's military successes were due to the novel use of armoured wagons against crusading Catholic knights. Around the square are the homes of rich burghers, spanning the period from late Gothic to baroque. On the north side is the Gothic **Church of the Transfiguration of Our Lord on Mt Tábor** (built in 1440-1512) with Renaissance gables and a baroque tower (1677).

The other imposing building on Žižkovo náměstí is the early Renaissance town hall (1521), now the **Museum of the Hussite Movement** (closed Monday), with the entrance to a visitable 650-metre stretch of the underground passages. You can visit the underground passages daily except Monday from April to October, but only when a group of 15 people forms. The passages, constructed in the 15th century as refuges during fires or times of war, were also used to store food and to mature lager.

The arch at Žižkovo náměstí 22, beside the old town hall, leads into Mariánská ulice and then Klokotská ulice, which runs south-west to the **Bechyně Gate**, now a small historical museum (closed Monday) which focuses on the life of the peasants. Kotnov Castle, founded here in the 12th century, was destroyed by fire in 1532; in the 17th century the ruins were made into a brewery which is still operating. The castle's remaining 15th-century round tower may be climbed from the Bechyně Gate museum for a sweeping view of Tábor, the Lužnice River and the surrounding area.

Places to Stay

Private Rooms & Pensions Though you can easily visit Tábor as a stopover between Prague and České Budějovice, there are several places to stay. Čedok (☎ 22 235) on třída 9 května has private rooms at US$18 double (no singles).

The Inforcentrum (☎ 23 401), Křižíkovo náměstí 505, corner of třída 9 května near the entrance to the old town, has private rooms at US$5 to US$20 per person.

If you arrive at night or on a weekend when these offices are closed, walk into town looking for pension signs. One place advertising such rooms is at třída 9 května 569, not far from the stations.

CZECH REPUBLIC

Hotels Hotel accommodation is expensive. The old Hotel Slavia, opposite the adjacent bus and train stations, has been done up and renamed *Hotel Bohemia* (☎ 22 827), Husovo náměstí 591. Prices have been increased four times to US$42 single or double without bath, breakfast included. For a room with private bath you'll pay a rip-off US$50/100 single/double (about six times what it was just a couple of years ago).

The other hotels are on 9 května, between the stations and the town centre. You first come to the red-brick, neo-Gothic *Slovan Hotel* (☎ 23 435), ulice 9 května 678, which charges US$16/32 for singles/doubles with shared bath (US$2 extra for a shower). Next is the modern *Palcát Hotel* (☎ 22 901), ulice 9 května 2471/2, a modern six-storey hotel where German tour groups always stay (US$37/57 single/double with shower and breakfast).

Places to Eat

A good place for a quick lunch is the *Pizza Restaurant*, Široká ulice 159, to the left off Palackého třída just before you reach Žižkovo náměstí.

A more pretentious choice would be the *Beseda Restaurant* next to the church on Žižkovo náměstí.

Entertainment

Tábor's two theatres, the *Městské Divadlo* and *Divadla Oskara Nedbala*, are next to one another on Palackého třída.

Getting There & Away

Tábor is on the main railway line between Prague and Vienna. The line from České Budějovice to Prague also passes through here. Local trains run to Pelhřimov.

To go from Tábor to Telč by train you must change at Horní Cerekev and Kostelec u Jihlavy, and although the connections are fairly good, the whole 107-km trip by local train takes three or four hours through unspoiled countryside. Otherwise take a bus to Jihlava (74 km) and another bus on to Telč (29 km) from there.

To go to Plzeň (113 km) or Brno (158 km) you're better off taking a bus. Eastbound buses to Jihlava and Brno leave only every couple of hours and the posted timetable bears numerous footnotes, so reconfirm your departure time at the information window.

Moravia

Moravia, the other historic land of the Czech Republic, is usually overlooked by tourists visiting Bohemia. This is an attraction in itself, but Moravia also has its own history and natural beauties, such as the karst area north of Brno. The theatres and art galleries of Brno, the capital, are excellent, and quaint towns like Kroměříž, Mikulov, Telč and Znojmo await discovery. The Moravian Gate between Břeclav and Ostrava is a natural corridor between Poland and the Danube basin. Heavy industry is concentrated in North Moravia, which is next to Polish Silesia, whereas fertile South Moravia produces excellent wines. Well placed in the geographical centre of the country, Moravia is a great place to explore.

TELČ

Telč (Teltsch) was founded in the 14th century by the feudal lords of Hradec as a fortified settlement with a castle separated from the town by a strong wall. The artificial ponds on each side of Telč provided security and a sure supply of fish. After a fire in 1530, Lord Zachariáš, then governor of Moravia, ordered the town and castle rebuilt in the Renaissance style by Italian masons. Profits from gold and silver mines allowed Lord and Lady Zachariáš to enjoy a regal lifestyle.

After the death of Zachariáš in 1589, building activity ceased and the complex you see today is largely as it was then. The main square of this loveliest of Czech towns is unmarred by modern constructions, and the fire hall at náměstí Zachariáše z Hradce 28 is poignant evidence of local concern to keep it that way. In 1992 Telč was added to UNESCO's 'world heritage' list. Surprisingly few visitors frequent the narrow, cobbled streets of the fairy-tale town of Telč.

Orientation & Information

The bus and train stations are a few hundred metres apart on the east side of town, a 10-minute walk along ulice Masarykova towards náměstí Zachariáše z Hradce, the old town square.

A left-luggage service is available at the train station 24 hours a day – ask the stationmaster.

There's an information office just inside the town hall.

Money The Česká Spořitelna, náměstí Zachariáše Hradce 21 (Monday and Wednesday 7.30 am to noon and 1 to 5.30 pm; Tuesday, Thursday and Friday 7.30 am to noon), changes travellers' cheques for 1% commission plus US$1 postage.

Post & Telephone The post office is on Staňkova, a block from the train station. The telephone section is open weekdays from 7.30 am to noon and 1 to 5.30 pm, Saturday 8 to 11 am.

Telč's telephone code is 066.

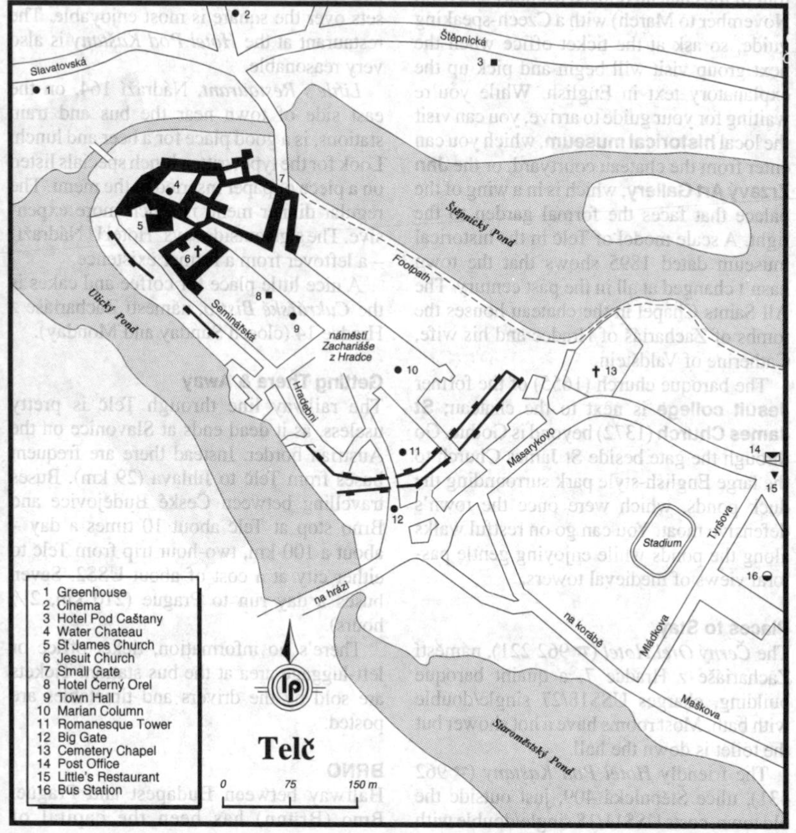

Things to See

Telč's wonderful old town square is surrounded on three sides by 16th-century Renaissance houses built on the ruins of their Gothic predecessors after the 1530 fire. This origin gave the square its basic unity with a covered arcade running almost all the way around it. Though from other eras, the 49-metre Romanesque **tower** east of the square and the baroque **Marian column** (1717) in the square itself do not detract from the town's character.

Telč's greatest monument is the splendid Renaissance **water chateau** (1568) at the square's western end. You can only go on a tour of the chateau (closed Monday and from November to March) with a Czech-speaking guide, so ask at the ticket office when the next group visit will begin and pick up the explanatory text in English. While you're waiting for your guide to arrive, you can visit the local **historical museum**, which you can enter from the chateau courtyard, or the **Jan Zrzavý Art Gallery**, which is in a wing of the palace that faces the formal garden to the right. A scale model of Telč in the historical museum dated 1895 shows that the town hasn't changed at all in the past century. The All Saints Chapel in the chateau houses the tombs of Zachariáš of Hradec and his wife, Catherine of Valdštejn.

The baroque church (1655) of the former **Jesuit college** is next to the chateau; **St James Church** (1372) beyond is Gothic. Go through the gate beside St James Church to the large English-style park surrounding the duck ponds, which were once the town's defensive moat. You can go on restful walks along the ponds while enjoying gentle pastoral views of medieval towers.

Places to Stay

The *Černý Orel Hotel* (☎ 962 221), náměstí Zachariáše z Hradce 7, a quaint baroque building, charges US$18/27 single/double with bath. Most rooms have a hot shower but the toilet is down the hall.

The friendly *Hotel Pod Kaštany* (☎ 962 431), ulice Štěpnická 409, just outside the old town, costs US$11/18 single/double with bath. This hotel tends to be partly occupied by school groups but four rooms are reserved for individuals. The walls are thin here – your neighbours will hear everything. There's a good beer bar attached.

If the Pod Kaštany is full there are several *Zimmer frei* signs advertising private rooms east along Štěpnická. Private rooms are also advertised on the houses at náměstí Zachariáše z Hradce 11, 32 and 53.

Places to Eat

The restaurant at the *Černý Orel Hotel* (closed Monday) is the best in town (try the fresh carp or trout from the local fish ponds) and dinner outside on their terrace as the sun sets over the square is most enjoyable. The restaurant at the *Hotel Pod Kaštany* is also very reasonable.

Little's Restaurant, Nádraží 164, on the east side of town near the bus and train stations, is a good place for a beer and lunch. Look for the typewritten lunch specials listed on a piece of paper inserted in the menu. The regular dinner menu is much more expensive. The sign outside says 'Hotel U Nádraží' – a leftover from a former existence.

A nice little place for coffee and cakes is the *Cukrářské Bistro*, náměstí Zachariáše z Hradce 14 (closed Sunday and Monday).

Getting There & Away

The railway line through Telč is pretty useless, as it dead ends at Slavonice on the Austrian border. Instead there are frequent buses from Telč to Jihlava (29 km). Buses travelling between České Budějovice and Brno stop at Telč about 10 times a day – about a 100-km, two-hour trip from Telč to either city at a cost of about US$2. Seven buses a day run to Prague (210 km, 2½ hours).

There's no information, ticket office or left-luggage area at the bus station. Tickets are sold by the drivers and timetables are posted.

BRNO

Halfway between Budapest and Prague, Brno (Brünn) has been the capital of

Moravia since 1641 and its large fortress was an instrument of Habsburg domination. The botanist Gregor Mendel (1822-84) established the modern science of heredity through his studies of peas and bees carried out at the Augustinian monastery in Brno. After the Brno-Vienna railway was completed in 1839, Brno developed into a major industrial centre.

Brno has a rich cultural life and its compact centre holds a variety of fascinating sights. Most of central Brno is a pedestrian zone which makes browsing around a pleasure. Brno hasn't been overwhelmed by tourism the way Prague has and you're still treated like a normal person, even in the centre of town. Although you can visit Brno in a very busy day, stay longer and delve deeper. If you're a city slicker, you'll like Brno.

Orientation

Brno's main train station is at the southern edge of the old town centre. Opposite the train station is the beginning of Masarykova, a main thoroughfare which trams and pedestrians follow into the triangular náměstí Svobody, the centre of town. The bus station *(autobusové nádraží)* is 800 metres south of the train station, beyond the Prior Department Store. To get to the bus station, go through the pedestrian tunnel under the train tracks, then follow the crowd along the elevated walkway.

There are two 24-hour left-luggage offices in Brno Railway Station, one upstairs opposite the lockers, and another downstairs by the tunnel to the platforms (a good little map shop which also carries train timetables is just opposite the downstairs office). The left-luggage office at the bus station is open daily from 6.15 am to 10 pm.

Information

Čedok is at Divadelní 3. CKM Student Travel is at Česká 11.

The Kulturní a Informační Centrum in the old town hall, Radnická 8, has computers which can answer almost any question. They know about hotel and pension prices and will help you make reservations (open weekdays from 8 am to 6 pm, weekends 9 am to 5 pm).

Motorists can turn to the Autoklub České Republiky (☎ 4221 5030), Bašty 8, or Autoturist (☎ 4321 1913), Pekařská 24.

Money The Komerční Banka has an office inside the train station which changes travellers' cheques for 2% commission with a US$1 minimum (open Monday from 7 am to noon, Tuesday to Friday 7 am to noon and 1 pm to 6 pm, weekends 7 am to 1 pm).

There's also Non-Stop Exchange in the train station which in theory is open 24 hours a day but they take 5% commission on travellers' cheques and give a lower rate.

The Komerční Banka has another exchange office at náměstí Svobody 6 (open weekdays 7.30 am to 5.30 pm).

Post & Telephone The telephone centre in the post office at the western end of the train station is open 24 hours a day. Brno's telephone code is 05.

Consulates The Consulate General of the Russian Federation, Hlinky 146 opposite the fairgrounds, is open Monday, Wednesday and Friday from 9 am to 1 pm.

Travel Agencies České Dráhy Travel Agency next to the international ticket office in the train station sells bus tickets to Western Europe (US$75 to Amsterdam, US$81 to London).

Čedok, Divadelní 3, sells international bus and train tickets (but not domestic train tickets or couchettes).

The Taxatour office in the train station (look for YMCA sign on their door) arranges rides in private cars to Western European cities at favourable rates (for example, Munich US$18, Stuttgart US$27, Bern US$33).

Visa Extensions The foreigners police, Kounicova 24, a northbound extension of Rašínova (Monday and Wednesday 8 am to noon and 1 to 4 pm, Tuesday 8 am to 1 pm, and Friday 7 to 11 am and noon to 3 pm),

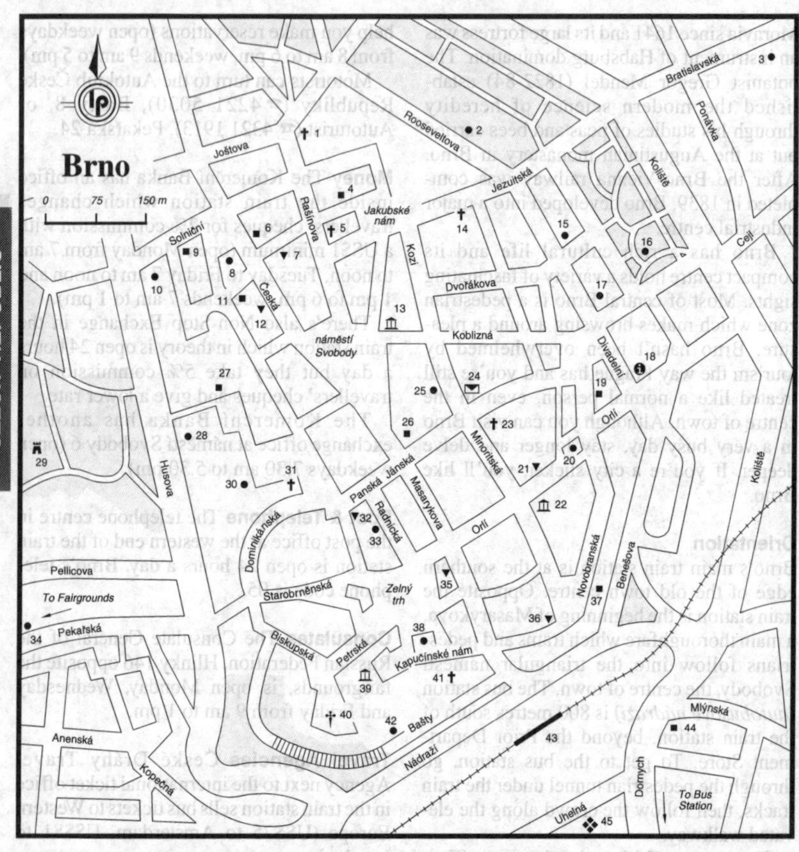

will have information about visa extensions. Also come here to report a lost passport or visa. Look for their separate entrance between the main police station and the post office.

Things to See

As you enter the city on Masarykova, turn left into Kapucínské náměstí to reach the **Capuchin monastery** (1651). In the ventilated crypt (closed Monday) below the church are the intact mummies of monks and local aristocrats deposited here before 1784. At the western end of Kapucínské náměstí is the recently restored Dietrichstein Palace (1760), with the **South Moravian Museum** (closed Monday).

The street in front of the monastery soon leads into Zelný trh and its colourful **open-air market**. Carp used to be sold from the waters of the baroque Parnassus Fountain (1695) at Christmas. The **Reduta Theatre**, also on Zelný trh, is where Mozart performed in 1767 and the operettas presented at the Reduta are still excellent.

On ulice Radnická, just off the northern side of Zelný trh, is Brno's 13th-century **old town hall**, which has a splendid Gothic

PLACES TO STAY

4 Hotel U Jakuba
6 Hotel Avion
9 Slavia Hotel
11 Bulharský klub
19 Astoria Hotel
26 Europa Hotel
27 International Hotel
37 Grand Hotel
44 Metropol Hotel

PLACES TO EAT

7 Pivnice Pegas
12 Stopkova plzeňská pivnice/Sputnik
21 Baroko Vinárna
32 Vinárna U zlatěho meče
35 Pizzera Sorento
36 Restaurace Gourmand

OTHER

1 St Thomas Church
2 Janáček Theatre
3 Radost Puppet Theatre
5 St James Church
8 CKM Student Travel
10 Beseda Concert Hall
13 Ethnographical Museum
14 Jesuit Church
15 Předprodej (Theatre Ticket Office)
16 City Art Gallery
17 Mahenovo Theatre
18 Čedok
20 Měnín Gate
22 Technological Museum
23 St John's Church
24 Main Post Office
25 Metro Night Club
28 Moravian Gallery of Applied Art
29 Špilberk Castle
30 New Town Hall
31 St Michael's Church
33 Old Town Hall
34 Autoturist
38 Reduta Theatre
39 South Moravian Museum
40 Cathedral of Sts Peter & Paul
41 Capuchin Monastery
42 Autoklub Česke Republiky
43 Main Railway Station
45 Prior Department Store

portal (1511) below the tower (which is well worth climbing for the small fee). Inside the passage behind the portal are a stuffed crocodile, or 'dragon', and a wheel, traditional symbols of the city. Legend tells how the dragon once terrorised wayfarers approaching the nearby Svratka River; the wheel was supposedly made by a cartwright in league with the devil.

Continue north and take a sharp left to **St Michael's Church** (1679) and the former Dominican convent. Facing the square on the far side of the church is the 16th-century **new town hall** with its impressive courtyard, stairways and frescos. Around the corner at ulice Husova 14 is the **Moravian Gallery of Applied Art** (closed Monday).

In the large park on the hill above this gallery is the sinister silhouette of **Špilberk Castle**, founded in the 13th century and converted into a citadel and prison during the 17th century. Until 1855 opponents of the Habsburgs were held here, including the Italian poet Silvio Pellico and other members of the Carbonari (an Italian secret political society which fought for the unification of Italy). Sections of the castle and the castle museum are closed for restoration but you can visit the casemates (closed Monday). There's a good view from the ramparts.

From the park surrounding the castle go south on Husova one block to Šilingrovo náměstí on the left. There look for an unmarked street in the south-east corner of the square which leads directly towards an old five-storey green building; this is Biskupská ulice which will take you up Petrov Hill to neo-Gothic **Cathedral of Sts Peter & Paul**, which is hidden behind high buildings. The cathedral, rebuilt in the late 19th century on the site of an older basilica, occupies the site where the city's original castle stood. The Renaissance **bishop's palace** adjoins the cathedral. In 1645 the Swedish general Torstensson who was besieging Brno declared that he would leave if his troops hadn't captured the city by noon. At 11 am the Swedes were about to scale the walls when the cathedral bell keeper suddenly rang noon. True to his word, the general broke off the attack; since that day the cathedral bells have always rung noon at 11 am.

From Petrov Hill descend Petrská into Zelný trh and continue on ulice Orlí to the **Technological Museum** (closed Monday),

CZECH REPUBLIC

another Brno curiosity. Buy a ticket for the Panorama, a rare apparatus installed here in 1890 which offers continuous showings of the wonders of the world in 3-D. Every couple of weeks the programme is changed so there are lots of regular visitors. Nearby on ulice Minoritská is **St John's Church** (rebuilt in 1733) with fine altarpieces, an organ and painted ceilings.

On nearby náměstí Svobody is a striking plague column (1680). At ulice Kobližná 1 in a corner of the square is the **Ethnographical Museum** (closed Monday) which has Moravian folk costumes and implements. Just north is the parish church, **St James** (1473), with a soaring nave in the purest Gothic style. This is Brno's most powerful church. **St Thomas Church** and the former **Augustinian monastery**, now an art gallery (closed Monday), are just north of St James.

Also worth seeing is the **City Art Gallery** (Dům umění), Malinovského náměstí 2, beside the Mahenovo Theatre. Excellent art exhibitions are sometimes staged in this gallery (closed Monday, free Wednesday).

Slavkov u Brna On 2 December 1805 the famous 'Battle of the Three Emperors' took place in the open, rolling countryside between Brno and Slavkov u Brna (Austerlitz). Here Napoleon Bonaparte, a product of emerging bourgeois capitalism, defeated the combined armies of Emperor Franz I (Austria) and Tsar Alexander I (Russia), defenders of the aristocratic, feudal past. The battle was decided at Pracký Kopec, a hill 12 km west of Slavkov u Brna where a monument was erected in 1912. After the battle Napoleon spent four days concluding an armistice at the baroque **chateau** (1705) in Slavkov u Brna.

Slavkov u Brna is 21 km east of Brno and is easily accessible by bus from Brno's autobusové nádraží (ask about times and platform numbers at the information counter). The chateau's historical exhibit on Napoleon's life is open Tuesday to Sunday from April to November. The decorated palace rooms and the gallery wing, which requires a separate ticket, are open daily from April to October. Unfortunately, Pracký Kopec is difficult to reach by public transport and hard to find.

Scenic Caves The caves, chasms and canyons of the Moravský Kras (Moravian Karst), 20 km north of Brno, have been created by the underground Punkva River. At Punkevní groups of 75 persons are admitted to the caves every 20 minutes. You walk one km through the deepest caves, admiring the stalactites and stalagmites, ending up at the foot of the Macocha Abyss. There you board a small boat for a 400-metre ride down the Punkva River out of the cave.

The visit to the Punkevní Caves takes 75 minutes (US$1.25 per person). The caves are open to the public all year, closing at 3 pm from April to September and at 1 pm from October to March. All tickets are usually sold out an hour before closing and in midsummer the trips will be fully booked for groups even earlier.

From Punkevní it's a 15-minute hike up to the top of the 138.7-metre-deep Macocha Abyss. Other caves to be visited in this area include Kateřinská, Balčárka and Sloupsko-Sošuvské. The Kateřinská Cave can be visited on a 30-minute tour (same hours as at Punkevní). Traces of prehistoric humans have been found in the caves.

To get there, take a train to Blansko, then walk over to the adjacent bus station. There's supposed to be a bus direct to the caves, leaving at 8 am and 11 am daily from May to September with connections back to Blansko in the afternoon, but it's automatically cancelled if there aren't at least 15 passengers. If this happens catch the Obůrka bus from stand No 12 at Blansko Bus Station to Nové Dvory, from which it's a pleasant 40-minute walk through the forest to Punkevní.

A so-called 'ecology train' carries motorists from the parking lot at Skalní Mlýn to the caves, but this service is of no use to anyone without a car because it's a 10-km walk along the highway from Blansko Railway Station to Skalní Mlýn. Buses listed on the board at the stop at Skalní Mlýn often don't show up, but it's not that hard to hitch back to Blansko.

It's also possible to take a bus from stand No 40 at Brno Bus Station to Jedovnice (29 km), departing every couple of hours. From Jedovnice follow the yellow hiking trail seven km to the Macocha Abyss via Kateřinská Cave.

The new, four-storey *Hotel Macocha* (☎ 0506 3203), Svitavská 35, right opposite the bus and train stations in Blansko, has 31 rooms at US$26 double with bath (no singles).

Places to Stay

The Czech Republic's most important international trade fairs take place in Brno in February, April, September and October. Before coming to Brno, check carefully that your visit does not coincide with one of these fairs, as hotel rates double at this time and all public facilities become very overcrowded. Fortunately, the hostel rates remain steady. In normal times, accommodation in Brno is good value compared to that in other Czech cities.

Camping *Autocamp Bobrava* (☎ 320 110) is just beyond Modřice, 12 km south of the city. Take tram No 2, 14 or 17 to the end of the line, then walk the remaining three km. Otherwise take a local train to Popovice Railway Station, 500 metres from the camping ground (get the times of returning trains before leaving Brno as no information is available at Popovice). Two-bed cabins are US$10, four-bed cabins US$15, while rooms in the motel are US$29 double. There's no hot water but the restaurant is good (open from May to September).

Hostels CKM Student Travel, Česká 11, knows of accommodation for students and hostellers in student dormitories, but these are only open during July and August.

The *Bulharský klub* (☎ 4221 1063), Skrytá 1, just around the corner from the CKM office, offers dorm beds at US$9 per person. This small pension in the centre of town is a good place to meet Eastern Europeans.

The *Ubytovna Teplárny a.s.* (☎ 571 919, extension 3500), Špitálka 11, off Cejl just east of the centre, offers comfortable triple rooms at US$3 per bed. This old four-storey building is opposite the factory with the huge pipe crossing the road. Walk east along Cejl to Cejl 52, then right on Radlas and right again on Špitálka.

South of the centre, the *Komárov Ubytovna* (☎ 339 341), Sladkého 13, rents beds in double rooms at US$8 per person. Take tram No 12 or 22 south to the end of the line, go through the underpass and follow Luzňá ulice east three blocks, then right on Lomená. The hostel is the tall modern building about two blocks down on your left. Both Čedok and CKM will book beds in this place.

North of the centre, the student dormitory at *Koleje Purkyňovy* (☎ 740 888), Purkyňova 93, block C-2, rents beds (US$7) in double and triple rooms from mid-July until the end of August. Take tram No 13, 16 or 22 northbound and ask someone where to get off.

Year-round you can get a room at *Vysokoškolské Koleje* (☎ 759 533), Kolejní 2, block K-1, on the northern side of the city, for US$12 double (no singles). This large student complex is readily accessible by taking tram No 13, 16 or 22 north to the end of the line, then trolleybus No 53 right to the hostel.

Private Rooms Čedok, Divadelní 3, arranges rooms in private homes for US$14 per person a night. Most private rooms are far from the centre but easily accessible on public transport. Čedok also arranges hostel accommodation at US$7 per person. These are always far from town.

Taxatour (☎ 4221 3348) in the train station arranges private rooms at US$15 per person in the centre, US$11 per person in the suburbs. It can also arrange accommodation in the *YMCA* on Hlinky ulice for US$8 per person.

Hotels The dumpy, old *Metropol Hotel*

CZECH REPUBLIC

(☎ 337 112), Dornych 5 behind the train station, is overpriced at US$27/39 single/double without bath, US$33/55 with shower, breakfast included.

In the centre of town is the *Astoria Hotel* (☎ 4232 1302), Novobranská 3, a pleasant old five-storey hotel with rooms at US$19/25 single/double without bath, US$22/37 with bath, breakfast included.

The *Europa Hotel* (☎ 4221 6333), Jánská 1/3, is rather run-down and it's big advantage is location and price: US$18/26 single/double (no rooms with bath). Try for a room that doesn't face the tram line.

The modern *Hotel Avion* (☎ 4221 5016), Česká 20, is reasonable at US$16/26 single/double without bath, US$24/36 single/double with bath.

A step up in price is the friendly *Hotel U Jakuba* (☎ 4221 0795), Jakubské náměstí 6, at US$32/45 single/double with shower. The hotel restaurant is good. The U Jakuba is clean, well-managed and relatively free of tram noise.

The *Hotel Pegas* (☎ 4221 0104), Jakubská 4, is a recently renovated old building on a quiet street right in the centre of town. Rooms with bath and breakfast are US$32/50 single/double.

Places to Eat

Self-Service *Bufet Sputnik*, Česká 1/3, has grilled chicken, draught beer, coffee, and strawberry milkshakes! It's a great place to fill your stomach if you don't mind eating standing up.

Jídelna Samoobsluha U tří križat, Minoritská 2 opposite St John's Church, is a self-service where you can at least sit down (closed weekends). There's a good local beer hall next door.

About the best ice-cream cones in town are dispensed by *Diana*, Česká 25, and there's a good takeaway pizza window next door.

Another cheap stand-up buffet is in the train station and there's a good supermarket in the basement of Prior Department Store behind the station on the way to the bus station – perfect if you need to stock up on groceries for a long trip.

Restaurants One of the 10 top places to eat in Eastern Europe is *Pivnice Pegas*, Jakubská 4, an attractive new private restaurant with an extensive menu in English. Their dark and light beer is brewed in two huge copper vats right on the premises and if you appreciate sizeable servings and hearty draught, you'll end up eating here more than once.

Stopkova plzeňská pivnice, Česká ulice 5 next to Sputnik, is a little more staid than Pegas but their menu (in German) is reasonable.

Pizzeria Sorento, Masarykovo 14, serves real pizza.

A good place to order a bottle of local wine with your meal is *Vinárna U zlatěho meče*, Mečová 3.

For more elegant dining try the *Restaurace Gourmand*, Josefská 14 (downstairs), which specialises in French cuisine and local wines at prices which are fair for what you get (closed Sunday).

Entertainment

Except in midsummer when the artists are on holidays, Brno's theatres offer excellent performances. In Brno the tickets aren't all cornered by scalpers and profiteers as they are in Prague, but you are expected to dress up a bit.

Opera, operettas and ballet are performed at the modern *Janáček Theatre* (Janáčkovo divadlo), Sady osvobození. This large theatre which opened in 1966 is named after composer Leoš Janáček, who spent much of his life in Brno.

The nearby neobaroque *Mahenovo Theatre* (Mahenovo divadlo) (1882), a beautifully decorated old-style theatre designed by the famous Viennese theatrical architects Fellner and Hellmer, presents classical drama in Czech and operettas.

Do try to see an operetta at the historic *Reduta Theatre* (1734), Zelný trh 3. The singing and dancing are excellent and the programmes enjoyable even if you don't understand Czech.

For tickets to the Janáček, Mahenovo and Reduta theatres, go to Předprodej, Dvořákova 11, a small booking office behind the Mahenovo Theatre (open weekdays from 12.30 to 5.30 pm, and Saturday from 9 am to noon). The staff are usually helpful to foreign visitors.

Also check the *Beseda Concert Hall* next to the Slavia Hotel which has been closed for renovations for some time.

If you're around on Sunday, don't miss the *Radost Puppet Theatre*, Bratislavská 32, which puts on shows at 10 am and 2.30 pm (Sunday only). It's kids' stuff but great fun if you haven't enjoyed puppets for a while.

The Kulturní a Informační Centrum, Radnická 8, has tickets to rock and folk concerts at a variety of venues. Drop in to peruse their leaflets and posters early in your stay.

Discos *Metro Night Club*, Poštovská 6, opposite the main post office, opens at 9 pm daily except Sunday and Monday.

Crazy Night Disco, Veveří 32, is just three blocks north of the city centre. Northbound trams Nos 3, 10, 13, 14, 16, 21 and 22 all stop here. It's a sharp modern place which attracts a young local crowd (daily from 9 pm; US$2 cover).

Things to Buy

Forte Music Store, Minoritská 1, has a good selection of local compact discs and they don't mind playing things for you. A recommended CD usually in stock here is *The Most Beautiful Folk Songs of Moravia* (EDIT 41 0034-2 731).

Getting There & Away

Bus The bus to Vienna (Mitte Bahnhof) departs from platform No 20 at the bus station twice a day (127 km, US$8 one way).

For shorter trips buses are faster and more efficient than the trains. A bus is better if you're going to Telč (96 km), Trenčín (134 km) or anywhere in South Bohemia.

Train All trains between Budapest and Berlin stop at Brno. If you're going to/from Vienna, change trains at Břeclav. To go to/from Košice, change trains at Přerov. Direct trains from Bratislava (141 km, two hours) and Prague (257 km, three hours) are frequent.

An overnight train with couchettes and sleepers runs between Brno and Košice. Reserve couchettes or sleepers at windows No 24 to 29 in the train station.

ČESKÝ TĚŠÍN

Český Těšín, a small northern Moravian town on the Olše River opposite Cieszyn, Poland, is a useful entry/exit point for those who enjoy the thrill of walking across borders while avoiding the hassle and expense of international train travel. Most of the people crossing the border here are Poles who come over with empty shopping carts and return home loaded down with cases of beer and alcohol.

Orientation

Two bridges, each with traffic in only one direction, link the towns; the Czech train station is about 500 metres from the bridges, the Polish station about a km away. Český Těšín Railway Station is much larger and more active than its counterpart on the Polish side. The left-luggage office is open 24 hours, except for three 30-minute breaks, and there's also a good self-service restaurant in the station.

For more information on Cieszyn turn to the Poland chapter of this book.

Money The Komerční Banka on the bridge leading into the Czech Republic from Poland changes travellers' cheques for the usual 2% commission (weekdays 7.30 am to noon, Thursday 8.30 am to noon and 2 to 5 pm). All the other exchange offices you see around Český Těšín change only cash, charge a similar commission and give a lower rate. One such office is Čedok, Hlavní třída 15.

Places to Stay & Eat
There are two reasonable hotels opposite the train station. The functional, three-storey *Hotel Slezský Dům* (☎ 57 141), Nádražní 10, costs US$16/24 a single/double with bath, while the imposing, five-storey *Hotel Piast* (☎ 55 651), Nádražní 18, is US$13 for a single without bath, US$25 for a double with bath. This is better value than the hotels on the Polish side.

U Huberta, Hlavní třída 3, a block dead ahead from the bridge leading into the Czech Republic from Poland, is a great introduction to the country's beers halls and meals are served. Czech beer is much cheaper than Polish brew, so drink up.

Getting There & Away
Railway service from Český Těšín is good; eight trains a day to Prague (397 km, five hours), 25 to Žilina (69 km, two hours) and eight to Košice (311 km, 4½ hours). For Brno (209 km) change at Bohumín or Česká Třebová.

Germany

Perhaps no other country in Western Europe has such a fascinating past, as well as history in the making – the reunification of Germany in 1990 was the beginning of another chapter. Much of this history is easily explored by visitors today, in a country of sheer beauty with many outdoor opportunities. There is a huge variety of museums, examples of architecture from most periods and a heavy emphasis on cultural activity. Infrastructure is extremely well organised, there is plenty of accommodation and the beer and wine is excellent.

Though it's now one country, the cultural, social and economic differences separating the former Germanys will take several years to disappear. Nevertheless the integration of the two is well advanced and visitors coming to Germany for the first time will not notice many big differences between them.

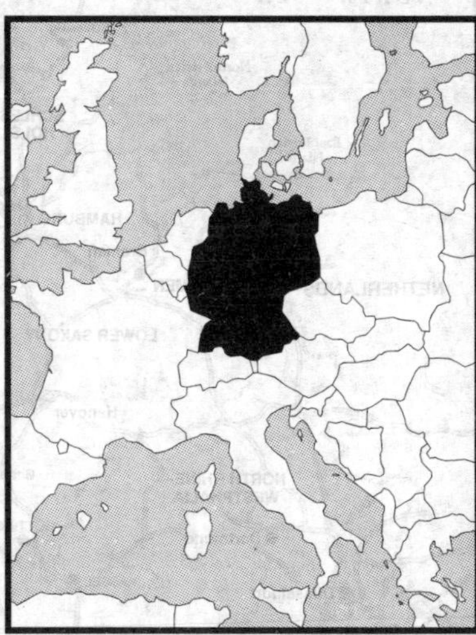

Facts about the Country

HISTORY

Events in Germany have often dominated the history of Europe. For many centuries, however, Germany was a patchwork of semi-independent principalities and city-states, preoccupied with internal quarrels and at the mercy of foreign conquerors. In the 18th and 19th centuries, these gradually came under the control of Prussia, a state created by the rulers of Brandenburg. Germany only became a nation-state in 1871, and, despite the momentous events that have occurred since then, many Germans still retain a strong sense of regional identity.

Ancient & Medieval History

Germany west of the Rhine and south of the Main was part of the Roman Empire, but Roman legions never managed to subdue the proud warrior tribes beyond. As the Roman Empire crumbled, these tribes spread out over much of Europe, establishing small kingdoms. The Frankish conqueror Charlemagne, from his court in Aachen, managed to forge a huge empire that covered most of Christian Western Europe. Inevitably, it broke up after his death in 814 AD.

The eastern branch of Charlemagne's Empire developed in 962 AD into the Holy Roman Empire, organised under Otto I (Otto the Great), and included much of present-day Germany, Austria, Switzerland and Benelux. The term 'Holy Roman' was coined in an effort to assume some of the authority of the defunct Roman Empire.

The house of Habsburg, ruling from Vienna, took control of the empire in the 13th century. By this stage the empire had already begun to contract, and eventually it was little more than a conglomerate of German-speaking states run by local rulers who paid mere lip service to the Habsburg emperor. A semblance of unity in northern Germany was

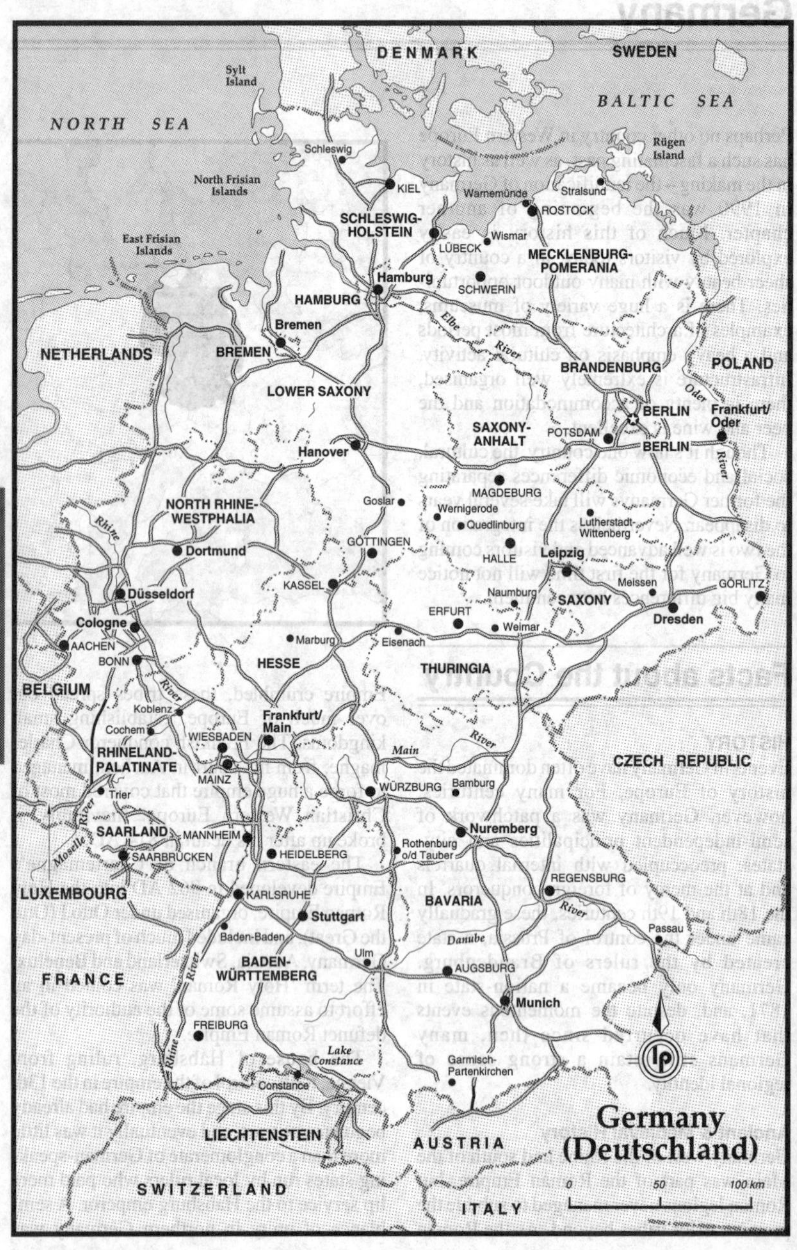

DENMARK
SWEDEN
Sylt Island
BALTIC SEA
NORTH SEA
Rügen Island
Schleswig
North Frisian Islands
KIEL
Stralsund
Warnemünde
ROSTOCK
SCHLESWIG-HOLSTEIN
East Frisian Islands
Wismar
LÜBECK
MECKLENBURG-POMERANIA
Hamburg
SCHWERIN
HAMBURG
Bremen
Elbe River
NETHERLANDS
BREMEN
BRANDENBURG
POLAND
LOWER SAXONY
Oder
BERLIN
Frankfurt/Oder
SAXONY-ANHALT
POTSDAM
BERLIN
Hanover
River
MAGDEBURG
Goslar
Wernigerode
NORTH RHINE-WESTPHALIA
Rhine
Quedlinburg
Lutherstadt-Wittenberg
GÖTTINGEN
Dortmund
HALLE
Leipzig
KASSEL
Meissen
GÖRLITZ
Düsseldorf
Naumburg
SAXONY
ERFURT
Dresden
Cologne
Weimar
AACHEN
Marburg
Eisenach
BONN
HESSE
THURINGIA
BELGIUM
River
Koblenz
Frankfurt/Main
Cochem
WIESBADEN
River
RHINELAND-PALATINATE
Main
CZECH REPUBLIC
MAINZ
Trier
WÜRZBURG
Bamburg
River
SAARLAND
MANNHEIM
Nuremberg
Moselle
Rothenburg o/d Tauber
SAARBRÜCKEN
HEIDELBERG
REGENSBURG
LUXEMBOURG
KARLSRUHE
BAVARIA
River
Stuttgart
Passau
Baden-Baden
Danube
Ulm
BADEN-WÜRTTEMBERG
AUGSBURG
FRANCE
River
Munich
FREIBURG
Rhine
Lake Constance
Garmisch-Partenkirchen
Constance
Germany (Deutschland)
LIECHTENSTEIN
AUSTRIA
SWITZERLAND
0
50
100 km
ITALY

maintained by the Hanseatic League created in 1358, a federation of German and Baltic city-states with Lübeck as its centre.

The Reformation

Things would never be the same in Europe after Martin Luther, a scholar from the monastery in Erfurt, nailed his 95 'theses' to the church door in Wittenberg in 1517. Luther proclaimed his opposition to a Church racket involving the selling of so-called indulgences, which absolved sinners from temporal punishment. In 1521 he was condemned by the Church and went into hiding in Wartburg castle in Eisenach. There he translated the Bible from the original Greek version into an everyday form of German. This Bible could be printed on the presses that had been developed by Gutenberg and read by the masses.

Luther's efforts at reforming the Church gained widespread support from the merchants, wealthy townsfolk and, crucially, several ambitious German princes. This protest against the established Church began the Protestant movement and the Reformation. The Peace of Augsburg in 1555 declared that the religion of a state would be determined by its ruler.

Meanwhile the established Church, which some people began to refer to as the 'Roman' Catholic Church, began a campaign against the spread of Protestantism, known as the Counter-Reformation.

Thirty Years' War

Tensions between Protestant and Catholic states across Europe led to the catastrophic Thirty Years' War (1618-48). Germany became the battlefield for the great powers of Europe, losing over one-third of its population and many of its towns and cities. The incessant fighting obliterated entire communities, and Germany was to take centuries to recover.

The Peace of Westphalia in 1648 established the rights of both faiths in Germany, but also sealed the political division of Germany. The German-speaking states remained a patchwork of independent principalities within the loose framework of the Holy Roman Empire, but were weakened further by the loss of important territories to other countries.

Prussia Unites Germany

In the 18th century, the Kingdom of Prussia, with its capital in Berlin, became one of Europe's strongest powers. Thanks to the organisational talents of Friedrich Wilhelm I (the Soldier King) and his son Friedrich II (Frederick the Great), it expanded eastwards at the expense of Poland, Lithuania and Russia.

In the early 19th century, the fragmented German states proved easy pickings for Napoleon. The Austrian emperor, Francis II, relinquished his crown as Holy Roman Emperor in 1806 following his defeat at Austerlitz. But the French never quite managed to subdue Prussia, which became the centre of stubborn German resistance. After Napoleon's disastrous foray into Russia, Prussia led the war that put an end to Napoleon's German aspirations in a decisive battle at Leipzig in 1813.

In 1815 the Congress of Vienna again redrew the map of Europe. The Holy Roman Empire was replaced with a German Confederation of 35 states; it had a parliament in Frankfurt and was led by the Austrian chancellor Klemens von Metternich. The Confederation was shaken by liberal revolutions in Europe in 1830 and 1848, but the Austrian monarchy continued to dominate a divided Germany.

The well-oiled Prussian civil and military machine eventually smashed this arrangement. In 1866, Otto von Bismarck (the Iron Chancellor) took Prussia to war against Austria, and rapidly annexed northern Germany. In 1871 after Prussia had defeated France, the Catholic, anti-Prussian states in southern Germany were forced to negotiate with Bismarck. The Prussian king, Wilhelm I, became *Kaiser* (German Emperor).

WW I & the Rise of Hitler

His son Wilhelm II dismissed Bismarck in 1890, but Germany's rapid growth overtaxed the Kaiser's political talents, leading to mounting tensions with England, Russia and France. When war broke out in 1914 Germany's only ally was a weakened Austria-Hungary.

The gruelling trench warfare sapped the nation's resources more quickly than those of its enemies. By late 1918 Germany was forced to sue for peace, and the Kaiser abdicated and escaped to Holland. Anger on the home front, which had been mounting during the fighting and deprivation, exploded when the troops returned home. A full-scale socialist uprising, based in Berlin and led by the Spartacus League, was put down and its leaders, Karl Liebknecht and Rosa Luxemburg, were murdered. A new republic, which became known as the Weimar Republic, was proclaimed.

The Treaty of Versailles in 1919 chopped huge areas off Germany and imposed heavy reparation payments. These proved virtually impossible to meet, and when France and Belgium occupied the Rhineland to ensure that payments continued, the subsequent hyperinflation and miserable economic conditions provided fertile ground for political extremists.

One of these was Adolf Hitler, an Austrian drifter and German army veteran, whose National (or Nazi) Socialist German Workers' Party staged an abortive coup in Munich in 1923. This landed Hitler in prison for nine months, during which time he wrote *Mein Kampf*.

From 1929, the worldwide economic depression hit Germany particularly hard, leading to massive unemployment, strikes and demonstrations. The Communist Party under Ernst Thälmann gained strength, but wealthy industrialists began to support the Nazis and the police turned a blind eye to Nazi street thugs.

The Nazis went from strength to strength in general elections and in 1933 replaced the Social Democrats as the largest party in the Reichstag. Hitler was appointed chancellor and a year later assumed absolute control as *Führer* (leader) of what he called the Third Reich (the 'third empire', the previous two being the Holy Roman Empire and Wilhelm I's German Empire).

WW II & the Division of Germany

From 1935 Germany began to rearm and build its way out of depression with strategic public works such as the autobahns. Hitler reoccupied the Rhineland in 1936, and in 1938 annexed Austria and parts of Czechoslovakia. Finally, in September 1939, after signing a pact with Stalin that allowed both a free hand in the east of Europe, Hitler attacked Poland, leading to war with Britain and France.

Germany quickly invaded large parts of Europe, but after 1943 began to suffer increasingly heavy losses. Indiscriminate bombing reduced Germany's centres to rubble and the country lost 10% of its population. Germany accepted unconditional surrender in May 1945, soon after Hitler's suicide. Among the horrors of WW II was the extermination of millions of Jews, Gypsies and others in history's first 'assembly-line' genocide. Camps were designed specifically to rid Europe of people considered undesirable according to racist Nazi doctrine.

At conferences in Yalta and Potsdam, the Allies redrew the borders of Germany, making it a quarter smaller than it had already become after the Treaty of Versailles 26 years earlier. Some 6.5 million ethnic Germans migrated or were expelled to Germany from their homes in eastern Europe, where they had lived for centuries. Germany was divided into four occupation zones and Berlin was occupied jointly by the four victorious powers.

In the Soviet zone, the (Communist) Socialist Unity Party (SED) won the 1946 elections and began a rapid nationalisation of industry. In June 1948 the Soviet Union stopped all land traffic between Germany's western zones and Berlin. This forced the Western allies to mount a military operation known as the Berlin Airlift, which supplied West Berlin by plane until the Soviets lifted the blockade in May 1949.

In September 1949 the Federal Republic

of Germany (FRG) was created out of the three western zones; in response the German Democratic Republic (GDR) was founded in the Soviet zone the following month, with Berlin as its capital.

From Division to Unity

As the West's bulwark against Communism, the FRG received massive injections of US capital in the postwar years, and experienced rapid economic development under the leadership of Konrad Adenauer. At the same time the GDR had to pay US$10 billion in war reparations to the Soviet Union and rebuild itself from scratch.

The better life in the West increasingly attracted skilled workers away from the miserable economic conditions in the East. As these were people the GDR could ill afford to lose, in 1961 it built a wall around West Berlin and sealed its border with the FRG. As the Cold War intensified, TV and radio stations in both Germanys beamed programmes heavy with propaganda to the other side.

Coinciding with a change to the more flexible leadership of Erich Honecker in the East, the *Ostpolitik* of FRG chancellor Willy Brandt allowed an easier political relationship between the two Germanys. In 1971 an agreement between the four occupying powers – the Soviet Union, the USA, the UK and France – formally accepted the division of Berlin. Many Western countries, but not West Germany itself, then officially recognised the GDR.

Honecker's policies produced higher living standards in the GDR, yet East Germany barely managed to achieve a level of prosperity half that of the FRG. After Mikhail Gorbachev came to power in the Soviet Union in March 1985, the East German Communists gradually lost Soviet backing. In May 1989 Hungary relaxed its border controls, allowing East Germans to escape to the West. Mass demonstrations demanding reforms similar to those in other Eastern European countries began in Leipzig and soon spread to other cities in the GDR. The East German government countered by prohibiting travel to Hungary, and would-be defectors began taking refuge in the FRG's embassy in Prague.

Gorbachev urged the East German Politburo to introduce reforms, but Honecker resisted. Forced to resign, Honecker was replaced by his security chief, Egon Krenz, who proved unable to rescue the regime. Promising free elections, Krenz cunningly chose 9 November (the anniversary of the Nazi pogrom Kristallnacht) to open the Berlin Wall. This prevented the day from being celebrated as a German national holiday. However, revelations of perks and corruption within the Communist leadership soon forced Krenz and his Politburo to step aside in favour of their reformist SED rival, Hans Modrow.

Opposition within the GDR had long been led by peace and human-rights activists who nevertheless had liberal-socialist sympathies, but the popular mood quickly shifted away from favouring reform to complete reunification with the West. Offering a fast-track unification plan with generous one-for-one exchange rates for the otherwise unconvertible East German currency, on 18 March 1990 FRG chancellor Helmut Kohl's Christian Democratic Union (CDU) easily won the first East German elections. The Communists – but also the citizen-based opposition groups who had been so instrumental in their downfall – were completely marginalised.

Leading economists had warned that attempts to rapidly integrate the two Germanys' fundamentally different economies would cause the collapse of many less efficient East German industries, but the GDR's new CDU prime minister, Lothar de Mazière, pushed monetary union forward to 1 July 1990. Kohl reassured West Germans that reunification would not lead to tax rises.

In September the two Germanys and the wartime Allies signed the Two-Plus-Four Treaty, ending the postwar system of occupation zones. Germany recognised its eastern borders, officially accepting the loss of territories annexed by Poland and the Soviet Union after 1945. On 3 October 1990, the German Democratic Republic was incorporated into the Federal Republic of Germany. In the ensuing national euphoria Kohl's CDU-led coalition soundly defeated the Social Democrat opposition in the all-German elections of 2 December 1990.

The 'Land in the Middle'

The social and economic costs of absorbing eastern Germany were grossly underestimated – even by many pessimists. East and West Germans, who began to refer to each other as *Wessis* and *Ossis* (westies and easties), discovered that their differences were greater than they had previously liked to believe.

Many uncompetitive and highly polluting eastern German industries had to be shut down altogether, causing the loss of millions of jobs. The government countered with enormous public spending, bringing about a 'unification boom' which delayed the onset of the international recession in Germany until late 1992.

Revelations that respected figures cooperated with the Stasi, the GDR's secret police, deepened public distrust of eastern Germany's 'new' democrats. Hundreds of former SED office holders and senior judges were charged with human-rights violations allegedly committed during the GDR years. Erich Honecker escaped manslaughter charges due to his declining health and died in exile in Chile in May 1994.

Despite continuing problems, eastern Germany's longer-term future looks promising. The region is receiving state-of-the-art technology that many parts of western Germany will have to wait years for. The year 1994 brought a turnaround, with social and economic conditions improving markedly. All foreign occupation troops once stationed on German soil, including over half a million Russian and Allied soldiers and their families, had withdrawn by late 1994.

Dislocation in the east and a general economic downturn throughout Germany have been exploited by neo-Nazi organisations. Although their support is too weak to win them more than a handful of parliamentary seats, attacks on immigrants and asylum-seekers by right-wing sympathisers have occurred repeatedly. Having regained its historical role as the 'land in the middle', Germany now finds itself torn between an inward-looking reunification process and the nation's support for further European integration.

GEOGRAPHY

Germany is a country of 356,866 sq km, and can be divided from north to south into several geographical regions.

The Northern Lowlands are a broad expanse of flat, low-lying land that sweeps across the northern third of the country from the Netherlands into Poland. The landscape is characterised by moist heaths interspersed with pastures and farmland.

In all senses of the word, the complex Central Uplands region divides northern Germany from the south. Extending from the Rhineland massifs marked by deep schisms to the Harz Mountains and the Bavarian Forest, the Central Uplands are Germany's heartland. The Rhine and Main rivers, important waterways for inland shipping, cut through the south-west of this region. With large deposits of coal and favourable transport conditions, this was one of the first regions in Germany to undergo industrialisation.

The Alpine Foothills take in the Swabian and Bavarian highlands from the Black Forest to Munich, and are largely drained by the Danube River. The landscape is typified by rolling subalpine plateaux and rounded, heavily forested mountain ranges with occasional peaks that rise above 1400 metres.

Germany's Alps lie entirely within Bavaria, and stretch along the Austrian border from the large, glacially formed Lake Constance to Berchtesgaden in Germany's south-eastern corner. Though lower than the mountains to their south, many summits are well above 2000 metres, rising dramatically from the Alpine Foothills to the 2966-metre Zugspitze, Germany's highest mountain.

GOVERNMENT

Germany has one of the most decentralised governmental structures in Europe, with a federal system based on regional states. With reunification, eastern Germany's six original (ie pre-1952) states of Berlin, Brandenburg, Mecklenburg-Vorpommern (Mecklenburg-Pomerania), Sachsen (Saxony), Sachsen-Anhalt and Thüringen (Thuringia) were re-established. In the context of the Federal Republic of Germany they are called *Bundesländer* (federal states). The Bundesländer in western Germany are Schleswig-Holstein, Hamburg, Niedersachsen (Lower Saxony), Bremen, Nordrhein-Westfalen (North Rhine-Westphalia), Hessen (Hesse), Rheinland-Pfalz (Rhineland-Palatinate), Saarland, Baden Württemberg and Bayern (Bavaria). Germans now commonly refer to the eastern states as the *neue Bundesländer* (new states) and to the western states as the *alte Bundesländer* (old states).

The Bundesländer have a large degree of autonomy in internal affairs and exert influence on the central government through the *Bundesrat* (upper house). The *Bundestag* (lower house) is elected by direct universal suffrage with proportional representation, though a party must have at least 5% of votes to gain seats. Federal government has alternated between the Christian Democrats (CDU, or CSU in Bavaria) and the Social Democrats (SPD), with the balance of power generally held by a small but influential liberal party, the Free Democrats (FDP). With Germany gradually pulling out of recession, Kohl's ruling CDU-led coalition won the second all-German elections in October 1994, though its majority in the new 672-seat Bundestag was reduced from 134 to a mere 10 seats. The SPD continued to dominate the Bundesrat.

In June 1991 the Bundestag voted to transfer the capital from Bonn to Berlin (although some administrative functions are to remain in Bonn). The move to Berlin should be completed in the year 2000.

ECONOMY

The Marshall Plan helped to produce West Germany's *Wirtschaftswunder* (economic miracle), which in the 1950s and 1960s turned the FRG into the world's third-largest economy. The trade unions and industrial corporations developed a unique economic contract by which the workers refrained from strikes in return for higher wages and better conditions. Important industries then and now include electrical manufacturing, precision and optical instruments, chemicals and vehicle manufacturing.

East Germany's recovery was even more remarkable considering the wartime destruction, postwar looting by the Soviet Union, loss of skilled labour, and isolation from Western markets. Although some of its own economic data may now be seriously questioned, the GDR was by any measure an important industrial nation, with major metallurgical, electrical, chemical and engineering industries.

At the time of unification, West Germany's per-capita income was almost three times that of the GDR. In 1991 and 1992 this situation worsened, as eastern Germany's export markets in the socialist Comecon trading bloc collapsed and its industries proved unable to compete elsewhere; industrial production in the east fell by 65%.

Under the Treuhandanstalt (Trust Agency) virtually all state-owned enterprises of the former GDR have been privatised, many with binding pledges for new investments. Rather than turning a profit, however, this massive sell-off has left liabilities of around DM300 billion.

Annual investments of around DM150 billion – almost half of all tax revenues in western Germany – have been devoted to welfare and badly needed infrastructure in the east. With public debt running at DM1.5 trillion, major tax rises have proved unavoidable to ease the enormous budget deficits. Industries in eastern Germany continue to struggle with low productivity levels, a problem set to worsen when in 1996 wages are raised to match fully those in the western states. In cash terms, eastern Germans buy 30 times more goods from the west than they manage to sell to them.

On the other hand, the per-capita level of company investment – one of the more telling long-term economic indicators – is now higher in the east than in western Germany. Taxpayer-funded spending has been pumped into everything from new roads, building construction and renovation, and ultramodern communications systems to education and the conversion from brown coal to cleaner natural gas. Despite continuing high unemployment, economic growth in eastern Germany during the last three years has averaged 7%, with the development of many new industries.

It will be at least a decade before the eastern German economy catches up to its western counterpart. Before WW II, northern Germany was the richest part of the country, but after the war the focus of technological excellence fell increasingly on the southern states of Bavaria and Baden-Württemberg, where many big names of German industry – Mercedes, BMW, Siemens – are based. A similar shift may well occur towards the east, but it may come too late to benefit many members of the present generation.

POPULATION & PEOPLE

There are 62 million people in western Germany and 16.5 million in eastern Germany, making the unified country the most populous European country apart from Russia-in-Europe. Germany's main native minority is the tiny group of Slavonic Sorbs, in the south-eastern corner. In political and economic terms, Germany is Europe's most decentralised nation, but considerable variation in population density exists. The Ruhr district in the northern Rhineland has Germany's densest concentration of people and industry, while Mecklenburg-Pomerania in the north-eastern corner is relatively sparsely settled. Roughly 75% of the population lives in urban areas.

Several million foreigners also live in Germany. Most are guest workers and their families from Turkey, Italy, Greece or the former Yugoslavia who arrived in the FRG from the early 1960s onwards to work in lower-paid jobs. Eastern Germany has fewer resident foreigners, though some of the roughly 200,000 workers who arrived in the GDR during the 1980s from 'fellow socialist' countries remain. In effect, Germany has become a nation of immigration, thus compensating for the extremely low birth rate among the established German population. (The number of Germans living in the country's eastern states has now dropped to levels last recorded in 1906!)

ARTS

Germany could never have made its major contributions to European culture without its meticulously creative population. Indeed Germans take their *Kultur* so seriously that visitors sometimes wonder how on earth they ever manage actually to enjoy it. The answer lies, perhaps, in a German musicians' proverb: true bliss is absolute concentration.

Architecture, Painting & Literature

The scope of German art is such that it could be the focus of an entire visit. Much of the artistic progress revolved around the Church, and this can be seen in artistic works and architecture. The first blossoming of the arts occurred during the Romanesque period (800-1200). Examples can be found at the Germanischisches Nationalmuseum in Nuremberg, Trier Cathedral and the churches of Magdeburg.

The Gothic style (1200-1500) is best viewed at the Freiburg Münster, Meissen Cathedral and the Marienkirche in Lübeck. Gothic painting and sculpture featured famous works, such as those produced by artists from the Cologne school of painters, and sculptors Peter Vischer and his sons.

The Renaissance was slower to develop in Germany than in Italy, but painting and graphic art flourished once it took hold. One of Germany's most famous draughtsmen, Albrecht Dürer of Nuremberg (1471-1528), became one of the world's finest portraitists. Another renowned visual artist was Lucas Cranach the Elder (1472-1553). During his 45 years in Wittenberg, Cranach's studio turned out hundreds of paintings and woodcuts. Though best known for his portraits, Cranach initiated the Lutheran school of painting.

The baroque period brought great sculpture, including works by Andreas Schlüter in Berlin. Balthasar Neumann's superb Residenz in Würzburg and the magnificent cathedral in Passau are foremost examples of baroque architecture.

Goethe & Schiller During the 18th-century Enlightenment, the Saxon court at Weimar attracted figures of European stature. Though born in Frankfurt/Main and educated at Leipzig, Johann Wolfgang von Goethe (1749-1832) moved to Weimar in 1775, spending the rest of his life there. Arguably the greatest of German writers, Goethe the poet, dramatist, painter, scientist and philosopher was perhaps the last European to achieve the Renaissance ideal of excellence in many fields. His greatest work, the drama *Faust*, is a masterful epic of all that went before him, as the archetypal human strives for meaning. Goethe characterised his literary works as 'fragments of a great confession'. The ghost of Goethe lives throughout Germany.

Goethe's close friend, Friedrich Schiller (1759-1805), was a poet, dramatist and novelist. His most famous work is the dramatic cycle *Wallenstein* (translated by Samuel Taylor Coleridge), based on the life of a treacherous Thirty Years' War general who plotted to make himself arbiter of the empire. Schiller's other great play, *William Tell*, dealt with the right of the oppressed to rise against tyranny. Large museums to both Schiller and Goethe exist in Weimar today.

The 19th & Early 20th Centuries Berlin too produced remarkable individuals, such as Alexander von Humboldt (1769-1859), an advanced thinker in environmentalism through his studies of the relationship of plants and animals to their physical surroundings. Humboldt's explorations of South America included a trek through the Amazon rainforest and studies of volcanoes and earthquakes. Humboldt's contemporary, the philosopher Georg Wilhelm Friedrich Hegel (1770-1831), created an all-embracing classical philosophy still influential today. His dialectical system influenced existentialism and Marxism.

The neoclassical period in Germany was led by Karl Friedrich Schinkel and the Munich neoclassical school. The romantic period looked even further back, to the Middle Ages, and is best exemplified by the paintings of Caspar David Friedrich.

The reaction to all of this looking back was impressionism and the popularity of Max Liebermann. New developments occurred through Art Nouveau, which made great contributions to German architecture. A wonderful example is Alfred Messel's Wertheim department store in Berlin.

Next came expressionism, with great names like Paul Klee and the Russian-born painter Vasili Kandinsky. This period also saw the development of the Bauhaus movement, founded in 1919 by Walter Gropius in an attempt to meld the theoretical concerns of architecture with the practical problems faced by artists and craftspeople. With the arrival of the Nazis, Gropius accepted a chair at Harvard.

Brecht In the 1920s, Berlin was the theatrical capital of Germany, and its most famous practitioner was the poet and playwright Bertolt Brecht (1898-1956). Born in Augsburg, in the 1920s Brecht moved to Berlin, where he began to develop Marxist concepts in theatre. His work was distinguished by the simplicity of its moral parables, its language and its sharp characterisation. Brecht revolutionised the theatre by detaching the audience from what was happening on stage, enabling them to observe the content without being distracted by the form. In 1933 Brecht fled the Nazis and lived in various countries, eventually accepting the directorship of the Berliner Ensemble in East Berlin, where his work has been performed ever since.

WW II & Beyond During the time of the Third Reich, the arts were devoted mainly to propaganda, with grandiose projects and realist art extolling the virtues of Germanhood. Max Ernst, resident in France and the USA, was a prominent exponent of dada and surrealism who developed the technique of collage.

Postwar literature in both Germanys was influenced by the Gruppe 47, a loose grouping whose members took a deliberately political stance. It included writers such as Günter Grass, whose modern classic, *Die Blechtrommel* ('The Tin Drum'), is about a young boy who stops growing in order to survive WW II.

Christa Wolf, an East German novelist and Gruppe 47 writer, maintained her independence while living in the GDR, and won high esteem in both Germanys. Wolf's 1963 story *Der geteilte Himmel* ('Divided Heaven') tells of a young woman whose fiancé abandons her for life in the West. Her 1976 novel *Kindheitsmuster* ('Patterns of Childhood') traces her own childhood under fascism.

Since the late 1980s, Patrick Süskind has been one of Germany's more popular young writers. Süskind's first novel, *Das Parfüm* ('The Perfume'), published in 1985, is the extraordinary tale of a psychotic 18th-century perfume-maker.

GERMANY

Music

Few countries can claim the impressive musical heritage of Germany. Much early music revolved around the Church, but the art developed rapidly in the 18th century. A partial list of household names includes Johann Sebastian Bach, Georg Friedrich Händel, Ludwig van Beethoven, Richard Wagner, Richard Strauss, Felix Mendelssohn-Bartholdy, Robert Schumann, Johannes Brahms and Gustav Mahler.

The two greatest baroque composers were born in Saxony in the same year. Johann Sebastian Bach (1685-1750) was born at Eisenach into a prominent family of musicians. From 1708 to 1717 he served as court organist at Weimar, moving to Leipzig in 1723 where he spent his remaining 27 years as city musical director. During his life, Bach produced some 200 cantatas, plus masses, oratorios, passions and other elaborate music for the Lutheran service, and sonatas, concertos, preludes and fugues for secular use.

Georg Friedrich Händel (1685-1759) left his native Halle for Hamburg at 18. Händel composed numerous operas and oratorios, including his masterpiece *Messiah* (1742). The birthplaces of both Händel and Bach are now large museums.

In the 19th century, the musical traditions of Saxony continued unabated with the songwriter Robert Schumann (1810-56), born at Zwickau. In 1843 Schumann opened a music school at Leipzig in collaboration with composer Felix Mendelssohn (1809-47), director of Leipzig's famous Gewandhaus Orchestra.

These musical traditions continue to thrive: the Dresden Opera and Leipzig Orchestra are known around the world, and musical performances are hosted almost daily in every major theatre in the country.

The Studio for Electronic Music in Cologne is a centre for cutting-edge developments in this field. Contemporary music is also popular: jazz, folk, rock and roll, new wave and much more can be found in every large city – the emphasis is often on beat and volume rather than melody. And traditional German oompah music is still popular with locals and tourists.

Porcelain

Germany has long been a world leader in porcelain production. The Meissen factory was the first in Europe to make white hard-paste porcelain. Factories in Fürstenberg and Nymphenburg gained a reputation for their vases, tableware and figurines. Excellent porcelain exhibits can be found in Meissen itself, Munich's Residenz and Frankfurt's Museum of Applied Arts.

CULTURE

Traditional Lifestyle

Once viewed as overly disciplined, humourless and domineering, today's Germans are generally more relaxed, personable and interested in enjoying life. Reunification has evidently strengthened this trend, as it seems to be spreading eastwards. English-speaking travellers readily identify with Germans, and find it easy to strike up conversations with them.

Despite their penchant for continual improvement and modernisation, upholding traditions is dear to the German heart. Hunters still wear green, master chimney sweeps get around in pitch-black suits and top hats, Bavarian women don the *Dirndl* (skirt and blouse), while their menfolk find suitable occasions to wear the typical Bavarian leather shorts, a *Loden* (short jacket) and felt hat.

Avoiding Offence

There are few real taboos left in modern Germany. Germans are generally not prudish people; millions regularly visit nude beaches (identifiable by the abbreviation FKK), and even public figures may sometimes express themselves in earthy Germanic terms.

Formal manners are still important, though perhaps less so than a decade or two ago. Except with very close friends, most Germans still use *Herr* and *Frau* in daily discussion. (In fact, the transition from the formal *Sie* to the informal *du* is often celebrated.) Similarly, professional titles are often used instead of surnames (eg *Herr Professor* or *Frau Doktor*). Germans always shake hands when greeting or leaving. Cheek kissing is standard between males and females who know one another. Eastern Germans are socially more conservative than western Germans, though the only events to which you really have to wear a tie are weddings and funerals.

The holocaust and WW II, while by no means taboo topics, should be discussed with tact and understanding in Germany. In western Germany these themes have been dealt with openly for decades, but Germans sometimes feel their country's postwar role as a model for peace continues to be underemphasised against its relatively short period under the Nazis. Germans understandably take great offence at the presumption that fascist ideas are somehow part of – or even compatible with – their national culture. The film *Schindler's List*, which deals with the holocaust with uncompromising frankness, was screened widely in Germany throughout 1994.

Sport

The Germans love their sports, both as participants and as spectators – one in three Germans belongs to some sort of sports club. The most popular sport is, of course, football (soccer). Cycling, swimming, skiing and, more recently, tennis (thanks to Boris Becker, Steffi Graf and Michael Stich) are becoming increasingly popular.

With the renewed interest in the environment, outdoor activities and sports are experiencing an astounding growth in popularity. The possibilities range from hiking to white-water rafting.

RELIGION

Most Germans belong to a church, and there are almost equal numbers of Catholics and Protestants: roughly speaking, Catholics predominate in the south, Protestants in the north and east. A majority of citizens pay contributions to their church, which the government collects along with their taxes, but in practice few Germans regularly attend church services.

Despite their bitter historical rivalry, conflict between Catholics and Protestants in Germany is a nonissue these days, but conflict *within* the two faiths is great. Catholics are concerned with old and new problems, such as abortion. Protestants are struggling with the church's involvement in political issues, like the environment.

In eastern Germany, the Protestant Church, which claims support among the overwhelming majority of the population there, played a major role in the overthrow of German Communism by providing a gathering place for antigovernment protesters. Despite the fall of Communism, however, active church membership remains even lower than in western Germany.

In 1933 some 530,000 Jews lived in Germany. Today Germany's Jewish citizens number around 40,000, with the largest communities being those in Berlin and Frankfurt.

There are also more than 1.7 million Muslims, most of them Turks.

LANGUAGE

It might be a surprise to know that German is a close relative of English. English, German and Dutch are all known as West Germanic languages. This means that you know lots of German words already – *Arm*, *Finger*, *Gold* – and you'll be able to figure out many others – *Mutter* (mother), *trinken* (drink), *gut* (good). A primary reason why English and German have grown apart is that when the Normans invaded England in 1066 they brought in many non-Germanic words. For this reason, English has many synonyms, usually with the more basic word being Germanic, and the more literary or specialised one coming from French; for instance, 'start' and 'green' as opposed to 'commence' and 'verdant'.

German is spoken throughout Germany and Austria and in much of Switzerland. It is also extremely useful in Eastern Europe, especially with older people. Although you will hear different regional dialects, the official language, *Hochdeutsch*, is universally understood. In some tourist centres, English is so widely spoken that you may not have a chance to use German, even if you want to! However, as soon as you try to meet ordinary people or move out of the big cities, especially in eastern Germany, the situation is rather different. Your efforts to speak the local language will be appreciated and will make your trip much more enjoyable and fulfilling.

Words that you'll often encounter on maps and throughout this chapter include: *Altstadt* (old city), *Bahnhof* (station), *Brücke* (bridge), *Hauptbahnhof* (main train station), *Markt* (market, often the central square in old towns), *Platz* (square), *Rathaus* (town hall) and *Strasse* (street). German nouns are always written with a capital letter.

Pronunciation

Unlike English or French, German has no real silent letters: you pronounce the **k** at the start of the word *Knie* (knee), the **p** at the start of *Psychologie* (psychology), and the **e** at the end of *ich habe* (I have).

Vowels As in English, vowels can be pronounced long, like the 'o' in 'pope', or short, like the 'o' in 'pop'. As a rule, German vowels are long before one consonant and short before two consonants: the **o** is long in the word *Dom* (cathedral), but short in the word *doch* (after all).

a	short, like the 'u' in 'cut', or long, as in 'father'
au	as in 'vow'
ä	short, as in 'act', or long, as in 'hair'
äu	as in 'boy'
e	short, as in 'bet', or long, as in 'day'
ei	like the 'ai' in 'aisle'
eu	as in 'boy'
i	short, as in 'in', or long, as in 'see'
ie	as in 'see'
o	short, as in 'pot', or long, as in 'note'
ö	like the 'er' in 'fern'
u	like the 'u' in 'pull'
ü	similar to the 'u' in 'pull' but with stretched lips

Consonants Most German consonants sound similar to their English counterparts. One important difference is that **b**, **d** and **g** sound like 'p', 't' and 'k', respectively, at the end of a word.

b	normally like the English 'b', but as 'p' at end of a word
ch	like the 'ch' in Scottish *loch*
d	normally like the English 'd', but like 't' at the end of a word
g	normally like the English 'g', but like 'k' at the end of a word, or like 'ch' in the Scottish *loch* at the end of a word when after 'i'
j	like the 'y' in 'yet'
qu	like 'k' plus 'v'
r	can be trilled or guttural, depending on the region

s	normally like the 's' in 'sun', but like the 'z' in 'zoo' when followed by a vowel
sch	like the 'sh' in 'ship'
sp, st	the **s** sounds like the 'sh' in 'ship' when at the start of a word
tion	the **t** sounds like the 'ts' in 'hits'
ß	like the 's' in 'sun' (written as '**ss**' in this book)
v	like the 'f' in 'fan'
w	like the 'v' in 'van'
z	like the 'ts' in 'hits'

Greetings & Civilities

Good day	*Guten Tag*
Hello (in southern Germany)	*Grüss Gott*
Goodbye	*Auf Wiedersehen*
Bye bye	*Tschüss*
Yes	*Ja*
No	*Nein*
Please	*Bitte*
Thank you	*Danke*
That's fine, you're welcome	*Bitte sehr*
Sorry (excuse me, forgive me)	*Entschuldigung*

Some Useful Phrases

Do you speak English?	*Sprechen Sie Englisch?*
Does anyone here speak English?	*Spricht hier jemand Englisch?*
I (don't) understand.	*Ich verstehe (nicht).*
Just a minute.	*Ein Moment!*
Please write that down.	*Können Sie es bitte aufschreiben?*
How much is it ?	*Wieviel kostet es?*

Useful Signs

Camping Ground	*Campingplatz*
Entrance	*Eingang*
Exit	*Ausgang*
Full, No Vacancies	*Voll, Besetzt*
Guesthouse	*Pension, Gästehaus*
Hotel	*Hotel*
Information	*Auskunft*
Open/Closed	*Offen/Geschlossen*
Police	*Polizei*
Police Station	*Polizeiwache*
Train Station	*Bahnhof (Bf)*
Rooms Available	*Zimmer Frei*
Toilets	*Toiletten (WC)*
Youth Hostel	*Jugendherberge*

Getting Around

What time does...leave?
Wann fährt...ab?
What time does...arrive?
Wann kommt...an?
What time is the next boat?
Wann fährt das nächste Boot?

next	*nächste*
first	*erste*
last	*letzte*
the boat	*das Boot*
the bus (city)	*der Bus*
the bus (intercity)	*der (Überland) Bus*
the tram	*die Strassenbahn*
the train	*der Zug*
I would like...	*Ich möchte...*
a one-way ticket	*eine Einzelkarte*
a return ticket	*eine Rückfahrkarte*
1st class	*erste Klasse*
2nd class	*zweite Klasse*

Where is the bus stop?
Wo ist die Bushaltestelle?
Where is the tram stop?
Wo ist die Strassenbahnhaltestelle?
Can you show me (on the map)?
Können Sie mir (auf der Karte) zeigen?
I'm looking for...
Ich suche...

far/near
weit/nahe
Go straight ahead.
Gehen Sie geradeaus.
Turn left.
Biegen Sie links ab.
Turn right.
Biegen Sie rechts ab.

Around Town

I'm looking for...	*Ich suche...*

a bank	*eine Bank*
the city centre	*die Innenstadt*
the...embassy	*die...Botschaft*
my hotel	*mein Hotel*
the market	*den Markt*
the police	*die Polizei*
the post office	*das Postamt*
a public toilet	*eine öffentliche Toilette*
the telephone centre	*die Telefonzentrale*
the tourist information office	*das Verkehrsamt*

beach	*Strand*
bridge	*Brücke*
castle	*Schloss, Burg*
cathedral	*Dom*
church	*Kirche*
hospital	*Krankenhaus*
island	*Insel*
lake	*See*
main square	*Hauptplatz*
market	*Markt*
monastery, convent	*Kloster*
mosque	*Moschee*
mountain	*Berg*
old city	*Altstadt*
palace	*Palast*
ruins	*Ruinen*
sea	*Meer*
square	*Platz*
tower	*Turm*

Accommodation

Where is a cheap hotel?	*Wo ist ein billiges Hotel?*
What is the address?	*Was ist die Adresse?*
Could you write the address, please?	*Könnten Sie bitte die Adresse aufschreiben?*
Do you have any rooms available?	*Haben Sie noch freie Zimmer?*
I would like...	*Ich möchte...*
a single room	*ein Einzelzimmer*
a double room	*ein Doppelzimmer*
a room with a bathroom	*ein Zimmer mit Bad*
to share a dorm	*einen Schlafsaal teilen*
a bed	*ein Bett*

How much is it per night/per person?
Wieviel kostet es pro Nacht/pro Person?
Can I see it?
Kann ich es sehen?
Where is the bathroom?
Wo ist das Bad?

Food

bakery	*Bäckerei*
grocery	*Lebensmittelgeschäft*
delicatessen	*Delikatessengeschäft*
restaurant	*Restaurant, Gaststätte*
breakfast	*Frühstück*
lunch	*Mittagessen*
dinner	*Abendessen*

I would like the set lunch, please.
Ich hätte gern das Tagesmenü bitte.
Is service included in the bill?
Ist die Bedienung inbegriffen?
I am a vegetarian.
Ich bin Vegetarierin (f)
Vegetarier. (m)

Time & Dates

today	*heute*
tomorrow	*morgen*
in the morning	*morgens*
in the afternoon	*nachmittags*
in the evening	*abends*

Monday	*Montag*
Tuesday	*Dienstag*
Wednesday	*Mittwoch*
Thursday	*Donnerstag*
Friday	*Freitag*
Saturday	*Samstag, Sonnabend*
Sunday	*Sonntag*

January	*Januar*
February	*Februar*
March	*März*
April	*April*
May	*Mai*
June	*Juni*
July	*Juli*
August	*August*
September	*September*
October	*Oktober*
November	*November*
December	*Dezember*

Numbers

0	*null*
1	*eins*
2	*zwei*
	zwo (telephone)
3	*drei*
4	*vier*
5	*fünf*
6	*sechs*
7	*sieben*
8	*acht*
9	*neun*
10	*zehn*
11	*elf*
12	*zwölf*
13	*dreizehn*
14	*vierzehn*
15	*fünfzehn*
16	*sechzehn*
17	*siebzehn*
18	*achtzehn*
19	*neunzehn*
20	*zwanzig*
21	*einundzwanzig*
22	*zweiundzwanzig*
30	*dreissig*
40	*vierzig*
50	*fünfzig*
60	*sechzig*
70	*siebzig*
80	*achtzig*
90	*neunzig*
100	*hundert*
1000	*tausend*
10,000	*zehntausend*
1,000,000	*eine Million*

Health

I'm...	*Ich bin...*
diabetic	*Diabetikerin* (f) *Diabetiker* (m)
epileptic	*Epileptikerin* (f) *Epileptiker* (m)
asthmatic	*Asthmatikerin* (f) *Asthmatiker* (m)
I'm allergic to antibiotics/penicillin.	*Ich bin gegen Antibiotika/Penizillin allergisch.*

antiseptic	*Antiseptikum*
aspirin	*Aspirin*
condoms	*Kondome*
constipation	*Verstopfung*
contraceptive	*Verhütungsmittel*
diarrhoea	*Durchfall*
medicine	*Medizin*
nausea	*Übelkeit*
sunblock cream	*Sunblockcreme*
tampons	*Tampons*

Emergencies

Help!	*Hilfe!*
Call a doctor!	*Holen Sie einen Arzt!*
Call the police!	*Rufen Sie die Polizei!*
Go away!	*Gehen Sie weg!*

Facts for the Visitor

VISAS & EMBASSIES

Americans, Australians, Britons, Canadians, New Zealanders and Japanese require only a valid passport (no visa) to enter Germany. Citizens of the European Union (EU) and some other Western European countries can enter on an official identity card. Unless you're a citizen of a Third World country you can probably stay up to three months.

German Embassies Abroad

Australia
119 Empire Circuit, Yarralumla, ACT 2600 (☎ 06-270 1911)

GERMANY

Canada
14th floor, 275 Slater St, Ottawa, Ont K1P 5H9 (☎ 013-232 1101)
New Zealand
90-92 Hobson St, Wellington (☎ 04-473 6063)
South Africa
180 Blackwood St, Arcadia, Pretoria 0083 (☎ 012-344 3854)
UK
23 Belgrave Square, London SW1X 8PZ (☎ 0171-235 5033)
USA
4645 Reservoir Rd, NW Washington, DC 20007-1998 (☎ 202-298 4000)

Foreign Embassies in Germany

German government bodies are gradually moving from Bonn to Berlin, but while the foreign ministry remains in Bonn, the main diplomatic missions of other countries will remain there too. Many embassies formerly located in East Berlin have closed or been demoted to consulates (see Berlin later in this chapter for details). Embassies in Bonn (telephone code 0228) include:

Australia
Godesberger Allee 105-107, 53175 Bonn (☎ 8 10 30)
Austria
Johanniterstrasse 2, 53113 Bonn (☎ 53 00 60)
Canada
Friedrich-Wilhelm-Strasse 18, 53113 Bonn (☎ 96 80)
France
An der Marienkapelle 1a, 53179 Bonn (☎ 36 20 31)
New Zealand
Bundeskanzlerplatz 2-10, 53113 Bonn (☎ 22 80 70)
Switzerland
Gotenstrasse 156, 53175 Bonn (☎ 81 00 80)
UK
Friedrich-Ebert-Allee 77, 53113 Bonn (☎ 23 40 61)
USA
Deichmanns Aue 29, 53179 Bonn (☎ 33 91)

CUSTOMS

Most personal items are duty-free. When entering Germany from another EU country, visitors can bring 300 cigarettes, 75 cigars, or 400 grams of tobacco; 1.5 litres of liquor more than 22% alcohol by volume or three litres of less than 22% alcohol by volume; five litres of wine; 75 grams of perfume and 0.33 litres of toilet water; and other products to a value of DM780.

From other European countries, duty-free allowances are 200 cigarettes, 50 cigars, or 250 grams of tobacco; one litre of strong liquor or two litres of less than 22% alcohol by volume; two litres of wine; 50 grams of perfume and 0.25 litres of toilet water; and other products to a value of DM115. Petrol reserves up to 10 litres are duty-free.

When entering from a non-European country, visitors can bring 400 cigarettes, 100 cigars, or 500 grams of tobacco; liquor, perfume and import restrictions are the same as for non-EU neighbours.

Tobacco products and alcohol may only be brought in by people aged 17 and over. There are no currency import restrictions.

MONEY

The German Mark, or Deutschmark (DM), consists of 100 pfennig (Pf). Germans refer to it as the Mark or D-Mark (pronounced 'day-mark'). The German economy is generally cash-based and, though this is changing, it's best to plan to use cash much of the time. The easiest places to change cash in Germany are banks and bank-operated booths at airports and train stations. Post offices often have money-changing facilities where rates tend to be better than at the bank.

Travellers' cheques are widely used and accepted, especially if issued in Deutschmark denominations. You'll usually get the full amount, though bank branches at borders often charge a small commission, and post offices charge a flat DM6-per-cheque fee for any cheques outside the postal financial system. A commission of up to DM10 (ask first!) is charged every time you change foreign currency into DM.

The most widely accepted travellers' cheques are American Express, Thomas Cook and Barclays. American Express charges no commission on its own cheques, but the exchange rates aren't great if the cheques have to be converted into DM. Eurocheques are widely accepted (up to DM400 per cheque).

Credit cards are not always accepted outside major cities, but are handy for emergencies. Hotels and restaurants often accept MasterCard, Visa and American Express. German banks prefer Eurocard, which is linked with Access and MasterCard, and in small towns you may have difficulty drawing cash with cards other than these three. Most over-the-counter cash advances against cards at major banks cost a flat DM10 per withdrawal, so it's better if you have automatic teller linkage (check fees and availability of services with your bank at home). Deutsche Verkehrs-Kredit Bank (DVB) offers the most convenient cash-for-card services and has offices at main train stations, but charges 1% commission or a minimum of DM7.50 (DM3 for small amounts) to change travellers' cheques.

Having money sent to Germany is fairly straightforward. American Express is a good bet and transfers to large commercial banks are also easy, although you may have to open an account. For emergencies, Western Union offers ready and fast international cash transfers through agent banks, but the commissions are costly.

Currency

Coinage includes one, two, five, 10, and 50 Pf, as well as DM1, DM2, and DM5. There are banknotes of DM5, 10, 20, 50, 100, 200, 500 and 1000. Beware of confusing the old DM5 and new DM20 banknotes, which are the same colour and have similar designs, although the DM20 note is larger, and watch out for counterfeit banknotes made on colour photocopy machines!

Exchange Rates

A$1	=	DM1.22
AS1	=	DM0.14
Dkr	=	DM0.26
C$1	=	DM1.21
1FF	=	DM0.29
Nethf1	=	DM0.89
NZ$1	=	DM0.80
Sfr	=	DM1.17
UK£1	=	DM2.50
US$1	=	DM1.65

Costs

Since reunification, inflation has been on the increase and the DM is losing some of its former strength. Rising interest rates, on the other hand, have begun to push up the value of the DM in relation to some currencies, increasing the cost of travelling in Germany. On the whole, though, food and accommodtion are still quite affordable by Western European standards. Prices have almost reached western levels in the cities of eastern Germany.

Tipping

Tipping is not widespread in Germany. In restaurants, service *(Bedienung)* is usually included but it is normal to round the bill up a bit if you're satisfied with the service. Do this as you pay, rather than leave money on the table. Taxi drivers, too, expect a slight tip. A tip of 10% is considered generous and is gratefully received.

Bargaining

Bargaining rarely occurs in Germany, but when paying cash for large purchases of more than, say, DM100, you could try asking for *Skonto*, which is a 3% discount. This doesn't apply to services like hotel and restaurant bills, however.

Consumer Taxes

Most German goods and services include a value-added tax *(Mehrwertsteuer)* which runs at an EU standard of 15%. Non-EU residents leaving the EU can have this tax refunded for goods (not services) bought, which is definitely worth it for large purchases.

Check that the shop where you're buying has the necessary customs forms which, together with the bills, must be stamped by German customs as you're leaving the country. You're not allowed to use the items purchased until you're out of Germany. Bus drivers and train conductors aren't likely to want to wait at the border while you're getting your paperwork stamped, so if you're travelling this way, ask the shop (or the tourist office) for the nearest customs authority that can do this beforehand. If you're leaving by air, have the paperwork stamped at the airport before you check in (you have to show the goods). The stamped forms, together with the bills, must be returned to the shop where the goods were bought. The shop will mail the refund, minus costs, to your home address.

Some 17,000 shops, including the biggest department stores, are affiliated with the Tax-Free Cheque Service, and carry a tax-free shopping label; this makes the procedure a lot easier. The shop will issue you a cheque for the amount of value-added tax to be refunded, which you can have stamped and cash in when leaving the country (or the EU, if you are moving on to another EU country). You can get literature at affiliated shops, some tourist offices, major hotels, airports and harbours.

CLIMATE & WHEN TO GO

The German climate can be variable, so it's best to be prepared for all types of weather throughout the year. That said, the most reliable weather is from May to October. This, of course, coincides with the standard tourist season (except for skiing). The shoulder periods can bring fewer tourists and surprisingly pleasant weather.

Eastern Germany lies in a transition zone between the temperate maritime climate of Western Europe and the rougher continental climate of Eastern Europe – continental and Atlantic air masses meet here. The mean annual temperature in Berlin is 11°C, the average range of temperatures varying from -1°C in January to 18°C in July. The average annual precipitation is 585 mm and there is no special rainy season. The camping season is May to September.

WHAT TO BRING

If you forget to bring it, you can buy it in Germany.

Standard dress can be casual, but should be fairly conservative. Jeans are generally accepted throughout the country. A layering system is best in Germany, where weather can change drastically from region to region and from day to night.

SUGGESTED ITINERARIES

Depending on the length of your stay, you might want to see and do the following things:

Two days
: Depending on where you enter the country, try and spend at least two days in either Berlin or Munich.

One week
: Divide your time between Berlin and Munich, and throw in a visit to Dresden or Bamberg.

Two weeks
: Berlin (including Potsdam), Dresden, Munich, Bamberg and Lübeck.

One month
: Berlin (including Potsdam), Dresden, Meissen, the Harz Mountains, the Moselle River, Munich, the Alps, Lake Constance and Bamberg or Lübeck.

Two months
: As for one month, plus Weimar, Regensburg, Passau, the Romantic Road, the Rhine valley, Cologne, and the North Frisian Islands.

TOURIST OFFICES

Tourism in Germany runs like the train system: very efficiently. Small and large tourist offices are incredibly helpful and well informed. Don't hesitate to make use of their services.

Local Tourist Offices

The German National Tourist Office (Deutsche Zentrale für Tourismus, DZT) is headquartered at Beethovenstrasse 69, 60325 Frankfurt/Main (☎ 069-7 57 20; fax 75 19 03). For local information, the office to head for in cities and towns in eastern and western Germany alike is the *Verkehrsamt* (tourist office) or *Kurverwaltung* (resort administration).

Tourist Offices Abroad

DZT representatives abroad include:

Australia & New Zealand
: German National Tourist Office, Lufthansa House, 9th floor, 143 Macquarie St, Sydney, NSW 2000 (☎ 02-367 3890)

GERMANY

Canada
: German National Tourist Office, 175 Bloor St East, North Tower, suite 604, Toronto, Ont M4W 3R8 (☎ 416-968 1570)

South Africa
: German National Tourist Office, c/o Lufthansa German Airlines, 22 Girton Rd, Parktown, Johannesburg 2000 (☎ 011-643 1615)

UK
: German National Tourist Office, Nightingale House, 65 Curzon St, London W1Y 7PE (☎ 0171-495 39 90/91)

USA
: German National Tourist Office, 52nd floor, 122 East 42nd St, New York, NY 10168-0072 (☎ 212-308 3300)
: German National Tourist Office, 11766 Wilshire Blvd, suite 750, Los Angeles, CA 90025 (☎ 310-575 9799)

There are also offices in Amsterdam, Brussels, Copenhagen, Madrid, Milan, Paris, Stockholm, Tokyo, Vienna and Zürich, and agencies in Chicago, Helsinki, Hong Kong, Moscow and Oslo.

USEFUL ORGANISATIONS

Allgemeiner Deutscher Automobil Club (ADAC)
: Am Westpark 8, 81373 Munich – Germany's main motoring organisation, with offices in all major cities (☎ 089-7 67 60)

Christlicher Friedensdienst eV
: Rendeler Strasse 9, 60385 Frankfurt/Main – organises cooperative work and study camps (not paid employment) for German and international youth, many of which are conducted in English (☎ 069-45 90 72)

Deutsches Jugendherbergswerk (DJH)
: Hauptverband, 32754 Detmold – coordinates all affiliated Hostelling International (HI) hostels in Germany (☎ 05231-7 40 10)

Studienkreis für Tourismus eV
: Dampfschiffstrasse 2, 82319 Starnberg – provides printed information in English on a range of organisations offering work camps or study schemes (not paid employment)

Verband Deutscher Gebirgs- und Wandervereine
: Reichsstrasse 4, 66111 Saarbrücken – German Climbing & Hiking Association, provides information about trails, shelters, huts etc, and addresses of local hiking associations (☎ 0681-39 00 70)

BUSINESS HOURS & HOLIDAYS

Shopping hours are generally from 8 or 9 am to 6.30 pm Monday to Friday, and from 9 am to 2 pm on Saturday, though times can vary in different parts of the country. On the first Saturday of each month, shops in many cities stay open at least until 4 pm ('long Saturday').

Banking hours are generally from 8.30 am to 1 pm and from 2.30 to 4 pm Monday to Friday (many stay open until later on Thursday). Government offices close for the weekend at 1 or 3 pm on Friday. Museum are generally closed on Monday; opening hours vary greatly, although many art museums are open later one evening per week.

Restaurants tend to open from 10 am to midnight, with varying closing days. Many of the cheap restaurants are closed on Saturday afternoon and Sunday, although fast-food stands and places in the train stations are open daily. Night bars are open from 9 pm to 4 am.

Germany has many holidays, some of which vary from state to state. Public holidays include New Year's Day; Good Friday to Easter Monday; 1 May (Labour Day); Whit Monday, Ascension Day, Pentecost, Whit Monday, Corpus Christi (10 days after Pentecost); 3 October (Day of German Unity); 1 November (All Saints' Day); 18 November (Day of Prayer and Repentance); and usually Christmas Eve to the day after Christmas. All shops and banks are closed on public holidays.

CULTURAL EVENTS

There are many festivals, fairs and cultural events throughout the year. Famous and worthwhile ones include:

January
: The carnival season (Shrovetide, known as *Fasching* in Bavaria) begins, with many carnival events in large cities, most notably Cologne, Munich, Düsseldorf and Mainz; the partying peaks just before Ash Wednesday.

February
: International Toy Fair in Nuremberg, International Film Festival in Berlin

March
: Frankfurt Music Fair; Frankfurt Jazz Fair; Thuringian Bach Festival; many spring fairs throughout Germany; Sommergewinn Festival in Eisenach

GERMANY

April
: Stuttgart Jazz Festival; Munich Ballet Days; Mannheim May Fair; Walpurgis Festivals – the night before May Day in Harz Mountains

May
: International Mime Festival in Stuttgart; Red Wine Festival in Rüdesheim; Dresden International Dixieland Jazz Festival; Dresden Music Festival (last week of May into first week of June)

June
: Moselle Wine Week in Cochem; Händel Festival in Halle; sailing regatta in Kiel; Munich Film Festival; International Theatre Festival in Freiburg

July
: Folk festivals throughout Germany; Munich Opera Festival; Richard Wagner Festival in Bayreuth; German-American Folk Festival in Berlin; Kulmbach Beer Festival; International Music Seminar in Weimar

August
: Heidelberg Castle Festival; wine festivals throughout the Rhineland area

September-October
: Munich's Oktoberfest, the world's biggest beer festival; Berlin Festival of Music & Drama

October
: Frankfurt Book Fair; Bremen Freimarkt; Gewandhaus Festival in Leipzig; Berlin Jazzfest

November
: St Martin's Festival throughout Rhineland and Bavaria

December
: Many Christmas fairs throughout Germany, most famously in Munich, Nuremberg, Berlin, Essen and Heidelberg

POST & TELECOMMUNICATIONS

Post

Post offices are generally open from 8 am to 6 pm Monday to Friday and main offices to noon on Saturday. Many train-station post offices stay open later.

Postal Rates Postcard rates are DM1 within Europe, DM2 to North America and Australasia; in Europe, sending a 20-gram letter costs DM1, a 50-gram letter DM2. Aerograms cost DM2, a 20-gram letter (by air to North America and Australasia) DM3. A 500-gram parcel to destinations outside Europe will cost you DM12 (surface) and DM24 (by air).

Receiving Mail Mail can be sent poste restante *(Postlagernde Briefe)* to the main post office in your city (no fee for collection). German post offices only hold mail for two weeks, so plan your drops carefully.

You can also have your mail addressed c/o American Express Travel Service in any large city. American Express holds mail for 30 days but won't accept registered mail or parcels. This service is free if you have an American Express card or travellers' cheques.

Telephone

Most pay phones in Germany accept only phonecards. These cards (available at any post office, many banks and some news kiosks) can be used throughout the country and are a good investment if you're making many calls or ringing abroad. With the DM12 card, call units cost DM0.30 each; with a DM50 card, only DM0.25 each, offering good value to talkative customers. Most post offices have pay phones. Locally, call units last for about five minutes (to other parts of Germany about 30 seconds to a minute).

To ring abroad from Germany, dial 00 followed by the country code, area code and number. You don't have to wait for a dial tone after the area code or international access code. Call units to EU countries and Germany's neighbours last 12 seconds, the rest of Europe about 10 seconds, the USA and Canada 7 seconds, and Australia and NZ 4.4 seconds.

If you want to talk to someone back home, you can call them from a pay phone and quickly give them your number so they can call you back; this is much cheaper than calling reverse charges. You can receive calls this way in phone booths indicated with a bell sign (if the number is actually indicated somewhere in the booth). A reverse-charge call or *R-Gespräch* from Germany is only possible to a limited number of countries, although in the eastern states (outside Berlin) these can still be arranged at post office *Ferngespräch* counters. For calls through the German operator, dial ☎ 0010. To reach the operator direct in the USA and Canada dial ☎ 0130 followed by 00 10 (AT&T), 00 12 (MCI), 00 13 (Sprint) or 00 14 (Canada). To Australia, dial ☎ 0130-80 06 61 for the Optus operator and ☎ 0130-80 00 61 for Telecom.

For international information call ☎ 0 01 18; for local information, call ☎ 0 11 88.

Fax & Telegram

The best places to send faxes and telegrams from are main post offices. Faxes (sending or receiving) are expensive; some shops and businesses offer fax services a little more cheaply. Telegrams can be sent through the post office, from many hotels, or by calling ☎ 11 31.

TIME

Germany is on Central European Time (GMT/UTC plus one hour), the same time zone as Madrid and Warsaw. Daylight-saving time comes into effect at the end of March, when clocks are turned one hour forward. At the end of September they're turned an hour back again. Times are usually indicated with the 24-hour clock, eg 6.30 pm is 18.30.

ELECTRICITY

Electricity is 220 V, 50 Hz. European standard two-pronged plugs are used.

LAUNDRY

You'll find a coin-operated laundry *(Münzwäscherei)* in most cities, though they are less common in the east. Some camping grounds and a few hostels also have them. Your best bet is to ask your hotel, hostel or camping ground manager. If you're staying in a private room, chances are your host will take care of your washing for a reasonable fee. Most major hotels provide laundering services for fairly steep fees.

WEIGHTS & MEASURES

Germany uses the metric system. Like other Continental Europeans, Germans indicate decimals with commas and thousands with points. Cheese and other food items are often sold per *Pfund*, which means 500 grams.

BOOKS & MAPS

The German literary tradition is strong and there are many works that provide excellent background to the German experience. These include Günter Grass' *The Tin Drum* and Thomas Mann's *Buddenbrooks*. Mark Twain's *A Tramp Abroad* is recommended for his comical observations of German life. For more cultural detail and insights into the German character, find a paperback edition of *The Germans* by the Canadian professor Gordon Craig.

The green *Michelin Guide* to Germany is strong on culture, but weak on practical travel details. A good collection of motoring itineraries is presented in *German Country Inns & Castles*, written by Karen Brown and published by Harrap, but it only concentrates on up-market accommodation.

Locally produced maps of Germany are among the best in the world. Most tourist offices have free city maps. The automobile clubs ADAC and AvD produce excellent road maps. More detailed maps can be obtained at most bookshops. The best city maps are made by Falkplan with a patented folding system.

MEDIA

Germany's cities can provide an overload of information, but away from major train stations and airports it's often difficult to obtain reading material of any kind in English.

Newspapers & Magazines

The most read newspapers in Germany are *Die Welt*, *Bild*, *Frankfurter Allgemeine*, Munich's *Süddeutsche Zeitung*, and the green-leaning *Die Tageszeitung (Taz)*. The most popular magazines are *Der Spiegel*, *Die Zeit* and *Stern*. The *International Herald Tribune* is available in most major cities, as are the international editions of *Time* and *Newsweek*.

Of special interest to Berlin visitors are the fortnightly magazines *Tip* and *Zitty*. The Berlin newspaper *Zweite Hand* (Second

Hand) comes out three times a week and carries classified listings. Throughout the paper, the word *biete* lists things being offered while *suche* indicates ads placed by people looking for something (see the Berlin section). In Hamburg, the weekly paper *Avis* publishes classifieds and the monthly *Szene* magazine covers culture and lifestyles.

Radio & TV

Germany's two main TV channels are ARD and ZDF, while a third, *Drittes Programm*, features regional programming. The best radio bets are the BBC World Service on varying AM and FM wavelengths (depending on the part of the country you're in).

FILM & PHOTOGRAPHY

Germany is a photographer's dream, whether in the Alps or the picturesque old towns. German film and photography equipment is among the best in the world and gear of all makes and types is readily available. Don't pay more than DM10 for a roll of 36-exposure slide film without shopping around first. Developing (if not included) will cost about DM6. Many 24-hour processing outlets also handle slides. The Porst chain offers specials with developing.

HEALTH

Germany is a clean and healthy nation, with no particular health concerns. No vaccinations are required to visit Germany, except if you're coming from certain Third World areas. Tap water is safe to drink everywhere.

Most major hotels have doctors available. In an emergency, look in the telephone book under *Ärztlicher Notdienst* (Emergency Doctor Service). Emergency health care is free for EU citizens with an E111 form, but otherwise, any form of treatment can be very expensive, so make sure you have travel insurance.

DANGERS & ANNOYANCES

Theft and other crimes against travellers are relatively rare. In the event of problems, the police are helpful and efficient. In most areas, the emergency number for the police is ☎ 110.

Be careful in crowded Berlin train stations, where pickpockets are often active. Don't allow anyone to help you put your luggage in a coin locker, especially at west Berlin's Zoo station. Once they've closed the locker, they might switch keys and later come back to pick up your things. Begging for small change is becoming prevalent in crowded city centres.

Africans, Asians and southern Europeans may encounter racial prejudice, especially in eastern Germany, where they have been singled out as convenient scapegoats for economic hardship (directed against immigrants, not tourists). People in eastern Germany are becoming used to foreigners, though a few may still feel a bit awkward in your presence.

WOMEN TRAVELLERS

Women should not encounter particular difficulties while travelling in Germany. The Lübeck-based organisation Frauen gegen Gewalt eV (☎ 0451-70 46 40), Marlesgrube 9, can offer advice if you are a victim of harassment or violence, in person (Tuesday from 5 to 7 pm, Friday from 10 am to noon) or by phone (Monday, Thursday and Friday from 10 am to noon, Tuesday from 5 to 9 pm). Frauenhaus München (☎ 3 54 83 11, 24-hour service ☎ 35 48 30) in Munich also offers advice, and Frauennotruf (☎ 76 37 37) at Güllstrasse 3 in Munich can counsel victims of assault. Many large cities have women-only cafés or teahouses (see the Munich section) and some offer ride services and flat-sharing services exclusively for women.

WORK

Reunification has made what was very difficult virtually impossible. Unemployment is running at historically high levels – in most western states it is near 10% and in eastern states 20% – so Germany is not what you'd call a prime job-hunting area. Citizens of the EU may work in Germany; otherwise no temporary work permits are available. Street artists and hawkers are widespread in the cities, though you should ask the municipal authority about permits.

To get an idea of the sorts of jobs available, check the *Stellenmarkt* (Employment Market) ads in the classified sections of big-city newspapers. Sometimes advertisers for unskilled labour are mainly interested in finding cheap workers and are not concerned whether or not you're legally authorised to work in Germany. Jobs are offered under the heading *Biete*, while people looking for work advertise themselves under *Suche*.

ACTIVITIES

The Germans are active outdoors people, which means there are plenty of facilities for like-minded visitors.

Cycling

Cycling is a favoured recreation. You'll often find marked cycling routes, and eastern Germany has much to offer cyclists in the way of lightly travelled back roads and a well-developed hostel network, especially in the flat, less populated north. Offshore islands like Amrum and Rügen are ready-made for pedal-powered travellers.

For details on Deutsche Bahn's Fahrrad am Bahnhof network and more tips, see Cycling in the following Getting Around section. Always have a good lock for your bike.

Hiking

Walking, hiking and climbing are among the most popular participant sports in the country. There are more than 100,000 km of marked trails throughout Germany and they are busy with hikers on fine weekends.

Verband Deutscher Gebirgs- und Wandervereine, the national hiking association, is at Reichsstrasse 4, 66111 Saarbrücken. It has lots of information on various itineraries, guides and clubs. Popular areas for hiking are the Black Forest, the Bavarian Alps and the Harz Mountains, but other good places are the Bavarian Forest, the so-called Saxon Switzerland area and the Thuringian Forest.

The Alps are the most popular area, and for good reason. Because of the trails (more than 10,000 km) and 50 mountain huts (with varying amenities), hiking the German Alps could be the focus of any trip. The best source of information is the Deutscher Alpenverein (☎ 089-2 11 22 40), Praterinsel 5, 80538 Munich. For alpine information, call ☎ 089-29 49 40.

Hikers' car parks *(Wanderparkplätze)* are ideal starting points for drivers wishing to embark on circuit hikes. See also Hiking in the following Getting Around section.

Joy Flights

For an experience with a difference, consider the special Lufthansa flights available from 40 airports in and around German cities. Flown by slow, angular 1930s Junkers JU-52 transport planes, these flights, though expensive, give breathtaking views of German cities in a 30-minute circuit. One way to cut the DM240 cost is to head to eastern Germany, where there are 20-minute flights (DM160). To book in advance, write or send a fax to Lufthansa Traditionsflug GmbH (fax 040-50 70 50 61), Box 630300, 22313 Hamburg. To enquire in Germany, call Frau Wirdemann (☎ 040-50 70 17 17) between 10 am and 1 pm or 2 and 2.30 pm on weekdays.

Skiing

The Bavarian Alps are the most extensive area for downhill and cross-country skiing and Garmisch-Partenkirchen is the most popular Alpine resort. Those who wish to avoid the glitz, glamour and prices there may want to try the Black Forest or the Harz Mountains.

Taking your own gear is cheaper, though usually impractical; all winter resorts have full rental facilities. Daily rates for good, full downhill kit start around DM30 and daily lift tickets cost at least DM25.

The skiing season generally runs from early December to late March. It's possible to ski all year on the higher runs of the Zugspitze near Garmisch-Partenkirchen. In the shoulder season, discounted ski package weeks are advertised by *Weisse Wochen* signs in tourist offices, hotels and ski resorts.

HIGHLIGHTS

Museums & Galleries

Germany is a museum-lover's dream. Munich features the huge Deutsches Museum and Nuremberg offers the country's biggest cultural collection in the Germanisches Nationalmuseum. Cologne's Römisch-Germanisches Museum is one of the finest of its type in the world. Frankfurt's Museumsufer (Museum Bank) has enough museums for any addict. The Dahlem Museum in Berlin and the Neue Meister Gallery in Dresden are among the chief art museums, but treasures of another sort are at Dresden's Grünes Gewölbe. Lesser known are the excellent special-interest museums including the oceanic museum and aquarium Meeresmuseum in Stralsund and the Pergamon museum of antiquities in Berlin.

Castles

Germany has castles of all periods and styles. If you're into castles, make sure to hit Heidelberg, Neuschwanstein, Burg Rheinfels on the River Rhine, Burg Eltz on the Moselle, the medieval Königstein and Wartburg castles, Renaissance Wittenberg Castle, baroque Jagdschloss Moritzburg and romantic Wernigerode Castle.

Historic Towns

Time stands still in much of Germany, and some of the best towns in which to find this flavour are Rothenburg ob der Tauber, Goslar and Regensburg. Meissen and Quedlinburg have a fairy-tale air, Weimar has a special place in German culture, and Bamberg and Lübeck are two of Europe's true gems. The old parts of many large cities also impart this historic feel.

Hotels & Restaurants

Some sleeping highlights include the hostels along the Rhine and Moselle rivers, in Rothenburg and in Nuremberg, and summer camping at 'the Tent' in Munich. The church-operated Verband Christlicher Hotels chain will remain good mid-range options through eastern Germany's hotel squeeze. The Hotel zum Ritter is in a 16th-century building on the main square in picturesque Heidelberg.

The restaurants along Frankfurt's Berger Strasse offer a cosmopolitan setting, and in Düsseldorf's lively city centre you can eat and drink on the pedestrian streets. In Weimar, Anno 1900 has a relaxed turn-of-the-century ambience and Leipzig wouldn't be the same without its Auerbachs Keller. Zur Letzten Instanz, Schwarzes Café and Café Voltaire are Berlin eateries you'll enjoy.

ACCOMMODATION

Accommodation in Germany is generally well organised, though since privatisation eastern Germany has been a little short on budget beds; private rooms are one option in these emergencies. If you're after a hotel or private room, head straight for the tourist office and use the room-finding service *(Zimmervermittlung)*, which usually costs DM3 to DM5. Staff will usually go out of their way to find something in your price range, although telephone bookings are not always available. The German Tourist Board associate ADZ Room Reservation Service (☎ 069-75 10 56), Corneliusstrasse 34, 60325 Frankfurt/Main is a national booking agency.

Accommodation usually includes breakfast. Look for signs saying 'Zimmer frei' (rooms available) or 'Fremdenzimmer' (tourist rooms) in house or shop windows of many towns. In official health spas, displayed prices usually include *Kurtaxe* (tourist tax) levies, but you should check (see the following Hostels section).

Camping

There are more than 2000 camping possibilities, so tenting it can be excellent. Most camping grounds are open from April to September, but several hundred stay open throughout the year. The best overall source of information is the Deutscher Camping Club, Mandlstrasse 28, 80802 Munich. Local tourist information sources can help too.

The range of facilities varies greatly, from quite primitive to ridiculously packed with amenities (and people). For camping on private property, permission from the landowner is required. If you can't find the landowner, check with the local police.

Many camping grounds in eastern Germany rent small bungalows, which are convenient if it's raining. But if you want to make camping your main form of accommodation, you'll probably need your own transport, since sites tend to be far from city centres.

Hostels

The youth hostel *(Jugendherberge)* situation in Germany is arguably the best in the world, which is to be expected of the country that pioneered the concept. There are more than 600 of them conveniently located throughout the country, ranging from big-city properties to excellent locations for the outdoors enthusiast.

Deutsches Jugendherbergswerk or DJH (☎ 05231-7 40 10, Hauptverband, 32754 Detmold), coordinates all affiliated Hostelling International (HI) hostels in Germany. The full DJH handbook, *Jugendherbergen in Deutschland,* is a detailed guide in which you can follow the basic details even if you don't know much German. It costs DM14.80 at hostels or from DJH offices and is the only full guide to all German hostels (at the back is a list of hostels for Switzerland, Austria and Luxembourg).

Almost all hostels in Germany are open all year. Visitors must be a member of a Hostelling International-affiliated organisation. If not, they must pay DM6 per night for a guest card and after six nights they receive full membership – not too bad a deal, considering that junior/senior membership for a German national costs DM18/30.

Hostels generally cost from DM17 to DM30 (in health-resort areas such as Sylt or Füssen you will pay just over DM2 extra per night as Kurtaxe). Camping at a hostel (where permitted) is usually half-price. If you don't have a hostel-approved sleeping sheet, it usually costs from DM4.50 to DM6.50 to hire one (some hostels insist you hire one anyway). Breakfast is usually included in the overnight price (a pot of coffee may be DM2 extra). Lunch or an evening meal could cost anything from DM4.50 to DM9.

Theoretically, visitors aged under 27 get preference, but in practice prior booking or arrival determines who gets rooms, not age. In Bavaria, though, the strict maximum age for anyone except group leaders is 27. Check-in hours vary, but you must usually be out by 9 am. You don't need to do chores at the hostels and there are few rules.

The *Jugendgästehäuser* (youth guesthouses) offer some recreational extras, bonus facilities, often freer hours and, occasionally, good single rooms for DM35 or less (you should expect compulsory sheet rental as well).

Pensions & Guesthouses

Pensions offer the basics of hotel comfort without asking hotel prices. Many of these are private houses with several rooms to rent, a bit out of the centre of town. Some proprietors are a little sensitive about who they take in and others are nervous about telephone bookings – you may have to give a time of arrival and stick to it (many well-meaning visitors have lost rooms by turning up late).

Cheap Hotels

Budget hotel rooms can be a bit hard to come by in Germany during the summer months, although there is usually not much seasonal price variation. The cheapest hotels only have rooms with shared toilets (and showers) in the corridor.

Expensive Hotels

Expensive hotels in Germany provide few advantages for their up-market prices. The best time to splurge on them is during weekends or lulls in trade-fair activity, when you can sometimes take advantage of a package deal or special discounts.

Long-Term Rentals

Rental of apartments (usually housing more than two people) is very popular in Germany. Have a look in newspaper classifieds for

Ferienwohnungen or *Ferien-Apartments*, although these can also be booked through the *Mitwohnzentrale* accommodation-finding services. Rates vary dramatically, but are typically lower than hotels and decrease with the length of stay.

FOOD

Germans are hearty eaters, but this is truly a meat-and-potatoes kind of country. Though vegetarian and health-conscious restaurants are starting to sprout, it's best to stop counting calories and cholesterol levels while in Germany. Many restaurants are more than happy to prepare something vegetarian if you give fair warning, and pizza outlets provide non-carnivores with alternatives.

Restaurants always post their menus outside with prices. Watch for daily specials chalked onto blackboards. Beware of early closing hours, and of the *Ruhetag* (rest day) at some establishments. Tipping is not necessary, although you might round up the bill as you're paying. Lunch is the main meal of the day; getting a main meal in the evening is never a problem, but you may find that the dish or menu of the day only applies to lunch.

A *Gaststätte* is somewhat less formal than a *Restaurant*, while a *Weinkeller* or *Bierkeller* would be fine for a lighter meal. Many town halls have an atmospheric restaurant, or *Ratskeller*, in the basement, serving traditional German dishes at reasonable prices. If you're on a low budget, you can get German sausages and beer at stand-up food stalls *(Schnellimbiss* or simply *Imbiss)* in all the towns. A *Konditorei* or *Stehcafé* is the place to indulge in that sinful German habit of coffee and cakes.

A good German breakfast usually includes rolls, butter, jam, cheese, several sliced meats, a hard-boiled egg, and coffee or tea. (Note that the German word for jam is *Marmelade*, and that marmalade is usually referred to as *Orangenmarmelade*.) Germans at home might eat their heaviest meal at noon and then have lighter evening fare *(Abendbrot* or *Abendessen*, consisting of cheeses and bread).

Cafés & Bars

Much of the German daily and social life revolves around these institutions, which are often hard to separate as both coffee and alcohol are usually served. They're great places to meet locals without spending too much money.

Snacks

The Schnellimbiss is the best place for snacks and quick meals. These places serve food ranging from doner kebabs to traditional German sausage and the food is usually quite reasonable and filling; often you stand up to eat.

Main Dishes

Sausage *(Wurst)*, in its hundreds of forms, is by far the most popular main dish. Regional favourites include *Bratwurst* (spiced sausage), *Weisswurst* (veal sausage) and *Blutwurst* (blood sausage). In Berlin, *Eisbein* (pickled pork knuckles) is the dish of choice. Other popular choices include *Rippenspeer* (spare ribs), *Rotwurst* (black pudding), *Rostbrätl* (grilled meat) and many forms of *Schnitzel* (breaded pork or veal cutlet).

Potatoes feature prominently in German meals, either fried *(Bratkartoffeln)*, mashed *(Kartoffelpüree)*, grated and then fried (the Swiss *Rösti)*, or as French fries *(Pommes Frites)*; a Thuringian speciality is *Klösse*, a ball of mashed and raw potato which is then cooked (a bit like a dumpling). In Baden-Württemberg, potatoes are often replaced by *Spätzle* – wide, flattened noodles.

Italian, Chinese and other ethnic cuisines are available as mid-price options.

Desserts

Germans are keen on rich desserts. A popular choice is the *Schwarzwälder Kirschtorte* (Black Forest cherry cake), which is one worthwhile tourist trap. Desserts and pastries are also often enjoyed during another German tradition, the 4 pm coffee break.

Fruit

Predictably in a meat-and-potatoes society, fruit is not available in great variety, but most groceries and markets have a fairly good, if expensive, fruit section.

Self-Catering

It's very easy and relatively cheap to put together picnic meals in any town. Simply head for the local market or supermarket and stock up on breads, sandwich meats, cheeses, wine and beer. Chains such as Penny-Markt and Norma can be good places to start, though they may lack a wide range.

DRINKS

Buying beverages can get very expensive. Be very careful at restaurants, and, if you like lots of liquids, make a point of buying your drinks in supermarkets.

Nonalcoholic Drinks

The most popular choices are mineral water and soft drinks. Nonalcoholic beers are becoming more popular and are quite good. Löwenbräu makes an especially tasty non-alcoholic beer that is frequently served on tap.

Alcohol

Beer is the national beverage and it's one cultural phenomenon that must be adequately explored. The beer is excellent and still relatively cheap. Each region and brewery has its own distinctive taste and body.

Beer-drinking in Germany has its own vocabulary. *Vollbier* is 4% alcohol by volume, *Export* is 5% and *Bockbier* is 6%. *Helles Bier* is light, while *dunkles Bier* is dark. Export is similar to, but much better than, typical international brews, while the *Pils* is more bitter. *Alt* is darker and more full-bodied. A speciality is *Weizenbier*, which is made with wheat instead of barley malt and served in a tall, half-litre glass with a slice of lemon.

Eastern Germany's best beers hail from Saxony, especially *Radeberger Pils* from near Dresden and *Wernesgrüner* from the Erzgebirge on the Czech border. *Berliner Weisse*, or 'Berlin white', is a foaming, low-alcohol wheat beer mixed with red or green fruit syrup. The breweries of Cologne produce their own specialities, and in Bamberg *Schlenkerla Rauchbier* is smoked to a dark-red colour.

German wines are increasing in popularity throughout the world, and for good reason. German wines are typically white, light and relatively sweet. As with beer, the cheaper wines are almost as cheap as bottled water or soft drinks, and quite good. Germans usually ask for a *Schoppen* of whatever – a solid wine glass holding 200 or 250 ml. A *Weinschorle* or *Spritzer* is white wine mixed with mineral water. Wines don't have to be drunk with meals. The Rhine and Moselle valleys are the classic wine-growing regions, but Franconian labels are becoming more popular. The *Ebbelwei* of Hesse is a strong apple wine with an earthy flavour.

ENTERTAINMENT

The German heritage is associated with high culture, and the standard of theatre performances, concerts and operas is among the best in Europe. Berlin is unrivalled when it comes to concerts and theatre, Dresden is famed for its opera, and Hamburg (by now) is synonymous with *Cats*.

Cinemas

Films are widely appreciated in Germany, but foreign films are usually dubbed into German. English-language subtitled options are limited to large cities like Munich, Hamburg and Frankfurt.

Nightclubs

Because of the German preference for pubs offering beer and conversation, nightclubs are not especially popular outside large cities. Many of these clubs are in international hotels, patronised by foreigners with money to burn. There are, however, exceptions, and any young local or tourist office can point you in the right direction.

Spectator Sports

Soccer is the sport of choice for the masses who like to watch rather than participate; almost every city or town has at least one team and stadium. The more genteel have taken to tennis since the international success of the best German players. Motor racing attracts huge and enthusiastic crowds, reflecting the Germans' special relationship with the automobile. Winter sports have always held a special place in the German heart.

THINGS TO BUY

Because of the general high costs in Germany, there are no true bargains but plenty of souvenirs. Among the better prospects here are the colourful heraldic emblems. There are also certain regional artefacts; of particular interest are cuckoo clocks from the Black Forest, the wines of various regions, and Bavarian wooden carvings. Art reproductions, books and posters are part of the cultural scene and are sold in some museums and speciality shops.

Getting There & Away

AIR

The main arrival/departure points for Germany are Frankfurt, Munich and Berlin – Frankfurt is Europe's busiest airport after Heathrow. Flights are priced competitively among all major airlines, but Germany's national carrier, Lufthansa, offers the most flexibility. The German charter company, LTU, also makes regular scheduled international flights.

Flights to Frankfurt are usually cheaper than to other German cities. Regular flights from Western Europe to Germany are usually more expensive than the train or bus, but not always: discount air tickets from London can be less than £100 return. Lufthansa alone has about 40 flights a day from the UK to Germany. It also flies from North America and Australia, but not from New Zealand (Air New Zealand provides direct flights via Los Angeles). Munich's new airport handles most main Lufthansa flights to and from southern Germany. Lufthansa's central reservation and flight information number is ☎ 01803-80 38 03 and can be dialled from anywhere in Germany at 23 Pf per minute.

It might be worth looking into the various fly/drive or flight/accommodation packages put together by travel agents or the airlines. Lufthansa often has special deals, particularly from the USA, and if you plan to hire a car, prices can be very attractive. A Lufthansa package offers flights to/from Frankfurt with connecting rail journeys to/from six other cities between Cologne and Nuremberg.

To and from the former Soviet Union, Lufthansa has regular connections with the Baltic States, Belorussia, Ukraine, Moscow and St Petersburg. It also flies from Düsseldorf to Prague and from Berlin to Prague, Budapest or Warsaw; there are many discount options.

An airport departure tax of DM6 to DM8 is included in ticket prices.

LAND

Bus

If you're already in Europe, it's generally cheaper to get to/from Germany by bus than it is by train or plane. Some of the coaches are quite luxurious, with toilet, air-con and snack bar. Advance reservations may be necessary, and any German travel agency should be able to tell you where to get them. Return fares are noticeably cheaper than two one-way fares.

Eurolines has a youth fare for those aged under 26 that saves around 10%. It operates daily services between London and Frankfurt which cost DM136/231 (adult one way/return), and four services a week (Thursday, Friday, Saturday and Monday) between London and Munich (DM146/282); Frankfurt-Paris tickets cost DM78/148. Other Eurolines services include Frankfurt-Warsaw and Munich-Prague (DM92/123), Munich-Paris (DM100/160), Munich-Budapest (DM95/145) and Munich-Győr (DM80/120). In Germany, Eurolines is represented by Deutsche Touring GmbH (☎ 069-7 90 30 or 7 90 32 51), Am Römerhof

17, 60486 Frankfurt/Main, though travel agents should be able to help you with tickets.

Train

The train is a good way to get to Germany if you're already in Western Europe, and is a lot more comfortable (if a bit more expensive) than the bus. But it is worth noting that, although the daytime services are frequent, rapid, and comfortable, overnight international trains are increasingly being made up from sleeping cars only, and the few seats are usually 2nd class.

The German word for train station is *Bahnhof*, often abbreviated *Bf;* the main train station is *Hauptbahnhof*, often abbreviated *Hbf*.

Berlin-Warsaw services via Poznań run several times a day (to and from Berlin Hauptbahnhof or Berlin-Lichtenberg); at least once daily these connect to Paris (the *Nord-Express* runs each evening through Berlin-Zoo). Three times a week the Berlin-Warsaw link carries the *Ost-West-Express* to and from Brest and Moscow.

There are several Berlin-Prague trains daily to and from Berlin Hauptbahnhof or Berlin-Lichtenberg (a few of these originate in or continue to Hamburg) and they run via Dresden.

Some of these continue to Vienna or Bratislava and Budapest and at least one train daily connects to and from Bucharest and Sofia. There are also a few direct Dresden-Prague services. There are direct afternoon and evening Munich-Prague services and some daily slow trains from Plattling in southern Bavaria through Bayerisch Eisenstein to Plzeň (Czech Republic).

Nuremberg is the hub station for picking up or jumping off services to and from Vienna (night services with sleeping cars are available). Most of these will run to and from Frankfurt/Main at intervals of two hours. There are direct Salzburg-Munich trains almost every half-hour, most of which connect to and from Vienna or with services to and from Zagreb and Budapest. Several direct trains run daily between Munich and Innsbruck (via Kufstein) and there are also connections available via Garmisch-Partenkirchen. You can also get trains to Bregenz in western Austria, from where you can connect for Switzerland. There are direct trains from Frankfurt to Basel and Konstanz and fast links between Stuttgart and Zürich (and further into Italy).

Eurail, Inter-Rail and Germanrail passes are not valid to Prague, but special seven-day excursion passes for round trips to Prague are available as extensions to Eurail and Germanrail passes. The best places to buy these extensions in Germany are the *Sonderverkehr* (rail pass) ticket counters and EurAide at Munich Hauptbahnhof and they are also available in the USA through some travel agents. The extensions in 1st/2nd class cost DM80/60 (youth tickets DM65/55, children DM40/30) and cover all supplements. See also Getting There & Away in Munich.

Train passes are also valid on some S-Bahns, such as Munich-Augsburg and the Rhine-Ruhr system encompassing Cologne, Düsseldorf and Bonn (but not Berlin). Beware: you cannot use other local transport (including U-Bahns) in this way.

Car & Motorbike

Germany is served by an excellent highway system from the rest of Western Europe. If you're coming from the UK, the best option (apart from the Channel Tunnel) is to take the car ferry or hovercraft from Dover, Folkestone or Ramsgate to Boulogne or Calais in France. You can be in Germany three hours after the ferry docks.

To and from the south, the main gateways are Munich, Freiburg and Passau, although the mountain autobahn Felbertauernstrasse takes you through Kufstein into Austria at Kitzbühel (and on to Trieste or Venice if you wish), giving superb Alpine views.

Heading for Poland during main holidays, you might find border delays, particularly during Easter at the main crossing of Frankfurt an der Oder.

To enter with a car or motorbike you must be third-party insured and have a Green Card.

Hitching & Ride Services

Hitchhikers should not have too many problems getting to and from Germany via the main highways. Aside from hitchhiking, the cheapest way to get to Germany from elsewhere in Europe is as a paying passenger in a private car. Leaving Germany, or travelling within the country, such rides are arranged by *Mitfahrzentrale* agencies in many German cities. You pay a reservation fee to the agency and a share of petrol and costs to the driver. The local tourist office will be able to direct you to several such agencies, or you can check the entry 'Mitfahrzentrale' in the Yellow Pages phone book. Most of those mentioned in this chapter belong either to the large Arbeitsgemeinschaft Deutscher Mitfahrzentralen (ADM – ☎ 1 94 40 in most cities) where you will pay DM47 from Hamburg to Amsterdam (DM90 to Paris), or the computer-equipped Citynetz Mitfahr-Service (☎ 1 94 44), which has booking fees up to DM33, and set prices from Frankfurt to Paris of DM36 (to Basel DM26).

GERMANY

SEA

If you're heading to/from the UK or Scandinavia, the port options are Hamburg, Cuxhaven, Lübeck and Kiel. The Hamburg-Harwich run carries a growing volume of passengers and a Newcastle-Hamburg ferry sails at least twice weekly from April to September. The Puttgarden-Rødbyhavn ferry is popular among those heading to Copenhagen (see the Hamburg Getting There & Away section for details). In eastern Germany, there are 10 ferries in each direction daily all year between Trelleborg (Sweden) and Sassnitz Hafen near Stralsund (see the Rügen Island section).

There is a daily service between Kiel and Gothenburg (Sweden). A ferry between Travemünde (near Lübeck) and Trelleborg (Sweden) runs four to eight times daily. Ferries also run several times a week between the Danish island of Bornholm and Sassnitz Hafen. Car-ferry service is also good from Gedser (Denmark) to Travemünde and to Rostock. Travemünde-Helsinki 24-hour high-speed runs are also available in summer. Baltic Express sails from Kiel (on Saturday only) to Stockholm and St Petersburg (with connections to Riga). See the Rostock, Warnemünde, Kiel, Stralsund and Rügen Island Getting There & Away sections for more details.

Getting Around

AIR

There are lots of flights within the country, but costs can be prohibitive compared to the train. Lufthansa, together with its charter subsidiary LTU, has the most frequent air services within Germany. Foreign airlines also offer services between major cities. There are several small airlines that offer services between regional cities, as well as to and from the North Frisian Islands.

BUS

As with the train system, the bus network in Germany is excellent and comprehensive. For trips of any distance, however, the train is faster and generally as cheap. Buses are better geared towards regional travel in areas where the terrain makes train travel more difficult.

Europabus, the motor-coach system of Europe's railways, operates within Germany as Deutsche Touring GmbH, a subsidiary of the German Federal Railways (Deutsche Bahn, DB). Europabus services include the Romantic and Castle roads buses in southern Germany, and a seven-day tour of eastern Germany (with an English-speaking guide) that leaves from Frankfurt and visits the key cities of Lutherstadt Wittenberg, Berlin, Potsdam, Dresden, Meissen and Hamburg for DM1695. See the Frankfurt and Romantic Road sections for details, or contact the Deutsche Touring GmbH main booking office (☎ 069-7 90 30), Römerhof 17, 60486 Frankfurt/Main.

TRAIN

The German train system is one of the best in the world. The eastern and western train systems have now been fully merged to form the Deutsche Bahn (DB), although fares on much of the former DR eastern network will remain lower for some time.

DB's InterCity Express (ICE) and the faster ICE Sprinter trains offer ultrarapid services and special fares apply. Travelling at speeds of over 250 km/h, ICE trains now dominate some long-distance routes between large cities, such as Frankfurt-Berlin (DM218/152 1st/2nd class) and Hamburg-Munich (DM324/218 1st/2nd class). ICE trains also run other major city-to-city routes such as Frankfurt-Nuremberg, but these routes are still mainly serviced by rather less rapid InterCity (IC) trains or the long-distance InterRegio express trains. For all IC trains a supplementary charge applies (DM6, or DM8 if purchased from the conductor); holders of Eurail, Inter-Rail and Germanrail passes do not pay supplements on ICE or IC trains. There are also slower D and E trains, which generally run regional and night services.

All larger train stations in Germany have coin-operated 24-hour luggage lockers (DM2 for small lockers; DM4 for large lockers). *Gepäckaufbewahrung* (left-luggage) counters are sometimes more convenient and charge similar rates.

Reservations

On holidays and in the busy summer season, reservations are recommended, particularly for sleeping compartments. Most night trains are equipped with 1st-class and 2nd-class sleeping compartments (four or six people per compartment), which must be booked at least one day beforehand; otherwise turn up on the platform and ask the conductor. The surcharge for the simplest 2nd-class D-train sleeping bunk is DM8 (or DM26 with sheets and other services); more expensive sleeping-car tickets are available for three or two-bed compartments, and also one-bed compartments in 1st class.

Passes & Discounts

In most cases, the least expensive way of riding Germany's trains is with some sort of rail pass; it also allows you to avoid the often long ticket queues.

The Germanrail Pass is available to anyone not resident in Germany, and entitles you to unlimited 1st or 2nd-class travel for five, 10 or 15 days within a one-month period. It costs US$178, US$286 and US$386 respectively (2nd class). A similar setup is the Germanrail Youth Pass, limited to 2nd-class travel by those aged between 12 and 25, which costs US$138, US$188 and US$238 respectively. The Germanrail Twin Pass for couples costs US$300, US$514 and US$662 respectively (2nd class). These passes can be obtained in the UK, Australia or the USA, and at all major train stations in Germany itself (passport required). They are valid on all trains, DB buses, and some river services operated by the Köln-Düsseldorfer Line. Of course, Inter-Rail and Eurail passes are also good within Germany.

The one-month Tramper Ticket, available to anyone under 22 and for students under 26 years of age, allows unlimited train travel within Germany and costs DM350 (or DM465 with ICE option). The Tramper Ticket works out cheaper per day than either the Inter-Rail or Eurail youth passes, so if you'll be travelling within Germany for four weeks or more it's your cheapest rail option – unless, that is, your Eurail or Inter-Rail pass has already been validated.

If you're over 26 years of age and intend travelling in Germany for longer than one month, the BahnCard may be a cheaper option than any rail pass. The basic 2nd-class BahnCard costs DM220 (DM110 for juniors, students and card-holders' spouses) and is valid for one year; it allows you to buy train tickets (including IC and ICE trains) and some regional bus tickets for half price. Remember that fares are lower on eastern Germany's rail network, so the BahnCard pays for itself more quickly during travel within western Germany.

Apart from youth, student and senior discounts on some tickets, there are various permanent and temporary reduced-rate ticket offers available. DB-accredited agents, such as Reise Welt and ABR, are often more helpful in explaining discount offers than the DB ticket offices themselves.

The Super-Sparpreis Ticket, a return ticket between any two stations in Germany (and also Salzburg in Austria), costs DM190. It remains valid for 30 days and allows stopovers and travel on ICE trains, and a second person can be included for DM90. You cannot use it on Friday, Sunday or public holidays. If arriving very late is not a problem, the Guten-Abend-Ticket is good value and is valid for unlimited train travel from 7 pm until 2 am. It costs DM49 in 2nd class and DM89 in 1st class (or DM59 in 2nd class and DM99 in 1st class with ICE option).

Many train stations now require passengers to buy tickets from vending machines for shorter distances – it's generally more convenient anyway. If you're travelling farther than anywhere indicated on the machine, press button X for the maximum fare and contact the conductor on board. Holders of the BahnCard should press the 'Kind' (child) button for a half-price ticket. Tickets can be bought from the conductor with a surcharge of DM5 (or DM10 for ICE trains).

Train tickets and passes are also valid on the S-Bahn (suburban train system) except in Berlin.

CAR & MOTORBIKE

German roads are excellent, and motorised transport can be a great way to tour the country. Prices for fuel vary from DM1.50 to DM1.65 per litre for unleaded super, and DM1.60 to DM1.75 per litre for leaded super. Avoid buying fuel at more expensive autobahn filling stations.

The autobahn system of motorways runs throughout Germany. Road signs (and most motoring maps) indicate national autobahn routes in blue with an 'A' number, while international routes have green signs with an 'E' number. Though very efficient, the autobahns are often busy, and literally present life in the fast lane. Tourists often have trouble coping with the very high speeds and the dangers involved in overtaking – don't overestimate the time it takes for a car in the rear-view mirror to close in at 180 km/h. Secondary roads are easier on the nerves, much more scenic, and still present a fairly fast way of getting from A to B.

Cars are less practical in the centre of most cities due to one-way streets and extensive pedestrian zones. Vending machines in the streets of many inner-city areas sell parking vouchers which must be displayed clearly behind the windscreen, but it's usually more convenient to leave you car at a central *Parkhaus* (car park) and proceed on foot. Most cities have automated car parks with signs indicating available space; rates are roughly DM18 per day or DM2.40 per hour.

Road Rules

Road rules are easy to understand and standard international signs are in use. The usual speed limits are 50 km/h in built-up areas (in effect as soon as you see the yellow nameboard of the town) and 100 km/h on the open road. The speed on autobahns is unlimited, though there's an advisory speed of 130 km/h; exceptions are clearly signposted. The highest permissible blood-alcohol level is 0.08% in western Germany and 0.05% in eastern Germany. Obey the road rules carefully: the German police are very efficient and issue heavy on-the-spot fines; speed and red-light cameras are in widespread use, and notices are sent to the car's registration address wherever that may be.

Rental

All of the major car-rental firms operate in Germany. There are many lower-priced packages, as well as smaller budget rental companies. Fly/drive packages can give excellent value for money; Lufthansa offers deals from US$25 per day if you book for longer than four weeks. Otherwise, shopping around upon arrival is preferable to making prior bookings. Larger companies such as Europcar and Autohansa offer very competitive weekend specials from around DM99 (for an Opel Corsa or a Renault Clio). Note that to hire you must usually be at least 21 (sometimes 23) years of age; some car-rental offices insist on payment by credit card or Eurocheque.

Purchase
Due to the costs and paperwork hassles involved, buying a car in Germany tends to be an unwise option. Experienced car dealers from Eastern Europe pick over the bargains, so it's a lot easier purchasing (and reselling) a vehicle in other Western European countries.

Within Germany, Berlin is one of the best places to shop around for used cars – if you know what to look for. Don't buy any vehicle without checking first that it has a current TÜV certificate of roadworthiness. The Berlin newspaper *Zweite Hand* has a separate car edition with thousands of listings each week. Opel Corsas – with more than a few years on the clock – can sometimes be snapped up for as little as DM3000. More novel are the GDR-built Wartburgs – the sturdier later models are good value at around DM2000 – and the absolutely no-frills Trabants from DM500 with TÜV.

BICYCLE
Radwandern (bicycle touring) is very popular in Germany. Favoured routes include the Rhine, Moselle and Danube rivers and the Harz Mountains. There are often separate cycling routes so you don't have to use the highways, and cycling is of course strictly *verboten* on the autobahns. If you plan to spend longer than several weeks in the saddle, buying a second-hand bike works out cheaper than renting a bike or bringing your own; good reconditioned models cost from DM300 to DM400. Hostel-to-hostel biking is an easy way to go, and route guides are often sold at local DJH hostels. There are well-equipped cycling shops in almost every town, and a fairly active market for used touring bikes.

A separate ticket must be purchased whenever you carry your bike on a train (DM5.40 for trips under 100 km on local trains; DM8.60 for trips over 100 km on local trains and all trips on other trains). The only rail pass that allows free transport of bikes is the Tramper Ticket. Bikes can be hired at many train stations; see DB's *Fahrrad am Bahnhof* brochures for lists of stations offering this service. Prices are around DM10 to DM15 per day; holders of rail passes or train tickets get a discount. See also Activities in the earlier Facts for the Visitor section.

HITCHING
Trampen (hitching) is considered an acceptable way of getting around in Germany and average waits are short. Don't waste time hitching in urban areas: take public transport to the main exit routes. It's illegal to hitch-hike on autobahns or their entry/exit roads, but service stations can be very good places to pick up a ride. Prepare a sign clearly showing your intended destination in German (eg 'München', not 'Munich'). You can save yourself a lot of trouble by arranging a lift through a *Mitfahrzentrale* (see Hitching & Ride Services in the earlier Getting There & Away section).

HIKING
Walking trails crisscross the German landscape. Two popular long-distance hiking trails are the 280-km Westweg from Pforzheim stretching south through the Black Forest to the Rhine, and the Rennsteig, a ridge path that runs 168 km from Eisenach through the Thuringian Forest. See also Activities in the earlier Facts for the Visitor section, and hiking information elsewhere in this chapter.

BOAT
Boats are most likely to be used for basic transport when travelling to or between the Frisian Islands, though tours along the Rhine and Moselle rivers are also popular. In summer there are frequent services on Lake Constance, but, except for the Constance to Meersburg and the Friedrichshafen to Romanshorn car ferries, these boats are really more tourist craft than a transport option. From April to October, excursion boats ply the lakes and rivers of eastern Germany and are an excellent, inexpensive way of seeing the country. Paddle-wheel

steamers operating out of Dresden are a fine way to tour the Elbe. Cruises are popular between Berlin and Potsdam (see Activities in the Berlin section).

LOCAL TRANSPORT

Local transport is excellent within big cities and small towns, and generally based on buses, trams, S-Bahn (suburban train system) and/or U-Bahn (underground train systems). Most public transport systems integrate buses, trams and trains; fares are determined by the zones or the time travelled – sometimes a combination of the two. Multiticket strips or day passes are generally available and offer far better value than single-ride tickets. See the individual Getting Around entries in this chapter for details.

Bus & Tram

Cities and towns operate their own local bus, trolleybus and/or tram services. In most places you must have a ticket before embarking, and stamp it once aboard (or pay a fine of around DM60 if caught without a validated ticket). Tickets are sold mainly by vending machines at train stations and tram or bus stops. Many bus drivers usually sell single-trip tickets as a service to forgetful passengers, but these are more expensive than tickets bought in advance.

Train

Most large cities have a system of suburban train lines called the S-Bahn. Trains on these lines cover a wider area than buses or trams, but tend to be less frequent. S-Bahn lines are often linked to the national rail network, and sometimes interconnect urban centres; rail cards or tickets are generally valid on these services (except in Berlin).

Underground

A few large cities, such as Berlin, Munich and Frankfurt, have an underground metro system known as the U-Bahn. Although fast and efficient, U-Bahns don't let you see where you're going, which can be quite disorienting.

Taxi

Taxis are expensive and, given the excellent public transport system, not recommended unless you're in a screaming hurry. (They can actually be slower if you're going to or from the airport.) For fast service, look up 'Taxi-Ruf' in the local telephone directory to find the nearest taxi rank. Taxis are metered and cost up to DM2.30 per km and DM4 flagfall; in some places higher night tariffs apply.

TOURS

Local tourist offices offer various tour options, from short city sightseeing trips to multiday adventure, spa-bath and wine-tasting packages. Apart from city tours, other good sources for organised tours in and around Germany are Europabus and Deutsche Bahn.

There are many other international and national tour operators with specific options. Your travel agent should have some details, and it's also worth contacting the German National Tourist Office in your home country. Many airlines also offer tour packages with their tickets.

Berlin

Berlin, the largest city in Germany, has more to offer visitors than almost any city in Europe. Divided by a 162-km wall until mid-1990, East and West Berlin remain separate and will continue to do so for some time – the West as an island of modern Western culture, parts of the East as cast-off ghettos until the sentiments and associations of the past are put aside. Despite plans to return the German government to Berlin, it will be years before the wounds of the Cold War are fully healed, and the reminders are everywhere of a 45-year insanity that in one way or another cost thousands of lives.

Such fresh and indelible scars do not disfigure the rugged tissue beneath – the might and scope of the Prussian achievement, the Berlin chic, the wit and the soul of its people.

This mighty city finally reached maturity in the 1920s, only to be bombed into rubble in WW II. Today, despite having lost a large part of its prewar population, its gross domestic product equals that of countries such as Ireland and Greece, and the city is once more being referred to as the *Hauptstadt*. Present-day Berliners, whose city was so often subjugated, would not presume to predict its future.

History

The first recorded settlement of the present Berlin was a place named Cölln (1237) around the Spree River south of Museumsinsel ('museum island'), although Spandau, the junction of the Spree and the ponded Havel River, is considered to be older. Medieval Berlin developed on the bank of the Spree around the Nikolaikirche and spread north-east towards today's Alexanderplatz. In 1432, Berlin and Cölln, which were linked by the Mühlendamm, merged.

In the 1440s, Elector Friedrich II of Brandenburg established the rule of the Hohenzollern dynasty, which was to last until Kaiser Wilhelm II's escape from Potsdam in 1918. Berlin's importance increased in 1470 when the elector moved his residence here from Brandenburg and built a palace near the present Marx-Engels-Platz (it is hoped that the palace will be reconstructed in its original baroque style).

During the Thirty Years' War Berlin's population was decimated, but the city was reborn stronger than before under the so-called Great Elector Friedrich Wilhelm in the mid-17th century. His vision was the basis of Prussian power, and it was he who sponsored Huguenot refugees seeking princely tolerance. The inscription on the western end of the Französischer Dom testifies to the Huguenots' gratitude to their benefactor, which they amply proved both by their industry and by opening an important link between Berlin and French high culture. The Great Elector's son Friedrich I, the first Prussian king, made the fast-growing Berlin his capital and his daughter-in-law Sophie Charlotte encouraged the development of the arts and sciences and presided over a lively and intellectual court. Friedrich II sought greatness through building and was known for his political and military savvy. All this led to the city being nicknamed *Spreeathen* ('Athens-on-Spree').

The Enlightenment arrived with some authority in the persons of G E Lessing and the thinker and publisher Friedrich Nicolai, who perhaps made Berlin a truly international city.

The 19th century began on a low note, with a French occupation from 1806 to 1813, and in 1848 a bourgeois democratic revolution was suppressed, somewhat stifling the political development that had been set in motion by the Enlightenment. From 1850 to 1870 the population doubled as the Industrial Revolution, spurred on by companies such as Siemens and Borsig, took hold. In 1871 Bismarck united Germany under Kaiser Wilhelm I. The population was almost two million by 1900.

Before WW I Berlin had become an industrial giant, but the war and its aftermath led to revolt throughout Germany. On 9 November 1918 Philipp Scheidemann, leader of the Social Democrats, proclaimed the German Republic from a balcony of the parliament (Reichstag) and hours later Karl Liebknecht proclaimed a free Socialist republic from a balcony of the City Palace. In January 1919 the Berlin Spartacists, Liebknecht and Rosa Luxemburg, were murdered by remnants of the old imperial army, which entered the city and brought the revolution to a bloody end.

On the eve of the Nazi takeover, the Communist Party under Ernst Thälmann was the strongest single party in 'Red Berlin', having polled 31% of the votes in 1932 (incidentally almost exactly the same as the 30% polled by Communists in the municipal elections in East Berlin in May 1990). Berlin was heavily bombed by the Allies in WW II and, during the 'Battle of Berlin' from November 1943 to March 1944, British bombers hammered the city every night. Most of the buildings you see today along Unter den Linden had to be reconstructed from the resultant ruins.

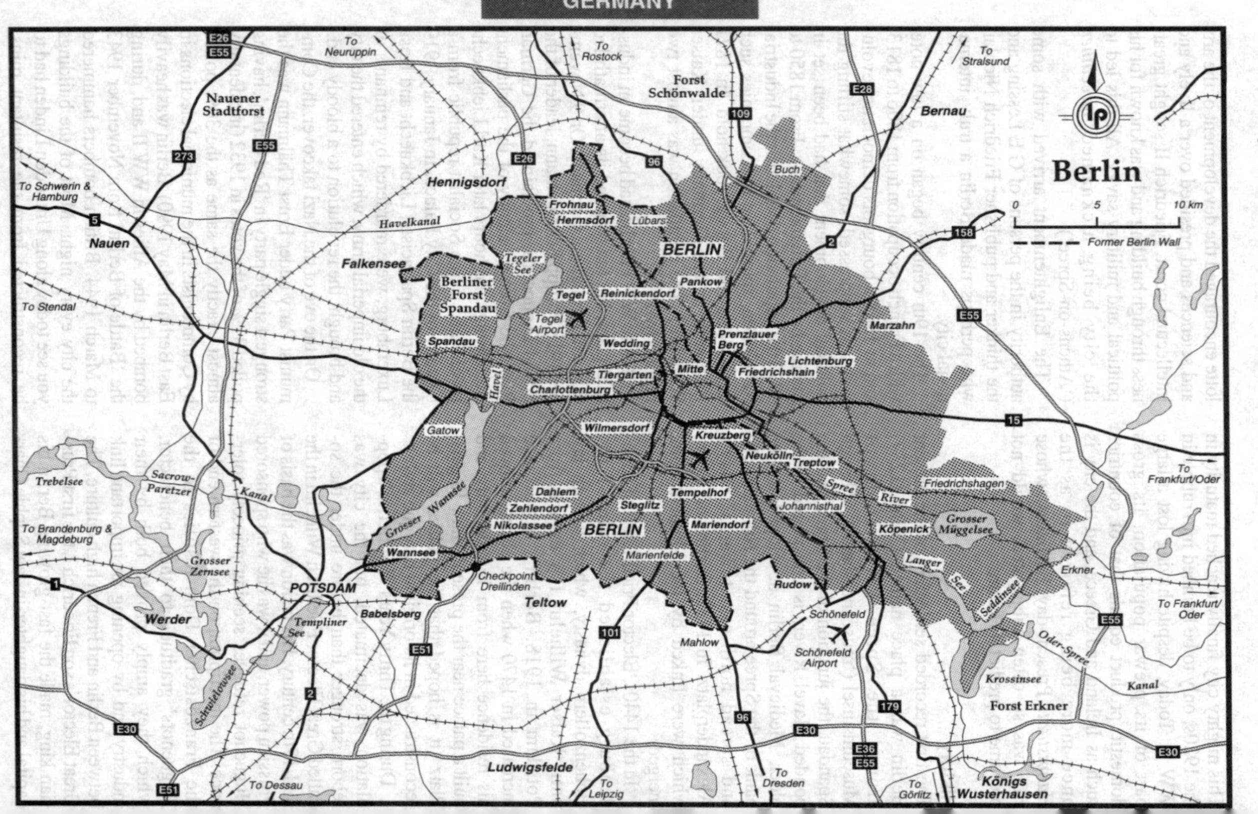
Berlin
0 5 10 km
Former Berlin Wall
To Neuruppin
To Rostock
To Stralsund
Forst Schönwalde
Bernau
Nauener Stadtforst
Buch
To Schwerin & Hamburg
Hennigsdorf
Frohnau
Hermsdorf
Lübars
BERLIN
Havelkanal
Nauen
Falkensee
Tegeler See
Berliner Forst Spandau
Tegel
Reinickendorf
Pankow
To Stendal
Tegel Airport
Marzahn
Spandau
Wedding
Prenzlauer Berg
Lichtenburg
Mitte
Friedrichshain
Tiergarten
Charlottenburg
Havel
Gatow
Wilmersdorf
Kreuzberg
Neukölln
Treptow
Trebelsee
Sacrow-Paretzer Kanal
Dahlem
Tempelhof
Spree
River
Friedrichshagen
To Frankfurt/Oder
Zehlendorf
Steglitz
Johannisthal
Grosser Wannsee
Nikolassee
BERLIN
Mariendorf
Köpenick
Grosser Müggelsee
To Brandenburg & Magdeburg
Wannsee
Marienfelde
Langer See
Grosser Zernsee
Checkpoint Dreilinden
Erkner
POTSDAM
Teltow
Rudow
Seddinsee
To Frankfurt/ Oder
Werder
Templiner See
Babelsberg
Schönefeld
Mahlow
Schönefeld Airport
Oder-Spree
Kanal
Krossinsee
Schwielowsee
Forst Erkner
Ludwigsfelde
To Dessau
To Leipzig
To Dresden
To Görlitz
Königs Wusterhausen
E26
E55
E28
E30
E36
E51
1
2
5
15
96
101
109
158
179
273

The Soviets shelled Berlin from the east, and after the last terrible battle buried 18,000 of their troops.

In August 1945, the Potsdam Conference sealed the fate of the city by agreeing that each of the victorious powers – the USA, Britain, France and the Soviet Union – would occupy a separate zone. In June 1948 the city was split in two when the three Western Allies introduced a western German currency and established a separate administration in their sectors. The Soviets blockaded West Berlin because of this, but an airlift kept it in the Western camp. In October 1949 East Berlin became the capital of the GDR. The construction of the Berlin Wall in August 1961 prevented the drain of skilled labour (between 1945 and 1961 three million East Germans had been lured westward by higher wages).

When Hungary decided to breach the Iron Curtain in May 1989, the GDR government was back where it had been in 1961, but this time without Soviet backing. On 9 November 1989 the Wall opened, and on 1 July 1990, when the Bundesrepublik's currency was adopted in the GDR, the Wall was being hacked to pieces. The Unification Treaty between the two Germanys designated Berlin the official capital of Germany, and in June 1991 the Bundestag voted to move the seat of government from Bonn to Berlin over the next decade at a cost of DM60 to 80 billion.

Orientation

Berlin sits in the middle of the region that from medieval times was known as the Mark, surrounded by the new *Bundesland* of Brandenburg; it is planned eventually to unite the two. Roughly one-third of the city's municipal area is made up of parks, forests (sections of the Berliner Forst), lakes and rivers. In spite of the WW II bombing, there are more trees here than in Paris and more bridges than in Venice. Much of the natural beauty of rolling hills and quiet shorelines is on the south-eastern and south-western sides of the city.

The Spree River winds across the city for over 30 km from the Grosser Müggelsee to Spandau. North and south of Spandau the Havel widens into a series of lakes from Tegel to Potsdam. A network of canals links the waterways to each other and the Oder River to the east and there are beautiful walks along some of them.

You can't really get lost within sight of the brooding and monstrous Fernsehturm (TV Tower). Unter den Linden, the fashionable avenue of aristocratic old Berlin, and its continuation, Karl-Liebknecht-Strasse, extend east from Brandenburger Tor (the Brandenburg Gate) to Alexanderplatz, once the heart of Socialist Germany. Some of Berlin's finest museums are here, on Museumsinsel in the Spree. The cultural centre is around Friedrichstrasse, which crosses Unter den Linden. South of here Berlin Mitte and Friedrichstadt are being restored and redeveloped. Some sections of the former wall have been left for public view and others are yet to be demolished. Around this area are the ugly scars of division (as well as the homeless population), although some Stadtbahn (S-Bahn) and Metro (U-Bahn) stations have been reopened after long disuse.

The ruin and modern annexes of Kaiser-Wilhelm-Gedächtnis-Kirche, the shattered memorial church on Breitscheidplatz a block away from Zoologischer Garten station, form the most visible landmark in west Berlin. The tourist office and hundreds of shops are in Europa-Center at the end of the square farthest from the station. The Kurfürstendamm (known colloquially as the 'Ku'damm'), west Berlin's most fashionable avenue, runs 3.5 km south-west from Breitscheidplatz. To the north-east, between Breitscheidplatz and the Brandenburger Tor, is Tiergarten, a vast city park which was once a royal hunting domain. The park area around the Spree has been chosen, appropriately, for the new national government complex, to be completed in the year 2000.

While in central Berlin, keep in mind that the street numbers usually run sequentially up one side of the street and down the other (important exceptions include Martin-

Luther-Strasse in west Berlin and Unter den Linden), although number guides appear on most corner street signs. Be aware, too, that a continuous street may change names several times, and that on some streets (Pariser Strasse, Knesebeckstrasse) numbering sequences continue after interruptions caused by squares or plazas. Some street and other names have been changed for political reasons and more will follow. The inner-eastern S-Bahn station that formerly was Marx-Engels-Platz is now Hackescher Markt.

Information

Tourist Offices The main office of Berlin-Touristen-Information (☎ 030-2 62 60 31) is at Budapester Strasse 45 in Europa-Center, west Berlin, and is open Monday to Saturday from 8 am to 10.30 pm, Sunday from 9 am to 9 pm. Room reservations cost DM5 per booking (singles/doubles from DM50/75 to DM300/1000). Another office (☎ 030-3 13 90 63) is in the hall of the Berlin-Zoologischer Garten station (Bahnhof Zoo) and is open from 8 am to 11 pm Monday to Saturday; the office at Tegel Airport (☎ 030-41 01 31) keeps similar hours. In east Berlin, go to the Berlin Hauptbahnhof office (☎ 030-2 79 52 09) in the station's main hall. It is an uncrowded place compared to the other two offices, offers full services, and is open from 8 am to 10.30 pm (Sunday 9 am to 9 pm).

Money Main post offices exchange travellers' cheques for a DM6 charge. American Express is at Uhlandstrasse 173-174 (open weekdays from 9 am to 5.30 pm, Saturday to noon). The office cashes American Express travellers' cheques without charging commission, but gives a very ordinary rate if you are converting (this office also offers a client-mail service). Another office is at Friedrichstrasse 172. Thomas Cook has exchange offices near the eastern end of Wittenbergplatz on Kleiststrasse and at Friedrichstrasse near Kochstrasse in Mitte.

The Deutsche Verkehrs-Bank (DVB) has an exchange office with a large yellow sign opposite the ticket windows in Friedrichstrasse train station (open weekdays from 8 am to 8 pm, and weekends from 9 am to 5 pm) and another facing Hardenbergplatz at Zoo station.

The Europa-Center Wechselstube on Breitscheidplatz buys and sells banknotes of all countries without any commission charge and you can easily compare the daily rate with the DVB or other exchange services around Zoo. Branches of the main German banks are not hard to find around Breitscheidplatz and the Kurfürstendamm.

Post & Telecommunications Postamt 12, at Goethestrasse 3 west of Zoo station (open weekdays from 8 am to 6 pm, Saturday to 1 pm), is the best place for international calls: line up at counter No 1 next to the cubicle. You can also call directly and quickly almost anywhere with a phonecard from the phones opposite the post office on the ground level of Zoo station. The post office there is open from 6 am to midnight (Sunday and holidays from 8 am) and there is a rough public fax. The poste restante is also at Zoo; letters should be clearly marked as 'Hauptpostlagernd', and addressed to you at 10612 Berlin 120, Bahnhof Zoo. Postamt 2 beside Alexanderplatz is also a handy telephone and postal centre, although it is open only from 8 am to 6 pm Monday to Friday and to 1 pm Saturday.

The telephone code for all of Berlin is 030. For local information or assistance dial ☎ 01188.

Consulates The following consulates are in Berlin:

Australia

Uhlandstrasse 181-183 in the Kempinski Plaza in west Berlin (☎ 8 80 08 80), open from 9 am to noon and 2 to 4 pm. New Zealand has no representation in Berlin as yet, and the Australians will only help those they call 'stressed New Zealanders' (lost or stolen passport, money, luggage etc).

Bulgaria

Leipziger Strasse 20 (☎ 2 00 09 22). Visas are issued between 2 and 4 pm on Thursday.

GERMANY

Canada
Friedrichstrasse 95, on the 23rd floor of the International Trade Centre (☎ 2 61 11 61 or 20 96 30 01), open weekdays from 9 am to noon

Czech Republic
Wilhelmstrasse 44 (☎ 2 00 04 81), open Monday to Friday from 8.30 am to 11 pm for visas (DM36 for Australians and New Zealanders, DM75 for Canadians)

France
Kurfürstendamm 211 (on the corner of Uhlandstrasse; ☎ 88 59 02 43). The office issues visas Monday to Thursday from 9 am to noon and on Friday from 9 to 11.30 am, although it's generally better to apply at other consulates, such as Bonn or Düsseldorf. You are asked to show identification as you enter.

Hungary
Unter den Linden 76 (☎ 2 29 16 66), open Monday to Friday from 9 am to noon. Visas (required by Australians and New Zealanders) cost DM50.

Poland
Unter den Linden 72 (☎ 2 20 25 51). Single-entry tourist visas, required by Canadians, Australians and New Zealanders, cost DM56.

Russia
Reichensteiner Weg 34-36 (☎ 8 32 70 04). The consular section is open from 9 am to 1 pm Monday, Wednesday and Friday, and from 2 to 5 pm Tuesday and Thursday. If you are booking tours to Russia, travel agencies will often take care of applications: a few private agencies will handle these quicker than Intourist, though generally at a higher price.

Slovakia
Friedrich-Engels-Strasse 91 (☎ 4 82 92 41; U2: Pankow, then tram No 53 to Nordendstrasse), open on Tuesday and Thursday from 8.30 am to noon.

UK
Unter den Linden 32-34 (☎ 2 20 21 31 or 20 18 40), open weekdays from 9 am to noon and 2 to 4 pm

USA
Clayallee 170 (U-Bahn: Oskar-Helene-Heim; ☎ 8 32 40 87 or 8 19 74 54 for consular services), open weekdays from 8.30 to 11.30 am and 1.30 to 3 pm (closed Wednesday afternoon). It's better to go in the afternoon when visa applications are not accepted and there is no queue.

Cultural Events The best information on current events, although it is in German only, is in the monthly magazine *Berlin Programm* (see the following Media section) where not an event nor day is missed. Berlin's galleries, theatres and orchestras distribute monthly guides that are available at the tourist offices, but only Deutsche Oper details its ticket prices.

Travel Agencies Reise Welt has several offices, the most convenient at Alexanderplatz 5 (others are at Schönefeld Airport and Bahnhofstrasse 18 in Köpenick). These are good places to buy train tickets very cheaply or make ferry and package reservations.

SRS Studenten Reise Service, at Marienstrasse 23 near Friedrichstrasse station, offers flights at student or youth (aged 25 or less) fares. It also sells the FIYTO youth and ISIC student cards (DM12; one photo is required). Jugendtourist is a travel service catering to young people and offers package tours here, there and everywhere. The office, on the east side of Berlin Hauptbahnhof station (out of the main tunnel and a few metres to the south), will gladly handle youth (to age 26) and student bookings and can issue ISIC cards if you have proper and recognisable student and personal ID.

Tourist information on Eastern European countries is available from several sources: Cedok (Czech Republic) on Jerusalemer Strasse near the east end of Leipziger Strasse; Ibusz (Hungary), centrally located at ground level in Haus Ungarn (Karl-Liebknecht-Strasse 7); and Polorbis (Poland), at Warschauer Strasse 5 (the Gromada Tourist office at Karl-Liebknecht-Strasse 7 may be handier). The Russian travel specialist Intourist and the Aeroflot office are together on Unter den Linden near the corner of Friedrichstrasse.

Travel agencies offering cheap flights advertise in the *Reisen* classified section of the popular magazine *Zitty*. One of the better discount operators is Alternativ Tours (☎ 8 81 20 89), Wilmersdorfer Strasse 94 (U-Bahn: Adenauerplatz), which specialises in unpublished, discounted fares to anywhere in the world. On Budapester Strasse north-east of the zoo are several agencies catering for exotic locations including the Middle East.

GERMANY

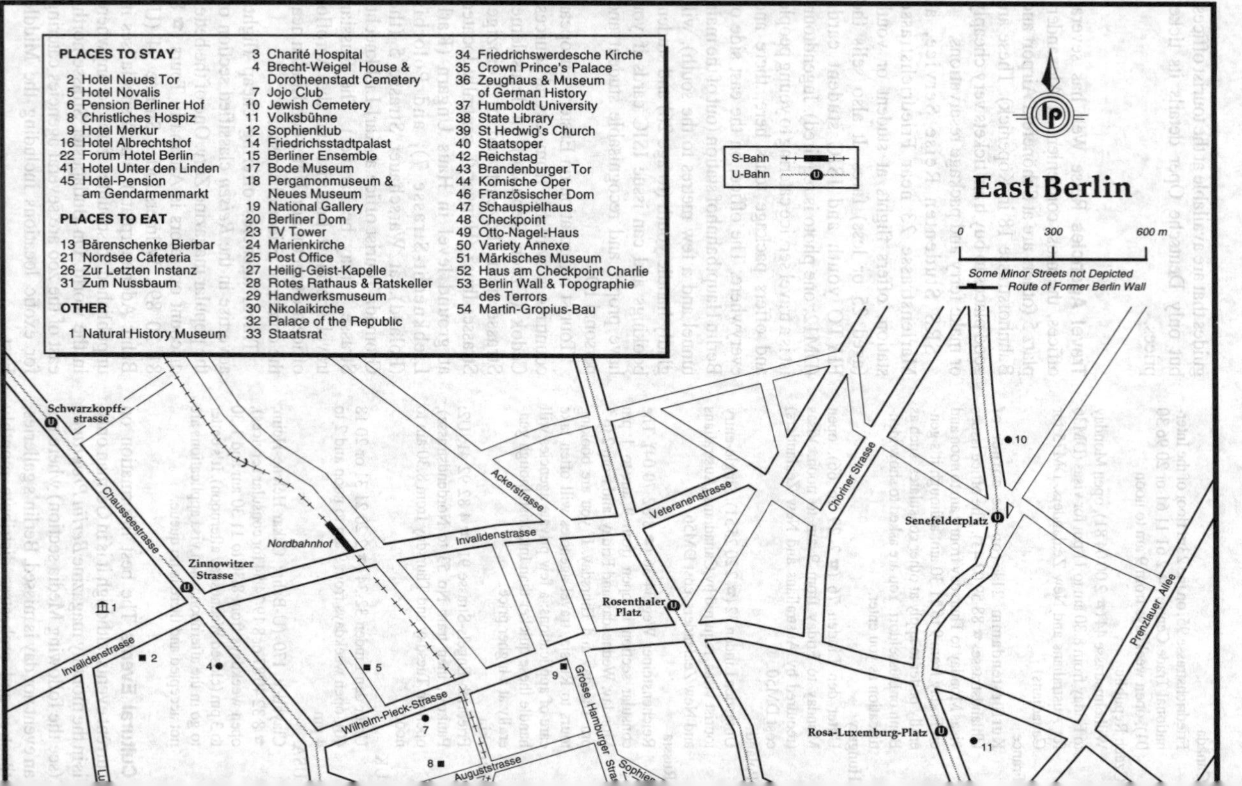

PLACES TO STAY
2 Hotel Neues Tor
5 Hotel Novalis
6 Pension Berliner Hof
8 Christliches Hospiz
9 Hotel Merkur
16 Hotel Albrechtshof
22 Forum Hotel Berlin
41 Hotel Unter den Linden
45 Hotel-Pension am Gendarmenmarkt
PLACES TO EAT
13 Bärenschenke Bierbar
21 Nordsee Cafeteria
26 Zur Letzten Instanz
31 Zum Nussbaum
OTHER
1 Natural History Museum
3 Charité Hospital
4 Brecht-Weigel House & Dorotheenstadt Cemetery
7 Jojo Club
10 Jewish Cemetery
11 Volksbühne
12 Sophienklub
14 Friedrichsstadtpalast
15 Berliner Ensemble
17 Bode Museum
18 Pergamonmuseum & Neues Museum
19 National Gallery
20 Berliner Dom
23 TV Tower
24 Marienkirche
25 Post Office
27 Heilig-Geist-Kapelle
28 Rotes Rathaus & Ratskeller
29 Handwerksmuseum
30 Nikolaikirche
32 Palace of the Republic
33 Staatsrat
34 Friedrichswerdesche Kirche
35 Crown Prince's Palace
36 Zeughaus & Museum of German History
37 Humboldt University
38 State Library
39 St Hedwig's Church
40 Staatsoper
42 Reichstag
43 Brandenburger Tor
44 Komische Oper
46 Französischer Dom
47 Schauspielhaus
48 Checkpoint
49 Otto-Nagel-Haus
50 Variety Annexe
51 Märkisches Museum
52 Haus am Checkpoint Charlie
53 Berlin Wall & Topographie des Terrors
54 Martin-Gropius-Bau
S-Bahn
U-Bahn
East Berlin
0 300 600 m
Some Minor Streets not Depicted
Route of Former Berlin Wall
Schwarzkopffstrasse
Chausseestrasse
Nordbahnhof
Zinnowitzer Strasse
Invalidenstrasse
Ackerstrasse
Veteranenstrasse
Choriner Strasse
Senefelderplatz
Rosenthaler Platz
Prenzlauer Allee
Wilhelm-Pieck-Strasse
Grosse Hamburger Strasse
Auguststrasse
Rosa-Luxemburg-Platz

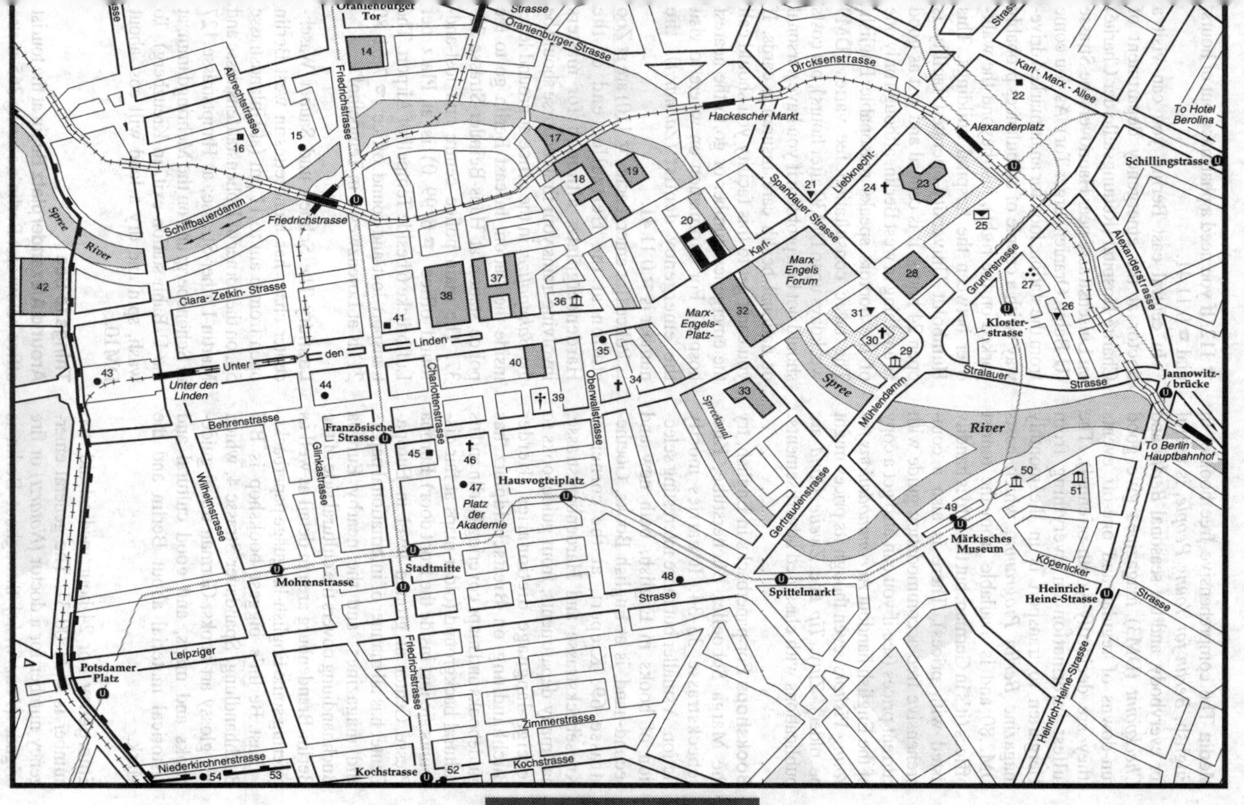

Oranienburger Tor
Oranienburger Strasse
Dircksenstrasse
Karl - Marx - Allee
To Hotel Berolina
Schillingstrasse
Alexanderplatz
Hackescher Markt
Albrechtstrasse
Friedrichstrasse
Schiffbauerdamm
Spree
River
Spandauer Strasse
Liebknecht-
Karl-
Marx Engels Forum
Grunerstrasse
Alexanderstrasse
Klosterstrasse
Clara- Zetkin- Strasse
Marx-Engels-Platz-
Unter den Linden
Stralauer Strasse
Jannowitzbrücke
Mühlendamm
Spreekanal
Oberwallstrasse
Behrenstrasse
Französische Strasse
Charlottenstrasse
Glinkastrasse
To Berlin Hauptbahnhof
Hausvogteiplatz
Platz der Akademie
Gertraudenstrasse
Märkisches Museum
Köpenicker Strasse
Wilhelmstrasse
Stadtmitte
Mohrenstrasse
Spittelmarkt
Heinrich-Heine-Strasse
Leipziger Strasse
Potsdamer Platz
Zimmerstrasse
Kochstrasse
Niederkirchnerstrasse

GERMANY

Media The comprehensive free booklet in English, *Berlin for Young People*, is useful for everybody, and the seasonal *Berlin* and *Checkpoint* (DM3) magazines give good run-downs of regular and one-off events (they are decidedly youth-oriented). The fullest information on everything from Tiergarten to transport is in the monthly magazine *Berlin Programm*, which costs DM2.80 and is available from the tourist offices (it's in German, but the info is handily listed with prices). There is also a comprehensive free accommodation guide with current prices (see if you can also get a copy of the English handout *Accommodations for Young Visitors*, even though its prices might be older). *Zitty*, *Tip* and *Zweite Hand* are publications with classified advertisements.

Bookshops For paperbacks in English, try the Marga Schoeller Bücherstube, Knesebeckstrasse 33-34. It carries mostly fiction. A smaller but more interesting selection of books in English, both new and second-hand, is at English Books, Goethestrasse 69. Kiepert, at the corner of Knesebeckstrasse and Hardenbergstrasse, has many departments, from guidebooks to foreign-language dictionaries. Herder Buchhandlung on Breitscheidplatz has guidebooks and maps covering Berlin and its cultural background (older maps at fair discounts are just inside the front door). Europa Presse Center at ground level in Europa-Center has all manner of international papers and magazines, and the nearby Europa Buchhandlung covers the cultural side of the Berlin-Brandenburg area in detail as well as offering some English-language paperbacks.

East Berlin's biggest bookshop is BU Buchhandlung, Spandauer Strasse 4, which has glossy art books, German travel guidebooks and maps, and good cultural and historical material about Berlin and the Mark.

Emergency For 24-hour medical aid, the number is ☎ 31 00 31. The general emergency number for a doctor *(Notarzt)* or fire brigade *(Feuerwehr)* throughout Berlin is ☎ 112. If you need a pharmacy out of hours, dial ☎ 0 11 41.

In central east Berlin, you can visit a doctor at the emergency department of Charité Hospital (Rettungstelle der Charité) on Luisenstrasse near Hannoversche Strasse (U-Bahn: Oranienburger Tor). As you come from the station, look for an unmarked driveway (with a couple of ambulances probably parked on the right), just beyond the walk-over between the hospital buildings. This Humboldt University-operated facility is open 24 hours. It is central and just as good as anything in west Berlin, although only one of the doctors speaks reasonable English. The basic consultation fee varies (DM9 weekdays up to DM30 after hours), but costs should not be a problem if you have personal or national health care insurance cards. If you can't get to this facility you should call the emergency number or go to the nearest hospital. For information on where to visit the emergency dentist *(Zahnarzt)*, the number is ☎ 0 11 41.

Police (for emergencies ☎ 110) are at Zoo station at the Hertzallee end of the Hardenbergplatz, although for matters involving trains your first recourse should be the *Bahnpolizei* in the office at ground level inside the station. In east Berlin go to the police station at Hans-Beimler-Strasse 27-37. The main police centre and lost-and-found office (☎ 6 99 0) is at Platz der Luftbrücke 6 beside Tempelhof Airport. The transport lost-and-found office (☎ 7 51 80 21) is at Lorenzweg 5 in Tempelhof.

Laundry The Schnell und Sauber Wasch-center chain has laundrettes in west Berlin open from 6 am to 11 pm (at Uhlandstrasse 53; on the corner of Hohenstaufenstrasse and Martin-Luther-Strasse; at Hauptstrasse 127 in Schöneberg; and on the Mehringdamm, at the U-Bahn station exit, in Kreuzberg). To wash, spin and dry a load will cost about DM10.

Things to See

Around Alexanderplatz Begin at the tourist office below east Berlin's soaring 365-metre

GERMANY

TV tower or Fernsehturm (1969). If it's a clear day and the queue isn't too long, pay the DM5 to go up the tower. It's open from 9 am to midnight (except some Mondays and Tuesdays, when it opens at 1 pm). The Telecafé at the 207-metre level revolves once an hour. The complex is being redeveloped at ground level as, oddly enough, a TV station with newsroom. Perhaps the pride of the GDR has not outlived its propaganda uses!

On the opposite side of the elevated train station from the tower is **Alexanderplatz** (or, affectionately, 'Alex'), named after Tsar Alexander I, who visited Berlin in 1805. The area was redesigned several times in the late 1920s but nothing was ever actually built because of the Depression. It was bombed in WW II and completely reconstructed in the 1960s. A redevelopment in line with Peter Behrens' 1929 vision of the Alexanderhaus and the Berolinahaus is now being attempted. The **World Time Clock** (1969) is nearby in case you want to check the time before making a telephone call home. The monumental red **Rotes Rathaus** (known as such for its appearance, not its politics) has been proudly restored and is once again the centre of Berlin municipal government.

Museum Island West of the TV tower, on an island between two arms of the Spree River, is the GDR's **Palace of the Republic** (1976) which occupies the site of the damaged baroque 'City Palace' that was demolished in 1950. During the Communist era, the People's Chamber (Volkskammer) used to meet in this showpiece (which faces Marx-Engels-Platz near the cathedral and the Lustgarten). In 1990 it was discovered that poisonous asbestos had been used in the construction, so this 'palace' too is expected to go, although nobody is volunteering to pay for the planned reconstruction of the palace.

On the southern side near the Spree bank is the former **Staatsrat** (Council of State) building (1964), with a portal from the old city palace incorporated in the façade. The modern white building just across the canal on the eastern side of Marx-Engels-Platz used to house the GDR foreign ministry and is intended to house that of united Germany in the future.

North across the busy avenue looms the great neo-Renaissance cathedral known as **Berliner Dom** (1904), the city's main Protestant church. The imposing edifice beside it is Karl Friedrich Schinkel's 1829 neoclassical **Altes Museum**, although only the rotunda area with its statues of the Greek divinities is open (daily except Monday; admission free). Behind this is the **Neues Museum** (1855), which is closed for rebuilding, but you can visit the adjacent 'old' **national gallery** (admission Tuesday to Saturday DM4, Sunday free; closed Monday), with sculpture by Johan Gottfried Schadow and Christian Daniel Rauch, and 19th and 20th-century paintings. Besides the Renoirs, Monets, Manets, Cézannes and Constables, you can take in the brooding and Romantic death images of Arnold Böcklin, the Prussian military scenes of Adolph Menzel and, in the 'Berlin' rooms, the works of Max Liebermann, Max Beckmann, Max Slevogt and Lovis Corinth. Perhaps the only better collection in Berlin is in the **Martin-Gropius-Bau** on Niederkirchnerstrasse.

The **Pergamon Museum** (admission Tuesday to Saturday DM4, Sunday free; closed Monday) is a feast of classical Greek, Babylonian, Roman, Islamic and Oriental antiquity. The world-renowned Ishtar Gate from Babylon (580 BC), the reconstructed Pergamon Altar from Asia Minor (160 BC) and the Market Gate from Greek Miletus (Asia Minor, 2nd century AD) are among the beautiful artefacts hauled from the Middle East. There's a good, reasonably priced self-service cafeteria outside. The **Bode Museum** (admission Tuesday to Saturday DM4, Sunday free; closed Monday) houses sculpture, paintings, coins and Egyptian art, although not all of the sections are open every day. (A day card covering the Pergamon, Bode and Altes museums, the Otto-Nagel-Haus and the Friedrichwerdersche Kirche costs DM8 and is available at all these museums).

Old Berlin The rebuilt 13th-century **Nikolaikirche** stands amid the interesting Nikolaiviertel quarter, conceived and executed under the GDR's Berlin restoration programme. Inside is a fascinating museum (admission DM3; open from Tuesday to Sunday 10 am to 6 pm) that exhibits relics of early Berlin, Cölln and the Mark and the remains of the church's interiors. Outside the church was erected a fountain displaying an imaginative seal of early Berlin, the city in medieval times being centred on the adjacent Molkenmarkt and the Mühlendamm crossing over the Spree. A statue of a dragon-slaying Sankt Georg overlooks the river. Another medieval church, **Marienkirche** (admission free; open Monday to Thursday from 10 am to noon and 1 to 4 pm, Saturday and Sunday from noon to 4 pm), is on Karl-Liebknecht-Strasse near the TV Tower. If you wish, go to the Sunday service at 10.30 am for a different experience of worship.

You can round off a medieval tour by inspecting the reconstructed vestiges of the **Heilig-Geist-Kapelle**, which mark the spot of the former Spandauer Tor and the earliest town wall, and the bombed-out shell of the **Franciscan Abbey** above the Klosterstrasse U-Bahn station on Gruner Strasse. The **Handwerksmuseum**, in the Nikolaiviertel on the Mühlendamm, has interesting displays of aspects of local working history and economic culture (DM2; closed Monday). Incredibly, the Berlin Museum is closed until 1998, but a new and better museum is promised, including a new wing to display the city's Jewish past. The **Hugenottenmuseum** (DM2), in Französischer Dom on Gendarmenmarkt, covers the Huguenot contribution to Berlin life.

Unter den Linden A stroll west on Unter den Linden takes in the greatest surviving monuments of the former Prussian capital (and hopefully the famous trees, if they do not fall in the name of U-Bahn redevelopment). All the captions may be in German at the **Museum of German History** in the former Armoury (or Zeughaus, 1706, by Andreas Schlüter), but the extensive collection of objects, maps and photos is fascinating (admission DM4; closed Wednesday). Be sure to see the building's interior courtyard with its 22 heads of dying warriors. The museum's development, which has caused the closure of the main historical collection, should be completed soon. Opposite the museum is the beautiful colonnaded **Unter den Linden** or Crown Prince's Palace (Kronprinzens Palais, 1732). Next to the museum is Schinkel's **Neue Wache** (1818), now the Memorial to the Victims of Fascism & Militarism (fortunately no longer guarded by helmeted goons). **Humboldt University** (1753), the next building to the west, was originally a palace of the brother of King Friedrich II of Prussia, and was converted to a university in 1810. Beside this is the massive **State Library** (1914). An equestrian **statue of Friedrich II** stands in the middle of the avenue in front of the university.

Across the street from the university, beside the **Old Library** (1780) with its curving baroque façade, is Wenzeslaus von Knobelsdorff's **State Opera** (Deutsche Staatsoper, 1743). Behind this site is the Catholic **St Hedwig's Church** (1773), which was modelled on the Pantheon in Rome.

Around Tiergarten At the western end of Unter den Linden (S-Bahn: Unter den Linden) is the **Brandenburger Tor**, or Brandenburg Gate (1791, by Karl Gotthard Langhans), a symbol of Berlin and once the boundary between East and West. The winged victory goddess and four-horse quadriga by Schadow are on top. The route of the Wall south from Pariser Platz to Potsdamer Platz is plain to see. At the open-air stalls around the gate you can buy GDR and Soviet military souvenirs and ever-smaller painted pieces of the Wall. Logic dictates, however, that genuine wall fragments, if you go in for that sort of thing, must be in limited supply. Compare prices before buying, and bargain. And mind the traffic – the Pariser Platz is now full of tour buses and vehicles of all sorts and is dangerous to cross (or use as a site for photography).

Beside the Spree River, just north of the Brandenburger Tor, is the **Reichstag** (1894), the German parliament until it was burned down on the night of 27 February 1933. At midnight on 2 October 1990 the reunification of Germany was enacted here. The restored Reichstag contains an excellent exhibition covering German history from 1800 to the present (admission free; closed Monday). All of the captions are in German, but a kiosk upstairs near the entrance to the exhibition rents a Walkman with a 45-minute guided tour in English, French or German for DM2. At ground level there's a good café. Between the Reichstag and the river is a small memorial to some of the 191 people who died trying to cross the Wall.

The huge city park, **Tiergarten**, stretches west from here towards Zoo station. It became a park in the 18th century and from 1833 to 1838 was landscaped with streams and lakes. Strasse des 17. Juni (named for the 1953 workers' uprising), which leads west from the Brandenburger Tor through the park, was known as the East-West Axis during the Nazi era, Hitler's showplace entrance to Berlin. On the north side of this street, just west of the gate, is a **Soviet War Memorial** flanked by the first Russian tanks to enter the city in 1945.

To the south, just beyond the memorial and straight ahead, is the angular **Berliner Philharmonie** (1963, by Hans Scharoun), diagonally across the street. This striking modern concert hall is unique in that the orchestra is completely surrounded by rows of seats. The **Musical Instruments Museum** (Kunstgewerbemuseum, 1984), Tiergartenstrasse 1 beside the Philharmonie (admission DM4, Sunday and holidays free; closed Monday), has a rich collection that is beautifully displayed. The red-brick **Mattäikirche** (1846) stands just south of the above-mentioned buildings in the centre of Berlin's new *Kulturforum*, and beyond it is the **New National Gallery** at Potsdamer Strasse 50 (admission DM4, Sunday and holidays free; closed Monday), with 19th and 20th-century paintings. This sleek gallery, built in 1968, is a creation of the architect Mies van der Rohe. The **State Library** (1976) across the street contains reading, periodical and exhibition rooms (closed Sunday).

The **Museum for Design** at Klingelhöferstrasse 13-14 near the Landwehrkanal is dedicated to the Bauhaus school (1919-33), which laid the basis for much contemporary architecture. It is housed in a building designed by its founder, Walter Gropius. Admission is DM4 (free on Monday) and the museum is closed on Tuesday.

North along Hofjäger-Allee from this museum is the **Victory Column** (Siegessäule, 1873), which commemorates 19th-century Prussian military adventures. It is topped by a gilded statue of the Roman victory goddess, Victoria, which is visible from much of Tiergarten. Just north-east is **Schloss Bellevue** (1785), built for Prince Ferdinand, brother of Friedrich II ('the Great'), and now an official residence of the President of Germany.

East along the Spree River is the **Kongresshalle** (1957), nicknamed the 'pregnant oyster' for its shape. The arched roof collapsed in 1980 but has since been rebuilt. The photo and art exhibits (often with Third World themes) inside are worth a look (closed Monday), but the main attraction is the soft seats where you can take a rest. You can board an excursion boat behind the building during the summer months.

Dorotheenstadt At the edge of east Berlin is the **Brecht-Weigel memorial house** at Chausseestrasse 125 (U-Bahn: Zinnowitzer Strasse or Oranienburger Tor), where the socialist playwright Bertolt Brecht lived from 1953 until his death in 1956. It can only be visited Tuesday to Friday from 10 to 11.30 am, Thursday from 5 to 6.30 pm and Saturday from 9.30 am to 1 pm in groups of eight people maximum with a German-speaking guide (admission free). Go into the rear courtyard and up the stairs to the right. The entrance is upstairs. Behind is **Dorotheenstadt Cemetery** with tombs of the illustrious

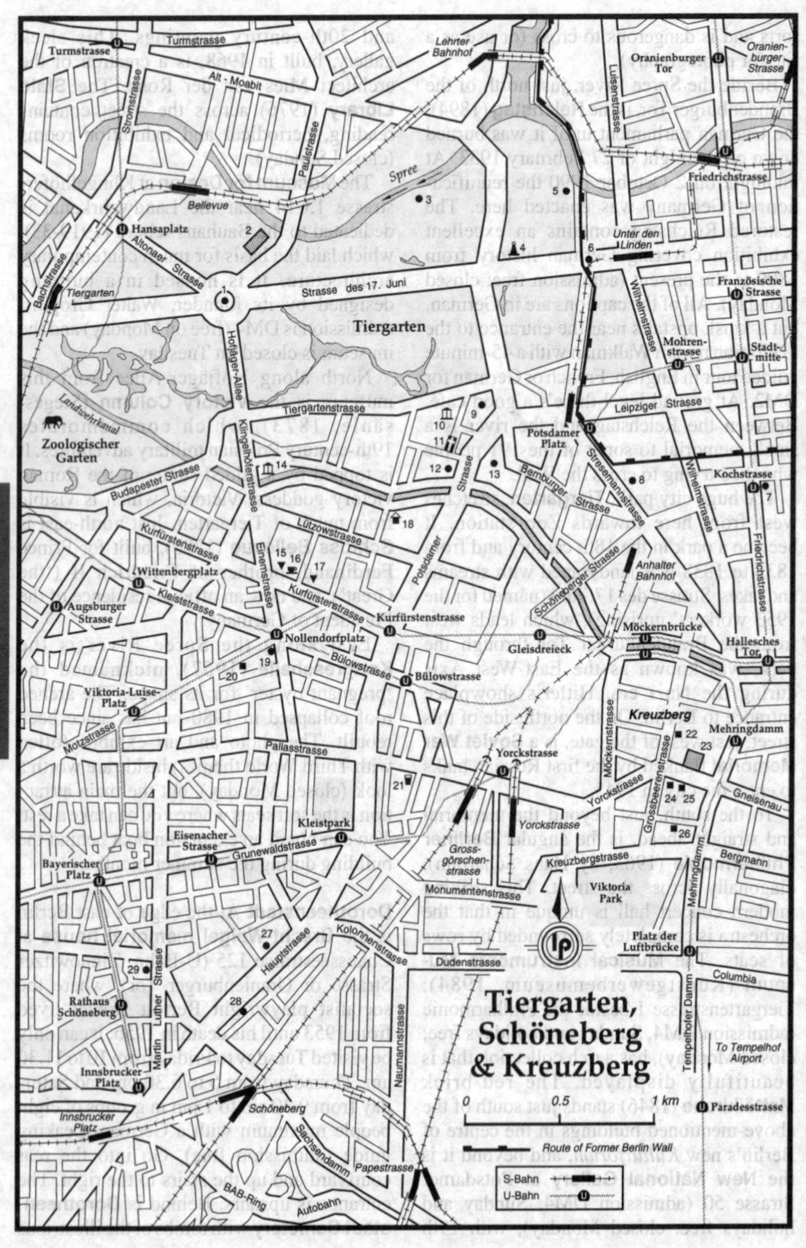

Tiergarten, Schöneberg & Kreuzberg
Turmstrasse
Lehrter Bahnhof
Oranienburger Tor
Oranienburger Strasse
Alt-Moabit
Stromstrasse
Paulstrasse
Luisenstrasse
Spree
Bellevue
Friedrichstrasse
Hansaplatz
Altonaer Strasse
Unter den Linden
Bachstrasse
Tiergarten
Strasse des 17. Juni
Wilhelmstrasse
Französische Strasse
Hofjäger-Allee
Mohrenstrasse
Stadtmitte
Landwehrkanal
Tiergartenstrasse
Leipziger Strasse
Zoologischer Garten
Klingelhöferstrasse
Potsdamer Platz
Stresemannstrasse
Budapester Strasse
Bernburger Strasse
Kochstrasse
Lützowstrasse
Kurfürstenstrasse
Einemstrasse
Potsdamer Strasse
Anhalter Bahnhof
Friedrichstrasse
Wittenbergplatz
Kleiststrasse
Augsburger Strasse
Schöneberger Strasse
Nollendorfplatz
Gleisdreieck
Möckernbrücke
Hallesches Tor
Bülowstrasse
Viktoria-Luise-Platz
Motzstrasse
Pallasstrasse
Kreuzberg
Mehringdamm
Yorckstrasse
Möckernstrasse
Grossbeerenstrasse
Gneisenau-
Kleistpark
Eisenacher Strasse
Grunewaldstrasse
Bayerischer Platz
Gross-görschen-strasse
Kreuzbergstrasse
Bergmann
Viktoria Park
Monumentenstrasse
Kolonnenstrasse
Hauptstrasse
Platz der Luftbrücke
Dudenstrasse
Columbia
Martin Luther Strasse
Rathaus Schöneberg
Naumannstrasse
Tempelhofer Damm
To Tempelhof Airport
Innsbrucker Platz
Schöneberg
Sachsendamm
Papestrasse
BAB-Ring
Autobahn
Paradestrasse
0
0.5
1 km
Route of Former Berlin Wall
S-Bahn
U-Bahn
GERMANY

PLACES TO STAY

18 Jugendgästehaus Berlin
20 Hotel Sachsenhof
22 Pension Kreuzberg
24 Hotel Pension Südwest
25 Riehmers Hofgarten Hotel & Noodle Company
26 Hotel Transit

PLACES TO EAT

15 Zum Ambrosius
16 Café Einstein
17 Spatz Steakhouse

OTHER

1 Victory Column
2 Schloss Bellevue
3 Haus der Kulturen der Welt
4 Soviet War Memorial
5 Reichstag
6 Brandenburger Tor
7 Haus am Checkpoint Charlie
8 Martin-Gropius-Bau
9 Philharmonie
10 Musical Instruments Museum
11 Mattäikirche
12 New National Gallery
13 State Library
14 Museum for Design
19 Metropol Disco
21 E&M Leydicke Bar
23 Rathaus Kreuzberg
27 Madhouse Ecstasy Disco
28 Odeon Cinema
29 Rathaus Schöneberg

going back to 18th century, such as the architect Schinkel, the philosopher Georg Friedrich Hegel, the poet Johannes Becher, and Brecht. There are two adjacent cemeteries here: you want the one closer to Brecht's house. The **Natural History Museum** (1810) nearby at Invalidenstrasse 43 (admission DM3; closed Monday) has a good collection of dinosaurs and minerals.

Terror & Division On Niederkirchnerstrasse behind a stretch of the Wall is the site of the former SS/Gestapo headquarters where the **Topographie des Terrors** exhibition (admission free; open until 6 pm daily) documents Nazi crimes, especially the 'Jewish solution'. A booklet in English costs DM1. A platform atop a high mound of rubble from the ruined buildings provides a good view of this desolate area. Diagonally opposite the Czech Consulate just north on the corner of Wilhelmstrasse and Vossstrasse is the site of **Hitler's bunker**. The Chancellery built here by Albert Speer in 1938 was demolished after the war, and the bunker below it (where Hitler shot himself on 30 April 1945) was completely effaced in the late 1980s when the Communists built the apartment complex that occupies the site.

The longest surviving stretch of the **Berlin Wall** is just across the bridge from the Schlesisches Tor terminus of the U1, about which the film *Linie 1* was made. As the Wall was being demolished in mid-1990, this 300-metre section was turned over to artists, who created a permanent open-air art gallery along the side facing Mühlenstrasse (the side facing the river is sprayed with graffiti).

All of the stations along the U6 line from Schwarzkopffstrasse south to Stadtmitte (excepting Friedrichstrasse) were below east Berlin and tightly sealed until mid-1990, although the U6 still rumbled through.

Nothing remains at the site of the famous **Checkpoint Charlie** except a plaque with an embarrassing attempt at English translation, but if you want to see where it stood, get off at Kochstrasse station and walk north on Friedrichstrasse. The structure at Friedrichstrasse 207-208 was, until 1990, the headquarters of all Western intelligence organisations in Berlin, and from here, or from the now-removed Allied guard trailer in the middle of the street nearby, photos were taken of everyone crossing the border. The Cold War atmosphere is perpetuated nearby in the **Haus am Checkpoint Charlie**, a fully commercial museum of donated escape memorabilia and photos, charging a damaging DM7.50 admission (if you are or can pose as a student, it's a mere DM4.50). Yet, such is the attraction of the Wall that it's crawling with customers daily from 9 am to 10 pm. The English translations here are marginally better.

GERMANY

Near the Magdalenenstrasse U-Bahn station is the former headquarters of the GDR Stasi (Staatspolizei or secret police). In Haus 1 at Ruschestrasse 59 (from the station around the corner to the right) is **Antistalinistische Aktion**, a museum of GDR memorabilia housed in the former executive suite of the Minister of State Security (admission DM5, students DM3; closed Monday). There isn't a lot to see in the museum but it's fun to wander around this complex, until recently one of the most tightly guarded of its kind in the world.

West Berlin The stark ruins of the **Kaiser-Wilhelm-Gedächtnis-Kirche** (1895) in Breitscheidplatz, engulfed in the roaring commercialism all round, marks the heart of west Berlin. The British bombing of 22 November 1943 left only the broken west tower standing. The former foyer (Gedenkhalle) below the tower may be visited from Tuesday to Saturday, 10 am to 4 pm. The modern church (1961) and its overwhelmingly blue stained glass is open to visitors from 9 am to 7 pm daily, except during services. Just beyond rises the gleaming **Europa-Center** (1965) with a rotating Mercedes symbol on top. North-east of Europa-Center on Budapester Strasse is the elephant gate to west Berlin's **zoo & aquarium** (admission for both DM15, students DM12, children DM7.50, or the zoo only DM10, 8 or 5). The zoo, 150 years old, is open daily.

GERMANY

Märkisches Ufer Several interesting sights can be covered from the Märkisches Museum U-Bahn station. The collections of the **Märkisches Museum** (admission DM3; open Tuesday to Sunday from 10 am to 6 pm) cover the early history of Berlin, and special features include a quite magnificent scale model of Berlin around 1750; a booklet is available in English. The interesting **variety annexe** at the entrance to the U-Bahn station to the west (DM2; closed Monday) brings back the atmosphere of long-gone theatres and the colourful cabaret, stage and magic shows of Berlin's 1920s and '30s. The brown bears housed in a pit in the park behind the main museum are the official mascots of the city (but it's sad to see such creatures boxed in one minute's walk from the underground train system in a huge city like Berlin). **Otto-Nagel-Haus**, Märkisches Ufer 16-18 on the Spree Canal nearby (admission DM4 or day card, closed Friday and Saturday), exhibits the work of the Berlin painter Otto Nagel (1894-1967) and his between-the-wars contemporaries.

Charlottenburg Built as a country estate for Queen Sophie Charlotte, **Schloss Charlottenburg** (1699) is an exquisite baroque palace on Spandauer Damm three km north-west of Zoo station (U-Bahn: Richard-Wagner-Platz). The palace was bombed in 1943 but has been completely rebuilt. Before the entrance is a baroque equestrian statue of Sophie Charlotte's husband, the first king of Prussia, Friedrich I (1700). Along the Spree River behind the palace are extensive French and English gardens (free admission), while the many buildings house an important group of museums.

In the central building below the dome are the former royal living quarters (admission DM3; closed Monday). The winter chambers of Friedrich II, upstairs in the new wing (1746) to the east, may be visited individually, or on a DM8 general admission ticket that takes in the **Schinkel Pavilion**, the neoclassical **Mausoleum** and the rococo **Belvedere** pavilion. The **Romantic Gallery** of the National Gallery is housed downstairs in the new wing (admission DM4, Sunday and holidays free; closed Monday).

In addition to these sights, three branches of the State Museum at Charlottenburg should not be missed (all are closed on Friday). The **Museum of Prehistory** (admission DM4, free on Sunday) occupies the west wing of the palace. Across the street at the beginning of Schlossstrasse are the **Egyptian Museum** collection (DM4, Sunday free), including the 14th-century BC bust of Queen Nefertiti, and the **Museum of Antiquities** (the same price and times), which has objects from ancient Greece and Rome displayed on four floors.

Huge crowds are often waiting for the guided tour of Charlottenburg Palace and it may be difficult to get a ticket. This is especially true on weekends and holidays. If you can't get into the main palace, content yourself with the façades and gardens.

Dahlem Museums A complex of museums that is worth all the others combined is the **Dahlem Museums**, Lansstrasse 8, Zehlendorf (U-Bahn: Dahlem-Dorf). Here is kept the better part of the former Prussian art collections amassed by Friedrich the Great, evacuated from Museumsinsel during WW II and never returned to east Berlin (DM4; closed Monday). The fantastic museum full of old master paintings as well as the sculpture, ethnographical exhibits and Indian, Oriental and Islamic art will knock you over; various admission prices apply. Arrive early in the morning and plan to spend the day there. A couple of blocks away is the **Botanical Garden**, Königin-Luise-Strasse 6-8 (open daily; DM4 admission).

Activities

Central Berlin may be crowded with roads, office buildings and apartments, but the south-east and south-west sections of the city are surprisingly green with forests, rivers and lakes. From April to October, tourist boats cruise the waterways, calling at picturesque villages, parks and castles. Food and drink are sold on board but they're moderately expensive, so take along something to nibble or sip.

Cruises Spreefahrt (☎ 3 94 49 54), in a kiosk by the riverside behind the Haus der Kulturen der Welt in Tiergarten (S-Bahn: Unter den Linden), offers circular cruises around Berlin from mid-April to September. Similar trips are offered by Reederei Heinz Riedel (☎ 3 92 40 60 or 3 94 21 80) whose kiosk is just downstream. From April to October its boats travel down the Spree to the Landwehrkanal, then through canals and under the bridges to Hansabrücke and back (departures daily; DM14). There are similar trips to Kottbusser Brücke, also from Haus der Kulturen der Welt (DM14), and lake tours from Wannsee past Potsdam and return (DM8.50).

Stern und Kreisschiffahrt (☎ 6 17 39 00) operates many different cruises all summer. A 3½-hour cruise from Jannowitzbrücke in east Berlin through Tiergarten to Schlossbrücke and back costs DM20 (DM25 by steamer) and is available several times daily from April to October. A one-hour spin around east Berlin's museums will set you back DM12.50 (May to October) and a 4½-hour voyage from Treptow in the east along the Spree and down to Havel to the castle of Cecilienhof in Potsdam is DM25 return (DM16 one way). Other cruises cover the Havel lakes from Wannsee and various canals.

Places to Stay

Things are tight east of the Tiergarten as hotels close, are demolished, or renovated into the exclusive class. This has diverted the attention of budget travellers to the west until the accommodation scene settles down. The tourist offices keep an excellent free accommodation booklet that you can use to survey and ring around the hotel and pension options. Further low-price options are in the handout *Accommodations for Young Visitors to Berlin + Brandenburg* – see if you can get a copy at one of the tourist offices.

Camping The camping facilities in Berlin are not good. There are several camping grounds in west Berlin charging DM7.50 per person plus from DM5.50 to DM8.50 per tent, but they're far from the city centre, crowded with caravans and often full. They cater almost exclusively to permanent residents who live in their caravans all year, and although you may be admitted if you're polite and persistent, they aren't really set up to receive casual tourists.

The only camping ground convenient to public transport is *Campingplatz Kohlhasenbrück* (☎ 8051737), Neue Kreisstrasse 36, in a peaceful location overlooking the

GERMANY

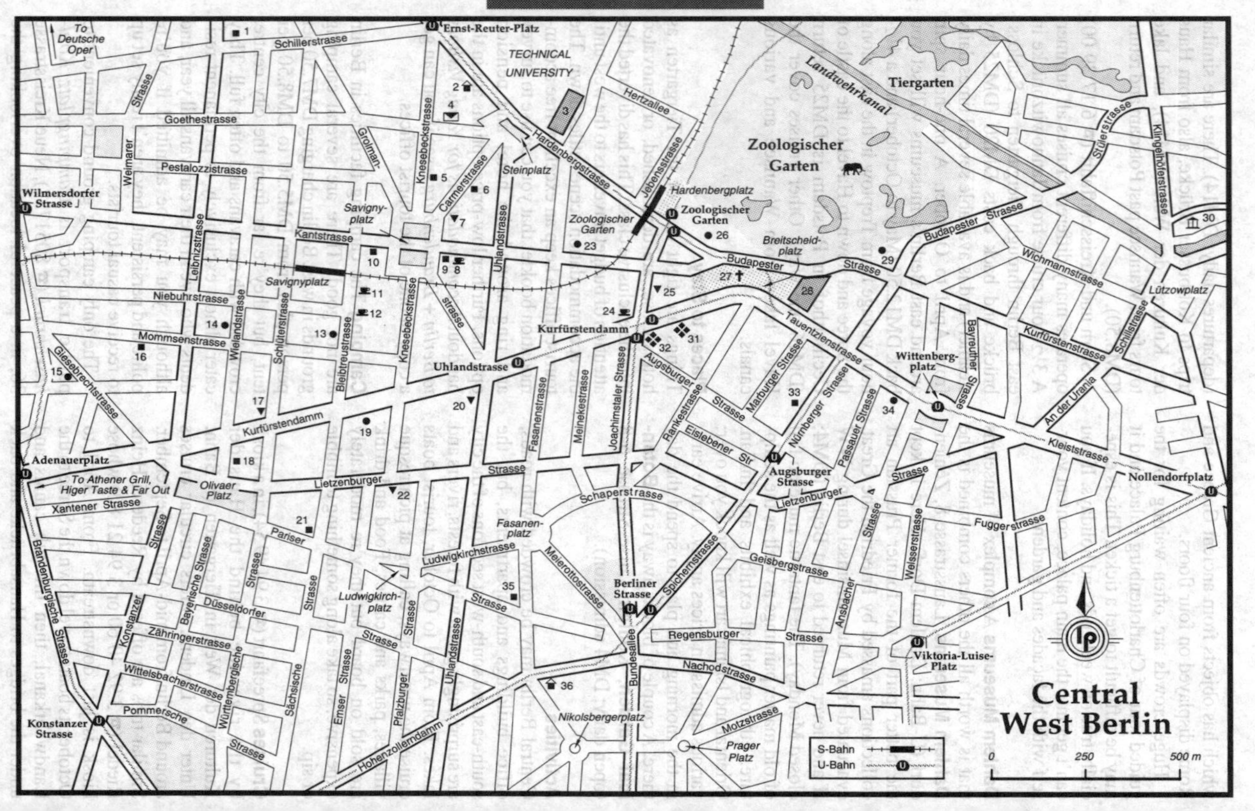
Central
West Berlin
0
250
500 m
S-Bahn
U-Bahn
Tiergarten
Landwehrkanal
Zoologischer
Garten
Hardenbergplatz
Zoologischer
Garten
Breitscheid-
platz
Wittenberg-
platz
Nollendorfplatz
Viktoria-Luise-
Platz
Lützowplatz
Savigny-
platz
Savignyplatz
Steinplatz
Ernst-Reuter-Platz
TECHNICAL
UNIVERSITY
Adenauerplatz
Olivaer
Platz
Fasanen-
platz
Ludwigkirch-
platz
Nikolsbergerplatz
Prager
Platz
Augsburger
Strasse
Berliner
Strasse
Konstanzer
Strasse
Wilmersdorfer
Strasse
Uhlandstrasse
Kurfürstendamm
To
Deutsche
Oper
To Athener Grill,
Higer Taste & Far Out
Schillerstrasse
Goethestrasse
Pestalozzistrasse
Weimarer
Strasse
Leibnizstrasse
Niebuhrstrasse
Mommsenstrasse
Wielandstrasse
Schlüterstrasse
Bleibtreustrasse
Knesebeckstrasse
Grolman-
strasse
Carmerstrasse
Kantstrasse
Hardenbergstrasse
Hertzallee
Jebensstrasse
Budapester
Strasse
Tauentzienstrasse
Fasanenstrasse
Meinekestrasse
Joachimstaler Strasse
Augsburger
Strasse
Rankestrasse
Eislebener
Str
Marburger Strasse
Nürnberger
Strasse
Passauer Strasse
Bayreuther
Strasse
Kurfürstenstrasse
Schillstrasse
Wichmannstrasse
Stülerstrasse
Klingelhöferstrasse
An der Urania
Kleiststrasse
Lietzenburger
Strasse
Fuggerstrasse
Geisbergstrasse
Ansbacher
Strasse
Welserstrasse
Spichernstrasse
Schaperstrasse
Meierottostrasse
Ludwigkirchstrasse
Regensburger
Nachodstrasse
Motzstrasse
Bundesallee
Giesebrechtstrasse
Xantener Strasse
Pariser
Brandenburgische Strasse
Konstanzer
Bayerische Strasse
Düsseldorfer
Zähringerstrasse
Wittelsbacherstrasse
Württembergische
Pommersche
Sächsische
Emser
Pfalzburger
Hohenzollerndamm

PLACES TO STAY

1 Hotelpension Brinn
2 Jugendgästehaus am Zoo
5 Pension Knesebeck
6 Hotelpension Bialias
9 Pension Peters
10 Hotel Crystal
16 Hotelpension Majesty
18 Hotelpensions Modena & Gloria
21 Hotelpension Pariser Eck
33 Pension Fischer & Hotelpension Nürnberger Eck
35 Pension Elton
36 Jugendgästehaus Central

PLACES TO EAT

7 Dicke Wirtin
8 Schwarzes Café
11 Zillemarkt
12 Café Bleibtreu
17 Beiz
20 Piccola Taormina
22 Loretta's Biergarten
24 Café Kranzler
25 Pizzeria Amigo

OTHER

3 School of Art Concert Hall
4 Post Office
13 Go In
14 Salsa
15 Kurbel Cinema
19 Big Eden
23 Theater des Westens
26 Filmzentrum Zoo-Palast
27 Kaiser-Wilhelm-Gedächtnis-Kirche
28 Europa-Center
29 Aquarium
30 Museum for Design
31 Wertheim Department Store
32 Ku'damm Eck Shopping Arcade
34 Kaufhaus des Westens (KaDeWe)

Griebnitzsee in the far south-west corner of Berlin. Bus No 118 from Wannsee S-Bahn station runs directly there. If the gate is locked when you arrive, just hang around until someone with a key arrives, and then ask for the manager at the caravan near the gate. It is open from March to October.

If Kohlhasenbrück is full, two km to the east along the Teltowkanal is *Campingplatz Dreilinden* (☎ 8 05 12 01) at Albrechts-Teerofen (open from 1 May to 30 September, bus No 118 from Wannsee).

Campingplatz Haselhorst (☎ 3 34 59 55) is near Spandau, two km north-west of Haselhorst U-Bahn station. Walk north on Daumstrasse to Pulvermühlenweg and then west to the canal.

Hostels The three DJH hostels in west Berlin fill up fast on weekends and throughout summer. Until early July, the hostels are often fully booked by noisy school groups. None of the hostels offers cooking facilities but breakfast is included in the overnight charge, and lunch and dinner are available. The hostels stay open all day throughout the year.

The only hostel within walking distance of the city centre is the impersonal 364-bed *Jugendgästehaus Berlin* (☎ 2 61 10 97), Kluckstrasse 3 in Schöneberg near Landwehrkanal (U-Bahn: Kurfürstenstrasse), which costs DM28 for juniors, DM35 for seniors.

The most pleasant location surely belongs to the modern 264-bed *Jugendgästehaus am Wannsee* (☎ 8 03 20 34), on Badeweg (not the nearby Wannseebad-Weg) on the lake Grosser Wannsee to the south-west of the city. The hostel is at most an eight-minute walk from Nikolassee S-Bahn station and direct trains to Zoo. Walk west out of the station over the footbridge, turn left at Kronprinzessinnenweg, and the hostel is soon in sight on the right. The cost is DM28 for juniors, DM35 for seniors, and the key deposit is DM20.

Jugendherberge Ernst Reuter (☎ 4 04 16 10), Hermsdorfer Damm 48, is in the far north of west Berlin. Take the U6 to Tegel, and then bus No 125 right to the door. The 110 beds are DM23 for juniors, DM28 for seniors.

It is a good idea to book west Berlin DJH hostels in writing with the Deutsches Jugendherbergswerk (☎ 2 62 30 24), Tempelhofer Ufer 32, 10963 Berlin, several weeks in advance. State precisely which nights you'll be in Berlin and enclose an international postal reply coupon so they can send back confirmation. You must give an address where the confirmation can be sent to. Otherwise you could just try calling a hostel to ask if they'll reserve a place for you.

Of the private hostels, the handiest is *Jugendgästehaus am Zoo* (☎ 3 12 94 10), Hardenbergstrasse 9a, three blocks from Zoo station, which charges from DM47/85 single/double and DM35 for dormitory beds, but there is no breakfast included. It's limited to people aged under 27, but the location is great if you get in. The giant *Jugendgästehaus Central* (☎ 87 01 88) at Nikolsburger Strasse 2 offers beds at DM32 and DM28 in two, three and multi-bed rooms with breakfast; the DM7 sheet charge is waived for stays longer than two nights. It helps if you are gregarious – there are more than 450 beds! Take the U1 to Hohenzollernplatz or the U9 to Güntzelstrasse.

Studentenwohnheim Hubertusallee (☎ 8 91 97 18) at Delbrückstrasse 24 offers discounts to students with a recognised card (singles/doubles/triples DM40/60/75), otherwise you pay DM70/90/100; all prices include breakfast. This establishment operates only from March to October. The *Studentenhotel Berlin* (☎ 7 84 67 20), Meininger Strasse 10 (U-Bahn: Schöneberg), operates like a youth hostel but you don't need a card. Bed and breakfast is DM37 per person in a double, DM33 per person in a quad. It's often full.

Hotel Transit (☎ 7 85 50 51), Hagelberger Strasse 53-54 (U-Bahn: Mehringdamm), a youth hotel crowded with young travellers, offers rooms from DM70/95 single/double, three-bed rooms at DM40 per person and multi-bed rooms at DM30 per person; a big breakfast is included. All rooms have a shower. The Transit sometimes fills up with school groups from March to May and in September and October, but in the other months it should have beds available.

From mid-June to August you can sleep in a big tent at the *Internationales Jugendcamp* (☎ 4 33 86 40) in northern west Berlin. From the U-Bahn at Tegel take bus No 222 (towards Lübars) four stops to the corner of Ziekowstrasse and Waldmannsluster Damm. The tents are behind the *Jugendgästehaus Tegel* (☎ 4 33 30 46), a huge, red-brick building opposite the bus stop. Beds in large communal tents are DM9 per person (blankets and foam mattresses provided) and check-in is after 5 pm (no curfew). Officially this place is only for those aged 14 to 23, but they don't turn away foreigners who are a little older. The maximum stay is three nights. Food can be purchased at the camp and a cheap breakfast is sold in the morning. Beds in the guesthouse's four-bed rooms go for DM35 each including breakfast.

One of the best places to stay in Berlin is the *Touristenhaus Grünau* (☎ 6 76 44 22), Dahmestrasse 6 in a quiet, attractive location beside the Dahme River in the quaint little town of Grünau. Take the S-Bahn to Berlin-Grünau, then any tram two stops towards Köpenick. It offers singles at DM60, doubles at DM95 and multi-bed rooms from DM120; there are communal facilities and a buffet breakfast. Though on the far south-east side of Berlin, transport to the city centre from here is good and there are hiking possibilities in the nearby Berlin city forest (Berliner Stadtwald).

Private Rooms Your best bet for private rooms is the Zimmervermittlung service at Berlin-Touristen-Information offices (see the Information section). Rooms start from DM50 per person in singles or doubles and you pay DM5 per booking. Sometimes the minimum stay is two nights.

Some of the rental rooms offered by the various Mitwohnzentrale agencies are available for only a few nights' stay. Most of these services have rooms or apartments starting about DM35 per person per day for a longer term (usually at least a month). It's best to call in and state your requirements, and the staff will try to help. For a week, singles/doubles start at about DM300/500 (a few are cheaper), but these can be hard to arrange on demand. *Mitwohnzentrale Ku'damm Eck* (☎ 1 94 45) on the 2nd floor of the Ku'damm Eck shopping arcade at Kurfürstendamm 227, has apartments from one to four beds. The office is open from 10 am to 6.30 pm Monday to Friday and from 11 am until 2 pm Saturday. *Erste Mitwohnzentrale* in Char lottenburg (☎ 3 24 30 31), Sybelstrasse 53 (U-Bahn: Adenauerplatz), has rooms for a minimum stay of two nights. It's open Monday to Friday from 9 am to 8 pm and Saturday from 10 am to 6 pm. *Mitwohnzentrale Mehringdamm 2.Domicil* (☎ 7 86 20 03) on the 3rd floor, Mehringdamm 72 in Kreuzberg, has rooms starting at slightly cheaper rates, although whole flats for short terms are almost impossible to locate. It's open weekdays from 10 am to 7 pm, Saturday from 11 am to 4 pm.

Long-Term Rentals If you'd like to spend some time in Berlin, look for someone willing to sublet their apartment. Many Berliners take off for extended holidays and are only too happy to have the bills paid while they're gone. The Mitwohnzentrale agencies handle many long-term rentals, and six months or more is usually no problem if the price suits you. Check the *Wohnungen* classified section in *Zitty* or *Zweite Hand*. The Mitwohnzentrale agencies (see Private Rooms above) charge 10 or 15% of the monthly rental rate, or about DM3 per person per day for short stays. If you're staying for under a month, you'll end up sharing a flat with others, a good way to meet people. Australians and New Zealanders who advertise for rooms often get quicker and readier responses by putting their nationality first in the ad ('Australian seeks room...').

Hotelpensions – West Berlin Mid-priced pensions and hotels do exist in west Berlin but they're all small, plain and uncommercial, so expect no luxury. Tourist offices don't book these rooms.

Rooms begin at around DM50/90 a single/double with shared facilities and some places charge extra for showers, though others offer a shower in the room. Breakfast can cost extra. Many are upstairs from shop fronts and some signs are hard to find; often you must ring to enter. There are a few big places, but many have 20 beds or less.

There are many places west of Zoo station and north of the Ku'damm. The excellent *Pension Knesebeck* (☎ 31 72 55), Knesebeckstrasse 86-87 just off Savignyplatz, has singles/doubles at DM75/125 (triples available). The *Hotelpension Bialias* (☎ 3 12 50 25) at Carmerstrasse 16 is about the biggest and rooms start at DM70/100 (showers extra). *Pension Peters* (☎ 3 12 22 78), upstairs at Kantstrasse 146, is one of the smallest, but good value starting at DM50/105. *Hotelpension Brinn* (☎ 3 12 16 05) at Schillerstrasse 10, also small and friendly, has good rooms at DM85/125 in attractive surroundings and relaxed buffet breakfasts. *Hotelpension Cortina* (☎ 3 13 90 59) at Kantstrasse 140 has plenty of rooms, which start at DM60/90. *Hotel Crystal* (☎ 3 12 90 47) at Kantstrasse 144 is large and reasonably priced from DM70/90.

Among the best offers around the Ku'damm is *Hotelpension Modena* (☎ 8 85 70 10) at Wielandstrasse 26, starting at DM55/95 and ranging up to DM120/170 with all facilities. Next door at No 27 is *Hotelpension Gloria* (☎ 8 81 80 60), offering similar variety and rates. *Hotelpension Majesty* (☎ 3 23 20 61), Mommsenstrasse 55, is one of the less expensive at DM50/100.

South of the Ku'damm are *Hotelpension Pariser Eck* (☎ 8 81 21 45), Pariser Strasse 19 (singles/doubles from DM50/90, showers extra for the cheapest rooms), and *Pension Elton* (☎ 8 83 61 55), Pariser Strasse 9 (from DM100/150). South of Breitscheidplatz are *Hotelpension Nürnberger Eck* (☎ 2 18 53 71), Nürnberger Strasse 24a (singles/doubles for DM75/120), and *Pension Fischer* (☎ 2 18 68 08) in the same building (from DM50/70, breakfast DM9 extra).

If you'd rather stay out in Kreuzberg, try *Pension Kreuzberg* (☎ 2 51 13 62), Grossbeerenstrasse 64, which has singles/doubles/triples for DM50/75/90 and multibed rooms for DM30 per person. The budget option on the edge of Schöneberg is *Hotel Sachsenhof* (☎ 2 16 20 74) at Motzstrasse 7, which has depressing rooms but a good breakfast buffet and starts at an affordable DM48/84.

The *Hotel Charlottenburger Hof* (☎ 32 90 70), Stuttgarter Platz 14, is large and still handy opposite Charlottenburg S-Bahn station (singles/doubles from DM65/100). A good breakfast is downstairs at Café Voltaire (from DM6 to DM8). A budget pension out in Spandau, and handy to Altstadt Spandau U-Bahn station, is *Hotel Hamburger Hof* (☎ 3 33 46 02) at Kinkelstrasse 6, where singles/doubles start at DM45/90.

Hotels – East Berlin The family-operated *Hotel Merkur* (☎ 2 82 82 97), at Elsässer Strasse 156, ranges from DM70/125 single/double to DM110/160 with bath and breakfast. It's a little overpriced for what you get, but has a few moderate family rooms. *Hotel Novalis* (☎ 2 82 40 08), Novalisstrasse 5 off Elsässer Strasse, is fairly central and starts at DM125/160 a single/double with all facilities, but has few beds. The *Christliches Hospiz* (☎ 28 49 70), Auguststrasse 82, has been undergoing renovation but promises to be a high-standard (although not cheap) hotel when it reopens. A little out of the city in Prenzlauer Berg, you could try *BCA Prenzlauer Berg* (☎ 4 23 28 05) at Storkower Strasse 114, where singles/doubles/triples cost DM65/90/130 and there are communal facilities on each floor. Take bus No 157 from Karl-Liebknecht-Strasse.

In the again-to-be-prestigious Charlottenstrasse, you can lash out a little at the *Gendarm Garni Hotel* (☎ 2 00 41 80) at No 60 (from DM150/170) and the *Hotel-Pension Charlottenhof* (☎ 23 80 60) at No 52 (from DM190/210). You are paying something for location (which is excellent), but most rooms have all facilities.

A small hotel accepting women only is *Frauenhotel Artemisia* (☎ 87 89 05) at Brandenburgische Strasse 18 in Wilmersdorf. It is not a budget outfit, however, charging from DM109/180 a single/double.

Expensive Hotels The 305-room *Hotel Unter den Linden* (☎ 23 81 10), near Friedrichstrasse train station, charges from DM150/195 a single/double up to suites costing over DM300, giving you a spot at No 14 on one of the world's famous avenues, though it's not beautiful to look at. The monstrous *Forum Hotel Berlin* (☎ 2 38 90) dominates Alexanderplatz with its almost 700 rooms. The prices start at DM225/275. The 346-room *Hotel Berolina* (☎ 2 40 95 41), at Karl-Marx-Allee 31 (U-Bahn: Schillingstrasse), charges DM165/205 for small rooms, DM205/245 for large ones. This three-star hotel is less comfortable and convenient than the other two (both four-stars). The smaller, renovated and well located *Hotel Albrechtshof* (☎ 28 40 30), Albrechtstrasse 8, starts expensively at DM195/245 a single/double with all facilities (S-Bahn: Friedrichstrasse).

One up-market west Berlin hotel deserves special attention. The 22 rooms at *Riehmers Hofgarten* (☎ 78 10 11), Yorckstrasse 83 in Kreuzberg (U-Bahn: Mehringdamm), cost DM200/240 a single/double, including a big breakfast. Bus No 119 from the Ku'damm passes the door. This elegant, eclectic edifice erected in 1892 will delight romantics, and it's a fun area in which to stay.

Places to Eat

There's a restaurant for every cuisine under the sun in Berlin – there are so many *Spezialitäten* that you will soon regard native fare as the real speciality. Yet among this variety is generally the best food available at (by local standards) reasonable prices. A cooked lunch or dinner at an unpretentious restaurant will cost less than DM15 if you order carefully.

Substantial snacks are available at the many *Schnellimbiss* stands around the city. In addition to German stand-bys like *Rostbratwurst* and *Currywurst*, most Imbiss stands also have doner kebab (usually DM4, though a mini-doner here and there costs about DM2.50) and mini-pizzas are often advertised for DM2. Many Schnellimbiss also offer smallish barbecued half-chickens (about DM5).

One Berlin treat to get acquainted with right away is a big DM1.50 cup of coffee dispensed by a coin-operated machine at many Eduscho and Tchibo coffee retailers around Berlin. You have to drink standing up and this deal isn't offered on evenings or weekends (even though the shop itself may be open) or by all outlets.

Breakfast Breakfast cafés are a Berlin institution catering to the city's late risers. In addition to canned music in a genteel setting, you can get a filling brunch of yoghurt, eggs, meat, cheese, bread, butter and jam for around DM12 (coffee extra). Some of the breakfasts are huge, so consider sharing one between two people. They also make a good lunch.

Typical of the genre are *Café Bleibtreu*, Bleibtreustrasse 45 (S-Bahn: Savignyplatz; breakfast from 9.30 am to 2 pm), and *Zillemarkt*, Bleibtreustrasse 48, which also has a special lunch menu from noon to 1 pm on weekdays.

Schwarzes Café, Kantstrasse 148 near Zoo station, serves breakfast any time and is open around the clock from 11 am Wednesday until 3 am Monday. This is one place to get off the street if you happen to roll into Berlin in the middle of the night. For coffee addicts, this place is a prayer answered – soup-sized bowls cost DM5. In Charlottenburg try *Café Voltaire* (see the following Vegetarian section). Many restaurants serve these 'breakfasts' until a rather civilised hour.

Cheap Eats Substantial, inexpensive meals are consumed in the food halls of the large west Berlin department stores, *KaDeWe* and *Wertheim*. At KaDeWe, the top floor is the 'gourmet floor'.

Pizzeria Amigo, Joachimstaler Strasse 39-40 near Zoo station (open daily from 11 am to 1 am), serves a wicked plate of spaghetti napoli or a pizza margherita for only DM6. It's self-service but the food is good and there's a fine place to sit down. *Piccola Taormina* on Uhlandstrasse in central west Berlin is a noisy warren of long benches serving fast, good-value pizzas (from the DM2 variety up to a quite filling DM18 if you prefer) and it is easy to escape for DM10 (including coffee). Locals like the style, and the waft along the nearby Ku'damm can be irresistible.

The *Athener Grill*, Kurfürstendamm 156 (U-Bahn: Adenauerplatz), has spaghetti, pizza, steaks, salads, Greek dishes and big mugs of draught beer at the lowest prices in town. It's self-service, but there are plenty of tables. It's open daily from 11 am to 4 am.

If even these cheap places are too expensive, you can enjoy a hot subsidised meal (DM5 to DM10) in a government cafeteria. They're open weekdays only and you clear your own table.

If you have a valid student card there's the *mensa* of the Technical University, Hardenbergstrasse 34 three blocks from Zoo station (open weekdays from 8 am to 5 pm), where you can fill up a tray for DM10.

The *Kantine* downstairs in Rathaus Charlottenburg, Otto-Suhr-Allee 100 close to Schloss Charlottenburg (U-Bahn: Richard-Wagner-Platz), serves non-employees from 2 to 2.30 pm only. It's in the basement inside the building, not the expensive Ratskeller outside. What's available is written on a blackboard at the far end of the counter.

The *Rathaus Casino* cafeteria on the 10th floor of Rathaus Kreuzberg, Yorckstrasse 4-11 (U-Bahn: Mehringdamm), is open weekdays from 7.30 am to 3 pm and offers cheap lunch specials (you can find a full meal and coffee for DM10), vegetarian dishes and great views. Everyone is welcome. (Nearby at Yorckstrasse 14 is an Eduscho outlet dispensing cheap coffee on weekdays.)

Almost any Arbeitsamt (employment office) you see in west Berlin will have a cheap *Kantine*. A good one is in Arbeitsamt IV at Charlottenstrasse 90 (U-Bahn: Kochstrasse); it's open weekdays from 9 am to 1 pm. Just walk straight in and take the lift on the left up to the 5th floor.

Only a little more expensive is the *Nordsee* cafeteria on the corner of Spandauer Strasse and Karl-Liebknecht-Strasse, which specialises in freezer-package fare that is nonetheless filling and locally popular. The *Noodle Company* at Yorckstrasse 83 in Kreuzberg is good value and has tasteful surroundings. The *Bärenschenke Bierbar*, Friedrichstrasse 124 (U-Bahn: Oranienburger Tor), is an unpretentious local pub serving meals from 10 am to 11 pm (closed Monday). Specialities include Schlachteplatte mit Blut und Leberwurst (a mixed meat plate typical of Berlin), Wildsuppe (venison soup) and Gebackener Camembert (fried cheese). There's a long bar here where you can chat with Berliners as you swill your beer.

German Cuisine Finding authentic German fare takes a little doing. One of the easiest places to experience a typical German meal is the *Ratskeller* (daily from 11 am to 1 am) below Berlin Rathaus just south of the TV tower (S/U-Bahn: Alexanderplatz). Prices are reasonable but the service tends to be slow. *Beiz*, Schlüterstrasse 38 off the Ku'damm (open daily from 6 pm to 2 am), is rather expensive. *Dicke Wirtin*, Carmerstrasse 9 off Savignyplatz, is an earthier Kneipe outfit offering goulash soup and beer. In summer, make for *Loretta's Biergarten*, Lietzenburger Strasse 89 behind the ferris wheel. More out of the way but full of atmosphere is *Zum Ambrosius*, Einemstrasse 14 (U-Bahn: Nollendorfplatz). The specials are marked on blackboards outside this rustic pub/restaurant. If Zum Ambrosius fails to please, try *Spatz*, a block away at Kurfürstenstrasse 56, a basement pub and steakhouse (opens at 6.30 pm daily except Sunday).

Cafés In the Berlin café culture the distinctions of pub, restaurant and bar become blurred and you can roll into most places, at most times, and order most things. But more along the lines of the *Konditorei*, and regarded as the top place for coffee and cakes, is *Café Kranzler* (open daily till midnight), on the corner of the Kurfürstendamm and Joachimstaler Strasse near Zoo station. Look for the circular pavilion up on the roof. It also serves a very good Berlin breakfast. Berlin's most elegant literary café is *Café Einstein*, Kurfürstenstrasse 58 (U-Bahn: Kurfürstenstrasse); it's open daily from 10 am to 2 am. This is a good place to go with friends if you want to talk.

Zum Trichter, Schiffbauerdamm 7 around the corner from the Berliner Ensemble (U and S-Bahn: Friedrichstrasse), is a favourite hang-out for actors and the literary crowd. It opens at 5 pm.

Counterculture pub-cafés with an earthy atmosphere are *Seifen und Kosmetik*, Schliemannstrasse 21 (S-Bahn: Prenzlauer Allee), and *Café Anfall*, Gneisenaustrasse 64 (S-Bahn: Südstern). Anfall opens only in the evening and has pretty wild décor and good, but loud, music, while Seifen und Kosmetik can offer a more laid-back afternoon if you wish. If you want to talk politics, try the café in the rear courtyard at Mehringhof, Gneisenaustrasse 2A in Kreuzberg (U-Bahn: Mehringdamm); it's closed Saturday. Another haunt is the café at Haus der Demokratie, on the corner of Behrensstrasse and Friedrichstrasse in Mitte.

A late-evening place to visit is *Café Arkade*, Französische Strasse 25 near Platz der Akademie (U-Bahn: Französische Strasse), which stays open until midnight. Here you can get excellent Viennese coffee, ice cream or drinks in a pleasant, relaxed atmosphere.

Vegetarian The Krishna snack bar *Higher Taste* at Kurfürstendamm 157 is an excellent specialist restaurant and exceptionally reasonably priced but is, like most of its type, closed on Sunday. Always open and a good café and restaurant for any purpose is *Café Voltaire* on Stuttgarter Platz opposite the Charlottenburg S-Bahn station. The speciality, though, is fresh food prepared while you wait (which is not hard to do as this interesting restaurant seems to be most things to most people – breakfast stop, all-nighter, or culture café-bar). The vegie menu is quite respectable and tasty.

Self-Catering If you are able to prepare your own food, start your shopping at the discount Aldi or Penny Markt chains, which have outlets throughout western and southern Berlin, or the less common Tip stores. You sometimes have to wait in long checkout queues and the variety of goods can sometimes be scant, but you will pay considerably less for the basic food items available.

Handy travelling food such as powdered fruit drinks and soups, dried and fresh fruit, bread, cheese, packaged salads, sandwich meats and chocolate bars are among the worthwhile items. They are also the cheapest places to buy beer and even some table wines. It is worth going between 9 and 11 am to get the best of the bargains, as they can run out fast.

Aldi is upstairs on Joachimstaler Strasse opposite Zoo station, at Uhlandstrasse 42 and on the corner of Kantstrasse and Kaiser-Friedrich-Strasse in Charlottenburg; Tip and Penny Markt are side-by-side near the corner of Hohenzollernstrasse and Martin-Luther-Strasse. Plus is another discounter, probably has more outlets and a slightly bigger range of goods, and often competes with the others on price.

Vegetarians could try the Einhorn buffets on Wittenbergplatz and on Mommsenstrasse near Bleibtreustrasse. For good-quality fruit and vegetables, though, consider the various street markets outside the city centre (see the later Things to Buy section).

Entertainment

Opera & Musicals East Berlin beats west Berlin hands down as far as opera and operetta go, and the best theatres are conveniently clustered near Friedrichstrasse. The productions are lavish with huge casts, and the best seats cost less than half the same tickets in west Berlin. Some theatres (such as the Metropol) give students and pensioners a 50% discount on unsold tickets 30 minutes before the performance. All performances are listed in the monthly magazine *Berlin Programm*, available at newsstands, hotels and tourist offices. Many of the theatres take Monday evening off and close from mid-July to late August.

Good seats for performances on the same evening are usually obtainable, and unclaimed tickets are made available an hour before the performance. The best way to get in is simply to start making the rounds of the box offices at about 6 pm. If there's a big crowd of people waiting at one theatre, hurry on to the next. You're allowed to move to unoccupied, better seats just as the curtain is going up. Berlin's not stuffy, so you can attend theatre and cultural events dressed as you please.

East Berlin's two opera houses are the *Staatsoper*, Unter den Linden 7 (the box office is open Monday to Saturday from noon to 6 pm, Sunday from 2 to 6 pm, tickets DM6 to DM125), and the *Komische Oper*, Behrenstrasse 55-57 at the corner of Glinkastrasse (U-Bahn: Französische Strasse); the box office at Unter den Linden 41 is open Monday to Saturday from noon until 90 minutes before the curtain (Sunday 1 to 4.30 pm), and tickets cost DM8 to DM70.

West Berlin's *Deutsche Oper* (1961), Bismarckstrasse 35 (U-Bahn: Deutsche Oper), is all glass and steel. Its box office opens Monday to Saturday from 11 am to 7 pm, Sunday from 10 am to 2 pm (tickets DM13 to DM135, but these include travel to and from the event on the U-Bahn).

Musicals and operettas are presented at the *Metropol-Theater* at Friedrichstrasse 101-102 directly in front of Friedrichstrasse station (box office opens Monday to Saturday from 10 am to 6 pm). It's not as famous as the operas, so tickets are easier to obtain – highly recommended! (Don't confuse this Metropol theatre with the Metropol disco in west Berlin.) Tickets range from DM8 to DM60.

Seats at west Berlin's *Theater des Westens*, Kantstrasse 12 near Zoo station, cost DM20 to DM76 most days, Friday and Saturday DM23 to DM84. The box office across the street is open Tuesday to Saturday from noon until 6 pm, Sunday from 2 to 4 pm. Though this beautiful old theatre (1896) has style and often features excellent musicals, it's hard to see much from the cheap seats.

The new *Friedrichstadt Palast*, Friedrichstrasse 107, offers vaudeville musical revues but it's often sold out (the box office is open daily from noon to 7 pm).

GERMANY

Theatre & Concerts Even if you speak little or no German, the *Berliner Ensemble*, Bertolt Brecht's original theatre, near the Friedrichstrasse station (box office opens Monday to Saturday from 11 am to 6 pm), is worth attending for its architecture and the musical interludes as well as the artistry of the classic Brecht plays. *The Threepenny Opera*, Brecht's first great popular success, premiered here in 1928. Tickets cost from DM6 to DM47.

East Berlin's wonderfully restored *Schauspielhaus* is on Platz der Akademie (U-Bahn: Stadtmitte). The box office opens Tuesday to Saturday from 2 to 6 pm. All seats at west Berlin's *Philharmonie*, Matthäikirchstrasse 1 (U-Bahn: Kurfürstenstrasse, then bus No 148), are excellent, so just take the cheapest. Do try to hear at least one concert at the Philharmonie. Other musical programmes are offered at the *School of Art Concert Hall*, Hardenbergstrasse 33. You can hear passion music and organ recitals regularly at the *Französischer Dom* on Gendarmenmarkt.

GERMANY

Cinemas If you want to see a movie, go on Tuesday or Wednesday ('cinema day', or *Kinotag)*, when tickets are half-price (DM6 or DM7). The *Filmzentrum Zoo-Palast*, Hardenbergstrasse 29a near Zoo station, contains nine cinemas (the film festival is held here). There are many other movie houses along Kurfürstendamm, but foreign films are dubbed into German. (If the film is being shown in the original language with German subtitles it will say 'O.m.U.' on the advertisement. If it's in English the ad will be marked 'engl. OF'.)

See movies in the original English at the *Odeon Theatre* (☎ 7 81 56 67), Hauptstrasse 116 (U-Bahn: Innsbrucker Platz, or S-Bahn: Schöneberg). There are three shows daily.

The *Kurbel Cinema* (☎ 8 83 53 25), Giesebrechtstrasse 4 off Kurfürstendamm (U-Bahn: Adenauerplatz), also usually has at least one film in English (seats DM12).

Youth Centres The nightlife scene in east Berlin is less slick but more authentic than that in west Berlin. Try the various youth cultural centres which offer a variety of entertainment possibilities under one roof. All are good places to meet people and they're relatively drug-free compared to west Berlin.

Podewil (☎ 24 74 96), at Klosterstrasse 68-70 south-east of Alexanderplatz (U-Bahn: Klosterstrasse), offers a mixed bag of film, stage and live music as well as a café, but what's on varies, so it is best to ring or call in for a coffee and check the monthly programmes that are posted at the door (the café is open from 8 am to 10 pm Monday to Friday and from 4 pm on Saturday). A counterculture place is *Jojo* (☎ 2 82 46 56), Elsässer Strasse 216 (U-Bahn: Oranienburger Tor), which includes a cinema, bookshop, theatre, music room, bar, disco and café. The DM5 entry price admits you to everything, but things don't start moving until 11 pm.

Checkpoint, Leipziger Strasse 55 (U-Bahn: Spittelmarkt), puts on a nightly programme of video, jazz, disco, cinema, theatre, dance, art gallery, bar, café and live music. Not everything is offered every night, so check the programme.

Discos & Clubs West Berlin has a reputation for its nightlife, and nothing happens until 10 pm. That's the time to stroll down the Ku'damm amid all the glitter. Before you get sucked into any of the tourist joints along the strip, take a look up Bleibtreustrasse and around Savignyplatz where the locals go.

West Berlin discos are wild and you have to put a big effort into keeping up with the scene. The favourite tourist disco is *Big Eden*, Kurfürstendamm 202 (open daily from 7 pm). Other than Friday and Saturday nights there's no cover charge, but they make up for it in the price of the drinks. *Society*, Budapester Strasse 42 opposite Europa-Center, is similar. *Zoo Club* at Nürnberger Strasse 49 is the late opener (from 10 pm to 7 am from Wednesday to Sunday).

If you'd rather dance with Berliners it's *Far Out*, Kurfürstendamm 156 (U-Bahn: Adenauerplatz). The entrance to this Bhagwan disco is beneath the bowling alley around the side of the building (open from 10 pm except Monday). You pay DM6 at the door, or DM10 on Friday and Saturday. For a slightly offbeat trip, try the *Metropol* (☎ 2 16 41 22), Nollendorfplatz 5 (U-Bahn: Nollendorfplatz), popular with gays and straights. The big disco operates Friday and Saturday nights from 10 pm, the small disco Sunday to Thursday from 10 pm. Rock concerts unroll at the Metropol around 7 pm, but they're often sold out.

One disco with live 'independent underground' music (hard rock or punk) is *Madhouse Ecstasy*, Hauptstrasse 30 in Schöneberg (U-Bahn: Eisenacher Strasse). It has top bands playing from 9 pm to dawn every Friday and Saturday night (cover charges vary, student discounts available). On other nights, you can dance in its Madhouse or Funhouse discos. Fascist skinheads are not admitted. Under-18s are to be out by midnight.

Pubs Many pubs offer live music and food. A cover charge of up to DM20 may be asked if there's live music, although some places only charge admission on Friday and Saturday nights. The *Sophienklub*, Sophienstrasse 6 off Rosenthaler Strasse (S-Bahn: Weinmeisterstrasse), has jazz nightly from 9 pm, with a special programme on Tuesday and Saturday nights. *Quasimodo*, Kantstrasse 12a near Zoo station (open from 9 pm, music from 10 pm), is a jazz cellar with live jazz, blues or rock every night. There are cover charges for 'name' acts.

For folk music, try *Go In*, Bleibtreustrasse 17 (S-Bahn: Savignyplatz), open daily from 8 pm. *Salsa*, Wielandstrasse 13, features Latin American and Caribbean music. It opens at 8 pm, has live music from 10.30 pm and offers free admission Sunday to Thursday (as well as happy hours from 8 to 10 pm). There is often live music at the *Irish Pub* in the basement of Europa-Center, where English-speakers often gather.

Berliner Kneipen Typical Berlin pubs (*Berliner Kneipen*) have their own tradition of hospitality and discourse – good food (sometimes small courses or daily soups only), good beer, good humour and *Schlagfertigkeit* (repartee). Today you can find this atmosphere in a few backstreet, unassuming-looking places (the tendency to add modern music is inevitable) and a handful of fine establishments maintain what is essentially a living and evolving tradition. Part of the charm of the following three venues is that each, in its own way, claims to be the oldest inn in Berlin.

The stories behind the historic *Zur letzten Instanz* ('The Last Resort') on Waisenstrasse (U-Bahn: Klosterstrasse or S-Bahn: Alexanderplatz) are many, but it should not be the last resort for food and atmosphere: a course of wholesome local fare, beer and coffee costs less than DM25. The pub claims traditions dating back to the 1600s and for good measure is next to a stretch of medieval town wall. The place got its present name 150 years ago when a newly divorced couple (we are told) came in from the nearby courthouse with their witnesses, but by the time they were ready to leave they'd decided to remarry the next day, at which one of those present exclaimed, 'This is the court of last resort!'

E & M Leydicke, Mansteinstrasse 4 (S/U-Bahn: Yorckstrasse) is one of the oldest pubs remaining open in Berlin (founded in 1877) and bottles its own liqueurs on the premises. It is open odd hours, for lunch and then from early evening until late, but is primarily a drinking place.

The inn *Zum Nussbaum*, associated in the past with the artist Heinrich Zille and the humorist Otto Nagel, has been re-established as part of the Nikolaiviertel (beside the church on the corner of Propststrasse near the Mühlendamm) and serves up good, reasonably priced fare while you examine some of Zille's sketches on the walls.

Sports From September to June, you can see football (soccer) every other Saturday at 3 pm at the *Olympic Stadium* – famous for the 1936 'Hitler Games' (U-Bahn: Olympia-

Stadion). There is also a small museum in the stadium.

On weekends, you're welcome to join in soccer and volleyball games on the field in front of the Reichstag.

Things to Buy

Tauentzienstrasse is the main shopping street for affluent west Berlin consumers. At the Wittenbergplatz end of this street is KaDeWe (Kaufhaus des Westens), an amazing, six-storey, turn-of-the-century department store which sells just about everything. Wertheim, Kurfürstendamm 232, west Berlin's second-largest department store, is less pretentious and less expensive. Shops selling discount cameras can be found along Augsburger Strasse near the Ku'damm. Meissner Porzellan, Unter den Linden 39, sells the famous Meissen porcelain, which is fun to look at but expensive to buy. Prices start at around DM100 per piece.

Second-hand clothes of all descriptions can be found at Made in Berlin, Potsdamer Strasse 106 (U-Bahn: Kurfürstenstrasse). You can find some pretty funky attire there! Otherwise, whatever you want in the way of clothes can be found at the street markets. A fine market surrounds the town hall in Schöneberg at John-F-Kennedy-Platz on Tuesday and Friday until late afternoon, and for the range and quality of food, drink, clothing and wares it is hard to beat in Berlin (take the U-Bahn to the adjacent Rathaus Schöneberg station). For fresh fruit and produce that is low-priced, try the Spandau Altstadt markets on Tuesday, Thursday and Friday from April until mid-November (U-Bahn: Rathaus or Altstadt Spandau).

There's an open-air flea market *(Trödelmarkt)* every Saturday and Sunday morning on Strasse des 17. Juni at Tiergarten S-Bahn station. Don't buy any GDR paraphernalia here, as you can get it much cheaper at the street market around the Brandenburger Tor. The markets on the Spree River bank across from Museumsinsel or in front of the university at the top of Unter den Linden are interesting, particularly for books, but these are mostly unpriced and you will need to bargain shrewdly or you might be ripped off at above-shop prices.

Second-hand cars are lined up on Stuttgarter Platz in Charlottenburg (just west of the S-Bahn station), on weekends, holidays and random weekdays as well. Prices start at about DM1500, but most of the respectable-looking second-hand Golfs and Corsas are in the DM3000 to DM5000 range. Varied information appears in the windows, and, although some offer service histories, it seems very much a case of *caveat emptor*. Perhaps it is better to ring around using the auto edition of *Zweite Hand* if you want a wide choice of marque or a particular car or features.

You can buy solid second-hand bicycles from about DM120 through the listings in *Zweite Hand*, although used touring models start at about DM230. Mehring Hof Fahrrad Laden (☎ 6 91 60 27), at Gneisenaustrasse 2a in Kreuzberg, is a handy showroom for good second-hand makes, and solid, three-gear models cost from about DM280. Fahrrad Station (see Bicycle Rental in the later Getting Around section) sells fully tested used machines from DM400.

For outdoors gear and camping equipment, investigate the range at Der Aussteiger, Schliemannstrasse 46 in Prenzlauer Berg, and compare with the big Alles für Tramper specialist store at Bundesallee 88 in west Berlin.

Getting There & Away

Bus The Funkturm bus station (U-Bahn: Kaiserdamm) is open from 5.30 am to 10 pm. Westkreuz S-Bahn station is within walking distance. Bayern Express-Berlinien bus (☎ 8 60 09 60) has buses to Amsterdam, Hanover, Munich, Nuremberg, Würzburg and Rothenburg ob der Tauber and has a DM99 fare to Frankfurt/Main (10 hours, under-27 discounts available). Tickets are available from most travel agencies in Berlin. Sperling GmbH (☎ 33 10 31) has services to Bremen, Düsseldorf, Goslar, Hamburg, Kiel, Lübeck and other cities in northern Germany.

Train The ticket and reservation offices at

Berlin Hauptbahnhof and Berlin-Lichtenberg train stations are far less congested than the one in Berlin-Zoologischer Garten. But beware that they (as well as Zoo) are being redeveloped around you as you leave or arrive – some arrangements are confusing, involving services that arrive at one station and link with services that leave from another – if you must link in this way, buy a local DM2.30 or DM3.50 ticket to connect, as rail passes are invalid on the Berlin S-Bahn (you could hop on the odd long-distance train that stops at Potsdam or Berlin-Schönefeld, though).

Conventional train tickets to and from Berlin are valid for all train stations in the city S-Bahn, which means that on arrival you may use the S-Bahn network (but not the U-Bahn) to proceed to your destination. Conversely, you can use the S-Bahn to go to the station from where your train leaves if you have a booked ticket. It's always best to board trains leaving Berlin at the originating station mentioned on your ticket.

Berlin Hauptbahnhof in east Berlin handles trains to the north (including cross-Baltic destinations such as Malmö), and some trains to Dresden and Prague. This station has more of the large DM3 lockers than Zoo and a DM4 per day left-luggage office (open from 6.15 am to 10.30 pm daily), exchange office (Monday to Friday 7 am to 10 pm, Saturday to 6 pm, Sunday 8 am to 4 pm), and a tourist office upstairs (see the earlier Berlin Tourist Offices section).

Berlin-Lichtenberg handles trains to all parts of northern Germany, south to Halle and Leipzig and many to Eastern Europe. This station is easily reached by S-Bahn or U-Bahn. The reservation office is open on weekdays from 6 am to 8 pm, on weekends from 8 am to 6 pm, and international tickets are easily purchased. The helpful attendants in the station information office speak good English and there's no crowd! The left-luggage room is always open (DM2 per piece per day) and there are coin lockers.

Trains to Poland and points farther east depart from Berlin Hauptbahnhof as well as Berlin-Lichtenberg. The left-luggage office at the Hauptbahnhof is closed from 1.30 to 3 am.

Zoo, on Hardenbergplatz, is the main train station in west Berlin for long-distance as well as U-Bahn and S-Bahn trains. This overcrowded station features coin lockers (DM2 or DM3 depending on the size, although at Zoo they are generally full) and a baggage station charging DM4 per item per day (it's not intended for left-luggage, rather it's a supplement to the locker set-up, as the larger lockers are few). There is a reservation office (long, slow queues), a train information office *(Zugauskunft)*, and a tourist office that makes hotel reservations. Outside on Hardenbergplatz is a local transit office with information where daily and weekly transport cards are for sale.

Bahnhof Friedrichstrasse or Alexanderplatz can be good places to dump your gear as big lockers cost only DM2 (though many will be out of order at any time). Trains between Poland and Western Europe pass through west Berlin, so you can get on or off at Zoo station. From there you can take the S-Bahn to Alexanderplatz or Berlin Hauptbahnhof.

Hitching You can hitch to Dresden, Hanover, Leipzig, Munich, Nuremberg and beyond from Checkpoint Dreilinden at Wannsee (S-Bahn: Wannsee, then walk less than a km up Potsdamer Chaussee and follow the signs to Raststätte Dreilinden). There's always a bunch of hitchhikers here, but everyone gets a ride eventually. Bring a sign showing your destination, and consider waiting until you find a car going right where you want to go.

There are several Mitfahrzentrale agencies in west Berlin, which charge from DM8 commission (to or from Leipzig or Rostock) to DM17 (to or from Stuttgart). The maximum amount payable to the driver is set and listed for German destinations (Magdeburg DM10, Freiburg DM47), while Paris can cost up to DM64 and Budapest DM56 (plus DM19 commission on both).

The ADM-Mitfahrzentrale office (☎ 31 03 31) is on the Vinetastrasse platform of the

U2 line at Zoo U-Bahn station and is open daily from 8 am to 8 pm. Another ADM office (☎ 2 42 36 42) is open daily at the Alexanderplatz U-Bahn station (as you cross from the U2 to the U8). Citynetz Mitfahr-Service (☎ 1 94 44) has offices open daily on the 2nd-floor shopping arcade of Ku'damm-Eck at Kurfürstendamm 227, at Sybelstrasse 53 and three other locations. Yet another Mitfahrzentrale agency is in Kreuzberg (☎ 2 16 60 21) at Yorckstrasse 57. The people answering the phone in these offices always speak good English, so don't hesitate to call around.

If you arrange a ride a few days in advance, be sure to call the driver the night before and again on departure morning to make sure he/she is still going.

Getting Around

Berlin is probably easier to drive around than many another metropolises, but you will still run into roadworks in the eastern parts for some time yet. You can park immediately west of the zoo for DM20 for the day and the going rate is about DM2 per hour for a few hours. Underground parking at similar rates is on Augsburger Strasse not far from Breitscheidplatz. The ring roads get you easily around the urban perimeter. Above-ground parking is easier to find in eastern areas and is generally cheaper. But using the efficient public transport network (or a bicycle) would be infinitely better.

To/From the Airport Most Eastern European and Third World carriers fly from Berlin-Schönefeld airport, next to Flughafen Berlin-Schönefeld station just outside the southern city limits. The S9 from Zoo station and Alexanderplatz runs to Schönefeld every 20 minutes from 4 to 1 am (or take the U7 to Rudow and bus No 171, also every 20 minutes). The more occasional S45 links Schönefeld and Tempelhof. Plans to make Schönefeld into the main Berlin gateway (at least until a single major international airport can be completed) have run into local opposition.

Berlin-Tegel (also called Otto Lilienthal), west Berlin's main commercial airport, six km north-west of Zoo station, receives most flights from Western Europe (bus No 109 from the Inter-Continental Hotel on the Kurfürstendamm via Zoo station, or bus 128 from the U6 at Kurt-Schumacher-Platz). These buses operate every 15 minutes from 5 am to midnight. Near the tourist office in the main hall at Tegel is a baggage storage office (open from 5.30 am to 10 pm) and a bank.

The Tempelhof airport receives mostly domestic flights (U-Bahn: Platz der Luftbrücke).

Public Transport The Berliner Verkehrs-Betriebe (BVG) operates an efficient suburban train (S-Bahn), metro (U-Bahn), ferry and bus system which reaches every corner of Berlin and the surrounding area and the network is constantly being extended. Trams exist only in east Berlin. The BVG ferry from Kladow to Wannsee operates hourly all year (except when there's ice or fog), with regular tickets, passes and transfers accepted. System maps are posted in all stations and most vehicles, and are available free from all ticket or information windows. You'll find the whole system easy to use.

There are two types of ticket, one for the whole Berlin network as far as Potsdam, and one for journeys exclusively within former East Berlin (if you are not sure, it's best to buy at a ticket window or check), each with normal and concession fares. Most stations now have orange ticket machines with English instructions, some of which accept DM5 coins or notes up to DM50, although you can often buy at a ticket window at the station entrance as well.

A single DM2.30 *(Kurzstrecke)* ticket (within the former East Berlin only, DM2) will take you three stops (with one change if necessary) on the train or about half a dozen stops on the bus; again, if in doubt, ask. The DM3.50 ticket (east Berlin DM3.10) allows unlimited transfers on all forms of public transport for two hours: in train stations validate the ticket as your train arrives to ensure full value.

A *Sammelkarte* with four trip-blocks of two hours each works out cheaply at DM12 (east Berlin DM10.50), and a 24-hour ticket costs DM13 (students DM6.50). The DM35 weekly pass is a good buy if you are travelling a lot.

If you are at a hotel or pension for a week or so, lean a little closer and ask the staff if there is a monthly pass available for loan at a small fee. It's less than legal, but many establishments offer this service to guests and you might get a week's travel for as little as DM30 all-up. Monthly passes cost DM82.

You validate your own ticket in a red machine *(Entwerter)* at the platform entrances to the S-Bahn and U-Bahn stations. If you're caught by an inspector without a valid ticket, there's a DM60 fine (random checks have been stepped up and no excuses are accepted). Cultural cringe is such that less than 1.5% of passengers ride illegally. First-class S-Bahn carriages are expected to be in use by 1996.

You can take a bicycle in specially marked cars on the S-Bahn or U-Bahn, but a DM2.30 fare must be paid. Monthly tickets allow you to take a bicycle with you free. You're not allowed, however, to take a bike on the west Berlin U-Bahn weekdays from 2 to 5.30 pm.

The S-Bahn differs from the U-Bahn in that more than one line uses the same track. Destination indicators on the platforms tell you where the next train is going. All trains to the east from Friedrichstrasse run to Alexanderplatz. The system is easy to use and route maps are posted in all carriages, but you have to pay attention. The next station (including an *Übergänge*, or place to change) is announced in most trains and even displayed at the end of carriages on some new trains. It's best, though, to know the name of the station before the one you need.

The double-decker buses offer great views from the upstairs front seats. One of the most popular double-decker routes is bus No 119, which runs from Grunewald to Kreuzberg via the Ku'damm.

The S-Bahn and U-Bahn lines close down between 1 and 4 am, but night buses run every 30 minutes all night from Zoo station to key points such as Rathaus Spandau, Alt-Tegel, Hermannplatz, Rathaus Steglitz, Mexikoplatz etc. Regular fares apply.

Bus drivers sell single tickets, but multiple, 24-hour, seven-day or monthly tickets must be purchased in advance. The seven-day ticket can only be purchased at the BVG information kiosk (open daily from 10 am to 6 pm) in front of Zoo station; the other passes are available from the orange machines in mass transit stations.

Taxi There's a taxi stand beside all main train stations. The basic flagfall tariff is DM3.80, then an additional DM1.93 per km. On Sunday and holidays it's DM2.10 per km, and baggage items cost various amounts: expect to pay up to DM1 flat rate if you have a rucksack or two bags. Some easy-to-remember numbers are ☎ 96 44, 69 02 and 21 02 02, though for faster response try the 'Taxi-Ruf' listings for your area in the telephone directory (for instance ☎ 8 81 52 20 for the Ku'damm-Uhlandstrasse area).

Car & Motorbike Rental All of the large car-rental chains are represented in Berlin, and their standard rates for the cheapest car begin around DM160 daily or DM850 weekly with unlimited km. Collision insurance begins around DM30 a day extra. Rental cars are often fully booked in Berlin, so advance reservations are advisable, and you may even get a better rate by booking from abroad. Weekends are usually the best times to rent.

Hertz (☎ 2 61 10 53), Budapester Strasse 39 at the Europa-Center, allows its cars to be driven into Poland but only with specific permission and restrictions. Its city-only weekend rates are much cheaper than its regular tariff at DM108 for small cars.

Budget/Sixt Rent-a-Car (☎ 2 61 13 57) at Budapester Strasse 18 offers standard economy rates of DM129 a day on Corsas, DM649 per week, km included, cards or Eurocheques only.

Europcar at Kurfürstendamm 178 has a

DM99 per day weekend offer, as does Avis in Europa-Center.

A good independent car-rental company is Allround Autovermietung (☎ 2 61 14 56), Zietenstrasse 1 (U-Bahn: Nollendorfplatz). Its cheapest cars are DM595 a week (unlimited km), DM300 deposit (credit cards only accepted from tourist customers). It's open weekdays from 9 am to 6 pm, Saturday to 1 pm.

Small companies offering discount car rentals advertise in the 'PKW – Vermietung' section of the classified newspaper *Zweite Hand*.

For motorbike rentals try Classic Rent (☎ 6 14 73 43) at Skalitzer Strasse 127 in Kreuzberg near Schlesisches Tor. Weekly rental rates vary from DM590 to DM950 and there is a deposit of DM1500 on cash rentals. The first 250 km are free. Another prospect is S7 Motorradvermietung (☎ 7 71 73 69) at Breite Strasse 22 in Steglitz, which starts around DM500 per week for 650cc models with a DM350 deposit.

Bicycle Rental Bicycles can be rented at Fahrradstation (☎ 2 16 91 77) at Möckernstrasse 92 in Kreuzberg and Gipsstrasse 7 in Mitte, which offers carefully inspected and maintained machines from DM25 per 24 hours for city use, DM110 per week, although a few three-geared models are available at DM15 and DM85. Most other bicycle shops in west Berlin will also rent out bikes, but not for less than 24 hours.

GERMANY

Brandenburg

The state of Brandenburg surrounds Berlin, and there are plans to merge the two before the year 2000. It's a flat region of lakes, marshes and rivers, and canals connect the Oder and Elbe rivers (utilising the Havel and Spree rivers, which meet at Spandau west of Berlin). The Spreewald, a marshy area near Cottbus, was inhabited by the Slavonic Sorbs right up until WW II. The electors of Brandenburg acquired the eastern Baltic duchy of Prussia in 1618, merging the two states into a powerful union called the Kingdom of Prussia. This kingdom eventually brought all of Germany under its control, leading to the establishment of the German Empire in 1871.

POTSDAM

Potsdam, on the Havel River just beyond the south-west tip of Berlin, became important in the 17th century as the residence of the Elector of Brandenburg. Later, with the creation of the Kingdom of Prussia, Potsdam became a royal seat and garrison town, and in the mid-18th century Friedrich the Great built many of the marvellous palaces in Sanssouci Park which visitors come to see today.

In April 1945, British bombers devastated the historic centre of Potsdam, but fortunately most of the palaces escaped undamaged (only the City Palace was badly hit). To make a point of their victory over German militarism, the victorious Allies chose the city for the Potsdam Conference of August 1945, which set the stage for the division of Berlin and Germany into four occupation zones.

Orientation & Information

Potsdam Stadt train station is just south-east across the Havel River. The next stop after Potsdam Stadt is Potsdam West, which is closer to Sanssouci Park; most trains also stop at Bahnhof Wildpark (closer still, but check). The centre and Sanssouci Palace are both reached from Hauptbahnhof by tram or bus (buy your ticket in advance at a kiosk or machine). You can walk from Schloss Cecilienhof to Glienicker Brücke (and bus No 116 to Wannsee) in about 10 minutes.

Potsdam-Information (☎ 0331-2 11 00), at Friedrich-Ebert-Strasse 5 beside Alter Markt, sells a variety of maps and brochures but is incredibly crowded. Its opening hours vary according to the season: in summer it is open on weekdays from 9 am to 8 pm, weekends from 9 am to 6 pm; from November to March its hours are weekdays from 9 am to 6 pm, weekends from 11 am to 3 pm. The

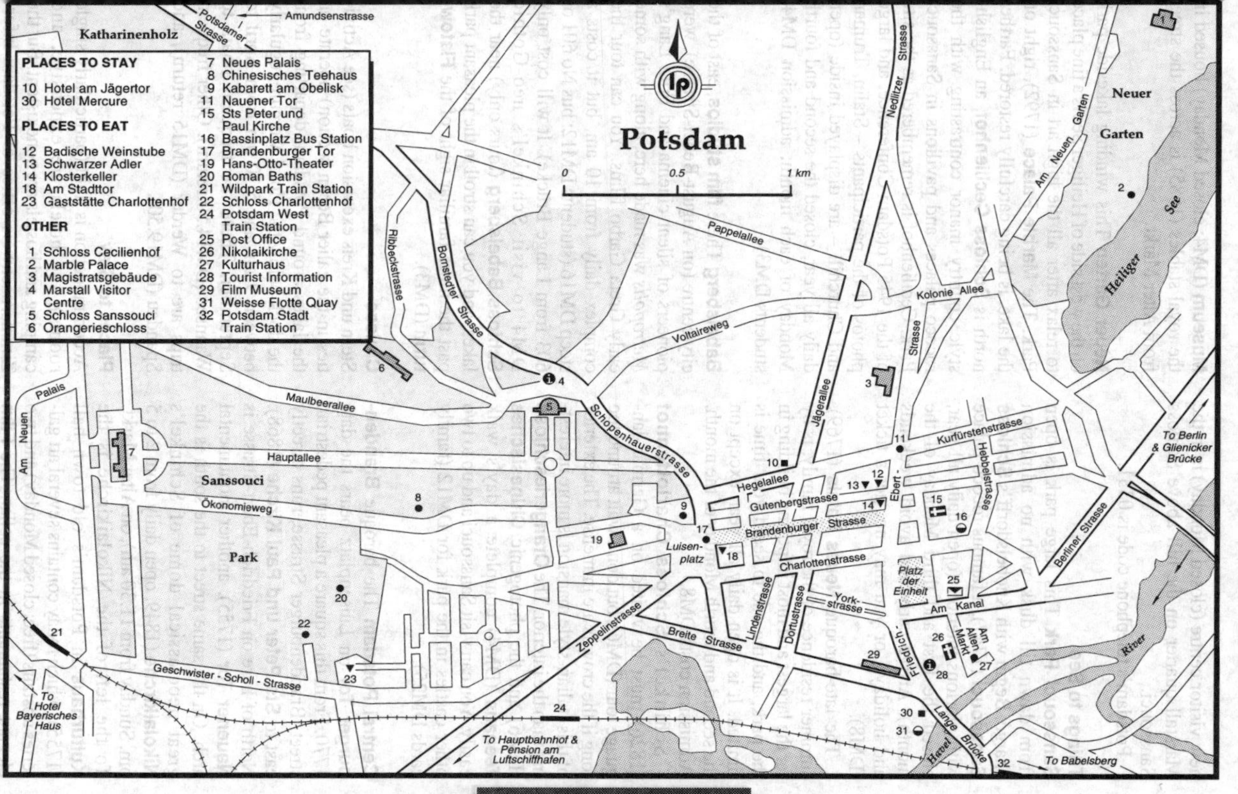
Potsdam
0
0.5
1 km
PLACES TO STAY
10 Hotel am Jägertor
30 Hotel Mercure
PLACES TO EAT
12 Badische Weinstube
13 Schwarzer Adler
14 Klosterkeller
18 Am Stadttor
23 Gaststätte Charlottenhof
OTHER
1 Schloss Cecilienhof
2 Marble Palace
3 Magistratsgebäude
4 Marstall Visitor Centre
5 Schloss Sanssouci
6 Orangerieschloss
7 Neues Palais
8 Chinesisches Teehaus
9 Kabarett am Obelisk
11 Nauener Tor
15 Sts Peter und Paul Kirche
16 Bassinplatz Bus Station
17 Brandenburger Tor
19 Hans-Otto-Theater
20 Roman Baths
21 Wildpark Train Station
22 Schloss Charlottenhof
24 Potsdam West Train Station
25 Post Office
26 Nikolaikirche
27 Kulturhaus
28 Tourist Information
29 Film Museum
31 Weisse Flotte Quay
32 Potsdam Stadt Train Station
Katharinenholz
Potsdamer Strasse
Amundsenstrasse
Neuer Garten
Heiliger See
Am Neuen Garten
Nedlitzer Strasse
Pappelallee
Kolonie Allee
Ribbeckstrasse
Bornstedter Strasse
Voltaireweg
Jägerallee
Strasse
Kurfürstenstrasse
Hebbelstrasse
Berliner Strasse
To Berlin & Glienicker Brücke
Am Neuen Palais
Maulbeerallee
Schopenhauerstrasse
Hauptallee
Sanssouci
Ökonomieweg
Park
Hegelallee
Gutenbergstrasse
Brandenburger Strasse
Ebert-
Luisen-platz
Charlottenstrasse
Lindenstrasse
Dortustrasse
York-strasse
Platz der Einheit
Am Kanal
Am Alten Markt
Friedrich-
Zeppelinstrasse
Breite Strasse
Geschwister - Scholl - Strasse
To Hotel Bayerisches Haus
To Hauptbahnhof & Pension am Luftschiffhafen
Havel
Lange Brücke
River
To Babelsberg

GERMANY

new visitor centre (closed Monday) is in the Marstall quarter on the hill above Schloss Sanssouci.

Potsdam's telephone code is 0331.

Things to See

Sanssouci Park This large park is open from dawn till dusk with no admission charge. Begin with Knobelsdorff's **Schloss Sanssouci** (1747), a famous rococo palace with glorious interiors (open daily all year, closed the first and third Monday of the month). Arrive early and avoid weekends and holidays, or you may not get a ticket (DM8).

The late-baroque **Neues Palais** (1769), summer residence of the royal family, is by far the largest and most imposing building in the park, and the one to see if your time is limited. It is open daily all year, except on the second and fourth Monday of the month. Admission costs DM8.

Schinkel's **Schloss Charlottenhof** (1826) must be visited on a German-language tour (DM6), but don't wait around too long if the crowds are immense. The exterior of this Italian-style mansion is more interesting than the interior. The **Orangerieschloss** (DM6) and the photogenic **Chinesisches Teehaus** (DM4) complete a day's walk easily. You can visit Sanssouci and up to two other castles in the park for DM12 (family cards DM25).

Central Potsdam The baroque **Brandenburger Tor** on Luisenplatz bears the date 1770. From this square a pleasant pedestrian street, Brandenburger Strasse, runs directly east to **Sts Peter und Paul Kirche** (1868). North of here on Friedrich-Ebert-Strasse is **Nauener Tor** (1755), another monumental arch. On the same street to the south is the great neoclassical dome of Schinkel's **Nikolaikirche** (1849, open daily from 2 to 5 pm, Sunday from 11.30 am), on Alter Markt. To the left of the Nikolaikirche is the **Kulturhaus** in Potsdam's old town hall (1755), which today contains several art galleries upstairs (free; closed Monday) and two elegant restaurants in the cellar. The **Film Museum** (DM4; closed Monday) housed in the royal stables (1685) is across the street from Alter Markt.

Neuer Garten This winding lakeside park on the west side of Heiliger See is a fine place to relax after all the high art in Sanssouci Park. The **Marble Palace** (1792), right on the lake, is being carefully restored. Farther north is **Schloss Cecilienhof**, an English-style country manor contrasting with the rococo palaces and pavilions in Sanssouci Park. Cecilienhof is remembered as the site of the 1945 Potsdam Conference, and large photos of the participants – Stalin, Truman and Churchill – are displayed inside (open daily all year, closed the second and fourth Monday of each month; admission DM4, students DM3).

Babelsberg These **film studios**, east of the city centre (on August-Bebel-Strasse), were pioneers of silent cinema and Fritz Lang's *Metropolis* was made here, along with some early Greta Garbo films. You can tour the complex daily from 10 am, but it costs a steep DM16 (students DM12; bus No 601 or 603 from Lange Brücke). It will cost only DM4 to visit Schinkel's neo-Gothic **Schloss Babelsberg** (tours only) near the lakes, and you can stroll in the pleasant park past the more familiar sight of the **Flatowturm** (DM3).

Cruises

Stern und Kreis excursion boats (see Activities in the ealier Berlin section) operate on the lakes around Potsdam, departing from the dock below the Hotel Mercure regularly between 9 am and 5.30 pm from April to September. There are frequent boats to Wannsee (DM14.50 return). Other frequent trips are to Werder (DM15 return), and Spandau (DM19.50).

Places to Stay

Accommodation is tight (particularly single rooms), the hotels are expensive, and camping and hostels are nonexistent. But the Zimmernachweis office of Potsdam-Information (see Orientation & Information) arranges private rooms in Potsdam from DM25 to DM50 (singles) or DM15 to DM30 per person. There are also apartments from DM25 to DM50 per person.

Pension One of the few places under DM100 is *Pension am Luftschiffhafen* (☎ 9 67 91 47), at Am Luftschiffhafen 1 off Zeppelinstrasse. For singles (in a double room) and doubles it charges DM95 and DM140. It is also the closest to Hauptbahnhof (or take tram No 94 or 96 from the city).

Hotels *Jugend- und Seminarhotel Potsdam* (☎ 97 23 25) has few singles but some doubles/multi-bed rooms (DM45/80/120). At Geschwister-Scholl-Strasse 51 south of Sanssouci Park, it is some compensation for the lack of a hostel. *Hotel Bayerisches Haus* (☎ 97 31 92), well located at Im Wildpark 1, is fair enough at the floor price of DM100/150 if you can get a room. The small and functional *Hotel am Jägertor* (☎ 2 18 34), Hegelallee 11 in the city centre, is overpriced at DM105/135 a single/double with shared bath, DM130/185 with private bath.

Rooms at the three-star *Hotel Schloss Cecilienhof* (☎ 3 70 50) in Neuer Garten begin at DM130/250 a single/double with bath and breakfast (up to DM230/380), and you get to sleep in one of Potsdam's most famous buildings. If you don't mind the price, have a travel agent book your room well in advance.

Places to Eat

The *Klosterkeller*, Friedrich-Ebert-Strasse 94 on the corner of Gutenbergstrasse, includes a grill bar (open weekdays from 8 am to 9 pm, weekends to 3 pm), a regular restaurant (daily from 11.30 am to late), a beer garden (May to September) and a night bar (Thursday to Saturday from 9 pm to 4 am). Prices are moderate and the place combines modern German décor with a traditional menu.

The *Badische Weinstube*, Gutenbergstrasse 90, often has good weekday lunch specials advertised in the window. *Am Stadttor* by the gate at the western end of Brandenburger Strasse has good lunch specials and offers a pleasant view. The *Gaststätte Charlottenhof*, just outside Park Sanssouci near Schloss Charlottenhof, offers much more elegant dining, if you have time.

For afternoon coffee and cakes, *Café Heider*, Friedrich-Ebert-Strasse 28 just across from Nauener Tor, is good.

Entertainment

The Besucherservice (☎ 2 80 06 93), in Theaterhaus on Am Alten Markt (closed Friday and Saturday afternoons, Sunday and Monday), has tickets for performances at the *Hans-Otto-Theater*, Zimmerstrasse 10, and the *Schlosstheater* in the Neues Palais. On Wednesday at 7.30 pm from July to mid-September, there are organ concerts at various churches in Potsdam (ask Potsdam-Information for locations).

The *Film Museum* opposite Alter Markt shows films from 2 or 3 pm each afternoon for DM6 (students DM4). The *Potsdamer Kabarett am Obelisk*, Schopenhauerstrasse 27, presents drama (in German) on contemporary themes at 8 pm from Wednesday to Sunday. Its ticket office (open weekdays from 8 am to 4.30 pm) is in the rear courtyard.

A local pub with an earthy atmosphere is the *Schwarzer Adler*, Gutenbergstrasse 91 (closed Tuesday and Sunday afternoon).

Getting There & Away

Bus Bassinplatz bus station is accessible from west Berlin on bus No 138 from Rathaus Spandau (hourly from 6 am to 8 pm) and bus No 113 from Wannsee (every 20 minutes from 5 am to 1 am).

Bus No 113 takes a roundabout route through Babelsberg, so if you're headed for Schloss Cecilienhof it is much faster to take bus No 116 from Wannsee to the Glienicker Brücke and walk from there.

Train Hourly S-Bahn trains run from Berlin-Wannsee to Potsdam Stadt, Potsdam West and Potsdam Hauptbahnhof, the most direct route by rail. If you arrive by S-Bahn from Berlin-Wannsee and want to go directly to the centre of town, get out at Potsdam Stadt. The Wannsee trains usually continue on to Potsdam Hauptbahnhof, off Zeppelinstrasse five km south-west of the centre of town. Going back, you won't need to validate tickets bought at platform machines.

There is no direct service to Flughafen Berlin-Schönefeld, but you can take the S45 from Westkreuz to the airport or change for the R1 regional train, which runs to and from Königs Wusterhausen, at Werder. All Berlin transit passes are valid for the trip to Potsdam by either S-Bahn or BVG transit bus, and for local trams and buses around Potsdam.

Trains between Hanover and Berlin-Zoo also stop at Potsdam Stadt. For Schwerin, take a train from Potsdam Hauptbahnhof to Stendal. Train connections from Potsdam south to Leipzig or Dresden are poor. To travel between Potsdam and Saxony, it's usually simpler to change at Berlin-Schönefeld.

GERMANY

Boat From April to October, large excursion boats ply between Wannsee and Potsdam (see also Activities in the Berlin section) from May to October.

Getting Around

Potsdam is part of Berlin's S-Bahn network and has its own trams and buses; these converge on Lange Brücke near Potsdam Stadt station. Comparable in price (DM2.50 per trip) are the summer excursion buses and trams around Sanssouci to Neues Palais, through the town centre to the park, or to Babelsberg. Most run direct from outside Potsdam Stadt station. For a taxi dial ☎ 87 91 29.

Saxony

The Free State of Saxony (Sachsen) includes the former districts of Dresden, Leipzig and Chemnitz (Karl-Marx-Stadt in Communist times). Germanic Saxon tribes originally occupied large parts of north-western Germany, but in the 10th century they expanded south-eastward into the territory of the pagan Slavs.

The medieval history of the various Saxon duchies and dynasties is complex, but in the 13th century the Duke of Saxony at Wittenberg obtained the right to participate in the election of Holy Roman emperors. Involvement in Poland weakened Saxony in the 18th century, and ill-fated alliances, first with Napoleon and then with Austria, led to the ascendancy of Prussia over Saxony in the 19th century.

In the south, Saxony is separated from Bohemia by the Erzgebirge, eastern Germany's highest mountain range. The Elbe River cuts north-west from the Czech border through a picturesque area known as the 'Saxon Switzerland' towards the old capital, Dresden. Leipzig, a great educational and commercial centre on the Weisse Elster River, rivals Dresden in historic associations. Quaint little towns like Bautzen, Görlitz and Meissen punctuate this colourful, accessible corner of Germany.

DRESDEN

In the 18th century the Saxon capital Dresden was famous throughout Europe as 'the Florence of the north'. During the reigns of Augustus the Strong (ruled 1694-1733) and his son Augustus III (ruled 1733-63), Italian artists, musicians, actors and master craftsmen, particularly from Venice, flocked to the Dresden court. The Italian painter Canaletto depicted the rich architecture of the time in many paintings which now hang in Dresden's Alte Meister Gallery alongside countless masterpieces purchased for Augustus III with income from the silver mines of Saxony.

In February 1945 much of Dresden was devastated by Anglo-American firebombing raids. At least 35,000 people died in this atrocity which happened at a time when the city was jammed with refugees and the war was almost over. In the postwar years quite a number of Dresden's great baroque buildings have been restored, but the city's former architectural masterpiece, the Frauenkirche, is still in the earliest stages of a laborious and enormously expensive reconstruction.

The Elbe River cuts a curving course between the low, rolling hills, and in spite of modern rebuilding in concrete and steel, this city invariably holds visitors' affection. With its numerous museums and many fine baroque palaces, a stay of three nights is the minimum required to fully appreciate Dresden.

Orientation

Dresden has two main train stations: Dresden Hauptbahnhof on the southern side of town and Dresden-Neustadt north of the river. Most trains stop at both, but the Dresden train station is more convenient unless you're staying in Neustadt; take tram No 11 to get to Postplatz near the Zwinger (see following Things to See section). Otherwise walk to town along Prager Strasse, the pedestrian mall directly in front of the Dresden train station.

Information

Dresden-Information (☎ 0351-4 95 50 25), at Prager Strasse 10 on the eastern side of the mall in front of the Dresden train station, sells maps and theatre tickets and has a service that finds private rooms. In summer it's open weekdays from 9 am to 8 pm, Saturday to 6 pm, and Sunday to 2 pm; the winter opening hours are Monday to Saturday from 9 am to 6 pm, and Sunday to 2 pm.

Dresden-Information's Neustadt office (☎ 0351-5 35 39) in the underpass below the Goldener Reiter statue is open Monday to Friday from 9 am to 6 pm, and Saturday, Sunday and public holidays to 4 pm.

There is a useful post office on Prager Strasse near the tourist office. The Deutsche Verkehrs Bank has a branch at the Dresden train station (open weekdays from 8 am to 7.30 pm and Saturday to 4 pm).

If you intend visiting two or more of Dresden's museums, then it's probably worth buying the combined one-day ticket for DM10 (students DM5) or the yearly ticket for DM30 (students DM15). This not only saves you money but allows you to bypass the often long ticket queues. You can buy these tickets at all museums where they are valid.

Dresden's telephone code is 0351.

Things to See

Altstadt A 10-minute walk north along Prager Strasse from the Dresden train station brings you into the Altmarkt area, the historic hub of Dresden. On the right you'll see the rebuilt **Kreuzkirche** (1792), famous for its boys' choir, and behind it the 1912 **Neues Rathaus** (New Town Hall).

Cross the wide Wilsdruffer Strasse to the **City Historical Museum** (closed Friday) in a building erected in 1776. North-west up Landhausstrasse is Neumarkt and the site of the once massive **Frauenkirche** (1738), Germany's greatest Protestant church, now in the early stages of a painstaking reconstruction expected to take almost two decades; the figure of Martin Luther silently watches the progress. On this same square is the interesting **Museum of Transport** (closed Monday).

Leading north-west from Neumarkt is Augustus Strasse with the 102-metre-long *Procession of Princes* mural depicted on the outer wall of the old royal stables. This street brings you directly to the Catholic **Hofkirche** (1755) where the organ is played each Saturday at 4 pm from May to October. Directly behind the Hofkirche are the remains of the Renaissance **Royal Palace**, which is also slowly being restored.

Most of Dresden's priceless art treasures are housed in two large buildings, the Zwinger and the Albertinum. To reach the **Albertinum** on Brühlsche Garten just off Terrassenufer, stroll east along the terrace overlooking the river. Here you'll find the **Neue Meister Gallery**, with renowned 19th and 20th-century paintings, and the **Grünes Gewölbe** (Green Vault), one of the world's finest collections of jewel-studded precious objects; both are closed Thursday and admission is DM7 (students DM3.50).

On the western side of the Hofkirche is

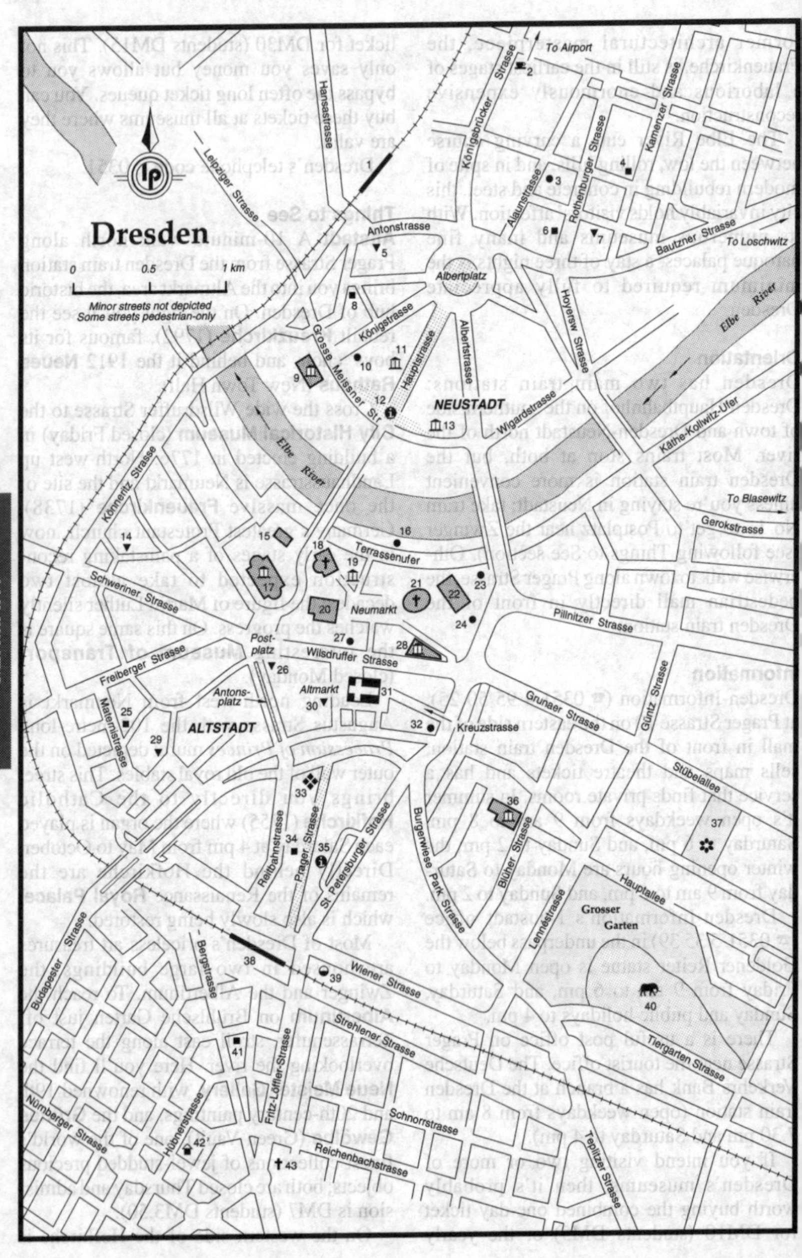
Dresden
0
0.5
1 km
Minor streets not depicted
Some streets pedestrian-only
To Airport
To Loschwitz
To Blasewitz
Hansastrasse
Leipziger Strasse
Königsbrücker Strasse
Rothenburger Strasse
Kamenzer Strasse
Alaunstrasse
Bautzner Strasse
Antonstrasse
Albertplatz
Königstrasse
Hauptstrasse
Grosse Meissner Str
Albertstrasse
Hoyersw Strasse
Elbe River
NEUSTADT
Wigardstrasse
Käthe-Kollwitz-Ufer
Könneritz Strasse
Gerokstrasse
Terrassenufer
Schweriner Strasse
Neumarkt
Pillnitzer Strasse
Post-
platz
Wilsdruffer Strasse
Freiberger Strasse
Antons-
platz
Altmarkt
Güntz Strasse
Grunaer Strasse
Maternistrasse
ALTSTADT
Kreuzstrasse
Stübelallee
Reitbahnstrasse
Prager Strasse
St Petersburger Strasse
Burgerwiese Park Strasse
Lennéstrasse
Blüher Strasse
Hauptallee
Grosser
Garten
Budapester Strasse
Bergstrasse
Wiener Strasse
Strehlener Strasse
Tiergarten Strasse
Fritz-Löffler-Strasse
Hübnerstrasse
Nürnberger Strasse
Schnorrstrasse
Reichenbachstrasse
Teplitzer Strasse
1
2
3
5
6
7
8
9
10
11
12
13
14
15
16
17
18
19
20
21
22
23
24
25
26
27
28
29
30
31
32
33
34
35
36
37
38
39
40
41
42
43

GERMANY

PLACES TO STAY

- 4 Hotel Stadt Rendsburg
- 6 Hotel Rothenburger Hof
- 8 Hotel Martha Christliches Hospiz
- 25 Hotel-Kongress-Business-Center
- 34 Hotel Königstein
- 41 Pension Rolle
- 42 Youth Hostel

PLACES TO EAT

- 2 Café Europa
- 5 Winzerstube Alt Dresden
- 7 Raskolnikov
- 11 Restaurant Kügelgenhaus
- 14 Topinambur/Umwelt-Zentrum
- 26 Buchara Terrassen-Restaurant
- 29 Gaststätte Zur Keule
- 30 Zum Goldenen Ring

OTHER

- 1 Dresden-Neustadt Train Station
- 3 Kulturzentrum Scheune
- 9 Japanisches Palais
- 10 ADM-Mitfahrzentrale
- 11 Museum of Early Romanticism
- 12 Dresden-Information & Goldener Reiter Statue
- 13 Museum of Folk Art
- 15 Semperoper
- 16 Sächsische Schiffahrts GmbH (Weisse Flotte)
- 17 Zwinger
- 18 Hofkirche
- 19 Museum of Transport
- 20 Royal Palace (Under Reconstruction)
- 21 Frauenkirche (Under Reconstruction)
- 22 Albertinum
- 23 Bärenzwinger
- 24 Jazzclub Tonne
- 27 Kulturpalast
- 28 City Historical Museum
- 31 Kreuzkirche
- 32 New Town Hall
- 33 Karstadt Department Store
- 35 Dresden-Information
- 36 Hygiene Museum
- 37 Botanical Gardens
- 38 Dresden Train Station
- 39 Bus Station
- 40 Zoo
- 43 Russian Church

Theaterplatz, with Dresden's glorious opera house, the neo-Renaissance **Semperoper**. The first opera house on the site opened in 1841 but burned down in 1869. Rebuilt in 1878, it was again destroyed in 1945 and only reopened in 1985 after the Communists invested millions in the restorations. The Dresden opera has a tradition going back 350 years, and many works by Richard Strauss, Carl Maria von Weber and Richard Wagner premiered here.

The southern side of Theaterplatz is occupied by the baroque **Zwinger** (1728), which houses no less than five major museums. The most important are the **Alte Meister Gallery** (closed Monday), with old masters including Raphael's *Sistine Madonna*, and the **Historisches Museum** (closed Monday), with a superb collection of ceremonial weapons. There are also the **Mathematics Salon** with old instruments and timepieces (open daily), the **Museum für Tierkunde** (closed Monday) with natural history, and the **Porcelain Collection** (closed Friday), all housed in opposite corners of the complex with separate entrances. The grey porcelain bells of the clock on the courtyard's eastern gate chime on the hour (you'll see the crowd waiting).

Anyone with a healthy interest in the human body should enjoy the unique **Hygiene Museum** (closed Monday), Lignerplatz 1, with fascinating interactive displays and transparent models of humans and animals.

Neustadt Neustadt is an old part of Dresden largely untouched by the wartime bombings, and since unification it has become the centre of the city's alternative scene. The **Goldener Reiter** statue (1736) of Augustus the Strong stands at the northern end of the Augustus Bridge, leading to Hauptstrasse, a pleasant pedestrian mall with the **Museum of Early Romanticism** (closed Monday and Tuesday) at No 13. On Albertplatz at its northern end there's an evocative marble monument to the poet Schiller. Other museums in the vicinity of the Goldener Reiter include the **Museum für Volkskunst** (Museum of Folk Art, closed Monday) at Grosse Meissner Strasse 1, and the **Japanisches Palais** (1737), Palaisplatz, with

GERMANY

Dresden's famous Ethnological Museum (closed Friday).

Places to Stay

Camping There are two camping grounds near Dresden. The closest is *Camping Mockritz* (☎ 4 71 82 26, open March to December), five km south of the city. (Take the frequent No 76 'Mockritz' bus from behind the Dresden train station.) It has bungalows, but like the camping ground itself they're often full in summer.

A more appealing choice, if more distant, is spacious *Camping Mittelteich Moritzburg* (☎ 035207-4 23; open April to mid-October) on a lake called Mittelteich, a 10-minute walk beyond Jagdschloss Moritzburg (see the following Around Dresden section). Tent sites cost DM3 plus DM4.50 per person, and four-person bungalows are DM60 per night. The lake is too murky to swim in, but rowing boats are available and the nearby park offers hours of restful walks – recommended.

Hostels Dresden's 75-bed *DJH hostel* (☎ 4 71 06 67), at Hübnerstrasse 11, is 10 minutes' walk south of the Dresden train station and charges DM18/23 for juniors/seniors. An excellent alternative is the *Jugendherberge Radebeul* (☎ 7 47 86), Weintraubenstrasse 12, in Radebeul, 10 km north-west of Dresden. The hostel has its own bar and charges DM16.50/19.50 juniors/seniors. It's easily accessible via the Dresden-Meissen S-Bahn (get off at the Radebeul-Weintraube train station), and on tram No 4 or 5.

Private Rooms Dresden-Information, Prager Strasse 10, finds private rooms priced from around DM30 per person (plus a DM5 service fee) and keeps a list of inexpensive pensions (priced from DM40/50 a single/double).

Hotels & Pensions If you want your own room anywhere near the centre of Dresden, it'll cost you.

Central Dresden's least expensive place is the 200-room *Hotel-Kongress-Business-Center* (☎ 4 84 50) at Maternistrasse 17, a short walk north-west of the Dresden train station. This converted former Communist party training centre offers no-frills singles/doubles/triples for DM70/80/110, and better rooms with shower, toilet and TV for DM125/150/180. To get a better deal, book ahead for the tiny *Pension Rolle* (☎ 4 71 70 63), at Lindenaustrasse 2a near the Dresden hostel. It charges DM80/110 for nice rooms with toilet, shower and TV overlooking leafy inner suburban gardens.

Neustadt's 20-room *Hotel Stadt Rendsburg* (☎ 5 15 51), built in 1884, is at Kamenzer Strasse 1, and offers basic singles/doubles with shared bath for DM65/95 including breakfast. The *Hotel Martha Christliches Hospiz* (☎ 5 67 60), at Nieritzstrasse 11 close to the Dresden-Neustadt train station, has four simple single rooms for DM75, but most other rooms are singles/doubles with private toilet and shower costing DM130/190. Also in Neustadt is the newly renovated *Hotel Rothenburger Hof* (☎ 5 02 34 34), Rothenburger Strasse 15-17, which has single/double rooms with shared bath for DM135/195.

In the pleasant suburb of Blasewitz, a few km east of the centre, are two reasonable budget options. The *Waldparkhotel* (☎ 3 44 41), at Prellerstrasse 16, has basic singles/doubles from DM70/100. For better value, try the *Pension Andreas* (☎ 33 77 76), Mendelssohnallee 40-42, whose rooms all come with toilet, bath and breakfast for DM85/140 a single/double. (If coming from the Dresden-Neustadt train station take tram No 6; from the Dresden train station take tram No 10 or 26 to Strassburger Platz, then change to an east-bound tram No 6.)

Along Prager Strasse near the Dresden train station are several large hotels: the *Hotel Bastei* (☎ 4 85 63 85), the *Hotel Königstein* (☎ 4 85 66 69) and the *Hotel Lilienstein* (☎ 4 85 63 72). Their rates are as similar as their 1960s-style architecture, and singles/doubles with shower, toilet etc cost from around DM150/180.

Dresden's most interesting up-market hotel is the *Hotel Schloss Eckberg* (☎ 5 25

71), a bit outside the city centre at Bautzner Strasse 134 (tram No 11). This romantic castle (1861) in a lovely park overlooking the Elbe has a few singles/doubles from DM160/200, and better doubles for DM235. Be sure to ask for a room in the castle – otherwise they might just put you in the boring modern annexe.

Places to Eat

Like most things eastern in Germany, Dresden's food scene has come a long way in a few short years. Particularly interesting are some of the eating (and drinking) places that have sprung up in Neustadt.

For starters, try the *Winzerstube Alt Dresden*, at Antonstrasse 19. It's a small place with simple, student-type fare, whose house speciality is Weinfleisch – meat fried with red wine and mushrooms for DM15.50. Worthy of high praise is the cuisine served at the previously mentioned *Hotel Rothenburger Hof*, ranging from creative vegetarian dishes to elegantly prepared game. Prices vary as widely as the menu: DM10 to DM34 per main course.

Neustadt's *Café Europa* at Königsbrücker Strasse 68 is a convenient place to drop in for a meal or a drink – come any time, it never closes. The ultra-alternative *Raskolnikov* at Böhmische Strasse 34 in Neustadt has salads (DM4) and pseudo-Russian dishes like borscht (DM5) scribbled on the blackboard menu. It stays open until very late, when the rickety tables in the rear garden are mostly taken by drunken artists and philosophers.

For something special, dine at the *Restaurant Kügelgenhaus* (☎ 5 27 91, open daily), at Hauptstrasse 13 below the Museum of Early Romanticism in Neustadt. It has a good range of local Saxon dishes, and there's a beer cellar below the restaurant.

Buchara Terrassen-Restaurant, south of the river on the Wallstrasse overlooking Antonsplatz, serves drinks and meals to tables on its large 1st-floor terrace. Also reasonable is the *Zum Goldenen Ring* (☎ 4 95 23 20) at Altmarkt 18 opposite the Kreuzkirche. The *Gaststätte Zur Keule* (☎ 4 95 15 44), below a cabaret at Sternplatz 1, is a lively beer hall that offers good, solid meals.

If you're in the mood for some soul food, hit the *Topinambur*, at Schützengasse 18 in an old building missed by WW II's bombs that now functions as an environmental centre. It has great wholemeal noodles, rice dishes, lentil burgers and salads all for under DM8. Everything – including the fruit juice – is made from organically grown produce.

Entertainment

Dresden's two largest theatres, the *Semperoper* and *Staatsschauspiel*, stand on opposite sides of the Zwinger. The *Staatsoperette*, Pirnaer Landstrasse 131, is in Leuben in the far east of the city (tram No 9, 12 or 14). You can buy tickets for all three theatres at the Zentrale Vorverkaufskasse in the Altstadler Wache, the stone building on Theaterplatz opposite the Semperoper, between the equestrian statue and the palace (open Monday to Friday from noon to 5 pm, and Saturday from 10 am to 1 pm). Many theatres close for holidays from mid-July to the end of August.

Dresden is synonymous with opera, and the performances at the Semperoper are brilliant. Dresden-Information sells tickets for the Semperoper (DM25 to DM55), but they're often booked well in advance. Otherwise, go to the Abendkasse (box office) at the theatre itself an hour before the performance, or stand outside the door with a small sign reading *Ich möchte eine Karte kaufen* (I'd like to buy a ticket).

The Staatsoperette is rarely sold out, as fewer tourists go there. A ticket at the entrance should set you back from around DM15 (students get a 50% discount), which is cheap for such performances.

A variety of musical events is presented in the *Kulturpalast* (☎ 4 86 63 33), which changes its programmes daily. The *Bärenzwinger* (☎ 4 95 14 09) at Brühlscher Garten in front of the Albertinum has live music, pantomime or cabaret acts most nights, and serves cheap drinks. The *Jazzclub Tonne* (☎ 4 95 13 54) on Tzschirnerplatz often offers live jazz on Friday and Saturday evenings; tickets are available at Dresden-Information. Dresden's International Dixieland Festival takes place every year in the first half of May.

For full details of what's going on in buzzing Dresden, buy the *Dresdener* magazine at any newsstand (DM2).

Getting There & Away

Dresden is just over two hours south of Berlin-Lichtenberg by fast train. The Leipzig-Riesa-Dresden service (120 km, 1½ hours) operates hourly. The double-decker S-Bahn trains run half-hourly to Meissen (40 minutes). There are also direct trains to Frankfurt/Main (six hours), Munich (7½ hours), Vienna (8½ hours), Prague (2¾ hours), Budapest (via Prague, 10½ hours), Warsaw (via Görlitz and Kraków, 11 hours) and Wrocław (Breslau in German, four hours).

Dresden-Klotzsche Airport can be contacted on ☎ 5 89 30 80. For train enquiries, call ☎ 4 71 06 00. At Königstrasse 10 there's an ADM-Mitfahrzentrale (☎ 5 02 22 31); some destinations and prices are (including fees): Berlin DM19.50, Hamburg DM46.50, Prague DM25 and Munich DM45.

Getting Around

Dresden's bus and tram-based transport network is surprisingly cheap. Fares are charged for the time travelled, not the distance – there are no zones. Seven-ride strip tickets cost DM6; stamp once for 10 minutes' travel, or twice for 60 minutes' travel. Weekly tickets cost just DM12 and are also valid for Loschwitz-area cableways to the east of town.

Taxi fares, on the other hand, are very expensive at DM3.90 flagfall and DM1.90 per km.

AROUND DRESDEN

Pillnitz Palace

From 1765 to 1918, Pillnitz Palace, on the Elbe east of Dresden, was the summer residence of the kings and queens of Saxony. The most romantic way to get there is by excursion boat from near Dresden's Augustus Bridge. Otherwise, take tram No 14 from Wilsdruffer Strasse or tram No 9 from in front of the Dresden train station east to the end of the line, then walk a few blocks down to the riverside and cross the Elbe on a small ferry operating throughout the year. The museum at Pillnitz (open from May to mid-October) closes at 5.30 pm, but the gardens, which stay open till 8 pm, and the palace exterior with its Oriental motifs are far more interesting than anything inside, so don't worry if you arrive too late to get in. In summer the Dresden Philharmonic Orchestra sometimes holds concerts here.

Jagdschloss Moritzburg

Like a French Renaissance chateau, this castle rises impressively from its lake 14 km north-west of Dresden. Erected as a hunting lodge for the Duke of Saxony in 1546, the palace was completely rebuilt in baroque style in 1730. Try to come during visiting hours, as it has an impressive interior. It is open Tuesday to Sunday from 10 am to 5 pm except during winter, when its opening hours are shorter; it is closed on Monday all year.

Behind the palace a huge park stretches out, and a walk through the woods is just the thing to clear a travel-weary head. Get a map from the information office (open in summer only) near the palace entrance and hike to **Fasanenschlösschen** (1782), a former hunting villa which is now a natural history museum (open daily from May to October). Then backtrack through the forest to the camping ground on Mittelteich where you can rent a rowing boat to tour the lake (see Dresden's Places to Stay section). There are buses to Moritzburg from the Dresden train station.

Elbe River Excursions

From May to November the Sächsische Dampfschifffahrts GmbH (☎ 0351-4 96 92 03) – which prides itself on having the world's oldest fleet of paddle-wheel steamers – has frequent services upriver from Dresden via Pirna and Bad Schandau to Schmilka. Local trains return to Dresden

GERMANY

from Schmilka-Hirschmühle opposite Schmilka about every half-hour until late in the evening, with stops all along the river. Boats run less frequently downriver as far as Meissen.

Between Pirna and Bad Schandau the scenery climaxes at the medieval **Königstein Castle** (1241) on a hill top to the west. Here the Elbe River has cut a deep valley through the hills with striking sandstone formations protruding from the banks. Three such rock pinnacles are Lilienstein (415 metres) and Pfaffenstein (427 metres), north and south of Königstein, and Bastei (305 metres), downriver near Rathen, all of which can be climbed.

Bad Schandau, a quaint resort town on the river's right bank, 40 km south-east of Dresden, is the starting point for the Kirnitzschtalbahn which runs the eight km to tiny Lichtenhainer Waterfall. From May to mid-October this narrow-gauge tram runs roughly hourly; during the rest of the year it runs every couple of hours on school days only. Hiking trails lead south from the falls up onto the ridge above the river, then they head west back to Bad Schandau through the Schrammsteine, a lovely walk of a couple of hours.

MEISSEN

Meissen, just 27 km north-west of Dresden, is a perfectly preserved old German town and the centre of a rich wine-growing region. In Albrechtsburg, the medieval quarter crowning a ridge high above the Elbe River, is the former ducal palace and Meissen Cathedral, a magnificent Gothic structure. Augustus the Strong of Saxony created Europe's first porcelain factory here in 1710. The cobbled streets of the lower town are a delight to explore.

Orientation & Information

Meissen straddles the Elbe, with the old town on the western bank; the train station is on the eastern bank. The train/pedestrian bridge behind the station is the quickest way across, and presents you with a picture-postcard view of the river and the Altstadt. From the bridge, continue up Obergasse then bear right through Hahnemannsplatz and Rossplatz to Markt, the town's central square.

The helpful Meissen-Information (☎ 03521-44 70) is just off Markt at An der Frauenkirche 3 in an old brewery. In summer the office is open Monday to Friday from 10 am to 6 pm, as well as Saturday and Sunday from 10 am to 2 pm; the shorter winter opening hours are from 9 am to 5 pm on weekdays only.

Meissen's telephone code is 03521.

Things to See

On Markt are the **town hall** (1472) and the 15th-century **Frauenkirche** (open 10 am to 4 pm daily from May to October). The church's tower (1549) has a porcelain carillon, which chimes every quarter-hour. It's worth climbing the tower (DM3) for fine views of Meissen's Altstadt; pick up the key from the *Pfarrbüro* (parish office), just up from the Weinschänke Vincenz Richter.

Various steeply stepped lanes lead up to the **Albrechtsburg**, whose towering medieval **cathedral** (open daily; DM3 or DM2 for students), with its altarpiece by Lucas Cranach the Elder, is visible from afar. Beside the cathedral is the 15th-century Albrechtsburg **palace** (open daily but closed all January; DM6, students DM4), a superb Renaissance construction below which Meissen stretches out as in a painting by Cranach himself.

Meissen has long been famous for its chinaware, with its easily distinguishable blue crossed-swords insignia. The Albrechtsburg palace was originally the manufacturing site, but the **porcelain factory** is now at Talstrasse 9, one km south-west of town. There are often long queues for the live workshop demonstrations (cost is DM5, students DM4), but you can view the fascinating porcelain collection in the museum upstairs at your leisure (another DM5, students DM4). For buying and browsing, visit the factory's porcelain shop downstairs, or its sales outlet at Markt 8.

Places to Stay

Meissen-Information has a free room-finding service; accommodation rates start at around DM25 per person.

Camping & Hostels *Campingplatz Scharfenberg* (☎ 45 26 80, open mid-April to November) is in a beautiful forest at Scharfenberg on the banks of the Elbe, three km south-east of Meissen. Two-person cabins cost DM42 per night; there's a small shop and a reasonable restaurant next door. Meissen's *DJH hostel* (☎ 45 30 65) is at Wilsdruffer Strasse 28, about 20 minutes' walk south of Markt (closed November to February). Beds for juniors/seniors cost DM13.50/19.50.

Hotels & Pensions A short way past the hostel, at Wilsdruffer Strasse 35, is the *Pension Plossenschänke* (☎ 45 22 54), a former school-holiday barracks. It has very basic rooms for the all-but-basic price of DM47 per bed. The *Pension Zum Schweizer Haus* (☎ 45 71 62), off Talstrasse at Rauhentalstrasse 1, has just four double rooms, all with private shower and toilet, and charges DM50/100 for one/two people. A very similar deal is offered by the *Haus Hartlich* (☎ 45 25 01), on the southern edge of town at Goldgrund 15.

If you can afford the extra, go to the 18-room *Pension Burkhardt* (☎ 45 81 98), at Neugasse 29 in a thoroughly renovated three-storey building about halfway between Rossmarkt and the porcelain factory. It has attractive rooms all with toilet, shower, phone and TV for DM60/100 a single/double; it's exceptionally good value for these parts.

Places to Eat

Meissen has many good restaurants where you can dine well on a budget. One is the large *Ratskeller* at Markt 1, which serves typical Saxon fare priced from DM12 to DM20 for main courses. On the way up to the Albrechtsburg is the *Gaststätte Winkelkrug* (☎ 45 25 28), Schlossberg 13 (closed Monday and Tuesday). It's in a quaint old building with many cosy corners, and you can eat from just DM8. For hearty meals to match its excellent selection of local wines, try the small *Probierstuben der Sächsischen Winzergenossenschaft* (☎ 73 32 93), seven minutes' walk north-east of the train station, at Bennoweg 9. It's often full, so make sure you book.

The *Zum Ritter* (☎ 45 20 28), at Elbestrasse 27 (closed Sunday), is an up-market pub decorated with knights' paraphernalia. In a similar vein is the *Weinschänke Vincenz Richter* (☎ 45 32 85), An der Frauenkirche 12, in an old wooden-beam house whose interior looks more like a museum – check the torture chamber. This expensive restaurant (closed Sunday and Monday) has a short food menu but the wine list is pages long.

Getting There & Away

Meissen is most directly accessible by the double-decker S-Bahn trains from Dresden (40 minutes) or Dresden-Neustadt train stations, but a more interesting way to get there is on the riverboats that run between May and September. Meissen is also on a less-transited train line running between Leipzig and Dresden via Döbeln; if you're coming from Leipzig this may be a quicker alternative than changing trains in Coswig or Dresden-Neustadt.

LEIPZIG

Leipzig is eastern Germany's second-largest city, and a major business and transport centre. Since medieval times it has hosted annual fairs, which during the Communist era provided an important exchange window between East and West. Since unification, however, Leipzig has struggled to maintain its status as a top 'fair city' against its well-established western rivals, Frankfurt/Main and Hanover.

Bach worked in Leipzig from 1723 until his death in 1750. Napoleon met with defeat near here in 1813, and it was in Leipzig that Georgi Dimitrov stood up to the Nazis in 1933 during the Reichstag Fire trial. Leipzig was always a major publishing and library centre; the city's Deutsche Bücherei houses some seven million titles, including every book published in German since 1913.

Though never as badly bombed as its Saxon rival Dresden, in recent years Leipzig has undergone a boom in building construction and reconstruction. Leipzig still has many fine old buildings and it's worth spending a day or two just visiting the city's museums.

Orientation

The Leipzig train station (1915), with 26 platforms, is the largest terminal station in Europe. If the few coin lockers are all taken, you can drop your pack off at the left-luggage room near the stairs at the station's western exit. It's open until 9.15 pm and charges DM4 for large items.

To reach the city centre head through the underpass below Willy-Brandt-Platz (formerly Platz der Republik) and continue south for five minutes; the central Markt square is just a couple of blocks south-west. Ring roads surround the old city centre, more or less where the former city walls once stood. The wide Augustusplatz (formerly Karl-Marx-Platz), three blocks east of Markt, is ex-socialist Leipzig, with the space-age lines of the university (1975) and concert hall (1983) juxtaposed against the functional opera house (1960). Leipzig's international fairgrounds are about three km south-east along Prager Strasse.

Information

Leipzig-Information (☎ 0341-7 95 90, open Monday to Friday from 9 am to 8 pm, and at weekends from 9.30 am to 2 pm) is at Sachsenplatz 1, between the main train station and the Altes Rathaus. Bear right after going through the underpass.

A helpful travel agency is the Bavaria Studentenreisebüro (☎ 0341-7 19 22 67), on the small square below the tall university building at Augustusplatz 9; it sells youth/student train and plane tickets.

Leipzig's telephone code is 0341.

Things to See

The Renaissance **Altes Rathaus** (1556) on Markt, one of Germany's largest town halls, houses the City History Museum (closed Monday). Behind it is the **Alte Börse** (1687), with a monument to Goethe (1903) in front. Goethe, who studied law at Leipzig University, called the town a 'little Paris' in his drama *Faust*. **St Nikolai Church** (1165), between Markt and Augustusplatz, has a remarkable interior.

Just south-west of Markt is **St Thomas Church** (1212), with the tomb of composer Johann Sebastian Bach in front of the altar. The Thomas Choir which Bach once led is still going strong. Opposite the church, at Thomaskirchhof 16, is the **Bach-Museum**. At the south-eastern corner of Leipzig's inner centre, the impressive baroque-style **Neues Rathaus** (New Town Hall), with its 108-metre tower, was completed as recently as 1905. Nearby at Dittrichring 24 in the former East German Stasi (secret police) headquarters (diagonally opposite the Schauspielhaus) is the **Museum Runde Ecke**, with exhibits outlining Stasi methods of investigation and intimidation. Leipzig's **zoo**, north-west of the train station, is renowned for its breeding of lions and tigers, and is open from 8 am to 7 pm in summer.

Leipzig has many fine museums, but its showpiece is the **Museum der bildenden Künste** (Museum of Plastic Arts) housed in former buildings of the Supreme Court of the Reich (1888), with an excellent collection of old masters downstairs. Upstairs you'll find the **Historische Räume im Reichsgericht** (Imperial Court Museum), where Georgi Dimitrov, the Bulgarian Communist leader, made such a fool of his prosecutors in the 1933 Reichstag Fire trial that he was acquitted; the hapless Dutch anarchist, Marinus van der Lubbe, was less fortunate. The museum is closed Monday, open from 1 to 9.30 pm Wednesday and 9 am to 5 pm other days.

Leipzig's most impressive sight is the **Völkerschlachtdenkmal** (Battle of Nations Monument), in Prager Strasse on the south-eastern outskirts of the city beyond the fairgrounds. This massive structure was erected in 1913 to commemorate the 1813

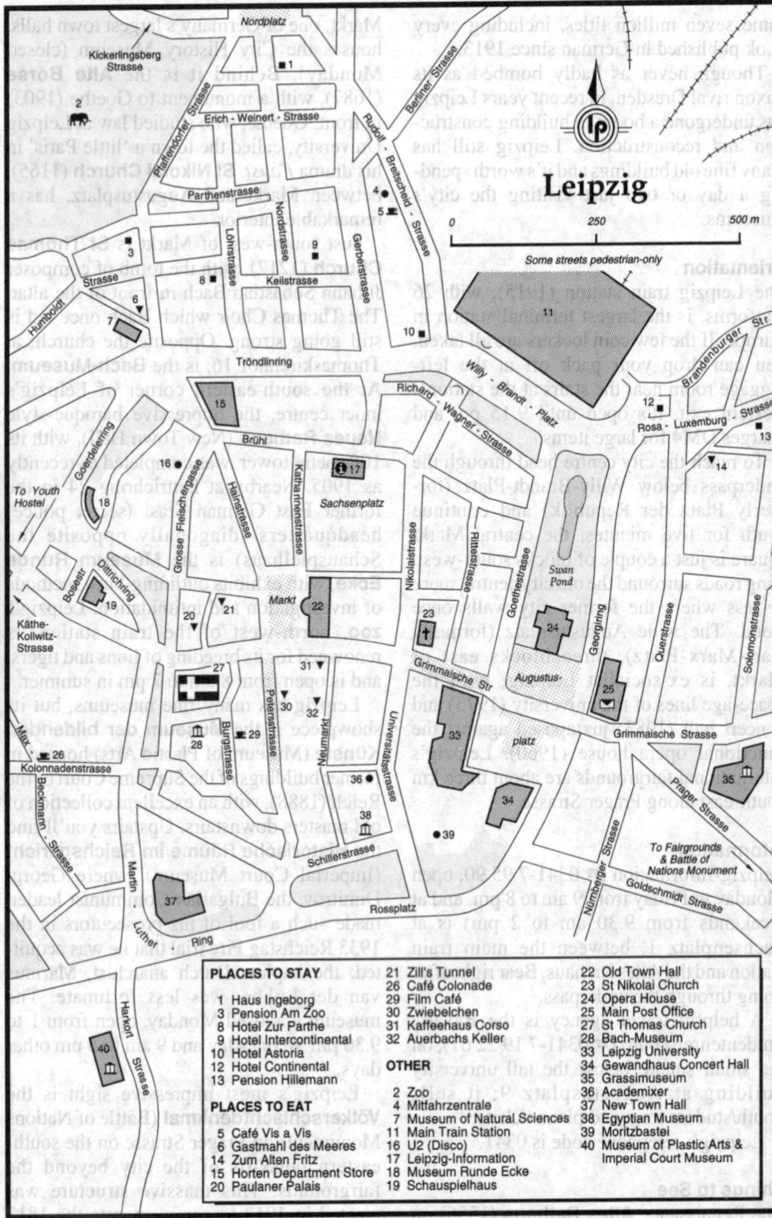
Leipzig
0
250
500 m
Some streets pedestrian-only
Nordplatz
Kickerlingsberg Strasse
Erich - Weinert - Strasse
Pfaffendorfer Strasse
Berliner Strasse
Rudolf - Breitscheid - Strasse
Parthenstrasse
Nordstrasse
Löhrstrasse
Gerberstrasse
Keilstrasse
Humboldt Strasse
Tröndlinring
Willy - Brandt - Platz
Richard - Wagner - Strasse
Brandenburger Str
Rosa - Luxemburg Strasse
Brühl
Goerdelerring
To Youth Hostel
Grosse Fleischergasse
Hainstrasse
Katharinenstrasse
Sachsenplatz
Nikolaistrasse
Ritterstrasse
Goethestrasse
Swan Pond
Bosestr
Dittrichring
Käthe-Kollwitz-Strasse
Markt
Grimmaische Str
Augustus-platz
Georgiring
Querstrasse
Solomonstrasse
Grimmaische Strasse
Petersstrasse
Burgstrasse
Neumarkt
Universitätsstrasse
Max
Kolonnadenstrasse
Beckmann - Strasse
Schillerstrasse
Prager Strasse
Nürnberger Strasse
To Fairgrounds & Battle of Nations Monument
Goldschmidt Strasse
Martin - Luther - Ring
Rossplatz
Harkort Strasse
PLACES TO STAY
1 Haus Ingeborg
3 Pension Am Zoo
8 Hotel Zur Parthe
9 Hotel Intercontinental
10 Hotel Astoria
12 Hotel Continental
13 Pension Hillemann
PLACES TO EAT
5 Café Vis a Vis
6 Gastmahl des Meeres
14 Zum Alten Fritz
15 Horten Department Store
20 Paulaner Palais
21 Zill's Tunnel
26 Café Colonade
29 Film Café
30 Zwiebelchen
31 Kaffeehaus Corso
32 Auerbachs Keller
OTHER
2 Zoo
4 Mitfahrzentrale
7 Museum of Natural Sciences
11 Main Train Station
16 U2 (Disco)
17 Leipzig-Information
18 Museum Runde Ecke
19 Schauspielhaus
22 Old Town Hall
23 St Nikolai Church
24 Opera House
25 Main Post Office
27 St Thomas Church
28 Bach-Museum
33 Leipzig University
34 Gewandhaus Concert Hall
35 Grassimuseum
36 Academixer
37 New Town Hall
38 Egyptian Museum
39 Moritzbastei
40 Museum of Plastic Arts & Imperial Court Museum

victory by combined Prussian, Austrian and Russian armies over Napoleon's forces. It is open daily from 9 am to 4 pm.

Places to Stay

Camping The *Campingplatz Am Auensee* (☎ 2 12 30 31), Gustav-Esche-Strasse 5, is in a pleasant wooded spot on the city's north-western outskirts (take tram No 10 or 28 to the end of the line at Wahren, then walk for eight minutes). Camping is DM8 per person plus DM5 for a car/tent site. There are also regular and A-frame bungalows for two people costing DM90 and DM55 respectively. Not quite so nice is the *Campingplatz Am Kulkwitzer See* (☎ 4 78 21 26), at Seestrasse south-west of the city centre in Miltitz.

Hostels The *Jugendherberge Leipzig* (☎ 47 05 30) at Käthe-Kollwitz-Strasse 62-66 is in the city's south-western sector. This large, prewar mansion with a pleasant garden at the back has four and six-person dorms at DM19/23.50 for juniors/seniors. Book in summer, as it fills quickly; you can get there on tram No 1 or 2 from the train station. There's also the small *Jugendherberge Am Auensee* (☎ 5 71 89), at Gustav-Esche-Strasse 4 on the lake near the previously mentioned camping ground, charging DM14/17 for juniors/seniors.

Private Rooms During fairs many of Leipzig's hotels raise their prices and it can be hard to find a room. Leipzig-Information runs a room-finding service for a DM5 fee, with singles/doubles from DM40/60. It also has a room-finding office at the train station near platform No 3 (open Monday to Friday from 9 am to 6 pm, and Saturday to noon), and at Leipzig-Halle Airport (open Monday to Friday from 7 am to 8 pm, Saturday from 8.30 am to 2.30 pm, and Sunday from 9 am to 6 pm).

Hotels & Pensions Easily the best value in town is the small *Pension Hillemann* (☎ 28 24 82), at Rosa-Luxemburg-Strasse 2, less than five minutes' walk east of the main train station. Here clean and cosy singles/doubles cost just DM40/80 (without breakfast). Also reasonable is the *Pension Prima* (☎ 6 34 81) at Dresdener Strasse 82, with simple rooms for DM50/85; breakfast is DM5 extra. It's two km east of the centre, but easily reached from Willy-Brandt-Platz by tram No 4, 6 or 20.

North-west of the station is the *Pension Am Zoo* (☎ 29 18 38), Pfaffendorfer Strasse 23, which charges DM55 for simple singles, and DM80/120 for single/double rooms with private shower. Not far away are the *Haus Ingeborg* (☎ 29 48 16), Nordstrasse 58, whose basic rooms with shared bath cost DM65/94, and the *Hotel Zur Parthe* (☎ 29 94 90), Löhrstrasse 15, with slightly better rooms for DM70/110.

In the up-market range, the *Hotel Continental* (☎ 21 65 90), at Georgiring 13 on the eastern side of the train station, charges DM159/209 for standard rooms. The Art-Deco *Hotel Astoria* (☎ 7 22 20), at Willy-Brandt-Platz 2 opposite the station's western hall, has singles/doubles from DM249/336. Behind it is the five-star high-rise *Intercontinental* (☎ 79 90), a palatial Japanese-built landmark at Gerberstrasse 15, whose cheapest rooms are DM290/320.

Places to Eat

Many of central Leipzig's cheaper eating houses have been forced out by privatisation and the continuing construction boom.

Always good for a filling feed is the restaurant on the 5th floor of the *Horten* department store, which has typical cafeteria food priced from about DM5 per plate. The *Zum Alten Fritz* (closed Sunday), a simple tavern at Chopinstrasse 6, offers good-sized meals from DM14.50. The *Café Colonade*, on the corner of Max-Beckmann-Strasse and Kolonnadenstrasse, serves sound dishes for less than DM15; there's a small beer garden out the back.

At Klostergasse 3-5 is the large *Paulaner Palais* (☎ 2 11 31 15), a Saxon-style beer hall serving hearty dishes from DM15 and daily three-course menus for DM21.50. The trendy and reasonably priced *Zwiebelchen*

GERMANY

(☎ 2 11 45 71), at Peterstrasse 1-13, serves salads, noodles and other dishes to outside tables that look out across the Markt square. For good seafood at reasonable prices, try the *Gastmahl des Meeres* (☎ 29 11 60, closed Sunday) at Pfarrendorfer Strasse 1 near the Naturkundemuseum (Museum of Natural Sciences).

Having survived WW II's bombs and later nationalisation, the *Kaffeehaus Corso* (☎ 28 22 33, open daily to 1 am) is back in business at Grimmaische Strasse 10, offering various breakfasts with Saxon cakes made in-house for DM13.20; for later meals there are plenty of salads or meaty main courses. Two other good cafés are the *Bachstübl* and the *Café Concerto* on Thomaskirchhof next door to the Bach-Museum.

Founded in 1525, the *Auerbachs Keller* (☎ 2 16 10 40), just south of the Altes Rathaus in the Mädler-Passage, is Leipzig's best restaurant. Look for the statues depicting scenes from Goethe's *Faust* near the entrance. (After carousing with students at the Auerbachs Keller, Mephistopheles and Faust left riding on a barrel.) *Zill's Tunnel* (☎ 20 04 46) just off Markt at Barfussgässchen 9 (open daily) is another of Leipzig's long-established culinary institutions, serving Saxon specialities from DM17.

GERMANY

Entertainment

Live theatre and music are major features in Leipzig's cultural offerings. With a tradition dating back to 1743, the *Gewandhaus* concert hall on Augustusplatz has Europe's longest-established orchestra – one of its conductors was the composer Mendelssohn. Leipzig's ultramodern *Opernhaus* is just across the square. The *Schauspielhaus* is a few blocks west of Markt, at Bosestrasse 1.

One of the best of Leipzig's surprisingly numerous cabarets is the *Academixer* (☎ 20 08 49) in Kupfergasse close to the university. The nearby *Moritzbastei* (☎ 29 34 86), at Universitätsstrasse 9 in a three-storey subterranean complex built into the old city walls, has blues, jazz and rock acts priced from just DM7 (DM4 for students).

Leipzig-Information sells tickets for practically all live performances.

The *Film Café*, Burgstrasse 9, is a café-pub popular among young Leipzigers. The *U2* disco, at Grosse Fleischergasse 12, is open daily from 9 pm. The *Café Vis a Vis*, located just north of the station at Rudolf-Breitscheid-Strasse 33, draws a largely gay clientele.

Getting There & Away

Leipzig's huge main train station has departures and arrivals to and from all important German cities as well as a number of other European cities. Leipzig/Halle Airport is halfway between the two cities; buses to the airport leave from in front of the main train station roughly every 45 minutes.

The local ADM-Mitfahrzentrale (☎ 2 11 42 22) is at Rudolf-Breitscheid-Strasse 39. For dirt-cheap car rentals, try the Ossi Autovermietung Fischer (☎ 3 40 39 10), at Altenburger Strasse 3, which rents GDR-era Trabant cars for DM25 per day with unlimited km.

Getting Around

Public transport in Leipzig is based on trams, with most important lines passing through Willy-Brandt-Platz beside the main train station. The S-Bahn circles the city's outer suburbs. The daily Citykarte ticket (valid 9 am to midnight) and the Sammelkarte (valid for six 10-minute rides within the central-zone) both cost DM5.

GÖRLITZ

Situated 100 km east of Dresden on the Neisse River, Görlitz emerged from WW II with its beautiful old town virtually undamaged. Today its Renaissance and baroque architecture is better preserved than that of any city its size in Saxony. Features of the Altstadt include the **town hall** (1537), the **Peterskirche** (1497), the 16th-century **Dreifaltigkeitskirche** on Obermarkt and the **Lange Läuben**, a row of opulent town houses built by medieval cloth merchants.

The telephone code for Görlitz is 03581.

Places to Stay & Eat

The *DJH hostel* (☎ 55 10), south of the station at Goethestrasse 17, charges juniors/seniors DM18.50/24.50. The tiny *Pension & Gaststätte Goldener Engel* (☎ 40 33 37), Hugo-Keller-Strasse 1, has a reasonable restaurant and offers simple singles/doubles for DM45/80. The *Hotel Prinz Friedrich Karl* (☎ 40 33 61) at Postplatz 9 has nice rooms with bath and shower for DM65/120. The *Restaurant Destille* (☎ 40 53 02), beside a medieval tower at Nikolaistrasse 6, serves local cuisine and has a few singles/doubles with shower and toilet for DM90/130.

Getting There & Away

Over a dozen daily trains run in either direction between Görlitz and Dresden (1 hour 40 minutes). Görlitz is also an important border-crossing point, and daily Frankfurt-Warsaw and Berlin-Kraków trains make a stop here before crossing into Poland (via the classic Neisseviadukt bridge, completed in 1847).

Thuringia

The state of Thuringia (Thüringen) occupies a basin cutting into the heart of Germany between the Harz Mountains and the hilly Thuringian Forest. The Germanic Thuringians were conquered by the Franks in 531 and converted to Christianity by St Boniface in the 8th century. The Duke of Saxony seized the area in 908 and for the next 1000 years the region belonged to one German principality or another. Only in 1920 was Thuringia reconstituted as a state with something approaching its original borders. Under the Communists the state was split into the districts of Erfurt, Suhl and Gera, but since 1990 it has been a single unit once again.

ERFURT

This trading and university centre, founded as a bishop's residence by St Boniface in 742, is the capital of Thuringia. Erfurt University, which dates back to 1392 and once counted Martin Luther as a student, has recently been re-established (almost 180 years after it was closed). Only slightly damaged during the war, Erfurt is a town of towers and flowers, with colourful burgher mansions gracing the well-preserved medieval quarter. Fortunately, industry has kept to the modern suburbs. Each summer the Erfurt Garden Exhibition (EGA) takes place in the south-western section of the city.

Orientation & Information

As you come out of the train station, turn left, then right and walk straight up Bahnhofstrasse. In a few minutes you'll reach Anger, a large square in the heart of the city. Continue straight ahead and follow the tram tracks along Schlösserstrasse past the town hall till you come to Domplatz, Erfurt's most impressive sight.

Erfurt has three information offices. Erfurt-Information (☎ 0361-2 62 67), Bahnhofstrasse 37, is on the corner of Bahnhofstrasse and Juri-Gagarin-Ring, halfway between the station and Anger. It's open Monday to Friday from 10 am to 6 pm, and Saturday to 1 pm. The main tourist office (☎ 0361-5 62 34 36) is at Krämerbrücke 3; its opening hours are Monday to Friday 10 am to 6 pm, Saturday to 4 pm, and Sunday to 1 pm. There's also a small information kiosk on Anger.

Erfurt's telephone code is 0361.

Things to See

The numerous interesting backstreets and laneways in Erfurt's surprisingly large Altstadt make this a nice place to explore on foot. Begin by visiting the **Angermuseum** (DM3 or DM1.50 students, free Wednesday, closed Monday), Anger 18, then take Schlösserstrasse north-west to Fischmarkt, the medieval city centre. Some interesting historical buildings such as the **town hall** (1873), the **Haus Zum Breiten Herd** (1584) and the **Haus Zum Roten Ochsen** (1562) surround this square.

The 13th-century Gothic **Dom St Marien** and adjacent **Severikirche** tower over

Domplatz in the centre of town and are particularly impressive when floodlit at night. The wooden stools (1350) and stained glass (1410) in the choir, and figures on the portals, make the cathedral one of the richest medieval churches in Germany. It is open until 5 pm Monday to Saturday and until 4 pm on Sunday. From here you can walk north-east up to **Petersburg**, the former site of a medieval church and abbey later converted into a fortress.

From Fischmarkt, the eastbound street beside the town hall leads to the medieval restored **Krämerbrücke** (1325), which is lined on each side with timber-framed shops. This is the only such bridge north of the Alps.

Places to Stay

Budget hotel accommodation is in critically short supply in Erfurt. Erfurt-Information may be able to find you a private room (from DM25 per person), but the number of singles is limited. The 110-bed *Jugendherberge Erfurt* (☎ 2 67 05), Hochheimer Strasse 12, is on the western side of the city (tram No 5 southbound to the terminus). It costs DM18/21.50 for juniors/ seniors (including breakfast); hot evening meals are DM7.

GERMANY

The tiny *Pension Schuster* (☎ 3 50 42), at Rubenstrasse 11 just outside the city centre, has rooms at DM60/80 for singles/doubles, but more often than not it's booked out. A better lower-budget option is the *Hotel Garni Daberstedt* (☎ 3 15 16), south-east of the central area at Buddestrasse 2, which charges DM60/100 for simple singles/doubles. (Take tram No 3 or 6 two stops from the station, then walk up Hässlerstrasse.)

The high-rise *Hotel Am Ring* (☎ 6 46 55 20), at Juri-Gagarin-Ring 148 next to the Museum für Thüringer Volkskunde, has twin two-bed apartments with shared toilet and shower rooms from DM65/95 single/double. The hotel was a workers' residence in socialist GDR days, but now features cable TV with porn movies. At Juri-Gagarin-Ring 154-156, nearby, is the *Hotel Thüringen* (☎ 6 46 55 12), a former youth tourist hotel with rooms from DM120/150.

Places to Eat

This is the place to try some local Thuringian cuisine – especially since few of the city's restaurants serve anything else.

The *Haus Zur Rose* (☎ 5 62 44 90), at Lange Brücke 28, has well-prepared specialities such as veal cutlets with fried beans and Thuringian dumplings (DM16) as well as salads and soups. It is closed on Sunday. On the corner of Michaelisstrasse and Augustinerstrasse is the *Zum Augustiner* (☎ 5 62 38 30), an old tavern filled with antiques and bric-a-brac where you can eat quite well for as little as DM11. The *Schmalztopf* on Domplatz is another popular pub with quite passable food. For a bit of a splurge, head for the *Gildehaus* (☎ 5 62 32 73) at Fischmarkt 13-16, where main courses average DM20.

A popular meeting place for young Erfurters is the *Café Spinnen-Netz*, on the corner of Turnierstrasse and Allerheiligenstrasse.

A *market* is held during the week on Domplatz.

Entertainment

Both rivalled and complemented by nearby Weimar, Erfurt's modest cultural scene includes the *Opernhaus* (☎ 5 12 21) on Theaterstrasse, with concert performances roughly every second night, and the *Theater Waldspeicher* (☎ 2 48 03) at Domplatz 18, famous for its puppet theatre. Tickets for most events can be bought at the main tourist office. Pick up the free monthly *Erfurt Live* and *In Erfurt & Weimar Aktuell* magazines for detailed information.

Getting There & Away

Erfurt is a major stop for both Frankfurt/Main to Berlin and Frankfurt/Main to Leipzig trains, and generally has good connections to most other large cities in Germany. Some train travel times are: Dresden 2¾ hours, Leipzig 1 hour 20 minutes, Berlin four hours, Eisenach one hour and Weimar 15 minutes.

Getting Around

Trams are the most convenient means of public transport in central Erfurt. Ticket prices are time-based; a 15-minute ticket costs DM1.20, while a one-hour ticket costs DM2. Day tickets cost DM4. There's also the Städtekarte for DM5.80, which is good for four hours of travel by bus, tram or train within and between Weimar and Erfurt.

WEIMAR

Not a monumental city, nor a medieval one, Weimar appeals to more refined tastes. As a repository of German humanistic traditions it's unrivalled, but these traditions are not always easily assimilated by a foreign visitor in a rush. The parks and small museums are meant to be savoured, not downed in one gulp.

Many famous men lived and worked here, including Lucas Cranach the Elder, Johann Sebastian Bach, Christoph Martin Wieland, Friedrich Schiller, Johann Gottfried von Herder, Johann Wolfgang von Goethe, Franz Liszt, Friedrich Nietzsche, Walter Gropius, Lyonel Feininger, Vasili Kandinsky, Gerhard Marcks and Paul Klee. The Bauhaus (Staatliches Bauhaus), which laid the foundations of modern architecture, functioned in the city from 1919 to 1925. Today Weimar is a centre for architecture and music studies.

Weimar is best known abroad as the place where the German constituent assembly drafted a republican constitution after WW I. The German republic which preceded the rise of fascism was therefore known as the Weimar Republic (1919-33), although you won't see much evidence of it here. The horrors of Buchenwald concentration camp (see the Around Weimar section) are well remembered, however.

Because of its historical significance to all Germans, Weimar has received particularly large handouts for the restoration of its many fine buildings. Weimar has been declared European Cultural City for 1999, and a range of (generously funded) cultural activities are planned for the years leading up to the major festivities.

Orientation & Information

The centre of town is just west of the Ilm River and a 20-minute walk south of the train station. Buses run fairly frequently between the station and Goetheplatz, from where it's a short walk east along small streets to Herderplatz or Markt.

Weimar-Information (☎ 03643-20 21 73), at Markt 10, is open from 10 am to 6 pm Monday, 9 am to 7 pm Tuesday to Friday, 9 am to 4 pm Saturday and 10 am to 4 pm Sunday and public holidays. The nearby Museum Ticket Office (☎ 03643-6 43 86), Frauentorstrasse 4, sells a combined ticket for eight of Weimar's museums (DM25, or DM15 for students).

Weimar's telephone code is 03643.

Things to See

City Centre A good place to begin your visit is on Herderplatz. The **Herderkirche** (1500) in the centre of the square has an altarpiece (1555) by Lucas Cranach the Elder, who died before he could finish it. His son, Lucas Cranach the Younger, completed the work and included a portrait of his father (to the right of the crucifix, between John the Baptist and Martin Luther). In front of this church is a statue of the philosopher and writer Johann Gottfried von Herder (1744-1803), who settled here in 1776.

A block east of Herderplatz towards the Ilm River is Weimar's major art museum, the **Schlossmuseum** (closed Monday) on Burgplatz. This large collection, with masterpieces by Cranach, Dürer and others, occupies three floors of the castle that was formerly the residence of the Elector of the Duchy of Saxony-Weimar.

Platz der Demokratie with the renowned music school founded in 1872 by Franz Liszt is up the street running south from the castle. This square spills over into Markt, where you'll find the neo-Gothic **town hall** (1841), and the **Cranachhaus** in which Lucas Cranach the Elder spent his last two years and died (in 1553).

West of Markt via some narrow lanes is Theaterplatz, with statues (1857) of Goethe and Schiller and the **German National Theatre**, where the constituent assembly, escaping the revolutionary climate in Berlin, drafted the constitution of the German Republic in 1919. Also on this square are the **Kunsthalle** and **Wittumspalais** (both closed Monday), the latter now a major museum dedicated to the poet Christoph Martin Wieland (1733-1813). Wieland, who moved to Weimar in 1772, was the first to translate Shakespeare's complete works into German.

There's a lively food and handicrafts **market** with occasional street theatre on Markt from Monday to Saturday.

Houses & Tombs From Theaterplatz, the elegant Schillerstrasse curves around to the **Schillerhaus** at No 12, now newly restored, with the modern **Schillermuseum** (1988) immediately behind it (closed Tuesday). Schiller lived in Weimar from 1799 to 1805.

Goethe, his contemporary, spent the years 1775 to 1832 here. The **Goethemuseum** (closed Monday), a block ahead and then to the right, is by far the most important of the many home-museums of illustrious former residents. There are two parts to this museum: to the right the personal quarters where Goethe resided, and upstairs an exhibition on his life and times. The immortal work *Faust* was written here.

The **Liszthaus** (closed Monday) is south on Marienstrasse by the edge of Park an der Ilm. Liszt resided in Weimar during 1848 and from 1869 to 1886, and here he wrote his *Hungarian Rhapsody* and *Faust Symphony*. In the yellow complex across the road from the Liszthaus, Walter Gropius laid the groundwork for all modern architecture. The buildings themselves were erected by the famous architect Henry van de Velde between 1904 and 1911 and now house the **Academy of Architecture**.

The tombs of Goethe and Schiller lie side by side in a neoclassical crypt in the **Historischer Friedhof** (Historical Cemetery), two blocks west of the Liszthaus. Behind the crypt is an onion-domed Russian Orthodox church (1862).

Parks & Palaces Weimar boasts three large parks, each replete with monuments, museums and attractions. Most accessible is **Park an der Ilm** which runs right along the eastern side of Weimar and contains Goethe's cottage. Goethe himself landscaped the park.

Several km farther south is the **Belvedere Park** with its baroque castle housing the **Rokokomuseum** and the **orangery coach museum** (both open from April to October, closed Monday). The surrounding park is beautiful and spacious, and could absorb hours of your time. In summer you can take bus No 12 from Goetheplatz straight to Belvedere.

Tiefurt Park, a few km east of the train station, is similar but smaller (palace closed Monday, and also Tuesday from November to March). Duchess Anna Amalia organised famous intellectual 'round-table gatherings' here in the late 18th century. Get here on bus No 3, which leaves hourly from Goetheplatz.

Places to Stay

Budget accommodation can get tight just about any time in Weimar. During the week the place is often busy (and noisy) with school excursion groups and the odd business traveller, while at weekends and on public holidays the city is a popular destination. Weimar-Information has lists of private rooms priced from DM20 to DM35 per person (plus DM3 booking fee).

Camping The closest camping ground is the *Campingplatz Oettern* (☎ 06453-2 64, open from May to November) in Oettern, seven km south-east of Weimar. It's in a scenic part of the Ilm Valley, with many walking trails.

Hostels Weimar is blessed with three hostels. The *Jugendherberge Germania* (☎ 20 20 76) at Carl-August-Allee 13 in the street running down from the station charges DM16.50/20.50 for juniors/seniors and serves hot meals for DM8. More central though much less comfortable is the *Am Poseckschen Garten* hostel (☎ 6 40 21) at Humboldtstrasse 17 near the Historischer Friedhof, charging DM16/19.50 for seniors/juniors. The *Jugendgästehaus Maxim Gorki* (☎ 34 71) is on the opposite side of the Historischer Friedhof at Zum Wilden Graben 12. All beds, whether in singles, doubles or dormitories, cost DM19.50/23.50 for juniors/seniors; take bus No 5 from the station.

Pensions To be sure of getting a room at any of these places book a day or so ahead. The tiny *Pension Savina* (☎ 60 07 97), at Rembrandtweg 13, has a few rooms with private bath and shower and charges DM55/98 a single/double. The *Gasthof Luise* (☎ 6 58 19), a quiet pub at Wielandplatz 3 a few minutes' walk up the road from the Am Poseckschen Garten hostel, has a few rooms with bath, toilet and telephone for DM85/150 a single/double; the restaurant downstairs is also good value. The *Gästehaus Zum Alten Zausel* (☎ 50 16 63) in Carl-Von-Ossietzky-Strasse offers simple doubles without breakfast for DM70. West of the centre but still conveniently close to town is the *Pension Am Berkaer Bahnhof* (☎ 20 20 10), Peter-Cornelius-Strasse 7, with singles/doubles for DM61/82, triples for DM123.

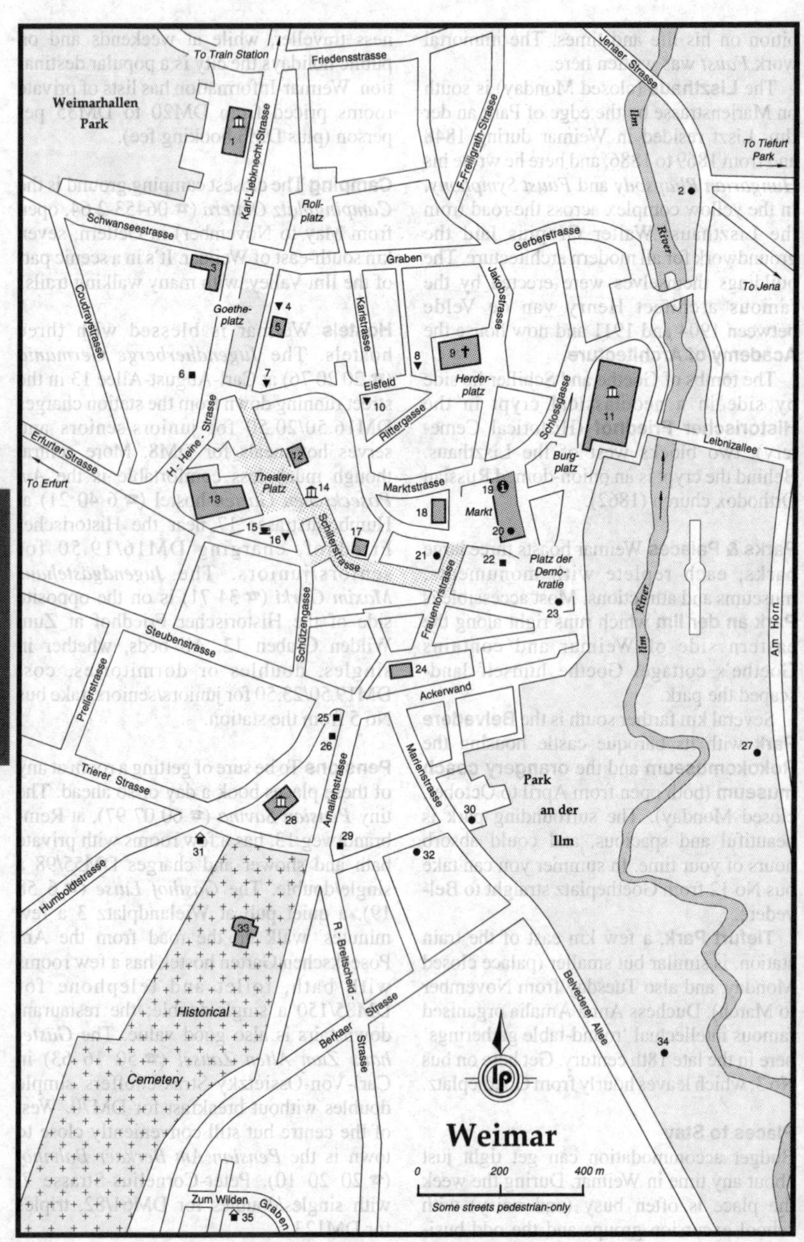
Weimar
To Train Station
Friedensstrasse
Weimarhallen
Park
Karl-Liebknecht-Strasse
F.-Freiligrath-Strasse
Jenaer Strasse
Ilm
To Tiefurt Park
Rollplatz
Schwanseestrasse
Graben
Gerberstrasse
River
Coudraystrasse
Goetheplatz
Karlstrasse
Jakobstrasse
To Jena
Eisfeld
Herderplatz
Rittergasse
Schlossgasse
Leibnizallee
Erfurter Strasse
To Erfurt
H.-Heine-Strasse
Theater Platz
Marktstrasse
Burgplatz
Markt
Schillerstrasse
Platz der Demokratie
Frauentorstrasse
Schützengasse
Steubenstrasse
Prellerstrasse
Ilm River
Am Horn
Ackerwand
Marienstrasse
Trierer Strasse
Amalienstrasse
Park an der Ilm
Humboldtstrasse
R. Breitscheid Strasse
Historical
Berkaer Strasse
Belvederer Allee
Cemetery
Zum Wilden Graben
0
200
400 m
Some streets pedestrian-only
GERMANY

PLACES TO STAY					
6	Hotel Russischer Hof	8	Zum Zwiebel	14	Wittumspalais
22	Hotel Elephant	10	Scharfe Ecke	17	Schillermuseum
25	Gasthof Luise	15	Theater-Café	18	Town Hall
26	Christliches Hotel Amalienhof	16	Studentenclub Schütze	19	Weimar-Information
29	Hübner's Hotel Am Stadtpark		**OTHER**	20	Cranachhaus
31	Youth Hostel Am Poseckschen Garten	1	City Historical Museum	21	Museum Ticket Office
35	Jugendgästehaus Maxim Gorky	2	Goethe-Schiller Archive	23	Franz Liszt Music School
	PLACES TO EAT	3	Post Office	24	Goethemuseum
4	Kasseturm	5	Mon Ami	27	Goethe's Cottage
7	Anno 1900	9	Herderkirche	28	Museum of Prehistory
		11	Schlossmuseum	30	Liszthaus
		12	Kunsthalle	32	Academy of Architecture
		13	German National Theatre	33	Goethe-Schiller Mausoleum
				34	Römisches Haus

Hotels On the eastern side of the square in front of the station at Brennerstrasse 42 is the *Hotel Thüringen* (☎ 9 94 23). Following a total overhaul, this place now charges DM105/160 for single/double rooms with toilet and shower. South-west of the city centre at Lisztstrasse 1-3 is the *Hotel Liszt* (☎ 5 40 80), with rooms from DM95/140. All rooms have bath, toilet and TV.

More central is the *Hotel Russischer Hof* (☎ 77 40) at Goetheplatz 2. It's been doing business since 1805, and has rooms with bath and breakfast priced from DM110/160. Nearing completion at the time of research, the 24-bed *Hübner's Hotel Am Stadtpark* (☎ 35 26) at Amalienstrasse 19 will offer double rooms only priced from DM120 with private shower. Not far from the Goethemuseum is the newly renovated *Christliches Hotel Amalienhof* (☎ 54 09), at Amalienstrasse 2, whose singles/doubles with mod cons cost DM125/186. For a bit of style, stay at Weimar's charming old classic, the *Hotel Elephant* (☎ 6 14 10). It's right in the heart of town at Markt 19, and offers rooms from DM170/230.

Places to Eat

The *Anno 1900* (☎ 50 13 37), at Geleitstrasse 12a in a restored turn-of-the-century winter garden, is surprisingly good value despite a posh ambience enhanced by live piano music. Few items on the menu are over DM20, and there are vegetarian dishes from as little as DM9. Nearby, at Eisfeld 2, is the *Scharfe Ecke* (☎ 24 30), with home-cooked cuisine and a wide range of beers (closed Monday and Sunday evenings). Farther down the way, at Teichgasse 6, is the *Zum Zwiebel* (☎ 50 23 75), a nice place to come with friends for a late meal and a drink.

Hard to pass is the *Theater-Café* (☎ 32 09) at Theaterplatz 1a, whose broad menu stretches from salads to Thuringian specialities served to outside tables bordering the quiet pedestrian square. The *Café Sperling* at Schillerstrasse 18 serves breakfasts, including numerous coffee variations, from 8 am daily.

Next to the Goethemuseum on Frauenplan is Weimar's best eating house, the *Zum Weissen Schwan* (☎ 6 17 15, closed Monday), with main courses priced from DM22. Its list of former patrons includes Goethe, Schiller and Liszt (though it's doubtful that they ever got to try the restaurant's New German Cuisine). Another Weimar institution is the *Felsenkeller* (☎ 6 19 41) at Humboldtstrasse 37, run by the local Felsenbräu brewery. The atmosphere is great, the beer is cheap, the food is good and well priced – no wonder it's often full.

GERMANY

Entertainment

The *German National Theatre* on Theaterplatz is the main stage of Weimar's cultural activities. As part of the 'European Cultural City 1999' programme, all of Goethe's theatrical works are to be performed here over the coming years. The youth centre *Mon Ami* (☎ 20 23 19), at Goetheplatz 11, has frequent but irregular classical, jazz and rock concerts. Tickets to the German National Theatre and other events can be bought at the theatre's own Besucherabteilung (☎ 75 53 34) or the tourist office.

The *Kasseturm*, in the round tower on Goetheplatz, and the *Studentenclub Schütze* just off Theaterplatz at Schützengasse 2 are two lively student pubs that serve cheap drinks.

Getting There & Away

Very few InterCity or EuroCity trains stop at Weimar, so for longer trips changing in Erfurt (just 22 km and 15 minutes away) may be quicker. There are direct InterRegio and D trains between Weimar and Berlin-Lichtenberg (DM38; 3½ hours), Frankfurt/Main (DM59; four hours and 20 minutes), Dresden (DM32; three hours), Halle/Leipzig (one hour) and Eisenach (one hour 20 minutes).

AROUND WEIMAR

Buchenwald

The Buchenwald museum and memorial are on Ettersberg Hill, seven km north-west of Weimar. You first pass the memorial with mass graves of some of WW II's 56,500 victims from 18 nations, including German antifascists, Jews, and Soviet and Polish prisoners of war. The concentration camp and museum are one km beyond the memorial. Many prominent German Communists and Social Democrats, Ernst Thälmann and Rudolf Breitscheid among them, were murdered here. On 11 April 1945, as US troops approached, the prisoners rebelled at 3.15 pm (the clock tower above the entrance still shows that time), overcame the SS guards and liberated themselves.

After the war the Soviet victors turned the tables by establishing Special Camp No 2, in which thousands of anti-Communists and former Nazis were worked to death. A new (and somewhat controversial) museum dealing with this post-1945 oppression is expected to open on the site in late 1995.

The Buchenwald museum and concentration camp are open every day except Monday from 9.45 am to 5.15 pm (8.45 am to 4.15 pm in winter). Buses run roughly hourly from bus stop No 31 on the lower side of the square in front of the station (DM1.60 each way).

EISENACH

Eisenach is a picturesque town on the edge of the Thuringian Forest. From the nearby Wartburg castle, the landgraves ruled medieval Thuringia. Richard Wagner based his opera *Tannhäuser* on a minstrel's contest which took place in the castle in 1206-07. Martin Luther was kept in protective custody here by the elector under the assumed name Junker Jörg after being excommunicated and put under the ban of the empire by the pope.

The first country-wide proletarian party, the Social Democratic Workers' Party, was founded in Eisenach by August Bebel and Wilhelm Liebknecht in 1869. Another first was the first automobile, produced in Eisenach in 1896. The town was formerly the manufacturing site of the now defunct East German car-maker Wartburg. Since unification the western giants Opel, Bosch and BMW have established new manufacturing plants here, thereby saving Eisenach's modest industrial base, along with the jobs and pride of many of its 44,000 inhabitants.

Orientation & Information

The train station and medieval Wartburg are on opposite sides of town. To get to the castle on foot from the station, follow Bahnhofstrasse west under the arch, cross the square and continue west on Karlstrasse to Markt. Two blocks west of Markt you'll find a steep signposted lane called Schlossberg which leads two km south-west through forest to the castle.

The friendly and well-organised Eisenach-Information (☎ 03691-48 95) is at Bahnhofstrasse 3-5 near the station; it's open Monday from 10 am to 6 pm, Tuesday to Friday from 9 am to 6 pm, and Saturday from 9 am to 2 pm. The room-finding service is free.

Eisenach's telephone code is 03691.

Things to See

The superb old **Wartburg** castle on a hill top overlooking Eisenach is world famous. Martin Luther translated the New Testament from Greek into German while in hiding here during 1521 and 1522, thus making an enormous contribution to the development of the written German language. You can only visit the castle's interior with a guided tour (most tours are in German), which includes the museum, Luther's study room and the amazing Romanesque great hall. Tours run every 15 minutes from 8.30 am to 4.30 pm (9 am to 3.30 pm in winter) and cost DM10 (students DM6); arrive early to avoid the crowds. Contact Wartburg-Information (☎ 7 70 73) at Am Schlossberg 2 for more information and English-speaking guides.

In town the **Thuringian Museum** in the former Town Palace (1751), Markt 24, has a collection of ceramics and paintings of local interest. It's currently closed for extensive renovations and will probably not reopen before late 1996; a small part of the collection is on display in the foyer (DM1). The interior of the **Georgenkirche** (rebuilt in 1676) on Markt has three balconies which run all the way around, plus a glorious organ and pulpit. Four members of the Bach family served as organists here between 1665 and 1797.

Up the hill from the Georgenkirche is the late-Gothic **Lutherhaus** (open daily; DM3 or DM1.50 for students), the reformer's home from 1498 to 1501. It contains original manually inscribed and illustrated works, as well as early printed editions of Luther's Bible translations. The **Bachhaus** (closed Wednesday; DM5, or DM4 for students), on Frauenplan, is where the composer was born in 1685. The **Gedenkstätte Parteitag 1869** (open Monday to Friday) nearby at Marienstrasse 57 has an interesting exhibit on the 19th-century workers' movements in Germany. It's now also the regional SPD office.

Places to Stay

Camping The nearest camping ground is the *Campingplatz Altenberger See* (☎ 03691-7 41 37), at Neubau 4, seven km south of town in Wilhelmsthal. Charges are DM5 for a site plus DM5 per person.

Hostels & Private Rooms There are two hostels in Eisenach: the 65-bed *Jugendherberge Erich Honstein* (☎ 73 20 12), at Bornstrasse 7 which charges DM14/17.50 for juniors/seniors, and the 102-bed *Jugendherberge Arthur Becker* (☎ 20 36 13), Mariental 24 in the valley below the Wartburg (DM16/19.50). For the latter, take the hourly No 3 bus from the station to the 'Liliengrund' stop.

Eisenach-Information can find you a private room from around DM25 per person.

Hotels & Pensions The cheapest place in the town centre is the *Hotel Burghof* (☎ 20 33 87), at Karlsplatz 24-26 next to the old city gate. The rather spartan rooms have hardly changed since GDR days, though you now pay a pricey DM55/110. Much better value is the small *Pension Kesselring* (☎ 73 20 49), at Hainweg 32, 10 minutes' walk up from Bachplatz, whose cosy singles/doubles with bath and toilet cost DM60/80. Also good value is the *Pension-Restaurant Shanghai*, at Karl-Marx-Strasse 16, which despite the rather distasteful new building has nice rooms with toilet and shower for DM60/120. At Mariental 26 (next door to the hostel) is the *Hotel Villa Karoline* (☎ 73 28 84). It's built in early Jugendstil form and offers simpler rooms for DM55/75 and rooms with private bath and toilet for DM90/120.

Places to Eat

For sit-down fast food, try the *Imbiss Oase* in Goldschmiedenstrasse: a fish fillet with chips costs just DM4.50 and half a chicken with salad goes for DM5.50. A convenient and reasonably priced eating place right in the heart of the old town is the *Alt Eisenach* (☎ 7 60 88), at Karlstrasse 51, where most main dishes are under DM15. Also good are the *Café-Restaurant Marianne* (☎ 7 53 66), Frauenberg 1 (enter the establishment from the small lane near the library), which serves large meals in pleasant surroundings, and the lively *Gaststuben Alt Nürnberg* (☎ 7 21 77), Marienstrasse 7, with three-course menus from DM18. For a coffee with home-made pastries, drop in at the *Café Lackner* on the corner of Frauenberg and Johannisstrasse.

In a wine cellar in an old monastery opposite the Georgenkirche is the *Brunnenkeller* (☎ 71 42 99), Markt 10, whose menu includes hearty Thuringian dishes like beef roulade with red cabbage and dumplings for DM14. It's open daily for lunch, and evenings until 1 am. The Malaysian-Chinese *Restaurant Shanghai*, downstairs at the previously mentioned pension, has complete menus with several courses from around DM20. The slightly up-market restaurant at the *Hotel Hellgrafenhof* (☎ 51 17), Katharinenstrasse 13, specialises in pizza, tortellini and other Italian food.

GERMANY

Getting There & Away

Eisenach has good train connections to Erfurt (56 km); through-trains running between Frankfurt/Main and Berlin-Lichtenberg also stop here.

Getting Around

Eisenach is eminently walkable. The No 10 shuttle bus runs from the train station up to the Wartburg roughly every 1½ hours between 1 May and 31 October.

Saxony-Anhalt

The State of Saxony-Anhalt (Sachsen-Anhalt) comprises the former East German districts of Magdeburg and Halle. Originally part of the duchy of Saxony, medieval Anhalt was split into smaller units by the sons of various princes. In 1863 Leopold IV of Anhalt-Dessau united the three existing duchies, and in 1871 his realm was made a state of the German Reich.

The mighty Elbe River flows north-west across Saxony-Anhalt past Lutherstadt Wittenberg and Magdeburg on its way to the North Sea at Hamburg. On the Saale River south of Magdeburg is Halle.

The Harz Mountains fill the south-west corner of Saxony-Anhalt and spread across into Lower Saxony to Goslar (see the Harz Mountains section for a map of the region). Quaint historical towns like Quedlinburg and Wernigerode hug the gentle, wooded slopes.

WERNIGERODE

Wernigerode is surrounded by the verdant foothills of the Harz Mountains. A romantic ducal castle rises above the old town, which reputedly contains something like 1000 half-timbered houses (in various states of repair). In summer this is a busy tourist centre attracting large throngs of German holiday-makers. It is also the northern terminus of the steam-operated, narrow-gauge Harzquerbahn, which has chugged 60 km south to Nordhausen for almost a century, and the line to Brocken, the highest mountain in northern Germany.

Orientation & Information

The bus and train stations are adjacent on the north side of the town. From Bahnhofsplatz, Rudolf-Breitscheid-Strasse leads south-east to Breite Strasse, which runs south-west to Markt, the old town centre. The tourist office (☎ 03943-3 30 35) is at Nicolaiplatz 1, just off Breite Strasse near Markt. Burgberg, Nussallee and Schlosschaussee all lead towards the fairy-tale castle on the hill at Agnesberg to the south-east.

Wernigerode's telephone code is 03943.

Things to See

Wander along the streets of the old town centre and admire the medieval brick-and-wood houses. The **Rathaus** (1544) on

Markt, with its pair of pointed black-slate towers, is a focal point. A block behind, the **Harz Museum** at Klint 10 features local and natural history (closed Sunday).

From Marktstrasse or Breite Strasse, you can join one of the two 'Bimmelbahn' wagon rides (DM2.50 one way) up to the neo-Gothic **castle**, though it's not a long climb. Built from 1862 to 1885 by Count Otto of Stolberg-Wernigerode, the castle's museum (entry DM6, students DM5; closed Monday) is worth visiting to see the chapel and great hall. For an extra DM2 you can climb the main tower and see parts of the castle's medieval predecessor, though the views of Wernigerode from the castle terrace are free.

Activities

There are plenty of short walks and day hikes nearby, foremost to the castle or to the inn Zur Harburg on the hill south of the town. The more serious might tackle the 30 km route (marked by blue crosses) from Mühlental south-east of the town centre to Elbingerode, Königshütte and the 18th-century wooden church and the remains of the medieval Trageburg castle at Trautenstein. More popular is the 11-km route (marked by red dots) past the rocks at Ottofelsen and the waterfall and inn at Steinerne Renne south-west of Wernigerode.

You can also take the steam train to the station at Drei-Annen-Hohne and from there select any of several short circle routes through the Hochharz National Park (or others from the main park entrance), the longest of which is 12 km. The tourist office has suggestions; you will need a good topographic sheet for some of them, but the KV Plan *Auto + Wanderkarte: Der ganze Harz* (DM9.80) is worth inspection.

The narrow-gauge Harzquerbahn train line runs south from the main station to Nordhausen (60 km, three hours) five times daily all year. Tickets (DM28 return) are available at the station. Rail passes are not valid. The other steam-train ride is to Brocken on the Brockenbahn, an adhesion train that connects with services from Wernigerode (2¾ hours; DM38 return). Nordhausen trains run direct to/from Halle. If you are a steam nut or just particularly taken by the mountains, the three-day steam-train pass at DM60, including connections (and the Selketalbahn, which runs from Gernrode), is fine value, as is the one-week pass at DM100.

Places to Stay

The tourist office arranges private rooms, free and by telephone if you wish, and Harz-Tourist-Service (☎ 2 32 34), at Burgberg 9b, handles bookings in the area. *Hotel zur Tanne* (☎ 3 25 54), Breite Strasse 59, charges only DM35/55 a single/double. The *Hotel zur Post* (☎ 3 24 36), Marktstrasse 17, is great value with rooms costing DM45/80 including breakfast (without shower). The *Hotel Schlossblick* (☎ 3 40 49), Burgstrasse 58 at Schöne Ecke, has similar rooms for DM60/75 or DM95/135 with all facilities. *Pension Schweizer Hof* (☎ 3 20 98) at Salzbergstrasse 13 should be the first choice for keen hikers, with route information and rooms from DM65/80. Your splurge choice could be the 16-room *Hotel Weisser Hirsch* (☎ 3 24 34), Marktplatz 5, from DM115/160.

Places to Eat

Good-value meals are served at the *Gaststätte zur Sonne*, Johannisstrasse 27 at Neuer Markt (closed Monday and from 2.30 pm Sunday), which has a full menu at DM13.50 per dish. For budget eats and take-away, visit *Kochlöffel* on the corner of Burgstrasse and Breite Strasse; burgers are DM4.50. The 'in' place to eat is the *Ratskeller* in the basement of the town hall on Markt.

Getting There & Away

The bus station is beside the main train station and the six daily buses to/from Bad Harzburg (50 minutes; DM5) use stop No 4; in Bad Harzburg you can connect with trains to Goslar, Hanover and Göttingen. Wernigerode is the end of the train line from Halberstadt (30 minutes), where you can connect for Quedlinburg, Magdeburg or

Berlin-Wannsee. You can get info and tickets at Reise Welt, Breite Strasse 37.

QUEDLINBURG

Unspoiled Quedlinburg has just celebrated 1000 years of existence and has quite stunning potential as a destination. Almost all the buildings in the centre are half-timbered, street after cobbled street of them, and they are slowly being restored. The main drawbacks at present are a shortage of transport and hotels, but it is worth visiting Quedlinburg before it becomes one of Germany's busiest tourist centres.

Orientation & Information

The centre of the old town is a 10-minute walk from the train station down Bahnhofstrasse. Take Heilig-Geist-Strasse to the left after the main post office, and follow it around into Steinbrücke and then to Markt. Quedlinburg-Information (☎ 03946-28 66) is at Markt 2.

The telephone code is 03946.

Things to See

The Renaissance **Rathaus** (1615) on Markt has its own Roland statue. However, the visitor's real focal point is the hill just south-west – the old castle district, known as **Schlossberg**. The area features the Romanesque **Church of St Servatii** (1129), or 'Dom' (closed Monday, admission DM5, students DM3), whose crypt dates back to the 10th century. In 1938 the SS confiscated the Dom to use it for their meetings as a 'Germanic solemn shrine'. The adjacent **Schlossmuseum** (closed Monday, admission DM2.50, students DM1) in the 16th-century castle has a good historical collection. The view of Quedlinburg from the castle is one of the most evocative in Germany.

Activities

To get in some hiking, take a bus or train 10 km south-west to Thale, at the mouth of the lovely Bode Valley in the Harz Mountains south of Quedlinburg. Here you'll find a cable car (closed Monday in winter) to Hexentanzplatz (the 'Witches' Dancing Ground' mentioned in Goethe's *Faust*), a trail up the valley and several caves. Outdoor stage performances are held in the amphitheatre nearby.

Places to Stay

Quedlinburg-Information has good private rooms from about DM30 and it is a good idea to ring ahead and book. The *Motel Quedlinburg* (☎ 28 55), Wipertistrasse 9, has singles/doubles for DM95/125. The historic 17th-century restored buildings of *Zum Schloss* (☎ 33 33), at Mühlenstrasse 22 by the castle and *Pension zum alten Fritz* (☎ 70 48 80), upstairs at Pölkenstrasse 18, make them both worth lashing out on. Zum Schloss has rooms from DM70/110; Zum alten Fritz has singles from DM60.

Getting There & Away

The easiest way to reach Quedlinburg is by train from Halle, though you must change at the isolated siding of Wegeleben; the link operates several times daily. Connections to Halberstadt (25 min) are by local trains, and from there you can ride to Wernigerode or Magdeburg.

MAGDEBURG

Magdeburg, on the Elbe River at a strategic crossing of transport routes from Thuringia to the Baltic and Western Europe to Berlin, was severely damaged by wartime bombing. It was rebuilt in steel and concrete, and of the old city only the cathedral and a few Romanesque churches remain. Accommodation is tight, so Magdeburg is perhaps best visited on a long day trip from Berlin. The city is now the capital of Saxony-Anhalt.

Orientation & Information

From the broad square in front of the train station, Wilhelm-Pieck-Allee leads east to a bridge over the Elbe, with Alter Markt a block back on the left. Magdeburg-Information (☎ 0391-5 41 47 04) is at Alter Markt 9.

The telephone code for Magdeburg is 0391.

GERMANY

Things to See

The centre of the old town is Alter Markt, with a copy of the bronze **Magdeburg Rider** figure (1240) of King Otto the Great facing the **Rathaus** (1698). Behind the Rathaus are the ruins of the 15th-century **Johanniskirche**, undergoing partial refurbishment after long being a memorial to the catastrophic bombing. To the north are arrayed the Romanesque **Wallonerkirche**, the ruins of **Magdalenkapelle** and the **Petrikirche**.

South of the bridge is the 12th-century Romanesque convent, **Unser Lieben Frauen**, now a museum (closed Monday; DM2, although you can enter the cloister and church free). Concerts are now held here in the name of Georg Philipp Telemann, a famous and prolific son. Farther south is the soaring Gothic **cathedral**, with its fine sculptures. Entry (from 10 am to noon and 2 to 4 pm only) is from the cloister. The **Kulturhistorisches Museum** (DM2, closed Monday) is on Otto-von-Guericke-Strasse at the corner of Danzstrasse. The original 'Rider' statue is kept here.

Places to Stay

There's no camping ground or hostel nearby, but you can get good private rooms from about DM40 through Magdeburg-Information for a DM3 fee. At Leiterstrasse 10 is *Magdeburger Hof* (☎ 3 38 81), a reasonable deal with singles/doubles at DM65/110. The small twin pensions *Schlee* and *Kieselbach* (☎ 4 86 71) at Stassfurter Strasse 26-28 are reasonable at DM50/100 (tram No 1 to Südring and walk under the expressway, third street on the right, then second right).

Getting There & Away

Trains to Berlin-Zoo take about 80 minutes direct or almost two hours via Potsdam Stadt. Others from Berlin-Wannsee carry on to Halberstadt (80 minutes). Magdeburg is on the main route from Rostock and Schwerin to Leipzig or Erfurt. Trains from Leipzig to Magdeburg run via either Halle or Dessau.

HALLE

The former state capital and largest city in Saxony-Anhalt, Halle is a surprisingly pleasant, untouristy place for a city that was the centre of the chemical industry in GDR days. Among the attractive and largely intact streets of the old town are churches and museums that justify a brief visit. Halle is also a university town, and a centre of modest cultural activities.

Orientation

To walk to the city centre from the main train station, head through the underpass and down the long pedestrian Leipziger Strasse past the 15th-century Leipziger Turm to Markt, Halle's central square.

Information

Halle-Information (☎ 0345-2 33 40) is in the unmistakable elevated gallery built around the Roter Turm in the middle of Markt. It's open weekdays from 9 am to 6 pm (from 10 am Wednesday), Saturday from 9 am to 1 pm, and Sunday from 10 am to 2 pm; opening hours are shorter in winter.

Halle's telephone code is 0345.

Things to See

In the centre of Markt is a statue (1859) of the great composer Georg Friedrich Händel. You can't miss **Marktkirche** (1529) with its four tall towers dominating the square. It's worth going inside to see the exquisitely decorated Gothic interior. Also on Markt is the **Roter Turm** (1506), a great red tower which is now an art gallery. Just south, at Grosse Märker Strasse 10, is the **City Historical Museum** (open daily).

Composer Georg Friedrich Händel was born in Halle in 1685, and his home at Grosse Nikolai Strasse 5 has been converted into a major museum, the **Händelhaus** (open daily), with a large collection of musical instruments. Händel left Halle in 1703 and, after stays in Hamburg, Italy and Hanover, spent the years from 1712 to 1759 in London where he achieved great fame. On Friedemann Bachplatz, a few blocks beyond the Händelhaus, is the 15th-century **Moritzburg** castle (closed Monday) with its art museum and Gothic chapel.

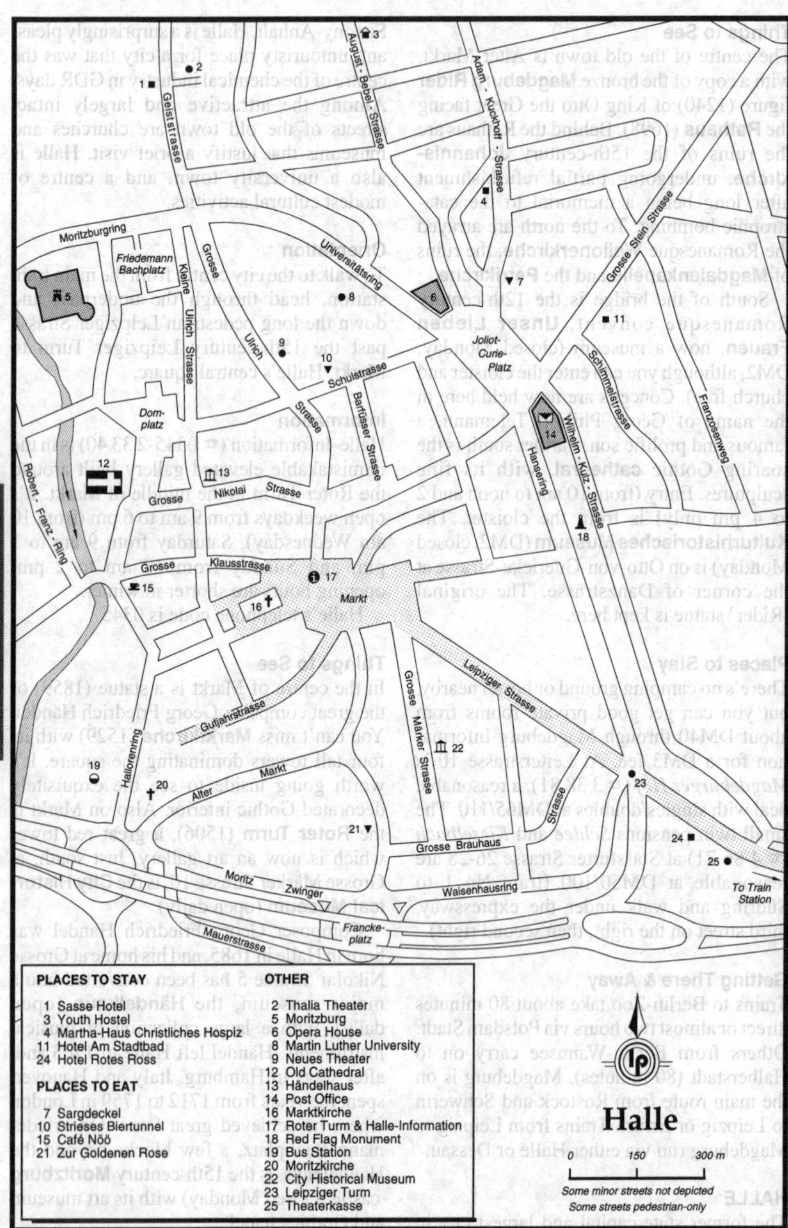
Halle
PLACES TO STAY
1 Sasse Hotel
3 Youth Hostel
4 Martha-Haus Christliches Hospiz
11 Hotel Am Stadtbad
24 Hotel Rotes Ross
PLACES TO EAT
7 Sargdeckel
10 Striese Biertunnel
15 Café Nöö
21 Zur Goldenen Rose
OTHER
2 Thalia Theater
5 Moritzburg
6 Opera House
8 Martin Luther University
9 Neues Theater
12 Old Cathedral
13 Händelhaus
14 Post Office
16 Marktkirche
17 Roter Turm & Halle-Information
18 Red Flag Monument
19 Bus Station
20 Moritzkirche
22 City Historical Museum
23 Leipziger Turm
25 Theaterkasse
August - Bebel - Strasse
Adam - Kuckhoff Strasse
Geiststrasse
Grosse Stein Strasse
Moritzburgring
Friedemann Bachplatz
Grosse Ulrich Strasse
Kleine Ulrich Strasse
Universitätsring
Joliot-Curie-Platz
Schimmelstrasse
Franzosenweg
Schulstrasse
Barfüsser Strasse
Domplatz
Hansering
Wilhelm - Külz - Strasse
Robert - Franz - Ring
Grosse Nikolai Strasse
Grosse Klausstrasse
Markt
Leipziger Strasse
Gutjahrstrasse
Grosse Märker Strasse
Hallorenring
Alter Markt
Grosse Brauhaus
Moritz Zwinger
Waisenhausring
Mauerstrasse
Francke-platz
To Train Station
0 150 300 m
Some minor streets not depicted
Some streets pedestrian-only

GERMANY

Places to Stay

Camping The closest camping is the municipal *Campingplatz* (☎ 34 00 85), which is at Pfarrstrasse near the Saale River on the northern edge of town; it's open from about mid-May until late September.

Hostels & Private Rooms The 72-bed *DJH hostel* (☎ 2 47 16), August-Bebel-Strasse 48a, charges DM18/24.50 for juniors/seniors. For private rooms (from DM30 per person plus a DM5 service fee), contact Halle-Information on ☎ 2 83 71.

Hotels It's lean pickings for budget accommodation in Halle. The *Pension Bett & Breakfast* (☎ 5 12 54), at Adolf-von-Harnack-Strasse 18 north of town, has just five rooms priced from DM75/110 a single/double. More central is the *Hotel Am Stadtbad* (☎ 50 32 70), Grosse Stein Strasse 64-65, where rooms cost DM80/120. The hall showers and toilets have been done up, but most rooms are rather shabby.

The *Hotel Rotes Ross* (☎ 3 72 71), Leipziger Strasse 76 between the train station and the centre of town, has a few simple singles for DM90, but its doubles (all with bath and toilet) cost an uncool DM198. The small *Sasse Hotel* (☎ 2 30 88), at Geiststrasse 22 near the Thalia Theater, has basic rooms priced from DM95/120 a single/double. The newly renovated *Martha-Haus Christliches Hospiz* (☎ 5 10 80), Adam-Kuckhoff-Strasse 5-8, offers rooms from DM130/190.

Places to Eat

For a bit of atmosphere, try the *Zur Goldenen Rose* (☎ 2 84 86) at Rannische Strasse 19 (closed Sunday). This 15th-century tavern serves sturdy Saxon specialities at affordable prices. The *Strieses Biertunnel*, around the corner from the Neues Theater on Schulstrasse, serves food until midnight and has many beers on tap. Another classic Halle pub is the *Sargdeckel*, Marthastrasse 28 near the Opernhaus, whose name (meaning 'coffin lid') was banned during the Weimar Republic for its supposed profanity. The lively *Café Nöö* (☎ 2 22 16 51) at Grosse Klausstrasse 11 near the old cathedral is a favourite haunt for Halle's students.

Entertainment

To find out what's on in Halle contact Theaterkasse (☎ 2 64 58), at Leipziger Strasse 82. Halle's main stage is the *Opernhaus* on Joliot-Curie-Platz, but there's also the *Neues Theater* at Grosse Ulrich Strasse 51 and the *Puppentheater* (☎ 2 49 62), which has regular puppet shows.

Getting There & Away

Just 40 km apart, Leipzig and Halle are linked by the hourly *Stadtexpress* shuttle trains. Halle is also on the route of fast trains from Rostock and Magdeburg to Leipzig or Erfurt, and also from Berlin-Lichtenberg or Berlin-Schöneweide to Erfurt and Eisenach. If you're coming from Dresden, you may have to change at Leipzig. Between Lutherstadt Wittenberg and Halle, you may have to take a local train (68 km, one hour).

NAUMBURG

Naumburg is one of those pretty little medieval towns for which Germany is famous. It is strategically located between Halle or Leipzig and Weimar and has frequent train services. The scenic Unstrut Valley lies to the north-west, and there are several hostels and camping grounds in the area. All of this makes Naumburg well worth including in a German itinerary.

Orientation & Information

The main train station (Naumburg/Saale) is 1.5 km north-west of the old town. You can walk into town along Rossbacher Strasse, visiting Naumburg's famous cathedral on the way. Alternatively, bus No 2 runs frequently from the main train station to Markt, Naumburg's central square.

Naumburg-Information (☎ 03445-20 16 14) is at Markt 6, and is open from 9 am to 6 pm Monday to Friday, to noon Saturday, and to noon Sunday in summer.

Naumburg's telephone code is 03445.

Things to See

Naumburg's picturesque **town hall** (1528) and Gothic **Stadtkirche St Wenzel**, built between 1218 and 1523, rise above Markt. The **City Historical Museum** (closed until mid-1995 for renovations) is on the eastern side of town at Grochlitzer Strasse 49-51.

In the ancient western quarter of the town stands the magnificent Romanesque **Cathedral of Sts Peter & Paul**, with its famous 13th-century statues of Uta and Ekkehard in the west choir. The cloister, crypt, sculpture and four tall towers of this great medieval complex are unique. The rather boring German-language tour is included in the admission price (DM3.50 or DM2 students), but if it's quiet, you can walk around on your own.

Places to Stay

Naumburg is one place in the east where you can find affordable accommodation. For a private room see Naumburg-Information; expect to pay around DM30 per person (plus a DM2 service fee) for somewhere central.

The *Camping Blütengrund* (☎ 20 27 11), 1.5 km north-east of Naumburg at the confluence of the Saale and Unstrut rivers, charges DM5 per person and DM3 for a tent site; there are also bungalows from DM40 per night.

Naumburg's large and well-equipped *Jugendgästehaus* (☎ 53 16), Am Tennisplatz 9, two km south of the town centre, has beds in double and four-person rooms at DM24/30.50 juniors/seniors. The *Jugendherberge Freyburg* (☎ 034464-2 95), Schlossstrasse 21a on the road up to the castle in Freyburg (see the following Around Naumburg section), has beds at DM15/19 for juniors/seniors. Five km south-west of Naumburg, in Bad Kösen, the *Jugendherberge Bad Kösen* (☎ 034463-5 97), at Bergstrasse 3, has beds for DM14/18.

In a quiet location by the Saale, 1.5 km south-east of Markt at Weichau 16, is the *Gasthof Alter Felsenkeller* (☎ 70 14 98) with simple singles/doubles for DM35/60, or DM60/90 with bath and toilet. The central *Caféhaus-Pension Kattler* (☎ 20 28 23), halfway between the cathedral and Markt at Lindenring 40, has nice rooms with toilet, shower and TV for DM50/100 (breakfast DM10 extra). Five minutes' walk north-east of the cathedral, the *Hotel Deutscher Hof* (☎ 70 27 12), at Franz-Ludwig-Rasch-Strasse 10, has rooms for DM70/110.

Getting There & Away

There are fast trains to Naumburg from Halle (one hour), Leipzig (one hour), Jena (45 minutes) and Weimar (45 minutes), and a local line to Artern via Laucha and Freyburg. Frankfurt/Main-Leipzig and Berlin-Munich InterCity trains stop in Naumburg.

AROUND NAUMBURG

Freyburg

Eight km north-west of Naumburg and easily accessible by train or bus, Freyburg lies in the lovely Unstrut Valley. The large medieval **Neuenburg** castle, now undergoing major restoration, stands on the wooded hill top directly above; the adjacent tower (closed Monday) offers a splendid view. Freyburg's vineyards are the second-most northerly in Europe (after those in England), and during the second weekend in September the town hosts eastern Germany's largest wine festival.

LUTHERSTADT WITTENBERG

Wittenberg is best known as the home of Martin Luther, but the Renaissance painter Lucas Cranach the Elder also lived here for 45 years. Wittenberg was a famous university town and the seat of the Elector of Saxony until 1547. It was at Wittenberg Castle in 1517 that Luther launched the Reformation, an act of the greatest cultural importance to all of Europe. A relaxed city, it can be seen in a day from a Berlin base, but is well worth a longer look.

Orientation & Information

There are two train stations. You'll probably arrive at Bahnhof Lutherstadt Wittenberg on the main line from Berlin to Leipzig or Halle. Bahnhof Wittenberg-Elbtor is a minor stop on a secondary line from Dessau. The city centre is a 15-minute walk from the station exit, between the two train lines and then under the tracks and into Collegienstrasse.

Wittenberg-Information (☎ 03491-22 39) is at Collegienstrasse 29. Wittenberg's telephone code is 03491.

Things to See

The **Lutherhaus** is a Luther museum inside the Lutherhalle, a former monastery yard at Collegienstrasse 54 (admission DM6; closed Monday). It contains an original room furnished by Luther in 1535. Luther moved into this monastic building in 1508 when he came to teach at Wittenberg University. The home of his friend and supporter, the humanist Philipp Melanchthon, nearby at Collegienstrasse 60, is also a museum (closed Friday, entry DM2).

In the Gothic **Stadtkirche St Marien** is a large altarpiece, begun by Lucas Cranach the Elder and finished by his son in 1555, showing Luther, Melanchthon and other Reformation figures in Biblical contexts, plus a self-portrait of Cranach the Elder. Luther married Katherina von Bora, a former nun, in St Marien in June 1525 and often preached here. In this church the first mass in the German language was celebrated in 1526. The baptismal font and marble tombstones in this church are remarkable. The **Luthereiche**, the site where Luther burnt his excommunication papers, is in the small garden at the corner of Lutherstrasse and Am Bahnhof.

Imposing monuments to Luther and Melanchthon stand in front of the impressive **Old Town Hall** (1535) on Markt. On one corner of Markt is the **House of Lucas Cranach the Elder**, Schlossstrasse 1, with a picturesque courtyard you may enter.

At the west end of town is **Wittenberg Castle** (1499) with its huge, rebuilt Gothic church (closed Monday). Luther nailed his *Ninety-five Theses* to the door of this church on 31 October 1517. His tomb may be viewed below the pulpit, and Melanchthon's tomb is opposite. From Wednesday to Sunday, you can climb the 289 steps of the 88-metre-high church tower for DM1.

Places to Stay

Accommodation is in short supply. Wittenberg-Information has private rooms from about DM40 per person (closed weekends), but the Fremdenverkehrsbüro (☎ 26 10) at Mittelstrasse 33 also books accommodation in and around the city and is handier to the main station.

The 104-bed *Otto Plättner Youth Hostel* (☎ 32 55) is housed upstairs in Wittenberg Castle (DM16.50 for juniors, DM22 for seniors, sheets DM6). *Gästehaus Lindemann* (☎ 34 27) at Friedrichstrasse 73 is a small but flexible outfit that charges from DM45/75 a single/double and can often arrange to collect you at the station if you call ahead (otherwise, jump on bus No 4 at the main post office).

The *Hotel Wittenberger Hof* (☎ 35 94), Collegienstrasse 56 beside the Lutherhalle, offers singles/doubles/triples with breakfast for DM70/119/149. The 40-room *Hotel Goldener Adler* (☎ 20 54), Markt 7, starts at DM78/90 a single/double without bath or breakfast.

Places to Eat

For German meals starting at less than DM9, try the *Café Topas* at the corner of Jüdenstrasse and Mauerstrasse (closed Saturday). The *Ratsschänke* at Markt 14 beside the town hall starts at DM11.50 with similar fare and is closed Monday.

Getting There & Away

Wittenberg is on the main train line to Leipzig and Halle, 90 minutes south of Berlin-Lichtenberg. All the Berlin trains stop at Schönefeld Airport. For train tickets and times, also ask at Reise Welt, Markt 12.

Mecklenburg-Pomerania

The state of Mecklenburg-Pomerania (Mecklenburg-Vorpommern) is a low-lying, postglacial region of lakes, meadows, forests and the beaches of the Baltic Sea (German: Ostsee) stretching across northern Germany from Schleswig-Holstein to Poland. Most of the state is historic Mecklenburg, and only the island of Rügen and the area from Stralsund to the Polish border traditionally belong to western Pomerania, or Vorpommern.

In 1160 the Duke of Saxony, Heinrich (Henry the Lion), conquered the region under the guise of introducing Christianity and made the local Polish princes his vassals. Germanisation gradually reduced the Slavonic element, and in 1348 the dukes of Mecklenburg became princes of the Holy Roman Empire. Sweden became involved in the area during the Thirty Years' War. In 1867 the whole region joined the North German Confederation and in 1871 the German Reich.

The offshore islands of Poel, Hiddensee and Rügen are still undiscovered paradises for outdoors people. Just keep in mind the very short swimming season (July and August only). Spring and autumn can be cold.

GERMANY

SCHWERIN

Almost surrounded by lakes, Schwerin is one of the most picturesque towns of eastern Germany and its popularity as a tourist attraction is rising. The town gets its name from a Slavonic castle known as Zaurin ('animal pasture') on the site of the present Schloss. This former seat of the Grand Duchy of Mecklenburg and contemporary capital of Mecklenburg-Pomerania is an interesting mix of 16th and 17th-century half-timbered town houses (many of which are being painstakingly renovated) and 19th-century architecture. It's also small enough to get around on foot.

Orientation & Information

Down the hill to the east of the train station is Pfaffenteich, the lake where you will find the pseudo-crenellated Arsenal. South of the lake is the town centre, focused on Markt. Farther south, around Alter Garten on the Schweriner See, are the monumental Marstall, the Schloss (the ducal castle), and the museums, parks and tour boats that will keep you entertained.

Schwerin-Information (☎ 0385-86 45 09) is at Am Markt 11. Schwerin's telephone code is 0385.

Things to See

Above Markt rises the tall 14th-century Gothic **cathedral** (Dom), where you can climb the 19th-century church tower (DM2) for the view. The cathedral is a superb example of north German red-brick architecture; another is the **Paulskirche**, which is being restored south of the train station.

South-east of Alter Garten over the causeway is Schwerin's neo-Gothic **Schloss** (closed Monday), on an island connected to the **Schlossgarten** by a further causeway. Admission to the superb interiors costs DM6. Behind is the **Technisches Landesmuseum**, which has exhibits of military history.

On the city side of the square is the **Staatliches Museum** (closed Monday, entry DM4, students DM2), which has an excellent collection of old Dutch masters including Frans Hals, Rembrandt, Rubens and Brueghel.

To the south-east of the Schlossgarten is the historic **Schleifmühle** mill quarter, where the road leads to Schwerin's **zoo**, which will be quite a surprise. Among the unexpected varieties of livestock are exotic birds such as pheasants and ostriches, great reptiles such as anacondas and boa constrictors, rare bison, polar bears and great cats. The zoo (DM5, children DM2) is open Monday to Friday in summer from 9 am to 5 pm (from October to April to 4 pm) and weekends all year to 6 pm. It is about three km south-east of Alter Garten (take bus 15 to the terminus).

The **Historisches Museum** at Grosser Moor 38 (DM2; closed Sunday) houses the town collection and the imposing annexe on Am Markt has a **print museum** (closed Monday) and exhibitions. Town **markets** are held on Schlachtermarkt in the old town behind the Rathaus.

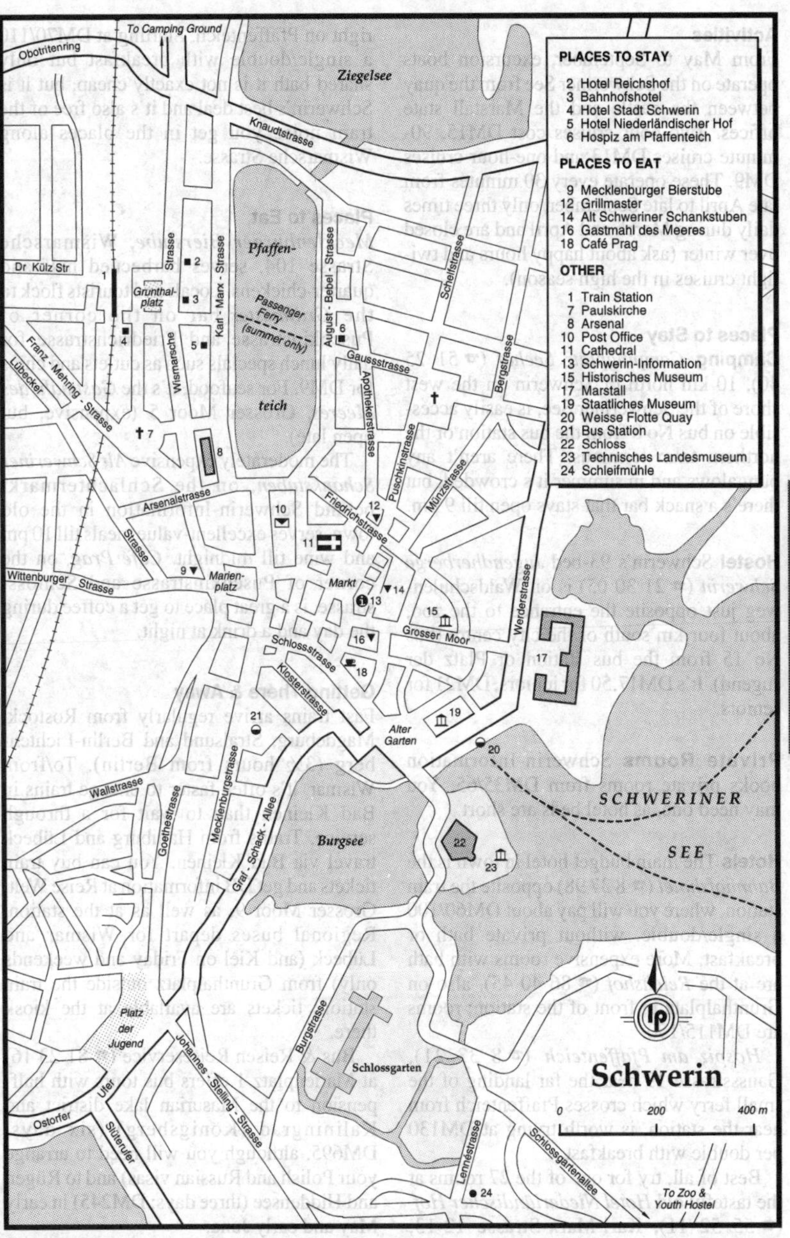

PLACES TO STAY
2 Hotel Reichshof
3 Bahnhofshotel
4 Hotel Stadt Schwerin
5 Hotel Niederländischer Hof
6 Hospiz am Pfaffenteich
PLACES TO EAT
9 Mecklenburger Bierstube
12 Grillmaster
14 Alt Schweriner Schankstuben
16 Gastmahl des Meeres
18 Café Prag
OTHER
1 Train Station
7 Paulskirche
8 Arsenal
10 Post Office
11 Cathedral
13 Schwerin-Information
15 Historisches Museum
17 Marstall
19 Staatliches Museum
20 Weisse Flotte Quay
21 Bus Station
22 Schloss
23 Technisches Landesmuseum
24 Schleifmühle
To Camping Ground
Obotritenring
Ziegelsee
Knaudtstrasse
Pfaffen-
teich
Passenger Ferry (summer only)
Dr Külz Str
Grunthal-platz
Wismarsche Strasse
Karl - Marx - Strasse
August - Bebel - Strasse
Schelfstrasse
Bergstrasse
Gaussstrasse
Apothekerstrasse
Franz - Mehring - Strasse
Lübecker Strasse
Puschkinstrasse
Münzstrasse
Arsenalstrasse
Friedrichstrasse
Werderstrasse
Wittenburger Strasse
Marien-platz
Markt
Grosser Moor
Schlossstrasse
Klosterstrasse
Alter Garten
Wallstrasse
Goethestrasse
Mecklenburgstrasse
Graf - Schack - Allee
Burgsee
SCHWERINER
SEE
Platz der Jugend
Burgstrasse
Schlossgarten
Johannes - Stelling - Strasse
Ufer
Ostorfer
Stüterufer
Lennéstrasse
Schlossgartenallee
To Zoo & Youth Hostel
Schwerin
0
200
400 m
GERMANY

Activities

From May to September, excursion boats operate on the Schweriner See from the quay between the castle and the Marstall state offices. Two-hour cruises cost DM15, 90-minute cruises DM13 and one-hour cruises DM9. These operate every 30 minutes from late April to late September, only three times daily during March and April and are closed over winter (ask about happy hours and twilight cruises in the high season).

Places to Stay

Camping *Campingplatz Seehof* (☎ 51 25 40), 10 km north of Schwerin on the west shore of the Schweriner See, is easily accessible on bus No 8 from the bus station or the northern tram terminus. There aren't any bungalows and in summer it's crowded, but there's a snack bar that stays open till 9 pm.

Hostel Schwerin's 93-bed *Jugendherberge Schwerin* (☎ 21 30 05) is on Waldschulenweg just opposite the entrance to the zoo, about four km south of the city centre (bus No 15 from the bus station or Platz der Jugend). It's DM17.50 for juniors, DM21 for seniors.

Private Rooms Schwerin-Information books private rooms from DM35/65. You may need one, as hotel beds are short.

Hotels The main budget hotel in town is the *Bahnhofshotel* (☎ 8 37 98) opposite the train station, where you will pay about DM60/100 a single/double, without private bath or breakfast. More expensive rooms with bath are at the *Reichshof* (☎ 86 40 45), also on Grunthalplatz in front of the station; rooms are DM115/150.

Hospiz am Pfaffenteich (☎ 8 33 21), Gaussstrasse 19 near the far landing of the small ferry which crosses Pfaffenteich from near the station, is worth trying at DM130 per double with breakfast.

Best of all, try for one of the 27 rooms at the tasteful old *Hotel Niederländischer Hof* (☎ 55 52 11), Karl-Marx-Strasse 12-13, right on Pfaffenteich. Starting at DM70/110 a single/double with breakfast but only shared bath it is not exactly cheap, but it is Schwerin's best deal and it's also free of the tram noise you get in the places along Wismarsche Strasse.

Places to Eat

Mecklenburger Bierstube, Wismarsche Strasse 104, serves barbecued half and quarter-chickens. Locals and tourists flock to the *Grillmaster* bar on the corner of Puschkinstrasse and Friedrichstrasse for daily lunch specials such as cutlets and chips for DM9. For seafood, it's the *Gastmahl des Meeres*, Grosser Moor 5 (expensive, but open late).

The moderately expensive *Alt Schweriner Schankstuben*, on the Schlachtermarkt behind Schwerin-Information in the old town, serves excellent-value meals till 10 pm and wine till midnight. *Café Prag*, on the corner of Puschkinstrasse and Schlossstrasse, is a great place to get a coffee during the day and a drink at night.

Getting There & Away

Fast trains arrive regularly from Rostock, Magdeburg, Stralsund and Berlin-Lichtenberg (3½ hours from Berlin). To/from Wismar, it's often faster to change trains in Bad Kleinen than to wait for a through service. Trains from Hamburg and Lübeck travel via Bad Kleinen. You can buy train tickets and get DB information at Reise Welt, Grosser Moor 9, as well as at the station. Regional buses depart for Wismar and Lübeck (and Kiel on Friday and weekends only) from Grunthalplatz outside the train station; tickets are available at the kiosk there.

Bus & Reisen Reiseservice (☎ 81 23 16) at Marienplatz 1 offers bus tours with half-pension to the Masurian lake district and Kaliningrad (Königsberg) (six days, DM695, although you will need to arrange your Polish and Russian visas) and to Rügen and Hiddensee (three days; DM245) in early May and early June.

WISMAR

Wismar, about halfway between Rostock and Lübeck, became a Hanseatic trading town in the 13th century. For centuries Wismar belonged to Sweden, and traces of Scandinavian rule can still be seen (and heard). It's less hectic than Rostock or Stralsund, and a pretty little town worth seeing for itself. It's also the gateway to Poel Island.

Information

Wismar-Information (☎ 03841-28 29 58) at Am Markt 11 has maps, brochures, stickers etc. Wismar's telephone code is 03841.

Things to See

Like many other German cities, Wismar was a target for Anglo-American bombers just a few weeks before the end of the war. Of the three great red-brick churches that once rose above the rooftops, only **St Nikolai** (closed Sunday and Monday) is intact. The massive red shell of **St Georgenkirche**, although partly restored, has been left as a reminder of the April 1945 raids, which drove a starving populace to burn what was left of a beautiful statue of George and the dragon. Cars now park where the 13th-century **St Marienkirche** once stood, although the great brick steeple (1339), also partly restored, still towers above.

Apart from this, it's hard to believe that Wismar's gabled houses were seriously bombed. Nearby in a corner of Markt are the graceful old **waterworks** (1602) and the **Rathaus** (1819). The town's historical museum (closed Monday) is in the Renaissance **Schnabbelhaus** at Schweinsbrücke 8 near St Nikolai and has many interesting exhibits on Wismar's past as a maritime Hanseatic power and a Swedish garrison town. Busy town **markets** are held on Tuesday, Thursday and Saturday on Markt.

Activities

To get out onto the Baltic Sea, board a Clermont Reederei boat to Kirchdorf on Poel Island, a very popular summer bathing resort for Germans. The trips operate from May to September (one hour; DM8). MS *Vaterland* operates 90-minute cruises from Alter Hafen (north-west of the town centre, past the Wassertor) at 11 am and 2 and 4 pm daily in summer.

Places to Stay

Wismar-Information arranges private singles and doubles from DM30 per person. *Hotel Altes Brauhaus* (☎ 21 14 16), Lübschestrasse 37, has rooms from DM90/140, and *Hotel Reingard* (☎ 61 34 95), Weberstrasse 18, has rooms from DM120/160; in both cases the off season is DM15 to DM20 cheaper, although in the high season the Reingard asks an extra DM15 for breakfast. The elegant *Hotel Alter Speicher* (☎ 61 47 61), Bohrstrasse 12, has most facilities; singles range from DM110 to DM150 and doubles from DM150 to DM220 all year.

Places to Eat

For some local seafood, try the *Fischrestaurant Seehase*, Altböter Strasse 6 (open weekdays from 11 am to 8 pm, Saturday to 3 pm). *Zum Weinberg* is a wine restaurant in the Renaissance house at Hinter dem Rathaus 3. The best-situated restaurant is the historic and exclusive-looking *Alter Schwede*, Am Markt 18. The local *Grillmaster* budget grill bar is at Lübsche Strasse 49; it's fast and filling for DM8 or less.

Getting There & Away

Trains run to/from Rostock every couple of hours, to/from Berlin-Lichtenberg and regularly to/from Schwerin; the trip should last 30 minutes, although there are often delays (see the Schwerin section). Trains to/from Lübeck and Hamburg travel via Bad Kleinen. There are daily buses to/from Lübeck, Kiel, Rendsburg and Hamburg from beside the train station. You can also get to Poel by bus several times a day. There are no lockers at the train station.

ROSTOCK

Rostock, the largest city in lightly populated north-eastern Germany, is a major Baltic port and shipbuilder. The giant shipyards on the estuary of the Warnow River were built from scratch after 1957. In the 14th and 15th centuries, Rostock was an important Hanseatic city trading with Riga, Bergen and Bruges. Rostock University, founded in 1419, was the first in northern Europe. The city centre along Kröpeliner Strasse retains the flavour of this period and much is being redeveloped, including the remains of the old city walls, the medieval churches and the local transit system. It's a popular tourist centre and the beach resort of Warnemünde is only 12 km north.

Orientation & Information

Rostock-Information (☎ 0381-4 92 52 60) is at Schnickmannstrasse 13-14, about two km from the train station. To get there, take tram No 11 or 12 outside the station and get off at the stop after the Rathaus and St-Marien-Kirche in the centre of town.

Rostock's main post office is adjacent to the Rathaus and the telephone code is 0381.

Things to See

Rostock's greatest sight is the 13th-century **St-Marien-Kirche**, which survived WW II unscathed. This great medieval brick edifice contains a functioning astronomical clock (1472), a Gothic bronze baptismal font (1290), a Renaissance pulpit (1574) and a baroque organ (1770) – all artistic treasures. Ascend the 207 steps of the 50-metre-high church tower for the view.

Kröpeliner Strasse, a broad pedestrian mall lined with 15th and 16th-century burgher houses, runs west from the **Rathaus** on Neuer Markt to the 14th-century **Kröpeliner Tor** (closed Saturday and Sunday mornings and on Monday) near a stretch of old city wall. Halfway along, off the south-west corner of Universitätsplatz, is the **Kloster 'zum Heiligen Kreuz' Museum** (closed Monday) in an old convent (1270); ask at the museum about visiting the convent church, which is being heavily renovated.

Rostock also has a good **Maritime Museum** (DM4; closed Monday) on the corner of Richard-Wagner-Strasse and August-Bebel-Strasse, near the **Steintor**, which is also worth seeing.

Places to Stay

The 85-berth *Jugendgästeschiff 'Traditionsschiff'* (☎ 71 62 24) is in a converted freighter on the harbour at Schmarl-Dorf between Rostock and Warnemünde (S-Bahn to Lütten Klein Station, then walk east and past the apartment blocks for 25 or 30 minutes, left at the three-way intersection and past the small lighthouse and the two car parks to the far gangway marked for the museum). It's more expensive than most hostels at DM25/31.50 for juniors/seniors, but the rooms and setting are pleasant – it's run more like a pension. But you are a long way from anything else, so shop first if you arrive late in the afternoon or evening.

Rostock-Information can book private singles/doubles from around DM30/60. Small but central and worth trying is *City-Pension* (☎ 4 59 08 29) at Krönkenhagen 3, with singles/doubles with private facilities from DM75/145.

Of the hotels, the eight-storey, 73-room *Hotel am Bahnhof* (☎ 3 63 31) opposite the train station is expensive at DM125/165 a single/double with breakfast. Even more expensive is the nine-storey, four-star *Hotel Warnow*, at Lange Strasse 40, from DM185/240.

Places to Eat

The plush *Ostseegaststätte*, Lange Strasse 9, specialises in seafood in the upstairs dining room, and there's a pizzeria downstairs. The service is good but it's not the cheapest place in town. The *Gastmahl des Meeres* opposite the Maritime Museum on August-Bebel-Strasse also specialises in seafood and is equally expensive.

For a late lunch, don't miss the *Rostocker Ratskeller* in the Rathaus building on Neuer Markt. Everything is half-price between 3 and 5 pm from Monday to Friday. The local stand-by is *Jimmy's Hamburger* at Kröpeliner Strasse 71, on the corner of Breite Strasse at Universitätsplatz (good burgers, big coffees for DM2.20), and *Café Meerschaum* across the street is the central breakfast and ice-cream spot.

Getting There & Away

There are direct trains to Rostock from Berlin-Lichtenberg and trains run to Stralsund, Wismar and Schwerin several times daily. Reise Welt at Lange Strasse in front of the Hotel Warnow sells DB tickets, as does the main station's ticket office.

There are two car-ferry trains a day between Berlin-Zoo and Copenhagen via Rostock. TR-Line ferries depart three times every day from Rostock to Trelleborg (Sweden). The crossing takes six hours and costs DM40 one way (students DM30, night trips are double the fare). A car can be transported for DM140 one way in summer season (30% more on night runs) and bicycles free. The Hansa/DFO ferries charge DM10 per person at most times except on Friday, Saturday and Sunday in summer (DM16). The vehicle price is DM130 on all runs, and bicycles are DM6 extra.

Getting Around

The double-deck S-Bahn has 1st (50% dearer) or 2nd class – be careful which one you get into and check exactly from which platform the next service will depart. The Rostock transit area, which includes Warnemünde, is divided into three zones and you pay DM1.80/2.80/3.40 for one/two/ three-zone single journeys (students half-price). There are DM10/13/16 day cards (concession DM7.50/10/12). The discounted after-9 am day card is excellent value at DM3.00/4.10/5.50. Local tickets are available at the machines at most tram stops and S-Bahn stations, or from the kiosk (open weekdays only) at Ernst-Barlach-Strasse near Steintor.

WARNEMÜNDE

Warnemünde, at the mouth of the Warnow River on the Baltic Sea just north of Rostock, is eastern Germany's most popular beach resort, though it's not as crowded as it used to be. S-Bahn trains (see Getting Around in the earlier Rostock section) connect Warnemünde to Rostock every 15 minutes on weekdays, every 30 minutes in the evenings, and hourly from midnight to dawn, so the town can easily be used as a base for day trips to Rostock, Wismar, Stralsund and even Schwerin. It's a good choice if you want to enjoy the comforts of city life while staying in what is ostensibly a small fishing village on the beach.

Information

Warnemünde has the same telephone code as Rostock: 0381. For currency exchange, there is a DVB Bank, Am Bahnhof in the station area near the ferry terminal, open Monday to Friday from 6 am to 7 pm, to 12.30 pm Saturday. Otherwise, you can exchange on the ferry if you are crossing to Scandinavia.

Things to See

Alter Strom, the old harbour, is a picturesque inlet still lined with quaint fishermen's cottages. One of these has been converted into a **museum** (open Wednesday to Sunday; DM3), on Alexandrinenstrasse just south of Kirchenstrasse, the church and the main square. The inlet is now being lined with tempting restaurants on the west side, while boats moored at the quay below sell fish and rolls, offer cruises, or present themselves as restaurants (some manage all three). The result is a pleasant atmosphere that can be experienced at little or no cost. The crowded **promenade** to the north, on the sea, is where German tourists congregate. Warnemünde's broad, sandy beach stretches west from the **lighthouse** (1898), and is chock-a-block with bathers on a hot summer's day.

Activities

Throughout the year (weather permitting), boats depart from near the mouth of Alter Strom on harbour cruises. Weisse Flotte at Am Strom 124 has crossings to Sweden on Tuesday, Thursday and Saturday for DM34 and to Copenhagen for DM64.

Places to Stay

The 69-bed *Erwin Fischer Youth Hostel* (☎ 5 23 03), at Parkstrasse 31 to the west of Richard-Wagner-Strasse, is DM17 for juniors, DM20.50 for seniors (the walk is 20 minutes west through the village centre from the S-Bahn at Warnemünde, so try getting off at Marienehe and catching the No 36 bus north). *Pension Zur Brücke* (☎ 5 24 48) at Alexandrinenstrasse 35 has a few singles all year from DM30 if you are lucky.

For a private room, try the *Kuramt Warnemünde Gästeservice* (☎ 5 11 42) on the corner of Wachtler Strasse and Heinrich-Heine-Strasse, in a corner of the park not far from the Neukauf supermarket. There is an info board with push-button screen, a coin telephone, and an office behind that is open capricious hours (Monday to Friday 9 am to noon and 1 to 3 pm, Tuesday 8 am to 6 pm with a similar lunch break). The private *Zimmervermietung Sixdorf* (☎ 5 23 77) at Parkstrasse 6 specialises in longer-term doubles and holiday flats. Otherwise, there are loads of private rooms along Parkstrasse. Just look for the 'Zimmer frei' signs in the windows.

The functional, 34-room *Promenaden-Hotel* (5 27 82), Seestrasse 5, has rooms from DM92/104 a single/double with shared bath, breakfast included; on weekends the rate drops to DM72/94 per night. *Hotel am Alten Strom* (☎ 5 25 81), Am Strom 60, has rooms starting at DM45/70 (shared facilities), ranging up to DM120/170, and *Hotel Stolteraa* (☎ 53 21) at Strandweg 17 offers similar facilities and prices.

Places to Eat

Eating in Warnemünde can be very expensive. In an emergency, you might try *Café zur Traube* at Alexandrinenstrasse 72. The food is uninspiring, but the prices are right. Also affordable are the daily fish specials at *Kettenkasten*, Am Strom 71. Try the lunch board posted outside the Promenade Hotel also. The growing speciality is Italian around Alter Strom, where daily specials are often reasonably priced.

Getting There & Away

It's easy to get to Warnemünde station on the double-decker S-Bahn from Rostock station (DM2.80; see Getting Around under Rostock). There is a car and train ferry service all year between the nearby Warnemünde terminal and Gedser in Denmark (DM10 one way, DM16 from June to August). Cars cost DM57 (in summer DM78 Sunday to Wednesday, DM117 from Thursday to Saturday). The ferry fits in with the Berlin-Copenhagen train schedule.

STRALSUND

Stralsund, an enjoyable city on the Baltic Sea north of Berlin, is nearly surrounded by lakes and the sea, which once contributed to its defence. Stralsund was a Hanseatic city in the Middle Ages and later formed part of the Duchy of Pommern-Wolgast. From 1648 to 1815 it was under Swedish control. Today it's an attractive old town with fine museums and buildings, pleasant walks and a restful, uncluttered waterfront. The island of Rügen is just across the Strelasund, and the ferry to Hiddensee leaves from here.

Orientation & Information

The old town and port are connected by causeways to their surrounds; the main train station is across the Tribseer Damm causeway, west of the old town. Neuer Markt is the south-western hub and the bus station is a few blocks south past the Marienkirche. Stralsund Stadtinformation (☎ 03831-25 22 51) is on Ossenreyerstrasse, near the northern focus of the old town at Alter Markt. Ask about the tourist pass (DM19.80, students DM9.80) that will admit you to the main attractions and summer organ concerts.

The post office is on Neuer Markt, opposite the Marienkirche. Stralsund's telephone code is 03831.

Things to See

On Alter Markt is the medieval **Rathaus**, where you can stroll through the vaulted and pillared structures and around to the impressive **Nikolaikirche**. Long-term restoration of

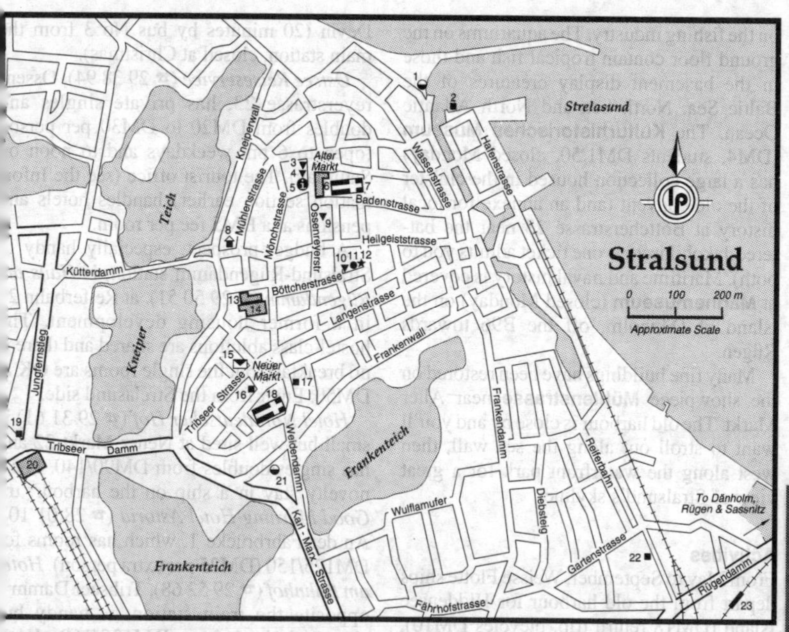

PLACES TO STAY

- 2 Hotel Astoria
- 8 Youth Hostel
- 16 Hotel Schweriner Hof
- 17 Hotel Norddeutscher Hof
- 19 Hotel am Bahnhof
- 22 Haus am Rügendamm

PLACES TO EAT

- 3 Getreidebörse Restaurant
- 4 Galerie-Café Duett
- 9 Teddy Bär
- 10 Bistro zum Speicher

OTHER

- 1 Weisse Flotte Quay
- 5 Tourist Information
- 6 Rathaus
- 7 Nikolaikirche
- 11 Kulturhistorisches Museum Annexe
- 12 Police
- 13 Meeresmuseum
- 14 Kulturhistorisches Museum
- 15 Post Office
- 18 Marienkirche
- 20 Main Train Station
- 21 Bus Station
- 23 Stralsund-Rügendamm Station

he church's magnificent painted medieval nterior is continuing, but parts are open in ummer on weekdays from 10 am to noon nd 2 to 4 pm, Saturday to noon and Sunday rom 11 am to noon. The 14th-century **Marienkirche** on Neuer Markt is a massive ed-brick edifice typical of north German Gothic architecture. You can climb almost 50 steps of the tower (DM2) for a sweeping view of Stralsund. Opening times are restricted.

On Mönchstrasse are two excellent museums. Stralsund's highlight is the fantastic **Meeresmuseum**, an oceanic complex and aquarium in a 13th-century convent church (closed Monday and Tuesday in winter, admission DM7). There's a large natural-history section and much information on the fishing industry. The aquariums on the ground floor contain tropical fish and those in the basement display creatures of the Baltic Sea, North Sea and North Atlantic Ocean. The **Kulturhistorisches Museum** (DM4, students DM1.50, closed Monday) has a large collection housed in the cloister of the old convent (and an annexe for local history at Böttcherstrasse 23 near the battered Jakobikirche – one ticket admits you to both). Maritime and naval history is covered at **Marinemuseum** (closed Monday) on the island of Dänholm, off the B96 towards Rügen.

Many fine buildings have been restored on the showpiece **Mühlenstrasse** near Alter Markt. The old harbour is close by and you'll want to stroll out along the sea wall, then west along the waterfront park for a great view of Stralsund's skyline.

Activities

From May to September, Weisse Flotte ships depart from the old harbour for Hiddensee Island (DM18 return trip, bicycles DM10), short crossings to Altefähr (DM3) and one-hour daily harbour cruises at 2.30 pm (DM6). You can book on ☎ 26 81 16 or buy tickets from the kiosk at the quay.

There are organ recitals on the 1659 instrument in the Marienkirche and in the Gothic splendour of the Nikolaikirche every other Wednesday in summer at 8 pm; the bill is occasionally filled by chamber music. The cost of performances at either church is DM7 (students DM4).

Places to Stay

No camping ground is handy and you should plan to camp on Rügen (see the following Rügen section). Stralsund's excellent 180-bed *Grete Walter Youth Hostel* (☎ 29 21 60) is in the 17th-century waterworks at Am Kütertor 1 (bus No 4 or 5 or 15 minutes' walk from the main station). It's DM17.50 for juniors, DM21.50 for seniors and is closed from mid-December to mid-January. Another *hostel* (☎ 27 03 58) is at Strandstrasse 21 off the Greifswald road in nearby Devin (20 minutes by bus No 3 from the main station, closed at Christmas).

Ostsee Reiseservice (☎ 29 38 94), Ossenreyerstrasse 23, has private singles and doubles from DM20 to DM30 per person (open to 6 pm weekdays and to noon on Saturday). The tourist office (see the Information section earlier) handles hotels and pensions at a DM5 fee per room.

A budget prospect, especially handy to Stralsund-Rügendamm station, is *Haus am Rügendamm* (☎ 29 50 51), at Reiferbahn 29 in a former housing development. The hostel-class ablutions are shared and there is no breakfast, but the single rooms are OK at DM50. Enter from the Strelasund side.

Hotel Norddeutscher Hof (☎ 29 31 61) is small but well sited at Neuer Markt 22 and has singles/doubles from DM90/140. For a novelty stay in a ship on the harbour: try *Good Morning Hotel Astoria* (☎ 28 01 10), An der Fährbrücke 1, which has rooms for DM125/150 (DM25 per extra person). *Hotel am Bahnhof* (☎ 29 52 68), Tribseer Damm 4 opposite the train station, is handy but elegant indeed from DM120/160. *Hotel Schweriner Hof* (☎ 2 68 20), at Neuer Markt 1 near Marienkirche, is fine if you can spare DM135/175 or up.

Places to Eat

For budget eating, go direct to the tiny *Bistro zum Speicher* on the corner of Böttcherstrasse and Filterstrasse, where the main dishes come in under DM10. Budget breakfasts or lunches are the business of *Teddy Bär*, a stand-up snack bar and café on the corner of Ossenreyerstrasse and Badenstrasse near the Rathaus. The *Getriedebörse* restaurant at Alter Markt 8 is a little more elegant, but there is a short vegetarian menu and daily fish specials are around DM10. *Galerie-Café Duett* next door has a steady local clientele for its budget lunches as well as beer and coffee.

Getting There & Away

Express trains run to/from Rostock (1½ hours, about 15 daily), Leipzig (5½ hours, 12 daily) and Berlin-Lichtenberg (thre hours, 15 daily; DM38). Connections to Hamburg (DM50.20) are regular. International trains between Berlin-Zoo and Stockholm or Oslo use the car ferry between Sassnitz Hafen and Trelleborg and Malmö (Sweden). Some trains to/from Sassnitz Hafen don't stop at Stralsund's main train station but instead call at Stralsund-Rügendamm on the south-east side of the city (some stop at both). Boarding for Sweden, use the cars labelled for Sassnitz Hafen and Malmö, as the train will split up at Sassnitz. Two or three daily connections to Stockholm (changing at Malmö) are available, some from Stralsund-Rügendamm only (see also Rügen Island, and the Getting There & Away section at the beginning of this chapter). About 20 daily trains run to Sassnitz (one hour) from Stralsund or Stralsund-Rügendamm, at least 10 daily run to/from Binz.

Train and ferry tickets can be booked at Reise Welt, at Alter Markt 10 next to the Rathaus.

Buses run to/from Bergen (two or three daily) and Sassnitz (three each weekday), stopping at the bus station by Frankenteich south of the city centre.

HIDDENSEE ISLAND

Hiddensee is a narrow island about 17 km long off Rügen's west coast north of Stralsund. No cars are allowed on Hiddensee and there are only two hotels, *Godewind* (☎ 038300-2 35) at Süderende 53, where prices start at DM40 per person, and *Lachmöwe* (☎ 038300-2 53), starting at DM45; both are at Vitte. There is no camping or hostels.

Weisse Flotte runs passenger boats from Stralsund to Neuendorf (DM9/15 one way/return), Vitte or Kloster villages (both DM12/18 one way/return) on Hiddensee up to three times daily. If you want to take a bicycle on this boat (DM10), check first. Large baggage costs DM1 a piece.

There are also ferries from Schaprode on Rügen's west coast across to Hiddensee. This is a shorter and cheaper crossing (DM9/14 one way/return) and bicycles are carried (but check first if you cross on Sunday).

RÜGEN ISLAND

Rügen Island, just north-east of Stralsund and connected by causeway, is Germany's largest island. At Stubnitz, six km north of Sassnitz, is the highest point on the island (118 metres), and steep **chalk cliffs** tower above the sea. The main resort area is around Binz, Sellin and Göhren on a peninsula on Rügen's east side. Rügen-Information-Service (☎ 038393-23 02) is at the train station in Binz and books rooms for clients in person only. In Sassnitz, the tourist office (☎ 038392-3 20 37) at Hauptstrasse 70 handles enquiries and also books private rooms.

Much of Rügen and surrounding waters is either national park area or protected nature reserves. Particularly sensitive are the **Bodden** inlet areas, which are popular with bird-watchers because of the variety of bird life that takes refuge there. Several maps are available, but Nordland's *Rügen mit Hiddensee* 1:75,000 sheet (about DM9 at most shops and tourist offices) is adequate for walking or cycling.

Places to Stay

Rügen has 18 camping grounds, the largest concentration of them at Göhren. For information about the individual sites, contact C & W Rohrdantz A Dirks KG (☎ 03838-2 22 05) at Industriegebiet Teschenhagen in Teschenhagen. The building is on route B96 about three km from Bergen.

In Binz, there's a *DJH hostel* (☎ 038393-3 25 97) at Strandpromenade 35. It's DM17 for juniors, DM20.50 for seniors (closed from November to mid-February). Another *hostel* (☎ 038393-3 28 45) is farther north at Prora-Ost, near the road to Sassnitz (bus from Binz).

In Binz, the small *Hotel-Pension Granitz* (☎ 038393-26 78) at Bahnhofstrasse 2 has doubles only from DM80, rising in high season; the *Vier Jahreszeiten* (☎ 038393-3 00 60) at Zeppelinstrasse 8 has some singles, but these start at DM70. The only place you will be reasonably certain of finding a room is at the 116-room, four-star *Rügenhotel*, Seestrasse 1, Sassnitz, above the ferry harbour.

Getting There & Away

Local trains run regularly from Stralsund to Sassnitz or Binz (one hour) on Rügen's north-east side. Both services pass Lietzow, 13 km before Sassnitz, where you may have to change trains. From Binz, a short narrow-gauge train continues to Göhren at Rügen's eastern tip. There are 10 ferries per day from Sassnitz to Trelleborg (Sweden) and return. The crossing takes four hours and costs DM10/20 one way/return (DM16/32 from Friday to Sunday in June, July and August). Cars and motorbikes are carried and cabins are available on night crossings. For bookings, call ☎ 2 22 67 or visit a travel agent (there is also a ticket kiosk on the street corner between Sassnitz station and the harbour).

If you are taking the train to/from the Sweden ferry, be sure of whether you need to walk between Sassnitz's main station and Sassnitz Hafen, which is 10 minutes down (or 20 minutes up) the hill, or whether your service takes you right to the quayside at Sassnitz Hafen (in the case of a split train you need to be in the appropriately labelled carriage). Local trains from Stralsund end at Sassnitz, while through services to/from Malmö connect with the ferry.

Bornholmstrafikken (☎ 038392-3 52 26) has four services a week (DM36 one way) between Neu-Mukran near Sassnitz and Rønne on Bornholm (Denmark)

See the Hiddensee Island section regarding transport from Rügen to Hiddensee.

Bavaria

For many visitors to Germany, Bavaria (Bayern) is a microcosm for the whole country. Here you will find fulfilled the Germanic stereotypes of Lederhosen, beer halls, oompah bands and romantic castles. Yet the Bavarians themselves are proudly independent and pursue a separate course from the rest of Germany in a number of ways, not least in the refusal of its youth hostels to accept any guests over the age of 26.

Bavaria was ruled for centuries as a duchy under the line founded by Otto I of Wittelsbach, and eventually graduated to the status of a kingdom in 1806. The region suffered amid numerous power struggles between Prussia and Austria and was finally brought into the German Empire in 1871 by Bismarck. The last king of Bavaria was Ludwig II (1845-86), who earned the epithet the 'mad monarch' for his obsession with building crazy castles at great expense. He was found drowned in Lake Starnberg in suspicious circumstances, and left no heirs.

Bavaria draws visitors all year. If you only have time for one part of Germany after Berlin, this is it. Munich is its capital and the heart and soul of the area. The Bavarian Alps, Nuremberg and the medieval towns on the Romantic Road are other important attractions. Try getting off the beaten track in a place like the Bavarian Forest for a taste of Germany away from the tour buses.

MUNICH

Munich (München) is the Bavarian mother lode. But this beer-belching, sausage-eating city can be as cosmopolitan as anywhere in Europe. Munich residents have figured out how to enjoy life and they're usually happy to show visitors. Just head to the Hofbräuhaus (or some other beer hall) and ask for advice on the Munich way of life.

There's much more to Munich, however, than beer halls. Decide on one of the many fine museums and take a leisurely look. The city is an ideal base for day trips to the great outdoors. On a clear day anywhere in Munich, the Bavarian Alps beckon. If the weather's good, head for the mountains; much of Munich can be seen on a rainy day, but clouds don't do the Alps justice.

Munich has been the capital of Bavaria since 1503, but really achieved eminence under the guiding hand of Ludwig I in the 19th century. It has seen many turbulent times, but this century has been particularly rough. WW I practically starved the city, and WW II brought bombing and more than 200,000 deaths.

Orientation

The main station is less than one km west of the centre of town. Though there's an extensive metro and S-Bahn system, old-town Munich is enjoyable for walking. Head east along Bayerstrasse, through Karlsplatz, and then along Neuhauser Strasse and Kaufingerstrasse to Marienplatz, the hub of Munich.

To the north of Marienplatz are the Residenz (the former royal palace), Schwabing (the famous student section) and the parklands of Englischer Garten. To the east is the Platzl quarter for beer houses and restaurants, as well as Maximilianstrasse, a fashionable street that's fun for strolling and window-shopping.

A few streets number sequentially up one side and back down the other (such as Rosenstrasse), and the renumbering of Sendlinger Strasse will cause confusion for a while yet.

Information

The main tourist office (☎ 089-2 39 12 56) is at the main train station, beside the south entrance near platform No 11. Its hours are 8 am to 10 pm from Monday to Saturday and 11 am to 7 pm on Sunday. Despite the efficiency of the staff, you should expect to stand in line during summer. The room-finding service costs DM5 and you must book in person or in writing.

During the week, it might be better to try the central city office at Sendlinger Strasse 1 near Rindermarkt (go upstairs to Room 213), open Monday to Thursday from 8.30 am to 6 pm, to 2 pm on Friday. The Munich airport office is open from Monday to Saturday, 8.30 am to 10 pm and from 1 to 9 pm on Sunday and holidays. There is all-day info available in English if you dial ☎ 23 91 61 (for museums and galleries) or ☎ 23 91 71 (for other sights).

Some of the printed tourist information will cost, but a current issue of the excellent *Young People's Guide to Munich* (DM1 from the tourist office) might be available free at the Jugendinformationszentrum. This useful office, at the corner of Paul-Heyse-Strasse and Landwehrstrasse, is open from noon to 6 pm Monday to Friday (until 8 pm on Thursday). From the Bayerstrasse exit at the main station, walk two blocks south on Schillerstrasse then two blocks to the west. You can select from the free material, some of which is multilingual or in English, on leisure, music and culture in Munich, budget youth transit and travel, environmental issues and work camps in Germany.

The train station also features another excellent source of information in English at EurAide (☎ 59 38 89), also near platform 11. It's a private information office run on behalf of Deutsche Bahn with more than just train information and seems more inclined than the tourist office to find the right accommodation at the right price (DM6 per booking). It's open daily from May to early October, from 7.30 am to 6 pm (to 4.30 pm only during May) and is closed for lunch, but a copy of its helpful newsletter is usually available at the door, even during winter. It also organises a few tours and has details on many more.

Money The main post office has lower commission rates than the DVB bank, which has two offices at Hauptbahnhof. American Express is at Promenadeplatz 6.

Post & Telephone Munich's central post office and telephone exchange is directly opposite the station at Bahnhofplatz 1, and is open daily from 6 am to 10 pm (from 7 am on weekends and holidays). The poste restante address is Postlagernd, 80074 München 32. The office in the station closes at 7 pm Monday to Friday, and at 2 pm Saturday and Sunday.

Munich's telephone code is 089.

Consulates Among the many consulates in the city are the British Consulate (☎ 3 81 62 80) at Amalienstrasse 62, the US Consulate

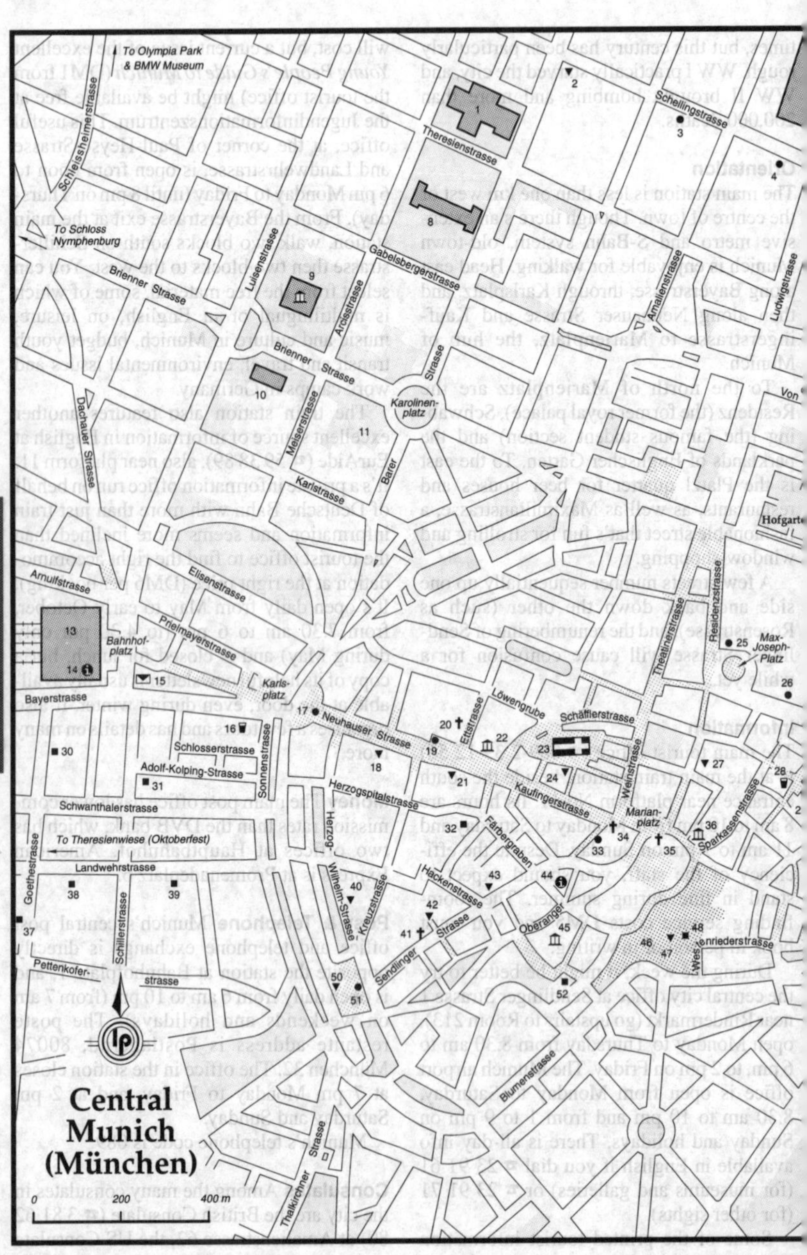
To Olympia Park
& BMW Museum
Schleissheimerstrasse
To Schloss
Nymphenburg
Brienner Strasse
Luisenstrasse
Arcisstrasse
Gabelsbergerstrasse
Theresienstrasse
Schellingstrasse
Amalienstrasse
Ludwigstrasse
Strasse
Brienner Strasse
Karolinen-
platz
Dachauer Strasse
Meiserstrasse
Barer
Karlstrasse
Von
Hofgarten
Arnulfstrasse
Elisenstrasse
Prielmayerstrasse
Bahnhof-
platz
Bayerstrasse
Karls-
platz
Neuhauser Strasse
Sonnenstrasse
Schlosserstrasse
Adolf-Kolping-Strasse
Schwanthalerstrasse
Herzogspitalstrasse
To Theresienwiese (Oktoberfest)
Landwehrstrasse
Goethestrasse
Schillerstrasse
Pettenkofer-
strasse
Herzog-
Wilhelm-Strasse
Kreuzstrasse
Löwengrube
Ettstrasse
Schäfflerstrasse
Weinstrasse
Theatinerstrasse
Residenzstrasse
Max-
Joseph-
Platz
Kaufingerstrasse
Marien-
platz
Sparkassenstrasse
Färbergraben
Hackenstrasse
Oberanger
Sendlinger
Strasse
Westenriederstrasse
Blumenstrasse
Thalkirchner
Strasse
Central
Munich
(München)
0
200
400 m

PLACES TO STAY

30 Jugendhotel Marienherberge
31 Pension Schiller
32 Hotel Arosa
37 Hotel Gebhardt
38 Pension Marie Luise
39 CVJM Jugendgästehaus
48 Hotel-Pension am Markt
52 Hotel Blauer Bock

PLACES TO EAT

2 Levantes Restaurant
18 Augustinerbräu
21 Zum Pschorrbräu
24 Nürnberger Bratwurst Glöckl am Dom
27 Alois Dallmayr
40 Art + Tart Vitamin Buffet
42 Bella Roma
43 Altes Hackerhaus
47 Löwenbräu Stadt Kempten
50 Höflinger

OTHER

1 Neue Pinakothek
3 Words' Worth Books
4 Anglia English Bookshop
5 University
6 Bike Rental
7 Chinesischer Turm
8 Alte Pinakothek
9 Glypothek
10 Staatliche Antikensammlungen
11 Amerika Haus
12 Staatsgalerie Moderner Kunst
13 Main Train Station
14 Tourist Information
15 Post Office
16 Mathäser Bierstadt
17 Karlstor
19 Richard Strauss Fountain
20 Michaelskirche
22 Deutsches Jagd- und Fichereimuseum
23 Frauenkirche
25 Residenz
26 Nationaltheater
28 Platzl Bühne
29 Hofbräuhaus
33 Sport Schuster
34 Peterskirche
35 Heiliggeistkirche
36 Spielzeugmuseum
41 Asamkirche
44 Tourist Information
45 Stadtmuseum
46 Viktualienmarkt
49 Deutscher Alpenverein
51 Sendlinger Tor
53 Deutsches Museum

(☎ 2 88 81) at Königinstrasse 5, and the Canadian Consulate (☎ 22 26 61) at Tal 29. The Czech consulate (☎ 95 01 24) is at Siedlerstrasse 2 (open 8.30 to 11 am only).

Travel Agencies ABR Reisebüro is in the main station building and has branches in the Starnberger Bahnhof subway (on the north side of Hauptbahnhof) that handle train-ticket sales (including under-26 discount TwenTickets). Studiosus Reisen is in the university quarter at Amalienstrasse 73 and handles student-oriented travel.

Bookshops Munich is one of the best German cities for stocking up on English-language reading material. Try the Anglia English Bookshop at Schellingstrasse 3, in the university area on a street filled with bookshops. Its range of paperbacks is hard to match elsewhere in Germany. Just down the street, you might also try Words' Worth Books in the courtyard at No 21a, which has guidebooks in English, but the best travel and cultural book range is at the multilevel Hugendubel branch opposite the Rathaus at Marienplatz (you can browse, lounge, or grab a coffee in civilised surroundings). For adventure travel, maps and more guides, turn to Geobuch at Rosental 6.

Emergency Medical help is available at the Kassenärztlicher Notfalldienst on ☎ 55 77 55; for ambulances dial ☎ 1 92 22. The police are at Hauptbahnhof on the Arnulfstrasse side, and their emergency number is ☎ 110.

Dangers & Annoyances Crime and staggering drunks leaving the beer halls are major problems in Munich. Watch valuables carefully around touristy areas and the seedy streets south of Hauptbahnhof. A common trick is to steal your gear if you strip off in the Englischer Garten.

Laundry Handy to the main station, and open from 6 am to 10 pm daily, is Prinz Münz-Waschsalon at Paul-Heyse-Strasse 21. Loads cost DM6 while drying is DM1 for 20 minutes, and the last wash must be in by 8 pm.

Things to See

The pivotal **Marienplatz** contains the towering neo-Gothic **Altes Rathaus** (old town hall) and the often-photographed **Glockenspiel** (carillon), which does its number at 11 am, noon and 5 pm (only at 11 am from 1 November to 30 April). Many other attractions are within easy walking distance.

Walking Tour Start at the Marienplatz. Two important churches are on this square: **Peterskirche** and, behind the Altes Rathaus, the **Heiliggeistkirche**. Head along the shopping street Kaufingerstrasse to the late-Gothic **Frauenkirche** (Church of Our Lady), the landmark church of Munich; the monotonous red brick is very Bavarian in its simplicity. Continue west on Kaufingerstrasse to **Michaelskirche**, Germany's grandest Renaissance church.

Farther west is the **Richard Strauss fountain** and then the medieval **Karlstor**. Double back towards Marienplatz and turn right onto Eisenmannstrasse which becomes Kreuzstrasse and Herzog-Wilhelm-Strasse. This ends at the medieval gate of Sendlinger Tor. Go down the left side of the shopping street Sendlinger Strasse to the **Asamkirche**. This remarkable church was totally designed by the Asam brothers and contains a unity rarely found in churches, which typically involve the input of many people in their development. It could have inspired some of Dame Edna Everage's less suitable outfits: with barely an unembellished surface to be found, it takes late baroque to its almost bizarre extreme.

Next, continue along Sendlinger Strasse, turn right on Hermann-Sack-Strasse and onto St-Jakobs-Platz and the **Stadtmuseum** (admission DM5; closed Monday), one of the better city museums in the country, with great exhibits on beer and brewing for adults, puppets for children and photography for Fuji fanatics. Walk around the left side of the museum and bear left onto Sebastiansplatz and Prälat-Zistl-Strasse. The **Viktualien-**

markt (food market), one of Europe's great markets, is nearby.

Residenz Easily found at Max-Joseph-Platz 3, this huge palace housed Bavarian rulers from 1385 to 1918 and features more than 500 years of architectural history. Along with the palace, restored after WW II, visit the **Residenz Museum**, an extraordinary array of 100 rooms including the Wittelsbach house's belongings, and the treasures of the **Schatzkammer** for a look at a ridiculous quantity of jewels, crowns and ornate gold. Admission to the Residenz is DM4 and it's open Tuesday to Sunday from 10 am to 4.30 pm; the Schatzkammer costs another DM4.

If this doesn't fulfil your passion for palaces, visit **Schloss Nymphenburg** (general admission DM6, castle and gallery only DM2.50) to the north-west of the city centre, the royal family's no less impressive summer home. There are several museums, including the ecologically oriented **Museum Mensch und Natur** (DM3; closed Monday). The surrounding park is worth a long, royal stroll.

Deutsches Museum If you visit just one museum in Munich (or even Germany), make it this one, south-east of the city centre. It's the world's largest science and technology museum, and is filled with anything but stuffy school-science projects. It's like a combination of Disneyland and the Smithsonian Institution all under one huge roof. You can explore anything from the depths of coal mines to the stars.

It's definitely too large to see everything (at 55,000 sq metres, it covers a whole island on the Isar and would require over 13 km of walking to see it all), so pursue specific interests. There's an excellent brochure, *Information for Your Visit*, which details times of free demonstrations. The museum's hours are 9 am to 5 pm daily (closed on important holidays) and admission is DM8 for adults and DM3 for students and children (free for those aged under six). A visit to the planetarium costs DM2 extra. To get to the museum, take the S-Bahn to Isartor, U1 or U2 to Fraunhoferstrasse, or tram No 18 to Deutsches Museum.

Neue Pinakothek At Barer Strasse 29 is this museum of mainly 19th-century painting and sculpture. Worth a look in its own right, it is most important to visit because of the famous works in the first 13 halls; these are refugees from the nearby **Alte Pinakothek**, which is sadly closed for renovation (probably until 1997). Dürer's Christ-like *Self-Portrait* and his *Four Apostles* should be on display, but you will be lucky to catch works such as Rogier van der Weyden's *Adoration of the Magi* and Botticelli's *Pietà*. It is best to check at the information desk before entering if you want to view particular works. Admission costs DM6 (free on Sunday and holidays) and the museum is closed on Monday.

Other Museums On Königsplatz, two museums are worth a look. The **Glyptothek** at No 3 and the **Staatliche Antikensammlungen** at No 1 feature one of Germany's best antiquities collections (mostly Greek and Roman stuff). To visit either museum costs DM5 (students DM3), both DM8 (DM4), or go on a Sunday when they're free; both are closed on Monday.

Also interesting is the **Staatsgalerie Moderner Kunst** at Prinzregentenstrasse 1. This gallery displays some of the great German and international contributions to modern art, including wild paintings by Munch, Picasso and Magritte, as well as funky sculpture and some pop art (admission DM5, students DM3, Sunday and holidays free; closed Monday).

BMW Factory To the north of the city is BMW's Munich factory at Peutelring 130. The excellent free tour (in English) takes visitors from raw metal to completed cars, and is conducted at 9.30 am and 1 pm on weekdays. The somewhat self-congratulatory museum is open daily (DM4.50, students DM3). Take the U2 to Scheidplatz and then the U3 or the U3 direct from Marienplatz to Olympiazentrum.

Olympiaturm If you like heights, go up the lift of the 290-metre tower Olympiaturm in the Olympia Park complex (DM5; open until midnight).

Dachau Don't miss this. Dachau was the very first Nazi concentration camp, built by Himmler in March 1933, and processed more than 200,000 prisoners, though it's not known exactly how many of these died. In 1933 Munich had 10,000 Jews. Only 200 survived the war. There are films in English daily at 11.30 am and 3.30 pm. A visit includes camp relics, a memorial, and a very sobering museum. It's open from 9 am to 5 pm every day except Monday, and admission is free. Take the S2 to Dachau and then bus No 722, which departs from Dachau station (you need a two-zone ticket to cover the journey).

Activities

Adventure Munich is the perfect place to plan adventurous outings. The Deutscher Alpenverein (German Alpine Club) headquarters is at Praterinsel 5 and can be very helpful with planning and information for mountain trips.

The Sport Schuster sporting goods store at Rosenstrasse 1-6 has five floors of everything imaginable for the adventurer, from simple camping gear to expedition wear, plus an excellent bookshop. It has a travel service on the 1st floor, offering various adventure outings.

Englischer Garten One of the largest city parks in Europe, this is a great place for strolling, especially along the Schwabinger Bach. Take liquid refreshment at the Chinesischer Turm beer garden or the nearby, less crowded Hirschau beer garden along the banks of the Kleinhesseloher See. The Englischer Garten is also the place to head for nude sunbathing with lots of company. It's not unusual for hundreds of naked people to be in the park on a normal business day, with their coats, ties and dresses stacked primly on the grass.

Festivals

Try to get to Munich for the Oktoberfest, one of the continent's biggest and best parties, running from the last Saturday in September to the first Sunday in October. Reserve accommodation well ahead. The Oktoberfest takes place at the Theresienwiese grounds south-west of Hauptbahnhof. There's no entrance fee, but most of the fun costs something. There are incredibly crazy carnival rides, food stands and, best of all, lots of beer tents.

Places to Stay

No-one older than 26 (unless travelling with children aged under 18) can stay in Bavarian youth hostels. This puts extra pressure on budget hotels and pensions, of which there are precious few in Munich. Reserve ahead when possible and arrive early in the day.

The tourist office accommodation guide costs 50 Pf.

Camping The most central location is *Campingplatz Thalkirchen* (☎ 7 23 17 07), south-west of the city centre at Zentralländstrasse 49, located close to the hostel on Miesingstrasse. It can be incredibly crowded in summer (it's closed from November to mid-March), but there's seemingly always room for one more tent. Take the U3 to Thalkirchen and bus No 57 to the last stop, 'Thalkirchen' (about 20 minutes from the city centre).

A bit farther from the city centre, but also more Bavarian, are *Waldcamping Obermenzing* (☎ 8 11 22 35) and *Langwieder See* (☎ 8 64 15 66); the latter has a great location but can only be reached by car on the autobahn towards Stuttgart. It is open from early in April to the end of October.

Hostels The youth hostels are only open to those aged 26 and under. The most central is the *Jugendherberge München* (☎ 13 11 56), north-west of the city centre at Wendl-Dietrich-Strasse 20 (U1: Rotkreuzplatz). It's one of the largest in Germany and is relatively loud and busy. Theft can be a problem but it's a great place to meet people. Beds cost from DM22.50.

Still decently close, and a better deal, is the more modern *Jugendgästehaus München* (☎ 7 23 65 50/60), south-west of the city centre in the suburb of Thalkirchen, at Miesingstrasse 4. Take the U3 to Thalkirchen, and then follow the signs. Per-person costs are DM24.50 in dorms, DM26.50 in triples and quads, DM28.50 in doubles, and DM32.50 in singles. Both hostels have a 1 am curfew.

Jugendherberge Burg Schwaneck (☎ 7 93 06 43) at Burgweg 4-6 is in the southern suburbs, 10 minutes' walk from the Pullach station on S-Bahn No 7. Dorm beds cost from DM18.50 (there are singles/doubles from DM21.50/24.50) and it's in a great old castle. Unfortunately for evening revellers, making the 11.30 pm curfew means catching a train from the centre at around 10.30 pm. Meals are available.

Munich's summer budget favourite is the *Jungendlager am Kapuziner Hölzl* (☎ 1 41 43 00) on In den Kirschen, near the Botanical Garden north of Schloss Nymphenburg. Nicknamed 'the Tent', it's only open from late June to early September, and there's an under-24 age limit that's rarely enforced. Take the U1 to Rotkreuzplatz and change to tram No 12 for the Botanischer Garten. It costs DM7 for a mattress, blanket, cooking facilities and some hot tea in the morning. More than 20,000 people take the Tent experience each summer.

Hotels Prices in Munich are higher than in most other parts of Germany. Accommodation services (see Information) can help, but even if you insist on the lowest price range, they won't find you anything cheaper than DM50 for a single or DM80 for a double.

The handiest budget hotel, the *CVJM Jugendgästehaus* (☎ 5 52 14 10) at Landwehrstrasse 13, is near the Hauptbahnhof. There are some dorm beds at DM32 and up and singles/doubles start at DM41/70. Prices are 15% higher for those aged over 27. Women aged under 26 can try the *Jugendhotel Marienherberge* (☎ 55 58 05) at Goethestrasse 9, with beds starting at DM25 and featuring singles/doubles for only DM35/60. *Haus International* (☎ 12 00 60) at Elisabethstrasse 87 has more than 500 beds in all and prices range from DM52 to more than DM80 for singles, DM98 to DM132 for doubles; dorm beds are about DM40 each.

There are plenty of fairly cheap, if seedy, options near the station. The best one is *Hotel Gebhardt* (☎ 53 94 46) at Goethestrasse 38, with bathless singles/doubles starting at DM60/85 (DM85/110 with bath). For a bed without breakfast or bath, head for *Pension Schiller* (☎ 59 24 35) at Schillerstrasse 11. Acceptable rooms start at DM45/65. The cramped *Marie-Luise* (☎ 55 42 30) upstairs at Landwehrstrasse 35 offers rooms from DM40/78. Phone for vacancies at the 11 am check-out time.

An ideal compromise of location, price and cleanliness is *Pension Haydn* (☎ 53 11 19) at Haydnstrasse 9. It's near the Goetheplatz U-Bahn station and within walking distance of the Hauptbahnhof (head south down Goethestrasse). Bathless rooms start at DM50/80. If they're full, head around Kaiser-Ludwig-Platz to *Pension Schubert* (☎ 53 50 87) upstairs at Schubertstrasse 1. Bathless rooms are DM50/85, while a fully equipped double isn't bad for DM95.

Munich's best location for the money is *Hotel-Pension am Markt* (☎ 22 50 14) at Heiliggeiststrasse 6, just off the Viktualienmarkt. Rooms start at DM56/98.

Clean, comfortable, central and reasonably spacious rooms can be found at *Hotel Blauer Bock* (☎ 23 17 80), Sebastiansplatz 9. Rooms with private shower and toilet start at DM95/140, or DM70/100 with communal facilities. Breakfast buffet is included and garage parking is available. Of a similar standard and price is *Hotel Arosa* (☎ 26 70 87), Hotterstrasse 2.

The best mid-price deal is the *Hotel Petri* (☎ 58 10 99), Aindorferstrasse 82. Rooms have distinctive old wooden furniture and a TV, plus there is a garden and a small indoor swimming pool, free for guests. Rooms with private shower and WC start at DM105/160.

Long-Term Rentals Lengthy stays are a bit uncommon in the centre of the city, but are more popular in the smaller Bavarian resort towns outside Munich. Check with the tourist office about stays of more than six days, and expect to pay DM300 per week or more.

Places to Eat

Eating cheaply in Munich is much like anywhere else in Germany. Go where the locals go – mostly to the less touristy beer halls and restaurants, or one of the many markets. At *Viktualienmarkt*, just south of Marienplatz, you can assemble a feast of breads and cheeses and fruit to take to Englischer Garten for DM10 or less per person. Make sure you figure out the price before buying, and don't be afraid to move on to another stall.

Student-card holders can fill up for less than DM4 at a university *mensa*, such as the busy site at Leopoldstrasse 13. Cheap eating is also available in various department stores in the centre. There's also a branch of the seafood chain *Nordsee* at Viktualienmarkt. A little more expensive but a change of scene is the restaurant and bar *Levantes* on Schellingstrasse near Barer Strasse. Cheap courses are available at the *CVJM Jugendrestaurant* in the hotel at Landwehrstrasse 13 until 11 pm (closed Sunday and Monday).

The beer halls like the *Hofbräuhaus* at Am Platzl are not particularly appetising or cheap for eating, unless you're just munching on a pretzel or a few sausages. Instead, head to one of the local Bavarian beer restaurants, where the company is just as lively, the beer just as cold, and the food generally much better in taste and quantity. On the Viktualienmarkt, find *Löwenbräu Stadt Kempten* at No 4 (closed Sunday). There, you'll get a half-litre of Löwenbräu for DM4.60 and food for DM10 to DM20.

The place to try for sausages, especially if you don't plan to make it to Nuremberg, is the *Nürnberger Bratwurst Glöckl am Dom* at Frauenplatz 9, in the shadow of the Frauenkirche. Here, the small Nuremberg sausages are served by the thousands day and night. Expect to pay about DM20 for eight sausages, sauerkraut and a couple of beers. It's closed on Sunday and holidays.

For a special picnic that's lots more expensive, call at the legendary *Alois Dallmayr* at Dienerstrasse 14, one of the world's great delicatessens. Try a little bit (100 grams should suffice) of anything from its huge international selection. The upstairs restaurant (☎ 21 35 100) is expensive, but if you can afford it, you can expect the best. Daily specials are DM12 to DM35 and there is an impressive cold buffet. Reservations are advised, especially at lunchtime.

Vegetarianism is catching on in this cosmopolitan, red-meat city. For a vegetable splurge, try *Art + Tart Vitamin-Buffet* at Herzog-Wilhelm-Strasse 25. There are lots of salads and creative concoctions that sell for less than DM3 per 100 grams. It's open Monday to Saturday to 10 pm.

Italian food is also a good deal in Munich. There are several *Bella Italia* restaurants in the city offering pizza or pasta dishes for less than DM10. *Bella Roma* in the Asam-Hof at Sendlinger Strasse 24-32 is reasonable while offering a good atmosphere.

Cafés With the exception of the ideally situated *Café am Dom*, upstairs at Marienplatz 1, stay away from the tourist-trap cafés around the Rathaus. A stand-up café and bakery with a good range of inexpensive meals (and some cheap and filling hot snacks) is *Höflinger* at the corner of Sendlinger-Tor-Platz and Sonnenstrasse. Another popular café is in the Stadtmuseum. A women-only teahouse, *Frauen Teestube*, is at Dreimühlenstrasse 1 on the corner of Isartalstrasse south of the city centre (closed Wednesday and Saturday).

Entertainment

Munich is one of the cultural capitals of Germany. Opportunities revolve around the *Nationaltheater* on Max-Joseph-Platz. It's the home of the Bavarian State Opera and the site of many cultural events (particularly during the opera festival in July). You can book (at least two weeks ahead) at Max-

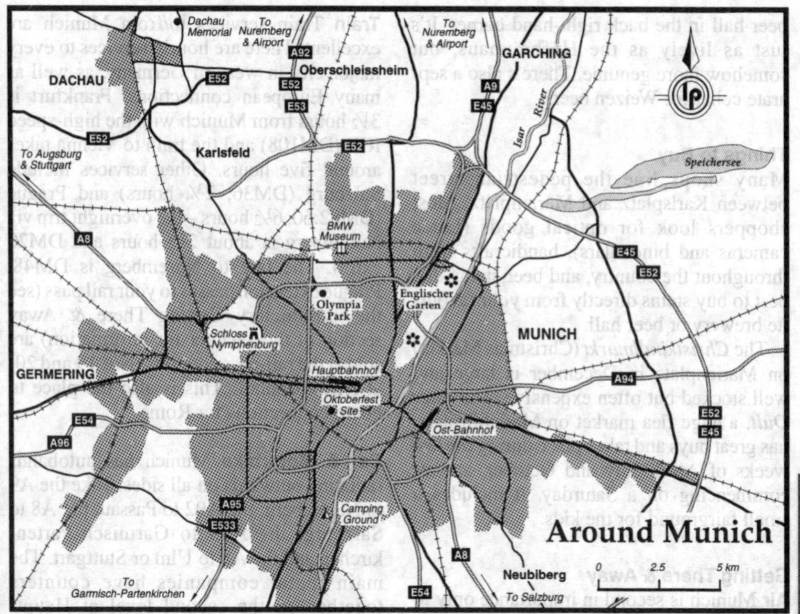

imilianstrasse from 11 to 6 pm Monday to Friday (1 pm Saturday) or dial ☎ 22 13 16.

Munich is also a hot scene for jazz, and the place to go is *Jazzclub Unterfahrt* (☎ 4 48 27 94) at Kirchenstrasse 96, near the Ostbahnhof station. It has live music from 9 pm (except Monday), and jam sessions open to everyone on Sunday nights.

The best two English-language cinemas are the *Europa-Kino* at Schwanthalerstrasse 2-6, and the cinema at Nymphenburger Strasse 31.

For other events and locations, pick up the *Monatsprogramm* for DM2.50 at any tourist office.

Beer Halls Beer drinking is the main form of entertainment in this city. Germans drink an average of 250 litres of beer each per year, while Munich residents average 350. Several breweries run their own beer halls around the city. The *Hofbräuhaus*, Am Platzl 9, is rightly the most famous and the most filled with tourists. It can really be good fun and a great chance to meet travellers and locals. Try at least one large, frothy, litre-mug (called a *Mass)* of beer before heading off to another beer hall. This is the hall where Hitler publicly announced his programme at a meeting on 20 February 1920.

Just across the plaza, check *Platzl Bühne* at Am Platzl 1. It features a Bavarian show every night at 8 pm except Sunday, and it's about the best value in the city for this type of entertainment.

There are two beer halls along Neuhauserstrasse, and both are much more subdued than the Hofbräuhaus. *Augustinerbräu* at No 16 is quiet and dark, but with decent food, while *Zum Pschorrbräu* at No 11 has loud entertainment, a wine cellar and probably the best food of the beer-hall scene.

Munich's blue-collar beer hall is the *Mathäser Bierstadt* at Bayerstrasse 5. This is the Löwenbräu brewery's beer hall and it's a favourite with locals. Head upstairs to the beer hall in the back right-hand corner. It's just as lively as the Hofbräuhaus, but somehow more genuine. There's also a separate cellar for Weizen beer.

Things to Buy

Many shops line the pedestrian street between Karlsplatz and Marienplatz. Most shoppers look for optical goods (Leica cameras and binoculars), handicrafts from throughout the country, and beer steins. It's best to buy steins directly from your favourite brewery or beer hall.

The *Christkindlmarkt* (Christmas Market) on Marienplatz in December is large and well stocked but often expensive. The *Auer Dult*, a huge flea market on Mariahilfplatz, has great buys and takes place during the last weeks of April, July and October, always commencing on a Saturday. It includes a small fairground for the kids.

Getting There & Away

Air Munich is second in importance only to Frankfurt for international and national connections. Flights will take you to all major destinations including London, Paris, Rome, Athens, New York and Sydney. Main German cities are serviced by at least half a dozen flights daily. The main carrier is Lufthansa (☎ 54 55 99), Lenbachplatz 1. For general flight information, the number is ☎ 97 52 13 13.

Bus Munich is linked to the Romantic Road (see the following Romantic Road section) by the Europabus Munich-Frankfurt service (daily from mid-March to late October). Eurail and Germanrail passes are valid for the bus, as is a Frankfurt-Munich train ticket; Inter-Rail gets a 50% discount. Enquire at Deutsche Touring GmbH (☎ 59 18 24) near platform 26 of the Hauptbahnhof. This is also the agent for Eurolines' twice-weekly bus services to Prague (DM69/123 one way/return), which take seven hours. For fare comparisons see the introductory Getting There & Away section at the beginning of this chapter.

Train Train services to/from Munich are excellent. There are hourly services to every major city in western Germany, as well as many European connections. Frankfurt is 3½ hours from Munich with the high-speed ICE (DM108) and the train to Vienna takes around five hours. Other services include Salzburg (DM36; 2¾ hours) and Prague (DM82.60, 6½ hours – the overnight trip via Nuremberg is about 2½ hours and DM20 extra). The fare to Nuremberg is DM48. Prague extension passes to your rail pass (see the introductory Getting There & Away section of this chapter for information) are sold at the rail-pass counters (Nos 19 and 20) at Hauptbahnhof. This is also the place to board connections for Rome.

Car & Motorbike Munich has autobahns radiating outwards on all sides. Take the A9 to Nuremberg, the A92 to Passau, the A8 to Salzburg, the A95 to Garmisch-Partenkirchen and the A8 to Ulm or Stuttgart. The main rental companies have counters together on the second level at Hauptbahnhof. The Mitfahrzentrale MC Share (☎ 1 94 40) is at Lämmerstrasse 4 off Hirtenstrasse to the north of the main train station and open daily to 8 pm. All up, you will pay DM52 to reach Berlin, DM40 to Frankfurt and DM64 to Hamburg. Comparable in price is the Citynetz Mitfahr-Service (☎ 1 94 44) at Amalienstrasse 87.

Getting Around

Walking is pleasant, even in the summer throngs, and the pedestrian sector leading from the main station to Marienplatz is useful (as are the subways under the main thoroughfares).

To/From the Airport Munich's new Flughafen Franz Josef Strauss is connected by S-Bahn to the Hauptbahnhof (the S8, DM12 with a single ticket). The service takes 40 minutes and runs almost around the clock. The airport bus leaves from the Kieferngarten station (U6) once or twice every hour until 11.40 pm (DM9, 25 or 30 minutes). Forget taxis (at least DM80!).

Bus & Train Getting around is easy on the excellent public transport network. Tickets are valid on the S-Bahn, U-Bahn, trams and buses and must be validated before use. Short rides cost DM1.60 and trips (with change) in the city inner zone *(Innenraum)* cost DM3.20 (up to DM16 for the five zones, though children pay no more than DM2.80 per trip). It's cheaper to buy a series of 12 tickets *(Streifenkarte)* for DM15. Validate at least two strips on the adult ticket for journeys over four stops. A day pass for the inner zone costs DM10 and covers most places of interest (except Dachau). The *Gesamttarifgebiet* day pass for DM20 covers the whole of Munich. The same day pass can be used by up to two adults and three children aged under 18, subject to time limits. For longer stays, consider the transferable monthly season ticket for DM49.

The U-Bahn ends around 12.30 am on weekdays and 1.30 am on weekends, but there are some later buses. Rail passes are valid on S-Bahn trains. Bicycles are forbidden from Monday to Friday during the morning and evening peak.

Car & Motorbike It's not worth driving in the city centre – many streets are pedestrian only. The tourist office map shows city parking places. Car rental is available from all main companies and their offices are together upstairs at Hauptbahnhof. Allround Autovermietung (☎ 7 23 23 43) at Boschetsriederstrasse 12 rents out some budget models and has motorbikes from DM869 per week (650cc) with insurance, but there is a DM2500 deposit on cash payments. The first 250 km is free.

Taxi Taxis are expensive (more than DM3 flagfall, plus DM2 per km) and not much more convenient than public transport. For a radio-dispatched taxi dial ☎ 2 16 10, or for local ranks check 'Taxi Ruf' listings in the Yellow Pages directory.

Bicycle The pedal is popular and you can rent from the Radius Radverleih depot on the north side of Hauptbahnhof or the bunker (closed Monday) just inside the main gate to Englischer Garten (DM10 for two hours, DM25 per day, DM50 deposit). To buy second-hand, or for repairs, try the small Mandy's Radklinik at Dreimühlenstrasse 20, open from noon to 6.30 pm weekdays and 9 am to 1 pm Saturday (follow Thalkirchner Strasse from Sendlinger Tor, turn south-west after the cemetery, then right at the cloister along Isartalstrasse, bearing right at the fork).

AUGSBURG

Augsburg was first a Roman centre and has an ambience like few places in Germany. Medium-sized by German standards, its vitality is matched only by bigger cities, and is reinforced by foreign influences and surges of immigration. For some it will be a day trip from Munich, for others an ideal base or a gate to the Romantic Road. Its tourist offices are at Bahnhofstrasse 7 (☎ 0821-50 20 70), open to 6 pm Monday to Friday, and at Rathausplatz, which is open on Saturday and Sunday until 1 pm. The telephone code is 0821.

Things to See

The tourist offices offer an excellent walking guide with three marked routes demanding up to three hours (to cover 2000 years of history!). You will quickly notice the onion-shaped towers, which spread through southern Germany after the pattern of the modest 16th-century **St Maria Stern Kloster** in Elias-Holl-Platz. More impressive in scale are those on the **Rathaus** (open to 6 pm daily), the adjacent **Perlachturm** and the soaring tower of **St Ulrich und Afra Basilika** (on Ulrichsplatz near the south edge of the old town), whose finely renovated interiors are dominated by the Hochaltar (Hans Degler, 1604). The **Dom Mariae Heimsuchung** on Hoher Weg north of Rathausplatz is more conventionally styled, although one of Martin Luther's more unconventional anti-papal documents was posted here after he was run out of town in 1518. He escaped from the tiny **Galluskirchlein** through one of the nearby north gates; strangely, this little chapel was to become Russian Orthodox. From an early stage, though, Augsburg was to enjoy religious freedom.

In this ecumenical spirit is the **Fuggerei**, an early type of old folks' home created by the merchant financier Jakob Fugger for good Catholics who had fallen on hard times – its work, and its **museum** (DM1) on Jakobsplatz, continue today. From later ages is the family home of the dramatist Bertolt Brecht on the stream at Am Rain 7, now given over as the **Bert-Brecht-Gedänkstätte** to a Brecht museum and the work of young artists (DM2.50, closed Monday and from 1 to 2 pm). The **Maximilianmuseum** at Philippine-Welser-Strasse 24 (DM4; closed Monday) contains Augsburg's art treasures.

Places to Stay & Eat

Campers can turn to *Campingplatz Augusta* (☎ 70 75 75) near the airport, half a km from the Augsburg Ost autobahn interchange north-east of the city (there are a few family rooms). Junior hostellers can seek beds at *Jugendherberge Augsburg* (☎ 3 39 09) at Beim Pfaffenkeller 3 inside the old town, for DM16.50.

Good budget rooms are available for DM50 or less just outside the city centre, and the tourist offices have a complete free guide. Perhaps the best value is at the combined *Hotel von den Rappen* (☎ 41 20 66) and *Pension Anita* at Äussere Uferstrasse 3, where modern bathless singles go for DM40 and singles/doubles with shower cost from DM60/80.

There is a vast range of food and drink. The old *Gaststätte am Roten Tor* (☎ 15 63 67), just inside the southern city gate, is congenial for mid-priced meals and wines or a DM50 splurge – it's best to book, and the restaurant is closed Monday. The city's Greek element comes in at the quiet and inexpensive pub eatery *Taverne Thessaloniki* on the corner of Am Fischertor and Georgenstrasse, where a little surprise arrives with your ale. More lively is the café and bar *Enchilada* behind the cathedral on Frauentorstrasse, while the coffee, cake and ice cream are very tempting at the choice *Café Dichtl*, on the corner of Bahnhofstrasse and Schrannenstrasse (closed Sunday in summer).

Getting There & Away

Augsburg is just off the autobahns north-west of Munich. Local trains from Munich (DM15.20, rail passes accepted) are frequent and fast trains take only 30 minutes at most times of day. There are also main-line links to Stuttgart and Nuremberg. There are a dozen or more train links to/from Füssen (DM25, direct or via Buchloe) daily.

ROMANTIC ROAD

The Romantic Road (Romantische Strasse) is a marketing concept linking a series of picturesque villages. Nevertheless, this is one occasion where it is well worth falling for the sales pitch and taking time to explore the area. The trip is one of the most popular in Germany. It's just a pity that the very thing that attracts everyone in the first place (peaceful countryside, unspoiled medieval village centres) is undermined by the presence of so many visitors. Claustrophobic summer weekends are best avoided.

Orientation & Information

The Romantic Road runs north-south through western Bavaria, from Würzburg to Füssen near the Austrian border, passing through Rothenburg ob der Tauber, Dinkelsbühl and Augsburg. It is possible to cover the route by car, train connections or local buses, but most people take the Europabus. Reservations are only necessary on peak-season weekends or for bicycle passage (DM10; three days' notice), but are wise any time in the tourist season. For information and reservations, contact Deutsche Touring GmbH (☎ 069-23 07 35), Mannheimer Strasse 4, Frankfurt, or its main office (☎ 7 90 32 56; fax 70 47 14) at Am Römerhof 17, 60486 Frankfurt/Main.

The best places for information about the Romantic Road are the tourist offices in Rothenburg (☎ 09861-4 04 92) at Markt 1, and in Dinkelsbühl (☎ 09581-9 02 40) at Marktplatz 1. In Füssen, the Kurverwaltung (☎ 08362-70 77) is at Augsburger-Tor-Platz (closed for lunch, Saturday afternoon and Sunday) with accommodation and other information, and there is an information office at Hohenschwangau castle.

Things to See

Rothenburg ob der Tauber Rothenburg is the main tourist attraction along the route. Granted the status of a 'free imperial city' in 1274, it's packed with cobbled streets and picturesque old houses and enclosed by towered walls, all of which are worth exploring. Crowded in summer, its museums open for short afternoon hours from November to March.

The **Rathaus** is on Markt, commenced in Gothic style in the 14th century but completed in Renaissance style. From the tower (DM1; open Saturday and Sunday afternoon only in winter) is a majestic view of the town, its walls and the Tauber River valley. According to legend, the town was saved during the Thirty Years' War when the mayor won a challenge by the Imperial general Tilly and downed more than three litres of wine at a gulp. The **Meistertrunk** scene is re-enacted by the clock figures on the tourist office building (eight times daily in summer), or in costumed ceremonies in the Rathaus hall during the Whitsun celebrations (mid to late May).

The fascinating and extensive **Mittelalterliches Kriminalmuseum** at Burggasse 3 south of Markt details crimes and displays brutal instruments of punishment from medieval times (DM5, students DM4). The **Puppen und Spielzeugmuseum** of dolls and toys at Hofbronnengasse 13, is the largest private collection in Germany (DM5, students DM3.50). The **Reichsstadt Museum** in the former convent (DM3) features the superb Rothenburger Passion in 12 panels (Martinus Schwarz, 1494) and the Judaika room, with a collection of gravestones with Hebrew inscriptions.

Dinkelsbühl This is another walled town of cobbled streets. South of Rothenburg, Dinklesbühl celebrates the **Kinderzeche** ('children's festival') in mid-July, commemorating a legend from the Thirty Years' War that the children of the town successfully begged the invading Swedish troops to leave Dinkelsbühl unharmed. The festivities include a pageant, re-enactments, lots of music and other entertainment. It is a pleasant walk of about an hour around the town's **walls** and its almost 30 towers.

Nördlingen The town of Nördlingen is enclosed by a circle of original 14th-century walls and you can climb the tower of the **St Georg Kirche** for a bird's-eye view. The town is also within the basin of the Ries, a huge crater created by a meteor more than 15 million years ago. It's one of the largest in existence (25 km in diameter) and was used by US astronauts to train for the exploration of the moon. The **Rieskrater Museum** gives details.

Füssen Füssen has a monastery, castle and splendid baroque architecture, but it is primarily visited for the two castles in nearby Schwangau associated with King Ludwig II. These castles provide a fascinating glimpse into the king's state of mind. Both are beautifully situated, overlooking mountains and lakes, and can only be visited by guided tour (35 minutes). Go early to avoid the crowds.

Hohenschwangau is where Ludwig lived as a child. More interesting is his own creation, **Neuschwanstein**, which was unfortunately unfinished at the time of his death in 1886. Even so, there is plenty of evidence of his twin obsessions: swans and Wagnerian operas. The fantastic pastiche of architectural styles inspired Walt Disney's Fantasyland castle.

From Füssen, take the bus from the train station (DM4.40 return), share a taxi (DM13, up to four people) or walk five km. Both castles are open daily from 8.30 am to 5.30 pm (from 10 am to 4 pm between 1 November and 31 March) and entry costs DM9 (students DM6) for each. There's a really great view of Neuschwanstein from the

Marienbrücke, south of the castle up Pöllat Gorge. From here you can hike up Tegelberg for even better panoramas.

Places to Stay

Tourist offices in most towns are very efficient at finding accommodation in almost any price range, although private rooms are rarely available for just a single night's stay. All the youth hostels listed below only accept people aged under 27.

Rothenburg ob der Tauber Camping is a km or two north of the town walls at Detwang, west of the road on the river. There are signs to *Camping Tauber-Idyll* (☎ 09861-31 77) and the bigger *Tauber-Romantik* (☎ 61 91). Both are open from March to September.

Rothenburg has two excellent youth hostels in historical buildings: *Rossmühle* (☎ 45 10) at Mühlacker 1, and the renovated *Spitalhof* (☎ 78 89) nearby. Beds start at DM18.50.

The tourist office books rooms for DM2 each, but not by phone and, at some places, for two nights minimum. At *Pension Hofmann* (☎ 33 71) at Stollengasse 29, singles/doubles with shower start at DM35/75. *Pension Raidel* (☎ 31 15), Wenggasse 3, has basic rooms in the old town for DM35/58 (doubles with shower from DM68). *Gasthof Butz* (☎ 22 01) at Kapellenplatz 4 has rooms with shower from DM44/85.

Dinkelsbühl Check the *youth hostel* (☎ 09851-95 09) at Koppengasse 10 for beds at DM16. *Pension Lutz* (☎ 94 54), Schäfergässlein 4, has a cheerful owner, excellent breakfasts, and singles/doubles from DM32 per person. The front façade of the *Deutsches Haus* (☎ 60 59), Weinmarkt 3, is one of the town's attractions; accordingly the singles/doubles inside start at DM135/210.

Nördlingen The *youth hostel* (☎ 09081-8 41 09) is at Kaiserwiese 1 and costs DM14.50. A hotel by the church with singles/doubles for DM30/60 is *Walfisch* (☎ 31 07), Hallgasse 15. The nearby *Zum Goldenen Lamm* (☎ 2 87 49) at Schäfflesmarkt 3 has doubles only for DM85 with bathroom.

Füssen The *youth hostel* (☎ 08362-77 54), Mariahilferstrasse 5, is by the train tracks, 10 minutes west of the station. Dorm beds cost DM17.50, curfew is at 10 pm and the hostel is closed from mid-November to Christmas. The pension *Haus Kössler* (☎ 73 04), Kemptener Strasse 42, has beds from DM40 to DM50 per person. The Kurverwaltung (see Orientation & Information earlier) has lists of private rooms (from DM25 per person) and vacant houses and apartments (from DM40 per person, from two to seven people), some of which have balconies and terraces with pleasant views of surrounding peaks. The lists, which are posted at the front door, give available dates (usually from the middle of May) and details for each listing, some of which specify minimum stays of two or three nights or more. In Füssen you will pay a resort tax of DM2.60 (per person, per night) on accommodation.

Places to Eat

It pays to picnic or eat takeaway, as most restaurants cater to the hordes of tourists.

Rothenburg ob der Tauber Large plates of pasta and pizza (DM8 to DM12) are served at *Pizzeria Roma*, Galgengasse 19, open daily to midnight. Virtually opposite is *Gasthof zum Ochsen* at No 26; fill up on standard German fare for DM7.50 to DM17 (closed Thursday). *Bräustüble*, Alter Stadtgraben 2, has daily specials comprising soup, main dish and salad for DM13.50 or DM15.50.

Füssen Grab fast food at *Pic Nic*, Bahnhofstrasse 2. *Pizzeria La Perla*, Drehengasse 44 in the pedestrian zone, has pizza and pasta from DM8 and salads from DM4 and is popular with families (closed from 2 to 6 pm and on Wednesday). *Gasthaus Torschänke*, Augsburger-Tor-Platz 2, is not bad for local food (it is closed Wednesday evening and Thursday).

Getting There & Away

Though Frankfurt is the most popular starting point for the Romantic Road, Munich is a better choice if you decide to take the bus (the stop is directly north of Hauptbahnhof). The buses heading south are often much more crowded than the ones heading north, making photography and sightseeing less comfortable. To start at the southern end, take the hourly train link from Munich (DM31) or Augsburg (DM25) to Füssen (2½ hours, some services change at Buchloe). Rail passes are valid on these lines. Rothenburg is linked by train to Würzburg and Munich via Steinach (you might need to change in Würzburg or Treuchtlingen), and Nördlingen to Augsburg (via Donauwörth).

Buses make the short trip between Steinach and Rothenburg station, and from Füssen train station to Garmisch-Partenkirchen and back (Monday to Friday twice each morning and afternoon, Saturday and Sunday at 8.05 am and 5.15 pm only). The bus also runs to Schloss Linderhof. The OVF Nuremberg-Rothenburg buses (No 8805) leave Nuremberg station daily at 8.45 am and return from Rothenburg at 4.33 pm. Berlinien Bus (☎ 030-3 30 00 10) has direct daily coaches to Rothenburg from Berlin (6½ hours for DM99 one way, DM115 return).

Getting Around

The Europabus service leaves daily in each direction between Frankfurt and Munich from mid-March to late October (one way DM105), and between Würzburg and Füssen (from mid-May to early October, DM85). Each route takes 11 hours and includes short stops in some towns, but it's silly to do the whole thing in one go, particularly as there is no charge for breaking the journey and resuming the next day. Eurail and Germanrail passes are valid and Inter-Rail gets 50% discount, Europass 30%, students under 27 10%, passengers over 60 50% (on one-way fares, with identification). Tickets are available for short segments of the trip.

Drivers just need to follow the special 'Romantische Strasse' signs. The most popular car or motorbike stretches are between Bad Mergentheim and Rothenburg, and Landsberg and Füssen.

The distances between towns make walking prohibitive, except for shorter stretches and hikes into the countryside. Cycling, however, is perfectly viable; machines can be rented from the train station in Rothenburg. Hitching is not very popular and is fairly frustrating compared to the rest of the country.

WÜRZBURG

The easy-paced and walkable city of Würzburg, on the River Main east of Frankfurt, is not very famous outside Germany. It should be – it is a centre of beautiful architecture and art, pleasantly sited and in an area of popular wines. It is worth two or three days just to get acquainted with the chief attractions.

Information

There are tourist offices outside the main train station on Röntgenring (☎ 0931-3 74 36), in Haus zum Falken on Markt in the city centre, and at the congress centre on Pleichtorstrasse. The main station office is open until 8 pm Monday to Saturday, but all are closed on Sunday.

The telephone code is 0931.

Things to See

Spread along Balthasar-Neumann-Promenade, the magnificence of the **Residenz**, a baroque masterpiece by Neumann, took a generation to build. The palace is on the UNESCO cultural heritage list, and is well worth the DM5 admission (students DM3). The open **Hofgarten** and **Rosenbach Park** behind are favourite spots. The **Dom St Kilian** interiors and the adjacent **Neumünster** in the old town continue the baroque themes of the Residenz.

The fortress **Marienberg**, across the river on the hill, is reached by crossing the 15th-century stone **Alte Mainbrücke** from the city. The fortress encloses the **Fürstenbau Museum** (costing DM3 and featuring the episcopal apartments) and the regional

GERMANY

Mainfränkisches Museum (DM3). It takes 15 or 20 minutes to make the climb from Zeller Strasse (any of three marked pathways), and perhaps an hour to stroll in and around the **well** and the **keep**. The museums (combined card DM5) are closed on Monday.

More practical is Neumann's fortified **Alter Kranen**, which serviced a dock on the river bank south of Friedensbrücke. Today it is the **Haus des Frankenweins**, where you can wander in and inspect, taste and buy Franconia's finest wines for DM2 or less by the glass and DM10 by the bottle. Medal wines start about DM20 and go well with the menu (from DM14) at the on-site restaurant. You can view the vines on the **Veitshöchheim cruises**, which depart hourly from Alter Kranen from 10 am in summer (about 40 minutes for DM8 one way, DM12 return), and you can take in the bishops' country palace **Schloss Veitshöchheim** (DM3; closed Monday and from October to March).

Würzburg's most important son is Wilhelm Conrad Röntgen, discoverer of the X-ray. The **Röntgen Gedächtnisstätte** at Röntgenring 8 is a tribute to his work and is open, free, from Monday to Friday.

Places to Stay & Eat

The only nearby camping ground is *Kanu-Club* (☎ 7 25 36) on the western bank of the River Main at Mergentheimer Strasse 13b (take tram No 5 from the train station). The hostel *Jugendgästehaus Würzburg* (☎ 4 25 90), on Burkarder Strasse below the fortress, charges DM25 for beds (juniors only, tram No 3 or 5 from the station).

You can book rooms in advance through the tourist office on ☎ 3 73 71. The budget pick for rooms with shower is *Hotel Dortmunder Hof* (☎ 5 61 63) at Innerer Graben 22 (singles/doubles from DM45/90). *Hotel am Markt* (☎ 5 25 51) at Markt 30 asks DM60/115 and is in the heart of the old town. *Hotel Meesenburg* (☎ 5 33 04) at Pleichtorstrasse 8 offers full facilities from DM85/120, and *Hotel Barbarossa* (☎ 5 59 53) at Theaterstrasse 2 offers the same for DM85/130 (both are about DM10 cheaper with shared toilet).

The *Burggaststätte* inside the fortress courtyard has DM11 daily specials, and the popular *Caféhaus Brückenbäck* at the fortress end of the old bridge starts at similar prices – both enjoy top locations. The pizza and pasta of the more relaxed *Bella Napoli da Luigi* at Neubaustrasse 16 range from DM10 to DM13.

Getting There & Away

Würzburg lies 80 minutes by train from Frankfurt and one hour from Nuremberg, and Frankfurt-Nuremberg and Hanover-Munich trains stop here several times daily. It is also handily placed if you want to join Europabus Romantic Road tours (2½ hours on the bus from Rothenburg or less than one hour by train via Steinach). The main bus station is next to the train station off Röntgenring. Berlinien Bus (☎ 030-3 30 00 10) runs daily from Berlin (5½ hours for DM90 one way, DM105 return).

BAMBERG

Tucked off the main routes in northern Bavaria, Bamberg is practically a byword for magnificence, an unwalled, untouched monument to the Holy Roman Emperor Heinrich II (who conceived it), to its prince-bishops and clergy and to its patriciate and townsfolk. Walk, behold, drink the unique beers, but experience Bamberg for at least a day. It is recognised as perhaps the most beautiful city in Germany, and one of the finest in Europe.

The tourist office (☎ 0951-87 11 54) is at Geyerswörthstrasse 3 on the island in the River Regnitz (closed Sunday). The telephone code is 0951.

Things to See

Bamberg's appeal rests in its sheer number of fine buildings, their jumble of styles and the ambience this helps create. Most attractions are spread either side of the River Regnitz, but the colourful **Altes Rathaus** is actually on it, built on twin bridges. The princely and ecclesiastical district is centred on Domplatz, where the Romanesque and Gothic **cathedral**, housing the statue of the chivalric king-knight, the *Bamberger Reiter*, is the biggest attraction. The **Diözesan Museum** in the cloister (DM2; closed Monday) represents one aspect of the city's past; the adjacent courtyard, the **Alte Hofhaltung** (partly Renaissance in style) contains the secular **Historisches Museum** (DM2, students free; closed Monday). The episcopal **Neue Residenz**, not as large as Würzburg's, is stately and superb within (DM3, students DM2; closed Monday) and the **Rosengarten** behind offers one of the city's fine views. Another view is from the tower of the castle **Altenburg** a few km away (take bus No 10 from Promenadestrasse and finish with a walk to the hilltop). There you can wander about freely during the day.

For refreshment and a very different taste, try the dark red, smoked *Schlenkerla Rauchbier*, preferably at the timbered and atmospheric 17th-century inn **Wirtshaus zum Schlenkerla** at Dominikanerstrasse 6 (DM3 for half a litre). The half-timbered houses around set the scene perfectly for this wonderful pub.

Above Domplatz is the former Benedictine monastery of St Michael at the top of Michaelsberg. The **Kirche St Michael** is a must-see for its baroque art and the herbal compendium painted on its ceiling. The garden terraces offer yet another great view as the city's splendours spread out agreeably before the eye. There is also the **Fränkisches Brauereimuseum** (open Thursday to Sunday from April to October; DM3), which shows how the monks brewed their robust *Benediktiner Dunkel* beer. This can be sampled (DM2.90 for half a litre) at Restaurant Michaelsberg next door (see Places to Stay & Eat).

Places to Stay & Eat

Camping options are limited to *Campingplatz Insel* (☎ 5 63 20), at Bug on the west bank of the Regnitz a few km south of the city, but the site is large and pleasant (DM10 per tent, DM6 per adult). The hostel *Jugendherberge Wolfsschlucht* (☎ 5 60 02) at Oberer Leinritt 70 (DM16.50, juniors only) is on the same bank but closer to town; turn south off Münchener Ring towards the clinic complex, then east at Bamberger Strasse, then north along the river.

Café-Gästehaus Graupner (☎ 98 04 00), Lange Strasse 5, has singles/doubles with shower from DM60/90, without DM50/80. *Hotel Alt-Bamberg* (☎ 2 52 66), in a quiet location at Habergasse 11, is great value at DM68/115 with all facilities. *Hotel Garni Hospiz* (☎ 20 00 11) at Promenadestrasse 3 is highly recommended at DM60/88 with all facilities (budget singles are only DM45) and *Gasthof Fässla* (☎ 2 65 16) at Obere Königsstrasse 21 is fine at DM58/98 and near the train station.

For breakfast, sandwiches or coffee and cake, try *Der Beck am Hauptwacheck* at the corner of Hauptwachstrasse and Promenade. Frankish food is on offer all over the city, but for atmosphere go straight to *Wirtshaus zum Schlenkerla* (see Things to See), where the daily staples start from DM11, or *Restaurant Michaelsberg*, where dishes are DM13 and up, bread and sausage DM6.50.

Getting There & Away

The most regular train connections to Bamberg are from Nuremberg (half an hour) or Würzburg (1¼ hours), though several through services run daily to Leipzig and there are daily trains from Munich and Berlin. The autobahn connection to Nuremberg is direct, but buses from anywhere else are few.

NUREMBERG

Nuremberg (Nürnberg) is the capital of the Franconia (Franken) region of northern Bavaria. Though the flood of tourists to this historical town never seems to cease, it's still worth the trip. The people of the city completely rebuilt Nuremberg after Allied bombs reduced it to rubble on the night of 2 January 1945. That includes the castle and the three old churches in the Altstadt, which were painstakingly rebuilt using the original stone.

Orientation & Information

The train station is right outside the city walls of the old town; the main artery, the mostly pedestrian Königstrasse, takes you through the old town and its main squares. The tourist office (☎ 0911-2 33 60) is in the station's main hall, open Monday to Saturday from 9 am to 7 pm. The main post office is at Bahnhofplatz 1 by the station. The telephone code for Nuremberg is 0911.

Things to See

The **Germanisches Nationalmuseum** on Kornmarkt (enter from Kartäusergasse), is the most important general museum of German culture. It shows works by German painters and sculptors, an archaeological collection, arms and armour, musical and scientific instruments and toys. More than a million items like these, and more, are on the museum's books. It's open Tuesday to Sunday from 10 am to 5 pm (to 9 pm Wednesday) and entry costs DM5 (students DM2).

The scenic **Altstadt** (old town) is easily covered on foot. The **Handwerkerhof**, a recreation of the crafts quarter of old Nuremberg, is walled in opposite the main station and opens from March to December. It's about as quaint as they can possibly make it, but the goods are overpriced. On Lorenzer Platz is the **St Lorenzkirche**, noted for the 15th-century tabernacle which climbs a pillar like a vine, all the way up to the vaulted ceiling.

To the north is the bustling **Hauptmarkt**. This is the site of the most famous *Christkindlmarkt* in Germany, lasting from the Friday before Advent to Christmas Eve. The church here is the ornate **Pfarrkirche Unsere Liebe Frau**; the figures around the clock go walkabout at noon. Near the Rathaus is the **St Sebalduskirche**, Nuremberg's oldest church (13th century), with the shrine of St Sebaldus.

It is a hard climb up Burgstrasse to the **Kaiserburg** castle area, but this location offers one of the best views of the city. You can visit the palace complex, chapel, well and tower on a DM3.50 ticket (students DM2.50). The walls spread west to the tunnel-gate of **Tiergärtnertor**, where you can stroll behind the castle into the garden zone.

Near Tiergärtnertor is the **Albrecht-Dürer-Haus**, where Dürer, Germany's Renaissance draughtsman, lived from 1509 to 1528. This house made it through WW II and features a large number of objects and effects from his life (entry DM4). At Karlstrasse 13-15, the **Spielzeugmuseum** (DM5) displays toys throughout the ages.

Much more sobering is a look at the role of Nuremberg during and after WW II. The city was a hotbed of Nazi activity and rallies before 1945. After the war, it was the site of the trials of Nazi war criminals. Nazi rallies were held in the fields at **Luitpoldhain**, where nowadays a tourist board-produced film, *Fascination and Force*, is shown between July and October. Get there by S-Bahn or U-Bahn to Dutzendteich, or tram No 9.

Places to Stay

Campingplatz am Stadion (☎ 81 11 22), Hans-Kalb-Strasse 56, is near the lakes in the Volkspark, south-east of the city centre (the U-Bahn No 1 from the main station takes you to Messezentrum, which is fairly close). It costs DM7 per person, DM10 per tent and DM5 per car, and is open from early in May to the end of September.

The excellent *Jugendgästehaus* (☎ 24 13 52) is in the historical Kaiserstallung next to the castle. Dorm beds including sheets cost DM25.50 (juniors only), and reception is open to 1 am. The cheapest option for those aged over 27 is the *Jugend-Hotel Nürnberg* (☎ 5 21 60 92) at Rathsbergstrasse 300 north of the city (take tram No 3). Dorm beds start at DM21 (DM23 with shower access) and there are singles from DM35 (DM40 with shower) and doubles from DM56 (DM66). The *Jugend + Economy Hotel* (☎ 9 26 20), south-west of the city centre at Gostenhofer Hauptstrasse 47, has games rooms and good facilities. Doubles start at DM117, singles DM69.

The most reasonable pension in the city centre is *Altstadt* (☎ 22 61 02), Hintere

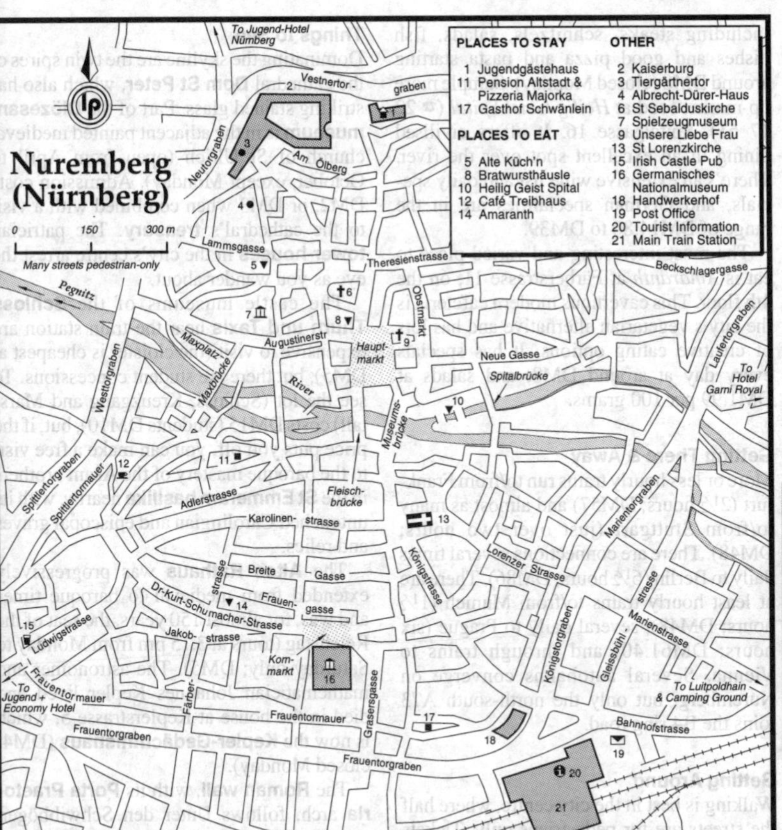

Ledergasse 4, with bathless singles/doubles from DM48/85. A better deal is the *Hotel Garni Royal* (☎ 53 32 09), Theodorstrasse 9, just to the east of the old city. This grand old building has a faux-marble hallway, ample parking round the corner. Spacious rooms start at DM43/78 with shower access (DM56/89 with *en suite* shower, extra beds available). Reception shuts at noon on Sunday and holidays, so call ahead. Near the station is *Gasthof Schwänlein* (☎ 22 51 62), Hintere Sterngasse 11, which has basic singles from DM43 to DM50, doubles from DM60 to DM80.

Places to Eat

Café Treibhaus, Karl-Grillenberger-Strasse, is a popular student bar, verging on the arty – hot, filling baguettes cost DM6.50 (there is usually free info on films and cultural events). The *Irish Castle Pub*, Schlehengasse 31, has pub food and is small and crowded with live music most nights.

Try Nuremberg's sausages at *Bratwursthäusle*, Rathausplatz 1 (closed Sunday). Interesting meat dishes (DM9.50 to DM24.80) can be chomped at *Alte Küch'n*, Albrecht Dürer Strasse 3. *Pizzeria Majorka*, Hintere Ledergasse 2, has a wide menu including steaks, schnitzels, salads, fish dishes and good pizza and pasta starting around DM8 (closed Monday). Sample more up-market food at *Heilig Geist Spital* (☎ 22 17 61), Spitalgasse 16. It offers civilised dining in an excellent spot over the river. There's an extensive wine list and daily specials, and German specialities are in the range of DM14.80 to DM39.

The most interesting and varied place to eat is *Amaranth* at Färberstrasse 11, on the 4th floor. This cavernous modern cafeteria is the city's vegetarian alternative and has lots of creative eating options. It has specials every day at around DM8, and salads at DM1.99 per 100 grams.

Getting There & Away

More or less hourly trains run to/from Frankfurt (2½ hours; DM57) and almost as many to/from Stuttgart (just over two hours; DM48). There are connections several times daily to Berlin (6½ hours; DM86). There are at least hourly trains to/from Munich (1½ hours; DM48), several daily to Prague (six hours; DM61.40) and through trains to Vienna. Several autobahns converge on Nuremberg, but only the north-south A73 joins the B4 ring road.

Getting Around

Walking is best in the city centre, where half the streets are for pedestrians only. Tickets on the efficient city bus, tram and U-Bahn system cost DM3.20 per journey in the central zone and day passes DM6.90. A roll of 10 tickets costs DM11.80.

REGENSBURG

Located on the Danube River, Regensburg has relics of all periods, yet lacks the packaged feel of some other German cities. Its Roman, medieval and later beauties escaped the fate of carpet bombing. Here, as nowhere else in Germany, you enter the misty ages between the Roman and the Carolingian.

The tourist office (☎ 0941-5 07 21 41) is in the Altes Rathaus and is open daily. The telephone code is 0941.

Things to See

Dominating the skyline are the twin spires of the cathedral **Dom St Peter**, which also has striking stained glass. Part of the **Diözesanmuseum** is in the adjacent painted medieval church of St Ulrich (open from April to October, except Monday). Admission costs DM2, or DM3 when combined with a visit to the cathedral's **treasury**. The patrician **tower-houses** in the city's centre arrest the eye as you wander about.

The castle museums of the **Schloss Thurn und Taxis** near the train station are expensive to visit (the cloister is cheapest at DM5), but there are student concessions. To see the lot (Schloss, Kreuzgang and Marstall) costs DM15 (students DM10), but, if the price puts you off, you can make a free visit to the baroque mastery of the Asam brothers in the **St Emmeram basilika** nearby, with its untouched Carolingian and episcopal graves and relics.

The **Altes Rathaus** was progressively extended from medieval to baroque times and was, for almost 150 years, the seat of the Reichstag (tours at 3.15 pm from Monday to Saturday only; DM5). The astronomer and mathematician Johannes Kepler lived and died in the house at Keplerstrasse 5, which is now the **Kepler-Gedächtnishaus** (DM4; closed Monday).

The **Roman wall**, with its **Porta Praetoria** arch, follows Unter den Schwibbögen onto Dr-Martin-Luther-Strasse and is the most tangible reminder of the ancient Castra Regina, whence the name 'Regensburg' comes. Ask at the tourist office for guides to the town's other attractions.

Places to Stay & Eat

Camp at the *Campingplatz* (☎ 2 68 39), Am Weinweg 40 (adults DM8.30 each, tent and car DM9.70). The *youth hostel* (☎ 5 74 02), Wöhrdstrasse 60, costs DM18.50 (for juniors only; closed from mid-November to mid-January). *Gaststätte Roter Hahn* (☎ 56 09 07) at Roter-Hahnen-Gasse 10 has singles/doubles from DM55/85 without bath and the restaurant downstairs caters for vegetarians. *Hotel Peterhof* (☎ 57 5 14) at

GERMANY

Fröhliche-Türken-Strasse 12 has rooms with bath from DM52/88 as well as budget rooms.

By the river is the *Wurstküche*, Goldene-Bärenstrasse, a 12th-century hut with a frantic turnover of grilled sausage and sauerkraut (from DM5; open daily to 7 pm). *Neue Filmbühne* at Bismarckplatz 9 is a café and breakfast and wine bar combined, with daily specials at around DM10.

Getting There & Away

Main-line trains run from Frankfurt through Regensburg on their way to Passau and Vienna (nine daily) and several Munich-Leipzig and Munich-Dresden services also pass through. The A3 autobahn runs north-west to Nuremberg and south-east to Passau, the A93 south to Munich and north towards Dresden.

PASSAU

The Danube River sweeps south-east and exits Germany at Passau, where it is joined by the rivers Inn and Ilz. Passau is a baroque delight, showing strong Italian influence, to bid you welcome or farewell to Germany. There are two useful tourist offices: at Rathausplatz 3 (☎ 0851-3 51 07, open weekdays and summer weekends), and the tourist centre for Passau and Upper Bavaria at the western building of the train station, which is especially useful for bicycle and boat travellers along the Danube.

The telephone code is 0851. If you have been hiking or pedalling hard, you will appreciate the laundrette at Neuburger Strasse 19.

Things to See & Do

The Italian essence has not doused the medieval feel and you can wander through the narrow lanes, tunnels and archways of the old town and monastic district to Ortspitze, where the rivers meet. Admire the view from the 13th-century **Veste Oberhaus** castle tower, which also contains a **cultural history museum** (closed Monday and all February; DM3). The baroque cathedral **Dom St Stephan** is impressive and houses the world's largest church organ (17,388 pipes). The 30-minute recitals daily (except Sunday) at noon between mid-May and October cost DM3 (students DM1), and you can get DM6 tickets to Thursday evening special concerts. There is also a **treasury** and **museum**. The **glockenspiel** at the colourful Rathaus tower sounds daily at 10.30 am and 2 and 7.25 pm, and the tower shows historical river floodmarks. In Kastell Boiotro, across the Inn footbridge from the city centre, is the **Römermuseum**, which covers the city's Roman period and archaeology (closed Monday).

Organised Tours

Return boat tours to Linz (Austria) are cheaper with Wurm + Köck. The 12-hour tours run from April to October, cost DM34, or DM38 (DM42) if you use the bus (train) on the trip back (passports are needed for all options), and depart daily at 9 am. The 45-minute city tour (from early in May) costs DM9. The tours use the pier at Rathausplatz outside the tourist office.

Places to Stay & Eat

There's camping at *Zeltplatz an der Ilz* (☎ 4 14 57), Halser Strasse 34, with a DM8 fee per adult and no tent price (over the Ilz river bridge with bus No 1, 2 or 3; no caravan facilities). Otherwise there are some top offers in great locations, starting with the youth hostel *Jugendherberge Passau* (☎ 4 13 51), which has the best view in town – it's in the castle, though that involves a climb. The price (juniors only) is DM16.50 and the full (DM27.50) or half (DM23) board adds up to good value.

Gasthof zum Hirschen (☎ 3 62 38), Im Ort 6 (or simply Ort, depending which sign you read), has singles/doubles without bath for DM30/60 and doubles with bath for DM70. There are good local dishes in the restaurant from DM11.50 and beer is DM3.20 for half a litre. Also in the old town are *Hotel zum König* (☎ 3 40 98), at Rindermarkt 2 by the Danube, with rooms from DM70/110, and *Pension Rössner* (☎ 20 35), Bräugasse 19, with rooms and breakfast for DM60/100.

For refined dining within muralled walls,

go to the *Passauer Ratskeller* (☎ 26 30), Rathausplatz 2 (most dishes from DM12 to DM25; open daily). A castle view is possible from *Chesa Pressi*, at Römerplatz 3, where the main courses range from DM20 to DM30. Schnitzel specials at *Bräustüberl* on Kleiner Exerzierplatz cost DM13 or less and there is hearty drinking at student prices.

Getting There & Away

Regional buses to/from Zwiesel, Grafenau and Bayerisch Eisenstein stop at the train station concourse outside the main post office and buses to/from Plattling use the stop on the lower level. Trains run direct to/from Munich, Regensburg and Nuremberg (you change at Plattling for the Bavarian Forest), Linz and Vienna.

Boat trips into Austria down the Danube River with DDSG (☎ 3 30 35), Im Ort 14a, offer multiple possibilities between April and October. The fares per person work out to about DM35 Passau-Linz (ASch248) and DM145 Passau-Vienna (ASch1032); downstream time is just over five hours to Linz.

There are several car parks in and near the centre of town but these vary in opening times and terms, so check before parking. Eight cycle routes converge here: the main Donauradweg runs along the Danube's south bank before crossing the hanging bridge, then the Ilz as you head east for Obernzell (Austria). The Inn River's track (north-east bank) crosses to the south at Innbrücke to shadow the Danube towards Engelhartzell.

BAVARIAN ALPS

While not quite as high as their sister summits farther to the south in Austria, the Bavarian Alps (Bayerische Alpen) rise so abruptly from the rolling hills of southern Bavaria that their appearance seems all the more dramatic.

Orientation

Stretching westwards from Germany's remote south-eastern corner to the Allgäu region near Lake Constance, the Bavarian Alps take in most of the mountainous country fringing the southern border to Austria. The year-round resort of Garmisch-Partenkirchen is Munich's favourite getaway spot, though nearby Mittenwald is a less hectic alternative. Other suitable bases from which to explore the Bavarian Alps are Berchtesgaden, the Tegernsee area, Füssen (see the Romantic Road section) and Oberstdorf.

Information

The Berchtesgaden tourist office (☎ 08652-50 11), directly opposite the train station in Königsseer Strasse, is open in summer from 8 am to 6 pm Monday to Friday, 8 am to 5 pm Saturday, and 9 am to 3 pm Sunday and public holidays. At other times of the year it is open Monday to Friday from 8 am to 5 pm, and Saturday from 9 am to noon.

In Garmisch-Partenkirchen, the tourist office (☎ 08821-18 06), on Richard Strauss Platz, is open Monday to Saturday from 8 am to 6 pm, and Sunday and holidays from 10 am to noon. In nearby Mittenwald, the tourist office (☎ 08823-3 39 81) is at Dammkarstrasse 3. It's open weekdays from 8 am to noon then from 1 to 5 pm, as well as Saturday and Sunday mornings.

Over in the western part of the Bavarian Alps, the down-to-earth resort of Oberstdorf has a tourist office (☎ 08322-70 00) at Marktplatz 7. It's open from 8.30 to 11.30 am then from 2 to 6 pm (shorter hours in winter). There's also a convenient room-finding service near the train station.

Things to See

Berchtesgaden Berchtesgaden is perhaps the most romantically scenic place in the Bavarian Alps. A tour of the **Salzbergwerk** (☎ 08652-6 00 20) is a must. Visitors change into protective miners' gear (including a broad leather 'bum belt') before descending into the depths of the salt mine for a tour. It's open daily from 8.30 am to 5 pm between 1 May and 15 October, and from 12.30 to 3.30 pm Monday to Saturday during the rest of the year. Admission is DM16 for adults and DM8 for children.

Outside Berchtesgaden is Hitler's former headquarters at **Obersalzberg**. The six-km

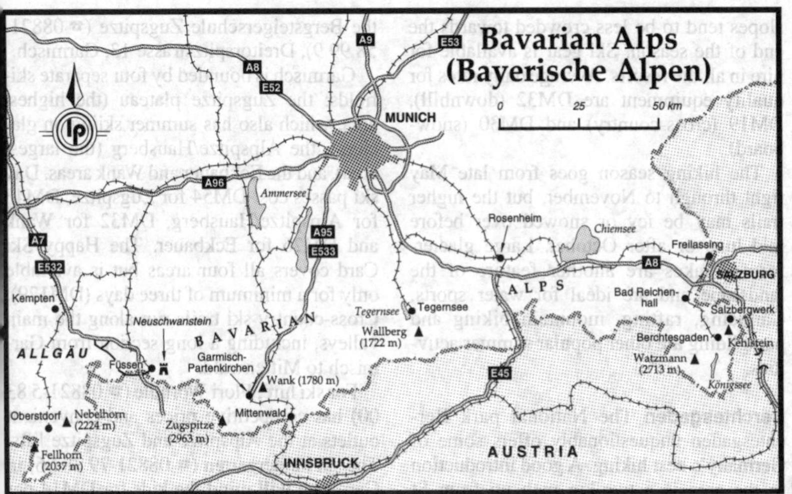

bus ride to the **Kehlstein** summit (open from late May to early October), also known as the Eagle's Nest, is one of the most scenic in Germany. Hitler turned Haus Wachenfels into a holiday house (which he called 'Berghof') for Nazi leaders, and then built Eagle's Nest as an elaborate retreat. It's reached from Berchtesgaden by getting to Obersalzberg-Hintereck (DM5.50 return by bus), taking a special bus to the Kehlstein car park (DM22 return) and then riding a lift 120 metres to the summit (DM4). On foot it's half an hour's brisk climb from the Kehlstein car park to the summit, from where the views and hiking possibilities make the effort worthwhile.

The Berchtesgaden area's other great attraction is the **Königssee**, a beautiful Alpine lake five km to the south (bus DM2.80 each way). There are frequent boat tours (DM16; 1½ hours) in all seasons across the lake to the quaint chapel at St Bartholomä. In summer boats continue to the far end of the lake.

Garmisch-Partenkirchen The huge **ski stadium** on the slopes right outside town has two ski jumps and a slalom course; it hosted more than 100,000 people for the Winter Olympics of 1936. Take a peek at the chapel of **St Anton**, at the edge of Partenkirchen, and then walk along **Philosophenweg** for great Alpine views.

Around Garmisch-Partenkirchen Garmisch can also be used as a base for excursions to crazy King Ludwig II's extravagant castles, Hohenschwangau and **Neuschwanstein**. Although they are most easily visited from Füssen (see the Romantic Road section for details), buses also run from the Garmisch train station (two hours each way; DM21.90 return).

Schloss Linderhof (open daily; DM7, students DM4) is 20 km west of Garmisch by road (bus fare is DM9.60 return).

Activities

For those with the time, energy and money, the Bavarian Alps are extraordinarily well organised for outdoor pursuits, though naturally skiing (or its increasingly popular variant, snowboarding) and hiking have the biggest following. The ski season usually begins in December and, given a cold, snowy winter, may continue well into April. The slopes tend to be less crowded towards the end of the season. Ski gear is available for hire in all the resorts. Average daily rates for quality equipment are DM32 (downhill), DM19 (cross-country) and DM30 (snowboard).

The hiking season goes from late May right through to November, but the higher trails may be icy or snowed over before mid-June or after October. Large glacier-formed lakes are another feature of the landscape and are ideal for water sports. Canoeing, rafting, mountain biking and paragliding are other popular summer activities.

Berchtesgaden The National park Berchtesgaden unquestionably offers some of Germany's best hiking. A good introduction to the area is a two-km path up from St Bartholomä beside the Königssee to the Watzmann-Ostwand, a massive 2000-metre rock face which has claimed the lives of scores of mountaineers attempting to climb it. Another popular hike goes from the southern end of the Königssee to the Obersee.

Berchtesgaden's main ski-field is the Jenner area at Königssee. Day ski-lift passes cost DM37. The Outdoor Club (☎ 08652-6 60 66), Bahnhofstrasse 11, rents out ski equipment and also offers guided climbs and hikes, mountain bike tours and rafting trips.

Garmisch-Partenkirchen A great short hike from Garmisch is to the Partnachklamm Gorge via a winding path above a stream and underneath waterfalls. Take the cable car to the first stop on the Graseck route and follow the signs.

An excursion to the Zugspitze summit, Germany's highest peak (2966 metres), is understandably the most popular outing from Garmisch. There are various ways up, including a return trip by rack-railway, summit cable car and Eibsee cable car for DM54, but the best option is hiking (two days). An excellent contoured hiking map showing all the trails is on sale locally and costs DM8.80. For information on guided hiking or courses in mountaineering call at the Bergsteigerschule Zugspitze (☎ 08821-58 99 9), Dreitorspitzstrasse 13, Garmisch.

Garmisch is bounded by four separate ski-fields: the Zugspitze plateau (the highest area, which also has summer skiing on glaciers), the Alpspitze/Hausberg (the largest area), and the Eckbauer and Wank areas. Day ski passes cost DM54 for Zugspitze, DM43 for Alpspitze/Hausberg, DM32 for Wank and DM26 for Eckbauer. The Happy Ski Card covers all four areas but is available only for a minimum of three days (DM129). Cross-country ski trails run along the main valleys, including a long section from Garmisch to Mittenwald.

For ski hire, Flori Wörndle (☎ 08821-5 83 00) has competitive prices and convenient outlets at the Alpspitze and Zugspitze lifts. The ski kindergarten (☎ 08821-79 78 56) in Garmisch will mind the kids for DM14 per day (plus lunch). For information and instruction in skiing (downhill) you can contact the Skischule Garmisch-Partenkirchen (☎ 08821-49 31), Am Hausberg 8, or (cross-country) the Skilanglaufschule (☎ 08821-15 16), Olympia-Skistadion.

Mountain biking is a great alternative to hiking. The Mountain-Bike-Schule Garmisch-Partenkirchen (☎ 08821-5 48 44) at Ludwigstrasse 22 rents out bikes (priced from about DM10 per day) and can advise you on biking routes. Regular rafting and canoeing trips on the surrounding mountain rivers are organised by Sportfreizeit Werdenfels (☎ 08824-81 62), Münchener Strasse 11, Oberau. It also offers an all-inclusive seven-day Active Week, including kayaking, paragliding, hiking and mountain biking for DM980.

Mittenwald Recommended hikes with cable-car access are to the Alpspitze (2628 metres), the Wank, Mt Karwendel (2384 metres) and the Wettersteinspitze (2297 metres). Day ski passes cost DM35 (Karwendel area) and DM30 (Kranzberg area). For skiing instruction, contact the Vereinigte Skischule (☎ 08823-15 85), Bahnhofstrasse 6. See Fahrradvermietung Frank (☎ 08823-12 93), Dammkarstrasse 39, for bike rentals.

Oberstdorf Like Garmisch, Oberstdorf is surrounded by towering peaks and offers some superb hiking. For a rewarding day walk, ride the Nebelhorn cable car to the upper station then hike down to the Gaisalpsee.

In-the-know skiers value Oberstdorf for its convenient, friendly and generally uncrowded skiing. There are two major skifields right beside the village: the Nebelhorn and Fellhorn/Kanzelwand areas. Day ski passes for the Nebelhorn cost DM46 and for the Fellhorn/Kanzelwand DM48 (including free use of adjoining lifts on the Austrian side). For ski hire and tuition, try the Erste Skischule (☎ 08322-31 10), Freiherr-von-Brutscher-Strasse 4.

The Eislaufzentrum (☎ 08322-21 20), behind the Nebelhorn cable-car station at Rossbichlstrasse 2-6, is one of the biggest ice-skating complexes in the country, with three separate rinks. Admission for individual skaters is priced from DM2, while skate hire costs as little as DM4.

Places to Stay

Most of the resorts have plenty of reasonably priced guesthouses and private rooms, though it's still a good idea to ring ahead and book accommodation. Tourist offices near the local train stations can help you find a room; otherwise look out for 'Zimmer frei' signs. During busy winter and summer seasons, some places levy a surcharge (usually DM5 per person) for stays of less than two or three days. Also, check whether the room price includes the local Kurtaxe, which is usually about DM3. If you plan a longer stay, check the tourist office's list of *Ferienwohnungen* (holiday apartments).

Berchtesgaden There are five camping grounds in the Berchtesgaden area (telephone code 08652); the nicest are up at Königssee: *Grafenlehen* (☎ 41 40) and *Mülleiten* (☎ 45 84); both cost DM8 per person plus a nightly DM7.50 site fee.

The *youth hostel* (☎ 21 90) is at Gebirgsjägerstrasse 52 and charges DM19.50 (including tourist tax and breakfast) for a bed. From the train station, take bus No 3 to Strub, then continue a few minutes on foot. The hostel closes from 1 November until 27 December.

The *Haus Ettl* (☎ 6 13 44), at Sunklergässchen 4, is a small guesthouse 10 minutes' walk from the station. Singles/doubles cost DM27/50. The *Hotel Watzmann* (☎ 20 55) is at Franziskanerplatz 2, just opposite the chiming church in the old town. Simple rooms cost DM33/66 (DM39/78 in summer) and DM44/78 with private shower (DM55/98 in summer). The hotel closes in November and December. Not far from the Jenner cableway, at Schönau am Königssee, the *Hotel Königssee* (☎ 65 80), Seestrasse 29, has simple rooms priced from DM34/59. It's also closed throughout November and December.

Garmisch-Partenkirchen The camping ground nearest to Garmisch (telephone code 08821), *Zugspitze* (☎ 31 80), is along highway B24. Take the blue-and-white bus outside the station in the direction of the Eibsee. Sites cost DM8, plus DM9 per person and DM5 per vehicle. Due to the chilly winters up here, camping is not recommended between November and April.

The *youth hostel* (☎ 29 80), at Jochstrasse 10, is in the suburb of Burgrain. It has beds for DM18.50 (including tourist tax) and an 11.30 pm curfew. It's closed in November and December. Take bus No 5, 6 or 7 from the station.

Two friendly budget places are the *Haus Buchwieser* (☎ 20 84) at Mitterfeldstrasse 2 (not to be confused with its more up-market namesake at Olympiastrasse 17), and *Haus Cenci* (☎ 7 86 50), next door at No 4. Both places have great balconies and cost around DM33 per person. Five minutes' walk from the station is the quiet *Hotel Schell* (☎ 29 89), at Partnachauenstrasse 3 (not Partnachstrasse). It has simple singles for DM40 and doubles with private shower from DM45 per person.

Mittenwald The camping ground closest to Mittenwald (telephone area code 08823) is

Am Isarhorn (☎ 52 16), north of town off the B2 highway. The local *youth hostel* (☎ 17 01) is in Buckelwiesen, four km outside Mittenwald. It charges DM15.50 per night and closes from 5 November until 26 December. One of the best deals in town is the cosy *Haus Schamriss-Eitzenberger* (☎ 83 65), Frühlingstrasse 17, with beds in singles or doubles for only DM25. The *Hotel Goldener Adler* (☎ 12 81), Innsbrucker Strasse 1, has nice singles/doubles for DM40/80.

Oberstdorf The local *camping ground* (☎ 08322-65 25) is at Rubinger Strasse 16, two km north of the station beside the train line. The *youth hostel* (☎ 22 25) is at Kornau 8, on the outskirts of town near the Söllereck cable car. Take the Kleinwalsertal bus (DM2.80) from the station and get off at Reute.

Geiger Hans (☎ 36 74), at Frohmarkt 5, has small rooms from DM33 per person. The *Paulaner Bräu* (☎ 49 66), at Kirchstrasse 1 right in the heart of the old town, charges DM35/70 for simple singles/doubles (DM44/88 with private shower). Also central is the *Gasthaus Binz* (☎ 44 55), in a quaint wooden tavern at Bachstrasse 14. Simple rooms are DM35 per person.

GERMANY

Places to Eat

Berchtesgaden Cheap choices are pretty limited in Berchtesgaden, but the *Balkan Grill* at Griesstätterstrasse 9 has main courses from DM12.50. The *Hubertus Stuben* next door to the Hotel Vier Jahreszeiten on Maximilianstrasse offers vegetarian as well as hearty meat dishes priced from around DM18.

Garmisch-Partenkirchen Most of the restaurants are clustered along the lanes around Marienplatz in the town centre. One of the cheapest places is the *Cafeteria Hans Bauer*, behind Marienplatz at Griesstrasse 1. It serves grilled chicken for DM5.90 and half-litre glasses of Löwenbräu for DM3.30, and has simple three-course meals for just DM8. It closes at 8 pm. One street farther back, at Sonnenstrasse 4, is the *Alpspitze*, a huge old four-storey inn which offers Bavarian delicacies like Schweinskopfsülze (DM14).

The spacious *Hofbräustüberl*, at Chamonixstrasse 2, serves hot meals until 10.30 pm, specialising in eastern-European grills. Some nights a folk band plays Bavarian oompah music here, but with generous main courses from DM14 to DM18 the prices are pretty reasonable. One of the best restaurants in town is *Isi's Goldener Engel* (☎ 08821-56 67 7), Bankgasse 5, complete with outside frescos and stags' heads. Featured on the menu are game dishes such as the deer loin and wild boar platter for two at DM80, but most other main courses are under DM20.

Mittenwald The *Gasthof Stern*, at Fritz Brösl Platz 2, has reasonably priced local dishes and you can order until 9 pm. The *Gasthof Gries*, at Im Gries 4, is also serves pretty good food.

Oberstdorf The large *Pauliner-Bräu* (see also Places to Stay) has a wide range of belly-filling selections priced from DM9.50. The restaurant is closed on Tuesday. The *Zum wilde Männle*, at Oststrasse 15, is a bit classier, but the extra you pay is worth it.

Getting There & Away

Berchtesgaden For the quickest train connections to Berchtesgaden it's usually best to take a Munich-Salzburg train and change at Freilassing. It's a 2½-hour (DM43) train trip from Munich, but less than an hour from Salzburg, although from there it's more convenient to take a bus or even a tour. Berchtesgaden is south of the Munich-Salzburg A8 autobahn.

Garmisch-Partenkirchen Garmisch is serviced from Munich by hourly trains (1½ hours; DM23). There's a special same-day return fare of DM30 on Tuesday, Thursday, Saturday and Sunday. The A95 is the direct road route. Trains from Garmisch to Innsbruck (DM27) pass through Mittenwald.

Getting Around

While the public transport network is very good, the mountain geography means there are few direct routes between main centres; sometimes a short cut via Austria works out quicker (such as between Garmisch and Füssen or Oberstdorf). Road rather than rail routes are often more practical. For those with private transport, the German Alpine Road (Deutsche Alpenstrasse) is a more scenic way to go – though obviously much slower than the autobahns and highways that fan out across southern Bavaria.

There are car-rental agencies in Berchtesgaden, Garmisch and Oberstdorf, but check first whether the company has a drop-off station near where you are heading. Avis (☎ 08821-55 06 6), Hindenburgstrasse 35, Garmisch, offers VW Polos at a special 'weekend' rate (ie Thursday evening until Monday morning) of just DM99 with unlimited km. Seven-day bus passes with unlimited travel on all regional (RVO) buses cost around DM35 and are a cheap and convenient way to explore the area.

BAVARIAN FOREST

Like the Harz Mountains to the north, the Bavarian Forest (Bayerischer Wald) is mostly visited by Germans, even though it's the largest continuous mountain forest in all of Europe. The forest is near the Czech border and a trip here has the feel of a new frontier compared to the rest of Germany. Go out of your way to get in some hiking, but don't get too excited about the downhill skiing possibilities. English is not very widely understood.

Orientation & Information

Most Germans agree that the ideal base for exploring the heart of the Bavarian Forest is Zwiesel, a valley town devoted to the forest surrounding it. Zwiesel's Kurverwaltung (☎ 09922-96 23) is in the Rathaus, about one km from the station at Stadtplatz 27. It has lots of free brochures, maps and helpful hints for exploring the area.

The tourist office (☎ 08552-4 27 43) for Grafenau is at Rathausgasse 1. For information about wildlife areas and trails, you can also turn to the Dr-Hans-Eisenmann-Haus (☎ 08558-13 00) at Neuschönau.

Things to See & Do

Zwiesel sits on the banks of the rushing Schwarzer Regen River, not far from peaks such as Grosser Arber (1456 metres), Grosser Falkenstein (1315 metres) and Grosser Rachel (1453 metres).

Near the Rathaus is an excellent **Waldmuseum** (Forest Museum) that covers the area's forests and its wood and glass products. Entry costs DM3 (students DM1) and opening times are Monday to Friday from 9 am to 5 pm, and Saturday and Sunday from 10 am to noon and 2 to 4 pm. Hours are slightly reduced in winter.

An essential excursion for the tour buses is to the **Bayerwald-Bärwurzerei Hieke** (☎ 09922-15 15), two km out on Frauenauer Strasse at No 80. It has no less than 26 Bavarian schnapps specialities that you can try as well as buy. There's also a background film in three languages.

Along with schnapps, glass is also an important product of the area. You can see locals blowing glass and purchase their wares in many places, such as at Zwieseler Kunstglasbläserei Gerhard Krauspe, Frauener Strasse 10, right in the centre of town.

Hiking & Skiing South of Zwiesel is a 130-sq-km national park. It's a paradise for the outdoors enthusiast and a refreshing respite from the more touristy Bavarian Alps or Black Forest.

The hiking is always good. There are several long-distance hiking routes, with mountain huts along the way. The most famous (and most difficult) is the Nördliche Hauptwanderlinie or E6 trail, a 180-km trek from Furth im Wald to Dreisessel. It's gorgeous and worth the 10 days it takes. The Südliche Hauptwanderlinie or E8 is its shorter sibling at 105 km, while the 50-km trek from Kötzting to Bayerisch Eisenstein near the Czech border is the quickest way to see lots of the Bavarian Forest. The approved map is the 1:50,000 *Fritsch Wanderkarte*

Mittlerer Bayerische Wald, which costs DM11.80, and its connecting sheets.

Cross-country skiing is available almost everywhere. Zwiesel's tourist office details routes leaving directly from town. For fairly sedate downhill skiing the Breitenau area, with the Geisskopf at 1097 metres and the Einödriegel at 1150 metres, has six lifts and lots of support facilities.

Places to Stay

Zwiesel is an ideal overnight base for day excursions. *AZUR Camping* (☎ 09922-18 47) is one km from the train station, near public pools and sports facilities. Head north from the station down Äussere Bahnhofstrasse and follow the signs. The small *youth hostel* (☎ 09922-10 61), Hindenburgstrasse 26, costs DM17 (juniors only, closed from the start of November to Christmas). If you want to stay in the middle of the Bavarian Forest, try the hostel *Waldhäuser* (☎ 08553-60 00) at Herbergsweg 2 near Neuschönau (DM18.50, juniors only). You can take a bus the 17 km from Grafenau train station.

Zwiesel is packed with pensions and apartments (prices include resort tax). One unique possibility is *Naturkost Pension Waldeck* (☎ 09922-32 72) at Ahornweg 23 (they'll pick you up at the train station), near Zwiesel's sports complex and with a nice view. This health-conscious pension features vegetarian cooking and is a great place for exploring the Hennenkobel mountains; it costs from DM47 to DM56 per person for half board.

If you want some flexibility, head to *Pension Bergfeld* (☎ 09922-95 53), Hochstrasse 45, which charges from DM52 per person. Nearby, the *Ferienhaus Bergfeld* (☎ 09922-26 36), Kolpingstrasse 9, charges DM53 to DM118 per person for apartments accommodating two to six people. Solicitous and excellent value is *Pension Haus Inge*, (☎ 09922-10 94), Buschweg 34, offering comfortable rooms with breakfast, private shower and toilet from DM31 to DM37 per person.

Places to Eat

Zwiesel has a genuine bargain in *The Big Chicken* at Bergstrasse 1. It's a family-oriented place, friendly and cheap; burgers are DM2.90 to DM9.95, and full meals are DM9 to DM12. It's closed on Friday. *Pfefferbräu Bräustüberl*, Regener Strasse 6 (closed Monday), has Bavarian food and cheap beer (the brewery is opposite) for DM3.50 per half-litre.

Try Balkan specialities at *Restaurant zum Nepomuk*, upstairs at Stadtplatz 30. Dishes start around DM10 and it has a salad buffet. *Zwieseler Hof Hotel-Restaurant*, Regener Strasse 5, has a comfortable ambience despite the plastic plants. The extensive menu (DM10.50 to DM24) includes fish, lamb and Bavarian dishes.

Getting There & Away

Zwiesel's little mountain trains (the route is pleasantly slow and scenic) run to/from Plattling (DM13) with connections to Munich, Nuremberg and Passau. The direct buses from Zwiesel to Passau work out cheaper than a change of trains at Plattling, but only run in the morning and late afternoon (early afternoon buses run only to/from Frauenau). Most trains run north to Bayerisch Eisenstein on the Czech border (DM4.40), with connections to Prague. A train ride from Zwiesel to Grafenau costs DM4.30, to Frauenau DM3. Various travel agents in Zwiesel offer cheap bus excursions to Prague. From Plattling, the A92 leads directly to Munich.

Baden-Württemberg

Baden-Württemberg is one of Germany's main tourist regions. With recreational centres like the Black Forest (Schwarzwald), Lake Constance (Bodensee), medieval towns such as Heidelberg and the health spa of Baden-Baden it's also one of the most varied parts of Germany.

The prosperous modern state of Baden-Württemberg was created in 1951 out of three smaller regions: Baden, Württemberg and Hohenzollern. Baden was first unified and made a grand duchy by Napoleon, who was also responsible for making Württemberg a kingdom in 1806. Both areas, in conjunction with Bavaria and 16 other states, formed the Confederation of the Rhine under French protection, part of Napoleon's plan to undermine the might of Prussia. Baden and Württemberg sided with Austria against Prussia in 1866, but were ultimately drafted into the German Empire in 1871.

STUTTGART

Stuttgart enjoys the status of being Baden-Württemberg's state capital and the hub of its industries. Lacking historical monuments, Stuttgart nevertheless attracts visitors with its impressive museums and air of relaxed prosperity. At the forefront of Germany's economic recovery from the ravages of WW II, Stuttgart started life somewhat less auspiciously, as a stud farm.

Orientation & Information

The main train station and the adjoining bus station are located immediately to the north of the central pedestrian shopping street,

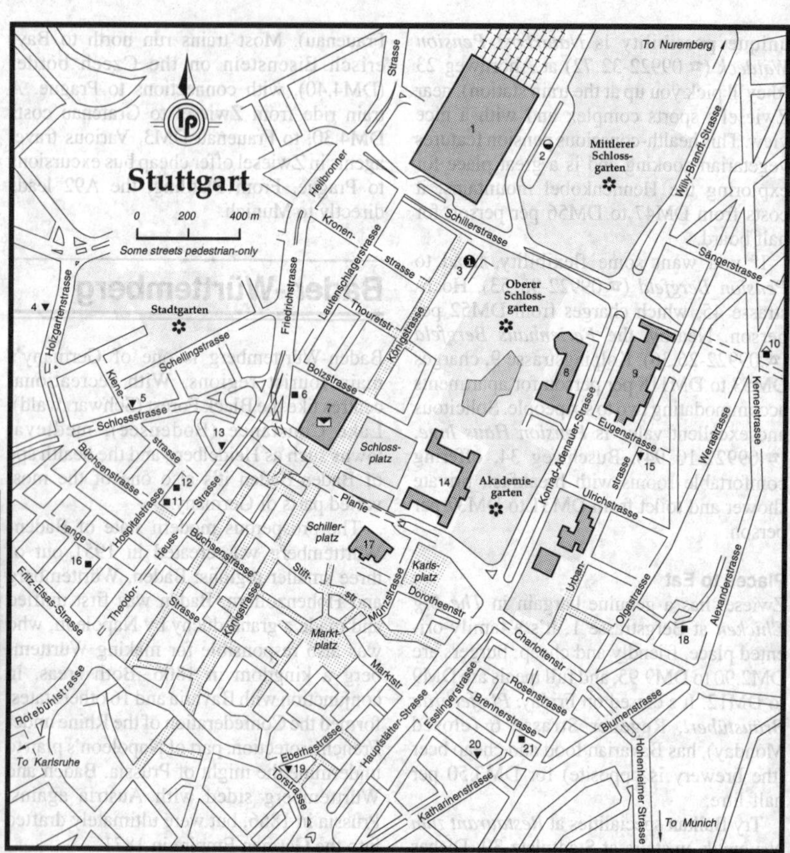

PLACES TO STAY		PLACES TO EAT		OTHER	
6	Pension Märklin	4	Mensa	1	Main Train Station
10	Youth Hostel	5	Uprising	2	Bus Station
11	Gasthof Alta Mira	13	Stuttgarter Kellerschenke	3	Tourist Office
12	Museumstube	15	Urbanstuben	7	Main Post Office
16	Hotel Wartburg	19	Oktave	8	Staatstheater
18	Wirt Am Berg	20	Weinstube Drei Mohren	9	Staatsgalerie
21	Hotel Dieter			14	New Castle
				17	Old Castle

Königstrasse. The tourist office (☎ 0711-2 22 82 40), Königstrasse 1a, is opposite the bus station. It's open Monday to Friday from 9.30 am to 8.30 pm, Saturday to 6 pm and Sunday from 11 am to 6 pm (1 to 6 pm between 1 November and 30 April). Room reservations incur no fee. The main post office is at Lautenschlagerstrasse 17, and there is a branch at the train station with longer opening hours (from 10 am to 11 pm daily).

Stuttgart's telephone code is 0711.

Things to See & Do

Stretching south-west from the Neckar River to the city centre is the **Schlossgarten**, an extensive strip of parkland and ponds, complete with swans, street entertainers and modern sculptures. At their northern edge the gardens take in the **Wilhelma** zoo and botanical gardens (DM8/4, open daily). At their southern end they encompass the sprawling baroque **Neues Schloss** (New Castle, now government offices) and the Renaissance **Altes Schloss** (Old Castle), housing the **Württembergisches Landesmuseum** (free; closed Monday). Adjoining the park, at Konrad-Adenauer-Strasse 30, you'll find the **Staatsgalerie** (free; closed Monday) housing Stuttgart's best art collection. The new section concentrates on modern art and has a good selection of works by Picasso; the old section has works from the Middle Ages to the 19th century.

Motor Museums The motor car was first developed by Gottlieb Daimler and Carl Benz at the end of the 19th century. The impressive **Mercedes-Benz Museum** (☎ 1 72 25 78) tells the story of their partnership and achievements via recorded commentary and numerous gleaming vehicles. It's open Tuesday to Sunday from 9 am to 5 pm (free; take S-Bahn No 1 to Neckarstadion), and is larger and more fun than the equivalent **Porsche Museum**, open Monday to Friday from 9 am to noon and 1 to 4 pm (free; take S-Bahn No 6 to Neuwirkshaus).

Better than either museum is a **factory tour** where you can view the whole production process from unassembled components to completed cars. Porsche does a free daily tour in English. It's often possible to join at short notice (☎ 8 27 53 84), but it's best to book at least six weeks ahead. Write to Porsche Besucherservice, Frau Schlegl, Postfach 400640, D-7000 Stuttgart. Mercedes-Benz also runs several free daily tours of its Sindelfingen plant (in English at 2.30 pm; no kids allowed). For bookings and information call ☎ 07031-90 24 93.

Places to Stay

Camping & Hostels You can camp at *Campingplatz Stuttgart* (☎ 55 66 96), by the river at Mercedesstrasse 40, just 500 metres from the Bad Cannstatt S-Bahn station. The *DJH hostel* (☎ 24 15 83), Haussmannstrasse 27, is a signposted 15-minute walk east of the main train station. Beds cost DM19.50/24.50 for juniors/seniors, reception is shut from 9 am to noon, and there is an 11.30 pm curfew. The *Jugendgästehaus* (☎ 24 11 32), south-east of the centre at Richard-Wagner-Strasse 2, charges DM35/60 for singles/doubles. (Take a No 15 Heumaden tram seven stops from the train station.)

Hotels & Pensions You'll need to book for the plain but central *Pension Märklin* (☎ 29 13 15), Friedrichstrasse 39, which charges DM40/80 for singles/doubles (without breakfast). The Greek-run *Hotel Dieter* (☎ 23 51 61), Brennerstrasse 40, has spartan rooms for 50/90. Rooms at the *Gasthof Alte Mira* (☎ 29 51 32), Büchsenstrasse 24, start at DM60/100 or DM75/125. The restaurant downstairs has Balkan specialities from DM11.50. Just around the corner at Hospitalstrasse 9 is the smaller *Museumstube* (☎ 29 68 10), with simple rooms from DM55/82.

The *Pension Schaich* (☎ 60 26 79), at Paulinenstrasse 16, has large and sunny rooms (soundproofed to combat the noisy overpass outside) for DM65/100, or DM75/110 with shower cubicle in the room. The *Wirt am Berg* (☎ 24 18 65), in a quiet backstreet at Gaisburgstrasse 12a, has simple rooms for DM70/110. At the *Hotel Wartburg* (☎ 2 04 50), Lange Strasse 49, all rooms have TV and radio, and parking is no problem. The simple singles/doubles for DM75/125 seem good value – until you start looking for the nonexistent hall shower.

GERMANY

Rooms with private bath and toilet cost DM145/240.

Places to Eat

Stuttgart is a good place to sample Swabian specialities like Linsen und Spätzle (lentils with noodles) or Maultaschen (meat and spinach inside pasta envelopes). For a really cheap feed, the university *mensas*, Holzgartenstrasse 11 and Pfaffenwaldring 45, have set menus for under DM4; student IDs are not regularly checked. Close to the university at Schlossstrasse 28 is *Uprising*, with interesting African dishes for around DM10; there's live reggae music on Friday and Saturday, but it's closed on Tuesday.

The *Punktum* cafeteria in the Treffpunkt cultural complex at Rotbühlplatz 28 (open Monday to Saturday to 11 pm) has salads from DM5.80 and a good range of vegetarian and Swabian food. The *Oktave* (☎ 24 55 45) in the basement of Ali's Brasserie at Eberhardstrasse 49 is popular with young Stuttgarters and has live bands several nights a week. The kitchen keeps cooking tasty Turkish treats until 5 am.

The *Stuttgarter Kellerschenke*, Theodor-Heuss-Strasse 2a, is downstairs in an unpretentious grey building and offers daily three-course Swabian menus from DM10 to DM16. It's open Monday to Friday from 10 am to midnight. The cosy *Urbanstuben*, on the corner of Urbanstrasse and Eugenstrasse, has predominantly vegetarian dishes from around DM20 and some excellent local wines. For some outstanding cuisine, dine at the *Weinstube Drei Mohren* (☎ 24 22 97), Pfarrstrasse 23. Main courses are priced between DM32 and DM43; it's closed Monday and Friday.

Entertainment

The Stuttgart area has dozens of theatres and live music venues. The *Staatstheater* (☎ 22 17 95) holds regular orchestral, ballet and opera performances. The *Theaterhaus* (☎ 40 20 70) at Ulmer Strasse 241 stages anything from serious theatre to jazz concerts to cabaret. The *Laboratorium* at Wagenburgstrasse 147 and the *Treffpunkt* (☎ 6 60 71 20) on Rotbühlplatz are also good for live jazz, folk or rock bands most nights. See the tourist office for ticket reservations.

Getting There & Away

Stuttgart has an international airport south of the city (now with direct S-Bahn access via the S2 and S3 from the main train station). There are frequent departures for all major German and many international cities, including ICE and IC trains, to Frankfurt (1⅓ hours), Berlin (six hours) and Munich (2¼ hours). The A8 from Munich to Karlsruhe passes Stuttgart, as does the A81 from Würzburg south to Lake Constance. There is an ADM-Mitfahrzentrale (☎ 6 36 80 36) at Lerchenstrasse 65.

Getting Around

On Stuttgart's public transport network single fares are DM1.60/2.50 for short/long trips within the central zone. A four-ride strip ticket for the central zone costs DM9 and a daily ticket is a whopping DM16.

AROUND STUTTGART

Tübingen

This gentle, picturesque university town, just 35 km south of Stuttgart, is a place to wander winding laneways past half-timbered houses and old stone walls. On **Marktplatz**, the centre of town, is the **town hall** with its ornate baroque façade and astronomical clock. The nearby late-Gothic **Stiftkirche** houses tombs of the Württemberg dukes and has excellent medieval stained-glass windows. From the heights of the Renaissance **Schloss Hohentübingen** (now part of the university) there are fine views over the steep, red-tiled rooftops of the old town.

The tourist office (☎ 07071-3 50 11) is on the way into town by the main bridge, Neckarbrücke.

Places to Stay & Eat There is a convenient *camping ground* (☎ 07071-4 31 45) at Rappenberghalde 61, while the *DJH hostel* (☎ 07071-2 30 02) can be found at Gartenstrasse 22/2. The *Hotel Am Schloss* (☎ 07071-9 29 40) at Burgsteig 18 has a few

GERMANY

simple singles/doubles from DM45/95 – very reasonable considering the central location. The *Markthalle Kelter* on the corner of Kelternstrasse and Schmiedtorstrasse is a food hall with various cheap takeaway stalls and restaurants. The *Collegium* on the corner of Collegiumsgasse and Lange Gasse has good-sized main dishes from DM13.

Getting There & Away Tübingen can easily be visited as a day excursion from Stuttgart, from where there are direct trains every two hours (DM32 return).

Schwäbisch Hall

The site of ancient saltworks dating back to pre-Germanic times, today Schwäbisch Hall is a household name throughout Germany – not so much because of the town's quaint medieval streetscapes but for the highly successful Schwäbisch Hall insurance and banking company that still maintains strong links with its tiny home base.

The tourist office (☎ 0791-75 13 75) is on **Marktplatz**, where you'll also find **Pfarrkirche St Michael**, begun in 1156, and the **town hall** (1735). The 15th-century **Keckenburg** on the eastern side of town by the river serves as the city museum.

Places to Stay & Eat The nearby *Campingplatz Steinbacher See* (☎ 0791-29 84; open April to mid-October) charges DM7 per person plus DM9 per site. The local *DJH hostel* (☎ 0791-4 10 50) at Langenfelder Weg 5 charges juniors/seniors DM18.50/23.50. The *Krone* (☎ 0791-60 22), next to Pfarrkirche St Michael at Klosterstrasse 1, offers singles/doubles priced from DM69/99 with shower and toilet, and from DM49/79 without. The *Gasthof Hirsch* (☎ 0791-23 22), at Sulzdorfer Strasse 14 near the Hessental train station, has simple rooms from DM35/70. A good place to eat is *Zum Grünen Baum* at Gelbinger Gasse 33, which serves main courses priced from DM10 (closed Sunday).

Getting There & Away Depending on available connections, there are two ways of reaching Schwäbisch Hall by train from Stuttgart: the quickest option is usually direct to the Schwäbisch Hall-Hessental station, then by public bus into town. The other alternative is to change trains in Heilbronn and continue to the main Schwäbisch Hall station, from where it's a 10-minute walk to Marktplatz.

HEIDELBERG

Although Heidelberg was all but destroyed by invading French troops in 1693, its magnificent castle and medieval town are irresistible drawing cards for most travellers in Germany. Mark Twain began his European travels here and recounted his comical observations in *A Tramp Abroad*. Britain's J M W Turner loved Heidelberg and it inspired him to produce some of his greatest landscape paintings.

With a sizeable student population (attending the oldest university in the country), Heidelberg is a surprisingly lively place for a city of only 140,000. But be warned: this place is chock-a-block with tourists during the high season (July and August), so try to avoid coming here then.

Orientation

Arriving in Heidelberg can be something of an anticlimax. Expectations of a quaint old town clash with the modern and less interesting western side of the city near the train station. To find out what this city is really all about continue down Kurfürsten-Anlage to Bismarckplatz, where the romantic old Heidelberg begins to reveal itself.

The Hauptstrasse is the pedestrian thoroughfare leading eastwards through the heart of the old city from Bismarckplatz via Markplatz to Karlstor. The two-km walk past old buildings, shops, bars and restaurants makes a nice introduction.

Information

The main tourist office (☎ 06221-2 13 41), directly outside the train station, is open from 9 am to 7 pm Monday to Saturday throughout the year, plus Sunday from 10 am to 6 pm from March to October and from 10 am

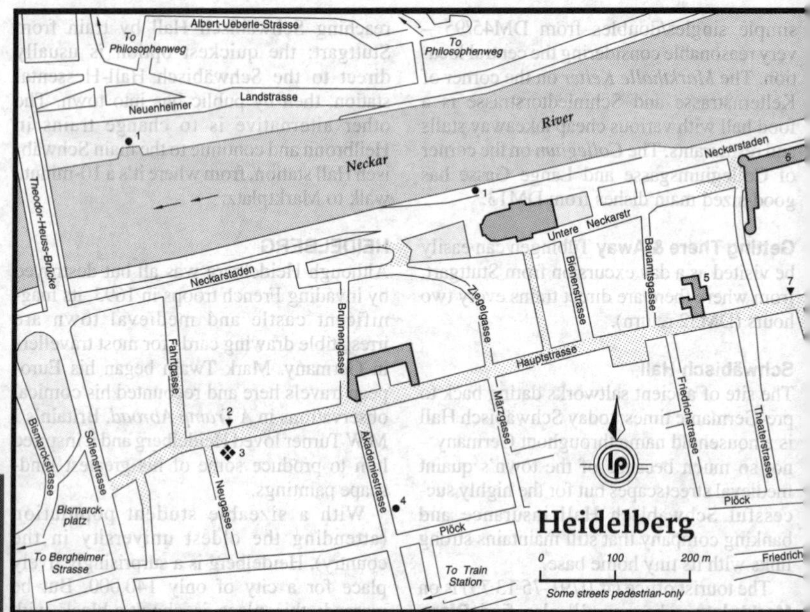

PLACES TO STAY

9 Hotel Vier Jahreszeiten
21 Hotel Zum Ritter
22 Jeske Hotel
24 Hotel Zum Pfalzgrafen

PLACES TO EAT

2 Mumtaz Mahal
7 Zum Güldenen Schaf
12 Sudpfanne
23 Simplicissimus
25 Mensa

OTHER

1 Docks for River Boats
3 Kaufhof Department Store
4 Institute of Natural Sciences
5 Palatinate Museum
6 Marstall
8 Gasthaus Zum Mohren
10 Schnookeloch
11 Goldener Reichsapfel
13 Zum Roten Ochsen
14 Zum Sepp'l
15 Town Hall
16 Heiligkeitskirche
18 Students' Jail
17 Punkt
19 Café Journal
20 Drugstore Café
26 University Library
27 Funicular Railway (Kornmarkt Station)
28 Castle

to 3 pm in November and December. It charges a DM4 room-finding fee.

There's also a smaller tourist office at the funicular train station not far from the castle. It is open from 10 am until 5 pm daily. The main post office is just to the right as you leave the train station. You can exchange foreign currency at the Deutsche Verkehrs-bank at the station and the money-changers in town.

Heidelberg's telephone code is 06221.

Things to See & Do

Heidelberg's large **castle** is one of Germany's finest examples of Gothic-Renaissance castles and the city's chief

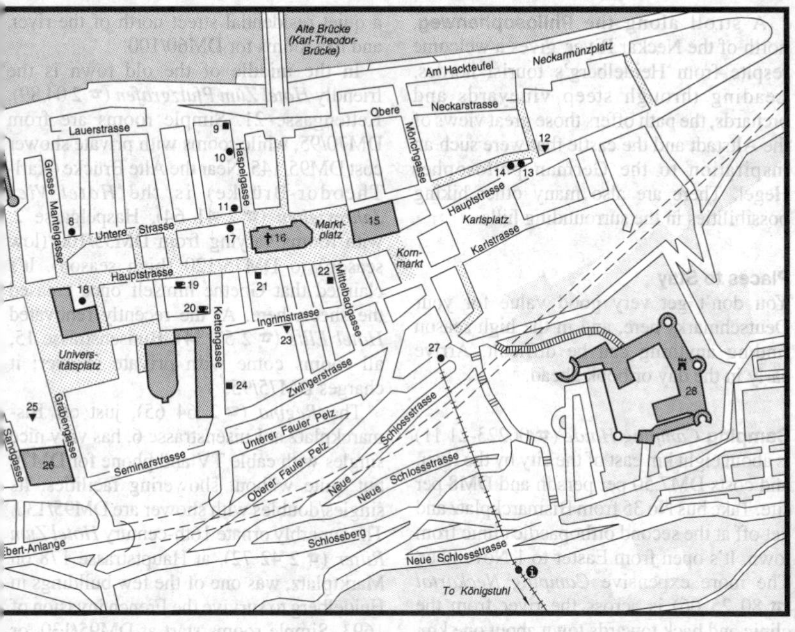

attraction. The building's half-ruined state actually adds to its romantic appeal. Seen from anywhere in the Altstadt, the striking red-sandstone castle dominates the hillside. It's open daily and admission is free if you just want to explore the grounds and garden terraces. There is a rather dull guided tour of the interior (DM4, students DM2). Make sure you see the **Grosses Fass** (Great Vat), an enormous 18th-century keg capable of holding 221,726 litres (DM1, students DM0.50, or part of the guided tour). The **Deutsches Apothekenmuseum** (German Pharmaceutical Museum) does a good job of recalling earlier times (DM3, students DM1.50). You can take the funicular railway to the castle from lower Kornmarkt station (DM4.50 return), otherwise it's an invigorating 10-minute walk up steep stone-laid lanes. The funicular continues up to the **Königstuhl**, where there's a TV and lookout tower; the return fare from Kornmarkt with a stop at the castle is DM7.

Dominating Universitätsplatz are the 18th-century **Alte Universität** (Old University) and the **Neue Universität** (New University). Head south down Grabengasse to the **University Library** and then down Plöck to Akadamiestrasse and the old **Institute of Natural Sciences**. Robert Bunsen, the inventor of the Bunsen burner, taught here for more than 40 years. The **Studentenkarzer** (students' jail) is on Augustinergasse, open daily (DM1, students DM0.70). From 1778 to 1914 this jail was used for uproarious students. Many 'convicts' passed their time by carving inscriptions and drawing on the walls. Sentences (usually two to 10 days) were earned for heinous crimes such as drinking, singing and womanising. The **Marstall** is the former arsenal, now a student refectory. The **Palatinate Museum** contains regional artefacts and works, plus the jawbone of 600,000-year-old Heidelberg Man (DM4, students DM2; closed Monday).

A stroll along the **Philosophenweg**, north of the Neckar River, gives a welcome respite from Heidelberg's tourist hordes. Leading through steep vineyards and orchards, the path offers those great views of the Altstadt and the castle that were such an inspiration to the German philosopher Hegel. There are also many other hiking possibilities in the surrounding hills.

Places to Stay

You don't get very good value for your Deutschmarks here, and in the high season finding anything can be difficult. Arrive early in the day or book ahead.

Camping *Camping Haide* (☎ 06223-21 11) is about eight km east of the city by the river, and costs DM7.50 per person and DM8 per site. Take bus No 35 from Bismarckplatz and get off at the second orthopaedic clinic from town. It's open from Easter to 1 November. The more expensive *Camping Neckartal* (☎ 80 25 06) is across the river from the clinic and back towards town about one km.

Hostels The local *DJH hostel* (☎ 41 20 66) is across the river at Tiergartenstrasse 5. The rates are DM19/24 for juniors/seniors (including breakfast). The doors are locked from 9 am to 1 pm, and there's an 11.30 pm curfew. To get there, take bus No 33 from the station or Bismarckplatz.

The veteran *Jeske Hotel* (☎ 2 37 33) is ideally situated at Mittelbadgasse 2. The Frau Jeske offers beds in simple rooms for just DM22 without breakfast. At that price the conditions are understandably spartan, but it's a great deal.

Hotels & Pensions With a few notable exceptions, the cheapies are well outside the old part of town. Many places have seasonally variable rates.

The *Kohler* (☎ 2 43 60), within walking distance of the station at Goethestrasse 2, has singles\doubles from DM60/80. The tiny *Astoria* (☎ 40 29 29), Rahmengasse 30, is in a quiet residential street north of the river, and has rooms for DM60/100.

In the middle of the old town is the friendly *Hotel Zum Pfalzgrafen* (☎ 2 04 89), Kettengasse 21. Simple rooms are from DM70/95, while rooms with private shower cost DM95/145. Near the Alte Brücke (Karl-Theodor-Brücke) is the *Hotel Vier Jahreszeiten* (☎ 2 41 64), Haspelgasse 2, with rooms varying from DM55/100 (low season) to DM75/120 (high season). It's claimed that Goethe himself once creased the sheets here. At the recently renovated *Hotel Elite* (☎ 2 57 34), Bunsenstrasse 15, all rooms come with private shower; it charges DM75/95.

The *Regina* (☎ 2 64 65), just off Bismarckplatz at Luisenstrasse 6, has very nice singles with cable TV and phone for DM70 but quite without showering facilities. Its singles/doubles with shower are DM95/130. The superbly ornate 16th-century *Hotel Zum Ritter* (☎ 2 42 72), at Hauptstrasse 178 on Marktplatz, was one of the few buildings in Heidelberg to survive the French invasion of 1693. Simple rooms start at DM95/130, or DM135/245 with private shower and toilet.

Places to Eat

You might expect a student town to have plenty of cheap eating, but unfortunately, free-spending tourists outweigh frugal scholars. If you can bluff your way into the *mensa*, a meal will only cost about DM3.50. For takeaways and picnics, seek out fast-food places and delicatessens along Hauptstrasse, though for cheaper sit-down food, Bergheimer Strasse, west of Bismarckplatz, is a better bet. There are also many student pubs (see Entertainment) with main courses from around DM13, though they tend to attract customers for the lively atmosphere rather than their culinary offerings.

The *Zum Güldenen Schaf*, a large old tavern at Hauptstrasse 115, has an extensive menu with local specialities priced from DM15. It's open daily until 1 am. The *Sudpfanne*, at Hauptstrasse 223, has similar cuisine from DM18.

The *Vegetarisches Restaurant*, Kurfür-

The main post office is on Leopoldsplatz. Baden-Baden's telephone code is 07221.

Things to See & Do
Baden-Baden's water was renowned back in Roman times. The ancient **Römische Badruinen** (Roman Bath Ruins) on Römerplatz are worth a quick look, but for a real taste of Baden-Baden head for the **Trinkhalle** at Kaiserallee 3. Here, in an ornate setting, the springs of Baden-Baden dispense curative drinking water (free with Kurkarte, open daily). Next door is the **Kurhaus** from the 1820s, which houses the opulent **casino** (guided tours every morning until 11.45 am; DM4).

The **Neues Schloss**, on the hill, has a good view and a small historical museum (open from Good Friday until October, closed Monday and Tuesday; DM2.50). The **Merkur Cable Car** takes you up to the 660-metre summit (DM5 return), from where there are fine views and numerous 'terrain treatment' trails, each with a specific gradient designed to therapeutically exercise your muscles. (Take bus No 5 from Leopoldplatz.) A good hiking/driving tour is to the wine-growing area of **Rebland**, six km to the west.

Spas On either side of Römerplatz are the two leading places where you can take the waters: the **Friedrichsbad** (☎ 27 59 21) at Römerplatz 1, and the **Caracalla-Therme** (☎ 27 59 40) at Römerplatz 11. A visit to one (or both) is an experience not to be missed.

The 19th-century Friedrichsbad is ornately Roman in style and offers two special bathing options: the Roman-Irish programme (DM25 with Kurkarte, DM23.80 for HI members) or the Roman-Irish Plus (DM34.20 with Kurkarte, DM32 for HI members).

Your two-odd hours of humid bliss consist of a timed series of hot and cold showers, saunas, steam rooms and baths that leave you feeling scrubbed, lubed and loose as a goose. The highlight of the Plus programme is the all-too-short soap-and-brush massage. At the end of the session they wrap you in a blanket for a half-hour's rest.

No clothing is allowed inside, and several of the bathing sections are mixed on most days, so leave your modesty at the reception desk. The Friedrichsbad is open Monday to Saturday from 9 am to 10 pm. Mixed bathing is on Wednesday and Saturday and from 4 pm on Tuesday and Friday.

The Caracalla-Therme, opened in 1985, has more than 1700 sq metres of outdoor and indoor pools, hot and cold-water caves ('grottoes') and whirlpools, showers and saunas. You're free to try any of these, but you must wear a bathing costume (not available for hire). Two-hour, three-hour and four-hour visits cost DM 28/24/32. It's open every day from 8 am till 10 pm, but the latest admission is two hours before closing time.

Places to Stay
Camping The closest camping is the *Campingplatz Adam* (☎ 07223-2 31 94), at Bühl-Oberbruch, about 12 km outside town, which charges DM9.50 per person plus DM9.50 for a tent/car site (summer prices). Take bus No 7135 from Leopoldplatz to the Bühl stop.

Hostel Baden-Baden has an appropriately ritzy *DJH hostel* (☎ 5 22 23) at Hardbergstrasse 34. From the station, take bus No 1 to Grosse-Dollen-Strasse and walk up the hill. It's about two km from the town centre and costs DM19/23.20 for juniors/seniors. The main hassle is the restricted check-in time: between 5 and 6 pm, and at 8 or 10 pm on the dot.

Private Rooms & Apartments Not everyone who comes to Baden-Baden is filthy rich, and a number of hotels and guesthouses in the town centre cater for less-well-to-do travellers. The tourist office can help you find cheaper private rooms or an apartment for longer stays. The prices given include breakfast and Kurtaxe.

Hotels & Pensions By Baden-Baden's standards, the *Hotel Löhr* (☎ 2 62 04) and the

GERMANY

Gästehaus Löhr (☎ 3 13 70) are a real bargain. Located in neighbouring buildings just off Augustaplatz at Adlerstrasse 2 and Stahlbadstrasse, the two are jointly managed. The reception is in the Café Löhr, at Lichtentaler Strasse 19. Rooms cost DM39/73 a single/double, or DM49/88 with private shower. Another good place is the *Hotel Zum Schützenhof* (☎ 2 40 88), at Baldbreitstrasse 1, where basic rooms cost DM49/98.

The *Hotel Am Markt* (☎ 2 27 47), Marktplatz 17, up by the Stiftskirche, charges DM52/92 for simple rooms, DM72/102 with private shower and DM119/134 with shower and toilet. The *Hotel Vier Jahreszeiten* (☎ 2 23 90), Lange Strasse 49, has large rooms, all with a shower unit in the corner, for DM59/98. Classier, but still affordable, is the *Hotel Römerhof* (☎ 2 34 15) at Sofienstrasse 25, where bright clean rooms with private shower and toilet cost DM74/148.

Places to Eat

Although Baden-Baden tends to live up to its pricey reputation, with a bit of backstreet reconnaissance you'll come up with an affordable place to eat.

For something cheap and tasty, go for *Hatip's Orientalisches Restaurant*, Gernsbacherstrasse 18. Stuffed aubergine with mince and rice costs DM9.50, and a half-litre of beer is just DM3.80. Another Eastern tip is the Indian *Namaskaar* (☎ 2 46 81) at Kreuzstrasse 1, with imaginative meat, fish and vegetarian dishes from DM19.

Locals favour the *Zum Nest* (☎ 2 30 76), Rettigstrasse 1, which serves up home-made noodles and some excellent risotto dishes (from DM17 with salad). It's closed on Tuesday. The *Weinstube im Baldreit*, on a small courtyard under the Stadtmuseum at Küferstrasse 3, also has some interesting culinary arrangements from DM 18. It's shut on Monday. The *Restaurant Badstüble* (☎ 93 80) in the Hotel Der Quellenhof at Sophienstrasse 27-29 has weekly and monthly specials, including a smorgasbord for DM35.

Getting There & Around

Baden-Baden is on the main north-south corridor. Trains leave every hour to most important destinations, including Frankfurt/Main (DM42), Freiburg/Basel (DM25/40), Heidelberg (DM19.40, direct or via Karlsruhe) and Stuttgart (DM29). The town is also close to the north-south A5 autobahn. Access the westward A8 at Karlsruhe.

The hub for city transport is Augustaplatz. One-zone single rides are DM2.50, while a 24-hour pass is DM6.

BLACK FOREST

There are lots of tourists and hikers roaming the Black Forest (Schwarzwald), but it's not hard to get away from the busy areas. Home of the cuckoo clock, the moniker 'Black Forest' comes from the dark canopy of evergreens. The fictional Hansel and Gretel encountered their wicked witch in these parts, but 20th-century hazards are rather more ominous. While superficially it seems as lush as ever, experts will tell you the Black Forest is being steadily destroyed by acid rain, ozone pollution and insect plagues. Enjoy it while you can.

Orientation & Information

The Black Forest lies east of the Rhine between Karlsruhe and Basel. It's roughly triangular in shape, about 160 km long and 50 km wide. Baden-Baden, Freudenstadt, Triberg and Freiburg act as convenient information posts for Black Forest excursions. Even smaller towns in the area generally have tourist offices.

Freudenstadt's tourist office (☎ 07441-86 40) is at Am Promenadeplatz 1. In Triberg, you'll find the tourist office (☎ 07722-95 32 30) at Luisenstrasse 10. (See also the previous Baden-Baden section and the Freiburg section that follows.)

Things to See

Though enjoying the natural countryside will be the main focus, there's still much history and culture to explore in the region.

Halfway between Baden-Baden and

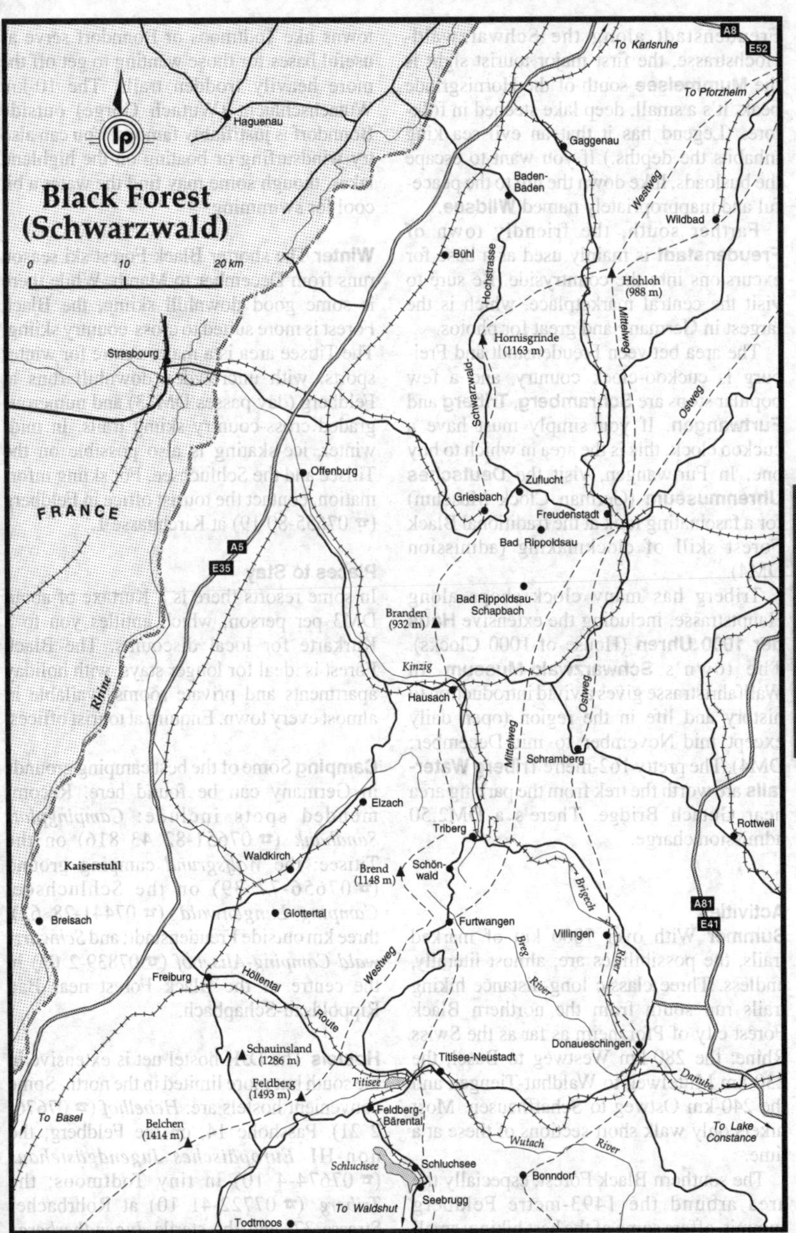

Black Forest
(Schwarzwald)
0
10
20 km
Haguenau
Strasbourg
FRANCE
Rhine
Kaiserstuhl
Breisach
To Basel
To Karlsruhe
A8
E52
To Pforzheim
Gaggenau
Baden-Baden
Wildbad
Westweg
Bühl
Hochstrasse
Hohloh
(988 m)
Mittelweg
Hornisgrinde
(1163 m)
Schwarzwald-
Ostweg
Offenburg
Zuflucht
Griesbach
Freudenstadt
Bad Rippoldsau
A5
E35
Bad Rippoldsau-
Schapbach
Branden
(932 m)
Kinzig
Hausach
Ostweg
Mittelweg
Schramberg
Elzach
Rottweil
Triberg
Waldkirch
Schön-
wald
Brend
(1148 m)
Brigach
Glottertal
A81
E41
Furtwangen
Villingen
Breg
River
River
Freiburg
Höllental
Route
Westweg
Schauinsland
(1286 m)
Donaueschingen
Titisee-Neustadt
Titisee
Danube
Feldberg
(1493 m)
Feldberg-
Bärental
Belchen
(1414 m)
To Lake
Constance
Wutach
River
Schluchsee
Schluchsee
Bonndorf
Seebrugg
To Waldshut
Todtmoos

Freudenstadt along the Schwarzwald-Hochstrasse, the first major tourist sight is the **Mummelsee** south of the Hornisgrinde peak. It's a small, deep lake steeped in folklore. (Legend has it that an evil sea king inhabits the depths.) If you want to escape the busloads, hike down the hill to the peaceful and inappropriately named **Wildsee**.

Farther south, the friendly town of **Freudenstadt** is mainly used as a base for excursions into the countryside. Be sure to visit the central marketplace, which is the largest in Germany and great for photos.

The area between Freudenstadt and Freiburg is cuckoo-clock country, and a few popular stops are **Schramberg**, **Triberg** and **Furtwangen**. If you simply must have a cuckoo clock, this is the area in which to buy one. In Furtwangen, visit the **Deutsches Uhrenmuseum** (German Clock Museum) for a fascinating look at the traditional Black Forest skill of clockmaking (admission DM4).

Triberg has many clock shops along Hauptstrasse, including the extensive **Haus der 1000 Uhren** (House of 1000 Clocks). The town's **Schwarzwald-Museum** in Wallfahrtstrasse gives a vivid introduction to history and life in the region (open daily except mid-November to mid-December; DM4). The pretty 162-metre **Triberg Waterfalls** are worth the trek from the parking area near Gutach Bridge. There's a DM2.50 admission charge.

Activities

Summer With over 7000 km of marked trails, the possibilities are, almost literally, endless. Three classic long-distance hiking trails run south from the northern Black Forest city of Pforzheim as far as the Swiss Rhine: the 280-km Westweg to Basel, the 230-km Mittelweg to Waldhut-Tiengen and the 240-km Ostweg to Schaffhausen. Most hikers only walk short sections of these at a time.

The southern Black Forest, especially the area around the 1493-metre Feldberg summit, offers some of the best hiking; small towns like Todtmoos or Bonndorf serve as useful bases for those wanting to get off the more heavily trodden trails. The 10-km Wutachschlucht (Wutach Gorge) outside Bonndorf is justifiably famous. You can also try windsurfing or boating on the highland lakes, though some may find the water a bit cool for swimming.

Winter The shorter Black Forest ski season runs from December to March. While there is some good downhill skiing, the Black Forest is more suited to cross-country skiing. The Titisee area is a major centre for winter sports, with uncrowded downhill runs at Feldberg (day passes DM33) and numerous graded cross-country skiing trails. In mid-winter, ice-skating is also possible on the Titisee and the Schluchsee. For skiing information, contact the tourist office in Feldberg (☎ 07655-80 19) at Kirchgasse 1.

Places to Stay

In some resorts there is a Kurtaxe of about DM3 per person, which entitles you to a Kurkarte for local discounts. The Black Forest is ideal for longer stays, with holiday apartments and private rooms available in almost every town. Enquire at tourist offices.

Camping Some of the best camping grounds in Germany can be found here. Recommended spots include: *Campingplatz Sandbank* (☎ 07651-82 43 816) on the Titisee; the *Wolfsgrund* camping ground (☎ 07656-77 39) on the Schluchsee; *Camping Langenwald* (☎ 07441-28 62), three km outside Freudenstadt; and *Schwarzwald-Camping-Alisehof* (☎ 07839-2 03) in the centre of the Black Forest near Bad Rippoldsau-Schapbach.

Hostels The DJH hostel net is extensive in the south but more limited in the north. Some convenient hostels are: *Hebelhof* (☎ 07676-2 21), Passhöhe 14, on the Feldberg; the non-HI *Europäisches Jugendgästehaus* (☎ 07674-4 10) in tiny Todtmoos; the *Triberg* (☎ 07722-41 10) at Rohrbacher Strasse 37; and the sterile *Jugendherberge*

Freudenstadt (☎ 07441-77 20) at Eugen-Nägele-Strasse 69 in Freudenstadt.

If you're hiking the Westweg, stop off at either the *Naturfreundehaus* (☎ 07226-23 8) in Plättig/Bühlerhöhe, or the *DJH hostel* (☎ 07804-6 11) in Zuflucht.

Hotels Many Black Forest hotels cater for higher-range budgets; however, some good deals for basic singles/doubles are: Seebrugg's *Pension Berger* (☎ 07656-2 38) along the Schluchsee (DM32/64); Triberg's *Hotel Bären* (☎ 07722-44 93), Hauptstrasse 10 (DM32/64); *Gasthaus Schwarzwaldstüble* (☎ 07722-33 24), at Obervogt, Huber-Strasse 25A (DM37 per person); Freudenstadt's central *Hotel Krone* (☎ 07441-25 59), Marktplatz 29 (DM35/70); and Schönwald's *Gasthof Schwarzwaldtanne* (☎ 07722-48 35) at Beethovenstrasse 7 (DM42/70).

Also in Freudenstadt is the *Hotel Dreikönig* (☎ 07441-8 32 99), at Martin-Luther-Strasse 3; rooms from DM35/68.

Places to Eat

Black Forest specialities include Schwarzwälderschinken (ham) and the much-imitated cherry cake. But restaurants are often expensive, so try to picnic whenever possible.

Along the main Talstrasse in the Glottertal region are the *Goldenen Engel* and the nearby *Hirschen*, both of which offer large serves from DM14.

In ultratouristy Titisee, try the *Hirschstüble* (☎ 07651-84 86), near the church at Im Winkel 3. It has healthy-sized main courses for around DM15 (and rooms for DM40/80). Farther north in Triberg, the *Krone*, Schulstrasse 37, has basic German dishes from DM12, while the *Peking Restaurant*, down at Hauptstrasse 1, serves quality Chinese cuisine from DM13 per main course.

In Freudenstadt the *Hotel Dreikönig* (☎ 07441-8 32 99), at Martin-Luther-Strasse 3, is great value with Greek dishes priced from DM11. Also good is *Gasthof Kaiser*, Schulstrasse 9, just off the main square (closed Saturday).

Getting There & Away

The north-south train route allows easy access to the region. Trains run very frequently between Karlsruhe and Basel, calling at Baden-Baden and Freiburg en route. There are also direct train connections to some of the hub towns from Strasbourg, Stuttgart and Constance. Road access is good too, with the A5 skirting the western side of the forest and the A81 the eastern side.

Getting Around

The rail network is surprisingly extensive for such a mountainous area. The most useful lines link Baden-Baden, Freudenstadt and Freiburg. One of the prettiest stretches runs between Freiburg and Titisee (DM8.60). Sightseers in a hurry should ask about the Schwarzwald-Rundfahrticket for DM35 that allows unlimited travel by train for one day (or two days if you start on a Saturday) within the Freiburg-Offenburg-Donaueschingen rail triangle.

Where rail fails to go, the bus system usually leads the way, but travel times can be slow in this rugged terrain. If you plan to spend several days in the southern Black Forest, consider the seven-day Südbaden Bus-Pass for DM35 (DM50 for two people) which is valid for the entire SBG network between Constance and Freiburg, and from Sulz right down to the Swiss border. Similar bus passes are available in other areas. Cycling is a good way to get about, despite the hills. Bikes can be hired at larger train stations.

Drivers enjoy flexibility in an area that rewards it. The main tourist road, the Schwarzwald-Hochstrasse (B500), runs from Baden-Baden to Freudenstadt and Triberg to Waldshut. Other thematic roads to explore are the Schwarzwald-Bäderstrasse (spa town route), Schwarzwald-Panoramastrasse (good views) and Badische Weinstrasse (wine route).

FREIBURG

The gateway to the southern Black Forest, Freiburg (full name: Freiburg im Breisgau) has a relaxed atmosphere accentuated by the city's large and thriving university community. Ruled for centuries by the Austrian Habsburgs, Freiburg has retained many traditional features, although major reconstruction was necessary following severe bombing damage during WW II. The monumental 13th-century cathedral is the city's key landmark.

Orientation

The city centre is a convenient 10 minutes' walk from the train station. Walk east along Eisenbahnstrasse to the tourist office, then continue through the bustling pedestrian zone to Münsterplatz, dominated by the red stone cathedral. All the sights are within walking distance of here.

Information

The tourist office (☎ 0761-368 90 90), Rotteckring 14, is open Monday to Saturday from 9 am to 9.30 pm, and Sunday and holidays from 10 am to 2 pm. Closure times from 1 October to 31 May are brought forward to 6 pm weekdays, 2 pm Saturday and noon Sunday and public holidays. Pick up the excellent official guide (DM6). The office has a free room-finding service. There's an information board showing accommodation just outside the entrance.

If you plan to hike in the Black Forest, contact the very helpful Schwarzwaldverein (Black Forest Club, ☎ 0761-2 27 94), at Bismarckallee 2a, for information on routes, mountain huts and maps.

The main post office, Eisenbahnstrasse 58-62, is open from 8 am to 8 pm on weekdays, to 6 pm on Saturday and 10 am to 3 pm on Sunday and holidays.

Freiburg's telephone code is 0761.

Dangers & Annoyances Steer clear of the drunks and beggars around the train station and the nearby Stühlinger Platz. They can become intimidating in the evening.

Things to See

The major sightseeing goal is the **Münster** cathedral, a classic example of high and late-Gothic architecture looming over Münsterplatz, Freiburg's active market square. Of particular interest are the stone and wood carvings, the stained-glass windows and the west porch. Ascend the tower to the stunning pierced spire (DM1.50) for great views of Freiburg and, on a clear day, the Kaiserstuhl and the Vosges. South of the Münster stands the picturesque **Kaufhaus**, the 16th-century merchants' hall.

Be sure to notice the pavement mosaics on the pedestrian laneways, but take care to sidestep the old drainage system, the **Bächle**, formerly used to clean beasts and combat fire. From the cathedral, wander south to the beautiful city gate, the **Schwabentor**, and peer into **Zum Roten Bären**, reputedly the oldest inn in Germany. The **University quarter** is north-west of the Martinstor and usually bustling with students. Along Bertoldstrasse, check the **Universitätskirche** (University Church) and then walk round the back to the picturesque Rathausplatz.

Near Augustinerplatz are the **Museum of Ethnology**, the **Museum of Natural History** and the **Augustiner Museum. The Museum of Prehistory** is in Columbipark, on the corner of Eisenbahnstrasse and Rotteckring. The city's museums are all closed on Monday and, except for the Augustiner Museum (DM4, students DM2), are free.

Activities

Schauinsland The popular trip by cableway to the 1286-metre Schauinsland peak is a quick way to reach the Black Forest highlands. Numerous easy and well-marked trails make the Schauinsland area ideal for day walks. From Freiburg take tram No 2 south towards Günterstal and then bus No 21 to Talstation. The five-hour hike to the Untermünstertal offers some of the best views with the fewest people; return to Freiburg via the train to Staufen and then take the bus.

Cable-car tickets cost DM11/18 single/return (DM8/14 for students and rail-pass holders). To avoid heading up into the fog, check the weather report on ☎ 1 97 03.

Places to Stay

Camping The most convenient spot is *Camping Hirzberg* (☎ 3 50 54) at Kartäuserstrasse 99. Take tram No 1 to Messeplatz (direction: Littenweiler), and then go under the road and across the stream. It charges DM6 per person, DM5 per tent and DM3.50 for cars, and is open from 1 April to mid-October. Farther north of the city are *Camping Breisgau* (☎ 07665-23 46) in Hochdorf (open all year) and the luxurious *Camping Tunisee* (☎ 07665-22 49).

Hostels & Private Rooms Out near Camping Breisgau, the rural *DJH hostel* (☎ 6 76 56), Kartäuserstrasse 151, is often full with groups of German students, so phone ahead. Take tram No 1 to Römerhof (direction: Littenweiler) and follow the signs

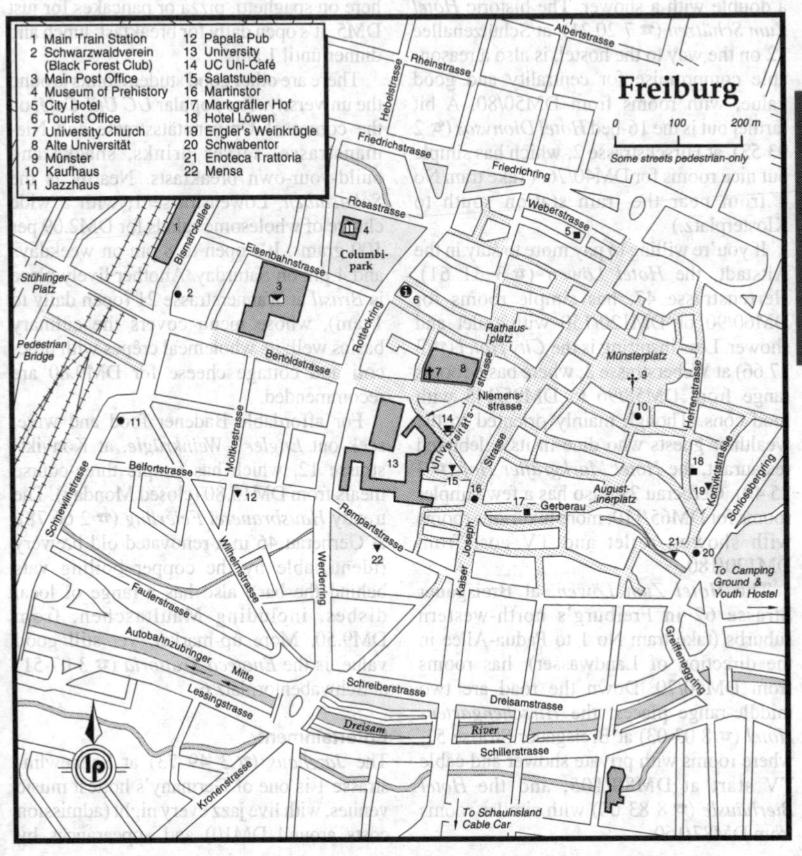

down Fritz-Geiges-Strasse. Beds cost DM19/24 for juniors/seniors. Reception is open all day and there is an 11.30 pm curfew.

The tourist office may be able to find a private room for you, but don't count on it.

Hotels & Pensions Finding an affordable room anywhere near the centre of town can be difficult – even Freiburg's students get frustrated.

The only central lower-budget option is *Pension Schemmer* (☎ 27 20), at Eschholzstrasse 63 behind the train station, where singles/doubles cost DM45/75, or DM80 for a double with a shower. The historic *Hotel Zum Schützen* (☎ 7 20 21), at Schützenallee 12 on the way to the hostel, is also a reasonable compromise for centrality and good value, with rooms from DM50/80. A bit farther out is the 16-bed *Hotel Dionysos* (☎ 2 93 53), at Hirschstrasse 2, which has simple but nice rooms for DM40/76. (Take tram No 4 from near the train station south to Klosterplatz.)

If you're willing to pay more to stay in the Altstadt, the *Hotel Löwen* (☎ 3 31 61), Herrenstrasse 47, has simple rooms for DM60/90 or DM120/150 with toilet and shower. Less inspiring is the *City Hotel* (☎ 3 17 66) at Weberstrasse 3, where basic rooms range from DM58/96 to DM95/145 with mod cons. Though mainly oriented to the wealthier guests who dine in its celebrated restaurant, the *Hotel Markgräfler Hof* (☎ 3 25 40), Gerberau 22, also has a few simpler rooms for DM65/110; more luxurious rooms with shower, toilet and TV cost from DM120/180.

The *Hotel Zum Löwen*, at Breisgauer Strasse 62 in Freiburg's north-western suburbs (take tram No 1 to Padua-Allee in the direction of Landwasser), has rooms from DM40/70. Down the road are two middle-range places: the *Hirschengarten-Hotel* (☎ 8 03 03) at Breisgauer Strasse 51, where rooms with private shower and cable TV start at DM80/105, and the *Hotel Bierhäusle* (☎ 8 83 00) with similar rooms from DM87/160.

Places to Eat

Being a university town, Freiburg virtually guarantees cheap eats. Take advantage of this while you can, as Black Forest food is more expensive.

The university-subsidised *mensas* at Rempartstrasse 18 (Monday to Saturday lunch only) and Hebelstrasse 9a (lunch and dinner) have salad buffets and other filling fodder. You may be asked to show a student ID when buying meal tickets (DM3.70), but it's worth a try.

The *Papala Pub*, at Moltkestrasse 30, is a typical Freiburg student hang-out with a slightly nostalgic 1970s feel. You can fill up here on spaghetti, pizza or pancakes for just DM5. It's open daily for breakfast, lunch and dinner until 1 am.

There are other good student joints around the university. The popular *UC Uni-Café*, on the corner of Universitätsstrasse and Niemanstrasse, serves drinks, snacks and build-your-own breakfasts. Nearby is the *Salatstuben*, Löwenstrasse 1, with a wide choice of wholesome salads for DM2.09 per 100 grams. It's open to 8 pm on weekdays and 4 pm on Saturday. Another lively place is *Brasil* at Wannerstrasse 21 (open daily to 1 am), whose menu covers the culinary basics well; its wholemeal crêpes with broccoli and cottage cheese for DM9.80 are recommended.

For affordable Badener food and wine, seek out *Engler's Weinkrügle*, at Konviktstrasse 12, which has simple three-course meals from DM15.80 (closed Monday). The trendy *Hausbrauerei Feierling* (☎ 2 66 78), at Gerberau 46 in a renovated old brewery (identifiable by the copper boiling vats behind the bar), also has a range of local dishes, including Maultaschen, from DM9.50. More up-market, yet still good value, is the *Enoteca Trattoria* (☎ 3 07 51) at Schwabentorplatz 6.

Entertainment

The *Jazzhaus* (☎ 3 49 73) at Schnewlinstrasse 1 is one of Germany's hottest music venues, with live jazz every night (admission costs around DM10) and appearances by internationally acclaimed artists. For a detailed programme, pick up a free copy of the monthly *Jazzhaus Journal* from the tourist office, university or cafés around town.

Freiburg is a great place to buy and taste the local wines of the Baden region. The best times for this are late June for the five days of *Weintagen* (Wine Days), or mid-August for the nine days of *Weinkost* (Wine Fare).

Getting There & Away

Freiburg lies directly on the north-south train corridor, and is therefore highly accessible. Trains frequently depart for Basel, Baden-Baden, Freudenstadt and Donaueschingen. The main A5 autobahn linking Frankfurt and Basel also passes Freiburg. This is an easy hitching route, but for more certainty call the Citynetz Mitfahr-Service (☎ 1 94 44) at Belfortstrasse 55. The nearest international airport is at Mulhouse/Basel in France (access via the A5/A36); airport buses (DM20; one hour) leave from the bus station beside the train station.

Getting Around

On the efficient local bus-and-tram network single rides cost DM2.50. The 24-hour Freiburger Stadtkarte allows unlimited travel with up to four children for two adults (DM9) or one adult (DM6.50), so it pays for itself after three rides. For longer stays, a Monday-to-Sunday ticket for DM18 will work out cheaper. For bicycle rental, try Fahradverleih Radhaus (☎ 28 08 32) at Turnseestrasse 10.

DANUBE RIVER

The Danube (Donau), one of Europe's great rivers, rises in the Black Forest. In Austria, Hungary and Romania it is a mighty, almost intimidating, waterway, but in Germany it's narrower and more tranquil, making it ideal for hiking, biking and motoring tours.

Orientation & Information

The Danube flows from west to east through Central Europe, finally finding an outlet in the Black Sea. In a nominal sense, Donaueschingen is the source of the river proper, though the Black Forest town of Furtwangen, on the Breg River, has a superior claim to being the true source of its waters – a rivalry that stimulates tourism to both places.

Donaueschingen has a tourist office (☎ 0771-85 72 21) at Karlstrasse 58 that is open weekdays, and also Saturday morning in summer. The Danube leads north-east through the large regional centres of Ulm and Regensburg. Ulm's tourist office (☎ 0731-6 41 61) is in an incongruous new building on Münsterplatz, and open Monday to Friday from 9 am to 6 pm as well as Saturday mornings. The river then sweeps south-east and leaves Germany at Passau (see the Regensburg and Passau entries in the Bavaria section).

Things to See & Do

Donaueschingen To mark the source of the Danube, the town has the **Donauquelle** (Danube Source) monument in the park of the Fürstenberg Schloss. This arbitrarily positioned pool points out that it's 2840 km to the Black Sea. However, the two tributaries that meet one km down the path, the Brigach and the Breg, actually rise farther from the Black Sea. Both these rivers are worth exploring.

Ulm *The* reason for coming to Ulm is to see the huge **Münster**, famous for its 161-metre-high steeple – the tallest anywhere in the world. Though the first stone was laid in 1377, it took just over 500 years for the entire structure to be completed. Only by climbing to the top (DM2.50) via the 768 spiralling steps do you fully appreciate the tower's astonishing height. The nearby **town hall**, adorned with frescos and an interesting astronomical clock, also demands inspection. Stroll past the **Schwörhaus** (Oath House) into the charming **Fischerviertel** – the old city's artisan quarter built along canals running into the Danube – then head downstream beside the river, with the old **Stadtmauer** (city walls) on your left.

Cycling The river's course can be followed by car, boat or on foot, but perhaps the most enjoyable way is by bicycle. The Donauradweg bike track now runs the entire length of the German Danube, from Donaueschingen to Passau and beyond into Austria. Local tourist offices and bookshops sell a German-language booklet, *Radwandern von Donaueschingen bis Passau* (DM16.80), which has detailed route maps and a list of budget accommodation in every town along the way.

Bikes can be hired at train stations in Ulm, Regensburg and Passau and returned to any of the others. It's also possible to send your pack ahead on the train. Donaueschingen's Southern Cross Independent Hostel (see Places to Stay & Eat) also rents bikes.

Places to Stay & Eat

Donaueschingen The excellent *Southern Cross Independent Hostel* (☎ 0771-33 27), Josefstrasse 13, is run by an ex-traveller who knows what backpackers want most: cheap, convenient and friendly accommodation. The hostel has a kitchen, a bar and several dorms with beds for DM15. The owner, Martin, also runs Southern Cross Travel on the premises, offering cheap worldwide flights.

A few doors up, at Josefstrasse 7-9, is the *Hotel Bären*, with singles/doubles for DM45/90. The *Hotel Ochsen* (☎ 0771-8 09 90), at Käferstrasse 18, has a few simple singles for DM45 and nicer singles/doubles/triples with private bathroom and cable TV priced from DM72/105/140.

The *SB Restaurant*, at Käferstrasse 16, is a good option for cheap food (Linsentopf DM8.50, Gulash DM4); it's open Monday to Friday. The *Zum Schützen*, at Josefstrasse 2, offers generous main courses priced from DM14.

Ulm The *DJH hostel* (☎ 0731-38 44 55) at Grimmelfinger Weg 45 charges juniors/seniors DM18.80/23.80 with breakfast. From the train station, take tram No 1 to Ehinger Tor, then bus No 4 to Schulzentrum, from where it's five minutes' walk. Across the river in Neu-Ulm are the *Gaststätte Max'l* (☎ 0731-78 60 5) at Maximilianstrasse 13 (singles/doubles DM35/70) and the *Rose* (☎ 0731-7 78 03) at Kasernstrasse 42a (singles/doubles DM40/80).

The *Rösch* (☎ 0731-6 57 18) at Schwörhausgasse 18 has singles/doubles priced from DM45/90. Even more central is the homely *Spanische Weinstube* (☎ 0731-6 32 97), right beside the Münster at Rabengasse 2, with rooms from DM49/85. It has a good restaurant downstairs. In the Fischerviertel, the *Allgäuer Hof* at Fischergasse 12 has basic dishes for around DM15, while the more up-market *Zunfthaus* at Fischergasse 31 offers local Swabian specialities.

Getting There & Away

Donaueschingen is on the Constance-Freiburg train route; Ulm is on the main Stuttgart-Munich train line. The Danube is shadowed by a series of roads, most notably the B311 (Tuttlingen to Ulm), the B16 (Ulm to Regensburg) and the B8 (Regensburg to Passau). North-south autobahns intersect at various points.

LAKE CONSTANCE

Lake Constance (Bodensee) is a perfect cure for travellers in landlocked southern Germany. The German side of this giant bulge in the sinewy course of the Rhine offers a choice of water sports, relaxation or cultural pursuits. The lake's southern side provides access to Switzerland and Austria.

The town of Constance (Konstanz) achieved historical significance in 1414 when the Council of Constance convened to try to heal huge rifts in the Church. The consequent burning at the stake of the religious reformer, Jan Hus, as a heretic, and the scattering of his ashes over the lake, failed to block the impetus of the Reformation.

Orientation & Information

The German side of Lake Constance features three often-crowded tourist centres in Constance, Meersburg and the island of Lindau. It's essentially a summer area, too often foggy or at best hazy in winter. In the low

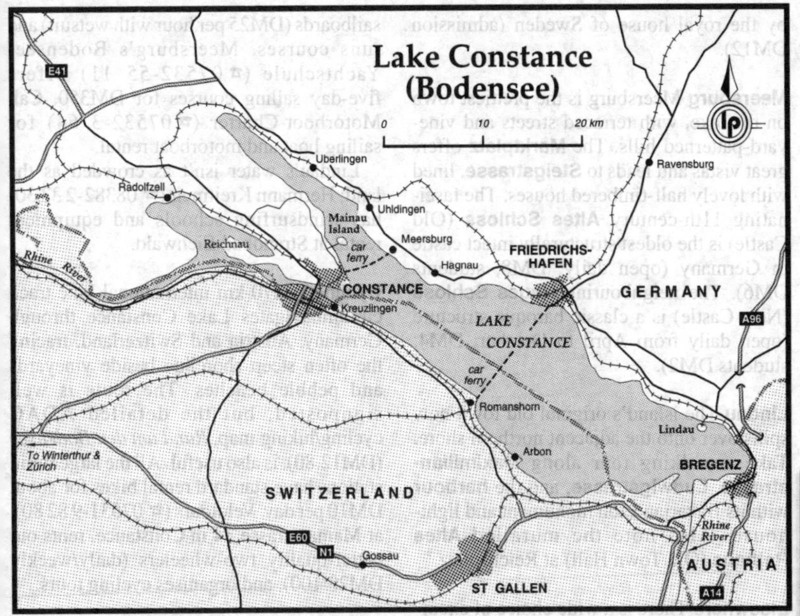

season, the pre-Lent Fasnacht celebrations can be lively, helped along by Constance's large student population.

In the west, Constance straddles the Swiss border, good fortune that spared it from Allied bombing in WW II. The tourist office (☎ 07531-28 43 76) is at Bahnhofplatz 13 (to the right as you leave the station). It's open weekdays between 9 am and 6 pm, and summer Saturdays to 1 pm.

Meersburg lies across the lake from Constance and is an ideal base for exploring the long northern shore. The helpful tourist office (☎ 07532-43 11 11) is up the steep hill on the Schlossplatz at Kirchstrasse 4. It's open Monday to Friday from 9 am to noon, and 2 to 5 pm. Nearby Friedrichshafen, the largest and most 'central' city on the lake's northern shore, has its own tourist office (☎ 07541-3 00 10) near the train station at Bahnhofsplatz 2.

Most of the German part of Lake Constance lies within Baden-Württemberg, but Lindau in the east is just inside Bavaria, near the Austrian border. The tourist office (☎ 08382-2 60 00), directly opposite the station, is open weekdays and Saturday mornings in summer.

Things to See

The lake itself adds special atmosphere to the many historic towns around its periphery, which can be explored by boat, bicycle and on foot.

Constance The town's most visible feature is the Gothic spire of the **cathedral**, added only in 1856 to a church that was started in 1052. The views from the top are excellent. Follow the walking tour of the historic centre prescribed in the tourist office leaflet, lingering in the **Stadtgarten** and the bohemian **Rheingasse** quarter. If you have time, head across the footbridge to **Mainau Island**, a peaceful tropical garden that was established by the royal house of Sweden (admission DM12).

Meersburg Meersburg is the prettiest town on the lake, with terraced streets and vineyard-patterned hills. The **Marktplatz** offers great vistas and leads to **Steigstrasse**, lined with lovely half-timbered houses. The fascinating 11th-century **Altes Schloss** (Old Castle) is the oldest structurally intact castle in Germany (open daily; DM8, students DM6). The neighbouring **Neues Schloss** (New Castle) is a classic baroque structure (open daily from April to October; DM4, students DM2).

Lindau The island's original old town now spills over onto the adjacent northern shore. Take a walking tour along **Maximilianstrasse**, **Ludwigstrasse**, and the **harbour** with its Bavarian Lion monument and lighthouse. Also note the muralled **Altes Rathaus** (Old Town Hall) at Reichsplatz.

Elsewhere There is a wide choice of excursions around the lake. Count Zeppelin was born in Constance, but first built his cigar-shaped balloons over in Friedrichshafen, an endeavour commemorated in that town's **Zeppelin Museum** (admission DM4; closed Monday). Überlingen features the astonishing **Cathedral of St Nicholas**, which boasts a dozen side altars and a wooden four-storey central altar dating from the 17th century. Another impressive baroque church can be found at Birnau.

Activities

Water Sports In season, the lake offers plenty of possibilities. In Constance, five public beaches are open from May to September, including the Strandbad Horn with nude bathing. See 3 UP (☎ 07531-2 31 17), Münzgasse 10, Constance, for equipment and courses.

Meersburg is perhaps a better base for watery pursuits, and some of the best windsurfers hang out here. The Surfschule Meersburg (☎ 07532-53 30) at Uferpromenade 37 is well organised and hires out sailboards (DM25 per hour with wetsuit) and runs courses. Meersburg's Bodensee-Yachtschule (☎ 07532-55 11) offers five-day sailing courses for DM350. Call Motorboot-Charter (☎ 07532-3 64) for sailing boat and motorboat rental.

Lindau's water isn't as crowded as the land; Hermann Kreitmeir (☎ 08382-2 33 30) has windsurfing schools and equipment rental at Strandbad Eichwald.

Cycling A 270-km international bike track circumnavigates Lake Constance through Germany, Austria and Switzerland, tracing the often steep shoreline beside vineyards and pebble beaches. The route is well signposted, but the detailed ADAC cycling/hiking map, *Rund um den Bodensee* (DM12.80), is also useful. All the larger train stations have standard rental bikes for about DM10 per day. Velotours (☎ 07531-9 82 80), at Mainaustrasse 34 in Constance, rents out better-quality two-wheelers (daily/weekly DM20/100), and organises cycling tours.

Places to Stay

The lake's popularity among German tourists pushes up accommodation prices; fortunately excellent hostel and camping facilities exist around the lake. See tourist offices for apartments and private rooms.

Camping Though there are many others along the shore, recommended camping grounds include the following: *Campingplatz Mainau* (☎ 07531-4 43 21) opposite Mainau Island near Constance; *Camping Hagnau* (☎ 07545-64 13), four km east of Meersburg (one of three camping grounds side by side); *Camping Seeperle* (☎ 07556-54 54) in Uhldingen-Seefelden, seven km west of Meersburg; and *Campingplatz Lindau-Zech* (☎ 08382-7 22 36), three km south-east of Lindau (1 April to 15 October).

Hostels The *DJH hostel* (☎ 07531-3 22 60) at Zur Allmannshohe 18 in Constance is open from March to October and costs DM17/23 for juniors/seniors. Take bus No 1 or 4 from the station. The *DJH hostel*

(☎ 07551-42 04), Alte Nussdorfer Strasse 26 in Überlingen, 15 km west of Meersburg, costs DM18.20/23.20. Lindau's hostel (☎ 08382-58 13) at Herbergsweg 11 is being rebuilt and will reopen in summer 1996 (juniors only). The Friedrichshafen *DJH hostel* (☎ 07541-7 24 04) is at Lindauer Strasse 3 (DM17.20/22.20).

Hotels In Constance, the *Pension Graf* (☎ 07531-2 14 86), close to the station at Wiesenstrasse 2, has tiny singles/doubles priced from DM46/85. Also central is the *Barbarossa* (☎ 07531-2 20 21), Obermarkt 8-12, with rooms with shower for DM55/98.

In Meersburg proper, the cheapest place is the cosy *Hotel Zum Lieben Augustin* (☎ 07532-65 11), in Unterstadtstrasse, which charges DM40/78 (showers DM2.50 extra). Not far out of town, the *Gasthaus zum Letzten Heller* (☎ 07532-61 49), Daisendorfer Strasse 41, has rooms priced from DM38/76 (great food, too).

In Lindau, the best deals on the island are the *Gästehaus Limmer* (☎ 08382-58 77), In der Grub 16, with rooms for DM34/66, and *Gasthof Inselgraben* (☎ 08382-54 81), at Hintere Metzgergasse 4-6, which has basic rooms with TV for DM50/90 (or DM40/70 without breakfast).

Places to Eat

You'll pay extra to eat anywhere overlooking the water, and the food rarely matches the prices.

In Constance, check the *Seekuh* at Konzilstrasse 4, a student-type bar that dishes up great food and company. Salads, pasta and pizza are priced from DM5 to DM10. It's open every evening until 1 am. The *Zur Wendelgard*, Inselgasse 5, has a good range of vegetarian meals for around DM18 (closed Monday). The Turkish *Sedir*, near the Münster at Hofhalde 11, is open daily, attracting a young clientele with its cheap and tasty böreks (flaky pastries) and pides (pizzas); you can eat here for as little as DM7.50. The university *mensa* also has cheap meals.

In Meersburg, the *Gasthof zum Bären*, at Marktplatz 11, has hearty main courses from DM14. A more up-market alternative, the *Alemannen-Torkel* (☎ 07532-10 67), in an old wine cellar at Steigstrasse 16-18, has Baden vintage wines and serves specialities priced from DM23 (open daily).

As far as dining out goes, Lindau can be the downfall of any budget traveller. For that cheaper picnic option, go to the *Früchtehaus Hannes*, In der Grub 36, which offers everything from fruit, vegetables, meats, fish, pastas and an array of ready-mixed salads. The touristy *Goldenes Lamm* on Paradiesplatz has filling main courses priced from DM16 and occasional live music.

Getting There & Away

Constance has train connections every one to two hours to Zürich, Donaueschingen (DM19.40) and Stuttgart (DM46). Meersburg is most easily reached by bus from Friedrichshafen (DM5.60), or by the car ferry from Constance (every 15 minutes all year; DM2, plus DM1.50 per bicycle). The car ferry between Friedrichshafen and Romanshorn (Switzerland) runs hourly in each direction (every two hours in winter). Lindau can be reached by train from Zürich (daily), Bregenz (hourly, 15 minutes), Ulm (via Friedrichshafen) and Munich (2½ hours).

Getting Around

Although trains link Lindau, Friedrichshafen and Constance, buses provide the easiest land connections. By car, the B31 hugs the northern shore of Lake Constance but it can get busy. The most enjoyable way to get around is on the ferries (☎ 07541-20 13 89), which from April to October call in several times a day at all the larger towns along both sides of the lake; the fare from Lindau to Constance is DM17.60 (3½ hours). There are concessions for holders of rail passes.

Rhineland-Palatinate

Rhineland-Palatinate (Rheinland-Pfalz) has a rugged topography characterised by thinly populated mountain ranges and forests cut by deep river valleys. Created after WW II from parts of the former Rhineland and Rhenish Palatinate regions, its turbulent history saw the area settled by the Romans and later hotly contested by the French and a variety of German states. The state capital is Mainz.

This land of wine and great natural beauty is still a secret spot for many travellers willing to get off the busy Rhine River tourist route. Instead of just riding the Rhine wave, head for the Moselle Valley, or become one of the few English-speaking travellers who visit the Ahr Valley, famous for its light and fruity red wines.

THE MOSELLE VALLEY

Exploring the vineyards and wineries of the Moselle (Mosel) Valley is an ideal way to get a taste of German culture, the people and, of course, the wonderful wines. Take the time to slow down and do some sipping.

There is, however, more to the Moselle than wine-making. The many historical sites and picturesque towns built along the river banks below steep rocky cliffs planted out with vineyards (they say locals are born with one leg shorter than the other so that they can more easily work the vines) make this one of the country's most romantically scenic regions. Though the entire route is packed with visitors from June to October, getting off the beaten path is always easy.

Orientation & Information

The German section of the Moselle Valley runs 195 km south-west from Koblenz to Trier. The river takes a slow, winding course, revealing new scenery at every bend.

At Koblenz, the tourist office (☎ 0261-3 13 04) is in the small, round building adjoining the bus area opposite the main train station. In the Moselle Valley proper, the staff in Cochem's tourist office (☎ 02671-39 71/72), on Endertplatz next to the bridge, are especially keen to please. In Bernkastel-Kues, the tourist office (06531-40 23) is at Am Gestade 5. Almost all other towns along the river have a visitor information centre; otherwise, people at the vineyards are usually full of ideas.

Things to See

Koblenz While not to be compared with Trier or Cochem, Koblenz is a nice enough place to spend half a day or so. The **Deutsches Eck** is a park at the sharp confluence of the Rhine and Moselle dedicated to German unity. Immediately across the Rhine is the impressive **Festung Ehrenbreitstein** fortress, which now houses the DJH hostel and the **Landesmuseum** (admission free).

Burg Eltz Not to be missed is a visit to Burg Eltz (open from April to November) at the head of the beautiful Eltz Valley. Towering over the surrounding hills, this superb medieval castle has frescos, paintings, furniture and ornately decorated rooms.

Burg Eltz is best reached by train to Moselkern, from where it's a 40-minute walk up through the forest. Alternatively, you can drive directly to the nearby car park. The interior can only be inspected with a tour (DM8, students DM5.50). Also worth seeing is the collection of artefacts in the **Schatzkammer** (DM2.50/1.50).

Cochem Cochem is one of those picture-postcard German towns with narrow alleyways and gates, and is a good base for hikes into the hills. For a great view, head up to the **Pinnerkreuz** with the chair lift on Endertstrasse. The trip up costs DM5.50 (DM8 return), and it's a nice walk back down through the vineyards. The famous **Reichsburg** castle is about 15 minutes' walk up the hill from town. There are regular tours (DM5 or DM4.50 students) between 9 am and 5 pm from mid-March to November; English translation sheets are available.

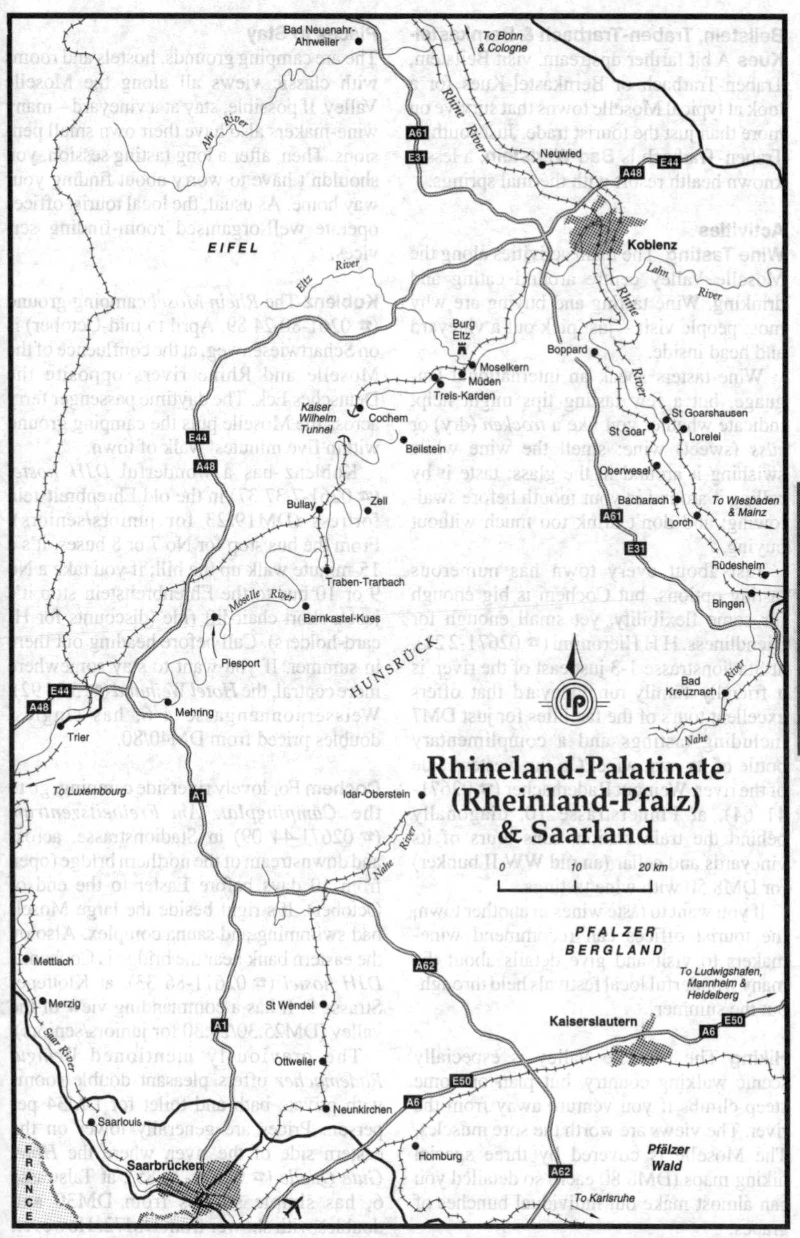
Rhineland-Palatinate
(Rheinland-Pfalz)
& Saarland
Bad Neuenahr-Ahrweiler
To Bonn & Cologne
Ahr River
Rhine River
A61
E31
Neuwied
A48
E44
Koblenz
EIFEL
Eltz River
Lahn River
Rhine River
Burg Eltz
Boppard
Moselkern
Müden
Treis-Karden
Kaiser Wilhelm Tunnel
Cochem
Beilstein
St Goarshausen
St Goar
Lorelei
Oberwesel
Bacharach
To Wiesbaden & Mainz
Lorch
E44
A48
Bullay
Zell
A61
E31
Rüdesheim
Bingen
Traben-Trarbach
Moselle River
Bernkastel-Kues
Piesport
HUNSRÜCK
Bad Kreuznach
River
Nahe
E44
A48
Mehring
Trier
To Luxembourg
A1
Idar-Oberstein
Nahe River
0
10
20 km
PFALZER BERGLAND
Mettlach
A62
To Ludwigshafen, Mannheim & Heidelberg
Merzig
St Wendel
Saar River
A1
Kaiserslautern
A6
E50
Ottweiler
E50
A6
Neunkirchen
Saarlouis
FRANCE
Homburg
Pfälzer Wald
Saarbrücken
A62
To Karlsruhe

GERMANY

Beilstein, Traben-Trarbach & Bernkastel-Kues A bit farther upstream, visit Beilstein, Traben-Trarbach or Bernkastel-Kues for a look at typical Moselle towns that survive on more than just the tourist trade. Just south of Traben-Trarbach is **Bad Wildstein**, a lesser known health resort with thermal springs.

Activities

Wine Tasting The main activities along the Moselle Valley centre around eating and drinking. Wine tasting and buying are why most people visit – just pick out a vineyard and head inside.

Wine tasters speak an international language, but a few tasting tips might help: indicate whether you like a *trocken* (dry) or *süss* (sweet) wine; smell the wine while swishing it around in the glass; taste it by rolling it around in your mouth before swallowing; and don't drink too much without buying.

Just about every town has numerous tasting options, but Cochem is big enough for some flexibility, yet small enough for friendliness. H H Hieronimi (☎ 02671-2 21), at Stadionstrasse 1-3 just east of the river, is a friendly family-run vineyard that offers excellent tours of the facilities for just DM7 including tastings and a complimentary bottle of its own wine. On the western side of the river, Weingut Rademacher (☎ 02671-41 64), at Pinnerstrasse 10, diagonally behind the train station, runs tours of its vineyards and cellar (an old WW II bunker) for DM8.50 with wine tastings.

If you want to taste wines in another town, the tourist offices can recommend wine-makers to visit and give details about the many wonderful local festivals held throughout the summer.

Hiking The Moselle Valley is especially scenic walking country, but plan on some steep climbs if you venture away from the river. The views are worth the sore muscles. The Moselle is covered by three special hiking maps (DM8.80 each) so detailed you can almost make out individual bunches of grapes.

Places to Stay

The are camping grounds, hostels and rooms with classic views all along the Moselle Valley. If possible, stay at a vineyard – many wine-makers also have their own small pensions. Then, after a long tasting session, you shouldn't have to worry about finding your way home. As usual, the local tourist offices operate well-organised room-finding services.

Koblenz The *Rhein Mosel* camping ground (☎ 0261-80 24 89, April to mid-October) is on Schartwiesenweg, at the confluence of the Moselle and Rhine rivers opposite the Deutsches Eck. The daytime passenger ferry across the Moselle puts the camping ground within five minutes' walk of town.

Koblenz has a wonderful *DJH hostel* (☎ 0261-7 37 37) in the old Ehrenbreitstein fortress (DM19/23 for juniors/seniors). From the bus stop for No 7 or 8 buses, it's a 15-minute walk up the hill; if you take a No 9 or 10 bus to the Ehrenbreitstein stop it's just a short chair-lift ride (discounts for HI card-holders). Call before heading out there in summer. If you want to stay somewhere more central, the *Hotel Weinand* (☎ 3 24 92), Weissernonnengasse 4-6, has singles/doubles priced from DM40/80.

Cochem For lovely riverside camping, go to the *Campingplatz Am Freiheitszentrum* (☎ 02671-44 09) in Stadionstrasse, across and downstream of the northern bridge (open from 10 days before Easter to the end of October). It's right beside the large Moselbad swimming and sauna complex. Also on the eastern bank near the bridge is Cochem's *DJH hostel* (☎ 02671-86 33), at Klottener Strasse 9. It has a commanding view of the valley (DM25.30/29.30 for juniors/seniors).

The previously mentioned *Weingut Rademacher* offers pleasant double rooms with private bath and toilet for DM34 per person. Prices are generally lower on the eastern side of the river, where the *Hotel Gute Quelle* (☎ 02671-74 85), at Talstrasse 6, has simple singles from DM30 and doubles with shower from DM72. However, at summer weekends and during the local wine harvest (mid-September to mid-October) you can forget about finding bargain accommodation anywhere.

Bernkastel-Kues In nearby Wehlen, the *Camping Schenk* (☎ 06531-81 76) is open from Easter to November. Bernkastel-Kues also has a nice *DJH hostel* (☎ 06531-23 95) at Jugendherbergsstrasse 1. The homy *Haus Konstanze* (☎ 06531-82 00), at Auf der Drift 30, charges DM38/73 for singles/doubles with private toilet, shower and balcony (great views!) and is 10 minutes' walk from the Altstadt.

Traben-Trarbach For campers, there's the *Rissbach* (☎ 06541-31 11, open April to mid-October) at Rissbacher Strasse 170. The *DJH hostel* (☎ 06541-92 78), at Am Letzten Hirtenpfad, has beds in small dorms for DM22.80/26.80 for juniors/seniors. The *Hotel Sonnenhof* (☎ 06541-64 51) at Kövinger Strasse 36 offers simple singles/doubles for DM39/68.

Elsewhere In Mehring, downstream from Trier, the *Gästehaus Weingut Schroeder* (☎ 06502-36 82), Bachstrasse 13A, charges from DM28 per person in rooms with private toilet, shower and TV. The *Pension Haus Sonnenschein* (☎ 02671-74 44), at Klosterstrasse 12 in the village of Ernst near Cochem, has singles/doubles priced from DM33/60. Brodenbach, on the lower Moselle, has a *DJH hostel* (☎ 02605-33 89) at Moorkamp 7.

Places to Eat

Good wine often means good food and this is true all along the Moselle, with dozens of inexpensive family places to choose from. The Moselle is also an ideal place for picnics – enjoying the peaceful river and countryside with good local food and wine.

Koblenz The *Salatgarten*, at Gymnasialstrasse 14, has literally dozens of self-serve salads for DM1.89 per 100 grams. It's closed from mid-evening and all day Sunday. The lively *Domino*, at Deichstrasse 3, offers plates of home-made noodles, large pizzas, and omelettes – all for no more than DM8.80. It has no wines but it does have some interesting bottled beers.

Cochem The *Zum Frölichen Weinberg*, at Schlauffstrasse 11, has main courses priced from DM12; the *Gute Quelle* (see Places to Stay) is not bad either. A good fast-food choice is *Kochlöffel* opposite the town hall at Am Markt 10; it has fresh salads from DM3.75, and half a chicken with French fries for only DM5.90.

Getting There & Away

It's most practical to begin your Moselle Valley trip from either Trier or Koblenz. If you have private transport and are coming from the north, however, you might head up the Ahr Valley and cut through the scenic High Eifel mountain area.

Getting Around

The Moselle can be explored on foot or by bike, car, boat or other public transport.

Bus The only scheduled bus service along the Moselle is between Trier and Bullay, about three-fifths of the way towards Koblenz. (In this section the train line is too far from the river for convenience.) The private Moselbahn (☎ 0651-2 10 75) runs seven daily buses in each direction (DM13.40, three hours each way); it's a highly scenic route, passing through numerous quaint villages along the way. Buses leave from outside the train stations in Trier and Bullay.

Train The trains running along the Moselle are frequent and convenient, even to the smallest towns, but they won't let you enjoy much of the beautiful scenery. The private Moselweinbahn line goes to Traben-Trarbach (change trains in Bullay).

Car & Motorbike Driving along the Moselle is also ideal, though drivers risk cramped necks (not to mention nervous passengers) from looking up at the majestic slopes. One possibility is to rent a car in either Koblenz or Trier and drop it off at the other end.

Hitchhiking is good, especially during summer, when the roads are crowded with friendly drivers. Just make sure that whoever picks you up hasn't spent too much time at one of the vineyards.

Bicycle The Moselle is a popular area among cyclists, and for much of the river's course there's a separate 'Moselroute' bike track. The ADFC map *Radtourenkarte Mosel-Saarland* (DM12.80) indicates optimum routes and is also useful for hiking. Touren-Rad (☎ 0261-9 11 60 16), at Hohenzollernstrasse 127, near the main train station in Koblenz, rents out quality mountain and touring bicycles. Its daily/weekend rates are DM15/28, and bikes can be returned in Trier or Bingen (on the Rhine, across the river from Rüdesheim). Larger train stations also have rental bikes; you can send luggage ahead on the train and drop off bikes at other stations.

GERMANY

Boat A great way to explore the Moselle is by boat. While much of the river's charm comes from its constantly winding course, this does make water travel particularly slow. To get from Koblenz to Trier using scheduled ferry services takes three days.

Between early May and mid-October, ferries of the Köln-Düsseldorfer (KD) Line (☎ 0221-2 58 30 11) sail daily from Koblenz to Cochem (DM35 one way). From Cochem, the Gebrüder Kolb Line (☎ 02673-15 15) runs boats upriver as far as Trier (DM71 one way) between April and early November. Various smaller ferry companies also operate on the Moselle.

Eurail and Germanrail passes are valid for all normal KD Line services and – something to consider when planning your itinerary – travel on your birthday is free. There are numerous other possible excursions, ranging from short return cruises to multiday wine-tasting packages.

TRIER

Trier is touted as Germany's oldest town. Although settlement of the site dates back to 400 BC, Trier was founded in 15 BC as Augusta Treverorum, the capital of Gaul, and was second in importance only to Rome in the Western Roman Empire. You'll find more Roman ruins here than anywhere else north of the Alps. There's a university too, and Trier can get pretty lively.

Orientation & Information

From the train station head west along Bahnhofstrasse to the Porta Nigra, where Trier's small and understaffed tourist office (☎ 0651-97 80 80) is located. From here walk Simeonstrasse's pedestrian zone to Hauptmarkt, the pivotal centre of the old city. Most of the sights are within this area of roughly one sq km. The main post office is just to the right as you leave the train station; there is another useful branch on Fleischstrasse.

Trier's telephone code is 0651.

Things to See

The town's chief landmark is the **Porta Nigra**, the imposing city gate on the northern edge of the town centre, whose origins date back to the 2nd century AD. You can pay DM4 (students DM2) to go inside, or better still, invest DM9 (students DM6) in a combined ticket to the city's other main sights. The **Rheinisches Landesmuseum** (Rhineland Museum), Weimarer Allee 1, is one of Germany's finest museums. It has a collection of Moselle artefacts and works of art dating from Palaeolithic, Roman and modern times (open from 10 am to 4 pm Monday, from 9.30 am Tuesday to Friday, from 9.30 am to 1 pm Saturday, and from 9 am to 1 pm Sunday). Admission (free) is via a new side entrance in the Palastgarten.

Trier's superb Romanesque **cathedral** shares a 1600-year history with the nearby and equally impressive **Konstantin Basilika**. Also worth a look are the ancient **Amphitheater**, the **Kaiserthermen** and **Barbarathermen** (Roman baths). The early Gothic **Dreikönigenhaus** on Simeonstrasse was built around 1230 as a protective tower: the original entrance was on the second level accessible only by way of a retractable rope ladder. History buffs and nostalgic socialists should seek out the **Karl Marx Museum**, in the house where the prophet was born on Brückenstrasse 10. The museum is open daily from 10 am to 6 pm (admission DM3, students DM2).

Places to Stay

The *Trier-City* municipal camping ground (☎ 8 69 21, open all year) is nicely positioned on the Moselle at Luxemburger Strasse 81. The *DJH hostel* (☎ 2 92 92) is at Maarstrasse 156 along the river and charges DM25.30 for both juniors and seniors.

Despite the hordes of tourists, hotels in Trier are still reasonably priced, but the cheaper rooms generally fill up first. The basic *Hotel Warsberger Hof* (☎ 7 51 31) at Dietrichstrasse 42 charges DM33/66 for singles/doubles, and also runs the larger *Jugendgästehaus* with beds for DM23. The *Handelshof* (☎ 7 39 33), Kellner-Strasse 1, next to the town hall in the south-western corner of the old town, has rooms for DM40/80. Worth paying a little extra for are the

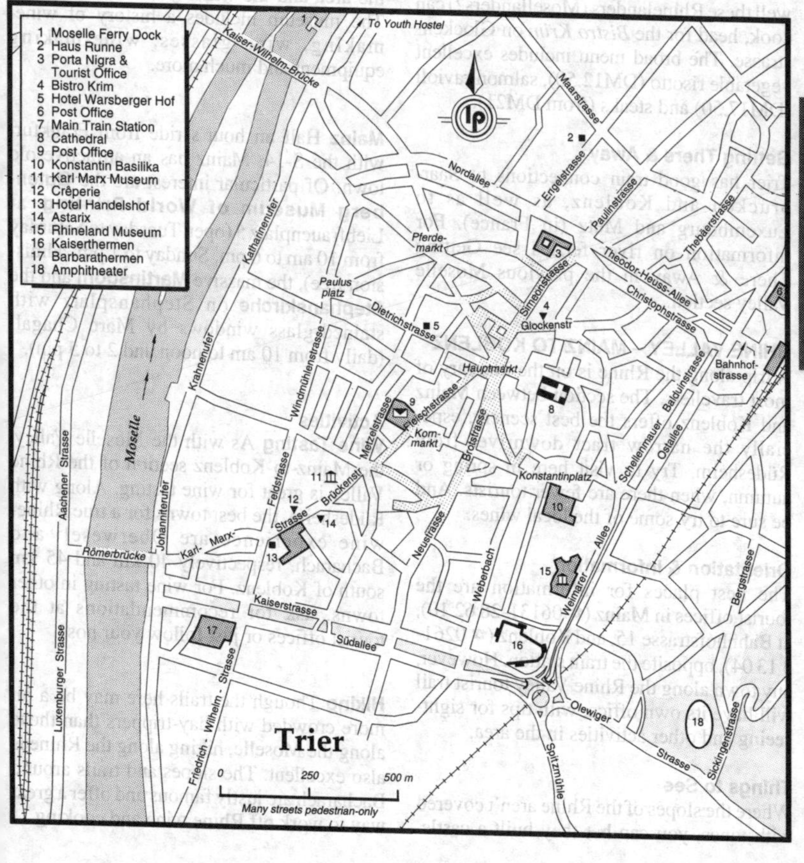

rooms at the *Haus Runne* (☎ 2 89 22) at Engelstrasse 35. Clean and sunny rooms with private toilet and shower cost just DM45/85 including breakfast.

Places to Eat

Trier is a great place to sample some Franco-German cooking. The *Crêperie* at Karl-Marx-Strasse 56 has excellent home-made sweet and savoury pancakes from DM3 to DM6.50. A favourite student hang-out is *Astarix*, down an arcade at Karl-Marx-Strasse 11. Made-to-order pizzas cost from DM7.80, and half a litre of Paulaner beer costs DM4.20. If you want to find out how well these Rhinelanders (Mosellanders?) can cook, head for the *Bistro Krim* on Glockenstrasse. The broad menu includes excellent vegetable risotto (DM12.50), salmon ravioli (DM17.50) and steaks (from DM21).

Getting There & Away

Trier has good train connections to Saarbrücken and Koblenz, as well as to Luxembourg and Metz (in France). For information on river ferries see Getting There & Away in the previous Moselle Valley section.

GERMANY

RHINE VALLEY – MAINZ TO KOBLENZ

A trip along the Rhine is on the itinerary of most travellers. The section between Mainz and Koblenz offers the best scenery, especially the narrow tract downriver from Rüdesheim. Try to visit here in spring or autumn, when there are fewer tourists. And be sure to try some of the local wines.

Orientation & Information

The best places for information are the tourist offices in Mainz (☎ 06131-28 62 10), at Bahnhofstrasse 15, and Koblenz (☎ 0261-3 13 04), opposite the train station. However, any town along the Rhine Valley tourist trail will have its own office, with tips for sightseeing and other activities in the area.

Things to See

Where the slopes of the Rhine aren't covered with vines, you can bet they built a castle. One of the most impressive is **Burg Rheinfels** in St Goar. Across the river, just south of St Goarshausen, is the Rhine's most famous, if somewhat overrated, sight: the **Lorelei Cliff**. Legend has it that a maiden sang sailors to their deaths against its base. It's worth the trek to the top of the Lorelei for the view, but try to get up there early in the morning before the hordes ascend.

Rüdesheim Although drunk on tourism, this town is worth visiting for the **Rheingau- und Weinmuseum** in the Brömserburg castle, which gives you some perspective of the area and the wines you'll be sampling. The museum includes a history of wine-making, wine glasses, wine-making equipment and much more.

Mainz Half an hour's ride from Frankfurt with the S-14, Mainz has an attractive old town. Of particular interest are the **Gutenberg Museum of World Printing** at Liebfrauenplatz 5 (open Tuesday to Saturday from 10 am to 6 pm, Sunday to 1 pm, admission free), the massive **Martinsdom** and the **Stephanskirche** on Stephansplatz with stained-glass windows by Marc Chagall (daily from 10 am to noon and 2 to 5 pm).

Activities

Wine Tasting As with the Moselle Valley, the Mainz-to-Koblenz section of the Rhine Valley is great for wine tasting. Along with Rüdesheim, the best towns for a true Rhine-wine experience are Oberwesel and Bacharach, respectively 40 km and 45 km south of Koblenz. For wine tasting in other towns, ask for recommendations at the tourist offices or just follow your nose.

Hiking Though the trails here may be a bit more crowded with day-trippers than those along the Moselle, hiking along the Rhine is also excellent. The slopes and trails around Bacharach are justly famous and offer a great way to work off Rhine wine and cooking.

Places to Stay

Camping Camping facilities line the Rhine, but amenities and views vary greatly. Good possibilities include: Oberwesel's *Schönburg* (☎ 06744-2 45, open April to October) right beside the river; Bacharach's *Sonnenstrand* camping ground (☎ 06743-17 52, open all year) beside the river at the southern end of town (can get windy); and St Goarshausen's *Auf der Loreley* (☎ 06771-4 30, open Easter to October) on the legendary rock.

Hostels There are excellent DJH hostels at Lorch (☎ 06726-3 07), Schwalbacherstrasse 54; Oberwesel (☎ 06744-70 46), Auf dem Schönberg; St Goarshausen (☎ 06771-26 19), Auf der Loreley – like the nearby camping ground it's right on the Lorelei, 100 metres from the lookout point (make sure you book!); Bacharach (☎ 06743-12 66), a legendary facility housed in the Burg Stahleck castle; and Rüdesheim (☎ 06722-27 11), Am Kreuzburg.

Hotels & Pensions In St Goar, try the *Hotel Zur Post* (☎ 06741-3 39) at Bahnhofstrasse 3 for basic but nice rooms in the old town (DM38/70 for singles/doubles). In Bacharach, the *Hotel Kranenturm* (☎ 06743-13 08), at Langstrasse 30 above an old town gate overlooking the Rhine, offers rooms with toilet and shower from DM42/84. Best value in Rüdesheim is the *Haus Felzen* (☎ 06722-24 30), Schmidtstrasse 23, with simple singles for DM35 and doubles with shower and toilet for DM80. Mainz has perhaps the least affordable hotels in western Germany – avoid staying there if you can.

For accommodation in Koblenz, see Places to Stay in the previous Moselle Valley section.

Places to Eat

Whether you put together a modest picnic by the river or dine in one of the numerous local restaurants, this is the time to savour some fine Rhine wine and food.

St Goar's *Zum Goldenen Löwen*, by the water at Heerstrasse 1, serves game and other specialities priced from DM22 (also have a look at the historic flood-level markings on the outside wall). In Rüdesheim, *Drosselmüller's Bierstube* at Oberstrasse 26 (near the chair-lift station) offers simple three-course meals priced from DM13. Avoid eating anywhere in Rüdesheim's aptly-named Drosselgasse (Strangle Lane), an oversold row of touristy shops and restaurants. In Mainz, the *Central* is good. It's at Rheinstrasse 27, near the cathedral, and has vegetarian and meatier dishes priced from DM9.

Getting There & Away

Koblenz or Mainz are the best starting points. The Rhine Valley is also easily accessible from Frankfurt on a long day trip, but that won't do justice to the region.

Getting Around

Each mode of transport has its own advantages and all are equally enjoyable. Try combining several of them by going on foot one day, cycling the next, and then taking a boat for a view from the river.

Boat The Köln-Düsseldorfer (KD) Line (☎ 0221-2 58 30 11) earns its bread and butter on the Rhine, with many slow and fast boats daily between Koblenz and Mainz. The most scenic stretch is between Koblenz and Rüdesheim; the journey downstream takes about 3½ hours (Rüdesheim-Koblenz, DM62.60) and about 5½ hours upstream (DM44 – the KD Line says it's cheaper because it's more popular). See Getting Around in the previous Moselle Valley section for information about discounts. Depending on demand, boats stop at riverside towns along the way.

Train & Bus Important train lines run on both banks of the Rhine. Providing you can get across the river easily, this increases the number of possible train connections.

Car Touring the Rhine Valley by car is also ideal. The route between Koblenz and Mainz is short enough for a car to be rented and returned to either one of these cities. There are no bridge crossings between Koblenz and Rüdesheim, but there are frequent ferries.

Saarland

In the late 19th century, Saarland's coal mines and steel mills fed the burgeoning German economy. Since WW II, however, the steady economic decline of coal and steel has made Saarland the poorest region in western Germany. Though distinctly German since the early Middle Ages, Saarland was ruled by France for several periods during its turbulent history. Reoccupied by the French after WW II, it only joined the German Federal Republic in 1959, after the population rejected French efforts to turn it into an independent state.

SAARBRÜCKEN

The Saarland capital of Saarbrücken has an interesting mixed French and German feel. Though lacking major tourist sights, this city of 200,000 is a 'real' place where people go about their daily business of living and working and where tourists are treated as individuals. It's also an easy base for day trips to some of the beautiful little towns nearby, such as Ottweiler and St Wendel.

Orientation & Information

The main train station is in the north-western corner of the old town, which stretches out on both sides of the Saar River.

The tourist office (☎ 0681-3 51 97) is to your left on the square as you leave the station. Its opening hours are from 9 am to 6 pm Monday to Friday, and to 3 pm Saturday. The room-finding service costs DM3. The main tourist office (☎ 0681-3 69 01), at Grossherzog-Friedrich-Strasse 1, just past the town hall, is open from 8 am to 6 pm Monday to Friday. For details of live music, theatre and other forthcoming cultural events get hold of the free monthly *Kakadu*.

The main post office is at Trierer Strasse 33, just right of the station exit. There's another branch in the town centre at Dudweilerstrasse 17, opposite its intersection with Kaiserstrasse.

Saarbrücken's telephone code is 0681.

Things to See & Do

Start your visit by strolling the lanes around the lively **St Johanner Markt** in the central pedestrian zone. A flea market is held here every second Saturday from April to November. Cross the 1549 **Alte Brücke** (Old Bridge) to **Schloss Saarbrücken**, the former palace on Schlossplatz designed by King Wilhelm Friedrich's court architect, Friedrich Joachim Stengel, in the 18th century. A modern central section was completed in 1989 and now houses the Museum of Regional History. More interesting is the **Abenteuer Museum** (Adventure Museum) in the **Altes Rathaus** (Old Town Hall) opposite the palace. It's a hotchpotch of weird souvenirs and photos collected since 1950 by the solo adventurer extraordinaire, Heinz Rox-Schulz. Unfortunately, the opening hours are rather limited: from 9 am to 1 pm Tuesday and Wednesday, from 3 to 7 pm Thursday and Friday, and from 10 am to 2 pm on the first Saturday each month.

The nearby **Ludwigsplatz** is a fine example of baroque architecture. The square, also Stengel's work, is dominated by the **Ludwigskirche**, an odd combination of a Lutheran church in a baroque setting. It keeps ridiculously inconvenient opening hours, so you may just have to peer through the glass doorway.

Places to Stay

The camping ground *Am Spicherer Berg* (☎ 5 17 80, open April to October), is out on the French border, south of the city; take bus No 12 to the ZF Gewerbegebiet or the Mercedes tower. The newly renovated *DJH hostel* (☎ 3 30 40) is at Meerwiesertalweg 31, half an hour's walk north-east of the station; otherwise take bus No 19 to Prinzenweiher. Beds cost DM23.80/27.80 for juniors/seniors in four-person dorms, or DM30.30/34.30 in two-person rooms.

Unfortunately, Saarbrücken has very few private rooms, and the many French day and weekend trippers keep hotel prices high. The cheapest alternative is *Hotel Schlosskrug* (☎ 3 54 48), Schmollerstrasse 14, on the edge of the lively area around Nauwieserplatz with single/double rooms from DM47/94. The *Gästehaus Weller* (☎ 37 19 03), at Neugrabenweg 8 near the DJH hostel, has basic rooms from DM39/59, and rooms with toilet, shower and TV for DM59/79.

Places to Eat

At Saarbrücken's eateries your taste buds get to visit France while enjoying hearty German servings.

In the central pedestrian zone try the *Gudd Stubb*, a tavern on the corner of Fröschgasse and Saarstrasse. Its menu ranges from filled pig's stomach with sauerkraut (DM14.50) to vegetarian versions of the Swabian speciality Maultaschen (DM11.80). The up-market *Weinstuben Hauck* (☎ 31919), at St Johanner Markt 7, has a formidable range of local Saarland and European wines, and fine food to complement every drop. There's a morning *market* at St Johanner Markt on Monday, Wednesday and Friday, and another on Ludwigsplatz on Tuesday, Thursday and Saturday.

You'll find most of the cheap restaurants and student pubs along the streets running off Nauwieserplatz. Perhaps the most popular hang-out is *Uff de Nauwies* on the corner of Nauwieserstrasse and Nassauerstrasse, with salads and pizzas from DM6.50 and beer on tap. The *Café Kostbar*, in an attractive backstreet courtyard at Nauwieserstrasse 19, is open daily from 10 in the morning to 1 am and offers dishes like chilli con carne and spaghetti pesto priced from DM7. As its German name implies, the creative *Auflauf* (☎ 3 11 68) at Johannisstrasse 17 specialises in oven-baked build-your-own soufflés for around DM13. Across the river, near Schlossplatz, is the *Tomate 2* (☎ 5 78 46), at Schlossstrasse 2. Its Italo-Alsatian cuisine changes daily, but staple options like risotto, fish soup and pasta are the order of the day.

Getting There & Away

Saarbrücken has a small international airport just 12 km from the city centre. There are hourly trains to the connecting cities of Mannheim, Koblenz, Mainz and Karlsruhe, and two direct trains to Paris each day. The international E50 autobahn connecting Mannheim with Metz in France passes close by Saarbrücken.

Getting Around

Saarbrücken is an easy place to explore on foot. Single-ride tickets on the bus-based city transport network cost DM2.80 (or DM10 for four) and a 24-hour pass costs DM7.50. Taxis are expensive at DM4 for flagfall plus DM2.30 per km.

Hesse

The Hessians, a Frankish tribe, were among the first people to convert to Lutheranism in the early 16th century. Apart from a brief period of unity in that same century under Philip the Magnanimous, Hesse (Hessen) remained a motley collection of principalities and, later, of Prussian administrative districts until it was proclaimed a state in 1945. Its main cities are Frankfurt, Kassel and the capital, Wiesbaden.

Along with being a transportation hub, the city of Frankfurt can also be used as a base to explore some of the smaller towns in Hesse that remind you that you're still in Germany. The beautiful Taunus and Spessart regions offer quiet village life and hours of scenic walks.

FRANKFURT/MAIN

They call it 'Bankfurt' and 'Mainhattan' and much more. It's on the Main (pronounced 'mine') River, and is generally referred to as Frankfurt-am-Main, or Frankfurt/Main, since there's another large city called Frankfurt (Frankfurt/Oder) near the Polish border.

Frankfurt/Main is the financial and geographical centre of western Germany, and the city hosts important trade fairs, including

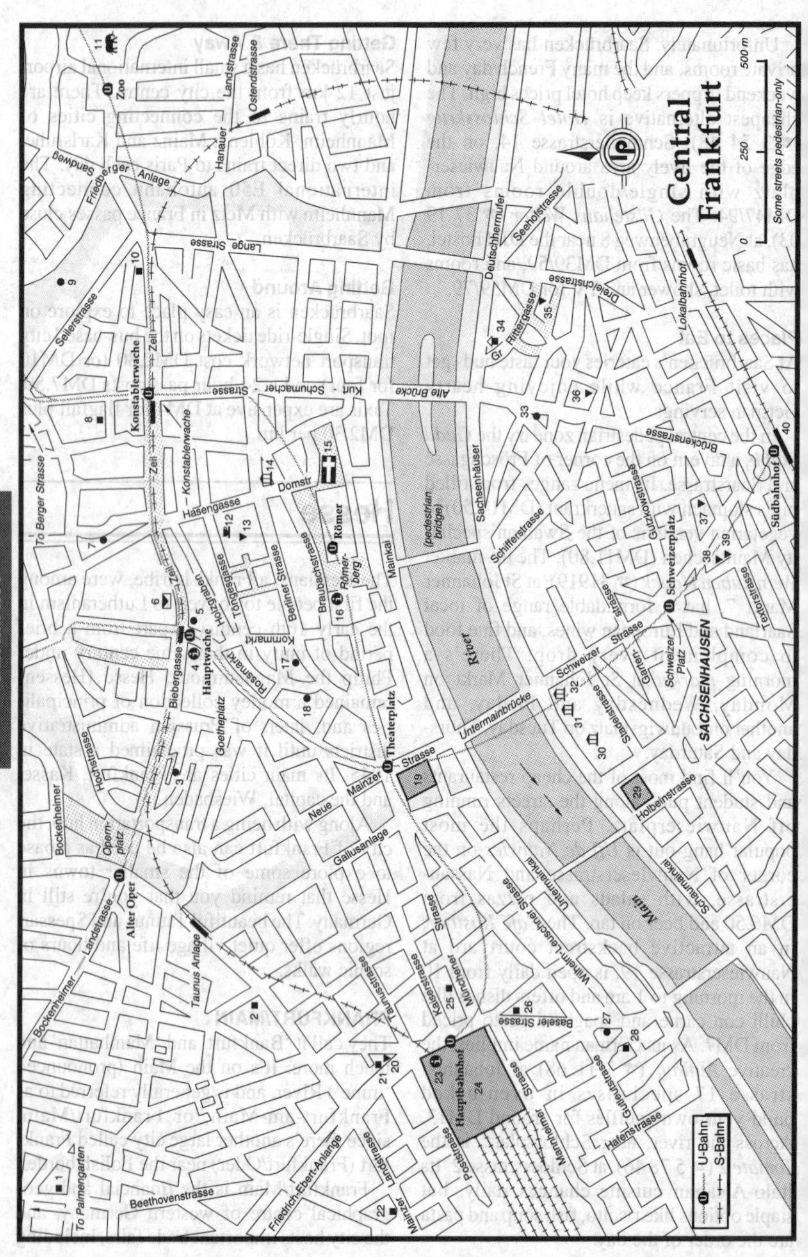
Central Frankfurt
Some streets pedestrian-only
0
250
500 m
U-Bahn
S-Bahn
To Palmengarten
To Berger Strasse
Bockenheimer Landstrasse
Beethovenstrasse
Friedrich-Ebert-Anlage
Mainzer Landstrasse
Taunus Anlage
Alter Oper
Opernplatz
Bockenheimer
Hochstrasse
Goetheplatz
Hauptwache
Biebergasse
Rossmarkt
Kornmarkt
Holzgraben
Töngesgasse
Hasengasse
Zeil
Konstablerwache
Seilerstrasse
Friedberger Anlage
Hanauer Landstrasse
Ostendstrasse
Zoo
Sandweg
Lange Strasse
Kurt Schumacher Strasse
Domstr
Berliner Strasse
Braubachstrasse
Römer
Römerberg
Mainkai
Theaterplatz
Neue Mainzer Strasse
Gallusanlage
Taunusstrasse
Kaiserstrasse
Münchener Strasse
Hauptbahnhof
Poststrasse
Mannheimer Strasse
Baseler Strasse
Gutleutstrasse
Hafenstrasse
Wilhelm-Leuschner Strasse
Untermainkai
Schaumainkai
Main
River
Untermainbrücke
(pedestrian bridge)
Alte Brücke
Deutschherrnufer
Seehofstrasse
Dreieichstrasse
Gr Rittergasse
Lokalbahnhof
Sachsenhäuser
Schifferstrasse
Gutzkowstrasse
Brückenstrasse
Schweizer Strasse
Schweizerplatz
Schweizer Platz
Stadelstrasse
Gartenstrasse
Holbeinstrasse
Textorstrasse
SACHSENHAUSEN
Südbahnhof
1
2
3
4
5
6
7
8
9
10
11
12
13
14
15
16
17
18
19
20
21
22
23
24
25
26
27
28
29
30
31
32
33
34
35
36
37
38
39
40

GERMANY

PLACES TO STAY					
1	Hotel-Pension Götz & Pension Sattler	35	Lorsbacher Tal	16	Tourist Office
2	Hotel Atlas	36	Tagtraum	17	Jazzkneipe
8	Hotel Colonia	37	Wolkenbruch	18	Goethe-Haus
10	Hotel Zeil	38	Zum Gemalten Haus	19	Frankfurt Oper
21	Hotel Adler	39	Wagner Adolf	23	Tourist Office
22	Hotel Glockshuber		**OTHER**	24	Main Train Station (Hauptbahnhof)
25	Hotel Apollo	3	Jazzkeller	27	Mitfahrzentrale
26	Hotel Wiesbaden	4	Hauptwache & Tourist Office	29	Städel Museum
28	Pension Wal	5	Sussman's Presse und Buch	30	Postal Museum
34	Haus der Jugend Youth Hostel	6	Main Post Office	31	Architecture Museum
	PLACES TO EAT	7	Sinkkasten	32	Film Museum
12	Café Mozart	9	Plastik	33	Negativ
13	Kleinmarkthalle	11	Zoo	40	Train Station (Südbahnhof)
20	Restaurant Panda	14	Museum of Modern Art		
		15	Cathedral		

the world's largest book, consumer-goods and musical-instrument fairs. Frankfurt's 650,000 inhabitants produce a disproportionately large part of Germany's wealth, and over 10% of the city's taxes are devoted to culture; here you'll find the richest collection of museums in the country.

Frankfurt is Germany's most important transport hub – for air, train and road connections – so you'll probably end up here at some point. Don't be surprised if you find this cosmopolitan melting-pot more interesting than you had expected.

Orientation

The airport is about 15 minutes by train south-west of the city centre. The main train station is on the western side of the city, but within walking distance of the old city centre.

The best way to walk into the old city from the train station is east along Taunusstrasse. This leads you to Goetheplatz and then to a large square called Hauptwache. The area between Hauptwache and the Römerberg, in the tiny vestige of Frankfurt's original old city, is the centre of Frankfurt. The Main River runs just south of the Altstadt, with several bridges leading to one of the city's livelier areas, Sachsenhausen. Its north-eastern corner, behind the DJH hostel (see Places to Stay) is known as Alt Sachsenhausen and is full of quaint old houses and narrow alleyways.

Information

Frankfurt's most convenient tourist office (☎ 069-21 23 88 49/51) is in the main train station, at the head of platform No 24. It's open Monday to Friday from 8 am to 9 pm (9.30 am to 8 pm weekends and holidays). The staff are efficient at finding (pricier) rooms, but there's a hefty service fee of DM5 plus a DM10 deposit on the room. Ask about the Frankfurt Card package for DM21, which covers admission to a number of main sights and travel by public transport.

In the centre of the city, the tourist office (☎ 069-21 23 87 08/09) at Römerberg 27 (in the north-western corner of the square) is open from 9 am to 6 pm Monday to Friday, from 9.30 am at weekends and on holidays. The Hauptwache shopping mall also has a tourist information office on level B (☎ 069-2 12 87 08/9).

The friendly head office of the German National Tourist Office (☎ 069-75 72 0) is north of the Hauptbahnhof at Beethovenstrasse 69. It's *the* place to visit if you're still planning your trip to Germany, as it has brochures of all areas of the country (open Monday to Thursday from 8 am to 4 pm, to 1 pm Friday).

The airport has no tourist office as such, but there are general information booths in arrival and departure halls B, on levels 1 and 2 respectively. For more information on Frankfurt Airport, see Getting There & Away later in this section.

Money The main train station has a branch of the Deutsche Verkehrs-Kredit Bank (☎ 069-2 64 82 01) near the southern exit at the head of platform No 1, which is open daily from 6.30 am to 10.30 pm; otherwise, use the money-exchange machine at the head of platform No 15. There are several banks at the airport, most of them open till about 10 pm, and exchange and automatic teller machines are dotted around the various arrival and departure halls.

Post & Telephone The main post office (☎ 069-90 90 10) is near Hauptwache at Zeil 108-110. It's open from 8 am to 8 pm Monday to Friday, and to 6 pm on Saturday; services are limited after 6 pm and on Saturday afternoons. The post office above the tourist office at the main train station is open from 6 am to 10 pm Monday to Friday, and 8 am to 9 pm on weekends and public holidays; the one at the airport (in the waiting lounge in departure hall B) is open from 6 am to 10 pm.

Frankfurt's telephone code is 069.

Bookshops Stock up on international magazines and newspapers at the Internationale Presse shop in the train station, at the head of platform No 15. Sussmann's Presse & Buch, on Hauptwache behind the orange-coloured Katharinenkirche, has a good selection of English-language books.

Emergency The Uni-Clinic (☎ 6 30 11), at Theodor Stern Kai 7 in Sachsenhausen, is open 24 hours a day. For medical queries you can contact the 24-hour doctor service on ☎ 1 92 92.

Dangers & Annoyances The area around the train station acts as a base for Frankfurt's sex and illegal drugs trades. Frequent police patrols of the station itself and the surrounding Bahnhofsviertel keep things under control, but it's nevertheless advisable to use 'big city' common sense.

Things to See & Do

Eighty per cent of the old city was wiped off the map by two Allied bombing raids in March 1944, and postwar reconstruction was subject to the demands of the new age. Rebuilding efforts were more thoughtful, however, in the **Römerberg**, the old central square of Frankfurt, west of the cathedral, where restored 14th and 15th-century buildings provide a glimpse of the beautiful city this once was. The old town hall, or **Römer**, is in the north-western corner of Römerberg and consists of three 15th-century houses topped with Frankfurt's trademark stepped gables.

East of the Römerberg, behind the Historical Garden (remains of Roman and Carolingian foundations), is the newly restored **cathedral**, the coronation site of the Holy Roman emperors from 1562 to 1792. It's dominated by the elegant 15th-century Gothic **tower** (completed in the 1860s) – one of the few structures left standing after the 1944 raids. The small **Wahlkapelle** (Voting Chapel) on the cathedral's southern side is where the seven electors of the Holy Roman Empire chose the emperor from 1356 onwards. The adjoining **choir** has beautiful wooden stalls. The cathedral is open from 9 am to noon and 2.30 to 6 pm (closed Friday morning).

Anyone with an interest in German literature should visit the **Goethehaus**, Grosser Hirschgraben 23-25. Goethe, arguably the last person to master all fields of human knowledge, was born in this house in 1749. It's open Monday to Saturday from 9 am to 6 pm, Sunday and public holidays from 10 am to 1 pm (shorter hours in winter) and costs DM4 (students DM3). The adjoining museum and library are undergoing major restoration and will reopen in 1996 – part of

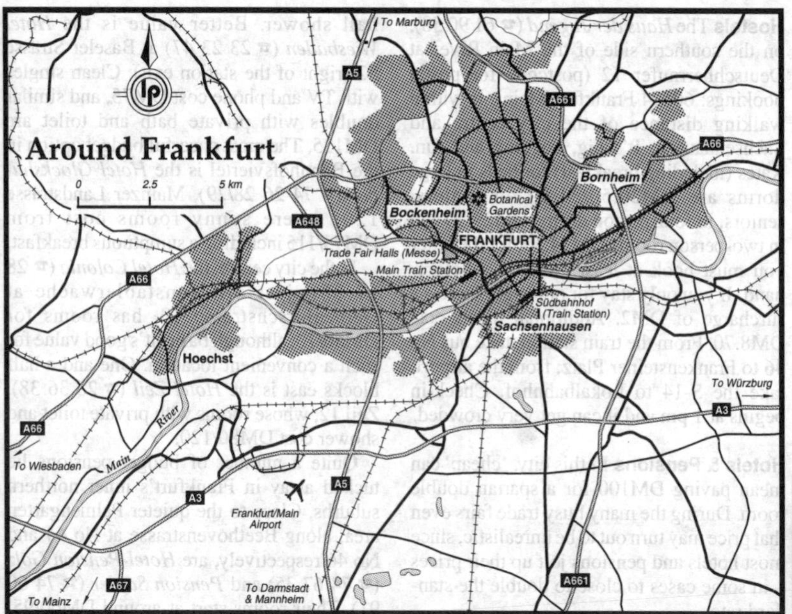

the collection is on display at the Städel Museum.

A bit farther afield, the botanical **Palmengarten** (admission free) and the creative **Frankfurt Zoo** (admission DM11 or DM5 for students) are perfect reliefs from the cosmopolitan chaos.

There's a great **flea market** along Museumsufer every Saturday till the early afternoon.

Museums Frankfurt has more top-ranking museums than any other German city. A recent addition is the **Museum für Moderne Kunst** (Museum of Modern Art), north of the cathedral at Domstrasse 10, featuring work by Joseph Beuys, Claes Oldenburg and many others; admission is DM7 (students DM3.50), but it's free on Wednesday.

A string of other museums lines the southern bank of the Main River along the so-called **Museumsufer** (Museum Row). Pick of the crop is the **Städel Museum** at Schaumainkai 63, with a world-class collection of works by artists from the Renaissance to the 20th century, including Botticelli, Dürer, van Eyck, Rubens, Rembrandt, Vermeer, Cézanne and Renoir, among many other greats. It costs DM8 (DM4 for students, free on Sunday and public holidays). Other interesting possibilities along the way include the **Deutsches Architekturmuseum** (Architecture Museum), the **Deutsches Filmmuseum** and the **Bundespostmuseum** (Postal Museum).

Places to Stay

Camping The only camping ground is *Heddernheim* (☎ 57 03 32, open all year) at An der Sandelmühle 35, in the Heddernheim district north-west of the city centre. It charges DM10 for a site and DM9 per person, and is a 15-minute ride on the U1, U2 or U3 from the Hauptwache (one zone) – get off at the Heddernheim stop.

Hostels The *Haus der Jugend* (☎ 61 90 58), on the southern side of the Main River at Deutschherrnufer 12 (postcode for postal bookings: 60594 Frankfurt/Main), is within walking distance of the city centre and Sachsenhausen. It's big, bustling and fun. Rates (including breakfast) for beds in large dorms are DM20.50/24.50 for juniors/seniors, in four-person dorms DM29.50 and in two-person rooms DM34.50; for the latter you must book at least three days beforehand. If you only stay for one night there's a surcharge of DM2. Additional meals cost DM8.70. From the train station, take bus No 46 to Frankensteiner Platz; from the airport, take the S-14 to Lokalbahnhof. Check-in begins at 1 pm and it can get very crowded.

Hotels & Pensions In this city, 'cheap' can mean paying DM100 for a spartan double room. During the many busy trade fairs even that price may turn out to be unrealistic, since most hotels and pensions jolt up their prices – in some cases to close to double the standard rate.

In order to experience the city in a more positive light, avoid staying in the sleazy Bahnhofsviertel around the main train station if at all possible. If you can't/won't take this advice, try *Pension Wal* (☎ 25 35 45), next to the station at Stuttgarter Strasse 9, with claustrophobic singles/doubles for DM52/85 (DM10/20 more during fairs). The *Hotel Apollo* (☎ 23 12 85), half a block from the main train station at Münchener Strasse 46, has more spacious singles for DM60 and doubles with shower for DM100, though its rooms smell of sour socks. Away from the sleaze but still within a few minutes' walking distance of the train station is the modern *Hotel Atlas* (☎ 72 39 46), at Zimmerweg 1, with simple singles/doubles from DM59/82 (or DM70/120 during fairs).

The *Hotel Adler* (☎ 23 34 55), on the 4th floor at Niddastrasse 65 just north of the station (access via the arcade next to the Restaurant Panda), has passable rooms for DM70/105 (DM90/180 during fairs). The doubles come with toilet and shower, the singles with private toilet and free use of a hall shower. Better value is the *Hotel Wiesbaden* (☎ 23 23 47) at Baseler Strasse 52 (right of the station exit). Clean singles with TV and phone cost DM75, and similar doubles with private bath and toilet are DM125. The most cheerful budget option in the Bahnhofsviertel is the *Hotel Glockshuber* (☎ 74 26 28/29), Mainzer Landstrasse 120, where sunny rooms cost from DM75/115 including a sumptuous breakfast.

In the city centre, the *Hotel Colonia* (☎ 28 17 88), just off Konstablerwache at Gelbenhirschstrasse 10, has rooms for DM50/70; although basic, it's good value for such a convenient location. One and a half blocks east is the *Hotel Zeil* (☎ 28 36 38), Zeil 12, whose rooms with private toilet and shower cost DM80/120.

Quite a number of budget pensions lie tucked away in Frankfurt's inner northern suburbs. Close to the quieter Palmengarten area, along Beethovenstrasse at No 44 and No 46 respectively, are *Hotel-Pension Gölz* (☎ 74 67 35) and *Pension Sattler* (☎ 74 60 91). Their rooms start at around DM60/95, but at those prices they're almost continuously full.

The friendly and clean *Pension Adria* (☎ 59 45 33), at Neuhausstrasse 21 in Nordend, has nice rooms overlooking garden lawns from DM57/110. The *Hotel Uebe* (☎ 59 12 09), at Grünebrugweg 3 near the Botanical Gardens in Westend-Nord, offers simple singles for DM55 and doubles with private shower for DM90. In the interesting Bornheim district north-east of town is the *Pension Zur Rose* (☎ 45 17 62) at Berger Strasse 238. Basic rooms go for DM60/100 or DM120/140 with shower and bath.

Places to Eat

The main train station is a good place to pick up a snack, but except for daytime bistros and the inevitable *McDonald's* restaurants the budget dining options within the inner city area are rather limited.

Known to locals as *Fressgasse* (Munch-Alley), the Kalbächer Gasse and Grosse Bockenheimer Strasse area, between Opernplatz and Rathenauplatz, has many cheap fast-food places with outdoor tables. The *Restaurant Panda* (☎ 23 35 79), Düsseldorfer Strasse 10, diagonally left across the road from the train station, is a straightforward Chinese restaurant with main dishes for around DM20. For snacks and picnic supplies you can go to the *Kleinmarkthalle* off Hasengasse. It's an active little city market with displays of fruit, vegetables, meats, fish and hot food. The nearby *Café Mozart* (☎ 29 19 54) at Töngesgasse 23 is popular for its cakes and coffee.

In Alt Sachsenhausen, the area directly behind the DJH hostel is filled with eateries and pubs. The apple-wine taverns in Sachsenhausen are good places to try typical Frankfurt snacks like Handkäse mit Musik (literally, 'hand-cheese with music', a round cheese soaked in oil and vinegar with lots of onions – the music comes later), and Grüne Sosse ('green sauce', a mixture of yoghurt, mayonnaise, sour cream and plenty of herbs served with potatoes and meat or eggs – Goethe's favourite food).

A particularly good apple-wine tavern in Alt Sachsenhausen is *Lorsbacher Tal* (☎ 61 64 59), Grosse Rittergasse 49. Two other worthwhile apple-wine taverns on the nearby Schweizer Strasse are *Wagner Adolf* (☎ 61 25 65), at No 71, and *Zum Gemalten Haus* (☎ 61 45 59), at No 67, a lively place full of paintings of old Frankfurt. Around the corner at Textorstrasse 26 is the organically inspired *Wolkenbruch* (☎ 62 26 12), which offers wholemeal pizzas and lentil burgers at wholesome prices. Another simple but good eating house in Sachsenhausen is the *Tagtraum* (☎ 61 87 57) at Affentorplatz 20, with nothing on the menu over DM15.

In the cosmopolitan Bornheim area north of the zoo, the *Café Gegenwart* (☎ 4 97 05 44), at Berger Strasse 6, is a stylish bar/restaurant serving traditional German dishes for DM11 to DM16.50; if the weather cooperates you can sit outside. The more way-out *Café Provisorisch* next door does particularly good breakfasts.

Over to the west in Bohemian Bockenheim, the *Diesseits* and the *Stattcafé*, diagonally opposite each other on the corner of Grempstrasse and Konrad-Brosswitz-Strasse, both offer vegetarian and meatier fare from around DM12, as well as a broad range of breakfasts (served until 4.30 pm). For more laid-back dining, try the *Pielok* (☎ 77 64 68), near the university at Jordanstrasse 3.

Entertainment

Frankfurt is a true *Weltstadt* – an 'international city' – with an exhaustive amount of evening entertainment.

Frankfurt's jazz scene is second to none, and the top acts perform at the *Jazzkeller* (☎ 28 85 37), Kleine Bockenheimer Strasse 18a, which is open Tuesday to Saturday from 9 pm to around 3 am. A less commercial alternative is the *Jazzkneipe* (☎ 28 71 73) at Berliner Strasse 70. Top bands perform at the *Sinkkasten* (☎ 28 03 85), just north of the city centre at Brönnerstrasse 5.

A popular live-music venue in Sachsenhausen is the misleadingly named *Negativ*, close to the DJH hostel at Walter-Korb-Strasse 1. Fashionable Frankfurters generally shun touristy Sachsenhausen, however, preferring the areas of Bockenheim, Nordend or Bornheim north of the river.

Sachsenhausen also has many *apple-wine taverns* (see Places to Eat earlier) where you can try the unique Ebbelwei (Frankfurt dialect for Apfelwein), which resembles spiked apple juice; it tastes weaker than cider but contains well over 5% alcohol by volume – beware!

A popular hang-out in Bornheim is *Mousonturm* (☎ 40 58 95 20), Waldschmidtstrasse 4, a converted soap factory that offers dance performances and politically oriented cabaret as well as a lively coffee shop. *Harvey's* (☎ 49 73 03), a restaurant on Friedberger Platz, is a favoured meeting place for Frankfurt's broadminded yuppie types.

The Nordend area, west of Bornheim, also attracts students and trendoids. *Grössenwahn* (☎ 59 93 56), Lenaustrasse 97, is a lively pub with good creative food for less than DM20. The young disco crowd goes to the up-market *Plastik* at Seilerstrasse 34 (open from 9 pm to 4 am, closed Tuesday and at weekends).

Ballet, opera and theatre are other strong points of Frankfurt's entertainment scene. For information and bookings, telephone either the Frankfurt Oper on ☎ 23 60 61 (Untermainanlage 11), or the Hertie concert and theatre-booking service on ☎ 29 48 48 (Zeil 90).

Things to Buy

There are no particular things you should buy in Frankfurt, though the shopping is excellent and it's an ideal place to satisfy any souvenir needs before boarding the plane or train home. Frankfurt's main shopping street is Zeil, particularly the section between the Hauptwache and the Konstablerwache. It's reputed to do more business than any other shopping district in Europe, but is generally expensive. More interesting areas for shopping are along Sachsenhausen's Schweizer Strasse and in Berger Strasse north-east of the city centre, where there are shops stocking all sorts of weird and wonderful stuff.

GERMANY

Getting There & Away

Air The airport, Flughafen Frankfurt/Main, is Germany's largest airport with the highest freight and second-highest passenger turnover in Europe. It's a complete town in itself and a claustrophobic maze, with two terminals linked by a high-tech elevated 'people mover'. Departure and arrival halls A, B and C are in the old Terminal 1, the western half of which handles Lufthansa flights; halls D and E are in the new Terminal 2, which opened to much fanfare in the autumn of 1994. Bus connections, are on level 1 of Terminal 1; train connections on level 0 (ground floor); and the S-Bahn on level -1. Good luck! For flight information, ring ☎ 69 03 05 11.

Bus Long-distance buses leave from the southern side of the main train station, where there's a Europabus office (☎ 23 07 35/6) open Monday to Friday from 7.30 am to 6 pm, and to 2.30 pm at weekends. It caters for most European destinations, but the most interesting possibility is the Romantic Road bus (rail passes accepted), which leaves daily at 8.15 am and costs DM117/211 one way/return for the full 11½-hour trip to Füssen; a one-day excursion to Rothenburg would set you back DM58/104. The Europabus head office is Deutsche Touring GmbH (☎ 7 90 30), Römerhof 17, 60486 Frankfurt.

Train The main train station handles more departures and arrivals than any other station in Germany (almost 1500 trains a day, with more than a quarter of a million travellers), so finding a train to or from almost anywhere is not a problem. The information office for train connections, tickets etc is at the head of platform No 9. For train information, call ☎ 1 94 19.

Car & Motorbike Frankfurt features the famed Frankfurter Kreuz, the biggest autobahn intersection in the country. The ADM-Mitfahrzentrale (☎ 23 64 44/5) is on Baselerplatz, three minutes' walk south of the train station. It's open Monday to Friday from 8 am to 6 pm, and Saturday till noon. A sample of fares (including fees) is: Berlin DM51, Hamburg DM49 and Munich DM39. The Citynetz Mitfahr-Service (☎ 1 94 44), at Homburger Strasse 36, has slightly cheaper rates.

Getting Around

To/From the Airport The S-Bahn No 15 runs between the airport and the main train station every 10 minutes; it takes 11 minutes and costs DM5.60, or DM4.20 outside peak hours. The S-14 continues to the Hauptwache every 20 minutes; it takes 15 minutes and charges the same price. Bus No 61 runs to/from the Südbahnhof in Sachsenhausen. Taxis charge about DM35 for the trip into town but are slower than the train.

Car & Motorbike Traffic flows smoothly in Frankfurt, but the extensive system of one-way streets makes it extremely frustrating to get to where you want to go. You're better off parking your vehicle in one of the many (expensive) car parks and proceeding on foot.

Public Transport Frankfurt's excellent transport network (FVV) integrates all bus, tram, S-Bahn and U-Bahn lines. A zonal system applies – the yellow zone covers the large central area of Frankfurt, but to get to or from the airport you need a two-zone ticket. The FVV has automatic ticket machines at virtually all stations and tram stops: a single trip costs DM2.80/5.60 for one/two zones, or DM2.20/4.20 outside peak hours. Trips of up to two km, irrespective of the zones, cost DM1.60 outside peak hours (DM2.30 otherwise). If you plan to do much city travelling, buy a 24-hour central-zone ticket for DM6, a three-day ticket for DM17, or the seven-day version for DM26.50 (DM17.50 for students); these tickets are also valid for the airport.

Taxi Taxis are slow compared with public transport and quite expensive at DM3.80 flagfall plus DM2.15 per km. There are taxi ranks throughout the city, or ring ☎ 23 00 01/33, 25 00 01 or 54 50 11.

MARBURG

Situated 90 km north of Frankfurt, Marburg is known for its charming Altstadt with the splendid **Elizabethkirche** and **Philipps-Universität**, Europe's first Protestant university (founded in 1527). Wander up to the museum in the **castle**, from where there are nice views of the old town.

Marburg's *DJH hostel* (☎ 06421-2 34 61) is at Jahnstrasse 1, about 10 minutes' walk upstream along the river from Rudolfsplatz in the Altstadt. Rates for juniors/seniors are DM19/23. For other budget accommodation drop in at the tourist office directly right as you exit the train station; it has a free room-finding service. At the *Café Local*, Steinweg 1, you can fill up on student food priced from DM7.50.

North Rhine-Westphalia

North Rhine-Westphalia (Nordrhein-Westfalen) was formed in 1946 from a hotchpotch of principalities and bishoprics, most of which had belonged to Prussia since the early 19th century. A quarter of Germany's population lives here. The Rhine-Ruhr industrial area is the country's economic powerhouse and one of the most densely populated conurbations in the world. Though the area is dominated by barren industrial cities connected by a maze of train lines and autobahns, some of the cities are steeped in history and their attractions warrant an extensive visit.

COLOGNE

Because of its location on a major crossroads of European trade routes, Cologne (Köln) was an important city even in Roman times. It was then known as Colonia Agrippinensis, the capital of the province of Germania, and had no less than 300,000 inhabitants. In later years it remained one of northern Europe's main cities (the largest in Germany until the 19th century), and it is still the centre of the German Roman Catholic church. Though almost completely destroyed in WW II, it was quickly rebuilt and many of its old churches and monuments have been meticulously restored.

It's worth making an effort to visit this city, if only for the famous cathedral, though there's much more to see.

Orientation

Situated on the Rhine River, the skyline of Cologne is dominated by the cathedral. The pedestrianised Hohe Strasse runs straight through the middle of the old town from north to south and is Cologne's main shopping street. The main train station is just north of the cathedral, within walking distance of almost everything. The main bus station is immediately behind the train station, on Breslauer Platz.

If you arrive by private transport, head for

GERMANY

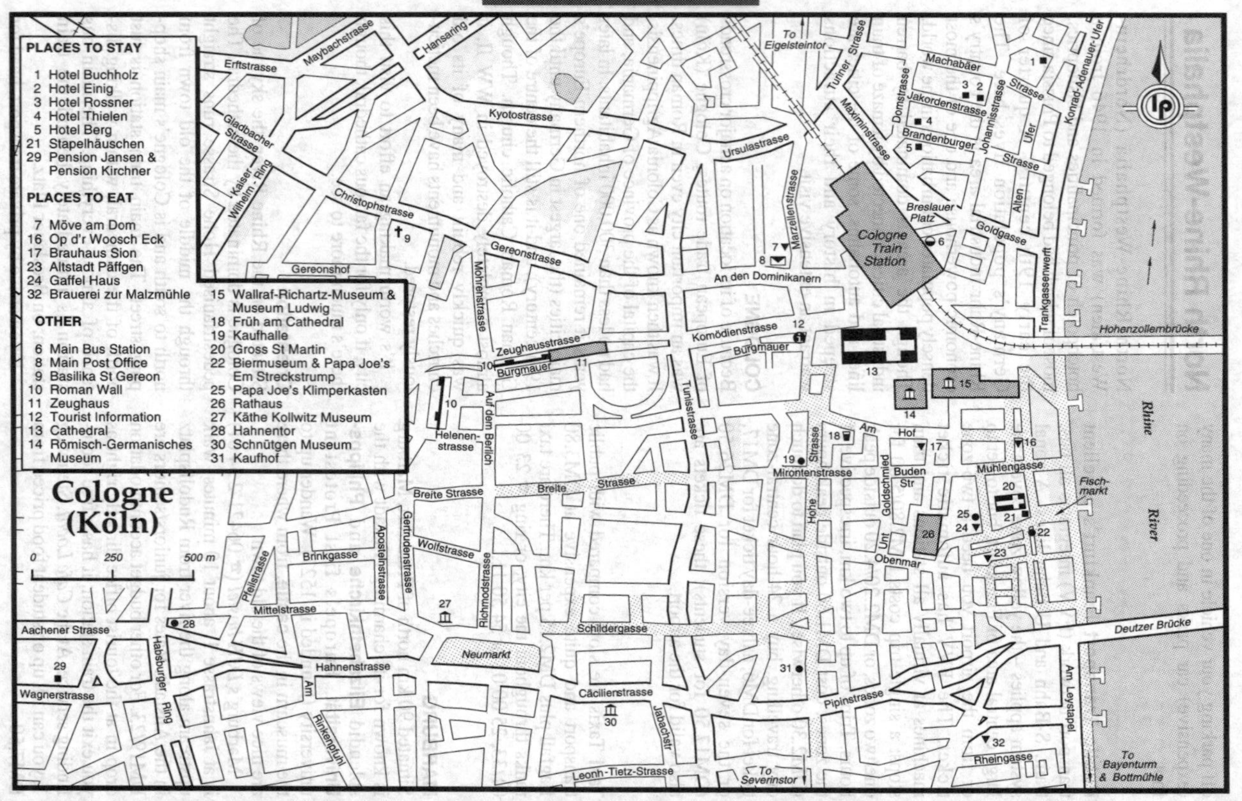
PLACES TO STAY
1 Hotel Buchholz
2 Hotel Einig
3 Hotel Rossner
4 Hotel Thielen
5 Hotel Berg
21 Stapelhäuschen
29 Pension Jansen & Pension Kirchner
PLACES TO EAT
7 Möve am Dom
16 Op d'r Woosch Eck
17 Brauhaus Sion
23 Altstadt Päffgen
24 Gaffel Haus
32 Brauerei zur Malzmühle
OTHER
6 Main Bus Station
8 Main Post Office
9 Basilika St Gereon
10 Roman Wall
11 Zeughaus
12 Tourist Information
13 Cathedral
14 Römisch-Germanisches Museum
15 Wallraf-Richartz-Museum & Museum Ludwig
18 Früh am Cathedral
19 Kaufhalle
20 Gross St Martin
22 Biermuseum & Papa Joe's Em Streckstrump
25 Papa Joe's Klimperkasten
26 Rathaus
27 Käthe Kollwitz Museum
28 Hahnentor
30 Schnütgen Museum
31 Kaufhof
Cologne
(Köln)
0
250
500 m
Erftstrasse
Maybachstrasse
Hansaring
To Eigelsteintor
Turiner Strasse
Machabäer Strasse
Konrad-Adenauer-Ufer
Domstrasse
Jakordenstrasse
Johannisstrasse
Brandenburger Strasse
Ufer
Maximinstrasse
Kyotostrasse
Gladbacher Strasse
Ursulastrasse
Marzellenstrasse
Kaiser-Wilhelm-Ring
Christophstrasse
Breslauer Platz
Alten
Goldgasse
Cologne Train Station
Trankgassenwerft
Gereonstrasse
Gereonshof
An den Dominikanern
Mohrenstrasse
Komödienstrasse
Burgmauer
Hohenzollernbrücke
Zeughausstrasse
Burgmauer
Tunisstrasse
Rhine
Helenenstrasse
Auf dem Berlich
Am Hof
Strasse
Mirontenstrasse
Goldschmied
Buden Str
Muhlengasse
Fischmarkt
Breite Strasse
Breite
Strasse
Hohe
Gertrudenstrasse
Apostelnstrasse
Wolfstrasse
Unt
Obenmar
River
Brinkgasse
Pfeilstrasse
Richmodstrasse
Mittelstrasse
Schildergasse
Deutzer Brücke
Aachener Strasse
Neumarkt
Habsburger Ring
Hahnenstrasse
Am
Wagnerstrasse
Cäcilienstrasse
Pipinstrasse
Am Leystapel
Rinkenpfuhl
Jabachstr
Rheingasse
Leonh-Tietz-Strasse
To Severinstor
To Bayenturm & Bottmühle

one of the many underground car parks in the city centre; a neat system of electronic signs indicates exactly how many parking spaces are left and where they are.

Information

The tourist office (☎ 0221-2 21 33 45) is conveniently located opposite the cathedral's main entrance, at Unter Fettenhennen 19. In summer it's open Monday to Saturday from 8 am to 10.30 pm, Sunday and public holidays from 9 am; from November to April, opening hours are from 8 am to 9 pm Monday to Saturday and 9.30 am to 7 pm Sunday and public holidays. Browse through the chained booklets before deciding which one to buy. *Monatvorschau*, the monthly what's-on booklet, is a good investment at DM2. The room-finding service, at DM5, is a bargain when the city is busy with trade fairs, but you cannot book by telephone.

Money The bank at the train station is open from 7 am to 9 pm, seven days a week. The station post office (open from 7 am to 9 pm Monday to Friday, 11 am to 8 pm Saturday and Sunday) cashes travellers' cheques but won't exchange cash. American Express is at Burgmauer 14 and Thomas Cook is at Komödienstrasse 7.

Post & Telephone The main post office is just opposite the train station on An den Dominikanern. It's open from 8 am to 6 pm Monday to Friday, to 1 pm Saturday.

Cologne's telephone code is 0221.

Bookshops Ludwig im Bahnhof, inside the main station, has newspapers and magazines from all over the world. For travel guides in English, try Herder Bücher at Komödienstrasse 11. Women can get additional reading matter from the Women's Cultural Centre at Moltkestrasse 66, which has a bookshop with a great selection of feminist publications. It's open Monday to Friday to 6.30 pm, Saturday to 2 pm.

Emergency You can call the police on ☎ 110; for fire and ambulance, ring ☎ 112. An on-call doctor can be contacted on ☎ 72 07 72.

Laundry Öko-Express Waschsalon (closed Sunday) is on the corner of Richard-Wagner-Strasse and Handelstrasse near Rudolfplatz. Washing costs DM6 per load, 10 minutes' drying DM1.

Things to See

Cologne has one of the most extensive old town centres in the country, and the cathedral (Dom) is its heart, soul, and tourist draw. Combined with the excellent museum next door, plan to spend at least one full day inside and around the Dom.

Dom First, head around to the south side of the Dom for an overall view. The structure's sheer size, with spires rising to a height of 157 metres, is overwhelming. Building began in 1248 in the French Gothic style. The huge project was stopped in 1560, but was started again in 1842, in the style originally planned, as a symbol of Prussia's drive for unification. It was finally finished in 1880. Strangely, it survived WW II's heavy night bombing intact and acquires a gilt appearance when photographed.

The Dom is open daily from 7 am to 7 pm. Invest DM1 in the informative *Cologne Cathedral* booklet sold at the tourist office. When you reach the transept, you'll be overwhelmed by the sheer size and magnificence of it all. The five **stained-glass windows** along the north aisle depict the lives of the Virgin and St Peter. Behind the high altar, see the **Magi's Shrine** (circa 1150-1210). On the south side, in a chapel off the ambulatory, is the 15th-century **Adoration of the Magi altarpiece**. The free guided tours are in German only, but get you into more parts of the Dom. They are held at 10 and 11 am, and 2.30 and 3.30 pm Monday to Friday, 10 and 11 am Saturday, and 2.30 pm Sunday; tours in English are on Wednesday at 2 pm and Saturday at 10.30 am and cost DM10.

For a fitness fix, pay DM3 (students DM1.50, open to 5.30 pm, to 3.30 pm only from October to April) to climb 509 steps up the Dom's south tower to the base of the stupendous steeple, which towered over all of Europe until the Eiffel Tower was erected. Look at the 24-tonne **Peter Bell**, the largest working bell in the world, on your way up. At the end of your climb, the view from the vantage point, 98.25 metres up, is absolutely stunning: with clear weather you can see all the way to the Siebengebirge mountains beyond Bonn. The cathedral **treasury**, just inside the north entrance (open to 5 pm Monday to Saturday, to 4 pm Sunday and daily from November to March, entry DM3), is pretty average. In the crypt, Cologne's archbishops are interred.

Outside on the cathedral forecourt, artists work on giant chalk reproductions of famous portraits in summer (a few Pfennig of appreciation are welcomed – 'Danke').

Other Churches There are many other churches worth a look, particularly Romanesque ones, that have been restored since WW II bombing. The most handsome from the outside is **Gross St Martin**, while the best interior has to be that of **Basilika St Gereon** on Christophstrasse, with its incredible four-storey decagon (open 9 am to noon and 3 to 6 pm daily; enter from Gereonkloster). A DM2 churches' guide is available at the tourist office.

Museums The **Römisch-Germanisches Museum**, next to the cathedral at Roncalliplatz 4, displays artefacts on all aspects of the Roman settlement and, on the 2nd floor, from the Rhine Valley. The highlights are the giant Poblicius grave monument and the *Dionysos mosaic,* around which the museum was built. Entry is DM5 and the museum is open daily to 4 pm (except Monday).

The **Wallraf-Richartz-Museum & Museum Ludwig** at Bischofsgartenstrasse 1 (DM8, open daily to 6 pm except Monday) is one of the country's finest art galleries and makes brilliant use of natural light. The 1st floor is devoted to the Cologne Masters of the 14th to 16th centuries, known for their distinctive use of colour. Farther along, look for familiar names like Rubens, Rembrandt and Munch. On the 2nd floor, the contemporary art collection provides a wonderful contrast. Catch some prime Kirchner, Kandinsky and Max Ernst, as well as pop-art works by Rauschenberg and Andy Warhol. The building also houses a unique photography collection from the former Agfa Museum in Leverkusen.

At Cäcilienstrasse 29, the former church of St Cecilia houses the **Schnütgen Museum**, an overwhelming display of church riches, including many religious artefacts and early ivory carvings (DM5, open to 4 pm daily except Monday). At the **Diözesanmuseum** on Roncalliplatz, admission is free to see the religious treasures (closed Thursday).

One museum is actually in a bank branch: the **Käthe Kollwitz Museum** at Neumarkt 18-24 (DM5, open to 8 pm Thursday, closed Monday) displays some of the sculpture and stunning black-and-white graphics of the great socialist artist. The **Zeughaus** on Zeughausstrasse, restored as the **Stadtmuseum** (DM5, closed Monday), has a scale model showing old Cologne and a fine arms and armour collection.

Activities

Guided Tours The summer daily city tour in English lasts two hours and departs from the tourist office at 10 and 11 am and at 1, 2 and 3 pm (from November to March at 11 am and 1 and 2 pm). The cost is DM23. The 'Cologne Bonbon', a tourist package costing DM26 and available at main hotels, is good value if you want to take a city tour and visit a few museums for free. You can make day package trips to nearby cities with KD Rhine Line (see Getting There & Away later in this section), with sections by bus or train, such as to Düsseldorf (DM76) or Amsterdam (Saturday or Sunday trips with canal-tour bonuses DM86).

Historical Walks You can give yourself a free tour of ancient and medieval Cologne by walking around its restored monuments with a free city-sites map from the tourist office. Starting from the cathedral's main door, you will see the remains of the arch of a Roman gate from the ancient north wall. If you walk west along Komödienstrasse over Tunisstrasse, you reach the Zeughaus museum, the Burgmauer side of which was built along the line of the Roman wall. On the pavement at the west end is a plaque tracing the Roman wall line on a modern street plan, which you can pencil on your map (other plaques are around the city pavements near Roman sites). Then continue west until you find a complete section of the north wall, which leads to a corner tower standing among buildings on the street corner at St-Apern-Strasse. Walk south one block and you come to another tower ruin near Helenenstrasse.

On the south wall of the Römisch-Germanisches Museum are the remains of the Roman harbour street that led to the Rhine bank and two Roman wells. You can also take a lift down and walk through the Roman sewer and see the remains of the palace of the Praetorium (entry on Kleine Budengasse; closed Monday) under the medieval town hall. The Rathaus itself is open from 7.30 am Monday to Friday (to 2 pm only on Friday); the façades, foyer and tower have been restored.

The city's medieval towers and gates complement its Romanesque churches and many have been restored for private use. The Bayenturm on the Rhine bank at the east end of Severinswall is almost completely rebuilt, but along the street to the west the vine-bedecked Bottmühle and the mighty main south gate of Severinstor have more of the original basalt and tuff stones. To the north-west along Sachsenring is the vaulted Ulrepforte tower-gate and a section of wall with two more towers. North of the city centre is the gate of Eigelsteintor on Eigelstein, suspended from which is a boat from the MS *Schiff Cöln*, which sank off Heligoland in 1914. The main west gate, Hahnentor, is at Rudolfplatz.

Festivals

Try to time a visit to Cologne during the wild and crazy period of the Cologne Carnival (Karneval), rivalled only by Munich's Oktoberfest. People dress in creative costumes, clown suits, as popular personalities, and whatever else their alcohol-numbed brains may invent. The streets explode with activity on the Thursday before the seventh Sunday before Easter. On Friday and Saturday evening the streets pep up, Sunday is like Thursday and on Monday *(Rosenmontag)* there are formal and informal parades, and much spontaneous singing and celebrating.

Places to Stay

Cheap accommodation in Cologne is not plentiful, but there are some good pensions around the city and you might get private rooms when trade fairs are not on. You'd be lucky to find a reasonably central hotel room for under DM60/90 a single/double.

Camping The most (though not very) convenient camping grounds are the municipal camping ground *Campingplatz der Stadt Köln* (☎ 83 19 66, open from May to at least the end of September) on Weidenweg in Poll, five km south-east of the city centre; and *Campingplatz Waldbad* (☎ 60 33 15), on Peter-Baum-Weg in Dünnwald, about 10 km from the city centre but open all year.

Hostels Cologne has two DJH hostels. The first, *Jugendherberge Köln-Deutz* (☎ 81 47 11), is at Siegesstrasse 5a in Deutz, a 15-minute walk east from Hauptbahnhof over the Hohenzollernbrücke or three minutes from Bahnhof Köln-Deutz. The cost for juniors/seniors is DM25/29, but the hostel is crowded and not very pleasant. The *Jugendgästehaus Köln-Riehl* (☎ 76 70 81) is north of the city in Riehl by the river at An der Schanz 14. It's much more enjoyable and the cost is a flat DM30.50. Take the U5, U16 or U18 to Boltensternstrasse.

Hotels Hotels in Cologne are expensive and prices increase by at least 20% when fairs are on. The cheapest rooms are usually taken, so count on paying DM10 to DM15 above the prices quoted here. If you have private transport, enquire about parking – a night in a car park will set you back DM25 or more (not all garages operate 24 hours). The tourist office room-finding service can help you with hotel rooms in the lower price range.

Excellent budget bets are the two pensions at Richard-Wagner-Strasse 18, *Pension Jansen* (☎ 25 18 75), with a few singles from DM35 to DM50 and doubles from DM40 to DM50 with breakfast, and *Pension Kirchner* (☎ 25 29 77), with similar singles and doubles starting at DM80. *Stapelhäuschen* (☎ 2 57 78 62) at Fischmarkt 1-3 in the middle of the Altstadt, has pleasant singles/doubles from DM45/106, but you'd be lucky to get in at those prices. Further south, you can try the church-operated *Gästehaus St Georg* (☎ 9 37 02 00) at Rolandstrasse 61, where rooms – when available – cost from DM46/86.

In the area north of the train and bus stations, try *Hotel Rossner* (☎ 12 27 03), Jakordenstrasse 19, with rooms from DM50/66. *Hotel Berg* (☎ 12 11 24), Brandenburger Strasse 6, has rooms from DM48/80. *Hotel Einig* (☎ 12 21 28), Johannisstrasse 71, offers rooms from DM60/80. *Hotel Brandenburger Hof* (☎ 12 28 89) at Brandenburger Strasse 2 and *Hotel Thielen* (☎ 12 33 33) at No 1 have rooms from DM60/80 but fill up quickly. All the cheap rooms have toilet and shower facilities out in the corridor. *Hotel Buchholz* (☎ 12 18 24) at Kunibertsgasse 5 has a few singles from DM55.

GERMANY

Places to Eat & Drink

Italian restaurants are generally Cologne's best value, as long as you stick to pizza and pasta, and most pubs serve decent meals for under DM20 if you don't get carried away by the menu. Cologne's beer halls serve cheap and filling (though often bland) meals to compliment their home brew (see under Entertainment). *Brauhaus Sion* at Unter Taschenmacher 9 is a big beer hall, packed most nights and for good reason: you'll eat your fill for well under DM20, including a couple of beers. *Brauerei zur Malzmühle*, at Heumarkt 6 off Am Malzbüchel south of the Deutzer Brücke feeder roads, is smaller but similar. Slightly more up-market and much more of a cosy pub, *Altstadt Päffgen* at Heumarkt 62 (the north or Salzgasse end) serves meals for about DM20. Another *Päffgen* is at Friesenstrasse 64-66, and *Gaffel Haus*, Alter Markt 20-22, is similar.

An interesting stand-up bar is *Metzgerei Schmidt* at Merowinger Strasse 34 near Chlodwigplatz; there you can actually get mini-steaks or cutlets and a selection from the salad buffet for DM10 or less. You can also take away your meat and salad or eat a solid breakfast for DM5.50. For good DM7 breakfasts (or wurst-and-salad lunches) near the train station, squeeze into *Möve am Dom* at Marzellenstrasse 11. The *Kaufhalle* department store on Hohe Strasse has a self-service cafeteria and the *Kaufhof*, towards the south end of Hohe Strasse, has a self-service restaurant on the 3rd floor with low-budget breakfasts. *Steakhaus am Dom* at Am Hof 48 (closed Tuesday) has splurge main courses from DM18, but your salads are included.

Op d'r Woosch-Eck, on the corner where Neugasse meets the greenery along the Rhine, is another worthwhile target: daily specials are DM11 or DM12. To put together a picnic, visit a *market*; the biggest is on Friday in Alter Markt. For hot DM15 vegetarian dishes and Indian curries, seek out *Bombay Palace* on the corner of Am Wiedenbach and Am Pantaleonsberg (closed Monday).

Entertainment

Evenings and weekends in the Altstadt are like miniature carnivals, with bustling crowds and lots of things to do. Beer is the beverage of choice and there are lots of places to enjoy it.

For excellent jazz, head for either *Papa Joe's Klimperkasten* at Alter Markt 50, or *Papa Joe's Em Streckstrump* at Buttermarkt 37. The first is large and lively, with a wonderful old pianola, whereas the second is more intimate.

The gay scene centres on the Belgisches Viertel around Bismarckstrasse.

Cologne's usual venue for rock concerts is *E-Werk*, a converted power station at

Schanzenstrasse 28-36 in Mülheim. It turns into a huge disco on Friday and Saturday nights (for information dial ☎ 62 10 91). For theatre programme information, ring ☎ 1 15 17; for concerts, exhibitions, special events, trade fairs etc, call ☎ 1 15 16. *Monatvorschau* (see Information) has full events listings, and Köln Ticket (☎ 28 01) at Roncalliplatz next to the museum has tickets and information (open Saturday to 2 pm).

Beer Halls Much as in Munich, beer reigns supreme in Cologne. There are more than 20 local breweries, all producing a variety called *Kölsch*, relatively light and slightly bitter. The breweries run their own beer halls and serve their wares in skinny glasses holding a mere 200 ml, but you'll soon agree it's a very satisfying way to drink the stuff. See Places to Eat & Drink or try *Früh am Cathedral* at Am Hof 12-14. For more of a choice in beers, the *Biermuseum* at Buttermarkt 39 (beside Papa Joe's) serves 39 varieties. Another favourite among connoisseurs is *Küppers Brauerei* at Alteburger Strasse 157 at Bayenthal south of the city (U-Bahn: Bayenthalgürtel). It has an interesting museum (open from 11 am to 4 pm Saturday only) .

Things to Buy

This is not the place to make big purchases, though a good souvenir might be a small bottle of *eau de Cologne*, which is still produced in its namesake city. Try the fancy Parfümerie Douglas at Domkloster 2, or find a cheaper version at the Kaufhof at Hohe Strasse 41.

Getting There & Away

Air Cologne/Bonn Airport has many connections within Europe and to the rest of the world. For flight information, ring ☎ 02203-40 40 01/2. The Lufthansa office (☎ 9 20 82) is in the city at Grosse Neugasse 2, though you should buy tickets at accredited agents (try at Am Hof 25, opposite Lufthansa City Centre).

Bus Deutsche Touring's Eurolines buses have overnight one-way tickets to/from Paris for DM69 (return DM120) and the journey lasts seven hours. The office is at the train station at the Breslauer Platz exit.

Train S-Bahn as well as main-line trains service Bonn (DM7.40) and Düsseldorf. Most trips to/from Aachen (hourly; DM17.20) take about one hour (via Düren is more direct). Other direct links are to Hanover (about three hours minimum), Dresden (three times daily, 8½ hours), Leipzig (six times daily, 6½ hours), Berlin (nine times daily, 7½ hours) and Frankfurt (regular trains, 2¼ hours).

Car & Motorbike The city is on a main north-south autobahn route and is thus easy for drivers and hitchhikers. The ADM Mitfahrzentrale (☎ 1 94 40) is at Trierstrasse 47 near Barbarossaplatz, and Citynetz Mitfahr-Service (☎ 1 94 44) is at Saarstrasse 22.

Boat One enjoyable way to travel to/from Cologne is by boat. The KD Line (for information ☎ 2 08 83 18), which has its headquarters in the city at Frankenwerft 15, has services all along the Rhine.

Getting Around

To/From the Airport Bus No 170 runs between Cologne/Bonn Airport and the main bus station every 15 minutes (DM7.20 for the 20-minute trip).

Public Transport Cologne offers a convenient and extensive mix of buses, trams and local trains – trams go underground in the inner city, and trains handle destinations up to 50 km around Cologne. Ticketing and tariff structures are complicated. The best ticket options are the one-day pass for DM9.50 if you're staying near the city (one or two zones), DM13.50 for most of the Cologne area (three zones), and DM19 including Bonn (six zones) and S-Bahn connections between the two (DM19/19/38 for the three-day versions). Single city trips cost DM1.80, 90-minute two-zone tickets are

DM2.80 and three-hour tickets (including Bonn) DM7.40.

Taxi Taxis cost DM3.40 flagfall plus DM2.20 per km; add another DM1 if you order by phone (☎ 28 82). There are taxi ranks on the city's larger squares.

DÜSSELDORF

More than 80% of Düsseldorf's Altstadt was destroyed in WW II, but it was reconstructed to become one of the most elegant and wealthy cities in all of Germany. Though not particularly strong in sights, the city, which is the capital of North Rhine-Westphalia, is a charming example of big-city living along the Rhine River.

Düsseldorf's telephone code is 0211.

Information

The tourist office (☎ 17 20 20) is towards the north side of Konrad-Adenauer-Platz, outside the main exit of the main train station. Across the road nearby is the main post office, at Konrad-Adenauer-Platz 1. A DVB bank is in the station's main hall, open to 9 pm daily. American Express is at Heinrich-Heine-Allee 14.

Düsseldorf's telephone code is 0211.

Things to See & Do

Upon arrival, head straight for the Königsallee, or 'Kö', a famed shopping, eating and drinking street that provides a perfect view of Düsseldorf's elegant lifestyle. Stroll north along the Kö to the **Hofgarten**, a large park in the city centre.

The city has several interesting museums, particularly art museums. These include the **Kunstmuseum Düsseldorf** at Ehrenhof north of the Oberkasseler Brücke (DM5, open to 8 pm Wednesday, closed Monday), with a comprehensive European collection, and the nearby **Glasmuseum Heinrich** next to the ramp. On Grabbeplatz are the **Kunstsammlung Nordrhein-Westfalen** at No 5 (DM8, students DM5, closed Monday), which has a huge collection of modern art, and the Kunstverein collections in the **Kunsthalle** at No 4 (DM5, closed Monday).

The **Goethe-Museum Düsseldorf** in Schloss Jägerhof, Jacobistrasse 2, pays tribute to the life and work of one of Europe's great men of letters. The collection and exhibits are large and complete, with books, first drafts, letters, medals and much more (DM4, closed Monday and Saturday morning). German-literature buffs will also want to visit the **Heinrich-Heine-Institut** at his house at Bilker Strasse 12-14, which documents the Düsseldorfer's career (open Tuesday to Saturday from 2 to 6 pm, Sunday from 11 am).

The old **Rathaus** building at Marktplatz has been restored and looks out onto the **statue of Elector Johann Wilhelm**, known affectionately in local speech as 'Jan Wellem'. The elector's mausoleum can be visited at the beautiful early-baroque **St Andreas Kirche** at the corner of Hunsrückenstrasse and Andreasstrasse, now in the care of a Dominican monastery. Another church worth visiting is **St Lambertus Basilika** on Stiftsplatz (closed Friday until noon). The reconstructed **Schlossturm** of the long-destroyed Residenz stands on Burgplatz as a forlorn reminder of the Palatine elector's glory.

Places to Stay

There are two camping grounds close to the city. *Campingplatz Nord Unterbacher See* (☎ 8 99 20 38) is at Kleiner Torfbruch in Düsseldorf-Unterbacher (S-Bahn No 707 to Düsseldorf-Eller, then bus No 735 to Kleiner Torfbruch). This is to the north of the lake – the camping ground to the south is private and does not accept tourists. *Camping Oberlörick* (☎ 59 14 01) is at Niederkasseler Deich 305 beside the Rhine in Düsseldorf-Lörick (U-Bahn No 70, 76, 705 or 717 to Belsenplatz, and then bus No 828 or 838). The trek to the Altstadt is very inconvenient from either camping ground.

The *Jugendherberge* and *Jugendgästehaus* (☎ 57 40 41) are at Düsseldorfer Strasse 1, cramped and overpriced (juniors/seniors DM25/29), but there are some private rooms from DM30.50 and it is one of the few budget options. With a DM2.80 ticket, take

PLACES TO STAY

10 Hotel Esser
18 Hotel Amsterdam
21 Hotel Komet
22 CVJM Hotel
24 Hotel Manhattan
25 Hotel Hillesheim
26 Hotel Diana

PLACES TO EAT

4 Brauerei im Füchschen
12 Im Goldenen Kessel
13 Zum Schlüssel
15 Ristorante Lago di Como
17 Maharadja

OTHER

1 Kunstmuseum
2 Glasmuseum Heinrich
3 Goethe Museum
5 Kunstsammlung
6 St Lambertus Basilika
7 Schlossturm
8 Kunsthalle
9 St Andreas Kirche
11 Rathaus
14 Zum Uerige
16 Heinrich-Heine-Institut
19 Main Post Office
20 Tourist Information
23 Train Station

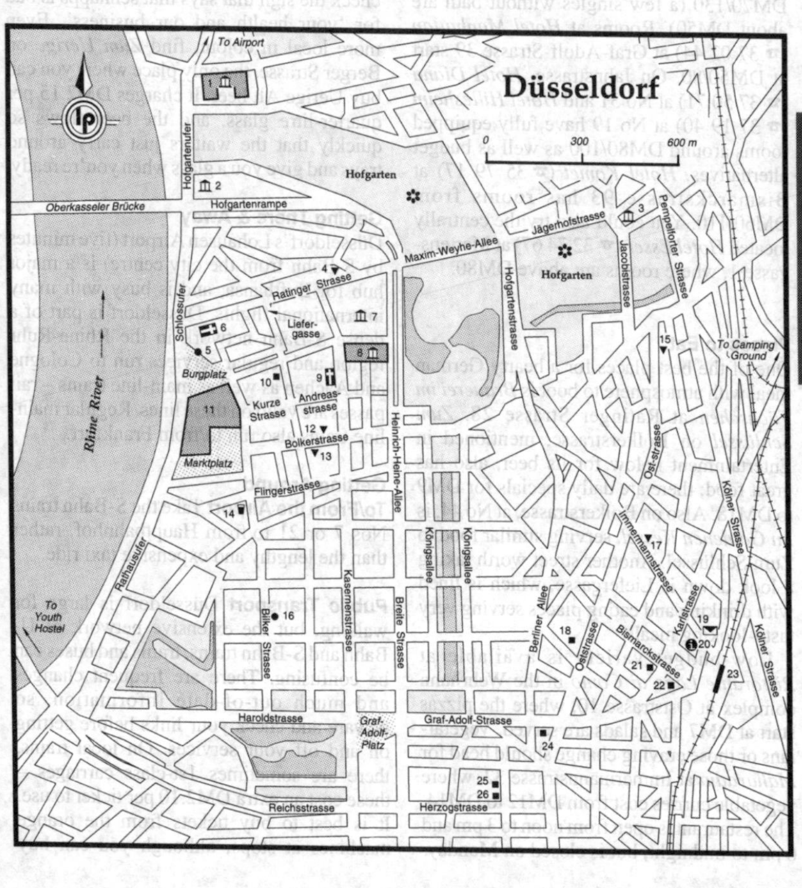

GERMANY

bus No 725 from stop 10 at Konrad-Adenauer-Platz towards Hafen and get off at Kirchplatz (about a seven-minute ride), crossing towards the church to the stop for bus No 835 or 836 over the Rhine bridge. About five minutes on this bus brings you outside the hostel, first stop off the bridge. On the return journey you change on the other side of Kirchplatz.

The YMCA's *CVJM-Hotel* (☎ 36 07 64) is at Graf-Adolf-Strasse 102, where basic singles/doubles start at DM58/100. Another option is *Hotel Amsterdam* (☎ 84 05 89) at Stresemannstrasse 20, with rooms from DM70/130 (a few singles without bath are about DM50). Rooms at *Hotel Manhattan* (☎ 37 02 44) at Graf-Adolf-Strasse 39 start at DM50/80. On Jahnstrasse, *Hotel Diana* (☎ 37 50 71) at No 31 and *Hotel Hillesheim* (☎ 37 19 40) at No 19 have fully equipped rooms around DM80/100 as well as budget alternatives. *Hotel Komet* (☎ 35 79 17) at Bismarckstrasse 93 has rooms from DM60/110. You could also try the centrally located *Hotel Esser* (☎ 32 74 67) at Mertensgasse 1, where rooms are above DM80.

Places to Eat

One of the best places for a hearty German meal with atmosphere to boot is *Brauerei im Füchschen* at Ratinger Strasse 28. *Zum Schlüssel* on Bolkerstrasse, mentioned in Entertainment below for its beer, also has great food; there are daily specials for DM9 to DM18. Also on Bolkerstrasse, at No 44, is *Im Goldenen Kessel*, serving similar food to Zum Schlüssel. Another street worth taking a look down is Liefergasse, which is lined with drinking and eating places serving very tasty-looking meals.

Low-budget variety is available at *Ristorante Lago di Como* in the Wehrhahn complex at Oststrasse 10, where the pizzas start at DM7 and salads are served. Vegetarians or those craving change should head for *Maharadja* at Immermannstrasse 32, where vegetable curries cost from DM12 to DM14. The restaurant is open from noon to 3 pm and 6 pm to midnight, but is closed on Monday.

Entertainment

Besides walking and museum-hopping, one of the best things to do in Düsseldorf is (surprise!) drink beer. There are lots of bars (for drinking and eating) in the Altstadt, affectionately referred to as the 'longest bar in the world'. On evenings and weekends, the best places overflow onto the pedestrian-only streets. Favoured streets include Bolkerstrasse, Kurze Strasse, Andreasstrasse and the surrounding side streets.

The beverage of choice is Alt beer, a dark and semisweet brew. Try Gatzweilers Alt in *Zum Schlüssel* at Bolkerstrasse 43-47, and check the sign that says that schnapps is bad for 'your health and our business'. Even more local in colour, find *Zum Uerige* on Berger Strasse, the only place where you can buy Uerige Alt beer. It charges DM2.15 per quarter-litre glass, and the beer flows so quickly that the waiters just carry around trays and give you a glass when you're ready.

Getting There & Away

Düsseldorf's Lohausen Airport (five minutes by S-Bahn from the city centre) is a major hub for Lufthansa, and is busy with many international flights. Düsseldorf is part of a dense S-Bahn network in the Rhine-Ruhr region and regular services run to Cologne and Aachen as well as main-line trains – rail passes are valid on these lines. Regular main-line trains also run to/from Frankfurt.

Getting Around

To/From the Airport Take the S-Bahn trains Nos 7 or 21 to/from Hauptbahnhof, rather than the lengthy and expensive taxi ride.

Public Transport Düsseldorf is large for walking, but the extensive network of U-Bahn and S-Bahn trains, trams and buses can be confusing. There are frequent changes and much out-of-date information, so beware and check your links before getting on and off your services. On local trains, there are sometimes 1st-class carriages – these cost an extra DM2.10 per ticket to use. It is best to buy tickets from the orange machines at stops, although you can buy tickets from bus drivers. Four-trip tickets for most zones and categories are also available and work out cheaper, but must be validated each time you board; there are also day cards. Short-trip tickets lasting 40 minutes cost DM1.70 for city services (four trips DM4.80) and a 90-minute ticket including a change for the city and the 'A' area costs DM2.80 (four trips or a day card DM8).

BONN

This friendly, relaxed city of 310,000 on the Rhine south of Cologne became West Germany's temporary capital in 1949. Since reunification, it threatens to sink into obscurity once more as the all-German parliament and government ministries shift back to Berlin.

Bonn was already settled in Roman times, and celebrated its 2000th anniversary in 1989. In the 18th century, it was the seat of the electors of Cologne, and some of their baroque architecture survived the ravages of WW II and the postwar demand for modern government buildings. Organise a day trip out here and to nearby Bad Godesberg, the spa town that forms one city with Bonn and houses most of its diplomats. If you are a classical music buff you will want to visit Bonn to pay homage to its most famous son, Ludwig van Beethoven.

Information

The tourist office (☎ 0228-77 34 66) is in an arcade at Münsterstrasse 20. Look carefully, because it's not well signposted. It's open from 8 am to 9 pm Monday to Saturday, 9.30 am to 12.30 pm Sunday (closes at 7 pm weekdays from November to March), and operates a DM3 room-finding service (DM5 for rooms over DM100). The range of brochures and free maps is second to none. A DM12 BonnCard will admit you to most main museums in the city for a day (see also Getting Around).

The bank in the train station operates Monday to Friday from 7.30 am to 6.30 pm, Saturday to 3 pm, Sunday 8.30 am to 1 pm. The main post office is on Münsterplatz.

The telephone code for Bonn and Bad Godesberg is 0228.

Foreign Embassies So long as the German foreign ministry remains in Bonn, most of the foreign embassies will remain here too. See the Facts for the Visitor section at the beginning of this chapter for a list.

Things to See & Do

City tours (summer only, at 10 am or 2 pm) cost DM16, smaller walking tours DM10.

The **Beethoven-Haus** is at Bonngasse 20 (open Monday to Saturday from 10 am to 5 pm, Sunday to 1 pm; DM5, students DM3). The composer was born here in 1770 and it contains much memorabilia concerning his life and music. In the front room on the 2nd floor, take a look at his last piano, specially made with an amplified sounding board to accommodate his deafness. The ear trumpets will make you wonder what kind of music he could have written with good hearing. The Beethoven Festival is held every three years (the next will be in 1995) and his music is performed at the **Beethovenhalle** on Fritz-Schroeder-Ufer by the Rhine and occasionally in the small chamber in his house.

The **Frauenmuseum** at Im Krausfeld 10 regularly changes its exhibitions on the lives and roles of women, but maintains a historical approach while favouring artistic expressions and perspectives. The museum costs DM5 to visit (students DM3), but is closed Monday; take tram No 61 to Rosenthal.

Sts Cassius and Florentinus, two martyred Roman officers who became the patron saints of Bonn, are honoured in the **Münsterbasilika** on Münsterplatz. It's one of the best examples of the unique Rhenish style of architecture in the transition from Romanesque to Gothic. The interior is mainly baroque.

The **Bundeshaus**, Germany's parliament building, started off as an education academy in the Bauhaus period but has since been extensively rebuilt and expanded. It's at Göresstrasse 15, south-east of the city centre on the Rhine. You would have to be particularly interested in German politics to take the (excellent) tour, which has to be booked in advance – contact the tourist office, or the Bundestag visitor service direct on ☎ 16 26 84. The recently opened **Haus der Geschichte der Bundesrepublik Deutschland** at Adenauerallee 250 covers the history of West Germany from 1949 (free entry; U-Bahn: Heussallee).

Places to Stay

The *Jugendgästehaus Venusberg* (☎ 28 99 70), Haager Weg 42, is inconvenient, large and loud, but beautifully located in the woods on Venusberg south of the city. A bunk costs DM30.50 including breakfast, and meals are available. Take bus No 621.

For the ultimate in German hostel elegance, head for the 90-bed *Jugendgästehaus Bad Godesberg* (☎ 31 75 16) in Bad Godesberg at Horionstrasse 60. Prices are identical to Venusberg. Take bus No 615 from this pretty town's train station to the 'Jugendgästehaus' stop. At both hostels, couples may be able to grab one of the rooms reserved for group leaders.

Bonn's hotels are not as pricey as you'd expect – DM65/95 should get you a single/double within easy walking distance of the city centre. Try *Hotel Kurfürstenhof* (☎ 63 11 66) on Baumschulallee 20 near the train station, with shower access and good breakfasts at DM63. *Eschweiler* (☎ 63 17 60), Bonngasse 7, right in the city centre just off Markt, or *Deutsches Haus* (☎ 63 37 77), Kasernenstrasse 19-21, just north of the centre (with a good, unpretentious restaurant), offer slightly cheaper rooms. Hotel prices in Bad Godesberg are even cheaper.

Places to Eat

Many pubs in Bonn serve decent food at decent prices. *Zum Gequetschen* at Sternstrasse 78, on the corner of Kasernenstrasse, is a cosy, Cologne-style beer establishment with main courses under DM20. Snack bars aren't hard to find, and there's a colourful *food market* on Markt in front of the Rathaus from 8 am to 6.30 pm Monday to Friday, to 2 pm Saturday. In the laid-back mood of the city is *Spitz*, a café and bar at Sterntorbrücke 10 that serves pasta and salad from DM12 every day.

Getting There & Away

Bonn makes for a pleasant day trip from Cologne or Düsseldorf, and it can even be seen by just jumping off the train for a few hours on your way through. There are more than 70 trains a day to/from Cologne in the north and Koblenz in the south. The KD Line (☎ 63 21 34 for the Bonn office at Brassertufer) also runs its Rhine cruises through Bonn.

Getting Around

Most of Bonn's sights are an easy walk from the station. The Bonn transit system is linked with Cologne's and a single train ride costs only DM7.40 (see the Cologne Getting Around entry for a pass covering both). A day pass for Bonn only costs DM9.80 (same price for a whole family), or there is the inclusive travel-and-museums BonnCard, valid on transport after 9 am (families DM24).

AACHEN

Aachen was already known in Roman times for its thermal springs. The great Frankish conqueror Charlemagne was so impressed by their revitalising qualities that he settled here and made it the capital of his kingdom in 794 AD. Ever since, Aachen has held special significance among the icons of German nationhood. It is now an industrial and commercial city of 260,000, and home to the country's largest technical university.

Orientation

Aachen's compact old centre is contained within two ring roads that roughly follow the old city walls. The inner ring road, or Grabenring, has different names all ending in '-graben', and encloses the old city proper. The main train station is in the south-eastern corner of the outer ring road, the Alleenring. The old city centre is a 10-minute walk away.

GERMANY

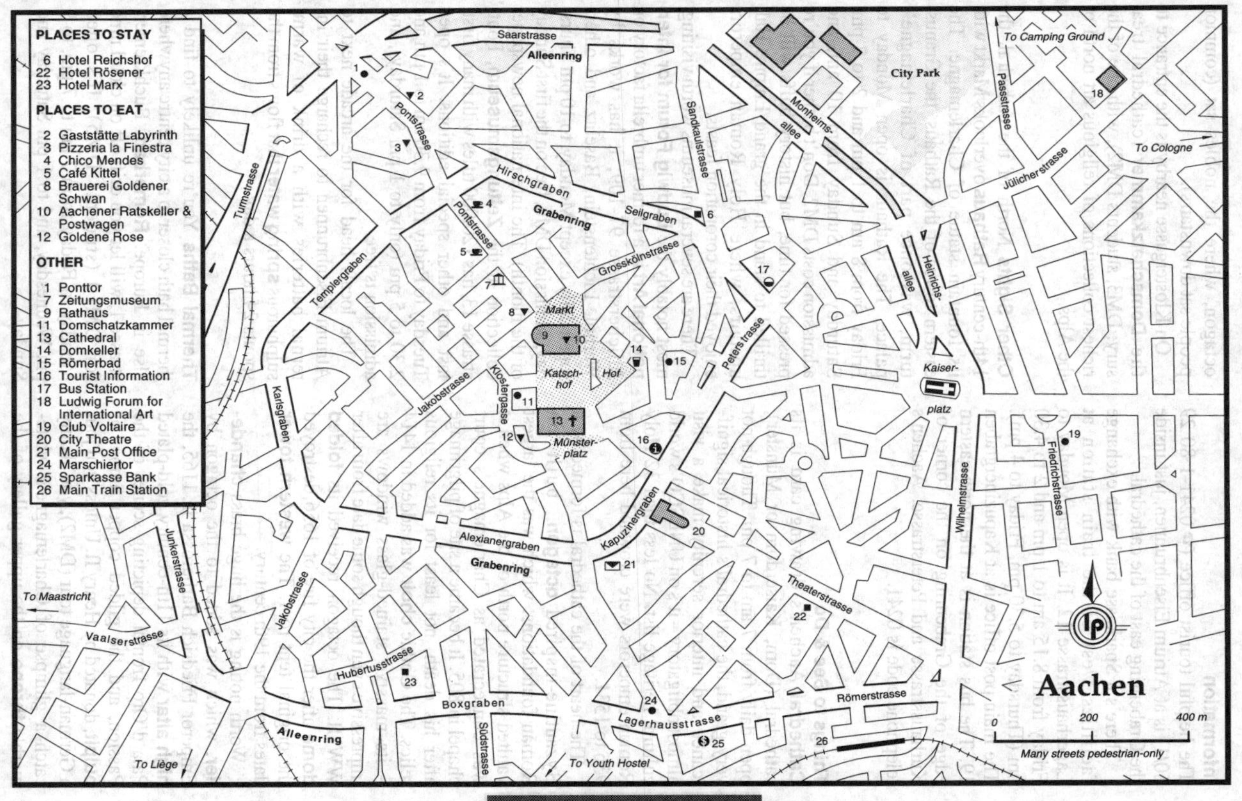
PLACES TO STAY
6 Hotel Reichshof
22 Hotel Rösener
23 Hotel Marx
PLACES TO EAT
2 Gaststätte Labyrinth
3 Pizzeria la Finestra
4 Chico Mendes
5 Café Kittel
8 Brauerei Goldener Schwan
10 Aachener Ratskeller & Postwagen
12 Goldene Rose
OTHER
1 Ponttor
7 Zeitungsmuseum
9 Rathaus
11 Domschatzkammer
13 Cathedral
14 Domkeller
15 Römerbad
16 Tourist Information
17 Bus Station
18 Ludwig Forum for International Art
19 Club Voltaire
20 City Theatre
21 Main Post Office
24 Marschiertor
25 Sparkasse Bank
26 Main Train Station
Aachen
0
200
400 m
Many streets pedestrian-only
To Camping Ground
To Cologne
City Park
Passstrasse
Jülicherstrasse
Saarstrasse
Alleenring
Monheims-allee
Sandkaulstrasse
Pontstrasse
Hirschgraben
Grabenring
Seilgraben
Grosskölnstrasse
Heinrichs-allee
Kaiser-platz
Peters trasse
Turmstrasse
Templergraben
Markt
Katsch-hof
Hof
Jakobstrasse
Klostergasse
Münster-platz
Karlsgraben
Friedrichstrasse
Wilhelmstrasse
Kapuzinergraben
Alexianergraben
Theaterstrasse
Junkerstrasse
To Maastricht
Vaalserstrasse
Jakobstrasse
Hubertusstrasse
Boxgraben
Römerstrasse
Lagerhausstrasse
Südstrasse
To Liège
To Youth Hostel

GERMANY

Information

The helpful tourist office (☎ 0241-1 80 29 50/1) is at Atrium Eisenbrunnen, just inside the Grabenring east of the cathedral.

There's a Sparkasse bank with exchange facilities west of the train station at Lagerhausstrasse 12. It is open Monday to Friday from 8.15 am to 1 pm and 2 to 4.30 pm (Thursday to 5.30 pm, Friday to 4 pm). The main post office is at Kapuzinergraben 19. The bus station is at the north-eastern edge of the Grabenring on the corner of Kurhausstrasse and Peterstrasse. Aachen's telephone code is 0241.

Things to See & Do

Cathedral Aachen's drawing card is its cathedral (Dom, Kaiserdom or Münster), open daily from 7 am to 7 pm. Though not very grand, the cathedral's historical significance and interior serenity make a visit almost obligatory – it's on UNESCO's world cultural heritage list. No less than 32 Holy Roman emperors were crowned here from 936 to 1531.

The heart of the cathedral is formed by a Byzantine-inspired **octagon**, built on Roman foundations, which was the largest vaulted structure north of the Alps when it was consecrated as Charlemagne's court chapel in 805. It became a site of pilgrimage after his death, not least for its religious relics. The Gothic **choir** was added in 1414 – its massive stained-glass windows are impressive even though some date from after WW II. The octagon received its **folded dome** after the city fire of 1656 destroyed the original tent roof. The **western tower** dates from the 19th century.

Worth noting is the huge brass **chandelier**, which was added to the octagon by Emperor Friedrich Barbarossa in 1165, the **high altar** with its 11th-century gold-plated Pala d'Oro frontal depicting scenes of the Passion, and the gilded copper ambo, or **pulpit**, donated by Henry II. Unless you join a German-language tour (DM2), you'll only catch a glimpse of Charlemagne's white-marble **throne** on the upper gallery of the octagon, where the nobles sat (common people sat downstairs).

On Klostergasse nearby is the entrance to the **Domschatzkammer** (cathedral treasury; DM3, students DM2), with one of the richest collections of religious art north of the Alps.

Other Sights North of the cathedral, the 14th-century **Rathaus** overlooks Markt with its fountain statue of Charlemagne. The eastern tower of the Rathaus, the Granusturm, was once part of Charlemagne's palace. The Rathaus is open Monday to Friday from 8 am to 1 pm and 2 to 7 pm, Saturday and Sunday from 10 am, and admission costs DM2. Don't bother if you're pressed for time, but history buffs will be thrilled to stand in the grand Empire Hall upstairs, where Holy Roman emperors enjoyed their coronation feasts.

There are several museums worth visiting, most notably the **Ludwig Forum for International Art** in a former umbrella factory on Jülicherstrasse 97-109; it has works by Warhol, Lichtenstein, Baselitz and others (open daily except Monday, to 10 pm Thursday, admission DM6, free on the first Sunday of the month). The international newspaper collection at the **Zeitungsmuseum**, Pontstrasse 13, has 120,000 titles with many first, last and other special editions. It's open Tuesday to Friday from 9.30 am to 1 pm and 2.30 to 5 pm (only to 1 pm Saturday), and admission is free.

The locals head for the arcade next to Atrium Eisenbrunnen to recharge their internal batteries with a drink of warm, sulphurous **spring water** that flows from the spouts 24 hours a day.

Thermal Baths You're unlikely to find a thermal bath closer to a city centre anywhere else in Europe. **Römerbad**, Buchkremerstrasse 1, will let you drift off on cloud nine for DM10 (students DM5). It's open Monday to Friday from 7 am to 7 pm, to 9 pm Wednesday, and to 1 pm Saturday and Sunday.

Places to Stay

The *camping ground* (☎ 15 85 02, open May to September) is in a great location just 10 minutes' walk north-east of the city centre, at the edge of the City Park at Passstrasse 85.

The *Colynshof* hostel (☎ 7 11 01), Maria-Theresia-Allee 260, is four km south-west of the train station on a hill overlooking the city. Catch bus No 2 to the Ronheide stop, or bus No 12 to the closer Colynshof stop at the foot of the hill. It costs DM18.50/22 for juniors/seniors, including breakfast, and other meals are available. The hostel is closed several weekends a year.

The tourist office has private rooms from DM30/50 single/double (fee DM3), but make sure they give you something that's within walking distance of the city centre. Don't be disappointed if the cheapest rooms are taken, even on a Monday in the low season. *Hotel Marx* (☎ 3 75 41), Hubertusstrasse 33-35, has singles/doubles from DM60/100, and an inner courtyard where you can park your car (a bonus in Aachen). *Hotel Rösener* (☎ 40 72 15), Theaterstrasse 62, has rooms from DM52/80. *Hotel Reichshof* (☎ 2 38 68) at Seilgraben 2 is central and rooms with all facilities start at DM80/130.

Places to Eat & Drink

Being a university town, Aachen is full of lively cafés, restaurants and pubs. *Café Kittel*, Pontstrasse 39, is a popular student hang-out with a lively garden out the back. It serves reasonably priced small meals including vegetarian dishes. The café *Chico Mendes* in the Katakomben Studentenzentrum, Pontstrasse 74-76, is excellent value and serves breakfast.

For authentic Italian food and a matching ambience, complete with a gaggle of Italian waiters shouting out their orders, head for *Pizzeria la Finestra*, Pontstrasse 123, where you can get mini-pizzas from DM3.50 and large ones from DM8.50. Diagonally opposite, at Pontstrasse 156-158, is *Gaststätte Labyrinth*, a rambling beer-hall-type place that lives up to its name. Good, filling meals range from DM8 to DM17.50, and the menu also lists several vegetarian dishes.

Brauerei Goldener Schwan, Markt 37, is a great old pub with most dishes from DM10 to DM24 and pizzas for around DM10. The jewel of Aachen's pub-restaurant scene is the *Aachener Ratskeller & Postwagen*, a 300-year-old pub-restaurant on the eastern side of the Rathaus underneath the Granusturm, with small, wooden rooms up and down several stairs, and a tremendous atmosphere. The Postwagen's prices are surprisingly reasonable, with a lunchtime dish of the day for around DM14.

Goldene Rose, facing the west side of the cathedral at Fischmarkt 1, is busy and boisterous with more than a touch of style, at slightly above-average prices. *Domkeller*, around the other side of the cathedral at Hof 1, is a pub with great atmosphere but, unfortunately, no food.

On Katschhof, the square between the cathedral and the Rathaus, there's a food-and-flower *market* on Tuesday and Friday from 8 am to 1 pm.

Entertainment

There are several discotheques in Aachen, mainly frequented by the young to the very young. The more mature crowd heads for *Club Voltaire*, Friedrichstrasse 9, which really starts swinging to funk and other Black music from midnight. The *City Theatre* (☎ 4 78 42 44 for bookings) on Theaterplatz has concerts and opera almost every night; the tourist offices can tell you what's on, or contact the Culture Office at Kapuzinergraben 12-14.

Getting There & Away

Aachen is well served by road and rail. Just north-east of town is the junction of the A4 autobahn between Maastricht/Heerlen and Cologne, and the A44 autobahn between Liège and Düsseldorf. There are fast trains almost every hour to Cologne (55 minutes; DM17.20) and Liège (50 minutes; DM13), and local trains every two hours to Maastricht (45 minutes; DM10.60).

Getting Around

Aachen's points of interest are clustered around the city centre, which is small enough to be covered easily on foot. Those arriving with private transport can dump their cars in one of the many car parks. City bus tickets bought from the driver cost DM1.10 (for short trips), DM2.30 or DM 2.80, depending on the distance. A batch of five tickets bought in advance (at the train station, machines, the bus station or tobacconists) costs DM9 (DM10.50 from bus drivers).

Bremen

The federal state of Bremen covers only 404 sq km and comprises the two cities of Bremen (the state capital) and Bremerhaven. In medieval times, Bremen was for a time Europe's northernmost archbishopric. The city was ruled by the Church until the 14th century, when a break was made and Bremen joined the Hanseatic League. Bremen was controlled by the French from 1810 to 1813, but went on to join the German Confederation in 1815. In 1871, the city was made a state of the German Empire. In 1949 Bremen was officially declared a Bundesland of the Federal Republic of Germany.

BREMEN

Bremen is, after Hamburg, the most important harbour in Germany, even though the open sea lies 113 km to the north. Its Hanseatic past and congenial Altstadt area around Am Markt and Domsheide make it an enjoyable place to walk, but, while exploring, make sure to drink a few Beck's beers.

Orientation & Information

The heart of the city is Am Markt, but the soul is the port, which provides about 40% of local employment. The tourist office (☎ 0421-30 80 00) is directly in front of the main train station. The staff are helpful and can provide an excellent brochure in English. There is also a booth at the new town hall opposite the smaller of the main Altstadt churches, Unser Lieben Frauen Kirche. The main hubs for trams and buses are in front of the Hauptbahnhof and Domsheide.

If you get lost in the Altstadt streets, look down – often there are stencilled arrows on the footpaths directing you to other sights. But don't walk with your head down, or you are likely to be knocked over by the local cyclists, who seem to claim the pedestrian areas (and just about any other ground) by proprietary right.

Bremen's telephone code is 0421. The main post office is on Domsheide.

Things to See & Do

Around Am Markt, take a look at the splendid and ornate **Rathaus**, the cathedral **St Petri-Dom**, which has a tower lookout (DM1) and museum (DM2, both closed Saturday afternoon and Sunday until 2 pm), and the large statue of **Roland**, erected in 1404 and Bremen's sentimental protector.

Walk down **Böttcherstrasse**, a re-creation of a medieval alley, complete with tall brick houses, shops, galleries, museums and restaurants. The **Paula-Becker-Modersohn-Haus** is at No 8, with works of the Worpswede contemporary painter Paula Modersohn-Becker, and the varied exhibits of the **Bernhard Hoetger Sammlung**; Hoetger's striking sculpture graces much of the Böttcherstrasse. The **Roselius-Haus** is at No 6, with medieval objects. There is a DM8 entry charge to the museums (students DM4). The **glockenspiel**, daily at noon, 3 and 6 pm, plays an extended tune from between rooftops and an adjacent panel swivels to reveal reliefs of fearless seadogs (the best known here being Columbus).

The nearby **Schnoorviertel** area features fishing cottages that are now a tourist attraction, with shops, cafés and tiny lanes.

An excellent walk encircling the Altstadt is along the **Wallanlagen**, parks stretching along the old city walls and moat. They're a peaceful break from the city. On a summer Saturday, look for the **flea market**, which might stretch a km or more along the north-east bank of the Weser, from beyond Burgermeister-Smidt-Brücke to the bridge at Balgebrückstrasse and the lawns to the south-east.

Along with Bremerhaven, 59 km downstream, Bremen has a large port system. The 75-minute **port tour** is excellent and costs DM12 per person.

One great reference around which to frame a Bremen trip is the **Fairy-Tale Road** from Bremen to Hanau, the birthplace of the Brothers Grimm (see the Fairy-Tale Road section later in this chapter for more information).

Places to Stay

The closest camping ground is at *Campingplatz Bremen* (☎ 21 20 02) at Am Stadtwaldsee 1. It's reasonably close to the university – take tram No 5 from the Hauptbahnhof to Kühlenkampfallee, then bus No 28 to the camping ground.

The city's hostel accommodation is *Jugendgästehaus Bremen* (☎ 17 13 69), on the Weser at Kalkstrasse 6, across from the Beck's brewery (take bus No 25 from the Hauptbahnhof to Faulenstrasse, or tram No 6). The cost is DM24.50/29 juniors/seniors.

Hotels in Bremen are expensive, but *Hotel*

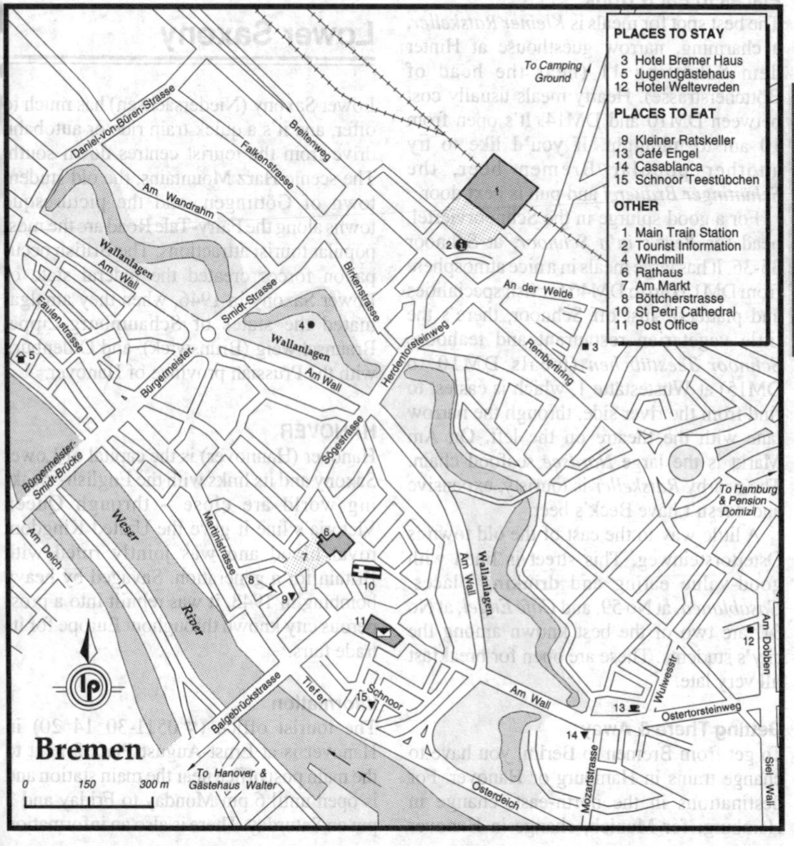

Garni Gästehaus Walter (☎ 55 80 27), Buntentorsteinweg 86-88, charges from DM40 to DM70 for a few singles and from DM70 for doubles. *Pension Domizil* (☎ 3 47 81 47) at Graf-Moltke-Strasse 42 is a little farther out but the dozen or so rooms all have a shower; singles/doubles start at DM78/110. To get there, take bus No 30 or 34 to Holler Allee, then walk. *Hotel Weltevreden* (☎ 7 80 15), Am Dobben 62, has rooms without bath for DM58/95. A good up-market option is *Hotel Bremer Haus* (☎ 3 29 40), Löningstrasse 16-20, where rooms cost from DM120/150.

Places to Eat & Drink

The best spot for meals is *Kleiner Ratskeller*, a charming, narrow guesthouse at Hinter dem Schütting 11 (near the head of Böttcherstrasse). Hearty meals usually cost between DM10 and DM14. It's open from 10 am to midnight. If you'd like to try another popular Bremen beer, the *Schüttinger Brauerei* and pub is next door.

For a good splurge in the Schnoorviertel, head for *Beck's in'n Schnoor*, at Schnoor 35-36. It has large meals in a nice atmosphere from DM15 (up to DM46 for fish specialities and platters). Just off Schnoor, there's the little vegetarian restaurant and teahouse *Schnoor Teestübchen* (meals DM10 to DM15) at Wüstestätte 1, which is easiest to find from the river side, through the narrow lane with the theatre on the left. On Am Markt is the large *Nordsee* seafood chain. The nearby *Ratskeller* is touristy, expensive and doesn't have Beck's beer.

A little way to the east of the old town is Ostertorsteinweg. This street is lined with good-value eating and drinking places. *Casablanca*, at No 59, and *Café Engel*, at No 31, are two of the best known among the city's students. These are open for breakfast till very late.

Getting There & Away

To get from Bremen to Berlin, you have to change trains in Hamburg or Hanover. For destinations in the north-east, change in Hamburg; for Munich, change in Hanover (occasionally Brunswick). For Amsterdam (from three to 3½ hours), change in Osnabrück. For Brussels (six hours), the best connections are via Cologne. Direct Frankfurt trains take about five hours.

Getting Around

Directly in front of the train station and tourist office, follow the tram route to Am Markt, and everything is within walking distance. The tram system is simple to follow on the map from the tourist office. Short trips cost DM1.50, a four-trip transferable ticket DM8.80 and a day pass DM6.50.

Lower Saxony

Lower Saxony (Niedersachsen) has much to offer, and it's a quick train ride or autobahn drive from the tourist centres down south. The scenic Harz Mountains, the old student town of Göttingen, and the picturesque towns along the Fairy-Tale Road are the most popular tourist attractions. The British occupation forces created the federal state of Lower Saxony in 1946, when they amalgamated the states of Schaumburg-Lippe, Braunschweig (Brunswick), and Oldenburg with the Prussian province of Hanover.

HANOVER

Hanover (Hannover) is the capital of Lower Saxony and its links with the English-speaking world are close – through Queen Victoria's line it gave the United Kingdom royal blood and was jointly ruled with Britain for a generation. Savaged by heavy bombing in 1943, it was rebuilt into a prosperous city known throughout Europe for its trade fairs.

Information

The tourist office (☎ 0511-30 14 20) in Hanover is at Ernst-August-Platz 2 next to the main post office near the main station and is open until 6 pm Monday to Friday and 2 pm on Saturday. There is also an information counter in the Rathaus. HannoverCard, valid after 9 am each day, costs DM14 for a day or DM22 for three days.

Hanover's telephone code is 0511.

Things to See

One way to pick out most city sights on foot is to follow the red line with its numbered attractions with the help of the *Red Thread Guide* from the tourist office. The chief attractions are the unique baroque parks of **Herrenhäuser Gärten**, especially **Grosser Garten** (DM3, accessible until 8 pm on summer evenings), and their museums outside of the city centre (take tram No 4 or 5). The **Fürstenhaus** (entry DM5, students DM3) shows what treasures remain from the Guelph palaces, and the **Wilhelm-Busch-Museum** of satirical art (DM6, closed Monday in winter) contains the work of that artist and others.

The **Sprengel Museum** (free entry, open to 10 pm on Tuesday, closed Monday) exhibits contemporary works, the highlights being Picasso and Max Beckmann, and the **Kestner-Museum** (DM2, Wednesday free; closed Monday) has antiquities, including a bust of the pharaoh Akhenaten. The entire old museum building has been encased by a modern shell. The **Niedersächsisches Landesmuseum**, Am Maschpark 5, has a varied collection covering regional prehistory, history and art. Entry is free and the museum is closed on Monday.

At Am Markt in the old town, the 14th-century **Marktkirche**, apart from its truncated tower, is characteristic of the northern red-brick Gothic style; the original stained-glass windows are particularly beautiful. The **Altes Rathaus** across the marketplace was built in various sections over a century. Around **Burgstrasse** some of the half-timbered town houses remain, as well as the **Ballhof**, originally constructed for badminton-type games of the 17th century, but the only plays there today are theatrical.

In the domed **Neues Rathaus** off Friedrichswall you can see four city models that show what has been lost and gained in the march of time (entry free), but on Breite Strasse the memorial ruin of the **Aegidienkirche**, smashed in 1943, speaks more eloquently. The peace bell inside was a gift from one of Hanover's sister-cities – Hiroshima.

Places to Stay & Eat

Hanover's *hostel* (☎ 1 31 76 74) is three km out of town at Ferdinand-Wilhelm-Fricke-Weg 1 and can be reached by U-Bahn (U3 or U7 from Hauptbahnhof to Fischerhof, then cross the river on the Lodemannbrücke bridge and turn right). The price for juniors/seniors is DM19/23.50.

The city centre has some affordable hotel options, such as *Hospiz am Bahnhof* (☎ 32 42 97), in sight of the main station at Joachimstrasse 2, with basic singles/doubles with breakfast from DM53/96 and access to a DM2 shower. Similar but bigger is *Hotel am Theilenplatz* (☎ 32 76 91), at Theilenplatz, with some rooms at DM63/120 without bath access. *Hotel Flora* (☎ 34 23 34), at Heinrichstrasse 36, has rooms with shared bathroom from DM50/80 (with private bathroom up to DM80/150).

Restaurant Gilde-Hof, Joachimstrasse 6 near Hauptbahnhof, has big serves of typical German food from DM10. If you've had your fill of this fare, try the slightly more expensive Turkish restaurant *Kreuzklappe*, on the corner of Kreuzstrasse and Kreuzkirchhof. *Block House* steaks sizzle in the pedestrian part of Ständehausstrasse and a *Nordsee* fish outlet is nearby in Karmarschstrasse.

Getting There & Away

Hanover is a major intersection of train lines. There are trains virtually every hour from 5 or 6 am to/from Hamburg, Munich, Frankfurt and Berlin. Approximate travelling times to these four cities are 1½, 4½ (overnight 6½), 2¼ and 3½ to four hours respectively.

If you are driving, Hanover is well positioned for autobahns to the same four cities. There are also good autobahn connections to Bremen, Cologne, Amsterdam and Brussels.

Getting Around
The city centre is best covered on foot, but from either end of Bahnhofstrasse the tram and U-Bahn networks are the handiest ways to reach beyond. Single journeys cost DM3.10, day passes DM9, but block tickets offer savings, and the tourist brochure *Travel Tips for Visitors* is vital reading.

FAIRY-TALE ROAD

The Fairy-Tale Road (Märchenstrasse), so called because of the number of legends and fairy tales which find their roots in this region, is definitely worth a day or two. The route begins at Bremen, passes near Hanover and then goes farther south to Göttingen, Kassel and Hanau. The stretch from Hanover to Göttingen is the most historical section of the route. Among the most interesting towns here are Hamelin (Hameln) of Pied Piper fame, Bodenwerder, where the great adventurer Baron von Münchhausen was at home, and the surprising town of Bad Karlshafen.

Information
Every town, village and hamlet along the Fairy-Tale Road has an information office of sorts. The office in Hamelin (☎ 05151-20 26 18) is most helpful. It is at Deister Allee 3, just outside the old town (there is also a counter in the Hochzeitshaus). In Bodenwerder, you will find the tourist office (☎ 05533-4 05 41) at Brückenstrasse 7. In Bad Karlshafen, you will find it in the Kurverwaltung (☎ 05672-10 91) by the 'harbour'. The office in Hamelin has a colourful map of the entire route.

The telephone codes for Hamelin, Bodenwerder and Bad Karlshafen are 05151, 05533 and 05672 respectively.

Things to See
Hamelin Among the most interesting sights is the so-called **Rattenfängerhaus** ('Rat Catcher's house') on Osterstrasse, the old town's main street. The house was built at the beginning of the 17th century. On the Bungelosenstrasse side is an inscription that tells how, in 1284, 130 children of Hamelin were led past this site and out of town by a piper wearing multicoloured clothes, never to be seen again. Also have a look at the **Rattenfänger Glockenspiel** at the Weser Renaissance **Hochzeitshaus** at the Markt end of Osterstrasse (daily at 1.05, 3.35 and 5.35 pm). More of the story is at the museum in the ornate **Leisthaus** (DM2, closed Monday). For the other beauties of Hamelin – the restored 16th to 18th-century half-timbered houses with inscribed dedications – stroll through the south-eastern quarter of the old town, around Alte Marktstrasse and Grossehofstrasse, or Kupferschmiedestrasse.

Bodenwerder The present-day **Rathaus** is said to be the house in which the legendary Baron von Münchhausen was born. The baron's fame was due to his telling of outrageous stories. Perhaps the most famous of these is how he rode through the air on a cannonball; this very cannonball can be seen today in the room dedicated to the baron in the Rathaus. Also interesting is the statue of the baron riding half a horse, in the garden outside the Rathaus. This was, of course, another of his stories.

There is a pleasant **walking track** along the Weser River in both directions from Bodenwerder.

Bad Karlshafen This place is simply unexpected. After passing through towns like Hamelin and Bodenwerder, the last thing you would expect is this whitewashed, meticulously planned, baroque village. Originally the city had been planned with an impressive harbour and a canal connecting the Weser River with the Rhine, in the hope of diverting trade away from Hanover and Münden in the north. The plans were laid by a local earl with help from Huguenot refugees. The earl's death in 1730 prevented completion of this project, but even today his incomplete masterpiece and the influence of the Huguenots is too beautiful to miss.

Places to Stay & Eat
In Hamelin the camping ground, *Fährhaus an der Weser*, is on Uferstrasse (☎ 6 11 67),

across the Weser River from the old town and 10 minutes' walk north, and the *DJH hostel* (☎ 34 25) is at Fischbeckerstrasse 33 (bus No 2 from the train station to Wehler Weg). In Bodenwerder, the *DJH hostel* (☎ 26 85) is on Richard-Schirrmann-Weg, above the valley on the eastern edge of the town. In Bad Karlshafen, the hostel *Hermann Wenning* (☎ 3 38) is at Winnefelderstrasse 7, a few minutes' walk from the train station near the river.

For a hotel in Hamelin, try *Hotel zur Börse* (☎ 70 80), Osterstrasse 41a, which has singles/doubles from DM67/125. *Hotel Altstadtwiege* (☎ 2 78 54), Neue Marktstrasse 10, has rooms from DM50/85. In Bodenwerder, the *Hotel Deutsches Haus* (☎ 39 25), Münchhausenplatz 4, has rooms from DM79/100.

For a gastronomic treat in Hamelin, you might try *Gaststätte Rattenfängerhaus* in the Rat Catcher's House, where you can lash out or order a DM11 daily special.

Getting Around

The easiest way to follow the Fairy-Tale Road is by car. The ADAC map of the Weserbergland covers the area in detail.

There are several local trains a day from Hanover to Hamelin and back (40 minutes), and from Hamelin's train station about a dozen buses a day (Nos 2612 to 2614, 40 minutes) to/from Bodenwerder. To/from Bodenwerder there are also Höxter buses, and Höxter-Kassel buses pass through Bad Karlshafen.

GÖTTINGEN

This leafy university town is an ideal stopover on your way north or south – it's on the direct train line between Munich and Hamburg. Almost one-quarter of Göttingen's population are students. The Brothers Grimm were professors here and a legion of notables including Otto von Bismarck were students. The prestigious Max Planck Institute is based here. You can make a quick exploration by hopping off and back on the train in the same day (locker DM4).

Information

The main tourist office (☎ 0551-5 60 00, closed from 1 pm Saturday and on Sunday) is just outside the main entrance to the train station, and a large post office is just to the left (north). There is another tourist office in the old Rathaus (at Markt 9), in a side room just off the main hall (open to 4 pm on Sunday in summer, to 1 pm Saturday and closed Sunday from November to March).

Göttingen's telephone code is 0551.

Things to See

In the old town, on the pedestrian **Prinzenstrasse**, the student population becomes immediately apparent. At Markt, make sure you see the beautifully decorated main hall in the old **Rathaus** and the **Goose Girl fountain** ('Gänseliese'), a tribute to Göttingen's favourite daughter. Her fame is due to her reputation as the most kissed girl in the world.

Next to the train station is a carefully presented **Zoological Museum** (in Berliner Strasse, but you enter from the back, through the driveway on the bus-station side). It is open on Wednesday from 6 to 8 pm, or on Sunday from 10 am to 1 pm.

The colourful **Junkernschränke** on the corner of Jüdenstrasse and Barfüsserstrasse, which dates from the 15th century, is well worth a photograph as perhaps the best of the old town's half-timbered buildings. You can walk on top of much of the old **town wall** along Bürgerstrasse, past the **Bismarckhäuschen**, an unlikely building where the Iron Chancellor spent salad days in 1832 and 1833 (open Tuesday 10 am to 1 pm, Thursday and Saturday 3 to 5 pm). A 12th-century **tower** remains on Turmstrasse.

Places to Stay

Campers have to go only a few km out of town to *Waldcampingplatz Eulenburg* (☎ 05522-66 11) at Scheerenberger Strasse 100. The *Jugendherberge Göttingen* (☎ 5 76 22) is less than friendly and a bit hard to reach at Habichtsweg 2. From the train station main entrance, head through the tunnel under Berliner Strasse to the right

GERMANY

(south) of the tourist office, take the first right to Groner-Tor-Strasse and cross it to the stop for route No 6; take this bus to the 'Jugendherberge' stop. The bed cost for juniors/seniors is DM19.50/24.

For pensions try *Hotel zum Schwan* (☎ 4 48 63) at Weender Landstrasse 23, which costs DM45/71 for a bathless single/double, or DM55/85 with bath.

In the centre of Göttingen, try *Central Hotel* (☎ 5 71 57), Jüdenstrasse 12, which has rooms for DM65/95, or *Gaststätte zur Rose* (☎ 5 70 50), Kurze Geismar Strasse 11, a small hotel with a few pleasant but bathless rooms for DM60/120. *Hotel Kasseler Hof* (☎ 7 20 81), at Rosdorfer Weg 26 near the edge of the old town, has rooms from DM56/108.

Places to Eat

Because it's a student centre, eating in Göttingen is fairly cheap and lively. Though the large *Zentralmensa*, through the arch off Weender Landstrasse, is good for cheap food to 3.30 pm weekdays (to 5.30 on Thursday), a better option with lots more flavour is *Zum Altdeutschen* at Prinzenstrasse 16, a student hang-out.

Nudelhaus, on the corner of Jüdenstrasse at Rote Strasse 13, has a huge selection of noodle-based dishes at very reasonable prices. Also popular with students is *Feuerstein* at Wendenstrasse 8a, on the corner of Mauerstrasse; it is open only from 5 pm on summer weekdays, but you can still order a full meal after midnight.

For a hearty meal, you can't go past *Zur Alten Brauerei*. If you are lucky, your eating may be accompanied by live music. The restaurant is in a courtyard behind the half-timbered building at Düstere Strasse 20 (under the gallery walkover and to the right at No 20a).

Getting There & Away

Trains constantly pass through on the Munich-Hamburg line. There are a few direct trains daily from Göttingen to Goslar in the Harz Mountains.

GOSLAR

Goslar is a centre for Harz Mountains tourism but has its own attractions and atmosphere, which attract summer tourists, but not too many. On a weekday or in May, it is one of the most relaxed and pleasant towns in Germany to visit.

Information

The tourist office (☎ 05321-28 46) is at Markt 7 and can help when the area's accommodation is packed. The Harzer Verkehrsverband (☎ 05321-22 00 31) through the big doors at Marktstrasse 45 has most information about Goslar as well as the Harz. The Goslar chapter of the Deutscher Alpenverein has an info point at Ski Maass at Bäckerstrasse 112. Streets in the old town number up one side, down the other.

Goslar's telephone code is 05321.

Things to See

The **Marktplatz** has several photogenic houses. Opposite the Gothic **Rathaus** there's one with a chiming clock depicting four different scenes of the history of mining in the area. It struts its stuff at 9 am, noon, 3 pm and 6 pm. The eagle on the **market fountain** goes back to the 13th century. For strolling, look at the **Schuhhof**, **Worthstrasse** and **Marktkirchhof** and buildings such as the **Kaiserworth**, an old textile guildhall decorated with the statues of emperors, and the **Bäcker-Gildehaus**.

The **Kaiserpfalz** is a restored Romanesque 11th-century palace now loaded with tour bus visitors. The 45-minute tour (DM3.50) is boring, but in the peaceful gardens behind is Henry Moore's sculpture **Goslarer Krieger**. More Romanesque architecture is on show at **Neuwerkkirche**, on Rosentorstrasse near the train, a cathedral in miniature that is being renovated inside.

For an excellent review of the history of Goslar and the geology of the Harz Mountains, visit the **Goslarer Museum** at Königstrasse 1, on the corner of Abzuchtstrasse (DM3.50, closed Monday). The mining history of the region is on show at the **Rammelsberger Bergbaumuseum**, about one km south of the town centre on Rammelsberger Strasse. You can go down into the mines on a variety of tours from DM6 to DM12. The **Zinnfiguren Museum** (Pewter Statuette Museum), in the courtyard at Münzerstrasse 11, has hundreds of painted figures in many different pretty settings. Entry costs DM3.50, and it's closed on Monday.

Places to Stay

The pretty *Jugendherberge* (☎ 2 22 40) is at Rammelsberger Strasse 25 behind the Kaiserpfalz (bus 'C' to Theresienhof from the train station). It charges DM18.50/22.50 for juniors/seniors with breakfast, and is often full of students.

A better option is *Hotel und Campingplatz Sennhütte* (☎ 2 25 02), three km south on Route B241 at Clausthaler Strasse 28. This is also reached by bus No 2434, getting off at the 'Sennhütte' stop. The few rooms are comfortable and start at DM30/60 a single/double (nice views). There are many trails leading away from the camping ground and into the mountains, including the one to Hahnenklee.

In town, a pension or Zimmer frei is the only inexpensive option. Try *Haus Bielitza* (☎ 2 07 44) at Abzuchtstrasse 11 at DM25/50 (shower DM3.50) or *Rüland* (☎ 2 51 62) at An der Abzucht 30, for singles at DM30 and doubles from DM50. You could lash out at the *Kaiserworth Hotel* (☎ 2 11 11) in the historic building at Markt 3 and enjoy the company of emperors for DM85/160.

Places to Eat

Most places are closed on Monday. About the only full plate under DM10 is at the schnitzel-and-chips *Kaiser Grill* at Hoher Weg 17. For a DM20 meal and some strong and tasty beer, head to *Gils Bräu Brauhaus Goslar* in the courtyard at Marstallstrasse 1. It offers daily luncheon and dinner specials in a brewery atmosphere, and even has two-litre portions of beer to go. It's the done thing to loll in the sunshine with coffee or ice cream on Marktkirchhof all afternoon; *Café Klatsch* is a panelled hangout on Marktstrasse that gets fuller as the evening approaches.

Getting There & Away

Goslar is best reached by train from Göttingen (about 1¼ hours); eight to 10 trains a day cover the route directly, and there are another 10 or so where you will need to change trains in Kreiensen. For information on getting to/from the eastern German Harz region, see the Quedlinburg and Wernigerode sections of this chapter.

WESTERN HARZ MOUNTAINS

Known mostly to Germans and Scandinavians, the Harz Mountains (Harzgebirge) don't have the peaks and valleys of the Alps, but they offer a great four-seasons sports getaway without some of the Alpine tackiness and tourism. The area provides one of the best opportunities in Europe to get off the crowded tourist tracks. Once there were many silver, lead and copper mines in the area, but these have been worked to the stage where most of them are no longer profitable.

Orientation & Information

Make sure to pick up the booklet *Grüner Faden für den Harz-Gast* ('Green Thread for the Harz Guest') from the tourist office in Goslar (DM3); the office also receives weather reports daily and winter snow information and can pass on important details in English. For outdoor activities, particularly in winter, you can pick up forms for detailing your adventure plans from Ski Maass in Goslar (see Information in the Goslar section); this is a good precaution if you don't know the area. Many mountain towns have tourist offices and their own Alpenverein and Harzclub offices, which are ideal places for further information, specific recommendations, itineraries, hiking partners and guided hikes.

Things to See

Hahnenklee is proud of its imitation of a Norwegian 'stave' **church**, but most remarkable is Clausthal-Zellerfeld's 17th-century wooden church **Zum Heiligen Geist**, at

Hindenburgplatz, which was built to accommodate over 2000 worshippers! Nearby, the technical university's **mineral collection** (open weekdays; DM1) is of particular interest to geology buffs. For a fine view, take the **Bergbahn** car up to the castle ruins above Bad Harzburg (DM4/7 one way/return if you have no resort card). The embarkation point is two km uphill from the train station, so you can promenade up among German wealth and ambition and check the array of furs and other luxury goods tucked away in this 'health' resort.

Activities

Hiking The Naturpark Harz is well organised for hikers, but its beauty doesn't suffer. Maps and information are abundant. Goslar has many highly recommended hikes just outside town, but the area up to and around the Granestausee (four or five km west of Goslar train station towards the town of Wolfshagen) is particularly scenic. Most of the hikes can be accomplished in a half-day and most are less than 10 km. You can hike the 15 km to Hahnenklee from Goslar without ever leaving the forest. From Goslar to Bad Harzburg you can pick up the medieval Kaiserweg route and follow it towards Walkenried, or turn back to Sennhütte via Langes Tal. From Bad Harzburg back to Altenau is a good 20 km stretch.

The excellent *Auto + Wanderkarte Harz* map (DM9.80) gives good information for hikers, as well as being a great driving map (make sure to ask for the newest version). Most trails are well marked and maintained, but it doesn't hurt to occasionally ask if you're heading the way you think you are. At any time of year and no matter what the current weather, be prepared for almost anything mother nature can throw at you.

Cycling The pedal has become popular in the Harz among those seeking a hilly hallenge. If the slopes get to you eventually, ou can get on any of the local buses, which vill carry your machine for only DM1. A ycle track follows the main road from Bad Iarzburg as far as the old border at Eckertal. All-Time Rent (☎ 05322-44 86) at Herzog-ulius-Strasse in Bad Harzburg has mountain ikes from DM30 a day or DM140 a week with helmet).

Skiing Downhill skiing is below average, ue to uninspiring slopes and inconsistent now conditions. Locals, however, are pas-ionate about cross-country skiing, and this s a better overall option. Most tourist offices ave an excellent brochure and map, *kilanglauf im Naturschutzgebiet Oberharz.* his gives details of about 10 different loops, anging from three to 15 km, with informa-ion on elevation, elevation changes, ifficulty and trailheads. One of the more onsistent and popular downhill resorts is Iahnenklee, with five nice runs (two of them 500 metres long) and three lifts (one a cable ar).

Rental equipment for both sports is easy o find. Downhill skis and boots or cross-ountry gear start at about DM20 a day.

Spas The Harz Mountains also offer many opular spas, but they don't come cheaply. Iahnenklee and Altenau have many places o stay with spa amenities, but it's best to stay omewhere cheaper and then ask the tourist ffice about paying separately to use private r public facilities. Hahnenklee's pump ouse is great for a splurge, with a sauna, ndoor swimming pool and standard spa menities.

Places to Stay

Many of the camping grounds are open all ear, but that doesn't mean the weather is uitable for camping, just that they cater for aravans. Hotel and guesthouse prices are igh. For extended stays, ask the tourist ffice about apartments or holiday homes, vhich become pretty good deals when taying for a week or more. In the resorts you will pay Kurtaxe as part of the price, or usually an extra DM2.50 or so at hostels.

Hahnenklee *Campingplatz am Kreuzeck* (☎ 25 70) is on the road two km north of Hahnenklee (bus from Goslar). The *Jugendherberge* (☎ 22 56) is at Steigerstieg 1 near the 'Bockswiese' bus stop on the road from Goslar (DM18/22 for juniors/seniors). The tourist office (☎ 20 14) at Rathausstrasse 16 can help you find a private room.

Altenau *Campingplatz Obertalsperre* (☎ 7 02) is on the B498 just north of town. The *Jugendherberge* (☎ 6 12) is at Auf der Rose 11 (seniors/juniors DM18/22). If you would like a private room, the Kurverwaltung (☎ 80 20) can help.

Bad Harzburg The *Campingplatz Wolfenstein* at Wolfsklippen on Ilsenburger Strasse east of the town is the only site that accepts tents (bus No 74 or 77 from the station). The hostel *Braunschweiger Haus* (☎ 05322-45 82) is at Waldstrasse 5 (bus No 73).

Clausthal-Zellerfeld The *DJH hostel* (☎ 05323-8 42 93) at Altenauer Strasse 55 is usually closed one weekend per month from mid-September to mid-June, so be certain of your plans.

Getting Around

The only effective public transport connection between the western and eastern areas of the Harz Mountains is the bus from Bad Harzburg (less than 15 minutes by train from Goslar) to Wernigerode. Bus No 77 runs several times every day in both directions (just under an hour; DM5). The bus stops on the far side of Am Bahnhofsplatz from the Bad Harzburg train station and next to the main station in Wernigerode (stop No 4).

Bus Nos 408 and 432 run Goslar-Altenau, and Nos 408 and 434 Goslar-Clausthal-Zellerfeld (No 434 via Hahnenklee).

GERMANY

Hamburg

The first recorded settlement on the present site of Hamburg was the moated fortress of Hammaburg, built in the first half of the ninth century AD. The city that developed around it became the northernmost archbishopric in Europe to facilitate the conversion of the peoples to the north. The city was burned down many times, but in the 13th century it became the Hanseatic League's gateway to the North Sea, and was second in importance and influence only to Lübeck. With the decline of the Hanseatic League in the 16th century, Lübeck faded into insignificance but Hamburg continued to thrive.

Hamburg strode confidently into the 20th century, but WW I stopped all incoming and outgoing trade, and most of Hamburg's merchant shipping fleet (almost 1500 ships) was forfeited to the Allies as reparation payment. In WW II, over half of Hamburg's residential areas and port facilities were demolished and 55,000 people killed in Allied air raids. Twenty-five years later, however, Hamburg was as good as rebuilt.

Today it is a sprawling port city and a separate state of Germany, with a stylish shopping district where you can shop for extended hours on Thursday evenings and on the first Saturday afternoon each month, numerous waterways (with more bridges than Venice), and even a beach (in Blankenese, Germany's most exclusive suburb).

Orientation

The main station, the Hauptbahnhof, is very central near Aussenalster lake and is fairly close to most of the sights. These are south of Aussenalster and north of the Elbe River, which runs all the way from the Czech Republic to Hamburg before flowing into the North Sea. The city centre features the Rathaus and two imposing landmarks – the TV Tower and the Köhlbrandbrücke, a huge suspension bridge that spans the Elbe River. The port is west of the city centre, facing the Elbe.

Information

The airport has a tourist office (☎ 040-3 0 51 24 0), open from 8 am to 11 pm daily o the arrivals level of terminal No 4.

The small tourist office in the Hauptbahn hof (☎ 3 00 51 23 0) at the Kirchenallee ex offers limited brochures and a room-findin service (DM3). It has great hours (7 am to 1 pm daily) and friendly, if overworked, staf There is another tourist office (☎ 040-3 0 51 22 0) at the Hanse-Viertel shopping centr on Poststrasse; it's open from 10 am to 6.3 pm Monday to Friday (until 8.30 pm o Thursday), 10 am to 3 pm on Saturday (to pm on a 'long' Saturday, to 4 pm in summer Sunday 11 am to 3 pm. There's also an offic (☎ 040-3 00 51 20 0) at St Pauli harbou between piers 4 and 5. It is open daily fror 9.30 am until 5.30 pm (S-Bahn: Landungs brücken).

The handy monthly information bookle *The Hamburger* (cost DM2) has an Englis version available at these offices or at news stands. The Hamburg Card, valid for the da of purchase and one (or two) more, cost DM10.80 (DM21) and offers small dis counts on some attractions. It is best to bu it at tourist offices: you can ask to see th leaflet that explains the discounts before yo buy. A youth activities information centre i at Holzdamm 53.

Money There is a DVB bank above th Kirchenallee exit of the Hauptbahnhof (ope 7.30 am to 10 pm daily), an exchang counter at the Altona train station (ope Monday to Friday 7.30 am to 3 pm and 3.4 to 7.30 pm, Saturday 9 am to 1.45 pm an 2.30 to 4.30 pm, closed Sunday), and Deutsche Bank counter at the airport (6.3 am to 10.30 pm daily). There are severa exchange shops scattered around the Haupt bahnhof. Most branches of banks are ope until 4 pm Monday to Friday (to 6 pm o Thursday) and are closed from 1 to 2.30 pm although in the city centre you will have fe problems. American Express is at Rathaus markt 5 (open Monday to Friday from 9 an to 5.30 pm, Saturday to noon).

Post & Telephone There's a small post office near the Kirchenallee exit of the Hauptbahnhof (open Monday to Friday from 7 am to 9 pm, Saturday from 8 am to 8 pm), where there is a poste restante counter. The main post office (telephone cubicles are downstairs as you enter) is on the corner of Dammtorstrasse at Stephansplatz. Hamburg's telephone code is 040.

Bookshops Dr Götze Land & Karte, Bleichenbrücke 9 in the Bleichenhof arcade (S-Bahn: Stadthausbrücke), claims to be the biggest specialist map-and-travel bookshop in Europe and has a smattering of guidebooks in English. A second, smaller shop is in the Wandelhalle shopping arcade at the Hauptbahnhof. The branch of Thalia Bücher on Spitalerstrasse within sight of the Hauptbahnhof has a civilised book café at the back of the shop and a large range of guidebooks (some in English).

Emergency The police are on ☎ 1 10; there are stations at the corner of Kirchenallee and Bremer Reihe outside the central station and at Spielbudenstrasse 31 off the Reeperbahn. For an ambulance, call ☎ 1 12; in other medical emergencies, contact the 24-hour medical clinic (☎ 4 68 47 17) at Eppendorf hospital on Martinistrasse (U-Bahn: Kellinghusenstrasse, or bus No 102). A medical emergency service is available (☎ 22 80 22), as well as a 24-hour first-aid service (☎ 24 82 81) and dental aid (after 7 pm ☎ 4 68 32 60, weekends and holidays ☎ 1 15 00).

Dangers & Annoyances The only two real problem areas are in the vicinity of the Hauptbahnhof and Kirchenallee (which is down-market and shows a pale red light), and the Reeperbahn. The station and the Reeperbahn are usually crowded, so there should be little danger so long as you keep moving and don't take pictures or ask too many questions.

Laundry Hamburg has several Waschcenter laundrettes, where a basic wash costs DM6, although to take away a dry load you will part with DM10. The most convenient is probably at Wandsbeker Chaussee 159, at the exit of the Ritterstrasse station on the U1. Another is reasonably central at Mühlenkamp 37 (bus No 108 from Rathausplatz).

Media For cultural events and lifestyle info, look for the monthly *Szene* magazine (DM5). For classified ads of all sorts, you can pick up a copy of the weekly paper *Avis* (DM3.50).

Things to See & Do

Altstadt Much of Hamburg's old city centre was lost in WW II, but it's still worth a walking tour. The area is filtered with wonderful canals (called 'fleets') running from the Alster to the Elbe.

The Altstadt centres on Rathausmarkt, where the large **Rathaus** and huge clock tower overlook the lively square. This is one of the most interesting city halls in Germany, and the 40-minute tour is worthwhile at DM2. It's in English hourly Monday to Thursday from 10.15 am to 3.15 pm, Friday to Sunday to 1.15 pm. The building has 647 rooms – six more than Buckingham Palace.

It is moving to visit the standing tower of the devastated **St Nikolai** on Ost-West-Strasse nearby. From there, walk a few blocks west to **Hauptkirche St Michaelis** and take the lift up the tower (DM4, children DM2, enter through portal No 3) for a great view of the city and the port. Inside, the beautiful interiors and the crypt (a donation of DM2.50 is requested) are open for viewing. The tower is open Monday to Saturday from 9 am to 6 pm and on Sunday from 11 am.

Port After exploring the Altstadt, stroll down to one of the busiest ports in the world. It boasts the world's largest carpet warehouse complex, while the Free Port Warehouses stockpile most spices from all continents.

The **port cruises** are admittedly touristy, but still worthwhile. Until you take one, you literally have no idea of the immensity of the world's shipping industry. There are many

PLACES TO STAY
5 Gästehaus Gurlitt
6 Steen's Hotel
7 Hotel-Pension Annenhof
8 Hotel St Georg
14 Eden Hotel
15 Hotel-Pension Zentrum
16 Hotel-Pension Kieler Hof
18 Hotel Fürst Bismarck
33 Auf dem Stintfang Hostel
PLACES TO EAT
3 Bäckerei von Altwörden
4 Blockhaus Restaurant
9 Essen und Trinken
13 Kantine am Schauspielhaus
19 Blockhaus Restaurant
20 Daniel Wischer Restaurant
25 Piceno
35 Fischerhaus Restaurnt
OTHER
1 TV Tower
2 Main Post Office
10 Streits Cinema
11 Tourist Information
12 Hauptbahnhof Train Station
17 Police
21 Gerhart-Hauptmann-Platz
22 Rathausplatz Bus Station
23 Rathaus
24 Cotton Club
26 Police
27 Schmidt Theater
28 Panoptikum
29 Operettenhaus
30 Bismarck Monument
31 Hauptkirche St Michaelis
32 St Nikolai Tower
34 Harry's Hafen Basar
36 Tourist Information
37 Greenpeace Headquarters
38 Free Port Warehouses
Schröderstiftstrasse
Bundesstrasse
Grindel
Planten un Blomen
Lagerstrasse
Karolinenstrasse
Hamburg Fairgrounds
Kleine Wallanlagen
Gorch-Fock-Wall
Feldstrasse
Grosse Wallanlagen
Glacischaussee
Holstenwall
Budapester Strasse
Holstenstrasse
Simon von Utrecht Strasse
Grosse Freiheit
Hein-Hoyer-Strasse
To Altona Train Station
Gross-neumarkt
Alter Steinweg
Reeperbahn
Helgoländer Allee
Zirkusweg
Ludwig-Erhard-Strasse
Herbertstrasse
Seewartenstrasse
Venusberg
Herrengraben
Bernhard-Nocht-Strasse
St-Pauli-Hafenstrasse
Ditmar-Koel-Strasse
Rambachstrasse
Neuer Neustädter Weg
Stubbenhuk
St-Pauli-Fischmarkt
To Fish Market
St Pauli Harbour
Johannis-bollwerk
Vorsetzen
Baumwall
Elbe
River

GERMANY

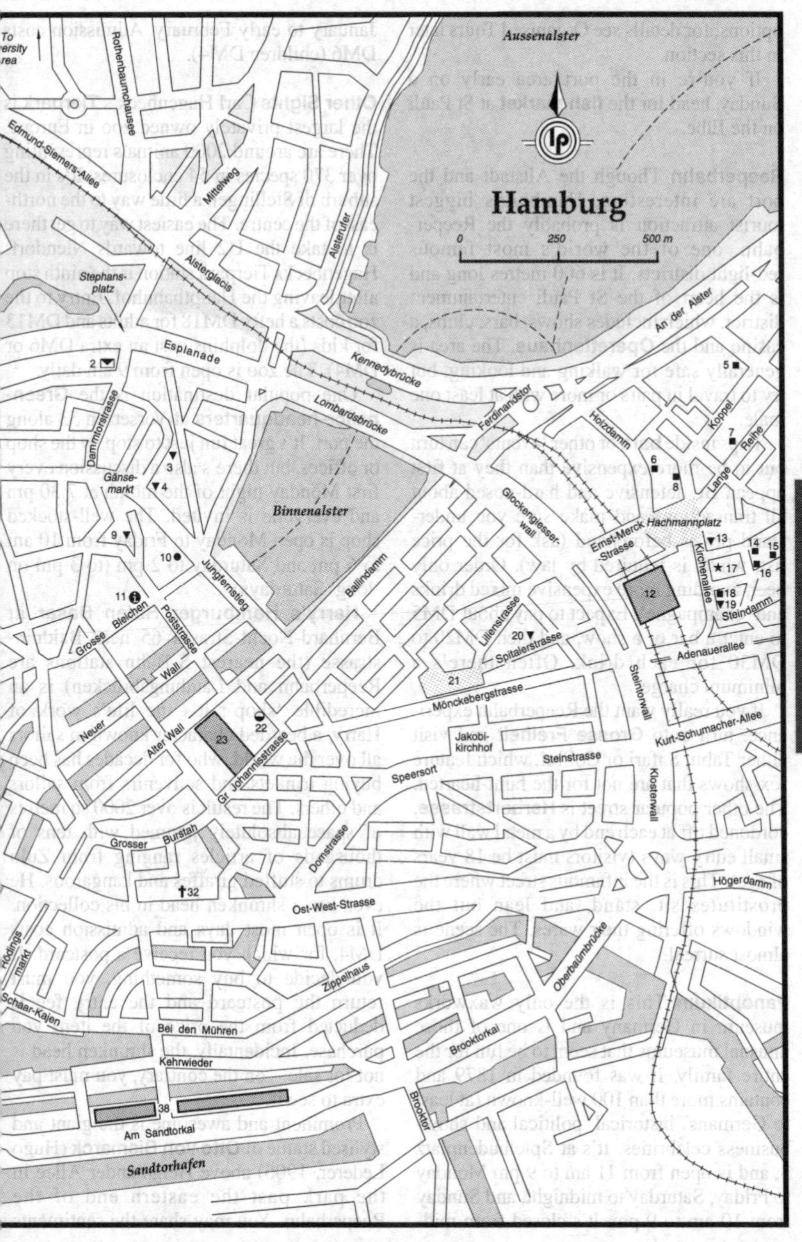
Hamburg
0
250
500 m
Aussenalster
Binnenalster
Sandtorhafen
To
ersity
rea
Rothenbaumchausee
Edmund-Siemers-Allee
Mittelweg
Alsterufer
Alsterglacis
Stephans-
platz
Esplanade
Kennedybrücke
Lombardsbrücke
Dammtorstrasse
Gänse-
markt
Jungfernstieg
Ballindamm
Ferdinandstor
An der Alster
Holzdamm
Koppel
Lange
Reihe
Glockengiesser-
wall
Ernst-Merck
Strasse
Hachmannplatz
Kirchenallee
Steindamm
Adenauerallee
Lilienstrasse
Spitalerstrasse
Steintorwall
Mönckebergstrasse
Kurt-Schumacher-Allee
Jakobi-
kirchhof
Steinstrasse
Speersort
Klosterwall
Grosse
Bleichen
Poststrasse
Neuer
Wall
Alter Wall
Gr Johannisstrasse
Grosser
Burstah
Domstrasse
Ost-West-Strasse
Högerdamm
Oberbaumbrücke
Hödings
markt
Schaar-Kajen
Zippelhaus
Bei den Mühren
Kehrwieder
Brooktorkai
Brooktor
Am Sandtorkai
1
2
3
4
5
6
7
8
9
10
11
12
13
14
15
16
17
18
19
20
21
22
23
32
38

GERMANY

options; for details see Organised Tours later in this section.

If you're in the port area early on a Sunday, head for the **fish market** at St Pauli on the Elbe.

Reeperbahn Though the Altstadt and the port are interesting, Hamburg's biggest tourist attraction is probably the Reeperbahn, one of the world's most famous red-light districts. It is 600 metres long and is the heart of the St Pauli entertainment district, which includes shows, bars, clubs, a casino and the **Operettenhaus**. The area is generally safe for walking and looking, but try to travel in pairs or more with at least one male.

Trips inside **bars** or other 'events' can turn out to be more expensive than they at first appear. Be defensive and hard-nosed about all transactions and make sure you understand prices beforehand (ask for the price list, which is required by law). Order only beer, avoiding more expensive mixed drinks and 'champagne'. Expect to pay about DM5 to enter a bar or a show, and then DM20 to DM30 for each drink. Often there's a minimum charge.

If you really want the Reeperbahn experience, turn onto **Grosse Freiheit** and visit either Tabu, Safari or Colibri, which feature sex shows that are not for the faint-hearted. The other popular street is **Herbertstrasse**, cordoned off at each end by a metal wall with small entry ways (visitors must be 18 years of age). This is the infamous street where the prostitutes sit, stand, and lean out the windows offering their wares. The scene is almost surreal.

Panoptikum This is the only waxworks museum in Germany and is one of those unusual museums that seem to be fun for the entire family. It was founded in 1879 and contains more than 100 well-known (at least to Germans) historical, political and show-business celebrities. It's at Spielbudenplatz 3, and is open from 11 am to 9 pm Monday to Friday, Saturday to midnight, and Sunday from 10 am to 9 pm. It's closed from mid-January to early February. Admission costs DM6 (children DM4).

Other Sights Carl Hagenbeck's **Tierpark** is the largest privately owned zoo in Europe. There are around 2000 animals representing over 370 species in 54 enclosures. It's in the suburb of Stellingen a little way to the north-east of the centre. The easiest way to get there is to take the U2 line towards Niendorf; Hagenbecks Tierpark station is the ninth stop after leaving the Hauptbahnhof. Entry to the zoo costs a hefty DM18 for adults and DM13 for kids (the dolphins cost an extra DM6 or DM4). The zoo is open from 9 am daily.

One popular destination is the **Greenpeace headquarters** at Vorsetzen 53 along the port. It's great fun just to stop by the shop or offices, but there's also a discussion every first Monday night of the month at 7.30 pm and everyone is invited. The well-stocked shop is open Monday to Friday from 10 am to 6 pm and Saturday to 2 pm (to 3 pm on 'long' Saturdays).

Harry's Hamburger Hafen Basar at Bernhard-Nocht-Strasse 65 near Balduinstrasse (the nearest S-Bahn stations are Reeperbahn and Landungsbrücken) is an incredible 'shop': it's the life's work of Harry, a bearded character known to sailors all over the world, who for decades has been buying trinkets and souvenirs from sailors and others. The result is over 2000 sq metres of space absolutely jammed with tens of thousands of articles ranging from Zulu drums to stuffed giraffes and kangaroos. He even has a shrunken head in his collection. It is open most days and admission costs DM4, for which you receive a postcard. If you decide to buy something, you must return the postcard and the entry fee is deducted from the price of the item you purchase. Incidentally, the shrunken head is not for sale – on the contrary, you must pay extra to see it.

Prominent and awesome is the giant and stylised statue of **Otto von Bismarck** (Hugo Lederer, 1906) above Helgoländer Allee in the park past the eastern end of the Reeperbahn. You may share the sentiments of the graffiti artists around the periphery, but they have problems climbing high enough to deface the prince himself.

Organised Tours

Basic city sightseeing tours in English depart four times daily (11 am to 4 pm) from Kirchenallee next to the Hauptbahnhof (DM24, children half-price) and last 1¾ hours; you can add a harbour cruise for an extra DM11. 'Fleet' cruises lasting two hours depart from Jungfernstieg three times daily and cost DM22 (children DM11), for which you get a multi-language guide brochure. The 50-minute Alster tour costs DM13; you can also cover the Alster lakes in stages hourly for DM1.50 each, DM9 one way, DM12 return. There are also canal and special summer cruises.

Port Cruises The Barkassen launch tours (70 minutes; DM15, half-price for children aged from four to 14) run all year from pier *(Brücke)* No 3. They depart half-hourly from 9 am to 5 pm from April to October, and hourly from 10 am to 4 pm from November to March. Tours with English commentary run daily at 11.15 am from March to November only. A one-hour HADAG steamer grand tour (DM15, children half-price) sails from pier No 2 half-hourly from 9 am to 6 pm Monday to Saturday, and 8.30 am to 6 pm on Sunday (the winter schedule is more limited). Other HADAG tour options are available in the leaflet at the pier or by telephone (☎ 3 11 70 70).

Places to Stay

Accommodation can be pricey, although you can find a range of options in *The Hamburger* (see Information) or the DM1 guide available from the tourist offices. The tourist office at the Hauptbahnhof charges DM6 to book rooms. Many hotels will accept reservations through the special booking number (☎ 3 00 51 10 4).

Camping Though inconvenient and catering mainly for caravans, the best camping option, *Campingplatz Buchholz* (☎ 5 40 45 32), is at Kieler Strasse 374. To reach Kieler Strasse from the Hauptbahnhof, take S-Bahn No 2 or 3 to Stellingen or Eidelstedt. It's better to get off the train at Hamburg-Altona station and then take bus No 183 towards Schelsen. It runs straight down Kieler Strasse, where there are also several other camping grounds.

Hostels Hamburg's two hostels are large. The first, *Auf dem Stintfang* (☎ 31 34 88), is convenient at Albert-Wegener-Weg 5 (U-Bahn or S-Bahn: Landungsbrücken) and offers a view of the port (juniors DM18.50, seniors DM22.50). *Horner Rennbahn* (☎ 6 51 16 71), supposedly a youth guesthouse, is less convenient at Rennbahnstrasse 100 (U3: Horner Rennbahn, walk 10 minutes north past the racecourse and leisure centre). You will find it overpriced at DM31 for a bed. The discount for stays of three nights or more will only apply if you book, not if you try to extend your stay. The independent youth hotel *Schanzenstern* (☎ 4 39 84 41) at Bartelsstrasse 12 (U-Bahn and S-Bahn: Sternschanze) has about 50 beds at DM58.50 per night.

Private Rooms Private rooms are hard to come by in Hamburg, and the price is unlikely to be a big saving on the more conveniently located budget accommodation around the Hauptbahnhof. You could try *Agentur Zimmer Frei* (☎ 41 20 70, 41 20 79) at Heimweg 3, an agency specialising in short-term private accommodation. For longer stays, see Long-Term Rentals.

Hotels The best budget hotels are along Steindamm, and a few blocks east of the Hauptbahnhof down Bremer Reihe (it's not the top end of town, though). On Holzdamm, try *Steen's Hotel* (☎ 24 46 42) at No 43 (from DM100/130 for singles/doubles with shared shower). A little closer to the Aussenalster, in a quiet street, is *Gästehaus Gurlitt* (☎ 24 30 11), Gurlittstrasse 38. It caters to a somewhat discerning clientele, as its prices would suggest: singles without bath for DM75, with DM125. Closer to the Hauptbahnhof,

Eden Hotel (☎ 24 84 80), Ellmenreichstrasse 20, has comfortable rooms, all with TV and telephone. Rooms with shared bathroom cost DM75/110, or DM150/200 with private shower and toilet. *Hotel St Georg* (☎ 24 11 41) at Kirchenallee 23 has rooms from DM85/125 and some multi-bed rooms; all prices include breakfast. *Hotel Fürst Bismarck* (☎ 2 80 10 91) at Kirchenallee 49 has rooms at DM115/175.

Pensions A handful of pensions (with not many more beds) are east of Kirchenallee. *Hotel-Pension Kieler Hof* (☎ 24 30 24), at No 15, has mostly doubles from DM95 and a few singles from DM58, breakfast included. *Hotel-Pension Annenhof* (☎ 24 34 26) is at Lange Reihe 23, with rooms for DM54/96. At Bremer Reihe 23 is *Hotel-Pension Zentrum* (☎ 2 80 25 28). The rooms are basic and the management is not overly friendly, but the place is clean and efficiently run, and the position and price are right: rooms cost from DM70/100 including breakfast. *Pension Sarah Petersen* (☎ 24 98 26) at Lange Reihe 50 is a very friendly place (DM79/95), but has only a few rooms.

Long-Term Rentals The tourist offices can help with long-term rentals, but for more options, contact the Mitwohnzentrale (☎ 39 13 73) at Lobuschstrasse 22. Several other agencies are in the Yellow Pages directory under 'Mitwohnvermittlung' and 'Wohnungs- und Zimmervermittlung'.

Places to Eat

City Centre Hamburg is one of the best spots in Germany for fish, but it doesn't come cheaply. For a splurge and a truly fishy Hamburg experience, head to *Fischerhaus* (☎ 31 40 53) at Fischmarkt 14. The food is just as good and the atmosphere almost so at any of the three *Daniel Wischer* locations, with specials costing less than DM10 and almost everything else less than DM15. The most convenient is at Spitalerstrasse 12 (250 metres from the Hauptbahnhof).

One of the best kept secrets in this part of town is *Kantine im Schauspielhaus*, downstairs in the Deutsches Schauspielhaus on Kirchenallee in front of the Hauptbahnhof. Officially it caters for actors and others working in the theatre, but anyone is welcome. With a new menu every day, and main courses from as little as DM7 on the right day, this place is simply too good to miss.

There is a wide variety of establishments around Gänsemarkt and Jungfernstieg near the Binnenalster lake. One lunchtime spot popular with locals is *Essen und Trinken*, in the arcade at Gänsemarkt 21, a vaguely buffet-style cooperative setup where you can choose from Greek, Italian, German and other dishes. In general, you should be able to put a meal together (main course and drink) for DM12 or DM15.

If you are looking for a more substantial meal, an excellent choice is *Blockhaus*. This is a Hamburg-based chain of steakhouses, which does a roaring trade for both lunch and dinner. The turkey breast *(Putenbrust)* steak is a real treat. The most convenient of its restaurants are on the 2nd floor of the Gänsemarkt Passage at Gänsemarkt, and at Kirchenallee 50, off Hachmannplatz by the Hauptbahnhof. Expect to pay about DM30 per person for a salad, steak and drink.

Also at Gänsemarkt, close to Dammtorstrasse, is the *Bäckerei von Altwörden*, a bakery which has expanded to cater for shoppers and workers in need of a warm drink and a filling, tasty snack. This is a great place for breakfast, but it is good at any time.

City Fringe The university area offers some cheap and unique dining options. Try the *Hindukusch* at Grindelhof 15. This friendly, family-run Afghan restaurant has lots of vegetarian dishes, and almost everything costs less than DM15. As a walk-in any time from breakfast on, *Herbert Neumann* at Grindelhof 11 turns on big coffees at DM2 and a variety of reasonably priced rolls and pastries.

If you are spending the evening around the Reeperbahn, *Piceno*, Hein-Hoyer-Strasse 8, serves up delicious Italian fare at very rea-

GERMANY

sonable prices. In the evenings it is always full of young people.

The lively Sunday fish market, near Landungsbrücken S-Bahn station on the banks of the Elbe River, is open from 6 to 9.30 am, with lots more than just fish. After you visit the market, head for one of the taverns with the locals for an early-morning beer.

Self-Catering If you are shopping, try one of the Penny-Markt budget groceries, eg on Baumeisterstrasse and at the corner of Lange Reihe and Schmilinskystrasse to the east of the main station, near the corner of Königstrasse and Holstenstrasse at the west end of the Reeperbahn, and at Thielbek 8. A Plus outlet is at Alter Steinweg 13 near Grossneumarkt, and good fresh fare is offered at Grossneumarkt on market days (Wednesday and Saturday, weather permitting).

Entertainment

The jazz scene is Hamburg is Germany's best, and it's definitely worth catching a show at the *Cotton Club*, near Grossneumarkt at Alter Steinweg 10. It opens at 8 pm and shows start at 8.30 pm, Monday to Saturday. On Sunday there's a daytime show from 11 am to 3 pm.

For an English-language fix, head for the plays at the *English Theatre* at Lerchenfeld 14. For kids (their language is more international) there's the personably presented *Theater für Kinder* at Max-Brauer-Allee 76 in Altona (tickets DM17). The *Streits* cinema, on Jungfernstieg near the corner of Grosse Bleichen, shows films in their original version every Sunday at 11 am. Half of Hamburg's expatriate English and American communities seem to show up, so you're well advised to come along a little early to get a ticket.

Hamburg has an excellent alternative and experimental theatre scene. In particular, *Kampnagelfabrik*, Jarrestrasse 20-26 (bus No 172 or 173), is highly thought of. *Schmidt Theater*, Spielbudenplatz 24 (S-Bahn: Reeperbahn), is much loved for its wild variety shows and very casual atmosphere.

The Andrew Lloyd Webber musical *Cats* is booked at the *Operettenhaus*, Spielbudenplatz 1 (S-Bahn: St Pauli), for a few years yet (tickets from DM70 to DM175; box office open from 11 am to 7 pm daily, closed from 2 to 3 pm weekends). The controversial *Neue Flora Theater*, on the corner of Alsenstrasse and Stresemannstrasse (S-Bahn: Holstenstrasse), is booked to host *Das Phantom der Oper* for several years (tickets from DM50 to DM200, open similar hours).

For central theatre or concert bookings, go to the Last Minute Theaterkasse (near the travel service counter) on the 2nd floor of the Alsterhaus shopping complex in Poststrasse, not far from the Hansa-Viertel tourist office; it's open Monday to Friday from 10 am to 6 pm (to 7 pm on Thursday), to 2 pm on Saturday, 4 pm on 'long' Saturdays.

Getting There & Away

Air Hamburg's international airport is growing in stature as Lufthansa continues to add services. Apart from links with other German cities, you can fly to/from Brussels, London, Paris, Manchester, Dublin, Oslo, Gothenburg, Stockholm, Helsinki and St Petersburg daily. SAS flies to/from Copenhagen. Airport buses (DM8) make the 25-minute trip to the airport from the Hauptbahnhof.

Bus International destinations which are not served directly by train from Hamburg, such as Amsterdam and London, are served by Eurolines buses. You can buy tickets from the travel agent on the 2nd floor of Hamburg-Altona station.

A very cheap option for getting to London is Rainbow Tours, which offers a weekend trip to London with accommodation included for DM99. Even if you don't use the return portion of the ticket, you will be hard pushed to find a cheaper one-way fare which includes your first night in London.

Train Hamburg's Hauptbahnhof is one of the busiest in Germany, although it does not handle all the through traffic. There are hourly trains to Lübeck, Kiel, Hanover and

Bremen, as well as good, direct connections to Berlin and Frankfurt (some stop at the airport, the super-fast ICE trains do not). There is an overnight train to Munich and another to Basel which continues to Milan. Hamburg-Altona shares the load of services north to/from Kiel (DM26), Husum and Westerland (DM57) and links with Denmark (Flensburg is the change point for some trains), and south to/from Hanover, though many trains also stop at the Hauptbahnhof. It is important to read the timetables clearly, or you can finish up at the wrong station at the wrong time. Hamburg-Harburg handles some regional services (for instance to/from Cuxhaven in East Friesland, the main port for Heligoland).

Car & Motorbike The autobahns of the E22 (Bremen-Lübeck) and E45 (Hanover-Kiel) cross south of the Elbe River, and the E45 runs through a tunnel beneath the Elbe near Altona. Three concentric ring-roads manage linking traffic. The Citynetz Mitfahr-Service (☎ 1 94 44) is at Gotenstrasse 19. The ADM Mitfahrzentrale (☎ 1 94 40) is at Lobuschstrasse 22 on the corner of Am Felde (U or S-Bahn: Altona, west from the square as you leave the station's Elbe exit).

Ferry Hamburg is 20 hours by car ferry from the English port of Harwich. Services vary according to the time of year and the weather, but are at least twice a week in either direction; check with Scandinavian Seaways (☎ 38 90 31 71). The Edgar-Engelhard-Kai terminal (☎ 38 90 30) is at Van-der-Smissen-Strasse, off Grosser Elbe Strasse, about two km west of St Pauli harbour (S-Bahn: Königstrasse, or, perhaps better, bus No 183 to/from the city centre). It is open Monday to Friday from 10 am to 5 pm, weekends just before departures only (you will have to exchange money before you reach the terminal or on board). The one-way passenger fare varies from DM84 to DM454, depending on the season, the day of the week and your cabin requirements. A car costs an extra DM50 to DM117, a motorbike DM40 to DM79, and a bicycle will cost DM19 in the high season but is free the rest of the year.

The busy train, car and passenger ferry from Puttgarden to Rødby (the quickest way to Copenhagen) goes every half an hour 24 hours a day, and takes one hour. If you're travelling by train, the cost of the ferry will be included in your ticket. From June to August, a car costs DM132/202 one way/return (DM96/153 on Sunday and Monday) including up to five people. The rest of the year, you pay only DM74/115. A motorbike including up to two people costs DM40/70, and a bicycle is DM5/10. A single passenger pays DM16 (DM10 from September to May) for a one-way ticket which is also valid for a return on the same day.

Getting Around

Public transport consists of buses, the U-Bahn and the S-Bahn. A day pass for travel after 9 am in most of the Hamburg area is only DM6.90 (including the surrounding area DM11.20) and there are various family passes. Single journeys cost DM2.30 for the city tariff area, DM3.60 for the city and surrounding area, and DM5.80 within the outer tariff area. Children cost a basic DM1.30 (for the Schnellbus or 1st-class S-Bahn the day supplements are DM1.60). A three-day travel-only pass is DM20, and weekly cards range from DM20.50 to DM43.50, depending on your status, in a complex of seven zones (check the diagrams with the oval-shaped areas marked in yellow). From midnight to dawn the night bus network takes over from the trains, converging on the main city bus station at Rathausmarkt. For details of the transport options with a Hamburg Card, see the Information section.

A taxi from the Hauptbahnhof to the airport should cost around DM40 (one easy number to use is ☎ 21 12 11). A better airport option is to use the shuttle bus that leaves at least once an hour from Kirchenallee directly in front of the Hauptbahnhof, or the express buses to/from the Ohlsdorf S/U-Bahn station.

Hamburg's bicycle tracks are extensive and reach almost to the centre of the city.

AROUND HAMBURG

The Altes Land area along the southern bank of the Elbe is a welcome relief from the city hustle and bustle and can be viewed from the city transit network or on one of the cruises to **Lühe**. The area was reclaimed from marshy ground by experts (the Dutch) in the Middle Ages, who then set about growing fruit. The area's jewels are probably the thatched and panelled **17th-century homes** around Jork (S3: Neugraben, then bus No 257 to Jork), although early in May the **orchards** are a brilliant sight.

The HADAG cruise to Lühe from St Pauli, lasting about 90 minutes, costs DM18 return and departs six times daily. In good weather there are extra services. You can pay supplements for an on-board feast. Family cards cost up to DM42.

Schleswig-Holstein

Schleswig-Holstein is Germany's northernmost state. Covering an area of 16,696 sq km, it borders Denmark at the lower end of the Jutland Peninsula. Among Schleswig-Holstein's many attractions are the North Frisian islands and the historical city of Lübeck.

Schleswig and Holstein began the long process of breaking away from Denmark with the help of Sweden in the mid-17th century. Only in 1773 were both finally free of their Danish masters. In 1815, Holstein joined the German Confederation, which resulted in Denmark trying to lure Schleswig back to the motherland.

Ever-increasing tensions finally led to two wars between Germany and Denmark, the first in 1848-50 and the second in 1864. After a short period under combined Prussian and Austrian rule, and yet another war, Austria was forced to accept Schleswig-Holstein's annexation by Bismarck's Prussia in 1866. Under the conditions of the Treaty of Versailles in 1919, North Schleswig was handed over to Denmark. Finally, in 1946, the British military government formed the state of Schleswig-Holstein from the Prussian province of the same name.

LÜBECK

Lübeck, a medieval town once known as the Queen of the Hanseatic League, was the capital of this association of towns which ruled trade on the Baltic Sea from the 12th to the 16th century. You will need a full day or more to explore this beautiful city and it is well worth the time.

Information

The tourist office in the train station (☎ 0451-7 23 00) is open Monday to Saturday from 10 am to 6.30 pm. Another office (☎ 0451-1 22 81 09), which handles accommodation bookings during the week, is in the Kanzleigebäude on Breite Strasse near the Rathaus, open Monday to Friday from 9.30 am to 6 pm, and Saturday and Sunday from 10 am to 2 pm (to 4 pm one Saturday per month). The central information office is at Beckergrube 95. Late on Thursday (to 8.30 pm) or at weekends, take booking enquiries to the Verkehrsverein office in Holstentor-Passage, just inside the arcade at the west end of Holstenstrasse.

Lübeck's telephone code is 0451, and the central post office is on Markt opposite the Rathaus.

Things to See

Most museums and attractions are free on Friday; the exception is the **Holstentor**, a fortified gate with huge twin towers, which serves as the city's portal, as well as its museum (DM4, closed Monday). Around Markt, the imposing **Rathaus** covers two full sides and the **Marienkirche** is on another side, with a stark reminder of WW II – a bombing raid brought the church bells crashing to the stone floor and the townspeople have left the bell fragments in place, with a small sign saying, 'A protest against war and violence'.

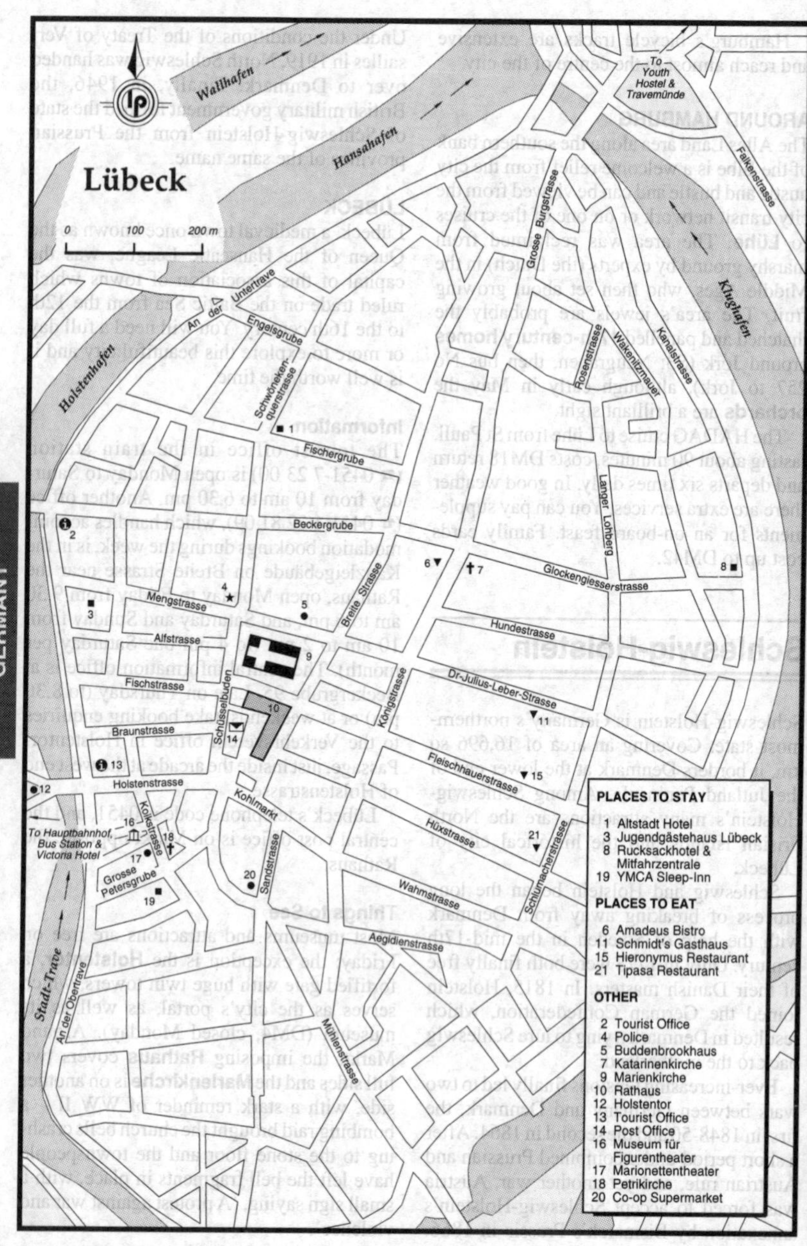
Lübeck
0
100
200 m
Wallhafen
Hansahafen
Holstenhafen
Stadt-Trave
To Youth Hostel & Travemünde
Falkenstrasse
Klughafen
Grosse Burgstrasse
Rosenstrasse
Wakenitzmauer
Kanalstrasse
Langer Lohberg
An der Untertrave
Engelsgrube
Schwönekenquerstrasse
Fischergrube
Beckergrube
Breite Strasse
Mengstrasse
Alfstrasse
Fischstrasse
Schüsselbuden
Braunstrasse
Holstenstrasse
Kohlmarkt
Kolkstrasse
Königstrasse
Glockengiesserstrasse
Hundestrasse
Dr-Julius-Leber-Strasse
Fleischhauerstrasse
Hüxstrasse
Schlumacherstrasse
Wahmstrasse
Aegidienstrasse
Sandstrasse
Mühlenstrasse
Grosse Petersgrube
An der Obertrave
To Hauptbahnhof, Bus Station & Victoria Hotel
PLACES TO STAY
1 Altstadt Hotel
3 Jugendgästehaus Lübeck
8 Rucksackhotel & Mitfahrzentrale
19 YMCA Sleep-Inn
PLACES TO EAT
6 Amadeus Bistro
11 Schmidt's Gasthaus
15 Hieronymus Restaurant
21 Tipasa Restaurant
OTHER
2 Tourist Office
4 Police
5 Buddenbrookhaus
7 Katarinenkirche
9 Marienkirche
10 Rathaus
12 Holstentor
13 Tourist Office
14 Post Office
16 Museum für Figurentheater
17 Marionettentheater
18 Petrikirche
20 Co-op Supermarket

To the north of the church is the **Buddenbrookhaus**, the family house where Thomas Mann was born and which he made famous in his novel *Buddenbrooks*. The literary works and philosophical rivalry of the brothers Thomas and Heinrich are commemorated here (entry DM4).

Lübeck's **Marionettentheater** (Puppet Theatre), on the corner of Kolk and Kleine Petersgrube, is an absolute must (closed Monday). Usually there is an afternoon performance for children (3 pm) and an evening performance for adults, but times vary. Afternoon seats cost DM7 and evenings DM12 or DM16. It is best to book: the box office is open Monday from 8 am to noon, Tuesday to Friday from 8 am to noon and 1.30 to 4 pm, and weekends in the afternoon only. The **Museum für Figurentheater**, a survey of all types of dolls and puppetry, is just around the corner from the theatre at Kleine Petersgrube 4. It is open daily from 9.30 am to 6 pm and entry is DM4 (students and children DM2).

The tower lift at the partly restored **Petrikirche** costs DM3 and affords a superb view over the Altstadt (open 9 am to 6 pm, closed Monday). You might consider a one-week admission pass to the main attractions: it's worth the DM15 cost (children DM7.50).

Places to Stay

Though a bit of a trek, the *camping* is excellent along the Travemünde shoreline. This area, on the mouth of the Trave River, is an international beach resort. The tourist offices have a list of camping grounds.

For budget accommodation, the small *Rucksackhotel* (☎ 70 68 92), Kanalstrasse 70, has beds in multi-bed rooms at DM19 to DM24, a few doubles at DM75, and a four-bed room at DM120; there are cooking facilities. It only has 28 beds, so you'd be wise to book ahead.

Lübeck has two DJH hostels. The excellent *Jugendgästehaus Lübeck* (☎ 7 02 03 99), Mengstrasse 33, is well situated in the middle of the old town, 15 minutes' walk from the train station (bus No 3 or 12 along An der Untertrave to Beckergrube). The cost for juniors/seniors is DM23/27.50, although there are multi-night discounts and some great singles and doubles costing DM27/32.50 per person, a few with a view of the Marienkirche. The other hostel, *Folke-Bernadotte-Heim* (☎ 3 34 33), is at Am Gertrudenkirchhof 4, a little outside the old town (same bus routes, past Burgtorbrücke). The cost here is DM18/22 for juniors/seniors. The cheapest place in town is the YMCA's *Sleep-Inn* (☎ 7 89 82) at Grosse Petersgrube 11 (DM15 per bed, DM40 per double, and there is a group room for DM30 per person). Breakfast is DM5 extra.

For something a little more up-market, try the *Hotel Victoria* (☎ 8 11 44), right by the main station at Am Bahnhof 17. Singles/doubles start at DM59/109. In the centre of town, *Altstadt Hotel* (☎ 7 20 83) is very well situated at Fischergrube 52. Singles without room facilities start at DM70, with facilities at DM95. Doubles start at DM110.

Places to Eat

The most popular restaurant among Lübeck's student population is *Tipasa*, Schlumacherstrasse 14. For atmosphere it is second to none. The menu includes a variety of meat, fish and vegetarian dishes as well as excellent pizzas. If you need a good brew, there are several beers on tap, including Guinness. Another place that is always crowded is *Schmidt's Gasthaus*, Dr-Julius-Leber-Strasse 60-62. The menu is similar to Tipasa's.

Hieronymus, at Fleischhauerstrasse 81, is an enormous restaurant spread over three floors of historic buildings. A filling main course from the impressive menu can cost anywhere from DM10 to DM40 or more. *Amadeus*, Königstrasse 26, is a great bistro with good music. It has a limited menu, but the prices are right. It is also a good place for breakfast (open from 10 am).

Save room for a dessert or a snack of marzipan, which was invented in Lübeck (local legend has it that the town ran out of flour during a long siege and resorted to grinding almonds to make bread). The best place for marzipan is *J G Niederegger* at

Breite Strasse 89, directly opposite the Rathaus.

Getting There & Away

Lübeck is close to Hamburg, with at least one train every hour (DM15.20). The trip takes from 40 minutes to a little over an hour depending on the train. Kiel is nearby, and there are numerous trains to/from Lübeck every day. All trains from Hamburg to Rostock make a stop in Lübeck. There is a left-luggage office near the entrance that charges DM4 per day for large baggage.

The regional bus services stop opposite the local buses, a brief stroll around the corner from the main train station. Kraftomnibusse services to/from Wismar arrive here, as well as Autokraft buses to/from Hamburg, Schwerin, Kiel, Rostock and Berlin. The private Mitfahrzentrale Einsteiger (☎ 7 10 74) is on the corner of Glockengiesserstrasse and Kanalstrasse, inside the Werkhof complex next to Rucksackhotel. The cost for a 1000-km journey is DM60, but trips in Schleswig-Holstein cost only DM1 for the service. The basic rate is 3 Pf per km.

Getting Around

Lübeck is easily walkable. If you plan to go to Travemünde, you'll find lots of transport options during the tourist season. Several buses link the city island with the train station from nearby Hansestrasse; a single journey costs DM2.50 on the island or to one stop beyond. Lübeck day-travel cards cost DM7.50 and include the Travemünde area, but the DM4 City-Karte does not.

KIEL

Kiel, the capital of Schleswig-Holstein, was seriously damaged by Allied bombing during WW II, but has since been rebuilt into a vibrant and modern city. Located at the end of a modest fjord, it has long been one of Germany's most important Baltic Sea harbours, and hosted Olympic sailing events in 1936 and 1972.

Orientation & Information

Kiel's main street is Holstenstrasse, a colourful, pedestrianised street a few hundred metres from the sea. It runs from St Nikolai church in the north to the tourist office in the south, although at this end the street is actually an undercover shopping mall. The tourist office at Sophienblatt 30 is reached by an overpass from the Hauptbahnhof – just follow the signs from within the station.

Kiel's telephone code is 0431.

Things to See

Kiel's most famous attraction is the **Kieler Woche** (Kiel Week) in the last full week in June, a week of festivities revolving around a yachting regatta attended by over 4000 of the world's sailing elite. Even if you're not into sailing, the atmosphere is electric – just make sure you book a room in advance if you want to be in on the fun.

If you want to experience Kiel's love for the sea in a less energetic fashion, you could take a ferry ride to the town of **Laboe** at the mouth of the fjord. Ferries leave every 90 minutes or so from a pier off Kaistrasse, no more than five minutes' walk from Hauptbahnhof. They take around one hour to reach Laboe, hopping back and forth across the fjord along the way. In Laboe, you can visit **U995**, a wartime U-boat on the beach, which is now a technical museum. Nearby is a **U-boat memorial** and a **navigation museum**.

Kiel is also the point at which the shipping canal from the North Sea enters the Baltic Sea. Some 60,000 ships pass through the canal every year, and the **locks** *(Schleusen)*, at Holtenau six km north of the city centre, are well worth a visit.

Finally, do not miss the **Schifffahrtsmuseum** (closed Monday), which contains an interesting collection of models and other maritime artefacts; admission is free.

Places to Stay

Kiel's *hostel* (☎ 73 57 23) is at Johannesstrasse 1 in the suburb of Gaarden, across the water from the Hauptbahnhof. To get there, take the Laboe ferry from near the train

GERMANY

station and get off at the first stop ('Gaarden'), from where it's a 10-minute walk. The other option is to take bus No 4, 24 or 34 from Sophienblatt by the tourist office to Kieler Strasse. The cost for juniors/seniors is from DM18/22.

In the budget-hotel range, *Touristhotel Schweriner Hof* (☎ 6 14 16), Königsweg 13, is the most centrally located. It has singles/doubles from DM60/105. *Rabe's Hotel* (☎ 66 30 70) at Ringstrasse 30 is also very central, with rooms from DM70/115.

In Gaarden, not too far from the DJH hostel, is *Hotel Runge* (☎ 73 19 92) at Elisabethstrasse 16. Rooms start at DM48/85 without shower, DM65/98 with.

Places to Eat

There are plenty of opportunities to eat at very reasonable prices. One of the best places is *Friesenhof*, at Fleethorn 9 in the Rathaus building. Daily lunch specials (from 11 am to 3 pm) cost about DM10, and tasty main courses start at DM15.

The *Klosterbrauerei* at Alter Markt 9 (at the northern end of Holstenstrasse) has a great atmosphere with prices to match. Around the hostel, the best value is found at the kebab and pizza places within walking distance.

Getting There & Away

There are numerous trains every day running to/from Kiel and Hamburg-Altona or Hamburg Hauptbahnhof. The trip takes from one to 1½ hours and costs DM26. To Lübeck, there are trains just about every hour (sometimes more often). The trip takes about 1¼ hours and costs DM19.40. Regional buses run to/from Lübeck, Schleswig and Puttgarden.

Langeland-Kiel (☎ 97 41 50) runs two or three ferries a day to Bagenkop on the Danish island of Langeland (not from early January to mid-February). The trip takes 2½ hours and the fare is DM7/11 one way/return except in July, when it is DM9/16 (bicycles DM19/33, cars DM18/34, rising to DM33/62 in July). The ferries leave from Oslokai.

The daily Kiel-Gothenburg ferry (11 or 12 hours) leaves Schwedenkai at 7 pm. From the beginning of November to the beginning of April, the fare is DM65/120 one way/return; from mid-June to the beginning of August, it costs DM160/260; the rest of the year, DM100/180. Bicycles are carried free. Sleeping berths vary in price from DM28 to DM560! For booking and information, call Stena Line on ☎ 90 99.

Color Line (☎ 97 40 90) ferries run direct to/from Kiel and Oslo almost every day from April to December, and generally every second day the rest of the year, although around Christmas there is a five-day break. Departures are at 1.30 pm on Tuesday, Thursday and Sunday, 4.30 pm other days, and the trip takes just under 20 hours. Fares start at DM122 (around 30% extra in summer) for a single bed in a four-bed cabin.

On all these ferries, occasional student discounts are available.

Getting Around

The bus station is conveniently located on Auguste-Viktoria-Strasse near the Hauptbahnhof. To get to the North-Baltic Sea Canal and the locks, take bus No 4 to Wik or bus No 41 from the bus station – the locks are only about five minutes' walk from the terminus.

SCHLESWIG

This peaceful town on the Schlei Fjord is worth a day trip if you can fit in all the attractions. It has a restored old centre a short walk south from the bus station on Königstrasse. In the old town is the tourist office (☎ 04621-81 42 26) in the historic building at Plessenstrasse 7 (a board posted next door covers local accommodation options). The telephone code is 04621.

Things to See

The Romanesque-Gothic **cathedral** and **Altstadt** are both well worth seeing, but **Schloss Gottorf** and its **Schleswig-Holstein Landesmuseum** collections of cultural history are a bigger attraction (cost is DM5, students DM2). They cover just about everything from prehistoric hunting to 19th-century arts and crafts, and afterwards you can stroll around the castle and its gardens.

More specific is the old Viking town of **Hedeby** (Haithabu), across the fjord from the town centre, marked only by the remains of its semicircular wall on the lagoon of Haddeby Noor. To make it all meaningful, visit the fascinating **Viking Museum** (DM4, closed Monday), which lies to the east of the B76. A Viking vessel has been partly reconstructed inside. More history, if you can handle it, is in a walk along the old dyke and wall complex of the **Danevirke** (Dannewerk), which runs from the walls of old Hedeby west to Hollingstedt. You can follow its twists for several km on worn trails.

Getting There & Around

The train station is linked by local bus to the town centre and there are trains to/from Kiel each day (DM13).

NORTH FRISIAN ISLANDS

The Frisian Islands reward those who make the trek with sunshine, sand dunes, sea and pure air.

Friesland itself covers an area stretching from the northern Netherlands along the coast up into Denmark. Many inhabitants speak Frisian dialects, very closely related to English but virtually incomprehensible if you hear them spoken. North Friesland (Nordfriesland) is the western coastal area of Schleswig-Holstein up to and into Denmark. The sea area forms the National Park of Wattenmeer, and the shifting dunes, particularly on the islands of Amrum, Föhr and Langeness, are sensitive and cannot be disturbed – paths and boardwalks are provided for strolling. Visiting cars are discouraged on Sylt, and wild and domesticated animals are protected by stringent regulation.

Orientation & Information

The most popular of the North Frisian Islands is Sylt, a resort known for its fresh air, spa facilities and water sports, while Föhr and Amrum are far more relaxed and less touristy. Not technically part of the Frisian Islands, Heligoland (Helgoland) lies 70 km out to sea and is a popular outing from the islands and a duty-free port.

Sylt's information office is Tourist Information Westerland (☎ 04651-2 40 01) next to the town's train station, though it's of little use unless you are booking spa facilities or accommodation in Westerland; private beds start at DM50. On Amrum, the friendly tourist office (☎ 8 65) faces one of the harbour car parks. The spa administrations *(Kurverwaltungen)* at the various resorts are also useful sources.

On Sylt, the telephone code for Westerland is 04651; for List the code is 04652 and for Hörnum 04653. For Amrum the code is 04682.

Things to See

Besides the sea, the beaches and the reed-roofed *Friesenhäuser*, there's little to see in the North Frisian Islands, but Sylt's **casino** is excellent. To get away from the often stifling summer crowds of Sylt, try Amrum or Föhr instead. On Amrum the remains of traditional Frisian life remain around the village of Nebel, particularly in the **churchyard** for sometimes unnamed sailors lost in hostile seas. The town **mill** is a small museum of local culture (DM1) and the **lighthouse**, the tallest in northern Germany at 63 metres, affords a spectacular view over the dunes from the south-west of the island and over to Sylt, Föhr and Langeness (DM2, open daily to 12.30 pm only).

Heligoland is a fun one or two-day excursion from the north coast. The island was used as a submarine base in WW II and it's still possible to tour the strong bunkers and underground tunnels. The island was heavily bombed in the war and all of the houses are new. Take a walk along Lung Wai ('long way'), filled with duty-free shops, and then up the stairway of 180 steps to Oberland for a nice view. There's also a scenic trail around the island, with lots of nature.

To get even farther away from it all, take the ferry from Heligoland to neighbouring **Düne**, a small island filled with beaches and

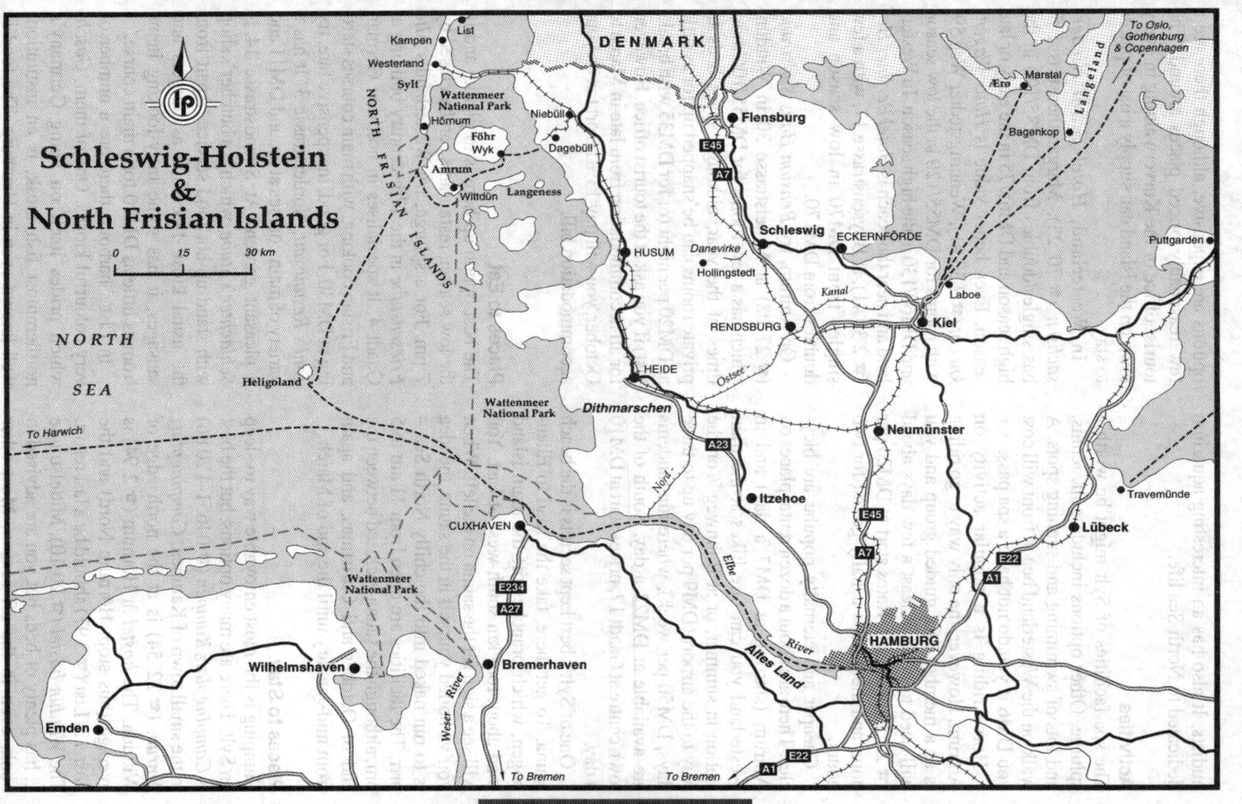
Schleswig-Holstein & North Frisian Islands
0 15 30 km
NORTH SEA
To Harwich
Heligoland
NORTH FRISIAN ISLANDS
List
Kampen
Westerland
Sylt
Hörnum
Wattenmeer National Park
Föhr
Wyk
Amrum
Wittdün
Langeness
Niebüll
Dagebüll
DENMARK
Flensburg
E45
A7
Schleswig
ECKERNFÖRDE
HUSUM
Danevirke
Hollingstedt
Kanal
RENDSBURG
Ostsee
HEIDE
Dithmarschen
Wattenmeer National Park
A23
Nord
Kiel
Laboe
Ærø
Marstal
Bagenkop
Langeland
To Oslo, Gothenburg & Copenhagen
Puttgarden
Neumünster
Itzehoe
Elbe
River
Altes Land
HAMBURG
Travemünde
Lübeck
E22
A1
CUXHAVEN
E234
A27
Wattenmeer National Park
Bremerhaven
Weser River
To Bremen
Wilhelmshaven
Emden

nudists. It also has an interesting aquarium dedicated to North Sea life.

Activities

The spa facilities of Sylt might be worth a splurge. Other options include golf, tennis, and lots of swimming and sunning spots. A walk on the Westerland beach front will cost you DM6 if you do not have a spa pass.

Horse riding is a popular activity on Amrum. However, the only way to go riding is as a member of a guided group and you will need to book at least a few days ahead (☎ 22 28 or 20 30). Rates start at DM20 per hour, and the groups usually go out for two hours.

Cheaper and eternally popular are bicycles. There are about a dozen rental places on Amrum (starting at DM7 a day) and in Westerland you can hire bikes at the train station in summer, or at Bahnweg 7 on the way to the airport (DM9 per day up to three days, DM50 per week), where fun tandems are available at DM22 a day. South of the town centre at Gaadt 17, prices start at DM10 a day.

One of Sylt's best kept secrets is the beach sauna. To get there, take the road to Ellenbogen, which branches off the main island road about four km south-west of List. You will see a sign for the sauna on the left. When you've boiled yourself in the sauna, the idea is to run naked into the chilly North Sea – brrr. The facilities are open from 11 am to 5 pm, although the sauna is closed between the end of October and Christmas, and again from mid-January until the end of March.

Places to Stay

Camping is the most enjoyable way to sleep on Sylt. There are many options, but the best is *Campingplatz Kampen* (☎ 04651-4 20 86) in the small town of Kampen. *Campingplatz Amrum* (☎ 22 54) is at the north edge of Wittdün. The *hostel* at Hörnum (☎ 2 94) is average (bus stop: Hörnum Nord) and the *hostel* at List (☎ 3 97) should be a last resort. The *Wittdün hostel* (☎ 20 10), Mittelstrasse 1, has plenty of beds but you are advised to book, even in the off season. Most other options are expensive, although there are a few reasonably priced places around. The tourist office or the Kurverwaltung in every town on the island can supply a list of places to stay.

In Westerland, *Hotel Garni Niedersachsen* (☎ 70 23), Margarethenstrasse 5, has singles/doubles from DM85/100 in the high season and DM65/75 in the early or late season. Even better value is *Haus Wagenknecht* (☎ 2 30 91), Wenningstedter Weg 59, with rooms for DM55/120 in the low season and DM60/130 in the high season. In Westerland and near the beach is *Hotel Berliner Hof* (☎ 2 30 41), at Boysenstrasse 17, with a few singles from DM70 in low season and doubles from DM170.

On Amrum, try *Pension Haus Südstrand* (☎ 27 08) at Mittelstrasse 30 in Wittdün, which has a few rooms for DM55/106 most times of the year, although spare beds in private rooms can be snapped up for as little as DM20 per night (or for DM35 with breakfast) if you ask at the tourist office. However, for all accommodation from late in March to October, you will pay 13% resort tax on your accommodation bill.

Places to Eat

The best option up here is to picnic, and in the low season, restaurants can be closed by 7 pm. For a splurge, try Westerland's *Alte Friesenstube* in the 17th-century building at Gaadt 4. It specialises in northern German and Frisian cooking, with main courses starting at DM30. For good, inexpensive fare, try *Toni's Restaurant*, Norderstrasse 3. It has a variety of main courses at around DM11 and a pleasant garden. At Strandstrasse 14 is *Schlachter's Stube*, which is a butcher's shop with stand-up hot food service. Apart from the usual kiosk fare such as burgers and sausages, it has some tasty-looking items from as little as DM10 for a main course.

In List's harbour, there are a number of very colourful kiosks. One of them, *Gosch*, which prides itself on being Germany's northernmost fish kiosk, is an institution, well known even in Hamburg. The food is delicious, and if you are not too hungry, it won't break your budget.

One of the nicest places on Sylt to sit with friends over a cockle-warming drink or a small meal is *Witthüs*. It is on the main island road about two km south of the town of Kampen, directly on the corner of the road which leads to Keitum.

There are not that many restaurants on Amrum, and many of them close out of season, but for local fare for lunch or dinner consider *Hotel Ual Öömreng* in Norddorf, or the relaxing teahouse atmosphere of *Burg Haus*, built on an old Viking hill-fort above the eastern beach at Norddorf.

Getting There & Away

Since Sylt is such a resort draw, it's fairly convenient to reach. Most people take the train directly from Hamburg-Altona station to Westerland. Between 13 and 18 trains make the three-hour trip every day. The fare is DM57.

If you are travelling by car, you will have to drive to the town of Niebüll near the Danish border and load your car onto a train. There is no need to reserve in advance: just turn up and they will make room for your car. There are 12 to 15 crossings in both directions every day. The cost is about DM120 return, depending on the size of the car. This price includes all passengers.

To get to Föhr and Amrum, you take the Sylt-bound train from Hamburg-Altona but get off in Niebüll. From Niebüll, you take a train to Dagebüll Hafen (DM8.70 one way, no rail passes as it is a private line). From Dagebüll Hafen, there is a fairly frequent ferry service to Föhr and Amrum. A day-return costs DM18 per person, which allows you to visit both islands. The trip to Amrum takes around two hours, stopping at Föhr on the way. There are also Heligoland-Hörnum ferries (DM42).

There are daily flights to/from Westerland airport from Hamburg, Munich and Berlin and several flights weekly from other German cities.

Getting Around

There is a reasonable bus service on Sylt, with buses running from Westerland north to List, south to Hörnum (DM5) and east to Keitum and Archsum around once every hour. On Amrum, a bus runs from the ferry terminal in Wittdün to Norddorf and back every 30 to 60 minutes, depending on the season (day passes are only DM5). The slow, fun inter-island option is one of the day-return cruises to Föhr (Wyk) and Amrum (Wittdün) from the harbour at Hörnum. You pass the shallow banks that attract seals and sea birds on the WDR tour boats for DM28. Similar Adler-Schiffe tours take in these islands and Langeness, and you can take a bicycle on board for DM6 or DM7.

Hungary

Only a short hop from Vienna, this romantic land of Franz Liszt, Béla Bartók, Gypsy music and the blue Danube welcomes visitors. You'll be enchanted by Budapest, once a great imperial city, and Pécs, the warm heart of the south. The fine wines, fiery paprika, sweet violins, good theatre and colourful folklore conspire to extend your stay. The friendly Magyars are very inviting.

The booming Hungary of the 1990s comes as a surprise to English-speakers whose image of the country often dates back to the repression and bleak poverty of the 1950s. Today's prosperous modern cities bustling with well-dressed inhabitants are a far cry from the grey façades and the leaden-faced peasants queuing for bread in old newsreels. Here you can have all the glamour and excitement of Western Europe at prices you can still afford. It's just the place to kick off an Eastern European trip.

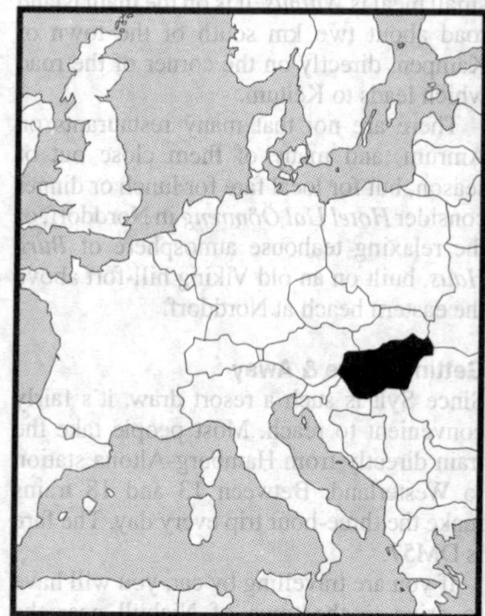

Facts about the Country

HISTORY

The Celts occupied Hungary in the final centuries BC but were conquered by the Romans in 10 AD. From the 1st to the 5th centuries all of Hungary west and south of the Danube (the area today known as Transdanubia) was included in the Roman province of Pannonia. The Roman legion stationed at Aquincum (Budapest) guarded the north-eastern frontier of the Empire. The epicurean Romans planted the first vineyards in Hungary and developed the thermal baths. In 408 the West Goths invaded the area, followed in 451 by Attila's Huns, then by the Lombards and Avars. From 795 Pannonia was part of the Carolingian Empire.

In 896 seven Magyar tribes under Khan Árpád swept in from beyond the Volga River and occupied the Danube Basin. They terrorised Europe with raids as far as France and Italy until they converted to Roman Catholicism in the late 10th century. Hungary's first king and patron saint, Stephen I (Szent István), was crowned on Christmas Day in the year 1000, marking the foundation of the Hungarian state. After the Tatars sacked Hungary in 1241, many cities were fortified.

Feudal Hungary was a large and powerful state which included Transylvania (now in Romania), Slovakia and Croatia. The medieval capital shifted from Székesfehérvár to Esztergom, Buda and Visegrád. Hungary's Golden Bull (1222), enumerating the rights of the nobility, is just seven years younger than the Magna Carta and universities were founded in Pécs (1367) and Buda (1389).

In 1456 at Nándorfehérvár (present-day Belgrade) Hungarians under János Hunyadi stopped a Turkish advance into Hungary and under Hunyadi's son, Matthias Corvinus, who ruled from 1458 to 1490, Hungary experienced a brief flowering of the Renaissance during a 'golden age'. Then in 1514 a peasant army that had assembled for a crusade against the Turks turned on the landowners. The serfs were eventually suppressed and their leader, György Dózsa, executed, but Hungary was seriously weakened. In 1526 the Hungarian army was defeated by the Turks at Mohács and by 1541 the Turks had occupied Buda.

For the next century the Kingdom of Hungary was reduced to a Habsburg-dominated buffer strip between Balaton Lake and Vienna with its seat at Pozsony (Bratislava). Continued Hungarian resistance to the Turks resulted in heroic battles at Kőszeg (1532), Eger (1552) and Szigetvár (1566). Though it was a Turkish vassal, the Principality of Transylvania was never fully integrated into the Ottoman Empire.

When the Turks were finally evicted in 1686 through the combined efforts of the Austrian and Polish armies, Hungary was subjected to Habsburg domination. From 1703 to 1711 Ferenc Rákóczi II, Prince of Transylvania, led the War of Independence against the Austrians, but the Hungarians were eventually overcome through force of numbers. During and after this war, the Habsburgs demolished any remaining medieval fortifications in order to deny their use to Hungarian rebels. Apart from the destruction, all the Turks left behind were a few bath houses in Buda and a couple of mosques in Pécs.

Hungary never fully recovered from these disasters. Most of the country's medieval monuments had been destroyed, and from the 18th century onwards Hungary had to be rebuilt almost from scratch.

The liberal-democratic revolution of 1848 led by Lajos Kossuth and the poet Sándor Petőfi against the Habsburgs demanded freedom for the serfs and independence. Although it was defeated in 1849, the uprising shook the oligarchy. In 1866 Austria was defeated by Bismarck's Prussia and the next year a compromise was struck between the Austrian capitalists and Hungarian landowners and a dual Austro-Hungarian monarchy formed. Although this partnership stimulated industrial development, it proved unfortunate in the long run because Hungary came to be viewed by its neighbours as a tool of Habsburg oppression. After WW I Hungary became independent from Austria, but the 1920 Trianon Treaty stripped the country of 68% of its territory and 58% of its population. These losses fuel resentment against neighbouring Romania, Slovakia and former Yugoslavia to this day.

In August 1919, a 133-day socialist government led by Béla Kun was overthrown by counter-revolutionary elements and thousands were killed, imprisoned or forced to flee the country. In March 1920, Admiral Miklós Horthy established a reactionary regime which lasted 25 years. Before WW II Hungary was an agricultural country with a third of the farmland owned by a thousand magnates while two million peasants had no land at all.

In 1941 the Hungarians' desire to recover their country's 'lost territories' drew them into war alongside the Nazis. Towards the end of the war hundreds of thousands of Jews living outside the capital were deported to Auschwitz, though there wasn't time to round up all those in the Budapest ghetto and about half survived. When Horthy tried to make a separate peace with the Allies in October 1944, the occupying Germans ousted him and put the fascist Arrow Cross Party in power. In December 1944 a provisional government was established at Debrecen and by 4 April 1945 all of Hungary had been liberated by the Soviet army.

(Horthy died in exile in Portugal in 1957, but in 1993 he was reburied in Hungary with eight cabinet ministers in attendance and the prime minister himself expressing admiration for the man who had eagerly joined in all of Hitler's wars of aggression against Hungary's neighbours.)

Post WW II

After the war the communists divided the large estates among the peasantry and nationalised the means of production, following the Stalinist line of collectivised agriculture and heavy industry. In February

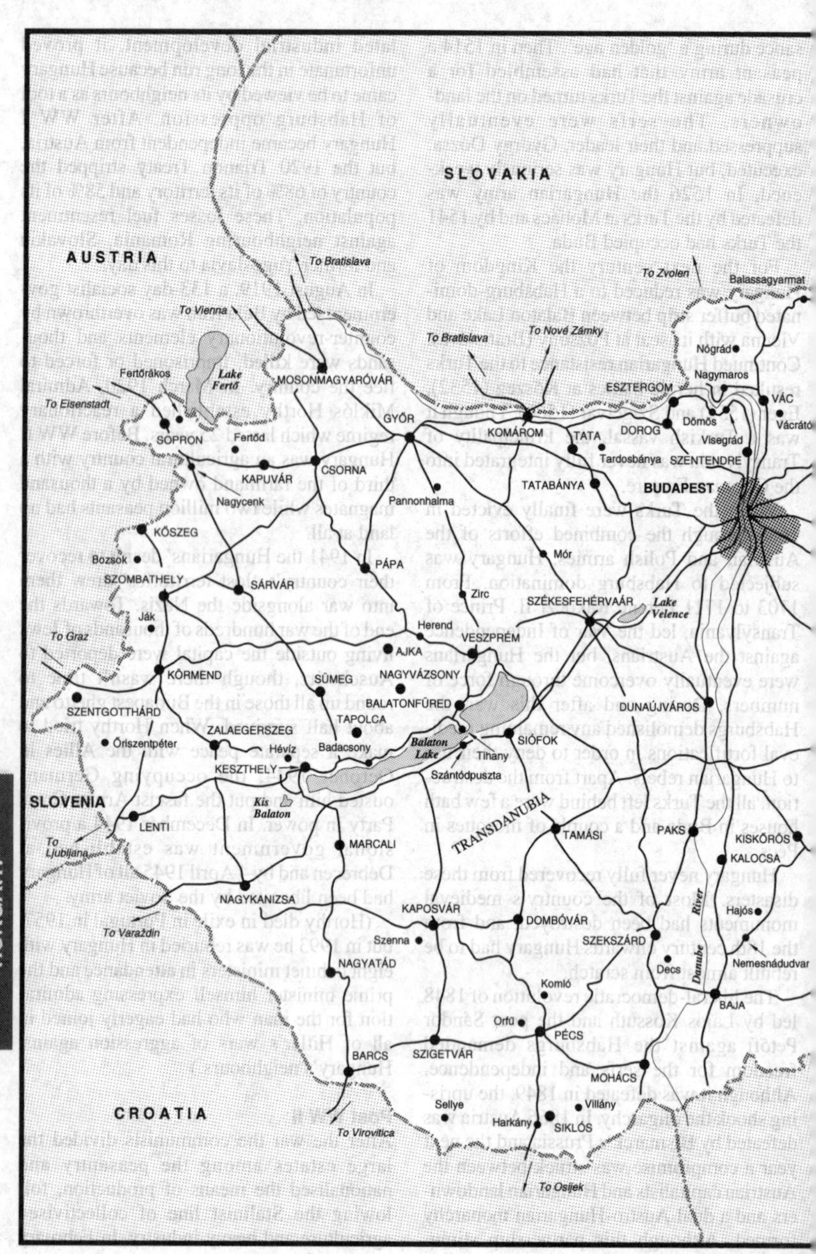
SLOVAKIA
AUSTRIA
SLOVENIA
CROATIA
TRANSDANUBIA
To Bratislava
To Vienna
To Eisenstadt
To Graz
To Ljubljana
To Varaždin
To Virovitica
To Osijek
To Zvolen
To Nové Zámky
Balassagyarmat
Nógrád
Nagymaros
ESZTERGOM
VÁC
Vácrátót
Dömös
Visegrád
DOROG
SZENTENDRE
BUDAPEST
KOMÁROM
TATA
Tardosbánya
TATABÁNYA
Fertőrákos
Lake Fertő
MOSONMAGYARÓVÁR
GYŐR
SOPRON
Fertőd
KAPUVÁR
CSORNA
Nagycenk
Pannonhalma
KŐSZEG
Bozsok
SZOMBATHELY
SÁRVÁR
PÁPA
Mór
Zirc
SZÉKESFEHÉRVÁR
Lake Velence
Ják
Herend
VESZPRÉM
AJKA
KÖRMEND
SÜMEG
NAGYVÁZSONY
SZENTGOTTHÁRD
BALATONFÜRED
DUNAÚJVÁROS
TAPOLCA
ZALAEGERSZEG
Őriszentpéter
Hévíz
Badacsony
Balaton Lake
Tihany
SIÓFOK
KESZTHELY
Szántódpuszta
Kis Balaton
LENTI
TAMÁSI
PAKS
KISKŐRÖS
KALOCSA
MARCALI
NAGYKANIZSA
KAPOSVÁR
DOMBÓVÁR
Danube River
Hajós
Szenna
SZEKSZÁRD
NAGYATÁD
Nemesnádudvar
Decs
Komló
BAJA
Orfű
PÉCS
SZIGETVÁR
BARCS
MOHÁCS
Sellye
Villány
Harkány
SIKLÓS

HUNGARY

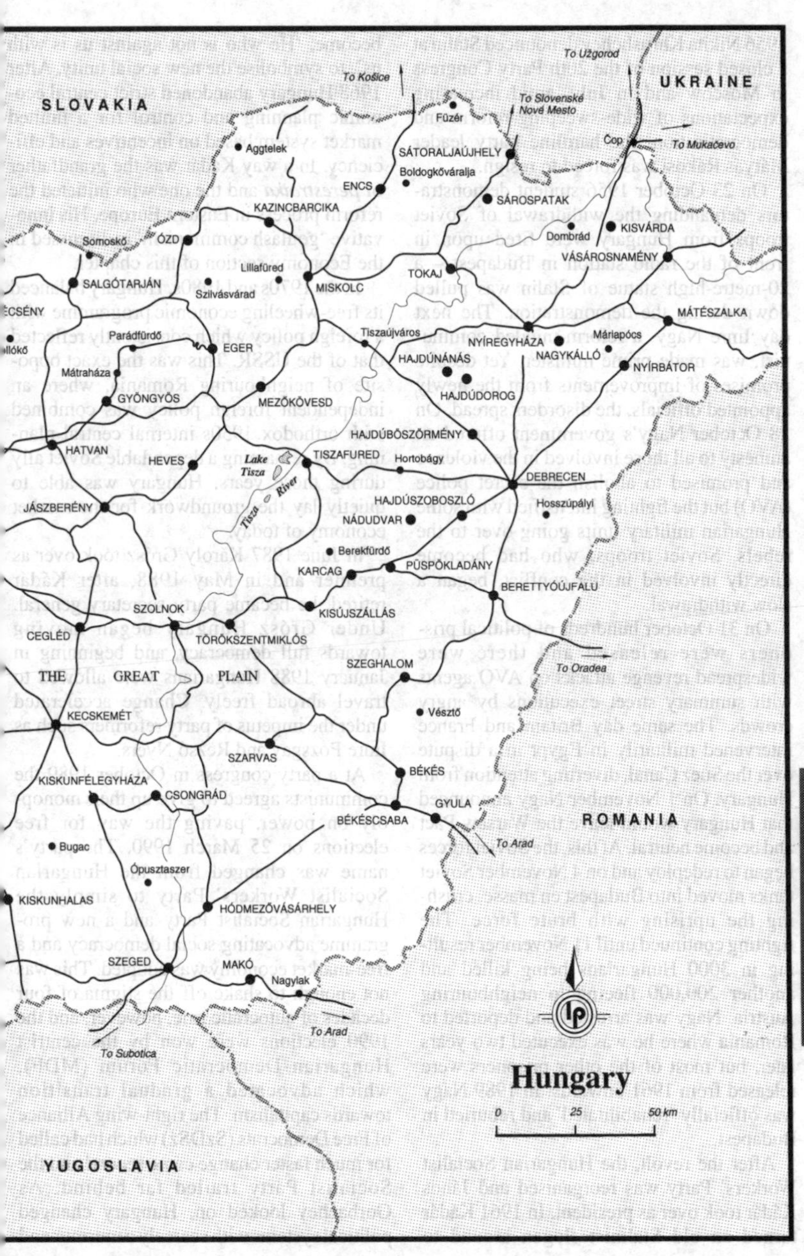
SLOVAKIA
UKRAINE
ROMANIA
YUGOSLAVIA
To Košice
To Užgorod
To Slovenské Nové Mesto
To Mukačevo
To Oradea
To Arad
To Arad
To Subotica
Füzér
Čop
Aggtelek
SÁTORALJAÚJHELY
Boldogkőváralja
ENCS
SÁROSPATAK
KISVÁRDA
Dombrád
KAZINCBARCIKA
Somoskő
ÓZD
VÁSÁROSNAMÉNY
Lillafüred
TOKAJ
MISKOLC
SALGÓTARJÁN
Szilvásvárad
ECSÉNY
MÁTÉSZALKA
Tiszaújváros
Máriapócs
Parádfürdő
NYÍREGYHÁZA
llókő
EGER
NAGYKÁLLÓ
HAJDÚNÁNÁS
NYÍRBÁTOR
Mátraháza
GYÖNGYÖS
MEZŐKÖVESD
HAJDÚDOROG
HAJDÚBÖSZÖRMÉNY
HATVAN
HEVES
Lake Tisza
TISZAFURED
Hortobágy
Tisza River
DEBRECEN
JÁSZBERÉNY
HAJDÚSZOBOSZLÓ
Hosszúpályi
NÁDUDVAR
Berekfürdő
KARCAG
PÜSPÖKLADÁNY
BERETTYÓÚJFALU
SZOLNOK
KISÚJSZÁLLÁS
CEGLÉD
TÖRÖKSZENTMIKLÓS
SZEGHALOM
THE GREAT PLAIN
Vésztő
KECSKEMÉT
SZARVAS
BÉKÉS
KISKUNFÉLEGYHÁZA
CSONGRÁD
GYULA
BÉKÉSCSABA
Bugac
Ópusztaszer
KISKUNHALAS
HÓDMEZŐVÁSÁRHELY
SZEGED
MAKÓ
Nagylak
Hungary
0
25
50 km

HUNGARY

1956 Nikita Khrushchev denounced Stalin at a closed session of the 20th Party Congress in Moscow and in July, amid increasing expectations of wide-sweeping reform and democratisation, the hardline party leader Mátyás Rákosi was forced to resign.

On 23 October 1956 student demonstrators demanding the withdrawal of Soviet troops from Hungary were fired upon in front of the radio station in Budapest – a 20-metre-high statue of Stalin was pulled down during the demonstration. The next day Imre Nagy, a reform-minded communist, was made prime minister. Yet despite promises of improvements from the newly appointed officials, the disorders spread. On 28 October Nagy's government offered an amnesty to all those involved in the violence and promised to abolish the secret police (AVO) but the fighting intensified with some Hungarian military units going over to the rebels. Soviet troops, who had become directly involved in the conflict, began a slow withdrawal.

On 31 October hundreds of political prisoners were released and there were widespread revenge attacks on AVO agents with summary street executions by angry crowds. The same day Britain and France intervened militarily in Egypt in a dispute over the Suez Canal, diverting attention from Hungary. On 1 November Nagy announced that Hungary would leave the Warsaw Pact and become neutral. At this, the Soviet forces began to redeploy and on 4 November Soviet tanks moved into Budapest en masse, crushing the uprising with brute force. The fighting continued until 11 November resulting in 3000 Hungarians being killed and another 200,000 fleeing to neighbouring Austria. Nagy was arrested and deported to Romania where he was executed two years later, but most of the other prisoners were released from 1961 onwards. In 1989 Nagy was officially 'rehabilitated' and reburied in Budapest.

After the revolt, the Hungarian Socialist Workers' Party was reorganised and János Kádár took over as president. In 1961 Kádár turned an old Stalinist slogan around to become, 'He who is not against us is with us', to symbolise the new social unity. After 1968 Hungary abandoned strict central economic planning and control for a limited market system based on incentives and efficiency. In a way Kádár was the grandfather of *perestroika* and the one who initiated the reform process in Eastern Europe. His innovative 'goulash communism' is discussed in the Economy section of this chapter.

In the 1970s and 1980s, Hungary balanced its free-wheeling economic programme with a foreign policy which consistently reflected that of the USSR. This was the exact opposite of neighbouring Romania, where an independent foreign policy was combined with orthodox 1950s internal central planning. By remaining a dependable Soviet ally during those years, Hungary was able to quietly lay the groundwork for the market economy of today.

In June 1987 Károly Grósz took over as premier and in May 1988, after Kádár retired, he became party secretary general. Under Grósz Hungary began moving towards full democracy, and beginning in January 1988 Hungarians were allowed to travel abroad freely. Change accelerated under the impetus of party reformers such as Imre Pozsgay and Rezső Nyers.

At a party congress in October 1989 the communists agreed to give up their monopoly on power, paving the way for free elections on 25 March 1990. The party's name was changed from the Hungarian Socialist Workers' Party to simply the Hungarian Socialist Party and a new programme advocating social democracy and a free-market economy was adopted. This was not enough to shake off the stigma of four decades of autocratic rule, however, and the 1990 elections were won by the centrist Hungarian Democratic Forum (MDF), which advocated a gradual transition towards capitalism. The right-wing Alliance of Free Democrats (SzDSz) which had called for much faster change came second and the Socialist Party trailed far behind. As Gorbachev looked on, Hungary changed political systems with scarcely a murmur and the last Soviet troops left Hungary in June 1991.

In coalition with two smaller parties, Democratic Forum provided Hungary with sound government during its painful transition to a full market economy. These years saw Hungary's northern and southern neighbours split apart along ethnic lines. Prime minister József Antall did little to improve relations with Slovakia and former Yugoslavia by claiming to be the 'emotional' and 'spiritual' prime minister of the large Hungarian minorities in those countries. In mid-1993 Democratic Forum was forced to expel István Csurka, a party vice president, after he made ultra-nationalistic statements which tarnished Hungary's image as a bastion of moderation and stability in a dangerous region. Antall died in December 1993 and was replaced by interior minister Péter Boross.

The economic changes of the past few years have resulted in declining living standards. In 1991 most state subsidies were removed leading to a severe recession exacerbated by the fiscal austerity necessary to reduce inflation and stimulate investment. This made life difficult for many Hungarians and in the May 1994 elections the Hungarian Socialist Party led by former communists won an absolute majority in parliament. This in no way implied a return to the past and Socialist leader Gyula Horn was quick to point out that it was his party which had initiated the whole reform process in the first place (as foreign minister in 1989 Horn played a key role in opening Hungary's border with Austria). All three main political parties advocate economic liberalisation and closer ties with the West but Hungarians have demonstrated that in future they want more consideration for the large majority which has yet to benefit from the changes.

GEOGRAPHY

Hungary (slightly bigger than Portugal) occupies the Carpathian Basin in the very centre of Eastern Europe and is not part of the Balkans. The 417-km Hungarian reach of the Danube River cuts through a southern extension of the Carpathian Mountains at the majestic Danube Bend north of Budapest. The Danube divides Hungary's 93,030 sq km in two: to the east is the Great Plain (Nagyalföld), to the west, Transdanubia (Dunántúl). The 579 km of the Hungarian portion of the Tisza River crosses the Great Plain about 100 km east of the Danube. The 'mountains' of Hungary are actually hills as they seldom exceed an elevation of 1000 metres (whereas mountains in Slovakia and Romania reach over 2000 metres). The highest peak is Kékes (1015 metres) in the Mátra Range north-east of Budapest.

Two-thirds of Hungary is less than 200 metres above sea level. The almost treeless Hungarian *puszta* (another name for the Great Plain) between the Danube and Romania is a harbinger of the steppes of Ukraine. Balaton Lake (covering 598 sq km) between the Danube and Austria reaches only 11.5 metres at its deepest point. The lake's average depth is three to four metres and the waters warm up quickly in summer. The over-use of nitrate fertilisers in agriculture has caused the ground water beneath Hungary's low-lying plains to become contaminated with phosphates and in recent years the government has had to expend great efforts to protect Balaton Lake from pollution by fertiliser runoff and sewage.

There are five national parks. The two on the Great Plain, Hortobágy and Kiskunság, preserve the environment of the open puszta while Bükk National Park north of Eger protects the Bükk Mountains, Hungary's largest continuous mountain range. North again is Aggtelek National Park with the country's largest caves. Fertő-tó National Park is near Sopron.

ECONOMY

In a way, Hungary was lucky not to have had the natural resources of Poland and Slovakia because without vast reserves of hard coal and iron ore the communists were never able to concentrate industrial development in heavy industry. The only metallic ore found here in significant quantities is bauxite of which Hungary is the largest European producer. After the 1956 political debacle, the emphasis shifted to light industry producing consumer goods.

Collectivised agriculture was introduced in Hungary between 1959 and 1961, and the country became a world leader in per capita grain and meat production. Hungary is self-sufficient in food, the main crops being barley, corn, potatoes, sugar beet and wheat. The collective farms have all been privatised but breaking them up into individual holdings has proved difficult.

Hungary was the first Eastern European country to move successfully towards an open marketplace; the economic reforms proposed by Mikhail Gorbachev in the late 1980s bore a distinct resemblance to those initiated by János Kádár two decades earlier. Kádár's 'New Economic Mechanism' combined central government planning with a market economy. Industrial plants and companies remained under state ownership but management was allowed wide discretionary power. The decentralised enterprises were required to compete and make a profit and those which consistently lost money had to declare bankruptcy. Foreign investment in joint ventures with state-owned firms was possible as early as 1972.

The competition resulted in an abundance of quality consumer goods with prices determined by actual costs or supply and demand rather than by state edicts. Numerous small, privately owned businesses such as bakeries, boutiques and restaurants had been functioning for years before 1990. Many Hungarians held after-hours jobs to supplement their incomes and taxation of this 'second economy' was an important source of government income. Yet despite providing this outlet for individual initiative, the communists restricted private enterprise to small family units cut off from credit and investment.

During the communist era two-thirds of Hungary's foreign trade was with the Soviet block and since the demise of the Moscow-based Council for Mutual Economic Assistance (Comecon) business has had to be reoriented towards the West. In 1990, 36% of Hungary's exports went to the European Community (now called the European Union – EU). In 1991 it was 47% and in 1992 it grew to 52%. In 1992 the European Free Trade Association (EFTA) countries accounted for another 20% of exports. Hungary became an associate member of the EU in 1991 with full membership envisioned by 2000, giving the country 10 years to prepare for unobstructed competition with the West.

In 1988 Hungary became the first Eastern European country to institute income tax and in June 1990 the Budapest Stock Exchange reopened after a hiatus of 42 years, Eastern Europe's first since the Stalin era. The stock market has not lived up to expectations due to the low return on stocks compared to other forms of investment and the turnover in government bonds on the exchange is 10 times the volume in stocks.

By mid-1994 Hungary had received US$7 billion in foreign investment, more than the rest of Eastern Europe combined. The USA has provided 40% of the investment, with Austria, Germany and France providing about 15% each. General Electric purchased the light-bulb manufacturer Tungsram in 1990 and General Motors, Suzuki, Audi and Ford have all set up automotive manufacturing plants in Hungary. Blue chips like the travel agency Ibusz, Danubius Hotels and Pick Salami have privatised in part by selling shares on the stock exchange, while Malév Hungarian Airlines has entered into a partnership with Italy's Alitalia. The private sector now accounts for almost 60% of the gross national product.

Yet despite all the investment, the Hungarian economy continues to contract, causing hardship and 13% unemployment. Tungsram has had to cut its workforce from 17,500 in 1990 to 10,400 in 1993 just to break even and the bus manufacturer Ikarus, which until 1989 produced 10% of all buses exported worldwide, has been forced to lay off thousands of employees to stay afloat.

Privatisation has proceeded slowly. In the three years following its founding in 1990, the State Property Agency only managed to sell off 20% of state-owned properties. Hungary has a US$24 billion hard-currency debt to Western creditors, the highest per capita debt in Eastern Europe, which absorbs 35% of export income. In 1993 inflation was running at 23% with a budget deficit of US$2 billion (7% of the gross domestic product).

Hungary is the fifth most visited country in the world with over 22 million 'tourists' a year, about half of them from former Yugoslavia and Romania.

Hungary gets 48% of its electricity from four Soviet-built VVER-213 440-megawatt nuclear reactors at Paks on the Danube River and much of the rest comes from generators powered by burning dirty brown coal.

The average wage in Hungary is US$350 a month, the second-highest in Eastern Europe (after Slovenia).

There's a joke making the rounds in Budapest which illustrates what Hungarians expect from the current economic reforms. As two Budapesters are walking across the Chain Bridge they notice the Hungarian prime minister below walking on the waters of the Danube.

'A miracle!' cries the first.

'Nonsense,' retorts the second, 'he just can't swim'.

POPULATION & PEOPLE

Neither a Slavic nor a Germanic people, the Finno-Ugrian Hungarians were the last major ethnic group to arrive in Europe during the period of the great migrations. Some 10,479,000 Hungarians live within their country, another five million abroad. The 1.7 million Hungarians in Transylvania constitute the second largest national minority in Europe (after the Albanians of Yugoslavia) and large numbers of Hungarians live in Slovakia, former Yugoslavia, Ukraine, the USA and Canada. Minorities within Hungary include Germans (1.6%), Slovaks (1.1%), South Slavs (0.3%) and Romanians (0.2%). The quarter of a million Hungarian Gypsies live mostly in the north-eastern corner of the country.

Religion-wise, 67.5% of the population is Catholic, 20% Calvinist and 5% Lutheran. Before WW II Hungary had 700,000 Jewish residents but now there are only about 80,000 (the largest Jewish community in Eastern Europe). Two-thirds of the people live in cities, over two million of them in Budapest. The next largest cities are Debrecen (215,000), Miskolc (195,000), Szeged (180,000), Pécs (170,000) and Győr (130,000). Hungary has the world's highest rates of suicide (48.4 per 100,000 men, 14.6 per 100,000 women) and abortion. Yet Hungary also has more poets per head than any country in Europe; 99% of the population is literate.

ARTS

Although the Renaissance flourished briefly in this region during the late 15th century, Hungary was isolated from the mainstream of European cultural development during the century and a half of Turkish rule which began in the mid-15th century. Then came domination by the Austrian Habsburgs until 1918 and, more recently, external interference from Nazi Germany and the USSR. Against this background, it's not surprising that Hungarian writers have struggled against oppression.

Hungary's greatest poet, Sándor Petőfi (1823-49), castigated both the privileges of the nobility and the plight of the common people. His poem *Talpra magyar* (Rise, Hungarian) became the anthem of the 1848 revolution in which he actively fought and died. Petőfi used the simple style of Hungarian folk songs to express subtle feelings and ideals.

An early colleague of Petőfi, novelist Mór Jókai (1825-1904), wrote historical works like *The Golden Age of Transylvania* (1852) and *Turkish World in Hungary* (1853) which are still widely read. The visual equivalent of Jókai's writings are the realist paintings depicting village life by the artist Mihály Munkácsy (1844-1900).

Hungary's finest 20th-century lyric poet, Endre Ady (1877-1919), attacked the narrow materialism of the Hungary of his time provoking a storm of indignation from right-wing nationalists. Later Ady went on to describe the pain and suffering of war. The work of novelist Zsigmond Móricz (1879-1942) portrays the human conflicts of provincial life, and the work of poet Attila József (1905-37) expresses the torments faced by individuals in the technological age.

Hungary's best known contemporary writer is the novelist György Konrád (1933-) whose family only escaped deportation to Auschwitz because someone sent them to Austria by mistake. Konrád's *A Feast in the Garden* (1985) is an almost autobiographical account of the fate of the Jewish community in the small eastern Hungarian town where he grew up.

Perhaps the finest Hungarian novel of recent years is *The Book of Memories* (1985) which journalist Péter Nádas (1942-) laboured over for 11 years. This massive, complex work explores the lives of three main characters from the turn of the century, the 1950s and the 1970s.

Music

Hungarian folk music is played on the bagpipes, hurdy-gurdy, bombard, *tambur* (lute), flute and *cymbalum*. In times gone by, villages which were too poor to buy an organ often used the bagpipes during church services. The cymbalum, a zither or dulcimer with strings that are struck, gave origin to the piano. The *taragot*, a single-reed oboe of Hungarian origin, has a haunting sound not unlike that of a soprano saxophone.

The famous Hungarian pianist and composer Franz Liszt (Liszt Ferenc in Hungarian) (1811-86) was fascinated by the music of the Gypsies and even wrote a book on the subject. His *Hungarian Rhapsodies* pulse with the wild rhythms of Hungarian Gypsy music.

Opera composer Ferenc Erkel (1810-93) attempted to transform Italian opera into a Hungarian operatic style through the use of the *verbunkos*, a Gypsy dance based on Western European dance music. In his opera *Hunyadi László* (1844), Erkel utilised the *csárdás*, the national dance of Hungary, which begins slowly but soon picks up as the couples whirl to syncopated rhythms. Erkel's 1861 opera *Bánk bán* captured the fiery nationalism of his time by portraying a 13th-century revolt against the queen's hated foreign court.

Both Liszt and Erkel incorrectly assumed that what they heard the Gypsy musicians of their time playing was Gypsy music, when in fact it was mostly adapted Hungarian folk music and nostalgic ballads written by 19th-century Hungarian nobles. Operetta composer Imre Kálmán (1882-1953) combined Liszt's Gypsy music with the Viennese waltz. Béla Bartók (1881-1945) and his colleague Zoltán Kodály (1882-1967) went beyond this urban 'Gypsy music' to collect genuine Hungarian folk music in remote villages and both integrated these folk songs and melodies into their own compositions.

Today folk music has largely disappeared in Hungarian villages as the lives of the peasants have been irrevocably changed. In Transylvania, however, folk music has survived as the Hungarian minority there seeks to preserve its identity by clinging to its traditional folk culture. The revival of folk music in Hungary in the 1970s drew inspiration from Transylvania and a journey there became *de rigueur* for all aspiring Hungarian folk musicians who later played at *táncház* (dance houses). The album *Blues for Transylvania* by Hungary's top folk group, Muzsikás, includes songs about conditions in Romania and the insecure position of the Hungarians living there.

Muzsikás' sound is appealing to Western ears because of the unique combination of traditional Hungarian instruments (bagpipes, buzuki, cymbalum, *duduk*, hurdy-gurdy, *kobsa*, shawm, tambur, Turkish horn), Western folk instruments (guitar, jews-harp, recorder) and classical instruments (cello, viola, violin, bass). Vocalist Márta Sebestyén's rich, earthy voice combines well with the group's lively folk rhythms.

Though Sebestyén's regular group is Muzsikás, she sings with many others including the Vujicsics Ensemble (pronounced voichich), which performs the spirited folk music of the Serbian and Croatian minorities living in southern Hungary. The skilfully arranged music of this professional group achieves its typical Balkan sound through the use of traditional instruments such as the tambur, *tapan* (a big drum hit at both ends with a stick), *okarina* (ceramic flute), bagpipes and *zurna* (flute), as well as the accordion, double-bass and violin.

Though Hungarian Gypsies are not a homogeneous ethnic group, their folk music is of a unified style. The original Gypsy musical tradition was mainly vocal and lively stick dances and slow lyrical songs relating the vicissitudes of life were accompanied only by snapping fingers, tapping pot lids, water cans or spoons – other musical instruments were not used. In the late 1960s young Gypsies began using the guitar as part of the Hungarian folk revival of the time. The best known contemporary Gypsy group, Kalyi Jag ('Black Fire'), sings mostly in Romany and uses household utensils alongside the double bass, oral bass, guitar and percussion.

Traditional Yiddish music is less known than Gypsy music but is of similar origin having once been closely associated with Central European folk music. Until WW I 'klezmer' dance bands were led by the violin and cymbalum, but the influence of Yiddish theatre and the first wax recordings inspired a switch to the clarinet which predominates today. In 1990 the Klezmer Band of Budapest was formed to revive this happy mix of jazz and the big band sound.

LANGUAGE

The Hungarians speak Magyar, a language only they understand. Of the languages of Europe only Finnish and Estonian are related. Though many older Hungarians understand German, this is one country where it's unusual to meet someone on the street who understands English. As usual, if you have trouble making yourself understood, try writing down what you want to say. Travel agency personnel usually do speak English.

Some useful words to learn are: *utca* (street), *körút* (boulevard), *út* (road), *tér* (square), *útja* (avenue), *sétány* (promenade) and *híd* (bridge). Public toilets (WC) are marked *női* for women, *férfi* for men. Hungarians put surnames before given names. Lonely Planet's *Eastern Europe Phrasebook* contains 72 pages of useful words and expressions in Hungarian.

The longest word in the Hungarian language (meaning something like 'for your unprofanability') is megszentségtelenithetetlenségeskedéseitekért.

Pronunciation

The Hungarian alphabet has 40 letters or combinations of letters. In addition the Roman letters 'q', 'w', 'x' and 'y' are used in foreign words. Hungarian words are pronounced as they're written, with each letter pronounced separately; there are no silent letters or diphthongs. An acute accent lengthens an unaccented vowel, and a double acute accent lengthens a vowel with a dieresis (for example, ű is a long version of ü). A plural is indicated by a final 'k' rather than an 's'. *Nem* indicates a negative. The stress is always on the first syllable.

c	'ts' as in 'hats'
cs	'ch' as in 'chair'
dz	'ds' as in 'roads'
dzs	'j' as in 'jump'
gy	'd' as in 'duty'
j	'y' as in 'yet'
ly	'y' as in 'yet'
ny	'n' as in 'onion'
s	'sh' as in 'shoe'
sz	's' as in 'see'
ty	't' as the first 't' in 'student'
zs	's' as in 'usual'

Greetings & Civilities

hello	*jó napot kivánok* (formal)
hello	*szia* (informal)
goodbye	*viszontlátásra*
goodbye	*viszlát* (informal)
good morning	*jó reggelt*
good evening	*jó estét*
please	*kérem*

thank you	*köszönöm*
thank you	*köszi* (informal)
I am sorry./ Forgive me.	*Bocsánat.*
excuse me	*elnézést*
yes	*igen*
no	*nem*

Small Talk

I don't understand.	*Nem értem.*
Could you write it down?	*Kérem, irja le?*
What is it called?	*Hogy hivják?*
Where do you live?	*Hol lakik ön?*
What work do you do?	*Mi a foglalkozása?*
I am a student.	*Diák vagyok.*
I am very happy.	*Nagyon boldog vagyok.*

Accommodation

youth hostel	*ifjúsági szálló*
camping ground	*kemping*
private room	*fizetővendégszoba*
How much is it?	*Mibe kerül?*
Is that the price per person?	*Ez az ára személyenként?*
Is that the total price?	*Ez a teljes ár?*
Are there any extra charges?	*Kell ezért plusszt fizetnem?*
Do I pay extra for showers?	*Kell fizetni külön a fürdőszóbáért?*
Where is there a cheaper hotel?	*Hol van egy olcsóbb szálloda?*
Should I make a reservation?	*Szükséges a helyfoglalás?*
single room	*egyágyas szoba*
double room	*kétágyas szoba*
It is very noisy.	*Nagyon zajos.*
Where is the toilet?	*Hol van a mosdó?*

Getting Around

What time does it leave?	*Mikor indul?*
When is the first bus?	*Mikor indul az első autóbusz?*
When is the last bus?	*Mikor van az utolsó autóbusz?*
When is the next bus?	*Mikor indul a következő autóbusz?*
That's too soon.	*Az túl korai.*
When is the next one after that?	*Mikor van a következő azután?*
How long does the trip take?	*Mennyi ideig tart a kirándulás?*
arrival	*érkezés*
departure	*indulás*
timetable	*menetrend*
Where is the bus stop?	*Hol van az autóbuszmegálló?*
Where is the train station?	*Hol van a pályaudvar?*
Where is the left-luggage room?	*Hol van a csomagmegőrző?*

Around Town

Just a minute.	*Rögtön.*
Where is ...?	*Hol van ...?*
the bank	*bank*
the post office	*posta*
the tourist information office	*túrista információs iroda*
the museum	*múzeum*
Where are you going?	*Hová megy?*
I am going to ...	*Megyek ...*
Where is it?	*Hol van ez?*
I can't find it.	*Nem találom.*
Is it far?	*Messze van?*
Please show me on the map.	*Kérem, mutassa meg a térképen.*
left	*bal*
right	*jobb*
straight ahead	*előre*
I want ...	*Akarok ...*
Do I need permission?	*Szükségem van engedélyre?*

Entertainment

Where can I buy a ticket?	*Hol vehetek jegyet?*
I want to refund this ticket.	*Vissza akarom váltani ezt a jegyet.*

HUNGARY

Is this a good seat? *Ez jó hely?*
at the front *elöl*
ticket *jegyet*

Food

I do not eat meat. *Nem eszem húst.*
self-service cafeteria *önkiszolgáló étterem*
grocery store *élelmiszerbolt*
fish *hal*
pork *disznó*
soup *leves*
salad *saláta*
fresh vegetables *friss zöldség*
milk *tej*
bread *kenyér*
sugar *cukor*
ice cream *fagylalt*
coffee *kávé*
tea *tea*
mineral water *ásványviz*
beer *sör*
wine *bor*
hot/cold *meleg/hideg*

Shopping

Where can I buy one? *Hol vehetem meg ezt?*
How much does it cost? *Mennyibe kerül?*
That's (much) too expensive. *Az túl drága.*
Is there a cheaper one? *Van ennél olcsóbb?*

Time & Dates

today *ma*
tonight *ma este*
tomorrow *holnap*
the day after tomorrow *holnap után*
What time does it open? *Mikor nyit?*
What time does it close? *Mikor zár?*
open *nyitva*
closed *zárva*
in the morning *reggel*
in the evening *este*
every day *naponta*

At what time? *Mikor?*
when? *Hányadikán?*

Monday *hétfő*
Tuesday *kedd*
Wednesday *szerda*
Thursday *csütörtök*
Friday *péntek*
Saturday *szombat*
Sunday *vasárnap*

January *január*
February *február*
March *március*
April *április*
May *május*
June *június*
July *július*
August *augusztus*
September *szeptember*
October *október*
November *november*
December *december*

Numbers

1	*egy*
2	*kettő*
3	*három*
4	*négy*
5	*öt*
6	*hat*
7	*hét*
8	*nyolc*
9	*kilenc*
10	*tiz*
11	*tizenegy*
12	*tizenkettő*
13	*tizenhárom*
14	*tizennégy*
15	*tizenöt*
16	*tizenhat*
17	*tizenhét*
18	*tizennyolc*
19	*tizenkilenc*
20	*húsz*
21	*huszonegy*
22	*huszonkettö*
23	*huszonhárom*
30	*harminc*
40	*negyven*

50	*ötven*
60	*hatvan*
70	*hetven*
80	*nyolcvan*
90	*kilencven*
100	*száz*
1000	*ezer*
10,000	*tir ezer*
1,000,000	*millió*

Facts for the Visitor

VISAS & EMBASSIES

Everyone entering Hungary must have a valid passport and in some cases also a visa. Nationals of the USA, Canada and most European countries do not require visas to visit Hungary. Citizens of Australia, Japan and New Zealand still require visas. If you hold a passport from one of these countries, check current visa requirements at a consulate or any Malév Hungarian Airlines office.

Visas are issued on the spot at Hungarian consulates upon receipt of between US$20 and US$25 and two photos. A double-entry tourist visa costs between US$30 and US$40 and you must have four photos. (If you know you'll be visiting Hungary twice, get a double-entry visa to avoid having to apply again somewhere else.) Some consulates charge US$5 extra for express service (10 minutes as opposed to 24 hours). Be sure to get a tourist rather than a transit visa. A tourist visa allows a stay of up to 90 days and can be used any time within three or six months. Visas are extended at local police stations for about US$10 (bring proof that you are staying in registered accommodation). A transit visa is only good for a stay of 48 hours, cannot be extended and costs the same price. On a transit visa you must enter and leave through different border crossings and must have a visa for the next country you visit. Visas are issued at highway border crossings and the airport for US$40 but this usually involves a wait of an hour or more. Visas are never issued on trains.

A notice on the visa form instructs you to report to police within 48 hours of arrival. If you're staying in a private room arranged by a Hungarian travel agency, or at a hotel or camping ground, this formality will be taken care of for you. The agency or hotel will stamp your visa form and write in the nights you stayed with them. If you're staying with friends, you're supposed to report to the police in person. Upon departure from Hungary, an immigration officer will scrutinise the stamps and if too many nights are unaccounted for, you'll have some explaining to do. Your visa serves as an exit permit and you can leave Hungary any time within the 90-day validity period. Those not needing a visa only have to register with the police and get a stamp if they stay longer than 30 days.

Hungarian Embassies Abroad

Australia

17 Beale Crescent, Deakin, ACT 2600 (☎ 062-82 3226)

suite 405, Edgecliffe Centre, 203-233 New South Head Rd, Edgecliffe, NSW 2027 (☎ 02-328 7859)

Canada

7 Delaware Ave, Ottawa, ON K2P OZ2 (☎ 613-232 1711)

1200 McGill College St, suite 2040, Montreal, PQ H3G 4G7 (☎ 514-393 3302)

102 Bloor St West, suite 1005, Toronto, ON M5S 1M8 (☎ 416-923 8981)

Netherlands

Hogeweg 14, 2585 JD The Hague (☎ 070-350 0404)

UK

35b Eaton Place, London, SW1X 8BY, England, (☎ 0171-235 2664)

USA

3910 Shoemaker St NW, Washington, DC 20008 (☎ 202-362 6730)

11766 Wilshire Blvd, suite 410, Los Angeles, CA (☎ 310-473 9344)

227 East 52nd St, New York, NY 10022 (☎ 212-752 0661)

MONEY

Unlike the situation in many other Eastern European countries, in Hungary travellers' cheques are a good way to carry money. You will need at least some cash hard currency in small bills to pay for visas and certain inter-

HUNGARY

national transportation tickets, and on weekends and holidays cash is much better than travellers' cheques.

Travel agencies like Ibusz charge 1% commission to change money but they may not accept travellers' cheques. Post offices are poor places to change money as they usually accept only cash and give a lousy rate. The Orszagos Takarékpenztár or OPT Bank (National Savings & Commercial Bank) offers good rates and charges no commission on travellers' cheques, though not all OPT branches deal in hard currency. We list the most convenient OTP Bank branches throughout this chapter. Be aware that the foreign exchange counter in banks often closes before the rest of the bank, so go at least an hour before the closing times listed herein.

Several flashy foreign exchange outlets have established themselves in Hungary. They advertise excellent rates without commission, but *only on exchanges over US$2250,* otherwise you get a rate 10% lower. This distinction is only mentioned in tiny letters at the bottom of their large exchange-rate boards, sometimes in Hungarian. At other times they'll loudly announce 'no commission' then pay a rate 10% lower than the banks or advertise their higher selling rate instead of the buying rate they'll pay you. You may want to take advantage of their long hours and fast service to change a few dollars upon arrival, to tide you over until you can get to an Ibusz office or a bank, but never change large amounts with them. Whenever changing money somewhere other than at a bank be sure to check both the rate and the commission before producing any funds.

Only change as much as you intend to spend, as changing excess forints back into hard currency is difficult. Some Ibusz and National Bank branches will do it but only up to half the amount you changed originally (US$100 maximum), provided this is verified by receipts bearing your passport number, and they will deduct 7% commission. Don't leave it until the last moment to change money back because if you have to take forints out of the country you'll only get about 60% of their value at banks abroad. To convert US dollar travellers' cheques into dollars cash also costs 7% commission.

For cash advances on Diners Club, MasterCard and Visa credit cards contact an Ibusz Bank (US$100 minimum). For American Express, go to the American Express office (☎ 251 0010) in Budapest.

Officially you're only allowed to import or export 1000 forints in notes not larger than 500 forints. Upon departure you could deposit Hungarian currency exceeding 1000 forints with customs against a receipt allowing you to pick it up at a savings bank on your next visit, less a 3% service charge. Banks in Vienna sell Hungarian currency at a nice discount.

It's senseless to make use of the black market to change money. The saving is only a couple of per cent, it's illegal and you are sure to be ripped off anyway. Anyone offering more than 10% over the current rate or trying to pay you with small notes is almost certainly a thief. Moneychangers like this will try to switch the counted money for a packet of cut paper, small bills or worthless Yugoslav banknotes at the last minute. If the person takes the money back from you after you have counted it, this is definitely his intention. These operators usually work in pairs. The second man will appear just as you're completing the transaction to cover the escape of the first by distracting you, perhaps by asking if you want to change more money with him.

With any luck, by the time you read this Hungary will have finally made its currency fully convertible, ending this fun and games.

Currency

The Hungarian forint is divided into 100 fillér. There are both old and new coins of one, two, five, 10, 20 and 200 Ft; old coins of 10, 20 and 50 fillér also exist (the old coins work better in vending machines and public telephones). Banknotes come in denominations of 50, 100, 500, 1000 and 5000 Ft.

Hungarian notes must be the most picturesque in Eastern Europe. The 50 Ft note bears the likeness of the 18th-century independence leader Ferenc Rákóczi II on the front and has mounted horsemen on the back. The 100 Ft note depicts the 19th-century revolutionary Lajos Kossuth and a horse cart, and for 500 Ft you get the poet Endre Ady and a nice view of Budapest. The 1000 Ft note features the composer Béla Bartók and a mother nursing a baby. The 5000 Ft note has Count István Széchenyi on the front and his mansion at Nagycenk on the back.

Exchange Rates

A$1	=	79.23Ft
AS1	=	9.79Ft
DM1	=	69.13Ft
Kč1	=	3.82Ft
Sk1	=	3.39Ft
UK£1	=	165.80Ft
US$1	=	106.64Ft

Costs

In 1993 Hungary experienced 23% inflation. However, you should still be able to get by on US$25 a day by staying in private rooms, eating in unpretentious restaurants and travelling 2nd class by train. Two or more people travelling together or those camping and eating only at self-services can spend less.

Hungary is still reasonable because it doesn't discriminate against Western tourists with a two or three-price system, as is the case in most other Eastern European countries. What you pay for a hotel room will be about the same as a Hungarian would pay. The 25% value-added tax (VAT) will have already been included in any price you're quoted.

Tipping

Hungarians routinely tip doctors, dentists, waiters, hairdressers and taxi drivers about 10%. In restaurants do this directly as you pay by rounding up the bill – don't wait to leave money on the table. If you feel you've been overcharged, you can make your point by paying exactly the amount asked and not a forint more.

CLIMATE & WHEN TO GO

Hungary has a temperate continental climate with Mediterranean and Atlantic influences. The winters can be cold, cloudy and humid, the summers warm. May, June and November are the rainiest months, although more rain falls in the west than in the east. Of the 2054 hours of sunshine a year at Budapest, 1526 occur in the period from April to September. July is the hottest month and January the coldest. The average annual temperature is 10°C.

SUGGESTED ITINERARIES

Depending on the length of your stay, you might want to see and do the following things in Hungary:

Two days
: Visit Budapest.

One week
: Visit Budapest, the Danube Bend and one or two of Győr, Kőszeg, Pécs, Kecskemét, Szeged or Eger depending on your next destination.

Two weeks
: Visit Budapest, the Danube Bend, Győr, Kőszeg, Hévíz, the north shore of Balaton Lake and one of Sopron, Pécs, Szeged or Eger depending on your next destination.

One month
: Visit all the places included in this chapter.

TOURIST OFFICES

The Hungarian Tourist Board, a branch of the Ministry of Industry & Trade, has established a chain of tourist information offices called Tourinform in many parts of Hungary and these are excellent places to ask general questions and pick up brochures.

If your query is about private accommodation, international train transportation or changing money, you should turn to a commercial travel agency, of which every Hungarian town has several. Ibusz is the largest travel company with over a hundred offices in Hungary plus representatives overseas (see the following list). Other national travel agencies with offices around the country include Cooptourist and Volántourist. Regional travel agencies in provincial centres (Dunatours, Balatontourist, Mecsek Tourist etc) are often more

HUNGARY

familiar with their own local area. The English-speaking staff in these offices are usually very courteous but keep in mind that they aren't paid to provide free information (although they often will if they have time).

The travel agency Express used to serve the youth and student market exclusively, but they now sell package tours more generally. They issue the ISIC student card (US$3) and sell reduced train tickets to students and all persons under the age of 26. Some Express offices also know about accommodation in student dormitories in July and August.

Ibusz Offices Abroad

Ibusz offices in countries outside Hungary include:

Netherlands
: Pampuslaan 1, 1382 JM Weesp (☎ 02940-30351)

UK
: Danube Travel, 6 Conduit St, London W1R 9TG (☎ 0171-493 0263)

USA
: One Parker Plaza, 4th floor, Fort Lee, NJ 07024 (☎ 201-592 8585)

Tourist Literature

One publication to get hold of is the monthly *Programme in Ungarn/in Hungary* which lists concerts, opera and ballet performances, musicals, puppet shows, circuses, sporting events, exhibitions, museums and many other events and attractions not only in Budapest but around the country. Also useful are the *Hotel* and *Camping* brochures published annually by the Ministry of Tourism. These list all the official accommodation establishments which replied to their questionnaire. The hotels are categorised according to the star system, so you have an idea of how much each should charge. These free publications are often available at the Ibusz offices abroad, at the Malév Hungarian Airlines' offices and inside Hungary itself at luxury hotels and tourist offices. Otherwise go to Tourinform, Sütő utca 2, Budapest (metro: Deák tér), which will have all three.

BUSINESS HOURS & HOLIDAYS

Grocery stores open weekdays from 7 am to 7 pm, department stores from 10 am to 6 pm. Most shops stay open until 8 pm on Thursday but on Saturday close at 1 pm. Post offices open on weekdays from 8 am to 6 pm, and on Saturday from 8 am to 2 pm. In Hungarian the word for 'open' is *nyitva* and that for 'closed' is *zárva*.

Most museums are closed on Monday and the days following public holidays (and a few also on Tuesday). Museum admission fees have doubled and tripled in the last few years though most are still under US$1. Students get into most museums for half-price. Many museums are free one day a week but the exact day varies from place to place and from year to year.

The public holidays are New Year's Day (1 January), Day of the 1848 Revolution (15 March), Easter Monday (March/April), Labour Day (1 May), Whit Monday (May/June), St Stephen's Day (20 August), Republic Day (23 October) and Christmas (25 and 26 December).

CULTURAL EVENTS

Among Hungary's most outstanding annual events are the Budapest Spring Festival (held in the last third of March), Hortobágy Equestrian Days (late June), Sopron Early Music Days (mid-June to mid-July), Pécs Summer Theatre Festival (June and July), Szentendre Summer Festival (July), Kőszeg Street Theatre Festival (July), Szombathely Bartók Festival (July), Debrecen Jazz Days (July), Szeged Open-Air Festival (mid-July to mid-August), Horse Festival at Szilvásvárad (early September), Eger 'Agria' Folk Dance Meeting and Wine Harvest Days (September), Budapest Arts Weeks (September) and Budapest Contemporary Music Festival (September).

On the first Sunday in June there's a Folk Art Fair in Győr. St Stephen's Day (20 August) is celebrated with sporting events, parades and fireworks. On the same day there's a Floral Festival in Debrecen and a Bridge Fair in nearby Hortobágy.

Formula 1 car races are held in August at

the Hungaroring near Mogyoród, just northeast of Budapest.

The Budapest Spring Fair held in the second half of May features industrial products and the Autumn Fair in the middle of September focuses on consumer goods. Every March there's a Touristic Exhibition at Budapest's Hungexpo Fair Centre. In 1996 Vienna and Budapest will co-host a World's Fair with the theme 'Bridges to the Future' celebrating the links between Austria and Hungary, past and present. Twelve million visitors are expected to attend the six-month event marking the 1100th anniversary of the Magyar conquest of Hungary.

POST

Mail sent c/o Poste Restante, GPO, H-1364 Budapest 4, Hungary, is held at the main post office, Petőfi Sándor utca 13, but they send letters back after only 15 days, so take care.

American Express cardmembers can have their mail sent c/o American Express, Deák Ferenc utca 10, H-1052 Budapest, Hungary. Mail is held there for 30 days.

TELEPHONE

You can make international calls on the old red coin phones though the new blue coin phones are much better, displaying the amount deposited and number dialled on a small screen. To call Western Europe is US$0.75 a minute, North America US$1.75 a minute and Australia US$2 a minute (there are no special times with reduced rates for international calls). If you use a coin phone have lots of old 10 and 20 Ft coins ready. The new coins either don't register or are counted as a lower denomination. Magnetic telephone cards can be used for international and local calls at card phones all around Hungary. The cards come in values of US$2.75 or US$6.75.

For overseas calls, dial the international access code 00, the two-digit country code, the city or area code and the local number. For domestic calls within Hungary, dial the inland access code 06, the city or area code and the local number.

You can also get straight through to an operator based in your home country by dialling the 'Country Direct' number from a public phone (charges are reversed and your coin will be returned). These are:

Australia Direct	☎ 00-800 06111
Britain Direct (BT)	☎ 00-800 04411
Britain (Mercury)	☎ 00-800 04412
Canada Direct	☎ 00-800 01211
New Zealand Direct	☎ 00-800 06411
USA Direct (AT&T)	☎ 00-800 01111
USA MCI	☎ 00-800 01411
USA Sprint Express	☎ 00-800 01877

To call Hungary from abroad dial the international access code, 36 (the country code for Hungary), the area code and the number. Important area codes include 1 (Budapest), 22 (Székesfehérvár), 26 (Szentendre and Visegrád), 33 (Esztergom), 34 (Komárom), 36 (Eger and Szilvásvárad), 46 (Miskolc), 48 (Aggtelek), 52 (Debrecen), 62 (Szeged), 72 (Pécs and Siklós), 76 (Kecskemét), 83 (Keszthely), 84 (Siófok), 86 (Balatonfüred and Tihany), 87 (Badacsony), 94 (Kőszeg and Szombathely), 96 (Győr) and 99 (Sopron and Fertőd).

As telephone calls are easily made from booths on the street we don't generally list the sort of special telephone centres included in other chapters. If you have any problem finding a reliable public telephone simply go to any post office and you'll have a choice of several phones.

TIME

Time in Hungary is GMT/UTC plus one hour. The clock is put an hour forward at the end of March and an hour back at the end of September. As in German, in Hungarian 1/2 8 means 7.30 and not 8.30 (quite a few English speakers arrive at appointments an hour late because of this distinction).

ELECTRICITY

The electric current is 220 V, 50 Hz, and the socket used is the two-pin variety.

WEIGHTS & MEASURES

Hungary uses the metric system.

BOOKS & MAPS

Books are good value in Hungary and many titles are available in English. While visiting Budapest be sure to pick up an indexed city map at a bookshop.

The *Magyarország Autóatlasza* (Cartographia, Budapest) contains twenty-three 1:360,000 road maps of Hungary plus small street maps of almost every village and town in the country. The complete index makes this a valuable reference for motorists or anyone spending much time in the country. Cartographia also publishes a yellow *Budapest Guide* with 38 maps of the city, a street index and descriptive information in English.

You won't find a better guidebook than Lonely Planet's *Hungary, a travel survival kit* by Steve Fallon; *Hungary: The Rough Guide* by Dan Richardson is also excellent. Hungarian bookshops should have *Budapest, A Critical Guide* by Andras Torok – highly recommended.

Hungary by Paul Ignotus (Ernest Benn, London, 1972) is a good history of the country which is often available at libraries. Ignotus presents the country's history in a very personal way by constantly referring to Hungarian literature.

A History of Modern Hungary by Jörg K Hoensch (Longman, London, 1988) covers the period from 1867 to 1986 in a balanced way. Reg Gadney's *Cry Hungary! Uprising 1956* (Weidenfeld & Nicolson, London, 1986) is an illustrated chronicle of the 13-day revolt. Nigel Swain's *Hungary: The Rise and Fall of Feasible Socialism* (Verso Publishers, London and New York) focuses on the events of 1989.

In his amusing little book *Do It Yourself, Hungary's Hidden Economy* (Pluto Press, London, 1981), János Kenedi describes the machinations he employed to build himself a house outside Budapest. Kenedi's gentle exposé of the foibles of human nature provides a delightful glimpse of everyday life as it was in communist Hungary.

MEDIA

Several English-language weekly newspapers are published in Budapest. The *Daily News* (Box 3, H-1426 Budapest) has been around since 1967, although it's only a weekly now. Even during the communist era the *Daily News* established a reputation for its candid, informative reporting – one of the first papers of the former-communist bloc to do so.

Budapest Week (Nagy Diófa utca 7, H-1072 Budapest) contains an 'About Town' section with a detailed calender of events, plus a complete listing of films in English showing at Budapest cinemas.

The Budapest Sun (Dózsa György út 84/a II, H-1068 Budapest) includes a 'Style' insert which is a complete travel guide to the city with up-to-date information on restaurants and clubs, plus another extensive weekly calender. A six-month subscription is US$70 in Europe or US$85 elsewhere (payment by Visa card accepted). Both the *Week* and the *Sun* also provide an interesting mix of local news and are well worth picking up.

The *Budapest Business Journal* is aimed at business people working in Budapest.

Two English-language magazines are *The Hungarian Quarterly* (Box 3, Budapest H-1426) and the *Hungarian Digest*.

FILM & PHOTOGRAPHY

All the major brands of film are readily available and you can have your film developed in one hour at a dozen locations in Budapest, including Kodak Express on Váci utca near Vörösmarty tér.

HEALTH

If you have a medical problem go to the county hospital *(megyei kórház)* in county seats or the town hospital *(városi kórház)* in smaller centres and ask for the outpatients clinic *(rendelő intézet)*. Hospitals also contain dental clinics.

First aid *(elsősegély)* attention in the case of an accident is free, but an examination *(orvosi vizsgálat)* by a doctor will be around US$15, an X-ray will cost US$10. First aid and ambulance service are free if your life is in danger or permanent bodily damage can result. Prescription drugs and all locally made medicines are inexpensive. A bilateral agreement between Britain and Hungary allows for free medical treatment for citizens of one country in the other.

Rather than trying to find your way in a large hospital where few people speak English, however, it's often simpler to go directly to a private general practitioner *(orvosi rendelő)*. Their offices usually display a red cross outside. Fees are still lower than in the West.

Thermal Baths

There are 154 thermal baths in Hungary, most of them open to the public. The Romans first developed the baths of Budapest, and the Turks and Habsburgs followed suit. The thermal lake at Hévíz is probably Hungary's most impressive spa, though public thermal pools at Budapest, Eger, Győr, Gyula, Harkány and Komárom are also covered in this book.

In Budapest, Danubius Travels (☎ 117 3652) beneath the elevated car park on Szervita tér can provide information about medical programmes at the spas and make reservations on the spot. For example, a stay at the Thermál Hotel in Hévíz begins at around US$522/812 single/double a week, including half-pension, medical examination, massage, sauna, use of thermal baths, fitness room etc. From mid-October to March prices are 25% lower.

WORK

Budapest is already saturated with English teachers but it's still possible to get teaching jobs in provincial centres. Don't expect to save up a lot of money for travelling this way; instead look upon it as a good excuse to spend a bit of time in one place getting to know about Hungary. To obtain a work permit you'll need copies of your birth certificate and school transcript or academic record officially translated into Hungarian (at US$10 a page). An AIDS test is also mandatory (free for ISIC student-card holders, otherwise about US$25). Your prospective employer must write a letter in Hungarian explaining why they are hiring you and not a Hungarian. Language schools often advertise in the English-language newspapers and making the rounds should produce leads. Your embassy may also have suggestions where you could apply.

ACTIVITIES

Water sports are concentrated around Balaton Lake, especially sailboarding at Balatonszemes and Killiántelep, and sailing at Balatonalmádi and Balatonboglár. Sailing boats and sailboards can be hired at many points around the lake. Motorboats are banned on the lake, so water-skiing is only possible at the FICC Rally Campground, Balatonfüred, where skiers are towed around a course by a moving cable.

Canoeing

There are many possibilities for canoeing or kayaking on the rivers of Hungary. The journey down the Danube from Rajka to Mohács (386 km) is fairly obvious but there are smaller, less congested waterways. For example, you can go down the 205 km of the Rába River from Szentgotthárd (on the Austrian border) to Győr. From Csenger near the far-eastern tip of Hungary, you can paddle down the Szamos and Tisza rivers to Szeged (570 km). A shorter trip would be from Gyula or Békés to Szeged (210 km) via the Koros and Tisza rivers. All of these places have train stations, making it easy to come and go, and there are many other possibilities.

Cycling

The possibilities for cyclists are many. The slopes of northern Hungary can be challenging, whereas Transdanubia is much gentler and the Great Plain monotonously flat (and in summer, hot). When planning your route, be aware that cycling is forbidden on motorways and main highways with a single-digit route number. Cycling is allowed on highways with two-digit numbers, although three-digit highways are preferable, as traffic is much lighter there. Bicycle touring is becoming very popular among Hungarians, which makes it all the nicer.

HUNGARY

The following train stations rent bicycles at US$3 for one day, US$4 for two days or US$5 for three days: Balatonaliga, Balatonalmádi, Balatonföldvár, Balatonfüred, Balatonlelle, Balatonmáriafürdő, Balatonszemes, Keszthely, Köszeg, Lébény-Mosonszentmiklós, Mosonmagyaróvár, Nagymaros, Nagymaros-Visegrád, Öttevény, Siófok, Szántód-Kőröshegy, Szécsény, Zamárdi and Zánka-Köveskál.

The Magyar Természetbarát Szövetség (Hungarian Nature-Lovers' Federation), Bajscy-Zsilinszky út 31, 2nd floor, suite 3, Budapest, sells a useful cycling atlas entitled *Hungary by Bicycle* for US$3.

Hiking

Though Hungary doesn't have high mountains, you can enjoy good hiking in the forests around Aggtelek, Visegrád and Badacsony. North of Eger are the Bükk Mountains and south of Kecskemét the Bugac puszta, both national parks with marked hiking trails. Before you go there, pick up detailed hiking maps in Budapest as these are not always available locally.

Horse Riding

The Hungarians have a passion for horses that goes back over 1000 years and the sandy puszta seems almost made for horse riding. To get in some horse riding yourself, contact Pegazus Tours (☎ 117 1644), Ferenciek tere 5, H-1053 Budapest. The staff speak English. Pegazus works with several ranches and can make advance reservations for rooms (about US$50/75 single/double with half-board in midsummer, less in the off season) and horses (US$10 an hour). Ask about the Sarlóspuszta Riding Centre at Tatárszentgyorgy between Budapest and Kecskemét (closed from November to February), one of Hungary's finest.

Going through Pegazus is the only sure way to arrange some riding because if you simply show up at a ranch in summer you may be told it's fully booked. It's cheaper, however, to ask staff at provincial tourist offices about riding possibilities in their area and then try to get them to call ahead to make reservations. Few of the ranches are on bus or train routes, however, so unless you have your own transport be prepared for some long taxi rides. Turn to the Bugac and Szilvásvárad entries in this chapter for more information on horse riding.

Courses

Each July and August, Debrecen University organises a summer school course on the 'Hungarian Language and Culture'. There are two-week, 60-hour and four-week, 120-hour courses. A programme of related events such as films, musical evenings, folk dancing and sightseeing accompanies the courses. Tuition, excursions and a tram pass are US$225 for two weeks or US$450 for four weeks, plus US$50 registration for either. Course materials are another US$50 to US$100. Accommodation in a three-bedded room with full board is US$125 for each two-week period. Applications close on 15 May. For advanced students, there's an 80-hour winter course (apply before 15 December). For more information, contact the Debreceni Nyári Egyetem (☎ /fax 52-329 117), Egyetem tér 1, H-4010 Debrecen, Hungary.

HIGHLIGHTS

Museums & Galleries

Budapest's Museum of Fine Arts shelters a huge collection of old master paintings. The Museum of Contemporary History in Budapest Castle mounts informative exhibitions on recent issues. Two galleries of note dedicated to individual Hungarian artists are the Kovács Margit Museum in Szentendre and the Csontváry Museum in Pécs.

Castles

Hungary's most famous castles are those which resisted being overwhelmed by Turkish armies: Eger, Kőszeg, Siklós and Szigetvár. Though in ruins, Visegrád Citadel symbolises the power of medieval Hungary.

Among Hungary's finest palaces are the Esterházy Palace at Fertőd, the Festetics Palace at Keszthely and the Széchenyi Mansion at Nagycenk.

Historic Towns

Many of Hungary's historic towns, including Eger, Győr, Sopron, Székesfehérvár and Veszprém, were rebuilt in the baroque style during the 18th century. Kőszeg is one of the few towns which retains a strong medieval flavour, and Szentendre on the Danube has a Balkan air. The greatest monuments of the Turkish period are in Pécs.

ACCOMMODATION

Camping

Hungary has from 140 to 150 camping grounds and these are the cheapest places to stay. Small, private camping grounds accommodating as few as six tents are usually preferable to the large, noisy, 'official' camping grounds. Prices vary from US$4 to US$12 for two adults at one, two and three-star camp sites. The sites around Balaton Lake are more expensive and an additional US$0.75 per person 'resort tax' is levied in some areas. Some sites on the Great Plain have poor drainage.

Most camping grounds open from mid-May to mid-September and rent small bungalows (from US$7) to visitors without tents. In midsummer the bungalows may all be taken, so it pays to check with the local tourist office before making the trip. Members of the International Camping & Caravanning Club (FICC) and holders of student cards usually get a 10% discount, although this varies. Freelance camping is prohibited.

Hostels & Student Dormitories

Despite the 23 hostels listed in the HI handbook, a YHA (Youth Hostels Association) card doesn't get you very far in Hungary. Excepting those in Budapest, most of the hostels are in places well off the beaten track which you're unlikely to visit unless you go there specifically because there is a hostel. The only year-round hostels are in Budapest.

Hostel beds cost about US$7 in Budapest and a bit less elsewhere. A YHA card is not required although you occasionally get 10% off with one. Some hostels give an additional 25% discount if you show a student card. Camping is not allowed. There's no age limit at the hostels, they remain open all day and are often good places to meet other travellers.

In July and August Hungary's cheapest rooms are available in vacant student dormitories where beds in double, triple and quadruple rooms begin around US$5 per person. There's no need to show a student or hostel card, and it usually won't get you any discount. Express offices can generally tell you which dormitories to try and they'll sometimes call ahead to reserve your bed. Most dorms will admit you without the mediation of Express, however, though it often seems to be at the discretion of the person holding the keys.

Tourist Hostels

There's another class of accommodation which is similar to Western hostels but not included in the HI handbook. A tourist hostel *(turistaszálló)* offers beds in separate dormitories for men and women. There are no rules (for example, there are no curfews, smoking and drinking are allowed in the rooms). Tourist hostels are found in many cities and most stay open all year. The overnight fee will be around US$3 and in winter you'll probably have a whole room to yourself.

Private Rooms

Private accommodation used to be the cheapest way to go in Hungary but high government taxation, agency commissions and inflation have caused private room prices to double and sometimes triple in recent years while hotel rates have remained more stable, making private rooms less of the good deal they once were. In many cases you can now get a room at a cheap hotel for close to what you'd pay to occupy the spare room in someone's flat. Rooms in student dormitories, hostels and bungalows at camping grounds are now often cheaper than private rooms.

Expect to pay from US$6 to US$15 single, US$10 to US$30 double depending on whether the room is 1st, 2nd or 3rd class. Private rooms at Balaton Lake are slightly more expensive. Single rooms are often hard to come by and you'll usually have to pay a 20% supplement if you stay only two or three nights.

Private rooms are assigned by travel agencies which take your money and give you a voucher bearing the address. The offices usually close at 4 pm on weekdays and 1 pm on Saturday, so you must arrive early. (Longer hours are common in summer.) If the first room you're offered seems too expensive, ask if they have a cheaper one. There are usually several agencies offering private rooms, so ask around if the price is higher than usual or the location inconvenient. The rooms only become available after 5 pm, so leave your bags at the station.

If you decide to take a private room, you'll share a house or flat with a Hungarian family. The toilet facilities are usually communal but otherwise you can close your door and enjoy as much privacy as you please. All 1st and some 2nd and 3rd-class rooms have shared kitchen facilities. In Budapest you may have to take a room far from the centre of town, but public transport is good and cheap.

In Budapest private individuals at the train stations or on the street in front of Ibusz offices may offer you an unofficial private room *(szoba)*. The prices these individuals ask are often higher than those asked at the agencies and you will have nowhere to complain in case of problems. Sometimes these people misrepresent the location or quality of their rooms to convince you to go with them. In resort areas watch for houses labelled *szobá kiado* or *Zimmer frei*, advertising the availability of private rooms.

Pensions

Small, privately owned pensions are popular with German-speaking visitors who like the personalised service and homy atmosphere. Most pensions have less than seven rooms and the restaurant that goes with them is their real moneymaker. Always ask to see the room first and ask if there is another if you're not completely satisfied as the rooms can vary considerably. Prices are about twice what you'd pay for a comparable private room (from US$25 double) but you can go straight there without wasting time at a travel agency and waiting until 5 pm.

You'll find pensions in main tourist areas like the Danube Bend, Balaton Lake, Sopron, and so on.

Hotels

Hungarian hotel rooms are usually more expensive than private rooms, but they are cheap by international standards (from US$12 single, US$15 double). A hotel may be the answer if you're only staying one night or if you arrive too late to get a private room. Two-star hotels usually have rooms with a private bathroom, whereas at one-star hotels the bathroom is usually down the hall.

If you want to be sure of finding accommodation in another Hungarian city, have a travel agency (such as Ibusz, Express, Cooptourist, Dunatours, Volántourist) reserve a hotel room for you. The staff will need a couple of days' notice, and in addition to the regular room rate you must pay the telex charges and a 10% commission. Still, if you're there in the busy summer season, it may be worth it.

FOOD

Hungary has a tasty national cuisine all of its own. Many dishes are seasoned with paprika, a red spice made from a sweet variety of red pepper which appears on restaurant tables beside the salt and pepper. Although paprika originated in Central America, the peasants of Szeged have been growing it since the early 18th century and it's now as important to Hungarian cuisine as the tomato is to Italian cuisine.

Hungarian goulash *(gulyás)* is a thick beef soup cooked with onions and potatoes. What we think of as goulash is here called *pörkölt*, meat stewed with onions and paprika. If sour cream is added to *pörkölt* it becomes *paprikás*. Pork is the most common meat dish. Cabbage is an important vegetable in Hungary, either stuffed in the Turkish fashion *(töltött káposzta)* or made into a thick cabbage soup *(káposzta leves)* that is popular among late diners. Other delicacies include goose-liver sandwiches and paprika chicken *(paprikás csirke)* served with tiny dumplings.

Fisherman's soup *(halászlé)* is a rich mixture of several kinds of boiled fish, tomatoes, green peppers and paprika. It's a full meal in itself. Balaton Lake pike *(süllő)* is generally served breaded and grilled.

Noodles with cottage cheese and tiny cubes of crisp fried bacon *(túrós csusza)* go well with fish dishes. Hungarian cream cheese *(körözött)* is a mixture of sheep cheese, paprika and caraway seeds. Strudel *(rétes)* is a typical layered pastry filled with apple, cherry, cabbage, curd or cheese. Look out for *lángos*, a huge Hungarian doughnut eaten with garlic salt, cheese and yoghurt.

Some dishes for vegetarians to request are *rántott sajt* (fried cheese), *rántott gomba* (fried mushrooms), *gomba leves* (mushroom soup), *gyümöles leves* (fruit soup), *sajtos kenyer* (sliced bread with melted cheese) and *túrós csusza* (cottage cheese crêpes). *Bab leves* (bean soup) sometimes contains meat. Pancakes *(palacsinta)* may be made with cheese *(sajt)*, mushrooms *(gomba)*, nuts *(dió)* or poppy seeds *(mák)*.

Of the two large supermarket chains, ABC and Csemege Julius Meinl, the latter is a bit more up-market and sometimes they sell take-away salads in plastic containers. Healthy brown bread is made from four to six different grains and is sprinkled with sesame, sunflower seeds and rolled oats. You can also find *kifli*, individual crescent rolls made from reform dough.

HUNGARY

Restaurants

Hungarian restaurants *(étterem* or *vendéglő)* are relatively inexpensive. Meal prices begin around US$2 in a self-service restaurant, US$3 in a local restaurant and US$6 in a tourist restaurant. Lunch is the main meal of the day. Some restaurants offer a set lunch or 'menu' on weekdays and this is usually good value. It consists of soup, a side salad, a main course and occasionally a dessert.

Restaurant menus are often translated into German and sometimes into English. The main categories are *levesek* (soups), *saláták* (salads), *előételek* (appetisers), *sajtok* (cheeses), *készéelek* (ready-to-serve meals which are just heated up), *frissensültek* (freshly prepared meals), *halételek* (fish), *szárnyasok* (poultry), *tészták* (desserts) – useful to know if you have to choose blindly from a Hungarian menu. If you're in a bit of a hurry, order something from the *készéelek* section and not a *frissensültek* dish which may take 20 minutes to prepare.

If garnishes *(köretek)* such as rice, pommes frites, *burgonya* (boiled potatoes) etc are individually listed in a separate section of the menu it probably means they're not included with the main plate and will cost extra, though the waiter should indicate this by asking which ones you want and not just add them to your order.

Occasionally, a sharp waiter will bring you a side salad or something else you didn't order with the intention of inflating your bill. If you don't really want it, just say *nem ezt rendeltem!* (I didn't order that!) and send it back. At other times you'll be charged extra for some dish you never got or a special brand of imported beer when all you wanted was ordinary Hungarian draught beer. If you ask for a *pohár* (glass) or a *korsó* (half-litre mug) by name and don't just say 'beer' they're less likely to try this trick. If the prices of the drinks aren't listed on the menu they'll be higher than you expect.

Always insist on seeing a menu with prices listed to get an idea how much your meal will cost and if you're sure a waiter is deliberately overcharging but it's only by 10 to 15%, just pay the exact amount without a tip and try not to let it spoil your meal. Some places add a 10% service charge to the bill which also makes tipping unnecessary. Honest, attentive waiters, on the other hand, deserve their 10% (tip as you pay). Mini rip-offs by waiters are routine at Budapest restaurants.

Many tourist restaurants feature Gypsy music after 6 pm and the musicians are accustomed to receiving tips. Give them 100 Ft and they'll move to the next table. At better restaurants it's obligatory to check in your coat (US$0.10).

A *csárda* is a traditional inn or tavern offering spicy fare and fiery wine. *Borozó* denotes a wine cellar, *söröző* a pub offering draught beer *(csapolt sor)* and sometimes meals. A *bisztró* is an inexpensive restaurant that is often self-service *(önkiszolgáló)*. *Büfés* are the cheapest places, although you may have to eat standing at a counter. Pastries, cakes and coffee are served at a *cukrászda*, while an *eszpresszó* is a café. A *bár* is a nightclub with music and dancing.

The Hungarian fast-food chains which sprang up in the 1980s are to be avoided for their dry, tasteless fare served on plastic plates. If there's anything worse than the US fast-food outlets it's City Grill, Dixie Chicken, Chips & Chicken and Paprika Aranybárány. In Hungary the ice cream is worth lining up for.

DRINKS

Hungarian wines match the cuisine admirably and the best wines have a Hungarian flag around the top of the bottle. The finest are those produced in the volcanic soils of Badacsony, Eger, Sopron and Tokaj. Southern Hungary (Pécs, Villány and Szekszárd) is also noted. One of the best Hungarian red wines is Egri Bikavér, and Tokaji Aszú is a very sweet golden-white wine of an almost liqueur consistency. Louis XIV of France called Tokaji Aszú 'the king of wines and wine of kings'. Medoc Noir is a strong, sweet red dessert wine. Others to watch for are Tihany Cabernet, Villány Pinot Noir, Soproni Kékfrankos, Badacsony Kéknyelű, Csopak Riesling and Móri Ezerjó (white). You can pick up a bottle of any of these at a local supermarket.

Also try the apricot, cherry or plum brandy *(pálinka)* which is to the Hungarians what schnapps is to the Germans. A shot before breakfast or dinner is in order. Mecseki and Hubertus are two Hungarian liqueurs.

Unicum, a semi-bitter herbal liqueur produced from 40 medicinal plants according to a secret recipe, has been the national drink of Hungary since 1790. Austrian emperor Joseph II christened the liqueur when he exclaimed *'Das ist ein Unikum!'* ('This drink is unique!'). Unicum comes in a round bottle and bears the brand name Zwack. It's not cheap: a 700-ml bottle costs US$12.

Though tourist restaurants often stock only Austrian beer as a way of justifying their high prices, Hungary does produce quality beer, one of the best of which is Dreher, brewed at Budapest. Many excellent German beers such as Kaiser are produced in Hungary under licence.

ENTERTAINMENT

Hungary is a paradise for culture vultures. In Budapest there are several musical events to choose from each evening and the best opera tickets seldom cost over US$10. Under the communists, culture was heavily subsidised by the state and many of the benefits remain. Unlike in Prague, tickets *are* available at normal prices and the friendly Hungarians usually go out of their way to help foreign visitors get seats. Besides the traditional opera, operetta and concerts, there are rock and jazz concerts, folk dancing, pantomime, planetarium presentations, movies, discos, floor shows and circuses to keep you smiling.

Excellent performances can also be seen in provincial towns such as Eger, Győr, Kecskemét, Pécs, Szeged, Székesfehérvár and Szombathely, all of which have fine modern theatres. Information about events is readily available at tourist offices. Some useful words to remember are *színház* (theatre), *pénztár* (ticket office) and *elkelt* (sold out).

In mid-June most theatres close for summer holidays, reopening in late September or October. Summer programmes especially designed for tourists, including operas, operettas and concerts, are twice as expensive as the programmes for regular subscribers in winter. On the other hand, there are many summer festivals from late June to mid-August, though the period from mid-August to late September is culturally dead.

Going to the movies in Hungary can be hit

HUNGARY

or miss as the programmes advertised outside may be coming attractions or even what's showing in some other cinema across town. To avoid unwelcome surprises, write down in Hungarian the name of the film you think you're going to see with a large question mark after it and show it to the ticket seller before you pay. Also be aware that many foreign films are dubbed into Hungarian, so again, try asking the ticket seller if the film is dubbed *(szinkronizált* or *magyarul beszélő)*, or only has Hungarian subtitles *(feliratos)* and retains the original soundtrack. If you and the clerk are unable to communicate, just wait at the ticket window until another patron comes along who either speaks a little English or is willing to try to understand. On the positive side, admission prices are extremely low in comparison with those in the West. The *Budapest Week* and the *Budapest Sun* provide comprehensive listings of what's on at Budapest's many cinemas with times, addresses and plot descriptions, but elsewhere around the country you're on your own. Unfortunately films by noted Hungarian directors like István Gaál, Miklós Jancsó, Zsolt Kezdi-Kovács, Károly Makk, Pál Sándor and István Szabó are likely to be in Hungarian with no subtitles (see them at a good art cinema at home).

THINGS TO BUY

Hungarian shops are as well-stocked as those in the West and the quality of the products is high. Food, alcohol, books and folk-music recordings are affordable and there is an excellent selection. Traditional products include folk-art embroidery and ceramics, wool carpets and wall hangings, bone lace, wooden toys, dolls, and Herend, Kalocsa or Zsolnay porcelain. If you might be interested in buying a painting, read Things to See in the Kecskemét section of this chapter.

Throughout Hungary, a Polish market is called a *Lengyel piac* though the vendors are as likely to be Ukrainians or Russians as Poles these days. These flea market-style events often occur in an open field near the edge of town and the locals usually know where.

In theory, visitors are only allowed to export US$50 worth of goods without receipts and not in commercial quantities. In practice, it's unlikely that you'll be asked to open your bags at the border. You can sometimes get a 25% discount from small private shops and street vendors if you offer to pay in cash hard currency, though you'll need small bills.

Getting There & Away

AIR

Malév Hungarian Airlines has direct flights to Budapest from Amsterdam, Athens, Beirut, Berlin, Brussels, Bucharest, Cairo, Cologne, Copenhagen, Damascus, Dresden, Frankfurt, Helsinki, Istanbul, Kaunas, Kiev, Larnaca, Leipzig, London, Madrid, Milan, Moscow, Munich, New York, Nuremberg, Paris, Prague, Rome, St Petersburg, Sofia, Stockholm, Stuttgart, Tel Aviv, Thessaloniki, Tirana, Trieste, Tunis, Vienna, Vilnius, Warsaw, Zagreb and Zürich.

Until recently Budapest's Ferihegy Airport handled all international flights but a new airport intended to receive tourist charters is under construction at Sármellék near Keszthely at the west end of Balaton Lake. There are no domestic flights in Hungary and there is no airport departure tax.

Malév has no student discounts on flights originating in Hungary but there is a youth fare available to persons aged 24 years or younger which is about 20% cheaper than the lowest discounted fare available to other passengers. It's available on one-way flights from Budapest: Amsterdam US$130, London US$190, New York US$385 high season, US$290 low season. Youth tickets to points in Europe can only be purchased one week in advance, to North America only three days in advance.

LAND

Budapest is well connected to all surrounding countries by road, rail, river and air. Trains arrive in Budapest from every neighbouring capital and in summer there's a hydrofoil service between Vienna and Budapest. Other major entry points by train are Sopron (from Vienna, Austria), Szombathely (from Graz, Austria), Pécs (from Zagreb, Croatia), Szeged (from Subotica, Yugoslavia), Miskolc (from Košice, Slovakia) and Sátoraljaújhely (from Slovenské Nové Mesto, Slovakia). By road there's bus service to/from all neighbouring countries, often the cheapest way to go. In Budapest, buses to/from Western Europe use the Erzsébet tér Bus Station while those serving Eastern Europe are from the Népstadion Bus Station.

Bus

To/From Western Europe There's a Eurolines bus service twice a week throughout the year from Rotterdam to Budapest via Amsterdam, Düsseldorf and Frankfurt/Main (1615 km, 24 hours, US$100 one way, US$162 return, with a 10% discount for those under 26 or over 59 years of age). From mid-June to mid-September the Amsterdam bus runs three times a week. Alternating services are operated by Dutch and Hungarian drivers. If you're a nonsmoker be sure to book the Hungarian bus as the Dutch drivers smoke continually and don't mind passengers following their example (whereas the Hungarian drivers don't allow smoking on their buses). Eurolines offers a special US$150 'Capital Tripper' fare to Amsterdam-Budapest-Prague-Amsterdam or vice versa. (A Slovak transit visa is required by some nationals.) The run from Amsterdam to Budapest is through Austria, so Czech and Slovak visas are not required. In Amsterdam tickets are sold by Budget Bus/Eurolines (☎ 020-627 5151), Rokin 10. In Budapest you can buy them at the Erzsébet tér Bus Station. In summer this bus is often full, so try to book ahead.

A similar service from Brussels to Budapest (1395 km, 20 hours, US$95 one way, US$157 return) also operates twice a week from June to September. Ask for information from the Europabus office (☎ 2-217 0025), Place de Brouckere 50, Brussels 1000.

Other international buses departing from Budapest's Erzsébet tér Bus Station include those to Florence (weekly, 1025 km, 17½ hours, US$62), Hamburg (two a week, 1215 km, 17 hours, US$79), Milan (two a week, 1080 km, 17 hours, US$65), Munich (three a week, 701 km, 10 hours, US$58), Paris (weekly, 1525 km, 23 hours, US$81), Prague (twice weekly, US$21), Rijeka (twice weekly, US$40), Rome (weekly, 1310 km, 22 hours, US$77) and Pula (weekly, US$40). It's best to reserve seats on these long-distance buses a few days in advance, especially in summer.

From June to September buses run between Budapest and London twice a week (1770 km, 29 hours, US$125 one way, US$200 return – half the price of a train ticket. In London check with National Express (☎ 0171-730 0202) at the Victoria Coach Station. In Paris enquire about Hungary-bound buses at the Gare Routiere Internationale Galliéni (☎ 4972 5151), Avenue du Général de Gaulle (metro: Galliéni).

A cheaper bus between London and Budapest is operated by Attila Tours (☎ /fax 0171-372 0470), suite 318, 36a Kilburn High Road, London NW6 5UA, departing from each end every Saturday morning (£60/100 one way/return). Smoking is not allowed on these buses. In Budapest, tickets are available from Attila Tours (☎ /fax 209 0923), suite 307, Karolina út 65 (tram No 49 from Deák tér to a railway bridge).

Also consider a low-cost bus tour with New Millennium Holidays (☎ 0121-711 2232), 20 High St, Solihull, West Midlands B91 3TB, England, UK. They have all-inclusive departures year-round to Alsópáhok near Keszthely.

To/From Austria Three buses travel daily between Vienna's Autobusbahnhof Mitte and Budapest's Erzsébet tér Bus Station, departing from Vienna at 7 am and 5 and 7 pm and from Budapest at 7 am, noon and 5 pm daily (254 km, US$23 one way, US$34 return). Smoking is not allowed on these buses. In Budapest you can make enquiries at the Erzsébet tér Bus Station and in Vienna at Blaguss Reisen (☎ 0222-50 1800), Wiedner Hauptstrasse 15, or at Autobusbahnhof Wien-Mitte.

To/From Romania The cheapest and easiest way by far to go from Hungary to Romania is by bus from Budapest's Népstadion Bus Station, Hungária körút 48-52 (metro: Népstadion). There are buses to Oradea/Nagyvárad (daily, 260 km, six hours, US$10), Arad (six a week, 276 km, seven hours, US$12), Timişoara/Temesvár (weekly, 327 km, eight hours, US$14), Cluj-Napoca/Kolozsvár (daily, 413 km, 9½ hours, US$19) and Brasov/Brassó (six a week, 790 km, 17½ hours, US$31). A return ticket is about 50% more than a one-way ticket.

The international ticket window at Népstadion Bus Station is open weekdays from 5.30 am to 6 pm, Saturday until 4 pm. On Sunday try paying the driver. The clerks at Népstadion speak no English, so study the posted timetables and then write down what you want. In this section the Hungarian names of the Romanian cities in question are provided as these are the ones you'll see written on the timetables. Tickets are easily purchased with forint – forget the train on these routes! Be aware, however, that there can be long delays at highway border crossings into Romania, though it's worse westbound than eastbound.

You will also find daily buses from Szeged to Arad (106 km, US$5) and Timişoara (157 km).

To/From Slovakia & Poland The bus from Budapest to Bratislava/Pozsony (200 km, US$9) runs only once a week (currently on Friday). More useful are the buses to Tatranská Lomnica/Tatralomnic (twice a week, 311 km, seven hours, US$13) and Zakopane (twice a week, US$15), on opposite sides of the Tatra Mountains, a route poorly served by train. The buses to Zakopane go via either Trstená (344 km, eight hours) or Łysa Polana (364 km, nine hours). All these leave from Népstadion Bus Station in Budapest.

To/From Former Yugoslavia & Turkey Other useful international buses from Népstadion Bus Station include those to Subotica/Szabatka, Yugoslavia (daily, 216 km, US$9) and Istanbul, Turkey (five a week, 1375 km, 25 hours, US$50). Tickets to Istanbul must be purchased with cash dollars and Romanian and Bulgarian transit visas are required. From Harkány, 22 km south of Pécs, you can catch a bus to Belgrade (US$19) three times a day.

You'll find frequent buses to Croatia and Slovenia from towns along the border, such as those from Pécs to Osijek (twice daily, 82 km, US$7), Barcs to Zagreb (five a day, 202 km, US$14), Nagykanizsa to Zagreb (twice daily, 176 km, US$9) and Lenti to Ljubljana (twice weekly, 235 km, five hours, US$12). With the border between Yugoslavia and Croatia closed, people from former Yugoslavia are forced to transit Hungary with bus changes in these towns.

Train

International railway fares from Hungary to other Eastern European countries are now from 10 to 15 times higher than they were in 1989. For instance, in 1989 a 1st-class fare from Budapest to Berlin cost US$10. Now you'll pay US$85 to cover the same distance in 2nd class. Similarly, from Budapest to Prague now costs US$55 in 2nd class, one way, compared with only US$6 in 1st class previously. Fares to Romania have also jumped spectacularly, making it essential to break your journey in border towns like Oradea or Arad if you're really serious about saving money. This is more of a problem if you buy your ticket in Hungary as tickets from Romania to Hungary are much cheaper: from Budapest to Bucharest is US$84 whereas from Bucharest to Budapest is US$31. This could change.

Other sample one-way 2nd-class train fares from Budapest are US$40 to Arad, US$27 to Belgrade, US$23 to Bratislava,

US$85 to Bucharest, US$22 to Košice, US$39 to Kraków, US$26 to Oradea, US$29 to Vienna, US$55 to Warsaw and US$30 to Zagreb. Bulgaria-bound, a ticket from Budapest to Sofia via Belgrade is US$54 but via Bucharest it's US$117! Before investing in a train ticket to any of these places, check the price of a bus along the same route. Train tickets to Western Europe have always been highly expensive. For example, from Budapest to Amsterdam is US$207 one way in 2nd class.

You can usually pay for international train tickets with Hungarian forint if you have an exchange receipt bearing your passport number. Otherwise hard currency in cash may be required (this seems to vary). The student travel agency Express has Eurotrain fares to Western Europe for persons aged under 26 years and 50% reductions to Eastern Europe for ISIC student-card holders (no student discounts to Western Europe). Inter-Rail passes (available only to European residents) are accepted in Hungary.

Hungarian students get a 33% discount on train journeys wholly within Hungary and it's sometimes possible to get such reduced tickets at Ibusz offices and train stations. If you do get such a reduction, the conductor will probably insist that you pay the 33% on the train and fine you US$3 for trying to use an invalid ticket. We've heard from several readers who had this experience.

Eurail passes are accepted in Hungary but it's almost impossible to use the train enough inside the country to get your per diem Eurail cost out of it. A good plan is to finish or begin your Eurail pass here, thus saving on high international fares to Western Europe while not having to count your days in Hungary. MÁV Hungarian Railways, Andrássy út 34, Budapest, can sell you a Eurail pass but at prices even higher than those charged outside Europe (see Getting There & Away in the main introduction to this book).

If you want to make a long trip across Western Europe, a much better deal than the Eurail pass is a regular one-way 2nd-class ticket. International train tickets are valid for two months and unlimited stopovers are allowed. For instance, if you pay US$220 to travel from Budapest to Lisbon you can have a leisurely two-month trip stopping in Vienna, Venice, Milan, Nice and Salamanca or anywhere else along that direct route you'd care to visit without any additional train costs. It costs US$300 to go via Vienna, Salzburg, Munich, Paris and Salamanca. After seeing Portugal you could buy another one-way ticket to some other remote corner of Europe and have a different two-month trip.

Unless otherwise stated, all of the 'name trains' listed following operate daily throughout the year and reservations are usually required. Second-class couchettes and 1st-class sleepers are almost always available. Though most of these trains have dining cars they're expensive, so take along some food and drink. Trains which originate in Hungary are less likely to be delayed than those transiting the country. Local unreserved trains are cheaper and easier if you just want to get across the border.

To/From Western Europe From Vienna, there are eight express trains a day to Budapest-Keleti via Hegyeshalom (270 km, three hours). These include the *Liszt Ferenc* from Dortmund (1365 km, 15 hours) via Nuremberg, the *Orient-Expressz* from Paris (1662 km, 21 hours) via Munich and the *Wiener Walzer* from Basel (1219 km, 15 hours) via Innsbruck, all via Vienna Westbahnhof. The Eurocity *Lehár* arrives at Budapest-Déli from Vienna Südbahnhof. In Vienna ask about special half-price return tickets between Vienna and Budapest on the *Lehár*. Seat reservations are not required on these trains but they're highly recommended unless you want to stand.

Several unreserved local trains travel between Vienna-Südbahnhof and Sopron (84 km, 1½ hours, US$10) via Wiener Neustadt or Ebenfurth. Sometimes you must change trains in these towns. One local train runs between Graz, Austria, and Szombathely (146 km, four hours) though there are six other trains if you change at Szentgotthárd, the Hungarian border station.

To/From Prague & Berlin From Prague to Budapest (616 km, nine hours) there's the *Pannónia* express train. From Berlin-Lichtenberg (993 km, 15 hours) to Budapest via Prague and Bratislava there are the daily *Hungária* and *Metropol* express trains which terminate in Hungary. The *Balt-Orient* and *Meridian* express trains also travel to Budapest from Berlin-Lichtenberg, Prague and Bratislava, then continue on to Romania or Bulgaria.

To/From Slovakia & Poland The *Báthory* express train runs daily from Warsaw to Budapest (837 km, 13 hours) via Katowice and Trenčín. The *Polonia* express train travels between Warsaw and Budapest via Žilina and Banská Bystrica. From western Poland there's the *Bem* express train to Budapest from Szczecin, Poznań and Wrocław via Trenčín. The *Varsovia* express train arrives from Gdynia/Gdańsk. These trains transit the Czech Republic as well as Slovakia, so beware of taking them if you require a Czech visa as the Czech border guards will put you off the train. Instead catch the *Cracovia* express train from Kraków to Budapest (599 km, 12 hours) via Košice and Miskolc which crosses eastern Slovakia.

The *Rákóczi* express train also runs from Košice to Budapest (270 km, 4½ hours) with an extension to/from Poprad-Tatry in summer. The two local trains a day between Košice and Miskolc (88 km, three hours) require no reservations. Otherwise, there are six unreserved local trains a day from Sátoraljaújhely, Hungary, to Slovenské Nové Mesto, Slovakia. These connect with trains to/from Miskolc on the Hungarian side and to/from Košice on the Slovak side.

To/From Romania & Bulgaria From Bucharest to Budapest (874 km, 15 hours) the *Balt-Orient, Dacia* and *Pannónia* express trains all travel via Arad. The *Karpaty* express train passes Arad, Szolnok, Miskolc and Košice on its way to Warsaw. The *Ovidius* express train runs from Constanţa to Budapest (1068 km, 17½ hours). Via Oradea, there's the *Claudiopolis* from Cluj-Napoca to Budapest (402 km, 7½ hours) and the *Corona* from Braşov to Budapest (1002 km, 14 hours).

Two local Hungarian trains a day also run between Oradea and Budapest-Nyugati (249 km, five hours, US$26 eastbound, US$18 westbound) and these are useful as no reservations are required. At last report their departure times were 6.05 am and 3.00 pm from Budapest-Nyugati and 7.27 am and 3.27 pm from Oradea. If coming from Romania, buy your open ticket from Oradea to Budapest at a CFR train ticket office well ahead (but not in Bucharest), as such tickets are not sold at Oradea Railway Station.

To/From Former Yugoslavia From Budapest to Croatia there are the *Adriatica, Agram, Drava* and *Maestral* express trains to Zagreb (394 km, seven hours) via Siófok. None of these are very convenient as they all put you in expensive Zagreb at odd hours. The *Drava* at least gets there in the early afternoon and conveys carriages to/from Ljubljana (500 km, 7½ hours) and Rome (25 hours).

A useful daily service connects Pécs directly to Zagreb (267 km, five hours, US$16), departing from Pécs in the early morning, Zagreb in the afternoon. Local trains run between Gyékényes and Koprivnica (15 km, 20 minutes, US$3) three times a day and between Nagykanizsa and Varaždin (72 km, 1½ hours) twice daily. None of these trains require reservations.

Yugoslavia-bound, you can take the *Avala, Beograd, Balkán, Hellas* and *Meridian* express trains from Budapest to Belgrade (354 km, six hours) via Subotica. The *Meridian* continues to Sofia (771 km, 15 hours) via Belgrade. Local unreserved trains shuttle between Szeged and Subotica (45 km, 1½ hours, US$2) three times a day.

To/From Moscow & China In the past, Star Tours (☎ 113 7062), József körút 45, Budapest, has sold tickets for the Trans-Siberian Railway, charging US$160/200 in 2nd/1st class from Budapest to Moscow (2110 km, two days) and US$350/440 from Moscow to Beijing (7865 km, five days). Payment in cash hard currency is required. In normal times they can make reservations for the Moscow-Beijing portion and you should be able to arrange everything in a week to 10 days.

Once you have your train ticket and reservations you can apply for a Chinese tourist visa (allow three days for processing), then a Russian transit visa (US$60) which you may be able to get in one day. If time is short, ask for the Russian train via Manchuria which eliminates the need for a Mongolian transit visa (another three days' processing). Three-day Ukrainian transit visas are usually available at the border for US$50.

If you want to stop in Moscow for a few days Star Tours can make the necessary reservations at US$60/70 single/double a night and up, payable in advance in cash. All transportation and hotel bookings must be confirmed before you can begin visa hunting. With Russia in political and economic chaos, it's often impossible for agencies like Star Tours to book any train travel to China at all, so it's much better to plan on doing the trans-Siberian trip westbound rather than eastbound (in other words, beginning in China itself).

Ibusz sells regular 2nd-class train tickets from Budapest to Kiev for US$102, to Moscow for US$136, but they cannot sell tickets to China. (In 1989 a 1st-class ticket from Budapest to Beijing with a sleeper was only US$90 total.)

Car & Motorbike

Some highway border crossings are only open to citizens of Hungary, Slovakia, Romania, Croatia and Yugoslavia but the crossings mentioned here (listed clockwise around the country) are open to everyone. In each case the name of the Hungarian border post is provided.

To/From Slovakia The border crossings are at Rajka (16 km south-east of Bratislava), Vámosszabadi (13 km north of Győr), Komárom (opposite Komárno), Parassapuszta (80 km north of Budapest via Vác), Balassagyarmat, Somoskőújfalu (just north of Salgótarján), Bánréve (45 km north-west of Miskolc), Tornyosnémeti (21 km south of Košice) and Sátoraljaújhely (opposite Slovenské Nové Mesto).

To/From Ukraine You may cross at Záhony (opposite Cop).

To/From Romania You have a choice of Csengersima (11 km north-west of Satu Mare), Ártánd (14 km north-west of Oradea), Gyula (66 km north of Arad) and Nagylak (between Szeged and Arad).

To/From Former Yugoslavia There are border crossings at Roszke (between Szeged and Subotica), Tompa (11 km north-west of Subotica) and Hercegszántó (32 km south of Baja).

To/from Croatia there's Drávaszabolcs (eight km south of Harkány), Barcs (right on the Dráva River), Berzence (23 km west of Koprivnica) and Letenye (between Nagykanizsa and Varaždin).

To/from Slovenia there's Rédics (eight km south-west of Lenti) and Bajánsenye (west of Zalaegerszeg).

To/From Austria You can cross at Rábafüzes (five km north of Szentgotthárd), Bucsu (13 km west of Szombathely), Kőszeg, Kópháza (just south of Sopron), Sopron (61 km south of Vienna) and Hegyeshalom (70 km south-west of Vienna).

On Foot

If you want to avoid the hassle or expense of getting an international train ticket, you can easily walk across the Danube bridge on the Hungarian/Slovak border at Komárom/Komárno, 100 km south-east of Bratislava. See the Komárom section in this chapter for details.

To/from Romania, the easiest place to cross on foot is Nagylak/Nădlac between Szeged and Arad. There are nine unreserved local trains a day from Szeged to Nagylak (47 km, 1¼ hours) near the border. After crossing into Romania you must walk or take a taxi six km to Nădlac, where you'll find four local trains a day to Arad (52 km, 1½ hours). See the Szeged section of this chapter for more information.

Slovenia-bound, take a train from Budapest to Zalaegerszeg (252 km via Tapolca, four hours by express train), then one of eight daily trains from Zalaegerszeg to Rédics (49 km, 1¼ hours) which is only two km from the main highway border crossing into Slovenia. From the border it's an interesting five-km downhill walk through Lendava to Lendava Bus Station where you'll have a choice of six daily buses to Ljubljana (204 km) and many more to Maribor (92 km).

RIVER

Hydrofoil

Hydrofoil service on the Danube from Budapest to Vienna operates daily from April to mid-October, twice daily from May to mid-September (282 km, 5½ hours). Fares are high at US$68 one way, US$100 return, but ISIC student-card holders get a 20% discount and children aged 15 years and under get a 50% discount. Eurail pass holders also pay 50%. Taking along a bicycle costs US$9 each way.

Bring along something to eat and drink and arrive early to get a good seat. The fare is supposed to include lunch but a favourite trick of the crew is to announce after departure that there wasn't time to load the food and then hand out small refunds. A short while later they're back selling sandwiches and drinks, but for a higher price.

In Vienna tickets are available from the Mahart Agency (☎ 1-505 5644 or 505 3844), Karlsplatz 2/8, A-1010 Vienna. In Budapest tickets are sold at the hydrofoil terminal on the river between the Erzsébet (Elizabeth) and Szabadság bridges or at Ibusz, Károly körút 3.

HUNGARY

Getting Around

BUS

Hungary's bright yellow Volán buses are a good alternative to the trains and bus fares are only about 15% more expensive than comparable 2nd-class train fares (expect to pay around US$1.50 an hour or US$3.75 per 100 km).

Taking buses is essential for crossing the southern part of the country, for instance, from Szombathely to Keszthely, Kaposvár, Pécs and Szeged. For short trips in the Danube Bend or Balaton Lake areas, buses are recommended. If you have a front seat, you'll see more from the bus than you would from the train, though you may be a little cramped. Seats on Volán buses are spaced far enough apart for you to be able to fit your pack between your knees, however. Tickets are usually available from the driver, but ask at the station to be sure. There are sometimes queues for intercity buses so it's wise to arrive at the bus stop early.

Bus timetables are clearly posted at stations and stops. Some footnotes you could see include *naponta* (daily), *hétköznap* (weekdays), *munkanapokon* (on workdays), *munkaszüneti napok kivételével naponta* (daily except holidays), *szabadnap kivételével naponta* (daily except Saturday), *szabad és munkaszüneti napokan* (on Saturday and holidays), *munkaszuneti napokan* (on holidays), *iskolai napokan* (on school days) and *szabadnap* (on Saturday).

TRAIN

The MÁV (Magyar Államvasutak) operates comfortable, reliable and not overcrowded railway services on 7769 km of track. Second-class train fares in Hungary are US$1.50 for 50 km, US$3.25 for 100 km, US$6.50 for 200 km or US$11.75 for 500 km. First class is 50% more but there's no price difference for express or local train tickets. You must watch out for express trains with compulsory seat reservations indicated on the timetables by an 'R' in a box. Seat reservations for these cost US$0.35 in the station or US$3.50 from the conductor. If you buy your ticket on the train rather than in the station, there's an additional US$2.50 surcharge.

An unlimited travel pass for all trains in Hungary is available at US$44/65 2nd/1st class for seven days, US$65/98 for 10 days. Reservation charges are additional, and since reservations are required on many express trains, this expensive pass doesn't give you the flexibility you might expect. It would only pay for itself if you stayed in Budapest and made a return trip to the farthest corners of the country every day.

If you'll be using trains extensively, you can buy a complete Hungarian timetable *(menetrend)* with an explanation of the symbols in a number of languages, including English, for US$3.50.

In all Hungarian train stations a yellow board indicates departures *(indul)* and a white board arrivals *(érkezik)*. Express trains are indicated in red, local trains in black. In some stations, large black-and-white schedules are plastered all over walls. To locate the table you need, first find the posted railway map of the country, which indexes the route numbers at the top of the schedules.

All train stations have left-luggage offices, many of which stay open 24 hours a day. You often have to go and pay the fee (US$0.70) at another office *(pénztár)*. A few large bus stations also have luggage rooms, but they generally close by 6 pm.

Routes

Most railway lines converge on Budapest. Some typical journeys with distances and travelling times by express train are Budapest to Győr (138 km, two hours), Sopron (210 km, three hours), Szombathely (236 km, 3½ hours), Pécs (229 km, three hours), Kecskemét (106 km, 1½ hours), Szeged (191 km, 2½ hours) and Miskolc (182 km, two hours). Some shorter trips by local train are Budapest to Székesfehérvár (67 km, one hour), Veszprém (112 km, two hours) and Siófok (115 km, two hours).

CAR & MOTORBIKE

The available fuels are 86 octane (normal), 92 octane (super), 98 octane (extra), 95 octane (Eurosuper unleaded) and diesel. A map indicating where unleaded fuel *(olommentes uzemanyag)* can be purchased should be posted at all filling stations. Stations selling unleaded petrol often display a white sign with a blue border on which a green and black petrol pump appears. Some station attendants try to make foreigners pay for fuel in hard currency but this is not compulsory and petrol coupons have been abolished. In the past fuel has been readily available. You're not allowed to enter Hungary with extra fuel in a spare tank.

The 24-hour all-Hungary number for road assistance is ☎ 088. The breakdown service for foreigners provided by the Magyar Autóklub is at ☎ 115 1220 (answered in English 24 hours a day).

Road Rules

Speed limits for cars are 60 km/h in built-up areas, 80 km/h on main roads, 100 km/h on highways and 120 km/h on motorways. For motorbikes the speed limit is the same as for cars except in built-up areas where the limit is 50 km/h. The beginning of a built-up area is indicated by a white rectangular sign bearing the town or village's name. At the end of the built-up area there's another such sign with a red diagonal line through the name. A green flashing light at intersections is the equivalent of a yellow warning light in other countries. Traffic is restricted in central Budapest and parking fees at garages in the city centre are high, so use public transport.

Rental

The Budapest addresses of Avis, Budget, EuroDollar, Europcar, Hertz and a few local car rental companies are listed under Getting Around in the Budapest section of this chapter.

To rent a car from Avis and Hertz is very expensive, beginning at US$38 plus US$0.38 a km, or US$118 a day with unlimited mileage for the cheapest car. Collision damage waiver (CDW) insurance is US$10

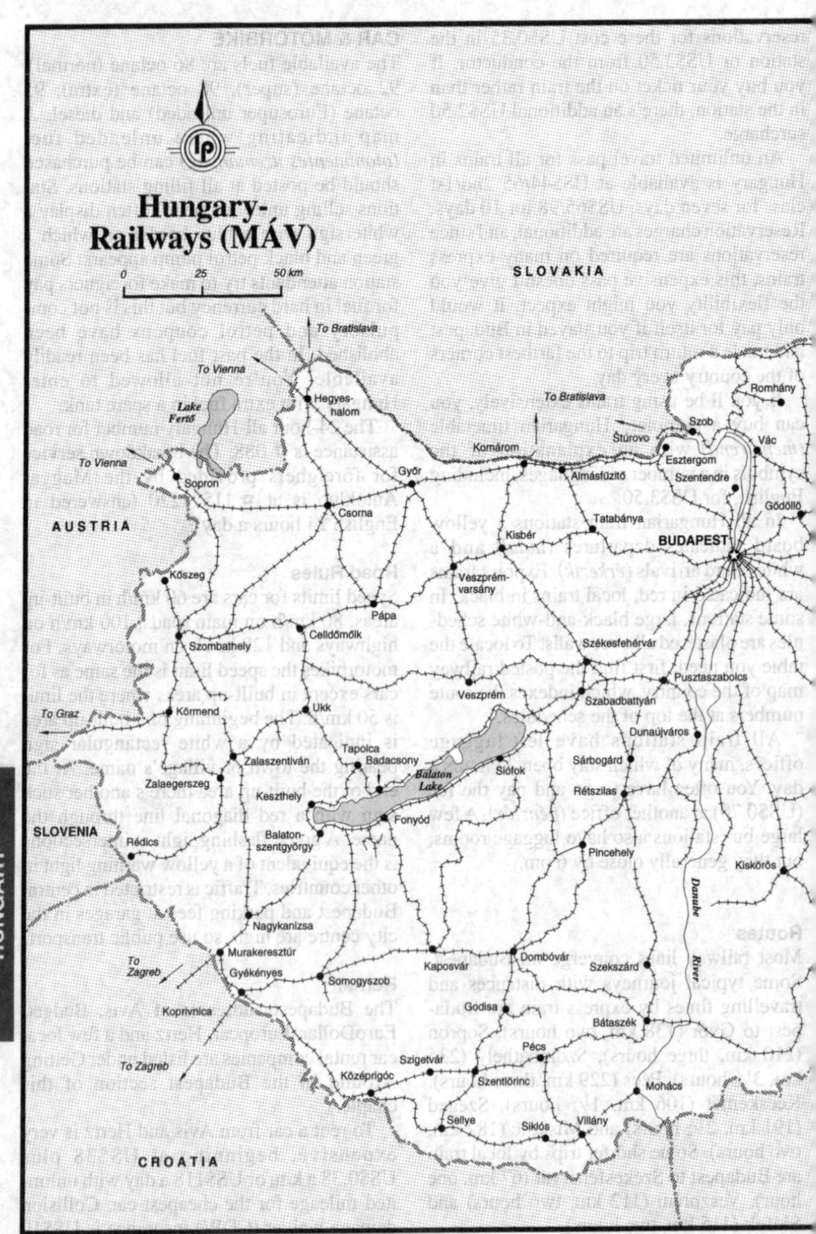
Hungary-
Railways (MÁV)
0
25
50 km
SLOVAKIA
AUSTRIA
SLOVENIA
CROATIA
To Bratislava
To Vienna
To Vienna
To Bratislava
To Graz
To Zagreb
To Zagreb
Lake Fertő
Hegyes-
halom
Sopron
Győr
Csorna
Komárom
Almásfüzitő
Štúrovo
Szob
Esztergom
Vác
Szentendre
Gödöllő
Romhány
Tatabánya
Kisbér
BUDAPEST
Veszprém-
varsány
Pápa
Kőszeg
Celldömölk
Szombathely
Székesfehérvár
Veszprém
Szabadbattyán
Pusztaszabolcs
Körmend
Ukk
Tapolca
Badacsony
Balaton
Lake
Siófok
Dunaújváros
Zalaszentiván
Zalaegerszeg
Keszthely
Fonyód
Sárbogárd
Rétszilas
Balaton-
szentgyörgy
Rédics
Pincehely
Kiskőrös
Danube
River
Nagykanizsa
Murakeresztúr
Gyékényes
Somogyszob
Kaposvár
Dombóvár
Szekszárd
Koprivnica
Godisa
Bátaszék
Pécs
Szigetvár
Középrigóc
Szentlőrinc
Mohács
Sellye
Siklós
Villány
HUNGARY

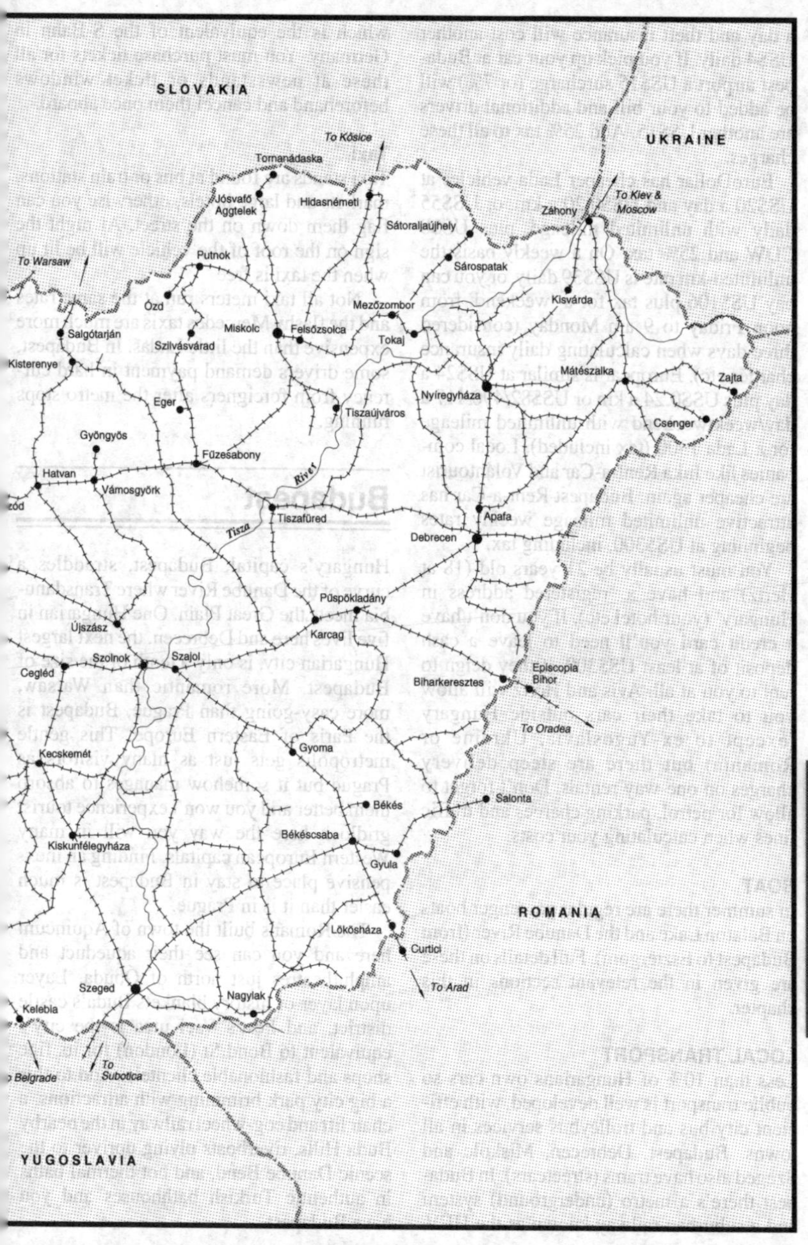
SLOVAKIA
UKRAINE
ROMANIA
YUGOSLAVIA
To Kósice
To Kiev & Moscow
To Warsaw
To Oradea
To Arad
To Subotica
Belgrade
Tornanádaska
Jósvafő Aggtelek
Hidasnémeti
Sátoraljaújhely
Sárospatak
Záhony
Kisvárda
Putnok
Ózd
Mezőzombor
Miskolc
Felsőzsolca
Tokaj
Salgótarján
Szilvásvárad
Kisterenye
Eger
Tiszaújváros
Nyíregyháza
Mátészalka
Zajta
Csenger
Gyöngyös
Füzesabony
Hatvan
Vámosgyörk
Tiszafüred
Tisza
River
Apafa
Debrecen
Püspökladány
Újszász
Karcag
Szolnok
Szajol
Cegléd
Biharkeresztes
Episcopia Bihor
Kecskemét
Gyoma
Békés
Salonta
Békéscsaba
Kiskunfélegyháza
Gyula
Lőkösháza
Curtici
Szeged
Nagylak
Kelebia
HUNGARY

a day and theft insurance will cost another US$4 daily. If you pick up your car at Budapest airport a US$15 surcharge (or 7%) will be added to your bill and additional drivers are another US$15. Add 25% tax to all these charges.

EuroDollar has cheaper Lada vehicles at US$20 a day and US$0.20 a km, or US$55 daily with unlimited mileage, plus US$8 CDW and 25% tax. On a weekly basis the unlimited-km rate is US$39 daily, or you can pay US$106 plus tax for a 'weekend' from noon Friday to 9 am Monday (considered three days when calculating daily insurance charges etc). Europcar is similar at US$24 a day plus US$0.24 a km or US$82/490/117 a day/week/weekend with unlimited mileage for a Lada 1300 (tax included). Local companies like Inka Rent-a-Car and Volántourist are cheaper again. Budapest Rent-a-Car has attractive unlimited mileage weekly rates beginning at US$300, including tax.

You must usually be 21 years old (18 at Hertz) and have a 'registered address in Hungary' (your hotel etc). If you don't have a credit card you'll need to leave a cash deposit of at least US$300, if they deign to rent to you at all. Avis and Hertz will allow you to take their cars outside Hungary (except to ex-Yugoslavia, Ukraine or Romania) but there are steep delivery charges on one-way rentals. Don't forget to allow for petrol, parking charges and traffic fines when calculating your costs.

BOAT

In summer there are regular passenger boats on Balaton Lake and the Danube River (from Budapest to Esztergom). Full details on these are given in the relevant sections in this chapter.

LOCAL TRANSPORT

Less than 10% of Hungarians own cars so public transport is well developed, with efficient city bus and trolleybus services in all towns. Budapest, Debrecen, Miskolc and Szeged also have trams (streetcars). In Budapest there's a metro (underground) system and a suburban railway known as the HÉV, which is the equivalent of the S-Bahn in Germany. You must purchase tickets for all these at newsstands or ticket windows beforehand and cancel them once aboard.

Taxi

Taxi stands are found at bus or train stations, markets and large hotels, otherwise you can flag them down on the street. At night the sign on the roof of the vehicle will be lit up when the taxi is free

Not all taxi meters run at the same rates and the flashy Mercedes taxis are much more expensive than the little Ladas. In Budapest, some drivers demand payment in hard currency from foreigners after the metro stops running.

Budapest

Hungary's capital, Budapest, straddles a curve of the Danube River where Transdanubia meets the Great Plain. One Hungarian in five lives here and Debrecen, the next largest Hungarian city, is only a tenth of the size of Budapest. More romantic than Warsaw, more easy-going than Prague, Budapest is the Paris of Eastern Europe. This gentle metropolis gets just as many visitors as Prague but it somehow manages to absorb them better and you won't experience tourist gridlock here the way you will in many Western European capitals. Finding an inexpensive place to stay in Budapest is much easier than it is in Prague.

The Romans built the town of Aquincum here and you can see their aqueduct and amphitheatres just north of Óbuda. Layer upon layer of history blankets Buda's castle district, and Pest's Váci utca is the city's equivalent to Bond St (London) for its fine shops and fashionable clientele. Add to this a big city park brimming with attractions, a chair lift and cog-wheel railway in the nearby Buda Hills, riverboats plying upriver to the scenic Danube Bend, and hot thermal baths in authentic Turkish bathhouses and you have Budapest.

The city has many fascinating aspects. Eastern Europeans come here to make money or get a taste of the West, while we Westerners revel in the nightlife, theatres, museums, restaurants and cafés. It's hard to get enough of Budapest. As the river descends from the Black Forest to the Black Sea, few cities are more striking than this 'Queen of the Danube'. Stay for a week or two, and when you leave there'll be one more person in love with Budapest.

Orientation

Budapest is 249 km south-east of Vienna, exactly halfway between Sofia and Berlin. The Danube is Budapest's main street, dividing historic Buda from commercial Pest (in Vienna the river is several km north-east of the centre). All eight bridges which cross the Danube at Budapest were destroyed in the war and later rebuilt. Most visitors will arrive at one of the three main train stations, Keleti (east), Nyugati (west) and Déli (south), all on the metro lines which converge at Deák tér on the northern edge of the city centre's shopping area. For information on left-luggage facilities at these stations see Train Stations under Getting There & Away following.

From Deák tér, Andrássy út (Budapest's Broadway because of its many theatres) runs north-east to City Park, while Károly körút, Múzeum körút and Vamház körút swing around to the Szabadság híd (bridge) and Gellért Hill. Important crossroads in the city are Baross tér before Keleti Railway Station, Blaha Lujza tér where Rákóczi út meets Erzsébet körút, and Moszkva tér just north of Déli Railway Station and Castle Hill. Óbuda is at the western end of the Árpád híd north of Buda, and Aquincum is north of the Árpád híd.

Information

Your best source of general information about Budapest and Hungary is Tourinform (☎ 117 9800), Sütő utca 2 (metro: Deák tér), which is open daily from 8 am to 8 pm. If your question is about train tickets and times, however, you'll get better answers at the nearby Ibusz offices at Károly körút 3/c (upstairs) or Károly körút 21.

The main Ibusz office, at Ferenciek tere 5 (metro: Ferenciek tere), supplies free travel brochures and the staff are very good about answering general questions. They also change money and rent private rooms.

Assistance for motorists is available at the Magyar Autóklub (☎ 115 1220), Rómer Flóris utca 4/a off Margit körút near Margit híd. A Magyar Autóklub travel agency is at Visegrádi utca 17 near Nyugati Railway Station.

Money As elsewhere in Hungary, the Orszagos Takarékpenztár, or OTP Bank, changes travellers' cheques without commission (get there at least an hour before closing to be sure the foreign exchange counter will still be open).

The OTP branch closest to Keleti Railway Station is at Rákóczi út 84 (open Monday 8.15 am to 6 pm, Tuesday, Wednesday and Thursday until 3 pm, Friday until 1 pm). The small private exchange office just inside Europa Cinema, Rákóczi út 82, often gives a better rate than the bank for cash, so check (open weekdays 9 am to 6 pm, weekends until 1 pm). The Ibusz office right inside Keleti Railway Station itself also changes travellers' cheques at a good rate weekdays from 8 am to 6.30 pm, Saturday until 1 pm.

The OTP branch with foreign exchange facilities closest to Nyugati Railway Station is at Tátra utca 10 (Monday 8.15 am to 6 pm, Tuesday to Thursday until 3 pm, Friday until 1 pm). The Ibusz Bank beside platform No 10 inside Nyugati (weekdays 8 am to 6 pm, Saturday until 3 pm) gives a good rate for travellers' cheques.

The OTP branch closest to Déli Railway Station is at Alagút utca 3, on the corner of Attila út (Monday to Thursday 8.15 am to 3 pm, Friday until 1 pm). Window No 4 in the Ibusz office downstairs at the entrance to the metro in Déli Railway Station (weekdays 8 am to noon and 12.45 to 6 pm, Saturday 8 am to 1 pm and 2 to 3 pm, Sunday 9 am to 12.30 pm) changes travellers' cheques without commission.

Near Erzsébet tér Bus Station is the OTP Bank, József nádor tér 10-11 (Monday 8.15 am to 6 pm, Tuesday to Thursday until 3 pm, Friday until 1 pm). The closest OTP branch to Deák tér is at Károly körút 1 (Monday to Thursday 8.15 am to 3 pm, Friday until 1 pm) (metro: Astoria).

The Ibusz Hotel Service, Petőfi tér 3 (metro: Ferenciek tere), changes travellers' cheques 24 hours a day at a rate only 2% lower than the bank rate.

The Kereskedelmi Bank, Váci utca 40 (Monday to Thursday 8 am to 1 pm, Friday until noon), will change dollar travellers' cheques into dollars cash for 3% commission. On the side of their building is a zany automat which changes the banknotes of 15 countries into forint 24 hours a day.

Another automatic currency exchange machine is outside the Kereskedelmi Bank, Károly kőrút 20 between Deák tér and Astoria.

The American Express office (☎ 251 0010) at Deák Ferenc utca 10, a block up from Vörösmarty tér towards Deák tér, changes its own travellers' cheques at a rate 3% lower than the banks. To convert US dollar travellers' cheques into dollars cash here costs 6% commission.

Ibusz at Keleti Railway Station will change excess forints back into hard currency if you have exchange receipts, but you will lose about 7%.

A few flashy private exchange offices around town deduct exorbitant 10% commissions. Others have huge signs reading 'no commission' but the 10% is already deducted from their rate. See Money in the chapter introduction for a warning about them. Most of the people offering to change money on the street are thieves.

Post & Telephone The main post office is at Petőfi Sándor utca 13 near Deák tér. Poste restante is held in a small office beside the post office boxes here (open weekdays from 8 am to 8 pm). You can mail parcels from a room on the opposite side of the main counters from poste restante and they sell boxes of varying sizes. The post office at Teréz körút

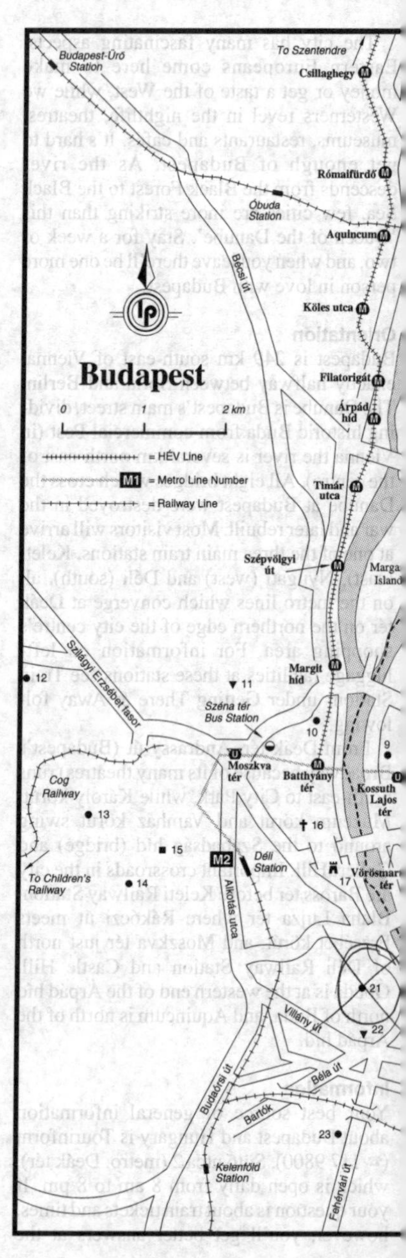

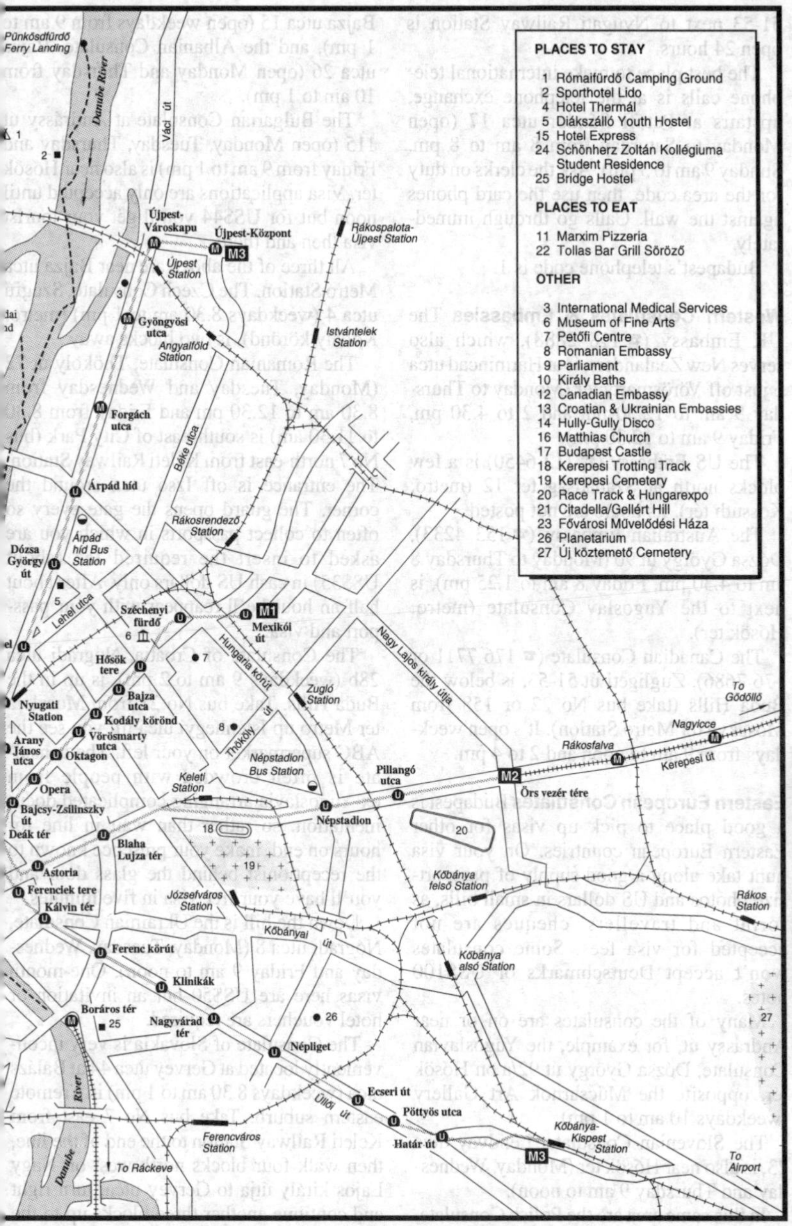
PLACES TO STAY
1 Rómaifürdő Camping Ground
2 Sporthotel Lido
4 Hotel Thermál
5 Diákszálló Youth Hostel
15 Hotel Express
24 Schönherz Zoltán Kollégiuma Student Residence
25 Bridge Hostel
PLACES TO EAT
11 Marxim Pizzeria
22 Tollas Bar Grill Söröző
OTHER
3 International Medical Services
6 Museum of Fine Arts
7 Petőfi Centre
8 Romanian Embassy
9 Parliament
10 Király Baths
12 Canadian Embassy
13 Croatian & Ukrainian Embassies
14 Hully-Gully Disco
16 Matthias Church
17 Budapest Castle
18 Kerepesi Trotting Track
19 Kerepesi Cemetery
20 Race Track & Hungarexpo
21 Citadella/Gellért Hill
23 Fővárosi Művelődési Háza
26 Planetarium
27 Új köztemető Cemetery
Pünkösdfürdő Ferry Landing
Danube River
Váci út
Újpest-Városkapu
Újpest-Központ
M3
Rákospalota-Újpest Station
Újpest Station
Gyöngyösi utca
Angyalföld Station
Istvántelek Station
Forgách utca
Béke utca
Árpád híd
Rákosrendező Station
Árpád híd Bus Station
Dózsa György út
Lehel utca
Széchenyi fürdő
M1
Mexikói út
Nagy Lajos király útja
Hősök tere
Hungária körút
Bajza utca
Zugló Station
Nyugati Station
Kodály körönd
Vörösmarty utca
Thököly út
To Gödöllő
Nagyicce
Rákosfalva
Kerepesi út
Arany János utca
Oktogon
Népstadion Bus Station
Pillangó utca
M2
Örs vezér tére
Opera
Keleti Station
Bajcsy-Zsilinszky út
Népstadion
Deák tér
Blaha Lujza tér
Astoria
Ferenciek tere
Kálvin tér
Józsefváros Station
Kőbánya felső Station
Rákos Station
Kőbányai út
Ferenc körút
Kőbánya alsó Station
Klinikák
Boráros tér
Nagyvárad tér
Népliget
Ecseri út
Üllői út
Pöttyös utca
Ferencváros Station
Határ út
Kőbánya-Kispest Station
To Ráckeve
To Airport
Danube River

HUNGARY

51-53 next to Nyugati Railway Station is open 24 hours.

The best place to make international telephone calls is at the telephone exchange, upstairs at Petőfi Sándor utca 17 (open Monday to Saturday from 8 am to 8 pm, Sunday 9 am to 3 pm). Ask the clerks on duty for the area code, then use the card phones against the wall. Calls go through immediately.

Budapest's telephone code is 1.

Western Consulates & Embassies The UK Embassy (☎ 118 2888), which also serves New Zealanders, is at Harmincad utca 6 just off Vörösmarty tér (Monday to Thursday 9 am to 12.30 pm and 2 to 4.30 pm, Friday 9 am to 12.30 pm).

The US Embassy (☎ 112 6450) is a few blocks north at Szabadság tér 12 (metro: Kossuth tér). Its hours are not posted.

The Australian Embassy (☎ 153 4233), Dózsa György út 90 (Monday to Thursday 8 am to 4.30 pm, Friday 8 am to 1.25 pm), is next to the Yugoslav Consulate (metro: Hősök tér).

The Canadian Consulate (☎ 176 7711 or 176 7686), Zugligeti út 51-53, is below the Buda Hills (take bus No 22 or 158 from Moszkva tér Metro Station). It's open weekdays from 9 am to noon and 2 to 4 pm.

Eastern European Consulates Budapest is a good place to pick up visas for other Eastern European countries. On your visa hunt take along a good supply of passport-size photos and US dollars in small bills, as forint and travellers' cheques are not accepted for visa fees. Some consulates won't accept Deutschmarks or US$100 notes.

Many of the consulates are on or near Andrássy út, for example, the Yugoslavian Consulate, Dózsa György út 92/a on Hősök tér, opposite the Műcsarnok Art Gallery (weekdays 10 am to 1 pm).

The Slovenian Consulate, Lendvay utca 23, is also near Hősök tér (Monday, Wednesday and Thursday 9 am to noon).

In this same area are the Polish Consulate, Bajza utca 15 (open weekdays from 9 am to 1 pm), and the Albanian Consulate, Bajza utca 26 (open Monday and Thursday from 10 am to 1 pm).

The Bulgarian Consulate at Andrássy út 115 (open Monday, Tuesday, Thursday and Friday from 9 am to 1 pm) is also near Hősök tér. Visa applications are only accepted until noon but for US$44 you'll get your tourist visa then and there.

All three of the above are near Bajza utca Metro Station. The Czech Consulate, Szegfű utca 4 (weekdays 8.30 am to 1 pm) (metro: Kodály körönd), is two blocks away.

The Romanian Consulate, Thököly út 72 (Monday, Tuesday and Wednesday from 8.30 am to 12.30 pm and Friday from 8.30 to 11.30 am) is south-east of City Park (bus No 7 north-east from Keleti Railway Station. The entrance is off Izsó utca around the corner. The guard opens the gate every so often to collect passports in which you are asked to insert the required fee (about US$35) in cash US dollars only. After about half an hour he'll reappear with your passport and visa.

The Consulate of Croatia, Nógrádi utca 28b (weekdays 9 am to 2 pm), is up in the Buda Hills. Take bus No 21 from Moszkva tér Metro up Istenhegyi utca till you see the ABC supermarket on your left. The consulate is often crowded with people from ex-Yugoslavia arranging complicated documentation, so rather than wait in line for hours on end, make your presence known to the receptionist behind the glass door and you'll have your free visa in five minutes.

Down the hill is the Ukrainian Consulate, Nógrádi utca 8 (Monday, Tuesday, Wednesday and Friday 9 am to noon). One-month visas here are US$50 but an invitation or hotel vouchers are required.

The Consulate of Slovakia is very inconveniently located at Gervey utca 44 at Balázs utca (weekdays 8.30 am to 1 pm) in a remote eastern suburb. Take bus No 7 east from Keleti Railway Station to the end of the line, then walk four blocks north-west on Nagy Lajos király útja to Gervey utca, turn right and continue another three blocks up to the consulate. This location is so poor it's hard to believe they'll stay there for long, so you might check the address with Tourinform before making the long trip out. Otherwise call them at ☎ 251 7973. They charge Australians US$20, Canadians US$45.

Trans-Siberian Consulates If you decide to take the Trans-Siberian Railway east from Budapest to China or Japan, you'll need a Russian transit visa. The Russian Consulate, Andrássy út 104 (open Monday, Wednesday and Friday from 10 am to 1 pm), takes a week or more to issue tourist visas (transit visas are quicker). You must have confirmed transportation reservations right through the Russian Federation, plus accommodation vouchers for each night to be spent in a Russian city.

The Chinese Embassy, Benczúr utca 17 – entry from Bajza utca (Monday, Wednesday and Friday from 2.30 to 5 pm), is only a block from the Russian Consulate. You must get your Chinese visa first.

If you take the Chinese train from Moscow to Beijing, you'll also need to visit the Mongolian Embassy in the Buda Hills at Bogár utca 14/c (bus No 11 from Batthyány tér Metro to the Bayer Hungaria building on Törökvész út). (The Russian train to Beijing doesn't pass through Mongolia.)

Travel Agencies The MÁV Hungarian Railways office, Andrássy út 35 (metro: Opera), has international train tickets and can make advance seat reservations for domestic express trains at the same price you'd pay at the station.

Skip the queue at MÁV by going to Ibusz, upstairs at Károly körút 3/c (metro: Astoria or Deák tér), which sells the same tickets and can also make seat reservations. Another Ibusz office at Károly körút 21 also has international train tickets and information. Ibusz sells international tickets for the same prices charged at the train stations and they're more likely to speak English and be helpful.

Express (☎ 111 6418), Zoltán utca 10 (metro: Kossuth tér), open Monday to Thursday from 8.30 am to 4.30 pm, Friday until 3 pm, sells Eurotrain tickets with a 30% discount on fares to Western Europe to persons under the age of 26. Express also has student fares with reductions of 25 to 50% on rail travel to other Eastern European countries. Another Express office at Semmelweis utca 4 (metro: Astoria) and Wasteels next to track No 9 at Keleti Railway Station also sells these tickets. You must have an ISIC card to get the student fare (no student fares are available on domestic tickets).

Keep in mind that all international train tickets must be paid for in cash hard currency unless you have an exchange receipt.

Express, Semmelweis utca 4, and the Express office at Keleti Railway Station sell the ISIC student card (US$3) but you must provide two photos and proof that you really are a student.

Panoráma Travel, Nyugati tér 7 (metro: Nyugati), has a bus to Munich four times a week (US$34). Other Panoráma buses run less frequently to Padua (US$35), Paris (US$64), Rimini (US$39), Stuttgart (US$55) and Zürich (US$66).

Kenguru (☎ 138 2019), Kőtfaragó utca 15 (Monday to Saturday 8 am to 6 pm) (metro: Blaha Lujza tér), arranges paid rides in private cars to many Western European cities. You pay the agency's fee plus a contribution to fuel costs. Sample charges are US$53 to Athens, US$36 to Berlin, US$62 to Amsterdam or Brussels, US$66 to Paris and US$73 to London. It's more pleasant than a long bus ride if you connect with the right driver. Enquiries from car drivers looking for paying passengers are most welcome here.

Jade Tours Imperial (☎ 112 8671) at Nyugati Railway Station (opposite Ibusz) offers organised sightseeing tours of Budapest and day trips to Balaton Lake and the Great Plain.

The Chosen Tours (☎ 166 5165) offers morning and afternoon tours focusing on Budapest's Jewish heritage daily except Saturday from mid-April to October. The 2½-hour ghetto walking tour (US$10) includes a stop at a kosher pastry shop while the 3½-hour bus tour (US$20) shows you

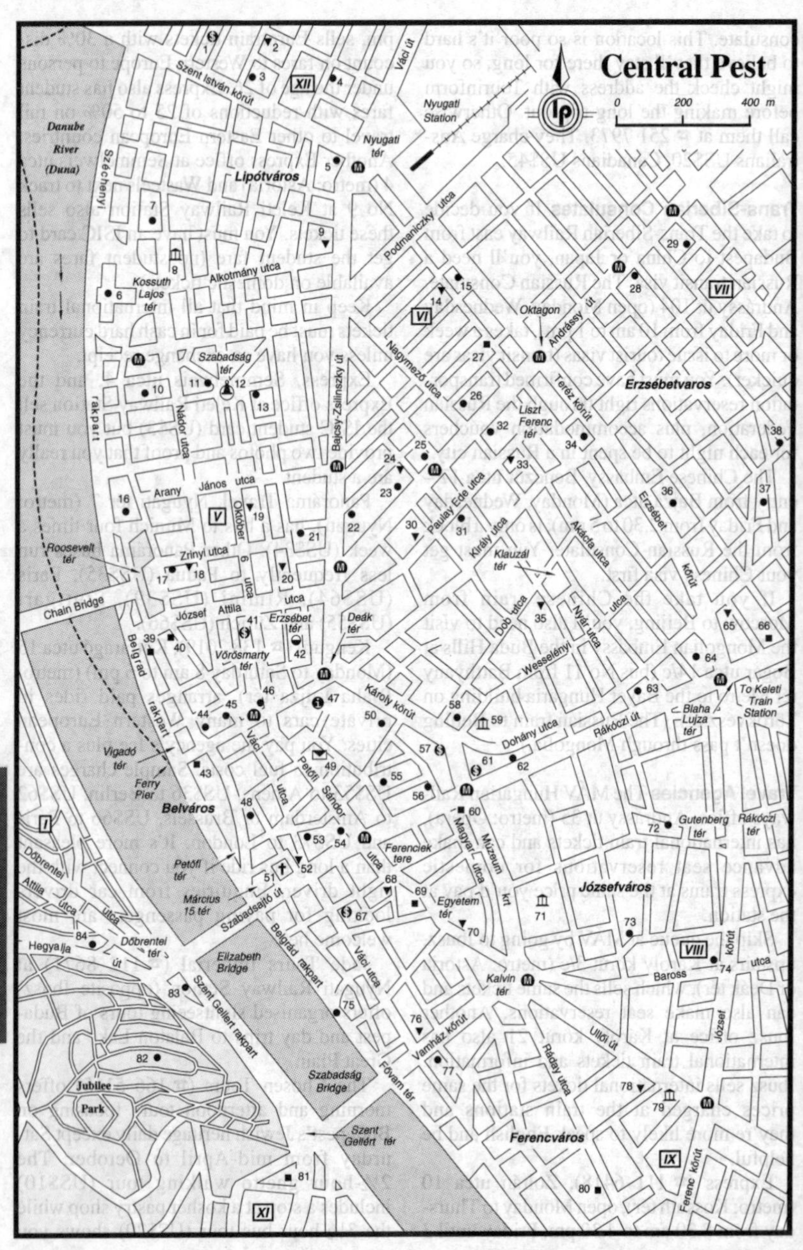
Central Pest
0
200
400 m
Danube River (Duna)
Széchenyi rakpart
Szent István körút
Váci út
XII
Nyugati Station
Nyugati tér
Lipótváros
Podmaniczky utca
Alkotmány utca
Kossuth Lajos tér
Szabadság tér
Nádor utca
Bajcsy-Zsilinszky út
VI
Nagymező utca
Oktagon
Andrássy út
VII
Erzsébetvaros
Teréz körút
Liszt Ferenc tér
Paulay Ede utca
Király utca
Akácfa utca
Erzsébet körút
Klauzál tér
Dob utca
Nyár utca
Wesselényi utca
Arany János utca
V
Október 6 utca
Roosevelt tér
Zrínyi utca
Chain Bridge
József Attila utca
Erzsébet tér
Deák tér
Vörösmarty tér
Belgrád rakpart
Károly körút
Dohány utca
Rákóczi út
To Keleti Train Station
Blaha Lujza tér
Vigadó tér
Ferry Pier
Belváros
Váci utca
Petőfi Sándor utca
Magyar utca
Múzeum krt
Gutenberg tér
Rákóczi tér
Józsefváros
I
Döbrentei
Attila út
Petőfi tér
Március 15 tér
Ferenciek tere
Egyetem tér
Szabadsajtó út
Hegyalja út
Döbrentei tér
Elizabeth Bridge
Szent Gellért rakpart
Kalvin tér
VIII
Baross utca
József körút
Üllői út
Ráday utca
Vámház körút
Fővám tér
Szabadság Bridge
Jubilee Park
Szent Gellért tér
Ferencváros
IX
Ferenc körút
XI

HUNGARY

PLACES TO STAY

27 Medosz Hotel
39 Forum Hotel
40 Atrium Hyatt Hotel
43 Duna Marriott Hotel
60 Astoria Hotel
66 Metropol Hotel
69 Ottó & Viktor's Hostel (Summer Only)
80 Strawberry Hostel (Summer Only)
81 Gellért Hotel

PLACES TO EAT

2 La Pampa Restaurant
9 Semiramis (Arab Restaurant)
14 Karcsi Ételbár
18 Duna Palota
19 Kisharang Étkezde
20 Number One Espresso
24 Morrison's Bar
30 Bohémtanya Vendéglő
33 No 1 Falafel Faloda
35 Salom Restaurant
52 Bölcs Bagoly Önkiszolgáló Étterem
65 Café New York
68 Vegetárium Restaurant
70 Alföldi Kisvendéglo
76 Stop Étterem
78 Kaltenberg Söröző

OTHER

1 OTP Bank
3 Vígszínház (Comedy Theatre)
4 Autóklub Travel Agency
5 Panoráma Travel
6 Parliament
7 Cooptourist
8 Ethnographical Museum
10 Express (Train Tickets)
11 Express (Youth Hostel Bookings)
12 Soviet Army Memorial
13 American Embassy
15 Volántourist
16 Academy of Sciences
17 Budapest Tourist
21 St Stephen's Basilica
22 Dunatours
23 Központi Jegyiroda (Ticket Office)
25 State Opera House
26 Fővárosi Operett Színház
28 Puppet Theatre
29 Czech Republic Embassy
31 Arany János Theatre
32 MÁV Hungarian Railways Office
34 Academy of Music
36 Madách Theatre
37 Szabadidőközpont (Almássy Cultural Centre)
38 National Theatre
41 OTP Bank
42 Erzsébet tér Bus Station
44 Pesti Vigadó
45 Jegyiroda Országos Filharmonia
46 American Express
47 Tourinform
48 Ibusz 24-Hour Office
49 Main Post Office
50 Merlin Jazz Club
51 Inner-City Parish Church
53 International Bookstore
54 Ibusz (Private Rooms)
55 Town Hall
56 Express (Main Office)
57 Kereskedelmi Bank
58 Ibusz (Train Tickets)
59 Jewish Museum
61 OTP Bank
62 Patyolat Laundromat
63 Map Store
64 Maxim Variete Night Club
67 Kereskedelmi Bank
71 National Museum
72 Kenguru Ride Service
73 Tilos Á Kávéház
74 Star Tours
75 Hydrofoil Terminal
77 Old Pest Market Hall
79 Museum of Applied Arts
82 Citadella
83 Rudas Baths
84 Rác Baths

the city through Jewish eyes. For Jews of Hungarian descent, The Chosen organises genealogical research and cemetery visits. The easiest way to make contact is by calling the number provided above (English is spoken).

Laundry Patyolat, Rákóczi út 8 (weekdays 7 am to 7 pm, Saturday until 1 pm) (metro: Astoria), is a self-service laundromat where you can wash up to five kg for US$3, plus another US$1 to dry. Laundry soap is supplied. Patience and the assistance of the women working here are required.

Another self-service laundromat is Mosoda, József nádor tér 9 (metro: Vörösmarty tér) (Monday, Wednesday and Friday 7 am to 3 pm, Tuesday and Thursday 11 am to 7 pm). This one has the advantage of a nice park opposite where you can sit and wait.

Bookshops Bestsellers, Október 6 utca 11 (metro: Arany János), specialises in books and magazines in English. Their slogan is, 'If we don't have it, we can order it'.

For general reading material in English, try the Antikvárium, Ferenciek tere 3 (metro: Ferenciek tere). Two second-hand bookshops which are even better are at Múzeum körút 15 and 35 near the National Museum (metro: Kálvin tér).

The International Bookstore, Váci utca 32 (metro: Ferenciek tere), has travel guidebooks and maps, plus Hungarian and foreign art books. You can buy Lonely Planet titles there.

In the arcade at Petőfi Sándor utca 2 is a bookshop which stocks maps of cities all across Europe. The newsstand at Petőfi Sándor utca 17 has English newspapers.

There's a self-service map shop at Nyár utca 1 (metro: Blaha Lujza tér). Another map shop with different maps is at Bajcsy-Zsilinszky út 37 (metro: Arany János utca).

Emergency International Medical Services (☎ 129 8423), Váci út 202 (metro to Újpest-Városkapu, then walk about three blocks south), is a private medical clinic open 24 hours a day. On the outside this place looks like a factory with two stone statues of workers standing watch. General examinations cost around US$28 from 8 am to 8 pm or US$39 from 8 pm to 8 am. Home visits are US$55. Common X-rays average US$16. The British Embassy refers people here and English is spoken.

A dental clinic specialising in treating foreigners is Dental Express (☎ 142 4257), Városligeti fasor 32 (metro: Bajza utca), open weekdays from 9 am to 7 pm.

If you need to register with the police or want to report a lost passport or visa, go to the foreigners' police at Andrássy út 12 (metro: Opera). It's open on Monday from 8.30 am to noon and 2 to 5 pm, Tuesday, Wednesday and Friday from 8.30 am to noon and Thursday from 2 to 5 pm. Ask about visa extensions here. English is spoken. To report accidents, crime or theft (for insurance purposes) you must go to the main police station at Deák Ferenc utca 16-18 near Deák tér (daily 8 am to midnight). Bring along a translator if you can.

Things to See

Buda Most of Budapest's medieval vestiges are in Castle Hill (Várhegy), the castle district of Buda. The easiest way to get there is to take the metro to Moszkva tér, cross the bridge above the square and continue straight up Várfok utca to Várhegy's **Vienna Gate**. A minibus marked 'Budavari Sikló' follows this same route from the bridge, shuttling every few minutes from Moszkva tér to Budapest Castle. Get off at the stop just after the Vienna Gate. Once through the gate, take a sharp right on Petermann biró utca past the National Archives to Kapisztrán tér. The **Magdalen Tower** is all that's left of a Gothic church destroyed in the last war. The white neoclassical building facing the square is the **Museum of Military History** (free Saturday), which you enter from the ramparts side straight ahead.

Walk south-east along Tóth Árpád sétány, the ramparts promenade, enjoying the views of the Buda Hills. The long black-and-white building below you is Budapest's Déli Railway Station. Halfway along the ramparts you'll catch a glimpse of the neo-Gothic tower of **Matthias Church** up Szentháromság utca. The church (rebuilt in 1896) has a colourful tiled roof outside, colourful murals inside and a museum which you enter through the crypt. Franz Liszt wrote the *Hungarian Coronation Mass* for the 1867 coronation here of the Austrian king Franz Josef and his wife Elizabeth as king and queen of Hungary. Organ concerts are held in the church on Sunday at 7 pm every couple of weeks throughout the year. Behind the Matthias Church is an equestrian statue of St Stephen (977-1038), Hungary's first king, and alongside the statue is the **Fisherman's Bastion**, a late 19th-century structure which offers great views of the parliament building and the Danube River.

From the **plague column** (1713) in front of Matthias Church, Tárnok utca runs south-east to the gate of the **Palace of Buda Castle**. The palace enjoyed its greatest splendour under King Matthias in the second half of the 15th century. Since then it has been destroyed and rebuilt three times, the last after WW II. Today the palace contains two important museums. The **National**

Gallery (free Saturday) has a huge collection of Hungarian works of art from Gothic to contemporary. The historical paintings by Mihály Munkácsy are worth noting. The **Historical Museum** (closed Tuesday, free Wednesday) shelters objects discovered during the recent reconstruction of the palace, plus a good overall display on Budapest through the ages.

From the castle terrace take the **funicular railway** (US$1) or walk down to the vehicular tunnel under Castle Hill at the Buda end of the **Chain Bridge** (Lánchíd), which was opened in 1849 and was the first bridge to be built across the Hungarian section of the Danube. In the park in front of the lower funicular station is the **Zero Kilometre Stone** for all highway distances in Hungary.

Go through the small pedestrian tunnel under the end of the Chain Bridge and take tram No 19 south along the right bank of the Danube. Get off at Móricz Zsigmond körtér, the second stop beyond the Gellért Hotel (1918). Walk back a little, round the corner to the left and board bus No 27 at Villányi út 5. This bus will take you right up to the Citadella on Gellért Hill.

A commanding fortress, the **Citadella** (now a hotel) was built by the Austrians in 1854 to control the rebellious Hungarians. The **Statue of Liberty** at the southern end of the Citadella commemorates the Soviet soldiers who died to liberate Hungary in 1945. The bronze soldier statue was pulled down during the 1956 uprising but replaced a year later. You'll see your most memorable views of Budapest and the Danube from this hill. At night with the city all lit up below you the views are rather spectacular. You can easily walk down from the Citadella to the Gellért Hotel.

Pest Industrialisation allowed Budapest to develop rapidly during the late 19th century and one of the nicest places to get a feeling for this period is **City Park**, north-east of the centre. Take the metro to Széchenyi Fürdő. This line, the oldest underground railway on the Continent, opened in 1896. You'll come out of the station right in the middle of the park beside the **Municipal Baths** (1913), behind which are an **amusement park**, the **Grand Circus** and the **zoo** (closed on Monday in winter).

Cross the busy boulevard to the south-east and you'll come to **Vajdahunyad Castle** (1896), a fascinating hotchpotch of replicas of actual buildings, many of them in what is now Romania. The **Agricultural Museum** (free on Tuesday) is housed in the castle (there's also a snack bar inside).

City Park's dominant feature is **Hősök tér** with a great monument erected in 1896 for the millennium of the Magyar conquest of Hungary. The Tomb of the Unknown Soldier is also here. On the south-east side of the square is the **Műcsarnok Art Gallery**, the most prestigious in the city, where important contemporary art shows are held (presently closed for reconstruction). On the other side of the square is the **Museum of Fine Arts** (1895), one of the richest of its kind in Europe (free Saturday). Here you'll see Hungary's major collection of foreign art, with prints and ancient sculpture on the ground floor, and European paintings on the 1st floor. The collection of Spanish paintings is one of the best outside Madrid.

From Hősök tér stately Andrássy út runs straight into the heart of Pest. To save yourself a long walk, take the metro to Opera. The **State Opera House** was built in the Italian neo-Renaissance style in 1884 and the tours (US$3) at 3 and 4 pm are worth taking, especially if you can't catch a performance. Many of the other great buildings along this section of Andrássy út also date from this time.

Proceed south-west on this fashionable avenue and round the corner onto Bajcsy-Zsilinszky út. You'll see the 96-metre-high neo-Renaissance dome of **St Stephen's Basilica** (1905) looming before you. The right hand of King St Stephen, founder of the Hungarian state, is kept in the chapel at the rear of the church, behind the altar. The ticket office just inside the basilica is charging admission to the treasury, not to the basilica itself. From July through to September organ concerts are held here every Monday at 7 pm (US$8).

Cross the square in front of the basilica and continue straight ahead for a block on Zrinyi utca, then right on Október 6 utca. Proceed straight ahead onto Szabadság tér with the National Bank (1905) to the right and the Television Company (also 1905) to the left. At the end of the square in front of the US Embassy is the **Soviet Army Memorial** (1945).

As you look up Vécsey utca from the memorial you see the great neo-Gothic silhouette of the **parliament building** (1904) on Kossuth Lajos tér. The exterior is impressive but individual tourists are not allowed inside.

The **Ethnographic Museum** (1896) also faces Kossuth Lajos tér. The Hungarian ethnographical collection here is fully captioned in English.

There's a metro station on the south side of Kossuth Lajos tér and for a good long view of the parliament building, take the metro for one stop to Batthyány tér, where you'll also find a large public market hall and some old churches. Note the very deep tunnel as the line dives under the Danube at this point. Built by the communists with Soviet assistance, this metro line opened in 1973.

Óbuda & Aquincum In 1872 three towns – Buda, Pest and Óbuda – united to form Budapest as the Austro-Hungarian emperor Franz Josef sought to create a rival to Napoleon III's Paris. Óbuda is most easily reached by taking the HÉV suburban railway from Batthyány tér Metro Station to Árpád híd mh. The **Vásárely Museum** greets you right outside the HÉV station. Go round the corner onto Szentlélek tér, which takes you to Fő tér, the beautifully restored centre of old Óbuda. **Óbuda Town Hall** is at Fő tér 3, but the most interesting building is the baroque **Zichy Mansion** (1752), Fő tér 1. At the back of the courtyard is an art gallery and the unique **Kassák Museum**, a tiny three-room exhibition with some real gems of early 20th-century avant-garde art.

Return to the HÉV and take a train three stops farther north to Aquincum vm. Aquincum was the key military garrison of the Roman province of Pannonia. A **Roman aqueduct** used to pass this way from a spring in the nearby park and remains have been preserved in the median strip of the modern highway alongside the HÉV railway line. The 2nd-century civilian **amphitheatre** is right beside the station. A few hundred metres away is a large excavated area and the **Aquincum Museum** (open from May to October, closed Monday). Don't miss the ancient musical organ with bronze pipes.

From Aquincum you have a choice of returning to Budapest or taking the HÉV on to Szentendre (see the Szentendre section). You can use regular yellow metro tickets as far as Békásmegyar on the HÉV, but to go to Szentendre you have to buy a special ticket which is checked by a conductor.

Other Museums Two museums in central Pest are worthy of special attention. The twin-towered synagogue (1859) on Dohány utca, the largest functioning synagogue in Europe and second largest in the world, contains the **Jewish Museum** (closed Saturday and from mid-October to mid-April). Sabbath services in the synagogue are on Friday evening and Saturday morning. The former Jewish ghetto extends behind this synagogue between Dohány, Kertész and Király streets, an area worth exploring. At the turn of the century a fifth of the population of Budapest was Jewish.

The **National Museum**, Múzeum körút 14-16 (metro: Kálvin tér), has Hungary's main collection of historical relics in a large neoclassical building (1847). Begin with the section on the ground floor, behind the cloakroom on the right, which covers the period up to the Magyar conquest. Behind the cloakroom on the left is the coronation regalia. These precious relics fell into the hands of the US troops in Germany in 1945 and were only restored to Hungary in 1978. Upstairs is a continuation of Hungarian history. The top floor contains a large natural history exhibit with dioramas to show the fauna in natural settings.

Most Budapest museums are closed on Monday and some are free on Saturday.

The Buda Hills If you have children with you, the Buda Hills are the place to take them. The variety of transportation opportunities makes visiting fun. Begin with a ride on the **cog railway** (fogaskerekű), which has been winding through pleasant wooded suburbs into the Buda Hills since 1874. The lower terminus of the cog railway is on Szilágyi Erzsébet fasor, opposite the circular high-rise Hotel Budapest and within walking distance from Moszkva tér Metro Station. The fare is one yellow metro ticket (daily, all year).

Near the upper terminus of the cog railway is Széchenyi-hegy Station of the **Pioneer Railway**, a 12-km scenic route opened in 1950, which operates hourly year-round daily except Monday (US$0.50). If Széchenyi-hegy Station looks closed, go in and knock on the ticket window – it may actually be open! Except for the engineer, this line is staffed mostly by children in order to interest them in transportation careers. Catch a train to János-hegy Station and walk up through the forest to the lookout tower on János-hegy (529 metres) with its 360° view. The **János-hegy chair lift** or *libegö* (operates daily, all year from 9.30 am to 4 pm, US$0.75) will take you down to Zugligeti út where you can catch bus No 158 back to Moszkva tér Metro Station.

If instead of getting out at János-hegy you stay on the Pioneer Railway to Hűvösvölgy Station, the northern terminus, you can catch tram No 56 back to Moszkva tér.

Margaret Island When your head begins to spin from all the sights, take a walk from one end to the other of Margaret Island (Margit sziget). Bus No 26 from beside Nyugati Railway Station covers the island or you can get there on trams No 4 or 6, which stop halfway across the unusual three-way bridge leading to Margaret Island. As you stroll among the trees and statues, you'll come across the ruins of two medieval monasteries, a small zoo, a rose garden, an open-air theatre, swimming pools, cafés and a pseudo-Japanese garden with hot spring pools (beside the Hotel Thermál). The island is such a relaxing, restful place you'll feel as if you're ages away from the busy city.

Cemeteries Budapest's most offbeat sight is **Kerepesi Cemetery** on Fiumei út near Keleti Railway Station. Beginning a century ago, it was the final resting place of Hungary's wealthiest and most prominent inhabitants. The evocative sculptured monuments scattered among the trees give Kerepesi Cemetery a unique, almost classical air which will enchant the wanderer. The most notable personages built themselves huge mausoleums which now stand alongside memorials to communists of yesteryear. Half the streets in Hungary are named after people buried here.

The graves of communists who died during the 1956 uprising are in the circular enclosure on the left side of the main avenue straight ahead from the entrance. The tombs of more recent communist leaders, János Kádár (1912-89) among them, are a block or two over to the right. All are marked only by their name, the dates of their birth and death and a gold (previously red) star. Farther back are the 19th-century mausoleums, including that of Ferenc Deák (1803-76), the politician who engineered the 1867 Austro-Hungarian 'compromise'.

In 1989 Imre Nagy (1896-1958), the man most closely associated with the 1956 revolution, was reburied in **Új köztemető**, Budapest's huge municipal cemetery on the far eastern side of town. Access to the municipal cemetery from Kerepesi Cemetery is fairly easy. As you leave Kerepesi, turn left on Fiumei út and walk south-east along the cemetery wall to the next tram stop (not the one near the cemetery entrance). Take tram No 28 south-east to the end of the line right at Új köztemető's gate. When you want to return to town, take bus No 95 from the cemetery gate direct to Keleti Railway Station or bus No 68 south-west to Kőbánya-Kispest metro.

Nagy and many other prominent figures

from 1956, plus approximately 2000 people liquidated between 1945 and 1956, lie in *parcelláz* 300 and 301 in the far north-east of the cemetery, a 30-minute walk from the entrance. The communists used this site to dump the bodies of executed 'traitors' in mass graves precisely because it was so remote. A map of the Új köztemető stands near the gate and the way is clearly signposted. At peak periods you can take a microbus marked *'temetójarat'* around the cemetery or hire a taxi at the gate. The site has become a *de rigueur* pilgrimage point for those interested in 1956.

Places to Stay

Camping The largest camping ground in Budapest is *Rómaifürdő* (☎ 168 6260), Szentendrei út 189, with space for 2500 guests, in a shady park north of the city. To get there take the HÉV suburban railway from Batthyány tér Metro Station to Rómaifürdő vm Station, which is within sight of the camping ground. The facility is open all year so it's up to you to decide if it's warm enough for camping. Cabins are available from mid-April to mid-October at US$11 double in 3rd category, US$17 double in 2nd category. They have 43 cabins in total, but they're often full. Use of the adjacent swimming pool, with lots of green grass on which to stretch out, is included, and nearby are a disco and several places to eat.

Up in the Buda Hills is *Hárshegy Camping* (☎ 115 1482) (open from Easter to mid-October), Hárshegyi út 7. Take bus No 22 from Moszkva tér Metro Station and watch for the signs on the right. Camping here costs US$3 per person, plus US$3 per tent. The 70 3rd-category duplex cabins without bath are US$13 single or double, US$19 triple. There are also six 2nd-category rooms with bath at US$36 single or double and 10 1st-category bungalows with bath at US$39 single or double.

A somewhat more convenient camping ground for those without their own transport is *Zugligeti Niche Camping* (☎ 156 8641), Zugligeti út 101, at the bottom station of the Buda Hills chair lift (take bus No 158 from Moszkva tér Metro Station to the end of the line). It's US$8 for two people to camp on one of the small hillside terraces. In addition, there's one on-site caravan at US$15 double, one bungalow at US$17 for two or three people and two rooms at US$22 double or US$33 for four persons. Their reception and buffet are in a couple of old Budapest trams parked at the entrance. Zugligeti Niche is open from April to mid-November and the friendly staff speak English.

Hostels The Express office (☎ 131 7777) booking hostel beds is at Szabadság tér 16, a block from Kossuth tér Metro Station (Monday to Thursday until 4 pm, Friday until 2 pm). The main Express office at Semmelweis utca 4 (metro: Astoria) also has information during business hours, though they don't make bookings. You can also go directly to the hostels. Hostel or student cards are not required at any of the hostels, although they'll sometimes get you a 10% discount and they're accepted as identification (eliminating the need to leave your passport at the reception). The two Express offices and all the hostels listed in this section are open year-round.

The *Bridge Hostel* (☎ 215 7604), Soroksári út 12, off Boráros tér, is a modern seven-storey building facing the Danube. A bed in a three-bedded room is US$6 and doubles with shared bath are US$12. They have a total of 180 beds so there should be something available. Get there on tram No 4 from Ferenc körút Metro Station to the last stop before the Danube, or just walk.

A popular 23-bed crash pad on the south-east side of the city is *Back Pack Guest House* (☎ 185 5089), Takács Menyhért utca 33. A place in a seven-bed dorm is US$5, in a five-bed dorm US$6, plus US$0.75 for linen (first night only) and US$1.25 for a filling breakfast. Double rooms are available in winter only. There's a kitchen, laundry, lockers, TV lounge and no curfew, but it's cramped (and very sociable). After a day of exploring Budapest everyone sits outside on the front steps and tries to decide where to go that night over a few beers. Worldwise managers Attila and Krisztina are super friendly and helpful (their docile red setter Alex is only friendly). Watch out, this place is a trap: if you like the backpackers scene you may find it hard to leave. Access is relatively easy on bus No 7 or 7a (black number) from Keleti Railway Station or Ferenciek tere Metro (get out right after the bus goes under a railway bridge and look for small green signs or ask).

Hotel Express (☎ 175 2528), Beethoven utca 7/9, several blocks south-west of Déli Railway Station (take tram No 59 for two stops), is US$19 single or double, US$23 triple with shared bath. The toilet and shower are down the hall and breakfast costs extra. There's a 10% discount for YHA cardholders.

One of Budapest's nicest yet least known places to stay is the *Youth Centre of Csillebérc* (☎ 156 5772), Konkoly Thege utca 21 in the Buda Hills. This huge complex is the former Pioneer Camp and it's in a quiet, wooded location. Both the official Hungarian Youth Hostel Association and the American School are based here. Csillebérc offers a 36-room hostel *(turistaszálló)* at US$11/14 single/double (20% discount with a YHA card but not on singles), eight four-bed bungalows with private bath at US$33, and camping at US$1.25 per person plus US$1.25 per tent (or US$2 per person if you sleep in one of their fixed dormitory tents). All of the above and the many sporting facilities are available year-round and are easily accessible on bus No 21 (red number) from Moszkva tér Metro to the end of the line, then bus No 90 to the first stop after the railway tracks (or a 10-minute downhill walk). The complex reception *(központ)* is open 24 hours a day. The restaurant is inexpensive, however, it closes at 8 pm.

Summer-Only Hostels In July and August private entrepreneurs rent vacant student dormitories from the government and turn them into hostels which they do their best to fill in order to make a profit. Competition is fierce and there are several rival hostel operators, so you can afford to shop around a bit. Beds average US$7 per person. Most of these hostels are open only in summer, so from September to June make sure a place is actually open before going far out of your way. Ask at Ibusz, Express or Tourinform, or call the hostel the night before. Functioning hostels always have receptionists who speak English, so if you get a monolingual Hungarian something's wrong. More Than Ways (see following) is the largest year-round operation, but their hostels are also the most crowded – great places to meet people.

In July and August backpackers are often approached at Keleti and Nyugati train stations by representatives from the different hostels offering free minibus rides to their hostels. This is fine but if you want a double room get a firm commitment that one is available that night, otherwise you could be stuck in a dormitory for days on end waiting for one to become available. The hostels rarely have single rooms, even if these are advertised in their brochures.

The most central hostel is *Ottó & Viktor's* (☎ 267 0311), Papnövelde utca 4-6, in the Apáczai Kollégiuma building just off Egyetem tér, a few minutes walk from Ferenciek tere or Astoria metro stations. Ottó and Viktor offer two, four and six-bedded rooms from late June to August only.

From late June to early September Széchenyi István Szakkollégium, Ráday utca 43-45, becomes *Strawberry Youth Hostel* (☎ 138 4766) with 60 rooms at US$9 per person in doubles, US$8 per person in triples, US$7 per person in quads. Nearby at Kinizsi utca 2-6 is another modern six-storey student residence which functions in exactly the same way, but opens and closes a little earlier. These places are within walking distance from Ferenc körút Metro Station and are a good bet in summer.

Most of the hostels belonging to the University of Technology are west of Ferenc körút Metro Station and in July and August it should be easy to find a bed here (though most function as regular student dormitories the rest of the year and are closed to travellers). One of the largest is the *Schönherz Zoltán Kollégiuma* (☎ 166 5422), Irinyi

József utca 42 (tram No 4 from Ferenc körút Metro Station to the second stop west of the Danube). In July and August only this 22-storey skyscraper offers hostel beds at US$6 per person with a disco on the premises.

Other summertime hostels in the large student residential area near Schönherz Zoltán Kollégiuma are *Kármán Tódor Kollégium* (☎ 181 2313), Irinyi József utca 9-11, *Martos* (☎ 181 2171), Sztoczek József utca 7 (doubles here are US$14), *Vásárhelyi* (☎ 185 2216), Kruspér utca 2-4 opposite Martos, *Rózsa Ferenc/Epitesz Kollégium* (☎ 166 6677), Bercsényi utca 28-30, and *Baross Gábor Kollégium/Landler* (☎ 185 1444), Bartók Béla út 17. These have mostly rooms with two to four beds.

If you're arriving in Budapest on a train from southern or western Hungary (or Vienna) which stops at Kelenföld Railway Station, jump off there and go through the underpass to the white 14-storey residence of *Komját Aladár Kollégium* (☎ 166 5355), Rimaszombati út 2. In July and August they offer rooms with two, three and four beds. The city centre is easily accessible from here on bus No 7 (red number).

More Than Ways The best news in years on the Budapest low-budget scene is the More Than Ways University Youth Hostels chain which operates eight hostels around Budapest in July and August. Towards the end of August seven of the hostels close and revert to their former lives as student dormitories but one hostel stays open year-round.

More Than Ways has its headquarters at the *Diakszálló Youth Hostel* (☎ 129 8644), Dózsa György út 152, a two-minute walk from Dózsa György út Metro Station. Although this 140-bed hostel is usually the most crowded (hordes of Western backpackers), they offer a free minibus transfer from there to any of their other hostels which still have beds available, so this is probably the best place to go first. The Diákszálló charges US$8/12 single/double or US$6 per person in dormitories of eight or 12 beds. The singles and doubles are almost always full in summer (but often available in winter).

HUNGARY

Donáti Youth Hostel (☎ 201 1971), Donáti utca 46, a five-minute walk from Batthyány tér Metro Station, has only 72 dormitory beds but it's open only in summer.

All the More Than Ways hostels are open 24 hours a day and you can check in any time, but you must depart by 9 am or pay for another night. There's no curfew and a YHA card is not required (the signs at the hostel entrances stating that a student or hostel card are required are only there to keep out undesirables). The More Than Ways hostels can be noisy and a little chaotic at times but they're fine if you only want a cheap place to crash and meet other travellers.

Private Rooms Reasonable value for accommodation in Budapest are the private rooms assigned by local travel agencies. They generally cost US$11/17 single/double or more plus US$1 to US$2 tax, with a 20% supplement if you stay less than four nights. To get a single or a room in the centre of town, you may have to try several offices. There are lots of rooms available and even in July and August you'll be able to find something. You'll probably need to buy an indexed city map to find your room.

Following is a list of various agencies, beginning with those closest to the transportation terminals. Most are open only during normal business hours so if you arrive late or on a weekend, try the Ibusz Accommodation Centre at Petőfi tér 3 (metro: Ferenciek tere) which never closes. If you arrive at Keleti Railway Station between 11.10 pm and 4.30 am when the metro isn't running, catch night bus No 78 from outside the nearby Grand Hotel to Erzébet hid. The centre's prices are higher than those of the following agencies, however, so only go there when the others are closed. Individuals on the street outside this Ibusz office will offer you an unofficial private room, but their prices are higher than those asked inside and there is no quality control.

You may also be offered a private room by entrepreneurs at the railway stations. These vary considerably and cases of travellers being promised an idyllic room in the centre of town, only to be taken to a dreary, cramped flat in some distant suburb are not unknown. Yet several readers report getting excellent rooms right on the metro from people outside the Ibusz office at Keleti Railway Station. You really have to use your own judgment here.

Near Keleti Railway Station The Ibusz office in Keleti Railway Station (open daily) has private rooms at US$9/11 single/double but there are few singles. Express opposite Ibusz also has private rooms.

Budapest Tourist at Baross tér 3, just beyond the overpass on the opposite side of the square from Keleti Railway Station, also arranges private rooms and changes money.

Near Nyugati Railway Station Ibusz at Nyugati Railway Station arranges private rooms. Also try Cooptourist and Budapest Tourist in the underground concourse at the entrance to the metro below Nyugati Railway Station. More rooms are for rent at Panoráma Travel, Nyugati tér 7, on the opposite side of the square from the station, and Volántourist, Teréz körút 38, also quite near Nyugati. A second Cooptourist office is in the opposite direction at Kossuth Lajos tér 13 near Parliament (metro: Kossuth tér).

Near Erzsébet tér Bus Station Dunatours at Bajcsy-Zsilinszky út 17 behind St Stephen's Basilica has reasonable rooms. To-Ma Tour, Október 6 utca 22, is expensive at US$17/20 single/double in the centre.

One of the largest offices in the city offering private rooms is Budapest Tourist, Roosevelt tér 5 (open until 6 pm on weekdays and Saturday mornings).

Near the Hydrofoil Terminal Some of Budapest's least expensive private rooms are available from Ibusz, Ferenciek tere 5 (metro: Ferenciek tere). They're open Saturday until 1 pm. The Ibusz 24-hour Accommodation Centre at Petőfi tér 3 is also within walking distance from both the hydrofoil and the bus station.

Near Déli Railway Station At Déli Railway Station private rooms are arranged by Ibusz, at the entrance to the metro, or Budapest Tourist, in the mall in front of the station. Also try Cooptourist, Attila út 107, directly across the park in front of Déli Railway Station.

Cheaper Hotels A hotel room will cost a bit more than a private room, though management doesn't mind if you stay only one night. There are no cheap hotels right in the city centre but the *Domnik Motel* (☎ 122 7655), Cházár András utca 3, directly behind a large church on Thököly út, is just two stops northeast of Keleti Railway Station on bus No 7 (black number). The 36 rooms with shared bath are US$18/22 single/double, breakfast included. This friendly pension is a convenient place to stay for a few nights.

The *Hotel Flandria* (☎ 129 6689), Szegedi út 27, is easily accessible on trams No 12 and 14 from Lehel tér Metro Station. Rooms with shared bath in this five-storey tourist hotel cost US$18/25 single/double including breakfast. They cater mostly to foreign groups.

One of the best deals in town if there are a few of you is the *Poscher Hotel* (☎ 149 0321), Kerekes utca 12-20, two blocks away from the Flandria. Also known as the Munkásszálloda Góliát, this huge 11-storey block accommodates workers as well as tourists. A room with four beds will cost US$11 for the room whether you're alone or in a gang of four. The atmosphere in the Poscher can be a little rough-and-ready at times – recommended for those who want to experience proletarian Budapest. There's a cheap self-service restaurant on the premises and check out *Club Viking* nearby at Kerekes utca 6.

If you've always dreamed of staying in a castle on the Danube you'll like the *Citadella Hotel* (☎ 166 5794) in the Citadel above Hotel Gellért (for public transport details see Things to See, above). The 11 twin rooms cost US$25/27 for singles/doubles without bath, US$28/36 with a leaky shower, and there are also 58 beds in 10-bed dormitories *(turistaszallas)* at US$6 per person. The dorms are usually booked by groups a week ahead so try calling well in advance for a reservation.

Several inexpensive places are accessible on the HÉV suburban railway line to Szentendre from Batthyány tér Metro Station. The first is the one-star *Hotel Polo* (☎ 250 0192), Mozaik utca 1-3 near the Filatorigat HÉV Station. You can't see the hotel from the station, but it's beside a service station, behind a long, white building which runs along the east side of the tracks. Doubles with shared bath are US$21, while the one room with private bath is US$32 (no singles). It's a new hotel built in 1987 and is in the same building as the local Volkswagen dealer.

Upriver beside the Danube is the *Sporthotel Lidó* (☎ 188 6865), Nánási út 67, a 10-minute walk from Rómaifürdő HÉV Station. Singles/doubles are available all year at US$17/26 with shared bath, breakfast included. Show your YHA card here for a 10% discount. The Sporthotel Lidó has a sauna, solarium, fitness room and tennis courts which are available to guests, and from May to September there's a ferry service from the embankment behind the hotel to Budapest.

The *Hotel Touring* (☎ 180 1595), Pünkösdfürdő utca 38, at the north-west end of Budapest, is an 11-storey workers' residence which has 65 rooms with shared bath reserved for tourists at US$19/20/25/30 single/double/triple/quad including breakfast – good value for small groups. It's a 10-minute walk from Békásmegyar HÉV Station (ask directions from the station). A regular Budapest transit ticket will take you here.

HUNGARY

More Expensive Hotels The old *Park Hotel* (☎ 113 5619), Baross tér 10, directly across from Keleti Railway Station, is US$31/41 single/double without bath, US$37/50 with shower (often full). The *Metropol Hotel* (☎ 142 1171), Rákóczi út 58 near Keleti (metro: Blaha Lujza tér), has singles/doubles at US$35/45 without bath, US$42/57 with bath.

A much better medium-priced hotel than these is the *Medosz Hotel* (☎ 153 1700), Jókai tér 9 in the theatre district. The 11 singles are US$31, the 53 doubles US$45, all with private bath and an excellent breakfast. There's no sign outside, so look for the modern 10-storey building marked 'háza' beside the 'Kolibri szinház' (metro: Oktogon).

Büro Panzió (☎ 115 1898), Dékán utca 3 at Retek utca, just a block off the north side of Moszkva tér, looks basic from the outside but the rooms (which cost US$38/48/60 single/double/triple with bath and breakfast) are comfortable and even luxurious (each with TV). Only a one-minute walk from the metro, this colourful place would be an excellent choice for the business traveller (fax, telex and photocopying on the premises) or anyone interested in value for money.

Places to Eat

Bottom End One of the few remaining self-service restaurants in Budapest is *Bölcs Bagoly Önkiszolgáló Étterem*, Váci utca 33 (metro: Ferenciek tere) (weekdays 11.30 am to 3 pm). It's always crowded with local office workers who appreciate a cheap lunch.

The *Városház Snack*, Városház utca 16, opposite the town hall at the back exit of the main post office, serves good food at reasonable prices. At lunchtime the place will be jammed with local office workers (weekdays 11 am to 7 pm).

The self-service *Önkiszolgáló Étterem* at Arany János utca 7, is open weekdays from 11.30 am to 4 pm only.

Another self-service place *Önkiszolgáló Étterem* is on the top floor of Skála Department Store directly opposite Nyugati Railway Station, accessible from the exterior terrace (open weekdays noon to 3 pm only).

One of the healthiest and least expensive places to eat in Budapest is *No 1 Falafel Faloda*, Paulay Ede utca 53 (metro: Opera or Oktogon). It's strictly vegetarian and you pay a fixed price to stuff a piece of pitta bread or fill a plastic container yourself from the great assortment of salad bar options. There's also a large selection of teas and a place to sit down in the loft. The bright, modern décor attracts a sharp young crowd (open weekdays from 10 am to 8 pm only).

The clean and attractive *Saláta Bár*, in a corner of the Grand Hotel Hungária, on Baross tér facing the overpass across the square from Keleti Railway Station, has fresh salad although you have to eat standing up. The attendant fills your plate so just ask for 10 dkg (100 grams) of three or four things you fancy. Because this place is connected to a top hotel the food is very good.

Look for the *lángos* (doughnut) stand in the circular open-air courtyard outside Keleti Railway Station, on the far left as you go from the station to the metro entrance. This may be the best bargain in Budapest (closed Sunday).

Cheap German-style sausage and beer are consumed standing up at *Gasztró Hús Hentesáru*, Margít körút 2, right opposite the first stop of trams Nos 4 and 6 on the west side of the Margaret Bridge (Monday 7 am to 6 pm, Tuesday to Friday 6 am to 7 pm, Saturday 6.30 am to 1 pm). Other Hús Hentesáru meat markets around Budapest offer the same sort of thing.

Central Pest The varied selection of regular restaurants listed following appear in geographical order across central Pest from north to south. Mexican food and other Latin American dishes are offered at *La Pampa*, Pannónia utca 7 off Szent István körút, behind the Vígszínház (metro: Nyugati tér).

Real Arab food is served at *Semiramis*, Alkotmány utca 20 near Nyugati Railway Station (there is additional seating upstairs). It's rather hidden halfway down the block.

The friendly *Karcsi Ételbár*, Jókai utca 20, a block back from Teréz körút four blocks from Nyugati Railway Station, serves very reasonable Hungarian meals and the menu posted outside also lists drinks! It doesn't serve lunch on weekends.

Kisharang Étkezde, Október 6 utca 17 (weekdays from 11 am to 8 pm, weekends 11.30 am to 3.30 pm), has excellent local fare at very reasonable prices. The menu is only in Hungarian and no English is spoken but just point at something on another table – the place is always crowded. Recommended. Next door is an excellent ice-cream place, if you still have room.

Dine in style at the restaurant upstairs in the *Duna Palota*, Zrínyi utca 5 (daily noon to 11 pm). This elegant palace erected in 1894 was formerly a military officers club. Complete food and drink menus are posted outside and prices are reasonable for a place like this.

The *Bohémtanya Vendéglő*, Paulay Ede utca 6 between Deák tér and the State Opera (metro: Bajcsy-Zsilinszky út), is an unpretentious but OK eatery that serves large portions. You may have to wait a while for a table. The menu is in English and German.

Morrison's Bar, Révay utca 25 next to the State Opera, serves meals although it's more of a drinking place.

There are two unpretentious kosher restaurants in what was the Jewish ghetto, north-east of Károly körút (metro: Astoria). The *Hanna Restaurant*, Dob utca 35 (open weekdays from 11.30 am to 4 pm only), is part of an active Jewish community centre occupying buildings which survived the war. A block or two away at Klauzál tér 2 is the more commercial *Salom Restaurant*.

The *Astoria Hotel*, Kossuth Lajos utca 19 (metro: Astoria), puts on a good self-service buffet breakfast (US$4) every morning from 7 to 10 am in the turn-of-the-century dining room.

Vegetarium, Cukor utca 3 just off Ferenciek tere (noon to 10 pm daily), is a full-service vegetarian restaurant with a comprehensive English menu which includes some macrobiotic items. It's not cheap but most readers report they enjoyed the friendly service, good food and smoke-free atmosphere. After 7 pm an acoustic guitarist sets the mellow scene (there's a music list on each table, allowing you to make requests). Look for Vegetarium's big red apple logo.

Cabar, Iranyi utca 25, around the corner from Vegetarium (metro: Ferenciek tere), has Israeli-style sawarma and felafel which you eat standing up. There's a self-service salad bar – you'll be charged by the weight of the food you select. On the corner near Cabar is a good ice-cream place called *Gelato*.

Abelino Pizzeria, Duna utca 6 (down a side street from Ferenciek tere), has reasonable oven-baked pizza and draught beer. The service here is good (closed Sunday and holidays).

Typical Hungarian meals are served at the *Alföldi Kisvendéglo*, Kecskeméti utca 4 (metro: Kálvin tér). The menu lists different prices for small portions *(zóna adag)* and large portions *(adag)*. The waiters sometimes serve foreigners who order large portions small portions, then charge for large portions, so you might be better off ordering a small portion in the first place. Got it?

Stop Étterem, Váci utca 86 at Fővám tér (metro: Kálvin tér), offers a good variety of fish, venison, pork, veal and poultry, plus four vegetarian selections. Prices are reasonable, the menu is in English, colour photos of many of the dishes are in the window and it's open almost 24 hours a day.

Kaltenberg Söröző, Kinizsi utca 30-36 (metro: Ferenc körút), combines substantial Hungarian meals, a German menu and the feel of one of the better US chain restaurants like Sizzlers. It's a reliable, medium-priced choice.

If you're not discouraged by the prospect of spending up to US$50 per person for dinner, *Gundel*, next to the zoo directly behind the Museum of Fine Art (metro: Széchenyi Fürdő), is probably Budapest's finest restaurant with a tradition dating back to 1894. It's not afraid to post the menu outside with prices (open daily from noon to 4 pm and 7 pm to midnight).

Castle District Expensive restaurants popular among tourists abound in the castle district, but weekdays from 11.30 am to 2 pm a self-service called simply the *Önkiszolgáló Étterem* functions inside the college at Országház utca 30. Take the elevator up to the 3rd floor.

A slightly better self-service *(önkiszolgáló étterem)* is above Fortuna Spaten, directly across the street from the Hilton Hotel on Fortuna utca, also open weekdays from 11 am to 2.30 pm.

The rather expensive *Régi Országház*, Országház utca 17, combines good wine with a medieval atmosphere.

Below Castle Hill A good little restaurant with regular table service inside the *Buda Concert Hall*, Corvin tér 8 (metro: Batthyány tér), directly below the Fisherman's Bastion on Castle Hill, serves lunch on weekdays from 7 am to 4 pm. It's worth the slight detour as the tourists up on the hill don't know this place.

The *Tabáni Kakas Restaurant*, Attila út 27, is a slightly up-market, old-style Hungarian restaurant.

Hearty Hungarian meals are served at *Söröző a Szent Jupáthoz*, Retek utca 16 a block north of Moszkva tér. The menu is posted outside in English and it's open 24 hours a day.

The *Marxim Pizzeria*, Kisrókus utca 23, a five-minute walk from Moszkva tér Metro (daily until 1 am), is popular among workers from the surrounding factories who appreciate the Gulag Pizza, not to mention the Lenin and Anarchism varieties. Mementos of the Stalin years hang from the walls and you can drown all your uncertainties in cheap Belgian beer.

Pizzeria Il Treno, Alkotás utca 15, serves real hand-tossed pizza in its upbeat location across the street from Déli Railway Station. Only a barbarian would want to put tomato sauce on the pizza here! The food is reasonable but drinks are priced on the high side. The self-service salad bar makes this place a good choice for vegetarians. *Banya-Tanya Vendéglő*, half a block up from Il Treno, is a good local place.

Yet another choice is *La Prima Pizzeria*, Margit körút 3 opposite the stop of tram Nos 4 and 6 on the west side of the Danube. They bake good pizza and, on weekdays from noon to 3 pm, offer a set three-course meal *(gyermek menü)*. There's also a self-service salad bar.

On your way to the Citadella you might stop for lunch at the *Tollas Bar Grill Söröző*, Móricz Zsigmond körtér 4, which offers grilled chicken and draught beer. Next door is a *Cukrászda* where you can get great cakes and ice cream. These places are right at the point where you change from tram No 19 to bus No 27, as described in the Things to See section above.

Óbuda A number of up-market restaurants are around Fő tér, Óbuda (HÉV suburban railway from Batthyány tér Metro to Árpád híd mh). The *Postakocsi Restaurant*, Fő tér 2, is one; *Sipos Halászkert*, Szentlelek tér 8, founded in 1930 by Károly Sipos, is another (try the fish soup). In the evening there will be Gypsy music at both places and you'll certainly break the budget if you eat at either. Menus are posted outside.

Even if you aren't prepared to pay the sort of prices listed on those restaurant menus, Fő tér is still fine for a romantic stroll at night and there's a good little bar, the *Kis Dreher Söröző*, on Harrer Pál utca just off Fő tér.

Cafés Like Vienna, Budapest is famous for its cafés and the most famous of the famous is the *Gerbeaud Cukrászda*, on the west side of Vörösmarty tér, a fashionable meeting place of the city's elite since 1870. In recent years it has become pretentious and overpriced.

If anything, *Cukrászda Művész*, Andrássy út 29, almost opposite the opera, is more elegant than Gerbeaud and has a better selection of cakes at lower prices.

Cheaper yet is *Perity mestercukrászat*, Andrássy út 37, with unbelievably rich desserts, great ice cream and drinks with prices clearly displayed (for a change).

The *Café New York*, Erzsébet körút 11 (metro: Blaha Lujza tér), has been a Budapest institution since 1895. The elegant turn-of-the-century décor glitters around the literati who still meet there. At least one visit must be made to the Café New York!

Number One Espresso, Sas utca 9 off Erzsébet tér (metro: Deák tér), is a good local pub with draught beer but no food (closed on Sunday).

A great place for cheap stand-up coffee and cakes is the *Jégbüfé*, Ferenciek tere 10 next to Ibusz (metro: Ferenciek tere). Write down the name of whatever it is you want and pay the cashier who will give you a voucher.

Up in the castle district, the perfect place for coffee and cakes is the crowded *Ruszwurm Café*, Szentháromság utca 7 near Matthias Church.

Beware of cafés in the centre that don't display the price of coffee – it will be double or triple what it costs everywhere else in the city. The places along Váci utca especially are becoming a rip-off.

Markets The old Pest market hall (presently closed for renovations) is on Fovam tér (metro: Kálvin tér). A large open-air street market (open Sunday) unfolds behind the large church above Lehel tér Metro Station.

A large supermarket (open Monday, Tuesday, Thursday and Friday from 6 am to 8 pm, Wednesday and Saturday from 7 am to 4.30 pm, Sunday from 7 am to 1 pm) is in the old market hall on the south side of Batthyány tér near the metro station. Stock up.

Entertainment

Opera & Operetta You should pay at least one visit to the *State Opera House* (1884), Andrássy út 22 (metro: Opera), to see the frescos and incredibly rich gilded decoration in the Italian Renaissance style. The box office is on the left-hand side of the building behind the tour office (closed on Saturday and Monday). Tickets are more expensive for Friday and Saturday night.

Budapest has a second opera house, the modern *Erkel Színház* at Köztársaság tér 30 near Keleti Railway Station. Tickets are sold just inside the main doors (Tuesday to Saturday 11 am to 7 pm, Sunday 10 am to 1 pm and 4 to 7 pm).

Operettas are presented at the *Fővárosi Operett Színház*, Nagy-mező utca 17, a block

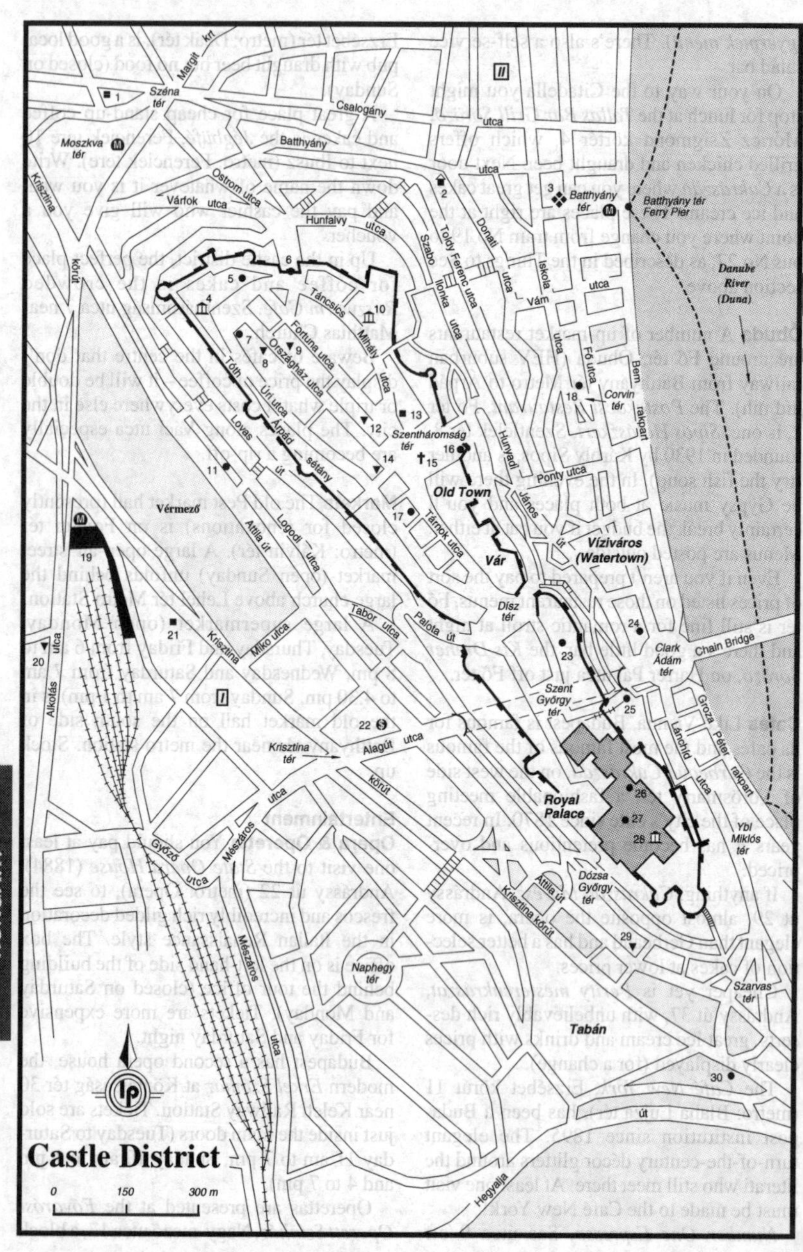
Margit krt
Széna tér
Csalogány
utca
Batthyány
Moszkva tér
Krisztina
Ostrom utca
Várfok utca
Hunfalvy utca
körút
Táncsics Mihály
Fortuna utca
Országház utca
Tóth
Úri utca
Árpád
Lovas
sétány
út
Szentháromság tér
Old Town
Vérmező
Attila út
Logodi utca
Tárnok utca
Vár
Tabor utca
Palota út
Miko utca
Krisztina
utca
Alkotás
Krisztina tér
Alagút utca
körút
utca
Mészáros
Győző utca
Mészáros
utca
Naphegy tér
Hegyalja
Szabo
Toldy Ferenc utca
Ilonka utca
Donáti utca
Iskola
Vám
utca
Fő utca
Batthyány tér
Batthyány tér Ferry Pier
Danube River (Duna)
Bem rakpart
Corvin tér
Hunyadi János út
Ponty utca
Víziváros (Watertown)
Dísz tér
Clark Ádám tér
Chain Bridge
Szent György tér
Groza Péter rakpart
Lánchíd utca
Royal Palace
Ybl Miklós tér
Dózsa György tér
Attila út
Krisztina körút
Szarvas tér
Tabán
út
Castle District
0
150
300 m

HUNGARY

PLACES TO STAY

1 Büro Panzió/Söröző a Szent Jupáthoz
2 Donáti Youth Hostel (Summer Only)
13 Hilton Hotel
21 Buda Penta Hotel

PLACES TO EAT

8 Önkiszolgáló Étterem
9 Régi Országház Restaurant
12 Fortuna Self-Service Restaurant (Upstairs)
14 Ruszwurm Café
20 Pizzeria Il Treno
29 Tabáni Kakas Restaurant

OTHER

3 Supermarket
4 Museum of Military History
5 National Archives
6 Vienna Gate
7 Magdalen Tower
10 Music History Museum
11 Cooptourist
15 Matthias Church
16 Fisherman's Bastion
17 Golden Eagle Pharmacy
18 Buda Concert Hall
19 Déli Train Station
22 OTP Bank
23 Várszinház (Castle Theatre)
24 Tram No 16
25 Funicular Railway
26 National Gallery
27 National Library
28 Historical Museum
30 Rác Baths

from the State Opera House. Tickets are sold inside and it's worth checking here in summer as there are often programmes.

Musicals are performed at the *Madách Theatre*, Eszsébet körút 31/33 (metro: Blaha Lujza tér). The Madách presents an interesting mix of rock operas, musicals and straight drama in Hungarian – it's worth checking.

Concerts A monthly *Koncert Kalendarium* lists all concerts in Budapest that month and most nights you'll have two or three to choose from. The motto of the Budapest Spring Festival in late March is '10 days, 100 venues, 1000 events' and you'll have a good selection of musical events each night. Budapest's main concert hall is the *Pesti Vigadó*, Vigadó tér 2 (metro: Vörösmarty tér). Other concerts are held at the *Academy of Music*, Király utca 64, on the corner of Liszt Ferenc tér (metro: Oktogon).

Circus The *Grand Circus*, Állatkerti körút 7 (metro: Széchenyi Fürdő), has performances on Saturday and Sunday at 10 am; Wednesday, Thursday, Friday and Saturday at 3 pm; and Wednesday, Friday, Saturday and Sunday at 7 pm (closed in summer). Although the matinées are occasionally booked out by school groups, there's almost always space in the evening. Advance tickets are sold at the circus itself (US$3).

Planetarium & Puppets Budapest's *Planetarium* (metro: Népliget) features exciting laser light shows to the accompaniment of rock music. There are usually shows held from Monday to Saturday at 7.30 and 9 pm. You can purchase tickets (US$4) at the door or from any Budapest ticket agency.

The *Puppet Theatre*, Andrássy út 69 (metro: Vörösmarty utca), presents afternoon shows designed for children and evening programmes for adults. There's a special adult performance on Monday at 6 pm. The shows are generally held at 3 pm on weekdays and at 11 am and 4 pm on weekends. It's closed all summer.

Táncház Authentic participatory folk-music workshops *(táncház* or 'dance house') are held once or twice a week at the *Sazbadidőközpont* (☎ 122 9870), Almássy tér 6, a couple of blocks from Blaha Lujza tér Metro Station. The famous Gypsy group Kalyi Jag sometimes plays here, and there are Greek, Bulgarian and Israeli dance workshops quite regularly.

From mid-September to the end of June the well-known Hungarian folk group Muzsikás runs a workshop at the *Fővárosi Művelődési Háza*, Fehérvári út 47, every Tuesday from 7 to 11 pm (admission costs US$0.75). On Wednesday during these same months there's a Balkan dance workshop here (admission costs US$1). You can get there on tram No 4 from Ferenc körút Metro

Station, south-west to the end of the line at Fehérvári út.

Most people come to the *táncház* evenings to learn the folk dances that go with the music (and of course you can dance too). These workshops have nothing to do with tourism and are a great opportunity to hear musicians practising and get involved in a local scene at next to no expense. You become part of the programme instead of merely watching others perform.

The Táncház Festival of Folk & Popular Music unfolds at the Népstadion on a Saturday evening during the last third of each March. This event is part of the Budapest Spring Festival.

Youth Scene The youth scene revolves around the *Petőfi Centre* (Fővárosi Ifjúsági Szabadidő Központ) in City Park (metro: Széchenyi Fürdő) where concerts by well-known international rock and blues groups are held a couple of times a month. It's great if you get tickets as the hall is small enough for you to really get close to the performers. The *táncház* evenings here give you the opportunity to learn folk dancing. Ask about Greek dancing *(görög táncház)* as this attracts oodles of young people who form massive circles and dance to the lively Greek folk music. Fan clubs dedicated to The Cure, Madonna, Metalica, Guns N' Roses, New Kids on the Block, Michael Jackson and others meet regularly in the centre and these are more fun than they sound. Those present spend the evening dancing to the music of their favourite stars in a small club room with subdued lighting and a bar, and videos are occasionally shown. Ask for the monthly Petőfi Centre programme at the information counter. The centre is easily accessible on trolleybus No 74 from in front of the synagogue on Dohány utca.

Blues, Jazz & Rock Clubs The *Merlin Jazz Club*, Gerlóczy utca 4, around the corner from Károly körút 28 (metro: Deák tér), has live music nightly from 10 pm.

From Tuesday to Saturday nights the *Made Inn Club*, Andrássy út 112 (metro: Bajza utca), presents live Latin American music, acoustic, pop or blues in a gentile setting. Thursday is a big night here (open daily 8 pm to 5 am).

Kávéház Tilos az Á, Mikszáth Kálmán tér 2, off Baross utca (metro: Kálvan tér), presents live blues or rock-and-roll groups from Thursday to Saturday nights and sometimes also on Wednesday. Some of the best music in Budapest is heard here. A block away at Krúdy Gyula utca 6 is *The Blues Pub* where you can also hear jazz.

Discos One of Budapest's top discos is *Globe* in City Park, across the street from the Municipal Baths (metro: Széchenyi Fürdő). Globe has a large modern dance floor – just the place to head when you start getting bored with the action at the nearby Petőfi Centre. It's open Friday, Saturday and Sunday from 9 pm to 4 am year-round (admission US$3).

Another very popular disco is *Hully-Gully*, Apor Vilmos tér 9, in the Buda Hills (tram No 59 five stops from Moszkva tér). The laser lighting, go-go girls and fair prices attract large crowds – almost nobody goes into *Randevu* next door. Hully-Gully is open daily from 9 pm to 5 am and the dress is informal.

Fortuna, Hess András tér 4, directly across the street from the Hilton Hotel in the castle district, functions as a disco after 10 pm from Thursday to Saturday during the school year. It's always packed with trendy Budapest youth and the music is good but they're selective about who they let in (try showing your ISIC).

Nightclubs Budapest's swankiest nightclub is *Maxim Variete* in the Emke Hotel, Akácfa utca 3 (metro: Blaha Lujza tér). The club's chorus line consists of 12 scantily dressed Maxim girls, and magicians, acrobats, singers and dancers, appearing in a Las Vegas-style extravaganza. Performances are at 10 pm and midnight daily (US$11 cover charge).

You'll find more of the same at the *Moulin Rouge Cabaret* (☎ 112 4492) beside the

Fővárosi Operett Színház (metro: Opera). The cabaret also functions as a disco and occasional rock concerts are held here too.

Summertime Entertainment From mid-June to mid-September most of the regular theatres will be closed for holidays. Among the programmes put on for tourists at this time is a special operetta staged at the *Arany János Theatre*, Paulay Ede utca 35 (metro: Opera). Tickets are US$11 to US$28.

Every Monday, Friday and Saturday from May to mid-October at 8.30 pm, the Folklór Centrum presents a programme of Hungarian dancing accompanied by a Gypsy orchestra at the *Fővárosi Művelődési Háza* (☎ 181 1360), Fehérvári út 47 (for public transport see Táncház above). This performance is one of the best of its kind in Budapest.

Also in summer, the 40 dancers of the Hungarian State Folk Ensemble perform at the *Buda Concert Hall* (☎ 201 5928), Corvin tér 8 (metro: Batthyány tér). The 1½-hour programmes begin at 7 pm every Tuesday, Wednesday and Thursday from April to October (but not in June). Both shows cost US$7 admission.

Every Wednesday at 8 pm year-round you can see Hungarian folk dancing at the stately *Duna Palota*, Zrínyi utca 5 just off Roosevelt tér in central Pest (US$6).

Ticket Agencies The busiest theatrical ticket agency is the Központi Jegyiroda, Andrássy út 18 (metro: Opera). They have tickets there to numerous theatres and events, although the best are gone a couple of days in advance.

For concert tickets try Jegyiroda Országos Filharmonia, Vörösmarty tér 1 (metro: Vörösmarty tér). Check out the zany elevator next to this office.

Music Mix, Váci utca 33 (metro: Ferenciek tere), has tickets to special events such as rock spectaculars, appearances by foreign superstars etc. Tickets here begin around US$20.

As you pursue your quest for tickets, you'll sometimes be told that everything is sold out. You usually get better seats by going directly to the theatre box office than you would by dealing with a ticket agency. Theatre tickets cost anywhere from US$2 to US$20.

Horse Races It should come as no surprise that the descendants of the nomadic Magyar tribes love horse racing. Races are held at the *Kerepesi Trotting Track*, Kerepesi út 9 near Keleti Railway Station (bus No 95 or trolley-bus No 80), throughout the year, beginning at 2 pm on Saturday (12 races) and 4 pm on Wednesday (10 races). Admission is US$0.50 and there's a large section where food and drinks are sold.

From mid-March to November regular horse races are held at the *Galopp Loversenypálya Race Track* on Albertirsai út, next to Hungarexpo, every Sunday beginning at 2 pm. From May to September horse races are also held here on Thursday, beginning at 4 pm. Each session lasts for about four hours (10 races). You can see the track and smell the horses from Pillangó utca Metro Station but the entrance is a 15-minute walk away (as you leave the station turn left, then left again onto Albertirsai út). It's great fun to observe this authentic local scene even if you aren't a gambler.

Thermal Baths Budapest is a major spa centre with numerous bathing establishments that are open to the public. Here the Danube follows the geological fault separating the Buda Hills from the Great Plain and over 40 million litres of warm mineral water gush forth daily from 123 thermal springs.

Begin your bathhouse tour with the *Gellért Baths* (enter through the side entrance of the eclectic hotel of the same name below Gellért Hill). Built in 1918, the thermal pools there maintain a constant temperature of 44°C and a large outdoor pool is open in summer. A price list two metres long is posted in English and German beside the ticket booth (entry costs US$3.50 for three hours, a tub bath for two people US$6, a cubicle US$1.50, a 30-minute massage US$4 etc). You must wear a bathing cap (supplied) in the swimming pool. Men and women are separated in the communal baths and if you're a couple paying extra for a two-person tub bath make sure you'll be allowed in together! Therapeutical services such as traction cure, ultrasonic, inhalation and short-wave treatments are available. Everything except the swimming pool is closed in the afternoon on weekends.

There are two famous bathing establishments near the Buda end of Erzsébet híd (Elizabeth Bridge). The *Rudas Baths* beside the river were built by the Turks in 1566 and retain a strong Islamic flavour. The Rudas Baths are open daily for men only (closed on Saturday afternoon and Sunday). Women should make for the *Rác Baths* at the foot of the hill, on the opposite side of the bridge. The Rác Baths are reserved for women on Monday, Wednesday and Friday and for men on Tuesday, Thursday and Saturday. Admission is US$1.25 at both these. Unlike the Gellért Baths which are accustomed to receiving tourists, all the posted information at the Rudas and Rác baths is in Hungarian. The resulting confusion is partly compensated for by their lower prices, so be persistent.

Everyone passing this way should seek out the *ivocsarnok*, or well room (closed weekends), which is below the bridge, within sight of the Rudas Baths. Here you can indulge in the drinking cure for a few coins. Pay the cashier who will give you a ticket which entitles you to a big mug of hot radioactive water.

The *Király Baths*, Fő utca 84 (metro: Batthyány tér), are genuine Turkish baths erected in 1570. Like at the Rác Baths there are alternate days for males (Monday, Wednesday and Friday) and females (Tuesday, Thursday and Saturday).

If you would rather bathe in ultramodern surroundings, try the *Hotel Thermál* on Margaret Island. The baths there are open to the public daily from 7 am to 8 pm, admission US$7. This includes the use of the three hot thermal pools and the sauna. A massage costs US$12. If you didn't bring your own bathing suit you'll have to buy one for US$12 (no rentals). This is Budapest's most luxurious bathing establishment by far.

The *Municipal Baths* right outside Széchenyi Fürdő Metro Station in City Park are US$1.25 admission for the whole day. A bathing cap must be worn in the swimming pool. These baths are less touristy than some of the others, yet large enough so that you won't stand out.

The easiest way to get to the baths is to take the metro to Batthyány tér, then tram No 19 south to Rácz, Rudas and Gellért, or walk north to Király. To go to Hotel Thermál, take bus No 26 from Nyugati Railway Station. There are lockers where you can leave your valuables. Some bath houses require you to wear a bathing suit while others do not. Have one with you and go with the tide. Most of the public baths hire out bathing suits and towels if you don't have your own. Unfortunately the baths are sometimes frequented by people whose interests go beyond getting clean, and friendly conversation should be approached with caution. Budapest's ornate public bathhouses are highly recommended.

Things to Buy

Before you do any shopping for handicrafts at street markets, have a look in the Folkart Centrum, Váci utca 14 (metro: Ferenciek tere), a large government store where prices are clearly marked. When you know what you want and are familiar with the prices, you'll be in a better position to bargain with street vendors.

Hanglemezek on the Danube side of Vörösmarty tér has compact discs of Hungarian folk music, including a few by Kalyi Jag and Muzsikás, amid all the tourist Gypsy music.

The Rózsa Gallery, Szentháromság utca 13 in the castle district (closed Monday), sells paintings by well-known Hungarian naive artists such as Kapolyi Makai Hedvig (born in 1940). Prices begin around US$300.

The philatelic shop at Szabad-Sajtó út 6 next to the John Bull Pub just off Ferenciek tere, sells cheap packets of Hungarian stamps.

In the far back corner of the Pest Market

on Fovam tér (metro: Kálvin tér), past the strings of paprika and garlic, are a couple of stands where vendors sell genuine Hungarian folk costumes, dolls, painted eggs, embroidered tablecloths etc. You can also get *lángos* (big flat Hungarian doughnuts) or hot sausages here. (This market is presently closed.)

Getting There & Away

Bus There are three important bus stations in Budapest. For buses to Western Europe and most points west of the Danube, try the Erzsébet tér Bus Station (metro: Deák tér). There's a left-luggage office inside the Erzsébet tér Bus Station which is open daily from 6 am to 6 pm.

Some buses for Eastern Europe and places east of the Danube depart from the Népstadion Bus Station, Hungária körút 48-52 (metro: Népstadion). Left luggage at Népstadion is in the office marked 'csomagmegőrző' below the stairway opposite platform No 6 (daily 6 am to 6 pm). Ring the bell.

Buses to the Danube Bend, including Esztergom and Visegrád, leave from the bus station next to Árpád híd Metro Station. For details of international bus and train services see the general Getting There & Away section in this chapter.

Train Budapest has three main train stations, all connected by metro. Keleti Railway Station (east) receives trains from Vienna Westbahnhof, Bucharest (via Arad), Belgrade, Poland, Košice, and northern Hungary.

Services from Bucharest (via Oradea), the Great Plain and the Danube Bend arrive at Nyugati Railway Station (west), also on the left bank of the Danube. Trains from Bratislava and Prague (via Štúrovo or Komárom) may use either Keleti or Nyugati.

Trains from Vienna Südbahnhof, Zagreb, Ljubljana, Pécs, Balaton Lake and western Transdanubia generally use Déli Railway Station (south) on the Buda side of the city. There are exceptions to the above, however, so be sure to check carefully which station you'll be using.

If you arrive in Budapest on a special summer train that continues through to another destination (Berlin to Bulgaria, for example), beware of missing the stop as the trains often don't go in to a main station, stopping instead at Köbánya-Kispest.

Train Stations When Keleti Railway Station opened in 1884 it was the most modern station in Central Europe. Keleti has somewhat better facilities than Nyugati. The domestic ticket windows are down the stairway from the end of tracks Nos 7 and 8. The international ticket office (with Hungarian-speaking staff) is in the main station hall next to track No 6 (allow one hour to purchase a ticket there in summer). The English-speaking staff at the nearby Ibusz office in Keleti sell the same international tickets and their queue is often shorter. The left-luggage office is also accessible from track No 6 (open 24 hours).

Nyugati Railway Station is a historic iron structure built in 1877 by the engineer Alexandre Gustave Eiffel of Paris. The ticket offices are in the main hall next to track No 13. The left-luggage office at Nyugati is near Ibusz on platform No 10 (open 24 hours). A 24-hour supermarket operates inside Nyugati.

At Déli Railway Station, both the international and domestic ticket windows are upstairs at the end of the platforms. The left-luggage office is on the outer side of the building, downstairs next to the taxi rank and behind Mister Minit (daily 4 am to midnight).

For currency exchange facilities in and around the stations see Money above. Don't take your eyes off your luggage for even a few seconds in any of these stations.

Getting Around

To/From the Airport There are two terminals several km apart at Budapest Ferihegy Airport, 16 km south-east of the centre. Malév Hungarian Airlines, Air France and Lufthansa flights use the new Ferihegy No 2

HUNGARY

terminal, while most other airlines fly out of the older Ferihegy No 1 terminal. Airport minibuses depart from the Erzsébet tér Bus Station every half-hour from 6 am to 9 pm (40 minutes, US$2.50) – buy your ticket from the driver. You can also get to Ferihegy Airport by taking the metro to Kőbánya-Kispest, then bus No 93 (red number) which stops at both terminals. Bus No 93 (black number) stops at Ferihegy No 1 only.

The Air Traffic and Airport Administration (LRI) operates a special eight-seater minibus which will take you between Terminal 1 and any address in Budapest for US$6 per person. This is much better than hassling with a taxi and is very convenient if you know exactly where you want to go upon arrival, though it's not the fastest way as each person is individually dropped off at their door. If you use this service to go to the airport allow an extra hour at least as they will drive around picking up other passengers. Ask for the LRI Airport Passenger Service in the Arrivals Hall or call ☎ 157 8555 to be picked up.

For flight information at the airport dial ☎ 157 2122.

Public Transport Budapest has three underground metro lines intersecting at Deák tér: line M1, the 'yellow' line from Vörösmarty tér to Mexikoi út; line M2, the 'red' line from Déli to Örs Vezér tér; and line M3, the 'blue' line from Újpest-Központ to Köbánya-Kispest. A possible source of confusion on M2 is that one stop is called Vörösmarty tér and another is Vörösmarty utca. The HÉV suburban railway, which runs north from Batthyány tér Metro Station, is in effect a fourth metro line.

Unlike in Prague and Bucharest where you can change from one metro line to another without paying again, in Budapest you must cancel (use) another ticket if you change trains at Deák tér. There's also a very extensive network of tram, trolleybus and bus services. On certain bus lines the same numbered bus may have a black or a red number. In this case, the red-numbered bus is the express which makes limited stops. An invaluable transit map detailing all services is available at metro ticket booths.

To use public transport you must buy tickets at a kiosk, newsstand or metro entrance. Yellow tickets valid on the metro, trams, trolleybuses, regular buses and HÉV (as far as the city limits) cost US$0.30 each. You must validate your ticket once aboard. You may carry two pieces of luggage without paying an extra fare. Teams of ticket inspectors are sometimes waiting at the top of the escalators at metro exits (no escape possible). Never ride without a ticket on the HÉV as tickets are always checked there. The metro operates from 4.30 am till just after 11 pm. Certain tram and bus lines operate throughout the night. After 8 pm you must board buses through the front doors and show your ticket or transit pass (a sensible security precaution).

Transit Passes A day ticket for all trams, buses, trolleybuses, HÉV and metro lines costs US$2.25. You must specify the day you wish to use the pass and it's good only from midnight to midnight, so buy one the day before. Three days costs US$4.50 (no photo required).

To buy transit passes *(bérletek)* for longer periods you must supply one passport-size photo and write the serial number of your photo card (US$0.75 extra) onto the pass. A seven-day pass *(hetibérlet)* costs US$6, 14 days *(kétheti bérlet)* is US$8 and one month *(havibérlet)* is US$13. The monthly pass is valid up to the fifth day of the following month. These prices are for transit passes valid on the entire system, including buses. A pass without buses included is a dollar or two cheaper.

Transit passes can only be purchased at a few main metro stations. At Keleti Railway Station transit passes can be purchased at the Pénztár in the circular open-air courtyard at the entrance to the metro. At Nyugati Railway Station look for the Bérletpénztár down the stairs opposite the end of platform No 1. At Deák tér transit passes are sold in the underground passageway beneath Károly körút, at the ticket window beside the

Transportation Museum. Transit passes are not sold at Déli Railway Station and you must go to Moszkva tér Metro Station.

Taxi Taxis aren't cheap and, considering the excellent public transportation network, they're a real extravagance. We've heard from several readers who were grossly overcharged by taxi drivers in Budapest, so taking a taxi in this city should be approached with caution. Not all taxi metres are set at the same rates and some are much more expensive than others. The shiny Western taxis with no name on the door and only a removable taxi sign on the roof are the most likely to cheat you. Instead try to use the smaller, older taxis with the company name painted on the doors. Reliable companies include City Taxi, 6 X 6, Főtaxi, Yellow Pages and Volántaxi. The rip-off taxis tend to park mostly at places frequented by tourists while the company taxis wait at markets and outlying metro stations where they're more likely to get Hungarian passengers. If you feel you are being grossly overcharged, insist on a receipt *(számla)* before paying, then tell Tourinform or your hotel what happened. Better still, just avoid using taxis altogether.

Boats to the Danube Bend Mahart riverboats operate on the Danube between Budapest and Visegrád three times a day from mid-May to early September. One service continues on to Esztergom. In April, early May and late September the boat runs to Visegrád and Esztergom on weekends and holidays only. Some boats go via Szentendre, others via Vác, making it possible to do a round trip on different arms of the Danube. The Szentendre route is the more scenic.

In Budapest the boats leave from below Vigadó tér (metro: Vörösmarty tér) on the left bank. Ask at the yellow ticket office (☎ 118 1223) on the riverside below the Duna Marriott Hotel. They all stop first near Batthyány tér Metro Station.

This five-hour scenic cruise is highly recommended for a running view of Budapest and the river. There's an open deck upstairs where you can sit; the fare for the full one-way trip is only US$2 (bicycles US$1.25).

In addition to the regular cruises described above, from June to early September Mahart runs a hydrofoil nonstop between Budapest and Esztergom (68 km, 1½ hours, US$6 one way) on weekends and holidays only, departing from Budapest in the morning and Esztergom in the afternoon. You'll see mostly foreign tourists on the hydrofoils – the locals (and occasional noisy school groups!) prefer to take the slower, cheaper boats.

Sightseeing Cruises From May to September there are two-hour Mahart cruises (US$3) on the Danube daily at noon and 7 pm. In April the lunchtime cruise operates on weekends and holidays only. You can buy your ticket and board the boat at the yellow ticket office by the river at Vigadó tér below the Duna Marriott Hotel (metro: Vörösmarty tér). Other more expensive cruises such as the 'Legenda' cruises (US$12) are heavily promoted, but try to find the much cheaper Mahart boat. The night lights of the city rising to the castle, parliament and the Citadella make the evening trip far more attractive than the afternoon cruises, and the timing doesn't conflict with the rest of your sightseeing. The views of Budapest are great.

Local Ferries From May to September BKV passenger ferries run every hour from 9 am to 7 pm between Boráros tér, beside Petőfi híd (Petőfi Bridge), and Pünkösofürdő, with 10 stops along the way. Buy tickets (US$1) once aboard. The ferry stop closest to the castle district is Batthyány tér, and Petőfi tér is not far from Vörösmarty tér, a convenient place to pick up the boat on the Pest side.

The ticket clerk at the Petőfi tér landing may try to convince you to sign up for the one-hour cruise (US$6) instead of taking the regular passenger ferry *(vonaljárat)*, but just study the posted timetable and insist on what you want. Rómaifürdő is a good place to get off the ferry as it's easy to return to Budapest on the HÉV from there.

Car Rental The main Avis office (☎ 118 4685) is at the multi-level parking facility at Szervita tér 8 (metro: Deák tér). Hertz (☎ 117 7533) is at Aranykéz utca 4-8, off Váci utca, a block from Vörösmarty tér. Also in the centre is Inka Rent-a-Car (☎ 117 2150), Bajcsy-Zsilinszky út 16 (metro: Deák tér), and Budapest Rent-a-Car (☎ 117 2129), Roosevelt tér 5 off Zrínyi utca.

Within walking distance from Ferenc körút Metro Station are Coop-Car/EuroDollar (☎ 113-1466), Ferenc körút 43, Europcar (☎ 113 1492), Üllői út 62, and Volántourist Rent-a-Car (☎ 133 4783), Vaskapu utca 16. Budget Rent-a-Car (☎ 155 0482) has an office upstairs in the Buda Penta Hotel on Krisztina körút next to Déli Railway Station.

Avis, Budapest, Budget and Hertz also have offices at both airport terminals while Europcar is at Ferihegy No 1 only. If you use an airport office you will be charged a special service surcharge of US$15 or 7% of the bill. Ask about other hidden extras such as collision insurance, theft insurance, 25% tax etc, which can add up to almost as much as the basic charge. Avis, Budget and Hertz are much more expensive than local companies like Budapest, Inka and Volántourist. EuroDollar and Europcar are medium-priced. See Getting Around in the chapter introduction for more information.

HUNGARY

The Danube Bend

Between Vienna and Budapest, the Danube breaks through the Pilis and Börzsöny mountains in a sharp S-bend. Here medieval kings once ruled Hungary from majestic palaces overlooking the river at Esztergom and Visegrád. East of Visegrád, the river divides into two branches, with Szentendre and Vác facing different arms. Today the historic monuments, easy access, good facilities and forest trails combine to put this scenic area at the top of any visitor's list. This is the perfect place to come on a Danube River cruise.

GETTING THERE & AWAY

You can reach the Danube Bend from Budapest by rail, road, and river. The HÉV suburban railway runs to Szentendre, and Nagymaros and Esztergom are served by local trains from Budapest's Nyugati Railway Station. Szentendre, Visegrád and Esztergom are accessible by bus from Budapest's Árpád híd Bus Station. All of these services are fairly frequent and in summer Mahart riverboats stop at most of the places described in this section.

SZENTENDRE

A trip to Szentendre (St Andrew), 20 km north of Budapest on an arm of the Danube, should not be missed. In the late 17th century Serbian merchants fleeing the Turks settled here, bringing a Balkan influence. Although most of them returned home in the 19th century, the Serbian appearance remained. In the early years of this century, Szentendre became a favourite of painters and sculptors, and the artists' colony is still alive and thriving today with numerous galleries exhibiting local artists' work.

In recent years Szentendre has become Hungary's main tourist centre and you'll see all the latest fashions displayed in front of the thousand and one boutiques and on the trendy tourists parading up and down the streets. The façades of many of the houses are obscured by clothing and embroidery hung up for sale and café tables extend far out onto the pavement with postcard racks marking territory. Nevertheless, a stroll through the winding streets between the city's exotic Orthodox churches, or along the Danube embankment, is still a most enjoyable experience.

Orientation & Information

From the Szentendre HÉV station, it's only a short walk up Kossuth Lajos utca to Fő tér, the centre of the old town. The Danube embankment (Duna-korzó) is a block east of this square. The riverboat terminal and camping ground are a couple of km farther north. There's no left-luggage office at Szentendre HÉV/bus station but there is a transportation museum, however.

Tourinform, Dumtsa Jenő utca 22, has brochures and information on other parts of Hungary, as well as Szentendre. It distributes free brochures in English which describe the sights of Szentendre in far more detail than is possible here.

The Magyar Autóklub has a small service facility in the public parking lot on Dunakanyar körút.

Money Beware of the tricky exchange offices on Fő tér which advertise no commission but give a rate 10% lower than the bank unless you change at least US$2250 (the small notices advising you of this are in Hungarian!).

Instead, patronise the OTP Bank, Dumtsa Jenő utca 6, just off Fő tér (Monday 8 am to 3 pm, Tuesday to Thursday 8 am to 2 pm, Friday 8 am to 12.30 pm).

If the OTP Bank is closed, head for Ibusz, Bogdányi utca 1, which is open longer hours and gives a rate only about 2% lower than the bank for travellers' cheques.

Things to See

Begin with Fő tér, which on July evenings becomes a stage for theatrical performances. Most of the buildings around the square date from the 18th century, as does the plague column (1763) in the centre and also (in one corner) the **Blagovesztenska Greek Orthodox Church** (1752).

In an alley off the east side of Fő tér is the **Kovács Margit Museum** at Vastagh György utca 1. It's the most delightful gallery in Szentendre and admission costs US$0.75. Margit Kovács (1902-77) based her decorative ceramic objects on Hungarian folk-art traditions, creating a style all of her own. Also be sure to see the **Ferenczy Museum**, Fő tér 6 beside the Greek Church, which displays the artwork of the Ferenczy clan, pioneers of the Szentendre artists' colony.

Narrow lanes lead up from Fő tér to the Catholic **parish church** (rebuilt in 1710) from where you get splendid views of the town. On Saturday and Sunday in July and August a large folk market is held here. The **Czóbel Béla Museum** is opposite the church. Just north is the tall red tower of **Belgrade Church** (1756), the finest of the Serbian churches. Beside the church is a museum of Serbian religious art.

Other art galleries worth seeing are the **Amos-Anna Museum**, Bogdányi utca 10, the **Kerényi Museum**, Ady Endre utca 6 on the way to Pap Island, and the **Barcsay Collection**, Dumsta Jenő utca 10 near Fő tér.

The **Ethnographic Open-air Museum** which is large and includes reconstructed farmhouses from around the country is about four km north-west of Szentendre. Buses from stand No 8 at the bus station run there only every couple of hours, but a minibus shuttle from the Tourinform office on Dumtsa Jenő utca will take you directly there almost whenever you want to go for US$1.25 return.

All of the museums are closed on Monday and a couple also on Tuesday. From November to March the open-air museum is closed and several other museums are only open on Friday, Saturday and Sunday.

Activities

In summer Ibusz rents bicycles at US$9 a day (shorter periods negotiable). Take the hourly ferry across to Szentendre Island and you'll have km of uncrowded cycling ahead of you.

The Wiking Restaurant on Duna-korzó just north of the centre rents jet skis at US$80 an hour.

Places to Stay

Camping *Aquatours Camping* (☎ 311 106), Ady Endre út 9-11, near the ferry landing just a short walk north of the centre, is a relaxing, quiet place to camp (US$2 per person, plus US$2 per tent) and they also have two single rooms (US$9) and four double rooms (US$14), all with toilet and shower, plus one four-bed house with toilet and kitchen (US$31). Ask the manager about canoe rentals (midsummer only). Aquatours is open from May to September.

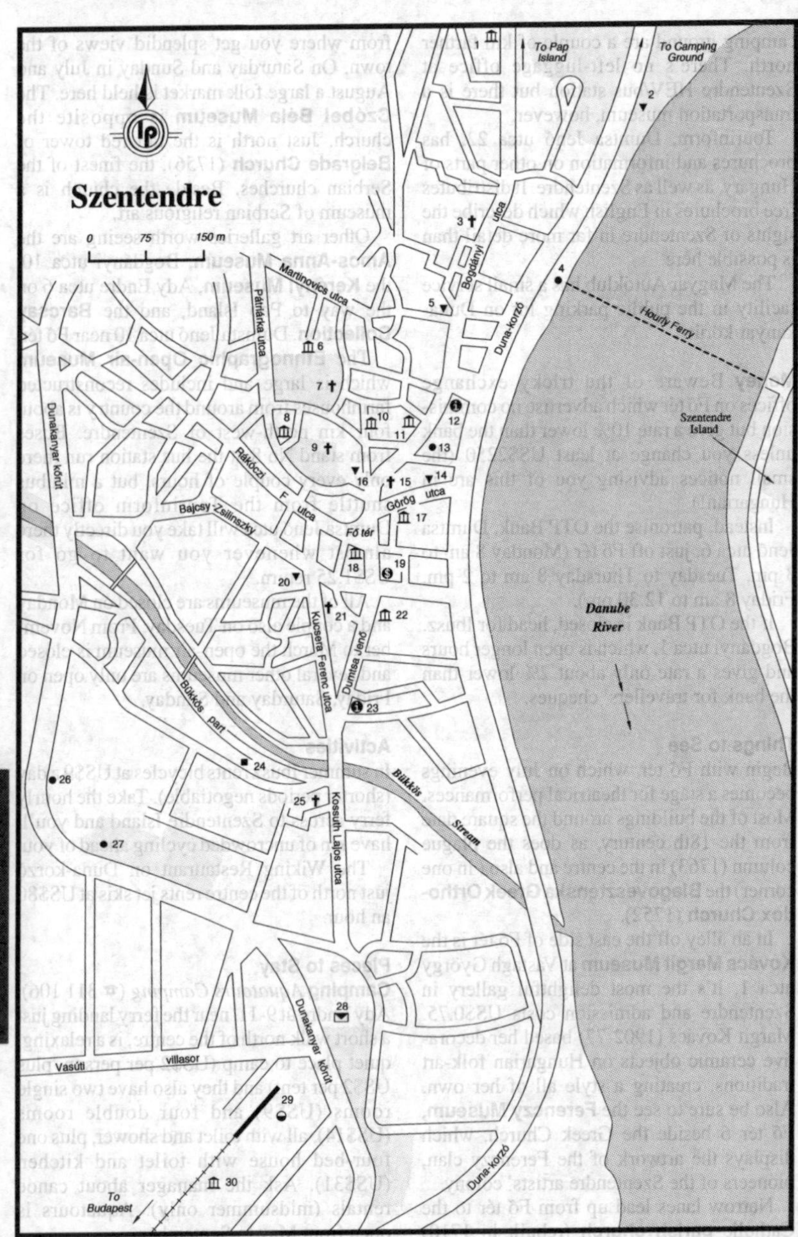

Szentendre
0
75
150 m
To Pap Island
To Camping Ground
Martinovics utca
Pátriárka utca
Bogdányi utca
Duna-korzó
Hourly Ferry
Szentendre Island
Dunakanyar körút
Rákóczi
F
utca
Görög
utca
Bajcsy-Zsilinszky
Fő tér
Danube River
Kucsera Ferenc utca
Dumtsa Jenő
Bükkös
part
Bükkös
Stream
Kossuth Lajos utca
Dunakanyar körút
Vasúti
villasor
To Budapest
Duna-korzó
1
2
3
4
5
6
7
8
9
10
11
12
13
14
15
16
17
18
19
20
21
22
23
24
25
26
27
28
29
30

PLACES TO STAY

24 Bükkös Panzió

PLACES TO EAT

2 Wiking Restaurant
5 Bárczy Fogadó
14 Surányi István Cukrászda
16 Angyal Borozó
20 Rab-Ráby Vendéglő

OTHER

1 Kerényi Museum
3 Preobraženska Church
4 Ferry to Szentendre Island
6 Serbian Art Museum
7 Belgrade Church
8 Czóbel Béla Museum
9 Catholic Parish Church
10 Vajda Lajos Museum
11 Amos-Anna Museum
12 Ibusz
13 Dunatours
15 Blagovesztenska Greek Orthodox Church
17 Kováks Margit Museum
18 Kmetty Museum
19 OTP Bank
21 Sts Peter & Paul Church
22 Barcsay Collection
23 Tourinform
25 Požarevačka Church
26 Magyar Autóklub Service Facility
27 Roman Sculpture Garden
28 Post Office
29 HÉV Railway & Bus Stations
30 Transportation Museum

Two km north of Szentendre near the Danube riverboat landing is *Pap-Sziget Camping* (☎ 310 697) run by Dunatours on Pap Island, just across the bridge from the Danubius Hotel bus stop. Camping is US$8 for two persons with tent and they also have 14 bungalows with bath at US$20 single or double, US$28 triple. The 20 motel rooms with shared bath are US$11 single or double, US$15 triple. All charges are plus US$1 tax per person per night, although the first night is free. Reception is open from 8 am to 4 pm only and you must check out by 10 am or you'll have to pay for another night. The overnight fee includes admission to the swimming pool next door and other facilities include a small supermarket, snack bar and restaurant. There's a disco here on weekends (ask about this when checking in and pitch your tent accordingly). This camping ground is open from May to September.

Private Rooms You can easily see Szentendre on a day trip from Budapest but the town also makes a good base from which to explore the Danube Bend. Dunatours (Idegenforgalmi Hivatal), Bogdányi utca 1, and Ibusz, Bogdányi utca 11, arrange private rooms. At US$15 double (no singles), Dunatours is about a dollar cheaper than Ibusz and in summer Dunatours is open weekends from 10 am to 6 pm.

Camping *Aquatours Camping* (☎ 311 106), Ady Endre út 9-11, near the ferry landing just a short walk north of the centre, is a relaxing, quiet place to camp (US$2 per person, plus US$2 per tent) and they also have two single rooms (US$9) and four double rooms (US$14), all with toilet and shower, plus one four-bed house with toilet and kitchen (US$31). Ask the manager about canoe rentals (midsummer only). Aquatours is open from May to September.

Two km north of Szentendre near the Danube riverboat landing is *Pap-Sziget Camping* (☎ 310 697) run by Dunatours on Pap Island, just across the bridge from the Danubius Hotel bus stop. Camping is US$8 for two persons with tent and they also have 14 bungalows with bath at US$20 single or double, US$28 triple. The 20 motel rooms with shared bath are US$11 single or double, US$15 triple. All charges are plus US$1 tax per person per night, although the first night is free. Reception is open from 8 am to 4 pm only and you must check out by 10 am or you'll have to pay for another night. The overnight fee includes admission to the swimming pool next door and other facilities include a small supermarket, snack bar and restaurant. There's a disco here on weekends (ask about this when checking in and pitch your tent accordingly). This camping ground is open from May to September.

Pensions & Hotels There are several small

pensions around town but all are quite expensive. The cheapest is the *Mini Hotel Apollo* (☎ 310 909), Méhész utca 3, off Dunakanyar körút on the north side of town, with six rooms at US$15/17 single/double. It's open year-round.

The 10-room *Hotel Fenyes* (☎ 311 882), Ady Endre utca 26, north of the centre, is US$15 single or double, US$22 triple with shared bath, and you can also camp in their garden. It's a good backup choice if the camping grounds are full or closed (open year-round). Next door is the more expensive *Danubius Hotel*.

Places to Eat

An ABC supermarket is next to the HÉV station if you want to give Szentendre's touristy restaurants a miss and have a riverside picnic.

Dixie Chicken, Dumtsa Jenő utca 16, is your standard greasy fast-food joint but they do have a salad bar and frozen yogurt, and you can sit in the back courtyard.

The *Régimódi Restaurant*, on Futó utca just down from the Kovács Margit Museum, occupies an old Szentendre house. *Angyal Borozó*, Alkotmány utca 4, posts an English menu outside. The *Bárczy Fogadó*, an old inn at Bogdányi utca 30, is more expensive.

Since 1974 Szentendre's best coffee, desserts and ice cream have been consumed standing up at *Surányi István Cukrászda*, Görög utca 4 (closed Monday and Tuesday). Hungarians flock here as it's one of the few places in town that charges normal prices.

Check to see if the lángos stall is open. These hot Hungarian doughnuts are one of the best deals in Szentendre but in winter the stall is only open on weekends. The stall is halfway up Váralja Lépcsö, a tiny alley between Fő tér 8 and 9 (closed Monday).

HUNGARY

Getting There & Away

Access to Szentendre couldn't be easier. Take the HÉV from Budapest's Batthyány tér Metro Station to the end of the line (21 km, 40 minutes). There are several trains an hour. If you have a Budapest transit pass show it to the clerk when buying your HÉV ticket to/from Szentendre and you'll get a discount.

Buses from Budapest's Árpád híd Bus Station also run to Szentendre frequently. Onward service to Visegrád and Esztergom is good.

From mid-May to early September, Mahart riverboats between Budapest and Visegrád stop at Szentendre three times daily. In April, early May and late September the boat only operates once a day on weekends and holidays. The landing *(hajóállomás)* is near Pap Island, a km north of the centre.

VISEGRÁD

Visegrád is superbly situated on a horseshoe bend of the Danube, between the Pilis and Börzsöny mountains. For hundreds of years the river was the border of the Roman Empire. After Tatar invasions in the 13th century, the Hungarian kings built a mighty citadel on a hill top with a wall running down to a lower castle near the river. In the 14th century a royal palace was built on the flood plain at the foot of the hills and the Angevin court moved here in 1323. For nearly two centuries Hungarian kings and queens alternated between Visegrád and Buda. The reign of the Renaissance monarch Matthias Corvinus in the 15th century was the period of greatest glory for Visegrád.

The destruction of Visegrád came with the Turks and later in 1702 when the Habsburgs blew up the citadel to prevent Hungarian independence fighters from using it as a base. All trace of the palace was lost until 1934 when archaeologists following descriptions in literary sources uncovered the ruins that you can visit today.

Things to See & Do

You can visit the **palace ruins** at Fő utca 27 daily except Monday throughout the year from 9 am to 4 pm. Some of the highlights are a red-marble fountain bearing the coat of arms of King Matthias in the Gothic courtyard and, on an upper terrace, a copy of the lion wall fountain, which is covered in winter. The original fountains are kept in the

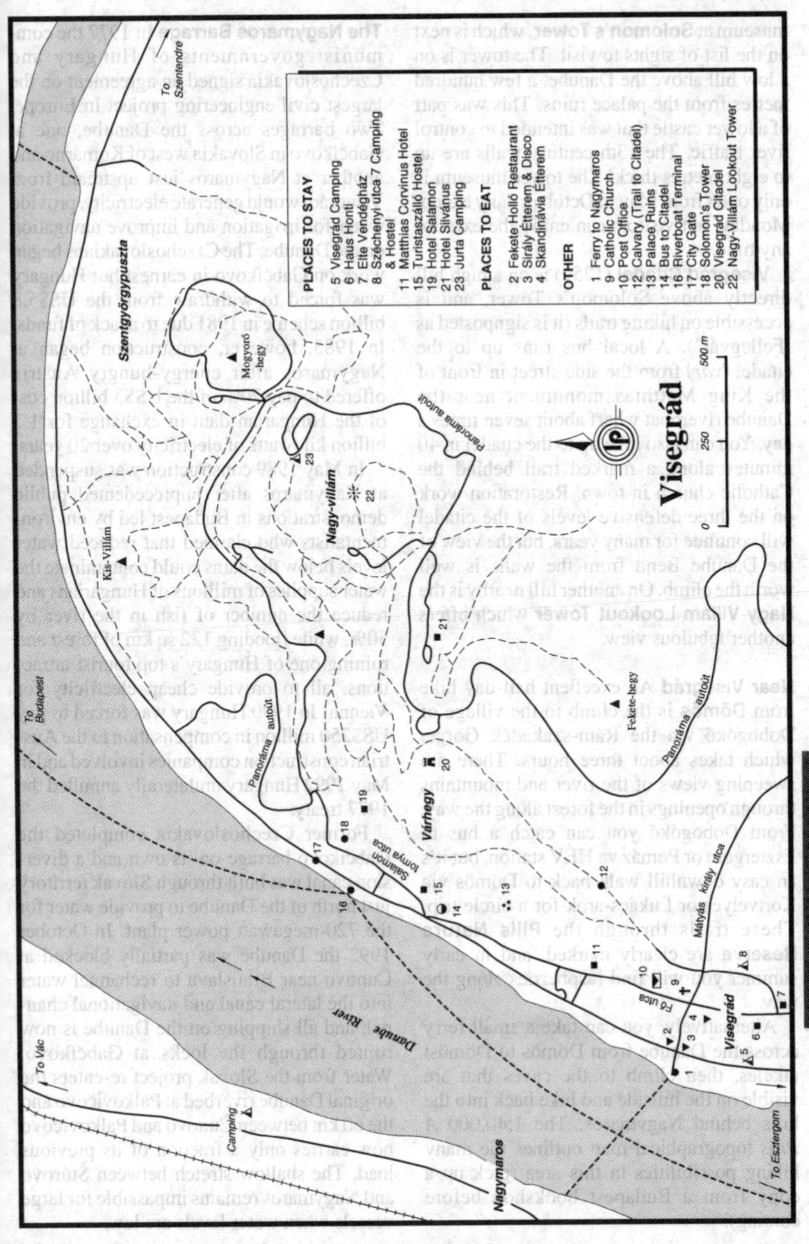
Visegrád
PLACES TO STAY
5 Visegrád Camping
6 Haus Honti
7 Elte Vendégház
8 Széchenyi utca 7 Camping & Hostel
11 Matthias Corvinus Hotel
15 Turistaszálló Hostel
19 Hotel Salamon
21 Hotel Silvánus
23 Jurta Camping
PLACES TO EAT
2 Fekete Holló Restaurant
3 Sirály Étterem & Disco
4 Skandinávia Étterem
OTHER
1 Ferry to Nagymaros
9 Catholic Church
10 Post Office
12 Calvary (Trail to Citadel)
13 Palace Ruins
14 Bus to Citadel
16 Riverboat Terminal
17 City Gate
18 Solomon's Tower
20 Visegrád Citadel
22 Nagy-Villám Lookout Tower
0
250
500 m
To Szentendre
Szentgyörgypuszta
Mogyoró-hegy
Panoráma autóút
Nagy-Villám
Kis-Villám
To Budapest
Várhegy
Salamon tornya utca
Fekete-hegy
Mátyás király utca
Fő utca
Visegrád
Danube River
To Vác
Camping
Nagymaros
To Esztergom

HUNGARY

museum at **Solomon's Tower**, which is next on the list of sights to visit. The tower is on a low hill above the Danube, a few hundred metres from the palace ruins. This was part of a lower castle that was intended to control river traffic. The 13th-century walls are up to eight metres thick! The tower museum is only open from May to October, daily except Monday, but visitors can enjoy the exterior any time.

Visegrád Citadel (1259) is on a high hill directly above Solomon's Tower, and is accessible on hiking trails (it is signposted as 'Fellegvár'). A local bus runs up to the citadel *(vár)* from the side street in front of the King Matthias monument near the Danube riverboat wharf about seven times a day. You can also hike up to the citadel in 40 minutes along a marked trail behind the Catholic church in town. Restoration work on the three defensive levels of the citadel will continue for many years, but the view of the Danube Bend from the walls is well worth the climb. On another hill nearby is the **Nagy-Villám Lookout Tower** which offers another fabulous view.

Near Visegrád An excellent half-day hike from **Dömös** is the climb to the village of Dobogókő via the Rám-szakadék Gorge, which takes about three hours. There are sweeping views of the river and mountains through openings in the forest along the way. From Dobogókő you can catch a bus to Esztergom or Pomáz va HÉV station, but it's an easy downhill walk back to Dömös via Kortvelyes or Lukács-arok for a circle trip. These trails through the **Pilis Nature Reserve** are clearly marked, and in early summer you will find raspberries along the way.

Alternatively, you can take a small ferry across the Danube from Dömös to Dömösi átkéles, then climb to the caves that are visible on the hillside and hike back into the hills behind Nagymaros. The 1:40,000 *A Pilis* topographical map outlines the many hiking possibilities in this area (pick up a copy from a Budapest bookshop before coming).

HUNGARY

The Nagymaros Barrage In 1977 the communist governments of Hungary and Czechoslovakia signed an agreement on the largest civil-engineering project in Europe. Two barrages across the Danube, one at Gabčíkovo in Slovakia west of Komárno and another at Nagymaros just upstream from Visegrád, would generate electricity, provide water for irrigation and improve navigation on the Danube. The Czechoslovakians began work on Gabčíkovo in earnest but Hungary was forced to withdraw from the US$5.8 billion scheme in 1981 due to a lack of funds. In 1985, however, construction began at Nagymaros after energy-hungry Austria offered to pay 70% of the US$3 billion cost of the Hungarian dam in exchange for 1.2 billion kilowatts of electricity over 20 years.

In May 1989 construction was suspended at Nagymaros after unprecedented public demonstrations in Budapest led by environmentalists who claimed that reduced water levels below the dams could contaminate the water supplies of millions of Hungarians and reduce the number of fish in the river by 50%, while flooding 122 sq km of forest and ruining one of Hungary's top tourist attractions, all to provide cheap electricity for Vienna! In 1990 Hungary was forced to pay US$250 million in compensation to the Austrian construction companies involved and in May 1992 Hungary unilaterally annulled the 1977 treaty.

Former Czechoslovakia completed the Gabčíkovo barrage on its own and a diversion canal was built through Slovak territory just north of the Danube to provide water for the 720-megawatt power plant. In October 1992 the Danube was partially blocked at Čunovo near Bratislava to rechannel water into the lateral canal and navigational channel, and all shipping on the Danube is now routed through the locks at Gabčíkovo. Water from the Slovak project re-enters the original Danube riverbed at Palkovičovo and the 60 km between Čunovo and Palkovičovo now carries only a fraction of its previous load. The shallow stretch between Štúrovo and Nagymaros remains impassible for large vessels when water levels are low.

The affair seriously damaged Hungary's relations with Czechoslovakia's successor state, Slovakia, and both countries have asked the International Court of Justice in The Hague to rule on the matter. Slovakia has condemned Hungary's violation of its treaty obligations while Hungary has objected to Slovakia's expropriation of international waters. Lately, Hungary has dropped its insistence that Gabčíkovo must be closed and the dispute now centres on how much water should be allowed to flow down the original Danube which marks the international boundary between the countries.

This whole controversy comes back to modern society's insatiable thirst for energy. Coal and nuclear-powered generators aren't very attractive either, and the problems created by acid rain and nuclear wastes are just as serious as the potential ecological consequences of a barrage at Nagymaros. Perhaps an idyllically beautiful yet threatened spot like Visegrád is just the place to sit and ponder these problems.

Places to Stay

Hostels & Camping There are two tourist hostels *(turistaszálló)* at Visegrád. One is at Salamon tornya utca 5 near the Danube riverboat landing, but the nicest is perhaps the one at Széchenyi utca 7 near the centre of the village. It's beside a small stream, back behind the church with the green tower, and you are also allowed to camp. Dorm beds are US$4 per person, while camping is US$1.25 per person plus US$2.25 per tent. This quiet, uncrowded site should be the first place you check, but both it and the hostel at Salamon tornya utca 5 are closed from October to April.

Motorists may prefer *Visegrád Camping* (☎ 328 102), by the highway just south of the Nagymaros ferry. Camping space is US$2 per person, US$1 per tent, plus US$0.75 per person tax, but no bungalows are available (open May to September).

Private Rooms Many houses along Fő utca have signs advertising 'Zimmer frei' ('room available'). One such is *Haus Honti*, Fő utca 66 next to a picturesque little stream. Also try the house at Fő utca 107 across the street.

Nearby at Fő utca 117 is the *Elte Vendégház* (☎ 328 165), a four-storey hotel with nine double rooms and 24 triples at US$9 per person (higher in July and August). It closes in winter.

Fanny Travel Agency, Fő utca 46 next to Skandinávia Étterem, has expensive private rooms.

Places to Eat

Skandinávia Étterem, Fő utca 48, has reasonable daily specials listed on a menu outside.

The *Fekete Holló* (closed Monday), a fish restaurant opposite the Nagymaros ferry on the Visegrád side, is touristy, so you're better off crossing the river to the *Maros Vendéglő* (closed Monday but open all year), near the Nagymaros ferry wharf on the Nagymaros side. The food is good, prices are moderate and in summer you can dine on a terrace overlooking the river. Check the ferry times carefully if you want to return late to Visegrád.

Getting There & Away

Buses between Budapest's Árpád híd Bus Station and Esztergom sometimes go via Visegrád but bus service is more frequent from stands Nos 1 and 2 at the Szentendre HÉV station. In summer some buses from the HÉV go all the way up to Nagy-Villám, so ask.

From mid-May to early September Mahart riverboats ply between Budapest and Visegrád three times a day. Twice daily there's service to Esztergom. In April, early May and late September the boat only operates on weekends and holidays.

Hourly ferries cross the Danube to Nagymaros. Don't panic if the large car ferry closes down early for the night as a smaller passenger launch usually takes its place. The Nagymaros-Visegrád ferry operates all year except when the Danube freezes over, but service is also suspended when fog descends, a common occurrence in winter. From Nagymaros Railway Station, just inland from the ferry wharf, there are trains to

Budapest-Nyugati about every hour (51 km, one hour).

ESZTERGOM

Esztergom, opposite Štúrovo in Slovakia, at the western entrance to the Danube Bend, is one of Hungary's most historic cities. The 2nd-century Roman emperor-to-be Marcus Aurelius wrote his famous *Meditations* while he was camped here. Stephen I, founder of the Hungarian state, was born and crowned at Esztergom, which was capital of Hungary from the 10th to the 13th centuries. After the Tatar invasion of 1241, the king and court moved to Buda but Esztergom remained the ecclesiastical centre of Hungary, as it is today. Originally the clerics lived by the riverbank and royalty, on the hill top above. When the king departed, the archbishop moved up and occupied the palace, maintaining Esztergom's prominence. In 1543 the Turks ravaged the town and much had to be rebuilt in the 18th and 19th centuries.

Orientation & Information

The train station is at the southern edge of town, a 10-minute walk south of the bus station. From the train station walk north on Baross Gábor út, then along Ady Endre utca to Simor János utca and the bus station. The ticket clerk at the train station holds luggage (open 24 hours) but no left-luggage service is available at the bus station. The three information offices are Komturist, Lörincz utca 6; Gran Tours, Széchenyi tér 25; and Express (☎ 313 113), Széchenyi tér 7. The Magyar Autóklub (☎ 311 908), Schweidel utca 5, is south of the centre near the train station.

HUNGARY

Money The OTP Bank on Bajcsy-Zsilinszky utca in the centre of town (open Monday from 8 am to 3.30 pm, Tuesday to Thursday 8 am to 2.30 pm and Friday 8 am to 12.30 pm) changes travellers' cheques.

Things to See

The bus station is a couple of blocks southeast of Széchenyi tér, the medieval market place, where the **town hall** (1773) is found. A block south is the **Inner City Parish Church** (1757), near a branch of the Danube that is lined by delightful little houseboats. Cross the footbridge to Primas Island and follow Gózhajó utca directly across to the riverboat landing on the main Danube channel.

Nearby stand the ruins of the **Mária Valéria Bridge**, the only bridge across the Danube between Budapest and Komárom. The retreating Germans blew up the bridge at the end of WW II but reconstruction is now underway with the reopening scheduled for 1995, to coincide with the centenary of the bridge's original construction. Hungary wants to open an international border crossing here but Slovakia is resisting for some reason. At present only citizens of the neighbouring countries can use the nearby ferry – this may change soon (see the following Getting There & Away section).

Continue north along the river and cross the bridge to **Víziváros Parish Church** (1738). Esztergom's famous **Christian Museum** (closed Monday) is in the adjacent **Primate's Palace** (1882). This is one of the best art collections in Hungary so don't miss it. A plaque on the side of the Primate's Palace bears the name 'József Mindszenty' and is dated 26 December 1948. Cardinal Mindszenty was arrested that day for refusing to allow the Catholic schools of Hungary to be secularised; in 1949 he was sentenced to life imprisonment for treason. Freed during the 1956 uprising, Mindszenty was soon forced to seek refuge in the US embassy in Budapest where he stayed until 1971. In 1974 Mindszenty was sacked as primate of Hungary for his criticism of the Pope's dealings with the communist regime and he died in Vienna in 1975. Nearby at Pázmany Péter utca 13 is the **Bálint Balassi Museum** (closed Monday) with objects of local interest. The lyric poet Bálint Balassi died defending Esztergom from the Turks in 1594.

You can't help noticing **Esztergom Cathedral**, the largest church in Hungary, which is on a high hill above the Danube. The building was rebuilt in the neoclassical

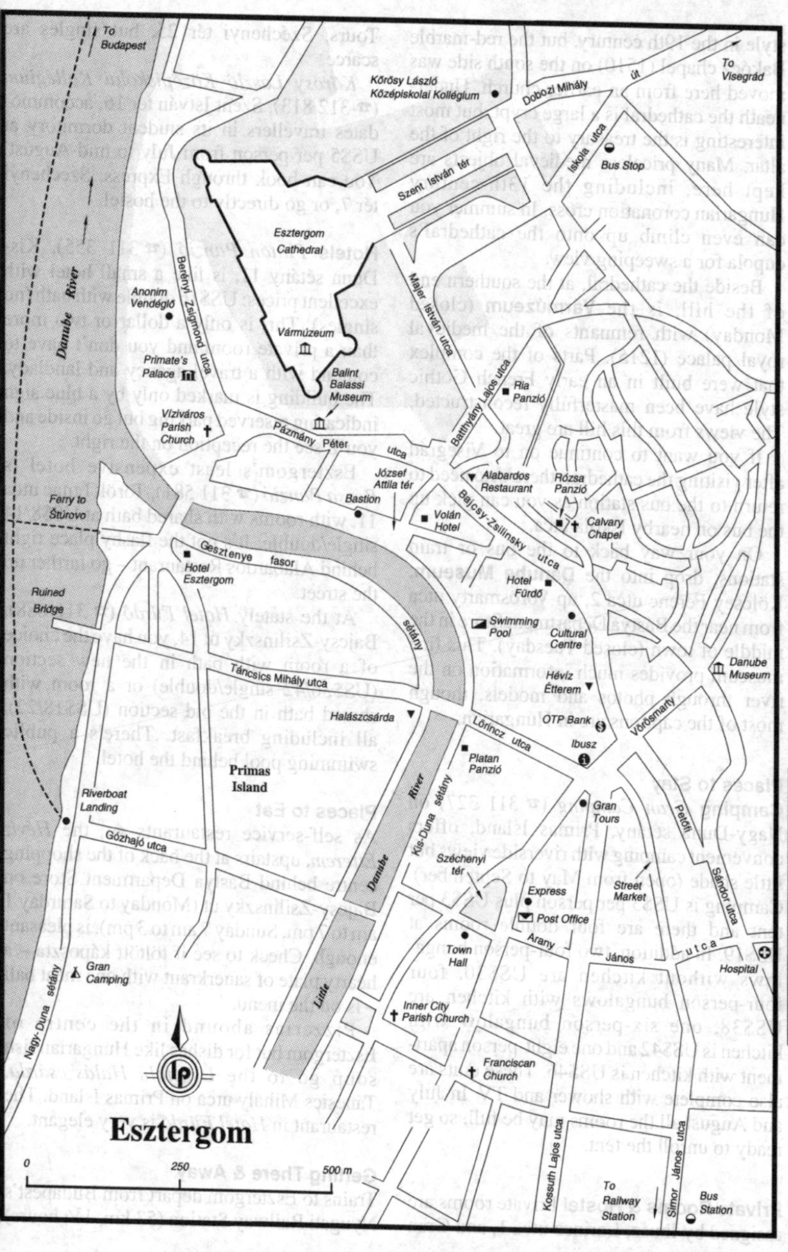
To Budapest
To Visegrád
Kőrösy László Középiskolai Kollégium
Dobozi Mihály út
Iskola utca
Bus Stop
Szent István tér
Esztergom Cathedral
Danube River
Berényi Zsigmond utca
Anonim Vendéglő
Vármúzeum
Primate's Palace
Majer István utca
Balint Balassi Museum
Víziváros Parish Church
Batthyány Lajos utca
Ria Panzió
Pázmány Péter utca
József Attila tér
Alabardos Restaurant
Rózsa Panzió
Bastion
Ferry to Štúrovo
Volán Hotel
Bajcsy-Zsilinsky utca
Calvary Chapel
Gesztenye fasor
Hotel Esztergom
Hotel Fürdő
Ruined Bridge
sétány
Swimming Pool
Cultural Centre
Danube Museum
Táncsics Mihály utca
Hévíz Étterem
Vörösmarty
Halászcsárda
Lőrincz utca
OTP Bank
Ibusz
Platan Panzió
Primas Island
Riverboat Landing
Danube River
Kis-Duna sétány
Gran Tours
Gőzhajó utca
Széchenyi tér
Petőfi Sándor utca
Street Market
Express
Post Office
Arany János utca
Town Hall
Hospital
Gran Camping
Little Danube
Nagy-Duna sétány
Inner City Parish Church
Franciscan Church
Esztergom
0
250
500 m
Kossuth Lajos utca
Simor János utca
To Railway Station
Bus Station

HUNGARY

style in the 19th century, but the red-marble Bakócz chapel (1510) on the south side was moved here from an earlier church. Underneath the cathedral is a large crypt, but most interesting is the treasury to the right of the altar. Many priceless medieval objects are kept here, including the 13th-century Hungarian coronation cross. In summer you can even climb up onto the cathedral's cupola for a sweeping view.

Beside the cathedral, at the southern end of the hill, is the **Vármúzeum** (closed Monday) with remnants of the medieval royal palace (1215). Parts of the complex that were built in an early French Gothic style have been masterfully reconstructed. The views from this hill are great.

If you want to continue on to Visegrád after visiting the cathedral, there's no need to return to the bus station as you can pick up the bus on nearby Iskola utca.

On your way back to the bus or train stations, drop into the **Danube Museum**, Kölcsey Ferenc utca 2, up Vörösmarty utca from near the Bástya Department Store in the middle of town (closed Tuesday). This fine museum provides much information on the river through photos and models, though most of the captions are in Hungarian.

HUNGARY

Places to Stay

Camping *Gran Camping* (☎ 311 327) on Nagy-Duna sétány, Primas Island, offers convenient camping with riverside views but little shade (open from May to September). Camping is US$3 per person plus US$3 per tent and there are four double rooms at US$19. In addition, two four-person bungalows without kitchen are US$30, four four-person bungalows with kitchen are US$38, one six-person bungalow with kitchen is US$42 and one eight-person apartment with kitchen is US$46. These units are also complete with shower and TV. In July and August all the rooms may be full, so get ready to unroll the tent.

Private Rooms & Hostel Private rooms are assigned by Ibusz, Lorincz utca 1, and Gran Tours, Széchenyi tér 25, but singles are scarce.

Kőrösy László Középiskolai Kollégium (☎ 312 813), Szent István tér 16, accommodates travellers in its student dormitory at US$5 per person from July to mid-August. You can book through Express, Széchenyi tér 7, or go directly to the hostel.

Hotels *Platán Panzió* (☎ 311 355), Kis-Duna sétány 11, is like a small hotel with excellent prices: US$16 double with bath (no singles). This is only a dollar or two more than a private room and you don't have to contend with a travel agency and landlady. The building is marked only by a blue sign indicating reserved parking but go inside and you'll see the reception on the right.

Esztergom's least expensive hotel is *Rózsa Panzió* (☎ 311 581), Török Ignác utca 11, with rooms with shared bath at US$8/14 single/double. It's not the flashy place right behind Alabardos Restaurant – go farther up the street.

At the stately *Hotel Fürdő* (☎ 311 688), Bajcsy-Zsilinszky út 14, you have the choice of a room with bath in the new section (US$36/42 single/double) or a room with shared bath in the old section (US$18/22), all including breakfast. There's a public swimming pool behind the hotel.

Places to Eat

As self-service restaurants go, the *Hévíz Étterem*, upstairs at the back of the shopping centre behind Bástya Department Store on Bajcsy-Zsilinszky út (Monday to Saturday 1 am to 7 pm, Sunday 7 am to 3 pm), is pleasant enough. Check to see if töltött káposzta – a hearty plate of sauerkraut with one meat ball – is on the menu.

Pizzerias abound in the centre of Esztergom but for dishes like Hungarian fish soup go to the *Úszófalu Halászcsárda*, Táncsics Mihály utca on Primas Island. The restaurant in *Hotel Fürdő* is very elegant.

Getting There & Away

Trains to Esztergom depart from Budapest's Nyugati Railway Station (53 km, 1¾ hours) about nine times a day. To go to western Transdanubia or Slovakia, take one of four daily local trains from Esztergom to Komárom (53 km, 1½ hours).

Unless you have a railway pass it's faster and more convenient to come by bus and you'll be dropped much closer to the centre of town. Bus services from Budapest's Árpád híd Bus Station are frequent. Buses from Budapest to Esztergom may travel via either Pilisvörösvár, which is the faster, more direct route, or via Visegrád, which is long, slow and scenic. Buses to Budapest run about every half-hour from 5 am to 8 pm, to Visegrád and Szentendre hourly from 6 am to 8.40 pm and to Sopron twice daily.

Mahart riverboats travel to/from Budapest once a day from mid-May to early September with a stop at Visegrád. In April, early May and late September this boat only operates on weekends and holidays. From June to August a nonstop Mahart hydrofoil glides between Budapest and Esztergom on weekends and holidays. All services leave Budapest in the morning and Esztergom in the afternoon, allowing day trippers several hours to visit the cathedral. For Esztergom-based tourists, there's a morning boat to Visegrád from mid-May to early September.

A ferry crosses the Danube to Štúrovo, Slovakia, 10 times a day from mid-February to December (US$0.50). In the past only citizens of Slovakia and Hungary were allowed to use this ferry and the nearest border crossing open to Western tourists was at Komárom. In early 1994 it was announced that the Esztergom-Štúrovo ferry would soon be made available to international travellers, so check.

Western Transdanubia

Beyond the Bakony Mountains, north-west of Balaton Lake, lies the Kisalföld, or Little Plain, which is bounded by the Danube and the Alps. Conquered by the Romans but never occupied by the Turks, this enchanting corner of Transdanubia is surrounded by a string of picturesque small towns with a decidedly European air. The old quarters of Sopron and Győr are brimming with what were once the residences of prosperous burghers and clerics, while Kőszeg offers an intact medieval castle, Szombathely has Roman relics, Fertőd a magnificent baroque palace and Pannonhalma a functioning Benedictine monastery. This region is also a convenient gateway to/from Austria and Slovakia.

GETTING THERE & AWAY

Many trains link Sopron to Austria and you can walk in/out of Slovakia via Komárom. From Budapest's Déli Railway Station there are trains to Komárom, Győr, Sopron and Szombathely. Rail links to/from the Danube Bend (Esztergom-Komárom) and Balaton Lake (Székesfehérvár to Komárom and Veszprém to Győr or Szombathely) are also good, though travelling south-east from Sopron and Szombathely is often easier by bus.

KOMÁROM

Komárom is the gateway to Hungary for visitors arriving from Komárno, Slovakia. Until 1920 these two towns were one. In antiquity the Romans had a military post called Brigetio here and the Habsburgs also fortified the area, although their fortresses ended up being used against them by Hungarian rebels during the 1848-49 War of Independence.

Komárom's position behind a large bridge across the Danube is of passing interest and there's a good camping ground next to the public thermal baths, within walking distance of the train station and border crossing. If you arrive in the late afternoon, this is a good place to stop for the night.

Orientation & Information

The train station (with a left-luggage office in a separate building next to the main station) is very near the highway bridge to/from Slovakia. Komturist is at Mártírok útja 19a in the centre of town. Walk straight south from the bridge to the first traffic lights and you'll find it a block to the left and on the right. A map of this vicinity is included in the Komárno section of the Slovakia chapter.

Money The OTP Bank, Mártírok útja 21 next to Komturist, cashes travellers' cheques on Monday from 8 am to 5 pm, Tuesday to Thursday from 8 am to 3 pm and Friday from 8 am to 2 pm. At other times you should be able to change cash at Ibusz Camping or at Hotel Thermál.

Things to See & Do

Right next to Hotel Thermál is a **thermal bathing complex** (open all year, US$1). To get to the thermal baths from the Danube bridge, go south for two blocks and then turn left on Táncsics Mihály utca, a 10-minute walk. A sauna and massage are available in addition to the big thermal pool.

Among the sights of Komárom are two large 19th-century fortifications that were built by the Habsburgs. The **Csillag Fortress** is near the river just north of the Thermál Hotel. You can see it from the train as you arrive from Budapest. The **Igmándi Fortress** is on the south side of town.

Places to Stay

Komturist (☎ 341 767), Mártírok útja 19a, should have private rooms at US$6 per person but they're usually fully booked.

The closest hotel to the Danube bridge is the *Beke Hotel* (☎ 340 333), Bajcsy-Zsilinszky út 8, a renovated two-storey building with rooms with shared bath at US$15 single or double.

Right next to the thermal baths is *Ibusz Camping* (☎ 342 551), on Táncsics Mihály utca. Apart from camping, they have bungalows with kitchen and private bath at US$23 for up to four people (often full).

The 39 rooms with bath at *Hotel Thermál* (☎ 342 447), Táncsics Mihály utca 38, cost US$19/22 single/double, breakfast included. Prices include admission to the thermal baths. Next to this attractive resort hotel is a camping ground that is open throughout the year. Motel-style units in the camping ground are US$10/12 single/double without bath or breakfast, but they're only available from mid-April to mid-October.

The newer and more luxurious *Hotel Karát* (☎ 342 222), Czuczor Gergely utca 54, two blocks from the baths, is US$23/25 single/double with bath and breakfast.

Getting There & Away

Train services from Komárom to Budapest (110 km, 1½ hours), Győr (37 km, 30 minutes) and Sopron (122 km, 1½ hours) are fairly frequent. (Most trains on this line depart from Budapest-Keleti but some use Budapest-Déli.) For the Danube Bend, catch a train to Esztergom (four daily, 53 km, 1½ hours), and for Balaton Lake take a train to Székesfehérvár (six daily, 82 km, 1½ hours).

Komárom is a convenient entry or exit point between Hungary and Slovakia. The highway bridge to Komárno, Slovakia, is just a five-minute walk from Komárom Railway Station and you can easily join the locals crossing between the two countries on foot. Both Hungarian and Slovakian passport controls are together at the Slovakian end of the bridge. Komárno is a much larger town than Komárom and the Slovakian train station is two km from the bridge. While travellers with backpacks will probably enjoy the walk, there's a bus between the two stations every couple of hours. Ask at the information counter in the stations for the departure time of the next bus and pay the driver.

On the Slovakian side you can easily catch a connecting local train to Bratislava (100 km), eliminating the need to buy an international train ticket. International trains usually cross the border here in the middle of the night and require compulsory seat reservations, so forget them. Turn to the Komárno section in the Slovakia chapter for more information.

GYŐR

Győr (Raab) is a historic city midway between Budapest and Vienna, in the heart of the Kisalföld at the point where the Mosoni-Danube, Rábca and Rába rivers

HUNGARY

meet. Győr-Sopron County is administered from here. In the 11th century, Stephen I established a bishopric here on what was the site of a Roman town named Arrabona. In the mid-16th century a strong fortress was erected at Győr to hold back the Turks.

Győr is Hungary's third-largest industrial centre, home to the Rába Engineering Works, which produces trucks and railway rolling stock. Despite this, the old town centre retains its charm. Less touristy than Esztergom, Sopron or Eger, Győr is well worth a visit.

Orientation

The neobaroque city hall (1898) towers above the train station. The left-luggage office at the train station (daily from 5 am to midnight) is next to the exit from one of the two tunnels under the tracks (the one closer to Budapest). This same tunnel leads directly through to the main bus station, which is just south of the train station. The old town is north, at the junction of the Rába and Mosoni-Danube rivers.

Information

Ciklámen Tourist is at Aradi vértanúk útja 22, a block from the train station.

The Magyar Autóklub (☎ 317 400), Bajcsy-Zsilinszky út 47, is a block east of the Express travel office.

Money If Győr is your first stop in Hungary you can change money at the MÁV Tours office upstairs from the main train station hall.

During banking hours you'll get a slightly better rate at the OTP Bank on Árpad út next to the Rába Hotel (Monday to Wednesday 7.45 am to 3 pm, Thursday until 5.30 pm, Friday until 1.30 pm). They change travellers' cheques without commission.

If both of the above are closed, try the Rába Hotel next to the OTP Bank or the reception at Hotel Klastrom which does accept travellers' cheques.

Post & Telephone The post office next to the train station is open weekend mornings (as well as during the week). Győr's telephone code is 96.

Things to See

If you follow Aradi vértanúk útja north to Becsi kapu tér, you'll find the enchanting **Carmelite church** (built in 1725) and many fine baroque palaces. On the far side of the square are fortifications that were built in the 16th century to stop the Turks. In the centre of Becsi kapu tér is a statue of the Romantic playwright Károly Kisfaludy (1788-1830).

Follow the narrow street north up onto Chapter Hill (Káptalan-domb), the oldest part of Győr. The large baroque **cathedral** (1639) on the hill was originally Romanesque, as you'll see if you look at the exterior of the apse. The baroque frescos on the ceiling are fine, but don't miss the Gothic chapel on the south side of the church which contains a glittering 14th-century bust of King St Ladislas. Opposite the cathedral is the fortified **bishop's palace** in a mixture of styles. Visit the garden.

The streets behind the cathedral are full of old palaces, and at the bottom of the hill on Jedlik Ányos utca is the outstanding **Arc of the Covenant Monument** (1731). A colourful open-air market unfolds on nearby Dunakapu tér. The view of the rivers from the adjacent bridge is good.

One of the nicest things about Győr is its atmospheric old streets, which seem not to have changed in centuries. Take a leisurely stroll down Apáca utca, Rákóczi Ferenc utca, Liszt Ferenc utca and Király utca where you'll see many fine buildings. The late Renaissance palace at Rákóczi Ferenc utca 6 was once a charity hospital. Go inside to admire the courtyards. Napoleon stayed in the house at Alkotmány utca 4 on 13 August 1809. It has now been turned into an art gallery.

Széchenyi tér is the heart of Győr and features a **Column of the Virgin** (1686) in the middle. **St Ignatius Church** (1641) is the finest church in the city with a superb pulpit and pews. Next door is the Benedictine Convent and next to it, at Széchenyi tér 9, is the **Széchenyi Pharmacy** (it is closed on

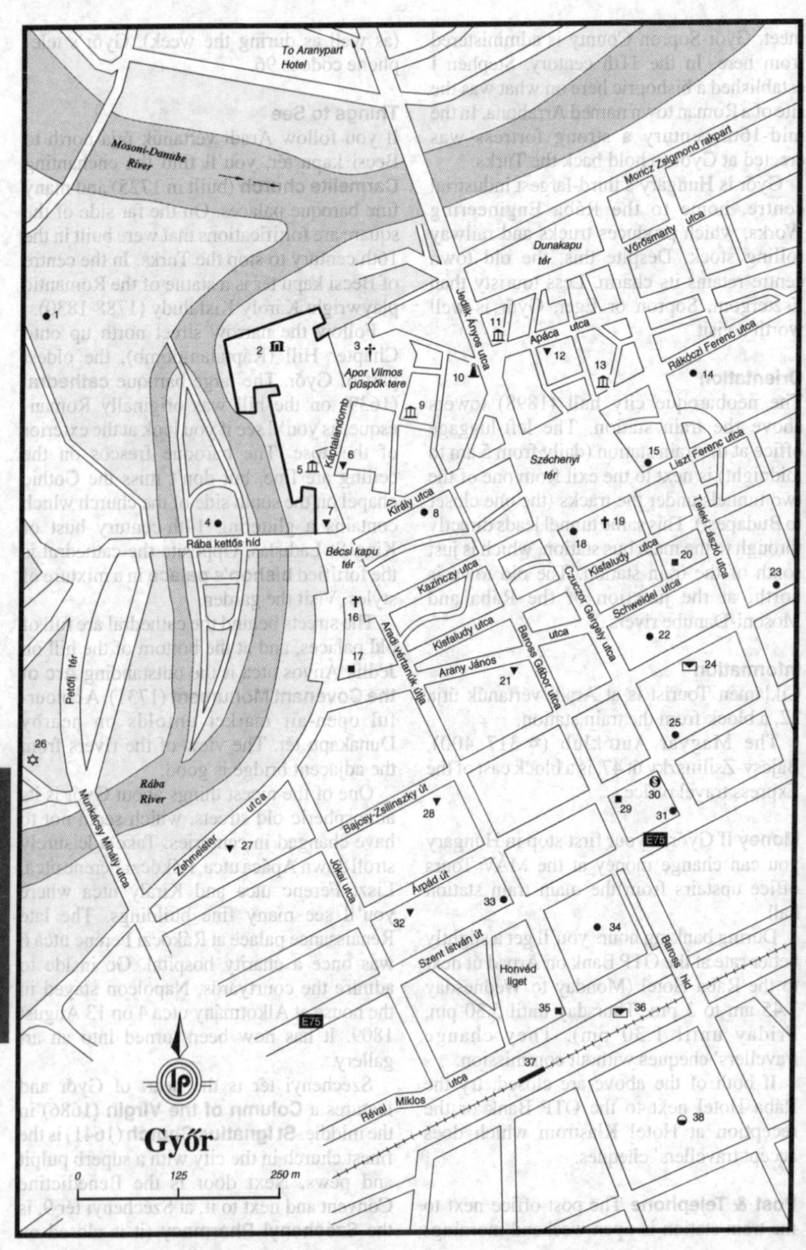
To Aranypart Hotel
Mosoni-Danube River
Moricz Zsigmond rakpart
Vörösmarty utca
Dunakapu tér
Jedlik Ányos utca
Apáca utca
Rákóczi Ferenc utca
Apor Vilmos püspök tere
Káptalandomb
Széchenyi tér
Liszt Ferenc utca
Király utca
Teleki László utca
Rába kettős híd
Bécsi kapu tér
Kisfaludy utca
Kazinczy utca
Czuczor Gergely utca
Schweidel utca
Kisfaludy utca
Baross Gábor utca
Arany János utca
Aradi vértanúk útja
Petőfi tér
Rába River
Bajcsy-Zsilinszky út
Zehmeister utca
Munkácsy Mihály utca
Jókai utca
Árpád út
Szent István út
Honvéd liget
Baross híd
Révai Miklós utca
E75
E75
Győr
0
125
250 m
1
2
3
4
5
6
7
8
9
10
11
12
13
14
15
16
17
18
19
20
21
22
23
24
25
26
27
28
29
30
31
32
33
34
35
36
37
38

PLACES TO STAY

17 Hotel Klastrom
20 Kertész Panzió
29 Rába Hotel
35 Hotel Szárnyaskerék

PLACES TO EAT

6 Várkapu Restaurant
7 Vaskakas Taverna
12 Halász Csárda
21 Szürkebarát Borozó
27 Rábaparti Étterem
28 Márka Étterem
32 Magyar Büfé

OTHER

1 Thermal Baths
2 Bishop's Palace
3 Cathedral
4 Jero Disco
5 Casemates Museum
8 Napoleon House
9 Borsos Miklós Collection
10 Arc of the Covenant Monument
11 Margit Kovács Collection
13 Xantus János Museum
14 Former Charity Hospital
15 Széchenyi Cultural Centre
16 Carmelite Church
18 Széchenyi Pharmacy
19 St Ignatius Church
22 Kisfaludy Theatre
23 Express
24 Main Post Office
25 Bartók Cultural Centre
26 Synagogue
30 OTP Bank
31 Ibusz
33 Ciklámen Tourist
34 City Hall
36 Post Office
37 Train Station
38 Bus Station

weekends) – a fully operating baroque institution! Cross the square to visit the **Xantus János Museum** (closed Monday), Széchenyi tér 5, which is in a palace that was built in 1743. Beside it at Széchenyi tér 4 is Iron Stump House, which still sports the beam into which itinerant journeymen would drive a nail. This building now houses the **Imre Patkó Collection** of paintings and African art, one of the best of Győr's various small museums (closed November to mid-March). You can enter it from the alley.

If you have a half day to spare, it's worth visiting **Pannonhalma Abbey**, on top of a 282-metre hill at the southern edge of the Kisalföld, 21 km south of Győr. Tours of the present Benedictine monastery (closed Monday) take you through the Gothic cloister (1486), into the Romanesque basilica (1225) and down to the 11th-century crypt. The 55-metre-high tower was erected in 1830 and the impressive Empire-style library (also included on the tour) dates from the same period. The visit concludes with a look in the one-room 'picture gallery'. Organ recitals are held in the church on Saturday afternoon about once a month. Pannonhalma is best approached from Győr by bus as the train station is a couple of km south-west of the abbey, although local trains between Győr and Veszprém do stop at Pannonhalma every couple of hours.

Activities

West of Rába River are Győr's well-maintained **thermal baths** (open daily May to September). If the first gate you come to is locked, follow the fence along until you reach the main entrance. A variety of large open-air pools are here, some with water as hot as 35°C.

Places to Stay

Camping *Kiskút-liget Camping* (☎ 318 986) is near the stadium, three km north-east of Győr (bus No 8 from beside the city hall). Camping is US$2 per person plus US$2 per tent and there are also 60 three and four-bed cabins at US$11, seven six-bed bungalows at US$28 and 25 three-bedded motel rooms at US$17 single, double or triple. The five four-bedded hotel rooms are US$22. The facilities for campers are in poor shape and there's often no hot water. They do have a restaurant and the site is open from mid-April to mid-October.

Hostels Express, Bajcsy-Zsilinszky út 41 (open weekdays 8 am to 3.45 pm), arranges accommodation in student dormitories year-round at US$9 single or US$5 per person in a four-bed dorm. In July and August ask about the huge student dormitories at Ságvári Endre utca 3 north of the river.

In summer you should be able to get a bed at *Kossuth Kollégium* (☎ 319 244), on the corner of Erkel Ferenc utca and Kossuth Lajos utca opposite an old synagogue. There are two dormitories here on diagonally opposite sides of the street, the one on Erkel Ferenc for men and the other on Kossuth Lajos for women. Both are only an eight-minute walk from the train station (via Munkácsy Mihály utca) or the centre of town (via Rába Kettos híd). Express can book you in here.

Private Rooms Private rooms are available at Ciklámen Tourist, Aradi vértanúk útja 22 near the train station (from US$15 double), and Ibusz, Szent István út 31 (from US$11/12 single/double). Singles are scarce and these offices close early.

Hotels The four-storey *Hotel Szárnyaskerék)* (☎ 314 629), Révai Miklós utca 5, directly opposite the train station, is US$17 double with shared bath (no singles).

A British reader wrote in recommending *Kertész Panzió*, Iskola utca 11, in the alley on the north side of Kisfaludy Theatre. A room with private bath and TV will be around US$20 double. A block away at Arany János utca 33, is *Kuckó Pension* (☎ 316 260).

The two-star *Hotel Klastrom* (☎ 315 611), Zehmeister utca 1, has 42 rooms with bath (US$44/46/69 single/double/triple, including breakfast) in the former Carmelite convent (1720). This is great if the price is right for you.

Hotel Aranypart (☎ 326 033), Áldozat utca 12, in Révfalu north of the centre, is a modern one-star sport hotel that charges US$17/18/26 single/double/triple without bath, US$19/20/30 with bath, breakfast included. Show a YHA card here and you'll receive a 10% discount. To get there, cross the bridge from Dunakapu tér, then continue straight ahead for about four blocks till you see the *Revesz Panzió*, Ságvári Endre utca 22, on the right. The Hotel Aranypart is down the next street on the left. Bus No 16 passes near the Hotel Aranypart from beside the city hall.

Places to Eat

For a cheap self-service meal you can't beat *Márka Étterem*, Bajcsy-Zsilinszky út 30 (weekdays 7 am to 5 pm, weekends 7 am to 3 pm).

The *Rábaparti Étterem*, Zehmeister utca 15, serves tasty Hungarian fare in an attractive, unpretentious locale at very reasonable prices.

The *Várkapu Restaurant*, Becsi kapu tér 7, has its dishes listed on a blackboard outside.

One of Győr's finest wine cellars is the *Szürkebarát Borozó*, Arany János utca 20 (closed Sunday). A stairway in the courtyard leads down into this vaulted restaurant. Only cold dishes are available at lunch. The ice-cream counter in this same courtyard is one of the best in Győr.

A typical inn near the market is the *Halász Csárda*, Apáca utca 4.

Cafés & Bars For coffee and cakes go to the *Cukrászda*, Baross Gábor út 30.

The *Magyar Büfé*, Árpád út 18, is a very friendly neighbourhood wine cellar where you can taste Balaton wine to your heart's content. Despite the name, no food is served here.

The *Metróz Csárda*, Dunakapu tér 3, is fine for having a glass of wine at the bar.

Entertainment

Győr has one of Hungary's most striking new theatres, the *Kisfaludy Theatre* on Czuczor Gergely utca. You can't miss the Vásárely mosaics covering the exterior walls! The box office is just inside. Győr's ballet company which performs here is internationally recognised.

At Kisfaludy utca 25 is the Országos Filharmonia (closed in summer), where you can enquire about concerts. Also try the *Széchenyi Cultural Centre*, Széchenyi tér 7.

Other events are staged at the *Bartók Cultural Centre*, Czuczor Gergely utca 17.

Jero Disco, in a large pavilion on an island in the river, is open daily except Monday and Wednesday from 10 pm to 4 am, Sunday 10 pm to midnight.

Győr's best disco is *Charlie M* in the Nádorváros district south of the railway line. It opens at 10 pm on weekends, you'll probably have to go by taxi.

Getting There & Away

Győr is well connected by express train to Budapest's Déli and Keleti train stations (131 km, two hours) and to Sopron (85 km, one hour). Other trains run to Szombathely (117 km, 1¾ hours) via Celldömölk. To go to Balaton Lake there's a secondary line with three or four slow local trains a day going south to Veszprém (79 km, 2¾ hours) via Pannonhalma.

To go to/from Vienna's Westbahnhof (126 km) you may have to change trains at Hegyeshalom since some express trains won't pick up passengers at Győr. Check with Ibusz well ahead (you could also hitch from Hegyeshalom). Another route to Austria is through Sopron. To go to/from Slovakia, walk across the bridge at Komárom.

Buses of possible interest include those to Balatonfüred (six daily, 99 km), Budapest (hourly, 123 km), Esztergom (two daily, 87 km), Hévíz (two daily, 214 km), Kecskemét (daily, 208 km), Pannonhalma (hourly or better, 21 km), Pécs (two daily, 241 km), Székesfehérvár (seven daily, 87 km) and Vienna (two daily, 122 km). To go to Fertőd you must take the Sopron bus to Kapuvár and change there for Fertőd.

SOPRON

Sopron (Ödenburg) sits right on the Austrian border, 217 km west of Budapest and only 69 km south of Vienna. In 1921 the town's residents voted to remain part of Hungary, while the rest of Bürgenland (the region to which Sopron used to belong) went to Austria, thus explaining the town's location in a narrow neck of land between Lake Fertő and the green eastern ridges of the Alps.

Sopron (the ancient Scarbantia) has been an important centre since Roman times. The Tatars and Turks never got this far, so numerous medieval structures have come down to the present day intact. In the horseshoe-shaped old quarter, still partially enclosed by medieval walls built on Roman foundations, almost every building is historic. This is Sopron's principal charm and wanderers among the Gothic and baroque houses are rewarded at every turn. Some of the buildings are now museums and you can peek into the courtyards of many others.

Orientation

From the main train station, walk north on Mátyás király utca, which becomes Várkerület after a few blocks. Várkerület and Ógabona tér form a loop right around the old town, following the line of the former city walls. Sopron's Fire Tower is between the northern end of Várkerület and Fő tér, the old town square. The bus station is on Lackner Kristóf utca off Ógabona tér. The left-luggage office in the main train station is open from 3 am to 11 pm. There's no left-luggage area at the bus station.

Information

Ciklámen Tourist is at Ógabona tér 8 on the corner of Lackner Kristóf utca. Express is at Mátyás király utca 7.

Money The exchange office in the train station changes only cash. Ciklámen Tourist, Ógabona tér 8, will change travellers' cheques until 3 pm weekdays, until 2.30 pm on Saturday, but they give a mediocre rate.

A better place to change money is the OTP Bank, Várkerület 96 (Monday to Wednesday 7.45 am to 3 pm, Thursday until 4.30 pm, Friday until 1 pm).

Things to See

The 61-metre-high **Fire Tower** above Sopron's north gate, erected after the fire of 1676, is the city symbol. You can climb up to the Renaissance loggia for a marvellous view of the city (closed Monday). What appears to be a Nazi bunker directly beside the Fire Tower is actually a museum (closed

HUNGARY

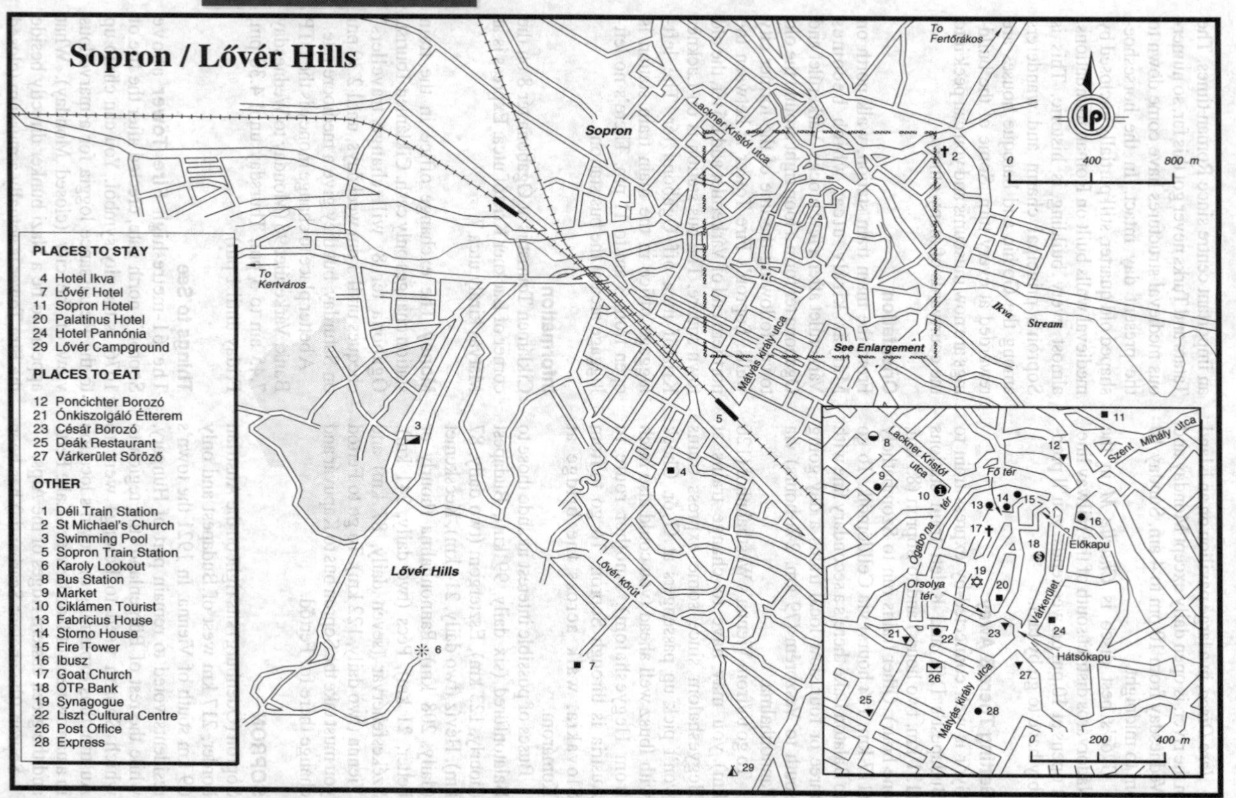
Sopron / Lővér Hills
To Fertőrákos
Sopron
Lackner Kristóf utca
Mátyás király utca
Ikva Stream
See Enlargement
To Kertváros
Lővér Hills
Lővér körút
0 400 800 m
Szent Mihály utca
Fő tér
Lackner Kristóf utca
Ógabo na tér
Orsolya tér
Előkapu
Várkerület
Hátsókapu
Mátyás király utca
0 200 400 m
PLACES TO STAY
4 Hotel Ikva
7 Lővér Hotel
11 Sopron Hotel
20 Palatinus Hotel
24 Hotel Pannónia
29 Lővér Campground
PLACES TO EAT
12 Poncichter Borozó
21 Önkiszolgáló Étterem
23 Césár Borozó
25 Deák Restaurant
27 Várkerület Sörözö
OTHER
1 Déli Train Station
2 St Michael's Church
3 Swimming Pool
5 Sopron Train Station
6 Karoly Lookout
8 Bus Station
9 Market
10 Ciklámen Tourist
13 Fabricius House
14 Storno House
15 Fire Tower
16 Ibusz
17 Goat Church
18 OTP Bank
19 Synagogue
22 Liszt Cultural Centre
26 Post Office
28 Express

Monday and from November to mid-March) where you'll see the excavated remains of a Roman gate which stood here long ago.

Fő tér, just beyond the tower, is the heart of the old town. In the centre of the square is the magnificent **Holy Trinity Column** (1701) and beyond this the **Goat Church** (1300), built by a goatherd with gold uncovered by his herd! In the adjoining building is the Gothic Chapter House of the former Benedictine monastery, now a museum (closed Monday) with stone carvings of the seven deadly sins.

Across the street from the Goat Church is the Esterházy City Palace, which is now a most interesting **Mining Museum** (closed Wednesday). Go inside to see the courtyard. There are several other museums on Fő tér. **Fabricius House** at No 6 is a comprehensive historical museum (closed from November to mid-March) with impressive Roman sculpture in the Gothic cellar. **Storno House** at No 8 is a famous Renaissance palace (1560) that is now a museum and art gallery. Both houses are closed on Monday.

Sopron's most unique museum is housed in the 14th-century **synagogue** (closed Tuesday) at Új utca 22. Jews were an important part of the community until their expulsion in 1526. Next to the **Orsolya Church** on Orsolya tér is a collection of religious art (open Monday, Thursday and Sunday from April to October).

Around Sopron To see some of Sopron's surroundings, take bus No 10 to **Kertváros** and climb the baroque stairway to the Hill Church. Better yet, you could take bus No 1 or 2 to the Lövér Hotel and hike up through the coniferous forest to the **Károly Lookout** for the view.

An hourly bus from the main bus station runs 10 km north to **Fertőrákos** where the mammoth halls and corridors of the old stone quarry are an impressive sight (open daily all year). In summer, concerts and operas are performed in the theatre which is in the largest chamber.

Nagycenk Nagycenk, 13 km south-east of Sopron, was once the seat of Count István Széchenyi (1791-1860), a notable reformer who founded the National Academy of Sciences, improved communications and wrote a series of books intended to convince the nobility to lend a hand in modernising Hungary. (The Chain Bridge in Budapest was one of his many projects.)

The baroque **Széchenyi Mansion** (1758) contains a memorial museum to Count István and a three-star hotel (☎ 99-60 061) with 19 rooms at US$65 double. The café just outside the restaurant (slow service) on the mansion grounds serves great ice cream. Other attractions in Nagycenk include the park with its long avenue of linden trees, the Széchenyi family mausoleum in the local cemetery, a three-km narrow-gauge steam railway to Fertőboz and a 60-horse stud farm. Nagycenk is accessible by bus and train.

Places to Stay

Sopron may be a convenient transit point but it's an expensive place to spend the night, so plan a morning arrival and afternoon departure if at all possible. For example, consider catching the 3 pm bus to Kőszeg where budget accommodation is more plentiful.

Camping No hostels or student dormitories exist and from mid-April to mid-October the cheapest accommodation around Sopron is available at the *Lövér Campground* (☎ 311 715), at Pócsi-domb, three km south of the station on Kőszegi út. Camping is US$3/5 single/double and the 129 bungalows here go for US$6/7/10/11 single/double/triple/quad. The atmosphere is friendly and welcoming (for a change). Take bus No 12 in the 'Lövérek fele' direction from either the bus or train stations right to the camping ground.

Private Rooms Ciklámen Tourist, Ógabona tér 8 (weekdays 7.30 am to 4 pm, Saturday 7.30 am to 3.30 pm), has private rooms (from US$15 double). Other private rooms are handled by Volántourist, Lackner Kristóf utca 1, and Ibusz, Várkerület 41 (from US$14 double). Sometimes in summer all rooms are full and singles will have to pay for a double.

You can also find a private room by taking bus No 1 from the train station to the Szieszta Hotel, Lövér körút 37, then walk back down the hill looking for houses with 'Zimmer frei' signs. There are quite a few near the hotel and around the public swimming pool. This procedure is often cheaper than dealing with Ciklámen Tourist.

Hotels Sopron's cheapest regular hotel is two-storey *Ikva* (☎ 332 032), József Attila utca 3-5, on the opposite side of the railway from the old town. It charges US$15 for singles/doubles without bath, US$21 with bath. As you leave the train station, turn left and keep left until you find the level crossing over the tracks. Turn left again and follow the main street up to the hotel.

Sopron's grand old hotel is the *Hotel Pannónia* (☎ 312 180), at Várkerület 75, which opened in 1893. A recent renovation has pushed prices out of sight and effaced much of the Pannónia's old-world flavour.

Places to Eat & Drink

For a tasteless self-service lunch go to *Önkiszolgáló Étterem* at the western end of Széchenyi tér (open from 7 am to 3 pm Monday to Saturday). The food is neither cheap nor good, so only eat here if you're pressed for time.

HUNGARY

A local restaurant with Hungarian flavour is the *Várkerület Söröző*, Várkerület 83. Césár Borozó, Hátsókapu 2, is more touristy; and, though a wine cellar, it serves meals. *Corvinus Pizzeria* on Fő tér, right in front of the Fire Tower, is only reasonably priced if you stick to the pizza.

The *Deák Restaurant*, Deák tér, on the corner of Erzsébet utca, specialises in game dishes like wild boar or venison, though fish is also on the menu. In the evening there's live music and the place is popular with Austrian border-jumpers. There's a large beer garden alongside.

Wine tasters repair to the *Gyógygödör Borozó*, Fő tér 4, opposite the Goat Church (closed Monday), or the *Poncichter Borozó*, Szentlélek utca 13, both great little wine cellars. Try the local Kékfrankos wine.

Entertainment

Posters in the window of the *Liszt Cultural Centre* on Széchenyi tér occasionally announce local events, though the adjacent gambling casino now seems to be the main focus of interest (open after 4 pm). Just around the corner on Petőfi tér is the *Petőfi Theatre*, with drama in Hungarian.

Getting There & Away

Express trains run to Budapest's Déli or Keleti train stations (216 km, three hours) via Győr and Komárom, and local trains run to Szombathely (64 km, 1½ hours) via Nagycenk.

Buses of interest from Sopron include one a day to Balatonfüred (160 km), five to Budapest (210 km), two to Esztergom (174 km), hourly or better to Fertőd and Fertőrákos, hourly to Győr (87 km), three daily to Hévíz and Keszthely (141 km), seven to Kőszeg (53 km), every half-hour to Nagycenk (13 km), daily to Pécs (287 km), two to Szekesfehérvár (174 km) and eight to Szombathely (73 km).

There's also a bus to Vienna from the bus station every morning except public holidays (69 km, 120 Austrian shillings in cash, forint not accepted).

A dozen daily trains run between Sopron and Wiener Neustadt (34 km, 45 minutes, US$4), while eight others use a different line to go to Ebenfurth (33 km, US$4). Trains straight through to Vienna Südbahnhof (84 km, 1½ hours, US$10) are rare so you'll probably have to change trains in one of these two towns to get to Vienna. Tickets to Austria must be purchased with cash hard currency, preferably shillings (forint are not accepted). Other trains go to Deutschkreuz (10 km), Eisenstadt (24 km) and Lackenbach (23 km) in Austria. When boarding for Austria at Sopron, be at the station an hour early to clear customs, which is in a separate hall to one side (customs controls are stricter than usual here).

Ticketing arrangements for both trains

and buses leaving Sopron for Austria are poor and you may be forced to buy your ticket directly from an Austrian conductor or driver who may demand Austrian shillings. If you know for sure you'll be catching a train from Sopron to Vienna, you ought to try to buy an open international ticket beforehand at an Ibusz office as the ticket offices at Sopron Railway Station are unable to carry out this simple transaction for some strange reason.

FERTŐD

Don't miss the 126-room **Esterházy Palace** (1766) at Fertőd, 28 km east of Sopron and readily accessible by bus. This magnificent Versailles-style baroque palace, easily the finest in Hungary, is open from 8 am to 4 pm all year (closed Monday). You must visit the palace with a guide. On Sunday there's a Haydn or Mozart concert in the music room (variably at noon or 5 pm).

Joseph Haydn was court musician to the princely Esterházy family from 1761 to 1790 and his *Farewell* symphony was first performed in the palace concert hall. A Haydn exhibition is included in the visit. The famous Habsburg queen Maria Theresa stayed in the palace in 1773 and three rooms are dedicated to her. Fertőd was the summer residence of the Esterházys (their winter residence was at Eisenstadt, Austria) and the large French Park behind the palace will help you to visualise the bygone splendour.

Places to Stay & Eat

You can spend the night in the palace. Clean, simple rooms in the *Kastélyszálló* on the 3rd floor are US$13/14 double/triple, US$18 for four, open all year. To find the hostel, look for the arrow near the ticket office that points up to the *szállóda*. For advance reservations have someone who speaks Hungarian call ☎ 370 971 for you. If you arrive to find the Kastélyszálló full don't let yourself be talked into staying at the Esterházy Panzió down the street as it's overpriced and full of drunks. One reader had a camera stolen from a locked room at the Panzió (she did say their restaurant was fine).

In the *Grenadier House* opposite the palace's rococo wrought-iron gate is a pleasant café (closed Monday) and there are several good restaurants in the village.

KŐSZEG

Kőszeg (Güns) is a lovely medieval town on the Austrian frontier among verdant hills between Sopron and Szombathely. Mt Írottkő (882 metres) right on the border south-west of Kőszeg is the highest point in Transdanubia. In 1532 the garrison of Kőszeg's 13th-century Jurisich Castle held off a Turkish army of 200,000 and this delay gave the Habsburgs time to mount a successful defence of Vienna, ensuring Kőszeg's place in European history. The houses along the street in front of the castle were erected in a saw-toothed design in order to give defenders a better shot at the enemy.

Jurisich tér, Kőszeg's jewel-box main square, hasn't changed much since the 18th century. It's a pleasant place where fruit and vegetables are left out on the street with little honesty boxes to collect the money. For its good facilities, pleasant atmosphere and wealth of things to see, Kőszeg is probably the nicest little town in all of Hungary.

Orientation & Information

The train station is a 15-minute walk south-east of the centre while buses stop just a block from Várkör. Kőszeg Railway Station doesn't have a regular left-luggage office but the staff will probably agree to hold your bags for the usual fee.

For information try Savaria Tourist, Várkör 69, or Express next door.

Money The OTP Bank, Kossuth Lajos utca 8, behind Hotel Irottkö (Monday 8 am to 5 pm, Tuesday to Thursday until 3 pm, Friday until 12.30 pm), changes travellers' cheques.

Things to See

The **City Gate** (1932) bears an exterior relief depicting the 1532 siege. In the 'General's House' next to the gate is a branch of the **Miklós Jurisich Museum** (closed Monday) which contains exhibits on trades with people such as the barber, shoemaker, hatter, book binder etc. One of the guards will probably follow you around carrying an ancient walkie-talkie they use to communicate. Ask if you may go out on the roof of the gate for the view.

The gate leads into Jurisich tér with the painted Renaissance façade of the **old town hall** at No 8. A Statue of the Virgin (1739) and the town fountain (1766) in the middle of the square adjoin two fine churches. The **Church of St Emerich** (1615) is closer to the gate. Behind it is **St James Church** (1403), a splendid Gothic building with medieval frescos. At Jurisich tér 11 is a baroque **apothecary**.

The other highlight of Kőszeg is **Jurisich Castle** (1263), now a historical museum (closed Monday). The courtyard and towers of this Gothic bastion have an almost fairytale air about them.

Other sights include the neo-Gothic **Church of the Sacred Heart** on Várkör (you can't miss it) and the baroque chapel on **Calvary Hill**, a 25-minute hike away.

Activities

Bicycles are for rent at the train station at

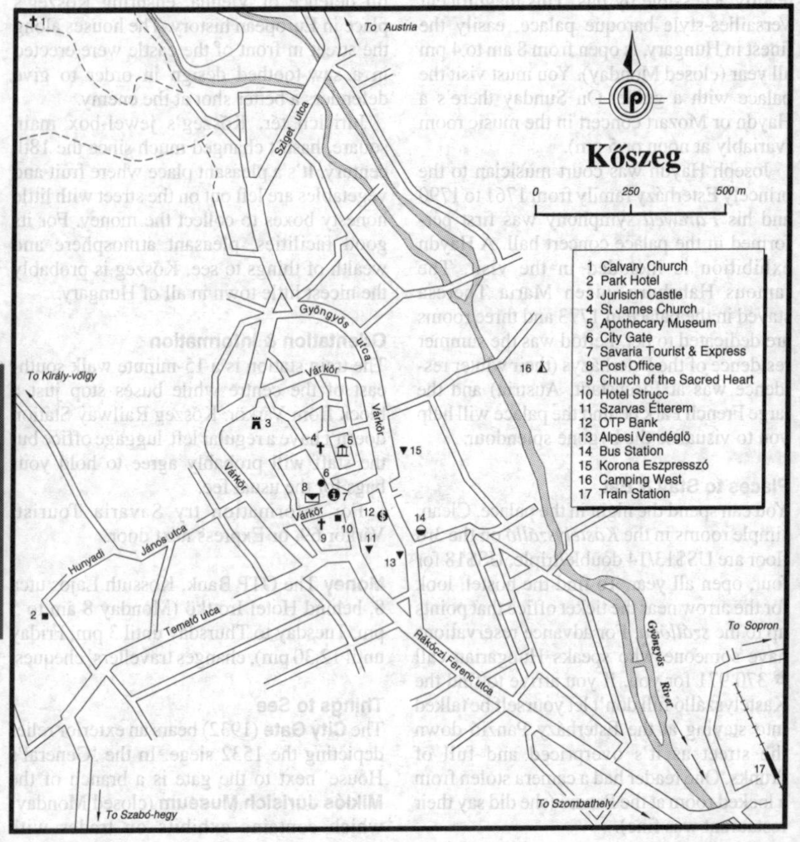

US$3 for 24 hours – ask the ticket clerk about this. Cycling along the quiet country roads south-west of town is fun.

Ask Savaria Tourist about the possibilities for horse riding at the riding school near Kőszeg.

Places to Stay

Camping & Hostels *Camping West* (☎ 360 981), Alsó körút 79, next to a public swimming pool *(strand/fürdő)* just across the river from the old town, is one of the nicest places to camp in western Hungary. It's just a five-minute walk east on Kiss János utca from Várkör. Camping is US$2 per person plus US$2 per tent and dormitory accommodation is available in their hostel *(turistaszálló)* at US$4 per person (open from mid-April to October).

The *turistaszálló* (☎ 360 227) next to Jurisich Castle (open from April to mid-October) has beds in an 18-bed dormitory at US$4. If it's occupied by a group you'll have to take one of the individual rooms at US$11/15 double/triple (no singles). Check-in time is 5 pm and check-out time is 8 am.

Private Rooms Savaria Tourist, Várkör 69, and Ibusz on Városház utca near the city gate both arrange private rooms.

Hotels The unpretentious two-storey *Hotel Strucc* (☎ 360 323), at Várkör 124 directly across the square from Savaria Tourist, is a fine old hotel with rooms at US$12/22/31 single/double/triple with bath, breakfast included. Ask if there's any hot water as you check in.

The *Park Hotel* (☎ 360 363) on Felszabadulás Park, just west of Kőszeg, is reasonable value at US$13 for singles/doubles without bath, US$21 with shower. A third person in the room is another US$4 and breakfast is US$2 per person extra. The Park is owned by the student travel agency Express and if you have a YHA card you'll get a 10% discount. It's open all year and there's a good restaurant on the premises. This large Victorian hotel is highly recommended to all travellers passing this way.

Places to Eat

The *Bécsikapu Söröző* on Rájnis utca, almost opposite St James Church, even has a menu in English! For large portions of tasty Hungarian food with draught beer, you can't beat it.

The *Alpesi Vendéglö*, Munkácsy utca 2, opposite the bus station (closed Sunday and Monday), is more expensive than the Bécsikapu but always crowded with wily Austrians who know a good meal when they taste one.

The *Szarvas Étterem*, Rákóczi Ferenc utca 15, has pizza in addition to the regular menu items.

After dinner, a drink at the bar in the castle is fun (open until midnight daily except Monday year-round).

For coffee and cakes you can't beat *Korona Eszpresszó*, Várkör 18 (daily 8 am to 6 pm).

Getting There & Away

There are frequent trains and buses from Szombathely and less frequent buses from Sopron (53 km). One morning bus goes to Keszthely (129 km).

The train between Szombathely and Kőszeg (18 km, 30 minutes) operates on an honesty system and you must punch your own ticket after boarding (there's a US$3 fine if you fail to do so).

SZOMBATHELY

Szombathely (Steinamanger), pronounced 'som-bat-eye', the seat of Vas County and a major crossroads in western Hungary, was founded as Savaria by the Roman emperor Claudius in 43 AD. It soon became capital of Upper Pannonia and an important stage on the Amber Road from Italy to the Baltic. Destroyed by an earthquake in 455 and pillaged by the Tatars, Turks and Habsburgs, Szombathely only regained its former stature when a bishopric was established here in 1777.

In 1945, just a month before the end of the war, US bombers levelled the town and it's a credit to Hungary that so much has been restored. Although off the beaten tourist

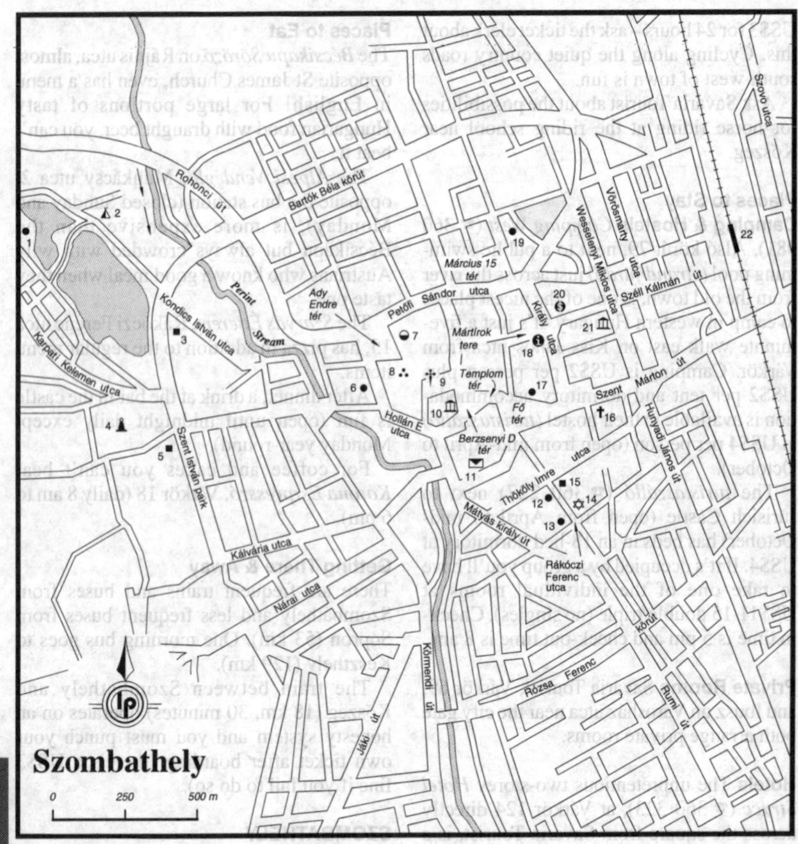

track, Szombathely may be a useful stop on your way around the country.

Orientation & Information

The train station is five blocks east of Mártírok tere along Széll Kálmán út. The bus station is on Petőfi Sándor utca, behind the cathedral. Szombathely's busiest square is Fő tér, a long block south of Mártírok tere. For left luggage in the train station ask at the window marked 'poggyász' inside the station hall (open 24 hours).

Savaria Tourist is at Mártírok tere 1. The Magyar Autóklub (☎ 313 945) has an office at Fő tér 19.

Money The OTP Bank at Király utca 10 next to Ibusz is open on Monday from 8 am to 5 pm, Tuesday to Thursday until 3 pm, and Friday until 1 pm.

Travel Agencies Railway information and tickets are available from MÁV Tours, Thököly utca 39 near the Isis Hotel.

Things to See

One of the most interesting things to see is

PLACES TO STAY

2 Camping Ground
3 Hotel Claudius
5 Liget Hotel
15 Isis Hotel

OTHER

1 Skansen
4 Liberation Memorial
6 Cultural Centre
7 Bus Station
8 Roman Ruins (Romkert)
9 Cathedral
10 Smidt Museum
11 Post Office
12 Temple of Isis
13 Szombathely Gallery
14 Synagogue
16 Franciscan Church
17 Magyar Autóklub
18 Savaria Tourist
19 Cultural & Sports Centre
20 Ibusz & OTP Bank
21 Savaria Museum
22 Train Station

the rebuilt neoclassical **cathedral** (1791) on Berzsenyi Dániel tér. Beside the cathedral are the excavated 4th-century **remains of Roman Savaria** (Romkert), including mosaics, roads and a medieval castle. On the other side of the cathedral is the baroque **bishop's palace** (1783), and beyond this on Hollán Ernő utca is the **Smidt Museum** (closed Monday), a fascinating assortment of small treasures collected by a local doctor before his death in 1975.

Head south to Rákóczi Ferenc utca to see the reconstructed 2nd-century **temple of the Egyptian goddess Isis**. A festival is held here in August. The **Szombathely Gallery** overlooking the temple is the best modern art gallery in Hungary (closed Monday and Tuesday). A plaque on the front of the **synagogue** (1881) opposite the Szombathely Gallery recalls the 4228 local Jews sent to Auschwitz in 1944.

Also worth visiting is the **Savaria Museum** (closed Monday) on Széll Kálmán út, which is especially strong on archaeology and natural history. There's a large Roman lapidarium (a collection of architectural fragments) in the basement.

On the western side of Szombathely is a major open-air **ethnographic museum**, or skansen (open from 10 am until 4 pm, closed on Monday), with 50 reconstructed folk buildings. It's on a lake near the camping ground (bus No 7 from the train station to the terminus).

Places to Stay

Camping From May to September you can stay at *Tópart Camping* (☎ 314 766) on Kondics István utca 4 by a lake west of town (bus No 7 from the train station to the end of the line). From the bus stop walk along the causeway across the lake. Bungalows here are US$14 single or double without shower, US$39 with shower. Camping is US$1.50 per person, US$2 per tent. There's a swimming pool nearby.

Private Rooms & Hostels Private rooms are assigned by staff at Savaria Tourist, Mártírok tere 1, and Ibusz, Széll Kálman út 3. In summer, Express, Király utca 12, may know of hostels. These tourist offices are next to one another.

Hotels The 35-room *Liget Hotel* (☎ 314 168), Szent István park 15, west of the city centre, offers motel-style accommodation at US$26/28 single/double with bath and breakfast (no singles). You can get there on bus No 7 from the train station.

Szombathely's nicest hotel by far is the turn-of-the-century *Hotel Savaria* (☎ 311 440), Mártírok tere 4 in the very centre of town. It's open all year but not cheap: rooms cost US$47/51 single/double with shower, US$33 double with shared bath, breakfast included.

Actually, Szombathely, unlike Rome, can be seen in a day and it may be better to go on to less expensive Kőszeg to spend the night.

Places to Eat

Szombathely's most elegant restaurant is in

HUNGARY

the *Savaria Hotel* on Mártírok tere. They don't sully their menu with prices.

For a less pretentious meal, try the *Gyöngyös Étterem*, Széll Kálmán út 8 nearby. It has a cheap 'menu' at lunchtime, but the food and service are always good. (It's closed on Monday).

The restaurant in the train station (not the stand-up 'bisztró') is also fine.

Entertainment

The concert hall is opposite the Szombathely Gallery, on Rákóczi Ferenc utca. Also visit the *Cultural & Sports Centre* and a second cultural centre, the *Megyei Müvelődési es Ifjusagi Központ* opposite the bus station.

If you have wheels, a popular night spot is *Ciao Amigo* out at the edge of town on the road to Kőszeg. Otherwise check out the *Garden Disco* in the Cultural & Sports Centre.

The symphony orchestra is based in the modern building opposite the Szombathely Gallery on Rakóczi Ferenc utca and concerts are advertised on the board outside.

Getting There & Away

Szombathely is only 13 km from the Austrian border and there are direct trains to/from Graz (146 km, three hours). Some of the Graz services involve a change of trains at the border (Szentgotthárd).

Express trains to Budapest-Déli (236 km, 3½ hours) go via Veszprém and Székesfehérvár. Other express trains run to Győr (117 km, 1¾ hours) via Celldömölk. There are frequent local trains to Kőszeg (18 km, 30 minutes) and Sopron (64 km, 1½ hours). To go to southern Transdanubia or Balaton Lake, take a bus to Keszthely (106 km) via Hévíz (three daily). There's also an early morning express train to/from Pécs (244 km, 4½ hours).

HUNGARY

Balaton Lake

In the very heart of Transdanubia, the 77-km-long Balaton Lake (Plattensee) is the largest freshwater lake in Central and Western Europe. The south-eastern shore of this 'Hungarian sea' is shallow and in summer the warm, sandy beaches are a favourite family vacation spot. Better scenery and more historic sites are found on the deeper north-western side of the lake.

North of the lake are the Bakony Hills and the extinct volcanoes of the Tapolca Basin. Several ruined castles, such as that at Sümeg, remind visitors that during the Turkish period the border between the Ottoman and Habsburg empires ran down the middle of the lake. The Turks maintained a lake fleet that was based at Siófok. Székesfehérvár and Veszprém, just north of the lake, are old historic towns full of monuments and one of Hungary's finest palaces is at Keszthely. The Benedictine crypt in Tihany Abbey is the oldest existing church in Hungary.

The many towns and villages along both shores have an organic connection to this ancient lake. This is wine-making country. Scenic railway lines encircle the lake and there are no less than 39 camping grounds on its shores. 'Zimmer frei' signs are everywhere. Balaton's very popularity is perhaps its main drawback, though the north-western shore is quieter than the south-eastern one.

To avoid pollution and public nuisances, the use of private motorboats is prohibited, making Balaton a favourite yachting centre. Continuous breezes from the north speed sailors and sailboarders along. Other common activities here are tennis, horse riding and cycling. Any local tourist office will be able to provide information on these activities and the thermal baths of Hévíz are nearby. If you want to spend some time in the area, get hold of the *A Balaton* 1:40,000 topographical map available at Budapest bookshops which illustrates the many hiking possibilities.

GETTING THERE & AWAY

Trains to Balaton Lake leave from Déli Railway Station and buses leave from the Erzsébet tér Bus Station in Budapest. If you're travelling north or south from the lake

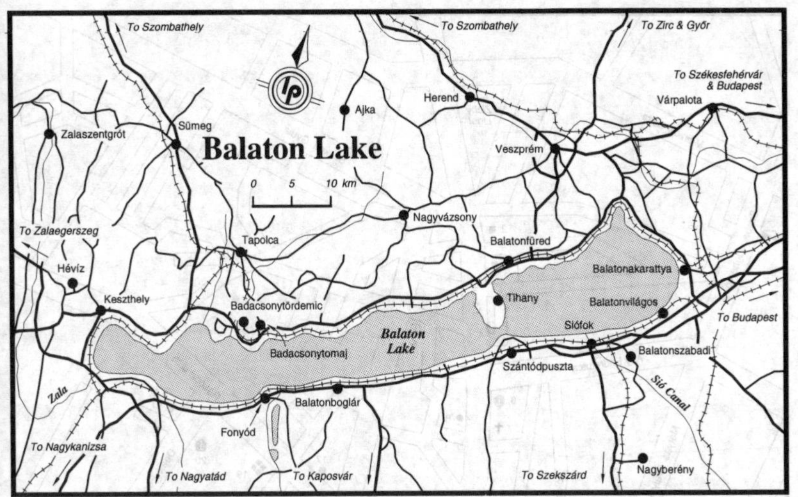

to/from towns in western or southern Transdanubia, buses are often preferable to trains.

GETTING AROUND

Railway service around the lake is fairly frequent. A better way to see Balaton Lake is by Mahart passenger ferry. These ferries operate on the route between Siófok, Balatonfüred, Tihany, Tihanyi-rév and Balatonföldvár from April to October. During July and August there is a ferry every couple of hours. During the main summer season, which is from mid-June to mid-September, ferries ply the entire length of the lake from Balatonkenese to Keszthely (five hours) with frequent stops on both shores. There are also car ferries across the lake between Tihanyi-rév and Szántódrév (from mid-March to mid-December), and Badacsony and Fonyód (from mid-April to mid-October). Fares are cheap: US$2 will take you anywhere. Of course, in winter there are no boats on the lake.

SZÉKESFEHÉRVÁR

Traditionally, Székesfehérvár (Stuhlweissenburg) is known as the place where the Magyar chieftain Árpád set up camp, therefore it's considered to be the oldest town in Hungary. In 972 the Grand Duke of Geza established his seat here and his son, Stephen I (later St Stephen), founded a basilica which became the symbol of royal power. Thirty-eight kings of early medieval Hungary were crowned at Székesfehérvár and 18 were buried in the basilica's crypt. It was here in 1222 that Andrew II proclaimed the Golden Bull, Hungary's first constitution.

The Turks captured Székesfehérvár in 1543 and used the basilica to store gunpowder. It exploded during a siege in 1601; by 1688 when the Turks left, the town was just an uninhabited field of ruins. The Habsburgs rebuilt Székesfehérvár in the 18th century, and around 1800 stones from the basilica ruins were used to erect the nearby Episcopal Palace. Only the foundations of the old coronation church are now seen, though the steeples of four huge baroque churches that were built after liberation from the Turks tower over the old town.

Today Székesfehérvár is the seat of Fejér County, a pleasant little town with a life of its own relatively unaffected by tourism. Although the town's not on Balaton Lake, everyone travelling between Budapest and

Székesfehérvár
Zichy Liget
Mészöly Géza
Szekpű Gyula
Szabadságharcos
Fő utca
Ady Endre utca
Rákóczi utca
Mátyás király körút
Jókai
Deák Ferenc utca
Városház tér
Várkörút
Palotai út
Kossuth utca
Budai útja
Piac tér
Prohászka Ottokár
Vörösmarty tér
Balatoni út
Horvát István
To Railway Station
To Railway Station
0
250
500 m
PLACES TO STAY
2 Magyar Király Hotel
18 Alba Regia Hotel
23 Rév Szálló
PLACES TO EAT
9 Korzo Söröző
15 Ősfehérvár Étterem
24 Viniczai Ice Cream Parlour
OTHER
1 Public Swimming Pool
3 Vörösmarty Theatre
4 OTP Bank
5 István Király Museum
6 Ibusz
7 Cistercian Church
8 Black Eagle Pharmacy
10 Törökudvar Turistaszálló
11 Franciscan Church
12 Albatours/Town Hall
13 St Stephen Cathedral
14 Bishop's Palace
16 Basilica Ruins
17 Express Travel Agency
19 Fehérvár Department Store
20 Cooptourist
21 Magyar Autóklub
22 Cinema
25 Post Office
26 Carmelite Church
27 St Stephen Monument
28 Bus Station
29 Market

HUNGARY

Balaton passes this way so it's included here for convenience. Székesfehérvár can also be seen as a day trip from Budapest.

Orientation & Information

The bus station is just outside the west wall of the old town, and the train station is a 15-minute walk south-east of the centre. If you arrive by train, march straight up Deák Ferenc utca, then turn left on Rákóczi utca and go through the city gate to Városház tér, the centre of town.

You can leave your bags in the office marked '*csomagmegorző*' next to 'Pénztár 5' inside the bus station (weekdays 8 am to 5 pm, Saturday 8 am to 2 pm). The left-luggage office inside the train station is open 24 hours.

Albatours is at Városház tér 6. The Magyar Autóklub (☎ 327 624) is at Deák Ferenc utca 2.

Money The OTP Bank on Várkapu utca off Fő utca (Monday to Thursday 7.45 am to 3 pm, Friday 7.45 am to 12.30 pm) changes travellers' cheques.

Things to See

Székesfehérvár is the sort of place you can visit at leisure – wander up and down the pedestrian promenades, Fő utca and Városház tér. The foundations of the 12th-century **royal basilica** where the coronations took place are on Koronázó tér, with St Stephen's sarcophagus to the right, just inside the gate. The 'garden of ruins' is only open from April to October, but you get a good view of it from the street.

Városház tér with the old town hall and **Episcopal Palace** (1801) is the heart of Székesfehérvár. As you stroll north on Fő utca you'll notice the Cistercian church on the left and next door the archaeological collection of the **István Király Museum**, Fő utca 6. The **Black Eagle Pharmacy** is across the street.

The István Király Museum, Országzászló tér 3, off Fő utca (closed Monday), has a small historical collection.

Places to Stay

Private Rooms Private rooms are available from Albatours, Városház tér 6 (US$11 double), and Ibusz, Fő utca on the corner of Ady Endre utca.

Hostels Express, Rákóczi utca 4, knows about accommodation in vacant college dormitories, available from July to mid-August only.

The *Törökudvar Turístaszálló* (☎ 324 975), Jókai utca 2 just off Városház tér, is a cheap dormitory open only in the evening.

Hotels The nine-storey *Rév Szálló* (☎ 327 015), Deák Ferenc utca 42, is a Hungarian workers' residence that accepts tourists. Here you pay US$13 for an adequate single, double or triple with a washbasin, but the shower and toilet are down the hall. This conveniently located, inexpensive hotel makes Székesfehérvár attractive as a stop-over on the way to/from Budapest.

If you crave luxury, the grand old *Magyar Király Hotel* (☎ 311 262), Fő utca 10, has rooms with private bath at US$37 single or double, breakfast included.

Places to Eat

Korzo Söröző, near the point where Fő utca merges with Városház tér, should satisfy your every need. You can get a huge cooked breakfast with lemon tea, mushroom omelette, bread, butter and jam, and for dinner there's fried cheese or mushrooms (for vegetarians) with cold Czech beer.

Also good is the *Ösfehérvár Étterem* (closed Sunday) on Koronázó tér, opposite the basilica ruins, which has a set lunch 'menu'.

Viniczai, Budai út 17, has some of the best ice-cream cones in town.

There's a pleasant restaurant upstairs in *Fehérvár Department Store* and a large supermarket downstairs. The regular restaurant in the train station is also good.

Entertainment

Check the *Vörösmarty Theatre* on Fő utca beside the Magyar Király Hotel.

Getting There & Away

There are buses from Székesfehérvár to Budapest's Erzsébet tér Bus Station (66 km) about every half-hour, to Balatonfüred (60 km) five times a day, to Veszprém (44 km) every hour, to Komárom (75 km) daily, to Győr (87 km) seven times a day, to Sopron (174 km) twice a day, to Siófok (43 km) seven times a day, to Keszthely (122 km) three times a day, to Hévíz (128 km) four times a day, to Pécs (153 km) three times a day, to Kecskemét (134 km) three times a day and to Szeged (206 km) five times a day.

Local trains between Budapest-Déli and Siófok or Baltonfüred stop at Székesfehérvár frequently. An express line from Budapest-Déli to Szombathely via Veszprém also passes here and there's a local line north to Komárom (82 km, 1½ hours).

BALATONFÜRED

Balatonfüred, an elegant spa town with the easy-going grace that highly commercialised Siófok lacks, is called the 'Mecca of cardiacs' for its curative waters. Located on the northern shore of Balaton Lake between Tihany and Veszprém, it has been the most fashionable bathing resort on the lake since 1772, when a medicinal bathing establishment was set up here. During the early 19th century it became an important meeting place for Hungarian intellectuals and the town still bears an aristocratic air.

Although Balatonfüred is a major spa, the mineral baths are reserved for patients being treated for heart disease, so casual tourists are out of luck. Yet because it's a health resort much is open throughout the year, so it's the best place to visit around the lake in the off season. In the past few years Balatonfüred has become overcrowded with Germans in midsummer.

Orientation & Information

The adjacent bus and train stations are a km north-west of the spa centre. The left-luggage office at the exit from the tunnel at the train station is open from 7.15 am to 9 pm. The small bus information office on the right as you leave the train station is helpful.

Buses to/from Tihany also stop near the ferry landing below the Round Church on Jókai Mór utca. Blaha Lujza utca runs from in front of the church directly into Gyógy tér where the visit begins.

Balatontourist is at Blaha Lujza utca 5.

Money The OTP Bank, Jókai Mór utca 15, next to the supermarket (Monday to Wednesday 7.45 am to 3 pm, Thursday until 5 pm, Friday until 1 pm), changes travellers' cheques.

Things to See

The heart of the spa is Gyógy tér with its **well house** (Kossuth Well), where travellers may freely fill their canteens with radioactive mineral water.

The park along the nearby lakeshore is worth a promenade. Near the wharf you'll encounter the bust of the Bengali poet Rabindranath Tagore before a lime tree that he planted in 1926 to mark his recovery from illness here. The poem 'Tagore' which he wrote for the occasion is reproduced on a plaque in English (the adjacent Hungarian plaque incorrectly identifies Tagore as a Hindi poet).

A little inland, diagonally opposite the **Round Church** (1841), is the **Jókai Museum**, formerly the house of novelist Mór Jókai (closed from November to February and Monday).

Places to Stay

Camping There's only one camping ground at Balatonfüred but it has a capacity for 3700 people. The *Füred Camping* (☎ 343 823), Széchenyi utca 24, is beside *Hotel Marina* on the lake, three km from the train station. Four-person bungalows here cost US$48 from mid-June to August, US$38 from May to mid-June and in early September, and a bargain US$21 in April and from mid-September to mid-October. To get a bungalow you have to arrive before reception closes at 7 pm. The only water-skiing on Balaton Lake is practised here using an electric-powered cable to tow skiers.

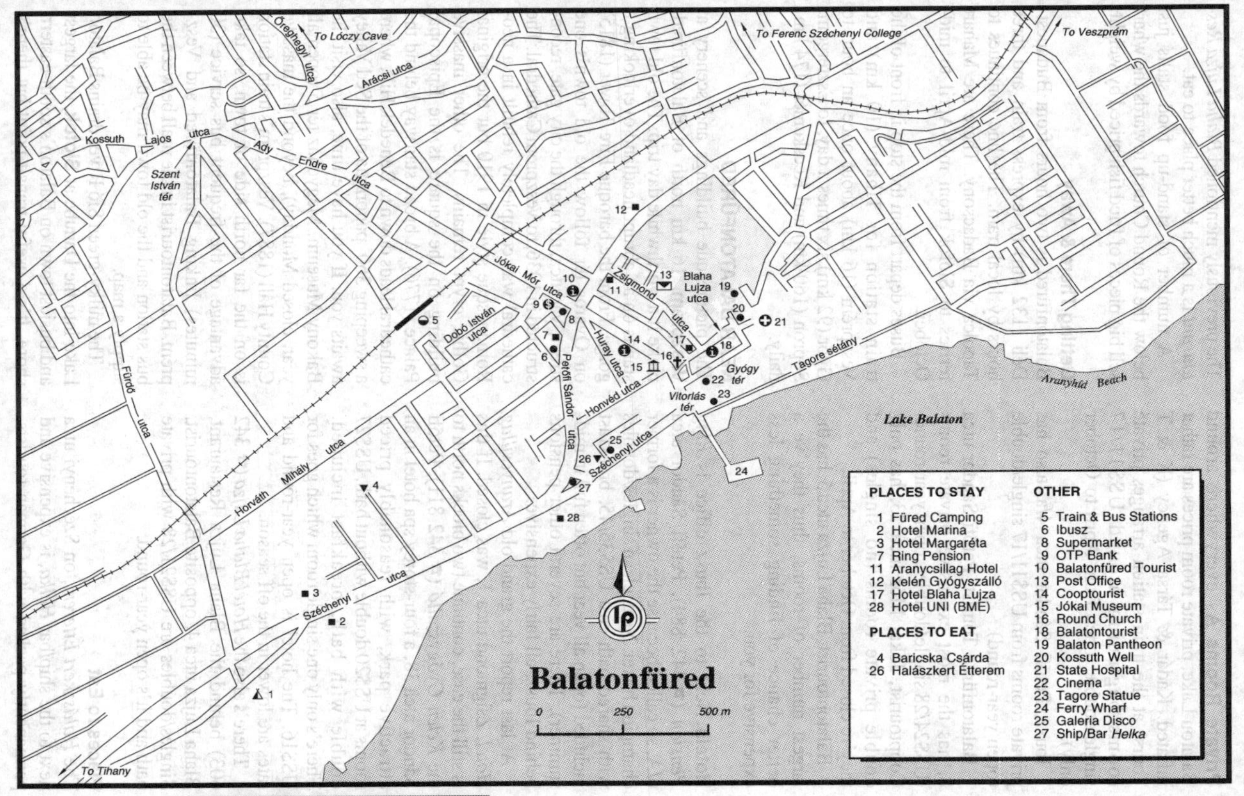
To Lóczy Cave
Öreghegyi utca
Arácsi utca
To Ferenc Széchenyi College
To Veszprém
Kossuth Lajos utca
Szent István tér
Ady Endre utca
Jókai Mór utca
Zsigmond utca
Blaha Lujza utca
Dobó István utca
Huray utca
Petőfi Sándor utca
Honvéd utca
Gyógy tér
Vitorlás tér
Tagore sétány
Aranyhíd Beach
Lake Balaton
Fürdő utca
Horváth Mihály utca
Széchenyi utca
To Tihany
Balatonfüred
0 250 500 m
PLACES TO STAY
1 Füred Camping
2 Hotel Marina
3 Hotel Margaréta
7 Ring Pension
11 Aranycsillag Hotel
12 Kelén Gyógyszálló
17 Hotel Blaha Lujza
28 Hotel UNI (BME)
PLACES TO EAT
4 Baricska Csárda
26 Halászkert Étterem
OTHER
5 Train & Bus Stations
6 Ibusz
8 Supermarket
9 OTP Bank
10 Balatonfüred Tourist
13 Post Office
14 Cooptourist
15 Jókai Museum
16 Round Church
18 Balatontourist
19 Balaton Pantheon
20 Kossuth Well
21 State Hospital
22 Cinema
23 Tagore Statue
24 Ferry Wharf
25 Galeria Disco
27 Ship/Bar Helka

Private Rooms As everywhere around Balaton Lake, private room prices are rather inflated. Kádár & Társa Agency (K & T Tours) at the train station arranges private rooms beginning around US$11/17 single/double (open from April to October only).

Ibusz, Petőfi Sándor utca 4/a, also has private rooms from US$11/17 single/double (open year-round).

Balatonfüred Tourist, Petőfi Sándor utca 8, has the most expensive private rooms (US$24/28 single/double), open year-round. Cooptourist, Jókai Mór utca 23, has only double private rooms (no singles) and they're closed from October to April.

Balatontourist, Blaha Lujza utca 5, has the largest number of rooms, thus they've a better chance of finding something less expensive for you.

Hotels Next to the Ibusz office is *Ring Pension* (☎ 342 884), Petőfi Sándor utca 6/A, so called because the owner is a former champion boxer. Neat, clean singles/doubles with shared bath cost US$35/45, breakfast included (open all year but often full in midsummer). There are several other pensions behind Ibusz, all fairly expensive.

At last report the grand old *Aranycsillag Hotel*, Zsigmond utca 1, was closed. If this is still the case, continue two blocks north to the *Kelén Gyógyszálló* (☎ 342 811), Petőfi Sándor utca 38, a four-storey spa hotel in an attractive park, with reasonably priced rooms at US$20 double without bath, US$27 double with bath, breakfast included. There's only one single room which goes for US$16. The hotel is open year-round and rates are lower in the off season.

There's also the *Hotel Blaha Lujza* (☎ 342 603) behind the Blaha Lujza Restaurant, Blaha Lujza utca 4, opposite Balatontourist. Singles/doubles are US$21/28 with private bath and it's open year-round.

Places to Eat

The *Halászkert Étterem*, on Széchenyi utca next to the ship/bar *Helka*, is expensive and permanently packed with German tourists. The previously mentioned *Blaha Lujza Restaurant* is a much better place to eat.

A number of stand-up food stalls just below the Round Church towards the wharf sell big pieces of fried fish priced by weight.

Getting There & Away

Balatonfüred is two hours from Budapest-Déli (132 km) by express train and three hours by local train. The line continues to Tapolca via Badacsony. There are Mahart ferries to Siófok from mid-April to mid-October.

Buses depart from the stop in front of the train station for Tihany (10 km) and Veszprém (16 km) about once an hour, to Győr (92 km) six times a day, to Esztergom, Sopron (160 km) and Kecskemét (174 km) daily.

NEAR BALATONFÜRED

The picturesque buildings and scenery at **Veszprém**, 16 km north of Balatonfüred, make it a worthwhile day trip. The old town stands on an abrupt headland overlooking a gorge. From the baroque Fire Tower (1815) on Ovaros tér follow the old town's one street, Vár utca, through the city gate, reconstructed in 1936, to Veszprém Cathedral. The cathedral was completely rebuilt in a neo-Romanesque style in 1910 but the original Gothic crypt remains. The other massive building on the square is the Episcopal Palace (1776). A broad stairway behind the cathedral leads down to Benedek Hill, where a sweeping 360° panorama of the Séd Valley awaits you. If you have time, also visit the Bakony Museum, Megyeház tér 5 (open all year, closed Monday), beyond the massive County Hall (1887). Veszprém's train station is on the far north side of town, so take advantage of the frequent bus service (30 minutes) linking Balatonfüred and Veszprém. Balatontourist in the mall between the bus station and the old town may be able to supply a map.

The milky-green Sió River drains Balaton Lake into the Danube at **Siófok**, the largest and busiest town on Balaton's south-eastern shore. It's a useful transit point but there's

HUNGARY

really no reason to stay. A strip of pricey high-rise hotels, six huge camping grounds, holiday cottages, tacky discos and a seamy nightlife attract big crowds of rowdy German and Austrian tourists. In midsummer bedlam reigns and the confused travel agency staff in charge of issuing private rooms won't even consider stays of one or two nights, and singles are unavailable. In winter Siófok is dead. However the town can be convenient if you're just passing through as the train and bus stations are adjacent in the centre of town and the lake boat terminal is only an easy 10-minute walk away. There's a cheap stand-up buffet in the bus station and the OTP Bank at Fő utca 188 across the street from the stations changes travellers' cheques weekdays from 7.45 am to 3 pm.

TIHANY

The Tihany Peninsula almost bisects the northern end of Balaton Lake. Consensus has it that this is the most beautiful place around and in summer Tihany gets more than its fair share of tourists. After a visit to the famous Benedictine Tihany Abbey, you can easily shake the hordes by hiking out past the hilly peninsula's inner lake, Belsó Lake, with its rare flora, fish and bird life. Külsó Lake has almost dried up.

Orientation

Tihany Abbey sits on a ridge above the Tihany ferry landing on the eastern side of the peninsula's high plateau. The village of Tihany is perched above Belsó Lake, just below the abbey. Lake boats also stop at Tihanyi-rév, the car ferry landing at the southern end of the peninsula.

Things to See & Do

Tihany's magnificent twin-towered **abbey church** (1754) is outstanding for its baroque altars, pulpit and organ, but pride of place goes to the 11th-century crypt at the front of the church. Here is found the tomb (1060) of the abbey's founder, King Andrew I. The earliest written relic of the Hungarian language, dating from 1085, was found here. In summer, organ concerts are given in the church.

The monastery beside the church has been converted into the **Tihany Museum** (open 9 am to 5 pm from March to October, closed Monday). An extensive lapidarium is in the museum basement. The view of Balaton Lake from behind the abbey is excellent.

The promenade Pisky sétány runs along the ridge north from the church to the Echo Restaurant, passing a cluster of folk houses which have now been turned into a small **open-air museum** (closed from November to April and every Tuesday). From the restaurant you can descend to the harbour or continue up on to green and red-marked hiking trails which pass this way. The red trail crosses the peninsula between the two lakes to **Csúcs Hill**, which offers fine views (two hours). The trail around Belsó Lake is very evocative at dusk. The trails are poorly marked but a delightful respite from the tourist trappings in the village.

Places to Stay & Eat

Tihany Tourist, Kossuth utca 11, opposite the last stop of the bus from Balatonfüred, rents private rooms at US$20 double (no singles), changes travellers' cheques at a fair rate and rents bicycles (US$4 for four hours). They're open from April to October and the staff are young and enthusiastic.

Balatontourist, Kossuth Lajos utca 22, directly below the monastery, opens shorter hours in summer only. Many houses around Tihany have 'Zimmer frei' signs, so in the off season you could try there.

The touristy *Rege Presso* beside the abbey offers a panoramic view from its terrace, but you would do better to eat at *Kecskeköröm Csárda*, Kossuth Lajos utca 19, a few hundred metres north-west on the main road, or just beyond at the *Fogas Csárda*, Kossuth Lajos utca 9. There are also a couple of pizzerias.

Getting There & Away

Buses cover the 11 km from Balatonfüred Railway Station about hourly. The bus stops at both ferry landings before climbing to the

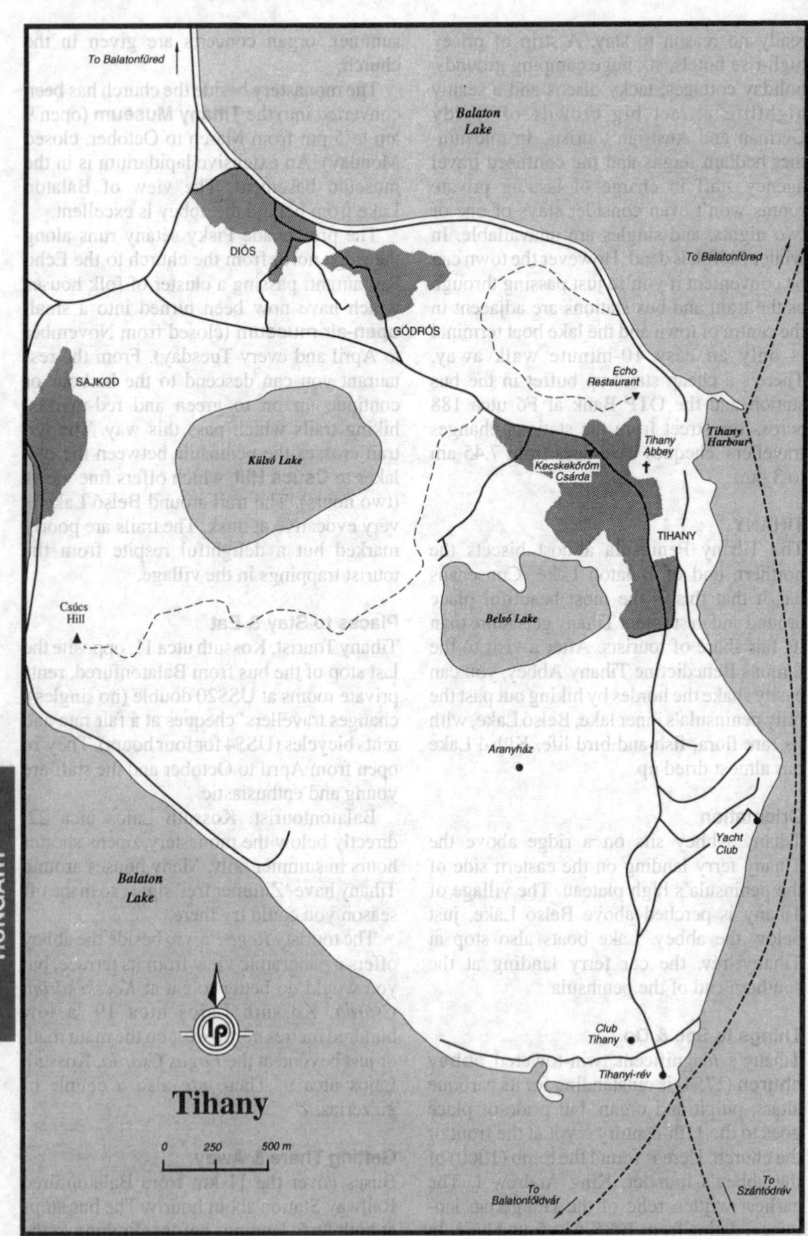
To Balatonfüred
Balaton Lake
DIÓS
GÓDRÓS
To Balatonfüred
SAJKOD
Echo Restaurant
Tihany Abbey
Tihany Harbour
Külső Lake
Kecskekőröm Csárda
TIHANY
Belső Lake
Csúcs Hill
Aranyház
Yacht Club
Balaton Lake
Club Tihany
Tihanyi-rév
Tihany
0
250
500 m
To Balatonföldvár
To Szántódrév

village of Tihany where it turns around and returns the same way.

The Balaton Lake ferries stop at Tihany from mid-April to mid-October. Catch them at the harbour below the abbey or at Tihanyi-rév, the car ferry terminal at the southern end of the peninsula. From April to November the car ferry crosses the narrow neck of Balaton Lake from Tihanyi-rév to Szántódrév frequently.

BADACSONY

Badacsony lies between Balatonfüred and Keszthely in a picturesque region of basalt peaks among some of the best hiking country in Hungary. Vineyards hug the sides of Badacsony's extinct volcanic cone (elevation 437 metres). The benign climate and rich volcanic soils make this an ideal wine-making area, and in summer hordes of drunken Austrian devotees of Bacchus cavort here. If you like your wine, Badacsony is for you.

From October to April all of the travel agencies, pensions and restaurants mentioned in this section are *closed*. You should still be able to find a room by looking for 'Zimmer frei' signs or asking around, but bring some food with you. The left-luggage office at the train station is open from 8 am to 8 pm. Ask at the ticket window.

Things to See & Do

An **art gallery** (open from May to October, closed Monday) near the train station displays the works of local painter József Egry (1883-1951), who lived here from 1918 onwards. Egry skilfully captured the beauty of Balaton at different times of day.

The beaten tourist track at Badacsony leads up through the vineyards to the **Borászati Wine Museum** (open from mid-May to September, closed Monday). You will pass some garish wine restaurants on the way, including one misleadingly labelled 'Bormúzeum'. The genuine museum isn't very interesting but the views of the mountain and lake are good.

The flat-topped forested massif overlooking the lake is just the place to escape the tipsy herd. If you'd like a running start on your hiking, catch one of the topless jeeps marked 'Badacsony hegyi járat', which leave Badacsony post office any time from 10 am to 8 pm from May to September whenever at least six paying passengers are aboard (US$2 per person). The jeep driver will drop you off at the Kisfaludy House Restaurant, where a large map outlining the well-marked trails is posted by the parking lot. There are numerous lookouts as well as a tall wooden tower that offers splendid views to the hiker.

Places to Stay

Private rooms are available from a number of agencies, including Balatontourist and Ibusz in the small shopping centre near the ferry wharf, Cooptourist hidden behind some food stalls between the post office and the ABC supermarket, and Miditourist on Park utca behind the train station. Singles are not available and doubles begin around US$15. There are several small pensions among the vineyards on the road above the railway line, a 10-minute walk from the station.

The closest camping ground (☎ 331 091; open from June to mid-September) is by the lake, just under a km west of the station. It's a casual place but be sure to bring mosquito repellent. Hotplates are available for cooking.

If all this sounds unappealing, you can easily see Badacsony as a stopover on your way around the lake.

Places to Eat

There are no cheap restaurants at Badacsony and the fried fare at the many food stalls near the train station is definitely second rate (although you might try the fried lake fish). Everything is sold by weight and the posted prices are for 100 grams. A better plan is to get picnic food at the ABC supermarket behind the food stalls and have a leisurely lunch by the lake or on top of the mountain. A good local dry white wine is Badacsony Kéknyelű.

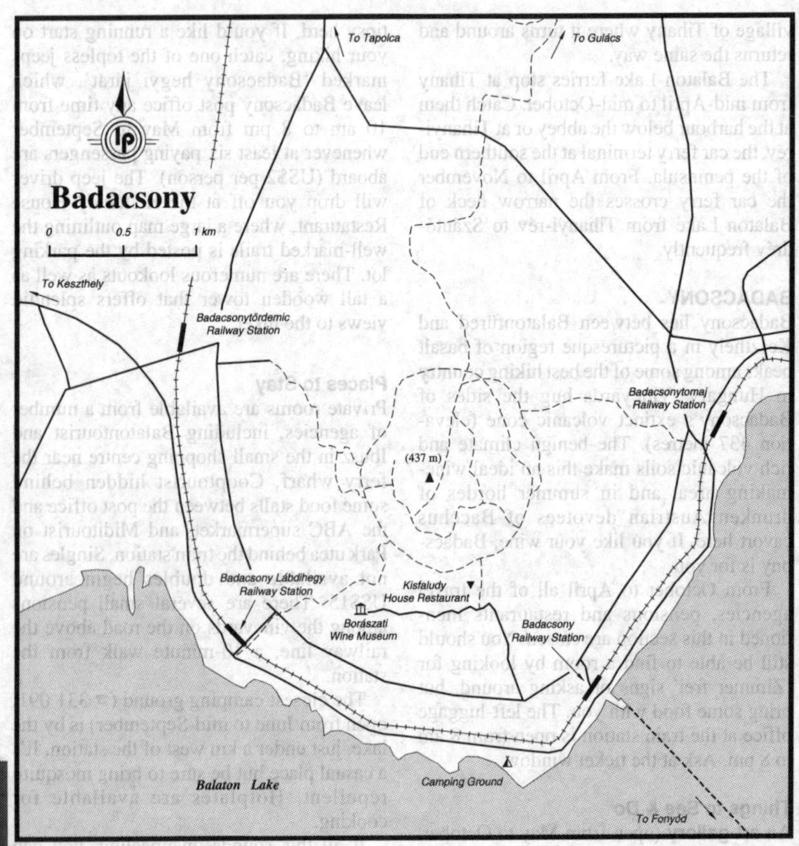

Getting There & Away

Badacsony vm Station is on the railway line from Budapest-Déli to Tapolca and Zalaegerszeg. To Keszthely the railway line follows a roundabout route via Tapolca, where you must change trains. There's often an immediate connection, however. If not, take a bus on to Keszthely, which would be a lot faster anyway.

There's a 'managed' pay-beach next to the ferry wharf in Badacsony but the swimming is better at Fonyód across the lake. Ferries between Badacsony and Fonyód are fairly frequent (from April to October) and in Fonyód you can get a connection to southern Transdanubia by taking a train direct to Kaposvár (53 km, one hour), then a bus on to Pécs from there.

A boat ride to Badacsony from Siófok or Balatonfüred is the best way to get the feel of Balaton Lake. Boats operate from June to mid-September. Ferries also travel to Keszthely at this time.

KESZTHELY

Keszthely (pronounced 'cast-eye') at the western end of Balaton Lake is a fairly large town that you'll pass through on your way from western to southern Hungary. It has a few attractions, good facilities and boat services on the lake from June to mid-September. Keszthely is the only town on Balaton Lake which has a life of its own; since it isn't entirely dependent on tourism, it's open all year. The abundance of budget accommodation makes Keszthely a natural stepping stone on your way around this part of Hungary.

Orientation

The bus and train stations are fairly close to the ferry terminal on the lake. The left-luggage office inside the train station is open 24 hours. From the stations follow Mártírok útja up the hill, then turn right on to Kossuth Lajos utca into town. The Festetics Palace is at the northern end of this street.

Information

Tourinform, Kossuth Lajos utca 28, is an excellent source of information on the whole Balaton area.

Money The OTP Bank, Kossuth Lajos utca 40 (Monday to Thursday 8 am to 2.30 pm, Friday 8 am to noon), changes travellers' cheques.

Post & Telephone An efficient public telephone office is at Kossuth Lajos utca 1 (Monday to Saturday 9 am to 7 pm). Keszthely's telephone code is 83.

Things to See

Keszthely's finest sight is the **Festetics Palace**, the former residence of the land-owning Festetics family, which was built in 1745 and greatly extended in 1887. The palace, now a museum, is open all year from 9 am to 5 pm except Monday. A highlight of the 101-room palace is the Helikon Library, but the entire complex is richly appointed and well worth seeing (though the hunting trophies show a lack of taste).

In 1797 Count Festetics founded Europe's first agricultural institute here and even today Keszthely is noted for its large Agricultural University. Part of the original school, the **Georgikon Manor**, Bercsényi Miklós utca 67, is now a museum (open from April to October, closed Monday) with antique farming equipment, and so on. It's only a couple of blocks from the palace. The **Balaton Museum** (closed Monday) is on Kossuth Lajos utca, towards the train station.

Places to Stay

Camping There are several camping grounds near the lake, all of which have bungalows. As you leave the train station, head south across the tracks and you'll soon reach *Sport Camping* (☎ 313 777) between the tracks and a road. Camping space is US$2 per person plus US$2 per tent plus US$0.75 tax. They also have four caravans for rent at US$8 double, plus US$0.75 tax, and a couple of bungalows from US$17 to US$22, plus tax. The mosquitoes are free. It's open from mid-May to September.

Twenty minutes farther south along the lakeshore is *Zalatour Camping* (☎ 312 728) with camping at US$2 per person plus US$3 per tent. Hot showers are US$1 each. Zalatour has 39 nice little bungalows which rent for US$10/11 double/triple from mid-June to August or US$6/8 from May to mid-June and in September. In addition there are 15 luxury apartments accommodating four people at US$35. Add US$0.75 per person tax to all charges. Unfortunately Zalatour has located its new reception building on the farthest possible side of the camping ground away from the train station, adding nearly 10 minutes walking time each way.

There's also *Castrum Camping* (☎ 312 120), Móra Ferenc utca 48 (open from April to October), a 20-minute walk north of the train station. It's expensive, far from the beach and intended mostly for visitors with cars.

Hostels The *Helikon Turistaszálló* (☎ 311 424), Honvéd utca 22, has three double rooms at US$7 per person and four 16-room dormitories at US$6 per person, breakfast included. You'll be welcomed warmly by the friendly family which runs this hostel (and also by their noisy dog) and it's a great deal

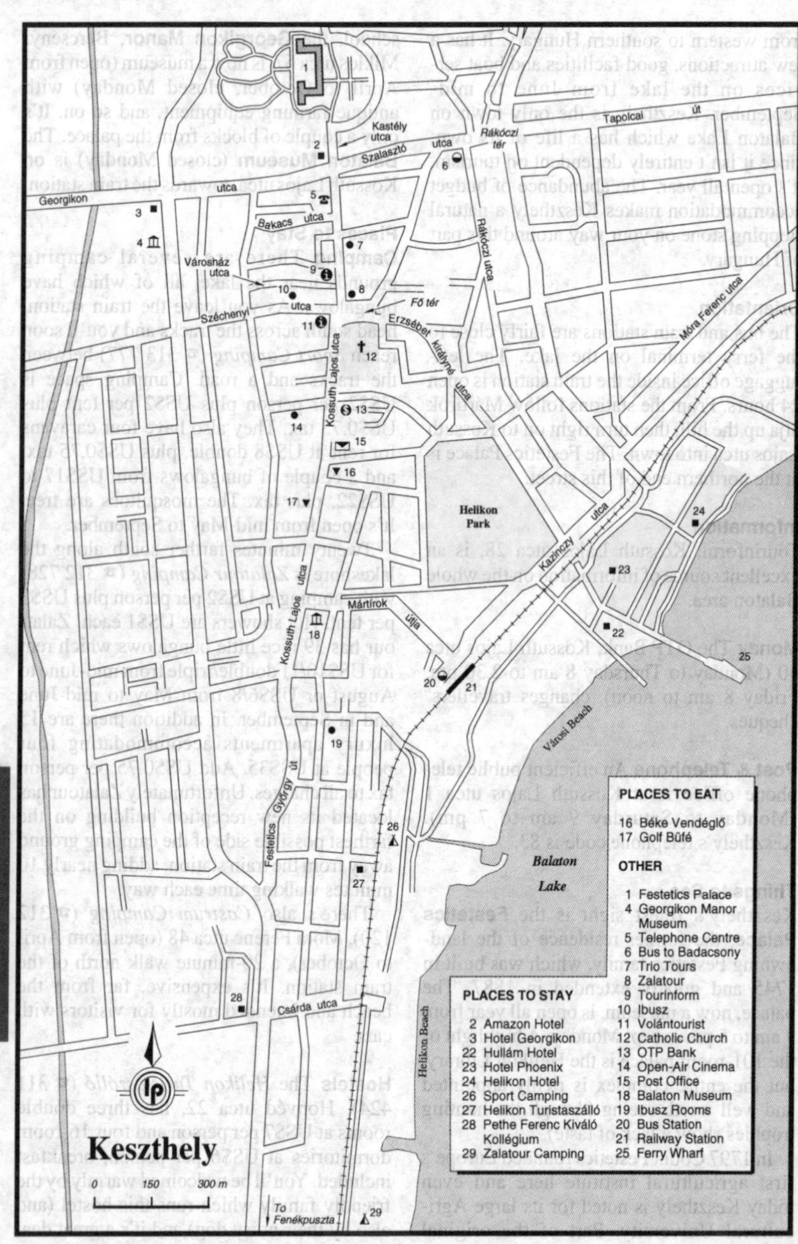

Keszthely
Kastély utca
Szalasztó utca
Rákóczi tér
Tapolcai út
Georgikon utca
Bakacs utca
Városház utca
Széchenyi utca
Fő tér
Erzsébet Királyné utca
Rákóczi utca
Móra Ferenc utca
Kossuth Lajos utca
Helikon Park
Kazinczy utca
Mártírok útja
Festetics György út
Városi Beach
Helikon Beach
Balaton Lake
Csárda utca
To Fenékpuszta
0 150 300 m
PLACES TO STAY
2 Amazon Hotel
3 Hotel Georgikon
22 Hullám Hotel
23 Hotel Phoenix
24 Helikon Hotel
26 Sport Camping
27 Helikon Turistaszálló
28 Pethe Ferenc Kiváló Kollégium
29 Zalatour Camping
PLACES TO EAT
16 Béke Vendéglő
17 Golf Büfé
OTHER
1 Festetics Palace
4 Georgikon Manor Museum
5 Telephone Centre
6 Bus to Badacsony
7 Trio Tours
8 Zalatour
9 Tourinform
10 Ibusz
11 Volántourist
12 Catholic Church
13 OTP Bank
14 Open-Air Cinema
15 Post Office
18 Balaton Museum
19 Ibusz Rooms
20 Bus Station
21 Railway Station
25 Ferry Wharf

HUNGARY

if you get one of the doubles (open year-round).

In July and August you can stay in the student dormitory at *Pethe Ferenc Kiváló Kollégium* (☎ 311 290), Festetics György út 5, for US$5 per person.

Private Rooms Private rooms are not such a bargain in Keszthely, but available from Ibusz, Széchenyi utca 1-3; Trio Tours, Kossuth Lajos utca 18; Zalatour, Kossuth Lajos utca 30; and Keszthely Tourist, Kossuth Lajos 25. Ask around as prices differ.

If all the travel agencies in the centre are closed when you arrive, try the special Ibusz private room agency at Római utca 2, a few blocks south-west of the train station, which should be open weekdays from 5 to 8 pm, Saturday 8 am to 8 pm, Sunday 9 am to 1 pm. Continue south on Múzeum utca behind the Balaton Museum.

If you're only staying one night, some of the agencies levy exorbitant surcharges, making it worthwhile to forgo their services and go directly to houses with 'Zimmer frei' signs where you may be able to bargain with the owners. One such 'Zimmer' sign is sometimes posted at Széchényi utca 2 just down from Ibusz (they take the sign in when they're full).

Hotels The 18th-century *Amazon Hotel* (☎ 312 248), Georgikon utca 1, is US$14/16 single/double without bath, US$24/26 with bath, breakfast included. At these prices it's often full, especially on Saturday nights, when wedding parties attending gala functions in the nearby palace occupy the place.

The next cheapest place is the *Hotel Georgikon* (☎ 315 730), on the corner of Bercsény Miklós utca and Georgikon utca, a renovated old manor which is US$42 double in summer, US$33 double in winter, breakfast included (no singles).

Places to Eat

The *Béke Vendéglő*, Kossuth Lajos utca 50, next to the post office, has a reasonable menu in German with several fish dishes and is open all year. It's popular among budget travellers of a dozen nationalities.

The *Golf Büfé*, Kossuth Lajos utca 95, serves grilled meats and pizza. They're only open in the evening after 6 pm and it's something of a youth hang-out. *Easy Rider*, Kossuth Lajos utca 79, also puts out a good beat in the evening.

For real oven-baked pizza and draught beer try *Pizzeria da Francesco*, Szabad nép utca 4 (the backstreet directly behind the main Ibusz office). In recent years da Francesco has become very touristy; colour photos of their offerings are displayed on boards outside without prices.

The *Bár Piccolo*, Szabad nép utca 9 near da Francesco, is just the place to stumble into after dinner, but watch the killer last step!

Entertainment

On Sunday at 8.30 pm from July to mid-August you can see Hungarian folk dancing in the back courtyard at the *Folk Centrum*, Kossuth Lajos utca 28.

Keszthely's top disco is *Club of Colours*, Sömögye dülő 1, three km east of the centre on the road to Badacsony. From mid-June to the end of August it's open nightly from 9 pm to 4 am; the rest of the year, Saturday only (US$2 cover).

Getting There & Away

Keszthely is on a branch line between Tapolca and Balatonszentgyörgy, so railway service is poor. Occasional fast trains arrive from Budapest-Déli (190 km, three hours) via Siófok. For Pécs take a train to Kaposvár, then change to a bus.

The morning train service from Keszthely to Szombathely involves changing trains at Tapolca and Celldömölk but the connections are good. At Tapolca you must go to the ticket window to get a compulsory seat reservation for the Celldömölk-Szombathely leg.

To go to Croatia, take a bus or train to Nagykanizsa where you'll find unreserved local trains to Varaždin (72 km, 1½ hours) twice a day, and buses direct to Zagreb (176 km, US$7), also twice a day.

A bus station with services to most of western Transdanubia adjoins the train station. Some buses for southern Transdanubia leave from in front of the Catholic church in the centre of town, so check carefully. The bus to Badacsony (marked Badacsonytomaj at the stop) leaves seven times a day from Szalasztó utca 20. Always scrutinise the yellow sign boards at the stops and be aware of footnotes. The office marked 'Váro' at Volántourist, Kossuth Lajos utca 43, has information on buses.

From the bus station in front of the Catholic church you can get buses to Budapest (185 km), Szombathely (106 km), Győr, Pécs (158 km) and Sopron (141 km), but most leave only in the very early morning. Buses to Hévíz (six km) from stand No 4 here are frequent. Buses to Sopron and Szombathely leave from the bus station next to the train station around noon.

Mahart ferries travel to Badacsony from June to mid-September. In July and August these boats continue on to Siófok.

HÉVÍZ

In a country with 1500 thermal baths there just had to be a real thermal lake. Lake Gyógy, the second-largest warm-water lake in the world, averages 30°C at the surface and red Indian water lilies blossom in it in summer. Eighty million litres of thermal water gush daily from a depth of one km at a rate of 1000 litres or one cubic metre a second, flushing the lake completely every two days. Radioactive mud from the lake bed is effective in the treatment of locomotor disorders. In winter the steaming waters, which never fall below 24°C, seem almost surreal.

Wooden catwalks have been built over the lake, allowing you to swim in comfort. The **lake baths** *(tófürdő)* are open all year from 8.30 am to 5.30 pm (admission US$2 for three hours, US$3 for all day). A 20-minute massage costs US$7 and a cabin US$2. The indoor **thermal baths** next to the lake function all year from 7 am to 4 pm daily. If you're addicted to the drinking cure, you can get a free fill-up here, but bring a cup.

Post & Telephone The post office is on Kossuth Lajos utca near the corner of Széchenyi utca and there are lots of public phones in front of the building.

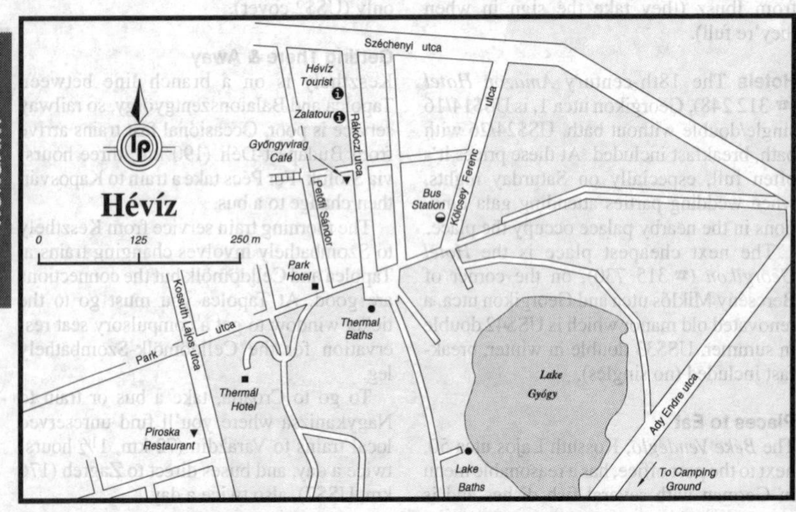

Places to Stay

The hotels of Hévíz cater mostly to Austrians on short trips who can afford to pay premium prices, or to people on packaged health tours. The camping ground is designed for motorists who pay a flat fee to occupy a large area, a system that works to the disadvantage of backpackers. The restaurants and cafés are also very touristy, so you're far better off staying in Keszthely, six km east, and visiting Hévíz for the day.

If you're determined to stay, your best bet is to visit the agencies renting private rooms, including Hévíztourist and Zalatour, both on Rákóczi utca, or Zala Volántourist in the bus station. Many houses with 'Zimmer frei' signs are along Kossuth Lajos utca though you may have to shop around for a good deal.

If you do want to stay at a Hévíz resort for a few days it's cheaper to book ahead through Danubius Travels, Szervita tér 8, Budapest. They have all-inclusive one-week packages at Hotel Thermál which are much cheaper than paying as you go.

Getting There & Away

Hévíz doesn't have a train station, but a bus goes to Keszthely (six km, 30 minutes) almost every half-hour and there are occasional services to Szombathely. Buses run to Badacsony twice daily, to Balatonfüred (73 km) three times daily, to Budapest (191 km) four times daily, to Pécs (164 km) twice daily and to Székesfehérvár (133 km) twice daily. There's no left-luggage office at the bus station.

Southern Transdanubia

Southern Transdanubia close to Croatia is characterised by rolling, forested hills and an almost Mediterranean climate. Near Mohács on the Danube in 1526 the Hungarian armies under King Louis II were routed by a vastly superior Ottoman force. As a result the gracious southern city of Pécs still bears the imprint of 150 years of Turkish rule. The good facilities in Pécs make it a perfect base for day trips to Siklós castles, the spas of Harkány and Sikonda, and hiking trails through the Mecsek Hills. Many people in transit between Croatia and Yugoslavia pass through here.

PÉCS

Pécs (Fünfkirchen), a large historical city in southern Hungary that lies between the Danube and Drava rivers, is the seat of Baranya County. The fine position on the southern slopes of the Mecsek Hills gives Pécs a relatively mild climate and the red-tiled roofs of the houses accentuate its Mediterranean flavour. Zsolnay porcelain and Pannónia champagne are made here. A less appealing activity is the uranium mining on the slopes just north-east of town.

For 400 years Sopianae (Pécs) was the capital of the Roman province of Lower Pannonia. Early Christianity flourished here in the 4th century and by the 9th century the town was known as 'Quinque Ecclesiae' for its five churches. In 1009 Stephen I, Hungary's first king, made Pécs a bishopric. The first Hungarian university (and the sixth in Europe) was founded here in 1367 and the city's humanistic traditions climaxed with the poet Janus Pannonius. City walls were erected after the Tatar invasion of 1241, but 1543 marked the start of 150 years of Turkish rule. The Turks left their greatest monuments in Pécs and these, together with imposing churches and a synagogue, over a dozen museums, possibilities for hiking through the Mecsek Hills, varied excursions and lively student atmosphere, make Pécs the perfect place to spend a couple of days. A direct rail link with Zagreb makes Pécs an excellent gateway city to/from Croatia.

Orientation

The bus and train stations are about three blocks apart on the southern side of the town centre. Find your way north to Széchenyi tér where 12 streets meet. Numerous city buses also run up this way (ask).

The left-luggage office in the main train station is in an obscure building at the far west end of platform No 1. The left-luggage

HUNGARY

office at the bus station closes at 6 pm, whereas the one at the train station is open around the clock.

Information

Tourinform, Széchenyi tér 9, has information on other parts of Hungary as well as Pécs and the staff are good about answering questions.

The Magyar Autóklub (☎ 324 729) is at Ferencesek utca 22.

Money The OTP Bank, Király utca 11, opposite the National Theatre (Monday to Wednesday 7.45 am to 3 pm, Thursday 9.15 am to 5.30 pm, Friday 7.45 am to 2 pm), changes travellers' cheques.

Post & Telephone The main post office is at Jókai Mór utca 10. You can make international telephone calls from there. Pécs's telephone code is 72.

Travel Agencies Advance train tickets and reservations are available at the MÁV ticket office, Rákóczi út 39/c.

Bookshops Corvina on Ferencesek utca between Széchenyi and Jókai squares has one of the best selections of books in English you'll find in Hungary.

Things to See

Széchenyi tér is the bustling heart of Pécs, dominated on the north by the former **Mosque of Gazi Kassim Pasha**, the largest Turkish building in Hungary. Now a Catholic church, Islamic elements such as the mihrab, a prayer niche on the south-eastern side, are easy to distinguish. Behind the ex-mosque is the **Archaeological Museum** with exhibits from prehistory up to the Magyar conquest. Informative summaries in English and German are displayed in each room.

From this museum go west along Janus Pannonius utca for a block to the **Csontváry Museum**, Janus Pannonius utca 11, dedicated to the surrealist painter-philosopher Tivadar Csontváry (1853-1919). His painting of the ruins of Baalbek, Lebanon (1905) is a masterpiece. On the corner opposite this museum is a good little wine cellar that is in front of the men's toilets.

Káptalan utca, which climbs east from here, is lined with museums. In a separate pavilion behind the **Endre Nemes Museum**, Káptalan utca 5, is the Erzsébet Schaár *Utca* or 'Street', a complete artistic environment in which the sculptor has set her whole life in stone. The **Vásárely Museum**, Káptalan utca 3, has 150 original examples of op art. Victor Vásárely, a longtime resident of southern France, was born in this house in 1908. Across the street is the **Zsolnay Porcelain Museum**, Káptalan utca 2, which has mostly Art-Nouveau pieces (captions are in German). A room downstairs in the same building contains sculptures by Amerigo Tot.

Return to Szent István tér and the tremendous four-towered **cathedral** (admission costs US$0.50). The oldest part of the building is the 11th-century crypt, but the entire complex was rebuilt in a neo-Romanesque style in 1881. In summer there are organ concerts in the cathedral on Friday evenings. Behind the **bishop's palace** (1770), next to the cathedral (and with a metallic statue of Franz Liszt leaning over the balcony), is a 15th-century **barbican** that remains from the old city walls.

In the centre of the southern portion of Szent István tér is an excavated 4th-century Roman Christian **mausoleum** with striking frescos of Adam and Eve, and Daniel in the lion's den, certainly a remarkable sight that is unique in Central Europe. Nearby at Apáca utca 14 are the ruins of a 4th-century Early Christian chapel. It's only open in summer but you can enter the courtyard and peek in through the windows any time.

On the east side of Szent István tér is the **Pannónia champagne factory** with a sales room just inside where you can purchase bottles of all the local wines and champagnes. It's possible to visit the factory and cellars if you come in the morning.

Follow your map south-west a few blocks from Szent István tér to the 16th-century

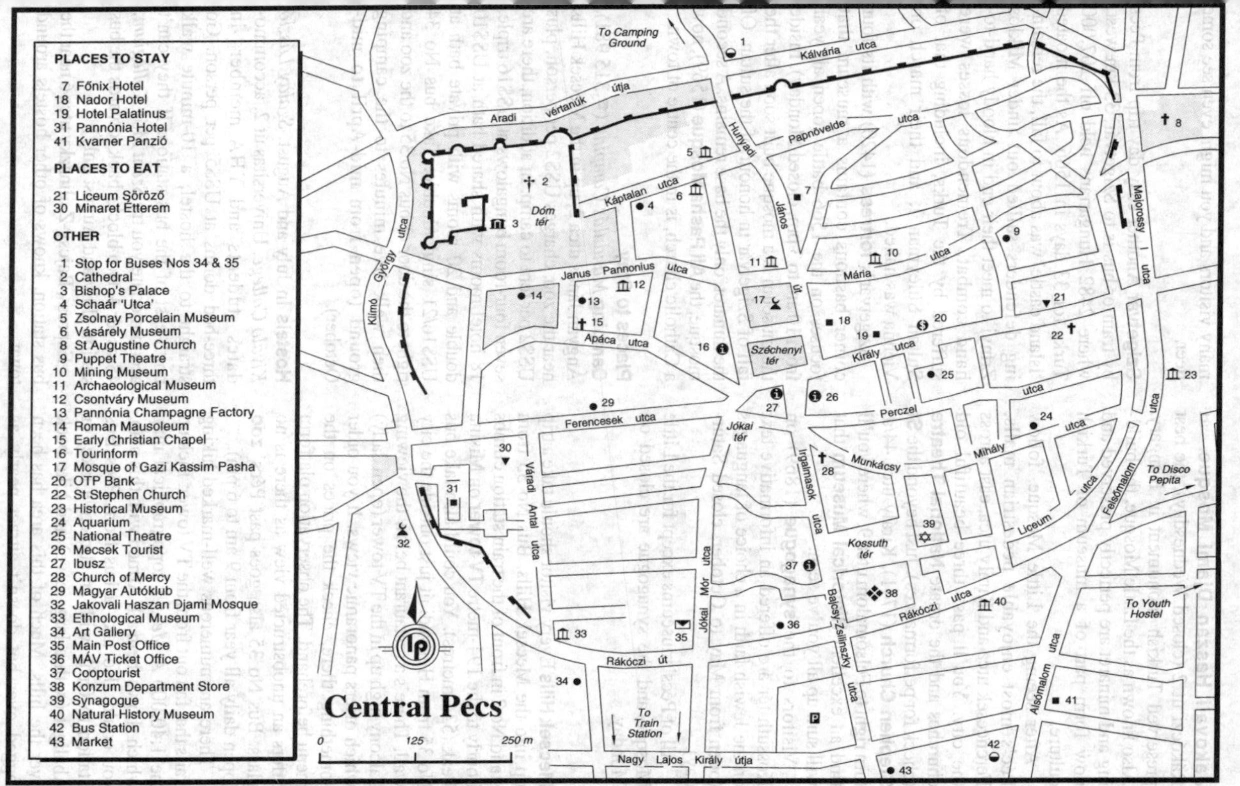
Central Pécs
PLACES TO STAY
7 Főnix Hotel
18 Nador Hotel
19 Hotel Palatinus
31 Pannónia Hotel
41 Kvarner Panzió
PLACES TO EAT
21 Liceum Sörözö
30 Minaret Étterem
OTHER
1 Stop for Buses Nos 34 & 35
2 Cathedral
3 Bishop's Palace
4 Schaár 'Utca'
5 Zsolnay Porcelain Museum
6 Vásárely Museum
8 St Augustine Church
9 Puppet Theatre
10 Mining Museum
11 Archaeological Museum
12 Csontváry Museum
13 Pannónia Champagne Factory
14 Roman Mausoleum
15 Early Christian Chapel
16 Tourinform
17 Mosque of Gazi Kassim Pasha
20 OTP Bank
22 St Stephen Church
23 Historical Museum
24 Aquarium
25 National Theatre
26 Mecsek Tourist
27 Ibusz
28 Church of Mercy
29 Magyar Autóklub
32 Jakovali Haszan Djami Mosque
33 Ethnological Museum
34 Art Gallery
35 Main Post Office
36 MÁV Ticket Office
37 Cooptourist
38 Konzum Department Store
39 Synagogue
40 Natural History Museum
42 Bus Station
43 Market
0 125 250 m
To Camping Ground
To Disco Pepita
To Youth Hostel
To Train Station
Kálvária utca
Aradi vértanúk útja
Hunyadi út
Papnövelde utca
Káptalan utca
János
Dóm tér
Klimó György utca
Janus Pannonius utca
Apáca utca
Mária utca
Széchenyi tér
Király utca
Majorossy utca
Ferencesek utca
Jókai tér
Perczel utca
Munkácsy Mihály utca
Irgalmasok utca
Kossuth tér
Liceum utca
Felsőmalom utca
Váradi Antal utca
Jókai Mór utca
Bajcsy-Zsilinszky utca
Rákóczi út
Rákóczi utca
Alsómalom utca
Nagy Lajos Király útja
HUNGARY

Jakovali Haszan Djami Mosque, at Rákóczi út 2 (closed Wednesday), the best preserved Turkish monument in Hungary. Also known as the Little Mosque, the building and minaret are perfectly preserved and now form part of a museum of Turkish culture.

After seeing the Little Mosque, follow Péc's most enjoyable pedestrian malls, Ferencesek utca and Király utca, east across the city. You'll pass three beautiful old churches and the ornate **National Theatre** (check for performances). Just beyond the **St Stephen Church** (1741), Király utca 44/a, turn right to Felsőmalom utca 9, where you'll find an excellent **Historical Museum** that will sum up all you've seen.

Visitors to the **synagogue** (1869) on Kossuth tér are offered an informative text on the Jewish faith in a choice of languages (open from May to October, closed Saturday).

All of Pécs' museums except for the Little Mosque and the synagogue are closed on Monday.

Mecsek Hills Every visitor should take a trip up into the Mecsek Hills. Bus No 35 from stand No 2 in front of the train station climbs hourly to the 194-metre **TV tower** on Misina Peak (534 metres). You could also take bus No 35 from Hunyadi út just outside the city wall. There's a restaurant below the viewing balcony high up in the TV tower (open daily) which offers panoramic views. If you order something there, check the prices on the menu beforehand. The observation platform offers an unobstructed view as there is no glass. Bus No 35 also goes past Pécs' **zoo** (open daily all year from 9 am to 6 pm).

There are numerous well-marked hiking trails that fan out from the TV tower. Pick up the 1:40,000 *A Mecsek* topographical map which shows them all. Armed with this map, you could also take a bus from Pécs Bus Station to Orfű (with an attractive lake) or Abaliget (with a large cave) and hike back over the hills. Much of this area has been logged over but doesn't attract nearly as many visitors and you might even see some deer.

Szigetvár Another easy day trip from Pécs by train or bus is to Szigetvár, 33 km west, where 2482 Hungarians held off 207,000 Turks for 33 days in 1566. As the moated 'island castle' was about to fall, the remaining defenders sallied out under Miklós Zrínyi to meet their end in bloody hand-to-hand combat. Tremendous losses were suffered by the Turks, including that of Sultan Süleyman I, and their march on Vienna was halted.

Szigetvár's **fortress** (1420) with its four corner bastions contains a museum that focuses on the 1566 battle (open all year from 10 am to 3 pm, closed Monday). Inside the museum is a mosque built soon after the fall of Szigetvár in honour of the sultan. Of the minaret, only the base remains. A second mosque, the **Ali Pasha Mosque** (1569), now a Catholic church, is in the centre of town.

Places to Stay

Camping *Mandulás Camping* (☎ 315 981), Ángyán János utca 2, up in the Mecsek Hills near the zoo, charges US$2 per person, plus US$2 per tent to camp. In addition, there are seven four-room bungalows at US$16 triple, 18 hotel rooms with shared bath at US$10 double and 20 rooms with private bath at US$16/21 single/double. Take bus No 34 right to the door or bus No 35 to the zoo and then walk five minutes to the camping ground (open from mid-April to mid-October).

Hostels In July and August, *Szalay László Kivalo College*, Universitas út 2, accommodates students and YHA members in three-bed dorms at US$5 per person. Go straight to the hostel, a 10-minute walk north-east of the bus station. If they can't accommodate you try *Szent Mór Kollégium*, 48-as tér 4, two blocks back towards the bus station (July and August only).

Express, Bajcsy-Zsilinszky utca 6 near the bus station, knows of other hostels around town.

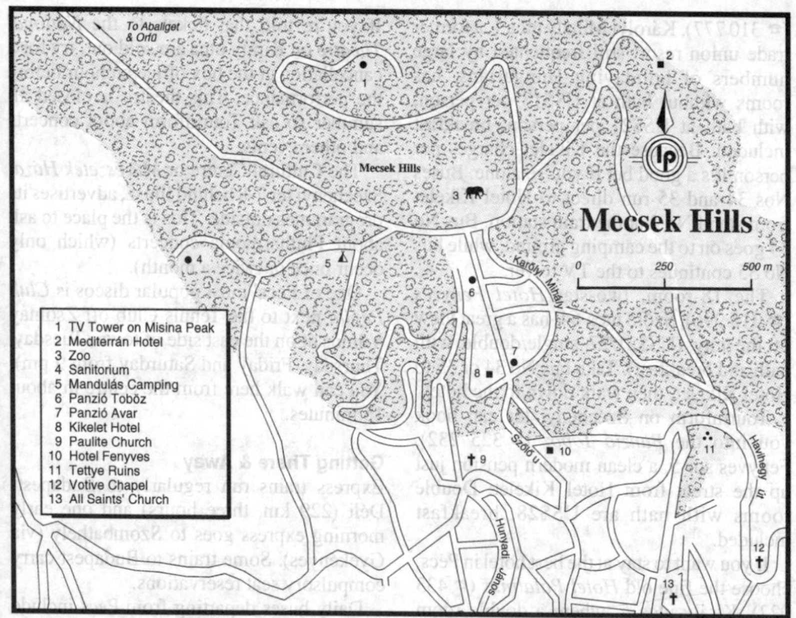

Private Rooms Mecsek Tourist and Ibusz, two offices that arrange private rooms, face one another at the southern end of Széchenyi tér. Cooptourist, Irgalmasok utcája 22, has more expensive private rooms. These offices close at 4 pm Monday to Thursday and 2 pm Friday, and they don't open on weekends. Unless you stay four nights there's a 30% surcharge on the first night. A tax of US$0.75 per person per night is charged on accommodation in the centre of town (US$0.50 outside the centre), but there's no tax on the first night.

Tourinform, Széchenyi tér 9, can book rooms at hotels and pensions.

Hotels *Kvarner Panzió* (☎ 326 495), Somogyi Béla utca 1, has a very convenient location diagonally opposite the bus station and its prices are also good: US$18 double with shower. There are only a few rooms but if you arrive by bus it only takes a few minutes to try for one. Ask to see the room.

The *Főnix Hotel* (☎ 311 680), Hunyadi János út 2, is a small, modern hotel where singles/doubles/triples with bath cost US$23/34/41, breakfast included. Their restaurant is good.

An excellent place to stay in Pécs is the *Hotel Laterum* (☎ 315 829), Hajnóczy utca 37-39, on the far west side of town. Take bus No 4 from the train station or the market on Bajcsy-Zsilinszky utca near the bus station to the end of the line at Uránváros. From the stop, the green four-storey hotel is visible behind an Afor petrol station. Rooms with shared bath are US$6 per person, with private bath US$8.50 per person, and there's an inexpensive self-service restaurant just off the hotel lobby. Most of the guests are Hungarian workers or student groups but tourists are welcome. Beware of rooms on the west side of the building which face the noisy disco above the restaurant.

Several slightly up-market places to stay are up near the TV tower. The *Hotel Kikelet*

(☎ 310 777), Károlyi Mihály utca 1, a former trade union resort still frequented by large numbers of holidaying Hungarians, has rooms without bath at US$13 per person, with bath at US$21 per person, breakfast included. Because the Kikelet charges per person it's a good bet if you're alone. Buses Nos 34 and 35 run direct to Hotel Kikelet from stand No 2 at the train station. Bus No 34 goes on to the camping ground, while bus No 35 continues to the TV tower.

The 18-room, two-star *Hotel Fenyves* (☎ 315 996), Szőlő utca 64, has a great view of the city (US$21/27 single/double with bath and breakfast). Take bus No 34 or 35 to Hotel Kikelet, then walk down to the hotel.

Tourinform on Széchenyi tér can book you into the *Panzió Toboz* (☎ 325 232), Fenyves sor 5, a clean modern pension just up the street from Hotel Kikelet. Double rooms with bath are US$28, breakfast included.

If you want to stay at the best hotel in Pécs, choose the fine old *Hotel Palatinus* (☎ 433 022), Király utca 5, where a double room with private bath and breakfast will cost US$58 (no singles). It's good for a splurge.

Places to Eat

One of the nicest places in town is *Minaret Étterem*, Ferencesek utca 35, which serves inexpensive meals in the pleasant courtyard of the old Franciscan monastery (1738).

Liceum Söröző, through the back courtyard at Király utca 35, also offers reasonable meals and its draught beer prices are good.

Fiaker Vendéglő, Felsőmalom utca 7 next door to the Historical Museum, is an unpretentious wine cellar with moderate meal prices and a few vegetarian selections such as mushroom stew (gombapörkölt).

A good local restaurant with table service and prices half those charged in the centre is *Csillag Vendéglő*, Hungária utca 27 (a westward continuation of Ferencesek utca). The menu is translated into German.

The local beer is called 'Szalon sör'.

Entertainment

Pécs has famous opera and ballet companies. If you're told that tickets to the *National Theatre* on Király utca are sold out, try for a cancellation at the box office an hour before the performance. This theatre is closed all summer so ask Tourinform about concerts and other events.

The Cultural Centre or *Művészetek Háza*, Széchenyi tér 7-8 behind Ibusz, advertises its programmes outside. This is the place to ask about Philharmonia concerts (which only occur once or twice a month).

One of Pécs' most popular discos is *Club Pepita* next to the Tennis Club off Zsolnay Vilmos út on the east side of town (Tuesday, Thursday, Friday and Saturday from 9 pm). You can walk here from the centre in about 15 minutes.

Getting There & Away

Express trains run regularly to Budapest-Déli (229 km, three hours) and one early morning express goes to Szombathely (via Gyékényes). Some trains to Budapest carry compulsory seat reservations.

Daily buses departing from Pécs include two to Hévíz (164 km), seven to Kaposvár (67 km), two to Kecskemét (176 km), hourly to Siklós (32 km), three to Siófok (122 km), one to Sopron (287 km) and six to Szeged (189 km, four hours). The bus is more direct than the train on all these routes.

Croatia-bound, a daily train runs between Pécs and Zagreb (267 km, five hours, US$16), leaving Pécs in the very early morning and Zagreb in the late afternoon. Buses run five times a day from Barcs to Zagreb (202 km, US$14) and there are also two afternoon buses a day from Pécs to Osijek (US$6 or DM10 in cash – pay the driver).

HARKÁNY

The hot springs at Harkány, 26 km south of Pécs, feature medicinal waters with the richest sulphuric content in Hungary. There's a large open-air thermal pool and you can also receive a mud bath which is said to alleviate various obscure afflictions. The baths are open to the public daily year-round.

Harkány is a major transit point for people

travelling between Croatia and Yugoslavia. The Drávaszabolcs/Donji Miholjac border crossing to/from Croatia is just eight km south of the town.

Information

Both Mecsek Tourist and Ibusz have offices at the entrance to the baths on Bajcsy-Zsilinszky utca, just up from the bus station.

The left-luggage office at the bus station is open Monday to Thursday from 8 am to 4 pm, Friday from 8 am to 2 pm.

Money The OTP Bank has a kiosk between the bus station and the baths changing travellers' cheques weekdays from 7.45 am to 3.30 pm (open May to September only).

Numerous individuals on the street near the bus station offer to change money, an indication of the proximity of Yugoslavia.

Places to Stay & Eat

Both Mecsek Tourist and Ibusz rent private rooms but for a one-night stay you may be better going to a hotel.

The *Baranya Hotel* (☎ 380 160), Bajcsy-Zsilinszky utca 5 opposite the baths, has doubles with shared bath at US$16, breakfast included (no singles). It's popular among transients from ex-Yugoslavia.

Before checking in at the Baranya check out the adjacent three-storey *Hotel Napsugár* (☎ 380 300), Bajcsy-Zsilinszky utca 7, which looks expensive but has 42 rooms at US$13/18 single/double with bath and breakfast.

Another block down the road is *Thermál Camping* (☎ 380 117), Bajscy-Zsilinszky utca 4. Camping here is US$3 per person plus US$3 per tent, and they also have 20 hotel-style rooms with shared bath at US$13 double, 26 rooms with private bath at US$19 double and 21 four-person bungalows with bath and kitchen at US$38 (open from mid-April to mid-October).

Getting There & Away

All buses between Pécs and Siklós stop here. Four buses a day link Harkány to Croatia, two to Osijek (87 km) and one each to Našice (71 km) and Slavonski Brod (125 km). Three buses a day run from Harkány to Belgrade (US$19). Since the border between Croatia and Yugoslavia closed in 1991, numerous travellers from former Yugoslavia have used Harkány as a transit point.

SIKLÓS

Siklós, south of the red wine-producing Villány Hills and six km east of Harkány, is the southernmost town in Hungary. On a hill top overlooking the surrounding farmland stands a well-preserved 15th-century **castle**, the only one in Hungary continuously in use since the Middle Ages, now a museum (open daily except Monday year-round). A section of the museum is dedicated to the 1848 Revolution and especially to the progressive lord of Siklós Castle, Casimir Batthyány, who freed his serfs in 1847. The tomb of this gentleman may be seen in the castle's Gothic chapel. There's also a small but excellent collection of 19th-century costumes.

Place to Stay & Eat

The *Hotel Központi* (☎ 352 513), Kossuth tér 4, just below the castle, is an old hotel with adequate rooms with shared bath at US$6 per person. The hotel restaurant is also reasonable.

The hotel and hostel in the castle itself have closed.

Getting There & Away

Siklós is connected to Pécs (32 km) by hourly bus (via Harkány), which makes it an easy day trip from Pécs.

The bus and train stations are on opposite sides of Siklós, each about a 10-minute walk from the castle which is visible from afar.

The Great Plain

South-eastern Hungary, the Great Plain (Nagyalföld), is a wide expanse of level puszta (prairie) drained by the Tisza River. This rich farming area bears barley, corn, oats, potatoes, rye, sugar beet and wheat.

Perhaps no other region of Hungary has a place in Hungarian folklore like the Great Plain. The poet Sándor Petőfi wrote of the puszta: *Börtönéből szabadult sas lelkem, Ha a rónak végtelenjét látom* (that his soul soars like an eagle released from a cage, every time he sees this endless plain). In the blazing heat of summer many have witnessed mirages shimmering over the blonde plains.

Visitors to the region are introduced to the lore of the Hungarian cowboys and their long-horned grey cattle or the nomadic shepherds and their tiny sheepdogs. Two national parks, Kiskunság in the Bugac puszta and Hortobágy in the Hortobágy puszta, preserve this unique environment. Kecskemét, Szeged and Debrecen are centres of the western, southern and eastern puszta.

KECSKEMÉT

Exactly halfway between Budapest and Szeged, near the geographical centre of Hungary, Kecskemét is a clean, healthy city famous for its potent *barack pálinka* (apricot brandy) and level puszta. It's known as the garden city of Hungary for the million fruit trees in the surrounding area; wine is also produced. Bács-Kiskun County is administered from here. Among Kecskemét's most renowned native sons are József Katona (1791-1830), author of the historical play *Bánk bán*, and the composer Zoltán Kodály (1882-1967).

Orientation & Information

The adjacent bus and train stations are on the north-eastern side of town. The left-luggage office at the train station is open from 7 am to 7 pm. From the train station follow the yellow brick pavement of Nagykőrösi utca to Szabadság tér and Kossuth tér, the centre of town.

Pusztatourist is between Szabadság tér and Kossuth tér. Express is upstairs at Dobó István körút 11.

The Magyar Autóklub (☎ 482 188) is at Jász utca 26.

Money The OTP Bank, Szabadság tér 5 next to the former synagogue (Monday to Wednesday from 7.45 am to 3.30 pm, Thursday until 4.30 pm, Friday to 1 pm), changes travellers' cheques without commission.

Post & Telephone The main post office on Katona József tér is open weekdays from 8 am to 7 pm, Saturday until 2 pm and holidays until noon. It is the best place from which to make international calls. Kecskemét's telephone code is 76.

Things to See

Kossuth tér is surrounded by historic buildings. Dominating the square is a massive Art-Nouveau **town hall** (1897) with a carillon that 'gives concerts' every hour on the hour. Half hidden among the bushes right in front of the town hall is a split stone cube bearing the inscription 'here broke the heart of Kecskemét's most famous son', for on this spot in April 1830 playwright József Katona died of a heart attack. Also in front of the town hall is a statue of the 19th-century politician Lajos Kossuth, who led the struggle for independence from Austria, and a monument bearing the distances to towns everywhere in Hungary.

Flanking the town hall are two fine churches: the neoclassical **Old Church** (1806) and the earlier **St Miklós Church** with a baroque calvary (1790) before the door. Close by on Katona József tér is the magnificent **Katona József Theatre** (1896) with a baroque statue of the Trinity (1742) standing in front of it.

Of the many other museums and art galleries around Kecskemét, the most interesting is the **Museum of Naive Artists** (closed Monday) in the 'Stork House' (1730), surrounded by a high white wall just off Petőfi Sándor utca. In the art gallery directly below the museum one can purchase original paintings almost as good as those on display upstairs at very reasonable prices. Next to this museum is a toy museum with all the pieces jumbled together in imaginative displays.

Places to Stay

Camping *Autós Camping* (☎ 329 358) is on

HUNGARY

Sport utca, on the south-western side of Kecskemét, nearly five km from the train station. City Busz No 101 and Volán buses Nos 1 and 11 run there from the train station. Camping costs US$2 per person plus US$2.50 per tent and there are 25 neat little bungalows with cooking facilities and cold showers at US$23 for up to four people. The restaurant here is good. Adjacent to the camping ground is an attractive public swimming pool (often empty) surrounded by manicured lawns. The camping ground is open from mid-April to mid-October.

Hostels About three blocks from the camping ground is Kecskemét's hostel, the *Gémpari és Automatizálási Műszaki Főiskola* or 'GAMP' (☎ 321 916), Izsáki út 10. A bed in a four-bedded room here is US$3. Officially it's only open in July and August but you can sometimes get in during other months. Buses Nos 1 and 11 from the train station run directly to this pleasant university complex south of the centre.

In summer you may be able to get a room in the *Tanítóképző Főiskola Lőveiklára Kollégiuma* (☎ 321 977), Jókai tér 4. In fact, it's worth trying this eight-storey student dormitory right in the centre of town any time – you could be lucky.

Private Rooms Pusztatourist (☎ 483 493), opposite the town hall on Kossuth tér (closed weekends) charges US$12 single or double for a private room for one night. Cooptourist, Ket templom köz 9, is slightly cheaper with singles for US$10. Also try Ibusz on Széchenyi tér opposite the Aranyhomok Hotel.

Hotels *Color Panzió* (☎ 324 901), Jókai utca 26, is a small pension with rooms above a chemist's at US$21 double (no singles).

Caissa Panzió (☎ 481 685), Gyenes tér 18, 5th floor, has 11 rooms varying in price from US$12/16 for singles/doubles without bath to US$20/26 with bath. Two larger rooms for up to five people are also available. The location is excellent so it is always worth a try.

The 45-room *Hotel Három Gúnár* (☎ 483 611), Batthyány utca 3, is expensive at US$32/38 single/double with bath and breakfast, but it has a certain charm and is minutes from the centre of town. A bowling alley and bar are in the hotel basement.

Two blocks south of the 'GAMP' hostel is the *Sport Szálló* (☎ 323 090), Izsáki út 15/a, a neat two-storey hotel with rooms with bath at US$20 single or double.

Places to Eat

If all you want is a fast feed the *Szalag Ételbár*, Petőfi Sándor utca 1, can provide it. Otherwise, eat elsewhere.

The *Jalta Restaurant*, Batthyány utca 2, right opposite the Hotel Három Gúnár, is a rather homy wine cellar with a menu in English and German. Their speciality is grilled meat and they have Kaiser beer on tap.

The *Kisbugaci csárda*, Munkácsy utca 10, serves regional dishes.

To taste the local wines go through the door marked *Borozó* at Rákóczi út 3 and take your choice from the row of pitchers on the counter. The price shown is for a litre and if you point to the smallest wine glass you'll pay a tenth of that. Drinking from these small glasses, you should be able to try all the wines for less than a dollar.

Entertainment

The ticket office of the *Katona József Theatre* on Katona József tér is on the side of the building (open Tuesday to Friday from 10 am to 1 pm and 5 to 7 pm). Operettas are often staged here.

Flash Dance Club on Liszt Ferenc utca north of the train station is a large modern disco open Wednesday to Sunday from 9.30 pm to 5 am. *Club Robinson*, Akadémia körút 2 (closed Monday and Tuesday) is similar.

Galaxis Disco Club, Szilády Károly utca 6, on a back street behind the concert hall (Wednesday to Sunday from 9 pm), isn't nearly as high-tech as the other places but it is a bit cheaper and right in the centre of town.

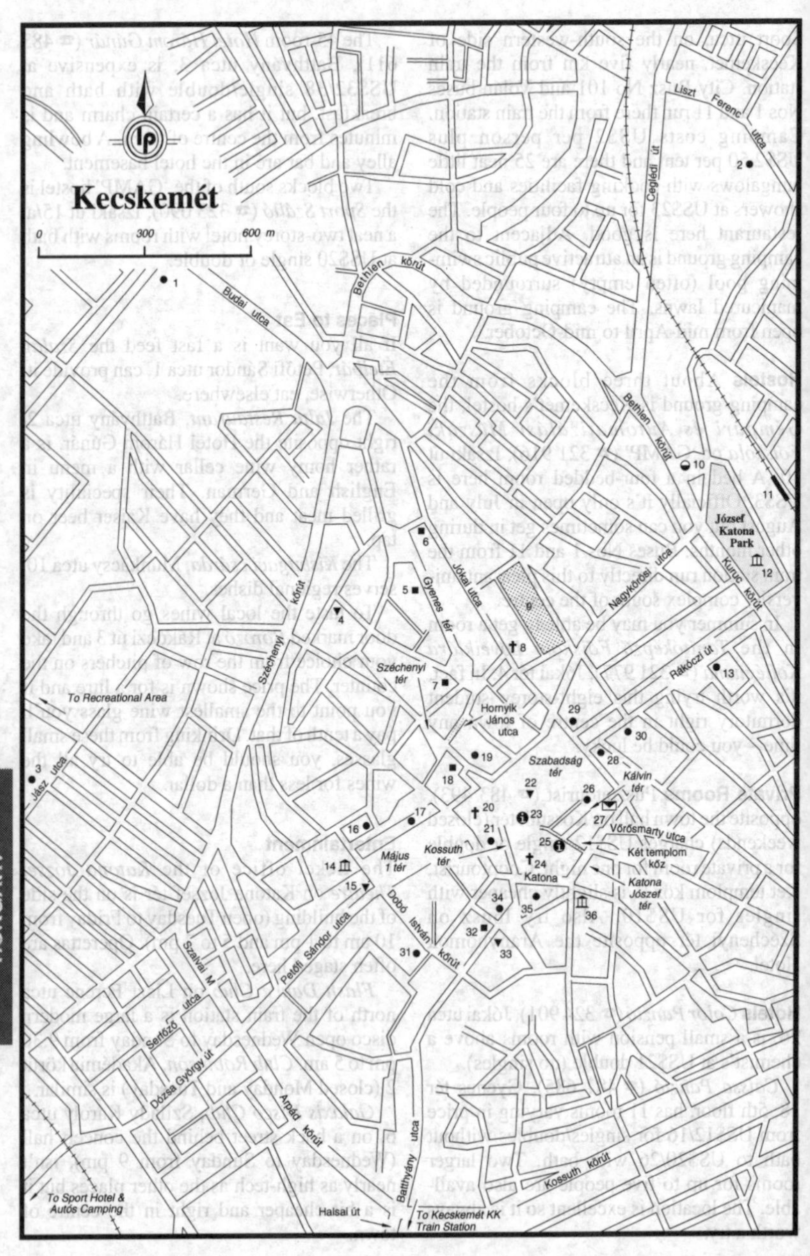

Kecskemét
0
300
600 m
Liszt Ferenc utca
Ceglédi út
Bethlen körút
Budai utca
Jókai utca
Gyenes tér
Széchenyi körút
Széchenyi tér
To Recreational Area
Hornyik János utca
Szabadság tér
Kálvin tér
Vörösmarty utca
Két templom köz
Katona József tér
Kossuth tér
Katona
Május 1 tér
Dobó István körút
Petőfi Sándor utca
Szalvai M. utca
Serfőző utca
Dózsa György út
Árpád körút
Batthyány utca
Halsai út
Kossuth körút
To Sport Hotel & Autós Camping
To Kecskemét KK Train Station
József Katona Park
Kuruc körút
Nagykőrösi utca
Rákóczi út
Jász utca
1
2
3
4
5
6
7
8
9
10
11
12
13
14
15
16
17
18
19
20
21
22
23
24
25
26
27
28
29
30
31
32
33
34
35
36

PLACES TO STAY

5 Caissa Panzió
6 Color Panzió
7 Tanítóképző Főiskola
18 Aranyhomok Hotel
32 Hotel Három Gúnár

PLACES TO EAT

4 Kisbugaci Csárda
15 Szalag Ételbár
22 Caffe Liberté
33 Jalta Restaurant

OTHER

1 Club Robinson
2 Flash Dance Club
3 Magyar Autóklub
8 Piarist Church
9 Market
10 Bus Station
11 Train Station
12 Museum
13 Városi Cinema
14 Museum of Naive Artists
16 Galaxis Disco Club
17 Concert Hall
19 Ibusz/Ottohon Cinema
20 Old Church
21 Town Hall
23 Pusztatourist
24 St Miklós Church
25 Cooptourist
26 Kodály School of Music
27 Main Post Office
28 Art Gallery
29 Former Synagogue
30 Borozó
31 Express
34 Arpád Cinema
35 Katona József Theatre
36 Photography Museum

Getting There & Away

Kecskemét is on the main railway line from Budapest-Nyugati to Szeged.

There are almost hourly buses to Budapest (85 km), every couple of hours to Szeged (86 km) and two a day to Pécs (176 km).

Buses run to Arad, Romania, about four times a week (191 km, US$11), but check with information. The bus to Subotica, Yugoslavia, is twice daily (130 km, US$6), but take the earlier one as the second one scheduled usually arrives from Budapest full. Tickets are available from the drivers.

Getting Around

There are two competing municipal bus systems. City Busz runs pink microbuses and tickets are available from the drivers. The larger Volán buses are about two forint more expensive and you must buy a ticket at a kiosk.

BUGAC

Bugac, an accessible corner of the 306-sq-km Kiskunság National Park south-west of Kecskemét, is a good place to get close to the Great Plain. Great herds of fork-horned Hungarian grey cattle and flocks of twisted-horned sheep *(racka)*, some black, some white, roam across the sandy puszta, while the adjacent juniper forest invites hikers.

Things to See & Do

The *Bugaci Csárda*, an eight-minute walk from Bugac-Felső Railway Station, is a very touristy folkloric restaurant where there's also a camping ground.

It's three km from the Csárda to Kiskunság National Park and the **Shepherd Museum** (closed from November to March and every Monday). The real reason to come is the **horse shows** which are performed daily at 1 pm in summer and more often when tour groups are present. You'll see real whip-snapping Hungarian cowboys working their horses and exciting 'five-in-hand' riding during which one man makes five horses gallop around a field at full speed while standing on the backs of the rear two horses.

You can see many fine animals in the nearby stables, so Bugac is a must for horse lovers. To get in some horse riding yourself you should make prior arrangements through Bugac Tours, Szabadság tér 1, Kecskemét.

Admission to the park and horse shows is US$1.50. Avoid the 30-minute horse-cart rides which are certainly not worth US$7 per person. The eight-minute helicopter rides are also a rip-off.

Getting There & Away

The fun way to get to Bugac is on the narrow-gauge railway from Kecskemét which rumbles 40 km south between vineyards, sunflower fields and apple orchards. The little carriages have hard wooden seats and a stove for heating in winter. This train departs from Kecskemét KK Railway Station, not the main station. To get there, walk south on Batthyány utca from the Három Gúnár Hotel and continue straight across a large bridge until you see the small station on the right. Get the 7.55 am train which reaches Bugac at around 9 am, but don't get off at Bugacpuszta or Bugac – you want Bugac-Felső. It's best to get the times of trains returning to Kecskemét before setting out as no information is available at Bugac-Felső.

If the return train times are inconvenient, catch a bus from the highway near the Bugaci Csárda to Kiskunfélegyháza (18 km), where there are frequent buses back to Kecskemét.

SZEGED

Szeged (Segedin), the paprika and 'Pick' salami capital of Hungary, straddles the Tisza River just before it enters Yugoslavia. The Maros River from Arad, Romania, enters the Tisza just east of the centre. In March 1879 a great flood burst upon Szeged, damaging almost every building in the city. Afterwards, the city was redesigned with concentric boulevards and radial avenues. Sections of the outer boulevard are named for cities which provided aid after the flood: Vienna, Moscow, London, Paris, Berlin, Brussels and Rome. Szeged is large and lively with lots of students, and in midsummer the city really comes to life for the famous Szeged Festival. It's the seat of Csongrád County and an important gateway to/from Yugoslavia and Romania.

Orientation

The train station is a 15-minute walk south of the centre, and the bus station is 10 minutes west of Széchenyi tér. Tram No 1 connects the train station to town. The left-luggage office at the train station is open from 4 am to 11 pm.

Information

Szeged Tourist is at Klauzál tér 7. The Magyar Autóklub is at Bartók tér 6. The Autóklub has a service centre opposite Rókus Railway Station.

Money The OTP Bank, Klauzál tér 5 (Monday from 7.45 am to 4.30 pm, Tuesday to Thursday until 3 pm, Friday until 11.30 am), changes travellers' cheques.

Post & Telephone A couple of public telephones are in the cramped main post office, Széchenyi tér 1 (weekdays 8 am to 7 pm, Saturday until 2 pm, Sunday until noon). Szeged's telephone code is 62.

Things to See

The one sight of Szeged not to be missed is the neo-Byzantine **Votive Church**, built between 1913 and 1930 in remembrance of the 1879 flood. The dome of this huge red-brick structure is 53 metres high, and the twin neo-Romanesque towers soar 92 metres. The church's cavernous interior is covered with frescos and the organ (1930) has 11,500 pipes.

Beside the church is the 13th-century **Demetrius Tower** remaining from the previous church, which was demolished to make room for the present one. The old **Serbian Church** (1745) behind the Votive Church provides a good contrast.

By the Belvárosi Bridge over the Tisza River is the **Móra Ferenc Museum** (closed Monday) in a huge neoclassical building (1896). Downstairs is a good collection of Hungarian painting (including several representations of the 1879 flood) and a new exhibit on the Avar people who occupied the Carpathian Basin from the 5th to 8th centuries (captions in English). The upper floor is dedicated to the folk art of the region. Behind this museum, in an **old gate** remaining from Szeged's 18th-century fortress, is a very informative city historical museum.

There are many fine buildings around Széchenyi tér in the centre of town, including the neobaroque **old town hall** (1883). In summer this park is Szeged's prettiest place.

Surprisingly, Szeged's most compelling sight is the **New Synagogue** (1903), a few blocks west of Széchenyi tér. The names of the many Jewish deportees from this area are inscribed in stone on the synagogue walls. This building with its great blue dome has a captivating Oriental atmosphere.

Places to Stay

Camping *Partfürdő Camping Ground* (☎ 430 843) is on Közép kikötő sor, right beside the river, opposite the city centre. You can see the tents from the Belvárosi Bridge. Camping is US$2 per person plus US$1.50 per tent and there are 26 hotel rooms at US$7/10/11 single/double/triple with shared bath. Guests have free use of the many swimming pools and one thermal pool in this area. This is your best bet for camping (open May to September).

A second camping ground, *Napfény Camping* (☎ 325 800), Dorozsmai út 2, is across a large bridge from Rókus Railway Station and the western terminus of tram No 1. In addition to camping, double rooms are available in a series of 20-room wooden barracks at US$9 with shared bath (available year-round). From May to August bungalows with kitchen and private bath are US$30 for three persons, US$37 for four. The modern hotel here has rooms at US$23/28 single/double with bath and breakfast.

Hostels In July and August the student dormitories of *Apáthy István College*, Apáthy István utca 4 right next to the Votive Church, and *Semmelweis Ignác College*, Semmelweis utca 4 between the train station and town, are opened as hostels. If Semmelweis is full, try *Ëotvös Loránd College*, Tisza Lajos körút 103 just around the corner. Go directly to the hostels or ask for information at Express, Kígyó utca 3. Some hostels in Szeged charge unusually high prices (US$18 double).

Private Rooms If you want a private room, your best bet is Szeged Tourist, Klauzál tér 7. During the Summer Festival it's open from 9 am to 7 pm daily and rooms are available. Ibusz, Klauzál tér 2, also has private rooms, but not as many.

Hotels The fine old two-star *Tisza Hotel* (☎ 478 278), Wesselényi utca 1 at Széchenyi tér, costs US$12/23 for singles/doubles without bath and US$31 double with bath. Beware of rooms directly above the disco.

If you arrive by bus you'll be within walking distance of *Sára Panzió* (☎ 314 920), Zákány utca 13, where rooms are US$17/23 single/double. If it's full there's a similar place around the corner at Pacsirta utca 17a.

Places to Eat

The *Boszorkanykonyha ételbár*, Híd utca 8, just off Széchenyi tér, is a cheap self-service. It's a little complicated because you have to pay first and get a ticket. Hang around until you see someone getting a plate of something you fancy and then point to it.

Festival Ételbár, in the modern building on Oskola utca directly across the street from the entrance to the Votive Church (daily 10 am to 9 pm), is a more expensive self-service with a pleasant terrace on which you can eat. It's easy since you pay at the end of the line.

Ciao Pizzeria, downstairs at Tisza Lajos körút 12 (daily from 11 am to midnight, Friday and Saturday until 2 am), has the best pizza in Szeged. It's real freshly baked pizza (not some microwave concoction) but order the 'maxi' size if you're at all hungry.

The *Virág Cukrászda*, Klauzál tér 1, opposite Szeged Tourist, serves great cakes and pastries. *Kis Virág* across the square is cheaper if you're willing to eat standing up. The ice cream is the best in town.

For a tasty treat upon arrival in Szeged look for the *lángos* shop (yellow sign) across the street from the train station and order a big Hungarian doughnut with cheese *(sajtos)*.

Entertainment

The *National Theatre* (built in 1883) is on Tanácsköztársaság útja on the corner of Vörösmarty utca.

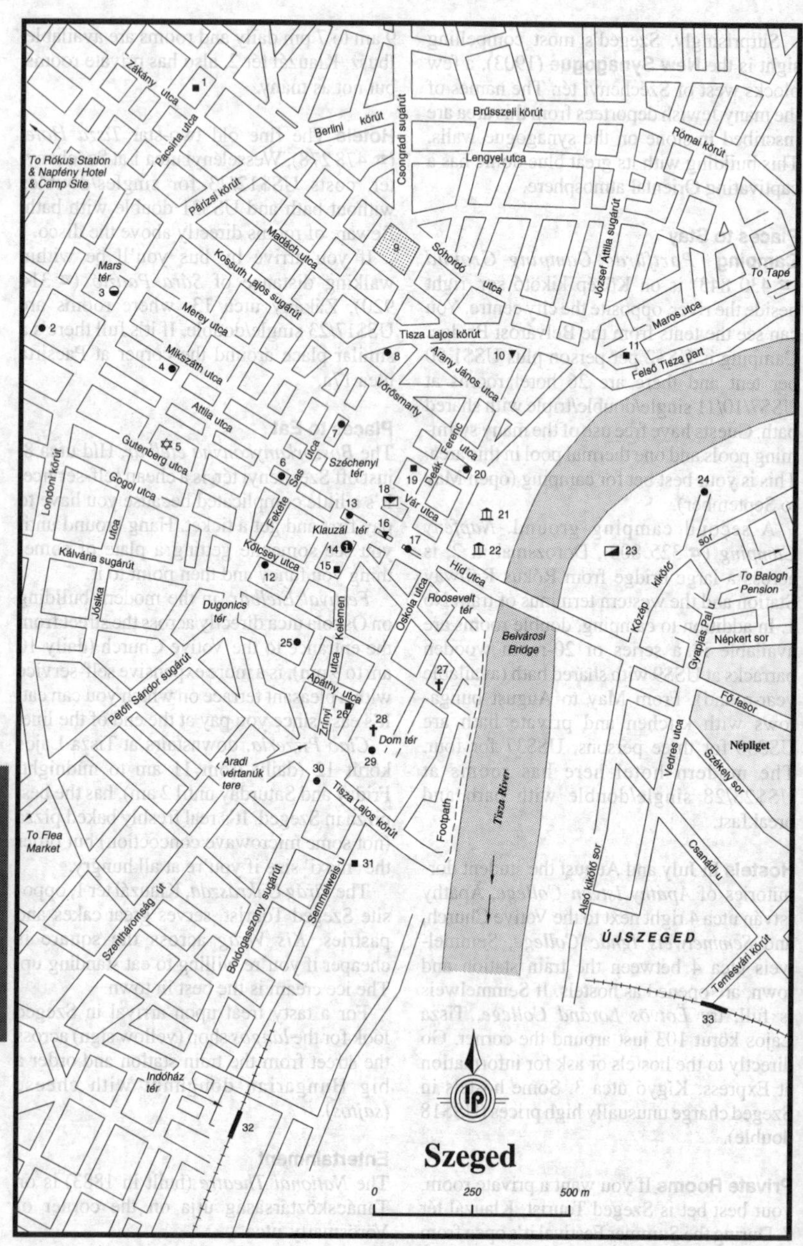
Zákány utca
Pacsirta utca
Berlini körút
Csongrádi sugárút
Brüsszeli körút
Római körút
Lengyel utca
To Rókus Station & Napfény Hotel & Camp Site
Párizsi körút
Madách utca
Kossuth Lajos sugárút
Sóhordó utca
József Attila sugárút
To Tapé
Mars tér
Merey utca
Maros utca
Tisza Lajos körút
Arany János utca
Felső Tisza part
Mikszáth utca
Vörösmarty
Attila utca
Gutenberg utca
Deák Ferenc utca
Széchenyi tér
Fekete Sas utca
Gogol utca
Londoni körút
Vár utca
Klauzál tér
Kölcsey utca
Kálvária sugárút
Híd utca
Roosevelt tér
Oskola utca
Dugonics tér
Jósika utca
Kelemen utca
Petőfi Sándor sugárút
Apáthy utca
Zrínyi utca
Dom tér
Aradi vértanúk tere
Tisza Lajos körút
To Flea Market
Semmelweis u
Szentháromság út
Boldogasszony sugárút
Indóház tér
Footpath
Tisza River
Belvárosi Bridge
Alsó kikötő sor
Közép kikötő sor
Gyapjas Pál u
To Balogh Pension
Népkert sor
Fő fasor
Vedres utca
Népliget
Székely sor
Csanádi u
ÚJSZEGED
Temesvári körút
Szeged
0
250
500 m

PLACES TO STAY

1 Sára Panzió
11 Hotel Hungária
15 Royal Hotel
19 Tisza Hotel
26 Apáthy István College
31 Semmelweis Ignac College

PLACES TO EAT

10 Ciao Pizzeria
16 Étél Bár

OTHER

2 Sing Sing Discoteque
3 Bus Station
4 Magyar Autóklub
5 New Synagogue
6 Express
7 Old Town Hall
8 Public Baths
9 Market
12 Reök Palace
13 Ibusz
14 Szeged Tourist
17 Festival Ticket Office
18 Main Post Office
20 National Theatre
21 City Museum
22 Móra Ferenc Museum
23 Public Swimming Pools
24 Partfürdő
25 University/Jaté Klub
27 Serbian Church
28 Votive Church
29 Site of Summer Festival
30 Heroes Gate
32 Szeged Train Station
33 Újszeged Train Station

The Szeged Summer Festival (held from mid-July to mid-August) unfolds on Dóm tér with the two great towers of the Votive Church as a backdrop. The open-air theatre here seats 6000 people. Main events include an opera, an operetta, a play, folk dancing, classical music, ballet and a rock opera. Festival tickets and information are available from Szabadtéri Játékok Jegyiroda (☎ 471 466), Deák Ferenc utca 30 (weekdays 10 am to 5 pm).

Daily organ concerts are given in the Votive Church during the festival period at 12.30 pm (US$1).

Jate Klub, Toldi utca 2 in the centre, is a student disco with live music Thursday to Saturday from 8 pm to 2 am.

Sing Sing Discotheque occupies a huge pavilion on Mars tér near the bus station. It's open Friday and Saturday from 10 pm to 4 am. Unlike some other clubs in this area, this one is safe.

Getting There & Away

Direct express trains travel from Budapest-Nyugati (191 km, 2½ hours) via Kecskemét.

Seven buses travel daily to Pécs (189 km), two daily to Eger (245 km), two daily to Győr (294 km), two daily to Siófok (224 km) and two daily to Debrecen (224 km). On most buses you pay the driver (but ask at the ticket window).

From mid-June to August, on Saturday and holidays only, a Mahart riverboat plies the Tisza River between Szeged and Csongrád (70 km, five hours), leaving Szeged in the early morning, Csongrád in the afternoon.

To/From Yugoslavia There are about two buses a day to Subotica (44 km, US$2.50 – pay the driver) but they're not listed on the departures board at the station and trying to get information about them is a struggle, so you're better off taking the train. (The people working at Szeged Bus Station seem to hate their jobs, so don't expect much help from them.)

Three local trains a day run to Subotica in Yugoslavia (45 km, 1½ hours, US$2). Buy your ticket at the train station.

To/From Romania There are daily buses to Arad (106 km, US$5) and Timişoara/Temesvár (157 km), departing from platform No 4 at the bus station (check with information). These buses are listed on the departures board.

Getting to Romania by train is complicated, as you must change at Békéscsaba (seven local trains a day go from Szeged to Békéscsaba, 97 km). This connection is not good. If you are adventurous and don't mind walking or hitching, you could take one of nine daily local trains from Ujszeged Station (across the Tisza River from central Szeged) to Nagylak (47 km, 1¼ hours), which is right on the Romanian border, halfway to Arad. The highway border crossing is near Nagylak Station and it's only a six-km walk from there to the first Romanian town, Nădlac, which has local trains to Arad four times a day (52 km, 1½ hours). Hitching from the border is easy.

Northern Hungary

Northern Hungary is the most mountainous part of the country. The southern ranges of the Carpathian Mountains stretch east along the Slovakian border in a 1000-metre-high chain of woody hills from the Danube Bend almost to the Ukrainian border. Miskolc is heavily industrialised but historic Eger offers an ideal base for sightseers and wine tasters. Day trips to the nearby Mátra and Bükk mountains are possible. Farther north, right beside Slovakia, are the caves near Aggtelek, Hungary's most extensive caves. To the east is the famous Tokaj wine-growing area.

EGER

Eger (Erlau), the seat of Heves County, is a lovely baroque city full of historic buildings. It was at Eger Castle in 1552 that 2000 Hungarian defenders temporarily stopped the Turkish advance into Europe and helped to preserve the Hungarian identity. The Turks returned in 1596 and captured the castle but were themselves thrown out by the Austrians in 1687. Later Eger was a centre for Ferenc Rákóczi's unsuccessful 1703-11 War of Independence against the Habsburgs.

It was the bishops and later the archbishops of Eger who built the town you see today. The many handsome 18th-century palaces and churches along Kossuth Lajos and Széchenyi streets deserve special attention. Eger possesses some of Hungary's finest examples of Zopf architecture, a late baroque-rococo style found only in Central Europe. Nineteenth-century railway builders left Eger to one side, so it retained its historic form and character.

Today Eger is more famous for its potent Egri Bikavér (Bull's Blood) red wine. Literally hundreds of wine cellars are to be seen in Szépasszonyvölgy (the Valley of Beautiful Women), just a 20-minute walk west of the cathedral.

Orientation & Information

The train station is a 15-minute walk south of town on Deák Ferenc utca, while the bus station is just above Széchenyi István utca, Eger's main drag. The left-luggage office at the train station is open from 6.30 am to 6.30 pm only (ask at the ticket window). At the bus station, the left-luggage office is only open as long as the ticket window functions (until 6 pm weekdays, 5 pm Saturday, 4 pm Sunday and holidays).

Tourinform, Dobó tér 2, can supply all the brochures you care to carry and the staff answer questions in fluent German.

The Magyar Autóklub (☎ 317 590) is nearby at Jókai utca 5.

Money To change a travellers' cheque go to the OTP Bank, Széchenyi utca 2 (weekdays 7.45 am to 3 pm).

Post & Telephone Both card and coin phones are available at the main post office, Széchenyi utca 22.

Eger's telephone code is 36.

Emergency If you have an urgent medical or dental problem try the county hospital *(megyei kórház)* near the Turkish minaret.

Things to See

The first thing you see as you come into Eger from the bus or train station is the huge neoclassical **cathedral** (1836) on Eszterházy tér. Opposite this is the rococo **Eszterházy Károly College** (1785). Buy a ticket just inside the college door to see the frescoed library in room No 48 on the 1st floor and the **Museum of Astronomy** (open Tuesday to Sunday from 9.30 am to noon) on the 6th floor of the tower at the back of

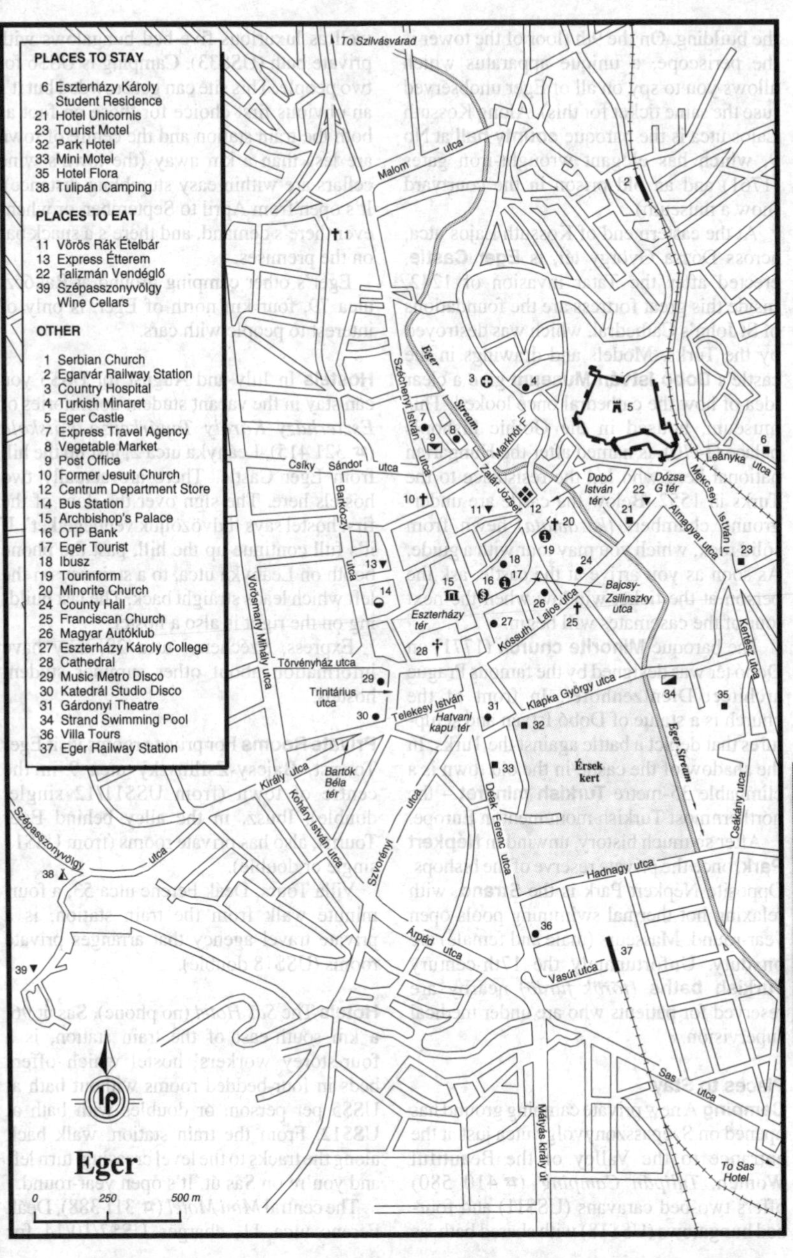
PLACES TO STAY
6 Eszterházy Károly Student Residence
21 Hotel Unicornis
23 Tourist Motel
32 Park Hotel
33 Mini Motel
35 Hotel Flora
38 Tulipán Camping
PLACES TO EAT
11 Vörös Rák Ételbár
13 Express Étterem
22 Talizmán Vendéglő
39 Szépasszonyvölgy Wine Cellars
OTHER
1 Serbian Church
2 Egarvár Railway Station
3 Country Hospital
4 Turkish Minaret
5 Eger Castle
7 Express Travel Agency
8 Vegetable Market
9 Post Office
10 Former Jesuit Church
12 Centrum Department Store
14 Bus Station
15 Archbishop's Palace
16 OTP Bank
17 Eger Tourist
18 Ibusz
19 Tourinform
20 Minorite Church
24 County Hall
25 Franciscan Church
26 Magyar Autóklub
27 Eszterházy Károly College
28 Cathedral
29 Music Metro Disco
30 Katedrál Studio Disco
31 Gárdonyi Theatre
34 Strand Swimming Pool
36 Villa Tours
37 Eger Railway Station
To Szilvásvárad
Malom utca
Eger Stream
Széchenyi István utca
Markhót F.
Csíky Sándor utca
Barkóczy utca
Zalár József
Dobó István tér
Dózsa G tér
Leányka utca
Mekcsey István utca
Almagyar utca
Bajcsy-Zsilinszky utca
Kossuth Lajos utca
Eszterházy tér
Vörösmarty Mihály utca
Törvényház utca
Trinitárius utca
Telekesy István
Hatvani kapu tér
Klapka György utca
Kertész utca
Csákány utca
Érsek kert
Király utca
Bartók Béla tér
Koháry István utca
Szvorényi
Deák Ferenc utca
Szépasszonyvölgy utca
Hadnagy utca
Árpád utca
Vasút utca
Sas utca
Mátyás király út
To Sas Hotel
Eger
0 250 500 m

the building. On the 9th floor of the tower is the periscope, a unique apparatus which allows you to spy on all of Eger unobserved (use the same ticket for this). Along Kossuth Lajos utca is the baroque **county hall** at No 9, which has elegant wrought-iron gates (1761) and an old prison in the courtyard (now a museum).

At the eastern end of Kossuth Lajos utca, across Dózsa György tér, is **Eger Castle**, erected after the Tatar invasion of 1242. Inside this great fortress are the foundations of St John's Cathedral, which was destroyed by the Turks. Models and drawings in the castle's **Dobó István Museum** give a clear idea of how the cathedral once looked. This museum, housed in the Gothic bishop's palace (1470), is named after the Hungarian national hero who led the resistance to the Turks in 1552. Below the castle are underground chambers *(kazamata)* hewn from solid rock, which you may tour with a guide. As soon as you arrive at the castle, ask the person at the ticket window when the next tour of the casemates will begin.

The baroque **Minorite church** (1771) on Dobó tér was designed by the famous Prague architect Dientzenhofer. In front of the church is a statue of Dobó István and sculptures that depict a battle against the Turks. In the shadow of the castle in the old town is a climbable 35-metre **Turkish minaret** – the northernmost Turkish monument in Europe.

After so much history, unwind in **Népkert Park**, once the private reserve of the bishops. Opposite Népkert Park is the **Strand**, with relaxing hot thermal swimming pools open year-round. Masseurs (male and female) are on duty. Unfortunately the 17th-century **Turkish baths** *(török fürdö)* nearby are reserved for patients who are under medical supervision.

HUNGARY

Places to Stay

Camping A new private camping ground has opened on Szépasszonyvölgy utca just at the entrance to the Valley of the Beautiful Women. *Tulipán Camping* (☎ 410 580) offers two-bed caravans (US$11) and four-bed bungalows (US$18) with shared bath, as well as luxurious five-bed bungalows with private bath (US$33). Camping is US$6 for two people. This site can get crowded but it's an obvious first choice for those on foot as both the train station and the centre of town are less than a km away (the town's wine cellars are within easy stumbling distance). It's open from April to September, or whenever there's demand, and there's a snack bar on the premises.

Eger's other camping ground at Rákóczi utca 79, four km north of Eger, is only of interest to people with cars.

Hostels In July and August for US$5 you can stay in the vacant student dormitories of *Eszterházy Károly Tanárkepzo Fóiskola* (☎ 321 415), Leányka utca 2, just up the hill from Eger Castle. There are actually two hostels here. The sign over the door of the first hostel says 'üdvözöljük vendégeiket'. If it's full continue up the hill, past the phone booth on Leányka utca, to a stairway on the left which leads straight back. The last building on the right is also a hostel.

Express, Széchenyi utca 28, may have information about other summer student hostels.

Private Rooms For private rooms visit Eger Tourist, Bajcsy-Zsilinszky utca 9 in the centre of town (from US$11/12 single/double). Ibusz, in the alley behind Eger Tourist, also has private rooms (from US$11 single or double).

Villa Tours, Deák Ferenc utca 53, a four-minute walk from the train station, is a private travel agency that arranges private rooms (US$18 double).

Hotels The *Sas Hotel* (no phone), Sas út 96, a km south-east of the train station, is a four-storey workers' hostel which offers beds in four-bedded rooms without bath at US$5 per person, or doubles with bath at US$12. From the train station, walk back along the tracks to the level crossing, turn left and you're on Sas út. It's open year-round.

The central *Mini Motel* (☎ 311 388), Deák Ferenc utca 11, charges US$7/10/14 for singles/doubles/triples. Lock your window in this single-storey building. The modern *Hotel Unicornis* (☎ 312 455) on Kossuth Lajos utca is US$13/14 single/double without bath, US$19/20 with bath. And finally, the *Tourist Motel* (☎ 310 014), Mekcsey István utca 2, is US$11 double (no singles). On summer weekends, accommodation in Eger is tight, so arrive early.

Places to Eat

Bottom End *Express Étterem*, Pyrker tér 4, just below the north-east side of the bus station parking lot, is a large self-service cafeteria open until 8 pm. You can take your own beer from the cooler here and if you dig deep enough you should find a cold one.

Some of Eger's cheapest food, including fried chicken or fish, barbecued ribs and sausages, are consumed standing up (weekdays from 10 am to 3 pm) at the various buffets upstairs in the indoor vegetable market on Katona István tér behind the main post office. No alcohol is served here.

At the attractive *Kondi Saláta Bár*, Széchenyi utca 2, you can get a deli-style lunch, or just coffee with delicious desserts, which you can carry out onto their terrace on a plastic tray.

Top End A good selection of places to eat is around Dobó tér. *Vörös Rák Etelbár*, Szent János utca 11 near Dobó tér, has a few inexpensive chicken and carp dishes, as well as the usual pork. Despite the name, don't expect to get any red lobster here.

Bajor Sörház, Bajsy-Zsilinszky utca 19, just off Dobó tér, offers up-market meals with big mugs of beer.

In summer you can dine at any of five rather touristy restaurants over the bridge at the north end of Dobó tér. They set their tables out on the square and there's even a keyboarder providing live music. Some of the restaurants here serve good traditional food while others are a rip-off. Vegetarians should check out the self-service *Salátabár* here.

The *Talizmán Vendéglő*, Kossuth Lajos utca 19, is a trendy wine cellar that's always packed with European tourists. The restaurant at the nearby *Hotel Unicornis* is cheaper. The *Kopcsik Cukrászda* across the street from Talizmán has a great selection of cakes which you can have with coffee on their terrace.

Many wine restaurants haunt the cellars of Szépasszony völgy utca. The most famous is the *Ködmön Csárda*, where live Hungarian folk music accompanies dinner. The menu is in Hungarian, but ask to see it anyway to get an idea of the prices. There are many other similar places and the noisiest is probably the best – great atmosphere. To get there, walk west on Telekesy István and Király streets. When you come to a fork in the road, go left down the incline and straight ahead.

Entertainment

The Gárdonyi Géza Theatre ticket office, Széchenyi utca 5, should know about local events.

Music Metro Disco is on the corner of Trinitárius utca and Törvényház utca. A block south on Trinitárius utca is the *Katedrál Studio Disco* where laser lights flash as you dance inside a huge baroque former church dating from 1782 (Thursday, Friday and Saturday from 10 pm).

Getting There & Away

Eger is connected to Budapest's Keleti Railway Station by express train (142 km, two hours). It can sometimes be quicker to take a local train to Füzesabony (17 km), where you can catch a connecting express train to Budapest.

Buses leave Eger's bus station to Budapest (128 km) about once an hour, to Szilvásvárad (24 km) about twice an hour, to Jósvafő/Aggtelek (2½ hours) once in the morning, to Szeged (245 km) twice a day and to Kecskemét (158 km) three times a day. The times are irregular so look at the posted schedule *(indul)* and then check them with information.

SZILVÁSVÁRAD

Just to the north of Eger are the Bükk Mountains, much of which fall within the

388-sq-km **Bükk National Park**. A good place to begin a visit to the forests of Bükk is the village of Szilvásvárad, 28 km north of Eger on the road to Aggtelek.

Szilvásvárad has the dual attraction of being an ideal base for hiking and the centre of horse breeding in Hungary, with some 250 prize Lipica horses in local stables. Horse riding can be arranged at about US$10 per hour, and in summer there are horse-cart rides, in winter horse-drawn sleigh rides.

Szilvásvárad also makes a good base for visiting the Aggtelek Caves as you can pick up the bus from Eger to the caves here and shave almost an hour off your travelling time in each direction.

Things to See

The best time to come to Szilvásvárad would be during the Lipicai Horse Festival in early September when the racecourse in the centre of town becomes the scene of major events. **Horse shows** *(lovasbemutató)* are also put on throughout the year, a couple of times a week in winter and almost daily in summer, in the smaller horse pavilion *(lovarda)* near the racecourse. Check on this as soon as you arrive.

From this pavilion, a chestnut-lined road leads up the Szalajka Valley to hiking trails into the hills. You can also ride on a **narrow-gauge railway** which takes 15 minutes to cover the five km about hourly from 9 am to 5 pm on weekends and holidays from April to October. On weekdays there are a couple of afternoon trains.

Among the varied attractions up the **Szalajka Valley** are waterfalls, a lake and an open-air museum of forest industries. From this museum you can climb to the **Istállóskő Cave** where evidence of habitation by early man was uncovered. Nearby **Istállós-kő** (958 metres) is the highest peak in the Bükk Mountains. Serious hikers can follow trails along the ridge all the way to Lillafüred near Miskolc. Some paved roads through the national park are now closed to motorised vehicles which makes this an excellent area for cycling. Eger Tourist and Tourinform in Eger sells a detailed map of this area.

Back in Szilvásvárad, you can see some of the famous Lipica horses in the stable adjoining the **Horse Museum** *(Lovaskiállítás)* at Park utca 8, next to Hotel Szilvás.

The **Orbán-Ház Museum** (closed on Monday), Miskolci út 58, at the north end of town, has exhibits on the flora and fauna of the Bükk Mountains in a typical farmhouse of this region dating from 1880. Opposite the museum is an impressive circular neoclassical **Lutheran church**.

Places to Stay & Eat

Camping *Hegyi Camping* (☎ 355 207), Egri út 36a, a five-minute walk from Szilvásvárad-Szalajkavölgy Railway Station, has neat bungalows at US$12/15/18 double/triple/quad. In addition, a US$0.65 per person per day resort tax is collected. This camping ground run by Eger Tourist is open from May to mid-October and there's a snack bar on the premises. (Freelance camping is not allowed in the national park.)

Hotels *Hotel Lipicai* (☎ 355 100), Egri út 14, a modern two-storey hotel, has rooms with bath and breakfast at US$10 per person.

The *Szalajka Vendéglő* (☎ 355 257), Egri út 2, has hotel rooms with shared bath at US$8/9 single/double, but it's usually full in summer. It serves substantial meals, often accompanied by live music, on the front porch.

At US$14/18 single/double the *Hotel Szilvás* (☎ 355 211), Park utca 6, a 40-room baroque palace overlooking a park in the centre of town, is a real bargain, but in summer it's usually full. This palace once belonged to Count Pallavicini whose family owned the entire region but after 1945 it became a trade-union holiday house.

Getting There & Away

Szilvásvárad is easily accessible from Eger by train (six daily, 31 km, one hour) or bus. Get on/off the train at Szilvásvárad-Szalajka völgy Station. In Eger the Szilvásvárad train stops at Egarvár Station, which you may find more convenient if you're making it a day

HUNGARY

trip. The Aggtelek bus to/from Budapest passes here.

AGGTELEK

Hungary's largest and most famous scenic caves are the **Baradla Caves** in Aggtelek National Park on the Slovakian border, north of Eger and Miskolc. The caves stretch 25 km underground, 18 km of which is in Hungary and seven km in Slovakia. The easiest way to get there is to take the morning Volán bus from Eger to Aggtelek (2½ hours, US$4). The same bus returns to Eger in the afternoon, allowing you plenty of time to see the Aggtelek caves. It doesn't, however, give you time to see the Jósvafö Caves. Alternatively, spend the night at Aggtelek and visit the three different sections of the caves. One reader commented that he didn't like the way the walking paths within the caves had been hacked out and cemented up.

Things to See & Do

The short tour at Aggtelek (one hour, US$1.75, students half-price, open year-round) includes recorded music in the 'concert hall'. There you will see beautiful karst formations and an underground lake. There's another entrance to the Baradla Caves near **Jósvafö**, six km east of Aggtelek, where you can go on different short tours (US$2, students half price). Two-hour trips (US$2.75) begin at **Vöröstó** between Aggtelek and Jósvafö, and in summer there's even an epic five-hour cave tour (US$9) during which visitors must carry lamps. All tours are led by Hungarian-speaking guides who only set out when 10 tickets have been sold, so you may have to buy the extra tickets when things are slow (the one-hour Aggtelek tour begins at 10 am, 1 and 3 pm even when fewer people are waiting).

Next to the Aggtelek entrance to the Baradla Caves is a **terrárium** with a small collection of local reptiles and insects (open mid-May to mid-September). **Hiking trails** begin behind this museum and even on a brief visit it's well worth climbing the hill for a view of the countryside. A trail marked with a green pine tree on a white base leads from here to the Jósvafö entrance (7½ km). The trail begins at the viewpoint above the cave entrance but soon swings right past a wooden electricity pole (don't charge straight up the hill on the main trail marked by blue triangles). You can swim in a small lake a five-minute walk from the Jósvafö entrance.

Places to Stay & Eat

The bus from Eger stops in front of the modern four-storey *Cseppkő Hotel* (☎ 343 075) at Aggtelek, where the 73 rooms with bath cost US$17/24 single/double including breakfast. The hotel has a restaurant with an English menu. The hotel reception changes cash only (no travellers' cheques).

Also at the Aggtelek entrance is pleasant *Baradla Camping* (☎ 343 073; open from mid-April to mid-October) with 3rd-class cabins at US$9 (two beds) and 1st-class bungalows at US$17. Camping is US$1.50 per person plus US$3 per tent.

The camping ground reception also controls the tourist hostel *(turistaház)* (US$3 per person) above the terrárium at the entrance to the caves (said to be open year-round). It has beds in eight-bed dorms at US$3 per person (plus 25% tax if you stay longer than one night). If you have a car there will be a parking fee. Cooking facilities are provided but you may have to walk to the end of the camping ground for a hot shower. The check-out time at the hostel is 10 am.

The *Tengerszem Szálló* (☎ 312 700) is a rustic 22-room lodge at the Jósvafö Caves, a km or so west of Jósvafö village. All the buses stop here.

Getting There & Away

Only one bus a day travels between Budapest, Eger and Aggtelek, leaving Budapest and Eger in the morning and Aggtelek in the afternoon. Buses travel from Aggtelek to Jósvafö every couple of hours and a morning bus goes from Miskolc to Aggtelek, returning to Miskolc in the afternoon. (Throughout Hungary, Aggtelek is listed on posted bus schedules as 'Jósvafö'.)

You can also come by train from Miskolc to Jósvafö-Aggtelek Railway Station where a bus is usually waiting to carry you the 22 km on to the caves at Aggtelek. At Miskolc look for one of the seven daily trains bearing the sign 'Tornanádaska'.

Though the caves in Aggtelek are only a five-minute walk from the Slovakian border, only Hungarians and Slovaks may cross here. There's a morning bus from Aggtelek to Rožňava in Slovakia, however, Westerners are not allowed to take it (the Hungarian government wants this changed, but for some reason the Slovakian government doesn't).

The nearest highway border crossing open to everyone is at Banréve, 30 km south-west, and if you don't have a car or bicycle you'll probably have to go all the way around via Miskolc to get to Košice.

MISKOLC

This large industrial city between Budapest and Košice often serves as a transit point between Hungary and Slovakia. Two unreserved local trains a day shuttle between Miskolc and Košice (84 km), and there are another six connections through Sátoraljaújhely/Slovenské Nové Mesto. At Tiszai pu Railway Station in Miskolc you should be able to change dollars or Deutschmarks in cash at the international ticket window No 7. If it's closed, use a coin to tap on the glass until someone comes.

A hundred metres from this train station is the *MTM Szálló* (☎ 340 043), to the right of the city buses and across a parking lot, with beds in four-bedded rooms at US$4 per person. In winter the rooms are tremendously overheated, so ask for one upstairs so you can open the window.

HUNGARY

Liechtenstein

Blink and you might miss Liechtenstein; the country measures just 25 km from north to south, and an average of six km from west to east. In some ways you could be forgiven for mistaking it for a part of Switzerland. The Swiss franc is the legal currency, all travel documents valid for Switzerland are also valid for Liechtenstein, and the only border regulations are on the Austrian side. Switzerland also represents Liechtenstein abroad, subject to consultation.

But a closer look reveals that Liechtenstein is quite distinct from its neighbour. The ties with Switzerland began only in 1923 with the signing of a customs and monetary union. Before that, it had a similar agreement with Austria-Hungary. Although Liechtenstein shares the Swiss telephone and postal system, it issues its own postage stamps.

Unlike Switzerland, Liechtenstein joined the United Nations (1990) and, in 1992, the European Economic Area (EEA). Switzerland's rejection of the EEA calls into question the viability of the open border between the two countries. Negotiations are under way, but the issue has not yet been resolved. Liechtenstein currently has no plans to follow other EEA states which are seeking full EU membership.

Liechtenstein is a prosperous country (though in September 1993 it suffered from an unusually high level of unemployment; 1.18% – 242 people!) and the people are proud of their independence.

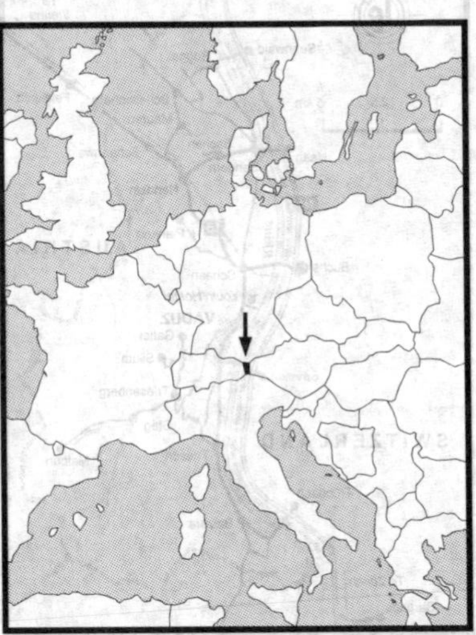

Facts about the Country

Liechtenstein was created by the merger of the domain of Schellenberg and the county of Vaduz in 1712 by the powerful Liechtenstein family. It was a principality under the Holy Roman Empire from 1719 to 1806 and, after a spell in the German Confederation, it achieved full sovereign independence in 1866. The modern constitution was drawn up in 1921. Even today, the prince retains the power to dissolve parliament and must approve every act before it becomes law. Prince Franz Josef II was the first ruler to live in the castle above the capital city of Vaduz. He died in 1989 after a reign of 51 years, and was succeeded by his son, Prince Hans-Adam II.

Liechtenstein has no military service – its minuscule army was disbanded in 1868. It is a country known for its wines, postage stamps, and its status as a tax haven.

Despite its small size, Liechtenstein has two political regions (upper and lower) and three distinct geographical areas: the Rhine valley in the west, the edge of the Tirolean Alps in the south-east, and the northern lowlands. The current population is 28,074 with a third of that total made up of foreign residents.

See the Switzerland chapter for details on entry regulations, currency etc.

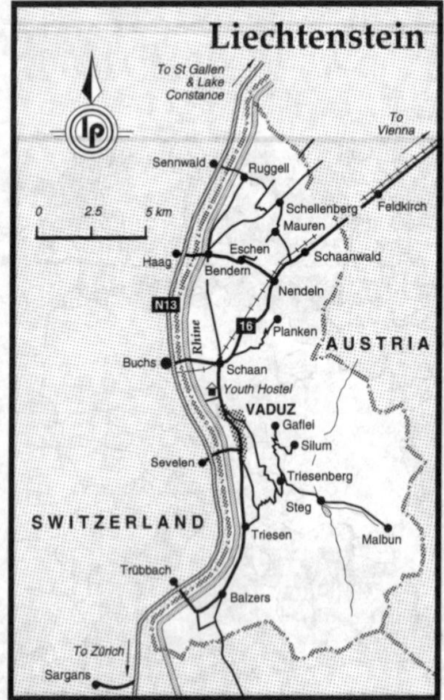

Getting There & Away

Liechtenstein has no airport (the nearest is in Zürich), and only a few trains stop within its borders (at Schaan). Getting there by postbus is easiest. There are approximately two buses an hour from the Swiss border towns of Buchs and Sargans which stop in Vaduz (Sfr3 single fare). There are hourly buses from the Austrian border town of Feldkirch, but you must change at Schaan to reach Vaduz (the Sfr3 ticket is valid for both destinations).

By road, route 16 from Switzerland passes through Liechtenstein via Schaan and terminates at Feldkirch. The N13 follows the Rhine along the Swiss/Liechtenstein border; minor roads cross into Liechtenstein at each motorway exit.

Getting Around

Postbus travel within Liechtenstein is cheap and reliable; all fares cost Sfr2 or Sfr3. The only drawback is that some services finish early; the last of the hourly buses from Vaduz to Malbun, for example, leaves at 4.25 pm (6.25 pm in summer). Get a timetable from the Vaduz tourist office.

Vaduz

The capital of Liechtenstein, with less than 5000 inhabitants, is really no more than a village.

Orientation & Information

Two adjoining streets, Städtle and Äulestrasse, enclose the town centre. Everything of importance is within this small area, including the bus station.

The Vaduz tourist office (☎ 075-232 14 43), Städtle 37, has a free room-finding service and information on the whole country. It is open Monday to Friday from 8 am to noon and 1.30 to 5.30 pm. Depending on demand, the office is also open from June to August for limited hours on weekends. Staff members are kept busy putting surprisingly dull souvenir entry stamps in visitors' passports (Sfr2). Pick up the excellent *Tourism Handbook*, which tells you everything you might want to know about the country.

The main post office, Äulestrasse 38, is open Monday to Friday from 8 am to 6 pm, and on Saturday from 8 to 11 am. Postal rates are the same as those in Switzerland. The post office has an adjoining philatelic section which is open similar hours. The telephone code for all of Liechtenstein is 075.

Bikes can be rented from Melliger AG (☎ 232 16 06), Kirchstrasse 10, for Sfr20 per day; they can be picked up the evening before rental begins.

LIECHTENSTEIN

Things to See & Do

Although the **castle** is not open to the public, it is worth climbing the hill for a closer look. There's a good view of Vaduz and the mountains, and a network of marked walking trails along the ridge. The **National Museum**, Städtle 43, has coins, weapons, folklore exhibits and an informative slide show in English of the history of Liechtenstein. The castle was closed in 1994 for lengthy renovations, so check with the tourist office to see if it has reopened.

The **State Art Collection** at Städtle 37 has worthwhile, temporary exhibitions; it is open daily, and entry costs Sfr3 (students Sfr1.50). The **Postage Stamp Museum**, next to the tourist office, contains 300 frames of national stamps issued since 1912. Located in just one room, it is free and open daily. Look out for processions and fireworks on 15 August, Liechtenstein's national holiday.

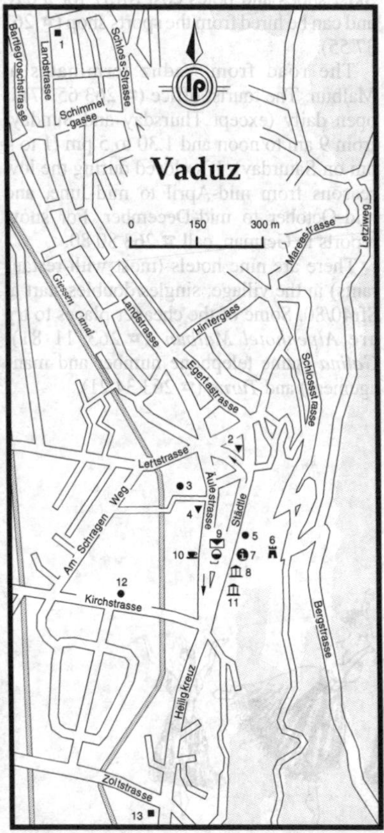

Places to Stay

The SYHA *Schaan-Vaduz Youth Hostel* (☎ 232 50 22), Untere Rütigasse 6, is open from March to November. Beds cost Sfr18, including breakfast. Reception is closed, and the hostel doors are locked, from 10 am to 5 pm. The hostel is a 30 minute walk from Buchs and a 10 minute walk from Schaan. Take the road to Vaduz and turn right at Marianumstrasse.

Check the tourist office hotel list for private rooms or cheaper accommodation outside Vaduz. *Hotel Falknis* (☎ 322 63 77), Landstrasse, is a 15 minute walk from the centre of Vaduz, towards Schaan. Reasonable singles/doubles are Sfr45/80, with a shower on each floor. *Gasthof Au* (☎ 232 11 17), Austrasse 2, is the only other budget option in Vaduz. Singles/doubles with private shower are Sfr70/100, or Sfr50/80 without; triples are Sfr120. Eating is pleasant and fairly inexpensive in its garden restaurant.

PLACES TO STAY

1 Hotel Falknis
13 Gasthof Au

PLACES TO EAT

2 Hotel Engel
4 Old Castle Inn
10 Café Amann

OTHER

3 Denner Supermarket
5 Liechtenstein State Art Collection
6 Vaduz Castle
7 Tourist Office
8 Postage Stamp Museum
9 Post Office & Postbus Station
11 Liechtenstein National Museum
12 Melliger AG

Places to Eat
Restaurants are pricey in Vaduz, so look out for lunchtime specials. *Hotel Engel*, Städtle 13, has good meals from Sfr14.50, with vegetarian choices. On Äulestrasse, try *Old Castle Inn*, (open daily), *Café Amann* (closed Sunday), or stock up in the *Denner* supermarket.

AROUND VADUZ
The lowlands (Unterland) of Northern Liechtenstein are dotted with small communities. There's little to do except enjoy the quiet pace of life and view the village churches. Pottery-making is demonstrated on weekdays at Schaedler Keramik (☎ 373 14 14) in **Nendeln** (admission free). The Rofenberg in **Eschen-Nendel** was formerly a place of public execution and is now the site of the Holy Cross Chapel. **Schellenberg** has a Russian monument, commemorating the night in 1945 when a band of 500 heavily-armed Russian soldiers crossed the border. They had been fighting for the German army, but they came to defect, not attack.

Triesenberg, on a terrace above Vaduz, commands an excellent view over the Rhine valley and has a pretty onion-domed church. There's also a museum devoted to the Walser community which journeyed from Valais (Switzerland) to settle here in the 13th century (admission Sfr2; students Sfr1). The Walser dialect is still spoken here.

Balzers, in the extreme south of the country, is dominated by the soaring sides of Gutenberg Castle. The interior of the castle is currently closed for renovations.

MALBUN
Liechtenstein's ski resort, Malbun, is nestled amid the mountains in the south-east. It has some good runs for novices (and two ski schools) as well as more difficult runs. A pass for all ski lifts and chair lifts costs Sfr19 (half a day), Sfr29 (one day) or Sfr120 (one week). Skis, shoes and poles cost Sfr37 for a day, and can be hired from the sports shop (☎ 263 37 55).

The road from Vaduz terminates at Malbun. The tourist office (☎ 263 65 77) is open daily (except Thursday and Sunday) from 9 am to noon and 1.30 to 5 pm (1 to 4 pm on Saturday). It's closed during the low seasons from mid-April to mid-June, and mid-October to mid-December. For snow reports in German, call ☎ 263 80 80.

There are nine hotels (most with restaurants) in the village; singles/doubles start at Sfr40/80. Some of the cheaper places to try are *Alpenhotel Malbun* (☎ 263 11 81), *Galina* (same telephone number and management) and *Turna* (☎ 263 34 21).

Poland

In both area and population, 312,683-sq-km Poland is one of the largest countries in Central Europe. It is just a bit smaller than reunified Germany and about the same size as the US state of New Mexico.

Always open to invaders from east and west, Poland has had a tumultuous past. The weight of history is on Kraków, the illustrious royal city; Gdańsk (Danzig), the former Hanseatic trading town where WW II began; Auschwitz, a reminder of the depths to which humanity can descend; and rebuilt Warsaw, symbol of the resilient Polish spirit. In 1939 Poland displayed great courage in being first to say 'no' to Hitler and half a century later it again changed the course of history by becoming the first Eastern European state to break free of communism.

Apart from the historical and cultural sides to this subtle land of Chopin and Copernicus, there's the gentle beauty of Baltic beaches, quiet north-eastern lakes and forests, and the majestic mountains in the south, all requiring time to be appreciated. Each of the separate regions of Poland has its own character: Mazovia (around Warsaw), Małopolska ('Little Poland', in the south-east), Silesia (in the south-west), Wielkopolska ('Big Poland', in the west), Pomerania (in the north-west) and Mazuria (in the north-east). Palpable differences remain between the areas once controlled by Austria, Germany and Russia; yet bound together by Catholicism, language, nationality and a common experience, Poland has a unity few other nations in the region can match.

In 1944 Stalin commented that fitting communism to Poland was like putting a saddle on a cow and now that the saddle has been removed, the pace of economic change goes faster in Poland than anywhere else in Eastern Europe. Though the full benefits of the changes are still in the future, Poland has already taken on new life as goods reappear in the shops and Polish small businesspeople spread their wares in the streets. The psychological change is tremendous.

For visitors, Poland is now a much nicer place than it was under communism. The shortages of food and drink are gone, it's much easier to find a cheap place to stay and most of the annoying paperwork previously involved in a visit (compulsory exchange, police registration, currency declarations, and, in many cases, visas) have been abolished. The old suspicion has also now disappeared and foreigners are accepted everywhere on the same footing as Poles. Of course prices have gone up, but tourists have been freed from the nuisance of having to deal on the black market to get fair value for their money and, compared to any Western European country, Poland is still excellent value. This is one of the only countries in Eastern Europe where you won't be charged two or three times more than the locals for hotel rooms. Once you have a visa (where required) there are few additional hassles.

Facts about the Country

HISTORY

In the 6th and 7th centuries AD the West Slavs pushed north and west and occupied most of what is now Poland. By the 10th century the leaders of the Polanian tribe in western Poland were uniting other Slavic tribes under their rule. Mieszko I adopted Christianity in 966, a date considered to mark the formation of the first Polish state, and in the year 1000 the Gniezno Archbishopric was founded. Boleslav the Brave took the title of king in 1025 and his descendant, Boleslav the Bold, consolidated the power of the Piast dynasty over a territory very similar to the Poland of today.

There was constant pressure from the west as the Germans pushed into Pomerania and Silesia, so, to be less vulnerable, from the 11th century onwards Polish kings were no longer crowned in Poznań but in Kraków. In the mid-12th century the country was divided into four principalities and a weakened Poland soon fell prey to invaders. In 1226 the Teutonic Knights, a Germanic mil-

itary and religious order, were invited to come to Poland by the Prince of Mazovia to subdue the restive Prussians of the north-east. Once the knights had subjugated the Baltic tribes they turned their attention to the Poles. The order set up a state in the lower Vistula area east of Gdańsk/Toruń, ruled from their castle at Malbork. Tatar invasions devastated southern Poland in 1241 and 1259. Though Poland was reunified in 1320, the knights held onto Pomerania and Prussia.

From the 14th to 17th centuries Poland was a great power. It's said that the 14th-century king, Casimir III the Great, last of the Piast dynasty, 'found a Poland made of wood and left one made of masonry'. His administrative reforms increased the significance of towns like Kraków, Lublin and Poznań. When Casimir died without an heir, the throne passed to the daughter of the King of Hungary, Princess Jadwiga, who in 1386 married the Duke of Lithuania, uniting the two countries under the Jagiello dynasty.

In 1410 the combined Polish, Lithuanian and Ruthenian (Ukrainian) forces under Ladislaus Jagiello defeated the Teutonic Knights at Grunwald, south of Olsztyn. After the Thirteen Years' War (1454-66) the Teutonic order was broken up and in 1525 the secular Duchy of Prussia became a fiefdom of the Polish crown. In 1490 King Casimir IV of Poland also assumed the Hungarian throne.

The early 16th-century monarch Sigismund I the Old brought the Renaissance to Poland and in 1543 Nicolaus Copernicus published his immortal treatise *De Revolutionibus Orbium Coelestium.* At a time when much of Europe was being torn apart by religious wars and persecutions, there was relative peace and tolerance in Poland. Lithuania and Poland were formally united as one country in 1569, to oppose Russian expansion, and the Polish-Lithuanian Commonwealth became the largest country in Europe, stretching from the Black Sea to the Baltic Sea.

After the death of Sigismund Augustus in 1572, the Jagiello dynasty became extinct and the Sejm (parliament) decided future kings would be elected by the entire gentry (about 10% of the total population), a system which greatly increased the power of the feudal nobility.

In the early 17th century Sigismund III, an elected king from the Swedish Vasa line, moved the capital from Kraków to Warsaw. Sigismund III also embroiled Poland in Swedish dynastic wars and, though the country successfully held off Sweden and Moscow for a time, in 1655 a Swedish invasion ('the Deluge') devastated Poland's towns. King Jan III Sobieski, builder of Warsaw's Wilanów Palace, led a crusade against the Turks which resulted in their removal from Hungary after 1683.

Weak leadership, constant wars and the domination of the gentry over the middle class led to the decline of Poland in the 18th century. In the first partition of Poland in 1772, Russia, Prussia and Austria took 29% of the national territory. Poland's last king, Stanislaus Poniatowski, tried to reverse the situation with reforms, but the powerful magnates resisted strongly, leading to civil war and a pretext for foreign intervention. In 1791 the king granted Poland a democratic constitution (the second in the world) but the magnates again revolted, leading to a second partition in 1793. A year later Tadeusz Kościuszko, a veteran of the American Revolution, led a war of independence against the invaders but was defeated in 1795. A subsequent third partition that year wiped Poland right off the map of Europe until 1918.

The oppressed Poles supported Napoleon, who set up a Duchy of Warsaw in 1807 from where he led his Grand Army to Moscow in 1812 (the beginning of a special Franco-Polish relationship which has continued until today). After 1815 Poland again came under tsarist Russia. There were unsuccessful uprisings against this in 1831, 1848 and 1864 with Poland's position worsening after each one. A Russification and Germanisation policy was enforced in the areas controlled by those powers; Poles were permitted to maintain their identity only in the Austrian-occupied part around Kraków.

The 20th Century

Poland was completely overrun by the Germans during WW I, but in 1919 a Polish state was again established by the Treaty of Versailles. Then the Polish military struck east and took big chunks of Lithuania, Belorussia and Ukraine, inhabited by non-Polish majorities, from a weakened Soviet Union. In 1926 Marshal Józef Piłsudski, ex-commander of the Polish Legions which had fought alongside Austria in WW I, staged a military coup and set himself up as dictator. Poland gained a measure of prosperity under Piłsudski, but by the time of his death in 1935 Poland had been ruined by the depression and soon fell victim to Hitler.

WW II began in Gdańsk (at that time the Free City of Danzig) where 182 Poles at Westerplatte held out for a week against the battleship *Schleswig Holstein*, Stuka dive bombers and thousands of German troops. To the west the Polish Pomorska Brigade of mounted cavalry met General Guderian's tanks – medieval lances against modern armour – in a final suicidal charge. Polish resistance continued for almost a month and German losses during the campaign were as great as subsequent losses during the 1940-41 invasions of Western Europe, the Balkans and North Africa combined. As these events took place in the west, the Soviet Union invaded from the east and took back the territories lost in the 1919-21 Polish-Soviet War. Poland had been partitioned for the fourth time.

During WW II Poland was the only country in Europe which never produced any quislings (collaborators) willing to serve in a German-dominated puppet government. The Nazi governor general, Hans Frank, ruled those areas not directly incorporated into the Reich, and Poles resident in the areas which had been annexed by Germany were deported east. Yet two resistance groups, the London-directed Armia Krajowa (Home Army) and the communist Gwardia Ludowa (People's Guard), later the People's Army, fought on inside Poland. In July 1944 the Red Army liberated Lublin and set up a communist-led provisional government.

Six million Poles – a fifth of the population – died during the Nazi terror, half of them Jews. During the Warsaw Ghetto uprising of 1943, some 70,000 poorly armed, starving Jews led by Mordechai Anielewicz held out against the full weight of the Nazi army for 27 days. The Warsaw uprising was begun on 1 August 1944 by the Home Army as Soviet forces approached the right bank of the Vistula River. The intention was to evict the retreating Germans from Warsaw and have a non-communist force in place to greet the Soviet army, but the uprising was premature. The Nazis brought up reserves to halt the Red Army in Praga across the river, then engaged the 50,000 Polish irregulars in house-to-house combat.

By 2 October, when the remaining partisans surrendered with honour, some 250,000 Poles had died, many of them civilians slaughtered en masse by SS troops. All the remaining inhabitants were then expelled from the city and German demolition teams levelled Warsaw street by street. The Soviet armies which entered the city three months later encountered only desolation. Ironically the Germans set the stage for a post-war communist Poland by physically eliminating the bulk of the non-communist resistance within the country.

At the Teheran Conference in November 1943, Churchill, Roosevelt and Stalin decided that everything east of the Odra (Oder) and Nysa (Neisse) rivers – which meant Silesia, Pomerania and Mazuria – was to be returned to Poland after centuries of German control. At the same time the Soviet Union was to get the eastern territories, reducing Poland's land area to four-fifths of the prewar size. Millions of people were dislocated by these changes which brought Poland's borders back to where they had been eight centuries earlier. Poland's postwar borders were guaranteed by the creation of the Warsaw Pact in 1955, and in 1970 Chancellor Willy Brandt signed a treaty accepting the Oder-Neisse border.

Recent History

After the war a Soviet-style communist

system was installed in Poland and the country was run according to five and six-year plans. The emphasis on heavy industry led to chronic shortages of consumer goods while the *nomenklatura* of party bureaucrats enjoyed many privileges. Intellectual freedom was curtailed by the security apparatus and individual initiative stifled. In 1956, when Nikita Khrushchev denounced Stalin at the Soviet 20th Party Congress, Bolesław Bierut, the Stalinist party chief in Poland, died of a heart attack!

In June 1956 workers in Poznań rioted over low wages, and in October, Władysław Gomułka, an ex-political prisoner of the Stalin era, took over as party first secretary. Gomułka introduced a series of superficial reforms reducing Soviet domination of Poland and freeing political prisoners, but the basic system continued unchanged. After the Arab-Israeli War of 1967, party hardliners used an 'anti-Zionist' purge to enforce discipline, but by December 1970 living conditions had declined to the point where workers in northern Poland went on strike over food price increases. When 300 of them were shot down during demonstrations, Edward Gierek replaced Gomułka as party leader and persuaded the strikers to return to work by promising sweeping changes.

Gierek launched Poland on a reckless programme of industrial expansion to produce exports which could be sold on world markets. Money to finance this was supplied by 17 capitalist governments and 501 banks, and by 1981 the country had run up a hard-currency debt of US$27 billion. Many of the ill-founded heavy industry schemes ended in failure as a recession in the West shrank the markets for Polish exports at the end of the 1970s.

This decade of mismanagement left Poland bankrupt. Living standards fell sharply as Poland was forced to divert goods to export from domestic consumption, to earn hard currency with which to service the debt. The election of a Pole to the papacy in October 1978, and the visit to Poland by John Paul II in June 1979, also changed the atmosphere in a country where the party was supposed to play the 'leading role'.

In 1980 a wave of strikes over sharp food price increases forced Gierek out and marked the emergence of Lech Wałęsa's Solidarity trade union which soon had 10 million members (a million of them also Communist Party members). Solidarity said all it wanted was self-management of the factories by workers' councils instead of central planning. At first the Polish government was conciliatory, recognising Solidarity in November 1980, and conceding to a five-day work week. In September 1981, many of Solidarity's demands for reduced central planning and greater worker control over enterprises were met.

Things soon got out of hand as union militants challenged government authority. Strikes and obstruction threatened Poland with economic collapse and a Soviet military intervention which could have led to a bloody civil war. On 13 December 1981 martial law was declared by General Wojciech Jaruzelski, who had become prime minister in February 1981, and thousands were interned as the government broke up the union. In October 1982 Solidarity was dissolved by the courts and by July 1983 martial law could be lifted.

A year after the imposition of martial law, General Jaruzelski introduced economic reforms of his own based on greater autonomy for state corporations. In April 1986, the government set in motion 'second stage' reforms providing for decentralisation, worker control of companies, greater competition, incentives, a market economy and some political pluralism. These initiatives lacked public support, and this showed when in a November 1987 referendum Poles cast a vote of no confidence in the communist government.

Meanwhile Solidarity had been biding its time, and in 1988 fresh strikes followed government attempts to remove food subsidies. The big pay increases won by the striking workers clearly revealed government weakness, and officials agreed to meet with Solidarity to discuss reform, realising that without a compromise Poland would explode.

In April 1989, nine weeks of round-table talks between Solidarity and the communists ended in an accord which legalised Solidarity and the other opposition groups. A 100-seat senate was to be created, giving Poland a two-house parliament for the first time since 1946. Both the senate and the new president would have veto power over a 460-seat Sejm, though these vetoes could be overridden by a two-thirds majority vote in the lower house. The Polish United Workers Party (PZPR) and allied parties were guaranteed 65% of the seats in the lower house, while the other 35% of the Sejm and the entire senate were to be chosen in Eastern Europe's first Western-style elections.

The sweeping Solidarity victory in the June 1989 elections soon caused the communist coalition to fall apart, and in August 1989 Tadeusz Mazowiecki was picked to head a Solidarity-led coalition, thus becoming the first non-communist prime minister of an Eastern European country in over four decades. Though General Jaruzelski had been elected to serve as a transitional president by parliament in July 1989, the communist era in Poland had come to an end, and the two-million-member Polish United Workers Party dissolved itself at its congress in February 1990.

The Mazowiecki government adopted a 'shock therapy' economic programme to switch Poland from a planned to a free-market economy. On 1 January 1990 price and currency exchange controls were removed, allowing both to find their real levels. During the first month, prices jumped 79% but the markets suddenly filled with products. Inflation was eventually brought under control as the złoty stabilised against Western currencies, though at the cost of wages losing 30% of their purchasing power in 1990 and industrial production falling by 25%. The Mazowiecki team also prepared for privatisation by cutting subsidies to overstaffed state industries, thereby sending unemployment up from zero to 7.5% in 1990.

In September 1990 General Jaruzelski stepped down and Lech Wałęsa was elected president three months later. Parliamentary elections with no allotted seats were held in October 1991, but Poland's system of proportional representation resulted in 29 political parties winning seats although only two got over 10% of the vote. In January 1992 Jan Olszewski formed a centre-right coalition government which was defeated after only five months in office and in July 1992 Hanna Suchocka of the centrist Democratic Union (UD) cobbled together a coalition of seven parties to become Poland's first woman prime minister.

Abortion had been legal in Poland since 1956 but parliament came under intensive lobbying from the Catholic Church and in January 1993 an anti-abortion law was pushed through by the Christian National Union, one of Suchocka's coalition partners. Abortion became illegal except in cases of incest, rape, deformed foetus or serious danger to the mother. Public opinion surveys showed a large majority of Poles against this move and the conservative politicians strongly resisted having the matter put to a referendum. Moderates did manage to have amendments attached to the law requiring that contraceptives be made available and that Polish schools begin providing sex education for the first time.

Political instability combined with lowered living standards and soaring unemployment had made the successive centrist governments highly unpopular among those hardest hit by economic austerity, especially pensioners, industrial workers and low-ranking civil servants. When Suchocka's government was defeated in a vote of no confidence over a labour dispute in May 1993, President Wałęsa ordered fresh elections to be held under a new rule restricting parliamentary representation to parties winning over 5% of the vote (8% for coalitions).

The parliamentary elections of September 1993 saw a strong swing to the left as voters abandoned the Catholic parties which had pushed through the anti-abortion and religious education legislation. Of the six parties represented in the new parliament, the largest was the Democratic Left Alliance (SLD), a party of ex-communist social democrats. Second place went to the Polish Peasant Party (PSL) whose leader, Waldemar Pawlak, became prime minister (and at age 34, the youngest to hold the post in Polish history), but the real power in the new parliament seems to be SLD leader Aleksander Kwaśniewski. The Solidarity-descended parties together obtained less than a quarter of the seats. The new government has promised to continue economic reform, but more slowly and with more attention for those most affected by the changes.

On 18 September 1993, the last 24 Russian soldiers left Poland by train, almost 54 years to the day after Stalin ordered his armies into the country on 17 September 1939.

GEOGRAPHY

Poland is divided into 49 provinces (voivodships) and 2383 local administrative units (gmina). It's a low, square-shaped country with sides about 550 km long with call of the mountains in the south. The Sudeten Mountains south of Jelenia Góra in Silesia are 280 km long and 50 km wide, with a medium height of 1200 metres culminating in Śnieżka (1605 metres). The Beskidy and Pieniny mountains in the Western Carpathians run along the Slovakian border north of the Tatras. The Bieszczady Mountains in the Eastern Carpathians are open grassy peaks which reach 1346 metres at Tarnica.

Poland's highest mountains are the rocky Tatras, a section of the Carpathian range that Poland shares with Slovakia. The Polish Tatras (150 sq km) are 50 km long and rise to Rysy (2499 metres), and the Slovakian Tatras (600 sq km) culminate in Gerlachovský Štít (2654 metres). Poland's lowest point is actually 1.8 metres below sea level in the Vistula delta.

Lowland predominates in central Poland, a land of great north-flowing rivers such as the Vistula, Odra, Warta and Bug. The entire drainage area of the 1047-km Vistula, the mother river of Poland, lies within Poland's boundaries and most of the rest of the country is drained by the Odra. Poland has more post-glacial lakes than any country in Europe except Finland. West of the Vistula is the Pomeranian lake district, and east are the picturesque Mazurian Lakes. The coastal plain along the broad, sandy, 524-km Baltic coast is spotted with sand dunes, bays and lakes, separated from the sea by narrow sand bars.

ECONOMY

After WW II, Poland was a patchwork of small farms with 38% of the economy in ruins and in the rebuilding process the emphasis was placed on heavy industry, leading to perennial shortages of consumer goods. Heavy industries include steel mills (at Warsaw, Kraków and Katowice), shipbuilding (at Gdańsk), mining machinery and chemicals. Textile production is centred at Łódź.

Zinc, lead, silver and copper are extracted in southern Poland. Poland is the fourth-largest producer of hard bituminous coal in the world, most of it from Silesia. This quality low-sulphur coal is mostly exported while dirty brown lignite is burned locally for electricity and to fuel industry. In 1990 Poland halted construction of its first nuclear power plant which was being built near Gdańsk using outmoded Soviet technology.

The communists sought increased production with scant regard to quality or cost, creating tremendous environmental problems. Some 20 million tonnes of toxic wastes are dumped in unregulated sites annually. The Odra and Vistula rivers discharge thousands and millions of tonnes of heavy metals, nitrogen, phosphorous, oil and highly toxic chloride compounds (PCBs) into the Baltic Sea every year, causing fish catches and tourism to plummet. Half the 813 towns and villages along the Vistula have no sewage-treatment facilities at all and 6000 factories also use the river as an open sewer.

In the south the steel mills and other coal-burning industries have caused severe air pollution, including the acid rain which is stunting Poland's forests and dissolving Kraków's medieval monuments. Heavy metals such as cadmium, copper, lead and mercury have contaminated the soil in the southern industrial zones, making fruits and vegetables inedible. The life span of the average Silesian is three years shorter than the national average and the infant mortality rate there is 30 per 1000 live births compared to 17 nationwide.

Poland is the world's second-largest producer of rye. Barley, oats, oilseed, potatoes, sugar beet and wheat are also important. Though an exporter of livestock and sugar, Poland still imports grain. Throughout the communist period Poland was unique in Eastern Europe in that most agricultural land was privately farmed by small holders. Today 76% of farm land is privately owned but 83% of these farms consist of less than 10 hectares, limiting productivity.

Until recently Poland exported machinery, coal, transportation equipment and chemicals to the former communist countries, particularly the USSR which supplied Poland with raw materials such as metals and phosphates for industry, plus 80% of its crude oil. Trading patterns changed rapidly after 1 January 1991 when Poland began accepting only hard currencies (not 'accounting roubles') for its exports and today Poland's largest trading partner by far is Germany, accounting for over a quarter of imports and exports, followed by the ex-Soviet states, the UK, Austria, Switzerland and Italy.

In December 1991 Poland became an interim associate member of the European Community (now the European Union, or EU) and the following March an interim trade agreement came into effect.

These moves are seen as the beginning of a 10-year transitional period which should see Poland fully integrated into the EU by the year 2002. By 1993, 58% of Poland's foreign trade was already with the EU, compared with just 32% in 1989. Though the EU maintains tariff barriers against Polish agricultural products, textiles, chemicals and steel, Poland has a trade surplus with the West.

Current Trends

In 1990 the Polish economy contacted 12%, followed by a further production drop of 7.5% in 1991. In 1992 this decline bottomed out and in 1993 Poland was the only Eastern European country to register net growth (of 5%). Production is still well below 1989 levels and real income has declined 25%, but things are getting better. Since 1989 two million new jobs have been created in the private sector and together new and privatised firms now account for 45% of the gross domestic product and over 60% of the total workforce.

Privatisation has moved fastest in the retail trade where 80% of the turnover is now in private hands. Most large industries are still state owned but construction, commerce and publishing are now largely in private hands. About 20 National Investment funds have been set up to facilitate the privatisation of larger firms. Shares have been distributed free to pensioners and civil servants, and for token amounts to others. With privatisation, employment in services has increased sharply as the importance of industry declines.

Initially Germany was the largest foreign investor in Poland, but the USA has now far surpassed the Europeans. In March 1991 Western governments forgave a big chunk of Poland's foreign debt, though at US$49 billion it remained the largest in the region by far. In March 1994 a group of Western commercial banks gave Poland additional relief by writing down another US$13 billion in defaulted loans by 43% on the condition that the remainder would be repaid.

In 1989 only half of the prices were based on supply and demand, in 1990 it was 90%, and in 1991, 100%. Deregulation at first led to soaring prices but inflation has been brought under control by strictly limiting government spending. Despite the economic rebound, by 1993 unemployment had reached 16%, or three million, and a third of the population was living in poverty. Much of the unemployment was linked to the loss of trade with the former Soviet bloc which has put heavy pressure on companies unable to adapt to Western markets. Unemployment may continue to rise as inefficient state monopolies are restructured or closed down, putting heavy pressure on both the government and people.

In mid-1993 a 22% value-added tax (VAT) was imposed (7% on energy, transportation, food and construction materials). For visitors, the economic changes still haven't affected the accommodation situation much, but a whole new generation of restaurants, bars and discos has appeared.

POPULATION & PEOPLE

Over half the 38,621,000 inhabitants of Poland live in towns and cities, the six largest of which are Warsaw (1,655,700), Łódź (850,000), Kraków (750,000), Wrocław (650,000), Poznań (600,000), Gdańsk (500,000) and Szczecin (425,000). The south-west is the most densely populated part, especially the area around Łódź and Katowice, while the north-east is the least populated. There's a serious housing shortage forcing many young families to live with in-laws. Literacy is 98%.

At the end of WW II 2,300,000 Germans were evicted from East Prussia, Pomerania and Silesia, their places taken by a further 2,000,000 Poles from the L'vov region of the Ukraine. Half a million Ukrainians, Belorussians and Lithuanians were resettled in the USSR. In the 18th century a third of the world's Jews lived in Poland but tragically few of Poland's 3.5 million prewar Jews survived the Nazis, and only five or six thousand Jews remain in Poland today.

These forced migrations and exterminations created a homogeneous population. Before the war, minorities accounted for 30% of the population of Poland. Today only 1.5% are minorities, mostly Ukrainians and Belorussians. Ten million Poles live abroad in North America, the former Soviet Union, France and Brazil, and Chicago is the second-largest Polish city in the world. Poles refer to the overseas Polish community as 'Polonia' and overseas Poles as 'Polonians'.

ARTS

Poland is a land of remarkable individuals, so many in fact that visitors often lose their way among the unfamiliar names. Apart from Copernicus and Chopin one soon becomes acquainted with Jan Matejko (1838-93), whose monumental historical paintings hang in galleries all around Poland. By creating dramatic visual images of decisive moments in Polish history, Matejko inspired his compatriots at a time when Poland was under foreign yokes.

A kindred spirit was the Romantic poet Adam Mickiewicz (1798-1855) who sought the lost motherland in his writings. Mickiewicz explored the ethical and moral problems of a Poland subject to Russia and held out the hope of eventual redemption, in the same way that Christ was resurrected.

Henryk Sienkiewicz (1846-1916) wrote historical novels which gave Poles a new sense of national identity and won the author a Nobel Prize. His book *The Knights of the Teutonic Order* published in 1900 makes fascinating reading in light of the Nazi attack on Poland four decades later.

One contemporary Polish writer who abandoned Socialist Realism in the 1950s is Kazimierz Brandys (1916-). His best known novel is *Rondo* which deals with theatrical life in Warsaw during WW II. Although written in 1976, it was only published in 1982 after Brandys went into exile in Paris.

Tadeusz Konwicki (1926-) also started out as a Stalinist but after Stalin's crimes were revealed in 1956 turned to depicting Polish life under a hollow system. Recent Konwicki works such as *The Polish Complex* (1982) and *Moonrise, Moonrise* (1987), both translated into English, again explore the theme summed up in the 1797 Polish national anthem: *Jeszcze Polska nie zginęła póki my żyjemy* (Poland has not yet perished as long as we live).

Music & Dance

Polish folk music goes back far beyond the

first written records of mid-16th century mazurka rhythms. Throughout Europe, most folk dances developed from medieval court dances. The *krakowiak* is an old folk dance from the Kraków region, while the mazurka, a spirited Mazovian folk dance similar to a polka, originated in central Poland. Danced by a circle of couples in three-four time with much improvisation, mazurkas were originally accompanied by goatskin bagpipes *(kozial)*.

The *polonaise* is a dignified ceremonial dance that originated as a formal march in the 16th century. During the 17th and 18th centuries the polonaise was used to open functions at the royal court. Arrayed according to their social station, the couples would promenade around the ballroom in three-four time, knees bending slightly on every third gliding step.

The Bohemian composer Jan Stefani (1746-1829), who spent most of his working life in Warsaw, created a unique sentimental style by writing over 100 polonaises for orchestra. Together with playwright Wojciech Boguslawski (1757-1829), Stefani wrote *Krakowiacy i Górale* (1794), a classical opera based on Polish folklore.

The romantic composer Frédéric Chopin (in Polish, Fryderyk Szopen) (1810-49) raised this dance music (mazurkas, polonaises and waltzes) to the level of concert pieces. Written at a time when central Poland was under Russian domination, Chopin's music displays the melancholy and nostalgia which became hallmarks of the Polish national style.

Stanisław Moniuszko (1819-72) 'nationalised' 19th-century Italian opera music by introducing folk songs and dances onto the stage. His *Halka* (1858) about a peasant girl abandoned by a young noble was the first Polish national opera, and many of Moniuszko's operatic characters now belong to Polish national 'mythology'. Chopin and Moniuszko are the forefathers of Polish art music.

The 20th-century composer Karol Szymanowski (1882-1937) strove to merge the traditions of Polish music with those of Europe. His ballet *Harnasie*, based on the folklore of the *Górale*, the highlanders of the Tatra Mountains, employed modern technical devices also used by the Russian Igor Stravinsky.

CULTURE

Poles greet each other by shaking hands much more than is done in the English-speaking world. Men also shake hands with women, though it's customary for the woman to extend her hand first. Poles bump into each other a lot and never apologise. They're not being rude, it's just what they're accustomed to.

If a Polish family befriends you, you'll be smothered with hospitality, in which case just submit and feel right at home going along with their suggestions. When the time comes, propose a toast to the health of the hostess, and be sure to take flowers and perhaps chocolates for the lady of the house whenever you're invited for dinner at a Polish home. Never arrive early for a dinner engagement, preferably arrive a little late, and be prepared to stay later than you'd planned. At the end of a meal always say *dziękuję* (thank you) as you get up, even in restaurants when you are sharing a table with strangers.

In this strongly Catholic country Easter is just as important as Christmas, and the most remarkable Easter event is the seven-day Passion Play at Kalwaria Zebrzydowska, 23 km south-west of Kraków. A re-enactment of Christ's entry into Jerusalem on Palm Sunday is followed by a crucifixion on Good Friday and a resurrection on Easter Sunday witnessed by hundreds of thousands of people. At times the crowd has become so excited that it has attempted to rescue Christ from the 'Roman soldiers'! Forty-two Calvary chapels representing the Stations of the Cross have been set up on this hilly site near the 17th-century Bernardine monastery. Of the few mystery cycles still performed in Europe, this is the oldest and most renowned – don't miss it if you're in Kraków around Easter.

On All Souls' Day (November 1) people

visit the cemeteries and adorn the graves with candles and flowers. In the mid-19th century, Poles adopted the custom of the Christmas tree from Western Europe. Before Christmas Eve dinner, hay is put under the tablecloth. When everyone is seated, each pulls out a blade of hay at random. To get a long blade signifies a long life, while a shorter one indicates a more complicated future. Traditionally an extra place is set at the table for an unexpected guest. There will be 12 courses, one for each of the 12 apostles. At midnight on Christmas Eve, a special mass is celebrated in all churches, while New Year's Eve is marked by formal balls.

RELIGION

In 966 AD Poland became the easternmost Roman Catholic country in Europe, while Russia and most of the Balkan countries converted to Eastern Orthodox Christianity. Archbishops are seated at Kraków, Poznań, Warsaw and Wrocław. The Polish Church often had a distant relationship with Rome until 1978, when a Pole was elected Pope. Today the overwhelming majority of Poles are fervent Catholics and on Sunday every church is full to overflowing. The Catholic university in Lublin (founded in 1918) and the Academy of Catholic Theology in Warsaw are leading church-controlled institutions. Częstochowa with its Black Madonna is one of the most important pilgrimage centres in Europe.

The narrow line between church and state has always been difficult to define in Poland. The church openly supported Solidarity throughout the years when it was banned, and the overthrow of communism was as much a victory for the Catholic Church as it was for democracy. It's no coincidence that Catholic religious instruction was reintroduced in the public schools just as the teaching of Marxist ideology was dropped. Legislation passed in 1993 requires both public and private radio and TV to espouse 'Christian values' in their broadcasts. The church has demanded the return of property confiscated not only by the communists but also by the Russian tsars!

LANGUAGE

English speakers are less common in Poland than in some other Eastern European countries – German and Russian are often more useful. While trying to make yourself understood you'll greatly increase comprehension by writing the word or message down on a piece of paper. A pocket English-Polish dictionary will come in handy; consider bringing one with you as they're often hard to find in Poland. Best of all, get a set of 'learn Polish' language tapes or records from your local library and listen to them a couple of times before leaving home.

The first words a visitor to Poland should learn are *proszę* (please) and *dziękuję* (thank you). Also be aware of *tak* (yes), *nie* (no), *dzień dobry* (good morning), *do widzenia* (goodbye), *wejście* (entrance), *wyjście* (exit) and *nieczynne* (closed). You'll quickly learn *remont* which means something like 'under repair'. You'll see this word posted frequently on museums, hotels and restaurants which close for extended renovations. Other common words are *nie ma* which mean something like 'nothing' or 'not available'.

Public toilets (or 'WC') are marked with a circle for women *(panie)* and a triangle for men *(panowie)*. When holding up fingers to indicate numbers in Poland, remember to begin with the thumb, otherwise you'll get one more item than you want.

Lonely Planet's *Eastern Europe Phrasebook* provides far more extensive coverage of the Polish language than is possible here and it's well worth taking along.

Pronunciation

Some of the 32 letters in the Polish alphabet are pronounced quite differently than they are in English.

c	'ts'
ć	'ch'
ci	'ch' (before a vowel)
cz	'ch'
ch	'kh'
dź	'j' as in 'jelly'
dż	'j' as in 'jelly'
dzi	'j' as in 'jelly' (before a vowel)

j 'y'
ł 'w'
ń 'ny' as in 'canyon'
rz 's' as in 'pleasure'
ś 'sh'
si 'sh' (before a vowel)
sz 'sh'
w 'v'
y 'i' as in 'sit'
ż 's' as in 'pleasure'
ź 's' as in 'pleasure'
zi 's' as in 'pleasure' (before a vowel)

The ogonek below ą and ę makes those vowels nasal. The vowels a, e, i, o and u are pronounced as in Italian or Spanish and r is always trilled. There are many refinements to the above which would take several pages to outline. In almost all Polish words, the stress falls on the next-to-last syllable.

When consulting indexes in Polish books or maps be aware that letters with acute, ogonek and overdot accents are considered distinct from the same letter without an accent, so if you don't find the word immediately, check further down the column. The nine accented letters are ą, ć, ę, ł, ń, ó, ś, ź and ż.

Greetings & Civilities

hello — *cześć* (very informal)
hello/good morning — *dzień dobry*
good evening — *dobry wieczór*
goodbye — *do widzenia*
please — *proszę*
thank you — *dziękuję*
excuse me/forgive me — *przepraszam*
yes — *tak*
no — *nie*

Small Talk

I don't understand. — *Nie rozumiem.*
Could you write it down? — *Czy mógł byś to zapisać?*
What is it called? — *Yak to się nazywa?*
Where do you live? — *Gdzie mieszkasz?*
What work do you do? — *Jaką wykonujesz pracę?*
I am a student. — *Jestem studentem.*
I am very happy. — *Jest mi bardzo przyjemnie.*

Accommodation

youth hostel — *schronisko młodzieży*
camping ground — *kemping*
private room — *kwatera prywatna*
How much is it? — *Ile to kosztuje?*
Is that the price per person? — *Czy to jest cena od osoby?*
Is that the total price? — *Czy to jest ostateczna cena?*
Are there any extra charges? — *Czy są jakieś dodatkowe opłaty?*
Do I pay extra for showers? — *Czy płacę dodatkowo za prysznic?*
Where is there a cheaper hotel? — *Gdzie jest tańszy hotel?*
Should I make a reservation? — *Czy mam zrobić rezerwację?*
single room — *pokój jednoosobowy*
double room — *pokój dwuosobowy*
It is very noisy. — *Jest bardzo głośny.*
Where is the toilet? — *Gdzie jest toaleta?*

Getting Around

What time does it leave? — *O której odjeżdża?*
When is the first bus? — *O której jest pierwszy autobus?*
When is the last bus? — *O której jest ostatni autobus?*
When is the next bus? — *O której jest następny autobus?*
That's too soon. — *To za wcześnie.*
When is the next one after that? — *O której jest następny po nim?*
How long does the trip take? — *Jak długo trwa podróż?*
arrival — *przyjazdy*
departure — *odjazdy*
timetable — *rozkład jazdy*

POLAND

Where is the bus stop?	*Gdzie jest przystanek autobusowy?*
Where is the train station?	*Gdzie jest stacja kolejowa?*
Where is the left-luggage room?	*Gdzie jest przechowalnia bagażu?*

Around Town

Just a minute.	*Chwileczkę.*
Where is...?	*Gdzie jest...?*
the bank	*bank*
the post office	*poczta*
the tourist information office	*informacja turystyczna*
the museum	*muzeum*
Where are you going?	*Dokąd idziesz?*
I am going to ...	*Idę do ...*
Where is it?	*Gdzie to jest?*
I can't find it.	*Nie mogę (tego) znaleźć.*
Is it far?	*Czy to daleko?*
Please show me on the map.	*Proszę pokazać mi to na mapie.*
left	*lewo*
right	*prawo*
straight ahead	*prosto*
I want ...	*chcę ...*
Do I need permission?	*Czy potrzebuję pozowolenie?*

Entertainment

Where can I buy a ticket?	*Gdzie mogę kupić bilet?*
Where can I refund this ticket?	*Gdzie mogę zwrócić ten bilet?*
Is this a good seat?	*Czy to jest dobre miejsce?*
at the front	*z przodu*
ticket	*bilet*

Food

I do not eat meat.	*Nie jadam mięsa.*
self-service cafeteria	*bar samoobsługowy*
grocery store	*sklep warzywniczy*
fish	*ryba*
pork	*wieprzowina*
soup	*zupa*
salad	*sałatka*
fresh vegetables	*świeża jarzyna*
milk	*mleko*
bread	*chleb*
sugar	*cukier*
ice cream	*lody*
coffee	*kawa*
tea	*herbata*
mineral water	*woda mineralna*
beer	*piwo*
wine	*wino*
hot/cold	*gorący/zimny*

Shopping

Where can I buy one?	*Gdzie mogę to kupić?*
How much does it cost?	*Ile to kosztuje?*
That's (much) too expensive.	*To jest zbyt drogie.*
Is there a cheaper one?	*Czy jest coś tańszego?*

Time & Dates

today	*dzisiaj*
tonight	*dzisiaj wieczorem*
tomorrow	*jutro*
the day after tomorrow	*pojutrze*
What time does it open?	*O której się otwiera?*
What time does it close?	*O której się zamyka?*
open	*otwarte*
closed	*zamknięte*
in the morning	*rano*
in the evening	*wieczorem*
every day	*codziennie*
At what time?	*O której godzinie?*
when?	*kiedy?*

Monday	*poniedziałek*
Tuesday	*wtorek*
Wednesday	*środa*
Thursday	*czwartek*
Friday	*piątek*
Saturday	*sobota*
Sunday	*niedziela*

January	*styczeń*
February	*luty*
March	*marzec*
April	*kwiecień*
May	*maj*
June	*czerwiec*
July	*lipiec*
August	*sierpień*
September	*wrzesień*
October	*październik*
November	*listopad*
December	*grudzień*

Numbers

1	*jeden*
2	*dwa*
3	*trzy*
4	*cztery*
5	*pięć*
6	*sześć*
7	*siedem*
8	*osiem*
9	*dziewięć*
10	*dziesięć*
11	*jedenaście*
12	*dwanaście*
13	*trzynaście*
14	*czternaście*
15	*piętnaście*
16	*szesnaście*
17	*siedemnaście*
18	*osiemnaście*
19	*dziewiętnaście*
20	*dwadzieścia*
21	*dwadzieścia jeden*
22	*dwadzieścia dwa*
23	*dwadzieścia trzy*
30	*trzydzieści*
40	*czterdzieści*
50	*pięćdziesiąt*
60	*sześćdziesiąt*
70	*siedemdziesiąt*
80	*osiemdziesiąt*
90	*dziewięćdziesiąt*
100	*sto*
1000	*tysiąc*
10,000	*sto tysięcy*
1,000,000	*milion*

Facts for the Visitor

VISAS & EMBASSIES

You must have a passport and in some cases a visa to enter Poland. Your passport must be valid six months after the expiry of the visa. You're supposed to obtain the visa at a consulate, although many travellers report success in buying one at the border. Still, it's cheaper to get the visa beforehand and you eliminate the possibility of problems with the border guards.

Citizens of Austria, Belgium, Denmark, Finland, France, Germany, Italy, Luxembourg, the Netherlands, Norway, Sweden, Switzerland and the USA do not require visas for a stay of up to 90 days; UK citizens can stay for six months. Other nationals should check with one of the Polish consulates listed in this section or at any LOT Polish Airlines office. By phone it's much easier to get through to LOT than to a consulate and they'll have the latest information in their computer.

Polish tourist visas cost about US$25 and two photos are required (US$35 at the border). Canadians are charged visa fees 50% higher than other nationalities due to a refusal by the Canadian government to lift visa requirements for Polish tourists wishing to enter Canada. In Eastern Europe visas are generally issued in 24 hours, with a one-hour express visa service available if you pay 50% more. Polish embassies in Western Europe tend to charge more for visas than those in Eastern Europe. For example, the Polish Embassy in Paris asks US$45 per entry. A multiple-entry visa valid for up to four entries costs four times the usual fee. Students who are 23 years of age and under are charged a reduced visa fee. A cheaper, 48-hour transit visa is also available (onward visa required).

If you apply to the consulate in your home country by registered mail it could be several weeks before you get your passport back. Ask about express service when you write in for the application forms. Some consulates only give seven-day visas if you apply by mail. Otherwise call one of the consulates listed below which are generally open weekday mornings. Some consulates are tremendously overcrowded or charge unusually high fees, so get your visa well in advance, allowing yourself the opportunity to try elsewhere if need be.

If you're asked how long you wish to stay in Poland when you apply for the visa, say one month even if you plan to stay less. That way you won't have to worry about visa extensions should you decide to stay a little longer. Since you must personally register with the police if you stay over a month, it's best to limit your stay to 30 days maximum though you can get a regular visa for a stay of up to 90 days. If you overstay your visa for any reason you'll be fined US$22 when you depart for every additional day.

Polish visas may be used any time within three or six months from the date of issue. If you have to extend your tourist visa within Poland, go to the local passport office *(biuro paszportowe)* on a weekday morning. Any tourist office will have the address. Extensions cost about US$35.

Polish Embassies Abroad

Australia
- 7 Turrana St, Yarralumla, Canberra, ACT 2600 (☎ 062-273 1208)
- 10 Trelawney St, Woollahra, Sydney, NSW 2025 (☎ 02-363 9816)

Canada
- 443 Daly St, Ottawa 2, ON K1N 6H3 (☎ 613-236 0468)
- 1500 Avenue des Pins Ouest, Montreal, PQ H3G 1B4 (☎ 514-937 9481)
- 2603 Lakeshore Blvd West, Toronto, ON M8V 1G5 (☎ 416-252 4171)
- 1177 West Hastings St, suite 1600, Vancouver, BC V6E 2K3 (☎ 604-688 3530)

Netherlands
- Alexanderstraat 25, 2514 JM The Hague (☎ 070-360 5812)

New Zealand
- 17 Upland Rd, Kelburn, Wellington (☎ 04-712 456)

UK
- 73 New Cavendish St, London W1N 7RB (☎ 0171-580 0476)
- 2 Kinnear Rd, Edinburgh EH3 5PE (☎ 31-552 0301)

USA
- 2640 16th St NW, Washington, DC 20009 (☎ 202-234 3800)
- 233 Madison Ave, New York, NY 10016 (☎ 212-889 8360)
- 1530 North Lake Shore Dr, Chicago, IL 60610 (☎ 312-337 8166)
- 3460 Wilshire Blvd, suite 1200, Los Angeles, CA 90010 (☎ 213-365 7900)

MONEY

One of the successes of the Mazowiecki government was the establishment of the złoty (zł) as a convertible currency. By legalising private currency trading (the former 'black market') in 1990 and allowing the country's currency to find its own value on the open market, Poland took a giant step along the road to economic reform.

You can pay for everything (except visas, duty-free goods and international transportation tickets) directly in Polish złoty with no exchange receipts and changing money is the easiest thing in the world, provided you have cash. You'll find private exchange offices known as 'kantory' all around Poland offering excellent commission-free exchange rates, but they rarely accept travellers' cheques. These offices stay open long hours, occasionally around the clock, and they're so numerous we don't usually bother listing them herein: when you need one you'll probably find one.

Travellers' cheques are not welcome in Poland. Only a few main banks will accept them and commissions *(prowizya)* of 1 to 2% with a minimum charge of US$2 to US$3 are standard. Main branches of the Narodowy Bank Polski (NBP) and the Polska Kasa Opienki or PKO Bank (also known as the Bank Pekao SA) change travellers' cheques, but you have to search for a branch willing to do it, line up and wait while they complete the paperwork. After that you'll get a rate lower that you'd have got in seconds without commission for cash at a private kantor. The PKO Bank is usually more efficient than the NBP and keeps longer hours. Most other banks simply refuse to change travellers' cheques at all, so bring cash if you possibly can.

Some Polish banks insist on seeing the original purchase receipt you got when you bought your travellers' cheques, even though such receipts are supposed to be carried separately for security. Rather than argue it's best to adopt a condescending attitude and humour these quaint officials by carrying your receipts together with your travellers' cheques (keep a record of the numbers elsewhere).

If you neglected to bring sufficient hard currency in cash, it's useful to know that the PKO bank will change dollar travellers' cheques into dollars cash for a half percent commission (minimum US$2). You can then take the cash dollars to any private kantor and buy złoty with no commission. The first chance you get, change enough travellers' cheques into dollars cash to cover your entire remaining stay in Poland (then guard the money with your life).

Credit cards are only accepted in Orbis hotels and expensive restaurants and shops which cater mostly to tourists. The best known cards are American Express, Visa, Diners Club, Eurocard and Access/MasterCard. In late 1990 an American Express office offering all the usual services opened in Warsaw.

Before you leave Poland it's usually no problem changing złoty back into hard currency at private exchange offices. Don't leave it to the last minute to do this, however, as some exchange offices right on the border may be unwilling to change back and the złoty is not recognised outside Poland. You might want to take the opportunity to pick up some Czech or Slovakian currency, to ease your entry into those countries. Poland's private exchange offices are also perfect places to unload all those leftover Turkish, Bulgarian and Romanian banknotes you've been carrying around!

You used to have to fill out a currency declaration upon arrival to inhibit you from changing the declared money on the black market. Now if they ask to see your money it's because they suspect that you may not have enough to support yourself while in Poland. Only cash in excess of US$10,000 must be declared in writing upon arrival. Keep any Polish or other Eastern European banknotes out of sight at the border, however, as they may still be forbidden to import/export.

Thanks to the deregulation of foreign exchange trading the black market in Poland is dead and if you change money with someone on the street, you're likely to get *less* than you would at a private exchange office and run the risk of being ripped off.

Currency

Poland may have a greater variety of banknotes in circulation than any other country. Depicted on the banknotes are the commander in chief of the International Brigades during the Spanish Civil War, Karol Świerczewski (50 złoty); 19th-century socialist activist Ludwik Waryński (100 złoty); Paris Commune commander in chief Jarosław Dąbrowski (200 złoty); 18th-century patriot Tadeusz Kościuszko (500 złoty); 16th-century astronomer Mikołaj Kopernik (1000 złoty); 10th-century king Mieszko I (2000 złoty); 19th-century composer Frédéric Chopin (5000 złoty); early 20th-century artist Stanisław Wyspiański (10,000 złoty); radium co-discoverer Maria Skłodowska-Curie (20,000 złoty); 18th-century geologist Stanisław Staszic (50,000 złoty); 19th-century opera composer Stanisław Moniuszko (100,000 złoty); author Henryk Sienkiewicz (500,000 złoty); author Wladyslaw Reymont (1,000,000 złoty), and composer/pianist Ignacy Jan Paderewski (2,000,000 złoty). The 200,000 note has been withdrawn.

When you first arrive, study Poland's banknotes carefully as the high denominations and great variety of bills can be confusing. The similar colour and appearance of the 200 and 20,000 and the 1000 and 100,000 notes doesn't help either! Watch out for counterfeit banknotes. Genuine notes have a watermark you can see if you hold the bill up to the light and the lettering on the

MARY BEERS

notes has a slightly elevated texture you can feel. Carefully check all bills of a half million złoty or more. Złoty banknotes printed before 1975 are worthless.

Exchange Rates

In 1981 one US dollar was worth 34 złoty; in 1986, 160 złoty; in November 1987, 310 złoty; in May 1989, 3750 złoty; and in July 1989, 6000 złoty. By late 1990 it was relatively stable at 9000 to the dollar, but by early 1994 it had devalued further to 22,000 to the dollar. Inflation was 251% in 1989, 586% in 1990, 70% in 1991, 45% in 1992 and 35% in 1993.

There's only one market exchange rate now, which is somewhere between what the old official and black market rates would have been. This makes accommodation cheaper while all other prices are still very manageable in hard currency terms. There's no systematic cheating in Poland and everyone pays the same price for food, accommodation, transport and admissions – quite a contrast to most other Eastern European countries where foreigners are often charged prices several times higher than those paid by locals.

A$1	=	16,896zł
AS1	=	2088zł
DM1	=	14,742zł
Kč1	=	815zł
Sfr1	=	17,459zł
Sk1	=	722zł
UK£1	=	35,354zł
US$1	=	22,740zł

Costs

You should be able to see Poland in relative comfort following the recommendations in this book for under US$25 per person per day. That includes a room at a budget-priced hotel, at least one meal a day at a regular restaurant, and admissions and 2nd-class transportation by train. Couples, families and small groups will spend less, and if you camp or sleep in hostels, and eat only at self-services you could easily end up spending under US$15 per person per day.

Museum admission fees are usually under US$1 (US$0.50 for students). Before congratulating yourself on how cheap it is, remember that Polish workers only make the equivalent of about US$200 a month.

Aside from being a bonanza for budgeteers, the low prices open other possibilities. If you're tired of travelling and want to hang out somewhere for a while, you can live very well in Poland on US$20 a day, provided you stay in one place. Ask any tourist office to find you a Polish language tutor, then just pass your time reading, writing, studying, painting or whatever. The friends you make during that time could end up being friends for life.

Tipping

Poles generally tip waiters, taxi drivers and hairdressers by rounding up the bill to the next even figure as they're paying. Rounding up by much over 10% is unusual but failing to round up at all suggests dissatisfaction with the service. Tips are never left on restaurant tables. If a 10% service charge is added to a restaurant bill there's no need to tip, although you could still round up slightly if it's only a small amount. Cloakroom and toilet attendants collect a small fee which is usually posted, otherwise put the equivalent of about US$0.10 in the bowl.

CLIMATE & WHEN TO GO

Poland has a moderate continental climate with considerable maritime influence along the Baltic coast, which makes conditions variable from year to year. Spring is a time of warm days and chilly nights, while summer (from June to August) can be hot. Autumn (September to November) brings some rain and there can be snow from December to March. In the mountains the snow lingers until mid-April. From around late October to February it gets dark around 5 pm.

The sea coast is the sunniest part of the country in summer; the Carpathian Mountains are sunnier in winter. July is the hottest month, February the coolest. Warsaw has average daily temperatures above 14°C from

May to September, above 8°C in April and October and below freezing from December to February. Expect Poland to be cooler and rainier than Western Europe.

In the mountains the ski season runs from December to mid-March, though between Christmas and New Year all the facilities will be packed. Spring (April and May) is a good time for sightseeing. Another major advantage of visiting Poland in spring is that the theatre and concert season will be in full swing, allowing you to see outstanding performances almost every night. Mountain hiking and camping are good and uncrowded in June and September; late August and early September are a relatively dry, sunny time to tour the Great Mazurian Lakes. To swim in the Baltic you'll have to come in July and August. The cities are visitable all year, and winter is sometimes even preferable as most theatres and concert halls are closed throughout summer.

SUGGESTED ITINERARIES

Depending on the length of your stay, you might want to see and do the following things in Poland:

Two days
: Visit Kraków.

One week
: Visit Kraków, Warsaw and Gdańsk.

Two weeks
: Visit Kraków, Zakopane, Warsaw, the Great Mazurian Lakes, Gdańsk and Wrocław.

One month
: Visit most of the places included in this chapter.

TOURIST OFFICES

Most cities have municipal tourist offices, such as Syrena in Warsaw and Wawel Tourist in Kraków, often identified by the letters IT *(Informacja Turystyczna)* on the door. These places are usually good sources of information and some also try to cover costs by selling various tickets and arranging private-room accommodation. Gromada, Juventur, Sports-Tourist and Turysta are tourism cooperatives catering exclusively to the domestic market. They don't usually arrange accommodation, sell train tickets or speak English.

Orbis is the largest travel agency in Poland with offices in cities and towns all around the country. Like commercial travel agencies in the West, its main functions are to make reservations, sell transportation tickets and book rooms at luxury hotels. Its staff will also give information if they're not too busy, and in most offices there's somebody who speaks English. They're not paid to provide free information, however, so don't hold it against them if they won't (try asking general questions about budget travel at an American Express office and see how far you get).

The Polish Tourists & Country-Lovers' Association (PTTK) has offices in towns and resort areas which often know about accommodation in city dormitories, camping grounds and mountain huts, and even have information on hitchhiking *(autostop)*. But English is seldom spoken, and what the staff tell you about facilities outside their immediate area may be unreliable. They often sell excellent indexed city or hiking maps of both their own and other areas, so always have a look inside whenever you see the letters PTTK.

Student Travel

Almatur is the Travel & Tourism Bureau of the Union of Polish Students. Its offices issue ISIC student cards (US$5) and know about student accommodation in July and August.

The ISIC (International Student Identity Card) card is valid in Poland for student reductions *(ulgowa)* on museum admissions and train or ferry tickets.

Almatur organises excellent weekly horse riding and sailing holidays which foreign students may join. In July and August there are Almatur International Camps of Labour in which participants work 46 hours a week as construction, agricultural, or forest labourers. After work there are excursions, sporting and cultural events etc. Get details from Orbis offices abroad or the Almatur office in Warsaw.

Orbis Offices Abroad

Orbis offices outside Poland include:

Netherlands
  Orbis, Leidsestraat 64 (upstairs)
  1017 PD Amsterdam (☎ 020-625 3570)
UK
  Polorbis, 82 Mortimer St, London W1N 7DE
  (☎ 0171-637 4971)
USA
  Orbis, 342 Madison Ave, suite 1512, New York,
  NY 10173 (☎ 212-867 5011)

USEFUL ORGANISATIONS

Every November the Polish globetrotters club, Travel-Bit (Box 258, 30-965 Kraków 69, Poland), organises a weekend meeting called OSOTT (Ogólnopolskie Spotkania Organizatorów Turystyki Trampingowej) to which all travellers are cordially invited. Every participant gets 15 minutes to show his/her slides and sessions have been known to continue until 5 am! Write at least two months in advance for the exact place and date of this years OSOTT.

The Exploration Society, another Polish travel club, meets in Warsaw every Friday afternoon at 6.30 pm. Call ☎ 022-227 436 or 022-224 870 for more information.

BUSINESS HOURS & HOLIDAYS

Banking hours are weekdays from 8 am to 1 pm with main branches open until 5 pm. Stores are generally open weekdays from 11 am to 7 pm, although this can vary an hour or two either way. Grocery stores open earlier and open Saturday until 1 pm. In smaller towns almost everything is closed on Sunday. Many businesses post their hours on the door.

Milk bars tend to open between 6 and 9 am and close between 5 and 8 pm. Restaurants stay open later. With privatisation and increased competition, businesses keep longer hours than they did.

Museums usually open at 9 or 10 am and close anywhere from 3 to 6 pm, with slightly shorter hours in winter. Most museums close on Monday, although a few maverick institutions close on Tuesday and occasionally both days. Most are also closed on days following public holidays. Most live theatres are closed on Monday and from the end of June to the end of September.

Public holidays in Poland include New Year (1 January), Easter Monday (March/April), Labour Day (1 May), Constitution Day (3 May), Corpus Christi (a Thursday in May or June), Assumption Day (15 August), All Saints' Day (1 November), Independence Day (11 November) and Christmas (25 and 26 December).

Independence Day commemorates 11 November 1918 when Poland reappeared on the map of Europe. Poland is a poor place to spend New Year's Eve as virtually every restaurant and bar except those in the luxury hotels will be rented out for private parties or closed.

As many as a dozen trade fairs and exhibitions a year are held in Poznań, the largest of which are the International Technical Fair in June and the Consumer Goods Fair in October. For information about the fairs contact: Poznań International Fair (☎ 061-692 592; fax 061-665 827), Głogowska 14, 60-734 Poznań. An international book fair is held in Warsaw in May.

CULTURAL EVENTS

Poland's many annual festivals provide the opportunity to experience the best in music, film and folklore amid an exciting cultural milieu. All the annual events referred to in the following paragraph are listed in the city sections under 'entertainment'; also ask at local tourist information offices.

Classical music festivals are held in Łańcut (May), Toruń (September) and Wrocław (December), while contemporary music festivals are held at Wrocław (February), Poznań (March), Zakopane (July), Warsaw (September) and Kraków (November). For organ music it's Kraków (April) and Gdańsk (July and August). Singing can be heard at Kraków (April), Opole (June), Gdańsk (from June to August), Sopot (August) and Wrocław (September).

Jazz festivals are held at Wrocław (May), Warsaw (October) and Kraków (September and October). Poland's leading folk festivals are those of Toruń (May), Żywiec (August) and Zakopane (August).

Film festivals are held at Kraków (May)

and Gdańsk (September). Annual street fairs take place in Poznań (June or July) and Gdańsk (June and August).

POST

Main post offices *(poczta)* are open from 8 am to 8 pm weekdays and in large cities one post office stays open around the clock. Always use airmail, even for parcels. Most mail boxes are red.

A good place to have mail sent is c/o Poste Restante, Poczta Główna, ulica Świętokrzyska 31/33, 00-001 Warszawa 1, Poland. Mail can be picked up there daily from 8 am to 8 pm at window No 12.

American Express card-holders can have mail sent c/o American Express Travel, Dom Bez Kantow, Krakowskie Przedmieście 11, 00-068 Warszawa, Poland. You must show your American Express card when collecting mail.

For the addresses of other potential mail drops, turn to Post & Telephone in the Kraków, Wrocław and Gdańsk sections of this book.

TELEPHONE

Improvements to Poland's antiquated telephone system have been announced several times, but as yet not much has materialised. It's said the Polish joke originated among people trying to communicate by phone.

The easiest way to make calls is with a phonecard purchased at a post office. These cards cost US$2 for 50 units or US$4 for 100 units, and are valid for domestic or international calls. Tokens (US$0.05) are used for local calls and some old phones still accept a C token for international calls.

Blue card telephones (often found outside post offices) can be used for all types of calls, though only half of them will be in actual working order at any given time and even those that do work only successfully make international connections one try in five. You'll often get a number you didn't dial or a busy signal which probably means that all the lines are engaged – try again.

In Warsaw and Zakopane the blue card phones work well, while in Poznań and Gdańsk they're hopeless. In Kraków card phones are so rare that the few that do exist always have a queue of people waiting. Card phones in hotel lobbies are the ones most likely to work and you've a better chance of getting though outside business hours.

If you place a call through an operator at a main post office it should go through right away, but will be more expensive than it would have been using a phonecard (US$4 for three minutes to Western Europe). The price of calls placed from hotels is much higher again than what you'd pay to call from a main post office.

To call Poland from abroad, dial the international access code (different from each country), then 48 (the country code for Poland), the area code (without the initial zero) and the number. Important area codes include 2 (with seven-digit phone numbers in Warsaw), 22 (with six-digit numbers in Warsaw), 12 (Kraków), 34 (Częstochowa), 56 (Toruń), 58 (Gdańsk and Gdynia), 59 (Łeba), 61 (Poznań), 71 (Wrocław), 81 (Lublin), 84 (Zamość), 89 (Olsztyn) and 165 (Zakopane).

Inside Poland, add 0 before the Polish area code for domestic intercity calls or 00 (the Polish international access code) before the country code for international calls.

TIME

Time in Poland is GMT/UTC plus one hour. Poland goes on summer time at the end of March when clocks are turned forward an hour. At the end of September they're turned back an hour.

ELECTRICITY

The electric current is 220 V, 50 Hz. A circular plug with two round pins is used.

BOOKS & MAPS

Bookshops and tourist offices in Poland sell excellent city and regional maps, often complete with indexes, for under US$2. Tram and bus routes are shown on the maps, which is handy. The *Samochodowa Mapa Polski* is the best map of the country. Also watch for the comprehensive, 316-page *Polska Atlas Samochodowy*.

Lonely Planet's *Poland – a travel survival kit* by Krzysztof Dydyński is easily the best travel guide to Poland. The information was compiled independently of *Eastern Europe on a shoestring* and it's well worth picking up if you'll be spending much time in Poland. *Poland: The Rough Guide* is also excellent. A traditional guidebook strong on art and history is *Nagel's Encyclopedia-Guide Poland* (Nagel Publishers, Geneva, 1986), though the practical information is scanty.

The Polish Way by Adam Zamoyski (John Murray, London, 1987) is a superb cultural history of Poland full of maps and illustrations which bring the past 1000 years to life. This book reads as smoothly as a novel though it's 100% factual.

The Struggles for Poland by Neal Ascherson (Michael Joseph, London, 1987) developed from a television series on Polish history in the 20th century. Ascherson provides much information on the formative 1930s and 1940s when the physical shape of modern Poland was decided.

Isaac Bashevis Singer's masterful novel *Shosha* gives some insight into the lives and attitudes of Polish Jews prior to WW II.

Mad Dreams, Saving Graces by Michael T Kaufman (Random House, New York, 1989) is a fascinating insider's look at Poland from the imposition of martial law in 1981 to the eve of the fall of Polish communism in 1988.

Kaufman, the *New York Times* correspondent in Warsaw those years, really brings to life Father Jerzy Popiełuszko, Marek Edelman (the only surviving leader of the Warsaw Ghetto Uprising), government movers and Solidarity shakers.

The Captive Mind is a collection of essays by Nobel Prize-winning Polish poet and novelist Czesław Miłosz, who left Poland in 1951 and now lives in California. Published in 1953, the book shows how intellectuals were co-opted by communism.

Poland, A Novel by James A Michener (Ballantine Books, New York, 1983) is a readable dramatisation of the history of Poland.

MEDIA

Poland's English-language weekly is *The Warsaw Voice*, published by the Polish Interpress Agency. To subscribe for 26 weeks send US$78 to: The Warsaw Voice, PO Box 28, 00-950 Warszawa 1, Poland. This well-written paper is hard to find outside Warsaw so grab it when you see it.

Poland Today Monthly (Aleje Stanów Zjednoczonych 53, 04-028 Warsaw, Poland), published every two months by the Polish Information Agency, presents a sanitised official picture of Poland. Annual subscriptions are US$29 to Europe, US$34 to North America and US$43 to Australia.

Of the British papers, the *Guardian* is cheaper and more readily available than the *Times* because it's printed in Frankfurt and on sale the same day.

HEALTH

Most foreigners have to pay for medical treatment, although in emergencies it's often free. Citizens of the UK receive free treatment if they can prove coverage back home. Speaking English often helps to jump hospital queues as Polish doctors are all keen to practise their English. In Warsaw call your consulate for the name of a private doctor experienced in treating foreigners. Orbis offices abroad can arrange stays at Polish health spas.

As of mid-1993 there were 130 AIDS victims and another 2500 HIV-positive persons in Poland, most of them infected as a result of sharing needles or syringes during drug abuse.

DANGERS & ANNOYANCES

Many Poles are chain smokers, so choose your seating in restaurants, bars and trains with this in mind.

Don't establish eye contact with the colourfully dressed women you see sitting on the pavement begging, often with small children, as they can quickly become aggressive.

While Poland is a lot safer than most large

US or Western European cities, be aware of your surroundings on lonely streets in big cities and watch out for pickpockets in crowded train stations, especially in Warsaw. Most of the violent crime is perpetrated by persons from the former Soviet Union, not Poles. Watch out for small groups of robust, poorly dressed men hanging around train stations or at street markets, and avoid men standing in front of private exchange offices, as you never know what they're up to. If you stay clear of types like this and keep your eyes open, you'll be okay.

It's unwise to leave money and valuables unattended in hotel rooms. Lock your luggage if you can. By removing the temptation you'll usually eliminate the danger.

Drunks can sometimes be a nuisance, especially for women, and about all you can do is try to steer clear of them. They're not usually dangerous.

If you go to the police to report a crime, expect to encounter indolence and indifference. In small towns English-speaking police are rare, so it's best to take along an interpreter. Be both persistent and patient, and once the police see you're not about to simply go away they'll go through the motions of making an investigation. Don't expect a lot: the police earn next to nothing and they can be rather cynical about a 'rich' foreigner complaining about losing a few dollars.

Clerks in self-services and fast-food outlets will sometimes cheat you out of small amounts (US$0.10 etc). Defend yourself by asking the clerk to write down the amount due on a piece of paper before you produce any money (offer him/her a pen and paper). Often you'll be able to see the amount rung up on the cash register.

ACTIVITIES

Zakopane, Poland's premier southern mountain resort, features hiking in summer and skiing in winter. With a little effort you could also get in some rafting on the Dunajec River near Zakopane. Hikers less interested in meeting their fellows along the trails should consider instead the Bieszczady Mountains south of Przemyśl.

Mikołajki in the Great Mazurian Lakes district of north-east Poland is a major yachting centre with boats available for rent. Canoeists and kayakers will be quite at home here, and this part of Poland is flat enough also to appeal to cyclists, as is most of northern Poland.

See Tours under Getting Around (later in this chapter) for information on tour packages built around the above activities and horse riding.

Courses

Since 1969, Jagiellonian University (fax 48-12-227 701), Rynek Główny 34, 31-010 Kraków, Poland, has organised a summer school of Polish language and culture in July and August. The three, four, and six-week courses are taught in English by university faculty members. Write for information well ahead.

HIGHLIGHTS

Nature

Poland excels in mountains, lakes and coast. Those wishing to commune with the Baltic will find the beaches of Łeba unending and the sand dunes inspiring. Mikołajki is a fine place to begin exploring the 3000 Mazurian lakes, while Zakopane is the launching pad for hikes into the Tatras, Poland's most magnificent mountain range. The Białowieska Forest in Poland's far east is home to the largest remaining herd of European bison and other wildlife. Each of these environments is distinct and equally worth experiencing.

Museums & Galleries

Warsaw's National Museum holds Poland's largest and finest art collection, though Kraków's Czartoryski Art Museum has individual works which are unsurpassed. The Musical Instruments Museum in Poznań will delight music lovers, as will Chopin's birthplace at Żelazowa Wola, 50 km west of Warsaw. Finally, the Auschwitz Museum at

Oświęcim is perhaps the most meaningful of them all.

Castles

Malbork Castle, one-time seat of the Teutonic Knights, is perhaps the largest surviving medieval castle in Europe, while another 14th-century castle at Lidzbark Warmiński is less known but equally impressive. For hundreds of years Kraków's Wawel Castle sheltered Polish royalty, most of whom are still buried in the adjacent cathedral. Lublin Castle intrigues us with its remoteness and memories of Nazi atrocities committed within its walls. True castle lovers will seek out Pieskowa Skała Castle and nearly a dozen others along the Eagles' Nests Route from Kraków to Częstochowa.

Palaces

It's not surprising that Poland's capital, Warsaw, contains Poland's two most magnificent royal palaces: the 17th-century Wilanów Palace and the 18th-century Łazienki Palace. In the countryside feudal magnates built splendid Renaissance, baroque and rococo palaces such as the Branicki Palace at Białystok, the Rogalin Palace near Poznań, and Łańcut Palace.

Historic Towns

Of all Poland's cities, only Kraków, the de facto capital till 1596, survived WW II relatively untouched. The historic cores of Poznań, Toruń and Gdańsk have been masterfully restored. All three grew rich from trade in the Middle Ages, as the homes of rich burghers around their central squares and the magnificent churches attest. Zamość in south-east Poland is unique as a perfectly preserved 16th-century Renaissance settlement.

ACCOMMODATION

Camping

There are hundreds of camping grounds in Poland, many offering small timber cabins which are excellent value. IFCC cardholders get a 10% discount on camping fees. Theoretically most camping grounds are open from May to September, but they tend to close early if things are slow. The opening and closing dates listed in official brochures (and this book) are only approximate. The yellow *Polska Mapa Campingów* map lists most camping grounds.

Hostels

Poland is the only country in Eastern Europe with hostels similar to those of Western Europe. Although there's no maximum age limit, persons under 26 years have priority. Children under 10 years cannot use the hostels. Groups larger than five persons must book a month in advance and Polish school groups crowd the hostels from mid-May to mid-June. Persons without YHA membership cards are readily accepted though they pay a little more. Many hostels are open only in summer although the main ones operate all year. The hostels are closed from 10 am to 5 pm and you must arrive before 9 pm.

All 1100 HI hostels in Poland are run by the Polskie Towarzystwo Schronisk Młodzieżowych (PTSM) and have a green triangle over the entrance. A large percentage are located in school buildings. They're categorised as 1st, 2nd or 3rd class, with overnight charges at 1st-class hostels costing about US$4 for members 26 and under, US$5 for members aged over 26, and US$6 for non-members. Second and 3rd-class hostels are about US$1 cheaper. Some hostels have kitchens where you can cook your own food. In cities where there's more than one hostel, if the first hostel you visit is full they may be willing to call around to the others to find you a bed.

International Student Hotels

In July and August the Polish student travel agency, Almatur, arranges accommodation in vacant student dormitories in 17 university towns. The Almatur hotels tend to be far from the centre of town and the addresses change annually, so you'll have to ask about them at local Almatur offices. You share a room of one to four beds and there are usually cooking facilities, cheap cafeterias and even disco clubs on the premises.

Accommodation costs about US$11 single, US$9 for a bed in a double or US$7 per person in a triple. If you take the triple rate you'll often have the room to yourself anyway.

Private Rooms

It's possible to stay in private rooms *(prywatny pokóy)* in Poland, though they're less common than in Hungary. A few municipal tourist offices *(Biuro Zakwaterowań)* arrange private rooms but their prices are sometimes high, almost what you'd pay for a budget hotel. The agencies classify the rooms according to 1st, 2nd or 3rd category. Singles are scarce and during busy periods all their rooms could be full.

Sometimes you're offered a private room by an individual on the street outside a tourist office or private room agency. Their prices may be lower and open to bargaining. In some cities like crowded Kraków and Gdańsk these 'black' rooms are good places to stay. Beware of rooms far from the centre of town.

Hotels

Hotels are graded from one to five stars, and unlike the Czech Republic and Slovakia where foreigners are charged double or triple, in Poland everyone pays the same price for rooms. Orbis hotels are all in the expensive, three and four-star category and a few hotels belonging to international chains such as Inter-Continental and Marriott are five-star. Municipal hotels are usually cheaper, and the PTTK has a chain of 'Dom Turysty' and 'Dom Wycieczkowy' which have hotel rooms and dorm beds. A country inn is called a *zajazd* or *gościniec*.

Hotel prices vary according to the season and these are different in the various regions of Poland. At Zakopane the high ski season is from mid-December to March, while in Poznań hotel rates increase dramatically at trade fair time. The low season runs from October to April in northern Poland and Wrocław, or from November to March in Kraków. In Warsaw hotel prices are the same throughout the year. Rooms booked from abroad through a travel agency or Orbis are much more expensive than what you'd pay locally.

Rates are usually posted on a board at hotel reception desks. Compare the price of a room with private bath to one with shared bath. Sometimes it's only a slight difference, other times it's a lot. If in doubt about the quality ask to *see* a room before checking in, in which case it's unlikely they'll give you their worst room. On arrival day, hotel rooms cannot be occupied until after noon, 2 or 4 pm, so leave your things at the station.

FOOD

Milk Bars

In Poland the word 'bar' is almost always used in the sense of snack bar or refreshment bar, and 'cocktail' means fruit cocktail or something similar. The cheapest places to eat in Poland are milk bars *(bar mleczny)* which are also good places to try local dishes not available at expensive restaurants. If you want an inexpensive fruit juice with your meal ask for *kompot*. Avoid the meat dishes at milk bars, however, as they're priced three or four times higher than anything else so most Poles don't take them and you could end up with something that's been on display for quite a while.

Milk bars are self-service *(samoobsługa)*. You either pay at the end of the line cafeteria-style or, more often, you pay first and get a receipt which you hand to the person dispensing the food. This can be confusing if you don't know the Polish name of whatever it is you want, but most cashiers are patient and will try to understand if you point to something someone else is eating. Try asking the person in line behind you what a particular dish is called. Sometimes you'll order the wrong thing, which adds to the excitement.

The cashiers at milk bars are often apprehensive about dealing with unpredictable foreigners and you yourself may be slightly intimidated by the unfamiliar food and surroundings. A smile and a sense of humour will go a long way here. You'll make yourself popular with milk bar staff by carrying your dirty dishes back to the counter, as you see others doing. Milk-bar lines usually move quickly, so don't be put off.

Some milk bars close on Saturday afternoons and all day Sunday. Breakfast is a bit of a problem as most milk bars only open at 9 am. Keep in mind that the difference in price between a fast-food stand and a 1st-class restaurant is much less in Poland than it is in the west. Eat at self-service cafeterias to save time, not money, and whenever you have the time to enjoy a proper meal, go to one of the better restaurants listed herein or any top-end hotel, not a milk bar. Now that milk bars have to make a profit they're having a hard time competing and it's sad to see them being replaced by US-style fast-food outlets serving bland unappetising fare on plastic plates.

Restaurants

Restaurants and coffee shops at the luxury Orbis hotels have the widest selection of dishes and the best service, although the atmosphere can be pretentious and even dull. These are the *only* places in Poland where you can get a reasonable English breakfast of ham and eggs with juice, but it's expensive at about US$5. Ask your hotel if they have some arrangement for breakfast vouchers. Elsewhere you may have to settle for soup.

Always ask to see the menu and have a look at the prices. Waiters who speak English or German and simply tell you what's available will charge extra for the service. If a waiter wants to be helpful, ask him or her to translate the menu or tell you what's available, as very few Polish restaurants offer everything listed. Soup is *zupy* and a main course is *dania*. Watch for the *obiad firmowy* (recommended meal) on restaurant menus.

When ordering seafood keep in mind that you will be charged by weight, and the price on the menu may only be for 100 grams. Expect to be charged extra for the bread, butter, sauces and vegetables with the meals. If beer prices aren't listed on the menu expect them to be much higher than usual. Beware of accepting things you didn't order, such as a sliced tomato salad, as this could be a ploy to double your bill. Also beware of waiters who come back five minutes after they've taken your order to tell you something isn't available. If you accept their suggestion of a substitute without asking to see the menu again and re-checking prices, your bill will be substantially increased. Many Polish waiters have worked out what 'Wow, that's cheap!' means and do their best to hear it less often.

In Polish restaurants it's customary to occupy any vacant seat, which can be a problem if you don't smoke. If you're wearing a coat you must deposit it at the coat check whenever there is one. It's also customary to round restaurant bills up to the next higher unit (but only in places with table service, not in milk bars). Write what you want to pay on the bill. If you feel you've been overcharged pay the exact amount asked and don't bother rounding up.

It may be cheap to eat in Poland (for tourists) but too often the quality reflects the price. Menus are usually only in Polish, occasionally in German and very seldom in English. Many things on the menu will not be available anyway, and whole categories such as soups and desserts may be unavailable. Salads are almost never fresh but pickled, and fresh fruit and vegetables are rare. Almost every dish includes some meat, so vegetarians will have a problem. Salt and pepper are usually not on the table, so you must either catch the waiter's attention or get up and search the other tables yourself.

The main meal in Poland is eaten at lunchtime. As a result, restaurants often close unexpectedly early (at 8 pm), forcing you to dine on cake and ice cream if you left it too late. Many restaurants have live music and 'dancing' after 7 pm, bringing food service to an end. It can also be hard to find an inexpensive restaurant open on Sunday, and many restaurants are closed for wedding receptions on weekends. The political changes in Poland have at least made it much easier to get a beer with your meal. Restaurant difficulties due to a poor supply situation may be understandable but the low level of service is not.

Cafés & Bars
Few restaurants serve dessert, so for cake and ice cream go to a *kawiarnia* (café). Alcohol is also served at these. Polish cafés are social meeting places where people sit around and talk. A *winiaria* is a wine bar. Polish ice cream *(lody)* is excellent.

Polish Specialities
Poland is a land of hearty soups such as *botwinka* (beet greens soup), *kapuśniak* (cabbage soup), *krupnik* (potato soup), *rosół* (bouillon with little dumplings stuffed with meat), *zacierka* (noodle soup) and *żurek* (sour cream soup). Many traditional Polish dishes originated farther east, including Russian borsch or *barszcz* (red beet soup), Lithuanian *chłodnik* (cold pink cream soup), *kołduny* (turnovers with meat) and *kulebiak* (cabbage and mushroom loaf).

Two world-famous Polish dishes are *bigos* (sauerkraut and meat) and *pierogi* (ravioli-like dumplings served with potatoes and cheese or sauerkraut and mushrooms). If you've got a strong stomach *fasolka po bretónska* (Brittany beans) is a heavy-duty dish, but don't consume a plate of it just before embarking on a long train trip as it may backfire and make you very unpopular.

A few special Polish dishes to watch for on restaurant menus are *kaczka* (roast duck) or *gęś* (goose) with apples, *zraz* (pound steak in cream sauce), *kotlet schabowy* (breaded pork cutlet), *golonka* (pea purée with pig's leg and sauerkraut), *flaki* (tripe Polish style) and sauerkraut with sausage and potatoes. *Zawijasy słowiańskie* is a meat roll of spicy stuffing wrapped in ham and deep fried. Beefsteak tartar is raw minced meat with a raw egg, sardine, chopped onions and seasoning. Only sample this at a 1st-class establishment where you can be sure of the quality. A favourite Polish fast food is *zapiekanka,* a long bread roll baked with onions, cheese and mushrooms on top.

Mushrooms *(grzyby)* have always been great favourites in Poland, either boiled, pan-fried, stewed, sautéed, pickled or marinated. Cucumbers are served freshly sliced and seasoned with honey, pepper or cream as a salad *(mizeria)*. *Ćwikła* is a salad of red beetroot with horseradish. Potatoes are made into dumplings, patties or pancakes *(placki ziemniaczane)*. *Kopytka* is chunks of dough served with a semi-sweet sauce – good for breakfast at milk bars. *Pyzy* is similar to *kopytka* except that the chunks are stuffed with meat. A traditional Polish dessert is *mazurek* (shortcake). In early summer you can get fresh strawberries, raspberries or blueberries with cream. Hot chocolate is called *kakao*.

DRINKS
Some restaurants have certain rooms in which alcoholic drinks are not served (beware of signs reading *sala bezalkoholowa)*. Alcoholism has long been a big problem in Poland and is getting bigger still. The minimum drinking age is 18 years.

Under the communists the only alcoholic beverage you could usually get was vodka. Now excellent beer in healthy half-litre bottles is available everywhere, though it's still hard to find it cold. If you don't say *zimne piwo* (pronounced 'jimne pivo') when ordering you'll automatically get it at room temperature, even in 1st-class restaurants. When ordering beer at restaurants always ask for Polish beer, unless the price of imported beer is clearly indicated on the menu. Otherwise you could end up paying 50% more for German or Czech beer than you would for an acceptable Polish equivalent such as Żywiec, Leżajsk, Okocim or Piast. Pool halls usually have bars where you can get a beer and other drinks at normal prices. Watch for the name *bilard*.

Red and black currant juices are popular nonalcoholic drinks. All wine is imported so pay attention to the price which may be for a glass, not a bottle. Vodka (served chilled) is the national drink, which the Poles claim was invented here. Other notable drinks include *myśliwska* (vodka flavoured with juniper berries), *śliwowica* (plum brandy) and *winiak* (grape brandy). The favourite Polish toast is *na zdrowie* (to your health), sometimes followed by a rendition of *Sto lat*, a popular hymn which means 'may you live 100 years'.

ENTERTAINMENT

A section near the back of the daily papers carries announcements of concerts, plays etc, plus cinema times and even museum hours. It doesn't take any knowledge of Polish to understand these listings, as Handel is Handel and Schubert, Schubert in any language. The name and address of the theatre are usually given, and a quick stop there to check the information and pick up tickets clinches the matter. When checking theatre listings it's important to check *both* local papers, as the list in one may be incomplete.

Discos are common in Poland, usually opening around 9 pm from Thursday to Saturday. Also ask about jazz clubs, operetta, opera, concerts, special events and so on at your hotel reception or at local tourist offices. Operetta performances will be in Polish, opera in the original language.

Cinemas

Movies are usually shown in the original language with Polish subtitles, and the admission is cheap. Unfortunately, most are Hollywood productions and films by outstanding Polish directors such as Andrzej Wajda, Krzysztof Zanussi and Waldemar Krzytek are a rarity. (One Hollywood film *about* Poland which you won't want to miss is Steven Spielberg's *Schindler's List*.)

Every year from mid-April to May there's a nationwide film festival called 'Konfrontacje' with 15 award-winning movies shown in the original language at selected cinemas around the country. A different film is shown each night during two 15-day cycles. This is one Polish institution other countries would do well to imitate!

THINGS TO BUY

Cepelia shops belonging to the Folk Art & Crafts Cooperatives Union sell authentic local handicrafts such as tapestries, rugs, embroidery, lace, hand-painted silks, sculptures in wood, pottery, paper cut-outs, folk toys, icons, glassware, wrought-iron objects, silver jewellery and amber necklaces. Works by living professional artists are sold at Desa shops. Amber necklaces are an excellent portable souvenir typical of Poland, and a good necklace shouldn't cost over US$25. If buying amber see the Malbork Castle exhibits first.

Desa shops have information on complicated Polish export regulations, so check before making large purchases. Basically, it's forbidden to take out any item manufactured before 9 May 1945, works of art and books included. Otherwise you're allowed to export goods from Poland up to a value of US$100 duty-free. Large quantities of crystal or amber will be scrutinised. Official sales receipts should be kept for valuable items.

Since 1989 the retail trade in Poland has come out of the shops into the streets with thousands of small pavement vendors displaying wares they often purchased on 'tourist' trips to other countries. Almost two-thirds of all music recordings sold in Poland are unauthorised 'pirate' copies.

Getting There & Away

AIR

The national carrier, LOT Polish Airlines, flies to Warsaw from Bangkok, Beijing, Cairo, Chicago, Damascus, Dubai, Istanbul, Larnaca, Montreal, Newark, New York, Singapore, Tel Aviv, Toronto and numerous European cities. In recent years LOT has retired its fleet of gas-guzzling, maintenance-intensive Tupolevs and Ilyshins and now flies mostly Western aircraft.

Regular one-way fares to Warsaw are not cheap: US$450 from Frankfurt/Main, US$535 from Amsterdam, US$550 from Paris and US$475 from London. Ask travel agents about special excursion and advance purchase excursion fares on LOT and note the restrictions. People aged 22 years and under get a 25% discount on flights from Western Europe.

LOT has 'Super Saver' fares from New York to Warsaw ranging from US$588 return in the low season to US$848 return in the high season. The minimum stay is seven days, the maximum one month. One-way fares are US$499 to US$1064. These prices are for midweek departures; weekend departures are about US$60 more per return ticket. In the USA call LOT for information on ☎ 800-223 0593 toll free (in Canada ☎ 800-361 1017).

A travel agency in the US specialising in Poland is Fregata (☎ 212-541 5707; fax 212-262 3220), 250 West 57th St, New York, NY 10107.

Bucket shops in Europe and Asia sell LOT tickets at deep discounts, usually on fares from Asia to Western Europe or vice versa with a free stopover in Warsaw. Ask around the budget travel agencies in Singapore, Penang, Bangkok, London and Amsterdam for deals.

Travel Agencies

Although Poland isn't a mecca for people in search of cheap long-distance flights, a few Polish travel agencies such as Sawa Tour, ulica Wspólna 65a, Warsaw, and World Computer Travel (☎ 061-481 342), ulica Dąbrowskiego 5, 60-848 Poznań, try to offer competitive fares. Of course, you could probably do better in Berlin, Amsterdam or London, but you'll have to add the cost of getting there and your expenses while shopping around and waiting for a reservation.

Departure Tax

The airport tax on international flights is US$10 at Warsaw, US$8 at Gdańsk and Kraków and US$7 at all other airports. There's no airport tax on domestic flights.

LAND

Bus

The cheapest way to travel to Poland from the UK, Holland and many other Western European countries is by bus, costing much less than a train or plane ticket. In Britain, the companies to call are Eurolines National Express (☎ 0171-730 8235), 52 Grosvenor Gardens, Victoria, London SW1W 0AC; Fregata (☎ 0171-734 5101), 100 Dean St, London W1V 6AQ; Fregata (☎ 0161-226 7227), 117 Withington Rd, Manchester MI6 7EU; and the Buchananan Bus Station, Killermont St, Glasgow. The Fregata bus leaves the Victoria Coach Station weekly year-round (three times a week from June to September). Fares from London to Warsaw are £70 one way, £110 return (30 hours) with reductions for those aged under 26 and over 59 years.

Budget Bus/Eurolines (☎ 020-627 5151), Rokin 10, Amsterdam, runs buses twice a week year-round from Amsterdam to Kraków, Warsaw and Gdańsk. All services depart from each end in the late afternoon and arrive at their destination by mid-morning (17 hours). The fare on all these services is US$88 one way, US$140 return (10% reduction for students and persons aged under 26 or over 59 years). For information on similar buses from Brussels to Warsaw (27 hours) contact Eurolines (☎ 217 0025), Place de Brouckere 50, Brussels.

Polish buses leave regularly for Western European cities and they're also cheaper than the train. Many of the companies selling international bus tickets are listed under the heading Travel Agencies in the main city sections of this chapter.

A Hungarian Volanbus runs daily between Budapest and Zakopane (nine hours, US$14).

Some Polish buses to Ukraine, Belorussia, Lithuania and Russia use border crossings still closed to Western tourists, so be sure to confirm that the border crossing you intend to use is in fact open to you when you pick up your visa (a list of places reliably open is provided under Car & Motorbike in this section).

To/From Lithuania Beware of travelling from Poland to Lithuania by train as the 425-km railway line from Warsaw to Vilnius via Grodno passes through Belorussia for 27 km and the Belorussian border guards come aboard and slap unsuspecting tourists with a US$30 Belorussian transit visa fee which is reportedly valid for a return trip. Avoid this rip-off by taking a bus from Poland direct to Lithuania. Orbis, Bracka 16, Warsaw, sells tickets for buses from Warsaw to Vilnius, otherwise catch one of the two morning buses (marked 'Wilno') to Vilnius from Suwałki in north-eastern Poland (209 km, US$7). They often sell out so make getting a ticket a priority. An unreserved local train leaves Suwałki every morning for Šeštokai, Lithuania, along a secondary line which also avoids Belorussia. Arrive at Suwałki in good time to get a ticket.

Train

It's important to keep in mind that there are three price levels for tickets on Polish trains. The most expensive are tickets to Poland bought in Western Europe. Avoid these by breaking your journey in the Czech Republic, from where you pay the much cheaper rate for travel between Eastern European countries. Cheaper still are domestic fares within Poland itself. You can easily take advantage of these by breaking your journey at the first city inside Poland (Poznań, Wrocław, Katowice, Kraków, Nowy Sącz etc). Many of the 'name trains' mentioned below have compulsory seat reservations available at Orbis offices and train stations. International tickets should be purchased in advance at Orbis.

Almatur sells discounted Eurotrain tickets for train trips to Western Europe to persons under 26 years. Holders of students cards are supposed to get a 25% discount on train tickets for travel within the Eastern European countries but you may be told that the reduction only applies if your student card was issued in Eastern Europe. Turn to the Warsaw and Kraków sections of this book for the addresses of the special Almatur offices handling these tickets. The Inter-Rail pass (sold to European residents only) is valid in Poland.

To/From Western Europe The *Ost-West* express train leaves Paris-Nord daily for Warsaw (22 hours) via Poznań. Portions of other trains from Ostend and the Hook of Holland are attached to the *Ost-West* somewhere in Germany, providing direct connections to/from London's Liverpool Street Station (29 hours from Warsaw). Amsterdam passengers join the train at Amersfoort and a one-way 2nd-class ticket from Amsterdam to Poznań is US$105. Only 2nd-class seats are available though the train also carries sleeping cars. At Rzepin you can change for Wrocław.

If you're coming from London, catch the morning train that goes straight through to Poland and not the evening train which involves a train change in Germany.

A through train from Basel, Switzerland, to Warsaw (25 hours) via Wrocław runs five times a week but only sleepers are available (no seats).

To/From Germany Many trains run between Berlin-Lichtenberg and Warsaw (569 km, eight hours) via Frankfurt/Oder and Poznań. The Eurocity *Berolina* covers the distance in only 6½ hours, leaving Warsaw in the morning and Berlin-Hauptbahnhof in the afternoon. If you really want to save money only get a ticket from Berlin to Rzepin, the first major junction inside Poland. There you could buy a cheap onward ticket with złoty and connect for Poznań, Wrocław or Kraków.

The nightly *Gedania* express with seats and sleeping cars runs from Berlin-Lichtenberg to Gdynia (10 hours) via Szczecin. An overnight train runs from Cologne to Warsaw (16 hours) via Poznań. Trains from Cologne to Kraków (24 hours) travel via Leipzig, Dresden and Wrocław. Another line goes from Frankfurt/Main to Warsaw (22 hours) via Leipzig, Dresden and Wrocław.

To/From the Czech Republic & Austria The overnight *Bohemia* express train between Prague and Warsaw (740 km, 12 hours) travels via Wrocław. Between Wrocław and Prague (339 km) the journey takes about six hours. The *Silesia* express travels via Katowice between Prague and Warsaw (10 hours). The *Baltic* express train runs overnight from Prague to Gdańsk (16 hours) via Wrocław and Poznań.

The *Sobieski* and *Chopin* express trains both travel from Vienna-Süd to Warsaw via Břeclav and Katowice, the *Sobieski* taking nine hours by day, the *Chopin* 11 hours by night in both directions (753 km).

To/From Slovakia, Hungary & Beyond From Budapest the overnight *Báthory* express train runs daily to Warsaw (837 km, 13 hours) via Komarno, Púchov and Katowice. The *Polonia* express from Belgrade goes via Budapest, Komarno, Žilina and Katowice to Warsaw (21 hours from Belgrade). Change at Katowice for Kraków. Both these trains are routed through a short stretch of the Czech Republic, so beware of taking them if you require a Czech visa as you'll be put off the train at the border.

A different route through Košice in eastern Slovakia is followed by the overnight *Cracovia* express train from Budapest to Kraków (598 km, 12 hours). The *Karpaty* express train from Bucharest to Warsaw (31 hours) also travels via Košice, Nowy Sącz and Kraków (missing Budapest).

To western Poland there's the *Bem* express train from Budapest to Szczecin (1027 km, 18 hours) via Žilina, Wrocław and Poznań.

In addition, there are three unreserved local trains a day which take 20 minutes to hop across the border between Plaveč, Slovakia, and Muszyna, Poland. On the Slovakian side, these trains connect with other local trains to/from Prešov and Poprad-Tatry. Ask about the unreserved *Poprad* fast train from Kraków to Muszyna which doesn't run every day.

To/From China Orbis, ulica Bracka 16, Warsaw, sells train tickets to Beijing, China, via the Trans-Siberian Railway. The one-way fare with a 2nd-class sleeper is US$125 – the best deal you're likely to get on this route anywhere. First class is about 50% more. Orbis will need a day or two to make all the necessary reservations, then you can start visa hunting. These fares could change, so if you're thinking of coming to Poland primarily to take advantage of these prices, try calling Orbis in Warsaw at ☎ 022-270 105 to check the current situation.

Car & Motorbike

The names of the Polish border posts at the main highway crossings into Poland are given below. Other highway border crossings may be restricted to local residents and closed to Western tourists.

To/From Germany You can cross at Kołbaskowo (20 km west of Szczecin), Świecko (at Frankfurt/Oder), Olszyna (24 km east of Cottbus) and Zgorzelec (at Görlitz).

To/From the Czech Republic You may cross at Jakuszyce (between Liberec and Jelenia Góra), Kudowa-Zdrój (43 km east of Kłodzko), Chałupki (12 km north of Ostrava) and Cieszyn (31 km east of Ostrava).

To/From Slovakia It's Chyżne (west of Zakopane), Łysa Polana (east of Zakopane), Piwniczna (31 km south of Nowy Sącz) and Barwinek (between Rzeszów and Prešov).

To/From the former Soviet Union You can use Medyka (14 km east of Przemyśl) to enter Ukraine, Terespol (opposite Briest) and Kuźnica Białostocka (between Białystok and Grodno) to enter Belorussia, and Ogrodniki (13 km north-east of Sejhy) to enter Lithuania. The line of cars waiting to cross at Ogrodniki can be several km long, in which case a detour via Belorussia may be worth the transit-visa fee.

On Foot

If you want to avoid the hassle or increasing expense of getting an international train ticket, consider walking across the border. From Germany you can easily walk across the bridge over the Neisse/Nysa River from Görlitz to Zgorzelec, where there are frequent onward train services to Wrocław (163 km). Turn to the Silesia section of this chapter for a complete description.

The best place to walk across the Czech/Polish border is between Cieszyn (Poland) and Český Těšín (Czech Republic), virtually one city cut in half by the Olza River. On the Czech side the onward train connections to/from Prague and Žilina are good. More information on this crossing is provided at the end of the Małopolska section of this book.

If you'd like to walk across to/from Slovakia, the easiest place to do it is at Łysa Polana with frequent bus service from Zakopane and one bus a day from Kraków. For more information turn to the Zakopane section in this chapter and the Vysoké Tatry section in the Slovakia chapter.

SEA

Ferries

Polferries offers regular year-round service to Świnoujście and Gdańsk from Denmark, Sweden and Finland. Any travel agent in Scandinavia will have tickets; in Poland ask at an Orbis office.

There are services to Świnoujście from Copenhagen, Denmark, five times a week (nine hours, US$43 one way), and from Ystad, Sweden, twice a day (seven hours, US$33 one way). The service to Świnoujście from Rønne on Bornholm Island, Denmark, runs weekly from June to August only (five hours, US$23 one way),

Ferries sail to Gdańsk from Oxelösund, Sweden, weekly from October to May, three or four times a week from June to September (19 hours, US$38 one way), and from Helsinki, Finland, twice a week (35 hours, US$44 from mid-August to June and US$66 one way from July to mid-August).

Reservations are recommended for car or cabin accommodation although deck space is almost always available. Return tickets (valid for six months) are 20% cheaper than two one ways. Holders of ISIC student identity cards and pensioners receive a 20% discount on ferry tickets. Other reductions are available to families of three or more persons. Bicycles are carried free.

The Corona Line runs car ferries from Karlskrona, Sweden, to Gdynia year-round. In July the service is daily and the rest of the year it's about three times a week (15 hours, US$37).

Getting Around

AIR

LOT Polish Airlines operates domestic flights daily from Warsaw to Rzeszów, Kraków, Wrocław, Poznań, Szczecin and Gdańsk. The fare from Warsaw on all these flights is US$35 one way during the week, US$30 on weekends, and there's a 50% discount for those aged 24 years and under. Standby fares are not available. You must check in at least 30 minutes before domestic flights and passports must be shown.

BUS

Long distances are better covered in Poland by train (PKP) than by bus (PKS). Buses are used mostly in mountainous areas, such as around Zakopane, or along routes where there are no direct train connections. Seats on long-distance buses can and should be booked ahead. Baggage is allowed aboard free of charge.

Always check the footnotes on posted bus schedules as some buses don't operate daily. First look at the *odjazdy* column on the departures board to pick a bus that might suit you. Then write down the destination and time, and show it to the person at information to confirm that this bus really will run. Try to buy a ticket (sometimes you can do this the day before, sometimes only on the same day), then check the board again to find out which platform your bus will leave from, locate the platform, and check that your bus is listed on the board there (if any). If you follow this procedure you'll have few problems with Polish buses. Often you can also buy the ticket from the driver.

When asking for the bus station, write PKS on a piece of paper; for the train station write PKP.

TRAIN
The Polskie Koleje Panstwowe (PKP) operates over 27,092 km of railway line allowing you to reach almost every town by rail. Express trains *(expresowy)* with seat reservations are the best way to travel. Direct trains *(pośpieszne)* are also fast and don't usually require reservations, but are much more crowded. Local trains *(osobowe* or *normalne)* are OK for short trips and never require reservations. Polish trains and buses usually run on time.

The best trains are the 'name trains' which usually run to and from Warsaw. To use one of these express trains you must reserve a seat, but reservations are easily made up to two months in advance in main train stations or at Orbis offices (US$1.50). On departure day, reservations can only be made at the train station. The name trains have Wars dining cars and comfortable compartments – even 2nd class is quite luxurious. We list these trains throughout this chapter – be sure to take them whenever possible. Intercity trains are being introduced in Poland, for example, the IC *Lech* which travels from Warsaw to Poznań in three hours (308 km) and the IC *Sawa*, *Krakus* and *Kościuszko* from Warsaw to Kraków in 2½ hours (325 km). On some of these trains a light meal is included in the price.

As in other European countries, train departures *(odjazdy)* are usually listed on a yellow board while arrivals *(przyjazdy)* are on a white board. Express trains are in red, local trains in black. Watch for the symbol R enclosed in a box, which indicates a fully reserved train. Departure boards also indicate whether a train offers both 1st and 2nd-class accommodation, plus the train number and departure track *(peron)*. The Polish railway system goes on its summer timetable (with extra services) around 1 June.

Tickets for express trains are 50% more expensive than tickets for local stopping trains, so make sure you've got the correct ticket for your train (by writing your destination and the departure time on a piece of paper to show the cashier, for example). Otherwise the conductor will charge you a supplement. In large stations, tickets for different trains are sometimes sold at different windows. Check the train number over the window to make sure you're in the right line and ask information. If you're forced to get on a train without a ticket, find the conductor right away and he/she will sell you one with only a small supplement instead of the heavy fine you'd pay if he/she found you first. Tickets *are* checked on Polish trains.

Both 1st-class and 2nd-class train travel is inexpensive with 1st class costing 50% more than 2nd class. Sample fares for a 100-km trip are US$2 in 2nd class by local train, US$3 in 1st class by local train, US$3 in 2nd class by direct train, US$4.50 in 1st class by direct train, US$4 in 2nd class by express train or US$6 in 1st class by express train.

A Polrailpass providing unlimited travel on trains throughout Poland is available from North American travel agencies through Rail Europe (not for sale in Poland). The passes come in durations of eight days (US$40/59 2nd/1st class), 15 days (US$45/69), 21 days (US$50/70) and one month (US$55/85). Persons aged under 26 years on the first day of travel can buy a 'Junior' pass for about 20% less. Seat reservation fees are not included.

Couchettes & Sleepers
Overnight trains are a good way of saving money in Poland while getting to your destination. A 2nd-class ticket and couchette are often less than the price of a hotel, and you arrive in the next city early in the morning. The attendant in the sleeping car sells soft drinks and coffee and express trains often carry good stand-up dining cars. You can't beat a breakfast of *flaki* (tripe) and coffee (US$1.75).

Second-class couchettes (US$9) contain six beds to the compartment, three to a side. First-class sleepers (US$19) have only two beds. There's a third type called 'special' 2nd-class sleeper which has three beds to the compartment (US$14). It used to be very hard to book these, involving over an hour in line at an Orbis office. Sharply increased prices have cut demand and most train stations are now computerised, allowing you to book your couchette or sleeper at the reservation window at any train station in minutes. Main stations have special 'Polres' offices to do this. Orbis, the Polish travel agency, also books couchettes and sleepers for the same price and its staff are more likely to speak English.

One reader commented that he found it cheaper to take a 1st-class seat on overnight trains rather than a 2nd-class couchette, and that he usually had the 1st-class seating compartment all to himself while the 2nd-class couchettes were full. This is probably only true during the middle of the week.

Train Stations

Train stations in Poland have good facilities: left-luggage rooms open round the clock, cafeterias, waiting rooms, newsstands, posted timetables etc. There are public toilets in all train stations (and in many other places) and you're expected to pay around US$0.10 to use them.

When you check your baggage at railway cloakrooms *(przechowalnia bagażu)* you must declare the value of the object in złoty

Polish Railways

and sign the form (have the amount written down on a piece of paper ready to show the clerk). You're charged 1% of the declared value which includes insurance. This makes it fairly expensive if you declare anything near the real value, though in small stations you can easily forgo the insurance and just pay the standard US$0.35 fee. If you say 'million' when the baggage handler asks you how much your bag is worth, you'll still pay under US$1. We've never heard of anyone actually losing luggage properly checked at a Polish train station. You pay the left-luggage charge when you pick the item up, not when you deposit it (useful to know if you arrive in the country with no Polish currency).

CAR & MOTORBIKE

Poland's 258,588 km of roads are generally narrow but in good condition and there isn't too much traffic. Over the next 15 years Poland is to build a 2000-km network of toll roads stretching from Gdańsk to the Czech border and Germany to Ukraine. The World Bank and Western banks have promised loans covering 65% of the US$5 billion cost.

To drive a car into Poland you'll need your driver's licence, the car registration card and liability insurance (the 'green card'). If your insurance isn't valid for Poland you must buy an additional policy at the border. The car registration number will be entered in your passport.

Always use 94-octane 'yellow' petrol or 98-octane 'red' (super), as the 86-octane 'blue' fuel can damage your engine. Unleaded 95-octane petrol *(benzyna bezołowiowa)* is becoming easier to find. If one station doesn't have unleaded fuel, ask them for the address of another which does.

In recent years petrol has become readily available at service stations around Poland, rendering obsolete such quaint communist inventions as petrol coupons purchased for hard currency and quick capitalist solutions like slipping the pump attendant a hard-currency tip.

Petrol stations are sometimes few, so plan ahead and expect queues, especially in the south. Elsewhere the lines at the fuel pumps are much shorter. Most petrol stations are open from 6 am to 10 pm (Sunday 7 am to 3 pm), though some work around the clock. You're allowed to import or export fuel up to a maximum of 10 litres in a spare tank.

When asking directions of people along the road, always write the place name on a piece of paper to avoid any misunderstanding. Car theft is a problem in Poland and most cars are fitted with alarm systems which go off at the slightest provocation. Drive carefully as Poland has the fourth highest incidence of motor-vehicle fatalities per capita in the world.

The Polski Związek Motorowy (Polish Motoring Association) with offices in all large cities can provide breakdown service *(pomoc drogowa)* and other assistance to motorists. If you're a member of an automobile club at home, bring along your membership card with an international letter of introduction, as this could entitle you to free breakdown service and legal advice from the PZM. The nationwide PZM emergency breakdown number is ☎ 981.

Road Rules

The speed limit is 110 km/h on expressways, 90 km/h on other open roads and 60 km/h in built-up areas. Motorcycles cannot exceed 90 km/h in any case. At the entrance to small towns, if the background of the sign bearing the town name is white you must reduce speed to 60 km/h. If the background is green there's no need to reduce speed.

Radar-equipped police are very active, especially in villages where you must slow down to 60 km/h, and speeding fines ranging from US$7 to US$32 are levied frequently. Approaching cars often flash their lights in warning. Seat belts are compulsory in the front seat. Parking tickets (US$7) are also common and having one person sitting in the car while the other pops into a shop doesn't exempt you.

Cyclists are not allowed to ride two abreast on highways.

Rental

Avis, Budget and Hertz/Orbis are now well represented in Poland. Their economy models begin around US$37 a day plus US$0.38 a km or US$100/550 daily/weekly with unlimited mileage. Add 5% tax and US$13 per day for compulsory loss damage waiver (LDW) insurance. If the car is stolen you may be charged US$100 or more despite having theft covered by the insurance. It's usually cheaper to prebook your car from abroad rather than just front up at an agency inside Poland.

The minimum age to rent a car is 21 years at Budget and Hertz, 23 years at Avis. Budget and Hertz allow you to drop the car off at any of their offices around Poland at no additional charge but their unlimited mileage cars cannot be taken out of Poland. Avis allows one-way rentals from Warsaw to Prague.

Some of the cars are in pretty poor shape so check the vehicle carefully before you drive off. If the lights aren't in order, for example, you could be fined. Insist on exchanging the car at the next rental office if you discover that they've unloaded a lemon on you.

If you had thought of renting a car in Berlin and driving it into Poland, think again as most German car rental agencies will not allow their vehicles to be taken to Poland. This is because of a report circulated by the Federal Office of Criminal Investigations in Wiesbaden concerning 'criminal organisations which have specialised in stealing new vehicles'. Call the car rental chains directly for the latest information.

HITCHING

Hitchhiking is a practical way of getting around and even Polish women regularly travel 'autostop'. There's even an official 'autostop' card complete with coupons for drivers available from PTTK offices!

Large commercial vehicles that pick up hitchhikers expect to be paid the equivalent of a bus fare but car drivers will also stop, leaving the question of payment at your discretion.

BOAT

Local Boats

A pleasant way to sightsee is from a ship, and local cruises on the Vistula River are offered at Kraków, Warsaw and Toruń. Other local river cruises are available at Gdańsk and Wrocław. The day excursion from Gdańsk or Sopot to Hel across the Gulf of Gdańsk is recommended. Most of these trips operate only in summer.

Enthusiasts for canal cruising by narrow boat won't want to miss a trip on the Elbląg Canal from Elbląg to Ostróda where the boats are carried up and down ramps on rail-mounted platforms. Also in north-eastern Poland, excursion boats of the Mazurian Shipping Company's White Fleet run daily from May to September between Giżycko, Mikołajki and Ruciane-Nida, while other tourist boats operate out of Augustów and Ostróda.

LOCAL TRANSPORT

Local buses, trolleybuses and trams cost about US$0.25 a ride, but tickets must be purchased in advance at kiosks or Ruch newsstands. Buy a bunch of them as drivers don't sell tickets. You punch the ticket as you board. Public transport operates from 5.30 am to 11 pm. Express buses *(pośpieszny)* are double fare, night buses after 11 pm triple fare. Luggage is an extra fare. Though tickets aren't checked often, you will receive a stiff fine if you're caught without one at a spot check.

Taxi

Since the Polish złoty became a 'hard' currency, taxis are a lot easier to find. There are always regular taxi stands in front of train stations and near markets, plus other strategic points around town. It's also possible to flag down taxis on the street. Beware of taxis waiting in front of the tourist hotels, and unmarked, unmetered 'pirate' taxis as these will try to overcharge. Always insist that the meter be turned on and carry small bills (otherwise you won't get proper change). If there's no meter agree on the price beforehand. Metered taxis operate on tariff No 1 from 6 am to 10 pm, tariff No 2 from 10 pm to 6 am. Make sure the meter is set to the correct level during the day.

Taxi meters have difficulty keeping up with inflation. At last report taxis charged from 400 to 600 times the meter fare. This could change as the meters are adjusted, so check by asking your hotel receptionist or any Polish acquaintance. Outside city limits and after 11 pm taxis charge double. Luggage and the number of passengers don't affect the fare. A short trip around town may cost US$2, while an hour-long search for a hostel including a 10-km drive out of town may cost up to US$10, tip included. It never hurts to round the fare up and if a driver is especially helpful in finding a cheap place to stay, tip generously.

TOURS

Of the package tours to Poland offered by travel offices abroad, the most interesting cater to special interests such as horse riding, skiing, yachting, health resorts etc, which are hard to organise on your own.

Almatur (☎ 022-262 639), ulica Kopernicka 23, Warsaw, offers one-week sailing trips on the Mazurian Lakes at US$135 per person. Horse riding in Silesia is US$132 for one week, US$197 for two weeks. These trips are intended mainly for young people and are only available in July and August.

Pegrotour (☎ 022-243 676), ulica Emilii Plater 47 (upstairs), opposite the Palace of Culture in Warsaw, arranges horse riding at Szczawno Zdroj in Silesia, 90 km from Wrocław. Their stable is three km from a train station with taxis to the door and it's open all year. Pegrotour packages cost about US$40 per person a day (double occupancy), half board and one hour in the saddle included. Additional riding is about US$5 an hour. Pegrotour can make all the arrangements for individuals who just walk into their Warsaw office.

The OZGT (☎ 089-275 156; fax 089-273 442), above tourist information at the High Gate in Olsztyn, runs regular 10-day canoe tours along the Krutynia canoe route from June to August and occasionally in spring and fall. The US$125 price includes canoe, food, lodging and a Polish-speaking guide. You can just show up at their Olsztyn office and hope they can fit you into one of their scheduled tours, or fax them before you leave for Poland and fit one of their departures into your schedule. Either way, it's worth the effort.

Orbis offices and private travel agencies around Poland offer organised city sightseeing tours in Warsaw, Kraków and other cities. The best of the Warsaw trips are to Wilanów Palace and Chopin's birthplace at Żelazowa Wola, while at Kraków you have the salt mines and Auschwitz-Birkenau to choose from. Most operate from mid-May to September only.

New Millennium Holidays (☎ 0121-711 2232), 20 High St, Solihull, West Midlands B91 3TB, England, offers low-cost bus tours from the UK to Gdynia and Zakopane year-round.

Warsaw

Warsaw (Warszawa), a city of nearly two million inhabitants, is almost equidistant from Berlin (590 km), Prague (620 km), Vienna (678 km) and Budapest (700 km). Viewed another way, Warsaw is almost the same distance from London (1590 km), Paris (1610 km) and Sofia (1660 km). The Vistula (Wisła) River cuts a curving course across Poland, from the Carpathian Mountains in the south to the Baltic in the north, and halfway down sits Warsaw, off-centre now that the country's borders have moved west.

The strategic location in the centre of the Mazovian lowland led to the site being fortified in the 14th century, and in 1596 King Sigismund III Vasa had the capital transferred here from Kraków. Warsaw has long resisted foreign domination: by the Swedes in the 17th century, tsarist Russia in the 19th century and Nazi Germany and the USSR in the 20th century.

Many of Warsaw's finest avenues, parks

and palaces were built in the 18th century, whereas the 19th century was a period of decay with the city as a mere provincial centre of the Russian Empire. Yet this was nothing compared to WW II when hundreds of thousands of residents were killed and all the survivors finally expelled before the city was levelled block by block. Before WW II a third of the population of Warsaw was Jewish but only a handful of Jews remain today.

In a way, Warsaw reborn from wartime destruction epitomises the Polish nation. The masterful rebuilding of old Warsaw and its harmonious union with the new symbolise the determination of the Polish people to develop and build without sacrificing an identity which has always been their greatest strength. You'll witness that identity in the museums and churches, but more directly in the surprisingly candid people. Warsaw is a fascinating layer cake you'll need several days to digest.

Orientation

If you're coming by train you'll probably arrive at Central Station beside the Palace of Culture & Science near the corner of Aleje Jerozolimskie and Marszałkowska. Dump your things in the baggage room and start hostel or hotel hunting using the listings in this section. More information on Central Station is given under Getting There & Away following. If you arrived by plane, the airport transportation possibilities are described under Getting Around.

Warsaw has many focal points but you'll soon become acquainted with Plac Zamkowy, the gateway to old Warsaw, and the Royal Way, which runs 10 km south-east from this square to Wilanów Palace with changing names: Krakowskie Przedmieście, Nowy Świat, Aleje Ujazdowskie, Belwederska, Jana Sobieskiego and also Aleja Wilanowska. Plan your sightseeing around this corridor.

Information

Tourist Offices Tourist information is available from the information-cum-souvenir shop marked 'IT' (☎ 635 1881) at Plac Zamkowy 1/13 in the old town. Stock up on maps of cities all around Poland here.

Just opposite Central Station is the Polski Związek Motorowy (Polish Motoring Association, ☎ 210 788), Aleje Jerozolimskie 63, where you should be able to buy a good indexed map of Warsaw.

If you'll be staying longer than a day or two it's a good investment to buy the indexed 48-page *Warszawa Plan Miasta* map book (US$3), available at bookshops all around Poland. It will make using public transport easy and will save you a lot of time and money.

Pick up a copy of the free monthly magazine *Warszawa, What, Where, When* at tourist information or at a luxury hotel. It includes an excellent centrefold map and current information about tourist facilities.

The Incoming Bureau at Orbis, ulica Marszałkowska 142, can answer questions about standard tourist facilities such as upmarket hotels, sightseeing excursions, river cruises, festivals and activities etc.

A map listing all hostels in Poland is available from PTSM (Polskie Towarzystwo Schronisk Młodzieżowych), at ulica Chocimska 28 near Łazienkowski Park, 4th floor, suite 426 (weekdays 8 am to 3 pm).

Money A convenient place to change travellers' cheques is the Bank Pekao SA, on the 3rd floor of the Marriott Hotel opposite Central Station (weekdays 9 am to 2 pm). Their commission is 2% with a US$2 minimum, and they'll change dollar travellers' cheques into dollars cash for half a per cent commission (minimum US$2).

The NBP Bank on Plac Powstańców Warszawy (upstairs), a couple of blocks from Central Station (weekdays 8 am to 6 pm, Saturday 8 am to 1 pm), changes travellers' cheques for 1.5% commission.

Of course, the numerous private exchange offices around town are much faster but they only accept cash. For exchange facilities at the airport and train station see Getting There & Away following.

American Express, located opposite Hotel

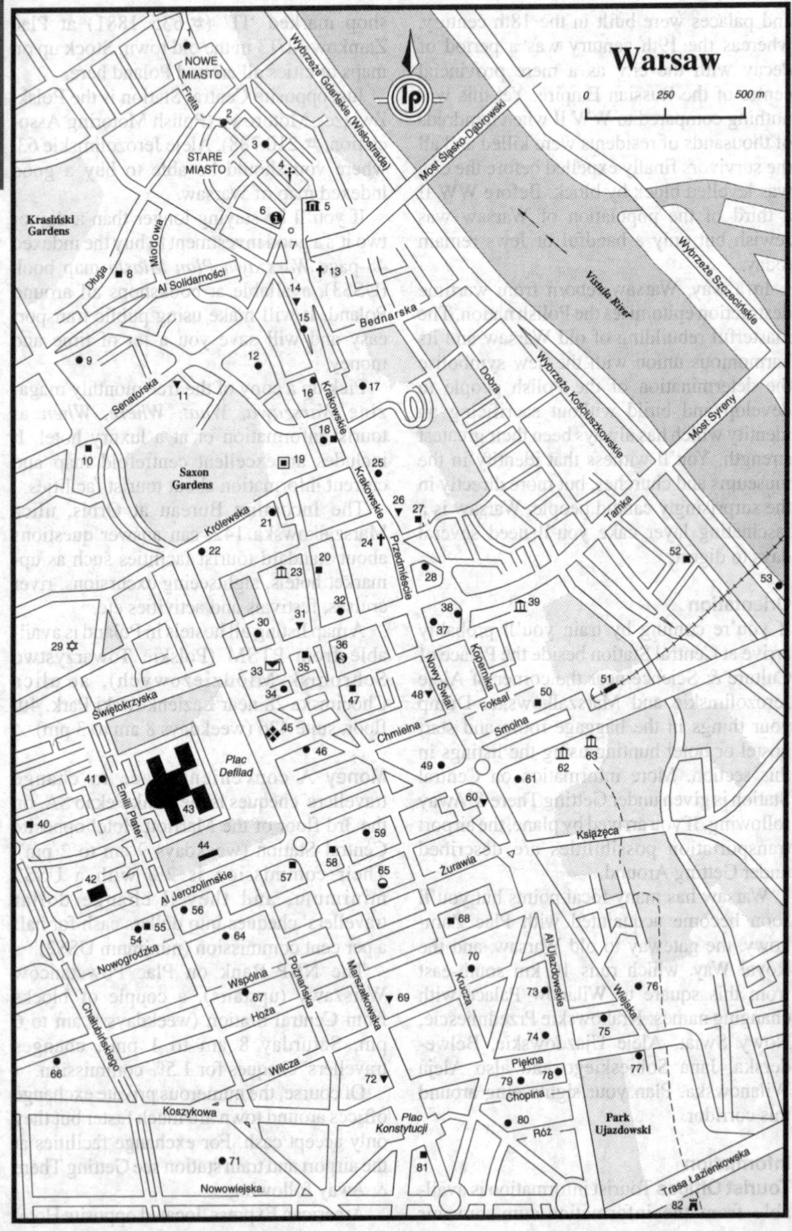
Warsaw
0
250
500 m
NOWE MIASTO
STARE MIASTO
Freta
Wybrzeże Gdańskie (Wisłostrada)
Most Śląsko-Dąbrowski
Vistula River
Wybrzeże Szczecińskie
Krasiński Gardens
Miodowa
Długa
Al Solidarności
Bednarska
Senatorska
Krakowskie
Krakowskie Przedmieście
Dobra
Wybrzeże Kościuszkowskie
Most Syreny
Saxon Gardens
Królewska
Tamka
Nowy Świat
Kopernika
Foksal
Smolna
Chmielna
Świętokrzyska
Plac Defilad
Emilii Plater
Al Jerozolimskie
Nowogrodzka
Książęca
Żurawia
Chałubińskiego
Poznańska
Wspólna
Hoża
Marszałkowska
Wilcza
Koszykowa
Plac Konstytucji
Nowowiejska
Krucza
Al Ujazdowskie
Wiejska
Piękna
Chopina
Róż
Park Ujazdowski
Trasa Łazienkowska

PLACES TO STAY

8 Pokoje Gościnne
10 Saski Hotel
18 Europejski Hotel
20 Hotel Garnizonowy
27 Hotel Harenda
35 Hotel Warszawa
40 Holiday Inn Hotel
47 Hotel Dom Chłopa
50 Smolna Youth Hostel
52 Hotel Belfer
55 Marriott Hotel
57 Metropol & Polonia Hotels
58 Forum Hotel
68 Grand Hotel
81 MDM Hotel

PLACES TO EAT

11 El Popo Restauracja Meksykańska
14 Pizzeria Giovanni
26 Uniwersytecki Milk Bar
31 U Matysiaków Restaurant
48 Familijny Milk Bar
60 Szwajcarski Milk Bar
69 Steak & Salad Bar Dolce Vita
72 Złota Kurka Milk Bar

OTHER

1 New Town Square
2 Barbican
3 Old Town Square
4 St John's Cathedral
5 Royal Palace
6 'IT' Tourist Information
7 Plac Zamkowy
9 Jewish Historical Institute
12 Wielki Opera House
13 St Anne's Church
15 Café Studio M
16 Kino Kultura
17 Radziwiłł Palace
18 American Express
19 Tomb of the Unknown Soldier
21 Zachęta Art Gallery
22 Orbis (Train Tickets)
23 Ethnological Museum
24 Church of the Holy Cross
25 University of Warsaw
28 Academy of Sciences
29 Synagogue
30 Klub Europa Voltaire
32 Antykwariat Warszawski
33 Post Office/ Telephone Centre
34 Filharmonia Concert Hall
36 NBP Bank
37 Wagon-lits Travel
38 Almatur
39 Chopin Museum
41 Akwarium Club/Pegrotour
42 Central Railway Station
43 Palace of Culture & Science
44 Śródmieście Railway Station
45 Department Stores
46 Bar Hybrydy
49 Orbis (International Tickets)
51 Powiśle Railway Station
53 Excursion Boats
54 LOT Polish Airlines
56 Polski Związek Motorowy
59 Kasy Teatralne
61 Former Party House
62 National Museum
63 Armed Forces Museum
64 Operetta
65 Pekaes Bus Office
66 Klub Medyków
67 Sawa Tour
70 Syrena Tourist Office
71 Politechnical University
73 Bulgarian Consulate
74 American Embassy
75 Canadian Embassy
76 Parliament
77 French Embassy
78 Hungarian & Yugoslavian Consulates
79 Romanian Consulate
80 Czech Republic Consulate
82 Ujazdów Castle

Europejski (weekdays 9 am to 5 pm, Saturday 10 am to 2 pm), is not a good place to change money. They change all types of travellers' cheques without commission, but give a lower rate than the banks. Ironically, they *do* charge commission to change cash. American Express will change dollar travellers' cheques into dollars cash but you lose about 3% on the transaction. There's an American Express automatic cash dispenser outside the office and clients' mail is held inside.

Post & Telephone Poste restante mail is held at window No 12 in the main post office, ulica Świętokrzyska 31/33 (daily 8 am to 8 pm). A 24-hour post and telephone centre functions in the same building.

There's a branch post office/telephone centre at Rynek Starego Miasta 15, but it's only open during business hours. They have some of the cheapest postcards in town and you can buy stamps right there.

Warsaw's telephone code is 02 with seven-digit numbers, 022 with six-digit numbers.

Western Embassies Embassy row stretches along Aleje Ujazdowskie between Aleje Jerozolimskie and Łazienki Park. The

American Embassy (☎ 283 041), Aleje Ujazdowskie 29/31, and the Canadian Embassy (☎ 298 051), ulica Matejki 1/5, are only a block apart, and the French Embassy (☎ 628 8401), Piękna 1, is just behind the Canadian Embassy.

The British Embassy is two blocks south of these, on the corner of Aleje Ujazdowskie and Aleje Róż, but only diplomatic business is dealt with there. British and New Zealand travellers must trek out to the British Consulate, ulica Wawelska 14 (weekdays 9 am to noon and 2 to 4 pm), in an inconvenient south-western suburb of Warsaw.

The Australian Embassy (☎ 176 081) is at ulica Estońska 3/5 on the east side of the Vistula (take any eastbound tram on Aleje Jerozolimskie and get off at the first stop across the river). They're open weekdays from 9 am to 1 pm.

Eastern Embassies Most of the Eastern European embassies are in the same area. The Bulgarian Consulate, Aleje Ujazdowskie 35 (open Monday, Wednesday and Friday 10 am to noon), issues tourist visas valid three months from the date of issue for US$32 and one photo, but you have to wait five working days. If you want a tourist visa on the spot it's a whopping US$70. Thirty-hour transit visas are always issued on the spot: US$22 for one entry, US$44 for two entries (no photos required).

Visas for the other Eastern European countries are more easily obtained. The Yugoslav and Hungarian consulates are side by side on Aleje Ujazdowskie, a block south of the American Embassy, and both are open Monday, Wednesday and Friday from 9 am to noon. Yugoslav visas are issued on the spot free of charge. Hungarian visas cost US$20 and two photos for one entry, US$33 and four photos for two entries, and are issued at once. Be sure to get a tourist and not a transit visa.

The Romanian Consulate, around the corner at ulica Chopina 10, keeps the same hours. Romanian visas are issued immediately at US$35 for Canadians, Americans, New Zealanders and Australians, and US$45 for British. No photos are required.

Nearby at ulica Koszykowa 18, on the corner of Aleje Róż, is the Czech Republic Consulate (Monday to Friday 9 am to noon). You'll receive a tourist or transit visa right away upon payment of US$23 and one photo for one entry, US$54 and one photo for multiple entries, though some nationalities are charged more (such as Canadians – US$48 for one entry). Transit visas are the same price.

The Slovak Embassy, ulica Litewska 6 off Aleja Jana Szucha (Monday, Wednesday, and Friday 9 am to noon), is three blocks south of the Czech Consulate. At last report they were charging exactly the same prices for exactly the same visas (but Slovakian visas are not accepted in the Czech Republic and vice versa).

Of the four former components of the USSR which have land borders with Poland, Lithuania is by far the easiest to visit. The Lithuanian Consulate, Aleje Szucha 5 (weekdays 10 am to noon and 2 to 4 pm), issues visas for US$20 plus US$7 for 24-hour express service (otherwise you must wait 10 days). Visas are free for US citizens and British nationals don't require visas. A Lithuanian visa is valid for two days transit through Latvia and Estonia, and stays in those countries can be extended upon arrival. See Getting There & Away in the introduction to this chapter for information of transportation to Lithuania.

At last report the Ukrainian Consulate was in temporary quarters at Aleja Szucha 7, next door to the Lithuanian Consulate. Ukrainian visas are US$50, but be prepared for all sorts of nasty communist-era requirements such as prepayment of rooms at expensive hotels.

The Consulate of the Russian Federation, ulica Belvederska 25, building C (Monday, Wednesday, Friday 8 am to noon), continues to enforce all the old USSR visa requirements, which makes independent travel to Russia a real drag. Check anyway, as things can only get better.

The Albanian Consulate, Słoneczna 15 across the park behind the Russian Embassy, is theoretically open weekdays from 8 to 10 am, but visiting them is usually a waste of time.

The Belorussian Embassy, Ateńska 67, is in an isolated suburb east of the Vistula.

Travel Agencies Student travel is handled by Almatur, ulica Kopernika 23 (weekdays 9 am to 5 pm, Saturday 10 am to 2 pm), and they're generally helpful. They'll be able to tell you about the International Student Hotels which are open in July and August only. Also ask about one-week Almatur sailing and horse-riding trips in July and August.

As many as 20 travel agencies in Warsaw sell international bus tickets from Poland to Western Europe and many such buses leave from the parking lot behind Central Railway Station. Service is more frequent from May to October.

Almatur, ulica Kopernika 23, has bus tickets to Amsterdam (US$91), Cologne (US$59), London (US$113), Paris (US$94) and Zürich (US$94).

Orbis, Bracka 16, sells bus tickets from Warsaw to Belgium, Britain, France, Germany, Holland, Italy, Norway, Spain and Sweden. This is the place to ask about buses to Vilnius, Lithuania.

Other companies with bus tickets to Western Europe include Anna Travel (☎ 255 389), on the top floor at Central Station (weekdays 8 am to 6 pm, Saturday 9 am to 3 pm), the Syrena Tourist Office, ulica Krucza 16/22, and Pekaes, ulica Żurawia 26.

International train tickets are available from Orbis, ulica Bracka 16. This is a good place to pick up discounted student train tickets to other Eastern European countries. Seat reservations for domestic express trains, sleepers and couchettes can also be booked at this Orbis office or at Central Station.

The Orbis office at Marszałkowska 142 also sells both domestic and international train tickets and it's sometimes less crowded. This is the only Orbis office that accepts Visa cards.

A special Almatur office at the University of Warsaw, Krakowskie Przedmiéscie 26/28, sells discounted Eurotrain international tickets to persons under 26 years (student card not required). This office (open weekdays from 9 am to 3.30 pm) is in room No 19, upstairs in the building to the right as you go through the gate. Eurotrain tickets are valid for two months.

Wagon-lits Travel, Nowy Świat 64, sells train and air tickets to points outside Eastern Europe.

Sawa Tour, ulica Wspólna 65a, can book cheap flights to anywhere departing from Berlin (they need a week to get the tickets).

Newspapers Klub MPK, ulica Marzałkowska 122 at ulica Sienkiewicza (next to Junior Department Store), has foreign newspapers and magazines.

Laundry Alba Self-Service Laundry, Anielewicza at Karmelicka (open weekdays from 9 am to 7 pm, Saturday 9 am to 1 pm), charges US$5 to wash and dry up to six kilos. You're asked to call ☎ 317 317 two days ahead to make a reservation. Bring your own detergent.

Things to See

The Old Town From Plac Zamkowy you enter the old city (Stare Miastro) along ulica Świętojańska. You'll soon come to 14th-century Gothic **St John's Cathedral**, and then the **Rynek Starego Miasta**, the old town square. Try to catch the 15-minute film at the **City Historical Museum**, Rynek Starego Miasta 42 (free Sunday, closed Monday), which unforgettably depicts the wartime destruction of the city. It's hard to believe that all the 17th and 18th-century buildings around this square have been completely rebuilt from their foundations. Stroll around, visiting the shops, galleries and restaurants.

Continue north a block on ulica Nowomiejska to the **barbican gate** (1548), part of the medieval walled circuit around Warsaw. Walk towards the river inside the walls a bit to find the city's symbol, the **Warsaw Mermaid** (1855). (Once upon a time a mermaid, Syrena, rose from the river and

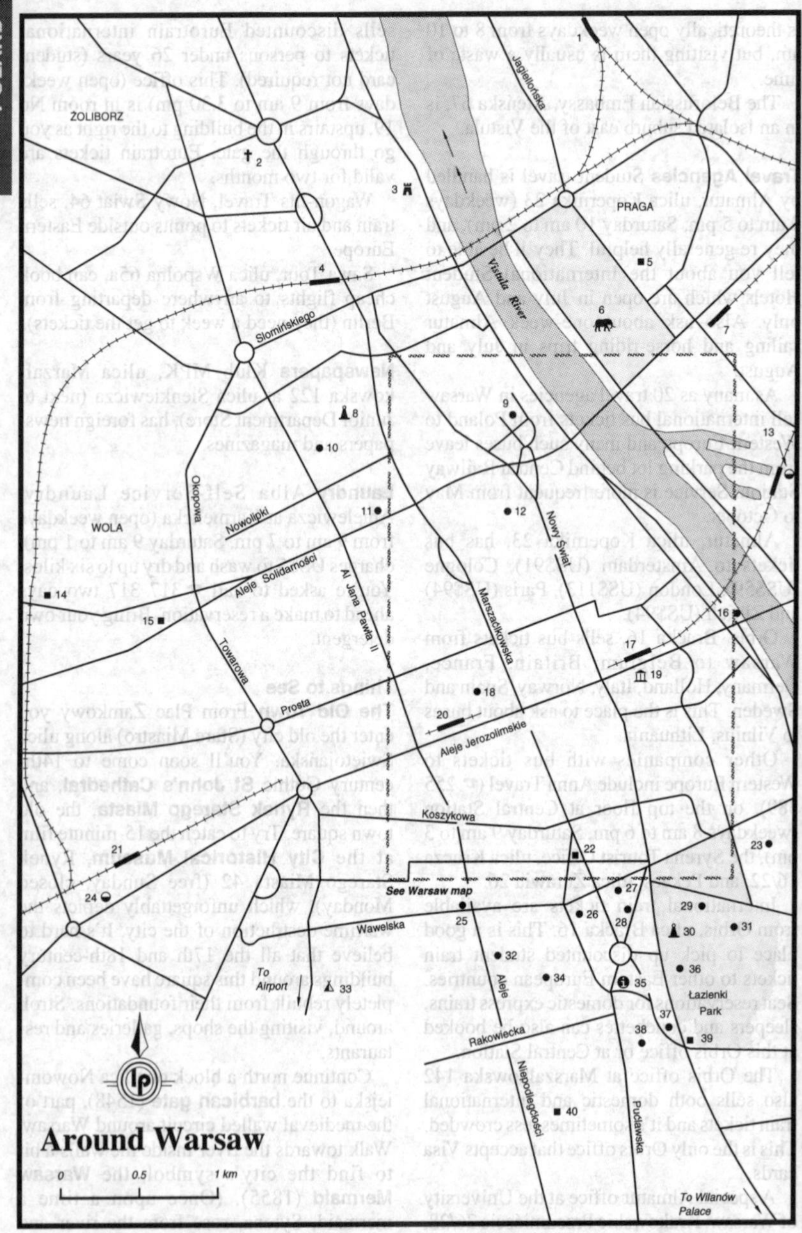

Around Warsaw

PLACES TO STAY

5 Nowa Praga Hotel
14 Hotel Syrena
15 Karolkowa Youth Hostel
22 MDM Hotel
33 Camping OST 'Gromada'
39 Hotel Uniwersytet Warszawski
40 Hotel Agra

OTHER

1 Praga Railway Station
2 Church of Św Stanisława Kostki
3 Citadel
4 Gdańska Railway Station
6 Zoo
7 Wileńska Railway Station
8 Warsaw Ghetto Monument
9 Old Town Square (Rynek)
10 Alba Self-Service Laundry
11 Warsaw Chamber Opera
12 Wielki Opera House
13 Stadion Bus & Railway Stations
16 Excursion Boat Landing
17 Powiśle Railway Station
18 Palace of Culture & Science
19 National Museum
20 Central Railway Station
21 Zachodnia Railway Station
23 Stadion 'Legia'
24 Central Bus Station
25 British Consulate
26 Disco Remont
27 Slovak Consulate
28 Lithuanian Consulate
29 Orangerie
30 Chopin Monument
31 Łazienki Water Palace
32 Disco Park
34 Disco Stodoła
35 Youth Hostel Association Office
36 Belvedere Palace
37 Russian Consulate
38 Albanian Consulate

told a fisherman, Wars, and his wife, Sawa, to found a city here.) Everything north of this wall is New Town (Nowe Miasto). Straight ahead on Freta, beyond several historic churches, is **Rynek Nowego Miasta** with more churches. At ulica Freta 5 is the Asian Gallery of the **Asia & Pacific Museum** (closed Monday) with interesting exhibitions. The delightful streets and buildings in both Old and New towns are best explored casually on your own without a guidebook.

The Royal Way On a tall pillar (1644) in the centre of Plac Zamkowy is a statue of King Sigismund III. The **Royal Castle** (1619) on the east side of the square developed over the centuries as successive Polish kings added wings and redecorated the interior. In 1945 all that remained was a heap of rubble but from 1971 to 1974 the castle was carefully rebuilt. The entrance is on the north side of the building, but castle tickets must be purchased at the Zamek Kasy Biletowe, around the corner on ulica Świętojańska (closed Monday, free Thursday, reduced admission Sunday). For US$1.50 you can see the 'Konmaty Pokoje Dworskie' (courtiers' lodgings) with the parliament chamber and historic paintings by Jan Matejko. To see the 'Apartamenty Królewskie' (king's apartments) with the Canaletto paintings a further US$3 must be paid (except on Sunday when you can see everything for US$2). Students get half price. A guided tour in English or French is US$7 extra. In summer demand outstrips supply, so arrive early and be prepared to wait.

On the south side of Plac Zamkowy is **St Anne's Church** (1454), one of the most beautiful churches in the city. Continue south on Krakowskie Przedmieście where there are many aristocratic residences, especially the **Radziwiłł Palace** (1643), on the left beside a church. The Warsaw Pact was signed in this building on 14 May 1955. Next to this palace is the elegant secessionist **Bristol Hotel** (1901) with the neoclassical **Hotel Europejski** (1877) across the street. Behind the Europejski are Saski Gardens with the **Tomb of the Unknown Soldier**, occupying a fragment of an 18th-century royal palace destroyed in WW II. The ceremonial changing of the guard here takes place Sunday at noon.

On the north side of the square is the massive **Wielki Opera House** (1833, rebuilt in 1965), while to the south is the modern Hotel Victoria Inter-Continental. On the west side of this hotel is the **Zachęta Art Gallery** (closed Monday) which often stages great art shows in summer. South a block beyond the circular **Evangelical Church** (1781) is the **Ethnological Museum** (closed Monday), ulica Kredytowa 1. This large museum has collections of tribal art from Africa, Oceania and Latin America, as well as Polish folklore.

From this museum follow ulica Traugutta east a block back to the Royal Way. Just around the corner on the right is the 17th-century **Church of the Holy Cross**. The heart of Frédéric Chopin is preserved in the second pillar on the left-hand side of the main nave of this church (though Chopin left Warsaw when he was 20 years old and died of tuberculosis in Paris aged only 39, he was a Polish nationalist to the end). In front of the 19th-century **Academy of Sciences** (Staszic Palace) nearby stands the famous statue (1830) of Polish astronomer Nicolaus Copernicus by the Danish sculptor Bertel Thorvaldsen. Below the Academy towards the river is the **Chopin Museum**, ulica Tamka 41 (closed Tuesday), with memorabilia such as Chopin's last piano and one of the best collections of Chopin manuscripts in the world. They'll play recordings of his music if you ask.

More Museums Return to the Royal Way and head south on Nowy Świat (New World Street), crossing Aleje Jerozolimskie (Jerusalem Avenue) to the former **Party House** (1951), where the Central Committee of the Polish United Workers' Party used to meet. In 1991 the top floor of this building became the Warsaw Stock Exchange. (After rising 820% in dollar terms in 1993, the Warsaw index crashed 50% in early 1994.)

The large building beside this on Aleje Jerozolimskie is the **National Museum** (closed Monday, free Thursday) which has a magnificent collection of paintings including *The Battle of Grunwald* by Jan Matejko. During WW II this huge painting was evacuated to Lublin and secretly buried. The Nazis offered a reward of 10 million Reichsmarks for information leading to its discovery but no-one accepted. After the war Matejko's work was uncovered and restored.

Towards the riverside next to the National Museum is the **Armed Forces Museum** (closed Monday and Tuesday) with a large assortment of old guns, tanks and planes on the terrace outside. A gate beyond the planes on the south side of this terrace opens into Park Kultury where a footpath leads south through the greenbelt all the way to Łazienki Park, a pleasant 25-minute walk (if the gate is locked you'll have to circle back around Party House).

The Royal Palaces Łazienki Park is best known for its 18th-century neoclassical **Water Palace** (closed Monday and during bad weather), summer residence of Stanislaus Augustus Poniatowski, the last king of Poland. This reform-minded monarch, who gave Poland the world's second written constitution in 1791, was deposed by a Russian army and a confederation of reactionary Polish magnates in 1792.

The **Orangerie** (1788) in the park is also well worth seeing for its theatre and gallery of sculpture (closed Monday). The striking **Chopin Monument** (1926) is just off Aleje Ujazdowskie but still within the park. On summer Sundays at noon and 5 pm excellent piano recitals are held here. Poland's Head of State resides in the neoclassical **Belvedere Palace** (1818), just south of the monument.

Six km farther south on bus No 180 or B (from the next intersection south of the massive Russian Embassy) is **Wilanów Palace** (1696), the baroque summer residence of King John III Sobieski who defeated the Turks at Vienna in 1683, ending their threat to Central Europe forever. In summer it's hard to gain admission to the palace (closed Tuesday, US$2) due to large groups and limited capacity, but even the exterior and 18th-century French-style park are worth the trip. One-hour guided tours in Polish begin every 15 minutes from 9.30 am to 2.30 pm but only 35 people are admitted each time, and on weekdays tour groups often pre-book all the tickets. Summaries in English and French are posted in most rooms. On Saturday, Sunday and holidays the palace is reserved for individuals so these are good days to come, but arrive early and be prepared to stand in line. Don't come on Tuesday or the day following a public holiday as not only the palace but also the park behind the palace will be locked. While you're at Wilanów the **Poster Museum** (Muzeum Plakatu) in the former royal stables beside the palace is worth a visit (closed Monday). There are two fancy restaurants between the bus stop and the palace where you could have lunch.

Other Sights Warsaw's **Palace of Culture & Science** (1955) near the Central Station is an impressive Stalin-era building with an elevator which will carry you up to the observation terrace on the 30th floor for a panoramic view (US$2). Poles often joke that this is the best view in the city because it's the only one which doesn't include the Palace of Culture itself! There's also a **Technical Museum** (closed Monday), several theatres and a congress hall in the palace. The large street market selling everything from imported beer to car tyres in the park around the palace and the large department stores, Junior, Wars and Sawa, on the east side of the Palace of Culture, are all good places to get a feel for the current state of Polish consumerism.

Most of the **Citadel** (1834) on the north side of the city is still occupied by the military; however, part of it may be visited through the Brama Straceń, the large gate near the middle of the Citadel wall on the river side. This large fortress was built by the Russians after a Polish uprising in 1830. There's a museum (closed Monday and Tuesday) and plaques recalling the Poles executed here by the tsarist forces a century or more ago. Buses Nos 118 and 185 stop near the Citadel entrance.

Within walking distance north-west of the citadel near Plac Wilsona is the **Church of Św Stanisława Kostki** with the red-granite tomb of Father Jerzy Popiełuszko in the yard. Prior to his murder by the secret police in October 1984 the 37-year-old priest had earned the enmity of communist hardliners by giving sermons in support of Solidarity. The government cooled the passions aroused by Father Popiełuszko's death by publicly trying and sentencing the four officers responsible to long prison terms. Don't miss the photo display on Father Popiełuszko's political activities inside behind the altar. Solidarity pins are sold at the church souvenir counter. Also in the churchyard is a moving memorial to those who died in Nazi death camps during WW II.

Activities

Organised Tours The 'Incoming Bureau' at Orbis, ulica Marszałkowska 142, books Orbis sightseeing tours, but this is more easily done at the reception desks of the Bristol, Europejski, Forum, Grand, Holiday Inn, Marriott, Sobieski and Victoria hotels. Five-hour city tours depart daily except Sunday, while the Wednesday tour to Wilanów Palace would ensure that you actually get inside and are shown around by a English-speaking guide. The tours cost anywhere from US$15 to US$19 per person and operate from mid-May to September.

Orbis and the hotels take bookings for the Sunday 'Polish landscape countryside tour'. For US$44 you visit palaces, farms, forests and villages, hear a live piano recital at Chopin's birthplace at Żelazowa Wola, 50 km west of Warsaw, and get a typical Polish lunch with vodka. (You can also get to Chopin's family home, now a museum, on your own by train from Warszawa Śródmieście Station to Sochaczew, then by bus No 6 hourly to Żelazowa Wola.)

Mazurkas Travel in the lobby of the Forum Hotel runs a very good four-hour city sightseeing tour daily year-round departing at 9 am (US$21). Included is the old town, the Royal Way and Wilanów Palace.

From May to September the Biała Flota runs six one-hour cruises a day (US$2) on the Warsaw reach of the Vistula River from a landing below the bridge at the east end of Aleje Jerozolimskie.

Festivals
Annual events worth asking about include the 'Złota Tarka' (Golden Washboard) Jazz Festival in June, the Mozart Festival from mid-June to mid-July, the Festival of Contemporary Music 'Warsaw Autumn' in September and the 'Jazz Jamboree' in late October.

Places to Stay

Camping From May to September one of the best places to stay in Warsaw is *Camping OST 'Gromada'* (☎ 254 391), ulica Żwirki i Wigury 32, south-east of town on the road in from the airport (bus No 175 between the airport and town stops at the gate). Tent space is US$2.50 per person and bungalows are US$8 a double or US$15 for four persons. Rooms in a large pavilion on the grounds are available for the same price when all the bungalows are full. The atmosphere is informal and welcoming.

Hostels The *hostel* (☎ 278 952) at ulica Smolna 30 is on the top floor of a large concrete building a few minutes' walk from Warsaw Powiśle Railway Station in the centre of the city. Go in the entrance with the green sign and up to the top of the stairs. It's dusty, crowded and 110 steps up, but the charge will be only US$4 and there are even two hot showers. Stow your gear in a locker during the day. The curfew is 11 pm.

The ulica Karolkowa 53a *hostel* (☎ 328 829), just off Aleje Solidarności, is less convenient. To get there catch a north or westbound tram No 1, 13, 20, 24, 26 or 27. Get off at the 'Centrum-Wola' department store, then walk back on the right and look for a three-storey building among the trees beyond Gepard Disco (which puts out a heavy beat all night). The baggage room is open from 6 am to 9 pm but the hostel itself is closed from 10 am to 5 pm.

Directly across the street from Camping Gromada are two 11-storey student dormitories at Żwirki i Wigury 95/97 and 97/99 which rent spare rooms in July and August at US$10/12 double/triple. Each building has its own individual reception so if the first one doesn't work out, try the next. For reservations call ☎ 222 407 weekdays from 9 am to 2 pm.

Private Rooms The Syrena Travel Office (☎ 628 7540), ulica Krucza 16/22, arranges accommodation in private homes for US$10/16 single/double. Although the office stays open till 7 pm daily you should try to get there before 4 pm. You cannot occupy the room until 6 pm, so leave your luggage at the station.

Cheaper Hotels The best of the regular hotels is the *Hotel Saski* (☎ 204 611), Plac Bankowy 1, on the square opposite Warsaw Town Hall. Rooms without bath are US$18/30 single/double; ask for one facing the interior courtyard, away from tram noise. You can usually get a US$2 per person reduction on the quoted rate by asking for a room without breakfast. This 141-bed hotel has real character and a fine location.

A few blocks away from the Saski is the *Pokoje Gościnne* of the Federacja Metalowcy (☎ 314 021), ulica Długa 29 near Stare Miasto. No English is spoken but the rooms are among the cheapest in Warsaw at US$10 single without bath, US$13/19 single/double with bath, and US$25 for a four-bedded room with bath.

The recently renovated *Hotel Harenda*, formerly the PTTK Dom Turysty Hotel (☎ 260 071), Krakowskie Przedmieście 4/6 opposite the Academy of Sciences, has rooms at US$16/25 single/double without bath, US$25/47 with bath. A bed in a three-bed room is US$9, a bed in a four-bed dorm US$6. The reception is up on the 2nd floor and the hotel is often full.

A few blocks west at ulica Mazowiecka 10 is the *Hotel Garnizonowy* (☎ 683 3569), an older hotel formerly reserved for military officers but now open to everyone. Rooms without bath or breakfast here are US$16/23/26 single/double/triple.

The *Hotel Belfer* (☎ 625 2600), ulica Wybrzeże Kościuszkowskie 31/33 on the Vistula Embankment, has singles/doubles at US$14/25 without bath, US$22/30 with ath. Some of the rooms on the upper floors ave excellent views of the river. Breakfast s US$3 extra. Occasionally there are water roblems with the showers only running for couple of hours in the evening. This nodern hotel was formerly Dom Nauczyciela ZNP, a hostel for visiting school eachers. It's complicated to reach by public ransport, so take a taxi the first time.

The seven-storey *Hotel Syrena* (☎ 321 56), ulica Syreny 23 off Górczewska, is on he far west side of Warsaw but there's a requent bus service. Singles/doubles are JS$13/24 without bath, US$31 a double with bath, breakfast included.

A similar but somewhat better place is the *Nowa Praga Hotel* (☎ 191 577), ulica Brechta 7, in a working-class neighbourhood ast of the zoo on the far east side of the river. The Nowa Praga charges US$13/20/21 for ingles/doubles/triples without bath, JS$16/29/35 with bath.

The four-storey *Hotel Uniwersytet Warszawski* (☎ 411 308), Belvederska 26/30, just south of Łazienki Park, has ingles/doubles with shared bath at JS$18/29, with private bath US$24/36, breakfast included. The cheaper rooms are usually full and the others are overpriced.

A few blocks west is the *Hotel Agra* (☎ 493 881), ulica Falęcka 9/11, at US$15/19/22 single/double/triple. Every two rooms hare a toilet and shower in this clean fourtorey hotel owned by Warsaw Agricultural University. Nearby at ulica Madalińskiego 38 is a large vegetarian restaurant.

Expensive Hotels Most of Warsaw's other hotels are in the luxury tourist bracket. Right opposite the Palace of Culture, a block from Central Station, is the old *Hotel Polonia* (☎ 628 7241), Aleje Jerozolimskie 45, at US$21/34 single/double without bath, US$31/52 with bath, breakfast included. The newer *Metropol Hotel* (☎ 294 001), ulica Marszałkowska 99, is similarly priced.

Hotel Dom Chłopa (☎ 279 251), Plac Powstańców Warszawy 2, is a modern hotel owned by the Polish travel agency Gromada. Rooms are US$23/41 single/double without bath, US$47 double with bath, breakfast included. The entrance is a little hard to find, around on the north side of this white fourstorey place, but the hotel itself is very convenient to everything.

Nearby is *Hotel Warszawa* (☎ 269 421), a three-star, 17-storey Stalinist erection at Plac Powstańców Warszawy 9, near the centre of town. It costs US$35/42 for singles/doubles without bath, US$42/57 with bath, breakfast included.

Jumping up-market, there's the four-star *Europejski Hotel* (☎ 265 051), Krakowskie Przedmieście 13. Erected in 1877, this was Warsaw's first modern hotel and Marlene Dietrich was once a guest. Be prepared for rates beginning at US$69/100 single/double for a small room, US$75/113 for a large room, all with bath and breakfast included. (The Europejski is soon to be renovated, which may mean you'll find it closed or the prices sharply increased.)

The five-star *Bristol Hotel* (☎ 625 2525), across the street at ulica Krakowskie Przedmieście 42/44, is also excellent, though the 209 rooms begin at US$180/220 single/double with breakfast. It's owned by the British Forte hotel chain which completed a US$36 million renovation in 1993. The US$27 Sunday brunch here (from noon to 5 pm) is superb with unlimited champagne and a buffet that includes smoked salmon, caviar, salads, cheeses, meats, six main dishes, sweets and coffee. Reservations are required.

Places to Eat

In the Old Town Many of Warsaw's tourist restaurants are on Rynek Starego Miasta, the old town square. Most famous is the *Bazyliszek Restaurant*, Rynek Starego Miasta 5 (upstairs), where game dishes like wild boar and venison are served. Sloppy dressers are not welcome. *Winiarnia Fukier*, Rynek Starego Miasta 27, is an up-market wine restaurant with old-world atmosphere. The *Kamienne Schodki Restaurant*, Rynek Starego Miasta 26, specialises in roast duck with apples (menu in English and German).

Another slightly pretentious place is the

Swietoszek Klub, ulica Jezuicka 6/8 just off Rynek Starego Miasta, with gourmet creations such as bline with black caviar and sour cream.

The *Zapiecek Restaurant*, Zapiecek at Piwna, posts its reasonable menu outside.

Several excellent, cheap places to eat are just north of Rynek Starego Miasto. *Bar Murzynek,* ulica Nowomiejska 3, is perfect for a plate of self-service spaghetti and a big bottle of Żywiec beer, or just coffee and cakes. The menu on the wall is in English, yet prices are low! The main clientele here is Polish students.

Pod Barbakanen, Mostowa 27/29 just north of the old town gate (Barbikan), is a cheap milk bar. *Pod Samsonem,* ulica Freta 3, serves more substantial meals. *Nowy Miasto*, Rynek Nowego Miasta 13, specialises in vegetarian food though the portions are a bit small.

One of Poland's most bizarre culinary concoctions is without doubt *El Popo Restauracja Meksykańska*, ulica Senatorska 27, not far from Plac Zamkowy. It offers a cuisine which could best be termed microwave Mexican, and the chef seems to have got his training out of a Mexican cook book which forgot to mention that south of the border French fries don't come with every meal. Even the name is wrong: Mexicans call parrots *papagayos*, not 'popos'. Still, for us *gringos*, it's good fun. The menu is in English and Spanish, the décor bright, the staff friendly and there's cold beer. Prices are high for Poland or Guadalajara but *no problema para Americanos ricos*. Vegetarians will get by here.

Along the Royal Way There are many places to eat at along this busy corridor. *Pizzeria Giovanni*, Krakowskie Przedmieście 37, serves real pizza at good prices. *Uniwersytecki Milk Bar*, Krakowskie Przedmieście 20, is easy since you pay at the end of the line.

The elegant *Staropolska Restaurant*, Krakowskie Przedmieście 8 beside Hotel Harenda, gives a taste of old Warsaw as you dine by candlelight (moderately expensive).

U Matysiaków, ulica Świętokrzyska 18 offers unpretentious meals with full tabl service (beer!) though there's little selection

Familijny Milk Bar, Nowy Świat 39, i cheap and open Sunday, and farther soutl near the National Museum is *Szwajcarsk Milk Bar*, Nowy Świat 5.

In the City Centre A cheap place to eat nea Central Station is *Milk Bar Srednicowy* Aleje Jerozolimskie 49.

For a big splurge indulge in the all-you can-eat buffet at the *Lila Weneda Restaurant* just beyond the casino on the 2nd floor of the 42-storey Marriott Hotel, Aleje Jerozol imskie 65, opposite Central Station (ente through the main entrance and take the lift). Lunch is US$11 (Monday to Saturday noor to 4 pm) and dinner US$15 (daily 4.30 pm to midnight). Sunday brunch (US$15) runs from noon to 5 pm while an orchestra plays. Each night there's a different theme Monday Indian, Tuesday Polish, Wednesday and Saturday Tex-Mex, Thursday Middle Eastern, Friday Oriental and Sunday international. You probably won't enjoy this place unless you're presentably dressed.

Steak & Salad Bar Dolce Vita, ulica Marszałkowska 68/70, is an attractive private self-service where you can get big mugs of draught beer and Polish specialties In summer there are tables out on the pavement – recommended.

Złota Kurka Milk Bar, Marszałkowska 55/57, down near the MDM Hotel on Plac Konstytucji, and *Bambino Milk Bar*, Krucza 21, beside Air France diagonally opposite the Grand Hotel, both offer typical Polish food at low prices.

Bars & Cafés In summer the tables come out onto Rynek Starego Miasta, especially in front of *Gessler* at No 19 where you'll hear more English than Polish spoken. At last report there were still a few public benches scattered around the square from which you could take in the scene for free.

The cafés on Rynek Nowego Miasta are less pretentious than those on Rynek Starego Miasta, and the *Kawiarna Nove Miasto* at

Rynek Nowego Miasta 15 often has a few musicians playing in the evening. *Bar Boruta*, ulica Freta 38 on the corner of Rynek Nowego Miasta, is also a good place to sit and chat over drinks in the evening.

Café Literacka, Krakowskie Przedmieście 87/89, just off Plac Zamkowy, becomes a pavement café in summer.

Café Studio M, Krakowskie Przedmiéscie 27, is an elegant café-cum-art gallery with additional seating upstairs.

Café Ambasador, Aleje Ujazdowskie 8, opposite the US Embassy, is just the place to sit and ponder the complexities of diplomatic life.

An all-night liquor store called *Delikatesy* functions at ulica Nowy Świat 53. Join the queue of hard-core alcoholics inside.

Entertainment

You'll find theatre, concert and cinema offerings in the daily newspapers. If you're after theatre tickets, go to Kasy Teatralne, Aleje Jerozolimskie 25, which has tickets for many events. The *Filharmonia* booking office is at ulica Sienkiewicza 12. If you're attending a concert in the smaller 'sala kameralna', enter by the ulica Moniuszki entrance on the other side of the building. Warsaw's National Philharmonic Orchestra is Poland's finest.

Tickets for the *Wielki Opera House*, Plac Teatralny, and the *Warsaw Operetta*, ulica Nowogrodzka 49 near Central Station, are sold at the theatres. The Wielki Opera is often sold out a few days in advance. You may have better luck at the smaller *Warsaw Chamber Opera*, at Al Solidariności 76b (in the back courtyard). The Kasy Teatralne handles its tickets.

Nightly at 8 pm from June to September there's a folklore show accompanied by traditional Polish cuisine in the restaurant at the *Europejski Hotel* (about US$16 per person). Reservations should be made in advance at the Europejski reception.

The *Akwarium Club*, Emilii Plater 49, across the street from the Palace of Culture, is the place for live jazz (nightly at 8 pm). There's no cover charge to sit downstairs.

The *Opus One Pub & Restaurant*, Plac Emila Młynarskiego, on the west side of Filharmonia Concert Hall, has live folk music every Thursday, live jazz every Friday, both from 10 pm to 1 am (admission US$4).

The cinema where you're the most likely to see quality films is *Kino Kultura*, ulica Krakowskie Przedmieście 21/23.

Discos On Friday, Saturday and Sunday there's a disco at *Bar Hybrydy*, ulica Złota 7/9 (downstairs), behind the department stores a block east of the Palace of Culture. At street level nearby is a good pub with food and drink all day.

Also central is *Klub Europa Voltaire*, ulica Szkolna 2/4, a block from the main post office. This glossy up-market disco opens at 10 pm on Thursday, Friday and Saturday; admission costs US$8.

A much larger locale with high-tech features such as strobe and laser lighting, artificial smoke etc, is *Gepard Disco* (☎ 321 857), Aleje Solidarności 128, west of the centre. The Fosters emblems are reassuring and people of all ages will feel comfortable here but the drinks are quite expensive, so have something before you arrive. It's open Thursday to Sunday from 7 pm till late; admission costs US$5.

Warsaw's three most popular student discos are a couple of km south of the Palace of Culture. *Remont*, on the corner of Aleje Armii Ludowej and Waryńskiego, functions from 9 pm to 4 am Thursday to Sunday. The cover charge is US$2 for students with ISIC, US$6 for others (includes one drink). *Stodoła*, ulica Batorego 10, about a km south-west of Remont, is open Friday and Saturday from 8 pm to 5 am; admission costs US$4. The liveliest of the student clubs is probably *Disco Park* at Aleje Niepodległosci 196, in the centre of a park about midway between Studoła and Remont. It's open Friday, Saturday and Sunday from 10 pm on, cover charge US$4 for men, US$2 for women. The crowd at all three places is mostly aged under 30 and drinks are normal-priced.

Also check the posters in the pedestrian

underpass in front of Warsaw University on Krakowskie Przedmieście for rock concerts, discos and happenings.

Spectator Sports Wednesday and Saturday at 5 pm you can often see soccer matches at the Stadion Wojska Polskiego 'Legia', ulica Łazienkowska 3 near Łazienki Park. Check the daily papers to make sure there's a game and cheer the local team, CWKS Legia.

Things to Buy

Good places to shop for souvenirs, amber jewellery, clothing etc, are Cepelia and Jubiler in the ulica Krucza 23/31 block, directly across from the Orbis Grand Hotel. Other shopping possibilities exist along Nowy Świat.

The Poles are noted graphic designers, and poster shops such as Galeria Plakatu, Rynek Starego Miata 23, offer real bargains. The store at ulica Nowomiejska 17 beside the barbican gate in the old town sells a greater variety of kitsch than you ever thought existed in Poland.

A better selection of genuine Polish handicrafts is available at Cepelia, ulica Chmielna 8 off Nowy Świat. For antiques try Desa, ulica Nowy Świat 51 (but ask about export restrictions).

Antykwariat Logos and Kosmos, Aleje Ujazdowskie 16 near the US Embassy, has a fascinating assortment of old books, maps, prints and paintings for sale (though exporting books printed before 1945 is officially prohibited).

Getting There & Away

Air The LOT Polish Airlines office is in the Marriott Hotel building on Aleje Jerozolimskie opposite the Central Railway Station.

Train International trains depart from Warsaw Central Station for Basel, Belgrade, Berlin, Bucharest, Budapest, Cologne, Frankfurt/Main, the Hook of Holland, Leipzig, Ostend, Paris, Prague and Vienna. These are described in the chapter introduction. Domestic expresses run to every part of Poland. For information on 'name train' expresses leaving Warsaw for cities around Poland turn to the section of this book dealing with the city you wish to reach. All these trains carry mandatory seat reservations.

Train Station Central Railway Station, Aleje Jerozolimskie 54, has four levels. Your train will arrive on the lowest level and you'll go up an escalator to a network of passageways where you'll also find a 24-hour, cash-only currency exchange and left-luggage office. Note carefully the two hours a day when the baggage room is closed *(przerwy)*. Beware of pickpockets on this crowded intermediate level. (Uniformed police patrol the station regularly, so if you're directly threatened, start screaming 'police' and you'll put your assailants on the defensive.)

Above this is the main station hall where you can buy domestic tickets and reserve couchettes to any city in Poland (long queues). The posted time-tables are easy to follow. Here you'll also find 24-hour stand-up coffee bars and a currency exchange (open 8 am to 10 pm daily) offering a slightly better rate than the offices downstairs in the passageways. This office will also change travellers' cheques but they take 10% commission (no commission on cash). On a balcony about this spacious hall are the international ticket windows and, on the opposite balcony, a travel agency which sells international bus tickets.

Reader Norm Mathews of Western Australia sent us this:

> I was robbed by pickpockets whilst boarding the train to Gdańsk. Two men hopped on before me, two after. I was jostled and lost the wallet in my hip pocket with day-to-day money. They tried to get at my waist belt but luckily it was under my jacket. The train moved off just after. I reported it to the conductor and later to the railway police in Gdańsk but they spoke no English and weren't interested. Later we heard of three other robbery episodes at Warsaw Central Station.

Reader Brian Moore of West Midlands, England, sent this:

One travelling companion had his pocket picked on the Warsaw-Kraków train by a well-organised pair. They had obviously selected their target at the Central Station. They followed him onto the train, one in front and one behind. As the target entered his carriage the first one bent down to pick up something whilst the one behind used the distraction to take his wallet and then bundled past as if in a hurry.

Bus The Central Bus Station serving western and southern Poland is on the west side of the city near Warsaw Zachodnia Railway Station.

For north-eastern Poland, including the Lake District, you must go to the Stadion Bus Station on the east side of the Vistula. An easy way to get there is to take a commuter train from Warsaw Śródmieście Railway Station in front of the Palace of Culture east to Warsaw Stadion Railway Station which adjoins the bus terminal.

Tickets for these buses are only sold at the stations and it's all a little complicated, so you're probably better off leaving Warsaw by train.

Getting Around

To/From the Airport The AirportCity 'linia specjalna' express bus runs to Terminal No 1 at the international airport from Aleje Jerozolimskie in front of Central Railway Station, every 20 minutes from 5.30 am to 10.30 pm (US$2, pay the driver). This bus also picks up near the hotels Bristol, Victoria and Forum (ask).

It's also possible to get there on bus No 175, which goes to Terminal No 1 from outside Central Station opposite the LOT office (punch a regular ticket). For the domestic airport take bus No 114 from Plac Trzech Krzyży at the south end of Nowy Świat. To get between the terminals (about three km) take either bus up ulica Żwirki i Wigury a few stops, cross the street and take the other bus back.

Airport Okęcie International Airport, 10 km south-west of central Warsaw, has arrivals downstairs, departures upstairs. Only change a small amount of money here as the exchange offices give a very poor rate. As little as US$1 should be enough to get into town if you're using public transport. Departing, there are no exchange facilities beyond passport control. The left-luggage office on the arrivals level is open 24 hours (US$3 per piece per day). To use bus No 114 or 175 to town you must purchase a ticket at a newsstand downstairs on the arrivals level inside the terminal building. Remember to get an extra ticket for your luggage. Both the AirportCity express bus and bus No 175 leave from the arrivals level (after dropping passengers at the upper departures level). A taxi from the airport to town will be US$20 (after bargaining).

Bus & Tram In Warsaw, city buses of the 100, 200, 300, 400 and 500 series and express buses with a letter instead of a number plus all trams and trolleybuses require only a single US$0.25 ticket (punch both ends). Suburban buses of the 700 and 800 series require two US$0.25 tickets, both punched at each end. Night buses of the 600 series operating between 11 pm and 5 am call for four US$0.25 tickets, all punched at both ends – a total of eight punches! Heavy baggage is an additional US$0.25 on all services.

You must purchase tickets at a newsstand (Ruch) before boarding the service, then validate them once aboard by punching them in a device near the door. Drivers don't sell tickets. You're liable for a stiff fine if caught without a valid ticket during a spot check.

Transit passes are available from the MZK Dział Sprzedaży Biletów office, ulica Senatorska 37 opposite the Saski Hotel, and at other locations. A one-day ticket *(bilet yednodniowy)* is US$1, a one-week ticket *(bilet tygodniowy)* US$5 and a one-month ticket *(bilet sieciowy)* US$13 (one photo required).

Watch out for pickpockets on crowded city buses and trams. Some are highly skilled and can easily zip open a bag you thought was in front of you. Don't become separated from your companion by people reaching between you to grab hold of the handrail. The pleasant looking young man who says hello may only be trying to distract you.

Metro Plans for a Warsaw underground railway were drawn up in 1925 but construction was interrupted by WW II. Work resumed in the 1960s but due to budgetary limitations progress has been slow and the metro still hadn't opened at press time. The initial north-south route linking Żurawia ulica in central Warsaw to Kabaty, a southern suburb, is scheduled to be completed by 1995 but it may take another 15 years for a second line to be built.

Taxi Some taxi drivers are friendly and just trying to make a living, while others will rip you off. Ask the driver to explain the meter system to you and judge his intentions by his response. At last report the meter reading was multiplied by 600, but this could change (any Warsaw resident should know the current multiplier). Beware of taxis parked at the Central Railway Station, the airport, the Palace of Culture, Plac Zamkowy and all the luxury hotels as they charge up to 1500 times the meter reading. Some taxis have new meters which show the exact fare. Avoid problems by making sure the meter is switched on.

Taxis with 'radio taxi 919' or 'super taxi 9622' on the side of the vehicle are far less likely to cause problems than unmarked 'pirate' taxis. If you take a taxi parked at a taxi stand you may be asked to pay double to allow the driver to return to the same stand (ask to be sure).

Car Rental The main Hertz office (☎ 211 360) is in the nine-storey car park at ulica Nowogrodzka 27, across the street from the Forum Hotel. Hertz also has desks at the Holiday Inn and Victoria Inter-Continental hotels. Avis (☎ 630 7316) and Budget (☎ 630 7280) both have reservations counters at the Marriott Hotel. All three companies are represented in the arrivals hall at Terminal No 1 at Okęcie International Airport. Turn to Getting Around in the introduction to this chapter for more information on car rentals.

There's a guarded parking lot between the Central Railway Station and the Holiday Inn Hotel.

Małopolska

Much of south-eastern Poland still bears a gentle bucolic air. Here in Małopolska ('Little Poland') you'll see people working the fields as they have for centuries, and long wooden horse carts along the roads. Until 1918 the region was divided into two parts. Everything north of the Vistula and a line drawn east from Sandomierz (including Lublin and Zamość) came under Russian control in 1815. South of this was 'Galicia' under the Habsburgs of Austria. Kraków remained semi-independent until 1846 when it was annexed by Austria. After an abortive uprising in 1863-64 tsarist Russia suppressed Polish culture in the territory it occupied, while the southern areas enjoyed considerable autonomy under the Austro-Hungarian Empire. In 1915 Germany evicted the Russians and in 1918 the whole area once again became Polish. The impact of this chequered history can still be seen.

While nearby industrial cities like Katowice and Łódź have little to offer the average tourist, nearly every foreign visitor makes it to Kraków, one of the great art centres of Europe. Some also join the hordes of Polish excursionists on their way to the mountains around Zakopane. There's much more to south-eastern Poland, however, such as the holy sanctuary of Jasna Góra at Częstochowa, perfectly preserved Renaissance Zamość, the superb baroque palace at Łańcut, and the horrors of Auschwitz, Birkenau and Majdanek. It's easy to lose the crowds in the unspoiled mountains along the southern border. Here is Poland to be savoured.

LUBLIN

Long a crossroads of trade, Lublin was an

important point of contact between Poland and Lithuania. In 1569 a political union of these kingdoms was signed here, creating the largest European state of the time. Beginning in the 17th century, Lublin saw repeated foreign invasions by Swedes, Austrians, Russians and Germans, culminating in the Nazi death camp at Majdanek. For a time in 1944 Lublin was capital of liberated Poland.

Somehow the compact old town (Stare Miasto) retains the flavour of this turbulent past with its narrow crumbling streets, defensive towers and ominously isolated castle, long a prison. During the 19th century the city expanded west to Plac Litewski and under the communists spectacular growth mushroomed in all directions. Many foreign students study at the Lublin Catholic University, Poland's oldest private university. Lublin is slightly off the beaten track so people are interested to meet you, which is half the reason for coming.

Orientation

The train station with its architecture echoing Lublin Castle is several km south of the city centre, so catch a trolleybus No 150 or bus No 13 to the 'centrum'. If you want one of the hostels on the west side of town, get out at the next stop after the Orbis Unia Hotel. The left-luggage office at the train station is open 24 hours. Left-luggage at the main bus station on Aleje Tysiąclecia is opposite stand No 11 (open daily from 6.30 am to 7 pm).

Plac Łokietka in front of Kraków Gate marks the boundary between the old and new towns. Go through the gate and you'll soon reach Rynek, the old market square. Krakowskie Przedmieście extends west from Kraków Gate, and most of Lublin's hotels, restaurants and large stores line this slightly decadent old avenue. The Orbis Unia Hotel, universities, parks and modern buildings are on Aleje Racławickie, its westward continuation.

Information

The tourist office (☎ 24 412) at ulica Krakowskie Przedmieście 78 (open weekdays 9 am to 5 pm, Saturday 10 am to 2 pm) sells good maps and is generally helpful.

In the old town, the PTTK, ulica Grodzka 3, may also provide information.

The Polski Związek Motorowy is at ulica Prusa 8 next to the PZM Motel. If you're having car trouble, this is the place to come.

Money To cash travellers' cheques you have a choice of the NBP Bank, Krakowskie Przedmieście 37, opposite Hotel Lublinianska (weekdays 8 am to 3 pm, Saturday 8 to 11.30 am), and the hectic PKO Bank, ulica Królewska 1 opposite Kraków Gate (weekdays 7.30 am to 6 pm, Saturday 7.30 am to 2 pm).

Post & Telephone The telephone centre on one side of the main post office, Krakowskie Przedmieście 48/50, is open around the clock.

Lublin's telephone code is 081.

Travel Agencies Orbis, ulica Narutowicza 31, sells international bus tickets to Western Europe, makes seat reservations on express trains and books couchettes.

Things to See

Old Town The 14th-century **Kraków Gate**, built to protect Lublin from Tatar invasions, is now the **City History Museum** (closed Monday and Tuesday). You'll get a good view of Lublin from the top floor. Rather than enter the old town straight away, go south-east a block on ulica Królewska to reach the baroque **cathedral** (1596). Beside the cathedral is the 19th-century neo-Gothic **Trinitarian Tower** with a religious art museum and another 360° panorama of Lublin, and below, a passage into the old city.

Walk straight ahead to Market Square (Rynek) with the 16th-century **Tribunal**, formerly the town hall, in the centre and many old town houses around. East of here at the end of ulica Złota is the beautiful **Dominican church**. It was rebuilt after the fire of 1575. In the first chapel to the right of the entrance is a large historical painting called *The Lublin Fire of 1719*.

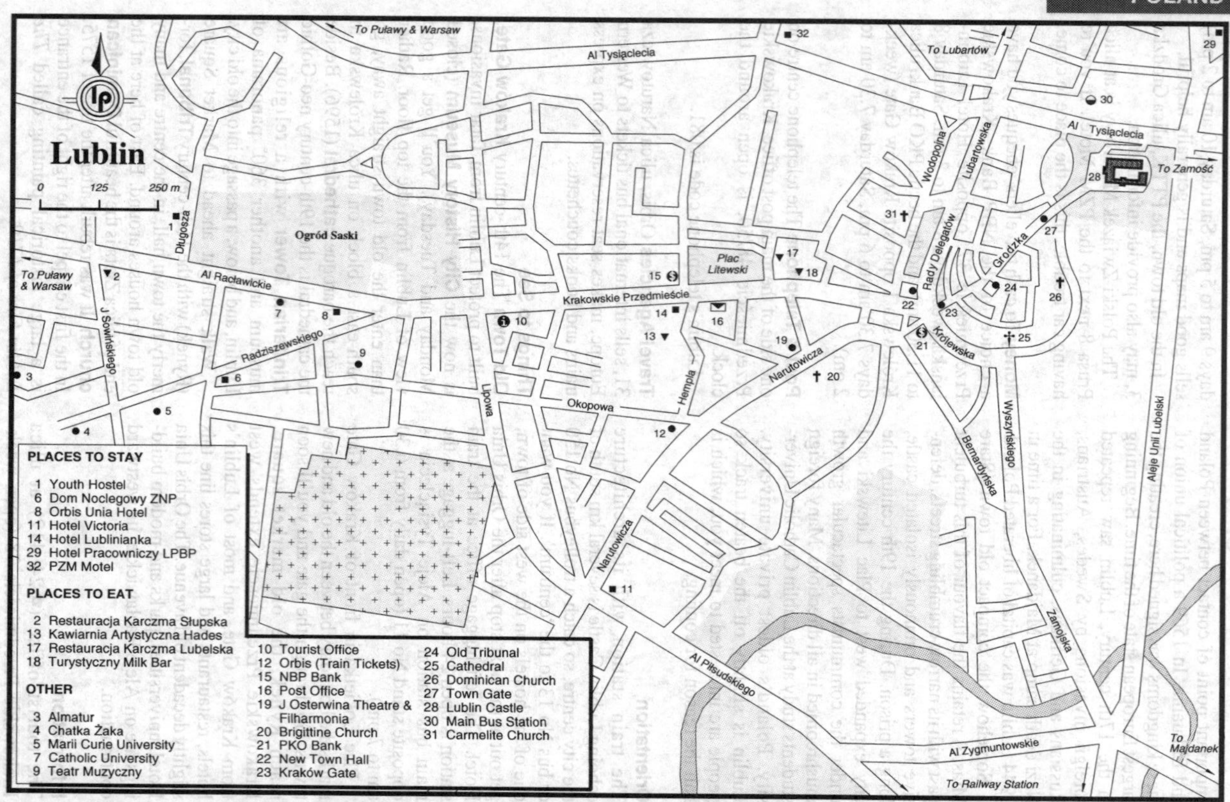
POLAND
Lublin
0
125
250 m
To Puławy & Warsaw
Al Tysiąclecia
To Lubartów
Długosza
Ogród Saski
To Puławy & Warsaw
Al Racławickie
J Sowińskiego
Radziszewskiego
Lipowa
Okopowa
Krakowskie Przedmieście
Plac Litewski
Hempla
Narutowicza
Wodopojna
Lubartowska
Rady Delegatów
Grodzka
Królewska
Al Tysiąclecia
To Zamość
Wyszyńskiego
Bernardyńska
Aleje Unii Lubelskiej
Zamojska
Al Piłsudskiego
Al Zygmuntowskie
To Majdanek
To Railway Station
PLACES TO STAY
1 Youth Hostel
6 Dom Noclegowy ZNP
8 Orbis Unia Hotel
11 Hotel Victoria
14 Hotel Lublinianka
29 Hotel Pracowniczy LPBP
32 PZM Motel
PLACES TO EAT
2 Restauracja Karczma Słupska
13 Kawiarnia Artystyczna Hades
17 Restauracja Karczma Lubelska
18 Turystyczny Milk Bar
OTHER
3 Almatur
4 Chatka Żaka
5 Marii Curie University
7 Catholic University
9 Teatr Muzyczny
10 Tourist Office
12 Orbis (Train Tickets)
15 NBP Bank
16 Post Office
19 J Osterwina Theatre & Filharmonia
20 Brigittine Church
21 PKO Bank
22 New Town Hall
23 Kraków Gate
24 Old Tribunal
25 Cathedral
26 Dominican Church
27 Town Gate
28 Lublin Castle
30 Main Bus Station
31 Carmelite Church

As you leave the church, turn right and continue north down the slope and through the Town Gate to **Lublin Castle**, which originated in the 14th century but assumed its present neo-Gothic form in 1826. During the war it was a Gestapo jail and 450 prisoners were murdered here just hours before Lublin was liberated in July 1944. There's a good view from in front of the castle and an impressive museum inside (closed Monday and Tuesday, free Saturday). One large painting by Jan Matejko depicts the union of Poland and Lithuania at Lublin in 1569. The 'devil's paw' *(czarcia łapa)* table in the museum recalls a legendary event at Lublin's Tribunal when a devil's court rendered a midnight verdict in favour of a poor widow. The Chapel of the Holy Trinity (1418) off the castle courtyard contains unique Byzantine-influenced frescoes, but is usually closed.

Majdanek Concentration Camp Just south-east of Lublin (buses Nos 28, 56, 153, 156 and 158 pass the site), Majdanek was the second-largest Nazi death camp in Europe. Here, where 360,000 human beings perished, barbed wire and watchtowers, rows of wooden barracks and the crematoria have been left as they were found in 1944. The immense concrete dome covering the ashes of the victims is a gripping memorial. Poles often leave bunches of flowers here.

As you arrive you'll see a massive stone monument by the highway. There's a sweeping view of the camp from there. The low modern building near the highway to the left of the monument contains a cinema where a documentary film is shown to groups (you have to be there before 2 pm to have any hope of seeing it). You can buy a site guide booklet in English here. The museum (closed Monday, admission free) is in the barracks to the right, outside the barbed wire fence on the west. Among the exhibits are three large buildings holding hundreds of thousands of pairs of shoes. The huge camp you see today is only a fraction of the facility the Nazis intended as part of their extermination programme. The Soviet army cut short their work.

Places to Stay

Camping If you have a tent try the *camping ground* (☎ 32 231; open from June to September) at ulica Słowinkowska 46 on the west side of the city, up beyond the Botanical Garden. Buses Nos 18 and 32 stop on a road behind the camping ground: find your way through a small woods, up a narrow lane and around the perimeter to the camping ground's main entrance. Simple, inexpensive bungalows are available, but they're often full.

Hostels Lublin's *hostel* (☎ 30 628) is at ulica Długosza 6 opposite Ogród Saski, not far from the Orbis Unia Hotel. It's difficult to locate the hostel as no sign faces the street, but just look for a low, yellow building between two large schools. The entrance is around on the north side at the very back – search.

In July and August your best bet is to head for the Almatur office (☎ 33 238), ulica Langiewicza 10, in the university district west of Dom Noclegowy ZNP. The staff arrange accommodation at *Dom Studencki 'Ikar'*, ulica Czwartaków 15, the fifth building west of their office. If Almatur is closed when you arrive, go directly to the hostel (US$3 per person).

Hotels The *Hotel Piast* (☎ 21 646), ulica Pocztowa 2, directly across the street from the main train station, is US$8/10 single/double, or US$14 for a four-bedded room. The entrance is around the side of this five-storey cube with the reception up on the 2nd floor. It's just a characterless place to crash, though perhaps worth a try if you happen to roll in late.

A slightly better place (though on the outside it looks worse) is the run-down, three-storey *Hotel BYT* (☎ 26 215), ulica 1-go Maja 16, with rooms at US$9 single or double. It's about two blocks from the train station.

Lublin's cheapest hotel is the *Hotel Pracowniczy LPBP* (☎ 774 407), ulica Podzamcze 7, a five-minute walk north-east of the main bus station. A double room in this nine-storey former workers dorm will set you back US$4. The main clientele is Ukrainian and Russian street-market vendors.

Dom Noclegowy ZNP (☎ 38 285), ulica Akademicka 4, also known as Dom Nauczyciela, is in a much nicer area close to the Orbis Unia Hotel beside the university (US$7/9 single/double with shared bath). If coming by bus from the train station, ask to be dropped near the Orbis Unia Hotel. This neat, eight-storey teachers' hotel is cheap but busloads of excited Polish tourists often fill the place. A good cinema and bar are behind the hotel and the biggest danger here – depending on who your neighbours are – is the radios found in every room.

Lublin's oldest hotel is the *Hotel Lublinianka* (☎ 24 261), ulica Krakowskie Przedmieście 56, which opened in 1900. Rooms here are US$13/19 single/double without bath, US$36 double with bath. The location is excellent. There used to be a cheap hotel nearby at Krakowskie Przedmieście 29 – check to see if they're reopened.

If you're driving you might consider the *PZM Motel* (☎ 34 232), ulica Prusa 8, on the north side of town. Rooms are US$9/15 single/double without bath, US$12/19 with bath, and breakfast costs US$2 per person extra. This place is owned by the Polish Automobile Association and there's a large auto service centre next door, but be prepared, this six-storey hotel is not all the name implies. Truck drivers often stay here.

Places to Eat

Turystyczny Milk Bar, ulica Krakowskie Przedmieście 29, is cheap. Another place in this vein is the *Staromiejski Milk Bar*, ulica Jezuicka 1 just inside the Kraków Gate in the old town.

The *Powszechna Restaurant* in the Lublinianka Hotel serves filling meals accompanied by good white wine and, in the evening, live music. The *Karczma Lubelska*, Plac Litewski 2, is another folksy restaurant.

The *Kawiarnia Artystyczna Hades*, ulica Peowiaków 12, downstairs in the Centrum Kultury w Lublinie, a block back from Hotel Lublinianka, is a private club where foreigners are always welcome. The bar opens at 10 am, the restaurant at 1 pm (menu in English and French), and on weekends there's usually live music (including jazz) and dancing. Sharp and modern yet reasonably priced, it's a little hard to find but worth the effort.

The restaurant in the *Orbis Unia Hotel*, Aleje Racławickie 18, is the best in Lublin and the only place in town where you can order eggs and toast for breakfast or be sure of a cold beer. Its menu is in English and French. The *Restauracja Karczma Słupska*, Aleje Racławickie 22, just west of the Orbis Unia Hotel, is a folkloric restaurant with live music in the evening (cover charge). It's open for dinner only (closed Wednesday).

The local Perła beer is not Poland's best, but it is cheap.

Cafés *Pod Czarcia Łapa*, ulica Bramowa between the Kraków Gate and the Tribunal, is an elegant café which plays on the devils' paw theme. Half a block away, *U Rajcy*, Rynek 2, is similar. *Café Trzosik*, ulica Grodzka 5a, also in the old town, is another nice place to sit.

Entertainment

For Filharmonia tickets check the ticket office at ulica Kapucyńska 7. Concerts are most likely on Saturday nights. Opposite the Brigittine Church just around the corner is the ticket office of the *J Osterina Theatre* (1886). Although it presents mostly drama in Polish, you might attend until the first intermission to see the theatre and sample the acting.

Teatr Muzyczny operettas are performed at the new theatre at ulica Skłodowskiej 5. Check the daily papers which list performances at all these theatres.

On the weekend there's usually a student disco at the *Chatka Żaka*, ulica Radziszewskiego 16 at Marii Curie University. Almost everything that's happening around Lublin is advertised on posters at the Chatka Żaka.

Getting There & Away

Bus Be aware that there are three bus stations in Lublin: the main bus station on Aleje Tysiąclecia, one near the main train station and another two km east of town. You don't need to bother with either of the latter to get out of town, but you need to be aware of them in case you happen to arrive at one. Frequent city buses link all stations to the 'centrum'.

Buses from the main bus station run west to Kazimierz Dolny (40 km) and Łódź (260 km), south-west to Kraków (269 km), Częstochowa (288 km) and Zakopane (376 km), south-east to Zamość (89 km) and north-west to Warsaw (161 km). Buses to Zamość leave from stands Nos 13, 14 and 15. It's always a good idea to buy an advance ticket with a reserved seat the day before, especially on weekends and holidays.

Train The *Bystrzyca* express runs daily between Lublin and Warsaw (175 km, three hours), leaving Lublin in the morning and Warsaw in the afternoon. Reservations are required. From Lublin there are overnight trains with sleepers to Gdynia and Wrocław (but not to Kraków). There is an overnight train with couchettes from Kraków. Two fast trains a day, the *Jadwiga* and *Jagiełło*, depart from Lublin for Kraków, one in the early morning and another in the afternoon (five hours via Radom).

Railway connections from Lublin to Zamość and southern Poland are poor because the lines were originally laid down before WW I when this area was under Russia while the area around Kraków was Austrian. Local trains to Zamość are painfully slow – take a bus.

ZAMOŚĆ

Zamość hasn't changed much since the 16th century when its chessboard street pattern was laid down by the Italian architect Bernardo Morando. The intact town square has an almost Latin American flavour with its long arcades and pastel shades.

Jan Zamoyski, chancellor and commander in chief of Renaissance Poland, founded Zamość in 1580 as an ideal urban settlement and impregnable barrier against Cossack and Tatar raids from the east. Its position on a busy trade route midway between Lublin and L'vov prompted merchants of many nationalities to settle here. Zamość's fortifications withstood Cossack and Swedish attacks in 1648 and 1656 but by the 18th century its military value had dwindled. Later it was used as a military prison.

The Nazis renamed Zamość 'Himmlerstadt' and expelled the Polish inhabitants from 292 nearby villages. Their places were taken by German colonists to create an eastern bulwark for the Third Reich. Surrounded by parks and totally unspoiled today, Zamość is unique in Eastern Europe. Unlike overpromoted cities like Prague, Zamość doesn't get a lot of Western visitors, which is refreshing.

Orientation

The bus and train stations are on opposite sides of Zamość, each about two km from the centre. From in front of the bus station take bus No 0, 22 or 59 to the centre of town. The left-luggage office at the bus station is next to the information counter. There's also left-luggage at the train station. The marketplace is on the north edge of the old town along ulica Przyrynek.

Information

The tourist information office (☎ 22 92) is in a corner of the old town hall directly off Rynek Wielki.

The Polski Związek Motorowy (☎ 34 71) is at ulica Peowiaków 9, a few blocks north-east of the old town. There's an auto service centre here.

Money Change travellers' cheques at the Bank Pekao SA, ulica Grodzka 2 (weekdays 7.30 am to 5 pm, Saturday 7.30 to noon).

Post & Telephone The post office and telephone centre is at ulica Kościuszki 9 (Monday to Saturday 7 am to 9 pm). Zamość's telephone code is 084.

Travel Agencies Orbis, ulica Grodzka 18, has information on trains and sells tickets.

The PTTK, ulica Staszica 31, can provide

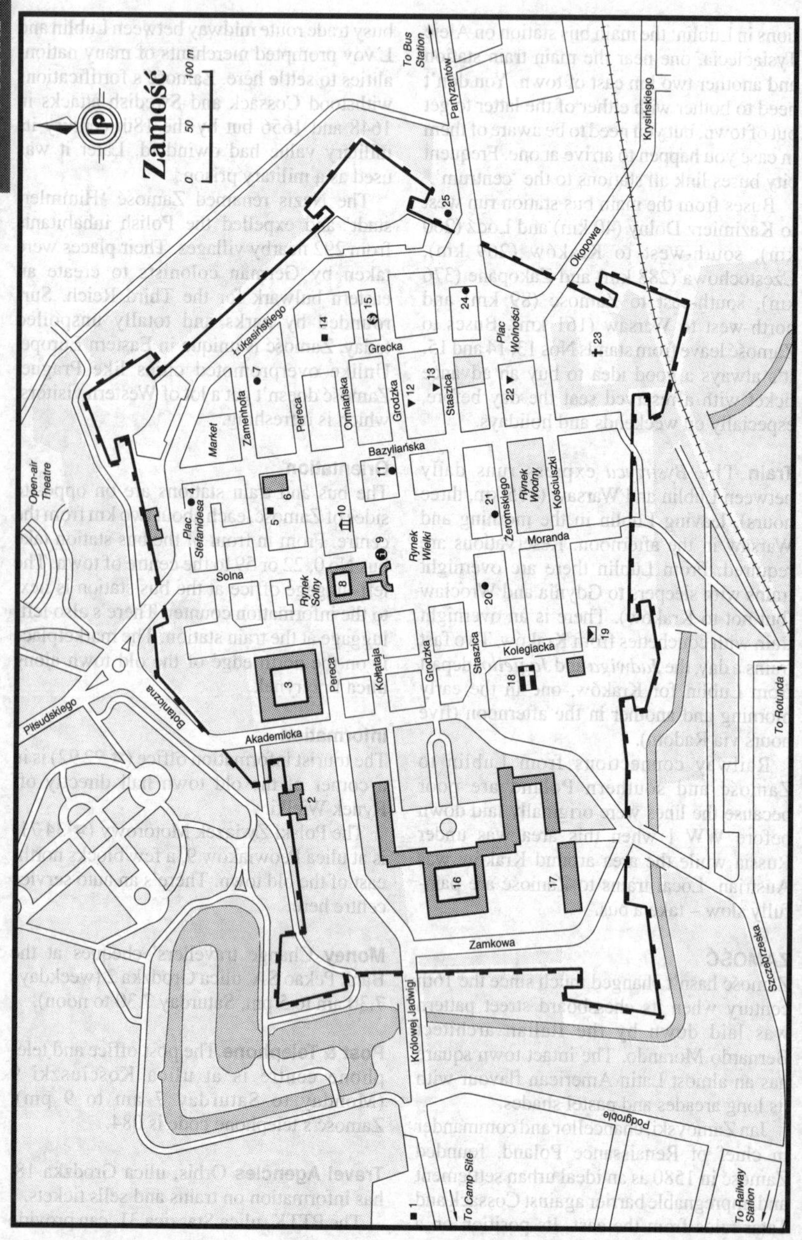
Zamość
0 50 100 m
To Bus Station
Partyzantów
Krysińskiego
Okopowa
Łukasińskiego
Grecka
Plac Wolności
Ormiańska
Pereca
Zamenhofa
Market
Grodzka
Staszica
Bazyliańska
Open-air Theatre
Plac Stefanidesa
Solna
Rynek Solny
Rynek Wielki
Żeromskiego
Rynek Wodny
Kościuszki
Moranda
Kolegiacka
Kołłątaja
Piłsudskiego
Botaniczna
Akademicka
Zamkowa
Szczebrzeska
Królowej Jadwigi
Podgroble
To Camp Site
To Railway Station
To Rotunda

PLACES TO STAY

1 Sportowy Hotel
5 PTTK Dom Wycieczkowy
14 Hotel Renesans

PLACES TO EAT

12 Bar Lech
13 Milk Bar Popularno
22 Restaurajca Centralka

OTHER

2 Old Lublin Gate
3 Former Academy
4 Market
6 Public Library
7 Jazz Club Kosz
8 Town Hall
9 Tourist Office
10 Museum
11 Orbis
15 Bank Pekao
16 Zamoyski Palace
17 Arsenal Museum
18 St Thomas' Cathedral
19 Post Office
20 PTTK Office
21 Royal Night Club
23 St Nicholas' Church
24 Cinema
25 Old L'vov Gate

an English-speaking guide for a four-hour city walking tour, including a visit to the passageways at the L'vov Gate, for US$30 per group.

Things to See

Zamość is a pleasant small town with all the sights an easy stroll apart. You'll want to begin on **Rynek Wielki**, an impressive square surrounded by Italian-style arcaded dwelling houses once owned by wealthy Greek and Armenian traders. The curving exterior stairway was added to the 16th-century **town hall** in 1768. The House 'Under the Angel' (1634), Ormiańska 24 on Rynek Wielki, is a **museum** (closed Monday) which presents the opportunity to see a good collection of historical paintings plus the interior of an Armenian merchant's house. Just off the south-west corner of this square, at ulica Staszica 37, the famous German revolutionary, Rosa Luxemburg, was born in 1870.

Continue west a bit to **St Thomas' Cathedral** (1598), a three-aisled Mannerist basilica. South-west of this church is the old **Arsenal** (1583), now a museum of old weapons (closed Monday). The nearby **Zamoyski Palace** (1585) lost much of its character when it was converted into a military hospital in 1831. North again on ulica Akademicka is the **former Academy** (1648). The fortifications opposite this building have been beautifully landscaped and made into a park extending east along the north side of Zamość to the **open-air theatre**.

Re-enter the town south from the theatre to see the old **synagogue** (1620), now a public library, on the corner of Zamenhofa and Bazyliańska. Do go inside. East on Zamenhofa you come again to the bastions of Zamość. Turn right and walk south towards **L'vov Gate** (1820) where you'll find a 16th-century bastion with endless passageways which groups may enter. Russians and Ukrainians often set up a street market near the gate.

Return to Rynek Wielki and follow ulica Moranda south from the square. Cross the park and go over the train tracks and a bridge till you get to the **Rotunda** (1831), a circular gun emplacement where the Nazis executed 8000 local residents. Today it's something of a Polish national shrine.

Places to Stay

Bottom End The *PTTK Camping* (☎ 24 99) on ulica Królowej Jadwigi, one km west of town, is US$2 per person to camp. There's plenty of shade, an appealing bar on the premises, and bungalows are available.

In summer the *Schronisko Turystyczne 'Relax'* (☎ 71 553), ulica Szczebrzeska 10 next to the zoo directly across the street from the train station, also operates as a basic dormitory-style hostel.

In July and August there's also a 50-bed *hostel* (☎ 79 125) in the school at ulica J Zamoyskiego 4, behind Hotel Jubilat a few blocks north of the bus station.

The *PTTK Dom Wycieczkowy* (☎ 26 39), beside the old synagogue at ulica Zamenhofa 13, isn't cheap at US$13 per person in three to eight-bed dormitories.

No private rooms are available in Zamość.

Middle The nicest place to stay is the modern 73-room *Hotel Renesans* (☎ 20 01), ulica Grecka 6 in the old city. A pleasant room with private bath is US$12/19/23 single/double/triple. Rooms at the Renesans have a shower but the toilets are down the hall. Try to get a room on the 2nd floor to be further away from the disco beat downstairs. Their breakfast is good value at US$3 per person extra.

The *Sportowy Hotel* (☎ 60 11), on ulica Królowej Jadwigi behind the stadium between the camping ground and town, has rooms at US$10/12 single/double with bath, US$4 per person in an eight-bed dorm, or US$29 double for an apartment. Most of the rooms at the Sportowy are dormitories with three to eight beds and it's usually booked by sports groups.

The unfriendly *Hotel Pracowniczy No 4* (☎ 51 64), ulica Młodzieżowa 6 just off ulica Partyzantów between the bus station and town, is a former workers' dormitory which rents rooms at US$10 double (no singles) or US$13 for a four-bedded room.

The three-storey, three-star *Hotel Jubilat* (☎ 64 01), Aleje Wyszyńskiego 52 right beside the bus station, is more expensive (US$24/33 single/double with bath and breakfast) and less convenient to the sights. These drawbacks mean it almost always has free rooms.

Places to Eat

Bar Lech, ulica Grodzka 7, has a self-service milk bar on one side, a stand-up beer bar on the other. You could try it for breakfast as it theoretically opens at 7 am.

Milk Bar Popularno, ulica Staszica 10, is open for lunch weekdays and it's easy since you pay at the end of the line.

The *Centralka*, ulica Żeromskiego 3, is a full-service restaurant with a menu in English (weird translations!). Try the żurek (cream soup with egg and sausage) and kotlet po zamojsku (pork roll). Prices are good and they're open late (for Zamość). An older crowd comes here to dance on Thursday, Friday and Saturday nights.

Around the corner from the Centralka is *Pizza Italiana*, ulica Bazyliańska 30, with barely passable pizza and ice cream.

If all else fails, try the restaurant in the *Renesans Hotel* which is open until 10 pm.

The local beer is Warka Hetman.

Entertainment

Royal Night Club, ulica Żeromskiego 22, offers disco dancing nightly except Monday from 8 pm to 3 am.

Jazz Club Kosz, in the rear courtyard at Zamenhofa 5, is a cosy little bar open from 1 pm daily, with a disco on Friday, Saturday and Sunday from 7 pm to midnight.

Piwnica Pod Arkadami, Staszica 25 on Rynek Wielki, is a subterranean students' hang-out.

Annual events include a jazz festival during the last week of May and an 'International Meeting of Jazz Vocalists' during the last weekend in September. In late June and early July theatrical performances (in Polish) are staged on the curving main stairway of the old town hall. If you decide to come to Zamość for any of these, call tourist information at ☎ 22 92 well in advance to verify the dates, then call one of the hotels for reservations.

Getting There & Away

There are trains and buses between Lublin and Zamość. The train takes over three hours to reach Zamość from Lublin on a roundabout route, so you're better off coming by bus as these run every half-hour and are faster.

Buses leave Zamość Bus Station for Lublin about every half-hour until 7.30 pm (89 km). There's one morning bus to Kraków (318 km, eight hours, US$9) and four buses to Warsaw (250 km). Some buses aren't listed on the departures board, and those that are listed aren't necessarily daily, so it pays to ask at information. If you want to continue south from Zamość plan your escape immediately upon arrival by booking an onward ticket as train service in this direction is terrible.

The three daily trains between Zamość and Kraków are all slow and inconvenient. One leaves around 5 am and the other two arrive in the middle of the night. About the only useful train leaving Zamość is the daily fast train to Warsaw, departing around 7 am and reaching Warszawa-Zachodnia Station five hours later. Check the times at Orbis.

It's possible to visit Zamość as a day trip from Lublin by bus if you get an early start and book your return bus ticket as soon as you arrive.

SOUTH-EAST POLAND

The south-eastern corner of Poland near Slovakia and Ukraine is off the beaten track but not without attractions. The border town of **Przemyśl** on the San River, just 14 km short of Ukraine, is sometimes used as an entry/exit point (buses to L'vov, 92 km). Six huge churches and their towers loom above the main town and there's the usual assortment of small hotels.

South-west of Przemyśl are the **Bieszczady Mountains**, beckoning youthful hikers in summer and cross-country skiers in winter. Youth hostels (summer only), tourist hostels and camping grounds (with cabins) make bases for exploring this sparsely populated region of enormous mountain pastures. A bus from Przemyśl to Ustrzyki Dolne, then another to Ustrzyki Górne, will bring you into the heart of the mountains. Costs in this area are very low.

The south-east's polished jewel is the magnificent Renaissance palace (1629) at **Łańcut**, 67 km north-west of Przemyśl on the road to Kraków. Now it's a Museum of Interior Decoration (closed Monday and Tuesday), worth getting off your bus to see. Lots of buses cover the 17 km from Łańcut to **Rzeszów**, the regional capital, with a few old streets and many ugly apartment blocks.

If you're arriving by train from Slovakia over the Muszyna border crossing you'll pass **Stary Sącz**, a sleepy little town of single-storey dwellings with high, sloping roofs lining the quiet, cobbled streets. For a place to stay you'll probably have to continue eight km north-east to **Nowy Sącz**, pronounced 'nove-sonch', which has an old town square, several hotels and a good restaurant in the *Panorama Hotel*.

KRAKÓW

Kraków (population 800,000) is the third largest city in Poland. Over a millennium ago Prince Krak founded a settlement on Wawel Hill, above a bend of the legendary Vistula River. Boleslav the Brave built a cathedral here in 1020 and transferred the capital here from Poznań shortly after. The kings of Poland ruled from Wawel Castle until 1596, but even afterwards Polish royalty continued to be crowned and also buried in Wawel Cathedral.

At this crossing of trade routes from Western Europe to Byzantium and from southern Europe to the Baltic, a large medieval city developed. Kraków was devastated during the 13th-century Tatar invasions, but rebuilt. In January 1945 a sudden encircling manoeuvre by the Soviet army forced the Germans to quickly evacuate the city, and Kraków was saved from destruction. Today Stare Miasto, the old town, harbours world-class museums and towering churches while Kazimierz, the now silent Jewish quarter, tells of a sadder recent history, and Auschwitz is close by (see the separate entry later in this chapter).

Kraków was a medieval students' town. Jagiellonian University, established at Kraków in 1364, is Poland's oldest; Copernicus studied here. It's still the second-largest university in Poland (after Warsaw) and 10% of the present population are higher education students. This is the one Polish city you simply cannot miss.

Reader Anne Small of Tauranga, New Zealand, who was in Kraków in 1992, sent us this:

> I'm not a 'spiritual' person but sitting enjoying rests in the city square in Kraków was one of the really special experiences in my life. There were no jarring Western influences and no architecture obtruded. The

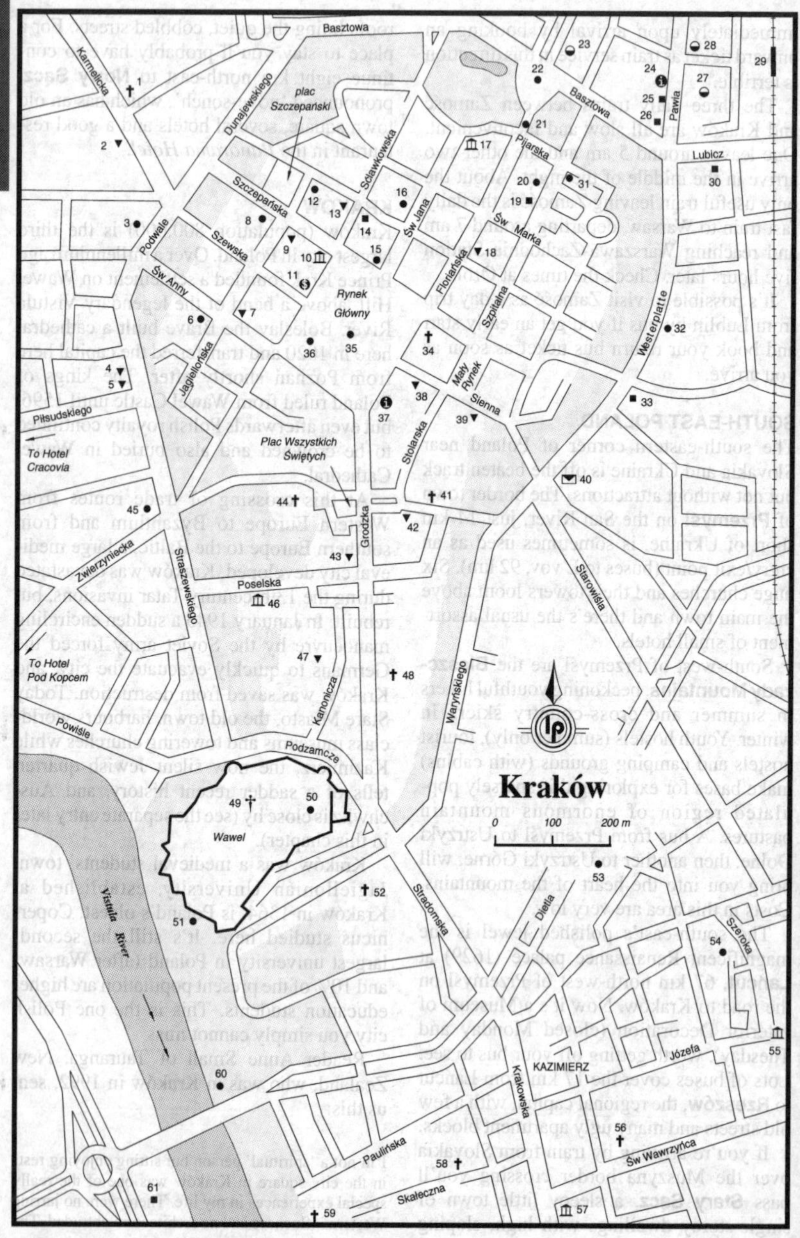
Basztowa
Karmelicka
Dunajewskiego
plac Szczepański
Sławkowska
Basztowa
Pijarska
Pawia
Lubicz
Szczepańska
Szewska
Podwale
Św Anny
Św Jana
Floriańska
Św Marka
Szpitalna
Rynek Główny
Westerplatte
Jagiellońska
Mały Rynek
Sienna
Piłsudskiego
To Hotel Cracovia
Plac Wszystkich Świętych
Stolarska
Grodzka
Starowiślna
Zwierzyniecka
Straszewskiego
Poselska
To Hotel Pod Kopcem
Kanonicza
Waryńskiego
Powiśle
Podzamcze
Wawel
Vistula River
Kraków
0
100
200 m
Stradomska
Dietla
Szeroka
Józefa
KAZIMIERZ
Krakowska
Św Wawrzyńca
Paulińska
Skałeczna

PLACES TO STAY

14 Hotel Saski
19 Hotel Pollera
25 Hotel Warszawski
26 Hotel Polonia
30 Hotel Europejski
33 PTTK Dom Turysty
61 Forum Hotel

PLACES TO EAT

2 Bar Rybny
4 Różowy Słoń Salad Bar
5 Bar Uniwersytecki
7 Pizzeria Grace
9 Bistro Piccolo
13 Lody u Jacka i Moniki
18 Żywiec Restaurant
38 Złoty Smok Self-Service
39 Jadłodajnia
42 Restauracja Orientalna Andalous
43 Balaton Restaurant
47 Café U Literató

OTHER

1 Carmelite Church
3 Księgarnia Elefant Bookshop
6 Collegium Maius
8 Stary Teatr
10 City Historical Museum
11 Bank Pekao SA
12 Strawberry Club
15 Orbis (Train Tickets)
16 Cartoon Gallery
17 Czartoryski Art Museum
20 Blue Box Disco
21 St Florian's Gate
22 Barbican
23 Bus No 100 & Jadłoderia Snack Bar
24 Tourist Office
27 Bus Station
28 Bus No 208 to Airport
29 Kraków Główny Station
31 Teatr Im J Słowackiego
32 Russian Consulate
34 Church of Our Lady
35 Cloth Hall (Sukiennice)
36 Town Hall Tower
37 Almatur
40 Post Office
41 Dominican Church
44 Franciscan Church
45 Filharmonia
46 Archaeological Museum
48 Sts Peter & Paul Church
49 Wawel Cathedral
50 Wawel Castle
51 Dragon Statue
52 Bernardine Church
53 Polski Związek Motorowy
54 Jewish Cemetery
55 Jewish Museum
56 Corpus Christi Church
57 Ethnographic Museum
58 St Catherine's Church
59 Pauline Church
60 Excursion Boats

cathedral meets the populace with its ground level entrances. Plenty of people but no crush of humanity and no groups of gawking tourists. I am so glad I took heed of the advice in your book and saw Kraków in that way because it could well be the last summer of innocence. I regret very much that I did not spend more than eight days in Poland.

Orientation

The main train and bus stations are next to one another just outside the north-east corner of the old town. There's no left luggage in the bus station but the left-luggage office at the adjacent train station is open 24 hours.

Ulica Pawia, with the tourist office and several hotels, flanks the stations to the west. To walk into town follow the crowds into the underpass on the corner of Pawia and Lubicz, then bear slightly right and lose yourself in the old streets until you come out on Rynek Główny, Kraków's glorious Market Square.

Trains on the Przemyśl-Wrocław line usually call at Kraków Płaszów Railway Station south of the city centre, not Kraków Główny. If there isn't a connecting train leaving immediately for the main station, take tram No 3 or 13 from ulica Wielicka, a few minutes' walk straight ahead from Kraków Płaszów, to 'Poczta Główna', the main post office on Westerplatte.

Information

There's an excellent tourist information office (☎ 220 471) at ulica Pawia 8, a few minutes' walk from the stations. They'll sell you maps and brochures, and direct you to the accommodation service next door. If you're staying longer than two days it's wise to invest in an indexed city map.

A poorly marked tourist information office is in the Cloth Hall on Rynek Główny, near the entrance to the National Museum (weekdays 9 am to 5 pm). They're seldom busy and good at answering questions.

The office of the Polski Związek Motorowy (☎ 220 215 or 223 490) is at ulica Dietla 67.

Kodak Express, Rynek Główny 41, does one-hour colour film developing.

Money Kraków's private exchange offices are open shorter hours than those in other major cities, but the one at Wawel Tourist, ulica Pawia 8, is open daily from 8 am until 8 pm.

To change travellers' cheques go to the Bank Pekao SA, Rynek Główny 31 (weekdays 7.30 am to 6.15 pm, Saturday 7.30 am to 1.45 pm), or the NBP Bank, ulica Basztowa 20 (weekdays 7.45 am to 1 pm).

Post & Telephone Mail addressed c/o Poste Restante, Poczta Główna, 30-960 Kraków 1, Poland, is collected at window No 1 in the main post office, Westerplatte at Starowislna.

American Express card-holders can receive mail addressed c/o American Express, Orbis, Hotel Cracovia, ulica Focha 1, 30-111 Kraków, Poland.

There's a crowded telephone centre in the main post office on Westerplatte, open weekdays 7.30 am to 9 pm, Saturday 8 am to 2 pm, Sunday 9 to 11 am.

Kraków's telephone code is 012.

Consulates There are five: the Austrian Consulate, ulica Św Jana 12, the German Consulate, ulica Stolarska 7, the US Consulate (☎ 229 764), ulica Stolarska 9, and the French Consulate, ulica Stolarska 15.

The Russian Consulate, Westerplatte 11 (Monday, Wednesday and Friday 8.30 am to noon), issues visas for US$20 and four photos, but one must first obtain an accommodation voucher from Orbis at the Hotel Cracovia (US$57/74 single/double a day and up). Interestingly, Orbis will also issue an 'open voucher' at US$30 for two weeks, US$60 for four weeks, which gets you nothing at all except the visa. The consulate may insist on seeing a Belorussian or Ukrainian visa if you plan to transit those countries on your way to Russia and such visas are only obtainable in Warsaw, so plan ahead.

Travel Agencies For bus tickets to Western Europe try Wawel Tourist, ulica Pawia 8, or Intercrac, Rynek Główny 14.

Dana Air Travel, ulica Szpitalna 40, and Fregata, ulica Szpitalna 32, sells cheap bus tickets to Western Europe and discounted air tickets to cities around the world.

Almatur, Rynek Główny 7 (upstairs on the 2nd floor from the courtyard), sells discounted Eurotrain tickets to Western Europe to persons aged under 26 years.

Both international and domestic train tickets, reservations and couchettes are available at regular prices from Orbis, Rynek Główny 41 on the north side of Market Square, and the staff speak English. From May to September, this same Orbis office offers rather rushed city sightseeing tours (three hours, US$15), plus day trips to the salt mines (five hours, US$15) and Auschwitz-Birkenau (daily, five hours, US$19).

Intercrac, Rynek Główny 14, runs daily sightseeing tours of Kraków (four hours, US$15), the Wieliczka salt mines (US$20) and Auschwitz (US$18). On Wednesday, Friday and Saturday nights they offer a typical Polish dinner with folk dancing at a local inn for US$25 per person including transfers. Ask about the 20% student discounts.

Bookshops Księgarnia Elefant, ulica Podwale 5/6, has books in English and the latest English-language newspapers.

For Carpathian Mountains hiking maps check the PTTK, ulica Jagiellońska 6, and Wierchy Sklep Górski, ulica Szewska 23, around the corner.

Things to See

Around Market Square You'll probably want to begin your visit on Rynek Główny, Kraków's wonderful Market Square, the largest medieval town square in Europe. It was here on 24 March 1794 that Tadeusz Kościuszko proclaimed a nationwide armed uprising to save Poland from partition. The 16th-century Renaissance **Cloth Hall** (Sukiennice) dominates the square and there's a large craft market under the arches. Upstairs is the National Museum (closed

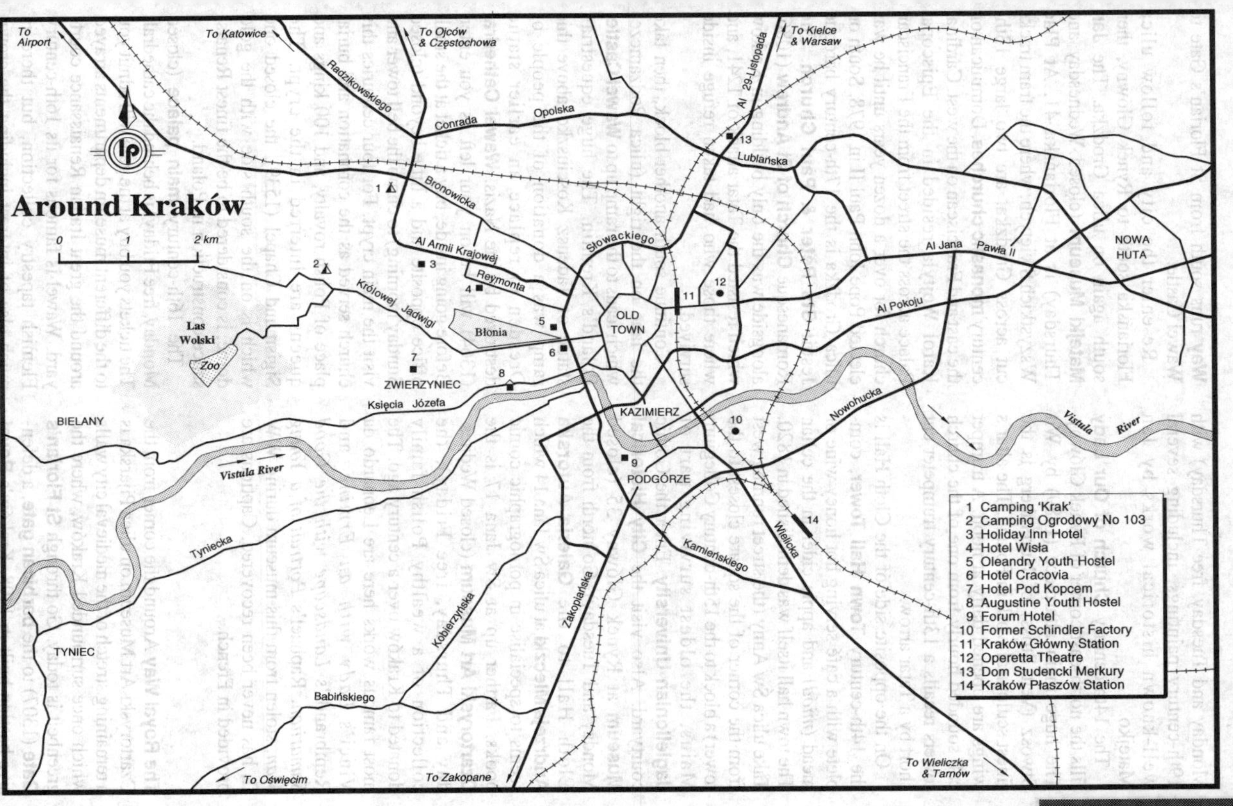
Around Kraków
0
1
2 km
To Airport
To Katowice
To Ojców & Częstochowa
To Kielce & Warsaw
To Oświęcim
To Zakopane
To Wieliczka & Tarnów
Radzikowskiego
Conrada
Opolska
Al 29-Listopada
Lublańska
Bronowicka
Al Armii Krajowej
Reymonta
Słowackiego
Al Jana Pawła II
Al Pokoju
Królowej Jadwigi
Błonia
Las Wolski
Zoo
ZWIERZYNIEC
Księcia Józefa
BIELANY
Vistula River
Tyniecka
TYNIEC
Babińskiego
Kobierzyńska
Zakopiańska
Kamieńskiego
Wielicka
Nowohucka
OLD TOWN
KAZIMIERZ
PODGÓRZE
NOWA HUTA
1 Camping 'Krak'
2 Camping Ogrodowy No 103
3 Holiday Inn Hotel
4 Hotel Wisła
5 Oleandry Youth Hostel
6 Hotel Cracovia
7 Hotel Pod Kopcem
8 Augustine Youth Hostel
9 Forum Hotel
10 Former Schindler Factory
11 Kraków Główny Station
12 Operetta Theatre
13 Dom Studencki Merkury
14 Kraków Płaszów Station

Monday and Tuesday, free Thursday) with 19th-century paintings, including several well-known historical works by Jan Matejko.

The 14th-century **Church of Our Lady** fills the north-east corner of Rynek Główny. The huge main altarpiece (1489) by Wit Stwosz (Veit Stoss) of Nuremberg is the finest sculptural work in Poland. The altar's wings are opened daily at noon. A trumpet call sounded hourly from one of the church towers recalls a 13th-century trumpeter cut short by a Tatar arrow.

On the opposite side of the Cloth Hall is the 14th-century **Town Hall Tower**, complete with a café serving hot honey wine or mead *(miód)* and apple cider in the cellar. The town hall itself was demolished in 1820. Take ulica Św Anny (the street running west from the corner of the square closest to the tower) a block to the 15th-century Collegium Maius, the oldest surviving part of **Jagiellonian University**. Enter the Gothic courtyard. Also visit the **City Historical Museum** at Rynek Główny 35 (closed Monday and Tuesday). Go north from the Cloth Hall to the **Galeria Autorska Andrzeja Mleczki** at ulica Św Jana 14 which seems to specialise in pornographic comic books. Farther up at Św Jana 17 is the **Czartoryski Art Museum** (closed Wednesday and Thursday, free Friday), the collection of a wealthy Polish family donated to Kraków over a century ago. The most famous works here are Leonardo da Vinci's *Lady with an Ermine* and Rembrandt's *Landscape with the Good Samaritan*. Raphael's *Portrait of a Young Man*, stolen from this museum during WW II, has never been recovered. Captions are provided in French.

The Royal Way Around the corner from the Czartoryski Art Museum on ulica Pijarska is a remaining stretch of the medieval city walls which once surrounded Kraków, where the greenbelt is today. Go through **St Florian's Gate** (1307) to the **barbican gate**, a defensive bastion built in 1498. Kraków's **Royal Way** runs south from St Florian's Gate to Wawel Castle.

Re-enter the city and follow ulica Floriańska south to Rynek Główny, then south again on ulica Grodzka. The **Jan Matejki Museum** (closed Wednesday and Thursday) is at Floriańska 41. At Plac Wszystkich Świętych, where the tram tracks cut across Grodzka, are two large 13th-century **monastic churches**, Dominican on the east and Franciscan on the west. Cardinal Karol Wojtyła resided in the Episcopal Palace across the street from the Franciscan church for over a dozen years until he was elected Pope John Paul II in 1978. South on ulica Grodzka is the 17th-century baroque Jesuit **Sts Peter & Paul Church**. The Romanesque **Church of St Andrew** (1086) alongside was the only building in Kraków which resisted the Tatar attack of 1241, and where those who had taken refuge inside survived.

Continue south another block, then take the lane on the right (ulica Podzamcze) which leads to the ramp up to **Wawel Castle**, Poland's Kremlin. The huge equestrian statue of Tadeusz Kościuszko above this ramp was a donation of the people of Dresden to replace an earlier statue destroyed by the Nazis. **Wawel Cathedral** (1364) will be on your left as you enter. Before going inside, buy a ticket at the small office opposite and a little beyond (closed Sunday morning) to climb the bell tower and visit the main crypt. For four centuries this church served as the coronation and burial place of Polish royalty, and 100 kings and queens are interred in the crypt. The Sigismund Chapel (1539), the closed one which is on the south side with the gold dome, is considered to be the finest Renaissance construction in Poland.

The 16th-century **main palace** (closed Monday, free Friday) is behind the cathedral. The tickets you buy at the gate will admit you to the different museum departments arrayed around the great Italian Renaissance courtyard. Wawel is famous for its 16th-century Flemish tapestry collection, but there is much else of interest including the crown ewels and armoury. The castle's greatest treasure is the 13th-century Piast coronation word, the 'Szczerbiec'. Many of the exhibits were evacuated to Canada in 1939 where hey sat out the war. Hans Frank, the Nazi governor general of Poland (later condemned to death at Nuremberg), resided in he castle during WW II. Keep in mind that he castle closes at 3 pm and a limited number of tickets are sold each day, so try to arrive before noon.

Wind your way down the back of Wawel Hill to the park along the Vistula River. Once upon a time a legendary dragon dwelt in a cave below the hill near the river. This fearsome creature had the nasty habit of feeding on fair maidens until Prince Krak put an end to his depredations by throwing him a burning sheep soaked in pitch which the greedy dragon ate, terminating his existence. A tacky **bronze dragon** now stands before the same cave breathing real fire, the creation of local sculptor Bronisław Chromy. Nearby you'll find the landing for **excursion boats** which operate on the Vistula River in summer, making scenic 1½ hour trips upriver to Bielany.

Kazimierz Founded in the 14th century by Casimir the Great, Kazimierz was settled by Jews a century later. To get there from the castle, walk south along the riverside and under the modern bridge to the 18th-century **Pauline Church**, which you enter through a small door in the high wall around the complex. Visit the crypt and then go east on ulica Skałeczna past Gothic **St Catherine's Church** (1373) to ulica Krakowska where you again meet the tram tracks. Follow these south a block to the **Ethnographic Museum** (closed Tuesday) in the old Kazimierz town hall. East across Plac Wolnica is Gothic **Corpus Christi Church**.

Ulica Józefa, the next street north of Corpus Christi, ends eastbound at a 15th century synagogue, now the **Jewish Museum** (closed Monday and Tuesday). The old **Jewish cemetery** at ulica Szeroka 40 is just north of here. Men must don a skull cap to enter. East of the cemetery you'll encounter another tram route which will take you back to the city centre (take tram No 3, 13 or 43).

Schindler's List During WW II the Germans relocated Kraków's Jewish population to a walled ghetto in Podgórze, just south of the Vistula River. Fifty years later the fate of these unfortunate people was unforgettably portrayed in Steven Spielberg's film *Schindler's List*. Interestingly, the Schindler factory is still there, unchanged since WW II, and in a glass showcase just inside the entrance is a small display about the Schindler episode. To get to the Krakowskie Zakłady Elektroniczne 'Telpod'. (Telpod Electrical Works), ulica Lipowa 4, follow the tram route south-east on Starowiślna from Kazimierz, turn left on Kącik (the second street south of the Vistula), go through a small tunnel under the train tracks and walk straight ahead on Lipowa. It's possible to look around the factory, but do ask permission first. (Many thanks to Andrzej Urbanik of Kraków for sending us photos and maps of the factory.)

As anyone who has seen the film will know, towards the end of the war Schindler moved his Jewish workforce to Moravia.

According to reader Larry Bailey of Huntington Beach, California, the new factory was at Březová nad Svitavou (formerly Brinnlitz), a village on the railway line from Brno to Česká Třebová. (This information arrived too late to be verified by the author.)

Nowa Huta Just east of Kraków is the industrial community of Nowa Huta with its ex-Lenin Steel Works, built by the communists in the early 1950s to balance the clerical/aristocratic traditions of the old capital. All of the raw materials have to be carted in. Far from acting as a bulwark of the regime, a May 1988 strike by 20,000 steelworkers here contributed greatly to that government's eventual fall. The tens of thousands of tonnes of carbon monoxide, sulphur dioxide and particulates emitted annually by the steel mill have seriously damaged Kraków's monuments but a restructuring programme is underway to cut both the workforce and pollution while improving the quality of the product by investing in new equipment.

Wieliczka The **salt mines** at Wieliczka, 13 km south-east, are a popular day trip from Kraków. Try to arrive before 2 pm to be sure of getting on a tour (open daily, 2½ hours, admission US$5, students and children US$3). Taking videos is an additional US$3.50. The basic charge includes a guided tour in Polish and you shouldn't have to wait over an hour for one to start. For a tour in English an additional US$22 per group must be paid. The tour in Polish can be rather tedious, so you might want to invest in the mine guide booklet in English sold at the souvenir shop.

You enter the mines down an elevator shaft, then follow a guide five km through the many chambers carved from solid salt. The mine's 11 levels of galleries stretch 300 km – some 20 million tonnes of rock salt were extracted over 700 years. According to a local legend the deposits were discovered in the 13th century by a Hungarian princess named Kinga whose lost ring was found in a block of salt extracted here. Thus it's not surprising that the largest underground chamber should be the **St Kinga Chapel**; it took 30 years to carve, measures 54 by 17 metres and is 12 metres high.

Another feature of Wieliczka is a health resort 200 metres below the surface where patients under medical supervision are treated for bronchial asthma and diseases of the respiratory tract. It's certainly a change of pace from museums and churches!

There are two train stations at Wieliczka. Due to an earthquake in 1992 which damaged the line (and the mine) most trains from Kraków terminate at Wieliczka Station. Wieliczka Rynek Station is about a km farther along, beyond the bus station. From Wieliczka Station follow the crowd south along the railway tracks until you see the bus station on your right. Walk through the bus station and continue a few minutes west up the hill to the mine. If the line has been repaired and your train continues to Wieliczka Rynek, stay on as it's closer. As you come out of Wieliczka Rynek Station turn right and go north through the park. Just beyond the red brick Miejski Dom Kultury turn left up the street to the mine. Either way follow any signs reading 'Kopalnia Soli Wieliczka'. The times of trains back to Kraków are posted at the mine ticket window. If these are inconvenient you can also return by bus No FB (ticket from the conductor) which departs from a stop on ulica Piłsudskiego, up the hill on the opposite side of Wieliczka Rynek Station from the mine. Bus No FB only goes as far as Kraków Płaszów Station from which you must take a tram on into Kraków.

Festivals

Kraków has one of the richest cycles of annual events in all of Poland. Ask about the Organ Music Days and Student Song Festival in April, the Polish Festival of Short Feature Films in May, the 'Kraków Days' and wreath-letting on the Vistula River in June, 'Music in Old Kraków' in August, the Folk Art Fair and the 'Solo-Duo-Trio' Festival of Small Jazz Groups in September, the 'Polonez' dancing contest in October, the Halloween Jazz Festival and the International Review of Modern Ballet held in November, and the exhibition of nativity scenes around Christmas.

During Easter week there's the famous week-long Passion Play at nearby Kalwaria Zebrzydowska; on Assumption Day(15 August) a solemn procession in folk costumes is held in the same village. The 'Kraków Days' are opened on Corpus Christi (a Thursday in May or June) by the 'Lajkonik', a legendary figure disguised as a Tatar riding a hobbyhorse!

Places to Stay

Kraków is Poland's premier tourist attraction and the city's hotels are expensive and heavily booked, so if you can skip a night by arriving in the morning or leaving in the afternoon, so much the better.

Camping From June to September *Camping 'Krak'* (☎ 372 122), in the far north-west corner of Kraków at the junction of the highways arriving from Katowice and Częstochowa, offers good camping facilities. The traffic noise here is considerable. The bar of the adjacent four-star motel is handy (bus No 238 from Kraków Railway Station).

A quieter camping ground is *Camping Ogrodowy No 103* (☎ 222 011), ulica Królowej Jadwigi 223, west of Kraków on the way to the zoo. Open from mid-May to September, it's US$4 per person to camp here and there's almost always space for tents (but no bungalows). Buses Nos 102, 134, 152, 452 and B all pass nearby.

Youth Hostels Both year-round HI hostels are west of the old town. The closest to the city centre is in a functional concrete building at ulica Oleandry 4 (☎ 338 822). Take tram No 15 from the train station to Hotel Cracovia. The hostel is on the street to the right of the tram line, west of the hotel. There are hot showers! Although this is the largest hostel in Poland it's often full in summer. Prices vary according to the size of the room and the staff may shift you around from one room to another charging a different price each time. We've heard of people being kicked out halfway through their stay because someone else had booked their bed! (The comments we receive from readers about this hostel are highly contradictory: some say it was the best hostel they stayed at, while others say it was the worst.) The hostel does serve a good breakfast. Upstairs in the building directly across the street from this hostel is the excellent and inexpensive *Oleandry Restaurant* – not the student dining hall downstairs.

There's a second, less expensive hostel (☎ 221 951) behind the large Augustine Church at Tadeusza Kościuszki 88, just west of the city (tram No 1, 2, 6 or 21, direction 'Salwator' to the terminus). Members stay in a functioning convent (mixed dorms!) overlooking the Vistula River. In summer it's also overcrowded. Ask about the direct bus to Auschwitz which leaves from across the street from this hostel around 8.30 am.

Both charge US$6 per person in a double room or US$4 for a bed in a six to 12-person dormitory, US$5 in a five-bed dorm. Everyone is welcome (no hostel card required).

Other Hostels The big, crowded *PTTK Dom Turysty* (☎ 229 566), ulica Westerplatte 15/16, an eight-minute walk from the stations, is a sort of glorified youth hostel. Singles/doubles are overpriced at US$19/24 without bath, US$28/34 with bath – you pay for the location. The only real reason to come here is if you're interested in a bed in one of the dormitories, which go for US$7 per person in a four-bedded room, US$6 in an eight-bedded room. Breakfast is US$2 extra. There's a noisy disco downstairs (open from 10 pm to 4 am).

Almatur (☎ 226 352), Rynek Główny 7 (upstairs on the 2nd floor from the courtyard), arranges accommodation in student dormitories at US$5 per person in two to seven-bedded rooms. Though many more beds are available in July and August they'll try to find something for you year-round.

The *Zaczek Student's Hotel* (☎ 335 477), Aleje 3 Maja 5 diagonally across the park from the Orbis Hotel Cracovia, is US$11 single, US$8 for a hard bed in a double, US$7 for a hard bed in a triple. This six-storey student residence belonging to Jagiellonian University is run as a regular hotel from July to September only. During other months the huge 'hotel' signs on the front of the building are only someone's idea of a joke. The Zaczek is a great place to stay if you want to meet Polish students, and there always seems to be a lot happening here. The 'Rotunda' disco is in the same building, and one of Kraków's HI hostels is just around the corner.

In July and August only the 11-storey *Dom Studencki Merkury*, Aleje 29-Listopada 48a, a couple of km north of the train station, operates as an international student hotel.

Private Rooms At ulica Pawia 8, near the

bus and train stations, is an office arranging stays in private homes for around US$8/13 single/double 1st class, US$6/10 in 2nd class. The rooms are often far from the city centre, so ask first. This office or the one next door can also help you find a hotel.

You may also be offered a private room by someone on the street outside. Ask them to point out the location on a good map of Kraków before agreeing to go.

Hotels The *Hotel Warszawski* (☎ 220 622), ulica Pawia 6, right next to the private room office, is about US$13/18/21 single/double/triple without bath, US$15/22/27 with bath. The more appealing *Hotel Polonia* (☎ 221 281), ulica Basztowa 23, just around the corner from the Warszawski, costs US$14/21/25 for singles/doubles/triples without bath, US$17/26/30 with bath. Ask for a room facing the quieter back garden. There's even an elevator that works! It's often full. The *Hotel Europejski* (☎ 220 911), ulica Lubicz 5 opposite the train station, is US$17/26/30 single/double/triple with bath.

To be sure of a room at one of these three hotels in summer you'll have to call ahead and make a reservation. The receptionists usually speak English, but you may have to call a couple before finding one with an available room. From September to May it should be enough to arrive before 2 pm to get a room on the spot. Beware of tram noise at these hotels.

The *Hotel Pollera* (☎ 221 044), ulica Szpitalna 30 in the old city, costs US$17/25/30 for singles/doubles/triples without bath, US$20/27/36 with bath, a satisfying breakfast included – quiet and good value.

A step up from these is the convenient *Hotel Saski* (☎ 214 222), ulica Sławkowska 3 just off Rynek Główny: US$22/34 for singles/doubles without bath, US$26/40 a single/double with bath.

The elegant old *Hotel Polski* (☎ 221 144), ulica Pijarska 17, charges US$22/32/35 single/double/triple without bath, US$29/41/50 with bath. For couples this is a good choice.

Right next to the Holiday Inn is the six-storey *Hotel Nauczycielska* (☎ 377 304), ulica Armii Krajowej 9, with 140 rooms with bath at US$18 single/double. If you don't mind commuting, this teachers' hotel is a good place to stay with a restaurant and disco on the premises.

The *Hotel Wisła* (☎ 334 922), ulica Reymonta 22, part of a large sports complex a km back towards town from the Nauczycielska, is also US$18 single or double, but it's not as convenient a place to stay.

By far the most unusual place to stay in Kraków is the *Hotel Pod Kopcem* (☎ 222 055), Aleje Waszyngtona, in a massive 19th-century Austrian fortress on a hill top overlooking the city. There's a cool forest surrounding the hotel, plus a coffee shop and restaurant. Room rates begin at US$31/35 single/double without bath, US$40/44 single/double with bath, breakfast included. There are only 36 rooms, so it might be worth calling ahead to make sure they'll have one for you. If you wanted to splurge once in Poland, this is it! Bus No 100 from Plac Matejki 2, opposite the barbican gate, ends in front of the hotel (hourly). Even if you're not staying, the Hotel Pod Kopcem merits a visit. There's a splendid view from the Kościuszki mound above the hotel.

Places to Eat

Around Market Square Privatisation has eliminated all of old Kraków's cheap proletarian milk bars but many excellent little places to eat have popped up in their place offering superior fare at prices any foreigner will find very affordable. Pushcart vendors sell obwarzanki, a doughnut-shaped pretzel or bagel which makes a tasty snack.

Złoty Smok (Golden Dragon), ulica Sienna 1, in a red brick building just off Rynek Główny, is a self-service for tourists with all prices clearly marked. Farther down the street, *Jadłodajnia*, ulica Sienna 11, provides basic fare to a local clientele.

For Polish haute cuisine try *Restauracja Staropolska,* ulica Sienna 4 (opens at 1 pm). Kraków's most exclusive restaurant is *Wierzynek*, Rynek Główny 15, allegedly founded in 1364. Since then the likes of Charles de Gaulle, Indira Gandhi and Mikhail Gorbachev have dined here. Drop by beforehand for reservations if you want to be sure of getting a table. The Wierzynek's immaculate service and excellent food are inexpensive by Western standards but you're expected to be neatly dressed.

The *Żywiec Restaurant*, ulica Floriańska 19, has a sharp, elegant appearance but the meals are substantial and inexpensive if you order correctly. There's a menu in English and the service is good.

West of Market Square *Bistro Piccolo*, ulica Szczepańska 2, is a great place to have a half chicken and chips.

The *Restauracja 'Cechowa'*, ulica Jagiellońska 11, is an old-style Polish restaurant with beer on tap. *Pizzeria Grace*, ulica Św Anny 7, serves good pizza at good prices. Vegetarians will like *Salad Bar Chimera*, ulica Św Anny 3 (downstairs), although it's weak on leafy green vegetables. The staff speak English.

Bar Rybny, ulica Karmelicka 16, dishes out huge pieces of fried fish at the counter.

The only genuine milk bar left in the centre of Kraków is *Bar Uniwersytecki*, on the corner of Piłsudskiego and Podwale (open daily).

Vegetarians will like *Różowy Stoń Salad Bar*, ulica Straszewskiego 24, where the salads are charged by weight.

The *Karczma Pod Blacha*, ulica Piastowska 22, just across the street from the western terminus of trams Nos 15 and 18, is a traditional inn serving typical Polish food (daily 10 am to 10 pm). There's sometimes folk dancing here.

A 24-hour convenience store (with beer) operates at ulica Szewska 10.

South of Market Square The *Restauracja Orientalna Andalous*, Plac Dominikański 6, offers North African dishes such as couscous.

For better Hungarian food than you'll get in Hungary try the *Balaton Restaurant*, ulica Grodzka 37 (menu in Polish only). The tipsy waiters tend to cause hilarity in the first hour, irritation and frustration the second hour.

North of the Old Town One of the best places for your money is *Jadłoderia Snack Bar*, Plac Matejki 3, next to the Grunwald monument just north of the barbican gate (Monday to Saturday 8 am to 8 pm, Sunday 10 am to 5 pm). The menu is in Polish and you must order at the counter, but just hang around and watch what others are getting. Huge plates of well-prepared food and cold beer are offered, and the dining area is tastefully decorated with modern art. It's just off the tourist track, so most of the patrons are locals.

Bar Smok next to the bus and train stations is neither cheap nor good but it does open at 6 am.

Dessert *Rio Bar Kawowy*, ulica Św Jana 2, has the best coffee in Kraków. Locate this place early in your visit.

For Kraków's top ice cream get in line at *Lody u Jacka i Moniki*, ulica Sławkowska 8.

Cafés *Jama Michalika*, ulica Floriańska 45, is the elegant turn-of-the-century café you'd expect to find in Kraków. Many famous artists and dramatists have sat on the forest green velvet couches surrounded by Art-Déco chandeliers, stained glass and dark wood. Certain nights there's a cabaret show at Jama Michalika. And as if that weren't enough, there's no smoking in the main section at the back. On a summers' day a nice place to sit outside and have a drink is the café straight through the arch at Rynek Główny 17. From the pavement café on Mały Rynek behind the Church of Our Lady you can watch the trumpeter in the church tower on the hour.

For coffee and ice cream you can't beat *Kawiarnia 'Alvorada'*, Rynek Główny 30. A less touristy place for coffee and cakes is *Kawiarnia U Zalipianek*, ulica Szewska 24. In summer you can relax on its open terrace facing a park.

There's a good little bar in the basement of *Galeria Krzysztofory*, ulica Szczepańska.

No sign faces the street but go down anyway. Jazz concerts sometimes happen here.

The *Café U Literatów*, ulica Kanonicza 7, has a nice garden where you can sit in summer.

The *Piwiarnia pod Beczkami*, ulica Dietla 46, between Wawel and Kazimierz, is just the place for a mug of cold Żywiec (the only woman in there is the barmaid).

Entertainment

Check the listings in the daily papers. One of the first things to do in Kraków is visit the *Filharmonia* booking office, ulica Zwierzyniecka 1 (weekdays 9 am to noon and 5 to 7 pm), for tickets to any concerts which happen to coincide with your stay. Don't be fooled by the price of the ticket; this orchestra ranks with the best in the world.

Teatr Im J Słowackiego, ulica Szpitalna, offers classical theatre, opera and ballet. It's worth attending a performance just to see the gilded interior of this splendid neobaroque theatre erected in 1893. The *Teatr Miniatura* is just behind and shares the same box office.

Kraków's *Operetta Theatre,* ulica Lubicz 48, is a 10-minute walk east of the train station. Lots of trams pass this theatre for the return trip.

Lighter Fare On Tuesday and Sunday nights there's jazz at the *Pod Jaszczurami Student Club*, Rynek Główny 8 (admission US$3, students US$1.50). *Jazz Club U Muniaka*, ulica Floriańska 3, has live jazz concerts on Friday and Saturday from 9.30 pm to 2 am.

Films and other events happen at the *Cultural Centre* (Pałac Pod Baranami), Rynek Główny 27. The *Institute Français de Cracovie*, ulica Św Jana 15, screens quality films (in French).

Discos Kraków's top disco is *Blue Box*, ulica Szpitalna 38 (open nightly, admission US$5). *Maxime*, ulica Floriańska 32, is another disco (dancing from 9 pm to 4 am, admission US$3). The cabaret show at *Feniks*, Św Jana 2, is also fun. The *Strawberry Club*, ulica Św Tomasza 1, is a sharp modern bar with a disco downstairs.

The *'Rotunda' Students' Cultural Centre,* ulica Oleandry 1 opposite the hostel near Hotel Cracovia, has a good disco from 8 pm on weekends. Posters outside Rotunda advertise special events.

Getting There & Away

Air The LOT Polish Airlines office is at ulica Basztowa 15 on the north side of the old town.

Bus Buses departing from Kraków Bus Station include one every half-hour to Zakopane (100 km), nine a day to Oświęcim (60 km), one daily to Lublin (269 km), two daily to Zamość (318 km), seven daily to Cieszyn (Czech border, 121 km) and one daily to Łysa Polana (Slovakian border, 109 km). In June, July and August there's a nonstop morning bus to Częstochowa (114 km). Always check the footnotes on the posted schedule and try to buy an advance ticket.

Train Kraków is on the main railway line between Przemyśl and Szczecin via Katowice, Opole, Wrocław and Poznań. Another important line through the city is Warsaw to Zakopane. The overnight *Cracovia* express train arrives direct from Budapest via Košice (Slovakia) and Nowy Sącz. Coming from Prague or Vienna you usually change at Katowice, although in summer there's a daily train direct from Vienna. From Germany there are direct trains from Berlin-Lichtenberg, Cologne, Frankfurt/Main and Leipzig.

The *Sawa* and *Tatry* express trains depart from Warsaw in the morning, reaching Kraków Główny (325 km) about three hours later. The return trips are in the evening. The *Krakus* and *Pieniny* express trains do the opposite, leaving Warsaw in the late afternoon and Kraków in the early morning. The *Kościuszko* departs from both ends in the afternoon while the *Małopolska* runs during the middle of the day. Reservations are required on these excellent trains which ensure fast, easy transport between the two cities.

The *Lajkonik* express train runs direct between Kraków Główny and Gdańsk (621 km, seven hours), leaving Kraków in the early morning and Gdańsk in the afternoon. This train also services Warsaw, Malbork, Sopot and Gdynia, and reservations are required.

Other fast trains departing from Kraków include the *Kasprowy* to Zakopane (147 km, 2½ hours), the *Giewont* to Częstochowa (two hours) and Zakopane and the *Jadwiga* and *Jagiełło* to Lublin (five hours). Reservations are not required on these.

There are seven trains daily between Kraków Główny and Oświęcim, four of them in the early morning and none during the middle of the day. To Wieliczka trains run about once an hour (every two hours in late morning). Carefully check the times beforehand.

Getting Around

Trams and city buses use the same US$0.25 tickets (punch both ends), so buy a bunch as soon as you arrive. Most places in the centre are easily accessible on foot.

To/From the Airport Balice Airport is 18 km west of Kraków on the road to Katowice. Bus No 208 from the train station runs directly there at least once an hour from 4.30 am to 10.30 pm (45 minutes).

Car Rental Hertz (☎ 371 120) is at Hotel Cracovia, ulica Focha 1. Budget (☎ 370 089) is at Motel Krak, ulica Radzikowskiego 99 on the north-west side of the city.

THE TATRA MOUNTAINS & ZAKOPANE

Poland is a flat, open land of lakes and rivers, but in the south the Sudeten and Carpathian mountain ranges break through the plains. The Tatra Mountains 100 km south of Kraków are the highest knot of these ranges with elevations averaging 2000 metres. Here, folded granite and limestone were shaped by glaciation to create a true Alpine environment. The Slovakian border runs along the ridges of these jagged Carpathian peaks.

The entire Polish portion of the range is included in Tatra National Park (217 sq km, entry US$0.50). Zakopane, the regional centre, is known as the winter capital of Poland due to its popularity as a ski resort. The noted Polish composer Karol Szymanowski lived at Willa Atma in Zakopane from 1930 to 1936. Because so many Polish tourists come here, everything is very well organised and there are lots of facilities. For summer visitors it's a chance to do some hiking and meet the Poles in an unstructured environment. Many students come here on holidays, and your conversations with them may be as memorable as the rugged landscape itself.

Orientation

Zakopane, nestling below Mt Giewont at an altitude of 800 to 1000 metres, will be your base. The bus and train stations are adjacent on the north-east edge of town. The left-luggage office in the train station is open around the clock but the bus station left luggage functions only from 7.30 am to 7 pm. If you want to leave your luggage somewhere in town, the cloakroom beside the restaurant in the PTTK Dom Turysty is open from 8 am to 9 pm.

From the train station, cross the street and take ulica Kościuszki past the bus station straight up into town. You'll pass Hotel Giewont on the right before reaching the post office, your reference point in Zakopane.

Ulica Krupówki, Zakopane's pedestrian mall, is always jammed with throngs of Polish tourists parading in trendy ski or hiking gear. The cable car to Mt Kasprowy Wierch is at Kuźnice, four km south of the stations. 'Rondo', a roundabout midway between the train station, or town, and Kuźnice, is another good reference point.

Information

The Centrum Informacji Turystyczny (☎ 12 211) is at ulica Kościuszki 23 in the five-storey Kolejarz Hotel next to the bus station. It claims to be open 24 hours a day!

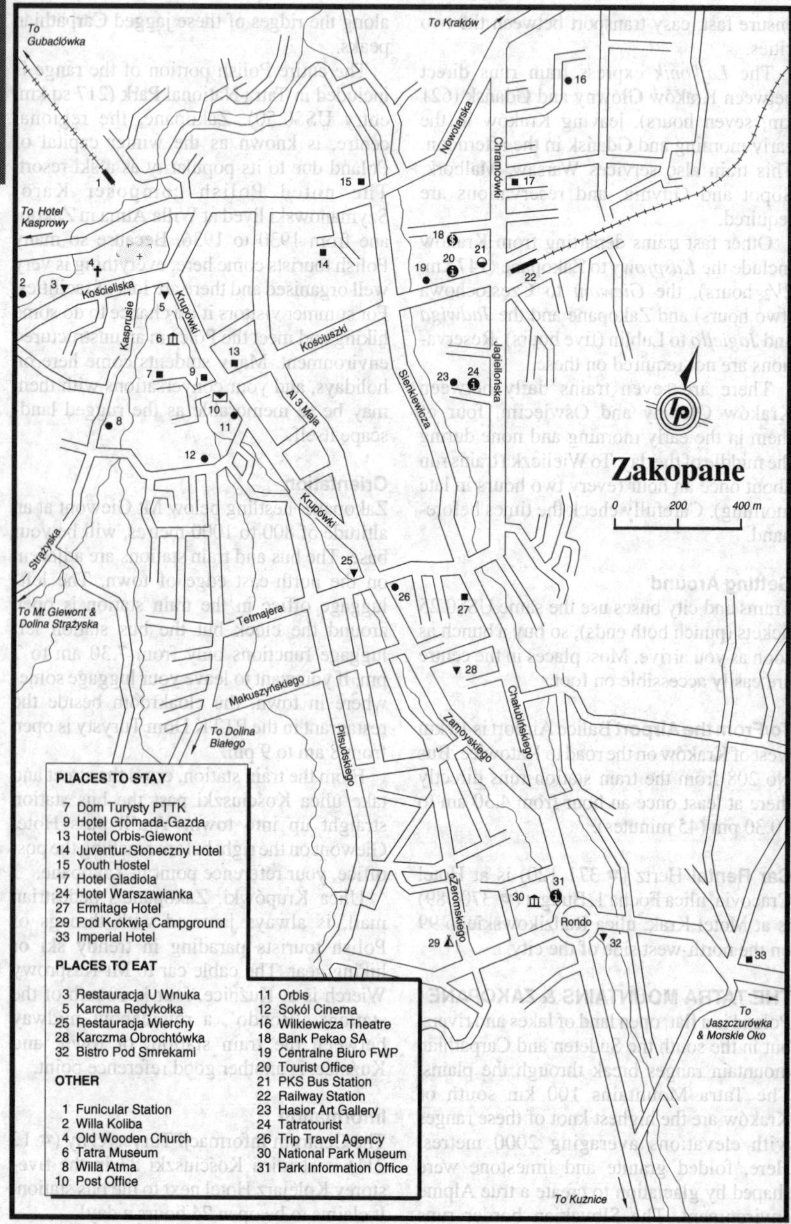
To Gubaćlówka
To Kraków
To Hotel Kasprowy
Kościeliska
Kasprusie
Krupówki
Nowotarska
Chramcówki
Kościuszki
Jagiellońska
Sienkiewicza
Al 3 Maja
Strażyska
To Mt Giewont & Dolina Strążyska
Tetmajera
Makuszyńskiego
To Dolina Białego
Piłsudskiego
Zamoyskiego
Chałubińskiego
Żeromskiego
Rondo
To Jaszczurówka & Morskie Oko
To Kuźnice
Zakopane
0
200
400 m
PLACES TO STAY
7 Dom Turysty PTTK
9 Hotel Gromada-Gazda
13 Hotel Orbis-Giewont
14 Juventur-Słoneczny Hotel
15 Youth Hostel
17 Hotel Gladiola
24 Hotel Warszawianka
27 Ermitage Hotel
29 Pod Krokwią Campground
33 Imperial Hotel
PLACES TO EAT
3 Restauracja U Wnuka
5 Karcma Redykołka
25 Restauracja Wierchy
28 Karczma Obrochtówka
32 Bistro Pod Smrekami
OTHER
1 Funicular Station
2 Willa Koliba
4 Old Wooden Church
6 Tatra Museum
8 Willa Atma
10 Post Office
11 Orbis
12 Sokół Cinema
16 Wilkiewicza Theatre
18 Bank Pekao SA
19 Centralne Biuro FWP
20 Tourist Office
21 PKS Bus Station
22 Railway Station
23 Hasior Art Gallery
24 Tatratourist
26 Trip Travel Agency
30 National Park Museum
31 Park Information Office

The Tatra National Park Information Office, ulica Chałubińskiego 44 at 'Rondo', sells good maps and can answer hiking questions, often in English. The National Park Museum, among the trees just behind this office, sells the same maps.

The PTTK office at Krupówki 12 arranges mountain guides from US$25 to US$50 a day per group depending on the difficulty of the hike. One guide, Mr Tadeusz Gąsienica (☎ 12 421), speaks perfect English and it would be worth calling him up beforehand to make sure he'll be available if you're sure you want a guide.

Money The only bank that will change travellers' cheques is the Bank Pekao SA, ulica Gimnazjalna 1, behind the bus station (open weekdays 10.15 am to 2.30 pm).

The currency exchange counter in the Hotel Giewont changes travellers' cheques on weekends, but deducts 5% commission.

Post & Telephone The telephone centre around the side of the main post office, on the corner of Kościuszki and Krupówki streets, is open weekdays from 7 am to 9 pm, Saturday 8 am to 9 pm and Sunday 8 am to noon. There are lots of blue card phones around town, and they work!

Zakopane's telephone code is 0165.

Travel Agencies Orbis (☎ 15 051), ulica Krupówki 22 beside the post office, books couchettes and sleepers on overnight trains (as does the ticket office at the train station). Orbis is also the American Express representative.

For bus tickets to Western Europe go to Trip Travel Agency, ulica Zamoyskiego 1.

Things to See & Do

Zakopane Founded in 1888, the **Tatra Museum** (closed Monday), ulica Krupówki 10, is hidden among the trees just down from the post office. Downstairs are displays on the folklore of the region including paintings on glass, peasant costumes, farm implements and dwelling interiors. Upstairs is natural history, including an excellent relief map of the Tatras.

From here walk down ulica Krupówki and turn left on ulica Kościeliśka to reach an old **wooden church** (1851) with a pioneer cemetery behind. If you continue west on ulica Kościeliśka you'll pass a number of traditional Zakopane-style houses, especially **Willa Koliba** (1892) across a wooden bridge to the right.

Return to the corner of ulica Krupówki and proceed west under the overpass to the **funicular railway** (built in 1938) up Mt Gubałówka (1123 metres). There's a fine view from the top (US$1.50 return trip) and a trail south-west along the ridge with spectacular mountain views on one side and quaint wooden farm houses on the other.

Kuźnice The work of Polish avant-garde artist Władysław Hasior can be seen at the **Hasior Art Gallery**, ulica Jagiellońska 7, up the hill from the train station (closed Monday and Tuesday).

For an introduction to the natural history of this area visit the **Przyrodnicze Museum of Tatra National Park** (open Tuesday to Sunday 9 am to 2 pm) in the forest just below 'Rondo' on the road up to the Kuźnice cable car.

Since it opened in 1935, almost every Polish tourist has made the **cable-car trip** from Kuźnice to the summit of **Mt Kasprowy Wierch** (1985 metres) where you can stand with one foot in Poland and the other in Slovakia. There's a great view from here, clouds permitting, and also a restaurant. Many people return to Zakopane on foot down the Gąsienicowa Valley, and the most intrepid walk the ridges all the way across to Morskie Oko Lake via Pięć Stawów, a very strenuous hike taking a full day in good weather.

In July and August the cable car operates from 7.30 am to 8 pm; in other months it's more like 8 am to 5 pm. Tickets cost US$4 for the return trip. When you buy a return-trip ticket you automatically get a reservation for a return two hours later. Advance cable-car tickets are sold at Orbis,

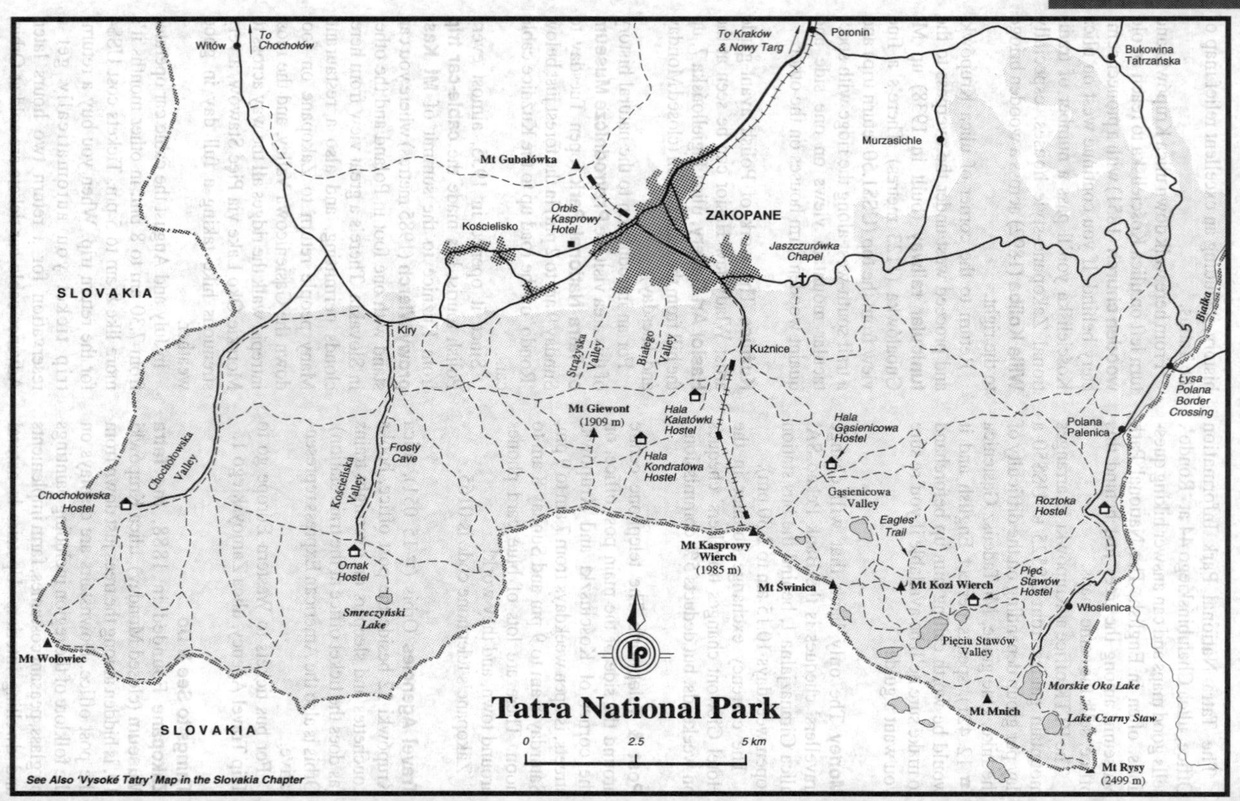
Tatra National Park
Białka
Łysa Polana Border Crossing
Bukowina Tatrzańska
Polana Palenica
Roztoka Hostel
Włosienica
Morskie Oko Lake
Lake Czarny Staw
Mt Rysy (2499 m)
Pięć Stawów Hostel
Mt Mnich
Pięciu Stawów Valley
Mt Kozi Wierch
Eagles' Trail
Murzasichle
Gąsienicowa Valley
Hala Gąsienicowa Hostel
Poronin
Jaszczurówka Chapel
Mt Świnica
Kuźnice
ZAKOPANE
To Kraków & Nowy Targ
Mt Kasprowy Wierch (1985 m)
Hala Kalatówki Hostel
Hala Kondratowa Hostel
Białego Valley
Mt Giewont (1909 m)
Strążyska Valley
Orbis Kasprowy Hotel
Mt Gubałówka
Kościelisko
Kiry
Frosty Cave
Ornak Hostel
Smreczyński Lake
Kościeliska Valley
To Chochołów
Witów
SLOVAKIA
Chochołowska Valley
Chochołowska Hostel
Mt Wołowiec
0 2.5 5 km
See Also 'Vysoké Tatry' Map in the Slovakia Chapter

ulica Krupówki 22 beside the post office. You can also usually get one at the terminal itself, though at busy times you risk running into a long line and having to wait an hour or more to go up, so it's best to book through Orbis the day before. In midsummer it may be faster to walk up (2½ hours).

Mountain Climbing One of the best things to do in Zakopane is to climb **Mt Giewont** (1909 metres), a jagged peak overlooking the town. From the cable-car terminus at Kuźnice follow the blue trail up the Kondratowa Valley past the *Hala Kondratowa Hostel* where refreshments are sold. From the cross on top of Mt Giewont (2½ hours from Kuźnice) you get a sweeping view of Zakopane and the Tatras, a truly magnificent spectacle on a clear day.

Return to Zakopane down the steeper red trail through the forested Strążyska Valley, along a foaming river beneath striking rock formations and past a flower-filled meadow, finishing at ulica Strążyska a couple of km south of the centre. The whole circle trip can be done in about six hours without too much difficulty.

Morskie Oko One of the highlights of a visit to Zakopane is the bus trip to Morskie Oko Lake, the largest lake in the Tatras (34.54 hectares in area and 53 metres deep). The name means 'eye of the sea' from a legendary tunnel said to connect the lake to the Adriatic. It's wise to book return bus tickets a few days in advance at the bus station, although tickets are often available on the bus itself (you want the 'Polana Palenica' bus). A couple of hours at the lake is enough.

From Polana Palenica it's still nine km (not steep) to the lake, though 20-passenger horse carts are available at US$4 per person to go up (two hours), US$3 to come down (one hour). It's best to pay each way separately so you can return whenever you like. Arrive early if want to be sure of finding a cart. At the lakeside is a large tea shop serving *bigos* (boiled cabbage).

A stone path runs around this mountain-girdled glacial lake – a lovely 40-minute stroll. You can climb to an upper lake, Czarny Staw, in another 20 minutes or so. **Mt Rysy**, the highest point in the Polish Tatras (2499 metres), rises directly above this upper lake. In late summer, when the snow has finally gone, you can climb it in about four hours from the tea shop. Lenin climbed Mt Rysy in 1913.

Side Trip West Take a bus (they depart frequently) west from Zakopane to **Chochołów**, an interesting village with large log farmhouses along the roadside for quite a distance. It's like an open-air museum of traditional architecture, except that all the houses are inhabited and the farming people have retained their age-old ways. There's a small museum (closed Monday and Tuesday) by the store opposite the church, and you can walk around the village.

On the way back to Zakopane get off at Kiry and walk up the **Kościeliska Valley** to the Hala Ornak Hostel. A broad stone road runs right up the valley. From the hostel you can climb the black trail to idyllic Smreczyński Lake in about 15 minutes. Buses from Kiry back to Zakopane are frequent.

Places to Stay

Camping The camping ground *Pod Krokwią* (☎ 12 256, open year-round), on ulica Żeromskiego between town and Kuźnice, has eight large bungalows, each containing several double and triple rooms (US$4 per person without bath, US$5 per person with bath), as well as camping space among the pines. The camping staff rents mountain bikes at US$9 a day and in winter you can rent skis to use on the ski slopes near Pod Krokwią from the outdoor shop on Rondo for about US$8.

Hostels Zakopane has a convenient year-round *hostel* (☎ 66 203) at ulica Nowotarska 45. From the train station walk straight up ulica Kościuszki to a bridge across a small stream. Here, turn right and follow ulica Sienkiewicza down to the corner of ulica Nowotarska, an easy 10-minute walk. You risk meeting large groups of preteens here.

The *Hotel Warszawianka* (☎ 63 261), ulica Jagiellońska 7/18, functions as a sort of hostel (sheets not provided and there's a 10 pm curfew), but they do have double rooms with shared bath at US$4 per person. They cater mostly to school groups and the signs outside are ambiguous, but look for a three-storey building between the road and the Hasior Art Gallery. The reception is inside: ring the bell at the counter and hope that someone's around. There are only hot showers when groups are present. In the basement is *Night Club Pstrąg* which opens at 8 pm.

Private Rooms People peddling private rooms often approach passengers getting off the buses from Kraków and lots of houses around Zakopane have *pokoje, noclegi* or *Zimmer frei* signs outside, indicating the availability of private rooms. You'll also see signs for new private *pensjonaty* all around Zakopane.

The tourist office (☎ 12 211), ulica Kościuszki 23 (open 24 hours a day), has private rooms at US$5 per person with shared bath, US$7 per person with private bath, but they only rent for stays of two nights or more. Some of the rooms are rather far from town.

Kozica Travel Bureau (☎ 12 212), ulica Jagiellońska 1, just across the park from the stations, rents private rooms at US$5 per person (one-night stays OK).

The Orbis office (☎ 15 051), ulica Krupówki 22, arranges room and board at small *pensjonaty* in Zakopane.

Holiday Hotels The Centralne Biuro Funduszu Wyzasów Pracowniczych (☎ 12 763), ulica Kościuszki 19, in Dom Wcyzasowy 'Podhale' just up from the bus station (Monday to Saturday 7 am to 4 pm), rents rooms in FWP holiday hotels around Zakopane. Rooms with bath and full board (three meals) cost US$14/26 single/double in 1st-class properties such as the *Hyry, Sienkiewiczówka* and *Roztoka*, while rooms with shared bath and full board are US$12/23 in 2nd-class places like the *Bristol, Postęp* and *Manru*. Without meals the rooms are about US$5 per person cheaper. A total of 11 hotels are available and the FWP office has a booklet with colour photos of each to help you choose. This is excellent value, so drop into their office as soon as you arrive.

Hotels The *Dom Turysty PTTK* (☎ 63 207), ulica Gen Zaruskiego 5, is a few minutes' walk from the post office along the road running towards the mountains. Rooms are US$10/18/27 single/double/triple with a bath tub, US$15 double with a shower, US$13 double without bath, or you can get a bed in dormitories with four beds (US$4), eight beds (US$3) or 28 beds (US$2.50). There's a restaurant in the building open from 8 am to 9 pm. Unfortunately, Dom Turysty is so swamped by excited groups of preteens that you should consider it as a last resort only. There's an 11 pm curfew.

At the modern three-star *Hotel 'Gromada-Gazda'* (☎ 15 011), ulica Zaruskiego 6 next to the post office, bright, clean rooms are expensive at US$22 single with toilet but no shower or US$35 double with bath, and breakfast included.

The *'Orbis-Giewont' Hotel* (☎ 12 011) across the street from the Gazda has rooms at US$13/18 single/double without bath, US$18/24 with bath, breakfast US$4 per person extra.

The *'Juventur-Słoneczny' Hotel* (☎ 66 253), ulica Słoneczna 2a off ulica Nowotarska, is a large modern hotel that caters mostly to students and young people (US$8/15 single/double without bath, US$12/23 with bath, breakfast included). It's only a block from Zakopane's hostel, so keep it in mind as the next place to try if you arrive to find the hostel full.

Comparatively few Westerners come here so prices are geared towards the Polish market which makes staying cheap if you shop around. Most hotels assume Westerners want a room with private bath and you have to specifically request one without bath. All accommodation rates are considerably lower in the off season, from October to mid-

December and April to May. During the ski season (from mid-December to March) prices double. Zakopane is one of Poland's most popular tourist centres (for Poles) and, despite the variety of accommodation available, on weekends and holidays everything could be full.

Mountain Huts There are a number of 'mountain huts' (large hostels) in Tatra National Park offering inexpensive accommodation for the hiker (US$4 per person in a dormitory or US$10 per person in a double room). All the huts serve basic meals. The hostels are in high demand at certain times and to protect the environment camping isn't allowed in the park (there are also bears!), so before setting out it's a good idea to check with the Biuro Obsługi Ruchu Turystycznego PTTK (☎ 12 429), ulica Krupówki 12 next to the Tatra Museum. It controls all the hostels and will know for sure which ones are open.

Alternatively, you could just take pot luck that there'll be a bed for you (don't arrive too late in this case). No-one is ever turned away though you may have to crash on the floor if it's very crowded. The huts often close for repairs in November so be sure to check that month. Otherwise they're open all year. The best weather for hiking is in August; until the end of May expect to encounter ice on the trails (boots required).

The easiest 'hut' to get to from Zakopane is the giant *Hala Kalatówki Hostel* (84 beds, US$10 per person, breakfast included), a 30-minute walk from the Kuźnice cable-car station (more like a hotel). Half an hour beyond Kalatówki on the trail to Giewont is the *Hala Kondratowa Hostel* (20 beds). For location and atmosphere it's great, but note the small size.

Hikers wishing to traverse the park could begin at the *Roztoka Hostel* (96 beds), accessible via the Morskie Oko bus. An early start from Zakopane, however, would allow you to visit Morskie Oko in the morning and continue through to the *Pięć Stawów Hostel* (70 beds), a couple of hours' walk on the blue trail over a high pass from Morskie Oko. Pięć Stawów (Five Lakes) is the highest (1700 metres) and by far the most scenically located hostel in the Polish Tatras.

A good day's walk west of Pięć Stawów is the *Hala Gąsienicowa Hostel* (100 beds), from which one can return to Zakopane. In midsummer the most crowded hostels are Pięć Stawów and Hala Gąsienicowa. In the western part of the park are the *Ornak* (75 beds) and *Chochołowska* (161 beds) hostels, connected by trail.

Places to Eat

Bottom End *Bar Fis* across the street from the bus station is a cheap self-service open from 8 am to 8 pm.

At a pinch the *Bar Semafor* in the train station (open daily 6.30 am to 10 pm) is not bad and serves a good bowl of flaki (tripe soup).

Several pizzerias, a Chinese restaurant and a host of snack bars have sprung up along ulica Krupówki during the past few years – take your pick.

Bistro Pod Smrekami at Rondo is the closest self-service to the camping ground.

Top End Zakopane's finest restaurant is in the *Hotel 'Orbis-Giewont'*, ulica Kościuszki 1 diagonally across from the post office. The menu is in English and German, the service good and there's even cold beer. Try a dish with bryndza (sheep cheese). The café serves a good breakfast. Though theoretically this place is open until 10 pm, the head waiter may deny you entry unless you have a reservation. *Restauracja Śwarna* (also known as Grill Bar 'Dom Podhala'), ulica Kościuszki 4, across the street from the Giewont, is less pretentious and offers a set regional meal of cream soup and pork cutlet. The *Karcma Redykołka*, on the corner of Kościeliska and Krupówki streets, is a rather touristy folkloric restaurant where the folk dances of the *górale* highlanders are performed some evenings at 8 pm (US$4 cover charge). A similar yet less touristy place is *Restauracja U Wnuka*, ulica Kościeliska 8, a block west of the old wooden church. This picturesque log edifice dating from 1850 and decorated with old glass folk paintings also contains a good café.

For regional dishes try the socialist-modern *Restauracja Wierchy*, ulica Tetmajera 2 at Krupówki. The menu is in English and German. From 8 pm to 2 am the Wierchy is a disco (US$3 admission, live music weekends).

A folklore-style restaurant worth seeking out is the *Karczma Obrochtówka*, ulica Kraszewskiego 10, a small street running between Zamoyskiego and Chałubińskiego streets halfway between 'Rondo' and town (coming from town, turn left at ulica Zamoyskiego 13a). Traditional Polish dishes are served in the basement of a large log house (Tuesday to Sunday noon to 10 pm). The menu is in English, French and German. This is perhaps the best of the various folkloric restaurants around Zakopane, though the beer is a little pricey. One reader reported that he had his four best meals in Poland here.

Cafés *Cocktail Bar Zakopiański*, Krupówki 40, is a good place to have ice cream out on the terrace and watch the passing parade.

Entertainment

Concerts occasionally take place at the *Ośrodek Kultury*, ulica Kościuszki 4, as advertised on posters outside.

Your most reliable entertainment option is probably a movie at *Kino Sokól*, ulica Orkana 2, next to the fire hall just off ulica Krupówki.

The Karol Szymanowski Musical Days in July and the Festival of Highland Culture in August are local events to ask about.

Things to Buy

Street vendors in Zakopane sell woollen sweaters, caps, gloves and socks at reasonable prices. Bargaining should get you 25% off the first price but check the quality carefully.

Cepelia below the Hotel Gromada-Gajda sells a variety of folk handicrafts, amber jewellery, icons etc.

Getting There & Away

The *Tatry* express train (for which reservations are required) takes just over six hours to cover the 472 km from Warsaw to Zakopane via Kraków, departing from Warsaw in the early morning, Zakopane in the afternoon. It's seasonal, so check to see if it's operating at the time you wish to travel.

Two unreserved fast trains operate daily to/from Kraków (147 km, 2½ hours), the *Kasprowy* departing from Kraków in the morning, Zakopane in the afternoon, the *Giewont* doing the opposite. The *Giewont* also serves Częstochowa departing from Zakopane in the early morning, Częstochowa in the afternoon. Several other trains also operate between Zakopane and Częstochowa (five hours).

Overnight trains with couchettes and sleepers run between Zakopane and Gdańsk, Wrocław, Poznań and Warsaw. In July and August there's an overnight train between Zakopane and Olsztyn.

From Kraków to Zakopane it's often shorter, faster and cheaper to take a bus (100 km, 2½ hours, US$3) instead of the train, but book advance tickets at the bus station. The bus driver may charge you a small amount for baggage. Two buses a day run between Zakopane and Lublin (a route poorly covered by train).

There's a direct Hungarian Volánbus daily from Zakopane to Budapest (364 km, nine hours, US$14), an excellent way to get from Poland to Hungary (Slovakian transit visa required by some). Get your ticket from the driver (reservations not possible).

Ask about buses direct to Poprad-Tatry, Poland.

To/From Slovakia Pedestrians may use the Łysa Polana highway border crossing off the road to Morskie Oko. All the Polana Palenica buses (eight daily in June and September, 13 daily in July and August, five daily the rest of the year) from Zakopane pass here. From Łysa Polana there's a road around to Tatranská Lomnica via Ždiar (30 km) with 15 buses a day. Pick up a few dollars worth of Slovakian crowns at an exchange office in

Zakopane to pay your onward bus fare as there's no bank on the Slovakian side of the border. The exchange office on the Polish side of the border gives a poor rate but they will take travellers' cheques. Southbound this route is easy but northbound you could find the Polana Palenica bus to Zakopane crowded with daytrippers from Morskie Oko (in which case hitch, as the taxi drivers want 20 times the bus fare).

Getting Around

There are buses to Kuźnice several times an hour from stand No 7 in front of the bus station. Buy your ticket (US$0.25) inside the terminal.

The minibuses you see parked opposite the stations operate like large taxis (you must charter the entire vehicle) and unfortunately they do not compete with buses.

THE DUNAJEC GORGE

Every year tens of thousands of people go rafting on the Dunajec River, along a stretch where the river cuts through the Pieniny Mountains just before turning north to flow up towards the Vistula. The river runs right along the Polish-Slovakian border here, winding through a lovely wooded gorge with high cliffs on both sides. The mix of deciduous trees and conifers makes for lovely colour patterns. This is not a white-water experience: the rapids are gentle and you won't get wet (accidents are unheard of).

The Dunajec Gorge is an easy day trip from Zakopane. First take a bus from Zakopane to Nowy Targ (frequent service, 21 km, 30 minutes, US$1), then one of the six daily Sromowce Niżne buses from Nowy Tary to Kąty (31 km, one hour, US$1), a couple of km east of Sromowce Wyżne. The landing at Kąty is fairly obvious with a large parking lot and entrance pavilion on the left.

The 2½ hour raft trips operate from mid-May to mid-September with boats leaving as soon as 10 people sign up (US$7 per person). If you arrive in the morning you're almost certain to be able to go (weather and water level permitting). Each 10-seat raft consists of five wooden coffin-like sections lashed together, guided by two boatmen dressed in embroidered velvet folk costumes. At the other end the sections are taken apart, loaded onto a truck and carried back to Kąty.

The trip ends at Szczawnica, a health resort, from whence you'll easily be able to catch one of the 25 daily buses back to Nowy Targ (35 km, US$1). They stop up on the main highway, a five-minute walk from the raft landing (not in the tourist bus parking lot near the landing). If you leave Zakopane just before 8 am and catch an onward bus to Kąty by 9 am, you'll easily be back in Zakopane in time for dinner.

Dunajec raft trips are also offered from Červený Kláštor in Slovakia, but the Slovakian trips are shorter and not as easily arranged.

OŚWIĘCIM

Auschwitz (Oświęcim) and Birkenau (Brzezinka), two deadly Nazi concentration camps 60 km west of Kraków, have been preserved as memorials to the 1.5 million people of 28 nationalities who perished here, the overwhelming majority of them Jews. From all Europe the fascists brought their

victims for slave labour purposes in the nearby armaments factories. Apart from the main camps there were 40 subcamps scattered throughout the area. As one group of starving prisoners became too weak to continue, they were led into the gas chambers, their places taken by new arrivals off the trains. It's difficult to conceive of the minds that could invent such a system. Children (especially twins) were held in the camps for medical experimentation.

Today the main Auschwitz camp contains a museum, information centre, cinema and restaurant, while the Birkenau camp has been left more or less as it was found. Due to their enormous historical significance, these camps are an essential part of any trip to Europe and something not to be missed. Yet you should be aware that many of the present inhabitants of Oświęcim are not overjoyed about the connotations associated with their town and it's role as a focus of 'death camp tourism', so it's best to be as considerate in your dealings with them as possible.

Orientation

Oświęcim Railway Station is about two km north of the main Auschwitz camp. Birkenau is three km north-west of Auschwitz or two km south-west of the train station. The left-luggage office at the train station is open 24 hours a day.

As you come out of the train station turn right and follow ulica Wyzwolenia south-west along the railway line, then head south on ulica Stanisławy Leszcsyńskiej to the 'muzeum', a 20-minute walk.

Things to See

Auschwitz Established in May 1940 in what used to be Polish army barracks, Auschwitz was the original extermination camp, though the number of people held here was much smaller than in some other camps such as nearby Birkenau. The museum occupies the various prison blocks, with different blocks dedicated to victims from different countries.

Over the years different groups have tried to exploit Auschwitz for their own purposes. The museum itself was conceived during the communist era as an anti-fascist exhibition and the fact that most of the victims were Jewish was played down (as all ethnic, racial or religious divisions were minimised under communism). The various national pavilions dedicated to the countries which lost citizens to Auschwitz were seen as a means of fostering international solidarity against fascism.

The Catholic Church has also been accused of attempting to 'use' Auschwitz and something of a cult has formed around Father Maximilian Kolbe, an inmate who voluntarily took the place of another Catholic prisoner sentenced to death in 1941. In 1982 Pope John Paul II dispensed with the usual requirement of verifiable miracles and abruptly declared Father Kolbe a saint even though prior to WW II he had been an ultranationalist who edited an anti-Semitic Catholic newspaper.

In 1984 a Carmelite convent was established right against the camp walls, sparking protests from Jewish organisations which considered its presence a sacrilege. In 1987 the Catholic Church agreed to move the convent within two years and when this deadline was not met, seven US Jewish activists climbed over the convent fence and staged a sit-in in July 1989. The beating and forcible eviction inflicted on the seven Americans and further delays led to much bitterness, and only in 1993 did the nuns finally agree to move to a new building about a km away after receiving a direct order to do so from the pope. The old building is still there, complete with its security fence and warning signs in English, just around the corner from the museum entrance in the opposite direction to the train station.

In the past the exhibitions at Auschwitz have been criticised by Jewish writers for giving undue prominence to the 75,000 Polish Catholics killed here at the expense of the Jewish dead. One Canadian reader of this book wrote that he was shocked when he suddenly realised that the thousands of individual ID photos of the dead on display at the museum were all Catholic Poles! This approach seems to be changing and pavilion No 27 dedicated to the 'suffering and struggle of the Jews' already presents Auschwitz with chilling accuracy as the place of martyrdom of European Jewry.

The Auschwitz Museum (admission free) opens daily at 8 am and closes at 7 pm in June, July and August; at 6 pm in May and September; at 5 pm in March and November; at 4 pm in April and October; and at 3 pm in December, January and February.

English-speaking guides can be hired at the museum information window, US$12 per group for one to 10 persons to visit Auschwitz, US$21 to visit both Auschwitz and Birkenau. The national pavilions are closed from October to April and can only be visited at that time with a guide (although pavilion No 27 is supposed to be open year-round). Pick up the guidebook which contains maps of the sites, plus information and photos.

Near the museum entrance is a flower shop if you'd like to leave a token.

The museum cinema (US$0.35) shows a 15-minute Soviet film taken just after the 1945 liberation. Ask when they'll be showing the English version. If you pay US$5 they'll schedule an English showing just for you, although the film's message is clear in any language.

Birkenau To grasp the real significance of this tragic site, Birkenau simply *must* be seen. The Auschwitz camp was originally intended to hold Polish political prisoners (like Father Kolbe) and it was at Birkenau that the extermination of large masses of Jews actually took place. Tour groups who are shown only Auschwitz with its cramped quarters and relatively small gas chamber and crematorium will get a totally false impression.

Birkenau surprises by its vast size. At the back of the camp is a monument flanked on each side by the sinister remains of much larger gas chambers and crematoriums, blown up by the retreating Nazis. Each gas chamber accommodated 2000 people and there were electric lifts to raise the bodies to the ovens. From the monument (1967) you'll have a view of the railway lines which brought victims to the wooden barracks stretching out on each side, almost as far as the eye can see. The camp could hold 200,000 inmates at a time.

In summer a bus runs direct from Auschwitz to Birkenau five times a day. There are also taxis (parked to the left as you leave the museum) which will drive you around Birkenau and back to the train station for about US$5. It's preferable to see it on foot but you'll need two or three hours at least.

Places to Stay & Eat

A Catholic institution, the *Centrum* (☎ 0381-31 000), ulica Św M Kolbergo 1, offers clean accommodation in a four-storey building next to the new Carmelite convent, about a km south-west of Auschwitz. There are seven two-to-five-bedded rooms at US$10 per person for bed and breakfast (students US$5). In the evening group discussions are sometimes held here.

A large self-service cafeteria, *Bar Smak*, is next to the museum entrance. The buffet in the train station is also inexpensive.

Getting There & Away

Oświęcim is fairly easy to reach. There are six local trains a day from Kraków Główny Station (1½ hours), 12 trains a day from Kraków Płaszów Station and 15 trains a day from Katowice (one hour). Check the times the day before as the services are irregular. Direct buses from Kraków (60 km, 1½ hours, US$2) pass the Auschwitz camp gate, although some terminate at a bus station on the opposite side of town (buses from there to the train station should pass the camp). The last bus back to Kraków leaves around mid-afternoon. There's fairly frequent bus service from the Auschwitz Museum to the train station. If there are a few of you, consider hiring a taxi at Kraków Bus Station for the excursion to Auschwitz and Birkenau (US$40 should be enough).

CZĘSTOCHOWA

Częstochowa (Tschenstochau) is the spiritual heart of Poland and pilgrims from every corner of the country come to Jasna Góra (Luminous Mountain) Monastery to worship the image of the Black Madonna, Poland's holiest icon. The best time to arrive is at dawn when the churches are overflowing with nuns in silent prayer. This could be the most sacred place you'll ever visit.

History

Częstochowa was first mentioned in 1220. In 1382 Duke Władysław of Opole invited the Paulites of Hungary to establish Jasna Góra Monastery, and the famous icon of the Black Madonna was brought from the east in 1384. The story goes that it had been painted at Jerusalem by St Luke. In 1430 the image was cut by invading Protestant Hussites and during restoration a scar from the sword blow was left on the Madonna's face as a reminder.

Early in the 17th century the monastery was fortified and subsequent Swedish (1655) and Russian (1770) sieges were resisted. Rebuilding took place after a fire in 1690, and centuries of patronage have increased the richness of Jasna Góra. Industry developed in the town at the end of the 19th century with the building of the railway from Warsaw to Vienna, and the communists built Częstochowa into a major industrial centre to balance the clerical influence at Jasna Góra. Today Częstochowa has a steel works with 30,000 employees, plus clothing, chemical and paper industries.

Orientation

The main train station (shown on our map) is undergoing renovation and the baggage room (open 24 hours except for three 30-minute breaks) has been moved several times recently – just keeping looking. Alternatively use the left-luggage office at information in the bus station (open from 7 am to 6 pm).

From the main train station, walk north a block to Aleje Najświętszej Marii Panny, locally known as Aleje NMP. Jasna Góra is on a low hill at the end of this important avenue, one km due west. If you're arriving in the early morning darkness you'll see a bright light high above the monastery.

A few local trains to Wrocław and Poznań use Częstochowa Stradom Railway Station on the south side of town (check).

Information

A very helpful tourist information office (☎ 41 360) is at Aleje NMP 65. It sells maps of many other cities in Poland.

The Polski Związek Motorowy (☎ 43 413 or 42 169), Aleje NMP 4, assists motorists.

Money The NBP Bank, Piłsudskiego 5 near the train station (weekdays 8 am to 1 pm, Saturday 8 to 11 am), changes travellers' cheques for 1.5% commission. The PKO Bank, Aleje NMP 19 (Monday to Saturday 8 am to 6 pm), also changes travellers' cheques.

The reception of the Orbis Patria Hotel will change travellers' cheques for 3% commission daily from 7 am to 7 pm.

Post & Telephone There's a telephone centre in the main post office next to the bus station (weekdays 7 am to 9 pm, weekends 8 am to 9 pm). Częstochowa's telephone code is 034.

Travel Agencies For express train tickets, couchettes and information try Orbis, Aleje NMP 40.

Things to See

Today **Jasna Góra Monastery** retains the appearance of a fortress, a vibrant symbol of Catholicism tossed in a secular sea. Inside the compound are two churches. The large baroque church you enter first is beautifully decorated, but the image of the Black Madonna is on the high altar of the smaller, less ornate church. It's hidden behind a silver curtain (1673) and only exposed during the frequent religious services. This makes it difficult to have a close look. Upstairs in the convent adjacent to the churches is the Sala

Rycerska where you can examine a copy of the icon up close.

There are also three museums to visit within the monastery's defensive walls (open daily). You can't miss the **Arsenal** (open 9 am to noon and 2 to 6 pm). The **600 Year Museum** (open 11 am to 4.30 pm), containing Lech Wałęsa's 1983 Nobel Prize, is just beyond. The **Treasury** or *Skarbiec* (open 9 am to noon and 3 to 5 pm) is rather hidden. It's above and behind the two churches and you enter from an outside terrace. You can also climb the monastery tower.

On weekends and holidays there are long lines to enter all three museums, and the crowds in the smaller church may be so thick you're almost unable to enter, much less get near the icon. A great 10-day pilgrimage on foot from Warsaw reaches here on Assumption Day (15 August).

The **City Museum** (closed Monday and Tuesday) in the old town hall (rebuilt 1908) on Plac Biegańskiego has an excellent historical collection and much information on the chain of ruined castles perched on top of sandstone crags along the 'Eagles' Nests Route' between Częstochowa and Kraków, once the border between Poland and Bohemia. The local **art gallery** (closed Monday and Tuesday) nearby at Aleje NMP 47 is also well worth visiting.

Places to Stay

Camping On the far side of the tour-bus parking lot behind the monastery is pleasant *Camping Oleńka No 76* (☎ 47 495; open from May to September). It's US$1.25 per person to pitch a tent, and rooms are US$4/7 single/double without bath, US$14/18/22 for three/four/five people with bath. There's a snack bar.

Summertime Hostels In July and August a seasonal *hostel* (☎ 43 121) functions in the three-storey school building at ulica Jasnagórska 84/90 (entry around back).

Also in July and August, it's possible to get a dorm bed for US$2 at the *Logos Foundation* (☎ 42 925), Aleje NMP 56, provided all the rooms are not occupied by groups. No bedding is provided.

Check with Almatur, Aleje NMP 37, for information on accommodation in student dormitories in summer. There's no office renting private rooms in Częstochowa (hopefully a landlady will find you).

Catholic Hostels *Dom Pielgrzyma* (☎ 43 302), the large building on the north side of the parking lot behind the monastery, has beds in double and triple rooms at US$10 per person (check-in from 3 to 8 pm, doors close at 10 pm). This church-operated facility is probably what you want if you came for strictly religious reasons.

Dom Rekolekcyjny, ulica Św Barbary 43 a couple of blocks south of Jasna Góra, also shelters pilgrims (doors closed from 10 pm to 5 am).

Hotels The three-storey *Hotel Centralny-Polonia* (☎ 44 067), at ulica Piłsudskiego 9 opposite the eastern exit from the train station, is US$12/20/25 single/double/triple without bath, US$22/28/35 with bath, breakfast included.

The *Hotel Miły* (☎ 43 391), nearby at ulica Katedralna 18, is US$10/12 double/triple without bath, US$14/15 with bath (no singles). It's often full.

A km south of Dom Rekolekcyjny is *Hotel Sportowy AZS* (☎ 55 247), ulica Św Andrzeja 8/10, in a neat white two-storey building. If you happen to arrive at Częstochowa Stradon Railway Station you'll find this hotel about halfway to the monastery. It's US$10/14 double/triple (no singles) and if there's no-one at the reception, check the back room downstairs. Since this place isn't often used by pilgrims, it's more likely to have rooms.

Places to Eat

Pizzeria La Bussola, Aleje NMP 16, services genuine pizza and beer, while *Restauracja Sir*, Aleje NMP 24, features Polish dishes.

Restaurajca Wiking, ulica Nowowiejskiego 10, has two sections: an up-market dining room facing the main street and a

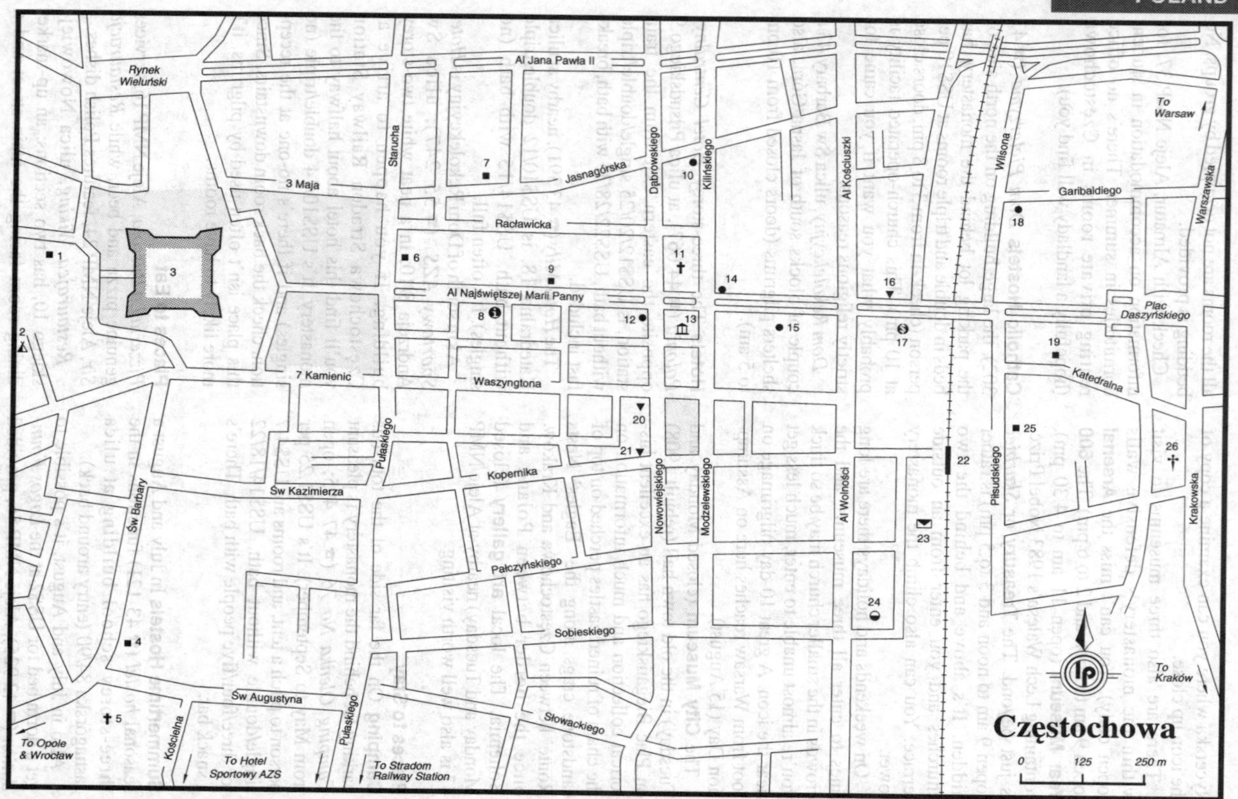
Częstochowa
0
125
250 m
To Kraków
To Warsaw
Warszawska
Krakowska
Plac Daszyńskiego
Katedralna
Garibaldiego
Wilsona
Piłsudskiego
Al Kościuszki
Al Wolności
Kilińskiego
Dąbrowskiego
Modzelewskiego
Nowowiejskiego
Jasnagórska
Al Jana Pawła II
Racławicka
Al Najświętszej Marii Panny
Waszyngtona
Kopernika
Pałczyńskiego
Sobieskiego
Słowackiego
Starucha
Pułaskiego
3 Maja
7 Kamienic
Św Kazimierza
Św Augustyna
Św Barbary
Kościelna
Rynek Wieluński
To Hotel Sportowy AZS
To Stradom Railway Station
To Opole & Wrocław
1
2
3
4
5
6
7
8
9
10
11
12
13
14
15
16
17
18
19
20
21
22
23
24
25
26

PLACES TO STAY

1 Dom Pielgrzyma
2 Camping Oleńka No 76
4 Dom Rekolekcyjny
6 Orbis Patria Hotel
7 Summer Youth Hostel
9 Logos Foundation
19 Hotel Miły
25 Hotel Centralny-Polonia

PLACES TO EAT

16 Pizzeria La Bussola
20 Restauracja Wiking
21 Bar Jedyny

OTHER

3 Jasna Góra Monastery
5 Church of St Barbara
8 Tourist Office
10 Theatre
11 Church of St Andrew
12 Art Gallery
13 City Museum
14 Orbis
15 Almatur
17 PKO Bank
18 Filharmonia Concert Hall
22 Railway Station
23 Post Office
24 Bus Station
26 Cathedral

cheaper bar with a few tables on the terrace around the side. Both serve Wiking Brok beer.

Farther up the same street is Częstochowa's last old fashioned milk bar, *Bar Jedyny*, ulica Nowowiejskiego 14.

Other than the *Orbis Patria Hotel* there's nowhere decent to eat up around the monastery. The tired staff of the cafeteria/bar adjacent to *Dom Pielgrzyma* dispense cheap, tasteless food to a pushy, queue-jumping crowd from 7 am to 9 pm.

A 24-hour convenience store is at Aleje NMP 67.

Getting There & Away

There are direct trains to Częstochowa from Warsaw (235 km, 3½ hours), Opole (95 km), Katowice (86 km, two hours), Kraków (two hours) and Zakopane (five hours). Local trains run almost hourly to Katowice where there are connections to Kraków and Wrocław. An overnight train with couchettes departs for Gdańsk-Sopot-Gdynia around 10 pm nightly year-round. Warsaw-bound trains from Budapest, Vienna and Prague also stop here.

The *Opolanin* express train runs daily all year between Częstochowa and Warsaw (three hours), departing from Warsaw in the late afternoon and Częstochowa in the morning. Reservations are required.

To go to Cieszyn (Czech border) you'll probably have to change trains at Katowice and Bielsko-Biała (allow six hours by local train, including the two changes). There's one morning train direct to Bielsko Biała (141 km, three hours).

Buses departing from Częstochowa include three daily to Kraków (114 km), three daily to Wrocław (176 km) and one a day to Zakopane (222 km).

BIELSKO-BIAŁA

On your way to/from the Czech Republic border at Cieszyn you may pass through Bielsko-Biała which has three daily trains to Kraków, 11 to Cieszyn, 30 to Katowice (55 km) and two express trains direct to Warsaw (376 km). From the train station a pedestrian bridge leads across to Bielsko-Biała Bus Station where you have a choice of 12 buses a day to Cieszyn (35 km) and 17 to Kraków (86 km).

Several large city maps are posted outside the bus and train stations. If connections force you to spend the night here the *PTTK Dom Wycieczkowy* (☎ 23 018), ulica Krasińskiego 38, about three blocks west of the bus station, has double rooms at US$8 and beds in six and seven-bed dorms at US$4 per person. It's closed from 10 pm to 6 am. There's also a year-round *hostel* (☎ 27 466) at ulica Komorowicka 25, about six blocks east of the train station. Otherwise all the hotels of Bielsko-Biała are expensive.

CIESZYN

The Polish border town, Cieszyn, sits in a verdant valley, separated from Český Těšín, Czech Republic, by the Olza River. The town has a quaint central square and some old churches but the only real reason to come here is to walk across one of the two one-way bridges linking the countries.

In Cieszyn the bus and train stations are adjacent about one km from the border, but the bus station has two sections a block apart. The left-luggage area at the train station is open 24 hours excepting two one-hour breaks. Ten trains a day link Cieszyn to Bielska-Biała and one goes on to Katowice, but there are none to points beyond. Buses move faster than the trains and you can choose from among 10 buses a day to Bielsko-Biała (35 km), 14 to Katowice (76 km) and six to Kraków (121 km).

Camping Olza is at Aleje Łyska 13, by the river a few blocks south of Rynek. At last report the old *Hotel 'Pod Brunatnym Jeleniem'*, Rynek 20, was closed for renovations and the other hotels of Cieszyn are expensive. You'll probably find a cheaper room in Český Těšín across the river (for more information turn to the Český Těšín section at the end of the Czech Republic chapter of this book).

The Bank Śląski, ulica Mennicza 1 just off Rynek (weekdays 8 am to 5 pm, Saturday 8 am to 1 pm), changes travellers' cheques, and there are several cash-only exchange offices around town. Change excess złoty into crowns at one of these before crossing over.

If you need a Czech visa, the nearest Czech consulate (☎ 518 576) is at ulica Pawła Stelmacha 21, Katowice.

Silesia

Silesia (Śląsk) in south-western Poland is the industrial heart of the country. Although Silesia accounts for only 6% of Poland's area, it provides a fifth of its wealth, including half its steel and 90% of its coal (8% of the world supply). The Upper Silesian Basin around Katowice, source of both the Vistula and Odra rivers, is densely developed, populated and polluted. Lower Silesia stretches north-west along the Odra past Wrocław. The fertile farming area between Opole and Wrocław is known as 'Green Silesia' while the coal-mining region of Upper Silesia is called 'Black Silesia'.

Silesia was originally inhabited by Slavic tribes, the largest of which, known as the Ślęzanie, gave their name to the region. Medieval Silesia was autonomous under Piast princes. In 1335 Silesia was annexed to Bohemia and from 1526 to 1742 it was under Austria's Habsburgs. Frederick the Great took Silesia for Prussia in 1742. Throughout the German period the large Polish minority was subjected to 'Germanisation'. After WW I Polish nationalist uprisings resulted in most of Upper Silesia going to Poland while Lower Silesia remained part of Germany until 1945. That year the German population was expelled and Silesia returned to Poland after a lapse of six centuries.

While tourists may not be attracted to the industrial wonders of Katowice and its vicinity, Wrocław is an old historic city with an intense cultural life. The Sudeten Mountains west of Kłodzko (the 'Góry Stołowe') and south of Jelenia Góra (Karkonoski Park Narodowy) lure hikers.

WROCŁAW

Wrocław (pronounced 'vrotslau'), historic capital of Lower Silesia, was German Breslau from 1742 until 1945. In the 13th century Wrocław had been capital of a local Piast dynasty, then the town passed from Bohemia to the Habsburgs and finally Prussia. During the final phase of WW II, the Nazis fortified the area and though surrounded, the 40,000 German soldiers at 'Festung Breslau' held out from 15 February to 6 May, only surrendering after Berlin fell on 2 May 1945. In the course of this 81-day siege 70% of the city was destroyed.

Immediately after the war, any German residents who hadn't already fled were deported and the ruins were resettled by Poles from L'vov in Ukraine. People in Wrocław still have a sentimental attachment to L'vov and you'll sometimes see historical displays on that city in the museums, or advertising for tourist trips to L'vov. Even the local beer brewed in Wrocław is called 'piwo Lwów' (though Wrocław's 'Piast' beer is better).

Today this enjoyable big city by the Odra offers good museums, historic buildings, concert halls, theatres, parks and over 120 canals, plus a picturesque central square and a memorable cluster of churches by the river. Wrocław is a lively cultural centre, a students' city, and the clubs are packed if anything's happening. It's all conveniently located so you can do most of your sightseeing on foot.

Orientation

Wrocław Główny Railway Station buzzes with activity 24 hours a day and most of the hotels are conveniently nearby. The left-luggage area inside the train station is open 24 hours. To walk to Rynek, the old market square, turn left on ulica Piłsudskiego and walk three blocks to ulica Świdnicka. Turn right and continue straight into town.

The addresses of buildings around the edge of the square are given as 'Rynek' while the block in the middle of the square is called 'Rynek-Ratusz'.

Information

The 'Odra' tourist information office, ulica Piłsudskiego 98, is below Hotel Piast I diagonally opposite the train station.

The PTTK tourist information centre, Rynek 38, is closed weekends and holidays.

The Polski Związek Motorowy, ulica Hauke-Bosaka 20, is the place to go for information if you're having car problems.

Money There are several exchange offices in the train station changing cash 24 hours a day. One is marked by a circular yellow sign next to the left-luggage office. Another with a red sign 'Kantor Korona' just a little farther down gives a slightly better rate. Compare.

To change a travellers' cheque you must go to the PKO bank, Plac Solny 16 (open weekdays 8 am to 5.30 pm, Saturday 8 am to 3 pm).

Post & Telephone Mail addressed to Poste Restante, ulica Krasiń-skiego 1, 50-415 Wrocław, Poland, is kept at window No 2 in the main post office at that address. A branch post office is at Rynek 28.

There's a telephone centre at ulica Malachowskiego 1, to the right as you leave the train station, which is open 24 hours a day. Wrocław's telephone code is 071.

Travel Agencies Orbis, at ulica Piłsudskiego 62, is where you go to purchase international train tickets, reserve seats, couchettes etc.

The Orbis offices at Rynek 29 and ulica Piłsudskiego 62 sell international bus tickets to Munich (twice weekly, US$50), Frankfurt/Main (twice weekly, US$50), Cologne (twice weekly, US$45), Amsterdam (twice weekly, US$75), Paris (three times a week, US$82), Brussels (twice weekly, US$75) and London (weekly, 27 hours, US$100). These services operate year-round and on return tickets the return portion is 50% cheaper than a one-way.

Haisig & Knabe, Rynek 45, also sells international bus tickets to many European cities, such as London, Vienna, Brussels, Lyon, Paris, Athens, Amsterdam, Geneva, Zürich, Rome and others. They also know about buses to Scandinavian cities departing from Poznań.

Bookshops Foreign books are available from the bookshop at Rynek 59. The map store at ulica Oławska 2, behind the Orbis office Rynek 29, has maps of many Polish cities. For hiking maps try the PTTK, ulica Wita Stwosza 15.

You can get the *Warsaw Voice* from the newsagent at Plac Kościuszki 21/23.

Things to See

The Old Town As you walk along ulica Świdnicka into town you'll pass **Corpus Christi Church** on the right and the neoclassical **Opera House** (1872) on the left. Next to the Monopol Hotel is **St Dorothy's Church**. When you reach the pedestrian underpass turn left a block to the Ethnographic and Archaeological **museums** (both

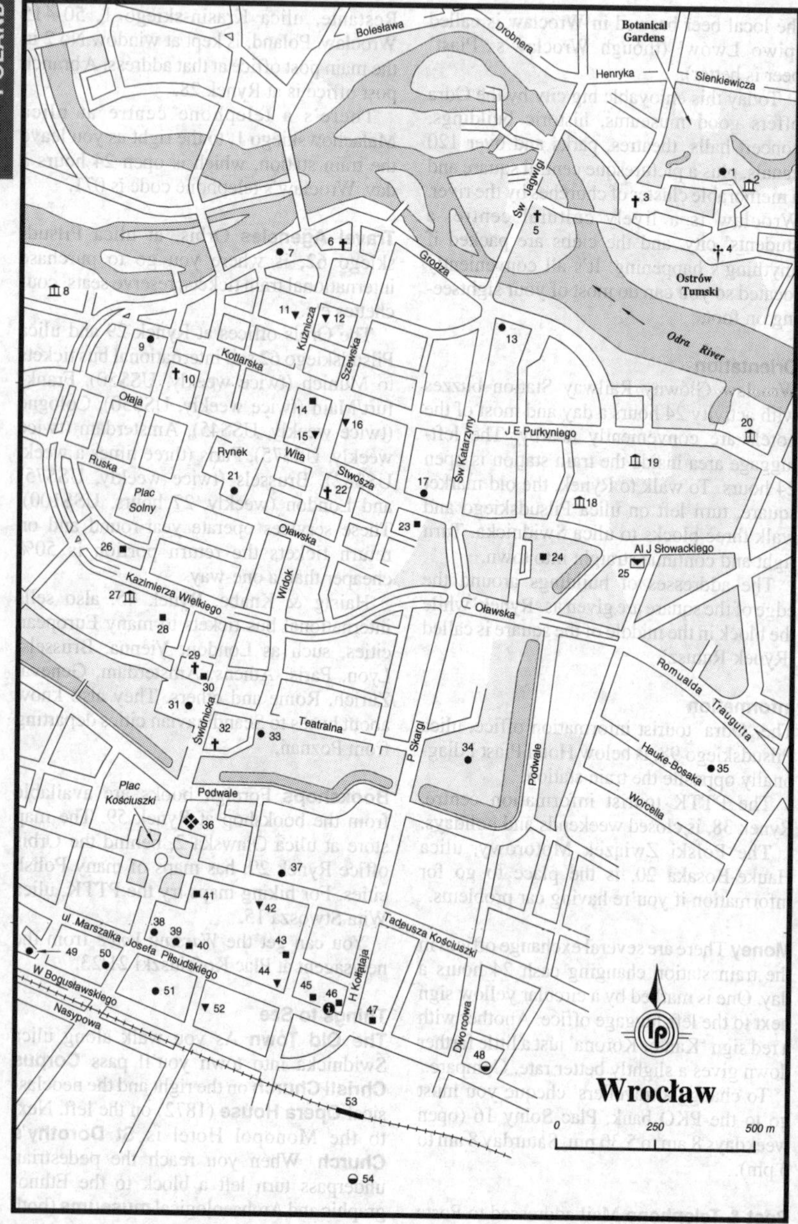
Wrocław
Botanical Gardens
Bolesława
Drobnera
Henryka
Sienkiewicza
Św Jagwigi
Grodza
Ostrów Tumski
Odra River
Kuźnicza
Szewska
Kotlarska
Oława
Ruska
Rynek
Wita Stwosza
Plac Solny
J E Purkyniego
Św Katarzyny
Oławska
Kazimierza Wielkiego
Widok
Al J Słowackiego
Romualda Traugutta
Hauke-Bosaka
Worcella
Świdnicka
Teatralna
P Skargi
Podwale
Plac Kościuszki
ul Marszałka Josefa Piłsudskiego
W Bogusławskiego
Nasypowa
Tadeusza Kościuszki
H Kołłątaja
Dworcowa
0
250
500 m

PLACES TO STAY

14 Teachers' Hostel
23 Hotel Saigon
24 Orbis Panorama Hotel
26 PTTK Stacja Turystyczna
28 DaiMen Hotel
30 Monopol Hotel
40 Hotel Polonia
41 Savoy Hotel
43 Hotel Piast II
45 Hotel Europejski
46 Hotel Piast I
47 Grand Hotel

PLACES TO EAT

11 Miş Milk Bar
12 Café Pod Kalamburen
15 Rancho Pizzeria
16 Café Studnią
42 Cyganeria Restaurant
44 Wzorcowy Milk Bar
52 Cocktail Bar

OTHER

1 Botanical Gardens
2 Archdiocesan Museum
3 Church of the Holy Cross
4 Cathedral
5 Church of the Virgin Mary on the Sands
6 Jesuit Church
7 Collegium Maximum
8 Arsenal (Military Museum)
9 Rura Jazz Club
10 St Elizabeth's Church
13 Market
17 Art Gallery
18 Museum of Architecture
19 Panorama Racławicka
20 National Museum
21 Ratusz (Town Hall)
22 Church of St Mary Magdalene
25 Post Office
27 Archaeological Museum
29 St Dorothy's Church
31 Opera House
32 Corpus Christi Church
33 Puppet Theatre
34 Bastion
35 Polski Związek Motorowy
36 Centrum Department Store
37 Pałacyk Student Club & Almatur
38 Orbis
39 Casino
46 Tourist Office
48 Old Bus Station
49 Teatr Polski
50 Happy 7 Night Club
51 Operetka Theatre
53 Railway Station
54 New Bus Station

are closed Monday and Tuesday). They have separate entrances but are in the same complex at ulica Kazimierza Wielkiego 34/35. Unfortunately, only Polish captions are posted in the Archaeological Museum, making the exhibits rather meaningless to foreigners.

Continue west again in the same direction and turn right across the street the first chance you get, then straight around into Plac Solny, the old salt market which is now a flower market and spills into Rynek, the medieval marketplace with its Renaissance and baroque burgher houses. Wrocław's Gothic **Ratusz** (town hall), built between 1327 and 1504, is one of the most intricate in Poland and now contains a museum (closed Monday and Tuesday, free Wednesday) in the arched interior. On the north-west corner of Rynek is 14th-century **St Elizabeth's Church** with its 83-metre tower. The two small houses on the corner, connected by a gate, are known as Hansel and Gretel.

Walk east from this church along the north side of Rynek and continue due east on ulica Wita Stwosza, with a digression to visit the Gothic **Church of St Mary Magdalene** on the right. Note the 12th-century Romanesque portal on the far side of the church.

Museums & Churches Keep straight on ulica Wita Stwosza till you reach the Orbis Panorama Hotel. The **Museum of Architecture** (closed Monday, free Wednesday) in the 15th-century convent across the street from the hotel has a scale model of Wrocław as it appeared in 1740.

In the park around behind this museum is the **Panorama Racławicka**, a huge 360° painting of the Battle of Racławice (1794) near Kraków during which the national hero, Tadeusz Kościuszko, led the Poles against Russian forces intent on partitioning Poland. Created by Jan Styka and Wojciech Kossak for the centenary of the battle in 1894, the painting is 120 metres long and 15 metres high. It was displayed at L'vov until 1939, then held in storage for over four decades due to political considerations (might have offended Poland's erstwhile Soviet allies) and only reopened at Wrocław in 1985. You're given headphones with an English or

German commentary, but they screech and the story is difficult to follow.

You may have difficulty getting panorama tickets (admission US$4, students US$2, closed Monday) as visitors are only admitted 17 times a day in groups of 40 persons, and tour groups often book all the showings a couple of days in advance. Check for tickets early during your stay. Someone standing at the door may offer to sell you a ticket purchased earlier which they cannot use.

Just east beside the park is the **National Museum** (closed Monday, free Thursday) with a large collection of masterpieces of medieval Silesian art. The Panorama Racławicka admission ticket is also valid for a same-day visit to this museum. Cross the bridge over the Odra beside the museum, taking a glance upstream at the **Most Grunwaldzki** (1910), the most graceful of Wrocław's 90 bridges.

On the north side of the river, turn left when the tram tracks bend right and walk west into Ostrów Tumski, an old quarter inhabited since the 9th century. In the 10th century the ducal palace was here. The chapels at the rear of the Gothic **Cathedral of St John the Baptist** deserve special attention, though they're usually kept securely locked. The **Archdiocesan Museum** (closed Monday) is at ulica Kanonia 12 between the cathedral and the **Botanical Gardens** (admission US$1.50). The gardens (established in 1811) are a lovely, restful corner of the city well worth seeking out.

West again from the cathedral is the two-storey Gothic **Church of the Holy Cross**. Keep straight and cross the small bridge to the 14th-century **Church of the Virgin Mary on the Sands** which has a stunning Gothic interior.

Southbound now, follow the tram tracks across another small bridge to the huge, red-brick **city market** (1908). Then follow the riverbank downstream a block or two till you reach a large **Jesuit Church** (1755) with the **Collegium Maximum** (1741) just beyond. Inside this ornate baroque building is the magnificent Aula Leopoldina, now used for formal university functions.

Parks & Zoo Take a taxi or tram No 1, 2, 4, 10, or 12 east to Wrocław's enjoyable **zoo** (US$1.50), Poland's oldest. In summer, **excursion boats** operate on a branch of the

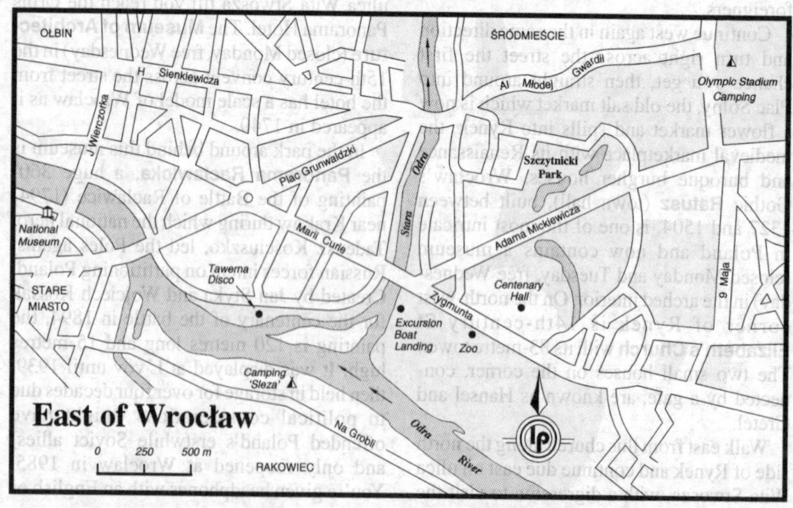

East of Wrocław

Odra several times a day from the landing beside the zoo.

Across the street from the zoo is a famous early work of modern architecture, **Centenary Hall** or 'Hala Ludova', erected in 1913 by the noted German architect Max Berg to commemorate the defeat of Napoleon in 1813. Enter to appreciate this great enclosed space. The steel needle beside the hall was the symbol of the 1948 Exhibition of the Regained Territories. The **Szczytnicki Park** beyond includes an attractive Japanese garden.

Circle Trip Provided there are no obstructions due to road works, tram No 0 makes a complete loop around Wrocław in about 45 minutes, the best city tour you'll ever get for US$0.25. You can pick it up in front of the train station.

Places to Stay

Camping Wrocław's *camping ground* (☎ 484 651) is near the Olympic Stadium across Szczytnicki Park from the zoo on the east side of the city (trams Nos 9, 16, and 17 pass the entrance). There's a row of simple, clean bungalows (US$4 per person), and from May to September foreigners wishing to pitch a tent (US$2 per person plus US$1 per tent) are *never* turned away. English and German are spoken.

Hostels The *hostel* (☎ 38 856) at ulica Kołłotaja 20, just behind the Grand Hotel, a few minutes' walk from the train station, is US$3 for the first night, US$2 for subsequent nights. Only dorm beds are available and it's usually full in midsummer but a good bet the rest of the year (open all year). The receptionist will hold your luggage until they open at 5 pm.

The PTTK runs a *Stacja turystyczna* (☎ 443 073) at ulica Szajnochy 11 (upstairs) just off Plac Solny in the old town. The hostel reception is only open from 5 to 9 pm and a bed in a six, 10, or 18-bed dormitory will be around US$4. It's open all year.

The *Ośrodek Zakwaterowań Nauczycieli* (☎ 443 781), ulica Kotlarska 42 right in the middle of town, is a teachers' hostel with rooms at US$10 single or double, or US$6 for a bed in a three-bed dorm, US$5 for a bed in a four-bed dorm. This place is really intended for teachers only but it will take others if space is available.

Almatur, ulica Kościuszki 34, will know about accommodation in student dormitories in summer.

Private Rooms Odra Tourist, ulica Piłsudskiego 98 opposite the train station, can arrange private rooms at US$7 per person. Before paying ask them to point out the location on their map.

Hotels Near the Station A whole row of relatively inexpensive hotels line ulica Piłsudskiego, to the left as you come out of the train station. The *Grand Hotel* (☎ 33 983), ulica Piłsudskiego 102 right across from the station, is US$14/20 single/double without bath, US$17/25 with bath, breakfast included. *Hotel Piast I* (☎ 30 033), just west on the next corner, is US$10/19 single/double without bath, US$23 double with bath.

The *Hotel Europejski* (☎ 31 071), at ulica Piłsudskiego 94/96, charges US$20/32 single/double for a 2nd-class room, US$27/40 for a 1st-class room, private bath and breakfast included in all. Quieter is the *Hotel Piast II* (☎ 445 447) around the corner at ulica Stawowa 13 (US$10/19 single/double without bath, US$23 double with bath, breakfast not included).

Hotel Polonia (☎ 31 021), ulica Piłsudskiego 66, is more expensive than any of the hotels just mentioned (US$24/36 single/-double with bath and breakfast). Wrocław's casino is beside the Polonia.

Rooms facing the street in the Grand, Piast I, Europejski and Polonia hotels get a lot of tram noise; the Piast II is on a quiet side street.

Hotels in Town The five-storey *Hotel Savoy*, Plac Kościuszki 19, is a bargain at US$10/13/15 single/double/triple with bath. It's free of tram noise.

The old three-storey *Hotel DaiMen*, ulica Kazimierza Wielkiego 45, has rooms with shared bath at US$16/22 single/double, including breakfast.

Of the four Orbis hotels the stylish *Monopol Hotel* (☎ 37 041), ulica Modrzejewskiej 2 beside the Opera House, is the most colourful (from US$22/35 single/double without bath, US$32/50 with bath, breakfast included). The Monopol was erected in 1890 and Hitler would stay here whenever he visited Breslau and would address the crowds from the balcony.

The *Hotel Saigon* (☎ 442 881), ulica Wita Stwosza 22/23, has rooms beginning at US$19/35 single/double with bath plus US$3 per person for breakfast (extra charge for a TV or king-size bed). This renovated five-storey hotel near the centre of town is a good medium-priced choice. Their Vietnamese restaurant is good.

Places to Eat

Near the Train Station Wrocław doesn't shine in the food department, and there's no good middle-level place to eat near the train station (*Mamma Mia Pizza* inside the train station itself is open 24 hours a day). The *Europejski* and *Polonia* hotels both have restaurants; ask what's available before struggling with the Polish/German menu.

Fast-food places have mushroomed in Wrocław in recent years and the numerous establishments of this kind along ulica Piłsudskiego near Hotel Polonia need no introduction. *Wzorcowy Milk Bar*, ulica Piłsudskiego 86, a block from the station (closed Sunday), would be great if they didn't tend to overcharge foreigners.

The *Cyganeria Restaurant*, ulica Kościuszki 37, looks bad at first – full of men drinking warm beer and vodka straight – but actually the food is quite good and the staff are friendly.

In the Old Town Most of the city's best eating and drinking places are conveniently located around Rynek. *Vega Bar Wegetariański*, Rynek Ratusz 27a, on the corner of Sukiennice behind the old town hall, has cheap cafeterias upstairs and down. Students feast on Polish peasant specialities here. You're supposed to return your tray to the counter. Look for a green building, part of the block in the middle of the square – it's worth taking a few minutes to locate.

Other cheap places around here include *Miś Milk Bar*, ulica Kuźnicza 48, a typical self-service, and *Rancho Pizzeria*, ulica Szewska 59/60. *Café Mona Liza*, Rynek 16/17, offers borsch, steak, and ice cream.

Zorba Bar, Przejście Garncarskie 8, hidden right in the middle of the block in the centre of Rynek, grills great souvlaki and other Greek dishes. It's visible through the passage at Rynek-Ratusz 15.

The *Piwnica Świdnicka Restaurant*, in a basement of the old town hall, serves reasonable meals in a medieval setting which dates back to the 14th century. Unfortunately, the cacophony of rock music directed at you from several directions obliterates most of the atmosphere (though some readers say they like it).

Spiż, Rynek-Ratusz 2, diagonally opposite the old town hall, is a subterranean German-style restaurant where they brew their own beer. The restaurant is up-market but a mug of their rich 13% brew or 12% pils in the wood-panelled bar should fit into almost anyone's budget and belly. You can even get huge one-litre mugs of rich black beer. The bar opens at 8 am and there's a beer garden on the square outside.

If you assumed from the American Express stickers in the window that the *Królewska Restaurant* at Dwór Wazów, Rynek 5, might be expensive, you'd be right. If price means anything to you at all, skip the meal and go upstairs to the very elegant café where you can get ice cream and a glass of wine for a more manageable sum. The elegant dining room in the *Monopol Hotel* is good for a splurge and there are even a few vegetarian dishes on the menu.

Cafés & Bars *Herbowa*, Rynek 19, is a teahouse serving excellent desserts. On weekend evenings it becomes a disco. *U*

Prospera, Rynek 27, is a billiard bar open around the clock.

Pod Papagami, ulica Sukiennice 9a, is a students pub which opens at 5 pm daily. It's a great place to go for a beer and unless there's live entertainment no cover charge is payable. The entrance is under the archway directly behind Spiż in the centre of Rynek.

Bar U Prasoła, Plac Solny 11 (through the archway), is open from noon to 11 pm. Avoid the *John Bull Pub*, Plac Solny 6, which is expensive and only for tourists. A 24-hour bottle shop is at Plac Solny 8/9.

Pod Kalamburen, ulica Kuźnicza 29a, is an elegant Art Nouveau-style café.

Cafe Studnią, ulica Szewska 19, is a students' bar with a good atmosphere. In the cellar below Cafe Studnią is the *Club 'Pod Studnią'* where there's sometimes live music. There's even a no-smoking section! The two bars are under separate management so you might have to enter the club through the yellow door around the corner on ulica Kotłarska.

There are three unpretentious places at the *Pałacyk Student Club*. The *Klub Samo Zycie* in the basement is a pub where a rock band is often playing. The billiard bar on the main floor is good for a game or just a drink and upstairs there's a lively disco.

The *Cocktail Bar*, ulica Komandorska 4a off Piłsudskiego, serves about the best coffee and ice cream in town.

Entertainment

Wrocław is a major cultural centre and during the winter season you'll have a lot to choose from. Check the listings in the morning papers, *Słowo Polskie* and *Gazeta Robotnicza*, or the evening paper, *Wieczór Wrocławia*.

At the *Operetka Theatre*, ulica Piłsudskiego 67, actors, actresses, costumes, music, scenery – everything is superb. The *Teatr Polski*, nearby at ulica Zapolskiej 3 off Piłsudskiego, also offers excellent performances in Polish. If Wrocław's *mime theatre* performs here during your stay, don't miss it. Also check *Filharmonia Hall*, ulica Piłsudskiego 17, and the *Opera House*, ulica Świdnicka 35. The architectural splendour of the opera complements the excellence of the performances.

The *Wrocławski Teatr Lalek*, Plac Teatralny 4, offers puppet theatre for kids several times a week at 10 and 11 am.

Annual musical events include the Festival of Polish Contemporary Music held in February, the 'Jazz of the Odra' jazz festival in May, the Flower Fair in July, the International Oratorio and Cantata Festival, 'Vratislavia Cantans', in September and the Days of Old Masters' Music held in early December.

Discos What Wrocław loses in the food department it more than makes up with its varied and lively nightlife. A good place to start is the *Klub Związków Twórćzyca*, Rynek Ratusz 24, Wrocław's most popular disco among the city youth (opens at 9 pm, US$5 admission). From noon to 9 pm the locale is an expensive-looking but reasonably priced restaurant with a menu in English.

A slightly older crowd frequents *Bachus Disco Club*, Rynek 16 (open from 4 pm to 5 am daily). It's downstairs through the café.

Be sure to attend any jam sessions at the *Rura Jazz Club*, ulica Łazienna 4. Great! This club is to move to a new location in the near future, so check the address at the tourist office.

On Friday and Saturday nights there's a disco at the *Pałacyk Student Club*, ulica Kościuszki 34 (8 pm to 3 am).

Wrocław's up-market disco is *Happy 7 Night Club* (☎ 442 332), ulica Świdnicka 53 (open daily from 10 pm, cover US$4). Dress sharp to feel comfortable here.

If you don't mind paying extra for taxi fares, *Bravo* in Centenary Hall (Hala Ludowa) is another popular disco. Halfway back to town from Bravo is the *Tawerna Disco*, ulica Wybrzeże Wyspiańskiego 40 (closed Sunday), across the street from the Politechnika Wrocławska.

Things to Buy

Wrocław's shopping is concentrated around

Plac Kościuszki and along ulica Świdnicka to Rynek. The largest of the department stores is Centrum, ulica Świdnicka 40 at Plac Kościuszki. Have a look around.

Cepelia, Plac Kościuszki 12, has an excellent selection of Polish handicrafts and some amber jewellery. Next door is the Philatelic Bureau at No 11 with some unusual bargains. Hitler stamps issued by the Nazi 'General Government' in Kraków are sold here. For antiques it's Desa, Plac Kośiuszki 16.

Pro Musica, Rynek 49, has Polish CDs and cassettes.

Getting There & Away

Train Main lines from Szczecin to Przemyśl (via Poznań and Kraków), and Warsaw to Jelenia Góra (via Łódź), cross at Wrocław. Other direct trains come from Gdynia or Gdańsk (via Poznań). There's service from Katowice (180 km), Poznań (165 km, three hours, US$5) and Rzepin (224 km) every couple of hours.

Several trains a day arrive from Berlin (329 km via Rzepin), Cologne, Frankfurt/Main and Hannover in Germany (via Dresden and Leipzig). The daily *Bohemia* express to/from Prague (339 km) arrives and departs in the middle of the night. Dresden and Prague are each about seven hours away.

The *Odra* express runs daily all year between Warsaw and Wrocław (390 km, five hours), departing from Warsaw in the afternoon and Wrocław in the early morning. Reservations are required.

Car Rental Orbis (☎ 34 780), Rynek 29, is the Hertz agent. Budget is represented by Haisig & Knabe (☎ 38 969), Rynek 45.

Vitesse (☎ 447 385), Plac Kościuszki 19 below the Savoy Hotel, also has rental cars.

GÖRLITZ TO ZGORZELEC

If you've got a taste for adventure and want to save a little money by walking in or out of Poland, the easiest border crossing for pedestrians to/from Germany is at Zgorzelec, 163 km west of Wrocław by train. Trains run between Wrocław and Zgorzelec every couple of hours with some services requiring a change of trains at Wegliniec. Only buy a ticket as far as Zgorzelec, the Polish border town, then walk across the bridge over the Nysa River to the neighbouring town of Görlitz where there are frequent trains to Dresden-Neustadt (102 km, US$10) and Berlin-Lichtenberg (212 km, US$20). If you have a Eurail pass Görlitz is the perfect place to begin using it.

Arriving from Western Europe, go out the main entrance from Görlitz Railway Station and head north up Berliner Strasse to Postplatz. Proceed east on Schützen Strasse (the street behind the main post office), turn right at the park and go down Am Stadpark to the bridge to Poland – an easy 15-minute walk. City maps are posted at Görlitz Railway Station and there's also a left-luggage office if you'd like to look around the old town. Don't miss medieval **Peter-Pauls Cathedral**.

You'll find several small exchange offices at the Polish end of the bridge where you can easily swap currencies (cash only). The train station in Zgorzelec is a 10-minute walk from the bridge. Go straight up the main street, turn right onto another main street and ask. You want Zgorzelec Station, not Zgorzelec Miasto Station which is farther away.

The only hotel in Zgorzelec is the five-storey *Hotel 'Pod Orłem'* (☎ 24 53), ulica Warszowska 17 between the bridge and Zgorzelec Railway Station. At US$22/40 single/double with bath and breakfast, it's expensive for Poland but good value compared to the places across the river. The pleasant *Görlitz Youth Hostel* (☎ 03581-406 510) is at Goethe Strasse 17. Go out the south exit from Görlitz Railway Station, turn left on Sattig Strasse, and walk east five minutes to Goethe Strasse where you turn right. As for hotels in Görlitz, the *Hotel Stadt Dresden* (☎ 03581-407 131), Berliner Strasse 37 opposite the station, is expensive at US$60/75/85 single/double/triple. A better bet is the old 28-room *Hotel Prinz Friedrich Karl/Monopol* (☎ 03581-403 361) on Postplatz in the centre of town. It's US$32/50 single/double with breakfast (shared bath).

Wielkopolska

Western Poland, or Wielkopolska ('Great Poland'), was the cradle of the Polish nation. Here on a plateau along the Warta River lived the Polanians, a Slavic tribe which gave its name to the whole country. In 966 Mieszko I, duke of the Polanians, was baptised at Gniezno. Mieszko's son, Boleslav the Brave, was crowned king in 1025, establishing the Piast dynasty which ruled Poland until 1370.

In 1253 Prince Przemyśl I granted Poznań municipal rights and the city became a regional centre. Wars in the 18th century seriously weakened Poland, and in 1793 Western Poland was annexed to Prussia. After Bismarck set up the German Empire in 1871, Germanisation and German colonisation became intense. Returned to Poland in 1919, the area was seized by the Nazis in 1939 and devastated during the liberation battles of 1945.

Today the rebuilt regional capital Poznań is a great industrial, commercial and historical city, well worth a stop on the way to or from Berlin. Gniezno can easily be visited on the way to Toruń, an enchanting old riverside town by the Vistula. Though the German influence is still evident, western Poland is as Polish as you can get.

POZNAŃ

Poznań (Posen), on the main east-west trade route between Berlin and Warsaw, has long been a focal point of Polish history. A wooden fort stood on Ostrów Tumski (Cathedral Island) in the 9th century, and from 968 to 1039 Poznań was capital of Poland. In 1253 Stare Miasto (Old Town) was founded on the left bank of the Warta River and it continued to play a major role in the life of the country. By the 15th century Poznań was already famous for its fairs, and despite Swedish assaults in the 17th century the city remained an important trading centre. In 1815 the Congress of Vienna created the Grand Duchy of Poznań under Prussian suzerainty, but after 1849 the Germans took direct control. From 1918 to 1939 Poznań was part of Poland and the 1945 battle to liberate the city lasted over a month.

The 1956 strike for higher wages by workers at the huge Cegielski Engineering Works was one of the first of its kind in Poland. The works, founded by Hipolit Cegielski in 1846 and still the city's largest employer, manufactures railway rolling stock, diesel engines and machinery. Since 1925 Poznań has been the site of Poland's largest international trade fairs, although the good restaurants, historic places and varied museums draw visitors all year. Poznań's Żytnia rye vodka is Poland's best.

Orientation

Poznań Główny Railway Station is a 20-minute walk from the centre of the city. The left-luggage area is upstairs in the main hall between tracks Nos 1 and 4 (open 24 hours). Exit the station from this hall and walk north to the second street, ulica Św Marcin, which you follow east. Turn left with the tram tracks at Aleje Marcinkowskiego, then right and straight ahead to Stary Rynek, the old town square.

If you want to catch a tram from the station to town, go out the exit beyond track No 6, buy a ticket at the Ruch kiosk beside the stop and board tram No 5 which will take you to the Rzymski Hotel.

Information

The tourist office (☎ 526 156) at Stary Rynek 59 is extremely helpful and sells maps. It has *IKS*, the monthly entertainment magazine which details everything that's happening.

The Polski Związek Motorowy, Cześnikowska 30 off Grunwaldzka, in a distant western suburb, assists motorists.

Money Glob-Tour in the main hall between tracks Nos 1 and 4 at the train station changes cash 24 hours a day. It also sells maps and the staff will answer general questions if they're not too busy. Two other exchange

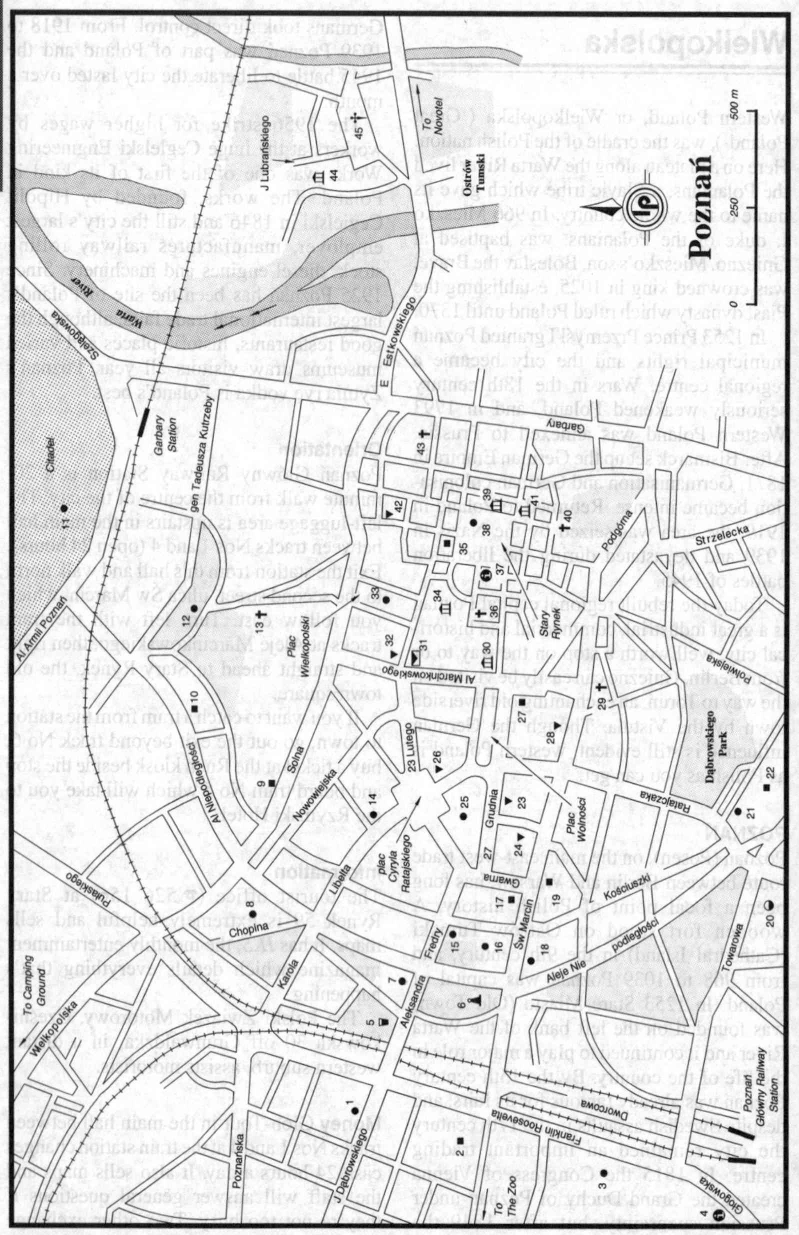
Poznań
0
250
500 m
Ostrów Tumski
To Novotel
J Lubrańskiego
Warta River
Szelągowska
E Estkowskiego
Garbary
Garbary Station
gen Tadeusza Kutrzeby
Cytadel
Al Armii Poznań
Strzelecka
Podgórna
Stary Rynek
Al Marcinkowskiego
Plac Wielkopolski
Solna
Nowowiejska
Al Niepodległości
Libelta
23 Lutego
Półwiejska
Dąbrowskiego Park
Ratajczaka
Plac Wolności
Grudnia
Gwarna
Kościuszki
plac Cyryla Ratajskiego
Fredry
Sw Marcin
Aleje Niepodległości
Towarowa
Pułaskiego
Chopina
Karola
Aleksandra
To Camping Ground
Wielkopolska
Poznańska
Dąbrowskiego
To The Zoo
Dworcowa
Franklin Roosevelta
Poznań Główny Railway Station
Głogowska

PLACES TO STAY

2 Orbis Mercury Hotel
9 Hotel Garnizonowy
10 Orbis Hotel
17 Lech Hotel
19 Wielkopolska & Savoy Hotels
22 Orbis Poznań Hotel
27 Rzymski Hotel
35 Dom Turysty PTTK

PLACES TO EAT

23 Smakosz Restaurant
24 Restauracja Indyjska
26 Pod Arkadami Milk Bar
28 U Marcina
32 Pekin Restaurant
42 Pizzeria Tivoli

OTHER

1 World Computer Travel
3 International Fairgrounds
4 Biuro Zakwaterowania
5 Stajenka Pegaza Pub
6 Solidarity Monument
7 Opera House
8 US Consulate
11 Commonwealth War Cemetery
12 Polish War Memorial
13 Carmelite Church
14 Studio Jack Disco
15 Agencja Eurostop
16 Palace of Culture
18 Filharmonia
20 PKS Bus Station
21 Musical Theatre
25 Polski Theatre 'Naród Sobie'
29 St Martin's Church
30 National Museum
31 Post Office
33 Vegetable Market
34 Decorative Arts Museum
36 Franciscan Church
37 Tourist Office
38 Old Town Hall
39 Musical Instruments Museum
40 Parish Church
41 Archaeological Museum
43 Dominican Church
44 Archdiocesan Museum
45 Cathedral

offices (cash only) are in the smaller station hall beyond track No 6.

The PKO Bank, Stary Rynek 44 (open weekdays from 8 am to 6 pm, Saturday from 10 am until 2 pm), changes travellers' cheques for 1.5% commission (US$3 minimum). Cash is changed at a better rate without commission.

The PKO Bank, ulica Masztalarska 8a, a block off the north-west corner of Stary Rynek (weekdays 7.30 am to 5 pm, Saturday 7.30 am to 1.30 pm), also changes travellers' cheques and their commission is slightly lower than that taken by the Stary Rynek office. You must go to 'Sala B', a small back office at the rear of a courtyard next to the main bank.

Post & Telephone The main post office is at ulica 23 Lutego 28. Avoid using the chaotic poste restante service here.

The telephone centre just outside the west exit from the train station is open daily from 7 am to 9 pm.

Poznań's telephone code is 061.

Consulates The US Consulate (☎ 529 586) is at ulica Chopina 4.

Travel Agencies Book domestic and international train tickets and couchettes at the Orbis office below the Orbis Poznań Hotel (weekdays 8 am to 6 pm, Saturday 8am to 2 pm).It also has international bus tickets from Poznań to Amsterdam, Barcelona, Brussels, London, Lyon, Madrid, Oslo, Paris, Vienna, and many German cities. This is a good place to get train information in English.

Agencja Eurostop (☎ 520 344), ulica Fredry 7, also has bus tickets to cities all across Europe and sells ISIC student cards.

World Computer Travel (☎ 481 342), at ulica J Dąbrowskiego 5A, has one-way flights to North America (US$500) and Melbourne, Australia (US$850), departing from Warsaw. They have a second office next to the US consulate.

Things to See

Museums There are half a dozen museums in the historic buildings on or near Stary Rynek. Begin with the one in the Renaissance **old town hall** (closed Thursday and Saturday) which will envelop you in Poznań's medieval past. The coffered ceiling in the vestibule dates from 1555. Every day at noon a bugle sounds and butting heraldic goats appear above the clock on the town hall façade opposite Proserpina's fountain (1766). The **Musical Instruments Museum** (closed Monday and Thursday, free Friday), Stary Rynek 45, is one of the best of its kind in Europe.

Nearby at the south-eastern corner of the square is the **Archaeological Museum** (closed Monday) in a 16th-century Renaissance palace. Make a side trip to the end of ulica Świętosławska from beside this museum to visit the baroque **parish church**, originally a Jesuit church. There's a peculiar **Military Museum** (closed Monday) full of little lead soldiers in one of the incongruous modern buildings in the very centre of Stary Rynek itself. Notice the art gallery opposite. There are two more museums, one literary (Stary Rynek 84) and the other political (Stary Rynek 3), on the west side of the square.

Go up ulica Franciszkańska from the latter to the beautiful 17th-century **Franciscan church**. In the Castle of Przemyśl on the hill opposite is the **Decorative Arts Museum** (closed Monday and Tuesday). Go around the church and west on ulica Paderewskiego to the **National Museum** (closed Monday), with Poland's best collection of Dutch and Spanish paintings.

Other Sights The historic centre of Poznań has a lot more to offer than just museums, most of which you'll be able to discover for yourself without a guidebook. However, a few sights just outside the centre deserve your attention.

Walk north from the National Museum to the end of Aleje Marcinkowskiego, then turn right, then left on ulica Działowa, the first street. You'll pass two old churches before reaching the striking **Polish War Memorial**, commemorating the Polish army's heroic resistance to the Nazi onslaught in 1939. Pass it and continue north on Aleje Niepodległości to the 19th-century Prussian **citadel**. Though Poznań fell to the Soviet army in January 1945, 20,000 German troops held out inside this fortress for another two months and the city was badly damaged by artillery fire. There's much to see around the citadel, including a couple of war museums (closed Monday), monuments to the Soviet liberators, and the **Commonwealth War Cemetery** (to the right). Many of the Soviet and Polish soldiers who died in the battle are buried along the hillside. The last name on the bronze plaque below the central obelisk is Marshall J Stalin.

Poznań's towering red-brick Gothic **cathedral** is at Ostrów Tumski on the east side of the Warta River. Any eastbound tram from Plac Wielkopolski will take you there. The Byzantine-style Golden Chapel (1841), mausoleum of Mieszko I and Boleslav the Brave, is behind the main altar. The **Archdiocesan Museum** (closed Sunday) at the north end of ulica Lubrańskiego near the cathedral is surprisingly rich.

Poznań's most compelling sight is the large bronze **monument** in the park beside the Palace of Culture, which you may have noticed on your way in from the train station. Erected in 1981 by supporters of the trade union Solidarity, the monument commemorates 'Black Thursday', 28 June 1956, when rioting by workers demanding higher wages was put down by force with as many as 70 killed and hundreds injured. The two huge crosses, bound together, symbolise the struggle of Polish workers for 'bread, peace and freedom', and the dates recall various popular upheavals: 1956 (Poznań), 1968 (Warsaw), 1970 (Gdańsk), 1976 (Radom), and 1980 (Gdańsk). Next to the monument is a statue of the Romantic poet Adam Mickiewcz.

Kórnik & Rogalin Each of these small towns 20 km south of Poznań boasts a large palace of the landed nobility in expansive parks. The two are similar, so unless you've got plenty of time or your own transport, one might be representative of the other. Kórnik is the easiest to reach with frequent bus service from Poznań. Buses between Kórnik and Rogalin run only a couple of times a day, but maybe you'll be lucky! There's a bus from Rogalin directly back to Poznań every couple of hours.

The 19th-century English-style country manor at Kórnik (closed Monday) was rebuilt on the site of an earlier palace by the famous Berlin architect Karl Friedrich Schinkel. A highlight at Rogalin is the small art gallery (closed Monday and Tuesday) hidden behind the 18th-century rococo palace. Its collection of 19th-century German and Polish paintings is quite good. Some of the oak trees in the surrounding park are almost nine metres around and 1000 years old. The three largest trees are named for the legendary brothers Lech, Czech and Rus who founded Poland, Bohemia and Russia.

Places to Stay

Poznań's hotels use the 12 annual trade fairs as a pretext for doubling prices, but when you ask what that week's trade fair is about they haven't a clue (typical themes include printing equipment, burglar alarms, medical equipment, computers, furniture, mining, agriculture, construction, packaging, advertising media and garbage collection). During the main trade fair in June all accommodation will be fully booked, so check the dates carefully before heading this way. The price increases are also in effect a few days before and after the fairs. One way to check the dates beforehand would be to call the Fair Agency (☎ 692 592) or Poznań tourist information (☎ 526 156).

Camping *Poznań-Strzeszynek Camping* (☎ 47 224), at ulica Koszalińska 15, is inconveniently located on the far north-west edge of Poznań (bus No 95). It's open from June to September.

Hostels The 56-bed *hostel* (☎ 663 680) is at ulica Berwińskiego 2/3, the tall yellow brick building opposite Kasprzaka Park. To get there leave the train station by the west exit and go left along ulica Głogowska till you come to the park (five minutes). The doors are locked at 9 pm.

Agencja Europstop (☎ 520 344), ulica Aleksandra Fredry 7 behind the Palace of Culture, may have information on International Student Hotels (open July and August).

Private Rooms The Przemysław Biuro Zakwaterowania (☎ 663 560 or 663 983), ulica Głogowska 16, can arrange accommodation in private homes at US$10/14 single/double. At trade fair times the prices double and the offices stay open extra long hours (normal hours are weekdays from 9 am to 6 pm, Saturday 10 am to 3 pm). Look for this office at the end of the long white building across from the west exit from the train station. If the first door you try is locked go to the next one along the row.

The Orbis Biuro Obsługi Cudzoziemców (BOC) office downstairs in the Orbis Poznań Hotel also has expensive private rooms at US$25/32 single/double, but only during the trade fairs.

Hotels The *Hotel Royal* (☎ 537 884), ulica Św Marcin 17 between the train station and the centre, through the archway and at the back of the courtyard, is US$13/19/22 single/double/triple with shared bath. There can be long waits to use the one communal shower.

The *Wielkopolska Hotel* (☎ 527 631), ulica Św Marcin 67, charges US$15/29 single/double without bath, US$29/33 with bath. The seven-storey *Lech Hotel* (☎ 530 151), ulica Św Marcin 74, is way overpriced at US$44/60 single/double with bath and breakfast.

Also good is the *Rzymski Hotel* (☎ 528 121), Aleje Marcinkowskiego 22, charging US$14/24 single/double without bath, US$23/32 with bath, breakfast included. In all of the above hotels except the Royal the rooms facing the street are noisy.

Dom Turysty PTTK (☎ 523 893) at Stary Rynek 91 (entry from Wroniecka 91), a 19th-century building right on Poznań's main square, is US$19/32 single/double without bath, US$22/38 with bath, US$7 per person in a five-bed dorm, US$5 per person in a seven-bed dorm (no breakfast). The location can't be beaten and the restaurant downstairs is good.

The *Hotel Garnizonowy* (☎ 492 671), a modern, 10-storey hotel on Solna just north of downtown, has rooms with bath at US$22/32 single/double. The Garnizonowy was originally intended to house military officers but it's now open to anyone.

The *Hotel Miejski Ósrodek Sportowy* (☎ 332 444), ulica Churałkowskiego 34, is a white four-storey sports hotel with rooms with shared bath at US$13 per person. The triple rooms have private bath. It's just beyond the stadium, south-east of the Orbis Poznań Hotel. From the train station follow our map east along Towarowa, which becomes Królowej Jadwigi, pass the Orbis Poznań, and look for the stadium on the right beyond the park after the next main street. Otherwise catch tram No 12 from the west side of the train station. There's a good snack bar upstairs in the adjoining gym.

Places to Eat

Old Town The *Stara Ratuszowa Wine Cellar*, Stary Rynek 55, is for real: you go down into the cellar to get wine. The downstairs restaurant is good for an atmospheric splurge.

Club Elite, in the basement of the old Weight House in the centre of Stary Rynek directly behind the old town hall, posts their menu outside in English and German. It's good for solid meat dishes.

Avanti Buffet, Stary Rynek 76, serves tasty platefuls of spaghetti but there's always a long line. The *Spaghetti Bar* on ulica Rynkova off the north-west corner of Stary Rynek is slightly cheaper.

Pizzeria Tivoli, ulica Wroniecka 13, serves pizza and beer until 11 pm. It's three blocks off the north end of Stary Rynek.

West of the Old Town There are several good places to eat in the streets and squares west of the old town. *Bistro Apetit*, Plac Wolności 1 below Hotel Rzymski, is a cheap milk bar.

Just two blocks west of here is the full-service *Smakosz Restaurant*, ulica 27 Grudnia 9, an old-style European restaurant with impeccable service, excellent food, good prices and an English menu. It's open till 11 pm.

Smak Coop, Św Marcin 73, and *Pod Kuchcikiem*, Św Marcin 75, both offer basic self-service meals with beer. *U Marcina*, Św Marcin 34, is a rather chic self-service popular with the city youth.

The *Restauracja Indyjska*, Kantaka 8/9, serves fairly expensive Indian curries and has cold beer to cool you down (open daily until midnight).

For an up-market Chinese meal there's the *Pekin Restaurant*, ulica 23 Lutego 29 opposite the main post office.

The *Pod Arkadami Milk Bar*, Plac Cyryla Ratajskiego 10, is great for a snack or a full meal. Whole groups of workers crowd in here – recommended.

Cafés & Bars When it's time for coffee, cakes and ice cream, stop at *Sukiennicza*, Stary Rynek 100. *Loger*, Stary Rynek 93, specialises in a sweet honey wine known as miód (mead). *Herbaciarnia*, Stary Rynek 68, is a place for having a pot of tea. *Pod Piwoszem*, ulica Wrocławska 12, off the south end of Stary Rynek, is a working man's pub with cold beer on tap. Lech is a good local beer to try here, but beware of the sweet, low-alcohol Czarna Perła beer. The *Stajenka Pegaza*, a small pub on ulica Aleksandra Fredry midway between the opera house and the train tracks, is a nice place to drop in after the opera or before going to a disco.

A 24-hour liquor store is at 27 Grudnia 13.

Entertainment

The *Opera House*, ulica Aleksandra Fredry 9, is in the park behind the Solidarity monument (ticket office open Tuesday to Saturday 1 to 7 pm, Sunday 4 to 7 pm).

Poznań's symphony orchestra plays at the *Filharmonia*, ulica Św Marcin 81 opposite the Palace of Culture. Check there for performances by the famous Poznań Boys' & Men's Philharmonic Choir which specialises in old music.

Also check the *Polski Theatre 'Naród Sobie'*, ulica 27 Grudnia, which presents plays in Polish.

The *Musical Theatre* next to the Orbis Poznań Hotel features Broadway shows like *Hello Dolly* and *Me and My Girl*.

St John's Fair in June or July and the Poznań Musical Spring in March are annual events to enquire about.

Discos Though you'll have a better selection of places to eat than in Wrocław, the nightlife in Poznań isn't as good.

Poznań's top disco is *Studio Jack* (☎ 520 522), ulica Działyńskich. It opens nightly with a billiard bar downstairs from 4 pm to 5 am and disco upstairs from 10 pm to 5 am.

Akumulatory, ulica Zwierzyniecka 7, in the 12-storey building directly across the street from the Orbis Mercury Hotel, is a students disco which opens at 9 pm.

Things to Buy

There's an Antykwariat (second-hand) bookshop at Stary Rynek 54, and Desa, Stary Rynek 48, has antiques plus old jewellery and paintings. Keep in mind that books and works of art produced before 1945 cannot be exported. Jubiler, Stary Rynek 40, has contemporary Polish amber jewellery. You can see more amber at Stary Rynek 81.

Księgarnia, ulica Gwarna at 27 Grudna near the Lech Hotel, has a large selection of cassettes and CDs. Also visit the large flower and vegetable market in Plac Wielkopolski in the old town.

Getting There & Away

Direct trains arrive at Poznań from Berlin (261 km), Copenhagen, the Hook of Holland (Hoek van Holland), Kiev, Moscow, Ostend and Paris abroad, and Ełk, Gdynia/Gdańsk, Kraków, Olsztyn, Rzepin, Szczecin, Toruń, Warsaw and Wrocław in Poland. As you see, it's quite a crossroads! If you're arriving in Poland from Western Europe via Berlin, stop here instead of going straight through to Warsaw.

The *Warta* and *Lech* express trains run daily all year between Warsaw and Poznań (311 km, 3½ hours). The *Warta* departs from Warsaw in the morning and Poznań in the late afternoon, whereas the *Lech* does the opposite. The Eurocity *Berolina* links Poznań to Berlin-Hauptbahnhof in just three hours, departing from Poznań in the morning, Berlin in the afternoon. Reservations are required on all these trains.

Buses to Kórnik and Rogalin leave frequently from the PKS bus station on Towarowa. First get a departure time from the Informacja window inside the station (offer them a piece of paper on which to write it down), then ask which gate *(stanowiska)* your bus leaves from as it's different every time. Gate numbers are also indicated by the blue footnotes on the white departures board posted in the station. Buy your ticket at any window, then go to the gate to check that your bus really is listed on the board there.

Getting Around

Tram tickets come in two varieties, one type valid for a single trip lasting up to 10 minutes, and another (costing double) for a 30-minute trip.

Car Rental The Hertz office (☎ 332 081) is at the Orbis Poznań Hotel, Plac Dąbrowskiego 1.

Taxi Taxis wait on ulica Rynkova, the street off the north-west corner of Stary Rynek. The fare will be 400 times the meter reading (if it hasn't been increased).

GNIEZNO

Gniezno, a small town 50 km east of Poznań, was the birthplace of the Polish nation. Here the legendary hero Lech found the white eagle now represented on the Polish flag. Already in the 8th century the Polanian tribe had their main fortified settlement at Gniezno, and in the 10th century, when Mieszko I converted to Christianity, a kingdom was established here. In the year 1000 Boleslav the Brave and the German emperor Otto III had a historic meeting at Gniezno. These events are retold in the **Museum of the Origin of the Polish State** (closed Monday) on Jelonek Lake, a little over a km west of the train station.

In the centre of town a bit back towards the station is the 14th-century Gothic **cathedral** with the silver sarcophagus (1662) of St Adalbertus on the main altar. The life story of this saint appears on the cathedral's famous Romanesque bronze doors (1170), inside below the tower. The Bohemian monk Adalbertus arrived at Gniezno in 996 on his way to the lands east of the mouth of the Vistula River where he intended to convert the heathen Prussians. Instead the tribesmen killed the monk, whose remains were bought back by Boleslav the Brave for their weight in gold. Pope Sylvester canonised Adalbertus in 999, elevating Gniezno to an archbishopric at the same time.

Getting There & Away

Gniezno is a day trip from Poznań or a stop on the way to Toruń. The town is on the main railway line from Wrocław to Gdynia via Poznań, Inowrocław and Bydgoszcz. Through trains from Poznań to Olsztyn via Toruń and Iława also pass here. Otherwise, to go from Gniezno to Toruń you must change at Inowrocław. Local trains to/from Poznań (52 km) are frequent and these stop at Poznań-Garbary Station as well as Poznań Główny.

TORUŃ

Halfway between Poznań and Gdańsk (or Warsaw and Gdańsk), Toruń (Thorn) was founded by the Teutonic Knights in 1233 and its position on the Vistula River at a crossing of trade routes made it an important member of the medieval Hanseatic League. The wealth this brought is reflected in Toruń's three towering Gothic churches. Two are near Rynek Staromiejski, the old town square in the merchants' quarter, while the third adjoins Rynek Nowomiejski, the new town square in the craftsmen's quarter. The ruins of the knights' castle can still be seen by the river between these two districts.

Fortunately medieval Toruń, still enclosed in surviving sections of the city walls, was not seriously damaged in WW II. It offers a chance to step briefly back in history without a lot of other tourists on your heels. Look for gingerbread *(pierniki)*, a local speciality made with honey using 18th-century moulds.

Orientation

There are several train stations in Toruń. Although Toruń Miasto is closer to the centre of town, most trains stop at Toruń Główny, the main station on the south side of the river. Here you'll find the left-luggage office and a restaurant between tracks Nos 2 and 3. Taxis park just outside this hall. To catch bus No 22 or 27 to town, go through the subterranean passage towards track No 4 and buy a ticket at the Ruch kiosk near the stop. Get off the bus at the first stop across the bridge and walk east from the stop, and within minutes you'll be on Rynek Staromiejski, the old town square. The main bus station is near the northern edge of town, an easy walk.

Information

Tourist Office Tourist information (☎ 10 931) is on the west side of the town hall building in the centre of Rynek Staromiejski. The enthusiastic staff here go out of their way to be helpful.

The PTTK Tourist Office (☎ 28 228), Plac Rapackiego 2, is at the west end of ulica Różana just by the passage into the old town. This PTTK office sells a good selection of maps from all over Poland but they aren't very good about answering questions, for this go to the town hall office.

The YHA has an information office selling hostel guidebooks at ulica Kopernicka 27 (weekdays 10 am to 1 pm).

The Toruń Automobile Club (☎ 28 691) is at Ducha Św 5 in the old town.

Money The Narodowy Bank Polski (NBP Bank), on Plac Rapackiego next to the PTTK office on the west side of the old town (weekdays 8 am to 5 pm, Saturday 8 to 11 am), changes travellers' cheques for 1.5% commission.

The PKO Bank, ulica Podmurna 81-83,

also changes travellers' cheques for the same commission (US$3 minimum) and it's far less crowded than the NBP Bank.

Post & Telephone The main post office and telephone centre is conveniently located at Rynek Staromiejski 15 (open weekdays 8 am to 8 pm, Saturday 8 am to 1 pm). At last report they still didn't have any card phones. Toruń's telephone code is 056.

Travel Agencies Seat reservations for express trains can be made at Orbis at ulica Żeglarska 31 on Rynek Staromiejski or at Toruń Główny Station.

Things to See

The Old Town Begin your sightseeing on Rynek Staromiejski with the **historical museum** (closed Monday) in the 14th-century old town hall, one of the largest of its kind in the Baltic states. From May to September you can climb the tower. The statue of Copernicus beside the town hall was erected in 1853. Don't miss the nearby **Oriental Art Museum** (free Sunday, closed Monday) in 15th-century Pod Gwiazdą house at Rynek Staromiejski 35, featuring a hanging wooden staircase dated 1697.

Just off the north-west corner of the square is 14th-century **St Mary's Church**, a typical Gothic hall church with all naves of equal height – but what a height! The presbytery, stained glass windows, organ (1609) and decoration of this church are fine.

Gothic **St John's Church**, on ulica Żeglarska south of Rynek Staromiejski, is remarkable for its soaring white interior and the richness of its altars. West at ulica Kopernika 15 from this church is the **birthplace of astronomer Nicolaus Copernicus** (born in 1473), now a museum dedicated to the man who moved the earth and stopped the sun (closed Monday). You must buy two tickets here, one to see the scale model of Toruń and another for the rest of the museum, though the two add up to under a dollar. Copernicus stayed in Toruń until his 17th birthday when he left to study in Kraków.

Go around the corner beyond the museum and walk straight down to the riverside. Here you'll see the **medieval walls and gates** which once defended Toruń. Walk east along the river past the castle ruins. To reach the ruins turn left, then left again on ulica Przedzamcze. The **Castle of the Teutonic Knights** was destroyed in 1454 but its massive foundations are visible. Early 14th-century **St James' Church** is off Rynek Nowomiejski in the north-east section of the old town. The flying buttresses on this church are rare in Poland.

If you're enchanted by Toruń's old Teutonic charm and have a good cheap place to stay, consider extending your stay by a day and visiting nearby Chełmo and Golub-Dobrzyń, both easily accessible by bus. **Chełmo**, near the Vistula 45 km north-west of Toruń, is completely surrounded by a 14th-century city wall protecting the same sort of picturesque central square and Gothic churches seen in Toruń. **Golub-Dobrzyń**, 43 km north-east of Toruń, has a red-brick castle erected by the Teutonic Knights.

Places to Stay

Camping Toruń's convenient camping ground makes this a good place to unroll the tent. *Camping 'Tramp'* (☎ 24 187; open year-round), near the south end of the highway bridge over the Vistula River, is a five-minute walk from Toruń Główny Railway Station. Bungalows are US$5 single or US$10 for up to four people, while hotel-style rooms in the building adjoining the restaurant are US$4/8 single/double. The public toilets and showers could do with a cleaning but camping is just US$2 per person. Bring mosquito repellent. The camping-ground restaurant is open till midnight.

Hostels Toruń's *hostel* (☎ 27 242) is at ulica Rudacka 15, across the river east of Toruń Główny Railway Station (bus No 13). The doors don't open until 5 pm.

The *PTTK Dom Wycieczkowy* (☎ 23 855), ulica Legionów 24, a continuation of ulica Uniwersytecka several blocks north of the

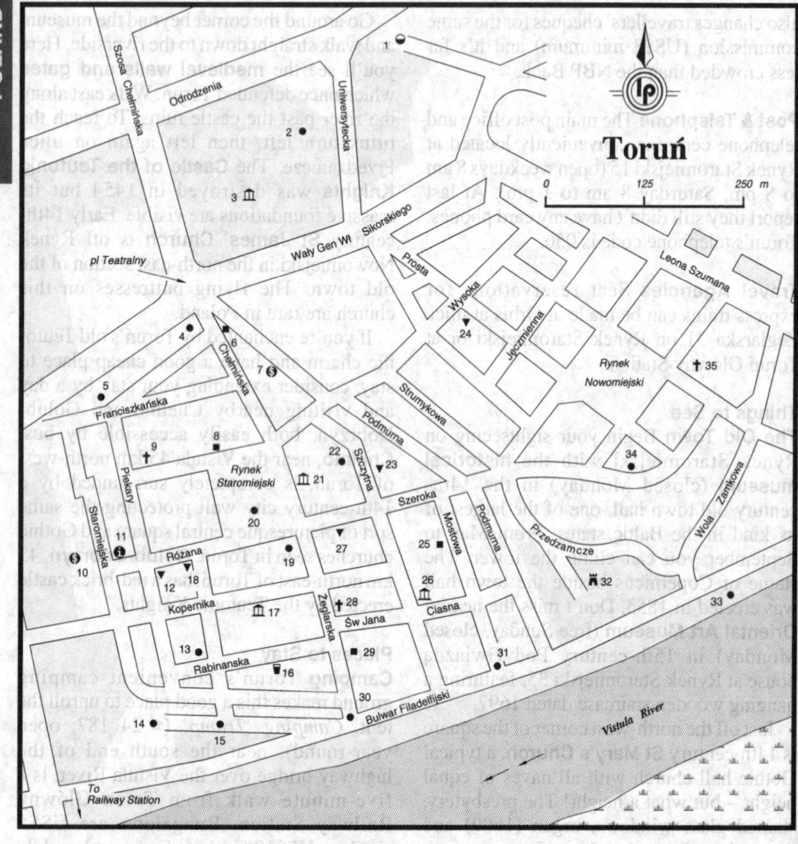

bus station, is a three-storey building in a pleasant suburb a 15-minute walk from the old town. Double rooms are US$12, a bed in a four-bed dormitory US$5, but it's sometimes fully booked by groups.

Hotels The old *Hotel Trzy Korony* (☎ 26 031), Rynek Staromiejski 21, is rather basic for US$10/14 single/double without bath or breakfast, though the location is great, right on the old town square. Don't stay here if you're a light sleeper as loud music from the downstairs bar continues late into the night.

The four-storey *Orzel Hotel* (☎ 25 024), ulica Mostowa 15 (US$10/16 single/double without bath, US$22 double with bath), is still cheap but nicer.

The *Hotel Polonia* (☎ 23 028), Plac Teatralny 5, a fine old four-storey hotel opposite the municipal theatre, is US$13 single or double, US$17 triple without bath, or US$16 single with bath (no doubles with bath). The rooms up on the top floor are about a dollar cheaper. The hotel restaurant is good.

For a mild splurge consider the *Zajazd Staropolski* (☎ 26 061), ulica Żeglarska 14,

PLACES TO STAY

6 Hotel Polonia
8 Hotel Trzy Korony
25 Hotel Orzeł
29 Hotel Zajazd Staropolski

PLACES TO EAT

12 Pizzeria
18 Bar Mleczny
23 Staromiejska Restaurant
24 Restauracja Hungaria
27 Pod Gołębiem Restaurant

OTHER

1 Bus Station
2 Ethnographic Park
3 Ethnographical Museum
4 Municipal Theatre
5 Copernicus University
7 PKO Bank
9 St Mary's Church
10 NBP Bank
11 PTTK Tourist Office
13 Kawiarna Pod 'Atlantem'/ Auto Club
14 Crooked Tower
15 Monastery Gate
16 Czarna Oberża Pub
17 Copernicus Museum
19 Orbis (Train Tickets)
20 Old Town Hall
21 Oriental Art Museum
22 Elana Klub
26 Archaeological Museum
28 St John's Church
30 Sailor's Gate
31 Bridge Gate
32 Castle Ruins
33 Excursion Boat Landing
34 Club 'Stary Browar'
35 St James' Church

a tasteful small hotel owned by the Polish travel agency Gromada. There are several different types of rooms with varying prices: back rooms are US$17/28 single/double while doubles with a street view go for US$32. Rooms with TV are about US$5 more and in midsummer all prices are increased about US$10. All rooms include bath and breakfast. The hotel restaurant has a nice open atmosphere and the menu is clearly written in German.

Places to Eat

There are three cheap places in a row on ulica Różana just off Rynek Staromiejski. *Bar Mleczny*, ulica Różana 1 (behind the ice-cream place on the corner), has genuine Polish dishes at low prices though it's difficult to order as you must point or just take a chance and pick anything on the menu. *Mini Bar Makary*, ulica Różana 3, has cheap spaghetti and lasagne, while the self-service pizza place at ulica Różana 5 serves assembly-line pizza covered with ketchup.

Restauracja Hungaria, Prosta 19, offers Hungarian cuisine at very reasonable prices. Their menu is in German and there's full bar service. Nearby at Prosta 20 is a place dispensing soggy self-service pizza to hordes of young Poles.

For more sedate dining with proper table service try *Pod Gołębiem*, ulica Szeroka 37. The *Staromiejska Restaurant*, at ulica Szczytna 4, is an up-market Italian restaurant.

Café & Gingerbread *Kawiarnia Pod 'Atlantem'*, Ducha Św 3 near the Copernicus Museum, is a nice informal place for coffee and cakes in plush surroundings. Authentic Toruń gingerbread can be purchased at *Kopernik*, ulica Żeglarska 25 near St John's Church. Join the queue of eager Polish tourists waiting to buy this treat.

Entertainment

The *Municipal Theatre* is on Plac Teatralny at the north entrance to the old town. Every second Friday at 7 pm there's a concert in the old town hall. Festivals include the Meeting of Folk Bands in May and the International Old Music Festival in September.

Bars & Discos *Pub Kuranty*, Rynek Staromiejski 29, is a popular drinking place for the town youth. Go through the café and down the stairs in back.

Czarna Oberża, ulica Rabiańska 9, is a German-style pub with billiard tables.

A mixed crowd frequents *Orion Night Club* (☎ 27 962), Plac Teatralny 7, which is open for drinks from 6 pm and functions as a disco from 10 pm to 5 am. The disco downstairs at the *Elana Klub*, ulica Szczytna 15, opens at 10 pm.

The *Club 'Stary Brower'*, ulica Browarna 1, is a students' bar with live music and disco dancing on Friday and Saturday nights. The downstairs bar opens around 5 pm nightly. There's no name outside – just look for the beer advertisements on what appears to be an 'old brewery'.

Getting There & Away

There are direct services from Gdańsk, Malbork, Olsztyn (via Iława), Poznań and Warsaw. Most trains to Warsaw carry mandatory seat reservations, so ask. Services between Gdańsk and Poznań require Toruń passengers to change trains, southbound at Bydgoszcz, northbound at Inowrocław.

The *Kujawiak* express train runs daily all year between Warsaw and Toruń (242 km, three hours), departing from Warsaw in the afternoon and Toruń in the morning. Reservations are required.

Buses to Chełmo and Golub-Dobrzyń depart from Toruń's bus station every hour or two. For more distant destinations you're probably better off taking a train, although one early morning bus does depart from Toruń for Gdańsk (181 km). The information and ticket windows inside the bus station are open from 6 am to 8.30 pm.

Pomerania

The Polish Baltic coast stretches 694 km from Germany to the Russian border, a region of rugged natural beauty where endless beaches and shifting dunes alternate with vast bays, lagoons and coastal lakes. Most of Pomerania (north-western Poland between the Vistula and Odra rivers) was part of Germany until 1945, though the area from Bydgoszcz to Gdynia belonged to Poland from 1918 on.

Here Baltic beach resorts such as Świnoujście, Łeba, Hel and Sopot join historic Gdańsk to put Pomerania on most Polish itineraries. Ferries from Denmark, Sweden and Finland call at Świnoujście and Gdańsk. Szczecin (Stettin), near the mouth of the Odra River, was once the main port of Berlin but the old town was largely destroyed in WW II and it's now just another seedy industrial city. Świnoujście is much nicer and nearby Międzyzdroje is the gateway to Wolin National Park. Słowiński National Park west of Łeba is another area of special interest to naturalists.

HISTORY

Northern Poland has long been a battleground between Poles and Germans. Poland never really controlled the Slavic tribes of western Pomerania, and beginning in the 12th century the area was absorbed by the margraves of Brandenburg. In eastern Pomerania the Germanic Teutonic Knights, invited here in 1226 to help subdue the restive Prussian tribes, played a similar role. From their castles at Malbork and Toruń, the knights defied the king of Poland until their defeat in the 15th century by combined Polish and Lithuanian forces. Although the Duchy of Prussia was a vassal of Poland in the 16th century, wars with Sweden and internal dissent weakened Poland's position in the 17th century.

In 1720 the Kingdom of Prussia reoccupied all of western Pomerania, and the first partition of Poland (1772) brought everything south as far as Toruń under Prussian control (Toruń itself wasn't annexed by Prussia until 1793). After the Congress of Vienna in 1815, Poland south-east of Toruń came under tsarist Russia, a situation that persisted until WW I. In 1919 the Treaty of Versailles granted Poland a narrow corridor to the sea, separating East Prussia from Pomerania. Since the Free City of Danzig (Gdańsk) was populated mostly by Germans, the Polish government built Gdynia from scratch after 1922.

In 1939 Hitler's demand for a German-controlled road and rail route across Polish territory to East Prussia and the incorporation of Danzig into the Third Reich sparked WW II. In 1945 the German inhabitants were

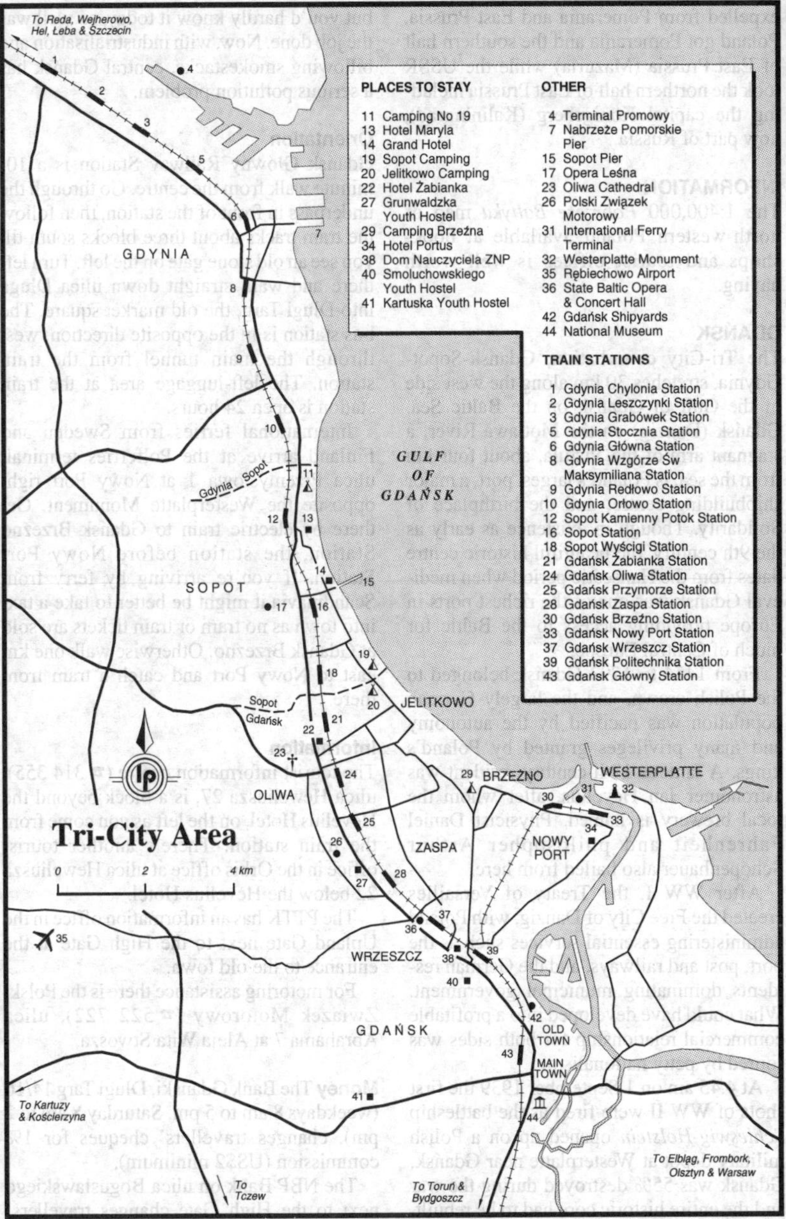
To Reda, Wejherowo, Hel, Łeba & Szczecin
PLACES TO STAY
11 Camping No 19
13 Hotel Maryla
14 Grand Hotel
19 Sopot Camping
20 Jelitkowo Camping
22 Hotel Żabianka
27 Grunwaldzka Youth Hostel
29 Camping Brzeźna
34 Hotel Portus
38 Dom Nauczyciela ZNP
40 Smoluchowskiego Youth Hostel
41 Kartuska Youth Hostel
OTHER
4 Terminal Promowy
7 Nabrzeże Pomorskie Pier
15 Sopot Pier
17 Opera Leśna
23 Oliwa Cathedral
26 Polski Związek Motorowy
31 International Ferry Terminal
32 Westerplatte Monument
35 Rębiechowo Airport
36 State Baltic Opera & Concert Hall
42 Gdańsk Shipyards
44 National Museum
TRAIN STATIONS
1 Gdynia Chylonia Station
2 Gdynia Leszczynki Station
3 Gdynia Grabówek Station
5 Gdynia Stocznia Station
6 Gdynia Główna Station
8 Gdynia Wzgórze Św Maksymiliana Station
9 Gdynia Redłowo Station
10 Gdynia Orłowo Station
12 Sopot Kamienny Potok Station
16 Sopot Station
18 Sopot Wyścigi Station
21 Gdańsk Żabianka Station
24 Gdańsk Oliwa Station
25 Gdańsk Przymorze Station
28 Gdańsk Zaspa Station
30 Gdańsk Brzeźno Station
33 Gdańsk Nowy Port Station
37 Gdańsk Wrzeszcz Station
39 Gdańsk Politechnika Station
43 Gdańsk Główny Station
GDYNIA
GULF OF GDAŃSK
Gdynia
Sopot
SOPOT
JELITKOWO
BRZEŹNO
WESTERPLATTE
OLIWA
ZASPA
NOWY PORT
WRZESZCZ
GDAŃSK
OLD TOWN
MAIN TOWN
Tri-City Area
0 2 4 km
To Kartuzy & Kościerzyna
To Tczew
To Toruń & Bydgoszcz
To Elbląg, Frombork, Olsztyn & Warsaw

expelled from Pomerania and East Prussia. Poland got Pomerania and the southern half of East Prussia (Mazuria) while the USSR took the northern half of East Prussia including the capital Königsberg (Kaliningrad), now part of Russia.

INFORMATION

The 1:400,000 *Pobrzeże Bałtyku* map of north-western Poland available at bookshops and tourist offices is well worth having.

GDAŃSK

The Tri-City conurbation, Gdańsk-Sopot-Gdynia, stretches 30 km along the west side of the Gulf of Gdańsk on the Baltic Sea. Gdańsk (Danzig) on the Motława River, a stagnant arm of the Vistula, about four km from the sea, is Poland's largest port, a major shipbuilding centre, and the birthplace of Solidarity. Though in existence as early as the 9th century, the beautiful historic centre dates from the Hanseatic period when medieval Gdańsk was one of the richest ports in Europe providing access to the Baltic for much of Central Europe.

From 1454 to 1793 Gdańsk belonged to the Polish crown, and the largely German population was pacified by the autonomy and many privileges granted by Poland's kings. A famous 17th-century resident was astronomer Jan Hevelius, after whom the local brewery is named. Physicist Daniel Fahrenheit and philosopher Arthur Schopenhauer also hailed from here.

After WW I, the Treaty of Versailles created the Free City of Danzig, with Poland administering essential services such as the port, post and railways, and the German residents dominating municipal government. What could have developed into a profitable commercial relationship for both sides was soured by petty nationalism.

At 4.45 am on 1 September 1939 the first shots of WW II were fired as the battleship *Schleswig-Holstein* opened up on a Polish military depot at Westerplatte near Gdańsk. Gdańsk was 55% destroyed during the war and the entire historic core had to be rebuilt, but you'd hardly know it today, so well was the job done. Now, with industrialisation and billowing smokestacks, central Gdańsk has a serious pollution problem.

Orientation

Gdańsk Główny Railway Station is a 10-minute walk from the centre. Go through the underpass in front of the station, then follow the tram tracks about three blocks south till you see an old stone gate on the left. Turn left there and walk straight down ulica Długa into Długi Targ, the old market square. The bus station is in the opposite direction, west through the main tunnel from the train station. The left-luggage area at the train station is open 24 hours.

International ferries from Sweden and Finland arrive at the Polferries terminal, ulica Przemysłowa 1 at Nowy Port right opposite the Westerplatte Monument. Get there by electric train to Gdańsk Brzeźno Station, the station before Nowy Port Station. If you're arriving by ferry from Scandinavia it might be better to take a taxi into town as no tram or train tickets are sold at Gdańsk Brzeźno. Otherwise walk one km east to Nowy Port and catch a tram from there.

Information

The tourist information centre (☎ 314 355), ulica Heweliusza 27, is a block beyond the Hevelius Hotel, on the left as you come from the train station. There's another tourist office in the Orbis office at ulica Heweliusza 22 below the Hevelius Hotel.

The PTTK has an information office in the Upland Gate next to the High Gate at the entrance to the old town.

For motoring assistance there is the Polski Związek Motorowy (☎ 522 722), ulica Abrahama 7 at Aleja Wita Stwosza.

Money The Bank Gdański, Długi Targ 14/16 (weekdays 8 am to 5 pm, Saturday 8 am to 2 pm), changes travellers' cheques for 1% commission (US$2 minimum).

The NBP Bank on ulica Bogusławskiego next to the High Gate changes travellers' cheques for 1.5% commission (weekdays 8 am to 3 pm, Saturday 8 am to noon).

Post & Telephone The poste restante office in Gdańsk is well hidden! As you leave the post office at Długa 22, turn right and count five doors. There's no name or number posted outside, but it's really there and on weekdays from 8 am to 8 pm you can pick up mail addressed c/o Poste Restante, 80-801 Gdańsk 50. Even if you don't want poste restante this office is worth seeking out for its five blue card phones which are seldom in use as few people seem to know about this place.

If you have an American Express card you can also have mail addressed c/o American Express, Orbis, ulica Heweliusza 22, 80-890 Gdańsk.

The telephone centre is at Długa 22 (weekdays 7 am to 9 pm, weekends 9 am to 5 pm). Gdańsk's telephone code is 058.

Travel Agencies Seats on express trains and couchettes can be booked at the Orbis office, ulica Heweliusza 22, or at the train station. They also have ferry tickets to Sweden and Finland.

Almatur, Długi Targ 11, sells international bus tickets from Gdańsk to Belgium, Britain, France, Germany, Holland and Italy. Orbis, ulica Heweliusza 22, and Gdańsk-Tourist, ulica Heweliusza 8, also sell international bus tickets to many Western European cities.

Things to See

Medieval Gdańsk was comprised of three quarters: the Old Town (Stare Miasto), the Main Town (Główne Miasto) and the Old Suburb (Stare Przedmieście). The principal streets of the Main Town run perpendicular to the port, which is reached through a series of gates. During their annual visits Polish kings entered the Main Town through the adjacent **High Gate** (1588) and **Golden Gate** (1614) and proceeded east along ulica Długa, the **Royal Way**.

Długi Targ (Long Market), the historic town square, is the very heart of old Gdańsk. The towering 15th-century **main town hall** on the corner of this square contains a good **Historical Museum** (closed Monday and Friday) in the buildings' coffered Gothic chambers and a great view from the tower. Behind Neptune's Fountain (1613) stands the **Artus Mansion** where local merchants once met. The Renaissance **Green Gate** (1568) at the east end of the square gives access to the old harbour on the Motława River. The excursion boats departing from the landing near the gate are highly recommended (see the Excursion Boats section that follows).

Two blocks north along the harbour is the Mariacka Gate with the **Archaeological Museum** (closed Monday) and through this gate is ulica Mariacka, the most picturesque street in Gdańsk, lined with 17th-century burgher houses. Follow it west to the Gothic **Church of Our Lady**, the largest brick church in Poland. You may climb the 78-metre tower for US$0.25.

Continue west on ulica Piwna (Beer Street!) to the Dutch Renaissance **Armoury** (1609), and take the street running north straight to Gothic **St Catherine's Church** in the Old Town. Opposite this church is the 14th-century **Great Mill**. Just behind St Catherine's is **St Bridget's Church** (1514), Lech Wałęsa's place of worship. At the back of the church are some Solidarity mementos including a memorial to Father Jerzy Popiełuszko. Solidarity and Wałęsa pins are sold at the souvenir counter inside the church.

Near Gdańsk On the north side of Gdańsk at the entrance to the **Gdańsk Shipyards**, just north-east of Gdańsk Główny Railway Station, is a tall **monument** with three steel crosses and anchors dedicated to 45 workers killed during a December 1970 strike. The monument, erected in 1980, stood here throughout the period of martial law. Nearby at the shipyard entrance is a souvenir stand selling Solidarność stickers, pins, T-shirts and even umbrellas.

Individuals are not allowed inside the shipyard but Almatur (☎ 312 403), Długi Targ 11, can organise guided tours at US$20

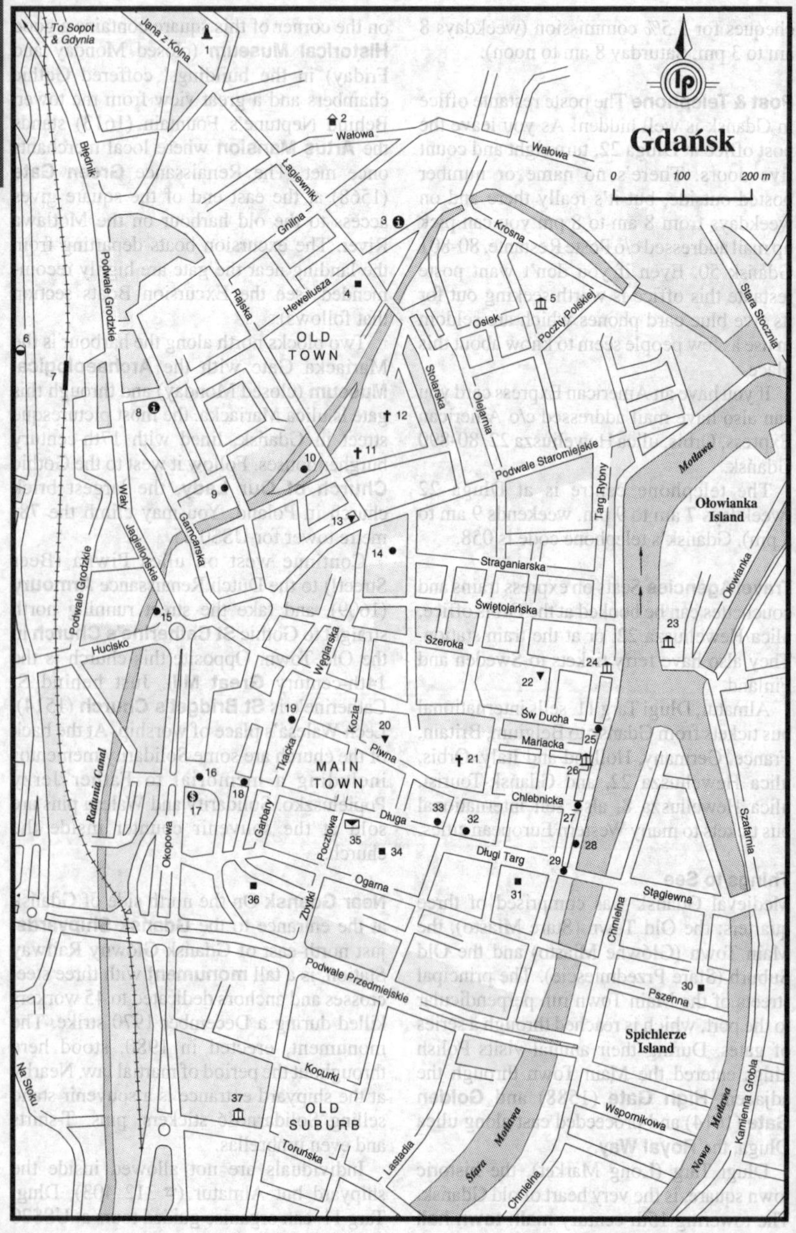
Gdańsk
0
100
200 m
To Sopot & Gdynia
Jana z Kolna
Wałowa
Wałowa
Łagiewniki
Gnilna
Krosna
Heweliusza
Rajska
Podwale Grodzkie
Błędnik
OLD TOWN
Osiek
Poczty Polskiej
Stara Stocznia
Stolarska
Olejarnia
Podwale Staromiejskie
Targ Rybny
Motława
Ołowianka Island
Ołowianka
Wały Jagiellońskie
Garncarska
Podwale Grodzkie
Hucisko
Straganiarska
Świętojańska
Szeroka
Węglarska
Św Ducha
Mariacka
Kozia
Tkacka
Piwna
MAIN TOWN
Chlebnicka
Radunia Canal
Garbary
Długa
Pocztowa
Długi Targ
Okopowa
Ogarna
Zbytki
Stągiewna
Chmielna
Szafarnia
Podwale Przedmiejskie
Pszenna
Spichlerze Island
Kocurki
Na Stoku
OLD SUBURB
Wspomnikowa
Toruńska
Lastadia
Stara Motława
Chmielna
Nowa Motława
Kamienna Grobla
1
2
3
4
5
6
7
8
9
10
11
12
13
14
15
16
17
18
19
20
21
22
23
24
25
26
27
28
29
30
31
32
33
34
35
36
37

PLACES TO STAY

2 Wałowa Youth Hostel
4 Orbis Hevelius Hotel
30 Novotel Hotel
31 Jantar Hotel
34 Hotel Zaułek
36 Dom Harcerza

PLACES TO EAT

13 Restauracja Tan-Viet
20 Pod Wieza
22 Pod Łososiem Restaurant

OTHER

1 Solidarity Monument
3 Tourist Office
5 Postal Museum
6 Bus Station
7 Gdańsk Główny Railway Station
8 Gdańsk-Tourist
9 Old Town Hall
10 Great Mill
11 St Catherine's Church
12 St Bridget's Church
14 Hala Targowa Market
15 Club Żak
16 High Gate
17 NBP Bank
18 Golden Gate
19 Armoury
21 Church of Our Lady
23 Museum Ship *Soldek*
24 Big Crane & Maritime Museum
25 Holy Ghost Gate
26 Mariacka Gate & Archaeological Museum
27 Chlebnicka Gate
28 Excursion Boats
29 Green Gate
32 Artus Mansion
33 Main Town Hall
35 Post Office
37 National Museum

per group of up to 25 people. Almatur must obtain special permission from the shipyard authorities, so you'll need to book at least five days in advance.

From the post office on ulica Długa walk south four blocks to the former Franciscan monastery (1514) in the Old Suburb, south of the Main Town. The monastery now houses the **National Museum** (closed Monday), ulica Toruńska 1 at Rzeźnicka, with porcelain and paintings. The highlight of this large collection is Hans Memling's *Last Judgment*.

At Oliwa between Gdańsk and Sopot is a soaring 13th-century **Cistercian cathedral** in a large park, with a museum (closed Monday) in the adjacent monastery. The cathedral's rococo organ (1788) is one of the best in Europe – ask about organ concerts (often weekdays at noon and Sunday at 3 pm). Get there on tram No 6, 12 or 15, or by electric train to Gdańsk Oliwa Station.

Excursion Boats From April to October excursion boats to Westerplatte (US$3 single, US$4 return, a third off for students) depart several times daily from the landing near Gdańsk's Green Gate. At the beginning and end of the season the 10 am and 2 pm departures to Westerplatte are the most likely to be operating. This is one of the best trips of its kind in Poland, allowing a fine cross-section view of Gdańsk's harbour. At **Westerplatte** a towering monument (1968) with sweeping views commemorates the heroic resistance of the Polish naval garrison here which held out for a week against ferocious attacks in September 1939. Bus No 106 also connects Gdańsk to Westerplatte.

From mid-May to September there are boats across the Baltic from Gdańsk to the fishing village of **Hel** on the Hel Peninsula (US$5 single, US$7 return). From June to August, boats go to Gdynia. Alternatively, take a boat from Gdańsk to Hel, then a second from Hel to Gdynia or Sopot. Be sure to get out on the water if you're in the area in season.

Places to Stay

Camping If you arrive on the international ferry from Scandinavia, the closest camping ground to the wharf is *Camping Brzeźna* (☎ 566 531), Aleje Józefa Hallera 234 (tram No 7 or 15 from the wharf).

Hostels There are four hostels in the Gdańsk area. Most convenient is the hostel (☎ 312 313) at ulica Wałowa 21, a large red-brick building set back from the road, only a five-minute walk from Gdańsk Główny Railway

Station. You have to ask for the key to use the showers (at the bottom of the back stairs next to the dining room). The reception is closed from 10 am to 5 pm.

The other three hostels are between Gdańsk and Sopot, too far to walk. First is the hostel (☎ 323 820) at ulica Smoluchowskiego 11 (take tram No 12 or 13 north from the train station).

The friendly Aleje Grunwaldzka 238/240 hostel (☎ 411 660) is in a small sports complex near Oliwa (open in July and August only). Take a northbound tram No 6, 12 or 15 to 'Abrahama' – ask someone where to get off.

The hostel (☎ 324 187) at ulica Kartuska 245 is about three km west of Gdańsk Railway Station (open July and August only). Catch a southbound tram No 10 or 12 outside the station, stay on to the end of the line, then walk west along the road about 10 minutes till you see a grey three-storey building with a gabled roof on the right.

Dom Harcerza (☎ 313 621), ulica Za Murami 2-10, is a large Boy Scout hostel with dormitory beds at US$5, double rooms with shared bath at US$12, doubles with private bath at US$25. The problem is, it's almost always full up with groups, but the excellent location right next to the old town makes it well worth trying anyway.

From June to September the student travel agency Almatur (☎ 314 403), Długi Targ 11 (open year-round weekdays 9 am to 5 pm, Saturday 9 am to 3 pm), rents rooms in student dormitories at US$10/15 single/double. The same office will book beds at local hostels.

Private Rooms Private rooms (US$10/16 single/double) are arranged by Gdańsk-Tourist (☎ 312 634), ulica Heweliusza 8 near the Gdańsk Główny Railway Station. A US$1 per person tax is charged the first night only and some of their rooms are in the old town. Freelancers on the street outside this office may have an unofficial private room to offer you, perhaps in the centre – bargain hard if their prices are higher than those asked inside.

The tourist office at Orbis in the Hevelius Hotel (weekdays 9 am to 5 pm, Saturday 10 am to 4 pm) has more expensive private rooms (US$16/22/29 single/double/triple), all in the centre of town. They have an album with colour photos of their rooms which you can thumb through.

Hotels The old *Jantar Hotel* (☎ 312 716), Długi Targ 19, has singles/doubles at US$18/26 without bath, US$37 double with bath, breakfast included. You couldn't ask for a more central location but it can be noisy due to the band playing downstairs.

The *Hotel Zaułek* (☎ 314 169), ulica Ogarna 107/108 (go into the courtyard), is cheap at US$6/9/12 single/double/triple and the location in the heart of old Gdańsk is fine, but it's usually fully booked weeks ahead.

One of Gdańsk's best bargains is the no-frills four-storey *Hotel Portus* (☎ 439 624), ulica Wyzwolenia 48/49, in Nowy Port. Plain rooms with shared bath are US$7 single or double. Take tram No 10 north from the train station and get out when you see the large Morski Dom Kultury on the right. The Portus will be just across the street. Otherwise it's a five-minute walk from Gdańsk Nowy Railway Station, or a 15-minute walk from the international ferry terminal. Many of the rooms are permanently occupied by Polish seamen but the staff are friendly to the very few travellers who happen to arrive. It's an interesting, totally untouristed area in which to stay.

Dom Nauczyciela ZNP (☎ 419 116), ulica Uphagena 28, is a school teachers' hotel which accommodates visitors at US$9/17/21 single/double/triple with shared bath, US$16/25/25 with private bath. This is good value but breakfast in the hotel restaurant is extra. It's a pleasant red-brick building a five-minute walk from Gdańsk Politechnika Railway Station.

The *Hotel Żabianka* (☎ 522 772), ulica Dickmana 14/15, is a functional five-storey hotel a five-minute walk from Gdańsk-Żabianka Railway Station in Oliwa. The reception is up on the 3rd floor. At US$16/18 single/double with bath and breakfast, it's fair value and they'll probably still have rooms when all the other places are full. Although convenient for those commuting by train, in about every other way the Żabianka is uninspiring and you get a lot of train noise here (ask for a room on the side facing west).

Places to Eat

Bottom End *Neptun Milk Bar*, ulica Długa 32-34, serves hearty, cheap cafeteria-style meals with no language problems since you pick up the food first and pay at the end of the line. It's a good place for breakfast since it opens at 7 am weekdays (closed Sunday). Unfortunately the choice for vegetarians is limited.

Meals at *Złoty Kur*, ulica Długa 4 near the Golden Gate, are also cheap. Cheap self-service pizza is dispensed at *Starówka*, ulica Długa 74.

Krewctka, ulica Elzbietańska 10/11 near the train station, is a cheap seafood self-service where you pay at the end of the line. It's worth going in just to see the long wooden mural of old Gdańsk along one wall.

Top End All of the up-market restaurants of Gdańsk are highly touristy and when ordering fish you must keep in mind that the menu price is probably only for 100 grams. The portion you'll be served could weigh anywhere from 200 to 300 grams, so to avoid getting a shock when you see your bill, ask first.

A picture of a salmon is in the window of *Pod Łososiem*, ulica Szeroka 52, Gdańsk's most famous seafood restaurant. The *Restaurant Retman*, ulica Stagiewna 1, across the bridge beyond the Green Gate, is another trendy seafood restaurant with prices somewhat lower than Pol Łososiem. Their menu is posted outside (in Polish).

The restaurant downstairs in the *Jantar Hotel*, Długi Targ 19, serves unpretentious, filling meals. After 7 pm a dance band plays for an older crowd and it's rather amusing to watch the action as you have dinner, just don't sit in that section or you'll be charged US$2 cover.

Pod Wieza, Piwna 51, is inexpensive as long as you stick to the traditional Polish meat dishes. Beware of the price of the beer.

The *Restauracja Tan-Viet*, ulica Podmłynska 1/5, diagonally opposite the Targowa market, is a rather expensive Vietnamese restaurant.

Artus beer, brewed by Hevelius Breweries, is Gdańsk's star suds.

Cafés The *Palowa Coffee House* in the basement of the main town hall on Długi Targ is a good place to sit and read, or eat cakes and ice cream. Sometimes it's reserved for tour groups. The *Cocktail Bar*, Długa 59/61, also has excellent coffee and ice cream. The *Café Nad Motława* next to the Chlebnicka Gate has a nice riverside terrace where you can sit and relax in summer. There are several romantic little bars and cafés along ulica Mariacka, such as *Podkolendrem* at No 38 and *Mariacka* at No 23.

Entertainment

Check the local papers and ask tourist information about events. The *Wybrzeże Theatre*, ulica Św Ducha 2, behind the armoury in the Main Town, presents mostly drama in Polish.

The *State Baltic Opera & Concert Hall*, Aleje Zwycięstwa 15, is near Gdańsk Politechnika Railway Station (take tram No 12 or 13 north from the train station). The opera ticket office is open weekdays from 10 am to 7 pm, Saturday 2 to 7 pm, and two hours before the performance. It's usually no problem getting in.

Gdańsk-Tourist, ulica Heweliusza 8, can reserve seats at the Musical Theatre in Gdynia.

Annual events to ask about include the Gdańsk Days in June, the International Choral Meetings from June to August, the International Festival of Organ and Chamber Music in July and August, the Dominican Fair in early August and the Festival of Polish Feature Films in September.

Lighter Fare *Club Zak* (☎ 314 115), the large red brick building on the corner of Wały

Jagiellońskie and Hucisko, is a student club which includes an art cinema, a jazz club, pool tables, an art gallery, a café (open from 5 pm to 2 am), two discos (both opening at 9 pm) and a pub with live music. The downstairs disco has a lower cover charge but it's better to go upstairs where a live band will be playing on Thursday, Friday and Saturday nights. Other nights there could be live jazz, plays and perhaps even a rock concert. Decent meals are served at the bar in the upstairs disco. Unaccompanied women should have no problems upstairs at Club Zak and everyone is welcome.

Kino Neptune, Długa 57, usually shows reasonable films and upstairs through the adjacent entrance are the smaller *Kameralne* and *Helikon* cinemas with different programmes.

Things to Buy

Cepelia, Długa 48/49, sells authentic folk items including costumed dolls, embroidered table cloths, inlaid jewellery boxes, amber necklaces, costume jewellery, wall hangings, icons, leather goods, bedspreads, ceramics, walking sticks, spinning wheels and more. Jubilar, Długa 15, also has amber necklaces and jewellery.

Getting There & Away

Bus Buses leaving Gdańsk Bus Station include hourly services to Krynica Morska (58 km) and Elbląg (59 km), five daily to Malbork (56 km), four daily to Lębork (81 km) and daily to Giżycko. To go to Łeba from Gdańsk you must first take a train to Gdynia and change to a bus there (or go by bus via Lębork).

Train All long-distance trains arriving in the Tri-City area call at Gdańsk, Sopot and Gdynia. Southbound trains usually originate in Gdynia while trains to Szczecin begin in Gdańsk.

Direct trains arrive at Gdynia/Gdańsk from Berlin-Lichtenberg (via Szczecin), Poznań, Szczecin, Wrocław, Warsaw (via Malbork) and Olsztyn (also via Malbork). Couchettes are available to Prague, Warsaw, Szczecin and Berlin.

The *Neptun, Słupia* and *Kaszub* express trains run from Warsaw to Gdańsk (333 km, 3½ hours) daily all year, with the *Neptun* departing from Warsaw in the morning and Gdańsk in the evening. The *Kaszub* and *Słupia* do the opposite, leaving Gdańsk in the morning and Warsaw in the late afternoon. The *Lajkonik* express train runs direct between Kraków Główny and Gdańsk (621 km, seven hours), leaving Kraków in the early morning and Gdańsk in the afternoon. All these trains also service Sopot and Gdynia, and reservations are required.

Ferry Large car ferries arrive at Gdańsk once or twice a week throughout the year from Oxelösund, Sweden, and Helsinki, Finland. The ferry from Karlskrona, Sweden, docks at Gdynia. Turn to Getting There & Away in the chapter introduction for a description of routes and fares.

Getting Around

To/From the Airport Bus No B to Rębiechowo Airport leaves from the stop on ulica Wały Jagiellońskie between Gdańsk-Tourist and the train station. Service is from 5 am to 6 pm with long gaps, so check the schedule posted at the stop well ahead.

Tram & Train Transport around the Tri-City area is easy. Tram lines carry you north from Gdańsk to Oliwa and Jelitkowo. To go to Westerplatte you can take a bus or boat. Cheap SKM electric commuter trains run constantly between Gdańsk, Sopot, Gdynia and Wejherowo (Inter-Rail valid). Frequencies vary from every six minutes during weekday rush hours to every half-hour on weekends. At Reda change for Hel. Commuter train tickets are sold at counters and you must punch your own ticket before going onto the platform. Tram tickets (sold at kiosks) are hard to find on Sunday or in outlying areas, so buy an adequate supply.

Car Rental The Avis Rent-a-Car agent in Gdańsk is Almatur, Długi Targ 11. Budget

(☎ 315 611) is at the Novotel Hotel, ulica Pszenna 1 two blocks east of Długi Targ, and at Rębiechowo Airport. Orbis (☎ 314 045) at Hotel Hevelius, ulica Heweliusza 22, is the Hertz agent.

SOPOT

Sopot (Zoppot), north of Gdańsk by electric train, has been Poland's most fashionable seaside resort since Napoleon's former doctor, Jean Haffner, erected baths here in 1823. During the interwar period, Sopot belonged to the Free City of Danzig, only fully joining Poland in 1945. Sopot has a greater abundance of budget accommodation than either Gdańsk or Gdynia, and the resort atmosphere makes for a pleasant stay. The resort hotels lining the wide, white sandy shores stretching north from Jelitkowo are expensive, but budget accommodation is also available. Unfortunately, the Vistula River flushes thousands of tonnes of pollutants into the Gulf of Gdańsk every year, so swimming here is definitely not recommended.

Orientation

Turn left as you leave the train station and in a few minutes you'll reach Bohaterów Monte Cassino, Sopot's attractive pedestrian mall which leads straight down to the 'molo', Poland's longest pier, jutting 512 metres out into the Gulf of Gdańsk. North of the pier and the Orbis Grand Hotel is a seaside promenade, while behind the town, west of the railway line, is a large forest.

Information

The tourist office is at ulica Dworcowa 4 near the train station.

Travel Agencies For train tickets with seat reservations, sleepers and couchettes try Orbis, Bohaterów Monte Cassino 49. They also have international bus tickets and ferry tickets to Scandinavia.

Places to Stay

Camping *Jelitkowo Campground* (☎ 532 731) is near the beach between Gdańsk and Sopot, a seven-minute walk from the northern terminus of trams Nos 2, 4 and 6. Twenty-five three-bed bungalows are available. It's open from May to September.

There's a cheaper camping ground, *Sopot Camping*, open June to August, at ulica Bitwy pod Płowcami 79, about one km north of Jelitkowo on the main highway. It doesn't have any bungalows but is closer to the beach.

Camping No 19 (☎ 518 011, extension 252) is a convenient five-minute walk from Sopot-Kamienny Potok Railway Station. The seven bungalows here are US$13 each (up to three people) but it can get crowded in the summer (open from May to September). A good bar with four pool tables is on the premises.

Hotels & Private Rooms The *Dworcowy Hotel* (☎ 511 525) near the Sopot Railway Station is US$7/12/15/18 single/double/triple/quad without bath or breakfast.

The Biuro Zakwaterowań beside the Dworcowy arranges stays in private rooms. In the off season they're closed weekends. If they can't help, hang around outside the office looking lost, baggage in hand, and wait until someone approaches you.

One of the few European-style pensions in Poland, *Pensjonat Irena* (☎ 512 073), ulica Chopina 36, in a large mansion just down the hill from Sopot Railway Station, is US$10/15/19 single/double/triple without bath or breakfast.

The 112-room, four-star *Orbis Grand Hotel* (☎ 510 041), by the pier right on Sopot Beach, is US$35/47 single/double and up with breakfast. During July and August these prices double. This neobaroque resort hotel built in 1926 hosts Sopot's gambling casino and it's becoming rather pretentious.

Hotels at Sopot-Kamienny Potok In front of Camping No 19 near Sopot-Kamienny Potok Railway Station is the *Hotel Miramar* (☎ 518 011), ulica Zamkowa Góra 25, formerly the PTTK Dom Turysty. Rooms with bath in the newer 'pavilion A' are US$19/30 single/double, while in the older 'pavilion B' they're US$17/28. Double rooms without bath are US$19 in both buildings and there is one single room without bath in pavilion A which costs US$8. Breakfast is included. There are also three, four, five and six-bed dormitories costing US$4 per person without breakfast. Though it does receive many groups and is very busy in the summer, the Miramar has 327 beds – hopefully including one for you. A disco called *Bungalow* is just down the street.

The *Maryla Hotel* (☎ 516 053), a couple of blocks away at ulica Sepia 22, is rather plush with a bar and restaurant on the premises. It sort of looks like a country club. Rooms with bath in the main building are US$19/25/32 single/double/triple and from June to August the adjacent 'camping bungalows' rent for US$16 double or US$22 for four persons without bath, US$29 for four with bath.

Next door to the Maryla is *Hotel Magnolia* (☎ 513 419), ulica Haffnera 100, with rooms at US$12/16/19 single/double/triple (shared bath).

Across the street from the Maryla and Magnolia is the 104-room *Sopot Lucky Hotel* (☎ 513 296), ulica Haffnera 81/85. It has rooms with bath at US$25/32/35 double/triple/quad (no singles). This modern three-storey building is a former holiday complex owned by the Gdynia shipyard.

All four hotels are on a hill a five-minute walk from Sopot-Kamienny Potok Railway Station and 10 minutes from the beach. Hotel prices at Sopot are greatly increased in July and August, so expect to pay considerably more than the rates quoted here at that time.

Places to Eat

The *Albatros Restaurant* in the Dworcowy Hotel not far from the Sopot Railway Station is one of the least expensive in town. The service is good and the portions large, but there may not be any printed menu so ask the waiter to write down the prices while ordering. The restaurant at *Pensjonat Irena* is also good and inexpensive.

Cafés The artists' club, *Spatif*, ulica Bohaterów Monte Cassino 54 (upstairs), has a great bar and meals are served, but this is a private club and the door is kept securely locked. If you knock you'll be scrutinised through a tiny window and only if the members present like what they see will you be admitted.

At the terrace at *Złoty Ul*, Bohaterów Monte Cassino 33, you'll be among visitors who like to sip as they sit and watch the passing parade. Sopot's most popular café among students is *Café Bazar*, Bohaterów Monte Cassino 5.

Entertainment

Summer activities centre around the open-air *Opera Leśna* in the forest, 15 minutes' walk straight west from Bohaterów Monte Cassino. The Opera and Musical Theatre Festival is held here in July and the International Song Festival during the last 10 days of August. Rock groups appear on the programme of the latter.

Plays in Polish are staged at the *Scena Kameralna*, Bohaterów Monte Cassino 55/57. *Kino Bałtyk*, Bohaterów Monte Cassino 28, is Sopot's best cinema.

For tickets to the Opera Leśna check with the Bałtycka Agencja Artystyczna-BART (☎ 510 115), ulica Kościuszki 61 a couple of blocks south of Sopot Railway Station. Orbis, Bohaterów Monte Cassino 49, may also have summer opera tickets.

Getting There & Away

All long-distance trains stop here.

GDYNIA

Gdynia (Gdingen), the northernmost of the Tri-City three, is the base for much of Poland's merchant and fishing fleet. Unlike Gdańsk which is on a river, Gdynia is a real Baltic port looking out onto the open sea, with sailors on the streets and seagulls flying above.

In 1922 the Polish parliament decided to build a port on the site of a small village here to give Poland an outlet to the sea at a time when Gdańsk was still the Free City of Danzig. With the help of French capital, Gdynia had become one of the largest ports

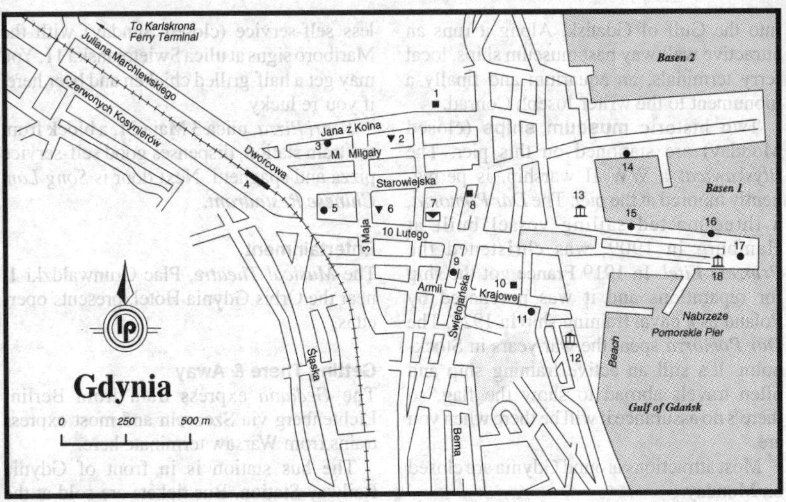

1 Hotel Garnizonowy
2 Dom Rybaka
3 Market
4 Gdynia-Gńówna Railway Station
5 Nord Turus
6 Sapri Pizza
7 Post Office
8 Hotel Lark
9 Orbis
10 Orbis Gdynia Hotel
11 Musical Theatre
12 Naval Museum
13 City Museum
14 Fishing Boats
15 Museum Ship *Bńyskawica*
16 Museum Ship *Dar Pomorza*
17 Joseph Conrad Monument
18 Oceanographic Museum & Aquarium

on the Baltic by the outbreak of WW II. Unlike most other towns along the north coast which are German in origin, Gdynia is Polish through and through.

Orientation & Information

Gdynia Railway Station shelters a left-luggage office and cash-only exchange facilities, both open 24 hours a day. The tourist information office (daily 9 am to 6 pm) in the train station is well hidden down near the PKS bus ticket window, beyond the video games to one side from the main station hall.

The ferry from Karlskrona, Sweden, arrives/departs from the Terminal Promowy, ulica Kwiatkowskiego 60, five km north-west of Gdynia Railway Station. Ask about the free shuttle bus between the terminal and Gdańsk when you book your ticket.

Post & Telephone There's a telephone centre in the main post office on ulica 10 Lutego (weekdays 7 am to 8 pm, Saturday 9 am to 5 pm, Sunday and holidays 11 am to 6 pm). If the main entrance is closed go in through the door around the corner on ulica Władysława IV.

Gdynia's telephone code is 058.

Travel Agencies Orbis, ulica Swiętojanska 36, has the usual international bus, train and ferry tickets, and can book couchettes.

Things to See

Sightseeing centres around Gdynia's broad main pier, Nabrzeże Pomorskie, pointing out into the Gulf of Gdańsk. Along it runs an attractive walkway past museum ships, local ferry terminals, an aquarium and finally a monument to the writer Joseph Conrad.

Two historic **museum ships** (closed Monday) are stationed on this pier. The *Błyskawica*, a WW II warship, is permanently moored at the pier. The *Dar Pomorza*, a three-masted sailing vessel built at Hamburg in 1909, was christened the *Prinzess Eitel*. In 1919 France got the ship for reparations and it was purchased by Poland as a naval training ship in 1929. The *Dar Pomorza* spent the war years in Stockholm. It's still an active training ship and often travels abroad to show the flag, so there's no assurance it will be there when you are.

Most attractions around Gdynia are closed on Monday.

Places to Stay

Private Rooms A good place to try first is Nord Turus (☎ 209 287), ulica Starowiejska 47 (entrance from ulica Dworcowa) near Gdynia Główna Railway Station, which arranges accommodation in private homes for US$5/9 single/double (higher in midsummer). It's open from 8 am to 6 pm Monday to Saturday.

Hotels The *Lark Hotel* (☎ 218 046), an old-style hotel conveniently located at ulica Starowiejska 1, is US$9/12/16 single/double/triple with shared bath. It's the kind of place a seaman might appreciate and the earthy atmosphere will also appeal to any rough-and-ready traveller looking to get off the beaten track.

If the Lark is fully booked try *Dom Rybaka* (☎ 208 723), ulica Jana z Kolna 27, a five-storey red-brick hotel with rooms at US$10/13 single/double.

The *Hotel Garnizonowy* (☎ 266 472), ulica Jana z Kolna 6, is a six-storey hotel formerly reserved for military personnel. Double rooms are US$19 (no singles).

Places to Eat

For cheap basic meals check out the nameless self-service (closed Sunday) with the Marlboro signs at ulica Swiętojanska 11. You may get a half-grilled chicken and beer here, if you're lucky.

Sapri Pizza, ulica 3 Maja 21, a block from the train station, dispenses good self-service pizza and spaghetti. Next door is *Song Lam Chinese Restaurant*.

Entertainment

The *Musical Theatre*, Plac Grunwaldzki 1, near the Orbis Gdynia Hotel, presents operettas.

Getting There & Away

The *Gedania* express train from Berlin-Lichtenberg via Szczecin and most express trains from Warsaw terminate here.

The bus station is in front of Gdynia Railway Station. Bus tickets are sold at the 'kasy PKS' near the train reservation windows inside the train station. Buses of possible use to visitors include those to Hel, Łeba and Świnoujście.

HEL

Hel, a real Baltic fishing village near the tip of the narrow peninsula separating the Gulf of Gdańsk from the sea, is the favourite day-trip destination for visitors to the Tri-City area.

Things to See & Do

The local **fishing museum** is in the old red church opposite the harbour. There's a beach on the bay just west of the harbour, or walk a little over one km across the peninsula to the sea beach.

Places to Stay & Eat

There are no hotels at Hel, though the PTTK Tourist Office, Generała Waltera 80 near the harbour, might be able to suggest a place to stay. Next to the PTTK is the *Kaszubska Bar* with big mugs of draught beer.

Getting There & Away

On summer mornings excursion boats to Hel leave from the end of the long wooden pier at Sopot, and less frequently from Gdańsk.

In Gdańsk buy tickets at the landing near the Green Gate on the waterfront. Upon arrival in Hel, buy your return ticket at the kiosk ashore right away as it closes as soon as the ship's capacity has been reached. There's a small bar aboard where you can get coffee or a beer and the open deck at the back makes for a very pleasant trip.

It's nice to take the boat over but they only allow 2½ hours at Hel, enough for a walk around town and a drink. If you want more time to enjoy the beach you can always get a train back. This is no problem as local trains run from Hel to Gdynia about four times a day, while the service from Hel to Reda (where there are immediate connections for Gdynia and Gdańsk) is seven times a day. The train trip to/from Gdynia takes over two hours while the boat needs only one.

ŁEBA

If you're looking for a Baltic beach resort you won't have to share with thousands of holidaying Polish workers and their families, where the small town ambience still prevails and the surrounding nature is relatively undisturbed, you won't go wrong by choosing Łeba (pronounced 'weba'). The beach here stretches in both directions as far as the eye can see, and only one old mansion breaks through the forest crowning the beachside sand dunes. Unlike the polluted waters around Gdańsk, you can swim in the open Baltic here. Łeba is too far to do as a day trip from Gdańsk – don't bother coming if you can't stay the night.

Orientation

Trains and buses from Lębork terminate at Łeba Railway Station two blocks west of ulica Kościuszki, Łeba's main drag. This shopping street runs north a few hundred metres, crosses the Chełst Canal, and ends in a park which you walk through to reach the sea. A town plan is posted outside the train station.

Things to See

Łeba is on a brief stretch of the Łeba River which joins Łebsko Lake to the sea. Just before dusk, people head down to the river mouth to join the fisher folk in watching the sunset. The river divides Łeba's beach in two. The town is nestled back out of the way behind the eastern beach, while the beach on the west side of the river is far less crowded. The broad white sands of this western beach stretch back 75 metres to the dunes – one of the best beaches on the entire Baltic.

Farther west of town and the river, a sand bar of white pine-covered dunes separates shallow Lake Łebsko from the Baltic. Here one finds **Słowiński National Park**, where the largest shifting sand dunes in Eastern Europe create a striking desert landscape. During WW II, Rommel's Afrika Korps trained in this desert, and a small Polish military base is still hidden among the dunes. V-1 rockets were fired at England from here, and you can still find what appear to be the old concrete launching pads.

The road into the park runs along the north shore of Lake Łebsko for 2.5 km to the Rabka park entry gate (pedestrians free, cars US$3), then another 4.5 km to Wydmy Ruchome where vehicular traffic ends. In July and August there are buses from Łeba to Wydmy Ruchome (seven km) every two hours. From the end of the road it's a two-km walk to a magnificent, 42-metre-high sand dune which simply must be climbed for a sweeping view of desert, lake, beach, sea and forest. You can return to Łeba on foot along the beach with perhaps a stop for a swim – something you can't do in the Sahara!

Places to Stay

Camping The *Intercamp* (☎ 61 206), a five-minute walk west from the train station (signposted), has camping space or rooms in a central building. In 1984 the International Camping and Caravanning Jamboree was held here. The facilities are good but there's little shade.

There are two more camping grounds a few hundred metres west of the Intercamp, to the right on ulica Turystyczna, and these have more shade and are closer to the beach. The first is *Camping 'Przymorze' No 21 'Leśny'*. The second is run by the PTTK and has lots of pretty little three-bed wooden cabins among the pine trees.

Camping No 21 and the Intercamp both have a bar and store, and all three are open from mid-May to mid-September. On a hot summer weekend every bed at Łeba will be occupied by people from the Tri-City area, so have your tent ready.

Private Rooms & Hotels The Przymorze Biuro Wczasów on Plac Dworcowy opposite the train station can arrange private rooms and provide general information.

Dom Wycieczkowy PTTK (☎ 661 324), ulica 1-go Maja 6 on the corner of ulica Kościuszki, just two blocks from the train station, has 28 rooms with private bath (but no hot water) at US$4 per person.

Pensjonat Angela (☎ 662 647), Plac Dworcowy 2 near the train station, is a new three-storey building, open only during the summer season. It's about US$8 per person. Ring the bell if it looks closed.

The three-storey *Hotel Morska* (☎ 661 468), beside the cinema between town and the beach, is US$10 single or double.

The *Dom Wypoczynkowy 'Kowelin'* (☎ 661 440), ulica Nad Ujścien 6, is an attractive four-storey building with 24 rooms with bath at US$8 per person. As you walk down ulica Kościuszki towards the beach, turn right after the small bridge over the canal. There's a restaurant downstairs in this former holiday home for workers from the copper mining industrial complex.

There are a number of other seasonal hotels and pensions around Łeba which the tourist office should know about.

Places to Eat

Try the *Restaurant Morska* in the hotel of the same name. You can't miss the *Karczma Słowińska Restaurant & Café*, ulica Kościuszki 28, overlooking the canal. Neither of these places is very good and there's nowhere to get breakfast before 9 am in Łeba, so it's best to buy groceries the night before.

Getting There & Away

Coming and going you'll probably transit Lębork, a town on the main railway line from Gdańsk to Szczecin, where you'll have to change for Łeba. Trains only run from Lębork to Łeba every three or four hours (28 km). If you're unlucky, check the bus station across the street from Lębork Railway Station where there are buses to Łeba every hour or so from platform No 3 (ticket from the office inside, US$0.75).

The *Słupia* express train runs daily all year between Warsaw and Lębork (409 km, five hours). It leaves Lębork in the very early morning and Warsaw in the late afternoon, travelling via Gdynia, Gdańsk and Malbork; reservations are required. Unfortunately neither schedule connects with a bus to/from Łeba, so unless you're willing to spend a night at the *Miejski Hotel* (☎ 21 903), ulica 10 Marca 9, Lębork, you can't use this train.

Trains between Lębork and Wejherowo (and the electric train line to Gdańsk) run every couple of hours. Several buses a day also go from Lębork to Wejherowo. A couple of buses a day go from Łeba direct to Gdynia (59 km).

MALBORK

From 1309 to 1457 Malbork (Marienburg) was the headquarters of the Teutonic Knights and one of the largest medieval fortified castles in Europe. The Teutonic Knights with their white robes and black crosses originated during the Third Crusade (1198), and with the Templars and Hospitallers became one of the three great military/religious orders of the time. In 1271 Monfort Castle in Palestine was lost and the order began searching for a new headquarters.

Construction of Malbork Castle began in 1276 and in 1309 the order's capital was shifted here from Venice. Constant territorial disputes with Poland and Lithuania finally culminated in the Battle of Grunwald in 1410. The order was defeated but continued to hold the castle until 1457. From 1772 to 1945 Malbork was incorporated into Prussia and extensive restorations were carried out in the years prior to WW I when Malbork was viewed as a romantic symbol of the glory of medieval Germany. After WW II the Polish authorities in turn continued the work to preserve this great monument of Gothic culture. The museum here was opened in 1960.

Orientation

As you leave the train station turn right and cut across the busy highway, then straight down ulica Kościuszki to the castle. Lots of taxis park in front of the train station, otherwise it's a 15-minute walk though the modern town. A left-luggage service is available at the train station.

Things to See

Malbork Castle, overlooking the Nogat River, an eastern arm of the Vistula, was badly damaged during WW II but has now been largely restored. It consists of the service facilities of the 15th-century Lower Castle (between the railway line and the main gate), the 14th-century Middle Castle where the Grand Master lived and the 13th-century High Castle.

The first courtyard features an outstanding museum of Polish amber. Three floors of exhibits are to be seen in the rooms around the second courtyard (High Castle). One hall contains a superb collection of inlaid antique weapons. In the far corner a passageway leads to the Gdanisko Tower. Yes, the gaping hole in the floor was the toilet.

At least four hours are required to explore this imposing monument (open from 8.30 am to 5 pm May to September, 9 am to 2.30 pm October to April, closed Monday). The compulsory, two-hour guided museum tour with a Polish-speaking guide in a group of up to 40 persons is US$3 per person. For a tour in English (or French or German) an additional US$30 per group must be paid. On Monday all the exhibition halls are closed but you're allowed to wander around the courtyards and corridors in relative peace for a US$0.50 fee. You must arrive at least three hours before closing time if you want to get on a tour.

The best view of Malbork Castle is from the train. Coming from Gdańsk it's on the right immediately after you cross the river; northbound towards Gdańsk it's on the left just beyond Malbork Station. Have your camera ready.

Places to Stay & Eat

The cheapest place to stay is the *Hotel Noclegownia PKP*, ulica Dworcowa 1a, just up the street from the train station as you head for the castle. It's the yellow brick building on the left just before the busy highway. A basic room with shared facilities will be US$4 per person and adjacent to this hotel is the self-service *PKP Bar Express* with cheap food.

Across the highway at ulica Kościuszki 43 is the functional, four-storey *Hotel Zbyszko* (☎ 25 11), a five-minute walk from the train station. At last report it was US$8 per person with shared bath but the hotel is gradually being renovated which could boost prices. The hotel restaurant may be worth patronising by daytrippers and there's also an inexpensive pizza place on the corner across the street at ulica Kościuszki 25.

The *Hotel Zamek* (☎ 27 38) offers rooms in a restored medieval building of the Lower Castle. At US$30/60 it's a splurge. The hotel restaurant (closed Monday) is a good place for lunch, however, but check their opening hours if you were thinking of having dinner there.

In July and August there's a *hostel* (☎ 25 11) in the big red school house at ulica Żeromskiego 45, a 10-minute walk from the station.

There's also a camping ground (open from June to August) on ulica Portowa about two km beyond the castle, away from the train station. The Hotel Sportovy (☎ 24 13) behind the camping ground has rooms and is open year-round.

Getting There & Away

It's quite easy to visit Malbork as a stopover between Warsaw and Gdańsk or vice versa using the half-dozen express trains which pass through every day. If you're travelling north from Warsaw you can arrive on the

Neptun, Posejdon or *Lajkonik* express trains in the morning and continue to Gdańsk on the *San, Stoczniowiec* or *Słupia* express trains (or a local train) in the afternoon. Southbound, leave Gdańsk on the *Słupia* or *San* express trains (or any local train) in the morning and carry on to Warsaw on the *Stoczniowiec, Lajkonik, Neptun* or *Posejdon* in the afternoon.

Ask an Orbis office to help you work out an itinerary using these trains with a stopover of three or four hours in Malbork. Malbork is 282 km and three hours by express train from Warsaw. Some trains are seasonal and reservations are required on all except the *San* and the *Stoczniowiec*. Ask Orbis to make the reservations for you and check the onward time as soon as you arrive in Malbork.

Otherwise visit Malbork as a day trip from Gdańsk (58 km) or on the way to/from Olsztyn. Sometimes to go between Malbork and Olsztyn (126 km) you must change trains at Elbląg or Bogaczewo or both; other times you change at Iława.

Mazuria

Mazuria stretches from the Vistula to the Russian, Lithuanian and Belorussian borders north of the Mazovian plain. Here the Scandinavian glacier left behind a typical postglacial landscape, and many of the 3000 lakes are linked by rivers and canals to create a system of waterways well favoured by yachtspeople. The winding shorelines with many peninsulas, inlets and small islands are surrounded by low hills and forests, making the picturesque lake districts of north-eastern Poland one of the most attractive and varied touring areas in the country. Add to this the many fascinating historical remains and the opportunity to venture into places which seldom see English speakers, and you'll have all the reasons you need to visit.

HISTORY

The historic regions of Warmia and Mazuria were the southern half of German East Prussia until 1945 (the northern half is now part of Russia). Originally inhabited by heathen Prussian and Jatzvingian tribes, the area was conquered in the 13th century by the Germanic Teutonic Knights who had been invited in by the Polish Prince Conrad of Mazovia in 1225. The intention was that the knights would convert the Baltic tribes and depart, but instead they created a powerful religious state on the north-east border of Poland.

The Battle of Grunwald, fought in 1410 just south-west of Olsztyn, turned out to be a pivotal showdown between the knights and the Polish Crown. The knights' defeat at the battle was followed by other long wars which led to the Treaty of Toruń (1466) which gave Warmia (Ermeland), the area between Olsztyn and Frombork, to Poland for over three centuries. It was during this period that the famous Polish administrator and astronomer lived in Warmia, and today we can follow the Copernicus Trail from Olsztyn to Lidzbark Warmiński and Frombork.

Mazuria came under the Hohenzollerns of Brandenburg in the 16th century and in 1772 Warmia was also annexed to the Kingdom of Prussia. In a 1918 plebiscite, Warmia and Mazuria voted to remain German while the area around Suwałki went to Poland. During WW II the Nazis militarised Mazuria, which became a base for Hitler's dreams of conquest. This policy brought seven centuries of German involvement in the area to an ignominious end. However, even today, Lutheran Protestantism is alive in central Mazuria whereas Warmia remains more stolidly Catholic.

OLSZTYN

Olsztyn, 177 km south-east of Gdańsk, is the capital of Mazuria and a regional transportation hub. For travellers, Olsztyn is important as a jumping-off point for Lidzbark Warmiński, Grunwald, the Elbląg Canal and the Great Mazurian Lake District rather than as a destination in itself. Though the food and

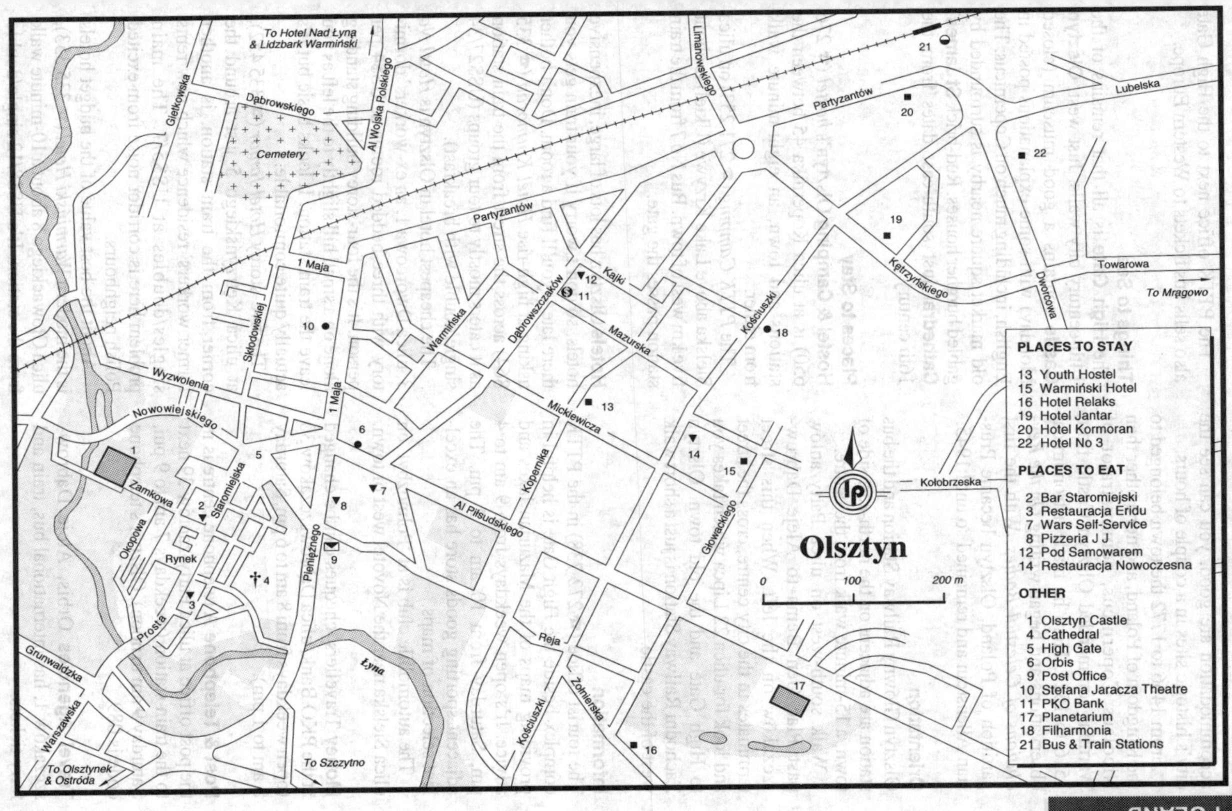
Olsztyn
0
100
200 m
PLACES TO STAY
13 Youth Hostel
15 Warmiński Hotel
16 Hotel Relaks
19 Hotel Jantar
20 Hotel Kormoran
22 Hotel No 3
PLACES TO EAT
2 Bar Staromiejski
3 Restauracja Eridu
7 Wars Self-Service
8 Pizzeria J J
12 Pod Samowarem
14 Restauracja Nowoczesna
OTHER
1 Olsztyn Castle
4 Cathedral
5 High Gate
6 Orbis
9 Post Office
10 Stefana Jaracza Theatre
11 PKO Bank
17 Planetarium
18 Filharmonia
21 Bus & Train Stations
To Hotel Nad Łyną & Lidzbark Warmiński
Gietkowska
Dąbrowskiego
Cemetery
Al Wojska Polskiego
Limanowskiego
Partyzantów
Lubelska
Partyzantów
1 Maja
Kajki
Towarowa
Kętrzyńskiego
Dworcowa
To Mrągowo
Skłodowskiej
Warmińska
Dąbrowszczaków
Mazurska
Kościuszki
Wyzwolenia
Nowowiejskiego
1 Maja
Mickiewicza
Kołobrzeska
Zamkowa
Staromiejska
Kopernika
Głowackiego
Okopowa
Rynek
Pieniężnego
Al Piłsudskiego
Prosta
Reja
Grunwaldzka
Łyna
Żołnierska
Kościuszki
Warszawska
To Szczytno
To Olsztynek & Ostróda

accommodation are good, you can see the city's historic sites in a couple of hours.

From 1466 to 1772 the town belonged to the Kingdom of Poland, and none other than Nicolaus Copernicus, administrator of Warmia, commanded Olsztyn Castle from 1516 to 1521. Here he made astronomical observations and began writing *On the Revolutions of Celestial Bodies*. With the first partition of Poland, Olsztyn became Prussian Allenstein and remained so until 1945.

Orientation

Olsztyn Główny Railway Station and the bus station are adjacent on the north-east side of town, a 15-minute walk from the centre.

Walk south-west on ulica Partyzantów past Plac Gen Bema to Aleje Dąbrowszczaków on the left. When this street terminates in the city centre, cross the street and look for ulica 22 Lipca which takes you to High Gate and the old town. Olsztyn Zachodni Railway Station is just a short walk west of the castle.

Information

The tourist office (☎ 272 738) in the PTTK complex beside the High Gate is helpful in providing maps of the Mazurian lakes and advice. It's open weekdays from 9 am to 4 pm, Saturday from 10 am to 2 pm. The adjacent sporting goods store has an excellent selection of maps.

The automobile club is at 'Polmozbyt' on ulica Sielska near the Novotel west of town.

Money Travellers' cheques can be changed at the PKO Bank, ulica Dąbrowszczaków 30 (open weekdays from 8 am to 6 pm, Saturday 8 am to 1 pm).

Post & Telephone A telephone centre is in the post office at ulica Party-zantów 39 next to the train station (weekdays 7 am to 9 pm, Saturday 9 am to noon). Olsztyn's telephone code is 089.

Travel Agencies Orbis, Aleje Dąbrowszczaków 1, has international bus, train and ferry tickets.

The PTTK office next to the High Gate also sells bus tickets to Western Europe.

Things to See

The **High Gate** is all that remains of the 14th-century city walls. Just west, **Olsztyn Castle** contains a good museum (closed Monday) with some explanations posted in English, including much on Copernicus. The old market square nearby is surrounded by gabled burgher houses. Red-brick **St James' Cathedral** just south-east dates from the 16th century.

Places to Stay

Hostel & Camping Olsztyn's *hostel* (☎ 276 650) is at ulica Kopernika 45 between the stations and town, an eight-minute walk from either.

The *PTTK Camping* (☎ 271 253) on ulica Sielska above Lake Krzywe (Ukiel) is about five km west of town. Bus No 7 from the train station passes the gate.

Hotels Olsztyn has lots of large, inexpensive hotels, so don't worry if your train gets you there late – you'll find a room. Don't bother asking at high-rise *Hotel Kormoran* (☎ 335 864) across the street from the train station as it caters mostly to tour groups (US$27/34 single/double with breakfast).

The cheapest hotel in Olsztyn is *Hotel No 3*, ulica Dworcowa 1, an ex-workers' dormitory with three-bedded rooms at US$4 per person. It's the four-storey building standing alone on a small hill slightly to the left as you leave the train station. It looks basic but it's actually quite comfortable.

The five-storey *Hotel Jantar* (☎ 335 452), at ulica Kętrzyńskiego 5 just around the corner from the train station, is another former workers' residence which now rents singles/doubles at US$5/7. The main problem here is corridor noise from excited Polish neighbours.

About the best value of the budget hotels is the modern *Warmiński Hotel* (☎ 335 353), ulica Głowackiego 8 about a 10-minute walk from the station. It's US$8/12 single/double for a room with shared bath, US$10/14 with shower.

Hotel Relaks (☎ 277 534), ulica Żołnierska 13a beside a large sports centre, is a comfortable six-storey hotel with singles/doubles with private bath at US$14/17. A few rooms with shared bath are US$10/12 double/triple.

If you'd like to be in the centre, the *Hotel 'Wysoka Brama'* (☎ 273 675) in the High Gate, ulica Staromiejska 1, is US$6/10 single/double with shared bath. The sign outside says 'Pizza Hotel', an indication of what is served in the hotel's basement.

Singles/doubles without bath or breakfast cost US$7/10 at the functional three-storey *Dom Wycieczkowy 'Nad Łyną'* (☎ 267 166), Aleje Wojska Polskiego 14. It's only a 10-minute walk from the train station via ulica Kolejowa (see the map).

Places to Eat

Wars Self-Service, Aleje Piłsudskiego 218 at the city end of Aleje Dąbrowszczaków, is cheap and has a place attached serving cakes, coffee and cold beer (one of the few places in Olsztyn you can get it).

Pizzeria J J, ulica Pieniężnego 18 just around the corner from the High Gate, has cheap self-service pizza. In the middle of the old town *Restauracja Eridu*, ulica Prosta 3-4, offers Islamic dishes. The *Bar Staromiejski* in the old town serves inexpensive Polish food till 8 pm.

Pod Samowarem, Aleje Dąbrowszczaków 26 between the stations and town, serves excellent inexpensive meals in its unpretentious dining room – it's also a good place to go if you only want a few drinks.

The *Restauracja Nowoczesna* on ulica Kościuszki behind Hotel Warmiński is a lot nicer inside than the plain exterior would imply. In fact, it's probably the most elegant restaurant in Olsztyn. The menu is in English and German.

For coffee, cakes and ice cream it's *Yogurcik Cocktail Bar*, ulica 22 Lipca 5.

Getting There & Away

There are direct trains to Olsztyn from Gdynia/Gdańsk (179 km via Malbork), Poznań (via Iława, Ostróda and Toruń) and Warsaw (237 km via Działdowo). If the timing doesn't allow you to use the Gdańsk train, you may have to change trains at Elbląg, Bogaczewo or Iława to travel between Malbork and Olsztyn (no direct buses). For Frombork or Kaliningrad you must change at Braniewo. For Lidzbark Warmiński change at Czerwonka (though the bus is much faster and more frequent on this route). For the Mazurian lakes look for a train to Ełk and get off at Giżycko, Mikołajki or Ruciane-Nida.

The *Kormoran* express train runs daily all year between Warsaw and Olsztyn (three hours), departing from Olsztyn in the morning, Warsaw in the afternoon. Reservations are required.

Numerous buses depart from Olsztyn, including nine daily to Elbląg (97 km), eight to Gdańsk (156 km), nine to Giżycko (120 km), eight to Kętrzyn (89 km), 43 to Lidzbark Warmiński (46 km) and four to Warsaw (213 km). Check the footnotes and ask at information, then try and purchase an advance ticket to be sure you selected a bus that really is going that day.

THE ELBLĄG CANAL

A fascinating excursion is a trip on the 81-km Elbląg Canal built in 1848-60 from Elbląg to Ostróda. The difference in water level between these towns is 100 metres, and to bridge this gap the boats pass through two locks and are carried up and down five slipways on rail-mounted platforms or 'ramps', a technical solution unique in Europe!

Theoretically, the excursion boats leave Elbląg for Ostróda at 8 am daily from mid-May to mid-September (11 hours, US$16) but captains often cancel the trip if not enough passengers are around. You should be OK from mid-June to August and on weekends. Bring your own food as what's sold on board is very expensive. (If the trip is cancelled consider going to Frombork instead.)

You can do the canal trip en route between

Gdańsk and Olsztyn, though you'll have to catch the 6 am bus from Gdańsk (59 km) in order to be there in time. Get out at the first stop after the canal in Elbląg, otherwise you'll have to walk back from the bus station. The boat dock is to the left as the bus crosses the bridge.

To do the canal as a day trip from Olsztyn involves a very early start. Check the 4.40 am train from Olsztyn to Elbląg (97 km) and the 9.06 pm train from Ostróda to Olsztyn (39 km), but remember, these times could change! In midsummer Orbis, ulica Dąbrowszczaków 1, Olsztyn, organises day excursions on the Elbląg Canal with bus transfers from Olsztyn (US$40).

It's probably better to spend the previous night in Elbląg and the *PTTK Dom Wycieczkovy* (☎ 24 307), ulica Krótka 5, is a good bet at US$5/8 single/double without bath. Otherwise there's the *Hotel Dworcowy* (☎ 27 011) opposite the bus/train station. The *PTTK camping ground* (☎ 24 307), ulica Panieńska 14, is right near the bridge over the canal. Elbląg was destroyed in WW II and the only reason to come is the canal trip.

THE COPERNICUS TRAIL

Though he was born in Toruń and studied at Kraków, astronomer Nicolaus Copernicus spent the last 40 years of his life in Warmia. From 1503 to 1510, Copernicus served as an adviser to his uncle, Bishop Łukasz Watzenrode, at **Lidzbark Warmiński**, episcopal seat of the Polish bishops who ruled the Duchy of Warmia under the Polish crown from 1466 to 1772. In the 14th century a strong castle was built here which the bishops later adopted as their residence, adding a neoclassical palace to the complex in the 17th century.

The vaulted chambers of the castle interior now house a world-class museum (closed Monday) with Gothic sculpture and painting in the grand refectory downstairs, a large art gallery and exhibition on the restoration of historic monuments upstairs. Also to be seen are a gilded chapel, old weapons in the cellars and a splendid arcaded interior courtyard. Just 46 km north of Olsztyn, Lidzbark Warmiński is an easy day trip by bus.

Frombork (Frawenburg), on the south-east shore of the Vistula Lagoon (Zalew Wiślany) between Lidzbark Warmiński and Gdańsk, was founded by colonists from Lübeck, Germany, in the 13th century. From 1512 to 1516, and again from 1522 until his death in 1543, Copernicus lived and worked in Frombork and his unmarked grave is in Frombork's red-brick Gothic cathedral (erected in 1388), beneath the aisle by the second pillar on the right as you stand below the organ.

On the opposite side of this pillar is a statue of the astronomer and in the former bishop's palace next to the cathedral is a Copernicus Museum (closed Monday). Just below Cathedral Hill is a tall statue of Copernicus which makes him look rather like Chairman Mao.

The easiest way to get to Frombork is by bus from Gdańsk (93 km – train connections from Gdańsk are bad). To/from Olsztyn (105 km) you must change trains at Braniewo. There isn't a lot of accommodation at Frombork, though you could try the *PTTK Dom Wycieczkowy* (☎ 72 51) in the park just west of Cathedral Hill which also serves meals. The year-round *hostel* (☎ 74 53), ulica Elbląska 11, is a couple of blocks west of the centre of town.

THE GREAT MAZURIAN LAKES

The Great Mazurian Lake District north-east of Olsztyn is a verdant land of rolling hills interspersed with glacial lakes, healthy little farms, scattered tracts of forest and many small towns. There are literally thousands of postglacial lakes to the north and south of Mikołajki. A fifth of the surface of this area is covered by water and another 30% by forest. Lake Śniardwy (110 sq km) is the largest lake in Poland, and Lake Mamry and adjacent waters total an additional 102 sq km. The large, clean lakes and abundant forests are an irresistible beacon for boaters, anglers and nature lovers. Polish tourists also arrive in great numbers though it's much less crowded after 15 August.

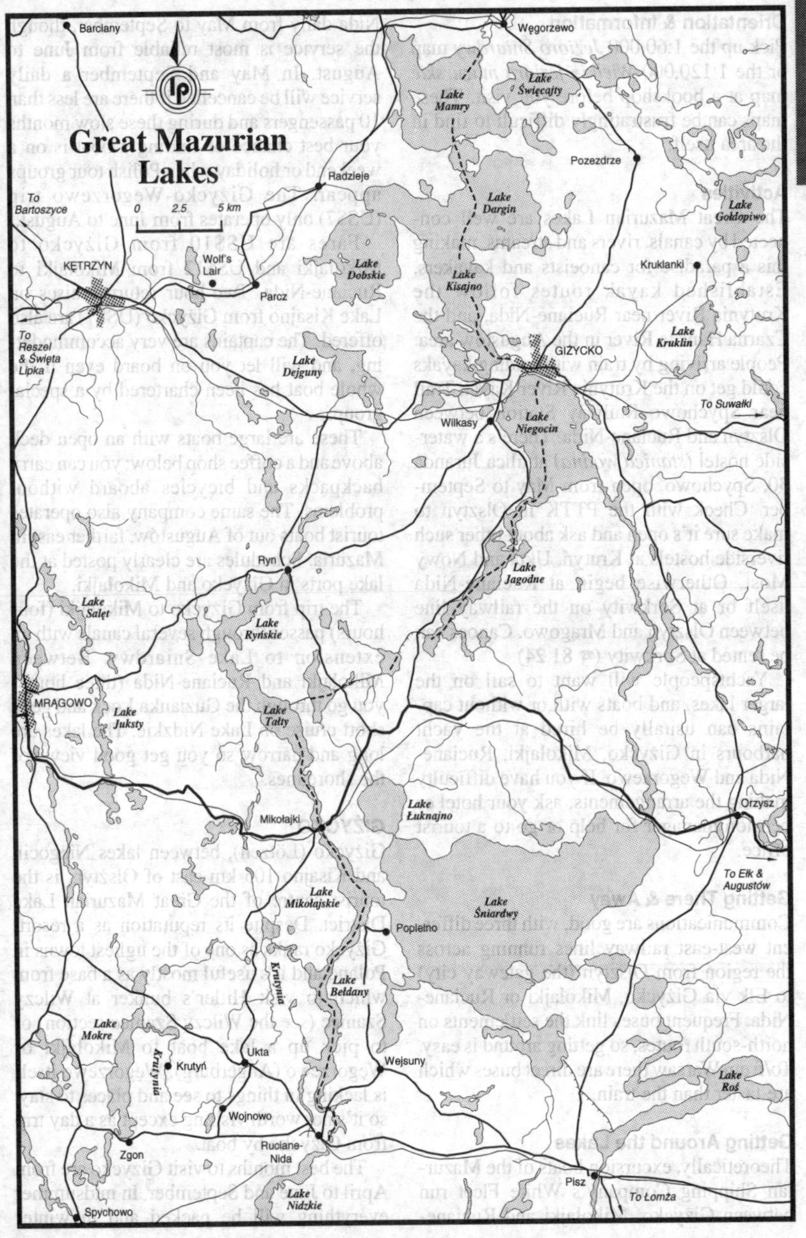
Great Mazurian Lakes
Barciany
Węgorzewo
Lake Mamry
Lake Święcajty
Pozezdrze
Radzieje
Lake Dargin
Lake Gołdopiwo
To Bartoszyce
0 2.5 5 km
KĘTRZYN
Wolf's Lair
Lake Dobskie
Kruklanki
Lake Kisajno
Parcz
To Reszel & Święta Lipka
Lake Kruklin
GIŻYCKO
Lake Dejguny
To Suwałki
Wilkasy
Lake Niegocin
Ryn
Lake Jagodne
Lake Salęt
Lake Ryńskie
MRĄGOWO
Lake Juksty
Lake Tałty
Lake Łuknajno
Orzysz
Mikołajki
To Ełk & Augustów
Lake Mikołajskie
Lake Śniardwy
Popielno
Lake Bełdany
Krutynia
Lake Mokre
Krutyń
Ukta
Wejsuny
Lake Roś
Wojnowo
Zgon
Ruciane-Nida
Pisz
To Łomża
Lake Nidzkie
Spychowo

Orientation & Information

Pick up the 1:60,000 *Jezioro Śniardwy* map or the 1:120,000 *Wielkie jeziora mazurskie* map at a bookshop before you visit. These maps can be frustratingly difficult to find in the area itself.

Activities

The Great Mazurian Lakes are well connected by canals, rivers and streams, making this a paradise for canoeists and kayakers. Established kayak routes follow the Krutynia River near Ruciane-Nida, and the Czarna Hańcza River in the Augustów area. People arriving by train with folding kayaks could get on the Krutynia River Kayak Trail near Spychowo Railway Station between Olsztyn and Ruciane-Nida. There's a waterside hostel *(stanica wodna)* at ulica Juranda 30, Spychowo, open from May to September. Check with the PTTK in Olsztyn to make sure it's open and ask about other such riverside hostels at Krutyń, Ukta and Nowy Most. Otherwise begin at Ruciane-Nida itself or at Sorkwity on the railway line between Olsztyn and Mrągowo. Canoes can be rented at Sorkwity (☎ 81 24).

Yachtspeople will want to sail on the larger lakes, and boats with or without captains can usually be hired at the yacht harbours in Giżycko, Mikołajki, Ruciane-Nida and Węgorzewo. If you have difficulty making the arrangements, ask your hotel or pension manager for help or go to a tourist office.

Getting There & Away

Communications are good, with three different west-east railway lines running across the region from Olsztyn (the gateway city) to Ełk via Giżycko, Mikołajki or Ruciane-Nida. Frequent buses link the settlements on north-south routes, so getting around is easy. To/from Warsaw there are direct buses which are faster than the train.

Getting Around the Lakes

Theoretically, excursion boats of the Mazurian Shipping Company's White Fleet run between Giżycko, Mikołajki and Ruciane-Nida daily from May to September, though the service is most reliable from June to August. In May and September a daily service will be cancelled if there are less than 10 passengers and during these slow months your best chance of finding a boat is on a weekend or holiday when Polish tour groups appear. The Giżycko-Węgorzewo trip (US$7) only operates from June to August.

Fares are US$10 from Giżycko to Mikołajki and US$12 from Mikołajki to Ruciane-Nida. Two-hour return cruises on Lake Kisajno from Giżycko (US$7) are also offered. The captains are very accommodating, and will let you on board even if the whole boat has been chartered by a special group.

These are large boats with an open deck above and a coffee shop below; you can carry backpacks and bicycles aboard without problems. The same company also operates tourist boats out of Augustów, farther east in Mazuria. Schedules are clearly posted at the lake ports in Giżycko and Mikołajki.

The trip from Giżycko to Mikołajki (four hours) passes through several canals with an extension to Lake Śniardwy. Between Mikołajki and Ruciane-Nida (three hours) you go through the Guzianka Lock and get a short cruise on Lake Nidzkie. The lakes are long and narrow so you get good views of the shorelines.

GIŻYCKO

Giżycko (Lötzen), between lakes Niegocin and Kisajno 105 km east of Olsztyn, is the tourist centre of the Great Mazurian Lake District. Despite its reputation as a resort, Giżycko ranks as one of the ugliest towns in Poland and it's useful mostly as a base from which to visit Hitler's bunker at Wilczy Szaniec (see the Wilczy Szaniec section) or to pick up a lake boat to Mikołajki or Węgorzewo (Angerburg). Węgorzewo itself is lacking in things to see and places to stay, so it's not worth visiting except as a day trip from Giżycko by boat.

The best months to visit Giżycko are from April to June and September. In midsummer everything will be packed and in winter there'll be nothing to do. If your time is limited give Giżycko a miss and head straight for Mikołajki.

Orientation & Information
The port on Lake Niegocin (26 sq km) is near the centre of town with the train station on the east and the yacht harbour on the west, a few hundred metres from either.

A large map of Giżycko is posted in front of the adjacent bus and train stations on Plac Dworcowy. Head up ulica Armii Krajowej to ulica Dąbrowskiego. The helpful staff at Orbis, ulica Dąbrowskiego 3, can answer questions and perhaps provide a map. Continue west on ulica Warszawska to Plac Grunwaldzki, the centre of town.

Post & Telephone The telephone centre is a few blocks inland from Hotel Wodnik on ulica 1 Maja (open weekdays 7 am to 9 pm, Saturday 8 am to 1 pm, Sunday 9 to 11 am).

Things to See
There's nothing much to see in Giżycko except perhaps a large 19th-century **fortress** on the west side of town which once guarded the narrow passage between the lakes. If you have time it's worth going beyond this fortress and cutting across the isthmus to the shore of Lake Kisajno near the Almatur and Sport hotels.

To rent a sailing boat capable of carrying four or five people will cost around US$14 a day in May and September, US$20 daily from June to August. In midsummer all the boats will be taken, so this is really only a tenable possibility in late spring and early fall. If you can't manage to rent a boat at Giżycko you may have better luck at nearby Wilkasy.

Places to Stay
Camping In July and early August Giżycko is overrun by Polish tourists, although those with a tent will always find a place to pitch it. If you go west on ulica Olsztyńska from Plac Grunwaldzki you'll reach the Łuczański Canal, across which is *Camping C1*, just before the railway tracks. At the Mazurski Yacht Club beyond the tracks is a small harbour where you can rent a sailing boat. In summer there's also camping here.

Private Rooms Centrum-Mazur (☎ 33 83) at Hotel Wodnik may be willing to find you a private room. Also ask them about boat rentals, though they only speak Polish and German and are only there weekdays from 8 am to noon. Otherwise the hotel desk clerk may be able to help you find a private room.

Gromada, ulica Warszawska 21 (weekdays 8 am to 3.30 pm), rents private rooms at US$4 per person.

Hostels In July and August ask about hostel accommodation in the school at ulica Mickiewicza 27, a block back from Hotel Wodnik. If this is closed the staff may be able to refer you to another hostel that's open.

You can usually rent a cheap room in the two-storey drivers' examination centre or *Ośrodek Egzaminowania Kierowćw* (☎ 25 30), Lotnicza 4, by the lake to the west of the Mazurski Yacht Club. The person in the small office at the level crossing over the train tracks here should know about this, otherwise just wait around the hostel itself until someone shows up. Rooms are US$5 per person.

Hotels The modern, four-storey *Hotel Wodnik* (☎ 38 71), ulica 3 Maja 2 just off Plac Grunwaldzki in the centre of town, offers clean, comfortable rooms with private bath at US$29/50 single/double from mid-May to mid-September, US$19/35 the rest of the year (breakfast US$4 per person extra). Foreign bus tour groups always stay at the Wodnik – it's their kind of place.

The *Hotel Garnizonowy*, ulica Olsztyńska 10a (behind the apartment buildings), is primarily intended for visiting military personnel and in the past they have not accepted tourists, though this could change. Ask, as a room here should be half what you'd pay at the Wodnik.

The *PTTK Dom Wycieczkowy* is between the train tracks and the lake right beside the Łuczański Canal, but on the town side across the canal from the camping grounds. It's closed in the off season.

Just beyond the bridge over the Łuczański Canal is *Motel Zamek* (☎ 24 19), ulica Moniuszki 1, with 12 rooms with bath at US$35 double. When it's cold outside, a log fire will be burning in the small bar at the reception.

Farther west a km or two is the stadium where a road leads off to the right towards Lake Kisajno and two hotels. The *COS Sport Hotel*, ulica Moniuszki 22, has inexpensive rooms. You can also camp here (bungalows available) and it's a quieter site than the one previously mentioned. The *Almatur Hotel* is nearby. When no groups are present the receptions of both hotels close early in the day, so don't expect to get a room if you arrive late. Boat rentals are possible.

Places to Eat

A couple of good self-service snack bars are right opposite the train station. The *Omega Bar*, ulica Olsztyńska 4, is a cheap self-service (open daily).

In the centre of town is the cavernous, socialist-modern *Mazurska Restaurant*, ulica Warszawska 2. In the evening there's sometimes live music here. For more familiar food and surroundings try *Pizza Nicola*, ulica Warszawska 14. The *Hotel Wodnik* has a reasonable restaurant with a German menu.

WILCZY SZANIEC

History buffs will certainly want to visit **Hitler's wartime headquarters**, the Wolfschanze or Wolf's Lair (Wilczy Szaniec in Polish), at Gierłóż, 30 km west of Giżycko or 10 km east of Kętrzyn. Hitler spent most of his time here from 24 June 1941 to 20 November 1944 and the base had its own train station and airfield surrounded by minefields, anti-aircraft guns and camouflaging.

The Germans blew up the Wolfschanze on 24 January 1945 and only cracked concrete bunkers remain, but it's significant as the site of the 20 July 1944 assassination attempt by Colonel Claus von Stauffenberg (a plaque now marks the spot). A heavy wooden table saved Hitler and as many people died and as much property was destroyed in the last year of war as during the first five combined.

Things to See & Do

Over 70 reinforced bunkers are scattered through the forest. A large map of the site is posted at the entrance and all the bunkers are clearly numbered: Bormann No 11, Hitler No 13, Goering No 16 etc. The roofs of the eight most important ones are eight metres thick! Bring along a torch (flashlight) if you want to explore inside the bunkers (although large signs warn you that it is dangerous to do so).

Admission to Wolfschanze is US$3 per person, plus another US$3 if you have to park a vehicle. English and German-speaking guides wait at the entrance and charge US$13 per group for a one-hour tour of the site. The guides also sell booklets about Wilczy Szaniec, priced according to language: Polish US$1, German US$2 and English US$3.

Some buses between Olsztyn and Kętrzyn pass the photogenic baroque church of **Święta Lipka** from which onward buses to Kętrzyn run hourly. It's well worth stopping to see the remarkable organ if you have the time.

Places to Stay & Eat

The recently renovated *Dom Wycieczkowy* (☎ 44 29) at the site is US$27 double with bath and breakfast (no singles). Rooms without bath are US$17 triple or US$23 for four persons, also including breakfast. The *Restaurant 'Michel'* behind the Dom serves reasonably good food. The hotel is open year-round but the restaurant is only open in summer. A basic *camping ground* is nearby – check in at the hotel reception.

Getting There & Away

Kętrzyn (Rastenburg), a large town on the railway line from Olsztyn to Ełk via Giżycko, is the starting point for most visits to Wilczy Szaniec. Trains from Kętrzyn to Węgorzewo pass right through the site but only stop at Parcz, two km east – walk back along the paved highway towards Kętrzyn. You can see Goering's bunker (No 16) from both the train and the road.

Eight buses a day on the route from Kętrzyn to Węgorzewo via Radzieje stop right at the gate. At Kętrzyn buy bus tickets in an office near the stop. From June to August city bus No 5 also runs hourly between Kętrzyn and the site.

MIKOŁAJKI

During summer the best gateway to the lakes for hikers and campers is Mikołajki (Nikolaiken), 86 km east of Olsztyn on a railway line to Ełk. Perched on a picturesque narrows crossed by three bridges, there are scenic views on all sides of this pearl of Mazuria. The red-roofed houses of Mikołajki stretch along the shore of narrow Lake Mikołajskie just north of the Mazurian Landscape Park and Lake Śniardwy. Wild horses are in the forests to the south. Lakes Ryńskie, Tałty, Mikołajskie and Bełdany together fill a postglacial gully 35 km long.

German tourism promoters have discovered Mikołajki and new developments are blossoming on all sides. Especially horrendous is the five-star Hotel Gołębiewski erected by a German company in 1992, a couple of km west of Mikołajki on the road to Olsztyn. The 280-room Gołębiewski comes complete with helicopter shuttles, disco, three restaurants, indoor swimming pool and an elderly clientele bused in from Germany. Thankfully, you can't see it from town.

Orientation & Information

The bus station is beside a large Evangelical church near the bridge in the centre of town. The train station, several blocks east down ulica Kolejowa, provides left-luggage service.

In late July ask about the International Festival of Country Music, or the 'Country Picnic', in nearby Mrągowo.

Post & Telephone The post office and telephone centre at ulica 3-go Maja 8 is open weekdays from 8 am to 6 pm and Saturday from 9 to 11 am.

Things to See

Europe's largest surviving community of **wild swans** is at nearby Lake Łuknajno. The 1200 to 2000 swans nest in April and May but stay at the lake all summer. The young birds are brown, the adults white. The 'Rezerwat Łuknajno' is about four km east of Mikołajki, beyond the Osiedle 'Łabędzia' suburb. Several observation towers beside the lake make viewing possible.

Activities

Mikołajki is an important yachting centre with a large Schronisko Żeglarskie (waterside hostel) overlooking the yacht harbour. Boats capable of carrying up to four people rent from around US$14 daily.

Agencja Sagit (☎/fax 16 470), Plac Wolności 3, can organise horse riding (US$13 an hour), buggy rides in the Pisz Forest (US$7 an hour for up to four people), yacht charter (US$13 to US$32 a day), canoe rental (US$7 a day), row boats (US$2 an hour) and waterskiing (US$7 an hour). In winter there's cross-country skiing. For those unfamiliar with sailing Sagit can organise lessons at US$4 an hour per group. In midsummer they should be able to get you a canoe, row boat or motorboat, but yacht rental at that time is difficult if you didn't reserve ahead. The Sagit office is open year-round (9 am to 4 pm in the off season, 8 am to 8 pm in summer) and the staff speak good English, so it's a good starting point.

Places to Stay

Camping *Camping 'Wagabunda'* (☎ 16 018), ulica Leśna 2, is across the bridge and two km west of town. In addition to camping space there are 60 neat little bungalows varying in price from US$16 for a four-bed unit without water to US$49 for a six-bed unit with private bath, They're open from April to October.

Hostels Ask about dormitory accommodation at the *Schronisko Żeglarskie* or waterside hostel (☎ 16 040), overlooking the yacht harbour (summer only).

In July and August a *hostel* functions in the Szkoła Podstanowa, a large school next to the tennis courts on ulica Labędzia.

Pensions & Hotels Pension owners in Mikołajki are forced to charge high prices in summer because from October to April the town is virtually empty. Unless you have a tent, it's risky to arrive late in the day in midsummer as you could be forced to pay a lot for your room.

Pensjonat Ada, ulica Kolejowa 8, and *Pensjonat Natalis* (☎ 16 311), ulica Kościuszki 2a (US$25 double), are side by side on the way from the train station into town.

About the cheapest hotel in Mikołajki is the *Hotel 'Żeglarsz'* (☎ 16 144), ulica Dąbrowskiego 2. It's next to the large red-brick building with circular windows you see on the right as you walk into town along ulica Kowalska from the train station. Rooms are US$7 per person, it's open all year and looks better inside than out.

The *Hotel Król Sielaw* (☎ 16 323), ulica Kajki 5, has rooms with shared bath at US$15 double, with private bath US$19 double (no singles). Breakfast is US$4 extra. This friendly little hotel is open year-round (except in November and December) and their restaurant is the most reliable eating place in town although the drinks at the bar are expensive.

Pensjonat 'Mikołajki' (☎ 16 437), ulica Kajki 18 near the centre of town, is Mikołajki's finest pension (US$16/32 single/double). The double rooms have private baths. A big breakfast is US$3 per person extra and other meals (US$7) are available, perhaps the best home cooking you'll get in Poland. The rooms are often fully booked but the owner speaks perfect English so call him up for reservations (open from April to October only).

Pensjonat 'Na Skarpie' (☎ 16 418), ulica Kajki 96, is one km beyond Pensjonat 'Mikołajki'. Some rooms have excellent lake views.

Agencja Sagit (☎/fax 16 470), Plac Wolności 3, books rooms at pensions around Mikołajki for US$22/44 single/double with breakfast from mid-June to mid-September, US$19/38 in spring and fall. Sagit handles bookings for *Pensjonat 'Tałty'* (☎ 16 398), four km north of town, which has four-person bungalows with cooking facilities at US$32 out of season, US$44 in season. Bungalows for up to six persons cost US$44 out of season, US$57 in season.

Places to Eat

All the tour groups eat at the *Restaurant Portowa* (open from May to September only) just above the lake-boat landing. The food is nothing special but prices are reasonable. Also keep in mind the *Król Sielaw* mentioned under Hotels above.

In summer tourists sit on the terrace of *Café Mocca* on ulica Kowalska just off the square and sip one of the 14 varieties of coffee. You can also get pizza here (but no alcohol).

Cold draught beer is on tap at *Mini-Bar Kufelek*, ulica Kajki 9. You probably won't see many tourists in there.

Entertainment

On summer weekends *Disco ABC* cranks up from 9 pm to 3 am in the basement of the big yellow schoolhouse building at ulica Kolejowa 6.

Things to Buy

Several small boutiques have sprung up in Mikołajki selling knockout amber jewellery with prices to match. Have a look at Bernstein, ulica 3-go Maja 17, and the two adjacent shops at ulica 3-go Maja 2/3. If you can resist buying amber here, you're safe from seduction in Poland.

Getting There & Away

There's only one bus a day to Ruciane-Nida (23 km) but there's bus service to Mrągowo every couple of hours (25 km) and several buses a day to Giżycko (31 km) and Suwałki (134 km). Buses to other points are rare. Trains run to Olsztyn (89 km) and Ełk (62 km) three times a day in either direction.

RUCIANE-NIDA

Hiking trails lead 23 km south from Mikołajki through the forest past many lakeside camping grounds to Ruciane-Nida (Rudschanny), in the heart of the Pisz Forest between picturesque Bełdany and Nidzkie lakes.

Lake Nidzkie (18.3 sq km) is considered the most beautiful of the Mazurian lakes for its small forested islands.

Ruciane-Nida is the right place to end a trip through the lake district by excursion boat, yacht, bicycle or foot as train service back to Olsztyn is good.

Orientation & Information

The adjacent bus and train stations are a five-minute walk from the lake-boat landing.

Places to Stay

Places to stay include the *PTTK Dom Wycieczkowy*, ulica Mazurska 16 (four-person cabin US$11), and *Pensjonat 'Bełdan'*, both north of the train station, and the more expensive *Orbis Pensjonat 'Kowaljik'* across the bridge. The 'Kowaljik' looks south down Lake Nidzkie. The *PTTK camping ground* is on Lake Nidzkie, a 20-minute walk south-west of the train station.

Getting There & Away

Train service to Olsztyn (90 km) and Ełk (70 km) is every couple of hours. There's a daily bus to Mikołajki via Ukta.

Slovakia

Europe's youngest country Slovakia only emerged from 74 years of junior partnership in Czechoslovakia in 1993. Though just half the size of the Czech Republic in area and population, Slovakia's strategic position as a bridge between Austria, Ukraine, Hungary and Poland ensures it a pivotal role in the new Europe.

The country has much to offer those who enjoy outdoor activities. The rugged High Tatra Mountains are an attraction of European stature and there's also the gentler natural beauty of the Malá Fatra near Žilina and the Slovenský raj east of Poprad. The possibilities for hikers are so numerous this book can only scratch the surface. In winter this is easily the best ski country in Europe when viewed in terms of value for money.

Slovakia is also rich in specific things to see. In East Slovakia a string of unspoiled medieval towns shelter Gothic artworks of the first order while Bratislava is a cosmopolitan city with a rich cultural life. There are 180 quaint castles and castle ruins in Slovakia, the largest of which are Spišský hrad, east of Levoča; Orava Castle, above the village of Oravský Podzámok, 28 km north of Ružomberok; and Trenčín Castle in West Slovakia.

Best of all, much of Slovakia is well off the beaten tourist track. The facilities are good, yet few visitors stray beyond the Prague-Bratislava-Budapest corridor. This certainly works to the advantage of the clever few willing to make the long detour east to see the magnificent mountain ranges along the Polish border and the 13th-century towns founded by Saxon Germans on what was then Hungary's eastern frontier.

The rural Slovaks are a people apart from the urbane Czechs and the peasant traditions of Slovakia are a clear transition from the more Germanised culture of Bohemia and Moravia to Ukraine. This background is evident in the folk costumes you'll see in remote Slovak villages on Sunday, the traditional meal of roast goose with potato pancakes and also the country's colourful handicrafts. For 1000 years Slovakia was Hungarian and many ethnic Magyars still reside here. You'll find the Slovaks an extremely warm, friendly people prepared to go out of their way to make sure you'll never regret including their country in your European tour.

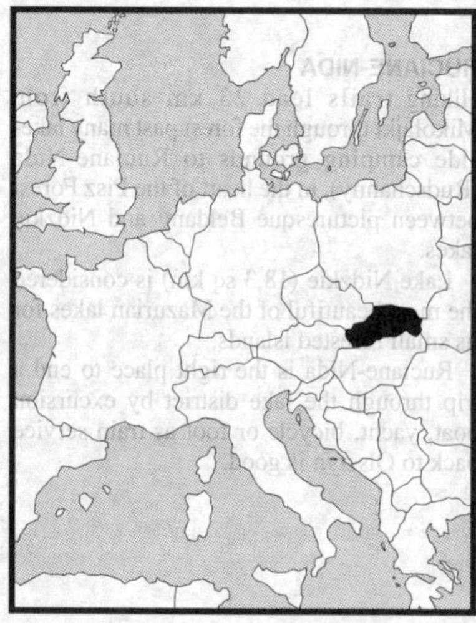

Facts about the Country

HISTORY

Slavic tribes occupied what is now Slovakia in the 5th century AD. In 833 the prince of Moravia captured Nitra and formed the Great Moravian Empire which included all of present Central and West Slovakia and Moravia in the Czech Republic. To counter Frankish influence from the west, the Great Moravian prince invited the Byzantine king

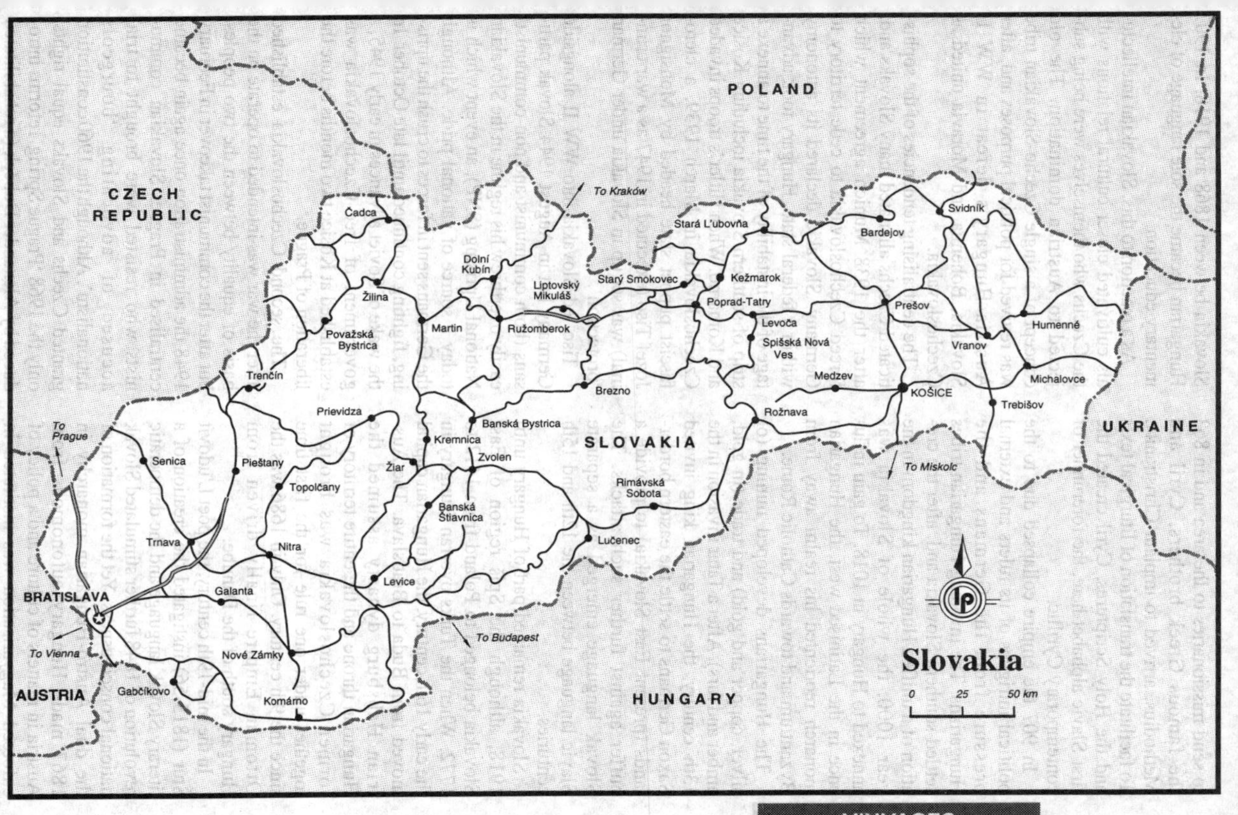
POLAND
CZECH REPUBLIC
UKRAINE
SLOVAKIA
HUNGARY
AUSTRIA
BRATISLAVA
To Prague
To Vienna
To Kraków
To Budapest
To Miskolc
Čadca
Žilina
Považská Bystrica
Trenčín
Dolní Kubín
Martin
Ružomberok
Liptovský Mikuláš
Starý Smokovec
Stará L'ubovňa
Kežmarok
Poprad-Tatry
Levoča
Spišská Nová Ves
Bardejov
Prešov
Svidník
Humenné
Vranov
Michalovce
Trebišov
KOŠICE
Medzev
Rožnava
Brezno
Banská Bystrica
Kremnica
Zvolen
Žiar
Banská Štiavnica
Prievidza
Topolčany
Nitra
Levice
Lučenec
Rimavská Sobota
Senica
Piešťany
Trnava
Galanta
Nové Zámky
Komárno
Gabčíkovo
Slovakia
0 25 50 km

to send missionaries to the area and in 863 the famous Greek brothers, Cyril and Methodius, arrived to implant Christianity. To facilitate the translation of liturgical texts and the Holy Scriptures, Cyril created the first Slavic alphabet here, the forerunner of contemporary Cyrillic.

In 907 the empire collapsed due to the political intrigues of its rulers and external pressure from the Germans and the Hungarians. The invading Hungarian tribes settled southern Slovakia and, after the creation of a unified Hungarian kingdom in the year 1000, the whole of Slovakia was annexed to Hungary in 1018. To gain influence in the Latinised west, the Hungarian monarch reoriented his realm away from Byzantium and towards Catholic Rome.

The Hungarians developed mining (of silver, copper and gold) and trade (in gold, amber and furs). After a Tatar invasion in the 13th century, the Hungarian king invited Saxon Germans to settle the eastern borderlands (present East Slovakia) to provide a buffer against further such attacks. The Slovak language emerged as a separate Slavic language between the 12th and 15th centuries.

Slovakia remained part of Hungary until 1918, although the Spiš region of East Slovakia belonged to Poland from 1412 to 1772. When the Turks overran Hungary in the early 16th century, the Hungarian capital moved from Buda to Bratislava. The Austrian Habsburg dynasty assumed the Hungarian throne and the entire territory of former Czechoslovakia was brought together under one rule for the first time since the 9th century. Only in 1686 was the Ottoman Empire finally driven from Hungary south of the Danube.

In the mid-19th century, the poet L'udovít Štúr (1815-56) instigated the creation of a literary Slovak language and the democratic revolution of 1848 further stimulated Slovak national consciousness. Yet the formation of the dual Austro-Hungarian monarchy in 1867 made Hungary autonomous from Austria in matters of culture and a policy of enforced Magyarisation was instituted in Slovakia between 1868 and 1918. In 1907 Hungarian became the sole language of elementary education.

As a reaction to this, Slovakian intellectuals cultivated closer cultural relations with the Czechs who themselves were being subjected to Austrian domination. The old concept of a single Czecho-Slovakian tribe was revived for political purposes and, after Austria-Hungary's defeat in WW I, Slovakia, Bohemia and Moravia united as Czechoslovakia.

The centralising tendencies of the sophisticated Czechs alienated many Slovaks and, after the 1938 Munich agreement which forced Czechoslovakia to cede territory to Germany, Slovakia declared its autonomy within a federal state. Hungary took advantage of the instability of the time to annexe a strip of southern Slovakia including Košice and Komárno. When Hitler's troops invaded Czechoslovakia in March 1939, a clero-fascist puppet state headed by Monsignor Jozef Tiso (executed in 1947 as a war criminal) was set up in Slovakia under German 'protection'.

Tiso led Slovakia into WW II alongside Germany but in August 1944 Slovak partisans (both communist and non-communist) easily overthrew his regime in the Slovakian National Uprising (SNP), an event which is today a source of national pride. Although the Germans sent in forces to crush the uprising, fighting continued until late October. In the wake of Soviet advances in early 1945, a government of free Czechoslovakia was established at Košice two months before the liberation of Prague.

The second Czechoslovakia established after the war was intended to operate on the basis of equality between the two peoples, but after the communist takeover in February 1948 the administration once again became centralised in Prague. Slovakian communists who resisted were brought to trial accused of advocating 'bourgeois nationalism'. Although the 1960 constitution granted Czechs and Slovaks equal rights, only the 1968 'Prague Spring' reforms introduced by Alexander Dubček (a rehabilitated

Slovakian communist) actually implemented this concept. In August 1968 Soviet troops quashed the democratic reforms and although the Czech and Slovakian republics theoretically became equal partners in a federal Czechoslovakia in 1969, the real power remained in Prague.

The fall of communism in Czechoslovakia in 1989 led to a resurgence of Slovakian nationalism and agitation for Slovakian autonomy. In February 1992 the Slovakian parliament rejected a treaty which would have perpetuated a federal Czechoslovakia.

The rift deepened with the June 1992 elections which brought to power the left-leaning Movement for a Democratic Slovakia (HZDS) headed by ex-boxer Vladimír Mečiar. The 150-seat Slovakian parliament was divided between the HZDS with 74 seats, the (ex-Communist) Party of the Democratic Left (SDL') with 29 seats, the Christian Democrats (KDH) with 18 seats, the ultra-nationalist Slovak National Party (SNS) with 14 seats and the Hungarian Minority Party (MKDH-E) with 14 seats. In July this parliament voted to declare sovereignty.

Mečiar held negotiations with his Czech counterpart Václav Klaus, with Mečiar calling for a loose confederation with a common currency, army and president, while Klaus insisted on a federation with a central government. By May 1992 unemployment was 11.8% in Slovakia compared to just 3.2% in Bohemia and Moravia, and only 10% of foreign investment had gone to Slovakia. To alleviate hardship, the Slovaks wanted to slow economic reform and, with both sides refusing to compromise, in August 1992 it was agreed that the federation would peacefully dissolve at the end of the year. Thus on 1 January 1993 the Czech and Slovak Federative Republic separated into two fully independent states.

With the economy in trouble, Mečiar lost the prime ministership in a parliamentary vote of no-confidence in March 1994 after it became apparent that his only clear policy was separation from Czechoslovakia. In September, however, his HZDS party won the general elections with 35% of the vote, and Mečiar looked set to form a new government. Slovakia faces an uphill struggle to keep economic pace with its neighbours in an increasingly competitive Europe.

GEOGRAPHY

Slovakia sits in the very heart of Europe straddling the north-western end of the Carpathian mountain range. This hilly 49,035-sq-km country (just a bit smaller than Nova Scotia, Canada) forms a clear physical barrier between the plains of Poland and Hungary. Almost 80% of Slovakia has an altitude of over 750 metres above sea level.

Slovakia south of Nitra is a fertile lowland stretching down to the Danube which forms the border with Hungary from Bratislava to Štúrovo/Esztergom. The Váh River joins the Danube at Komárno and together they flow south-east to the Black Sea.

Žilina is caught between the Beskydy of Moravia and the Malá Fatra (Little Fatra) of Central Slovakia, and to the east are the Vysoké Tatry (High Tatra). At 2655 metres Gerlachovský štít (Gerlach in German) is the highest of the mighty peaks in this spectacular alpine range which Slovakia shares with Poland. The Nízke Tatry (Low Tatra) are between Poprad-Tatry and Banská Bystrica.

There are five national parks: Malá Fatra (east of Žilina), Nízke Tatry (between Banská Bystrica and Poprad-Tatry), Vysoké Tatry (north of Poprad-Tatry), Pieniny (along the Dunajec River) and Slovenský raj (near Spišská Nová Ves). In this book we provide practical information on visiting all of these parks except Nízke Tatry.

ECONOMY

For centuries this was a backward agricultural area from which people sought to escape through emigration (nearly two million people of Slovak origin live in the USA today). In 1918 Slovakia united with the far more advanced Czech lands, stimulating limited industrial development. During WW II, however, most existing Slovakian factories were adapted to the needs of the German war effort and later the communists developed arms production into a key industry; in fact, 65% of former Czechoslovakia's military production came from Slovakia. Attempts since 1989 to convert these plants to other uses have led to widespread unemployment in Central Slovakia and created severe problems for Slovakia's heavy engineering and metallurgy industries. In early 1994 unemployment in Slovakia stood at 14.4% and inflation was 25% a year.

Under the communists, agriculture was neglected and the natural connection of the farmers to their land was disturbed by Soviet-style collectivisation. State subsidies kept production and consumption high but since 1990 agricultural output has plummeted as subsidies were removed and the purchasing power of the general public reduced. Slovakia's cooperative farms are now owned by those who work on them and the state farms are soon to be privatised but as yet private farms account for only 4% of the land.

Heavy industry was developed throughout former Czechoslovakia, with Slovakia being industrialised almost from scratch. By 1989 Slovakia accounted for a fifth of former Czechoslovakia's industrial output with oil refineries at Bratislava, textile mills at Bratislava, Trenčín, Žilina and Prešov, cement works at Banská Bystrica and an iron works at Košice. In 1991 the chemical industry alone accounted for 67.5% of industrial production, textiles 16% and leather and shoe-making a further 8%.

The heavy industry concentrated here is experiencing the biggest difficulties in Eastern Europe today due to a combination of lost markets in the former Soviet bloc and intense protectionism in Western Europe which is keeping out Slovakian chemicals, iron, textiles and agricultural products. Not only is Slovakia unable to sell its armaments in Europe but Western countries also object to sales to the Third World. Inefficient, debt-ridden companies without saleable products are not prime candidates for privatisation and the choice between endless state subsidies and mass bankruptcy is daunting. And to make matters worse, trade between Slovakia and the Czech Republic has plummeted. This is a much bigger problem for Slovakia which relies on the Czech Republic for 40% of its trade than it is for the Czechs who only conduct 20% of their foreign business with Slovaks.

The big investors in Slovakia to date have been Austria, Germany, the USA and the Czech Republic, in that order. Slovakia offers investors competitive advantages in the form of a highly trained workforce (over 10% of Slovakian workers have a university education and 36.4% are high school graduates) and low wages (averaging just US$200 a month), but some Western investors claim there are many bureaucratic obstacles to doing business here. The Slovakian government defines its goal as a 'socially oriented' market economy.

Slovakia's first nuclear generating station was built at Jaslovské Bohunice near Trnava in the 1970s and a second plant is nearing completion at Mochovce east of Nitra. These Soviet-designed VVER-440 facilities supply nearly half of Slovakia's electricity but the safety of the Jaslovské Bohunice facility has been questioned.

The Gabčíkovo hydroelectric project on the Danube west of Komárno became highly controversial after Hungary backed out of the joint project in 1989 due to environmental considerations. By October 1992 the Danube River had been partially diverted near Bratislava and in November the power plant and navigational route at Gabčíkovo were put into operation (turn to the Visegrád section in the Hungary chapter for more information). Gabčíkovo produces enough electricity to cover the needs of every home in Slovakia and the canal allows even the largest river vessels to reach Bratislava year-round.

POPULATION & PEOPLE

Slovakia has a population of 5,354,000 of which 85.6% are Slovaks, 10.7% Hungarians, 1.5% Gypsies and 1% Czechs. The 600,000 ethnic Hungarians live mostly in southern and eastern Slovakia. The September 1992 Slovakian constitution guarantees

SLOVAKIA

the rights of minorities and three-quarters of Hungarian children receive schooling in their mother tongue. For historical reasons, some antagonism exists between Slovaks and Hungarians but leaders on both sides have tried to minimise confrontations.

Eighty thousand Slovakian Gypsies managed to escape Nazi extermination because the Germans didn't actually occupy Slovakia until after the uprising in late 1944 and there wasn't time to send them to Auschwitz. The communists gave the Gypsies homes and jobs, and most of them now lead normal lives, though their nomadic culture has been destroyed in the process. Lately, as heavy industrial jobs disappear, many Slovakian Gypsies have migrated to the Czech Republic. As elsewhere in Eastern Europe, there is much prejudice against Gypsies.

Slovakia's Jews weren't as lucky as the Gypsies and beginning in March 1942 60,000 of them were deported to Nazi death camps in Poland by the Slovakian fascists while another 30,000 were rounded up in the Hungarian-occupied part of southern Slovakia. Many of those who survived emigrated to Palestine after the war and the number of Jews in Slovakia today is very small.

Catholics are in a majority but Evangelicals are also numerous and in East Slovakia there are many Greek Catholics and Orthodox believers. Religion is taken rather more seriously by the folksy Slovaks than it is by the secular Czechs.

The largest cities are Bratislava (440,000), Košice (236,000), Žilina (97,000), Nitra (91,000), Prešov (89,000), Banská Bystrica (87,000) and Trnava (73,000).

ARTS

Music

Traditional Slovakian folk instruments include the *fujara* (a two-metre-long flute), the *gajdy* (bagpipes), and the *konkovka* (a strident shepherd's flute). Folk songs helped preserve the Slovak language during the millennium of Hungarian control and in East Slovakia the ancient folk traditions are still a living part of village life. The songs tell of love, lament, anticipation and celebration as vigorous dancing dispels the uncertainty of life.

The locally available compact disc *Spievajme si, dievky* (OPUS 9157 2186) by the female folk choir Vajana makes a good souvenir, although the songs are highly orchestrated and not pure folk music.

LANGUAGE

Although many people working in tourism have a good knowledge of English, in rural Slovakia very few people speak anything other than Slovakian. German is probably the most useful non-Slavic language to know.

An aspect of Slovakian nationalism is pride in the language and Slovaks can get a little hot under the collar when Slovak is given short shrift in comparison with other Slavic languages. As a visitor, you won't be taken to task if you mix your 10 words of Czech with your five words of Slovak, but any effort to communicate in the language of the land will be most appreciated.

Pronunciation

The 43 letters of the Slovak language are pronounced similarly to those of Czech. In words of three syllables or less the stress falls on the first syllable. Longer words generally also have a secondary accent on the 3rd or 5th syllable. The number of syllables is the same as the number of vowels (a, á, ä, e, é, i, í, o, ó, u, ú, y, ý), semi-vowels (l, l', r) or diphthongs (ia, ie, iu, ou, ô). Letters and diphthongs pronounced somewhat differently from their English equivalents include the following:

c 'ts' as in 'cats'
č 'ch' as in 'chain'
dz 'ds' as in 'pads'
dž 'j' as in 'jaw'
ia 'yo' as in 'yonder'
ie 'ye' as in 'yes'
iu as in 'you'
j 'y' as in 'yet'
ň 'ni' as in 'onion'
o 'wo' as in 'won't'

ou	‘ow’ as in ‘know’
š	‘sh’ as in ‘show’
y	‘i’ as in ‘machine’
ž	‘z’ as in ‘azure’

Greetings & Civilities

hello	*ahoj*
good morning	*dobré ráno*
good day	*dobrý deň*
good evening	*dobrý večer*
goodbye	*dovidenia*
please	*prosím*
thank you	*d’akujem*
excuse me/ forgive me	*prepáčte mi/ odpuste mi*
I am sorry.	*Ospravedlňujem sa.*
yes	*áno*
no	*nie*

Small Talk

I don’t understand.	*Nerozumiem.*
Could you write it down?	*Môžeš mi to napísat’?*
What is it called?	*Ako sa do volá?*
Where do you live?	*Kde bývaš?*
What work do you do?	*Čo robíš?*
I am a student.	*Som študent.*
I am very happy.	*Som vel’mi šťastný.*

Accommodation

youth hostel	*mládežnícka ubytovňa*
camping ground	*kemping*
private room	*súkromné izby*
How much is it?	*Kol’ko to stojí?*
Is that the price per person?	*Je to cena za jednu osobu?*
Is that the total price?	*Je to celková cena?*
Are there any extra charges?	*Sú tam ešte iné položky?*
Do I pay extra for showers?	*Platím zvlášť za sprchu?*
Where is there a cheaper hotel?	*Kde tu je lacnejší hotel?*
Should I make a reservation?	*Môžem si to rezervovat’?*
single room	*jednolôžková izba*
double room	*dvojlôžková izba*
It is very noisy.	*Je to vel’mi hlučné.*
Where is the toilet?	*Kde je toaleta?*

Getting Around

What time does it leave?	*O ktorej to odchádza?*
When is the first bus?	*Kedy ide prvý autobus?*
When is the last bus?	*Kedy odchádza posledný autobus?*
When is the next bus?	*Kedy ide ďalšď’ autobus?*
That’s too soon.	*To je vel’mi skoro.*
When is the next one after that?	*Kedy ide najbližší spoj po tomto?*
How long does the trip take?	*Ako dlho trvá výlet?*
arrival	*príchod*
departure	*odchod*
timetable	*cestovný poriadok*
Where is the bus stop?	*Kde je autobusová zastávka?*
Where is the train station?	*Kde je vlaková stanica?*
Where is the left-luggage room?	*Kde je úschovňa batožín?*

Around Town

Just a minute.	*Počkajte chvíl’u.*
Where is ... ?	*Kde je ... ?*
the bank	*banka*
the post office	*pošta*
the tourist information office	*turistické informácie*
the museum	*múzeum*
Where are you going?	*Kam ideš?*
I am going to ...	*Ja idem do ...*
Where is it?	*Kde to je?*
I can’t find it.	*Nemôžem to nájsť’.*
Is it far?	*Je to d’aleko?*
Please show me on the map.	*Prosím, ukážte mi to na mape.*
left	*vl’avo*
right	*vpravo*
straight ahead	*rovno*
I want ...	*Ja chcem ...*
Do I need permission?	*Potrebujem povolenie?*

Entertainment

Where can I buy a ticket?	*Kde si môžem kúpit' lístok?*
Where can I refund this ticket?	*Kde môžem vrátit' lístok?*
Is this a good seat?	*Je to dobré miesto?*
at the front	*vpredu*
ticket	*lístok*

Food

I do not eat meat.	*Ja nejem mäso.*
self-service cafeteria	*samoobslužný bufet*
grocery store	*potraviny*
fish	*ryba*
pork	*bravčovina*
soup	*polievka*
salad	
šalát	
fresh vegetables	*čerstvá zelenina*
milk	*mlieko*
bread	*chlieb*
sugar	*cqkor*
ice cream	*zmrzlina*
coffee	*káva*
tea	*čaj*
mineral water	*minerálka*
beer	*pivo*
wine	*víno*
hot/cold	*horúci/studený*

Shopping

Where can I buy one?	*Kde to môžem kúpit'?*
How much does it cost?	*Kol'ko to stojí?*
That's (much) too expensive.	*To je vel'mi drahé.*
Is there a cheaper one?	*Kde to kúpim lacnejšie?*

Time & Dates

today	*dnes*
tonight	*dnes večer*
tomorrow	*zajtra*
the day after tomorrow	*pozajtra*
What time does it open?	*Kedy otvárajú?*
What time does it close?	*Kedy zatvárajú?*
open	*otvorené*
closed	*zatvorené*
in the morning	*ráno*
in the evening	*večer*
every day	*každý deň*
At what time?	*O ktorej?*
when?	*kedy?*

Monday	*pondelok*
Tuesday	*utorok*
Wednesday	*streda*
Thursday	*štvrtok*
Friday	*piatok*
Saturday	*sobota*
Sunday	*nedel'a*

January	*január*
February	*február*
March	*marec*
April	*apríl*
May	*máj*
June	*jún*
July	*júl*
August	*august*
September	*september*
October	*október*
November	*november*
December	*december*

Numbers

1	*jeden*
2	*dva*
3	*tri*
4	*štyri*
5	*pät*
6	*šest'*
7	*sedem*
8	*osem*
9	*devät'*
10	*desat'*
11	*jedenást'*
12	*dvanást'*
13	*trinást'*
14	*štrnást'*
15	*pätnást'*
16	*šestnást'*
17	*sedemnást'*
18	*osemnást'*

19	*devätnásť'*
20	*dvadsat'*
21	*dvadsat'jeden*
22	*dvadsat'dva*
23	*dvadsaťtri*
30	*tridsat'*
40	*štyridsat'*
50	*pät'desiat*
60	*šest'desiat*
70	*sedemdesiat*
80	*osemdesiat*
90	*devät'desiat*
100	*sto*
1000	*tisíc*
10,000	*desat'tisíc*
1,000,000	*milión*

SLOVAKIA

Facts for the Visitor

The official separation of Slovakia and the Czech Republic only occurred in January, 1993, and much of the practical information contained in the Facts for the Visitor section of the Czech Republic chapter also applies to Slovakia. Rather than repeat information, in this section we've tried to focus on differences between the countries. For this reason, you should read the previously mentioned part of the introduction to the Czech Republic chapter even if you have no intention of going there.

VISAS & EMBASSIES

At last report entry requirements were the same as for the Czech Republic (visas not required by most Europeans and US citizens, though the latter can only stay 30 days without a visa). Visas cost US$25 for Australians and New Zealanders, or US$50 for Canadians, and two photos are required. The visa consists of a full-page stamp in your passport and two separate sheets (make sure the clerk doesn't forget to give you these), one of which should include your photo. Slovakian visas cannot be used to visit the Czech Republic, nor vice versa, and if you have only a Czech visa you'll be refused entry at the Slovakian border. Don't count on getting your Slovakian visa at the border.

Slovakian Embassies Abroad

Australia
: 47 Culgoa Circuit, O'Malley, Canberra, ACT 2606 (☎ 062-90 1516)

Canada
: 50 Rideau Terrace, Ottawa, ON K1M 2A1 (☎ 613-749 4442)

Netherlands
: Parkweg 1, 2585 JG The Hague (☎ 070-355 7566 or 355 8097)

UK
: 25 Kensington Palace Gardens, London W8 4QY (☎ 0171-243 0803)

USA
: 2201 Wisconsin Ave NW, Washington, DC 2000 (☎ 202-965 5161)

MONEY

Currency

Slovakia's currency is the Slovakian crown, or *Slovenská koruna* (Sk). It is worth about 10% less than the Czech crown. In late 1993 Slovakia issued its own distinctive currency with coins of 10, 20 and 50 hellers (halierov) and 1, 2, 5 and 10 crowns (Sk). Banknotes come in denominations of 20, 50, 100, 500, 1000 and 5000 crowns. The old Czechoslovakian notes and coins are now worthless.

The easiest place to change a travellers' cheque is at a branch of the Všeobecná Úverová Banka (General Credit Bank) or the Investičná Banka (Investment Bank) where you'll be charged a standard 1% commission. Satur offices (see Tourist Offices) deduct 2% and may only accept cash. Post office exchange windows never change travellers' cheques and take 2% weekdays and 3% weekends to change cash. Banks often give a slightly better rate for travellers' cheques than for cash.

If you'll be arriving from Poland you might think about purchasing a small amount of Slovakian currency at a Polish exchange office to make your entry easier (keep them out of sight at the border). Poland-bound, you can easily get rid of excess crowns at any Polish exchange office, at a loss of about 10%. Otherwise, it's best to spend all your Slovakian currency before you leave.

Exchange Rates

A$1	=	23.40Sk
DM1	=	20.42Sk
Ft1	=	0.30Sk
Kč1	=	1.13Sk
UK£1	=	48.97Sk
US$1	=	31.5Sk
zł100	=	0.139Sk

Costs

Because Slovakia has been slower to privatise than the Czech Republic it's likely to remain a bargain for travellers far longer than its neighbour, whatever the economic logic of the situation. You'll find food, admissions and transport cheap and accommodation manageable except in Bratislava. The value-added tax (VAT) in Slovakia is 25%.

CLIMATE & WHEN TO GO

Slovakia experiences hot summers and cold winters. The warmest, driest and sunniest area is the Danube lowland east of Bratislava. Due to the altitude there are really only two seasons in the High Tatra Mountains with spring and fall each lasting less than two weeks. The High Tatras also experience the highest rainfall.

SUGGESTED ITINERARIES

Depending on the length of your stay, you might want to see and do the following things in Slovakia:

Two days
: Visit Bratislava.

One week
: Visit Košice, Levoča and the Tatra Mountains.

Two weeks
: Visit most of the places included in this chapter.

TOURIST OFFICES

The old Czechoslovakian tourism monopoly Satur (called Čedok until early 1994) is well represented in Slovakia. Turn to them whenever you require the assistance of a commercial travel agency. Other commercial travel agencies with offices around Slovakia include Tatratour and Slovakoturist. CKM Student Travel also has offices in most towns. In Bratislava the Bratislava Information Service (BIS) is an excellent source of general information on both city and country.

BUSINESS HOURS & HOLIDAYS

Public holidays in Slovakia are New Year's Day (1 January), Three Kings Day (6 January), Easter Friday and Easter Monday (March/April), Labour Day (1 May), Liberation Day (8 May), Cyril and Methodius Day (5 July), Feast of the Assumption (15 August), SNP Day (29 August), Constitution Day (1 September), All Saints Day (1 November) and Christmas (from 24 to 26 December).

Things are really quiet in Slovakian towns from Saturday afternoon to Monday morning as the locals evacuate to their cottages in the country. Don't plan on doing any business at this time although most museums will be open. All grocery stores *(potraviny)* are shut tight from noon Saturday until Monday morning and even the kiosks are closed.

CULTURAL EVENTS

The Bratislava Lyre in May or June features rock concerts. During June or July folk dancers.from all over Slovakia meet at the Východná Folklore Festival, 32 km west of Poprad-Tatry. The Bratislava Jazz Days are held in September.

POST

Mail addressed c/o Poste Restante, 81000 Bratislava 1, Slovakia, can be picked up at window No 6 in the main post office, námestie SNP 34, weekdays from 7 am to 8 pm, Saturday 7 am to 1.30 pm.

American Express card-holders can have their mail sent c/o Tatratour, Frantiákánske námestie 3, 81509 Bratislava, Slovakia.

TELEPHONE

The telephone system isn't quite as good as the one in the Czech Republic and it's sometimes hard to get even local calls through. Calls are most easily placed from main post offices or telephone centres although you

SLOVAKIA

can also make them from blue coin phones on the street. A three-minute telephone call from Slovakia will cost about US$3.50 to the UK, US$6.50 to the USA or Australia.

To call Slovakia from abroad, dial the international access code, 42 (the country code for Slovakia), the area code and the number. Important area codes include 7 (Bratislava), 89 (Žilina or Vrátna), 91 (Prešov), 92 (Poprad-Tatry), 95 (Košice), 819 (Komárno), 831 (Trenčín or Trenčianské Teplice), 935 (Bardejov), 965 (Spišská Nová Ves), 966 (Levoča or Spišské Podhradie) and 969 (Starý Smokovec, Štrbské Pleso or Tatranská Lomnica). When dialling from within Slovakia you must add a 0 before the area code.

TIME

In Slovakia time is GMT/UTC plus one hour. At the end of March Slovakia goes on summer time and clocks are set forward an hour. At the end of September they're turned back an hour.

ELECTRICITY

The electric current is 220 V, 50 Hz.

WEIGHTS & MEASURES

The metric system is used in Slovakia.

HEALTH

Thermal Baths

Public thermal swimming pools exist at Trenčianské Teplice and Komárno. Most of Slovakia's other spas are reserved for patients under medical supervision, but Slovakoterma, Radlinského 13, 800 00 Bratislava, can organise stays at health resorts such as Bardejovské Kúpele and Trenčianské Teplice. New Millennium Holidays (☎ 0121-711 2232), 20 High St, Solihull, West Midlands B91 3TB, England, UK runs inexpensive bus tours from the UK to Trenčianské Teplice from May to October.

ACTIVITIES

Hiking

Slovakia is one of Eastern Europe's prime hiking areas and full information is provided in the sections of this chapter devoted to Malá Fatra, Vysoké Tatry and Slovenský raj.

Rafting

For information on rafting on the Dunajec River in Pieniny National Park turn to the section on the Dunajec Gorge. The hiking is also good here.

Skiing

Slovakia contains some of Europe's top ski resorts and this really is the place to come skiing on a budget. The ski season runs from December to April in the Vysoké Tatry, Nízke Tatry and Malá Fatra. Quality ski gear is hard to find in Slovakia though you can usually rent the local variety at very competitive rates. Sometimes the waits at the ski lifts can be excruciatingly long. The runs are colour coded: black (difficult), red (moderate) and blue (easy).

Cycling

Slovakia offers some of the best cycling terrain in Eastern Europe with uncrowded roads and beautiful scenery. East Slovakia especially is prime cycling territory. Several places at the Vysoké Tatry resorts rent mountain bikes and the possibilities there are endless.

HIGHLIGHTS

Museums & Galleries

Epicureans will enjoy Bratislava's wine museum. The Šarišské Museum at Bardejovské Kúpele has one of the best collections of reassembled traditional dwellings in Eastern Europe. The Slovak National Uprising Museum in Banská Bystrica, a 'political' museum built by the communists, survives because of the crucial period it documents in Slovakia's history. Finally, at the museum of the Tatra National Park at Tatranská Lomnica, you have the rare opportunity of stepping out the door and exploring the very things you saw in the exhibits.

Castles

Spišský hrad, in remote Spišské Podhradie,

is the largest castle in the country, and Trenčín Castle is well known as having been perhaps the most strategic. Bratislava Castle had to be rebuilt from the ground up after wartime destruction.

Historic Towns

Three of Slovakia's most picturesque historic towns are Bardejov, Košice and Levoča. Old Bratislava is also lovely.

ACCOMMODATION

Since 1990, hotel prices for Slovaks have remained fairly steady while those for foreigners have doubled and tripled. Much of the accommodation information in the introduction to the Czech Republic chapter also applies here.

Hostels

CKM Student Travel often has information on hostels and can often make advance bookings at CKM 'Juniorhotels' in Bratislava, Banská Bystrica, Horný Smokovec (Vysoké Tatry) and Jasná pod Chopkom (Nízke Tatry). A hostel card is not required but it should get you a discount at these. In July and August vacant student dormitories are often converted into temporary hostels and CKM is the most likely to know.

FOOD

Once again, check the introduction to the Czech Republic chapter for general information on eating out here. As in the Czech Republic, always insist on seeing a menu with prices listed before ordering a meal at a regular restaurant.

The Slovaks serve their meals with paprika and *halušky* (small dumplings topped with grated cheese and bits of bacon). A real treat to watch for is *palačinky so zavareninou* (peach pancakes). *Langoše* is a large round fried donut with garlic and oil brushed on which makes a great snack. It's usually possible to get fairly good salads in Slovakia.

DRINKS

Two-thirds of former Czechoslovakia's vineyards are on the southern and eastern slopes of the Little Carpathian Mountains north of Bratislava. Slovakian wine is good and cheap and there are also some excellent sparkling wines.

Getting There & Away

AIR

Czechoslovak Airlines (ČSA) flies from Bratislava to Prague several times a day with immediate connections twice a week to Chicago, Montreal, New York and Toronto. ČSA links Bratislava directly to Moscow once a week.

From Prague, ČSA flies daily to Bratislava (US$66), Poprad-Tatry (US$77) and Košice (US$87). Weekdays there are also flights from Bratislava to Košice (US$54). These overpriced services are mostly intended for international passengers connecting with long-haul ČSA flights in Prague.

In addition, a local carrier called Tatra Air has daily flights from Bratislava to Košice and Zürich.

A US$2.50 airport tax is charged on all flights except Bratislava-Košice.

LAND

Bus

There's a bus several times a day from Vienna (Mitte Busbahnhof) to Bratislava (64 km, two hours, US$9). For more information on international buses turn to Getting There & Away in the Bratislava section.

Eurolines has a weekly bus year-round between Amsterdam and Bratislava (22 hours, US$86 one way, US$139 return) via Brussels and Vienna (Czech transit visa not required). A 10% reduction is available to those aged under 26 or over 59 years. Tickets are available from Budget Bus (☎ 020-627 5151), Rokin 10, Amsterdam, and Europabus (☎ 2-217 0025), Place de Brouckere 50, Brussels.

Train

To/From Western Europe Vienna (Südbahnhof) to Bratislava is a 64-km hop done

SLOVAKIA

four times a day (two hours, US$8). All trains to/from Germany pass through Prague and a Czech transit visa is required by some nationals.

To/From Eastern Europe Bratislava is linked to Budapest (215 km, three hours, US$23) by the *Hungária, Balt-Orient* and *Pannónia* express trains from Budapest-Keleti and the *Metropol* express train from Budapest-Nyugati, all via Štúrovo. From Budapest, the morning Eurocity *Hungária* and the afternoon *Metropol* are your best bet because the *Balt-Orient* and *Pannónia* often arrive late from Romania. Ask about reservations when you book your ticket.

Surprisingly, there are no direct trains from Bratislava to Poland and all connections are via the Czech Republic. Several express trains pass through West Slovakia between Hungary and Poland, for example the *Bem* to Wrocław, Poznań and Szczecin, and the *Polonia* to Katowice and Warsaw, both passing Žilina in the middle of the night. The *Báthory* express train, which travels between Warsaw and Budapest via Katowice, calls at Trenčín in the middle of night in both directions. Reservations are mandatory on all these trains and you should avoid them if you require a Czech visa as they transit the Czech Republic for a short distance and you could be put off at the Czech border.

Train services from East Slovakia to Poland and Hungary avoid the Czech Republic. The *Rákóczi* express train shuttles daily between Budapest and Košice (270 km, 4½ hours, US$22), continuing to Poprad-Tatry on certain days (ask). The *Rákóczi* leaves Budapest-Keleti in the early morning, Košice in the late afternoon. Reservations are optional. The *Cracovia* express train from Budapest-Keleti to Kraków transits Košice around midnight northbound, around 4 am southbound. The *Karpaty* express train to Kraków and Warsaw passes Košice during the day, but northbound it often arrives late from Romania and southbound it only goes to Hatvan (not Budapest). Reservations are required on both the *Cracovia* and *Karpaty*.

Unreserved local trains run three times a day between Muszyna, Poland, and Plaveč, Slovakia (16 km, 20 minutes). In Plaveč there are train connections to/from Prešov (54 km, 1½ hours) and Poprad-Tatry (61 km, two hours); from Muszyna trains run to Nowy Sącz (50 km) and (less frequently) to Kraków (217 km). Approximate times of this cross-border train are given in the Prešov section.

Unreserved local trains connect Košice and Miskolc, Hungary, twice a day (88 km, 2½ hours, US$9). Six times a day there are unreserved local trains between Slovenské Nové Mesto, Slovakia, and Sátoraljaújhely, Hungary, with connections to/from Košice and Miskolc.

Both daily trains to/from Moscow, the *Dukla* to/from Prague and the *Slovakia* to/from Bratislava (2325 km, 44 hours), pass through Košice. From Košice 2nd-class fares are from US$46 to Kiev and US$66 to Moscow.

Car & Motorbike

Some highway border crossings are only open to citizens of Slovakia, Hungary and Poland, though this could change. The following crossings (listed clockwise around the country) are open to everyone. In each case, the name of the Slovakian border post is provided.

To/From Poland You can cross at Trstená (west of Zakopane); Javorina (east of Zakopane); Mníšek nad Popradom (31 km south of Nowy Sącz); and Vyšný Komárnik (between Rzeszów and Prešov).

To/From Ukraine You can cross at Vyšné Nemecké (94 km east of Košice).

To/From Hungary The border crossings are at Slovenské Nové Mesto (opposite Sátoraljaújhely); Hraničná pri Hornáde (21 km south of Košice); Král' (45 km northwest of Miskolc); Šiatorská Bukovinka (just north of Salgotarjan); Slovenské Ďarmoty,

Šahy (80 km north of Budapest); Komárno (opposite Komárom); Medved'ov (13 km north of Győr); and Rusovce (16 km southeast of Bratislava).

To/From Austria The only crossing is at Petržalka (at Bratislava).

On Foot

Walking in and out of Slovakia is cheap, easy and fun. By crossing on foot you avoid the hassle of buying an expensive international ticket and end up with a memorable experience.

To/from Poland, the most convenient place to cross is at Łysa Polana/Javorina between Starý Smokovec and Zakopane. Turn to the Vysoké Tatry section of this chapter and Zakopane in the Poland chapter for a description of how it's done.

To/from Hungary, you can easily walk across the bridge over the Danube River between Kormárno and Komárom. This route is described in the Kormárno section of this chapter and the Komárom section in the Hungary chapter.

To/from Austria, you could hitch towards Vienna from Bratislava and a few details of the route are provided in the Bratislava section.

Getting Around

BUS

Buses are more expensive than trains and on weekends bus services are more sharply reduced than rail services. Plan on doing most of your travel by train with side trips by bus. Bus tickets in Slovakia cost US$0.50 for 25 km, US$1 for 50 km, US$2 for 100 km and US$4 for 200 km.

When trying to decipher posted bus schedules beware of departure times bearing footnotes you don't completely understand as these buses often don't show up. Check the time at the information window whenever possible. It is helpful to know that *premáva* means 'it operates' and *nepremáva* means 'it doesn't operate'.

TRAIN

The Slovak Republic Railways or Železnice Slovenskej republiky (ŽSR) provides efficient service at low rates. Most of the places covered in this chapter have been selected precisely because they're on or near the main railway line between Bratislava and Košice. By express train from Bratislava it's 123 km and 1¾ hours to Trenčín, 203 km and three hours to Žilina, 344 km and five hours to Poprad-Tatry, 370 km and 5½ hours to Spišská Nová Ves and 445 km and 6½ hours to Košice.

Most train stations in Slovakia have a left-luggage office where you can check your bag for US$0.20.

CAR

Rental

Europcar has offices in Bratislava and Košice, as well as at Bratislava airport (US$10 service charge at this outlet). Their cheapest Škodas begin at US$40 a day plus US$0.40 a km, or US$98/480 daily/weekly with unlimited mileage, 25% tax included. A weekend rate of US$128 runs from 3 pm Friday to 9 am Monday with unlimited mileage. Add about US$10 daily for collision insurance and another US$10 for theft coverage. Europcar allows one-way rentals between Bratislava and Prague or Košice at no additional charge.

Also check Budget, Hertz, Pragocar and other car rental agencies in Bratislava as their rates could well be lower (ask the Bratislava Information Service for a list of companies).

Bratislava

Bratislava (Pozsony in Hungarian, Pressburg in German) is Slovakia's largest city. Here the Carpathian Mountains, which begin at the Iron Gate of Romania, finally come to an end. As you arrive at the main train station, you'll see vineyards on the slopes of

SLOVAKIA

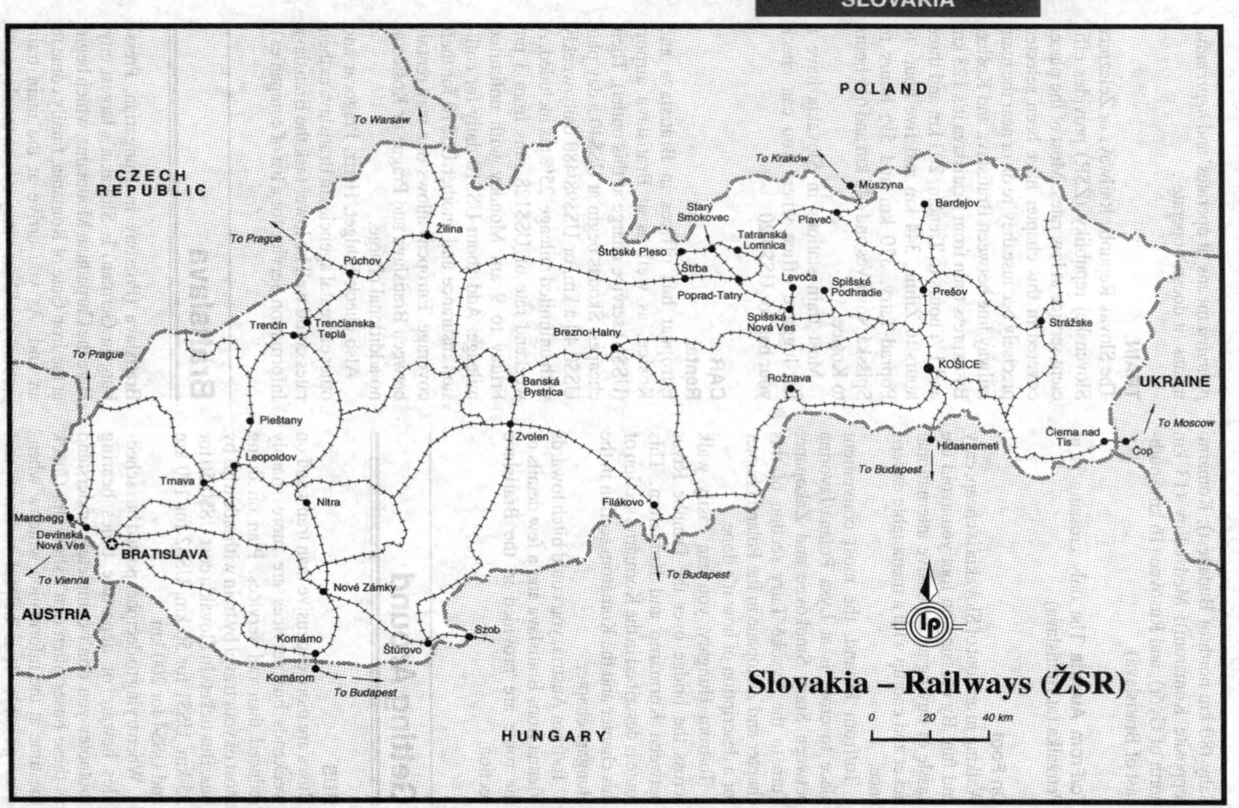

POLAND
CZECH REPUBLIC
UKRAINE
AUSTRIA
HUNGARY
To Warsaw
To Kraków
To Prague
To Prague
To Moscow
To Vienna
To Budapest
To Budapest
To Budapest
To Budapest
Žilina
Púchov
Trenčín
Trenčianska Teplá
Piešťany
Leopoldov
Trnava
Nitra
Marchegg
Devínska Nová Ves
BRATISLAVA
Nové Zámky
Komárno
Komárom
Štúrovo
Szob
Banská Bystrica
Zvolen
Filákovo
Brezno-Halny
Starý Smokovec
Tatranská Lomnica
Štrbské Pleso
Štrba
Poprad-Tatry
Levoča
Spišské Podhradie
Spišská Nová Ves
Muszyna
Plaveč
Bardejov
Prešov
KOŠICE
Rožnava
Hidasnemeti
Strážske
Čierna nad Tis
Čop
Slovakia – Railways (ŽSR)
0
20
40 km

the Little Carpathian Mountains which meet the Danube River here. The Austrian border is almost within sight of the city and Hungary is just 16 km away.

Founded in 907 AD, Bratislava was already a large city in the 12th century. Commerce developed in the 14th and 15th centuries and in 1467 the Hungarian Renaissance monarch Matthias Corvinus founded a university here, the Academia Istropolitana. The city became Hungary's capital in 1541, after the Turks captured Buda, and remained so for nearly three centuries. Between 1563 and 1830, 11 Hungarian kings and seven queens were crowned in St Martin's Cathedral. Bratislava flourished during the reign of Maria Theresa of Austria (1740-80) and some imposing baroque palaces were built. In 1918 the city was included in the newly formed Republic of Czechoslovakia and since 1969 it has been the capital of the Slovak Republic.

Many beautiful monuments survive in the old town to tell of this glorious past under Hungarian rule, and Bratislava's numerous museums are surprisingly rich. Franz Liszt visited Bratislava 15 times, and the opera productions of the Slovak National Theatre rival anything in Europe. Bratislava isn't at all as swamped by Western tourism as Budapest and Prague (except on weekends when the Austrians invade), and if you can find a reasonable place to stay it's well worth a couple of days.

Orientation

Bratislava's main train station, Hlavná stanica, is several km north of town. Tram No 1 runs from the lower level at this station to námestie L Štúra near the centre. A few trains also use stanica Bratislava-Nové Mesto, less conveniently located on the north-eastern side of the city.

Hviezdoslavovo námestie is a convenient reference point, with the old town to the north, the Danube to the south, Štúrova ulica to the east and Bratislava Castle to the west. The main bus station *(autobusová stanica)* is in a convenient modern building on Mlynské nivy, a little over one km east of Štúrova ulica. The left-luggage office at the bus station is open weekdays from 5 am to 10 pm, weekends 6 am to 6 pm. The left-luggage area at Hlavná stanica is open 24 hours.

Information

General information about the city is supplied by the Bratislava Information Service or BIS (☎ 333 715), Panská 18 (open weekdays from 8 am to 6 pm, Saturday from 8 am to 1 pm). They sell an indexed city map and are very helpful. *Kam v Bratislave* (Where in Bratislava) available at BIS provides detailed information about what's on around Bratislava.

Map freaks can go to the source and buy maps of almost anywhere in Slovakia at Slovenská Kartografia, Pekná cesta 17 off Račianska (eastbound tram No 3, 5 or 11). Geodézia Bratislava, Pekná cesta 15, has topographical maps of western Slovakia.

Money The Všeobecná Úverová Banka has a poorly marked exchange office at Hlavná stanica open daily from 7.30 am to 6 pm. It's hidden to one side of the corridor, around behind the 'Internationale Kasse' on the opposite side of the main hall from the left-luggage office. Their rate is as good as anything in town and they take the usual 1% commission on cash and travellers' cheques.

The Všeobecná Úverová Banka upstairs in the bus station is open Monday to Thursday from 8 am to noon and 1 to 5 pm, Friday 8 am to noon.

The Všeobecná Úverová Banka, námestie SNP 14 (weekdays 8 am to 5 pm, Saturday 8 am to noon), also charges 1% commission to change travellers' cheques.

An automatic currency-exchange machine able to convert the banknotes of 14 countries is outside the Slovenská Štátna Sporitel'ňa, Štúrova ulica 11 near the ČSA office (accessible 24 hours).

Post & Telephone Mail addressed c/o Poste Restante, 81000 Bratislava 1, can be collected at window No 6 at the main post office námestie SNP 34 (open weekdays from 7 am

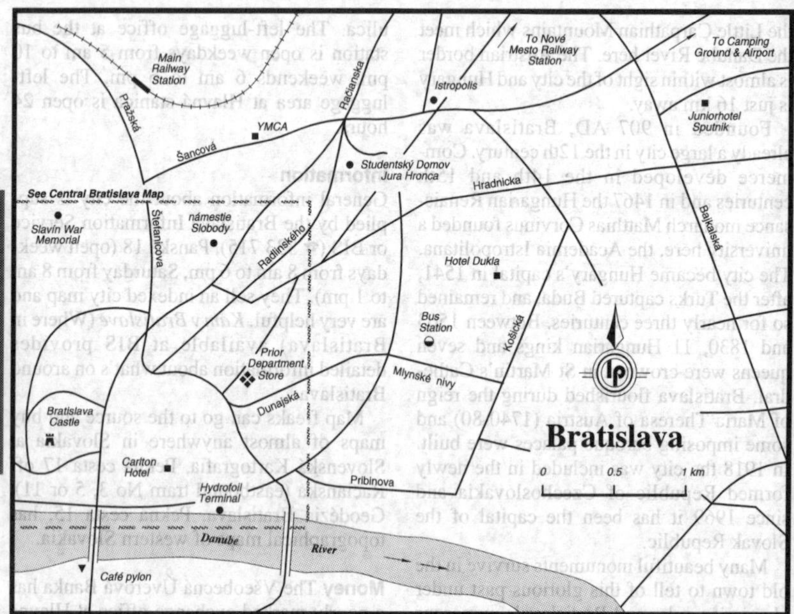

to 8 pm, Saturday 7 am to 1.30 pm). Letters from abroad are held one month. To mail a parcel you must go to the office marked 'podaj a výdaj balíkov' through the next entrance at námestie SNP 35.

It is possible to make international telephone calls at Kolárska ulica 12 (open 24 hours a day).

Bratislava's telephone code is 07.

Embassies The American Embassy (☎ 335 932) is at Hviezdoslavovo námestie 4 (weekdays 8.30 am to noon and 2 to 4 pm).

The British Embassy (☎ 364 420; open weekdays from 8.30 am to 12.30 pm and 1.30 to 5 pm) and the French Embassy (☎ 361 727) are in the same building at Grösslingová 35. The Croatian Embassy is nearby at Grösslingová 47.

The Czech Embassy is at Panenská 33, off Hodžovo námestie (Monday and Wednesday 9 am to noon and 2 to 4 pm, Tuesday and Thursday 9 am to noon).

Nearby are the Hungarian Embassy, Palisády ulica 54 (open Monday, Wednesday and Friday from 9 am to noon), and the Embassy of Bulgaria, Kuzmányho 1 off Palisády ulica (open Monday, Wednesday and Friday from 9 am to noon).

Also in this area is the Russian Embassy, Maróthyho ulica 3 off Palisády ulica (Monday, Wednesday and Friday 9 am to 1 pm), and the Romanian Embassy, Fraňa Krála 11 (Monday, Wednesday and Friday 9 am to noon).

The Polish Embassy, Hummelova 4, is in the residential area north-west of Bratislava Castle. To get to the Polish Embassy (open Monday to Friday from 9 am to 12.30 pm), take trolleybus No 213, 216 or 217 from Hodžovo námestie to 'Hummelova'.

In the same neighbourhood as the Polish Embassy is the Ukrainian Embassy, Radvanská ulica 35 (Monday, Wednesday and Friday from 9 am to 1 pm), which issues one-month tourist visas for US$50.

Travel Agencies CKM Student Travel, Hviezdoslavovo námestie 16, sells HI hostel cards (US$6) and ISIC student cards (US$7). If you're under 26 years old, ask CKM about Eurotrain tickets for reduced international train travel to Western Europe.

The American Express representative in Bratislava is Tatratour (☎ 335 852), Františkánske námestie 3.

Staff at Slovakoterma, Radlinského 13, can arrange stays at health spas throughout Slovakia (from US$50/80 single/double all-inclusive).

For information on travel to the former USSR visit Intourist, Ventúrska 2 (weekdays 8 am to 4 pm).

Bookshops Knihy Slovenský, on the corner of Rybárska brána and Laurinská, sells useful hiking maps.

Visa Extensions Any visa or passport enquiries should be directed to the foreigners' police, conveniently located at Svoradova ulica 11 (Monday, Tuesday, Thursday and Friday 7 am to noon, Wednesday 8.30 am to noon and 1 to 5 pm).

Things to See

Begin your visit with the **Slovak National Museum** (1928) opposite the hydrofoil terminal on the river. The museum features anthropology, archaeology, natural history and geology exhibits – notice the large relief map of Slovakia. A little farther up the riverfront is the ultramodern **Slovak National Gallery** (admission US$1.50), Bratislava's major art collection with a good Gothic section. The gallery building itself is interesting because of the daring incorporation of an 18th-century palace into the design.

Backtrack slightly to námestie L Štúra where, on the corner of Mostová, you'll find the Art-Nouveau **Reduta Palace** (1914), now Bratislava's concert hall. Go north up Mostová to the neobaroque **Slovak National Theatre** (1886) on the right with Ganymede's Fountain (1888) in front.

Crowded, narrow Rybárska brána penetrates the old town to Hlavní námestie, at the centre of which is Roland's Fountain (1572). To one side is the old town hall (1421), now the **Municipal Museum** with torture chambers in the casemates and an extensive collection housed in finely decorated rooms. You enter the museum from the picturesque inner courtyard where concerts are held in summer.

Leave the courtyard through the east gate and you'll be on a square before the **Primate's Palace** (1781). Enter to see the Hall of Mirrors where Napoleon and the Austrian emperor Franz I signed a peace treaty in 1805. In the municipal gallery on the 2nd floor are rare English tapestries (1632). St George's Fountain stands in the courtyard. On Saturday the palace is crowded with couples being married, but it's still open to visitors. Just beyond this palace is the **Hummel Music Museum**, Klobučnícka 2, in the former home of the German composer and pianist Johann Hummel (1778-1837).

Return through the old town hall courtyard and turn left into Radničná 1 to get to the **Museum of Wine Production** (closed Tuesday) in the Apponyi Palace (1762). Buy the museum guidebook in English if you're at all interested in the subject. Next head north on Františkánske námestie to the **Franciscan Church** (1297). The original Gothic chapel (1297) with the skeleton of a saint enclosed in glass is accessible through a door on the left near the front. Opposite this church is the **Mirbach Palace** (1770), Františkánske námestie 11, a beautiful rococo building which houses a good art collection.

From the palace continue around on narrow Zámočnícka ulica to the **Michael Tower** (closed Tuesday), which has a collection of antique arms. There's a great view from the tower. Go north through the tower arch into the old barbican, out the north gate and across the street, to the **Church of the Holy Trinity** (1725), an oval edifice with fine frescos.

Return to the Michael Tower and stroll down Michalská to the **Palace of the Royal**

Chamber (1756) at Michalská 1. Now the university library, this building was once the seat of the Hungarian parliament. In 1848 serfdom was abolished here, marking the end of feudalism in Hungary.

Take the passage west through the palace to the Gothic **Church of the Clarissine Order** with a unique pentagonal tower (1360) supported on buttresses. Continue west on Farská, then turn left into Kapitulská and go straight ahead to the 15th-century coronation church, **St Martin's Cathedral**. Inside is the bronze statue (1734) of St Martin cutting off half his robe for a beggar.

Castles on the Danube The busy motorway in front of St Martin's follows the moat of the former city walls. Construction of this route and the adjacent bridge was rather controversial as several historic structures had to be pulled down and vibrations from the traffic have structurally weakened the cathedral. Find the passage under the motorway and head up towards Bratislava Castle, built above the Danube on the southernmost spur of the Little Carpathian Mountains. At the foot of the hill is the **Decorative Arts Museum** (closed Tuesday).

Since the 9th century, **Bratislava Castle**

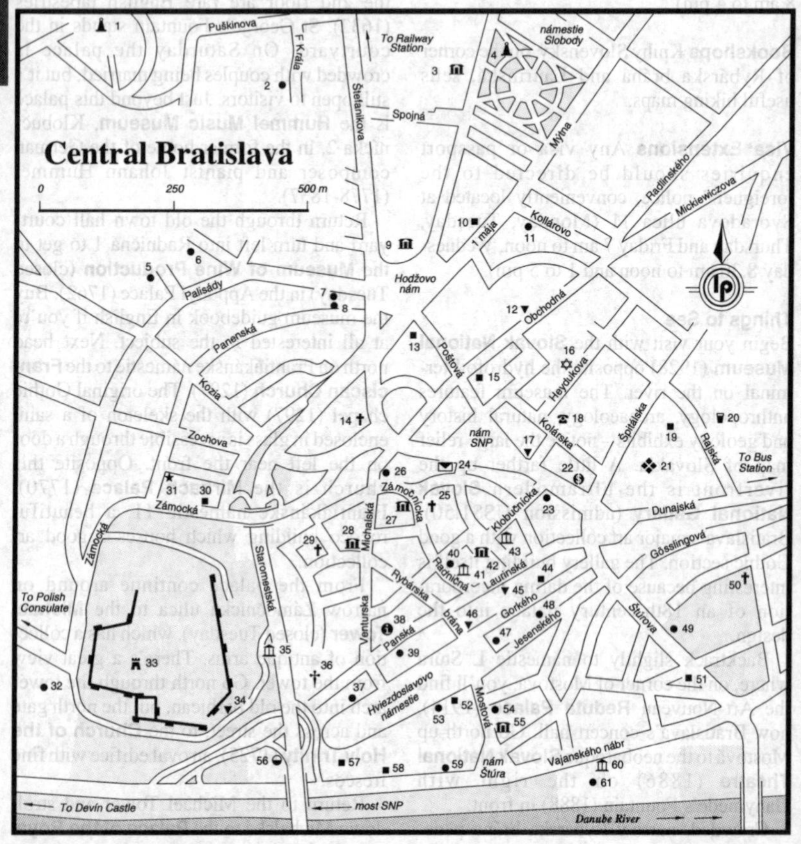

has been rebuilt several times; it served as the seat of Hungarian royalty until it finally burnt down in 1811. Reconstructed between 1953 and 1962, the castle now houses a large historical museum. Climb up to the castle for a great view. The Slovakian National Parliament meets in the modern complex that overlooks the river, just beyond the castle.

As you return from the castle, take a stroll on one of the pedestrian walkways across the sweeping **most SNP** (SNP Bridge) (1972) over the Danube. On the far side you can take a lift (US$0.50) up one of the pylons to an expensive café that sits 80 metres above the river. Even the toilets have a view.

Below the Bratislava end of most SNP is a city bus terminal where you can catch city bus No 29 west along the Danube to the Gothic ruins of **Devín Castle** (open from May to October, closed Monday), which is on a hill where the Morava and Danube rivers meet. The castle withstood the Turks but was blown up in 1809 by the French. Stay on the bus to the end of the line and walk back to the castle. Austria is just across the rivers from Devín.

From the 1st to 5th centuries AD, Devín and Bratislava castles were frontier posts of the Roman Empire, manned by the 14th Legion. In the 9th century Devín Castle was a major stronghold of the Great Moravian Empire, and today both castles are regarded as symbols of the Slavic peoples who maintained their identity despite centuries of foreign rule.

Post-Communist Bratislava To see a bit of the Bratislava built by the communists, head north from the Michael Tower across Hodžovo námestie to the baroque **Grassalkovich Palace** (1760), previously the House of Pioneers. Continue north-east

PLACES TO STAY

- 10 Hotel Tatra/Kino Tatra
- 13 Hotel Forum
- 15 Palace Hotel
- 19 Hotel Kyjev
- 30 Chez David Pension
- 44 Gremium Pension/Café
- 51 Krym Hotel
- 52 Carlton Hotel
- 57 Hotel Danube
- 58 Hotel Devín

PLACES TO EAT

- 12 Picco Pizza
- 17 Cukráreň Jezbera
- 34 Modrá Hviezda Restaurant
- 45 Diétna Jedáleň
- 46 Food Market

OTHER

- 1 Slavín War Memorial
- 2 Romanian Embassy
- 3 Archbishop's Summer Palace
- 4 Site of the Klement Gottwald Monument
- 5 Russian Embassy
- 6 Bulgarian Consulate
- 7 Hungarian Consulate
- 8 Czech Embassy
- 9 Grassalkovich Palace
- 11 nová scéna
- 14 Church of the Holy Trinity
- 16 Synagogue
- 18 International Telephone Office
- 20 Charlie's Pub
- 21 Prior Department Store
- 22 Všeobecna Úverová Banka
- 23 Old City Market
- 24 Main Post Office
- 25 Franciscan Church
- 26 Michael Tower
- 27 Mirbach Palace
- 28 Palace of the Royal Chamber
- 29 Church of the Clarissine Order
- 31 Foreigners' Police
- 32 Slovak National Parliament
- 33 Bratislava Castle
- 35 Decorative Arts Museum
- 36 St Martin's Cathedral
- 37 CKM Student Travel
- 38 Bratislava Information Service
- 39 City Art Gallery
- 40 Old Town Hall
- 41 Museum of Wine Production
- 42 Primate's Palace
- 43 Hummel Music Museum
- 47 Slovak National Theatre
- 48 Pokladňa Kassa (Theatre Ticket Office)
- 49 ČSA Airline Office
- 50 Hungarian Church
- 53 American Embassy
- 54 Slovenská filharmonia
- 55 Reduta Palace
- 56 Bus to Devín Castle
- 59 Slovak National Gallery
- 60 Slovak National Museum
- 61 Hydrofoil Terminal

towards námestie Slobody, previously known as Gottwaldovo námestie. An impressive monument to Klement Gottwald (1980), the man instrumental in implanting communism in Czechoslovakia, once stood on the platform in the north-west corner of the square but the massive marble figures of Gottwald and others were destroyed during the political upheaval of late 1989. Some of the new buildings on the square belong to the **Technical University**. On the western side of námestie Slobody is what used to be the **archbishop's summer palace** (1765), now the seat of the Government of the Slovak Republic.

If you go west down Spojná and north up Štefánikova ulica 25, you'll come to the former **Lenin Museum**, now an art gallery. Continue north a little, then head west up the steps of Puškinova towards the **Slavín War Memorial** (1965). This is where 6847 Soviet soldiers who died in the battle for Bratislava in 1945 are buried. There's a good view of modern Bratislava from here.

Unless otherwise noted, all of Bratislava's galleries and museums are closed on Monday.

Hiking

To get out of the city and up into the forested Little Carpathian Mountains, take trolleybus No 213 north-east from Hodžovo námestie to the end of the line at Koliba, then walk up the road to the **TV tower** on Kamzík Hill (440 metres) in about 20 minutes. Here an elevator (US$0.50) lifts you to a viewing platform overlooking three countries. The revolving café just below the platform has no food but the drinks are quite affordable. The tower is closed on Monday from October through to February.

Maps posted at the tower outline the many hiking possibilities of this area. For example, head north from the Koliba EXPO Restaurant near the tower down a road closed to vehicular traffic to 'Lanovka'. When you get to a main road at the foot of the hill, turn right to reach a favourite weekend picnic area for Bratislava locals. Bus No 33 runs back to town from here (ask the driver where you have to change to trolleybus No 212 to return to Hodžovo námestie).

Places to Stay

Hostels Staff at CKM Student Travel, Hviezdoslavovo námestie 16, may be able to tell you about summer hostels and perhaps reserve a bed for you at the *Juniorhotel Sputnik* (☎ 294 167) at Drieňová 14 in the eastern suburbs (tram No 8, 9 or 12 or bus No 34, 38 or 54). The Juniorhotel Sputnik, a modern hotel beside a large pond, is open all year and comfortable double rooms are US$14 per person for YHA or student-card holders (or several times that for others). Ask if breakfast is included. This place is often full up with groups.

The *YMCA* (☎ 498 005), on the corner of Šancová and Karpatská, has 13 doubles at US$13, six triples at US$20 and one five-bedded room at US$33 but they're often full. It's conveniently located just an eight-minute downhill walk from the main train station, so you could always give it a try upon arrival.

In July and August the 12-storey *Študentský Domov Jura Hronca* (☎ 497 721), Bernolákova ulica 1, about five blocks east of the main train station, rents beds in doubles at US$7 per person. There's a swimming pool and disco (audible throughout the building). Ask CKM about this gigantic student dormitory or just go there direct.

Študentský domos 'Mladá Garda' (☎ 253 136), Račianska 103, north-east of town (tram No 3, 5, 7 or 11), provides accommodation in this large student dormitory complex from July to mid-September only. The communal showers are hidden way down in the basement.

Private Rooms Satur, Jesenského 1-3, arranges private room accommodation for about US$10/15 single/double. The rooms are 20 minutes by tram from the centre.

Your best all-round accommodation stop is the Bratislava Information Service, Panská 18, which rents private rooms near the centre at US$15/18 single/double and knows about cheaper hotels out in the suburbs where rooms begin around US$6 per person. In July and August they can tell you about student hostels where beds cost from US$3 to US$6 per person.

Reditour (☎ 335 174), Ursulinská 11, next to the Primate's Palace, has pricey private rooms at US$13 per person.

Hotels With the closure of the Carlton Hotel for reconstruction and the upgrading of the Palace Hotel, the already critical budget hotel situation in downtown Bratislava has become almost hopeless. The only moderately priced hotel in the centre is now the *Krym Hotel* (☎ 325 471), Šafárikovo námestie 7 (US$23/35 single/double without bath, US$28/45 with bath), but it's noisy and usually full.

Better is the *Gremium Pension* (☎ 321 818), Gorkého 11, at US$20/31 single/double including breakfast. Considering the alternatives and the excellent location it's a good bet if you can get one of the five rooms.

In the splurge category is *Chez David Pension* (☎ 313 824), Zámocká 13, a clean, modern hotel on the site of the old Jewish ghetto directly below the castle. The eight double rooms are US$52/65 single/double with bath and breakfast – the right choice if price isn't a big consideration.

The white, two-storey *Športhotel Trnávka* (☎ 223 497), Nerudova 8, next to a small stadium north-east of town, is seedy and the rooms are small but at US$12/16/23 single/double/triple with shared bath it's good value. Get there on trolleybus No 215 from Cintorínska ulica near Hotel Kyjev or trolleybus No 219 eastbound from Palárikova ulica just down the hill from the train station. On Friday and Saturday nights ask for a room away from the disco. In winter there's the constant sound of water trickling through the ancient radiators. It's often crowded with people from the former USSR waiting for onward visas.

Ask the Bratislava Information Service about the *Hotel Ineks* (☎ 277 2195), Nobelova 16 north-east of the centre, which sometimes rents rooms at US$6 per person. Going directly there is risky as they're often closed and it's a long way to go for nothing (BIS can sell you a map to help you find the place). Also ask BIS about the *Clubhotel*, Odbojárov 3 off Vajnorská, which also has a tendency to close at the most unexpected times.

The hostel of the *Institute for Adult Education in the Building Industry* or 'Ústav Vzdelávania v Stavebníctve' (☎ 372 060), Bardošová 33, on a hill 1.5 km north-west of the main train station, is not breathtaking value at US$17 per person but the accommodation is good. This place is often full, so ask someone to help you call ahead before going there (take trolleybus No 212 from Hodžovo námestie).

Zlaté piesky There are bungalows, a motel, a hotel and two camping grounds at Zlaté piesky (Golden Sands), which is near a clear blue lake seven km north-east of Bratislava. Trams No 2 (from the main train station) and No 4 (from the city centre) terminate right at Zlaté piesky. You can hire rowing boats and sailboards here in summer and there are also tennis courts.

As you cross the bridge from the tram stop you'll see *Hotel Flora* (☎ 257 988) on your left. Double rooms here are US$27 with shower (no singles) and the hotel restaurant is open until 10 pm daily. Next to the Flora is a lakeside camping ground (☎ 257 373) with 50 four-bed cottages without bath at US$18 for the unit and 20 three-bed bungalows with private bath at US$31. Tent camping is possible and the facility is open from mid-April to mid-October. A second, poorer camping ground with run-down three-bed bungalows at US$20 triple is nearby (but not on the lake). Camping here is handled at the reception but the bungalows are controlled by *Motel Evona Zlaté Piesky* (☎ 257 365) a couple of minutes away. The 35 double rooms with bath at the motel are US$22 (no singles). Motel Evona is open year-round but the bungalows are only available from mid-May to September.

Places to Eat

Budget One of the few places to get an early

breakfast is *Cukráreň Jezbera*, námestie SNP 11, which opens at 6.30 am Monday to Saturday, 8 am Sunday. The stand-up buffet in the basement, which you enter from around the corner, opens an hour later and not at all on weekends. On weekends the upstairs section of the Jezbera is a good choice for lunch or dinner and the menu is in English.

The *Food Market* found on the corner of Hviezdoslavovo námestie and Rybárska brána (open daily from 9 am to 10 pm), caters for a dozen cuisines at individual counters in the stand-up section or you can sit down and order spaghetti or pizza in the adjacent full-service restaurant.

The *Diétna Jedáleň Restaurant*, Laurinská 8, is a great place for lunch (open weekdays only from 11 am to 4 pm). Ask the person in line behind you to translate the menu. It's self-service but you can get beer and there's a pleasant dining room where you sit down to eat. Note the floral arrangements hanging from the walls. Next door is the similar *Vegetariánská Jedáleň* which keeps identical hours.

Another self-service vegetarian restaurant is in the passageway at Obchodná 68 (Monday to Thursday 11.30 am to 3.30 pm, Friday 10 am to 3 pm only). It's one of the least expensive places to eat in Bratislava and really is vegetarian!

The pizzas served at *Picco Pizza*, Obchodná 45 (closed Sunday), are small and dry (most people douse them in ketchup), and the drinks expensive. An excellent beer garden is directly behind Picco but unfortunately you can't get takeaway pizza to carry back there. A stand adjacent to Picco sells *piróžky*, a sweet Slovakian doughnut.

At the bus station, the *Bistro Express* on the outer back side of the station facing the buses is much better than the self-service inside the station itself.

In summer check out the *Občerstvenie Beer Garden* at námestie SNP 28/30.

Top End A slightly up-market but still affordable place for a better meal is the *Korzo Restaurant*, Hviezdoslavovo námestie 11. Gypsy musicians occasionally play here.

A wine restaurant worth trying is *Vináreň Vel'ký františkáni*, Frantiákánske námestie 10, in the old monastery beside the Mirbach Palace. Other typical smoky wine-cellars, known as *pod viechou*, where Gypsy music is often played, are found in Baštová and Zámočnícka alleys near the Michael Tower.

The *Modrá Hviezda Restaurant*, Beblavého ulica 14 on the way up to the castle, features local dishes such as cheese pie. The menu is in English.

Chez David Kosher Restaurant, Zámocká 13 directly below the castle, is up-market but not intolerably so. Carp served in the Jewish manner is a speciality.

Stará Sladovňa, Cintorínska 32 (daily until 11 pm), between the Prior Department Store and the bus station, is a large, modern restaurant complex-cum-beer hall dating back to 1872 but reconstructed in 1980 as an eating and drinking place for the masses. The service is variable, the menu only in Slovak and the waiters will tell you the cheaper dishes are unavailable, then bring you things you didn't order merely to inflate your bill. Treat Stará Sladovňa strictly as a drinking place and eat elsewhere.

Cafés *Espresso Cukráreň*, Hviezdoslavovo námestie 25 (closed Monday), is just the place for coffee and cakes.

Another good coffee, cakes and ice-cream place is *Atlantis*, Stúrovo 13 (daily until 9 pm). They have Bratislava's best ice cream and on Sunday afternoon the queue runs out the door and down the pavement.

The *Gremium Art Galerie Café*, Gorkého 11, is the place to sip a pseudo-intellectual cup of Viennese coffee *(Viedenská káva)* without having to be pretentious. The atmosphere is good.

Entertainment

Opera and ballet are presented at the *Slovak National Theatre* (1886), on Hviezdoslavovo námestie (often closed Sunday). The local opera and ballet companies are outstanding. Tickets are sold at the 'Pokladňa

Kassa' office (open weekdays from noon to 6 pm) on the corner of Jesenského ulica and Komenského námestie, behind the National Theatre. An hour before the performance begins ticket sales are at the theatre itself, but they're usually sold out by then, especially on weekends.

The *nová scéna*, Kollárovo námestie 20, presents operettas, musicals – and drama in Slovak – so you have to check. The ticket office is open weekdays from 12.30 to 6 pm and an hour before the performance but they're usually sold out *(vypredané)*.

The *Slovenská filharmonia* is based in the neo-rococo Reduta Palace (built in 1914) on Palackého on the corner of Mostová, across the park from the National Theatre. The ticket office (open weekdays from 1 to 5 pm) is inside the building.

The PKO Predpredaj Vstupeniek, Hviezdoslovo námestie 24, has tickets for special events such as rock concerts.

The *Štátne Bábkóvé Divadlo*, Dunajská 36, puts on puppet shows for kids, usually at 9 or 10 am and sometimes again at 1 or 2 pm. It's good fun.

There's often something happening at Dom Kultury, námestie SNP 12.

Charlie's Pub, Špitálska 4 near Hotel Kyjev (daily from 4 pm to 4 am), is like a disco without the dancing (and without the cover charge). It's probably the most popular meeting and drinking place in town for the city youth.

Discos *Danglár Klub VŠVU-Friedl*, Hviezdoslavovo námestie 18 (downstairs through the smaller entrance to one side), is a student club open weekdays from 11 am to 3 am, weekends 6 pm to 3 am. Friday nights from 8 pm to midnight there's live jazz here (US$1 cover charge on Friday, other nights US$0.50). Apart from the bar and friendly staff, Danglár is a good place to eat and the kitchen stays open until midnight. Prices are reasonable. On Saturday night the locale is often booked by wedding parties.

Klub Rock-Pop-Jazz, Jakubovo námestie 12, a few blocks east of Hotel Krym, is one of the best places near the centre (opens at 8.30 pm).

MM Night Club 'Dimitrovec', on Nobelova (tram No 3, 5, 7 or 11 north-east to Vinohrady Railway Station), is a laser disco open daily from 8 pm to 5 am (US$2 cover). It's spacious and has four bars, but only expensive small cans of beer are available so you ought to have a couple of drinks at the adjacent *Queen's Pub* before going in.

Cinemas In the same complex as Charlie's Pub, Špitálska 4, are cinemas Marilyn and Charlie, Bratislava's best art cinemas. Other cinemas in the centre include Kino Mladosť, Hviezdoslavovo námestie 17, Kino Mier, Grösslingová ulica 23, Kino Slovan, námestie SNP 14, Kino Tatra, námestie 1 mája 5, and Kino Hviezda, námestie 1 mája 9. Near the train station, there's a cinema at the YMCA, Karpatská 2. Films are shown in the original language with Slovak subtitles and admission prices are low.

SLOVAKIA

Getting There & Away

Bus At Bratislava's main bus station you can usually buy your ticket from the driver, but check first at the information counter. Advance tickets may be purchased for the buses marked 'R' on the posted timetable. The footnotes on this timetable are in English.

Ten express buses a day run to Prague (one hour faster than the train for about the same price) and there are 13 buses a day to Komárno (104 km). Other buses leaving Bratislava include six to Košice (402 km), four to Bardejov (457 km), three to Prešov (429 km) and two each to Banská Štiavnica and Tatranská Lomnica.

Six buses a day connect Vienna (Mitte Busbahnhof) to Bratislava (63 km, US$9). In Bratislava buy your ticket for this bus at the ticket window inside the bus station.

Other international buses posted at the bus station are those to Brussels (weekly, US$72), Budapest (three a week, US$9), Cologne (weekly, US$96), Frankfurt (weekly, US$88), Kraków (two a week,

US$12), London (weekly, US$108), Munich (weekly, US$52), Paris (weekly, US$75), Salzburg (weekly, US$38), Sofia (two a week, US$47), Stockholm (weekly, US$119) and Thessaloniki (weekly, US$85). Tickets may be purchased for crowns at any of the ticket windows in the bus station or at the adjacent office with the yellow sign 'Obchodná agentúra'. If you require a Czech visa beware of buses which transit that country as you could be 'bumped off' at the border.

Trains All express trains between Budapest and Prague call at Bratislava. Train services from Košice to Bratislava (via Poprad-Tatry, Žilina and Trenčín) are fairly frequent and couchettes are available on the night train.

If you can't find a reasonable place to stay in Bratislava, go to the train station and book a couchette or sleeper to Košice (445 km) or Prague (398 km) for that night. Don't forget that you'll need a regular train ticket along with the couchette ticket. In total a 1st-class sleeper and ticket shouldn't cost you more than you would have had to pay for a hotel room anyway.

There are four local trains a day between Vienna (Südbahnhof) and Bratislava Hlavná stanica (64 km, 1½ hours, US$8). One nightly train departs for Moscow but there's no direct service to Poland. International train tickets are available at Hlavná stanica.

Two local trains a day run from Bratislava Nové Mesto Station to Györ, Hungary (90 km, two hours, US$9), via Rajka. The ticket office in Nové Mesto Railway Station will only sell you a ticket as far as the border (US$0.50) and you must pay the Hungarian conductor the balance. Otherwise buy a through ticket at Hlavná stanica or from Satur the day before.

Walking into Hungary or Austria If you don't want to bother getting an international train ticket, take a local train or bus to Komárno and walk across the bridge to Komárom in Hungary. See the Komárno section for details.

The Austrian border is about four km beyond most SNP along Viedenská cesta. Take bus No 47 from Hodžovo námestie southbound across the bridge and get off at the next stop after high-rise Hotel Incheba. Walk two km to the border, clear customs and stick out your thumb: Vienna is 64 km west.

Boat From mid-April to September, Raketa hydrofoils ply the Danube between Bratislava and Vienna twice a day for US$19 one way, US$30 return (1¼ hours). In October the service is only daily. Children aged 15 years and under and students pay half-price. Tickets and information are available at the hydrofoil terminal in Bratislava. In late summer the service can be interrupted because of low water levels.

It makes an interesting day trip if your visa allows you to return to Slovakia; a day in Vienna is probably enough, especially considering how outrageously expensive it is. The scenery between Bratislava and Vienna is surprisingly dull and there are no boats downriver to Budapest, a much more scenic trip.

Getting Around

Public transport around Bratislava is based on an extensive tram network that is complemented by buses and trolleybuses. Orange automats at tram and trolleybus stops sell tickets, but make sure that the green light is on before inserting any coins.

Tourist tickets *(turistické cestovné lístky)* valid for 24 hours (US$1), 48 hours (US$2) or seven days (US$3) are sold at the DPHMB office in the underground passageway below Hodžovo námestie (weekdays from 7 am to 6 pm). At Bratislava Hlavná stanica these tickets are sold at the window marked 'Cestovné Lístky' next to the taxi stand in front of the station. The validity of the ticket begins immediately upon purchase, so only buy one when you need it.

Bratislava's taxis all have meters and they're far less likely to try to overcharge you than those in Prague. Downtown Bratislava is small enough for you to be able to walk almost anywhere.

To/From the Airport Airport buses leave from the ČSA office, Štúrova ulica 13 (three or four a day, US$0.20). You can also get to Ivanka International Airport on city bus No 24 from the train station (eight km).

Car Rental Budget Rent-a-Car is represented by Tatratour, Františkánske námestie 3. Pragocar (☎ 333 233) is at Hviezdoslovo námestie 14 (in the courtyard) and Europcar (☎ 340 841) is in the lobby of nearby Hotel Danube. Hertz has a desk in the lobby of Hotel Forum. Hertz and Europcar also have desks at Ivanka airport.

West Slovakia

KOMÁRNO

This Danube border town opposite Komárom, Hungary, is a convenient entry/exit point for travellers in transit between Slovakia and Hungary. Frequent trains with low domestic fares run between these twin cities and their respective capitals, Bratislava and Budapest, and it costs nothing to walk across the massive river bridge erected in 1892. By coming this way you not only avoid the hassle and expense of an international train ticket but you have a chance to compare conditions on both sides of the border up close.

Three-quarters of the inhabitants of Komárno are Hungarian and it's mostly Hungarian you hear spoken in the shops. Komárno serves as the cultural and political centre of the large Hungarian community in south Slovakia, and all street signs in Komárno are written in Slovak and Hungarian. Across the river in Komárom they're in Hungarian and German. Of the twin cities, Komárno is by far the more interesting and less touristy, although you don't have the thermal baths found in Komárom.

As at Komárom, the Habsburgs erected impressive fortifications here between 1541 and 1592 to hold back the Turks, who never managed to capture the town. The defensive system was rebuilt and greatly expanded during the Napoleonic wars. The large shipyards at Komárno founded in 1898 build both river and ocean-going vessels.

Orientation

The bus and train stations in Komárno are close to one another. To get to the border from the stations, walk due south on Petöfiho ulica to the end of the street, then left a block and right at Azia Centrum Department Store. Continue south past Hotel Európa to the bridge, a 20-minute walk from the stations. The left-luggage office in the train station is open irregularly (try your luck with one of the coin lockers).

Slovakian and Hungarian customs are together on a peninsula in the middle of the river. For conditions on the Hungarian side, turn to the Komárom section in the Hungary chapter.

Information

Money The Všeobecná Úverová Banka has an exchange office on Tržničné námestie midway between hotels Európa and Danubius, just as you come into town from the bridge. They change travellers' cheques for 1% commission weekdays from 7.30 am to noon and 1 to 5 pm.

The VUB also runs an exchange office right next to customs on the bridge itself (open 7 am to 6 pm and 7 pm to 6 am daily). Their rate for cash is as good as any in town.

The exchange office in the post office behind Hotel Európa will change excess crowns into forints weekdays from 8 am to noon and 2 to 6 pm and Saturday 8 am to noon. They deduct 2% commission weekdays, 3% on Saturday.

Post & Telephone The main post office directly behind Hotel Európa contains a telephone centre open weekdays from 8 am to 6 pm and Saturday 8 am to 1 pm. Komárno's telephone code is 0819.

Things to See

The two tall towers of **St Andrew's Church** (1734) on Palatínova ulica are visible from afar. Directly opposite the church is the

SLOVAKIA

Danube Museum (closed Sunday and Monday) with a small historical collection and one room of paintings. East on Palatínova is námestie gen Klapku with several attractive monuments and the **town hall** (1875). East again in the same direction is the massive 18th-century **fortress** near the junction of the Váh and Danube rivers. It's still occupied by the military and is inaccessible.

Komárno's most interesting museum (closed Monday) is the one dedicated to composer Ferenc Lehár and novelist Jókai Mór which is right next to the approach to the bridge to Hungary. Admission includes the adjacent 18th-century Serbian Orthodox church with its interesting woodcarvings.

Places to Stay

Your best bet is the *Hotel Danubius* (☎ 44 91), Dunajské nábrežie 12, on the corner of Lehárova ulica (US$10 single or double without bath). As you're walking north across the bridge from Hungary you'll see a yellow three-storey building down on the right with the words 'Spoločenský dom' on the roof. This is the hotel.

The 57 rooms at *Hotel Európa* (☎ 42 51),

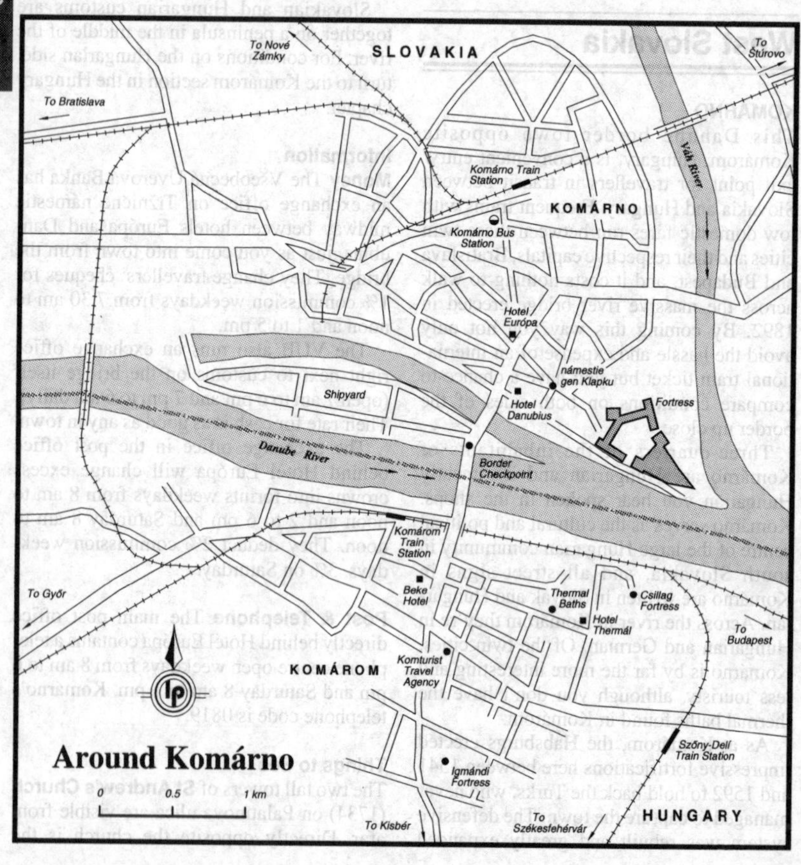

náměstie Štefánika 1, are overpriced at US$22/36/45 single/double/triple with bath and breakfast. Rooms with only a shower and no toilet are a few dollars cheaper. This undistinguished, three-storey building on the road to the bridge is only 500 metres from the border.

Places to Eat

Pizzeria Rigoletto in the sharp, modern Mestské Kultúrne Stredisko, Hradná 1, has inexpensive pizza and beer. *Restaurant Lehár* facing the park next to Hotel Danubius is also said to be good. *Zlata Ryba*, Lehárova ulica 12 next to Hotel Danubius (closed Sunday), is a very cheap stand-up buffet.

Getting There & Away

Eight buses a day run between Bratislava and Komárno (104 km). Otherwise take one of the six local trains to/from Bratislava Nové Mesto Railway Station (94 km, two hours). A list of all trains leaving Komárno is posted at the Hotel Európa reception.

Bus and train services north from Komárno to Trenčín and Žilina are very poor and you're probably better going through Bratislava. Theoretically there are three buses a day to Trnava and one to Trenčín but the departures board bears numerous confusing footnotes, so check with information (if it's open).

A bus to the Hungarian train station across the river leaves from in front of the train station five times a day.

TRENČÍN

For centuries, here where the Váh River valley begins to narrow between the White Carpathians and the Strážov Hills, Trenčín Castle guarded the south-west gateway to Slovakia and one of the routes from the Danube to the Baltic. Laugaricio, a Roman military post – the northernmost Roman camp in Central Europe – was established here in the 2nd century AD. A rock inscription at Trenčín dated 179 AD mentions the stay of the Roman 2nd Legion and its victory over the Germanic Kvad tribes.

The mighty castle which now towers above the town was first mentioned in 1069 in a Viennese illustrated chronicle. In the 13th century the castle's master, Matúš Čák, held sway over much of Slovakia and in 1412 Trenčín obtained the rights of a free royal city. The present castle dates from that period, and although both castle and town were destroyed by fire in 1790, much has been restored. Today Trenčín is a centre of the textile industry.

Orientation & Information

From the adjacent bus and train stations walk west through the park and take the Tatra Passage under the highway to Mierové námestie, the main square.

Information is available from Satur, Hviezdoslavova 2 (upstairs).

Money The Všeobecná Úverová Banka, Mierové námestie 37 opposite the Tatra Passage, changes travellers' cheques Monday to Thursday from 7.15 to 11 am and 2 to 5 pm, and Friday from 7.30 to 11.30 am only.

Post & Telephone The telephone centre in the main post office, Mierové námestie 21, is open weekdays from 7.30 am to 8 pm, Saturday 8 am to 2 pm, Sunday 8 am to noon.

Trenčín's telephone code is 0831.

Things to See

At the south-western end of Mierové námestie are the baroque **Piarist Church** and the 16th-century **town gate**. The **art gallery** (closed Monday) in the former Piarist convent next to this church features works by local artists, especially the realist painter M A Bazovský.

A covered stairway from the corner of the square opposite the Piarist Church leads up to the Gothic **parish church** and the entrance to **Trenčín Castle** (open daily all year). The so-called 'Well of Love' on the first terrace is a fantastic construction that is 70 metres deep. Above is the castle's great central tower which provides a sweeping view of the whole area. At night the castle is

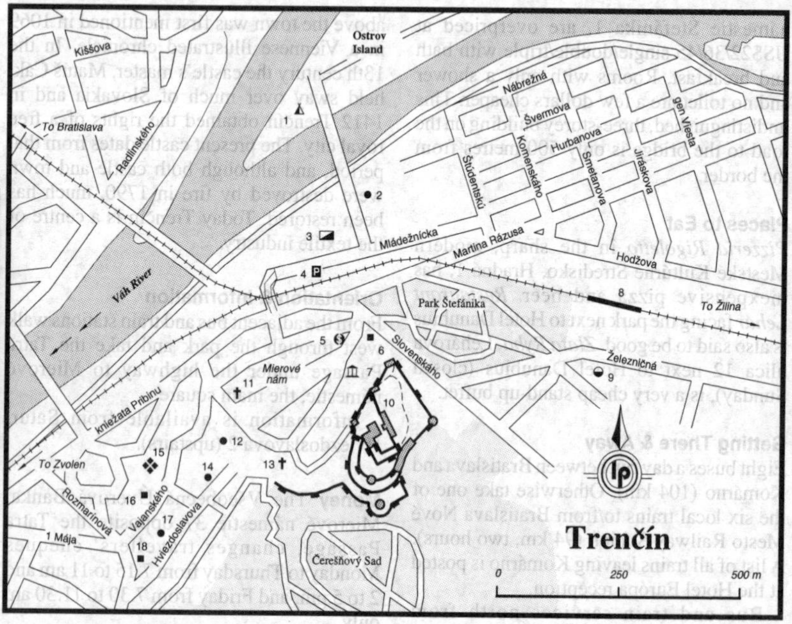

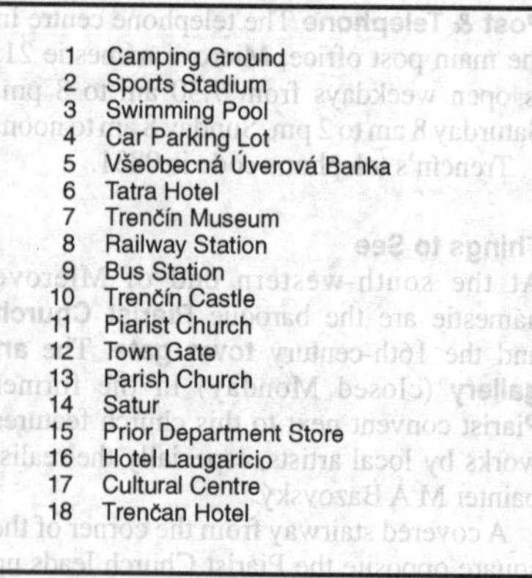

1 Camping Ground
2 Sports Stadium
3 Swimming Pool
4 Car Parking Lot
5 Všeobecná Úverová Banka
6 Tatra Hotel
7 Trenčín Museum
8 Railway Station
9 Bus Station
10 Trenčín Castle
11 Piarist Church
12 Town Gate
13 Parish Church
14 Satur
15 Prior Department Store
16 Hotel Laugaricio
17 Cultural Centre
18 Trenčan Hotel

illuminated with fairy tale green and purple lights.

The famous Roman inscription of 179 AD is behind the Tatra Hotel at the north-eastern end of Mierové námestie and not directly accessible from the castle. The **Trenčín Museum** (closed Monday), Mierové námestie 46, is next to the Tatra Hotel.

Places to Stay

Camping The *Vodácky Klub Ostrove Camping Ground* (☎ 34 013) is on Ostrov, an island in the Váh River, opposite the large sports stadium near the city centre. Camping is US$1 per person, US$1.50 per tent, and nice little two and four-bed cabins are US$3 per person. Singles are accommodated for the same price aboard the ex-hydrofoil *Raketa*, now permanently moored at the camping ground. Though the rooms are often full, this place is well worth trying if you arrive between June and August.

Hotels Rooms at the nine-storey *Hotel Laugaricio* (☎ 37 841), on Vajanského námestie, next to the Prior Department Store on the edge of the old town, a 10-minute walk from the train station, cost US$17 single without bath, US$34 double with bath.

The basic old *Trenčan Hotel* (☎ 33 117), Braneckého 7, just around the corner from the Hotel Laugaricio, costs US$18/23 triple/quad (no singles or doubles). Use of the communal showers is US$1.50.

Getting There & Away

All express trains on the main railway line from Bratislava to Košice via Žilina stop here. The *Báthory* and *Bem* express trains to/from Poland stop at Trenčín in the middle of the night but reservations and (in some cases) a Czech visa are required. Take a bus to go to/from Brno (134 km).Trenčín

TRENČIANSKE TEPLICE

Trenčianske Teplice, a spa in a narrow valley 14 km north-east of Trenčín, is a worthwhile day trip and an alternative place to stay. Hiking trails lead into the green hills flanking the resort and there's a **thermal swimming pool** open to the public at the Zelená žába (Green Frog) Restaurant on the hillside just above the spa (open daily until 6 pm from May to September, US$0.50).

Also visit the 'hamman', an exotic neo-Moorish bathhouse (1888) in the middle of town. The five hot sulphur springs at the spa are used to treat rheumatic and nervous system diseases. There are many attractive parks and from June to September a varied cycle of musical programmes is presented at Trenčianske Teplice. You can buy the circular spa wafers (and see them being made) at Kúpel'né Oblátky, ulica Masaryka 14.

Places to Stay

The *Hotel Jalta* (☎ 29 91), a modern five-storey hotel near the train station, is US$21/33 single/double with bath.

The Satur office (☎ 23 61) inside the Liečebny dom Pol'nohospodárov Spa House, ulica 17 novembra 14, has private rooms, but there's a minimum stay of one week (cost is US$42/56 a single/double for the week).

Getting There & Away

Trenčianske Teplice is accessible via a six-km branch line from Trenčianska Teplá on the main railway line between Trenčín and Žilina. Electric tram-type trains shuttle back and forth about once an hour.

Central Slovakia

ŽILINA

Žilina, midway between Bratislava and Košice, at the junction of the Váh and Kysuca rivers, is the gateway to the Malá Fatra Mountains. Since its foundation in the 13th century at a crossing of medieval trade routes, Žilina has been an important transportation hub, a status that was confirmed with the arrival of railways from Košice in 1871 and Bratislava in 1883. Though the third largest city in Slovakia, it's still a pleasant, untouristy town with an attractive main square and many interesting shops.

Orientation

The adjacent bus and train stations are near the Váh River on the north-eastern side of town, a five-minute walk from Mariánske námestie, Žilina's old town square. Another five minutes south from Mariánske námestie is Štúrovo námestie, with the Cultural Centre and the luxurious Hotel Slovakia.

Information

Satur (☎ 48 512) is at Štúrovo námestie 3, but don't expect much from them.

CKM Student Travel, Hodžova ulica 8, is just off Mariánske námestie.

Tatratour, Mariánske námestie 21, is the American Express representative.

Money The Všeobecná Úverová Banka, Na bráne 1, changes travellers' cheques (weekdays from 7.30 to 11 am and 1 to 5 pm, Wednesday 7.30 am to noon only).

Post & Telephone The telephone centre in the post office next to the train station is open weekdays from 7 am to 8.30 pm, Saturday 7 am to 3 pm, Sunday 8 am to 2 pm.

Žilina's telephone code is 089.

Things to See

Žilina's central square with its picturesque church and covered walkway all around could have been lifted straight out of Mexico. Other than this, the only sight worth seeking out is the **Regional Museum** (closed Monday) in the Renaissance castle *(zámok)* across the river in Budatín, a 15-minute walk north-west from the train station. As you come out of the train station, turn right and go straight ahead for a few minutes, then go right under the train tracks and straight again till you reach the bridge over the river. The white castle tower is visible from there.

Places to Stay

The *Metropol Hotel* (☎ 29 300), right opposite the train station, is the least expensive at US$8 per person without bath – a triple is the same price as three singles. The rooms have a sink and double doors which keep out corridor noise but use of the communal showers is US$0.50 extra. They almost always have rooms.

Also opposite the train station is the more up-market *Hotel Polom* (☎ 21 152) which charges US$18/26 for singles/doubles with private bath and breakfast. Žilina's casino is here.

The *Športklub Hotel* (☎ 22 164), Na strelnici 1, beyond the stadium on the back side of the train station, has rooms at US$8 per person. You check in at the restaurant.

If these places are full, you can always resort to the recently renovated *Hotel Slovan* (☎ 20 556), Kmetova 2, behind the Prior Department Store, back towards the train station (US$25/30 double/triple with bath, TV and breakfast, no singles).

Places to Eat

If you want to eat standing up, try the *Potravinárske Centrum L'udová Jedáleň* in a white four-storey building on a corner near the bus station. It serves hearty breakfasts of goulash soup and beer from 5 am weekdays, from 6 am Saturday (closed Sunday).

The trendy *Vegetariánska Reštaurácia*, Mariánska námestie 11, is fine for what it is, though some of the dishes are pretty unimaginative (for example, lentils and rice with a fried egg).

Non-vegetarians may prefer the *Reštaurácia na bráne*, Bottova 10. The beer hall downstairs and the wine restaurant upstairs are mostly drinking places, but the menu is extensive.

In summer the tables come outside at the *Záhradná Reštaurácia*, ulica Hurbana 24 (through the alley), and it becomes a great place to sit at picnic tables and guzzle draught beer.

Piccollo Pizzeria, Zaymusova 4 near Satur, is a new private place with a nice back terrace where you can down pseudo-pizza and cheap red wine to the beat of rock music.

Getting There & Away

Žilina is on the main railway line from Bratislava to Košice via Trenčín and Poprad-Tatry, and is served by fairly frequent express trains. Most trains between Prague and Košice also stop at Žilina. Express trains from Žilina take six hours to reach Prague (466 km), 1½ hours to Trenčín (80 km), three hours to Bratislava (203 km), two hours to Poprad-Tatry (141 km) and three hours to Košice (242 km).

There are several buses a day to Brno (134 km), but none to Prague.

To/from Poland, if you don't require a Czech visa you can take a local train from Žilina to Český Těšín (69 km) and walk across the border (see the Český Těšín section in the Czech Republic chapter). If you do need a separate Czech visa you will have to avoid that route and go via Poprad and the Javorina/Łysa Polana border crossing to Zakopane.

Both of the express trains between Hungary and Poland which call at Žilina in the middle of the night, the *Bem* and the *Polonia*, also transit the Czech Republic and require mandatory seat reservations.

THE MALÁ FATRA

The Malá Fatra (Little Fatra) Mountains stretch 50 km across north-western Slovakia; Vel'ký Kriváň (1709 metres) is the highest peak. Two hundred sq km of this scenic range, north of the Váh River and east of Žilina, are included in the Malá Fatra National Park. At the heart of the park is Vrátna, a beautiful mountain valley enclosed by forested slopes on all sides.

Noted for its rich flora, the Vrátna Valley has something for everyone. The hiking possibilities vary from easy tourist tracks through the forest to scenic ridge walks. There are plenty of places to stay and eat, though in midsummer accommodation is tight. The valley is an easy day trip from Žilina. In winter Vrátna becomes a popular ski resort and has many lifts operating.

Information

The Mountain Rescue Service (Horská Služba), on the access road to Hotel Boboty, can provide detailed information on the park.

Things to See & Do

The bus from Žilina enters the Vrátna Valley just south of Terchová where it runs through the **Tiesňavy Pass** which has rocky crags on both sides. One rock resembles a person praying (look back after you've gone through the pass).

Stay on the bus until **Chata Vrátna** (750 metres) where detailed maps of the area are posted. From just above Chata Vrátna, a two-seater chair lift climbs 770 metres to the Snilovské sedlo (1520 metres), a saddle midway between Chleb (1647 metres) and Vel'ký Kriváň (1709 metres). Take along a sweater or jacket as it will be a lot cooler on top. The chair lift (US$2 return) only runs if at least 20 people are present – no problem in summer when there may be a queue. In rain the chair lift doesn't operate at all as there's no protection.

From Snilovské sedlo you can follow the red trail south-east along the mountain ridges past Hromové (1636 metres), then north-east to Poludňový grúň (1460 metres) and Stoh (1608 metres) to the **Medziholie Pass** (1185 metres) right below the rocky summit of **Vel'ký Rozsutec** (1610 metres). An orange trail skirting the side of Stoh allows you to avoid a 200-metre climb. From Medziholie it's easy to descend another green trail to **Štefanová**, a picturesque village of log houses with private rooms available (ask around). You can do the hike from Snilovské sedlo to Štefanová via Medziholie in about four hours. Other possible hikes from Snilovské sedlo are the blue trail to Starý Dvor via the ridges (three hours) and the red trail west to Strečno Railway Station via the Starý hrad castle ruins (6½ hours).

A good alternative if the chair lift isn't operating, or you don't have much time, is to take the yellow trail from Chata Vrátna to **Chata na Grúni** at 970 metres (45 minutes). This mountain chalet has 30 beds and a restaurant but it's often closed or full. From Chata na Grúni the blue trail descends to Štefanová (45 minutes), where you can get buses back to Žilina.

Places to Stay & Eat

No camping is allowed in the Vrátna Valley. The nearest camping grounds are at Nižné Kamence, three km west of Terchová, and at Varín, both on the way to/from Žilina.

Chata Vrátna (☎ 95 223), a large wooden chalet at 750 metres elevation with 88 beds, is usually full up with hikers in summer and skiers in winter. In spring and late autumn, groups of school children pack the dormitories. Regular hotel rooms at Chata Vrátna are US$15/19/22 double/triple/quad, while the *turistická ubytovňa* dormitory is US$4 to US$7 per person. A good self-service restaurant faces the bus stop below the hotel.

Chata pod Sokolím on the hillside above Reštaurácia Starý Dvor has 60 beds and a large restaurant. The view from here is great. It it's closed try *Pension Vahostav* about a km farther up the valley.

The *Chata Pod Skalným Mestom* (☎ 95 363), a few minutes up the green trail in Štefanová village, charges US$14 per person for bed, breakfast and dinner. A few hundred metres beyond is the similar *Chata Pod Lampá Šom*. Both are open year-round.

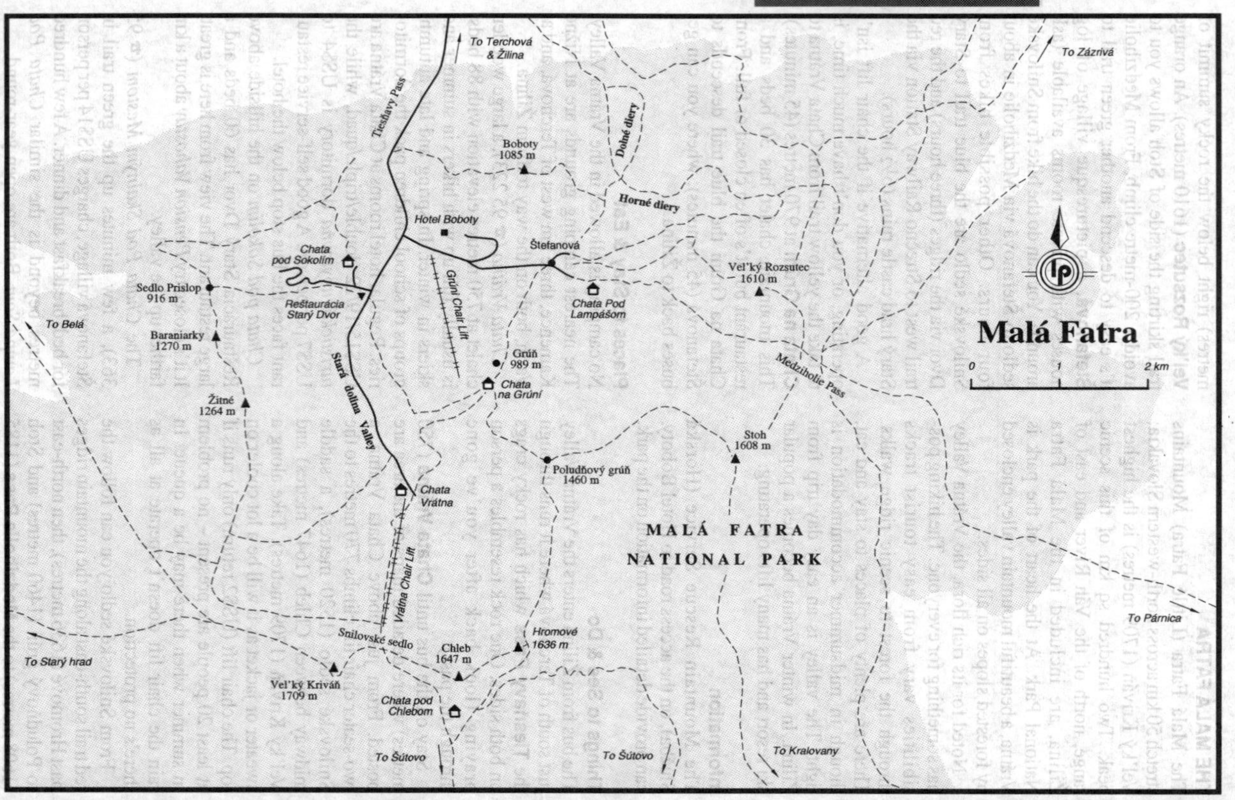
Malá Fatra
0
1
2 km
To Terchová & Žilina
To Zázrivá
Tiesňavy Pass
Boboty 1085 m
Dolné diery
Horné diery
Hotel Boboty
Štefanová
Chata pod Sokolím
Sedlo Prislop 916 m
Reštaurácia Starý Dvor
Grúni Chair Lift
Chata Pod Lampášom
Veľký Rozsutec 1610 m
To Belá
Baraniarky 1270 m
Grúň 989 m
Chata na Grúni
Medziholie Pass
Stará dolina Valley
Žitné 1264 m
Stoh 1608 m
Poludňový grúň 1460 m
Chata Vrátna
MALÁ FATRA NATIONAL PARK
Vrátna Chair Lift
To Párnica
Snilovské sedlo
Hromové 1636 m
Chleb 1647 m
To Starý hrad
Veľký Kriváň 1709 m
Chata pod Chlebom
To Šútovo
To Šútovo
To Kralovany

Reštaurácia Štefanová (☎ 95 325) at Štefanová rents cabins in the forest at US$5 per person year-round except in November.

The *Hotel Boboty* (☎ 95 227), a fairly luxurious mountain hotel, a five-minute walk up from a bus stop near Štefanová, costs US$19/29 single/double with shower and breakfast (higher in midsummer). The hotel also has a sauna, swimming pool and restaurant.

Getting There & Away

A bus from Žilina to Chata Vrátna, 32 km east (US$1), leaves from platform No 10 at the Žilina Bus Station about once an hour. The bus travels via Krasňany, which has a natural history museum, and Terchová, where a folk festival is held in July.

If you come on a day trip, check the times of afternoon buses returning to Žilina from Štefanová at the information counter in Žilina Bus Station before setting out.

East Slovakia

East Slovakia is one of the most attractive touring areas in Eastern Europe. In one compact region you can enjoy superb hiking in the High Tatra Mountains, rafting on the Dunajec River, historic towns such as Levoča and Bardejov, the great medieval castle at Spišské Podhradie, the lovely spa of Bardejovské Kúpele and city life in the capital Košice. The proximity of Ukraine gives the region an exotic air. Getting around is easy with frequent trains and buses to all these sights plus easy access to Poland and Hungary. In spite of all these advantages, exciting East Slovakia is still well off the beaten track.

THE VYSOKÉ TATRY

The Vysoké Tatry (High Tatras) are the only truly alpine mountains in Central Europe and one of the smallest high mountain ranges in the world. This 27-km-long granite massif covers 260 sq km, forming the northernmost portion of the Carpathian Mountains. The narrow, rocky crests soar above wide glacial valleys with precipitous walls. At 2655 metres, Gerlachovský štít (Mt Gerlach) is the highest mountain in the entire 1200-km Carpathian Mountains, and several dozen other peaks exceed 2500 metres.

Enhancing the natural beauty packed into this relatively small area are 30 valleys, almost 100 glacial lakes and bubbling streams. The lower slopes are covered by dense coniferous forests. From 1500 to 1800 metres altitude, there's a belt of brushwood and knee pines, and above this are alpine flora and bare peaks. (In short, the Slovakian High Tatras is the most appealing mountain resort area in Eastern Europe.)

Since 1949 most of the Slovakian portion of this jagged range has been included in the Tatra National Park (TANAP), the first national park to be created in former Czechoslovakia, which complements a similar park in Poland. A network of 600 km of hiking trails reaches all the alpine valleys and many peaks. The red-marked Tatranská Magistrála Trail follows the southern crest of the Vysoké Tatry for 65 km through a striking variety of landscapes. The routes are colour-coded and easy to follow. Park regulations require you to keep to the marked trails and refrain from picking flowers. A park entry fee of US$0.50 is collected in July and August.

Orientation

The best centre for visitors is Starý Smokovec, a turn-of-the-century resort that is well connected to the rest of the country by road and rail. Tram-style electric trains run frequently between the three main tourist centres in the park: Štrbské Pleso (1320 metres), Starý Smokovec (990 metres) and Tatranská Lomnica (850 metres). At Poprad-Tatry these trains link up with the national railway system. Buses also run frequently between the resorts. Cable cars, chair lifts and a funicular railway carry you up the slopes to hiking trails which soon lead you away from the throng. During winter, skiers flock to this area which offers excellent facilities.

All three main train stations have left-

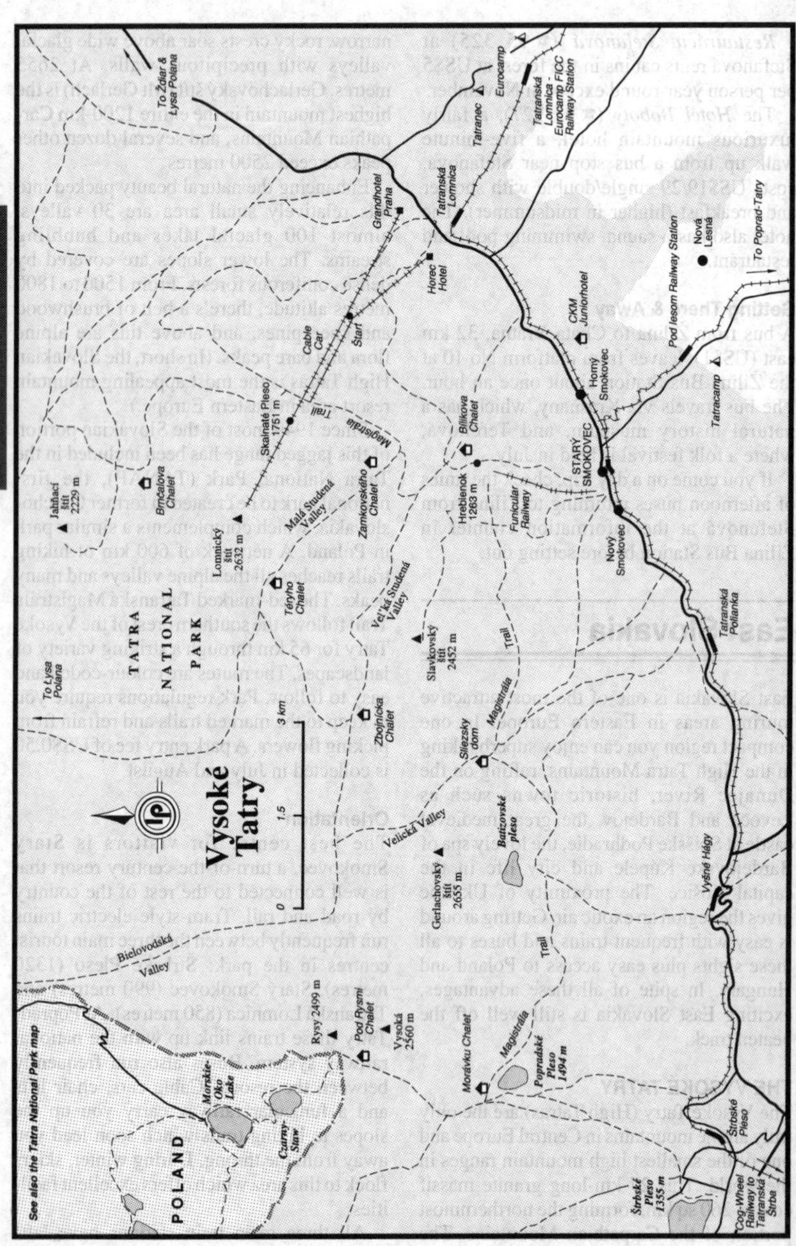
See also the Tatra National Park map
POLAND
Morskie-Oko Lake
Czarny Staw
To Ždiar & Lysa Polana
To Lysa Polana
TATRA NATIONAL PARK
Vysoké Tatry
0
1.5
3 km
Bielovodská Valley
Rysy 2499 m
Pod Rysmi Chalet
Vysoká 2560 m
Morávku Chalet
Magistrála
Popradské Pleso 1494 m
Gerlachovský štít 2655 m
Batizovské pleso
Velická Valley
Sliezsky dom
Trail
Zbojnícka Chalet
Slavkovský štít 2452 m
Téryho Chalet
Veľ'ká Studená Valley
Lomnický štít 2632 m
Jahňací štít 2229 m
Brnčalova Chalet
Zamkovského Chalet
Malá Studená Valley
Skalnaté Pleso 1751 m
Magistrala Trail
Cable Car
Štart
Horec Hotel
Grandhotel Praha
Tatranská Lomnica
Tatranec
Eurocamp
Tatranská Lomnica - Eurocamp FICC Railway Station
Hrebienok 1263 m
Bilíkova Chalet
Funicular Railway
STARÝ SMOKOVEC
Horný Smokovec
Nový Smokovec
CKM Juniorhotel
Tatracamp
Pod lesom Railway Station
Nová Lesná
To Poprad-Tatry
Tatranská Polianka
Vyšné Hágy
Štrbské Pleso
Štrbské Pleso 1355 m
Cog-Wheel Railway to Tatranská Štrba
SLOVAKIA

luggage offices, with those at Starý Smokovec and Tatranská Lomnica open 24 hours a day and the one at Štrbské Pleso Station open from 5 am to 10.30 pm.

Information
A helpful Satur office (☎ 27 10) is just above the train station at Starý Smokovec. Another main Satur office is upstairs in a building near the Tatranská Lomnica Railway Station. At Štrbské Pleso, Satur has a counter in the post office up the hill from the train station.

Our Vysoké Tatry map is intended for initial orientation only. Buy a proper *Vysoké Tatry* hiking map at a bookshop as soon as you arrive in Slovakia. Good maps are also usually available at hotels or newsstands inside the park. When buying your Tatras hiking map, make sure you get one with summer hiking trails and not the winter ski routes.

Money The Všeobecná Úverová Banka in the commercial centre above the bus station in Starý Smokovec changes travellers' cheques for 1% commission (open Monday to Thursday 7.30 to 11.30 am and 1.30 to 4 pm, Friday 7.30 am to noon).

The bank in the building next to Tatranská Lomnica Railway Station doesn't accept travellers' cheques.

Post & Telephone The telephone centre in the post office near Starý Smokovec Railway Station (ask directions to *'pošta')* is open weekdays from 7 am to 8 pm, Saturday 7 am to 6 pm, Sunday 8 am to noon.

The telephone code at all three High Tatras resorts is 0969.

Climate When planning your trip, keep in mind the altitude. At 750 metres the camping grounds will be too cold for a tent from October to mid-May. By November there's snow, and avalanches are a danger from November to June when the higher trails will be closed (ask someone to translate the *achtung* notices at the head of the trails for you). Some of the highest passes can have snow as early as September! Beware of sudden thunderstorms, especially in the alpine areas where there's no protection, and avoid getting lost if clouds set in. It's worth noting that the assistance of the Mountain Rescue Service is not free. July and August are the warmest (and most crowded) months, and August and September are the best for high-altitude hiking. Hotel prices are at their lowest from April to mid-June, the months with the longest daylight hours.

The TANAP horská služba (mountain rescue) office next to Satur in Starý Smokovec can give you a weather report for the next day.

Things to See

Above Starý Smokovec From Starý Smokovec a funicular railway (at 1025 metres) carries you up to **Hrebienok** (1280 metres), a ski resort with a view of the Vel'ká Studená Valley. The funicular railway (built in 1908) is closed in April and November and every Friday morning, but if it's not running it takes less than an hour to walk up to Hrebienok (green trail).

From Hrebienok the red Magistrála Trail carries you down to several waterfalls, such as Studenovodské vodopády and Obrovský vodopád.

For great scenery follow the blue trail to Zbojnícka Chalet in the Vel'ká Studená Valley (three hours). Beyond Zbojnícka the blue trail climbs over a 2428-metre pass and descends to the Polish border.

The green trail leads north to Téryho Chalet in the Malá Studená Valley (three hours). The Zamkovského (formerly Nálepkova) Chalet is just off the Magistrála, only an hour from Hrebienok up the same trail. The round trip from Hrebienok to Zamkovského, Téryho and Zbojnícka back to Hrebienok would take about eight hours. The trail from Téryho to Zbojnícka is one way, only in that direction.

Štrbské Pleso Take a morning train to the famous ski resort Štrbské Pleso and its glacial lake (at 1355 metres). Swimming is possible in summer. After a look around this smart health and ski resort, take the

Magistrála Trail up to **Popradské Pleso**, an idyllic lake at 1494 metres elevation (a little over one hour). In Štrbské Pleso the Magistrála begins near Hotel Patria, where a pedestrian bridge crosses the main road at the entrance to Helios Sanatorium. Have lunch at the Morávku Chalet right next to Popradské Pleso. From here the Magistrála zigzags up the mountainside towards Sliezsky dom and Hrebienok. A better bet is to hike up the blue trail from Popradské Pleso to the Hincovo lakes in another hour and a half.

SLOVAKIA

Via Tatranská Lomnica A recommended round trip begins with a morning train from Starý Smokovec to Tatranská Lomnica. In 1937 a **cable car** able to carry 30 people at a time began operating, going from the resort up to **Skalnaté Pleso** (1751 metres); an extension to Lomnický štít (2632 metres) was completed in 1941. As soon as you arrive, visit the cable-car station near the Grandhotel Praha in Tatranská Lomnica to pick up tickets (US$2 one way) for the ride to Skalnaté Pleso. The cable car (closed Tuesday) is very popular with tourists, so you have to get to the office early to book the trip.

In 1973 a second, smaller cable-car line (closed Monday) with four-seat cabins was built to Skalnaté Pleso via Štart from above the Horec Hotel in Tatranská Lomnica. It doesn't operate when there's too much wind (at last report this cable car was closed for reconstruction).

While you're waiting for your departure time to roll around, visit the **Museum of Tatra National Park**, a few hundred metres from the bus station at Tatranská Lomnica (open weekdays from 8.30 am to 5 pm, weekends from 8 am to noon). The exhibition on the natural and human histories of this area is excellent.

There's a large observatory at Skalnaté Pleso and a smaller cable car (US$4 return) to the summit of **Lomnický štít** where you get a sweeping view of the entire High Tatra Range. If you're lucky the service will be running, the sky will be clear and you won't have to wait too long to go. You're only allowed 30 minutes at Lomnický štít and if you miss your car down you'll have to wait around until another car has room for you (maximum capacity 15 persons). From Skalnaté Pleso it's only two hours down the Magistrála Trail to Hrebienok and the funicular railway back to Starý Smokovec.

If you visit the High Tatra Mountains during a peak period when the place is overflowing with tourists, you can do the Skalnaté Pleso-Hrebienok trip in reverse. It's a lot easier to get in the cable car at Skalnaté Pleso for a ride down than at Tatranská Lomnica for a ride up. Hundreds of people may be waiting to get on at Tatranská Lomnica.

Activities

In summer Satur offers several interesting bus excursions from the Vysoké Tatry resorts. The weekly trip to the Demänovská jaskyňa Caves near Liptovský Mikuláš also includes a chair-lift ride to Chopok Peak (2024 metres) in the Nízke Tatry (US$13). Rafting on the Dunajec River is offered four times a week from June to September (US$13). You can make bookings at Satur offices in any of the three High Tatras resorts but the trips don't happen unless at least 30 people sign up.

Mountain Climbing You can reach the summit of Slavkovský štít (2452 metres) in nine hours on a round trip via the blue trail from Starý Smokovec. Rysy Peak (2499 metres), right on the Polish border, is about nine hours away on a round trip from Štrbské Pleso (via Popradské Pleso and Pod Rysmi Chalet). These you can do on your own, but to scale the peaks without marked hiking trails (Gerlachovský štít included) you must hire a mountain guide. Members of recognised climbing clubs are exempt from this requirement.

The TANAP horská služba (mountain rescue) office in Starý Smokovec charges US$65 per day for a mountain guide for up to five people.

Places to Stay

Camping There's no camping within the Tatra National Park. The nearest commercial camping ground to Starý Smokovec is the *Tatracamp* (☎ 24 06) near the Pod lesom Railway Station, three km down the road to Poprad-Tatry. Six-person bungalows cost US$30 (open from June to September).

There's also a camping ground at Tatranská Štrba (open from May to September) below Štrbské Pleso.

Three camping grounds are a couple of km from Tatranská Lomnica (near the Tatranská Lomnica-Eurocamp Railway Station on the line to Studený Potok). The largest of these is the *Eurocamp FICC* (☎ 967 741), a five-minute walk from the train station, with 120 four-person luxury bungalows with private bath at US$49, plus regular hotel rooms with shared bath at US$17 double (no singles). Camping is US$3 per person, US$3 per tent. The Eurocamp features restaurants, bars, shops, a supermarket, a swimming pool, tennis, sauna, disco, hot water and row upon row of parked caravans. One reader wrote in with lavish praise for the folkloric Kolibar Restaurant here. The 1975 rally of the International Camping & Caravaneering Federation was held here. This place is open all year.

An eight-minute walk south of the Eurocamp is the less expensive *Športcamp* (☎ 967 288) where camping is US$2 per person plus US$2 per tent. Bungalows here are US$19 for up to four persons or US$24 for five persons, but in summer they're usually taken (open year-round).

Halfway between the Eurocamp and Tatranská Lomnica is the *Tatranec Campground* where bungalows are also available, but there's no train station nearby so it's more for people with cars.

Chalets Up on the hiking trails are eight mountain chalets *(chata)* but given the popularity and limited capacity of this area, the chalets could all be full in midsummer. Staff at the TANAP horská služba (mountain rescue) office next to Satur in Starý Smokovec will be able to tell you if a certain chalet is open and may even telephone ahead to see if there's a place for you. Many of the chalets close for maintenance in November and May. Although food is available at the chalets, you should take along some of your own supplies.

Basically, the chalets come in three varieties, as explained in the following examples. The *Morávku Chalet* (1500 metres, 82 dorm beds) on Popradské Pleso and *Sliezsky dom* (1670 metres, 79 dorm beds) are large mountain hotels. To stay at Morávku is US$9 per person in three, four and six-bed dorms. Sliezsky dom (☎ 23 545) is US$34/45 double/triple (no singles) in individual rooms with toilet and shower, or US$11 per person in a six to 12-bed dorm. Breakfast and dinner at both Morávku and Sliezsky dom cost US$8 per person for the two.

Bílikova (1255 metres, 68 beds), *Zamkovského* (1475 metres, 20 beds) and *Brnčalova* (1551 metres, 52 beds) are rustic wooden buildings on the Magistrála Trail. Bílikova is only five minutes from Hrebienok and room prices have been jacked up to US$32 double, so you'd be well advised to hike one hour down into the forest and stay in four-bedded rooms at the much friendlier Zamkovského Chalet which is US$10 per person with breakfast and dinner. Brnčalova is US$9 per person including breakfast and dinner in four, six and 12-bed dorms.

Pod Rysmi (2250 metres, 19 beds), *Zbojnícka* (1960 metres, 16 beds) and *Téryho* (2015 metres, 21 beds) are high mountain chalets built of stone. Pod Rysmi is US$8 per person including breakfast and dinner in the one 19-bed dorm, while both Zbojnícka and Téryho are US$9 per person in their dorms including breakfast and dinner. These three places make perfect bases for alpine exploration, but make sure they're open and available before you set out.

Satur in Starý Smokovec handles chalet bookings at Sliezsky dom and Morávku. Slovakoturist (☎ 20 31), just above the Pekná vyhliadka Railway Station in Horný Smokovec, a 10-minute walk east from Satur in Starý Smokovec, can reserve beds at all eight of the chalets.

Actually, staying at a chalet is a far better mountain experience than a hotel room at one of the resorts and it's cheaper. You're also more likely to meet interesting local people at the chalets and you'll have ample time in the evening to chat. Leave your backpack at a left-luggage office at a train station and carry basic essentials in a day pack.

Reader Tony English of Sunderland, England, sent us this:

> One of the best things I did in Slovakia was to climb Mt Rysy on the Polish border. The day I climbed up there the Pod Rysmi hut was being resupplied with food and booze and there was considerable rivalry as to who had carried the heaviest pack up to the hut. Two porters astonishingly managed to carry in packages weighing 75 kg. The strength and courage needed to carry in such a load, tied to a special backpack frame, up steep snow-covered slopes and over rocky scrambles, is quite mind boggling. There was a good atmosphere in the hut that night!

Private Rooms Satur doesn't have any private rooms at Starý Smokovec but can arrange rooms with families in the village of Nová Lesná for US$11/17 double/triple. Unless you have a car this is not convenient. Slovakoturist (☎ 20 31) in Horný Smokovec has private rooms at US$13/18 double/triple (no singles).

Private rooms are advertised by *Zimmer frei* signs outside numerous houses in Ždiar village on the north side of the High Tatras and easily accessible from Poprad-Tatry or Starý Smokovec on the Łysa Polana bus. Several small restaurants and pensions are also here. Ždiar is a pretty little village with sheep grazing in the fields and it makes a good base for exploring the High Tatras from this less-frequented side.

Hotels Many of the hotels you see in this area are owned by the trade unions and are only open to their members. Other hotels are reserved for groups. Hotel prices are almost double in the high seasons (mid-December to February and mid-June to September) as compared to the low seasons (March to mid-June and October to mid-December). Be aware that most prices quoted in this section are those charged in the low season.

Staff at the Satur office (closed on Saturday afternoon and Sunday) near the train station at Starý Smokovec will help you to find a room. Satur controls many hotel rooms around Smokovec, so it's sometimes easier to go there for a booking than to tramp around looking on your own. The staff can arrange rooms in all categories from low budget to deluxe.

Smokovec If the price doesn't deter you, you'll like the three-star *Grandhotel* (☎ 21 54) at Starý Smokovec. This majestic turn-of-the-century building has a certain elegance the high-rise hotels lack. Since many of the 83 rooms (both single and double) have shared bath, it's not as expensive as you might think. In the low season it's US$18/28 single/double without bath, US$28/44 with bath; in the high season you'll pay US$29/45 without bath, US$48/74 with bath. Breakfast and use of the indoor swimming pool are included.

The nearby *Hotel Crocus* (☎ 27 41) just above the train station at Starý Smokovec is overpriced at US$16/31/46 single/double/triple without bath but with breakfast. This hotel may be cheaper if booked through Satur.

The *Park Hotel* (☎ 23 42), a circular five-storey hotel that opened just above the Nový Smokovec Railway Station in 1970, charges US$22/35 single/double including breakfast in the low season, or US$37/58 without breakfast in the high season. All 96 rooms have private bath. Avoid the hotel restaurant.

The log cabin-style *Hotel MS 70* (☎ 20 61), just west of the Park Hotel, is one of the least expensive around at US$6/12 single/double with shared bath.

One of the best deals at Starý Smokovec is *Pension Vesna* (☎ 27 74), a white two-storey building behind the large sanatorium opposite Nový Smokovec Railway Station. Spacious rooms with shared bath and private balcony are US$8 per person and there's a kitchen where you can cook. There's a short-cut through the sanatorium grounds to get there (ask).

Another inexpensive hotel at Starý Smokovec is the four-storey, B-category *Hotel Šport* (☎ 23 61; US$8/18 single/double with shared bath), a five-minute walk east from Starý Smokovec train station. It's popular with noisy youth groups and the hotel restaurant is not recommended.

Pension Pol'ana (☎ 25 18), across the street from the Sports Centrum at Pekná Vyhliadna Railway Station, is US$8/13 single/double with shared bath. The rooms are small but comfortable, each with a sink, and many also have a balcony. The cosy little bar downstairs serves a spicy bowl of tripe soup. The Pol'ana is often full.

The cheapest place to stay at if you have a YHA or ISIC card is the *CKM Juniorhotel Vysoké Tatry* (☎ 26 61), just below the Horný Smokovec Railway Station. The regular charge will be around US$10 per person including breakfast. Students and youth-hostel card-holders should get a 50% discount if they book direct (not through an agency). Guests are accommodated in half a dozen single-storey pavilions spread around the hotel grounds. The hotel is open all year, but it's often full with noisy school groups.

Tatranská Lomnica *Hotel Lomnica* (☎ 967 251), an older two-star hotel with quaint folk architecture between the train and bus stations in Tatranská Lomnica, is expensive at US$21/27 double/triple without bath, US$28/36 with bath, breakfast included (no singles). Only one or two rooms with bath are available.

The newer *Hotel Horec* (☎ 967 261), a five-minute walk up the hill from the train station, is US$22 double without bath, US$24 with bath, breakfast included (no singles).

One of Slovakia's most romantic hotels is the 91-room *Grandhotel Praha* (☎ 967 941), built in 1905, up the hill beside the cable-car terminal. In the high season singles/doubles with bath cost US$47/72, or US$28/43 in the low season, bath and breakfast included. By all means stay there if price isn't a big consideration and you want to go in style.

Štrbské Pleso The 11-storey *Hotel Panorama* (☎ 92 111) next to the Prior Department Store, above the Štrbské Pleso Railway Station, costs US$17/26 single/ double without bath, US$20/31 with bath, breakfast included. This hotel has 42 single and 50 double rooms.

The 150-room *Hotel Patria* (☎ 92 591), a huge A-frame hotel overlooking the lake, a 10-minute walk uphill from the train station, costs US$43 double (no singles).

Hotel FIS (☎ 92 221) opposite the huge ski jumps, five minutes beyond the Patria Hotel, is US$20/29 single/double with bath. The FIS is a modern sports hotel and both it and ski jumps were built for the 1970 International Ski Federation world championships.

Places to Eat

Almost all the hotels and chalets of this region have their own restaurants.

Just above the bus station at Starý Smokovec are two adjacent restaurants. The *Tatranská Kúria* is a folk-style restaurant but it's nothing special. The neighbouring *Reštaurácia Tatra* is cheaper, better and more likely to be open. They even have a vegetarian section in their menu. If you'd like to splash out, there's the elegant restaurant in the *Grand Hotel* (you're expected to dress up).

Pizza Piccola, right beside the Tatranská Lomnica Railway Station, has a great variety of pizzas. Right next door is the *Slovenská Reštaurácia* with national dishes. The *Vínna Pivnička* in Hotel Lomnica serves light local meals and cold beer.

There's an excellent self-service restaurant in *Prior Department Store* next to Štrbské Pleso Railway Station (open daily from 8 am to 5.45 pm).

Entertainment

The *Stella Bar* between Satur and Starý Smokovec Bus Station operates as a disco

Friday, Saturday and Sunday from 8 pm to 2 am. There's also a disco at the *Park Hotel*.

Getting There & Away

Bus There are regular express buses from Bratislava to Tatranská Lomnica via Nitra, Banská Bystrica and Starý Smokovec.

From Starý Smokovec there are 15 buses a day to Łysa Polana (38 km, one hour), 26 to Ždiar, seven to Levoča (38 km), three to Bardejov, four to Prešov, six to Žilina, five to Trenčín, three to Bratislava and two to Brno.

The Hungarian Volánbusz bus from Budapest to Tatranská Lomnica runs twice a week (311 km, seven hours, US$13).

Train To come by train, take one of the express trains running between Prague or Bratislava and Košice and change at Poprad-Tatry (couchettes are available). There are frequent narrow-gauge electric trains between Poprad-Tatry and Starý Smokovec (13 km).

Alternatively, get off the express train at Tatranská Štrba, a station on the main line from Prague to Košice, and take the cog-wheel railway up to Štrbské Pleso (there are over 20 services daily), which climbs 430 metres over a distance of five km. Also known as the 'rack railway', this service opened in 1896.

The booking offices in Starý Smokovec and Tatranská Lomnica train stations can reserve sleepers and couchettes from Poprad-Tatry to Prague, Karlovy Vary, Brno and Bratislava.

To/From Poland For anyone interested in walking between Slovakia and Poland there's a highway border crossing near Javorina, 30 km from Tatranská Lomnica via Ždiar by bus. The Slovakian bus to/from Starý Smokovec is never crowded and the bus stop is just a hundred metres from the border (bus times posted). On the Polish side buses can be full up with people on excursions between Morskie Oko Lake and Zakopane, so this route is easier southbound than northbound.

You'll find a bank at Łysa Polana on the Polish side where you can change money, but there's no Slovakian bank at Javorina. The rate offered at the border is about 10% worse than you'll get in Zakopane. Southbound travellers should buy a few dollars worth of Slovakian crowns at an exchange office in Poland to pay the onward bus fare to Starý Smokovec or Poprad, as this may not be possible at the border. Northbound, excess crowns are easily unloaded at exchange offices in Poland (at a loss). (See the Tatra Mountains section in the Poland chapter of this book for information on conditions on the Polish side.)

A bus direct to Zakopane leaves Starý Smokovec Bus Station weekdays at 7 am (60 km, US$3 one way, pay the driver). This bus isn't listed on the posted schedule but Satur knows about it. Also ask Satur about its excursion buses to Zakopane and Kraków.

Getting Around

You can experience virtually every type of mountain transportation here: funicular railway, cog-wheel or rack railway, narrow-gauge electric trains, cable cars and chair lifts. The most used are the electric trains which run from Poprad-Tatry to Starý Smokovec (13 km) and Štrbské Pleso (29 km) about every half-hour. Trains also travel from Starý Smokovec to Tatranská Lomnica (six km) every 30 minutes. These trains make frequent stops along their routes; when there isn't a ticket window at the station, go immediately to the conductors upon boarding and buy your ticket from them.

POPRAD-TATRY

Poprad-Tatry is a modern industrial city with little to interest visitors. However, it's an important transportation hub that you'll pass through at least once. The electric railway from here to Starý Smokovec was built in 1908 and was extended to Štrbské Pleso in 1912.

Money Change travellers' cheques at the Všeobecná Úverová Banka, ulica Mnohel'ova 9, next to Hotel Satel two blocks from the train station (weekdays 7 am to noon and 1 to 5 pm, Wednesday 7 am to noon only, Saturday 8 am to noon).

Places to Stay & Eat

If you arrive late, you could stay at the old *Hotel Európa* (☎ 092-32 744; US$6/8 single/double with shared bath) just outside the Poprad-Tatry Railway Station. The hotel restaurant is quite good (the menu is in German).

Getting There & Away

Bus There are buses to almost everywhere else in Slovakia from the large bus station next to the train station. Banská Bystrica (124 km), Łysa Polana (via Starý Smokovec), Červený Kláštor, Levoča (26 km), Spišské Podhradie (41 km), Bardejov (125 km) and Prešov (84 km) are most easily reached by bus. Ask about buses to Zakopane, Poland.

Train Poprad-Tatry is a major junction on the main railway line from Bratislava or Prague to Košice. Express trains run to Žilina (141 km, two hours) and Košice (101 km, 1½ hours) every couple of hours. Electric trains climb 13 km to Starý Smokovec, the main Vysoké Tatry resort, every half-hour or so. A feeder railway line runs north-east to Plavec (61 km, two hours by local train) where you can get a connection to Muszyna, Poland, three times a day (see the Prešov section for approximate times).

DUNAJEC GORGE

Pieniny National Park (21 sq km), created in 1967, combines with a similar park in Poland to protect the nine-km Dunajec River gorge between the Slovakian village of Červený Kláštor and Szczawnica, Poland. The river here forms the international boundary between the two countries and the 500-metre limestone cliffs are impressive.

At the mouth of the gorge is a 14th-century fortified **Carthusian monastery**, now a park administrative centre and museum with a good collection of statuary and old prints of the area (open daily from May to September, closed Sunday and Monday from October to April).

From June to mid-September, Dunajec raft trips (US$6) depart from two locations at Červený Klášstor: a landing opposite the monastery and a second landing a km upriver west of the village. A raft only sets out when 12 passengers gather and when business is slow you may have to wait around for the quorum to be reached. From the downriver terminus you can hike back to the monastery in a little over an hour, or rent a bicycle (US$4) and peddle back. Actually, the rafting operation on the Polish side is larger and better organised, so you might wait to do your rafting there (see under Dunajec Gorge in the Poland chapter for details). The raft trip in Slovakia is much shorter than the one in Poland.

Even if you don't go rafting, it's still worth coming to Červený Kláštor to hike along the riverside trail through the gorge on the Slovakian side (no such trail exists on the Polish side). In midsummer a US$0.30 'trail fee' is charged to enter the national park but this fee includes a brochure in English.

Places to Stay

Just across a small stream from the monastery is a camp site that is open from mid-June to mid-September. No bungalows are available here.

A couple of km up the road to Vel'ký Lipník from the monastery is the *Hotel Dunajec* with some bungalows across the road. A few km farther along in the same direction is the more up-market *Dunajec Motorest* camping ground with more bungalows (often full in summer).

Near Lesnica, a bit inland from the downriver end of the gorge where the raft trips end, is the inexpensive *Pieniny Chata* (☎ 0963-97 530) which is often full in summer. In this case the hostel manager has two rooms for rent in his private residence at US$12 double including a terrific breakfast.

Getting There & Away

Direct buses go to Červený Kláštor from Poprad-Tatry. Although Poland is just across

SLOVAKIA

the river, there's no official border crossing here, so you must take a bus from Červený Kláštor to Stará L'ubovňa (25 km), and then a train to Plavec (16 km), where a local train goes to Muszyna, Poland (16 km) three times a day (see Getting There & Away in the Prešov section). From Muszyna there are Polish trains to Nowy Sącz (50 km) and Kraków. Check connecting train times beforehand. There are also buses from Stará L'ubovňa to Bardejov, Prešov, and Košice. Alternatively use the Łysa Polana crossing directly to Zakopane.

SPIŠSKÁ NOVÁ VES

Spišská Nová Ves, the administrative centre of the Spiš region, is a modern city with a history dating back to 1268. The long central square is nice to walk around and the many large apartment complexes built here by the communists are impressive. Spišská Nová Ves makes a good base from which to visit Levoča, Spišské Podhradie and nearby Slovenský raj National Park.

Orientation

The bus station is about 200 metres west of Spišská Nová Ves Railway Station. A 24-hour left-luggage office is available at the train station.

Money You can change travellers' cheques at the Všeobecná Úverová Banka, Letná ulica 33 (Monday 9 am to 4 pm, Tuesday to Friday 9 am to 5 pm).

Post & Telephone There's a telephone centre in the main post office, Štefánikovo námestie 7 opposite Dom Kultury (Monday to Saturday from 7 am to 8 pm, Sunday 8 am to 4 pm).

Spišská Nová Ves's telephone code is 0965.

Things to See & Do

Just south-west of Spišská Nová Ves is **Slovenský raj** (the Slovak Paradise), a national park created in 1988, with cliffs, caves, canyons, waterfalls and 1896 species of butterflies. This mountainous karst area is accessible via **Čingov**, eight km west of Spišská Nová Ves by bus. The closest train station to Slovenský raj is **Spišske Tomášovce**, less than an hour from Tomášovský

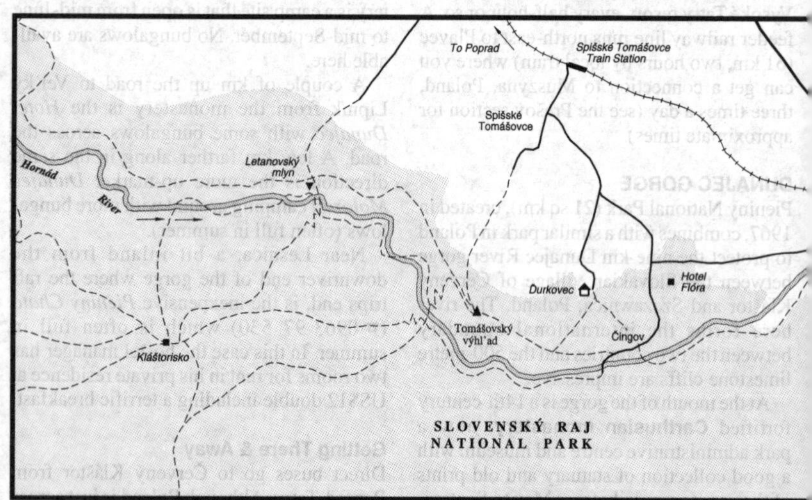

výhl'ad on the green trail. Only local trains stop at this station.

From Čingov (elevation 494 metres) the blue trail leads up the Hornád River gorge, passing below Tomášovský výhl'ad, to Letanovský mlyn. The trail up the river is narrow and there are several ladders and ramps where hikers can only pass one by one. This can cause delays if you happen to meet a large group at such a place and during peak periods hikers are only allowed to travel in an upstream direction from Čingov (returning over the mountain).

A km beyond Letanovský mlyn, a green trail leaves the river and climbs sharply to **Kláštorisko** (elevation 755 metres) where there's a restaurant (☎ 0965-90 307), open daily year-round, with cabins at US$5 per person. If you'd like to stay there, call ahead to check availability in midsummer. From Kláštorisko you can follow another blue trail back down the ridge towards Čingov.

From Čingov to Kláštorisko via Letanovský mlyn and the gorge takes a good three hours and to return to Čingov down the ridge takes another two hours, so a minimum of at least six hours are required to do this entire circuit, lunch at Kláštorisko included.

Places to Stay

The modern, 10-storey *Metropol Hotel* (☎ 22 241), Štefánikovo námestie 2 next to Dom Kultury, three blocks south of the train station, charges US$16/25 single/double with shower and breakfast.

The *Šport Hotel* (☎ 26 753), on ulica T Vansovej, next to the Zimný Štadión, is US$6 per person with shared bath. From Hotel Metropol continue south a few blocks and you'll see this neat, clean five-storey building off to the left. The hotel restaurant is reasonable.

Satur opposite Dom Kultury near the Metropol knows of private rooms, but at US$9 per person with breakfast they're no bargain.

Čingov The *Hotel Flora* (☎ 91 129), a large three-storey establishment at Čingov, has rooms at US$13/25 single/double with bath. Cheaper accommodation is available at the *Chatová osada Ďurkovec* on a hill about a 20-minute walk from the bus stop at Čingov. There's also camping at Ďurkovec, which is good as camping is not allowed in the park itself. There are many other places to stay at Čingov, so ask around.

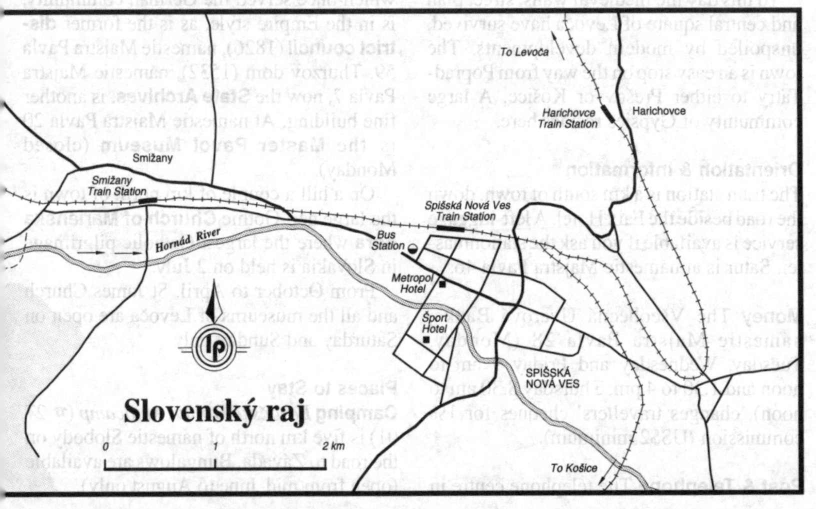

SLOVAKIA

In Spišské Tomášovce, about a km south of the train station, is a large 65-bed *Ubytovnacie zariadenie* 'Touristic hut' (☎ 91 184).

Getting There & Away

Spišská Nová Ves is on the main railway line from Žilina to Košice with trains from Poprad-Tatry (26 km) every hour or so. All trains stop here. A feeder line runs 13 km north to Levoča with services every two or three hours.

Buses leave Spišská Nová Ves for Čingov every couple of hours. There are morning buses to Spišské Podhradie, Tatranská Lomnica, Starý Smokovec and Štrbské Pleso.

LEVOČA

In the 13th century the king of Hungary invited Saxon Germans to colonise the Spiš region on the eastern borderlands of his kingdom as a protection against Tatar incursions and to develop mining. One of the towns founded at this time was Levoča (Leutschau), 26 km east of Poprad-Tatry. Granted urban privileges in 1271, the merchants of Levoča grew rich in the 14th century.

To this day the medieval walls, street plan and central square of Levoča have survived, unspoiled by modern developments. The town is an easy stop on the way from Poprad-Tatry to either Prešov or Košice. A large community of Gypsies resides here.

Orientation & Information

The train station is a km south of town, down the road beside the Faix Hotel. A left-luggage service is available if you ask the stationmaster. Satur is at námestie Majstra Pavla 46.

Money The Všeobecná Úverová Banka, námestie Majstra Pavla 28 (Monday, Tuesday, Wednesday and Friday 9 am to noon and 1.30 to 4 pm, Thursday 8.30 am to noon), changes travellers' cheques for 1% commission (US$2 minimum).

Post & Telephone The telephone centre in the post office at námestie Majstra Pavla 42 is open weekdays from 7 am to 8 pm, Saturday 8 am to 1 pm.

Levoča's telephone code is 0966.

Things to See

Bastions and 15th-century walls greet the traveller arriving by bus at námestie Slobody. The old town begins just through **Košice Gate** with the **new Minorite church** (1750) on the left.

Námestie Majstra Pavla, Levoča's central square, is full of things to see. In the 15th-century **St James' Church** (closed Monday, admission US$1) is a gigantic Gothic high altar (1517) by Master Pavol, one of the largest and finest of its kind in Europe. The Madonna on this altar appears on the new 100 Sk banknote. Next to St James is the Gothic **town hall**, enlivened by Renaissance arcades, today the **Museum of the Spiš Region** (closed Monday). Beside the old town hall is a 16th-century cage where prisoners were once exhibited.

There's an **art museum** (closed Monday) in the 15th-century house at námestie Majstra Pavla 40. While you're there have a peek in the courtyard of námestie Majstra Pavla 43. The **Evangelical church** (1837), which once served the German community, is in the Empire style, as is the former **district council** (1826), námestie Majstra Pavla 59. Thurzov dom (1532), námestie Majstra Pavla 7, now the **State Archives**, is another fine building. At námestie Majstra Pavla 20 is the **Master Pavol Museum** (closed Monday).

On a hill a couple of km north of town is the large neo-Gothic **Church of Mariánska hora** where the largest Catholic pilgrimage in Slovakia is held on 2 July.

From October to April, St James Church and all the museums of Levoča are open on Saturday and Sunday only.

Places to Stay

Camping *Levočská Dolina Autocamp* (☎ 27 01) is five km north of námestie Slobody on the road to Závada. Bungalows are available (open from mid-June to August only).

Autocamping Starý mlyn (☎ 36 51), with deluxe bungalows and a restaurant on the premises, is more convenient, about five km west of Levoča on the road to Poprad.

Hotels Your best bet is the 25-room *Hotel Faix* (☎ 23 35), Probstnerova cesta 22, between the train station and the old town. Rooms in this recently renovated hotel are US$11/14 single/double with shared bath, US$14/21 with private bath. The hotel restaurant is good.

The *Hotel Barbakan* (☎ 43 10), Košická 15, offers comfortable rooms with private bath (US$35/38 for singles/doubles) in a newly renovated building in the centre of town. Hotel guests are required to purchase US$6 per person in compulsory meal coupons to ensure that they won't stray from the restaurant.

An even more expensive place is the Austrian-owned *Hotel Satel*, námestie Majstra Pavla 55. Tourism development plans call for Levoča to be converted into the 'Slovak Prague' so there'll probably be a few more up-market establishments around town by the time you get there.

SLOVAKIA

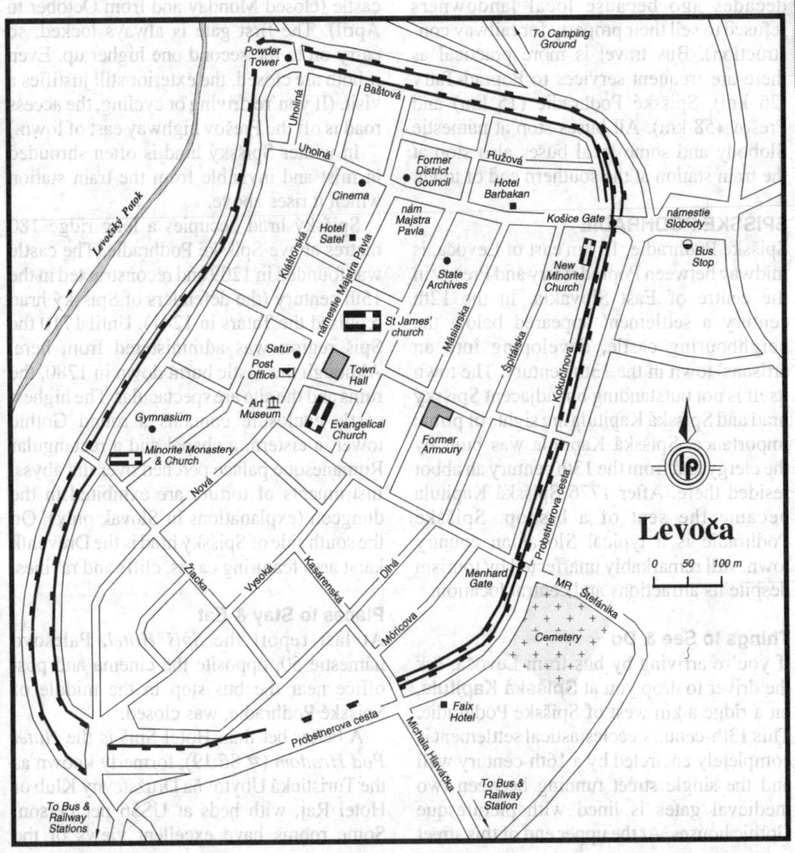

Places to Eat

Levoča's best restaurant is the *Restaurant u 3 Apostolov*, námestie Majstra Pavla 11. For coffee and cakes go to *Mliečne Lahodky*, námestie Majstra Pavla 9.

A reader wrote in recommending a vegetarian restaurant which recently opened at Vholňa 3, just off the north-west corner of the main square behind the cinema.

Getting There & Away

Levoča is connected by 11 daily local trains to Spišská Nová Ves, a station 13 km south on the main line from Bratislava to Prague and Košice (the main line bypassed the town decades ago because local landowners refused to sell their property for railway construction). Bus travel is more practical as there are frequent services to Poprad-Tatry (26 km), Spišské Podhradie (15 km) and Prešov (58 km). All buses stop at námestie Slobody and some local buses also stop at the train station at the southern end of town.

SPIŠSKÉ PODHRADIE

Spišské Podhradie, 15 km east of Levoča, is midway between Poprad-Tatry and Prešov in the centre of East Slovakia. In the 12th century a settlement appeared below the neighbouring castle, developing into an artisans' town in the 13th century. The town itself is not outstanding but adjacent Spišský hrad and Spišská Kapitula are sights of prime importance. Spišská Kapitula was built by the clergy and from the 13th century an abbot resided there. After 1776 Spišská Kapitula became the seat of a bishop. Spišské Podhradie is a typical Slovakian country town, still remarkably unaffected by tourism despite its attractions and central location.

Things to See & Do

If you're arriving by bus from Levoča, ask the driver to drop you at **Spišská Kapitula**, on a ridge a km west of Spišské Podhradie. This 13th-century ecclesiastical settlement is completely encircled by a 16th-century wall and the single street running between two medieval gates is lined with picturesque Gothic houses. At the upper end of this street is magnificent **St Martin's Cathedral** (1273) with twin Romanesque towers and a Gothic sanctuary. Inside are three folding Gothic altars (1499) and, near the door, a Romanesque white lion. Unfortunately, the church is often closed. On opposite sides of the cathedral are the seminary and the Renaissance bishop's palace (1652).

On the opposite side of Spišské Podhradie is **Spišský hrad** (Zipser Burg), the largest castle in Slovakia. Spišský hrad is directly above and east of the train station, a km south of Spišské Podhradie's bus stop. Cross the level crossing over the tracks near the station and follow the yellow markers up to the castle (closed Monday and from October to April). The first gate is always locked, so carry on to the second one higher up. Even if both are closed, the exterior still justifies a visit. (If you're driving or cycling, the access road is off the Prešov highway east of town.)

In winter Spišský hrad is often shrouded in mist and invisible from the train station which it rises above.

Spišský hrad occupies a long ridge 180 metres above Spišské Podhradie. The castle was founded in 1209 and reconstructed in the 15th century (the defenders of Spišský hrad repulsed the Tatars in 1241). Until 1710 the Spiš region was administered from here. Although the castle burnt down in 1780, the ruins and the site are spectacular. The highest castle enclosure contains a round Gothic tower, a cistern, a chapel and a rectangular Romanesque palace perched over the abyss. Instruments of torture are exhibited in the dungeon (explanations in Slovak only). On the south side of Spišský hrad is the Dreveník karst area featuring caves, cliffs and ravines.

Places to Stay & Eat

At last report the *Spiš Hotel*, Palešovo námestie 50, opposite the cinema and post office near the bus stop in the middle of Spišské Podhradie, was closed.

A better bet than Hotel Spiš is the *Hotel Pod Hradom* (☎ 86 19), formerly known as the Turistická Ubytovňa Družstevný Klub or Hotel Raj, with beds at US$6 per person. Some rooms have excellent views of the castle. It's a red three-storey building behind some apartment blocks on a backstreet, a five-minute walk from the bus stop.

The only restaurant in Spišské Podhradie is the one in Hotel Pod Hradom and its menu consists of pork chops with potatoes and not much else. The supermarket you pass on the way from the post office to the train station has large quantities of a few items.

Getting There & Away

A secondary railway line connects Spišské Podhradie to Spišské Vlachy (nine km), a station on the main line from Poprad-Tatry to Košice. Departures are scheduled to connect with the Košice trains. You can leave your bags at the left-luggage office in the Spišské Podhradie Railway Station (ask the stationmaster).

Buses from Prešov (43 km), Levoča (15 km), Spišská Nová Ves (25 km) and Poprad-Tatry (41 km) are quite frequent.

PREŠOV

This busy market centre, 36 km north of Košice, is the centre of the Slovakian Ukraine, the breadbasket of Slovakia. Prešov (Preschau) received a royal charter in 1374 and, like Bardejov to the north and Košice to the south, was once an eastern bulwark of the Kingdom of Hungary. In June 1919 a Slovak Soviet Republic was proclaimed at Prešov, part of a larger socialist revolution in Hungary. This movement was quickly suppressed by the big landowners, whose holdings were threatened, and in 1920 the region was incorporated into Czechoslovakia. The accommodation situation is poor but you may wish to stop off when travelling between Košice and Bardejov.

Orientation & Information

Hlavná ulica, Prešov's central square, is a 20-minute walk north up Masarykova from the adjacent bus and train stations (or take trolleybus No 4 to/from 'železničná stanica').

The left-luggage office at Prešov Railway Station is open 24 hours except for two half-hour breaks. Satur is at Hlavná ulica 1.

Money The Všeobecná Úverová Banka, Masarykova 13 just south of Prior, changes travellers' cheques for 1% commission (open weekdays from 7.30 am to 12.30 pm and 1.30 to 5 pm, Wednesday from 7.30 am to 12.30 pm only).

The Investičná Banka, Hlavná ulica 82, changes travellers' cheques Monday and Friday from 8 am to 1.30 pm, and Tuesday, Wednesday and Thursday from 8 am to noon and 1.30 to 3 pm.

Post & Telephone There's a telephone centre in the post office at Masarykova 2 opposite Prior (daily 6 am to 10 pm).

Prešov's telephone code is 091.

Things to See

The most imposing structure in the city is 14th-century **St Nicholas Church** with its Gothic structure and baroque organ and altars. Behind it is the **Evangelical church** (1642). To one side is the **Prešov Museum** (closed on weekend afternoons and every Monday), inside Rákóczi House, Hlavná ulica 86. In addition to the archaeology, history and natural history displays, there's a large fire-fighting exhibit. The Slovak Soviet Republic was declared on 16 June 1919 from the iron balcony of the **old town hall** (1533), Hlavná ulica 73.

Places to Stay

The nine-storey *Penzión ZPA* (☎ 23 206), Budovatelská 14, is about the only inexpensive option. The 40 rooms with bath in this pleasant workers hostel are US$9 single or double. It's about a 10-minute walk from the train station: walk north on Masarykova and turn left on Škultétyho ulica which crosses the railway line. The second street on the left is Budovatelská. Expect some noise from the adjacent Victoria Night Club on Friday and Saturday nights. Actually the music probably won't bother you as much as the drunken dancers leaving.

Prešov has two high-rise tourist hotels, the cheaper of which is the eight-storey Interhotel Šariš (☎ 46 351) at US$22/42/53/triple with bath and breakfast. The 39-room *Dukla*

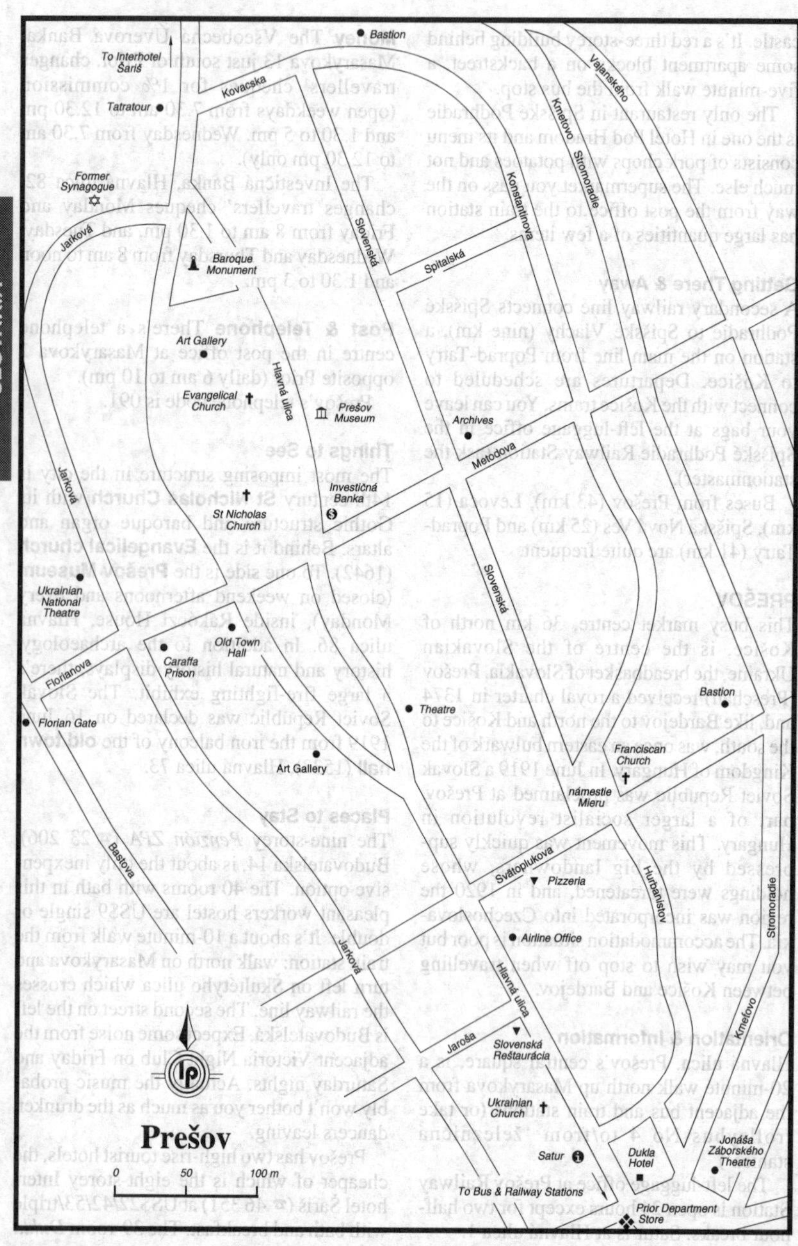
Prešov
0
50
100 m
Bastion
To Interhotel Šariš
Kovacska
Tatratour
Vajanského
Kmeťovo Stromoradie
Konštantínova
Former Synagogue
Jarková
Slovenská
Spitalská
Baroque Monument
Art Gallery
Hlavná ulica
Evangelical Church
Prešov Museum
Archives
Metodova
Investičná Banka
St Nicholas Church
Slovenská
Ukrainian National Theatre
Old Town Hall
Caraffa Prison
Florianova
Florian Gate
Theatre
Bastion
Art Gallery
Franciscan Church
námestie Mieru
Baštova
Svätoplukova
Pizzeria
Hurbanistov
Stromoradie
Airline Office
Hlavná ulica
Jarková
Jaroša
Slovenská Reštaurácia
Kmeťovo
Ukrainian Church
Satur
Dukla Hotel
Jonáša Záborského Theatre
To Bus & Railway Stations
Prior Department Store

SLOVAKIA

Hotel (☎ 22 741), Hlavná ulica 2, charges US$22/33 single/double without bath, US$26/46 with bath. This five-storey hotel erected in 1952 just isn't worth it.

Satur, Hlavná ulica 1, has no private rooms.

Places to Eat

The *Slovenská Reštaurácia*, Hlavná ulica 13 (closed Sunday), has a fairly reasonable menu (in Slovak).

You can get more familiar fare at *Pizzeria*, Svätoplukova 1 (closed weekends and after 7 pm).

The *Hotel Dukla* does a good buffet breakfast for US$4.

Entertainment

The *Jonáša Záborského Theatre* is opposite the Dukla Hotel. Also check the *Ukrainian National Theatre* (1894), Jarková 77, for plays in Ukrainian. To see a movie check Kino Klub in Odborový Dom Kultúry opposite Interhotel Šariš and Kino Panoráma, Masarykova ulica 7 opposite the main post office.

Getting There & Away

Trains north to Bardejov (45 km, 1¼ hours) and south to Košice (33 km, 45 minutes) are frequent enough, but bus travel is faster on these routes (25 buses a day to Bardejov). You'll want to take a bus to go to Spišské Podhradie (43 km, 17 daily), Levoča (58 km, 19 daily), Poprad (84 km, 19 daily) and the Vysoké Tatry resorts.

To/From Poland The daily *Cracovia* and *Karpaty* express trains between Kraków and Hungary stop at Prešov (reservations required). You can also pick these trains up at Košice, although the *Cracovia* passes in the middle of the night and the *Karpaty* is often late.

An easier route to Poland involves taking a local train from Prešov to Plaveč (54 km, 1½ hours) on the Polish border, and then one of three daily local trains 16 km to Muszyna in Poland itself. At last report, these unreserved trains left Plaveč northbound at 7.52 am and 2.18 and 4.16 pm and Muszyna southbound at 8.35 am and 1.15 and 4.50 pm (these times could change). Any one of the 18 daily buses from Prešov to Stará L'ubovňa will also drop you in Plaveč. From Muszyna there are Polish trains to Nowy Sącz and Kraków. Unless you're lucky with connections, such a trip will probably end up taking all day.

BARDEJOV

Bardejov received municipal privileges in 1320 and became a free royal town in 1376. Trade between Poland and Russia passed through the town and in the 15th century the Bardejov merchants grew rich. After an abortive 17th-century revolt against the Habsburgs, Bardejov's fortunes declined, but the medieval town survived. In late 1944 heavy fighting took place at the Dukla Pass into Poland, 54 km north-east of Bardejov on the road to Rzeszów (the wrecks of a few tanks and planes can be photographed from the road). Since 1954 the town plan and the former Gothic-Renaissance houses of wealthy merchants lining the sloping central square have been carefully preserved. Much of the town walls, including the moat, towers and bastions, remain intact today. Jas shoes are made in Bardejov.

Orientation & Information

The combined bus and train station (with a left-luggage office open daily from 7 am to 7 pm) is a five-minute walk from Radničné námestie, the town's main square. Satur is at Radničné námestie 46.

Money The Všeobecná Úverová Banka, Kellerova 1, changes travellers' cheques weekdays from 7.30 to 11 am. The exchange office of the Investičná Banka, Radničné námestie 36, is open Monday to Thursday from 7.30 to 11.30 am and 12.30 to 2.30 pm, Friday 7.30 am to noon.

Post & Telephone The telephone centre in the main post office, Dlhý rad 14, is open weekdays from 7.30 am to 9.30 pm, Saturday 7.30 am to 8 pm and Sunday 8 to 11 am.

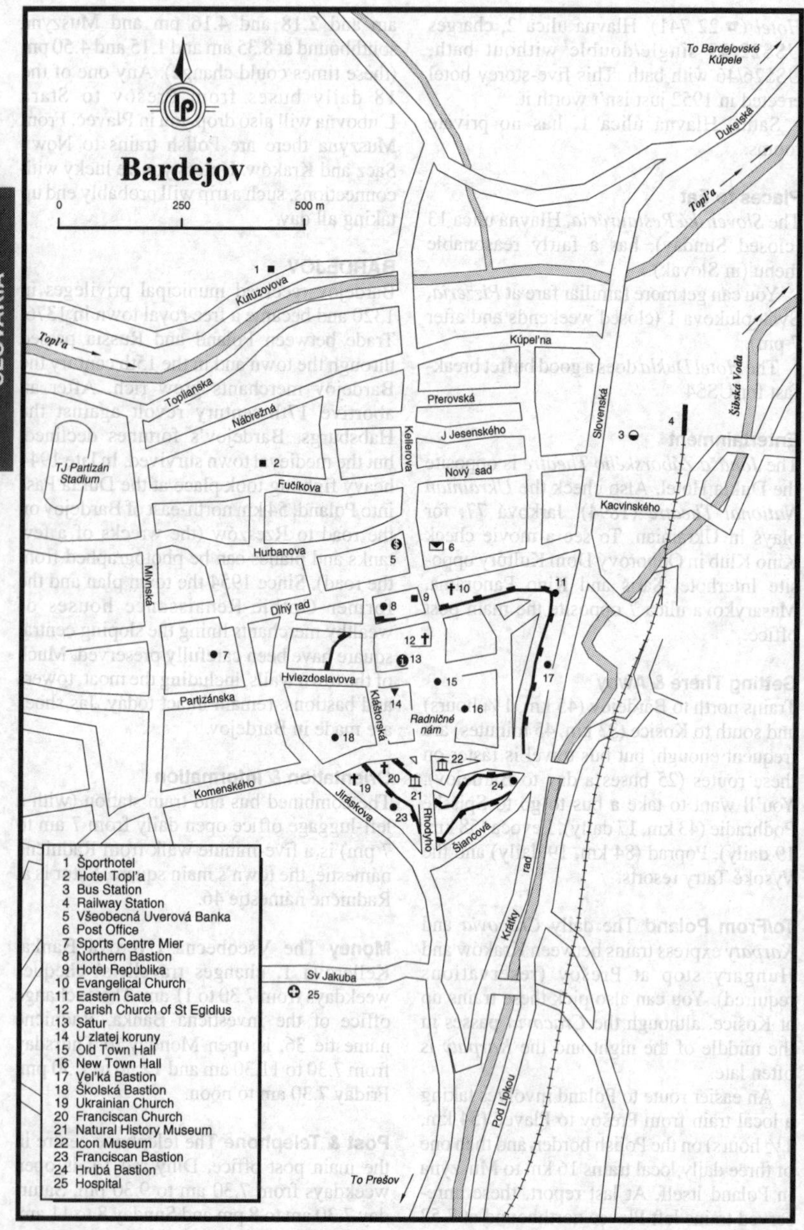
Bardejov
0
250
500 m
To Bardejovské Kúpele
Dukelská
Topl'a
Šibská Voda
Kutuzovova
Topl'a
Toplianska
Nábrežná
TJ Partizán Stadium
Fučíkova
Hurbanova
Mlynská
Dlhý rad
Hviezdoslavova
Partizánska
Komenského
Klaštorská
Jiráskova
Rhodyho
Šiancová
Radničné nám
Kellerova
Kúpel'na
Přerovská
J Jesenského
Nový sad
Kacvinského
Slovenská
Krátky rad
Pod Lipkou
Sv Jakuba
To Prešov
1 Športhotel
2 Hotel Topl'a
3 Bus Station
4 Railway Station
5 Všeobecná Uverová Banka
6 Post Office
7 Sports Centre Mier
8 Northern Bastion
9 Hotel Republika
10 Evangelical Church
11 Eastern Gate
12 Parish Church of St Egidius
13 Satur
14 U zlatej koruny
15 Old Town Hall
16 New Town Hall
17 Vel'ká Bastion
18 Školská Bastion
19 Ukrainian Church
20 Franciscan Church
21 Natural History Museum
22 Icon Museum
23 Franciscan Bastion
24 Hrubá Bastion
25 Hospital

Things to See

The 14th-century **Parish Church of St Egidius** is one of the most remarkable buildings in the country, with no less than 11 tall Gothic altarpieces, built from 1460 to 1510, all with their own original paintings and sculptures. The structural purity of the church and the 15th-century bronze baptismal font are striking.

Near this church is the **old town hall** (1509), the first Renaissance building in Slovakia, now a museum (closed Sunday and Monday) with more altarpieces and an historical collection. Two **museums** (closed Monday) face one another on ulica Rhodyho at the southern end of the square. One has an excellent natural history exhibit, the other a collection of icons. A fourth museum at Radničné námestie 13 contains a display of deer antlers hardly worth seeing.

Places to Stay

The B-category *Hotel Republika* (☎ 27 21), right next to the parish church, is fine for one night at US$9/14/17 single/double/triple with shared bath. This place was built in 1947.

The smaller C-category *Hotel Topl'a* (☎ 40 41), Fučíkova 25, about six blocks west of the bus station, is US$11/18/22/25 single/double/triple/quad – poor value. There's a cheap beer hall just downstairs.

The *Športhotel* (☎ 49 49), ulica Kutuzovova 31, a modern two-storey hotel overlooking the Topl'a River, has 20 rooms with bath at US$8 per person.

Places to Eat

Restaurant U Floriána, Radničné námestie 44, is one place to eat. Around the corner at Hviezdoslavovo 2 is *U zlatej koruny* where you can get a fast lunch.

Getting There & Away

Local trains run between Bardejov and Prešov (45 km, 1¼ hours), but if you're coming from Prešov or Košice, buses are faster. If you want to go to the Vysoké Tatry, look for a bus to Poprad-Tatry (125 km, 12 daily); three times a day there are buses direct to Starý Smokovec. Four times a day buses go as far as Bratislava (453 km) and twice daily there's a bus to Žilina (278 km).

To go to Poland, take a Stará L'ubovňa bus west to Plaveč (34 km, 13 daily) where you can pick up a local train to Muszyna, Poland (three daily). Turn to Getting There & Away in the Prešov section for more information on the train to Muszyna. There are buses from Bardejov direct to Krosno, Poland (US$3), via Svidník, a couple of times a week but these are not listed on the main departures board, so ask at information.

BARDEJOVSKÉ KÚPELE

Just six km north of Bardejov is Bardejovské Kúpele, one of Slovakia's most beautiful spas, where diseases of the alimentary and respiratory tracts are treated. From the late 18th century, Bardejovské Kúpele was one of the most popular spas in Hungary and was frequented throughout the year by European high society. After WW II the communist authorities rebuilt the spa. Most of the hotels at the spa are reserved for patients undergoing medical treatment and the two that do accept tourists, the Mineral and Mier, have unusually high prices for foreigners, so you're better off making it a day trip.

Things to See & Do

Don't come to Bardejovské Kúpele expecting to enjoy a hot-spring bath because it's impossible unless you've booked a programme with Slovakoterma in Bratislava. Everyone is welcome to partake of the drinking cure, however, and crowds of locals constantly pace up and down the modern **colonnade** (1972), where an unending supply of hot mineral water streams from eight different springs (bring your own cup).

Near the colonnade is the **Šarišské Museum** dedicated to local history and ethnography. Alongside this is Slovakia's best **skanzen**, a fine collection of old farm buildings, rustic houses and wooden churches brought here from villages all over Slovakia. Both museum and skanzen are open daily except Monday all year.

Cukráreň Domino in the shopping mall

opposite Hotel Mineral sells *oplátky* (spa wafers), a local treat not to miss. Domino also dispenses *grog* (rum with hot water).

Getting There & Away

There's no train station, but Bardejovské Kúpele is connected to Bardejov by the city buses Nos 1, 2, 6, 7, 10 and 11. Some long-distance buses for places as far away as Bratislava begin here.

KOŠICE

Košice (Kassa in Hungarian) is the second-largest city in Slovakia and capital of the eastern portion of the republic. Before WW I Košice was a Hungarian city where Slovak was seldom heard and the historic and ethnic influence of nearby Hungary remains strong. The Transylvanian prince Ferenc Rákóczi II had his headquarters at Košice during the Hungarian War of Independence against the Habsburgs from 1703 to 1711. The town became part of Czechoslovakia in 1918 but was recovered by Hungary from 1938 to 1945. From 21 February to 21 April 1945, Košice served as the capital of liberated Czechoslovakia. On 5 April 1945 the Košice Government Programme was announced here, outlining the future socialist development of the country.

Although now a major steel-making city with vast new residential districts built by the communists, there is much in the old town to interest visitors. Churches and museums abound, and there's an active State Theatre. The city is a good base for excursions to other East Slovakian towns. Daily trains between Kraków and Budapest stop here, making Košice the perfect beginning or end to a visit to Slovakia.

Orientation

The adjacent bus and train stations are just east of the old town, a five-minute walk down Mlynská ulica. This street will bring you into námestie Slobody, which becomes Hlavná ulica both north and south of the square. Much of your time in Košice will be spent on this colourful street. Large indexed city maps are posted at various locations around town.

The left-luggage office *(úschovňa)* in the train station is open 24 hours, except for three 45-minute breaks (note the times of these).

Information

Satur (☎ 622 3123) is in the Slovan Hotel, Rooseweltova 1.

There are no Hungarian, Polish or Ukrainian consulates in Košice, so be sure to get your onward visas beforehand in Bratislava.

Money The Investičná Banka exchange office upstairs in the train station is open weekdays from 7.30 am to 5 pm (no commission).

The Všeobecná Úverová Banka, Hlavná ulica 112 (Monday to Thursday 7.30 to noon and 1 to 5 pm, Friday 7.30 am to noon), changes travellers' cheques for 1% commission.

The reception at Hotel Slovan, Rooseweltova 1, will change travellers' cheques at a reasonable rate from 8 am to 10 pm daily. A large sign says this service is for hotel guests only but they'll usually make an exception of the few English-speakers who stray in.

Post & Telephone There's a 24-hour telephone centre in Poštova 2, about 500 metres north of the train station at the end of the park. Košice's telephone code is 095.

Travel Agencies Satur, Rooseweltova 1, reserves sleepers and couchettes and sells international train tickets. The 'Pokladnica Ares' office upstairs in the train station also arranges these tickets.

Satur, Rooseweltova 1, has international bus tickets to Athens, Cologne, Düsseldorf, Istanbul, London, Milan, Munich, Rome, Salzburg, Stockholm, Stuttgart and Zürich. Many of these buses actually leave from Bratislava and some transit the Czech Republic (check visa requirements). Prominent Travel Agency, Mlynská ulica 18, Tatratour, Alžbetina ulica 6, and Autoturist,

Továrenská 1, also sell international bus tickets.

For reduced student and under-26 train tickets to places outside Slovakia try the 'Medzinárodná Pokladnica' window upstairs in the train station.

CKM Student Travel, Alžbetina ulica 11, also has international train tickets with student and youth discounts and they sell ISIC student and hostel cards.

The American Express representative in Košice is Tatratour (☎ 24 872), Alžbetina ulica 6.

Bookshops Petit, Hlavná ulica 41, and Kníhkupectivo, Hlavná ulica 38, have a good selection of hiking maps and town plans.

Visa Extensions The Úradovňa Cudzineckej Polície a Pasovej Služby, across the street from the huge Okresný Úrad Košice/Mestský Magistrát building on trieda Slovenského Národného Povstania (Monday and Wednesday 10 am to noon and 12.30 to 6 pm, Tuesday, Thursday and Friday 7 am to noon), is the place to apply for visa extensions, complete police registration or report a lost passport or visa. Several trams pass here (ask).

Things to See

Košice's top sight is the **Cathedral of St Elizabeth** (1345-1508), a magnificent late-Gothic edifice a five-minute walk west of the train station. In a crypt on the left side of the nave is the tomb of Ferenc Rákóczi (tickets are sold at the adjacent Urban Tower). Duke Rákóczi was exiled to Turkey after the failed 18th-century Hungarian insurgency against Austria and only in 1905 was he officially pardoned and his remains reburied here.

Beside the cathedral is the 14th-century **Urban Tower**, with a museum of metalwork. On the opposite side of the cathedral is the 14th-century **St Michael's Chapel** and the **Košice Programme House**, Hlavná ulica 27, where the 1945 National Front programme was proclaimed. The building dates from 1779 and is now an art gallery (closed Monday) with a large collection by local painter Július Jakoby (1903-85).

Most of Košice's other historic sites are north along Hlavná ulica. In the centre of the square is the ornate **State Theatre** (1899) with a musical fountain in front. Beside it at Hlavná ulica 59 is the rococo former **town hall** (1780), now a cinema, and north of the theatre is a large **plague column** (1723). The Jesuit and Franciscan churches are also on the square. Farther north at Hlavná ulica 88 is the **Slovak Technical Museum** (closed Monday and Saturday).

The **East Slovak Museum** (1912) is on námestie Maratónu mieru at the northern end of Hlavná ulica. The 1st and 2nd floors are dedicated to archaeology and prehistory. Don't miss the Košice Gold Treasure in the basement, a hoard of over 3000 gold coins dating from the 15th to the 18th centuries and discovered by chance in 1935. In the park behind the museum building is an old wooden church.

Walk back along Hlavná ulica to the State Theatre and take the narrow Univerzitná ulica beside the Jesuit church east to the **Miklušova Väznica**, ulica Pri Miklušovej Väznici 10. This connected pair of 16th-century houses once served as a prison equipped with medieval torture chambers and cells. If the houses are closed, ask for the keys at the **Zoology Museum** beside the nearby church. The Zoology Museum is housed in the Executioner's Bastion, part of Košice's 15th-century fortifications.

Most museums and galleries in Košice are closed on Sunday afternoon and Monday.

Places to Stay

Camping South of the city is the *Autocamping salaš Barca* (☎ 58 309). Take tram No 3 south along Južná trieda from the train station until the tram turns left at an underpass, then walk west on Alejová (the Rožňava Highway) for about 800 metres till you see the camping ground on the left. It is open from 15 April to 30 September and there are cabins (US$10/14 double/triple or US$24 for five beds) and tent space (US$1 per person, US$1 per tent). The cabins are

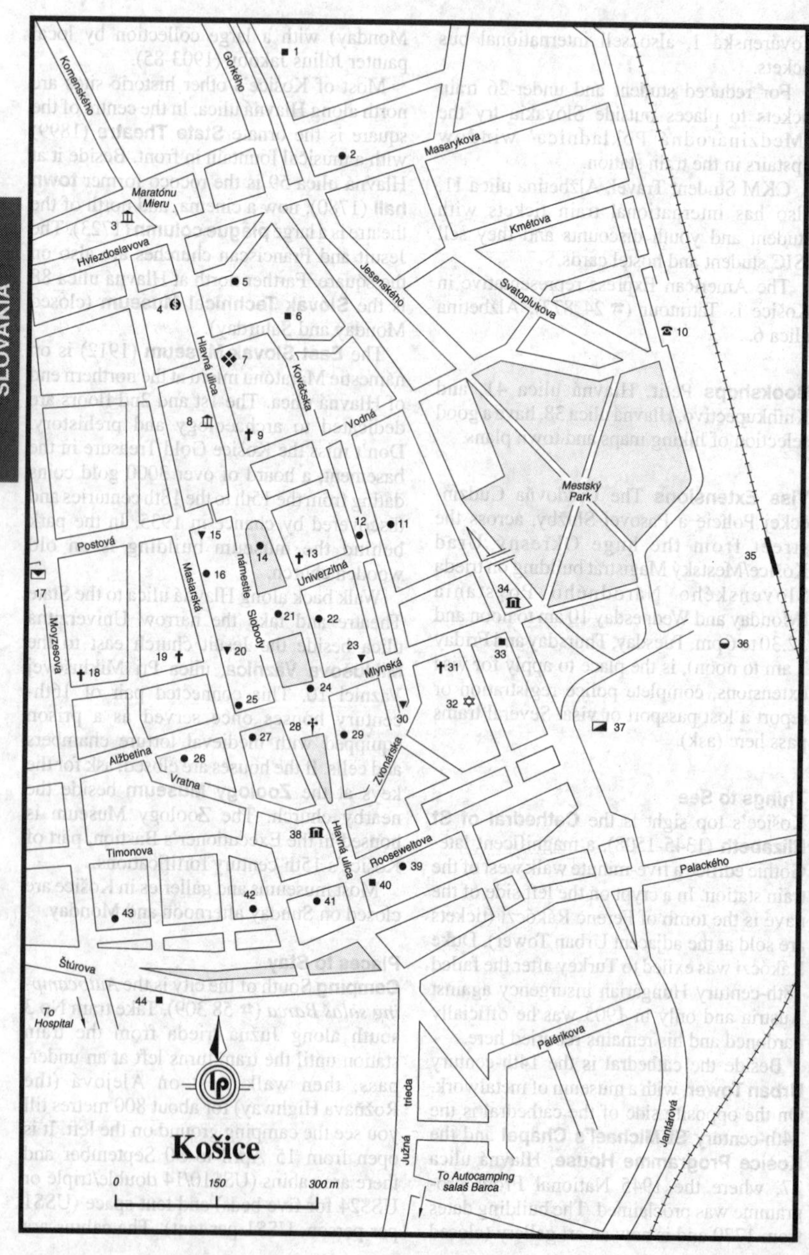

Komenského
Gorkého
Masarykova
Maratónu Mieru
Hviezdoslavova
Kmétova
Jesenského
Svatoplukova
Hlavná ulica
Kováčska
Vodná
Mestský Park
Postová
Maslarská
námestie Slobody
Univerzitná
Moyzesova
Mlynská
Zvonárska
Alžbetina
Vratna
Timonova
Rooseweltova
Palackého
Štúrova
To Hospital
Palárikova
Jantárová
Južná trieda
To Autocamping salaš Barca
Košice
0
150
300 m
1
2
3
4
5
6
7
8
9
10
11
12
13
14
15
16
17
18
19
20
21
22
23
24
25
26
27
28
29
30
31
32
33
34
35
36
37
38
39
40
41
42
43
44

available year-round and there's a restaurant on the premises.

Hostels CKM Student Travel, Alžbetina ulica 11, arranges hostel accommodation year-round. For example, they can book you in to the *Domov Mládeže* (☎ 429 334), Medická 2, on the west side of town, at US$6 per person in two and three-bedded rooms (student card not required). If CKM is closed when you arrive you could try going directly there. CKM can also make advance bookings for you at other hostels and budget hotels around Slovakia.

PLACES TO STAY

1 Hutník Hotel
6 Hotel Coral
33 Hotel Európa
40 Slovan Hotel
44 TJ Metropol Turistická Ubytovná

PLACES TO EAT

15 Aida Espresso
20 Piváreň U Dominikánov
23 Grill Dětva
30 Reštaurácia Ajvega

OTHER

2 Dom kultúry
3 East Slovak Museum
4 Všeobecná Úverová Banka
5 Autoturist
7 Prior Department Store
8 Slovak Technical Museum
9 Franciscan Church
10 Pošta 2 Telephone Centre
11 Executioner's Bastion
12 Miklušova Väznica
13 Jesuit Church
14 Plague Column
16 Ursuline Convent
17 Main Post Office
18 Ukrainian Church
19 Dominican Church
21 State Theatre
22 Former Town Hall
24 Urban Tower
25 CKM Student Travel
26 Art Gallery
27 Tatratour
28 Cathedral of St Elizabeth
29 Košice Programme House
31 Evangelical Church
32 Former Synagogue
34 Jakub's Palace
35 Railway Station
36 Bus Station
37 Swimming Pool & Sauna
38 Forgach Palace
39 Bábkové Divadlo
40 Satur
41 ČSA Airline Office
42 Thália Hungarian Theatre
43 Dom Umenia Concert Hall

Hotels Because Košice is not a major tourist centre, hotel prices are lower than those in Bratislava but Satur in the *Slovan Hotel* has no private rooms.

The recently renovated *Hotel Európa* (☎ 622 3897), a grand old three-storey building just across the park from the train station, costs US$15/26/35 single/double/triple with shared bath.

The *Hotel Coral* (☎ 622 6819), Kasárenské námestie 5 behind the Prior Department Store, is good value at US$12/24 single/double. Every two rooms in this new five-storey building share a shower.

The *TJ Metropol Turistická Ubytovňa* (☎ 55 948), Štúrova 32, is an attractive sports complex with cheerful rooms with shared bath at US$9/11/15 single/double/triple. It's an easy walk from town but is often full with groups. You get a lot of tram noise here in the very early morning.

The proletarian *Hotel Strojár* (☎ 54 406), Južná trieda 93, has double and triple rooms with a bathroom shared between every two rooms at US$6 per person. Apartments are US$19 double. This workers' dormitory is a little run-down but usually has rooms. Get there on tram No 3 from the stations.

The 12-storey *Hutník Hotel* (☎ 37 780), Tyršovo nábr 6 (US$18/28 single/double with bath), is there as a last resort.

Places to Eat

One of the cheapest and best places to eat at is *Grill Dětva*, Mlynská ulica 8. You'll be served tasty wholesome meals promptly (ask for the English menu). You can get a good breakfast here.

Reštaurácia Ajvega, Orlia 10, is an inexpensive, friendly vegetarian restaurant with an English menu. The portions are large but the meals are only so-so and carnivores would do well to eat elsewhere.

The *Zdroj Grill*, Hlavná ulica 83, offers succulent barbecued chicken which you eat standing up. The *Veverická Grill*, Hlavná ulica 95, is good for grilled meats and fish.

A local beer hall worth checking out is *Piváreň U Dominikánov*, Mäsiarska ulica 15 near the market.

A better restaurant for more leisurely dining is the *Zlatý ducat*, Hlavná ulica 16 (upstairs). You'll find less expensive wine (vináreň) and beer (piváreň) restaurants are downstairs. The *Madárská Hungarian Restaurant*, Hlavná ulica 65 (closed on Sunday), features a bright, attractive décor, an extensive menu, good food and a relaxed atmosphere – recommended. It's in Levoča House, a 16th-century warehouse reconditioned into a restaurant, café and nightclub.

Aida Espresso on Poštová ulica through the passage at Hlavná ulica 74 (daily 9 am to 10 pm) has the best ice cream in town (and perhaps the best in Eastern Europe).

Entertainment

The *State Theatre* on námestie Slobody is currently closed for renovations. In the meantime performances are being held at *Dom kultúry* near the Hutník Hotel.

The *Thália Hungarian Theatre* and the *State Philharmonic Dom Umenia* are both in the south-west corner of the old town, but performances are only held once or twice a week. Recitals are sometimes given at the Konzervatórium, Hlavná ulica 89.

The *Bábkové Divadlo*, Rooseweltova ulica 1, puts on puppet shows for children weekday mornings and Sunday afternoon.

You can buy theatre tickets from the box office at Štúdio SMER, Hlavná ulica 76.

Cinemas include Kino Tatra, Hlavná ulica 8, and Kino Slovan, Hlavná ulica 59.

The first Sunday in October runners from many countries participate in an International Marathon Race for Peace here.

Discos Try the *Hacienda Disco Club*, Hlavná ulica 65.

The *Valtická Vináreň*, Hlavná ulica 97, functions as a disco Friday and Saturday from 9 pm to 2 am, but it's better known as a pub open nightly until 11 pm. If there are any English-speaking beer drinkers in town you'll probably find them here.

Things to Buy

Úľuv, Hlavná ulica 76, has a good selection of local handicrafts.

A large street market operates along ulica Cyrilometodejská from the Ukrainian to the Dominican churches.

Getting There & Away

Train Two morning trains depart from Košice for Kiev (1013 km, US$46) and Moscow (1880 km, US$66). Tickets for these trains must be purchased from Satur before 10 am the day before.

Overnight trains with sleepers and couchettes are available between Košice and Prague (708 km), Brno (493 km), Bratislava (445 km), Děčín (807 km), Karlovy Vary (897 km), Plzeň (896 km) and Frantiákovy Lázně (1081 km). Daytime express trains connect Košice to Prague (via Poprad-Tatry and Žilina) and Bratislava (via Banská Bystrica or Žilina).

Bus For shorter trips to Prešov (several an hour, 36 km), Bardejov (14 daily, 77 km, 1¾ hours), Bardejovské Kúpele (six daily, 83 km) and Spišské Podhradie (eight daily, 64 km), you're better off taking a bus. A bus to Užgorod, Ukraine (200 km, three hours, US$3), leaves Košice on Tuesday, Thursday and Saturday at 7 am.

To/From Poland The daily *Cracovia* and *Karpaty* express trains between Hungary and Kraków pass through Košice (reservations required). Northbound the *Cracovia* travels overnight, the *Karpaty* in the late afternoon. A ticket Košice-Kraków costs US$17. For information about unreserved local trains to Poland, see the sections on Prešov and Bardejov.

There's a bus from Košice to Nowy Targ early every Thursday and Saturday morning, to Rzeszów every afternoon. Both are US$5 and you pay the driver. Check the exact times with information as they're not listed on the departures board.

To/From Hungary Local trains run the 88 km from Košice to Miskolc, Hungary (2½ hours, US$9), via Hidasnémeti every morning and afternoon. This is an easy way to cross the border as no reservations are required. If you take the morning train, get a ticket right through to Budapest (if you're going there!) as you will only have five minutes to change trains at Miskolc and no time to change money and buy another ticket.

Alternatively, there are six unreserved local trains a day between Slovenské Nové Mesto, Slovakia, and Sátoraljaújhely, Hungary, with connections to/from Košice and Miskolc.

The *Rákóczi* express train links Košice to Budapest (270 km, 4½ hours, US$21) daily, departing from Budapest-Keleti in the morning, Košice in the late afternoon (reservations optional).

There's a bus from Košice to Miskolc on Wednesday, Friday and Saturday at 6.30 am (84 km, US$3). Book your ticket the day before at window No 1 in the bus station.

Car Rental Autoturist (☎ 622 4066), Továrenská 1, represents Europcar.

Switzerland

Switzerland (Schweiz, Suisse, Svizerra) offers its fair share of clichés – irresistible chocolates, kitsch cuckoo clocks, yodelling Heidis, humourless bankers – but plenty of surprises, too. The visitor will find a flavour of Germany, France and Italy, but always seasoned with a unique Swissness.

Goethe described Switzerland as a combination of 'the colossal and the well-ordered', a succinct reference to the indomitable and majestic Alpine terrain set against the tidy, efficient, watch-precision towns and cities. The combination of these elements provides a peerless attraction. Unfortunately, high costs may prompt you to rush through the whole landscape faster than you would like.

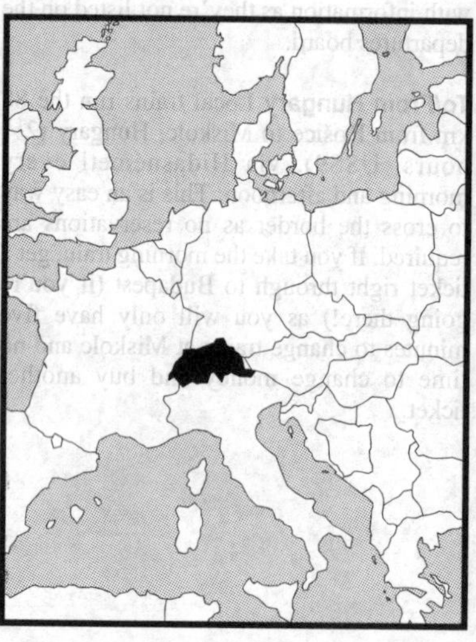

Facts about the Country

HISTORY

The first inhabitants of the region were a Celtic tribe, the Helvetii. The Romans appeared on the scene in 107 BC by way of the St Bernard Pass, but owing to the difficulty of the terrain their attempted conquest of the area was never decisive. They were gradually driven back by the Germanic Alemanni tribe which settled in the 5th century. Burgundians and Franks also settled the area, and Christianity was gradually introduced.

The territory was united under the Holy Roman Empire in 1032 but central control was never very tight, allowing neighbouring nobles to contest each other for local influence. That was all changed by the Germanic Habsburg family, which became the most powerful dynasty in Central Europe. Habsburg expansion was spearheaded by Rudolph I, who gradually brought the squabbling nobles to heel.

The Swiss Confederation

Upon Rudolph's death in 1291, local leaders saw a chance to gain independence. The forest communities of Uri, Schwyz and Nidwalden formed an alliance on 1 August 1291. Their pact of mutual assistance is seen as the origin of the Swiss Confederation, and their struggles against the Habsburgs is idealised in the familiar legend of William Tell. Duke Leopold responded by dispatching a powerful Austrian army in 1315 which was routed by the Swiss at Morgarten. The effective action of the union soon prompted other communities to join. Lucerne (1332) was followed by Zürich (1351), Glarus and Zug (1352), and Bern (1353). Further defeats of the Habsburgs followed at Sempach (1386) and Näfels (1388).

Encouraged by these successes, the Swiss gradually acquired a taste for territorial expansion themselves. Further land was seized from the Habsburgs. They took on Charles the Bold, the Duke of Burgundy, and defeated him at Grandson and Morat. Fribourg, Solothurn, Basel, Schaffhausen

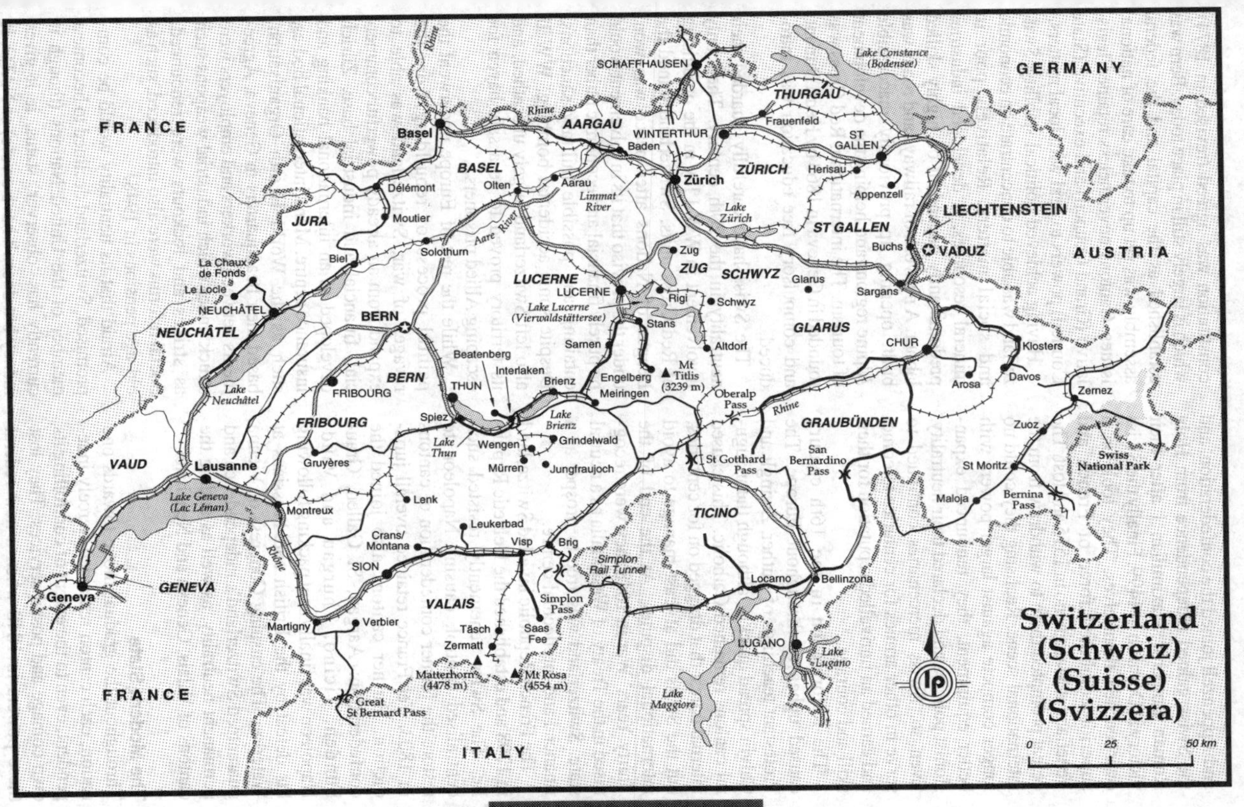

SWITZERLAND

and Appenzell joined the confederation, and the Swiss gained independence from Holy Roman Emperor Maximilian I after their victory at Dornach in 1499. Finally the Swiss over-reached themselves. They took on a superior combined force of French and Venetians at Marignano in 1515 and lost. The defeat prompted them to withdraw from the international scene. Realising they could no longer compete against larger powers with better equipment, they renounced expansionist policies and declared their neutrality. Even so, Swiss mercenaries continued to serve in other armies for centuries to come, and earned an unrivalled reputation for their skill and courage.

The Reformation in the 16th century caused upheaval throughout Europe. The Protestant teachings of Luther, Zwingli and Calvin spread quickly, although the inaugural cantons remained Catholic. This caused internal unrest that dragged on for centuries, but the Swiss did at least manage to avoid international disputes. At the end of the Thirty Years' War in 1648 they were recognised in the Treaty of Westphalia as a neutral state. Switzerland was free to prosper as a financial and intellectual centre.

The French Republic invaded Switzerland in 1798 and established the Helvetic Republic. The Swiss vehemently resisted such centralised control, causing Napoleon to restore the former confederation of cantons in 1803. Yet France retained overall jurisdiction. Further cantons also joined the confederation: Aargau, St Gallen, Graubünden, Ticino, Thurgau and Vaud. Napoleon was finally sent packing following his defeat by the British and Prussians at Waterloo. The ensuing Congress of Vienna guaranteed Switzerland's independence and permanent neutrality, as well as adding the cantons of Valais, Geneva and Neuchâtel.

The Modern State

Throughout the gradual move towards one nation, each canton remained fiercely independent, even to the extent of controlling its own coinage and postal services. They lost these powers in 1848 when a new federal constitution was agreed (revised in 1874), which is largely still in place today. Bern was established as the capital and the federal assembly was set up to take care of national issues. Cantons nevertheless retained legislative (Grand Council) and executive (State Council) powers to deal with local matters.

Having achieved political stability, Switzerland was able to concentrate on economic and social matters. Relatively poor in mineral resources, it developed industries predominantly dependent on highly skilled labour. A network of railways and roads was built, opening up previously inaccessible Alpine regions and helping the development of tourism. The international Red Cross was founded in Geneva in 1863 by Henri Dunant, and compulsory free education was introduced.

The Swiss have carefully guarded their neutrality in the 20th century. Their only involvement in WW I lay in the organising of Red Cross units. Switzerland joined the League of Nations after peace was won, under the proviso that its involvement would be purely financial and economic rather than entailing any possible military sanctions. Despite some accidental bombing, WW II also left Switzerland largely unscathed, and its territory proved to be a safe haven for escaping Allied prisoners.

While the rest of Europe underwent the painful process of rebuilding from the ravages of war, Switzerland was able to expand from an already powerful commercial, financial and industrial base. Zürich developed as an international banking and insurance centre. Many international bodies, such as the World Health Organisation, based their headquarters in Geneva. Agreements between workers and employers were struck under which industrial weapons such as strikes and lockouts were renounced. Social reforms were also introduced, such as old-age pensions in 1948.

Afraid that its neutrality would be compromised, Switzerland declined to become a member of the United Nations (though it currently has 'observer' status, ie it gives money but doesn't have a vote) or NATO. It did, however, join EFTA (the European Free Trade Association). In the face of other EFTA nations applying for EU (European Union, then known as the EC) membership, Switzerland finally made its own application in 1992. As a prelude to full EU membership Switzerland was to join the EEA (European Economic Area), yet the government's strategy lay in ruins after citizens rejected the EEA in a referendum in December 1992. Switzerland's EU application has consequently been put on ice; in the meantime the government has been laying the groundwork for closer integration with the EU, in the hope that the people will eventually come round.

DEFENCE

Despite the fact that Switzerland has managed to avoid international conflicts for over 400 years, every able-bodied male undergoes national service at age 20. Each remains in the reserves, keeping his rifle and full kit at home. During this time, he must serve regular refresher courses and be ready for recall if the country is threatened. Since national service began, there has never been a complete recall, not even during the nervous days of WW II. The reserves stint is to be reduced to 22 years from 30 years, thereby reducing the army to about 400,000-strong.

In the last 55 years, Switzerland has made comprehensive preparations against attack. Besides the civilian army, a whole infrastructure is in place to repel any invasion. Roads and bridges have built-in recesses for explosives so that they can be immediately sabotaged to thwart an invading army. All new buildings must have a substantial air-raid capacity, and underground car parks can be instantly converted to bunkers. Fully equipped emergency hospitals, unused yet maintained, await underneath ordinary hospitals. It's a sobering thought, as you explore the countryside, to realise that those apparently undisturbed mountains and lakes hide a network of military installations and storage depots. The message that comes across today is the same as that dealt out by the country's fearless mercenaries of centuries ago: don't mess with the Swiss.

GEOGRAPHY

Mountains make up 60% of Switzerland's 41,295 sq km. The land is 45% meadow and pasture, 24% forest and 6% arable. Farming of cultivated land is intensive and cows graze on the upper slopes in the summer as soon as the retreating snow line permits.

The Alps occupy the central and southern regions of the country. The Dufour summit (4634 metres) of Monte Rosa is the highest point, although the Matterhorn (4478 metres) is more well known. A series of high passes in the south provide overland access into Italy. Glaciers account for an area of 2000 sq km, most notably the Aletsch Glacier which at 169 sq km is the largest valley glacier in Europe.

The St Gotthard Massif in the centre of Switzerland is the source of many lakes and rivers, such as the Rhine and the Rhône. The Jura Mountains straddle the northern border with France. These mountains peak at around 1700 metres and are less steep and less severely eroded than the Alps.

Between the two mountain systems is the Mittelland, also known as the Swiss Plateau, a region of hills crisscrossed by rivers, ravines and winding valleys. This area has spawned the most populous cities and is also where much of the agricultural activity takes place.

GOVERNMENT

The modern Swiss Confederation is made up of 23 cantons; three are subdivided, bringing the total to 26. Each has its own constitution and legislative body for dealing with local issues. The Jura achieved full cantonal status as late as 1979.

National legislative power is in the hands of the Federal Assembly which consists of two chambers. The lower chamber, the National Council, is elected by proportional representation with one member per 22,000 people. The upper chamber, the States Council, is composed of 46 members, two per full canton. The Federal Assembly elects seven members to form the Federal Council, which holds executive power. All elections are for a four-year term except the posts of president and vice-president of the Confederation, which are rotated annually. The vice-president always succeeds the president, meaning the governing body is not dominated by any one individual.

Under the 1874 constitution, laws can actually be influenced directly by the Swiss people, provided enough signatures can be collected from active citizens: 50,000 to force a full referendum on proposed laws, and 100,000 to initiate legislation. Citizens regularly vote in referenda on national, local and communal issues. Surprisingly for such a democratic people, women only won the right to vote in federal elections in 1971, and in some cantons women gained a local vote only in the last few years. A few cantons still vote by a show of hands in an open-air parliament called the *Landsgemeinde*.

ECONOMY

Switzerland has a mixed economy with the emphasis on private ownership. The only industries nationalised outright are telecommunications, post and some railways. Other than municipal enterprises, everything else is in private hands and operates according to capitalist principles, with the occasional subsidy thrown in. A good proportion of the wealth generated is channelled back into the community via social welfare programmes. The system is very efficient (though price-fixing cartels are a problem); even so, Switzerland is not immune from world recession. Unemployment, previously virtually unknown, has crept to around 5%. Inflation was expected to keep below 2% in 1994 and 1995.

In the absence of other raw materials, hydroelectric power has become the main source of energy. Chemicals, machine tools and watches and clocks are the most important exports. Silks and embroidery, also important, are produced to a high quality. Swiss banks are a magnet for foreign funds attracted by political and monetary stability. Tourism is the country's third-biggest industry and the Swiss aim to make things as easy as possible for visitors (especially to spend money!). Swiss breakthroughs in science and industry include vitamins, DDT, gas turbines and milk chocolate. They also, for their sins, developed the modern formula for life insurance.

POPULATION & PEOPLE

With a population of 6,910,800, Switzerland averages 166 inhabitants per sq km. The Alpine districts are sparsely populated, meaning that the Mittelland is densely settled, especially round the shores of the larger lakes. Zürich is the largest city with 343,000 inhabitants, next comes Basel (172,000), Geneva (167,00) and Bern (150,000). Most of the people are of Germanic origin as reflected in the breakdown of the four national languages spoken (see the Language section). Over 17% of people living in the country are residents but not Swiss citizens; the foreign influx started after WW II, particularly from southern Europe.

ARTS

Switzerland does not have a very strong tradition in the arts, even though many foreign writers and artists have visited and settled, attracted by the beauty and tranquillity of the mountains and lakes. Among them were Voltaire, Byron and Shelley. Paul Klee is the best-known native painter. He created abstract works which used colour, line and form to evoke a variety of sensations. The 18th-century writings of Rousseau in Geneva played an important part in the development of democracy. Carl Jung, with his research in Zürich, was instrumental in developing modern psychoanalysis.

Arthur Honegger is the only Swiss composer of note. Despite that, music is strongly emphasised with a full symphony orchestra in every main city. Gothic and Renaissance architecture are evident in urban areas, especially Bern. Rural Swiss houses vary according to region, but are generally characterised by ridged roofs with wide, overhanging eaves, and balconies and verandahs which are usually enlivened by colourful floral displays.

CULTURE

Traditional Lifestyle

In a few mountain regions such as Valais, people still wear traditional rural costumes, but dressing up is usually reserved for festivals. Every spring hardy herders climb to Alpine pastures with their cattle and live in summer huts while tending their herds. They gradually descend back to village level as the grassland is grazed. Both the departure and the return is a cause for celebrations and processions. Yodelling and playing the alp horn are also part of the Alpine tradition, as is Swiss wrestling.

Avoiding Offence

In general the Swiss are a law-abiding nation; even minor transgressions such as littering can cause offence. Always shake hands when being introduced to a Swiss, and again when leaving. Formal titles should also be used (*Herr* for men and *Frau* for women). It is also customary to greet shopkeepers when entering their shops. Public displays of affection are OK, but are more common in French Switzerland than in the slightly more formal German-speaking parts. Attitudes to homosexuality are reasonably tolerant (the gay age of consent is 16).

Sport

Shooting and gymnastic clubs are popular with male adults. The interest in shooting is a spillover from the need to maintain a minimum standard with service weapons while in the reserves. Mountaineering, skiing and fishing are also favourite pastimes, but the number one activity is hiking.

RELIGION

Protestantism and Roman Catholicism are equally widespread, though the concentration varies between cantons. Strong Protestant areas are Bern, Vaud and Zürich, whereas Valais, Ticino and Uri are mostly Catholic. Some churches are supported entirely by donations from the public, others receive state subsidies.

LANGUAGE

Located in the corner of Europe where the German, French and Italian language areas meet, the linguistic melting pot which is Switzerland has three official federal languages: German (spoken by about two-thirds of the population), French (18%) and Italian (10%). A fourth language, Rhaeto-Romanic, or Romansch, is spoken by 1% of the population, mainly in the canton of Graubünden. Derived from Latin, it's a linguistic relic which, along with Friulian and Ladin across the border in Italy, has survived in the isolation of mountain valleys. In 1938, Romansch was recognised as an official national (though not federal) language by referendum.

For a rundown on German, turn to the Language section in the Germany chapter. Though German-speaking Swiss have no trouble with standard High German, they use Swiss German, or *Schwyzerdütsch*, in private conversation and in most nonofficial situations. Swiss German covers a wide

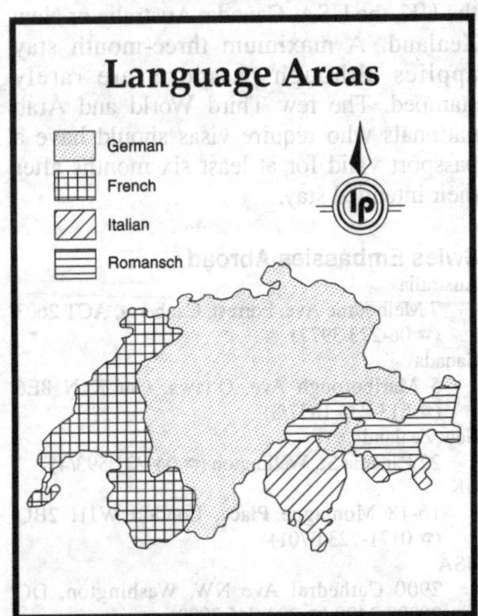

variety of melodic dialects that can differ quite markedly from High German. Visitors will probably note the frequent use of the suffix *-li* to indicate the diminutive, or as a term of endearment.

You will have few problems being understood in English in the German-speaking parts of Switzerland. However, it is simple courtesy to greet people with the Swiss-German *Grüezi* (Hello) and to enquire *sprechen Sie Englisch?* (do you speak English?) before launching into English. In French Switzerland you shouldn't have too many problems either, though the locals' grasp of English is likely to be less complete than that of German speakers. Italian Switzerland is where you will have the greatest difficulty. Most locals speak some French and/or German in addition to Italian. English has a lower priority, but you'll still find that the majority of hotels and restaurants have at least one English-speaking staff member.

SWITZERLAND

Facts for the Visitor

VISAS & EMBASSIES

Visas are not required for passport holders of the UK, the USA, Canada, Australia or New Zealand. A maximum three-month stay applies although passports are rarely stamped. The few Third World and Arab nationals who require visas should have a passport valid for at least six months after their intended stay.

Swiss Embassies Abroad

Australia
7 Melbourne Ave, Forrest, Canberra, ACT 2603 (☎ 06-273 3977)
Canada
5 Marlborough Ave, Ottawa, Ont K1N 8E6 (☎ 613-235 1837/8)
New Zealand
22 Panama St, Wellington (☎ 04-721 593/4)
UK
16-18 Montague Place, London W1H 2BQ (☎ 0171-723 0701)
USA
2900 Cathedral Ave NW, Washington, DC 20008-3499 (☎ 202-745 7900)

Foreign Embassies in Switzerland

See the relevant city sections for details. Bern has all the embassies (there isn't one for New Zealand: its consulate and mission is in Geneva). Consulates can be found in many other towns, particularly Geneva and Zürich.

DOCUMENTS

British citizens may travel on a one-year British Visitors' passport. If you're driving, a European driving licence is OK but other nationals should have an International Driving Permit.

CUSTOMS

Visitors from Europe may import 200 cigarettes, 50 cigars or 250 grams of pipe tobacco. Visitors from non-European countries may import twice as much. The allowance for alcohol is the same for everyone: one litre of spirits plus two litres below 15%. Tobacco and alcohol may only be brought in by people aged 17 or over.

MONEY

Currency

Swiss francs are divided into 100 centimes (usually called *Rappen* in German-speaking Switzerland). There are notes for 10, 20, 50, 100, 500 and 1000 francs, and coins for five, 10, 20 and 50 centimes, as well as for one, two and five francs.

All major travellers' cheques and credit cards are equally acceptable. Virtually all train stations have money exchange facilities which are open daily, and many offer Visa card cash advances. Shop around when changing: commission charges are gradually being introduced (though they're not widespread yet) and exchange rates can vary. Hotels usually have the worst rates. To get money sent to Switzerland, an international money order is cheap and easy. Swiss banks are reluctant to handle computer transfers for non-customers: all you need to open an account is a passport and a home address. There are no charges at the Swiss end for American Express' Moneygram transfer system.

Exchange Rates

A$1	=	Sfr1
C$1	=	Sfr1
DM1	=	Sfr0.83
NZ$1	=	Sfr0.76
UK£1	=	Sfr2.07
US$1	=	Sfr1.40

Costs

Prices are higher in Switzerland than in anywhere in Europe outside Scandinavia, and VAT (see the following Consumer Taxes section) will increase expenses. Some travellers can scrimp by on under Sfr40 a day after buying a railpass. This is survival level – camping or hostelling, self-catering when possible and allowing nothing for nonessentials. If you want to stay in pensions and have the odd beer, count on spending twice as much. Taking cable cars is a major expense; if you're fit enough, walk instead.

Tipping

Tipping is rarely necessary as hotels, restaurants and bars are required by law to include a 15% service charge in bills (though locals often 'round-up'). Even taxis normally have a charge included. Prices are fixed, but people have successfully haggled for lower hotel rates in the low season.

Consumer Taxes

On 1 January 1995, VAT (MWST) on goods and services replaces the old 'turnover' tax which applied only to goods. The rate was expected to be 6.5% (though it may be lower for hotel bills). At the time of research, it was not clear if nonresidents would be eligible for a refund: if you plan on making big purchases, ask.

If you're driving to Switzerland, see the Getting There & Away section for important information about paying the motorway tax.

CLIMATE & WHEN TO GO

Ticino in the south has a hot, Mediterranean climate, and Valais in the south-west is noted for being dry. Elsewhere the temperature is typically 20 to 25°C in summer and 2 to 6°C in winter, with spring and autumn hovering around the 7 to 14°C mark. Summer tends to bring a lot of sunshine, and most rain falls in the spring and autumn. You will need to be prepared for a range of temperatures dependent on altitude.

Look out for the *Föhn*, a hot, dry wind that sweeps down into the valleys and can be oppressively uncomfortable. It can strike at any time of the year. Daily weather reports covering 25 resorts are displayed in major train stations. Switzerland is visited throughout the year – December to April for winter sports, and May to October for general tourism and hiking. Alpine resorts all but close down in May and November.

WHAT TO BRING

Take a sturdy pair of boots if you intend to walk in the mountains, and warm clothing for those cold nights at high altitude. Hostel membership is invaluable, and it's cheaper to join before you get to Switzerland.

SUGGESTED ITINERARIES

Depending on the length of your stay, you might want to see and do the following things:

Two days
: Visit the sights in Geneva and take a trip on the lake. Don't miss Chillon Castle in Montreux.

One week
: Visit Geneva and Montreux. En route to Zürich, spend a couple of days exploring Interlaken and the Jungfrau Region.

Two weeks
: As above, but spend longer in the mountains. Detour to Bern, Basel and Lucerne.

One month
: As above, but after Zürich, explore St Gallen and eastern Switzerland before looping down to take in Graubünden, Ticino and Valais.

Two months
: As above, but take your time. Visit Neuchâtel and the Jura from Bern.

TOURIST OFFICES

The Swiss National Tourist Office (SNTO) abroad and local tourist offices *(Verkehrsbüro)* in Switzerland are extremely helpful and have plenty of literature to give out to you, including maps (nearly always free).

SWITZERLAND

Somebody invariably speaks English. Local offices can be found everywhere tourists are likely to go, and will often book hotel rooms and organise excursions.

If staying in resorts, ask the local tourist office if there's a Visitor's Card, as these are good for useful discounts.

Tourist Offices Abroad

Australia
: Swiss Consulate General, 3 Bowen Crescent, Melbourne 3004 (☎ 03-867 2266)

Canada
: SNTO, 154 University Ave, Toronto, Ont M5H 3Z4 (☎ 416-971 9734)

UK
: SNTO, Swiss Centre, Swiss Court, London W1V 8EE (☎ 0171-734 1921)

USA
: SNTO, Swiss Center, 608 Fifth Ave, New York, NY 10020 (☎ 212-757 59 44)

The SNTO also has offices in Los Angeles, Chicago, Paris, Rome, Munich and Vienna.

USEFUL ORGANISATIONS

Swiss Alpine Club
: Schweizer Alpenclub (SAC), Helvetiaplatz 4, CH-3005 Bern (☎ 031-351 36 11)

Swiss Automobile Club
: Automobil-Club der Schweiz (ACS), Wasserwerkgasse 39, CH-3000 Bern 13 (☎ 031-311 77 22)

Swiss Camping & Caravanning Federation
: Schweizerischer Camping und Caravanning-Verband (SCCV), Habsburgerstrasse 35, CH-6004 Lucerne (☎ 041-23 48 22)

Swiss Hotel Association
: Schweizer Hotelier-Verein (SHV), Monbijoustrasse 130, CH-3001 Bern (☎ 031-370 41 11)

Swiss Invalid Association
: Schweizerischer Invalidenverband, Froburgstrasse 4, CH-4600 Olten (☎ 062-32 12 62)

Swiss Youth Hostel Association (SYHA)
: Schweizerischer Jugendherbergen, Schaffhauserstrasse 14, CH-8042, Zürich (☎ 01-482 35 44)

BUSINESS HOURS & HOLIDAYS

Most shops are open from 8 am to 6.30 pm, Monday to Friday, with a 90-minute or two-hour break for lunch at noon. Some are closed on Monday morning and Wednesday afternoon, and some towns have late opening on Thursday. Banks are open Monday to Friday from 8.30 am to 4 pm with some local variations. National holidays are 1 January, Good Friday, Easter Monday, Ascension Day, Whit Monday, 25 and 26 December. Some cantons observe 2 January, 1 May (Labour Day), Corpus Christi, All Saints Day and 1 August (National Day).

CULTURAL EVENTS

Numerous events take place at a local level throughout the year, so it's worth checking with the tourist office. Most dates vary from year to year. This is just a brief selection:

January
: Costumed sleigh-rides, Engadine

February
: *Carnival*, Basel

March
: *Engadine Skiing Marathon*, Graubünden

April
: Landsgemeinde meetings in Appenzell, Hundwil (or Trogen), Sarnen and Stans (last Sunday of the month)

May
: *May Day*, especially St Gallen and Vaud

June
: *Geneva Rose Week*
: *Combats des Reines* (cow fighting; yes, the cows fight each other!), lower Valais
: *International June Festival of the Arts*, Zürich

July
: *Montreux Jazz Festival*

August
: *National Day*
: Swiss wrestling, Emmental
: *Geneva Festival*

September
: *Knabenschiessen* shooting contest, Zürich

October
: Vintage festivals in wine-growing regions such as Morges, Neuchâtel and Lugano

November
: Open-air markets including the Onion Market in Bern

December
: *St Nicholas Day* (6 December)
: *Escalade festival*, Geneva

POST

Postcards and letters to Europe cost Sfr1/0.80 *prioritaire/non prioritaire*; to elsewhere they cost Sfr1.80/0.90. The term 'poste restante' is widely understood although you might prefer to use the German term, *Postlagernde Briefe*. Mail can be sent to any town with a post office and is held for 30 days, but you need to show your passport in order to collect it. American Express also holds mail for one month for people who use its cheques or cards.

Post office opening times vary but typically are Monday to Friday from 8 am to noon and 2 pm to 6.30 pm, and Saturday from 8 am to 11 am. The larger post offices offer services outside normal hours (daily lunchtime and evening), but some transactions are subject to a Sfr1 to Sfr2 surcharge.

TELEPHONE

Nearly all post offices have telephones. Hotels can charge as much as they like for telephone calls, and they usually charge plenty (even for direct-dial). Even in payphones the minimum charge is a massive Sfr0.60. Calls within Switzerland are 60% cheaper on weekdays between 5 pm and 7 pm and between 9 pm and 8 am, and throughout the weekend. International calls to Europe are cheaper from 9 pm to 8 am on weekdays, and throughout the weekend. You can dial to just about anywhere worldwide. Phonecards *(Taxcard)* are available for Sfr10 and Sfr20.

TIME

Swiss time is GMT/UTC plus one hour. Daylight-saving time comes into effect at midnight on the last Saturday in March, when the clocks are moved forward one hour; they go back again on the last Saturday in September.

ELECTRICITY

The electric current is 220 V, 50 Hz. Sockets are a pain: the standard Continental plug, with two round pins, can be used in the Swiss three-pin socket. But not if, as is common, the socket is recessed to receive the Swiss six-sided plug. International adapters don't fit these – it's best to buy and fit a Swiss plug on arrival.

LAUNDRY

There is no shortage of coin-operated or service laundrettes in cities. Expect to pay around Sfr10 to wash and dry a five-kg load. Many hostels also have washing machines, and prices are usually slightly cheaper.

WEIGHTS & MEASURES

The metric system is used. Note that cheese and other foods may be priced per 100 grams rather than per kg (a futile attempt to cushion the shock of the high prices?). Like other Continental Europeans, the Swiss indicate decimals with commas and thousands with points.

BOOKS & MAPS

For more detail, refer to Lonely Planet's *Switzerland – a travel survival kit*. The SNTO sells camping and hiking guides in English, and other books and maps on Switzerland. *Living and Working in Switzerland* by David Hampshire (paperback) is an excellent practical guide for those doing what the title suggests. *Why Switzerland?* by Jonathan Steinberg looks at the country's history and culture, and enthusiastically argues that Switzerland is *not* a boring country. Fiction about Switzerland is surprisingly scarce, but Anita Brookner won the Booker Prize in 1984 for *Hotel du Lac*, a novel set around Lake Geneva.

Michelin covers the whole country with four maps. The *Landeskarte der Schweiz* (Topographical Survey of Switzerland) series is larger in scale and especially useful for hiking. Kümmerley & Frey maps are also good for hikers. All these maps are widely available in Switzerland.

MEDIA

The BBC World Service broadcasts on medium wave (1296 and 648 kHz), and American Forces Network is on the FM band (101.8 mHz). Swiss Radio International (3985, 6165 or 9535kHz) broadcasts in English at 6 am, 8 am and 1 pm. English-language newspapers are widely available and cost around Sfr3 to Sfr4.

FILM & PHOTOGRAPHY

You may photograph anything anywhere

you're allowed to go. Film is cheaper than in Austria at around Sfr6.50 for Kodak Gold and Sfr16.50 for Kodachrome (36 exposures). The Inter Discount chain has the lowest prices.

HEALTH

No inoculations are required for entry to healthy Switzerland. All medical treatment must be paid for, whether in cantonal or university hospitals or private clinics. Charges are high, so medical insurance is strongly advised. Remember that the air is thinner at high altitude. Take things easy above 3000 metres, and if you start feeling light-headed, come down to a lower altitude. Call ☎ 144 for an ambulance (most areas).

WOMEN TRAVELLERS

Women travellers should experience no special problems. Some older Swiss men believe that a woman's place is in the home (under Swiss marriage laws, wives weren't granted equal rights until 1988!), however, the independence of female travellers is respected.

DANGERS & ANNOYANCES

Crime rates may be low but don't neglect security. There are a lot of young drug addicts in Switzerland who may cause problems where they congregate in groups in cities. Emergency telephone numbers are police, ☎ 117, fire brigade, ☎ 118, motoring assistance, ☎ 140. Take special care in the mountains: helicopter rescue is extremely expensive (make sure your travel insurance covers Alpine sports).

WORK

Officially, only foreigners with special skills can work legally but people still manage to find work in ski resorts – anything from snow clearing to washing dishes. Hotel work has the advantage of including meals and accommodation. In theory, jobs and work permits should be sorted out before arrival, but if you find a job once there, the employer may well have unallocated work permits. The seasonal 'A' permit *(Permis A, Saisonbewilligung)* is valid for up to nine months, and the elusive and much sought-after 'B' permit *(Permis B, Aufenthaltsbewilligung)* is renewable and valid for a year. Many resort jobs are advertised in the Swiss weekly newspaper, *Hotel & Touristik Revue*. Casual wages are higher than in most other European countries.

ACTIVITIES

Water Sports

Water-skiing, sailing and windsurfing are possible on most lakes. Courses are usually available, especially in Graubünden and central Switzerland. There are over 350 lake beaches. Anglers should contact the local tourist office for a fishing permit valid for lakes and rivers. The Rotsee near Lucerne is a favourite place for rowing. Rafting is possible on many Alpine rivers including the Rhine and the Rhône. Canoeing is mainly centred on the Muota in Schwyz canton and on the river Doubs in the Jura.

Skiing

There are dozens of ski resorts throughout the Alps, the Pre-Alps and the Jura, incorporating some 200 ski schools. Those resorts favoured by the package-holiday companies do not necessarily have better skiing facilities, but they do tend to have more diversions off the slopes, in terms of sightseeing and nightlife.

Equipment can always be hired at resorts; charges average about Sfr35/20 per day for downhill/cross-country gear. You can buy new equipment at reasonable prices. It's also worth looking around for ski dumps, as the Swiss are so affluent they tend to throw away perfectly usable equipment.

Ski passes (around Sfr45 for one day; multi-day passes are cheaper per day) allow unlimited use of mountain transport. Beginners could save money by buying ski coupons instead (where available) if they only want to try a couple of experimental runs.

Hiking & Mountaineering

There are 50,000 km of designated footpaths

with regular refreshment stops en route. Bright yellow signs marking the trail make it difficult to get lost; each gives an average walking time to the next destination. Zermatt is a favourite destination for mountaineers, but you should never climb on your own, or without proper equipment. For information contact the Swiss Alpine Club (see the Useful Organisations section earlier in this chapter).

HIGHLIGHTS

Endless beautiful vistas greet you in this country. The views from Shilthorn or its neighbour, Jungfrau, are unforgettable. Zermatt combines inspiring views of the Matterhorn and fine skiing. Be sure to take a boat trip: Lake Lugano reveals the sunny side of Switzerland's Italian canton, and Lake Thun offers snowcapped scenery and several castles. Excursions are also excellent on lakes Lucerne and Geneva.

The Château de Chillon near Montreux is justifiably the most famous castle in Switzerland. Picturesque town centres include Bern, Lucerne, St Gallen and Stein am Rhein. Zürich, Basel and Geneva are bursting with fine museums and art galleries. Lausanne features a unique collection of bizarre 'outsider' art.

ACCOMMODATION

Camping

There are about 450 camping grounds, which are classified from one to five stars depending upon their amenities and convenience of location. Charges per night are around Sfr5 per person plus Sfr3 to Sfr5 for a tent, and maybe the same for a car. Many sites offer a slight discount if you have a Camping Carnet. Free camping is not actively encouraged and should be discreet.

Hostels

There are 80 official Swiss Youth Hostels *(Jugendherberge, auberge de jeunesse, allogio per giovanni)* spread throughout the country, which are automatically affiliated to the international network. Most Swiss hostels (including *all* those mentioned in this chapter except Lugano) include breakfast in the price; most also add an extra Sfr2.50 for the first night's stay only (exceptions are the hostels in Bern, Geneva, Lugano and Vaduz). It is the full *first night's charge* that is quoted in this chapter. Sheets are nearly always included, and some places have double or family rooms available (with single or bunk beds). Membership cards must be shown. Nonmembers pay a Sfr7 'guest fee' to stay in Swiss hostels; six of these add up to a full membership card. However, you're better off paying a one-off fee of Sfr30 for international membership, or becoming a member in your country of residence should be even cheaper.

Hostels do get full, and telephone reservations are not accepted. Write, or use the excellent telefax service. Under this system, Swiss hostels will reserve ahead to the next hostel for you but you must give specific dates. The cost is Sfr1.50 plus a Sfr13.50 refundable deposit, and you must claim your bed by 9 pm. A map, giving full details of all hostels on the reverse, including fax numbers, is available free from hostels and some tourist offices.

Hotels

Swiss accommodation is geared towards value for money rather than low cost, so even bottom-of-the-range rooms are fairly comfortable. High-season prices can be 10% (towns) to 40% (Alpine resorts) higher than in the low season, but exactly when the high season occurs varies from region to region. Hotels are star-rated. Prices start at around Sfr60 for a basic double room. Count on at least Sfr10 more for a room with a shower. Rates generally include breakfast, which tends to be a buffet in mid-price and above hotels. Note that some train stations have hotel information boards with a free telephone.

Other Accommodation

'Hotel Garni' means bed and breakfast without any extra meals being available. Private houses in rural areas sometimes offer inexpensive rooms: look out for signs saying

Zimmer frei ('room(s) vacant'). Some farms also take paying guests. Self-catering accommodation is available in holiday chalets, apartments or bungalows. Local tourist offices have full lists of everything on offer in the area. The Swiss Alpine Club maintains around 150 mountain huts at higher altitudes.

FOOD

The Swiss emphasis on quality extends to meals. Basic restaurants provide simple but well-cooked food although prices are generally high. Many budget travellers rely on picnic provisions from supermarkets, but even here prices can be a shock with cheese costing over Sfr20 a kg!

The main supermarket chains are Migros and Coop; larger branches have good quality self-service restaurants, which typically open to around 6.30 pm on weekdays and to 4 pm on Saturday. These, along with EPA department store restaurants, are usually the cheapest places for hot food, with dishes starting at around Sfr7. Likewise at university restaurants *(mensas)*; when mentioned in this chapter they are open to everyone. Buffet-style restaurant chains, like Manora and Inova, offer good food at low prices. The food is freshly cooked in front of you, and you can sometimes select the ingredients yourself.

In restaurants the best value is a fixed-menu dish of the day *(Tagesteller, plat du jour,* or *piatto del giorno)*. Fast-food joints are proliferating. Some wine bars *(Weinstübli)* and beer taverns *(Bierstübli)* serve meals. Main meals are eaten at noon. Cheaper restaurants (except pizzerias) tend to be fairly rigid in when they serve. Go to a hotel or more up-market restaurant for more flexible, later eating. Dedicated vegetarian restaurants can be hard to come by, though many places offer non-meat choices.

Swiss food borrows characteristics from its larger neighbours. Breakfast is of the continental variety. *Müsli* (muesli) was invented in Switzerland at the end of the 19th century but few people seem to eat it in its country of origin. Soups are popular and often very filling. Cheeses form an important part of the Swiss diet. Emmental and Gruyère are combined with white wine to create *fondue*, which is served up in a vast pot and eaten with bread cubes. *Raclette* is another cheese dish, served with potatoes. *Rösti* (fried, shredded potatoes) is German Switzerland's national dish. A wide variety of *Wurst* (sausage) is available. Veal is highly rated throughout Switzerland. In Zürich it is thinly sliced and served in a cream sauce *(Geschnetzeltes Kalbsfleisch)*. *Bündnerfleisch* is dried beef, smoked and thinly sliced. Swiss chocolate, excellent by itself, is often used in desserts and cakes.

DRINKS

Mineral water is readily available but tap water is fine to drink. Note that milk from Alpine cows contains a high level of fat.

Alcohol licensing laws in Switzerland aren't very restrictive – you're more likely to be restricted by the high prices. Fortunately, beer and wine prices in supermarkets aren't too bad. In bars, lager beer comes in 0.5 or 0.3-litre bottles or on draught *(vom Fass)* with measures ranging from 0.2 to 0.5 litre.

Wine is considered an important part of the meal even though it is rather expensive. Local wines are generally good but you may not have heard of them before, as output can not even meet domestic demand so they are rarely exported. The main growing regions are the Italian and French-speaking parts of the country, particularly in Valais and by Lake Neuchâtel and Lake Geneva. Both red and white wines are produced, and each region has its own speciality (eg Merlot in Ticino). There is also a choice of locally produced fruit brandies, often served with or in coffee.

ENTERTAINMENT

Cinemas usually show films in the original language. Check posters for the upper-case letter: E/d/f indicates English with German and French subtitles. In French Switzerland you might see instead 'VO', signifying 'original version'. Nightlife is not all it could be in the cities, and where it does exist, it is expensive. Geneva is the best place for late nightclubs *(boîtes)*, although Zürich is also lively. In ski resorts the 'après ski' atmosphere can keep things lively until late. Listening to music is popular. Classical, folk, jazz and rock concerts can be found in all major cities.

THINGS TO BUY

Watches and chocolates are on many people's lists. Swiss army knives range from simple blades (Sfr10) to mini toolboxes (Sfr100 or more). A grotesquely tacky cuckoo clock with a girl bouncing on a spring will set you back at least Sfr20, a musical box anything upwards of Sfr30. Should you want a cowbell to warn people of your arrival, one with a decorative band will cost from Sfr5 to a fortune depending on the size. Look for textiles and embroidery around St Gallen, and woodcarvings in Brienz.

Getting There & Away

AIR

The main entry points for flights are Zürich and Geneva. Each has several nonstop flights a day to major transport hubs such as London, Paris and Frankfurt. Both airports are linked directly to the Swiss rail network. Basel airport is another busy centre, even though it is actually on the French side of the border at Mulhouse. Bern has a small airport with some international flights (eg direct to/from London's Stansted airport by Air Engiadina). Swissair luggage check-in facilities are at major Swiss train stations. There is no airport departure tax to pay when flying out of Switzerland.

LAND

Bus

The international bus service to Switzerland is minimal. Buses go to both Zürich (once or twice a week, via Basel) and Geneva (approximately every other day) from London's Victoria Coach Station. The journey takes 21 hours and costs £99 (£89 for those under 26). Geneva also has bus connections to Chamonix and Barcelona (see Geneva for details). Eurolines' representative in Zürich is Marti Travel (☎ 01-221 04 72), Usteristrasse 10.

Train

Located at the heart of Europe, it is not surprising that Switzerland has excellent and frequent train connections to the rest of the Continent. Zürich is the busiest international terminus. It has five direct trains daily to Vienna (takes eight hours). There are several trains a day to both Geneva and Lausanne from Paris, and journey time is three to four hours by super-fast TGV. Paris to Bern takes 4½ hours by TGV. Most connections from Germany pass though Zürich or Basel. Nearly all connections from Italy pass through Milan before branching off to Zürich, Lucerne, Bern or Lausanne. Reservations on express trains are subject to a surcharge of Sfr4 to Sfr22, depending on the day and/or service.

Car & Motorbike

Roads into Switzerland are good despite the difficulty of the terrain, but special care is needed when negotiating mountain passes. Some, such as the N5 route from Morez (in France) to Geneva are not recommended if you have not had previous experience. Upon entering Switzerland you will need to decide whether you wish to use the motorways. There is a one-off charge of Sfr30 if you do. Organise this money beforehand, since you might not always be able to change money at the border. Better still, buy it in advance from SNTO or a motoring organisation. The sticker (called a vignette) you receive is valid for a year and must be displayed on the windscreen. A separate fee must be paid for trailers and caravans (motorcyclists must pay, too). Some Alpine tunnels incur additional tolls.

BOAT

Basel can be reached by Rhine steamer from Amsterdam or other towns en route. The total journey time is more than four days. Switzerland can also be reached by steamer from several lakes: from Germany via Lake Constance (Bodensee in German); from Italy via Lake Maggiore; and from France via Lake Geneva.

Getting Around

AIR

Internal flights are not of great interest to the visitor, owing to the excellent ground transport. Crossair, a subsidiary of Swissair, is the local carrier, and links major towns and cities several times daily.

BUS

Yellow postbuses are a supplement to the rail network, following postal routes and linking towns to the more inaccessible regions in the mountains. In all, routes cover some 8000 km of terrain. They are extremely regular, and departures tie in with train arrivals. Postbus stations are next to train stations.

TRAIN

The Swiss rail network covers 5000 km and is a combination of state-run and private lines. Trains are clean, reliable, frequent and as fast as the terrain will allow. Prices are high, though the travel passes mentioned above will cut costs. All fares quoted are for 2nd class; 1st-class fares are about 65% higher. In general, Eurail passes are not valid for private lines and Inter-Rail gets 50% off. All major stations are connected to each other by hourly departures, but services stop from around midnight to 6 am.

Train stations invariably offer luggage storage, either at a counter (Sfr2 to Sfr5 per piece) or in 24-hour lockers (Sfr2 to Sfr5). They also have excellent information counters which give out free timetable booklets and advice on connections. Single train tickets are often valid for two days and it is possible to break the journey on the same ticket, but tell the conductor of your intentions. Train schedules are revised yearly, so double-check details before travelling.

CAR & MOTORBIKE

Be prepared for winding roads, high passes and long tunnels. Speed limits are 50 km/h in towns, 120 km/h on motorways, 100 km/h on semi-motorways (roadside rectangular

SWITZERLAND

TRAVEL PASSES

Swiss public transport is a fully integrated and comprehensive system incorporating trains, buses, boats and funiculars – some say it's the most efficient network in the world. Various special tickets are available to the tourist to make the system even more attractive.

The best deal for people planning to travel extensively is the Swiss Pass, entitling the holder to unlimited travel on Swiss Federal Railways, boats, most Alpine postbuses and also on trams and buses in 30 towns. Reductions of 25% apply on funiculars and mountain railways. Passes are valid for four days (Sfr200), eight days (Sfr250), 15 days (Sfr290) and one month (Sfr400) – prices are for 2nd-class tickets.

The Swiss Card allows a free return journey from your arrival point to any destination in Switzerland, 50% off rail, boat and bus excursions, and reductions on mountain railways. The cost is Sfr130 (2nd class) or Sfr160 (1st class) and it is valid for a month. The Half-Fare Card is a similar deal minus the free return trip. The cost is Sfr85 for one month or Sfr125 for one year. The Swiss Flexi Pass allows free, unlimited trips for three days out of 15. The cost is Sfr200 for 2nd class. All these cards are best purchased before arrival in Switzerland from SNTO, as they can be purchased at only a few major transport centres once you're there.

Regional passes are available for free travel on certain days and for half-price travel on other days within a seven or 15-day period, but they are only valid within that particular region. Swiss Pass and Swiss Card holders can get free Family cards (Sfr20 otherwise) from SNTO or Swiss train stations for free travel for minors accompanied by at least one parent. ■

pictogram shows a white car on a green background) and 80 km/h on other roads. Don't forget you need a vignette to use motorways and semi-motorways (see the Getting There & Away section). Mountain roads are good but stay in low gear whenever possible, and remember that ascending traffic has right of way over descending traffic, and postbuses always have right of way. Snow chains are recommended in winter. Some minor Alpine passes are closed from November to May; the tourist office can provide details or ring ☎ 163. Use dipped lights in *all* road tunnels.

The Swiss Touring Club operates a 24-hour breakdown service on ☎ 022-3 58 00. Switzerland is tough on drink-driving, so don't risk it; the BAC limit is 0.08%, and if caught exceeding this limit, you face a large fine or imprisonment.

Rental

One-way drop-offs are usually free of charge within Switzerland, though collision damage waiver may cost extra. Rates for Hertz and Avis are similar (eg from Sfr199 unlimited mileage from noon Friday to 9 am Monday). Budget and Europcar are slightly cheaper, but look to local operators for the lowest prices (the tourist office will have details). Overall, pre-booked rates are less than in Italy and Austria, more than in Germany and about the same as in France.

BICYCLE

Despite the hilly countryside, cycling is popular in Switzerland. Cycles can be hired from most train stations and returned to any station with a rental office. Cost is Sfr19 per day or Sfr76 per week. Bikes can be transported on normal trains but not on InterCity or EuroCity trains. The SNTO issues three free, useful booklets on cycling holidays, concentrating on the Pre-Alps, the Midlands, and from the Rhine to Ticino.

HITCHING

Although illegal on motorways, hitching is allowed on other roads and can be fairly easy. At other times it can be quite slow. Indigenous Swiss are not all that sympathetic towards hitchers, and you'll find that most of your lifts will come from foreigners. A sign is helpful. Make sure you stand in a place where vehicles can stop. To try to get a ride on a truck, ask around the customs post at border towns.

WALKING

Walking is popular, and an exhilarating activity in rural areas. The SNTO shows the way with its *Switzerland Step by Step* booklets detailing 100 walks to mountain lakes, over mountain passes, and from town to town.

BOAT

All the larger lakes are serviced by steamers, for which rail passes are usually valid. A Swiss Navigation Boat Pass costs Sfr35 and entitles the bearer to 50% off fares of the main operators. It is valid year-round, but few boats sail in winter.

LOCAL TRANSPORT

City Transport

All local city transport is linked together on the same ticketing system and you should buy tickets before boarding. One-day passes are usually available and are much better value than paying per trip. There are regular checks for fare dodgers; those found wanting pay an on-the-spot fine of Sfr40 to Sfr50.

Taxis are always metered and tend to wait around train stations. Beware – they are expensive!

Mountain Transport

There are five main modes of transport used in steep Alpine regions. A funicular *(funiculaire* or *Standseilbahn)* is a pair of counter-balancing cars drawn by cables. A cable car *(téléphérique* or *Luftseilbahn)* is dramatically suspended from a cable high over a valley. A gondola *(télécabine* or *Gondelbahn)* is a smaller version of a cable car except that the gondola is hitched onto a continuously running cable once the passengers are inside. A cable chair *(télésiège* or *Sesselbahn)* is likewise hitched onto a cable but is unenclosed. A ski lift *(téléski* or *Schlepplift)* is a T-bar hanging from a cable, which the skiers hold onto while their feet slide along the snow.

In practice, the terms 'gondola' and 'cable car' are more or less interchangeable, and T-bars are gradually being phased out.

TOURS

Tours are booked through local tourist offices. The country is so compact that excursions to the major national attractions are offered from most towns. A trip up to Jungfraujoch, for example, is available from Zürich, Geneva, Bern, Lucerne or Interlaken. Most tours represent reasonable value.

Bern

Founded in 1191, Bern (Berne in French) is Switzerland's capital and fourth-largest city. The story goes that the city was named after the first animal killed by the founder, Berchtold V, when hunting in the area. That animal was a bear, and even today the bear remains the heraldic mascot of the city. Despite playing host to the nation's politicians, Bern retains a relaxed, small-town charm. A picturesque Old Town contains six km of covered arcades and 11 historic fountains, as well as the descendants of the city's first casualty who perform tricks for tourists. The world's largest Paul Klee collection is housed in the Museum of Fine Arts.

Orientation

The compact centre of the old town is contained within a sharp U-bend of the River Aare. The main train station is within easy reach of all the main sights and has bicycle rental (daily from 6.10 am to 11.45 pm), Swissair check-in, showers (expensive) and washing machines.

Most shops are shut on Monday morning, Wednesday afternoon, and have extended hours on Thursday.

Information

Tourist Office The Offizielles Verkehrsbüro Bern (☎ 031-311 76 76) is in the train station and is open daily from 9 am to 8.30 pm. From 1 October to 31 May it shuts two hours earlier and Sunday hours are from 10 am to 5 pm. Services include hotel reservations (Sfr3 commission charge) and excursions. Its free booklet, *This Week in Bern*, contains much practical and recreational information.

Money & Post The SBB exchange office is in the lower level of the train station, open daily from 6.15 am to 8.45 pm (9.45 pm in summer). The Schweizerische Volksbank down the passage may have better rates.

The main post office (Schanzenpost 1) is at Schanzenstrasse; it is open Monday to Friday from 7.30 am to 6.30 pm and on Saturday from 7.30 am to 11 am. The telephone code for Bern is 031.

Foreign Embassies Most embassies are south of Kirchenfeldbrücke, including: the British Embassy (☎ 352 50 21), Thunstrasse 50; the US Embassy (☎ 357 70 11), Jubiläumsstrasse 93; the Canadian Embassy (☎ 352 63 81), Kirchenfeldstrasse 88; and the Australian Embassy (☎ 351 01 43), Alpenstrasse 29. A few, like the French Embassy (☎ 351 24 24), Schosshaldenstrasse 46, and the German Embassy (☎ 359 41 11), Willadingweg 83, are a little farther east. As Bern is Switzerland's capital city, many other embassies are here; the tourist office has a full list.

Travel Agencies Kehrli & Oeler Reisebüro (☎ 311 00 22), Bubenbergplatz 9, is the American Express travel service representative. The budget and student travel agency SSR has two offices: Falkenplatz 9 (☎ 302 03 12), and Rathausgasse 64 (☎ 312 07 22). Both are open Monday to Friday only.

Bookshops Stauffacher, Neuengasse 25, has many English-language books. Check Rathausgasse or Kramgasse for second-hand books.

Emergency The police emergency number is ☎ 117. The university hospital (☎ 632 21 11) is on Friboursgstrasse.

Things to See & Do

Walking Tour The city map from the tourist office details a picturesque walk through the old town. The core of the walk is Marktgasse and Kramgasse with their covered arcades and colourful fountains. Dividing the two streets is the **Zeitglockenturm**, a clock tower on which revolving figures herald the chiming hour. Congregate a few minutes before the hour on the east side to see them twirl. Originally a city gate, the clock was installed in 1530. The **Einstein House**, Kramgasse 49, is where the physicist developed his special theory of relativity (Sfr2). Spend a few minutes here (though time being relative, it may seem longer).

The unmistakably Gothic, 15th-century **cathedral** *(Münster)*, is noted for its stained-glass windows and elaborate main portal. Just over the River Aare are the **bear pits** *(Bärengraben)*. Bears have been at this site since 1857, although records show that as far back as 1441 the city council bought acorns to feed the ancestors of these overgrown pets. Up the hill is the **Rose Garden**, which has 200 varieties of roses and an excellent view of the city.

Parliament Well worth a visit are the Bundeshäuser, home of the Swiss Federal Assembly. There are free daily tours when the parliament is not in session. Arrive early and reserve a place for later in the day. A multilingual guide takes you through the impressive chambers, and highlights the development of the Swiss constitution.

Museums There is no shortage of museums. The **Museum of Fine Arts** *(Kunstmuseum)*, Hodlerstrasse 8-12, holds the Klee collection and an interesting mix of Italian masters, Swiss and modern art. It is open Tuesday from 10 am to 9 pm, and Wednesday to Sunday from 10 am to 5 pm; entry costs Sfr6 (students Sfr4).

Many museums are grouped together on the south side of the Kirchenfeldbrücke. The best here is the **Bern Historical Museum** *(Bernisches Historisches Museum)*, Helvetiaplatz, open Tuesday to Sunday from 10 am to 5 pm (admission Sfr5, students Sfr3, free on Saturday). Highlights include the original sculptures from the Münster doorway depicting the Last Judgment, Niklaus Manuel's macabre *Dance of Death* panels, and the ridiculous codpiece on the William Tell statue upstairs.

Also worthwhile is the **Natural History Museum** *(Naturhistorisches Museum)* on Bernastrasse, with animals depicted in realistic dioramas. It is open Monday from 2 to 5 pm, Tuesday to Saturday from 9 am to 5 pm, and Sunday from 10 am to 5 pm (Sfr3, Sfr1.50 for students, free on Sunday).

Market An open-air vegetable, fruit and flower market is at Bundesplatz in the morning on Tuesday and Saturday.

Organised Tour A two-hour city tour by coach (Sfr19) goes nowhere you can't walk yourself, but the commentary is informative. Get details from the tourist office.

Places to Stay

Camping To get to *Camping Kappelenbrücke* (☎ 901 10 07), take postbus No 3 or 4 from the train station to Eymatt. It's open year-round and reception is shut from 1 to 4 pm. Cost is Sfr6 per person and Sfr6 each for a car and tent. Near the river but south of town is *Camping Eichholz* (☎ 961 26 02), Strandweg 49. Take tram No 9 from the station. The site is open from late April to the end of September, and costs are Sfr5.50 per person, tents Sfr4, cars Sfr2, and vans Sfr9. Two-bed rooms may also be available.

Hostel The SYHA *hostel* (☎ 311 63 16), Weihergasse 4, is in a good location below Parliament (signposted). It is usually full in summer, when a three-day maximum stay applies. Reception is shut from 9.30 am to 3 pm (summer) or 5 pm (winter), but bags can be left in the common room during the day. Beds are Sfr15, breakfast Sfr6, and lunch and

SWITZERLAND

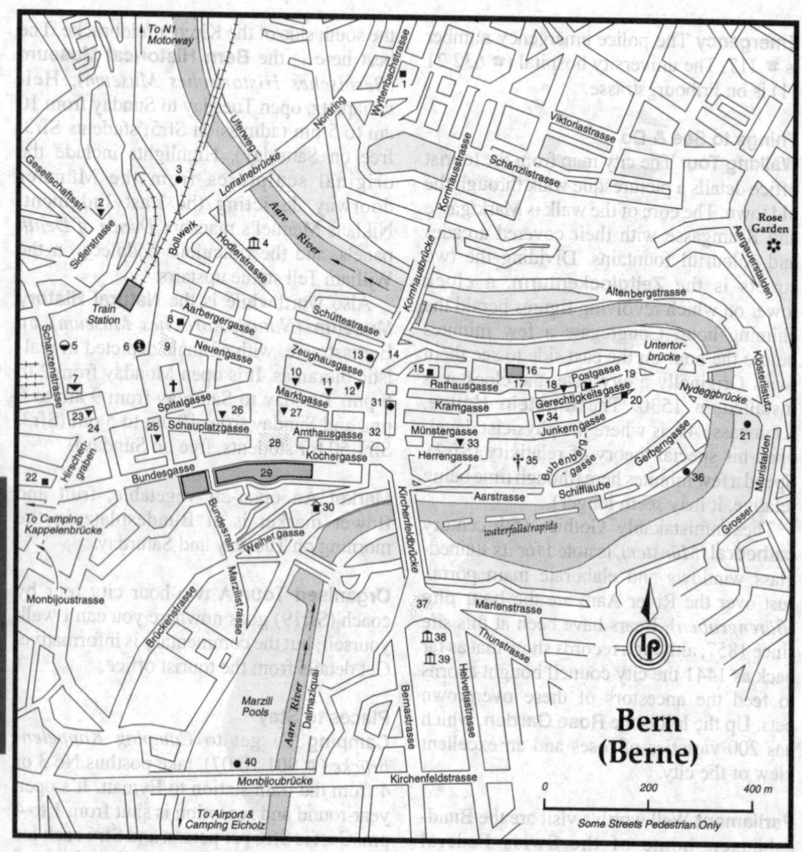

dinner are Sfr10.50 each. There are lockers, a midnight curfew, and washing machines at Sfr3 to wash and Sfr3 to dry.

Hotels There's a limited choice of budget rooms in Bern. *Bahnhof-Süd* (☎ 992 51 11), Bümplizstrasse 189, to the west of town beyond the autobahn, has singles/doubles with hall showers from Sfr50/80 without breakfast. To get there, take bus No 13 from the city centre. Take bus No 20 from Bahnhofplatz for *Marthahaus Garni* (☎ 332 41 35), Wyttenbachstrasse 22A. It's a friendly place with comfortable rooms and two TV lounges. Singles/doubles start from Sfr55/90 and triples/quads from Sfr120/130. Showers are in the hall. Convenient for the train station is *National* (☎ 381 19 88), Hirschengraben 24. It has good-for-the-price singles/doubles with hall shower from Sfr51/88, or Sfr80/106 with private shower and WC.

In the Old Town in an 18th-century building is *Hospiz zur Heimat* (☎ 311 04 36), Gerechtigkeitsgasse 50, with singles/doubles for Sfr62/92, and triples/quads for Sfr123/164, all with hall showers. Rooms with shower are around Sfr25 extra. *Golde-*

PLACES TO STAY		18	Klötzlikeller	14	Kornhausplatz
		23	Bubenberg Vegi	16	Rathaus
1	Marthahaus Garni	25	Manora	17	Rathausplatz
8	Hotel Krebs	26	Della Casa	21	Bear Pits
15	Goldener Schlüssel	27	Mazot	24	Bubenbergplatz
19	Hospiz zur Heimat	33	Menuetto	28	Bundesplatz
20	Goldener Adler	34	Ratskeller	29	Parliament
22	National			31	Zeitglockenturm
30	SYHA Hostel	**OTHER**		32	Theaterplatz
				35	Cathedral
PLACES TO EAT		3	Reithalle	36	Wasserwerk
		4	Museum of Fine Arts	37	Helvetiaplatz
2	Mensa	5	Bus Station	38	Bern Historical Museum
10	Migros and GD Restaurant	6	Tourist Office	39	Natural History Museum
11	EPA	7	Post Office	40	Dampfzentrale
12	Brasserie Anker	9	Bahnhofplatz		
		13	Kornhauskeller		

ner Schlüssel has singles/doubles for the same price. Rooms are clean and reasonably spacious in both places.

Goldener Adler (☎ 311 17 25), Gerechtigkeitsgasse 7, offers similar rooms but with a TV: Sfr105/140 with private shower or Sfr75/130 without. Another good choice for mid-price accommodation is *Hotel Krebs* (☎ 311 49 42), Genfergasse 8, near the train station. Singles with shower, WC, and TV are expensive at Sfr120, but the corresponding doubles are a much better deal at Sfr145; the family room for four costs Sfr235.

Places to Eat

The *EPA* department store, between Marktgasse and Zeughausgasse, has meals from Sfr6.50 in its self-service restaurant. *Migros* supermarket at Marktgasse 46 has a cheap self-service restaurant on the 1st floor. On the same floor is *G D Restaurant* with local dishes from Sfr9.50; it's open Monday to Friday from 8.30 am to 7.30 pm (9.30 pm on Thursday), and Saturday from 8 am to 4 pm. Also good value is the university *mensa*, Gesellschaftsstrasse 2, on the 1st floor. Meals cost around Sfr8 to Sfr10, with reductions for students. It is open Monday to Friday from 11.30 am to 1.45 pm and (not on Friday) from 5.45 to 7.30 pm. The café downstairs keeps longer hours for drinks and snacks.

Apero, on the 1st floor in the train station, has daily specials from Sfr8 to Sfr15, and terraced seating overlooking the square. *Manora*, Bubenbergplatz 5a, is a busy buffet-style restaurant with tasty dishes for Sfr9 to Sfr16. The pile-it-on-yourself salad is Sfr4.50 to Sfr9.50 per plate. Nearby is *Café Bubenberg Vegi*, 1st floor, Bubenbergplatz 8, which has terrace seating and good vegetarian food for Sfr11 to Sfr18. It is open Monday to Saturday from 7 am to 10 pm. Slightly more expensive but also recommended for vegetarian food is *Menuetto* (☎ 311 14 48), Münstergasse 47, open daily except Sunday from 8.30 am to 10 pm.

Several pleasant restaurants with outside seating line Bärenplatz, though there's little to choose between them. Go to *Mazot* at No 5 to try Swiss specialities such as Rösti (Sfr10.50) and fondue (Sfr18). *Restaurant Brasserie Anker* at Zeughausgasse 1 has fondues for the same price. Its front section is more popular with beer drinkers – just Sfr3.60 for half a litre.

The dingy exterior of *Della Casa* (☎ 311 21 42), Schauplatzgasse 16, hides a good-quality restaurant within. The local speciality, *Bärner Platte* (a selection of meats with sauerkraut and beans), is served here but it is expensive (Sfr36). If you're lucky, you can find it on the excellent three-course daily menu for Sfr19.50 (different menu lunch and dinner). It is open Monday to Friday from 8.30 to 11.30 pm (menu to 9 pm) and Saturday from 8.30 am to 3 pm.

For good-quality fish and meat dishes (Sfr15 to Sfr40) in a calm setting, try the *Ratskeller* at Gerechtigkeitsgasse 81 (open daily). Downstairs it has a cheaper Weinkeller with live music on Tuesday. *Klötzlikeller* (☎ 311 74 56) is a lively and atmospheric wine cellar at Gerechtigkeitsgasse 62, also with occasional live music. Menus (cheapish to mid-price) change periodically in which food and wine from different regions are featured. It is open Tuesday to Saturday from 4 pm till after midnight.

Entertainment

On Monday, cinemas cost Sfr9 instead of the usual Sfr12. Open-air swimming pools, such as those at Marzili, are free (open May to September). A favoured activity in the summer is to walk upriver then float in the swift current of the Aare back to Marzili.

There are various late-night clubs in the centre but entry and drink prices are high. Young people with fewer francs go to places like *Wasserwerk*, Wasserwerkgasse 5. There's a bar, disco (Sfr8) and live music (Sfr18 to Sfr25). On Tuesday bands play for free, though there is a collection. *Dampfzentrale*, in Marzili, is a venue for jazz and other music, plus art exhibitions. The *Reithalle*, Shuttzenmattestrasse, is a centre for alternative arts, offering reasonable admission prices for dance, theatre, cinema, and live music, as well as a bar, restaurant and women's centre. The place looks a bit seedy, and there have been safety problems in the past. Nowadays, however, it is said to be safe and almost respectable.

Kornhauskeller (☎ 311 11 33), Kornhausplatz 17, is a traditional beer hall with live music nightly. Entry is free but the middle-of-the-road music can yield more pain than pleasure, depending on the band. Monday is Swiss folklore night (Sfr5). Food can get pricey, but the daily menus for around Sfr15 are better value. It is open Tuesday to Saturday from 11.30 am to around midnight. Occasionally on Sunday it has a jazz matinee (entry around Sfr15).

Getting There & Away

Air There are daily flights to/from London, Paris, Lugano, Munich, Brussels and other European destinations from the small airport.

Bus Postbuses depart from the west side of the train station.

Train There are at least hourly connections to most Swiss towns, including Geneva (Sfr47, takes 1¾ hours), Basel (Sfr33, 70 minutes), Interlaken (Sfr24, 50 minutes) and Zürich (Sfr42, 1½ hours).

Car & Motorbike There are three motorways which intersect at the northern part of the city. The N1 is the route from Neuchâtel in the west and Basel and Zürich in the north-east. The N6 connects Bern with Thun and the Interlaken region in the south. The N12 is the route from Geneva and Lausanne in the south-west.

Getting Around

To/From the Airport Belp airport is 10 km south-east of the city centre. A bus run by Crossair links the airport to the train station (Sfr12). It takes 20 minutes and is coordinated with flight arrivals and departures.

Bus Getting around on foot is easy enough if you're staying in the city centre. Bus and tram tickets cost Sfr1.40 or Sfr2.20, but you're better off buying daily tourist cards valid for unlimited travel. One, two or three-day passes cost Sfr5, Sfr7 or Sfr10. A 24-hour card costs Sfr6 and is valid from first use. Buy single-journey tickets at stops and daily cards from the tourist office or the public transport office at Bubenbergplatz 5.

Taxi Many taxis wait by the station. The cost is Sfr6 plus Sfr2.50 to Sfr2.80 per km depending on factors like the number of passengers, the time of day, or the district.

(Or if it's raining? If the driver has a hang-over?)

AROUND BERN
There are some excellent excursions close to Bern. **Fribourg**, 30 minutes away by train (Sfr9.80), provides an old town-centre, fine views and a well-presented Art & History Museum. Farther south is **Gruyères**, about an hour away from either Fribourg or Montreux. It has a 13th-century castle on the hill, and next to the train station is a dairy (☎ 029-6 14 10) offering daily free cheese-making tours. About 30 km west of Bern is **Murten**, a historic walled town overlooking a lake (hourly trains from Fribourg and Bern).

Neuchâtel

Neuchâtel is just inside the French-speaking region of Switzerland, on the north-west shore of the lake that shares its name. It's a relaxing town and offers easy access to the mountain areas of the Jura.

Orientation & Information
The train station (Gare CFF) changes money daily from 5.30 am to 10 pm. A post office is just opposite (Poste, 2002 Neuchâtel 2). The old part of town is less than one km away down the hill along Ave de la Gare. Place Pury is the hub of local buses. The tourist office (☎ 038-25 42 42) is between Place Pury and the port, at Rue de la Place d'Armes 7, and is open Monday to Friday from 9 am to noon and 1.30 to 5.30 pm, and on Saturday from 9 am until noon (opening hours are extended in summer). Pick up a copy of its walking tour of the town centre. Neuchâtel's area code is 038.

Things to See
The centrepiece of the old town is the **castle** and the adjoining **Collegiate Church**. The castle dates from the 12th century and now houses cantonal offices. The church contains a striking cenotaph of 15 statues dating from 1372. Nearby, the **Prison Tower** (entry Sfr0.50) offers a good view of the area and has interesting models showing the town as it was in the 15th and 18th centuries.

One of the town's several museums, the **Musée d'Art et d'Histoire**, 2 quai Léopold Robert, is especially noted for three 18th-century clockwork figures. Unfortunately they are only activated on the first Sunday of each month. Entry is Sfr7, or Sfr4 for students, and the museum is shut on Monday.

Six km to the east of town at Marin (take bus No 1 from Place Pury) is **Papiliorama**, open daily (Sfr8) in the Marin Centre, with over 1000 butterflies of all sizes and hues. The tourist office has information on nearby walking trails and boat trips on the lake.

Places to Stay & Eat
The SYHA *hostel* (☎ 31 31 90), Rue du Suchiez 35, is two km from the town centre; take bus No 1 to Vauseyon and then follow the signs. It is a small, pleasant, family-run place with good evening meals and a laundry service. Beds are Sfr20.50 and it closes from mid-December to mid-February.

Marché (☎ 24 58 00) is ideally placed in the town centre at Place des Halles 4. Ask for a room overlooking the square. Singles/doubles for Sfr65/90 vary in size; each has a TV but no shower. An extra bed in the room costs Sfr25. *Hôtel du Poisson* (☎ 33 30 31), Ave Bachelin 7, Marin, has singles/doubles for Sfr41/76.

Self-service restaurants are at *Coop*, Rue de la Treille 4, and *EPA*, opposite the tourist office. There is also a *Migros* supermarket on Rue de l'Hôpital. Opposite Migros is the *Crêperie*. If you don't like thin pancakes you'll think this place is a load of crêpe, because that's all it serves – but they're very tasty with many sweet or savoury fillings.

Café du Cerf, Rue de l'Ancien 4, has good oriental food (from Sfr12 to Sfr25), and lots of different beers for evening drinkers. You can eat upstairs, too, in the more formal part.

Getting There & Away
There are hourly fast trains to Geneva (70 minutes, Sfr41), Bern (35 minutes, Sfr15.80)

SWITZERLAND

and many other destinations. Postbuses leave from outside the station.

Getting Around

Local buses cost Sfr1.50 to Sfr2.40, or Sfr7 for a 24-hour ticket.

Jura Mountains

Less visited by tourists, this area to the north and west of Lake Neuchâtel can be slightly cheaper than the rest of Switzerland. The mountains are less rugged than the Alps and are ideal for hikers, with over 2000 km of maintained and marked footpaths. Horse riding is also a popular activity. In the winter, hiking gives way to cross-country skiing, for which some of the groomed trails are lit. It is also an important area for watch-making and there are several museums devoted to this industry, most notably in **La Chaux de Fonds** and **Le Locle** (both museums shut on Monday).

SWITZERLAND

Orientation & Information

The largest town in the region and also the highest in Switzerland (1000 metres) is La Chaux de Fonds, 20 km north-west of Neuchâtel. The tourist office (☎ 039-28 13 13) is in the Espacité building on Ave Léopold Robert. Opening hours are similar to Neuchâtel. For snow reports, ring ☎ 039-28 75 75. The area code for La Chaux de Fonds is 039.

Places to Stay & Eat

All the places mentioned here are in La Chaux de Fonds. There's a camping ground (☎ 23 25 55) on the edge of the wood, two km south of the station. The SYHA *hostel* (☎ 28 43 15) is closed from late October to late December and has beds for Sfr21.50. It's 15 minutes' walk from the station, at Rue de Doubs 34. Opposite the station, on Rue Daniel Richard, is *Garni de France* (☎ 23 11 16), with singles/doubles from Sfr41/62 (reserve ahead).

About 200 metres to the right of the station is a *Migros* with a restaurant. *La Pinte Neuchâteloise* on Rue du Grenier offers a range of food (including fondue) for all budgets (closed Tuesday).

Getting There & Away

La Chaux de Fonds and Le Locle are connected to each other, as well as to Neuchâtel, by rail. A network of postbuses connects the smaller towns and villages in the region, although departures can be infrequent.

Geneva

Geneva (Genève, Genf, Ginevra) is Switzerland's third-largest city, comfortably encamped on the shore of Lake Geneva (Lac Léman). Geneva belongs not so much to French-speaking Switzerland as to the whole world. It is truly an international city, a place where belligerants worldwide come to settle their differences by negotiation. One in three residents are non-Swiss and many world organisations are based here, not least the United Nations (the European headquarters). Unfortunately, the presence of so many businesspeople, bankers and diplomats means that prices for food and accommodation can be high.

After gaining respite from the Duke of Savoy in 1530, Geneva was ripe for the teachings of John Calvin two years later; it soon became known as the Protestant Rome, during which time fun became frowned upon. Thankfully this legacy barely lingers and today Geneva offers a varied nightlife. In 1798 the French annexed the city and held it for 16 years before it was admitted to the Swiss Confederation as a canton in 1815.

Orientation

The River Rhône runs through the city, dividing it into *rive droite* (north of the Rhône) and *rive gauche* (the south). Conveniently in the centre of town on the north side is the main train station, Gare de Cornavin. To the south of the river lies the old part of town, where many important buildings are located. In the summer, Geneva's most visible landmark is the Jet d'Eau, a 140-metre-high fountain on the southern shore.

Information

Tourist Offices The busy tourist office (☎ 022-738 52 00) is in the train station, open Monday to Saturday from 9 am to 6 pm. From mid-June to mid-September it's open daily from 8 am to 8 pm (6 pm weekends). Hotel reservations cost Sfr5. There's another office (☎ 311 98 27) in the old town at Place du Molard.

The Centre d'Accueil et de Renseignements (CAR) (☎ 731 46 47) has tourist and accommodation information. It is based in a yellow bus at the entrance to the Gare de Cornavin and is open daily between 8.30 am and 11 pm, but only between mid-June and mid-October.

Anglo-Phone (☎ 1 575 014) is a premium-rate (Sfr2 a minute from anywhere in Switzerland) information line, and produces an events magazine for Lake Geneva; both are in English.

The area code for Geneva is 022.

Money & Post Exchange counters in Gare de Cornavin are open daily from 6.45 am to 9.30 pm. The best rates for cash seen while researching this edition were in an exchange office at 9 Rue de Chantepoulet.

The main post office is at 18 Rue du Mont Blanc, 1211 Genève 1. Unless specified otherwise, poste restante will end up here. It is open Monday to Friday from 7.30 am to 6 pm, and Saturday from 7.30 to 11 am.

The telephone code for Geneva is 022.

Foreign Consulates Foreign consulates in Geneva include:

Australia
    56-58 Rue de Moillebeau (☎ 734 62 00)
Canada
    1 Pré de la Bichette (☎ 733 90 00)
France
    11 Rue J Imbert Galliox (☎ 311 34 41)
Italy
    14 Rue Charles Galland (☎ 346 47 44)
New Zealand
    28A Chemin du Petit-Saconnex (☎ 734 95 30)
UK
    37-39 Rue de Vermont (☎ 734 12 04)
USA
    1-3 Ave de la Paix (☎ 738 76 13)

Travel Agencies American Express (☎ 731 76 00) is at 7 Rue du Mont Blanc, near many other travel agents and airline offices. The budget and student travel agency SSR (☎ 617 58 11) is at 3 Rue Vignier (closed Saturday).

Bookshops Elm Book Shop (☎ 736 09 45), 5 Rue Versonnex, has English-language books. Librairie des Amateurs, 15 Grand Rue, and Librairie Prior, Rue de la Cité 6, both have English-language second-hand books from Sfr2. Artou (☎ 731 87 65), 8 Rue de Rive, is good for travel books.

Medical Services The Cantonal Hospital (☎ 383 33 11) is at 24 Rue Micheli du Crest. Permanence Médico Chirurgicale (☎ 731 21 20), 21 Rue de Chantepoulet, is a private clinic, open 24 hours a day. Dental treatment (☎ 733 98 00) can be obtained between 7.30 am and 8 pm (6 pm weekends) at 60 Ave Wendt. Ring ☎ 735 81 83 for a legal advice service.

Things to See & Do

Walking Tour The centre of the city is so compact that it is easy to see most of the main sights on foot. Start a scenic walk through the Old Town at the **Île Rousseau**, noted for a statue in honour of the celebrated free thinker.

Turn right along the south side of the Rhône until you reach the 13th-century **Tour d'Île**, once part of the medieval city fortifications. Walk south down the narrow, cobbled Rue de la Cité until it becomes Grand Rue. On each side are a variety of interesting buildings, including Rousseau's birthplace at No 40. Grand Rue terminates at **Place du Bourg-de-Four**, the site of a medieval marketplace which now has a fountain and touristy shops.

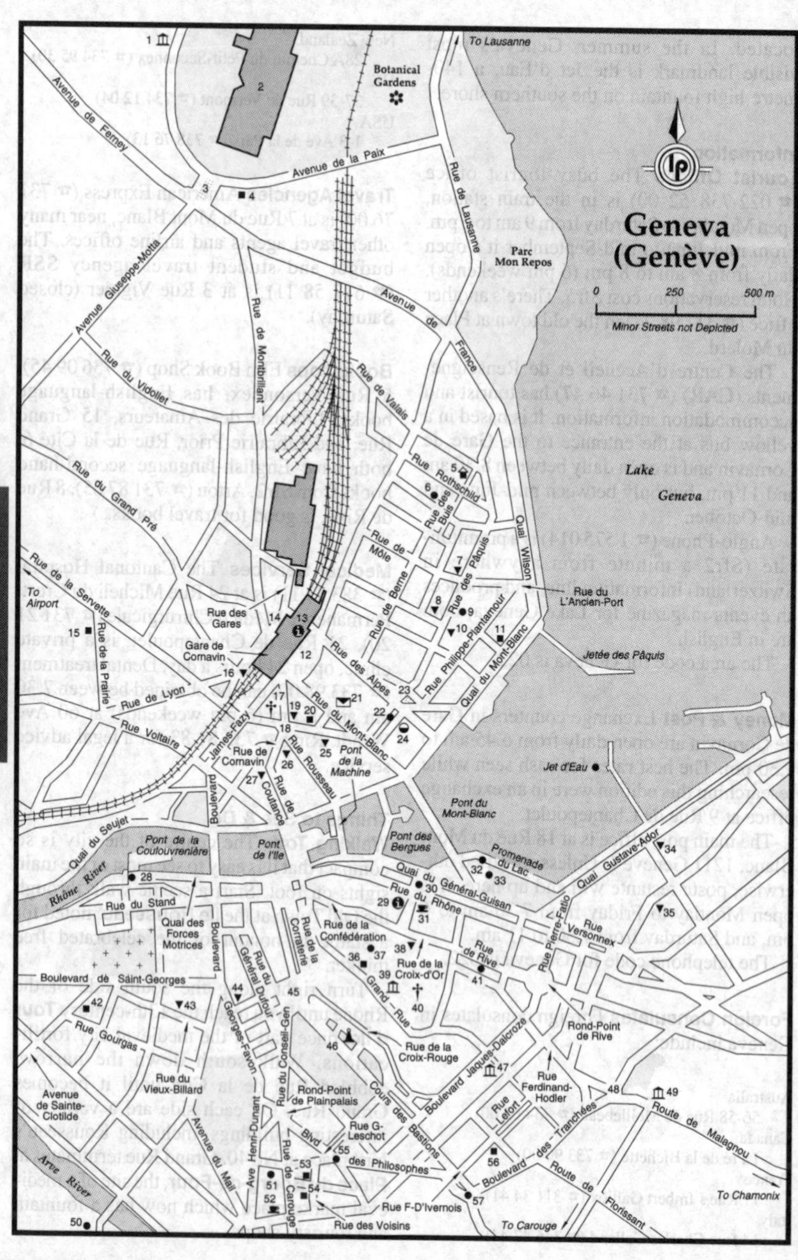

SWITZERLAND

PLACES TO STAY

4 Centre Masaryk
5 SYHA Hostel
11 Hôtel de la Cloche
15 Pension de la Servette
20 Hotel Lido
36 Hôtel le Chandelier
42 Hôtel le Grenil
53 Centre Universitaire Zofingien
54 Hôtel le Prince
56 Hôtel Saint Victor

PLACES TO EAT

7 Migros
8 Le Blason
10 Auberge de Savièse
16 l'Oasis Bleu
19 La Siesta
25 Miyako
26 Restaurant Manora
27 Auberge de Coutance
31 Café du Centre
34 l'Amiral
35 Dent de Lion
38 EPA
43 Le Bleu Nuit
44 Cave Valaisanne et Chalet Suisse

OTHER

1 Red Cross & Red Crescent Museum
2 Palais des Nations
3 Place des Nations
6 Léman (car rental)
9 Horizon Motos (motorbike rental)
12 Place de Cornavin
13 Tourist Office
14 Place du Reculet
17 Notre-Dame
18 Place des 22 Cantons
21 Post Office (Genève 1)
22 Place Dorcière
23 Place des Alpes
24 International Bus Terminal
28 l'Usine
29 Tourist Office
30 Place du Lac
32 CGN Ticket Booth
33 Jardin Anglais
37 Alhambar
39 Maison Tavel
40 Cathedral St Pierre
41 Artou (Bookshop)
45 Place Neuve
46 Reformation Monument
47 Museum of Art & History
48 Place Emile Guyénot
49 Museum of Natural History
50 Centre Sportif des Vernets
51 SSR (Travel Agency)
52 Café Universal
55 Place des Philosophes
57 Place Edouard Claparède

The centre of town is dominated by the partially Romanesque, partially Gothic **Cathedral St Pierre**. John Calvin preached here from 1536 to 1564. There is a good view from the tower, which is open daily to 5.30 pm (entry Sfr2.50). The cathedral is on an important archaeological site which is of only limited general appeal (entry Sfr5, students Sfr3, closed Monday).

Nearby, the **Promenade des Bastions** is a pleasant park which contains a massive monument to the Reformation. The giant figures of Bèze, Calvin, Farel and Knox are flanked by smaller statues of other important figures, and depictions in relief of events instrumental in the spread of the movement.

Perhaps the best walk is along the shores of the lake. At weekends in the summer the water is alive with the bobbing white sails of sailing boats. On the lakefront near the old town, the **Jardin Anglais** features a large clock composed of flowers. Close by is the **Jet d'Eau**, the waters of which shoot up with incredible force (200 km/h, 1360 horsepower) and, depending on the whims of the wind, spray spectators who venture out on the pier. Colourful flower gardens and the occasional statue line the promenade on the north shore of the lake leading to two relaxing parks. Well worth a visit is the **Botanical Gardens** (Jardin Botanique) which, among other attractions, features exotic plants, llamas and an aviary. Entry is free and it is open daily from 7 am to 7.30 pm.

Museums Geneva is not a bad place to get stuck on a rainy day as there are plenty of museums, many of which are free. The most important is the **Museum of Art and History** (Musée d'Art et d'Histoire), 2 Rue Charles Galland, with a vast and varied collection including paintings, sculpture, weapons and archaeology. The nearby **Museum of Natural History** (Musée d'Histoire Naturelle), Route de Malagnou, has dioramas, minerals and anthropological displays. In the old town, **Maison Tavel**, 6 Rue du Puits Saint Pierre, is notable for a detailed relief map of Geneva covering 35 sq metres.

All these museums are free and open Tuesday to Sunday from 10 am to 5 pm.

By the United Nations is the **International Red Cross & Red Crescent Museum**, a vivid multimedia illustration of the history of those two humanitarian organisations. It's open Wednesday to Monday from 10 am to 5 pm (entry Sfr8, or Sfr4 for students and senior citizens).

United Nations The European arm of the UN is housed in the former home of its deceased parent, the League of Nations, and is the focal point for a resident population of 3000 international civil servants. The hour-long tour of the interior is fairly interesting if a touch expensive at Sfr8 (students Sfr6). There is no charge to walk around the gardens where you'll find a towering grey monument coated with heat-resistant titanium. It was donated by the USSR to commemorate the conquest of space.

The gardens are open Monday to Friday from November to March and daily from April to October. Guided tours are from 10 am to noon and 2 to 4 pm, and from 9 am to noon and 2 to 6 pm during July and August. You need to show your passport to gain admittance.

Excursions In France, **Mont Salève** yields an excellent view of the city and Lake Geneva. Take bus No 8 to Veyrier and walk across the border. The cable car up costs Sfr14.20 return and runs daily in summer, infrequently in winter. **CERN**, on the French border (take your passport) near Meyrin, is a research laboratory into particle physics, and has a free exhibition open Monday to Saturday from 10 am to 5 pm. Get there on bus No 15 from the station.

Activities There are several sports centres in the city. Centre Sportif des Vernets (☎ 343 88 50), 4 Rue Hans Wilsdorf, has swimming (Sfr3) and ice skating and is open daily except Monday from 9 am. Swimming in the lake is possible at Genève Plage on the south shore and Pâquis Plage on the north shore.

Festivals The Geneva Festival in the second weekend of August is a time of fun, fireworks and parades. L'Escalade on 11 December celebrates the foiling of an invasion by the Duke of Savoy in 1602.

Places to Stay

Camping The most central camping ground, *Sylvabelle* (☎ 347 06 03), 10 Chemin de Conches, is reached by bus No 8 from Gare de Cornavin or Rond-Point de Rive. Four-person bungalows are available and camping is Sfr5 per person, Sfr4 per tent and Sfr3 per car. The eccentric owner opens up the camp when she feels like it, which is never in winter.

Seven km east of the city centre on the southern lakeshore is *Camping Pointe à la Bise* (☎ 752 12 96), 1222 Vesenaz; it costs Sfr5 per person, plus tents from Sfr6. Take bus E from Rive. Seven km farther east and five minutes' walk from the last stop on bus E is *Camping D'Hermance* (☎ 751 14 83), Chemin des Glerrets. It costs Sfr8 per person, including tent. Both sites are open from 1 April and include car parking.

Hostels A good selection of dormitory beds is listed in the *Young People Info* leaflet issued by the tourist office, including some that take women only.

North of the Rhône The SYHA *hostel* (☎ 732 62 60), 28-30 Rue Rothschild, is big, modern and busy with helpful and knowledgeable staff. Dorms are Sfr20 and there are a few family rooms and doubles (Sfr70) for couples. Three-course dinners are Sfr10.50, and there's a TV room, laundry and kitchen facilities. The hostel is closed from 10 am to 5 pm (to 4 pm from 15 June to 15 September) and there is a midnight curfew.

Centre Masaryk (☎ 733 07 72), 11 Ave de la Paix, has dorms for Sfr25 with an 11 pm curfew. Singles/doubles/triples cost Sfr38/64/90 and you can get your own key for late access. Get there by bus No 5 or 8 from Gare de Cornavin.

South of the Rhône *Cité Universitaire*

(☎ 346 23 55), 46 Ave Miremont, has 500 beds, but dorms (Sfr14 without breakfast) are only available from 1 July to mid-September. Take bus No 3 from Cornavin to the terminus at Champel, south of the city centre. Singles/doubles cost Sfr38/52 or Sfr32/46 for students, likewise without breakfast. A double studio with kitchen, WC and shower costs Sfr60. Reception is open from 8 am to noon and 2 pm (6 pm on weekends) to 10 pm.

Centre Universitaire Zofingien (☎ 329 11 40), 6 Rue des Voisins, has well-equipped rooms which are excellent value even if they are slightly cramped. Each room has a WC, shower, sink and small cooker. Singles/doubles/triples are Sfr48/72/90, with breakfast.

Hotels As befits an international city that receives many important visitors on unlimited expense accounts, there is no lack of high-class, high-cost hotels. The following are some of the more affordable options.

North of the Rhône *Hôtel de la Cloche* (☎ 732 94 81), 6 Rue de la Cloche, is small, old-fashioned, friendly, and liable to be full unless you call ahead. Big singles/doubles with hall shower are Sfr45/75; doubles with shower cubicle in the room are Sfr80. *Pension de la Servette* (☎ 734 02 30), 31 Rue de la Prairie, is a little old and dilapidated but the rooms are large enough. Singles/doubles/triples are Sfr35/50/75. *Hôtel Lido* (☎ 731 55 30), 8 Rue de Chantepoulet, has a better ambience, decent-sized rooms, and genial staff. Singles/doubles with private shower, WC, TV and radio start at Sfr75/120, and there are a couple of cheaper rooms for Sfr65/110 using a hall shower.

There's not much to choose between the tourist-class hotels clustered round the train station. *Bernina* (☎ 731 49 50), *Astoria* (☎ 732 10 25) and *Excelsior* (☎ 732 09 45) all have comfortable singles/doubles with shower or bath and WC for around Sfr110/150. *Hôtel Suisse* (☎ 732 66 30), 10 Place de Cornavin, is the pick of them, with a nice swirling staircase and better appointed rooms, but it's also more expensive, starting at Sfr140/165 for singles/doubles.

South of the Rhône To get to *Hôtel Saint Victor* (☎ 346 17 18), 1 Rue Lefort, take bus No 8 or 3 from Cornavin. It's convenient for the museums, in a building that's a bit past its prime. Singles/doubles start at Sfr50/75.

Hôtel le Grenil (☎ 328 30 55) is at 7 Ave Sainte Clotilde. Singles are overpriced at Sfr90 upwards but there are also doubles/triples/quads from Sfr120/125/140. Dormitory beds at Sfr25 are only for people under 26 (in theory: smile nicely if you're a little older). Night owls will appreciate the reception being open 24 hours. *Hôtel le Prince* (☎ 329 85 44/5), 16 Rue des Voisins, has comfortable if smallish rooms with a TV, telephone and shower. Singles/doubles are Sfr75/95, and breakfast costs Sfr6. It has an inexpensive restaurant (closed Sunday).

Hôtel le Chandelier (☎ 311 56 88), 23 Grand Rue, has all the same amenities as places like the Bernina and Astoria, plus the added character of a 300-year-old building. Singles are Sfr80 to Sfr150, doubles Sfr130 to Sfr190, and it's Sfr30 for an extra bed. The more expensive rooms are very spacious. Parking can be a bit of a problem.

Places to Eat

Eating is generally cheaper north or west of Gare de Cornavin, or south of the old town in the vicinity of the university. Fondue and raclette are widely available. Also popular is perch caught from the river, but it is likely to set you back at least Sfr20 unless you can find it as a plat du jour. There is a small fruit and vegetable market open daily on Rue de Coutance. *Migros* supermarket on the corner of Rue des Pâquis and Rue de Môle has a self-service restaurant. See the following Entertainment section for more places to eat.

North of the Rhône *Restaurant Manora*, 4 Rue de Cornavin, is buffet-style with tasty daily dishes from Sfr9 and salad from Sfr3.90. Always popular, it is open daily to 9.30 pm (9 pm Sunday). *La Siesta*, Place de

Cornavin, is convenient for inexpensive Italian food. Round the back of the station is *l'Oasis Bleu* (☎ 738 38 28), 4 Place de Montbrillant, open daily from 9 am to midnight. It's ideal for a quick chomp between trains, or for more leisurely consumption of snacks, Mediterranean food and vegetarian specialities.

Two informal bistro-style restaurants are near each other on Rue des Pâquis. *Le Blason* (☎ 731 91 73) at No 23 has plats du jour for Sfr12 and Sfr14 and is open daily (closed lunchtime on weekends). *Auberge de Savièse* at No 20 has lunchtime plats du jour for the same price, and Swiss specialities such as fondue from Sfr17. Opening hours are Monday to Friday from 9 am to midnight, and Saturday from 3 pm to midnight.

Take advantage of the international flavour of Geneva to vary your diet. The streets off Rue du Mont Blanc are good places to explore for cheapish Mexican, Chinese and Oriental food. *Auberge de Coutance* (☎ 732 79 19) is recommended for exquisite specialities from Sfr20, including duck delicacies. It's an atmospheric below-ground restaurant at 25 Rue de Coutance (closed Saturday evening and Sunday). *Miyako* (☎ 738 01 20), 11 Rue de Chantrepoulet, is expensive but the quality is excellent. This Japanese restaurant has three-course business lunches from Sfr27, and a full evening meal will cost around Sfr50 (closed Sunday).

SWITZERLAND

South of the Rhône For the cheapest eating in the old town, make for the restaurant in the *EPA* department store on Rue de la Croix d'Or. Meals are Sfr6 to Sfr10. *Le Zofage*, downstairs in the Centre Universitaire Zofingien (see Places to Stay), has a choice of plats du jour for just Sfr10.50 (Sfr8.50 for students) and is open daily from 7 am to midnight.

Café du Centre, 5 Place du Molard, has outside seating in a pleasant square near the old town. Office staff relax here after work over a coffee or a beer. The lunchtime plat du jour costs around Sfr14 on weekdays (open daily from 6 am to 2 am). *Dent de Lion*, 14 Rue des Eaux-Vives, is a vegetarian self-service place, open Monday to Friday from 9 am to 3 pm and 6 to 10 pm. The plat du jour is Sfr14.

More up-market is the large and popular *Cave Valaisanne et Chalet Suisse* (☎ 328 12 36), 23 Blvd Georges Favon. It's an excellent place to try fondue (starting at Sfr17.90); the scent of bubbling cheese inside could give a mouse palpitations at 20 paces. It's open from 11 am to 1 am daily. Another good place for those with slightly larger budgets is *l'Amiral* (☎ 735 18 08), 24 Quai Gustave Ador, near the Jet d'Eau. The 'menu du touriste' is fillet of perch with salad and dessert for Sfr28.

Entertainment

Geneva has a good selection of nightclubs but unless you have money to burn, steer clear. *Bolero*, 21 Grand Rue, has varied music (not house or techno) and is open Wednesday to Sunday after 10 pm. You cash in the entry fee (around Sfr15) for drinks.

L'Usine (☎ 781 34 90), 4 Place des Volontaires, is highly recommended for alternative arts. A converted old factory (hence the name), it is now a centre for cinema, cabaret, theatre, concerts and homeless art objects. It has a good restaurant with inexpensive daily menus; beer is cheap in the bar, too (Sfr4 for half a litre). It's all closed on Monday; otherwise it's open till well after midnight. *Alhambar* (☎ 312 30 11), 1st floor, 10 Rue de la Rôtisserie, has food, drinks and live music (closed Monday). *Au Chat Noir* (☎ 343 49 98), 13 Rue Vautier, is a jazz club with interesting murals and music every night.

Café Universal, 26 Blvd du Pont d'Arve, is French and smoky, with food and theatrical patrons (closed Sunday, Monday, and in July and August). A good British/Irish meeting place is *Post Café*, 7 Rue de Berne, with draught cider and Guinness. Another sociable place, with inexpensive food, is *le Bleu Nuit*, 4 Rue du Vieux Billard, open daily till late.

Getting There & Away

Air Geneva airport is an important transport hub and has frequent connections to every major European city. Enquire at Swissair (☎ 799 59 99) about youth-fare bargains (age under 25); the office is just to the left of the station on Rue de Lausanne, open Monday to Friday from 8.30 am to 6 pm.

Bus International buses depart from Place Dorcière (☎ 732 02 30), off Rue des Alpes. There are three buses a week to both London (Sfr150) and Barcelona (Sfr90). There are several buses a day to Chamonix (Sfr47).

Train There are more or less hourly connections to most Swiss towns; Zürich takes 3 hours (Sfr73), as does Interlaken Ost (Sfr60), both via Bern. There are regular international trains to Paris (Sfr82 by TGV, reservations essential), Hamburg (Sfr270), Milan (Sfr71) and Barcelona (Sfr103). Gare des Eaux-Vives is the station for Annecy and Chamonix. To get there from Gare de Cornavin, take bus No 8 or 1 to Rond-Point de Rive and then tram No 12.

Car & Motorbike Lyons is 130 km by motorway to the west. The N1/E4 from Lausanne and the north, and the E21 from the south-east, also lead directly into Geneva. Toll-free main roads follow the course of these motorways.

Léman (☎ 732 01 43), 6 Rue Amat, has low rates: Group 'A' cars are Sfr175 with unlimited mileage for the weekend (from noon Friday to 9 am Monday). Horizon Motos (☎ 731 23 39), 22 Rue des Pâquis, has motorbikes (from Sfr110, unlimited mileage weekend rates) and mountain bikes.

Boat Compagnie Générale de Navigation (CGN) (☎ 311 25 21) by the Jardin Anglais operates a steamer service to all towns and major villages bordering Lake Geneva, including those in France. Most boats only operate between May and September, such as those to Lausanne (3½ hours, Sfr27 one way or Sfr44 return) and Montreux (4½ hours, Sfr33 one way or Sfr53 return – but get a day card instead for Sfr47). CGN also has 80-minute excursions on the lake for Sfr17. Both Eurail and Swiss passes are valid on CGN boats.

Getting Around

To/From the Airport Getting from Cointrin airport is easy with 100 trains a day into Gare de Cornavin (takes six minutes, Sfr4.40). Bus No 10 (Sfr2) does the same trip.

Bus A combination of buses, trolleybuses and trams makes getting around just as easy. There are ticket dispensers at bus stops. A ticket valid for one hour costs Sfr2; a book of six such tickets costs Sfr11, while a book of 12 costs Sfr20. Day passes are also available for the city and canton network. One, two or three-day passes cost Sfr8.50, Sfr15 or Sfr19. A day pass only for the city costs Sfr5. Passes are available from the tourist office or from Transports Publics Genevois at the lower level of Gare de Cornavin (by the yellow escalators) or at Rond-Point de Rive.

Taxi The cost for taxis is Sfr5 per person plus Sfr2.50 per km.

Bicycle The bike rental office at Gare de Cornavin is open daily from 7 am to 8 pm. It has a leaflet showing cycle routes in and around the city.

Boat In addition to CGN (see the previous Getting There & Away section) smaller companies operate excursions on the lake between April and October but no passes are valid. Ticket offices and departures are along Quai du Mont Blanc and by Jardin Anglais. Trips range from half an hour (Sfr10, several departures a day) to two hours (Sfr25), with commentary in English.

Around Lake Geneva

LAUSANNE

Capital of the canton of Vaud, this hilly city is Switzerland's fifth-largest, with 123,000 inhabitants. Water sports and Alpine scenery are big attractions, as well as one of Europe's most unusual art collections.

Orientation & Information

There is a tourist office in the train station, open daily: 1 May to 30 June from 2 to 8 pm; 1 July to 15 October from 10 am to 9 pm; and 16 October to 30 April from 3 to 7 pm. There is bicycle rental (summer only) and money changing facilities in the station. The main post office is by the station. The cathedral, shopping streets and Place St François (the main hub for local transport) are up the hill to the north.

The main tourist office (☎ 021-617 14 27), 2 Ave de Rhodanie, is by the picturesque harbour of Ouchy. Opening hours are: 1 April to mid-October, Monday to Saturday from 8 am to 7 pm, and Sunday from 9 am to noon and 1 to 6 pm; mid-October to 31 March, Monday to Friday from 8 am to 6 pm, and Saturday from 8.30 am to noon and 1 to 5 pm. Pick up a free copy of the excellent *Lausanne Official Guide*, which lists everything from consulates to local walking tours.

SWITZERLAND

Things to See & Do

The fine Gothic **cathedral** was built in the 12th and 13th centuries and has an impressive main portal and attractive stained-glass windows. The church and tower are open daily.

The **Musée de l'Art Brut**, 11 Ave de Bergières, should not be missed. It's a fascinating amalgam of art created by untrained artists – the mentally unhinged, eccentrics and incarcerated criminals. Some of the images created are startling, others merely strange. Biographies and explanations are in English and the collection is open Tuesday to Friday from 10 am to noon and 2 to 6 pm, and on Saturday and Sunday from 2 to 6 pm. Entry costs Sfr6, or Sfr4 for students.

Lausanne is the headquarters of the International Olympic Committee, so it is perhaps inevitable that there's a museum devoted to the games. The lavish **Musée Olympique**, 1 Quai d'Ouchy, is open daily except Monday (Sfr12, students Sfr9), and tells the story using videos, archive film, interactive computers and memorabilia.

The large **Palais de Rumine** contains several museums. The most important one is the Musée cantonal des Beaux-Arts, exhibiting many works by Swiss artists, and temporary exhibitions (entry around Sfr7). The other museums in the building are free and cover natural history and other sciences (closed Monday).

The lake provides plenty of sporting opportunities. Vidy Sailing School (☎ 617 90 00) offers courses on windsurfing, waterskiing and sailing, as well as equipment rental. For less athletic entertainment, try a tour of the nearby wine-growers' cellars, centering on Lavaux and Chablais to the east and La Côte to the west. Get details from the tourist office.

Places to Stay

Year-round lakeside camping is possible at *Camping de Vidy* (☎ 624 20 31), just to the west of the Vidy sports complex. The SYHA *hostel* (☎ 616 57 82), 1 Chemin du Muguet, Ouchy, can be reached by bus No 1 from the train station, or it's a 20-minute walk if you get on the lake side of the station and head right down Ave Mont d'Or. Dorms cost Sfr22.50 per night and dinners cost Sfr10.50. Reception is closed from 9 am to 5 pm and a curfew comes into effect at 11.30 pm.

Newly opened in 1993, *Jeunotel* (☎ 626 02 22), 36 Chemin du Bois de Vaud, offers no-frills accommodation in dorms (Sfr20), singles/doubles (Sfr50) or triples/quads (Sfr20 per person). Rooms with private shower cost a little more. The self-service restaurant serves cheap meals; if you want breakfast add Sfr6. *Villa Cherokee* (☎ 647 57 20), 4 Chemin de Charmilles, is family-run and has singles/doubles from Sfr35/60 without breakfast. To get there, take bus No 2 from the train station and get off at Presbytère.

The best mid-price deal is *Hôtel d'Angleterre* (☎ 616 41 45) on the Quai d'Ouchy. It's a stately old building and has large, comfortable rooms with TV and views of the lake. Singles/doubles are Sfr130/170 with shower or Sfr75/120 without (cheaper in winter).

Places to Eat

There is a *Migros* restaurant below Place de la Riponne at Rue Neuve, but you're better off heading for the buffet-style *Manora*, 17 Place St François, open daily to 10.30 pm. There's a good choice of vegetables, salad and fruit, and main dishes are around Sfr10. *Café de l'Everche*, 4 Rue Louis Curtat, by the cathedral, has a lunch and evening two-course menu for Sfr13 and a pleasant garden round the back. It is open daily from 7 am to midnight.

Restaurant *Au Couscous* (☎ 312 20 17), 2 Rue Enning, on the 1st floor, has a wide menu including Tunisian, vegetarian and macrobiotic food. Lunch specials are around Sfr14; evening dining is a little more expensive and it's open daily to 1 am.

Getting There & Away

There are three trains an hour from Geneva, the journey takes 40 to 50 minutes and costs Sfr18.60. Most trains from Bern to Geneva go via Lausanne. For boat services, see the Geneva section. Trains to Interlaken Ost go either via Bern (Sfr49) or the scenic route via Montreux (Sfr51).

MONTREUX

Centrepiece of the so-called Swiss Riviera, Montreux offers marvellous lakeside walks and access to the ever-popular Château de Chillon.

Orientation & Information

The train station and main post office are on Ave des Alpes, which down to the south leads to Place de la Paix and the main streets of Grand Rue and Ave du Casino. The tourist information office (☎ 963 12 12) is a few minutes away on the lakefront to the north of Place du Marché; it is open Monday to Friday from 9 am to noon and 1.30 to 6 pm, and on Saturday from 9 am to noon. Hours are extended in the summer, when the place is open daily.

Things to See

Montreux is known for the **Château de Chillon** (pronounced 'Sheeyon'), which receives more visitors than any other historical building in Switzerland. Occupying a stunning position right on Lake Geneva, the fortress caught the public imagination when Lord Byron wrote about the fate of Bonivard, a follower of the Reformation, who was chained to the fifth pillar in the dungeons for four years in the 16th century. Byron etched his own name on the third pillar.

The castle, still in excellent condition, dates from the 11th century and has been much modified and enlarged since then. Allow at least two hours to view the tower, courtyards, dungeons and numerous rooms containing weapons, utensils, frescos and furniture.

Entry costs Sfr5.50 for adults, Sfr4.50 for students and Sfr2 for children, and the castle opens daily at 10 am (9 am from April to September). The closing time varies through the year: it is 4.45 pm from November to February; 5.30 pm in March and October; 6.30 pm in April, May, June and September; and 7 pm in July and August.

The castle is a pleasant 45-minute walk along the lakefront from Montreux (15 minutes from the hostel), or it's also accessible by train or bus No 1.

Montreux's other claim to fame is the **Jazz Festival** in early July. The programme is announced at the end of April and tickets are available shortly afterwards from the Montreux tourist office or from branches of the Swiss Bank Corporation throughout Switzerland.

Nearby Vevey, to the west, has several interesting museums and is easily reached by bus No 1.

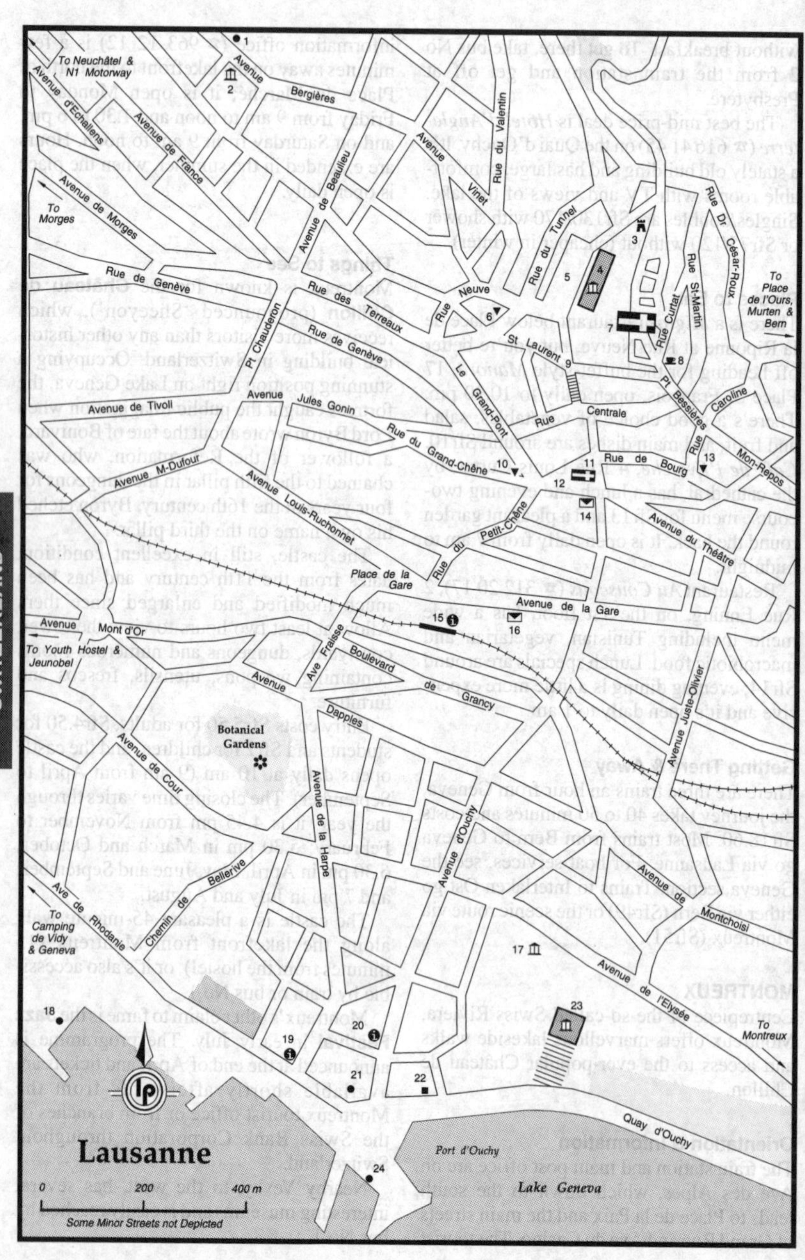

SWITZERLAND

PLACES TO STAY

22 Hôtel d'Angleterre

PLACES TO EAT

6 Migros Supermarket & Restaurant
8 Café de l'Everche
10 Manora
13 Restaurant Au Couscous

OTHER

1 Palais de Beaulieu
2 Musée de l'Art Brut
3 Castle St Marie
4 Palais de Rumine & Museum of Fine Arts
5 Place de la Riponne
7 Cathedral
9 Place de la Palud
11 St François Church
12 Place St François
14 Post Office
15 Main Train Station
16 Main Post Office
17 Musée de l'Elysée
18 CGN Head Office
19 Tourist Office
20 Regional Tourist Office
21 Ouchy Metro
23 Olympic Museum
24 CGN Boat Departure Point

Places to Stay

The SYHA *hostel* (☎ 963 49 34) is at 8 Passage de l'Auberge, Territet, 30 minutes' walk along the lake to the east from the tourist office. It's nicely situated near the waterfront and newly refurbished, although the trains clattering overhead will ensure you won't sleep in. Dorms are Sfr24.50 and doubles are Sfr64. Near the casino in Montreux, the *Élite* (☎ 963 67 33), 25 Ave du Casino, has singles/doubles from Sfr55/85, or Sfr75/115 with shower. *Hostellerie du Lac* (☎ 963 21 71), 12 Rue du Quai, has rooms with high ceilings, big balconies and views of the lake. Doubles start from Sfr80, or Sfr125 with private shower, and there's a discount for single occupancy. Prices for both are slightly lower in winter. *Villa Germaine* (☎ 963 15 28), 3 Ave de Collonges, Territet, is the same price year-round. Singles/doubles start at Sfr50/80.

Places to Eat

The tourist office produces a list of restaurants. *Migros* supermarket on Ave du Casino has a self-service restaurant, open Monday to Friday until 6.30 pm, and Saturday until 5 pm. *Restaurant City*, 37 Ave des Alpes, is also self-service with meals for around Sfr12. The main advantage of this place is the sunny terrace overlooking the lake (open daily).

Brasserie des Alpes, 23 Ave des Alpes, serves good, cheap French and Italian fare (from Sfr12), and it's open daily to around midnight. On the lake along Rue de Quay, check *Restaurant le Palais*, decked out in fake inlays, looking like a low-budget version of the Taj Mahal. It's fairly pricey, with Oriental food for around Sfr25 to Sfr35, but the weird patio and posey patrons make up for the expense (closed Monday).

Getting There & Away

Hourly trains run to/from Geneva and take 70 minutes (Sfr27). From Lausanne, there are three trains an hour (Sfr7.80) which take around 25 minutes. Slow local trains continue eastwards from Montreux to stop at Territet for the hostel, and Chillon for the castle. Interlaken can be reached via a scenic rail route, with changeovers at Zweisimmen and Spiez. The track winds its way up the hill for an excellent view over Lake Geneva. For boat services, see Getting There & Away in the Geneva section.

Valais

The dramatic Alpine scenery of Valais (Wallis in German) once made it one of the most inaccessible regions of Switzerland. Nowadays the mountains and valleys have been opened up by an efficient network of roads, railways and cable cars. It is an area of great natural beauty, and naturally enough, each impressive panorama has spawned its own resort. Skiing (47 listed centres) in the winter and hiking in the summer are primary pursuits, but angling, swimming, mountaineering, even tennis, are widely enjoyed.

Valais is also known for its *Combats des Reines* (*Kuhkämpfe* in German) – cow fights organised in villages to determine which beast is most suited to lead the herd up to the summer pastures. They usually take place on selected Sundays through the summer from April, accompanied by much celebration and consumption of Valaisan wine. The combatants rarely get hurt. There is a grand final in Aproz on Ascension Day, and the last meeting of the season is at the Martigny Fair in October.

SION

Sion, the capital of the Lower Valais, merits a perusal en route from Montreux to Zermatt. Its historical pre-eminence (the Bishops of Sion formerly held the powers of temporal princes) is hinted at by the two ancient fortifications that dominate the town: Tourbillon Castle, and on the neighbouring hill, the Valère church. Either provides a fine view of the Rhône valley. The regional museums of Valais are here too; get details from the Sion tourist office (☎ 027-22 85 86), Place de la Planta. The regional tourist office (☎ 027-22 31 61), 16 Rue Pré-Fleuri, can help you plan excursions to other attractions in the Valais.

If you want to stop over, there's a SYHA *hostel* (☎ 027-23 74 70), Rue de l'Industrie 2, behind the station (exit left and turn left under the tracks). All trains on the Lausanne-Brig express route stop at Sion.

ZERMATT

Skiing, hiking and mountaineering are the main attractions in this resort, all overseen by the Matterhorn, the most famous peak in the Alps.

Orientation & Information

The massive Matterhorn stands sentinel at the end of the valley. Zermatt is car-free except for electric taxis, and there are few street names. The centre of the resort is to the right of the train station.

The tourist office (☎ 028-66 11 81), beside the train station, is open Monday to Friday from 8.30 am to noon and 2 to 6 pm, and Saturday from 8.30 am to noon. During the summer and winter high season it is also open Saturday afternoon and Sunday. Next-door is a travel agent which changes money. The mountain guides office *(Bergführerbüro)* (☎ 67 34 56) on the main street near the post office is another good information source. Some hotels and restaurants close during the low season which falls in May, June, and mid-September to mid-November.

Activities

Zermatt has many demanding slopes to test the experienced skier; beginners have fewer possibilities. Spring is a popular time as the higher runs are opening up, but in early summer the snow is still good and the lifts are much less busy. There are excellent views of mountain panoramas, including Mt Rosa and the Matterhorn, from the network of cable cars and gondolas.

The cog-wheel railway to Gornergrat (3100 metres) is a particular highlight. The Klein Matterhorn is topped by the highest cable station in Europe, at 3820 metres, and provides access to summer skiing slopes. It is possible to ski into Italy from here along the Ventina route but don't forget to take your passport. There are footpaths to and from many of the cable-car terminals. A day pass for all rides costs Sfr60, and ski coupons are available. Ski shops open daily for rental – allow Sfr30 per day for skis and stocks and Sfr14 per day for boots.

A walk in the cemetery is a sobering experience for would-be mountaineers, as numerous monuments tell of deaths on Mt Rosa and the Matterhorn. Also wander round the traditional Valais wooden barns in the Hinter Dorf area, just north of the church.

Places to Stay & Eat

Camping Spiss (☎ 67 39 21), to the left of the train station, is open from June to September and charges Sfr7.50 per day.

The SYHA *hostel* (☎ 67 23 20) is rather rule-orientated but has an excellent view of the Matterhorn. Turn left at the church, cross the river and take the second right. Dorm beds at half-board cost Sfr36.50. Laundry loads cost Sfr8. The doors stay open during the day, but a curfew comes into effect at 11.30 pm. The hostel is shut during May, and from the end of October to mid-December.

Opposite the train station and popular with mountaineers is *Hotel Bahnhof* (☎ 67 24 06), with dorms for Sfr26 and singles/doubles for around Sfr42/72, without breakfast. Guests have use of a communal kitchen and there is no curfew or daytime closing. *Hotel Gabelhorn* (☎ 67 22 35), in the Hinter Dorf area of the village, is small and family-run, costing from Sfr40 per person.

Most other places increase prices by about 40% in the high season: *Hotel Garni Malva* (☎ 67 30 33), overlooking the east side of the river, costs from Sfr36 to Sfr53 per person; add about Sfr15 per person for a private shower.

North Wall Bar, near the hostel, is one of the cheapest and best bars in the village, popular with resort workers. It has ski videos, music, good pizzas from Sfr9 and beer at Sfr4 for half a litre. The bar is closed during the low season, otherwise it's open daily from 6.30 pm to midnight. Just down the hill, the more expensive *Papperla Pub* is also popular.

Beyond the church on the main street, *Restaurant Weisshorn* and the *Café du Pont* next door are both good places for food. Also recommended is *Walliser Kanne*, by the post office, which has pizzas, fondue, fish dishes and Valais specialities from Sfr10 to Sfr20.

Getting There & Away

Hourly trains depart from Brig at 23 minutes past the hour up to at least 7.23 pm, calling at Visp en route. The steep and scenic journey takes 80 minutes and costs Sfr33 one way, or Sfr53 return. It is a private railway; Eurail passes are not valid, Inter-Rail earns 50% off and the Swiss Pass is good for free travel. The only way out is back, but if you're going to Saas Fee you can divert there from Stalden-Saas.

As Zermatt is car-free, you need to park cars at Täsch (Sfr4.50 per day) and take the train from there (Sfr6.20). Parking is free in Visp if you take the Zermatt train (for details, ☎ 23 13 33).

SAAS FEE

In the valley adjoining Zermatt, Saas Fee may not have the Matterhorn, but there are plenty of other towering peaks to keep you occupied.

Orientation & Information

The village centre and ski lifts are to the left of the bus station, which contains a post office. High season is from mid-December to mid-April. The tourist office (☎ 028-57 14 57), opposite the bus station, is open in the high season Monday to Friday from 8.30 am to noon and from 2 to 6.30 pm, Saturday from 8.30 am to 7 pm, and Sunday from 4 to 6 pm. During the low season, weekend opening is reduced depending on demand.

Activities

Saas Fee is surrounded by an impressive panorama of 4000-metre peaks and rivals Zermatt as a summer skiing centre. There is also ski mountaineering along the famous Haute Route to Chamonix. The highest metro in the world operates all year to Mittelallalin at 3500 metres, where there's an ice pavilion explaining interesting facts about glaciers.

A general lift pass costs Sfr50 for one day. Ski rental prices are as for Zermatt. The tourist office has a map of summer walking trails. Even in winter, 30 km of marked footpaths remain open.

Places to Stay & Eat

The summer *camp ground* (☎ 57 14 57) costs Sfr4 per person plus Sfr3 for a tent. The *Albana* has beds in shared rooms with shower from Sfr24, including a great breakfast. It shuts at the end of April and reopens in early July. It's a good idea to book in advance in winter. Reception is in the adjoining *Hotel Mascotte* (☎ 57 27 24), which has singles/doubles for Sfr70/140 with private WC and shower. In the south of the village, convenient for the ski lifts, is *Garni Feehof*

(☎ 57 33 44), with reasonable singles/doubles for around Sfr44/88.

Eat pizza at *Boccalino* near the ski lifts. *Restaurant Vieux Chalet*, off the main street, is good for snacks and meals and sometimes has live music. In the extreme north of the village, *Restaurant Alp Hitta* (☎ 57 10 50) has a relaxed atmosphere, raclette for Sfr6, fondue from Sfr18 and other dishes from Sfr12. It is open daily from 8 am to 1.30 am, except during the low season when it closes down. The restaurant manages two to four-person apartments, each with a small kitchen, which are available all year. The price of Sfr35 per person includes breakfast.

Getting There & Away

Saas Fee cannot be reached by train. Hourly buses depart from Brig via Visp, take one hour and cost Sfr30 for a one-month return.

Like Zermatt, Saas Fee is car-free. Park at the entrance to the village, where daily charges are Sfr12 in the garage or Sfr10 outside (discount with the Guest Card, supplied by your hotel in Saas Fee).

OTHER RESORTS

The best known resort in west Valais is **Verbier,** with 400 km of ski runs. Ski passes cost Sfr55 for one day or Sfr324 for a week. Lesser known resorts can have perfectly adequate skiing yet be much cheaper. Ski passes in **Leukerbad,** for example, north-east of Verbier, are Sfr36 (students Sfr30) for one day or Sfr186 (students Sfr148) for a week. Leukerbad is also a health spa with the added attraction of hot springs.

Ticino

Situated south of the Alps and enjoying a Mediterranean climate, Ticino (Tessin in German) gives more than just a taste of Italy. Indeed, it belonged to Italy until the Swiss Confederation seized it in 1512. The people are darker skinned than their compatriots, and the cuisine, architecture and vegetation reflect that found farther south. Italian is the official language of the canton. Many people also speak French and German but you will find English less widely spoken than in the rest of Switzerland. The region offers mountain hikes and dramatic gorges in the north, water sports and relaxed, leisurely towns in the south.

Warning: From autumn 1995 *all* telephone numbers in Ticino will have seven digits; the area code for the whole canton will be 091.

LOCARNO

Locarno lies at the northern end of Lake Maggiore. Switzerland's lowest town, at 205 metres above sea level, it enjoys the country's best climate.

Orientation & Information

The centre of town is the Piazza Grande where the main post office can be found. The tourist office (☎ 093-31 03 33) is nearby at Largo Zorzi, adjoining the Kursaal. It has brochures on many parts of Switzerland. From March to October, it's open Monday to Friday from 8 am to 7 pm, and Saturday and Sunday from 9 am to noon and 1 to 5 pm. From November to February, opening hours are Monday to Friday from 8 am to noon, and 2 to 6 pm.

Five minutes' walk away is the train station, where money exchange counters are open daily from 5.45 am to 9 pm, and bikes can be rented daily from 7 am and returned up to 11.30 pm.

Things to See

The principal attraction is the **Madonna del Sasso**, up on the hill with a good view of the lake and the town. The sanctuary was built after the Virgin Mary appeared in a vision in 1480. It contains some 15th-century paintings, a small museum and several distinctive statue groups. There is a funicular from the town centre, but the 20-minute walk up is not demanding (take Via al Sasso off Via Cappuccini) and you pass some shrines on the way.

In the town, as well as exploring the Italianate piazzas and arcades, there are a couple of churches worth a look, including the 17th-century **Chiesa Nuova** on Via Cittadella, with an ornate ceiling complete with frolicking angels.

Locarno has more hours of sunshine than anywhere else in Switzerland, just right for strolls round the lake. **Giardini Jean Arp** is a small lakeside park off Lungolago Gius Motta, where sculptures by the surrealist artist are scattered among the palm trees and tulips.

Places to Stay

Delta Camping (☎ 31 60 81) is expensive at Sfr20 minimum per site, rising to Sfr45 from 1 June to 31 August.

Pensione Città Vecchia (☎ 31 45 54), Via Toretta 13, off Piazza Grande (head up the hill by the sign for 'Innovazione'), is a friendly, private hostel without curfew or daytime closing. Beds are Sfr20 with your own sleeping bag, or Sfr24 if you need sheets. Dorms (using hall showers) vary in size but the price doesn't change. Optional breakfast is Sfr4. It is only open from 1 March to 31 October. The new owners in 1995 aren't expected to change the style of the place. The old owners, meanwhile, have opened a place called *Albergo Reginetta* (☎ 32 35 53), not far away at Via della Motta 8. Singles/doubles are Sfr40/80, or Sfr34/68 without breakfast.

Convenient for the station is *Garni Montaldi* (☎ 33 02 22), Piazza Stazione, with singles/doubles for Sfr56/112 with shower and TV. Reception is also here for *Stazione*, an older, slightly noisier building to the rear where singles/doubles are Sfr38/76, also with shower. Stazione closes for the winter.

Hotel Ristorante Zurigo (☎ 33 16 17), Via Verbano 9, offers comfortable accommodation overlooking the lake. Gold-coloured metal bedsteads, tastefully arranged pictures and patterned tiled floors give the rooms some style. Prices start at Sfr83/116 for a single/double in winter, rising to Sfr139/169 in summer. All rooms have cable TV and private shower/WC. The restaurant serves good, mid-price food.

Places to Eat

The *Coop* supermarket on Piazza Grande has a self-service restaurant. *Inova*, Via Stazione 1, by the train station, has good self-service dishes from Sfr7.90 and help-yourself salad plates from Sfr3.80 to Sfr9.50. It is open daily to 10 pm. *Trattoria Campagna Ristorante*, Via Castelrotto, west of St Antonio church, has a *piatto del giorno* (dish of the day) for Sfr13, and pizza and pasta from Sfr9.50 It is open every day until midnight.

Try fish specialities (from Sfr28) in the upstairs section at *Ristorante Cittadella*, Via Cittadella 18. *Ristorante Centenario* (☎ 33 82 22), Lungo Lago 17, is acknowledged as the best restaurant in Ticino, but its French cuisine is extremely expensive (closed on Sunday and Monday).

Getting There & Away

The St Gotthard pass provides the road link (N2) to central Switzerland. There are trains every two hours from Brig, passing through Italy en route. The cost is Sfr47 and it takes around three hours. You change trains at Domodossola across the border, so bring your passport.

One-day travel passes for boats on Lake Maggiore cost Sfr9 to Sfr17 depending upon the area they're valid for on the lake. For more information, contact Navigazione Lago Maggiore on ☎ 31 18 65. There is a regular boat and hydrofoil service from Italy.

BELLINZONA

The capital of Ticino is a city of castles. It is set in a valley of lush mountains, and stands at the southern side of two important Alpine passes, San Bernardino and St Gotthard.

Orientation & Information

Postbuses arrive one block in front of the train station on Via C Molo. The money-exchange counter in the station is open daily from 6 am to 9 pm. The tourist office (☎ 092-25 21 31), Via Camminata 2, Palazzo Civico, is open Monday to Friday from 8 am to noon and 1.30 to 6.30 pm, and Saturday from 9 am to noon. To get there, turn left out of the station and walk for 10 minutes, passing the main post office (6500 Bellinzona 1) on the way.

Things to See

The three medieval castles which dominate the town are testimony to Bellinzona's historical importance, based on its key location at the crossroads of major Alpine routes. All the castles are well preserved, free to enter, and offer fine views of the town and surrounding mountains.

Castel Grande, dating from around the 6th century, is the largest and most central; **Castello di Montebello** is slightly above the town. Both are open daily. Quite a trek up the hill is the smaller **Castello di Sasso Corbaro**, open from 1 April to 31 October from 9 am to noon and 2 to 5 pm (closed Monday). There are no buses up there but it's easy to beg a lift back down again from the car park. Each castle has a small museum covering history and archaeology (Sfr2, students Sfr1, closed Monday); if you want to see them all, buy a combined ticket for Sfr4 (students Sfr2).

The **Santa Maria delle Grazie** church in the town features an impressive 15th-century fresco of the Crucifixion, similar to that in Lugano.

Places to Stay

The *camp ground* (☎ 29 11 18), Bosco di Molinazzo, costs from Sfr4.60 per person, Sfr4 per tent and Sfr8 for a camper van. The few budget hotels in town fill quickly. Two places to try near the station are *Metropoli* (☎ 25 11 79), Via Ludovico il Moro, with singles/doubles from Sfr40/80, and *San Giovanni* (☎ 25 19 19), Via San Giovanni 7, with singles/doubles for Sfr45/88, all using a hall shower. Ideally situated is *Croce Federale* (☎ 25 16 67), Viale Stazione 12, with singles/doubles/triples for Sfr90/120/150. All rooms have shower, WC and TV.

Places to Eat

Cheap self-service restaurants are at *Coop*, on Via H Guisan, the nearby *Migros*, and *Inova*, in the Innovazione department store on Viale Stazione. You could also try *Ristorante l'Arcada*, Piazza Collegiata 1, or *Birreria Corona*, opposite the tourist office at Via Camminata 5. All these places are closed on Sunday.

Speranza (☎ 26 19 39), Via Pedemonte 12, by the station on the east side of the tracks, is a great place for mid-price food. Personal service is paramount – there's not even a written menu; instead, the staff explain the dishes to you (closed Monday, Tuesday, and in July and August).

Getting There & Away

Bellinzona is on the train route connecting Locarno (Sfr6.20, takes 20 minutes) and Lugano (Sfr9.80, 30 minutes). It is also on the Zürich-Milan route. Postbuses head north-east to Chur (Sfr5 supplement applies even with travel passes). You need to reserve your postbus seat the day before on ☎ 25 77 55. There is a good cycling track along the Ticino River to Lake Maggiore and Locarno.

LUGANO

Switzerland's southernmost tourist town offers an excellent combination of lazy days, watery pursuits and hillside hikes.

Orientation & Information

The old town lies down the hill to the east of the train station, which offers daily money-exchange and bike rental. About 15 minutes' walk away, the tourist office (☎ 091-21 46 64) overlooks Lake Lugano, on Riva G Albertolli 5. Opening hours are Monday to Friday from 9 am to 6 pm (6.30 pm between 1 July and 30 September). On Saturday between April and October it is open from 9 am to 5 pm. These hours are subject to change depending on demand.

The main post office is in the centre of the old town on the corner of Contrada di Verla and Via della Posta. The Italian Consulate (☎ 22 05 13) is at Via Monte Ceneri 16.

Things to See & Do

Winding alleyways, pedestrian-only piazzas and colourful parks make Lugano an ideal town for walking around. The **Santa Maria**

SWITZERLAND

degli Angioli church, Piazza Luini, has a vivid fresco of the Crucifixion by Bernardino Luini dating from 1529.

The **Thyssen-Bornemisza Gallery**, Villa Favorita, Castagnola, is a famous private art collection, covering every style from abstract to photorealism, though the Old Masters are on loan in Spain. Admission is expensive at Sfr12 for adults or Sfr8 for students, and it might only be open from Friday to Sunday. For people who want a more affordable taste of art, the **Cantonal Art Museum**, Via Canova 10, has a worthwhile modern selection. Entry costs about Sfr5 (students Sfr3), depending on exhibitions (closed Monday).

The **Lido**, east of the Cassarate River, offers a swimming pool and sandy beaches for Sfr5 a day, and it's open daily from 1 May to mid-September. A tourist fishing permit for Lake Lugano costs Sfr50 and is valid for 10 days. A boat tour of the lake is a very enjoyable excursion. There are boat and bus departures approximately every 90 minutes to nearby Melide, where **Swiss Miniatur** displays 1:25 scale models of national attractions (Sfr10, children Sfr6; closed in winter, otherwise open daily).

The tourist office has hiking information, and even conducts free guided walks of the town on Tuesday in the summer (reserve the day before). There are excellent hikes and views from **Monte San Salvatore** and **Monte Brè.** The funicular from Paradiso up Monte San Salvatore operates from March to November only and costs Sfr10 to go up or Sfr14 return. To get up Monte Brè, you can take the year-round funicular from Cassarate which costs Sfr10 to go up or Sfr15 return.

Places to Stay

The relaxed SYHA *hostel* (☎ 56 27 28), Via Cantonale 13, is a hard 20 minutes' walk uphill from the train station (signposted), or take bus No 5 to Crocifisso (Sfr1.50). Beds are Sfr14 plus (if required) Sfr2 for sheets and Sfr6 for breakfast. It also has private rooms from Sfr18 per person. Reception is shut from 1 to 3 pm and curfew is at 10 pm. The hostel has private grounds and a swimming pool and closes from 31 October to late March.

Close to the train station is *Hotel Montarina* (☎ 56 72 72), Via Montarina 1, with beds in large dorms for Sfr20 (excluding sheets), singles/doubles from Sfr46/76 and triples/quads for Sfr105/140, all without breakfast. It's convenient but not as friendly as the hostel. Reception is open from 9 am to 9 pm and there's no curfew. It closes from 31 October to about two weeks before Easter.

Hotel Restaurant Pestalozzi (☎ 22 95 95), Piazza Indipendenza 9, offers a range of singles/doubles from Sfr48/90, up to Sfr86/144 if you want private bath and WC. *Zurigo*, along the road at Corso Pestalozzi 13, also has rooms with various facilities, all starting at Sfr55/90. It has plenty of off-street parking spaces.

Around the bay in Paradiso is *Victoria au Lac* (☎ 54 20 31), Via General Guisan 3, which sometimes has space when places in town are full. It's slightly aged but comfortable enough and very atmospheric; singles/doubles are around Sfr55/90, or Sfr90/120 with shower. Parking is no problem, and it's open from April to October.

Places to Eat

There is a large *Migros* supermarket and restaurant on Via Pretorio opposite Via Emilio Bossi. The *EPA* department store on Piazzetta San Carlo also has a cheap restaurant. Similarly priced, *Ristorante Inova*, up the stairs on the north side of Piazza Cioccaro, has excellent buffet-style food (open daily to 10 pm). Also good and cheap for Italian and vegetarian food is *Pestalozzi* (see Places to Stay), open daily from 6 am to 11 pm.

As you might expect, pizza and pasta abound. On the south side of Piazza Cioccaro is the large *Sayonara*. It has the usual selection, as well as local dishes (open daily). *La Tinera*, Via dei Gorini, off Piazza della Riforma, is also good for Ticinese food, and has meals for Sfr10 to Sfr25. At lunch you may have to queue to be seated (closed Sunday).

Getting There & Away

Lugano is on the same road and rail route as Bellinzona. There is a daily postbus service to St Moritz (one in winter, three in summer), which costs Sfr53 (plus a Sfr5 supplement, even if you have a travel pass) and takes four hours. You need to reserve your seat the day before at the train information counter in the station, or by phoning ☎ 21 95 20. Buses leave from the bus station on Via S Balestra, though the St Moritz bus calls at the train station. A seven-day regional holiday ticket costs Sfr86 and is valid for all regional public transport including funiculars and boats on Lake Lugano.

Graubünden

Once upon a time, tourists in Switzerland were a summer phenomenon. Then, in 1864, the owner of the Engadiner Kulm Hotel in St Moritz offered four English summer guests free accommodation if they returned for the winter. He told them they were missing the best time of the year. Although dubious, the English were unable to refuse a free offer. They returned, enjoyed themselves, and winter tourism was born.

Today Graubünden (Grisons, Grigioni, Grishun) has some of the most developed and best known winter sports centres in the world, including Arosa, Davos, Klosters, Flims, and, of course, St Moritz. Away from the international resorts, Graubünden is a relatively unspoiled region of rural villages, Alpine lakes and hilltop castles. The people speak German, Italian or Romansch.

CHUR

Chur is the cantonal capital, yet retains a small-town feel. It has been continuously inhabited since 3000 BC.

Orientation & Information

Money exchange is possible in the train station daily from 5.50 am to 9.15 pm. Five minutes' walk straight ahead down Bahnhofstrasse is Postplatz. To the right is a post office (PTT 7002, Chur 2) and to the left is the tourist office (☎ 081-22 18 18), Grabenstrasse 5, open Monday to Friday from 8 am to noon and 1.30 to 6 pm, and Saturday from 9 am to noon. Pick up a free copy of the walking tour of the centre of town. The regional tourist office (☎ 22 13 60), Alexanderstrasse 24, has information on the whole canton but it's only open on weekdays. Chur's area code is 081.

Things to See

Chur has an attractive old town with 16th-century buildings, fountains and alleyways. The murals of ordinary people on various façades are by Robert Indermaur. Augusto Giacometti designed three of the windows in the 1491 **Church of St Martin**. In the impressive **cathedral**, built from 1150, take note of the crypt, the high altar and the carved heads on the choir stalls. The **Kunstmuseum** on Postplatz is closed Monday and contains modern art, including a generous gathering of stuff by the three Giacomettis. Note also the sci-fi work by local artist, HR Giger, who created the monsters in the *Alien* films. Entry costs Sfr5 (students Sfr3). If you like sci-fi themes, visit Giger's creatively decorated bar at Comercialstrasse 23.

Places to Stay

Camp Au (☎ 24 22 83), to the north of town by the sports centre, costs Sfr5 per person and from Sfr4 for a tent. The SYHA *hostel* (☎ 22 65 63), Berggasse 28, is up the hill to the east, 15 minutes' walk from the tourist office. This rustic hostel is very intimate: each bunk comprises at least five mattresses side by side! Beds cost Sfr19, curfew is at 10 pm, and reception shuts from 10 am to 5 pm during which time the doors are locked. The hostel is closed from around November to March.

There are no particularly cheap hotels in town. The central *Franziskaner* (☎ 22 12 61), Untere Gasse, has adequate singles/doubles from Sfr50/90. A better deal is *Rosenhügel* (☎ 22 23 88), up the hill to the south at Malixerstrasse 32. Prices start at

Sfr45/90. Greater comfort can be found at *Hotel Drei Könige* (☎ 22 17 25), Reichsgasse 18. Singles/doubles are Sfr90/140 with shower or Sfr70/115 without. There's free parking nearby and it also stages occasional concerts.

Places to Eat

Cheap restaurants are at *Coop* on Bahnhofstrasse and at *Migros* on Gürtelstrasse. *Bierschwemme*, Malixerstrasse 1, has simple but good-value food from Sfr7.50. The two-course daily menu for Sfr9.80 is only available from 11 am to 1 pm and 6 to 8 pm (open daily to midnight). *Calanda Restaurant* on Postplatz has meals and daily menus from about Sfr12, including vegetarian choices. It's also a popular venue with evening drinkers.

For well-prepared food in a wooden environment (the décor, not the company), go to *Hotel Stern*, opposite Drei Könige on Reichsgasse. Main dishes are around Sfr30, or you can splash out on the eight-course gourmet menu at Sfr138 for two. Lunchtime eating is cheaper, with three menus (one vegetarian) from Sfr15 including soup.

Entertainment

At night the hectic, crowded *Churchill Pub* on Grabenstrasse is where the local youth go to drink, pose and play pool.

Getting There & Away

Postbuses leave from the depot above the train station, including the express service to Bellinzona (reserve ahead on ☎ 22 38 23). There are rail connections to Davos, Klosters and Arosa, and fast trains to Sargans (the station for Liechtenstein, only 25 minutes away) and Zürich (85 minutes, Sfr36). Chur can be visited on the Glacier Express route (see St Moritz below).

ST MORITZ

This resort needs little introduction. Playground of today's international jet-setters, the curative properties of its waters have been known for 3000 years.

Orientation & Information

St Moritz exudes health and wealth. The train station near the lake rents bikes and changes money from 6.50 am to 8.10 pm daily. Just up the hill is the post office and five minutes farther on is the tourist office or Kurverein (☎ 082-3 31 47) at Via Maistra 12. It's open Monday to Friday from 9 am to noon and 2 to 6 pm, on Saturday morning, and also on Saturday afternoon during the high season. To the south-west, around the lake from the main town, St Moritz Dorf, lies St Moritz Bad. Not much stays open during November, May and early June.

Activities

In the St Moritz region there are 350 km of downhill runs, although the choice for beginners is limited. A one-day ski pass costs Sfr51, and ski and boot rental is about Sfr43 for one day. There are also 160 km of cross-country trails (equipment rental Sfr20) and 120 km of marked hiking paths.

Numerous other sporting activities are on offer: golf (including on the frozen lake in winter), tennis, squash, fishing, horse riding, sailing, windsurfing and river rafting, to mention just a few. Inevitably, however, they are expensive. The tourist office has a price list. Buying a health treatment in the spa is another way to spend money, or you could pop into the two museums.

Places to Stay

The *Olympiaschanze* camping ground (☎ 3 40 90) is one km south-west of St Moritz Bad; it is open from early June to mid-September.

The *Stille Youth Hostel* (☎ 3 39 69), Via Surpunt 60, St Moritz Bad, is 30 minutes' walk round the lake from the tourist office, and has excellent facilities. Half-pension per person prices are Sfr38 in four-bed dorms and Sfr48 in double rooms. Laundry costs Sfr4 per load. Reception is closed from 9 am to 4 pm, curfew is 10 pm and the hostel closes in the low season. If it's full, try the *Sporthotel Stille* (☎ 3 69 48) next door. Per person prices start at Sfr45 in summer or Sfr69 (for half-board) in winter.

Hotel prices fluctuate according to the season, reaching a peak from around mid-December to mid-February, and these are the prices quoted below. The summer high season, July and August, isn't quite so expensive. In some places in winter you must take half-board. *Bellaval* (☎ 3 32 45), right by the train station on the south side, has singles/doubles from Sfr65/126. St Moritz Bad has the cheaper options, such as *Hotel Bernina* (☎ 3 60 22), Via dal Bagn, charging from Sfr80/160 half-board (Sfr50/100 in summer for B&B).

Most of the hotels in the centre of St Moritz Dorf sport four or five stars. The best three-star choices are close together on Via Veglia: *Hotel Eden Garni* (☎ 3 61 61) at Sfr110/200 and *Hotel Languard Garni* (☎ 3 31 37) at Sfr115/210.

SWITZERLAND

Places to Eat

The cheapest restaurants are in St Moritz Bad. There is a *Coop* in Via dal Bagn. Its self-service restaurant, *Bellevue*, is next door and has menus from Sfr8.50. Beside it is *Al Tavolo*, offering food for a range of prices. The popular *Hotel Sonne*, Via Sela 11, close to the hostel, serves pasta, salads and tasty pizzas (after 5 pm) from Sfr11.50. It is open daily from 7 am to midnight.

In Dorf, look for lunch specials or go to *Hotel Steinbock*, opposite the post office, where meals start at Sfr15. Try an expensive taste of the highlife at the top of the Corviglia funicular by sampling the truffles, caviar and desserts at *la Marmite* (☎ 3 63 55). Queue or reserve ahead in season.

Getting There & Away

To Lugano, three postbuses run daily in summer, one in winter: you must reserve a seat the day before on ☎ 3 30 72, and the route incurs a Sfr5 supplement. A train-and-bus combination will get you to Landeck in Austria for Sfr47.

At least nine daily trains travel south to Tirano in Italy with connections to Milan. The famous Glacier Express connects St Moritz to Zermatt via the 2033-metre Oberalp Pass, taking 7½ hours to cover 290 scenic km and crossing 291 bridges (Sfr112). Some drink glasses in the dining car have sloping bases to compensate for the hills – but you must remember to keep turning them around! Beware of the Sfr6 reservation fee that's payable only on some trains on both routes.

AROUND ST MORITZ

The Engadine Valley, running north-east and south-west of St Moritz, offers a combination of plush resorts and unspoilt villages. In the latter category are **Guarda** and **Zuoz**, where you can see homes displaying traditional sgraffito designs (patterns scratched on wall plaster) that are characteristic of the Engadine. The annual cross-country ski marathon between Maloja and Zuoz takes place on the second Sunday in March. The route crosses ice-covered lakes and passes by St Moritz lake. Trains and buses run regularly along the Engadine Valley.

Flora and fauna abound in the 169 sq km of the **Swiss National Park** (open June to October). The park information centre (☎ 082-8 13 78), Zernez, has details of hiking facilities. Trains to Zernez from St Moritz cost Sfr10.60.

OTHER SKI RESORTS

In the Davos/Klosters region there are 320 km of ski runs, mostly medium to difficult, including one of the hardest runs in the world, the Gotschnawang. **Arosa** is another top-notch resort, easily reached by a scenic train ride from Chur. Most other ski resorts in Graubünden have predominantly easy to medium runs. Ski passes average Sfr45 for one day (cheaper by the week).

Zürich

Zürich started life as a Roman customs post until it graduated to the status of a free city under the Holy Roman Empire in 1218. Today, Switzerland's most populous city offers an ambience of affluence and plenty of cultural diversions. Banks and art galleries will greet you at every turn, in a strange marriage of finance and aesthetics.

The city's reputation as a cultural and intellectual centre began after it joined the Swiss Confederation in 1351. Zwingli helped things along with his teachings during the Reformation. The city's intellectual and artistic tradition continued during WW I with the influx of luminaries such as Lenin, Trotsky, Tristan Tzara, Hans Arp and James Joyce. On the financial side, Zürich's status as an international industrial and business centre is thanks in no small part to the efforts in the 19th century of the energetic administrator and railway magnate, Alfred Escher.

Orientation

Zürich is 409 metres above sea level at the northern end of Lake Zürich. The city centre is ranged on either side of the Limmat River. Like many Swiss cities, it is compact and conveniently laid out. The main train station (Hauptbahnhof) is on the west bank of the river, close to the old centre.

Information

Tourist Offices The main tourist office (☎ 01-211 40 00), Bahnhofplatz 15, arranges car rentals and excursions. From April to October it is open Monday to Friday from 8.30 am to 9.30 pm, and Saturday and Sunday from 8.30 am to 8.30 pm; from November to March it closes an hour earlier on weekdays and two hours earlier on weekends. There is an airport branch in Terminal B (☎ 01-816 40 81), open daily from 10 am to 7 pm. Maps of Zürich and lists of hotels cost Sfr1 to Sfr3.

The Swiss National Tourist Office headquarters (☎ 01-288 11 11) is located at Bellariastrasse 38, and has information on the whole of Switzerland. It's open Monday to Friday from 8 to 11.45 am and 1 to 5 pm.

Money & Post There's no shortage of choice when exchanging money in this banking city. Banks are open Monday to Friday from 8.15 am to 4.30 pm, except Thursday when they are open until 6 pm. The exchange office by platform 16 in the Hauptbahnhof is open daily from 6.30 am to 10.45 pm.

The main post office is Sihlpost (☎ 01-296 21 11), Kasernenstrasse 95-97. It is open Monday to Friday from 6.30 am to 10.30 pm, and Saturday from 6.30 am to 8 pm. Like many other Swiss post offices, it also has extended trading hours but some transactions are subject to a small surcharge during these times. There's also a post office at the Hauptbahnhof.

The telephone code for Zürich is 01.

Consulates Consulates in town include the following:

Austria
 Minervastrasse 116 (☎ 383 72 00)
Germany
 Kirchgasse 48 (☎ 265 65 65)
South Africa
 Basteiplatz 7 (☎ 221 11 88)
UK
 Dufourstrasse 56 (☎ 261 15 20)
USA
 Zollikerstrasse 141 (☎ 422 25 66)

Travel Agents SSR is a specialist in student, youth and budget fares. There are two branches, at Leonhardstrasse 10 (open Monday to Friday) and at Bäckerstrasse 40 (open Monday afternoon to Saturday morning), or call ☎ 297 11 11 for telephone sales. Globetrotter (☎ 211 77 80), Rennweg 35, also has worldwide budget fares, and a travel noticeboard and magazine. American Express (☎ 211 83 70), Bahnhofstrasse 20, is open Monday to Friday from 8.30 am to 5.30 pm and Saturday from 9 am to noon.

Bookshops For foreign titles, you always pay more in francs than the cover price. Stäheli English Bookshop (☎ 201 33 02), Bahnhofstrasse 70, has many books, and during May sells off old stock very cheaply. It is open Monday to Friday from 9 am to 6.30 pm and Saturday from 9 am to 4 pm. English and French-language books are also available at Librairie Poyot, Bahnhofstrasse 11. The Travel Book Shop (☎ 252 38 83), Rindermarkt 20, has a huge selection of

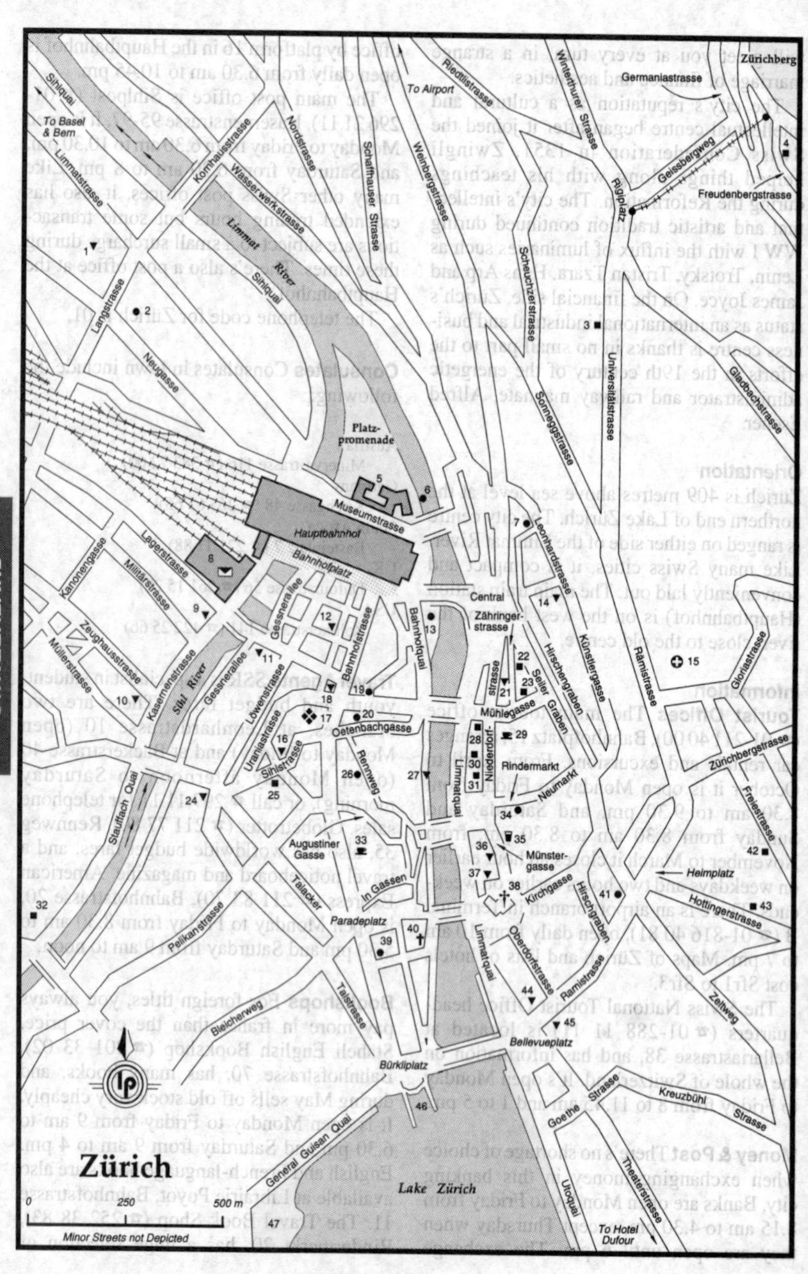

SWITZERLAND

PLACES TO STAY

3 Hotel Poly
4 Justinusheim
22 Martahaus
23 Scheuble
25 Vereinhaus Glockenhof YMCA
28 Splendid
30 City Backpacker
31 Rothus
32 St Georges
42 OASE Evangelisches Haus
43 Foyer Hottingen

PLACES TO EAT

1 Restaurant JOSEF
9 Clipper Restaurant
10 Bernerhof
11 Migros City
12 Bistretto
14 Mensa Polyterrace
16 Hiltl Vegi
18 Manora
21 Rheinfelder Bierhalle
24 EPA
27 Stadtküche
29 Café Zähringer
36 Bodega Española
37 Mère Catherine
44 Bistretto
45 EPA

OTHER

2 Speed-Wash Laundry
5 Swiss National Museum
6 Limmat Boat Terminus
7 SSR (Travel Agency)
8 Post Office
13 Coop (Supermarket)
15 Cantonal Hospital
17 Jelmoli Department Store
19 Billettzentrale Ticket Agency
20 Stäheli English Bookshop
26 Globetrotter Travel Agency
33 Café Münz
34 Travel Bookshop
35 Casa Bar
38 Grossmünster Cathedral
39 American Express
40 Fraumünster Church
41 Kunsthaus (Art Gallery)
46 Lake Steamers Landing Stage
47 Arboretum

English-language travel books and can order anything you want. It also runs the map shop next door.

Emergency For medical and dental help, ring ☎ 261 61 00. The Cantonal University Hospital (☎ 255 11 11), Ramistrasse 110, has a casualty department. There is a 24-hour chemist at Bellevue Apotheke (☎ 252 56 00), Theaterstrasse 14. The police (☎ 216 71 11) are at Bahnhofquai 3.

Dangers & Annoyances Crime and drug-addiction have grown apace in Zürich in recent years. Crime still isn't high by international standards, but keep alert.

Things to See & Do

Walking Tour The pedestrian streets of the old town on either side of the Limmat contain most of the major sights. Features to notice are winding alleyways, 16th and 17th-century houses and guildhalls, courtyards and fountains. Zürich has 1030 fountains and the locals insist the water is drinkable in them all. Don't be surprised if a waiter heads for the nearest fountain if you ask for tap water in a restaurant!

The elegant **Bahnhofstrasse** was built on the site of the city walls which were torn down 150 years ago. Underfoot are bank vaults crammed full of gold and silver. Zürich is one of the world's premier precious metals markets but the vaults (for some reason) aren't open to the public.

The 13th-century tower of **St Peter's Church**, St Peterhofstatt, has the largest clock face in Europe (8.7 metres in diameter). The **Fraumünster Church** nearby is noted for the distinctive stained-glass windows in the choir created by Marc Chagall, completed when he was 83. Augusto Giacometti also did a window here, as well as in the **Grossmünster Cathedral** across the river where Zwingli preached in the 16th century. The figure glowering from the south tower of the Grossmünster is Charlemagne.

Informative guided walks around the old town, organised by the tourist office in summer, last around two hours and cost Sfr16 (Sfr8 for students). Walks around the Zürichsee (Lake Zürich) are pleasant. The concrete walkways give way to trees and lawns in the Arboretum on the west bank. Look out for the flower clock face at nearby Bürkliplatz. On the east bank, the Zürichhorn park has sculptures and a new (disappointing) Chinese Garden (Sfr4).

Museums The most important of many is the **Museum of Fine Arts** (Kunsthaus) (☎ 251 67 65), Heimplatz 1. The large permanent collection ranges from 15th-century religious art to the various schools of modern art. Swiss artists Füssli and Hodler are well represented, as are the sculptures of Alberto Giacometti. It is open Tuesday to Thursday from 10 am to 9 pm, and Friday to Sunday from 10 am to 5 pm. Entry costs Sfr4 (students Sfr3) except on Sunday when it's free. Temporary exhibitions always cost extra. Look out also for the numerous private galleries round the city.

The **Swiss National Museum** (Schweizerisches Landesmuseum), Museumstrasse 2, has a definitive section on church art, plus weapons, coins, costumes and utensils all housed in a pseudo-castle built in 1898. Opening hours are Tuesday to Sunday from 10 am to 5 pm and entry is free.

Zoo The large zoo has 2500 animals from all around the world; it's open daily from 8 am to 6 pm (to 5 pm November to February). Entry costs Sfr10 (students Sfr5) and you can get there by tram No 5 or 6. The zoo backs on to Zürichberg, a large wood ideal for walks away from the noise of the city.

Festivals Most shops are shut on the third Monday in April when Zürich's spring festival, *Sechseläuten*, is held. Guild members parade down the main streets in historical costume and then adjourn to the local bars. Another local holiday is *Knabenschiessen*, celebrated during the second weekend of September. Events revolve around a shooting competition for 12 to 16-year-old boys.

The Zürich Carnival, *Fasnacht*, is noted for mobile bands of lively musicians and a large, costumed procession. The carnival commences with typically Swiss precision at 11.11 am on 11 November, though the biggest parades are in February. The International June Festival concentrates on music and the arts, and the International Jazz Festival takes place at the end of October.

Places to Stay

Accommodation can be a problem, particularly from June to August. Cheaper hotels fill early. Book ahead if you can, or use the information board and free phone in the train station. The tourist office can sometimes get lower rates (Sfr5 booking fee). Private rooms are virtually nonexistent.

Camping *Camping Seebucht* (☎ 482 16 12) is on the west shore of the lake, four km from the city centre, at Seestrasse 559. It is well signposted and can be reached by bus No 161 or 165 from Bürkliplatz. It has good facilities including a shop and café, although it is only open from 1 May to 30 September. Prices are Sfr5 per person (20% discount with a Camping Carnet), tent Sfr6 and camper van Sfr10.

Hostels Some of the places mentioned are not strictly hostels, but they appear here because they offer dorm beds as well as comfortable private rooms.

The SYHA *hostel* (☎ 482 35 44) is at Mutschellenstrasse 114 in Wollishofen: take tram No 6 or 7 to the Morgental stop. There's no curfew and you can check in from 11 am to 1 am. Dorm beds are Sfr27.50. Dinner costs Sfr10.50 and there are laundry facilities (Sfr8 to wash and dry).

More convenient is *City Backpacker* (☎ 251 90 15), Schweizerhofgasse 5, newly opened in April 1994. Small dorms without breakfast are Sfr29 and singles/doubles are Sfr65/75. Kitchens and showers are in the hall. Reception is closed from 11 am to 2 pm. Also ideally central is *Martahaus* (☎ 251 45 50), Zähringerstrasse 36. Singles/doubles/triples cost Sfr60/90/105, and Sfr30 gets you a place in a six-bed dorm which is separated into individual cubicles by partitions and curtains. There is a comfortable lounge and breakfast room, and a shower on each floor.

Book ahead (telephone reservations OK), particularly for single rooms.

Foyer Hottingen (☎ 261 93 15), Hottingerstrasse 31, is run by nuns. The sisters of the cloth believe that single men always cause problems, so they only accept women, married couples and families. Such people reckon this is a very nice place to stay, an opinion that is probably not totally uninfluenced by the absence of noisy young men. Singles/doubles are Sfr50/80, and triples/quads are Sfr95/105. Dorms (with lockers) start from Sfr22. Showers cost Sfr1 and there's a midnight curfew. Telephone reservations are accepted.

OASE Evangelisches Haus (☎ 252 39 81) is at Freiestrasse 38, off Hottingerstrasse. It's mainly geared towards students but anybody can stay. Christian faith is promoted but not obligatory. Singles/doubles are Sfr61/102, and dorms (only in the summer and perhaps Easter) with canvas beds are Sfr27.

Justinusheim (☎ 361 38 06), Freudenbergstrasse 146, is a student home. It has up to 30 beds available during summer and Easter holidays, but few vacancies the rest of the year. Singles/doubles/triples vary in size and price, starting at Sfr35/70/90. It's just a few paces away from the woods of Zürichberg, and has a terrace with good views of Zürich and the lake. Take tram No 10 from the Hauptbahnhof to Rigiplatz and then the frequent Seilbahn to the top (city network tickets are valid).

Vereinhaus Glockenhof YMCA (☎ 221 36 73), Sihlstrasse 33, takes men only, and singles cost from Sfr40 without breakfast. Reception closes at 7.45 pm weekdays, 3.30 pm Saturday and 1.30 pm Sunday. It has a cheap café open to all, with daily menus, and breakfast for Sfr5.50.

Budget Hotels *Hotel Splendid* (☎ 252 58 50), Rosengasse 5, offers a choice of old or new rooms in the old town. Either type is good value, with singles/doubles/triples for Sfr55/90/120 (hall showers). Optional breakfast is Sfr8 and there's live piano music nightly in the bar downstairs. *Hotel St Georges* (☎ 241 11 44), Weberstrasse 11, is quiet and comfortable and has a lift; singles/doubles are Sfr65/95 using hall showers.

Dufour (☎ 422 36 55), Seefeldstrasse 188, has acceptable singles/doubles for Sfr55/70, again using hall showers, and without breakfast. Reception in the bar downstairs is open daily from 9 am to midnight. Get there by tram No 2 or 4.

Hotel Poly (☎ 362 94 40), Universitätsstrasse 63, has fresh singles/doubles for Sfr100/110 using hall showers. Rooms from Sfr110/140 are bigger and have a TV and private shower. Get a very substantial discount on these rates by booking through the tourist office.

Mid-Range Hotels In the city centre, *Hotel Limmathof* (☎ 261 42 20), Limmatquai 142, has modern fittings but it's a bit stingy with space. Singles/doubles with bath or shower are Sfr100/130, and triples/quads are both Sfr190. The nearby *Alexander Guesthouse* (☎ 251 82 03), Niederdorfstrasse 40, costs from Sfr90/130 for a similar standard.

Goldenes Schwert (☎ 252 59 40), Marktgasse 14, has singles/doubles from Sfr110/150 with private bath/WC. The staff thoughtfully (and significantly) lay out ear plugs in each room. Reception is opposite in the *Hotel Rothus*, where rooms using hall shower are Sfr70/110. The three-star *Hotel Scheuble* (☎ 251 87 95), also in the old town at Mühlegasse 17, has singles/doubles starting at Sfr110/140.

Places to Eat

Zürich has hundreds of restaurants serving all types of local and international cuisine. The Zürich speciality, *Geschnetzeltes Kalbsfleisch* (thinly sliced veal in a cream sauce), will probably set you back at least Sfr20. Fast-food stands offer Bratwurst and bread from around Sfr4.50. There is a large *Coop* opposite the Hauptbahnhof.

Self-Service *Mensa Polyterrace*, Leonhardstrasse 34, is next to the Seilbahn (funicular) top station. Large and busy, it has good meals costing Sfr9.50 (Sfr7.50 for ISIC holders) including vegetarian options. It's open Monday to Friday from 11.15 am to 1.30 pm and 5.30 to 7 pm, and every second Saturday from 11.30 am to 1 pm. From mid-July to late September it's open for lunch only. There is a café upstairs which is also popular. Just along the road, there is another *mensa* in the university building, Rämistrasse 71, open Monday to Friday, 7.30 am to 8 pm, and alternate Saturdays to the Polyterrace.

Food is just as cheap in *Stadtküche*, Schipfe 16, one of several government-subsidised kitchens (weekday lunches only). The *EPA* department stores at Sihlporte and Stadelhoferstrasse have a cheap restaurant, or you could try *Silberkugel*, below ground by the station, or *Migros Restaurant* in the Migros City shopping centre. The Vilan department store on Bahnhofstrasse has a good *Manora* buffet-style restaurant. *Bistretto* offers cheap Italian food and a salad bar. There are branches at Schweizergasse and Kruggasse; both are open daily.

Other Budget Restaurants *Clipper Restaurant*, Lagerstrasse 1, is basic and busy with good-value if simple food. Seating opens on to the pavement making it nice and cool in the summer. Most main dishes cost as little as Sfr9 to Sfr13. The cheap beer (Sfr4 for half a litre) attracts many local drinkers. It is open daily from 10 am to 11.30 pm.

Bernerhof, Zeughausstrasse 1, has satisfying, filling food in an unpretentious environment. Several daily menus from Sfr10.80 (including soup) are available midday and evening. The restaurant is open daily from 8 am (weekdays), 9 am (Sunday) or 3 pm (Saturday) until midnight. Food stops around 9 pm, when the locals sit around drinking and playing board and card games.

Rheinfelder Bierhalle, Niederdorfstrasse 76, has all-day menus including soup starting from Sfr12.50, and the beer's cheap too (Sfr3.80 for half a litre). Opening hours are 9 am to midnight daily.

Vegetarian Vegetarians will have a field day in the meat-free environment of *Hiltl Vegi* (☎ 221 38 70), Sihlstrasse 28, on two floors. It has a wide menu including tofu schnitzel (Sfr17.50), curry (16.50), soya spaghetti bolognese (Sfr15.20), salads from Sfr10.50 and varying lunchtime specials. It is open Monday to Saturday from 6.30 am to 9 pm, and Sunday from 11 am to 9 pm. *Café Zähringer* on Spitalgasse serves up organic food to alternative types, and it's a good place to linger in the evening for a coffee or game of chess (closed Monday).

Mid-Range Restaurants *Mère Catherine* (☎ 262 22 50), Nägelhof 3, is a popular French restaurant in a small courtyard. The food is tasty but not cheap unless you choose the lunchtime menus from Sfr13 (not available Sunday). Quality Spanish fare (Sfr18 to Sfr40) is at *Bodega Española* (☎ 251 23 10), on the 1st floor at Münstergasse 15. It has a good selection of Spanish wines from Sfr31 a bottle.

Splurge on French food amid the mirrors and gleaming metal of *Brasserie Lipp Restaurant* (☎ 211 11 55), Uraniastrasse 9 (opposite Billettzentrale on the map). Its elegant clientele are attracted by a wide choice of sumptuous dishes in the Sfr20 to Sfr35 range (open daily). *Restaurant JOSEF* (☎ 271 65 95), Gasometerstrasse 24, greets mainly youngish diners. There are interesting and varied daily specials (Sfr20 to Sfr30), and reservations are usually necessary in this small place. It's closed Sunday.

Entertainment

Zürich has numerous cafés where you can linger over a coffee. Try the entertaining *Café Münz* (☎ 221 30 27), Münzplatz 3, where Jean Tinguely mobiles hang from the ceiling. It is open Monday to Friday from 6.30 am to 7 pm (9 pm on Thursday), and Saturday from 8 am to 5 pm.

Many late-night pubs, clubs and discos are in Niederdorfstrasse and adjoining streets in the old town. This area is also a red-light district. On Sunday you might come across devout parishioners parading through the sin-sodden streets chanting hymns to anyone who can't avoid listening. The *Casa Bar*, Münstergasse 30, is a lively pub with live jazz from 8 pm. During summer, the *Comedy Club* performs plays in English – get information and tickets from the Jelmoli department store on Uraniastrasse.

Pick up the free weekly events magazine *Züritip* from the tourist office. Tickets for most events can be obtained from the *Billettzentrale* (☎ 221 22 83), Werdmühleplatz, off Bahnhofstrasse; it's open Monday to Friday from 10 am to 6.30 pm, Saturday to 2 pm. It is a government agency with minimal commission charges, and closes in July and August when activities in the arts die down. Cinema prices are reduced to Sfr9.90 every Monday from their normal price of around Sfr15. Films are usually in the original language.

Alternative arts are centred in *Rote Fabrik* (☎ 481 98 11 for music, ☎ 482 42 12 for theatre), Seestrasse 395, not far from the hostel. It has concerts most nights ranging from rock and jazz to avant-garde (Sfr15 to Sfr20), original-language films (Sfr10), plus theatre and dance. It's worth going along simply to enjoy the laid-back atmosphere in the bar area.

Getting There & Away

Air The major gateway of Kloten airport is 10 km north of the city centre and has several daily flights to/from all important destinations. Swissair has an office in the Hauptbahnhof which is open Monday to Friday from 8 am to 6 pm, Saturday to 4 pm. For Swissair reservations around the clock, call ☎ 258 34 34.

Train The busy Hauptbahnhof has direct trains to Stuttgart (Sfr61), Munich (Sfr87), Innsbruck (Sfr63) and Milan (Sfr66) as well as to many other international destinations. There are also hourly departures to most Swiss towns, eg Lucerne (50 minutes, Sfr18.60), Bern (70 minutes, Sfr42) and Basel (65 minutes, Sfr29).

Car & Motorbike The N3 approaches Zürich from the south along the shore of Lake Zürich. The N1 is the fastest route from Bern and Basel and the main entry point from the west. The N1 also services routes to the north and east of Zürich.

Hitching Zürich's Mitfahrzentrale (☎ 261 68 93) is at Leonhardstrasse 15. This agency links drivers and hitchers, but only for international journeys (Sfr10 to Sfr15 commission). It's open Monday to Friday from noon to 2 pm.

Getting Around

To/From the Airport Don't take a taxi if you can help it; trains are about a tenth of the price at Sfr4.70 (five an hour, takes 10 minutes).

Public Transport There is a comprehensive and unified bus, tram and S-Bahn service in the city, which includes boats on the Limmat River. All tickets should be bought in advance from dispensers at stops. The variety of tickets and zones available can be confusing. Short trips (up to five stops) cost Sfr1.90, but it's worth getting a 24-hour pass for Sfr6.40 (press the blue key and return symbol), covering all the central zone. Getting to the airport involves travel in two zones (Sfr9.40 for a 24-hour pass). A 24-hour pass valid for unlimited travel within the whole canton of Zürich costs Sfr25.20, including extended tours of the lake.

Lake steamers leave from Bürkliplatz, departing hourly from the end of March to late October (Swiss Pass and Eurail valid, Inter-Rail 50% discount). For boat information, phone ☎ 482 10 33.

Other Transport Taxis in Zürich are expensive even by Swiss standards, at Sfr6 plus Sfr2.90 per km. Bicycle rental in the Hauptbahnhof is open from 6 am to 7.40 pm. City bikes are available free of charge (take passport) for the day; get details from the tourist office. The tourist office also has a list of car-parking spaces near the central pedestrian zone.

Central Switzerland

This is the region which many visitors think of as the 'true' Switzerland. Not only is it rich in typical Swiss features – mountains, lakes, tinkling cowbells, Alpine villages and ski resorts – but it is also where Switzerland began as a nation 700 years ago. The original pact of 1291, signed by the communities of Uri, Schwyz and Nidwalden, can be viewed today in the Bundesbriefarchiv hall in Schwyz town centre.

LUCERNE

Ideally situated in the historic and scenic heart of Switzerland, Lucerne (Luzern in German) is an excellent base for a variety of excursions, yet it also has a great deal of charm in its own right, particularly the medieval town centre.

SWITZERLAND

Orientation & Information

The medieval town centre is on the north bank of the River Reuss. The train station is nearby on the south bank; extensive station facilities below ground level include daily bike rental (from 7 am to 7 pm) and money exchange.

Exit left for the tourist office (☎ 041-51 71 71), Frankenstrasse 1, which is open Monday to Friday from 8.30 am to 6 pm and Saturday from 9 am to 5 pm. From 1 November to 31 March it closes at 1 pm on Saturday and for two hours at noon on weekdays.

In front of the train station is the boat landing stage, and close by is the main post office (Luzern 1, Hauptpost). Across the river is American Express (☎ 50 11 77) at Schweizerhofquai 4, open weekdays and Saturday morning.

Things to See

The picturesque old-town centre offers 15th-century buildings with painted façades and the towers of the city walls. Some of these towers can be climbed for good views of the town and the lake. Be sure to walk along the two covered bridges, **Kapellbrücke** (built in 1333, and newly reopened after fire damage in 1993) with its water tower that appears in just about every photograph of Lucerne, and **Spreuerbrücke**. Both contain a series of pictorial panels under the roof.

The poignant **Lion Monument**, carved out of natural rock in 1820, is dedicated to the Swiss soldiers who died in the French Revolution. Next to it is the fascinating **Gletschergarten** (Glacier Garden), Denkmalstrasse 4, where giant glacial potholes prove that 20 million years ago Lucerne was a subtropical palm beach. The potholes can be perused from Tuesday to Sunday, and admission costs Sfr7 (students Sfr5). Also worth a look is the nearby **Bourbaki Panorama**, Löwenstrasse 18, an 1100-sq-metre circular painting of the Franco-Prussian war. Entry is Sfr3 (Sfr1.50 students). A ticket for both is Sfr8.

The large and widely acclaimed **Transport Museum**, Lidostrasse 5, contains trains, planes and automobiles, is open daily and costs Sfr15 (students Sfr11, reductions with railpasses). It's more fun than it sounds; get there on bus No 2 from Bahnhofplatz. A three-day general museum pass costs Sfr25. There's a fine **view** of the town and lake from the Gütsch Hotel; walk uphill for 20 minutes or take the Gütschbahn (Sfr2).

Lucerne hosts the annual **International Festival of Music** from mid-August to mid-September. Details are available from the Internationale Musikfestwochen (☎ 23 35 62), Hirschmattstrasse 13, CH-6002 Lucerne. **Sedel** (☎ 36 63 06), near the hostel behind Rotsee, is a former women's prison which holds rock concerts at the weekend.

Excursions

There are a number of scenic cruises on the lake, ranging from one hour to Hermitage (Sfr8.80 return), to six hours to Flüelen (Sfr37 return). Eurail passes are valid on all boat trips and Inter-Rail gets you half price. Also popular are trips to the nearby mountains; inevitably they are expensive, but ask about special reduced-price deals in winter.

An excellent route is to take the lake

steamer to Alpnachstad, the cog railway (closed in winter) up Mt Pilatus (2100 metres), the cable car down to Kriens and the bus back to Lucerne. The total cost for this jaunt is Sfr67.20. Mt Titlis (3020 metres) can be reached by train from Engelberg (Sfr26.80 return) and then by a series of cable cars (Sfr66 return), but the tourist office's all-in guided tour (Sfr75 from Lucerne) is cheaper. A combination steamer, cog railway and cable-car excursion up Mt Rigi (1800 metres) costs Sfr73.20. There are reductions on all these prices with rail passes.

Places to Stay

Hotels provide a Visitor's Card, valid for useful discounts.

Camp Lido (☎ 31 21 46), Lidostrasse 8, is on the north shore of the lake and east of the town. It is open all year and charges Sfr5 per person, Sfr2 per tent and Sfr3 per car.

The modern SYHA *hostel* (☎ 36 88 00) is at Sedelstrasse 12, 15 minutes' walk north of the city walls. You can get there by bus No 1 or (preferably) No 18 from the train station. Dorm beds are Sfr26.50, doubles are Sfr67 and dinners are Sfr10.50.

Reception is shut from 10 am to 2 pm

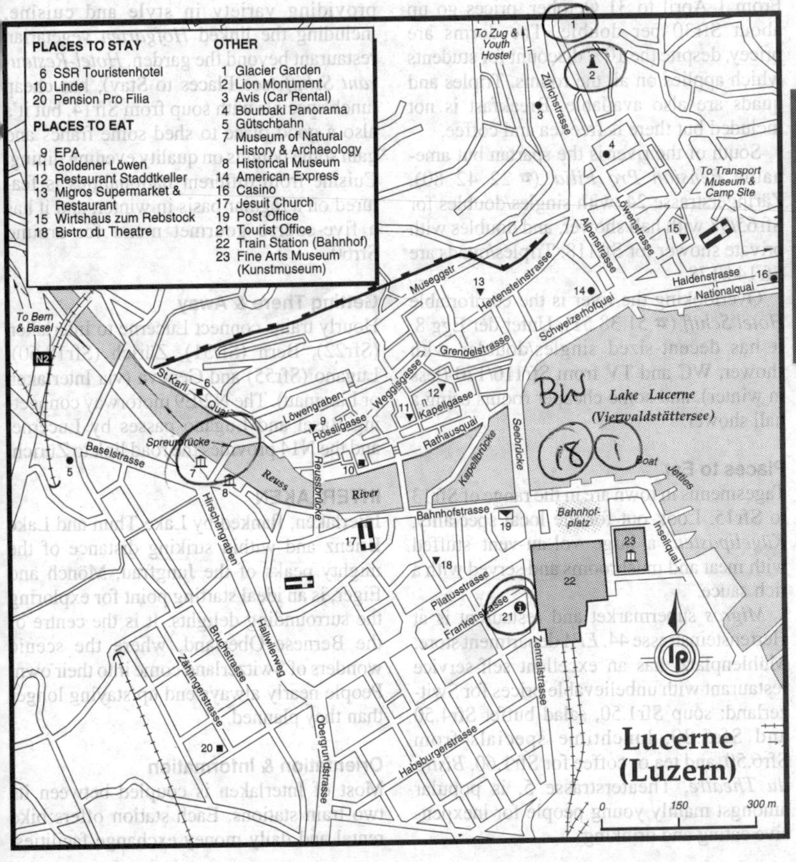

when the doors are also locked. Curfew is at 12.30 am.

The small *Linde* hotel (☎ 51 31 93), Metzgerrainle 3, off Weinmarkt, has basic singles/doubles for Sfr39/78 with hall showers and without breakfast. It has an excellent central location but check-in is not possible on Sunday as the restaurant is closed.

SSR Touristenhotel (☎ 51 24 74), St Karli Quai 12, has large dorms for Sfr33, and doubles for Sfr94 with private shower/WC, Sfr72 without, or Sfr62 in bunk beds. Single occupancy of doubles is possible in winter for Sfr57, Sfr46 and Sfr41 respectively. From 1 April to 31 October, prices go up about Sfr30 per double. The dorms are pricey, despite the 10% discount for students which applies on all the rooms. Triples and quads are also available. Breakfast is not included but there is free tea and coffee.

South of the river is the spartan but amenable *Pension Pro Filia* (☎ 22 42 80), Zäringerstrasse 24, with singles/doubles for Sfr65/98 with hall shower, and doubles with private shower for Sfr118. Triples/quads are Sfr144/178.

Overlooking the river is the comfortable *Hotel Schiff* (☎ 51 38 51), Unter der Egg 8. It has decent-sized singles/doubles with shower, WC and TV from Sfr116/170 (less in winter), and some cheaper rooms using a hall shower.

SWITZERLAND

Places to Eat

Tagesmenus in town are in the range of Sfr13 to Sfr15. Look out for the local speciality, *Kügelipasteti*, a large vol-au-vent stuffed with meat and mushrooms and served with a rich sauce.

Migros supermarket and restaurant is at Hertensteinstrasse 44. *EPA* department store, Mühlenplatz, has an excellent self-service restaurant with unbelievable prices for Switzerland: soup Sfr1.50, salad buffet Sfr4.50 and Sfr5.80, lunchtime specials from Sfr6.50, and tea or coffee for Sfr1.60. *Bistro du Theatre*, Theaterstrasse 5, is popular amongst mainly young people for inexpensive eating and drinking.

Goldener Löwen, Eisengasse 1, is small, quiet and open daily. Main courses, including Swiss specialities, start at around Sfr15. At the other extreme, *Restaurant Stadtkeller* (☎ 51 47 33), Sternenplatz 3, has two folklore shows a day to allow you to yodel with your mouth full. Dishes cost from Sfr15 at lunch and Sfr30 in the evening, plus Sfr6 for the show (show without food is Sfr10). Reservations are usually necessary. Live music replaces the full show from November to mid-March.

Wirtshaus zum Rebstock (☎ 51 35 81), St Leodegar Strasse, has daily specials from Sfr14 to Sfr30. There are several eating areas providing variety in style and cuisine, including the linked *Hofgarten* vegetarian restaurant beyond the garden. *Hotel-Restaurant Schiff* (see Places to Stay), has cheap lunch specials with soup from Sfr14, but it's also a good place to shed some francs and gain some pounds on quality evening dining. Cuisine from different nationalities is featured on a regular basis in winter, and it has a five-course gourmet menu for around Sfr60.

Getting There & Away

Hourly trains connect Lucerne to Interlaken (Sfr22), Bern (Sfr31), Zürich (Sfr18.60), Lugano (Sfr55) and Geneva (via Interlaken or Langnau). The N2/E9 motorway connecting Basel and Lugano passes by Lucerne, and the N14 provides the road link to Zürich.

INTERLAKEN

Interlaken, flanked by Lake Thun and Lake Brienz and within striking distance of the mighty peaks of the Jungfrau, Mönch and Eiger, is an ideal starting point for exploring the surrounding delights. It is the centre of the Bernese Oberland, where the scenic wonders of Switzerland come into their own. People nearly always end up staying longer than they planned.

Orientation & Information

Most of Interlaken is coupled between its two train stations. Each station offers bike rental and daily money exchange facilities,

Bus No 1.
Reception 5.00pm

and behind each is a boat landing for boat services on the lakes. The main shopping street, Höheweg, runs between the two stations. You can walk from one to the other in 20 minutes.

The tourist office (☎ 036-22 21 21), Höheweg 37, is nearer to Interlaken West and it's open Monday to Friday from 8 am to noon and 2 to 6 pm, and Saturday from 8 am to noon. During July and August, hours are extended. The office charges Sfr5 for hotel reservations and has lists of private rooms from Sfr35 per night, but the minimum stay for these is three days; the minimum for apartments is one week. The main post office is near the Interlaken West station at Marktgasse 1 (CH-3800).

The telephone code for Interlaken is 036.

Things to See & Do

Numerous hiking trails dot the area surrounding Interlaken, all with signposts giving average walking times. The funicular up to **Harder Kulm** (Sfr19 return) yields an excellent panorama and further prepared paths. There are worthwhile boat trips to several towns and villages round the lakes. Eurail passes are valid on all boats and Inter-Rail is good for 50% off the fare. On **Lake Thun**, both the towns of Spiez (Sfr20 return by steamer, Sfr14.40 by train) and Thun (Sfr29.20 return by steamer, Sfr24.80 by train) have a castle. Other resorts offer water sports. A short, Sfr5.40 boat ride from Interlaken are the **St Beatus Höhlen** (St Beatus Caves), with some impressive stalagmite formations and a small museum. Combined entry is Sfr10, or Sfr9 for students. The department store dummies in a 'realistic reconstruction of a prehistoric settlement' are a laugh. Photography is prohibited in the caves as it holds up the guided tour – not that that stops anybody. The caves can also be reached from Interlaken by bus or a 90-minute walk, and are open daily from 9.30 am to 5 pm.

Lake Brienz has a more rugged shoreline than its neighbour, and fewer resorts. Brienz itself (Sfr23.20 return by steamer, Sfr11.20 by train) is the centre of the Swiss wood-carving industry and close to the Freilichtmuseum Ballenberg, a huge open-air park displaying typical Swiss crafts and houses. The park is open daily from mid-April to the end of October, and admission costs Sfr12 (students Sfr10).

Places to Stay

Hotels provide a Visitor's Card, valid for useful discounts.

There are five camping grounds close together north-west of Interlaken West. *Alpenblick* (☎ 22 77 57), on Seestrasse by the Lombach River, costs Sfr5 per person, from Sfr8 per tent and Sfr4 for a car. Just along the road by the lake is *Manor Farm* (☎ 22 22 64), which is more expensive but has more facilities. Both are open all year.

The SYHA *hostel* (☎ 22 43 53), Aareweg 21, am See, Bönigen, is 25 minutes' walk round the lake from Interlaken Ost, or you can take bus No 1. It has an excellent location by the lake, with swimming facilities. Beds in large dorms are Sfr23.10 and dinner is Sfr10.50. The reception shuts between 9 am and 5 pm but the communal areas stay open. There is a 1 am curfew, and the hostel is closed from 1 November to 31 January.

More central and more sociable is *Balmer's Herberge* (☎ 22 19 61), Hauptstrasse 23, 15 minutes' walk (signposted) from either station. Excellent communal facilities include a reading room, games room, music room and videos every night. The staff also organises various excursions and rents bikes. There's a great atmosphere and it's a refreshing change of style from SYHA hostels, even if it's too much like an American summer camp at times. Dorms are Sfr17, showers are Sfr1, optional sheet rental is Sfr4, and there is a choice of dinners nightly for Sfr5 to Sfr10. Doubles, triples and quads are also available. Sign for a bed during the day and check in at 5 pm. During busy periods, people aged over 30 are charged Sfr19 in dorms. *Balmer's Tent*, one km farther south, takes care of the summer overflow.

The *Alp Lodge* annex of the Bellvue Hotel (☎ 22 47 48), Marktgasse, usually has cheap rooms (from Sfr24 per person) but the new owner may close it down. *Hotel Garni Bären* (☎ 22 76 76) also on Marktgasse is good value. Old-fashioned singles/doubles for Sfr45/90 use a hall shower; doubles with a bath (Sfr110) are especially spacious and have a sofa. A few metres on the right from Interlaken West is *Touriste Garni* (☎ 22 28 31); standard singles/doubles start at Sfr48/80.

Hotel Splendid (☎ 22 76 12), Höheweg 33, offers three-star comfort with well-presented singles/doubles for around Sfr100/170 with private shower/WC or Sfr70/110 without. Rooms have tea and coffee-making facilities. *Hotel Europe* (☎ 22 71 41), near Interlaken Ost station at Höheweg 94, offers similar comfort and prices, and rates come down in winter.

SWITZERLAND

Places to Eat

The *Migros* self-service restaurant, above the supermarket on Bahnhofstrasse by Interlaken West, is open Monday to Friday from 7.30 am to 6.30 pm, Saturday to 4 pm. A good place for cheap Italian food is *Pizzeria Mercato*, off Höheweg round the back of Chalet Hotel, open to at least midnight (closed Tuesday in winter).

Anker Restaurant, Marktgasse 57, is inexpensive for Swiss and Italian food. There is a games room around the back, and occasional live bands in winter (closed Thursday). The *Hotel Europe* (see Places to Stay) has tasty two-course menus for Sfr13 (Sfr18 on Sunday), and a three-course vegetarian menu for Sfr17; other dishes cost Sfr15 to Sfr25.

Weisses Kreuz on Höheweg (opposite Buddy's Pub) is the place for vegetarians to head, with tagestellers for Sfr13.50. A good place for traditional food (for about Sfr30) is *Gasthof Hirschen*, on the corner of Hauptstrasse and Parkstrasse. Another good mid-price choice is the restaurant in the *Hotel Metropole*, by the tourist office. The hotel also has the *Panoramic Bar/Café* on the 15th floor – it's worth going up for a drink or snack to admire the view and to walk round the balcony.

Entertainment

Evening entertainment in Interlaken encompasses the casino with its folklore show, and several discos round town. Good places for a drink are *Buddy's Pub*, Höheweg 33, and (assuming the new owner doesn't change it) the *Riverside Bar* on Marktgasse.

Getting There & Away

Trains to Lucerne depart hourly from Interlaken Ost. Trains to Brig (Sfr36) and to Montreux (via Bern or Zweisimmen) depart from Interlaken West or Ost. Main roads go to Lucerne, Bern and to the west via Zweisimmen. For vehicles, the only way south through the mountains without a big detour is to take the car-carrying train from Kandersteg, south of Spiez.

JUNGFRAU REGION

The views keep getting better the further south you go from Interlaken, and it's a fine region for hiking and skiing. The telephone code for the whole area is 036.

Grindelwald

Only 40 minutes by train from Interlaken Ost (Sfr8.40 one way, Sfr16.80 return) is Grindelwald, a busy resort under the north face of the Eiger. In the First region there are 90 km of hiking trails above 1200 metres. Of these, 48 km stay open in winter. In winter, the First is also the main skiing area, with a variety of runs stretching from Oberjoch at 2486 metres, right down to the village at 1050 metres. The cable car from Grindelwald-Grund to Männlichen, where there's more good views and hikes, is the longest in Europe (Sfr26 up, Sfr40 return). Grindelwald can be reached by road.

The tourist office (☎ 53 12 12) is in the centre by the Sportzentrum; it's open daily in summer, and weekdays and Saturday morning from October to June. It is 200 metres up from the train station.

Places to Stay & Eat Grindelwald has several camping grounds and a SYHA *hostel* (☎ 53 10 09), which is at Terrassenweg, 20 minutes' climb from the train station. Dorm beds are Sfr24.60. Kitchen facilities are available. Reception is shut from 9 am to 5 pm and the hostel closes completely from one week after Easter for five weeks, and from the end of October to mid-December. Close to the hostel is the *Naturfreundehaus* (☎ 53 13 33), which has dorms from Sfr26.10 (closed in low season). Other dorms are listed in the tourist office leaflet.

In the centre of the village, just off the main street (signposted), is *Lehmann's Herberge* (☎ 53 31 33), with two, four and six-bed rooms, plus one single, all for just Sfr40 per person. At the same turning on the main street is *Hotel Tschuggen* (☎ 53 17 81), with attractive singles/doubles for Sfr75/150 with private bath/shower, and some cheaper rooms using a hall shower. Next door is *Ristorante Mercado*, about the cheapest place to eat in this pricey village. Pizza and pasta start from Sfr11 and lunch specials are around Sfr15. Nearby, *Restaurant Rendezvous* also has decent daily specials (from Sfr12). There's a *Coop* supermarket opposite the tourist office.

A good mid-price choice for both food and accommodation is *Fiescherblick* (☎ 53 44 53), on the eastern side of the village.

Lauterbrunnen Valley

This valley is the other fork branching from Interlaken into the mountains. The first village reached by car or rail is **Lauterbrunnen**, known mainly for the Staubbach Falls cascading down outside the village, and the more impressive and farther Trümmelbach Falls, spitting its spray in a chute inside the mountain (Sfr8 entry, open April to November). Find out more from the tourist office (☎ 55 19 55) on the main street.

Above the village (via funicular) is Grütschalp, where you switch to the train to **Mürren** (Sfr7.80), a skiing and hiking resort. The ride yields tremendous unfolding views across the valley to the Jungfrau, Mönch and Eiger peaks. Mürren's efficient tourist office (☎ 55 16 16) is in the sports centre. Forty minutes' walk down the hill from Mürren is tiny **Gimmelwald**, relatively undisturbed by tourists.

Gimmelwald and Mürren can also be reached from the valley floor by the Stechelberg cable car, which runs all the way up to **Schilthorn** at 2971 metres. From the top there's a fantastic 360-degree panorama, and film shows will remind you that James Bond performed his stunts here in *On Her Majesty's Secret Service*. The return cable fare is a wallet-withering Sfr78.40, but there may be low season or first/last ascent of the day discounts.

Places to Stay & Eat Gimmelwald and especially Lauterbrunnen are bargains for accommodation, but Mürren is more touristy and therefore more expensive.

Lauterbrunnen *Camping Schützenbach* (☎ 55 12 68) and *Camping Jungfrau* (☎ 55 38 18) both have cheap dorms and bungalows in addition to camping. *Matratzenlager Stocki* (☎ 55 17 54) has a sociable atmosphere, kitchen facilities, and dorms beds for Sfr11 (without breakfast). *Chalet im Rohr* (☎ 55 21 82) has singles/doubles for around Sfr24 per person (access to kitchen but no breakfast).

Eating on the cheap is less easy. Stock up in the *Coop*, or try the *Hotel Jungfrau* for daily plates from Sfr12, or the two-course weekday special for Sfr15.50.

Gimmelwald The *Mountain Hostel* (☎ 55 17 04) is diminutive and decaying, but is still a great place to stay (phone first to make sure it's open, and arrive early in the day). Dorms (no breakfast) are just Sfr8.50, with kitchen facilities, but minimal showers. It's by the cable-car station. Up the hill a bit is *Mittaghorn* (☎ 55 16 28), with loft beds (in the summer) for Sfr25, singles/doubles for Sfr55/60 and triples/quads for Sfr85/105, including breakfast. The food is excellent in the café, but it's only for guests (who must pre-order). Anybody can go there for drinks (beer is Sfr4 for an 0.58-litre bottle). There's another café by the Mountain Hostel, and an adjoining shop open just a few mornings a week. Some families in the village offer private rooms.

Mürren Staying in the village costs around Sfr80 per person, but there are two cheaper pensions about 30 minutes' walk up the hill: *Suppenalp* (☎ 55 17 26), with dorms for Sfr29 with breakfast, and *Sonnenberg* (☎ 22 11 27), with dorms at half-board for Sfr45. In Mürren is *Hotel Edelweiss* (☎ 55 26 12), with rooms for Sfr90/160. It also has reasonable food from Sfr12, and good views from the south-facing terrace (restaurant closed Tuesday). The small *Staegerstübli*, next to the Coop supermarket, has daily specials from Sfr14, salad plates for Sfr12.50 and fondue from Sfr18. It's open daily.

Jungfraujoch

The trip to Jungfraujoch by railway (the highest in Europe) is excellent. Unfortunately, the price is as steep as the track and is hardly worth it unless you have very good weather – call ☎ 55 10 22 for forecasts in German, French and English. From Interlaken Ost, trains go via Grindelwald or Lauterbrunnen to Kleine Scheidegg. From here, the line is less than 10 km long but took 16 years to build. Opened in 1912, the track powers through both the Eiger and the Mönch with wonderful views from two windows blasted in the mountainside, before terminating at 3454 metres at Jungfraujoch.

On the summit, there is free entry to the **ice palace** (a maze cut in a glacier). From the terrace of the Sphinx Research Institute (a weather station) the panorama of peaks is unforgettable, including the Aletsch Glacier to the south, and mountains as distant as the Jura and the Black Forest. Take warm clothing and sunglasses (for glacier walking). There's a self-service restaurant in the complex.

From Interlaken Ost, journey time is 2½ hours each way and the fare is Sfr146 (Eurail no reduction, Inter-Rail Sfr73, Swiss Pass Sfr99). There's a cheaper (or more accurately, less exorbitant) 'good morning ticket' of Sfr110 (rail cards no reduction, Swiss Pass Sfr86) if you depart at 6.34 am or (1 November to 30 April only) 7.37 am, and you have to leave the summit by noon. The last train back in the summer is at 6 pm. Allow at least three hours at the site.

Other Destinations

Marvellous views and hikes compete for attention from various other vantage points in the Jungfrau region, such as **Schynige Platte**, **Wengen** (where there's dormitory accommodation) and **Kleine Scheidegg**.

Skiing is a major activity in the winter months, with a good variety of intermediate runs plus the demanding run down from the Schilthorn. Ski passes cost Sfr48 or Sfr50 per day, or Sfr130 for a minimum three days in the whole Jungfraujoch region.

Northern Switzerland

This part of the country is important for industry and commerce, yet it is by no means lacking in tourist attractions. Take time to explore Lake Constance, the Rhine and the picturesque town centres of the region.

BASEL

Basel (Bâle in French) joined the Swiss Confederation in 1501. Although an industrial city, it retains an attractive old town and offers many interesting museums. The famous Renaissance humanist, Erasmus of Rotterdam, was associated with the city and his tomb rests in the cathedral.

Orientation & Information

Basel's strategic position on the Rhine at the dual border with France and Germany has been instrumental in its development as a commercial and cultural centre. On the north bank of the Rhine is Kleinbasel (Little Basel), surrounded by German territory. The old town and most of the sights are on the south bank in Grossbasel (Greater Basel).

The main tourist office (☎ 061-261 50 50) is by the Mittlere bridge at Blumenrain 2, Schifflände, open Monday to Friday from 8.30 am to 6 pm, and Saturday from 8.30 am to 1 pm. Two km south is the main SBB

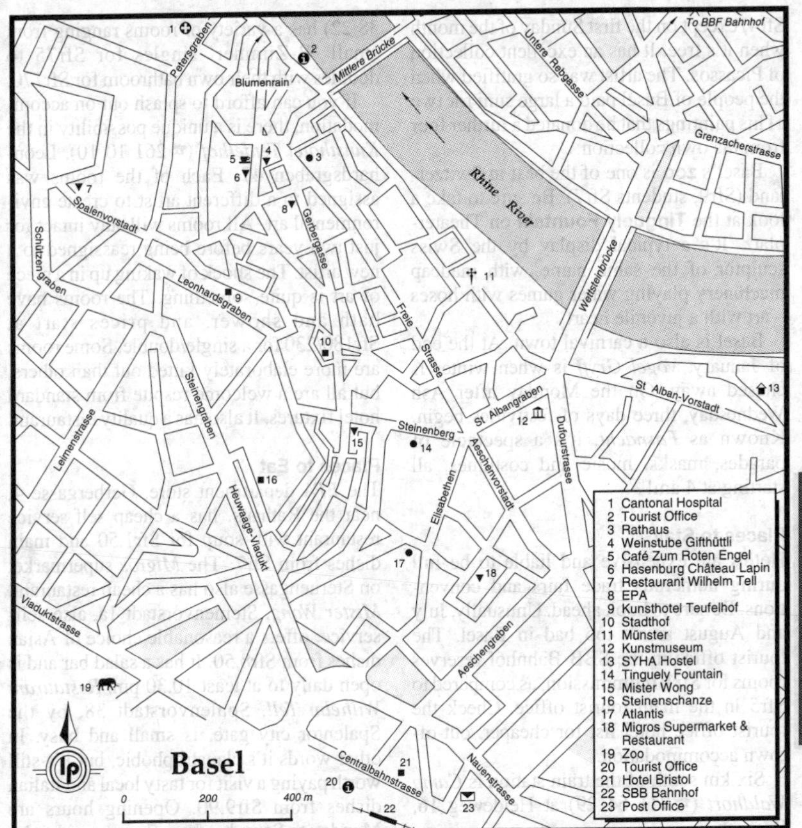

Bahnhof which has daily bike rental, money exchange (6 am to 9 pm daily), a grocery store (6 am to 10 pm daily) and another tourist office (☎ 271 36 84), open Monday to Friday from 8.30 am to 6 pm, and Saturday from 8.30 am to 12.30 pm. Its opening hours are extended between April and September to 7 pm weekdays, 1.30 to 6 pm Saturday, and (between June and September) Sunday from 10 am to 2 pm.

A convenient post office is just outside the station. Address poste restante to: Basel 2, Gartenstrasse, CH-4002 Basel.

The telephone code for Basel is 061.

Things to See & Do

The tourist office has free guides to walks through the old town, taking in cobbled streets, colourful fountains and 16th-century buildings. The restored **Rathaus** is very impressive and has a frescoed courtyard. The 12th-century **Münster** (cathedral) is another highlight with its Gothic spires and Romanesque St Gallus doorway.

Of the many museums, the most important is the **Kunstmuseum**, St Albangraben 16, with a good selection of religious, Swiss and modern art. It is open Tuesday to Sunday from 10 am to 5 pm, and costs Sfr6 (students

Sfr4) except on the first Sunday of the month when it's free. It has an excellent collection of Picassos. The artist was so gratified when the people of Basel paid a large sum for two of his paintings that he donated a further four from his own collection.

Basel's **zoo** is one of the best in Switzerland (Sfr9, students Sfr7). Be sure to take a look at the **Tinguely Fountain** on Theaterplatz. It's a typical display by the Swiss sculptor of the same name, with madcap machinery playing water games with hoses – art with a juvenile heart.

Basel is also a carnival town. At the end of January, *Vogel Gryff* is when winter is chased away. On the Monday after Ash Wednesday, three days of festivities begin. Known as *Fasnacht*, it's a spectacle of parades, masks, music and costumes, all starting at 4 am!

Places to Stay

Hotels are expensive and liable to be full during numerous trade fairs and conventions. Be sure to book ahead. Unusually, July and August aren't too bad in Basel. The tourist office in the SBB Bahnhof reserves rooms for Sfr10 commission, as compared to Sfr5 in the main tourist office. Check the tourist office hotel list for cheaper, out-of-town accommodation.

Six km south of the train station is *Camp Waldhort* (☎ 711 64 29) at Heideweg 16, Reinach.

The SYHA *hostel* (☎ 272 05 72) is fairly near the centre of town at St Alban Kirchrain 10. Dorm beds are Sfr24.50 and double rooms are Sfr35 per person. Reception is shut from 11 am to 2 pm, when the doors are also locked. The 12.30 am curfew is brought forward to midnight in winter.

In the old town, *Stadthof* (☎ 261 87 11), Gerbergasse 84, has basic singles/doubles from Sfr50/100 without breakfast. Not far from SBB Bahnhof is *Steinenschanze* (☎ 272 53 53), Steinengraben 69, which has singles/doubles with private shower/WC for Sfr90/125. The price for students is reduced to 50% for the first three nights. By the station, the three-star *Hotel Bristol* (☎ 271 38 22) has a variety of rooms ranging from small 'B-Zimmer' singles for Sfr75 to doubles with their own bathroom for Sfr170.

If you can afford to splash out on accommodation, there is a unique possibility in the *Kunsthotel Teufelhof* (☎ 261 10 10), Leonhardsgraben 47. Each of the rooms was assigned to a different artist to create environmental art. All rooms will stay intact for just two years before being reassigned to a new artist. The shock of waking up in a piece of art is quite something. The rooms have bath and shower, and prices start at Sfr180/230 for a single/double. Some rooms are more elaborately kitted out than others, but all are a welcome respite from standard hotel fixtures. It also has a quality restaurant.

Places to Eat

The *EPA* department store, Gerbergasse 4, near the Rathaus, has a cheap self-service restaurant with soup for Sfr1.50 and main dishes from Sfr7. The *Migros* supermarket on Sternengasse also has a cheap restaurant. *Mister Wong*, Steinenvorstadt 1a, also self-service, offers a reasonable choice of Asian dishes from Sfr8.50. It has a salad bar and is open daily to at least 10.30 pm. *Restaurant Wilhelm Tell*, Spalenvorstadt 38, by the Spalentor city gate, is small and busy. In other words it's claustrophobic, but it's still worth paying a visit for tasty local and Italian dishes from Sfr9.90. Opening hours are Monday to Saturday from 7 am to midnight.

For Basel specialities in a typical ambience, try *Weinstube Gifthüttli* (☎ 261 16 56), Schneidergasse 11. It has daily lunch and evening menus from Sfr12 to Sfr20 (closed Sunday). Opposite is the slightly more down-to-earth *Hasenburg Château Lapin*. Vegetarians should check the environmentally-sound *Café Zum Roten Engel* in the adjoining courtyard (outside tables). It serves organic vegetarian food for around Sfr12.50 to Sfr15. Good breakfasts are also available.

Entertainment

For evening entertainment, try *Atlantis* (☎ 272 20 38), Klosterberg 13. It has live music daily (mainly rock, jazz and R&B), and entry costs between Sfr5 and Sfr25.

Getting There & Away

Basel is a major European rail hub. All trains to France go from SBB Bahnhof where you pass the border controls in the station. There are four to five trains a day to Paris (Sfr72) and connections to Brussels and Strasbourg. Trains to Germany (border controls on the train or in the station) stop at BBF Bahnhof on the north bank; local trains to the Black Forest stop only at BBF, though fast EC services stop at SBB too. Main destinations along this route are Frankfurt (Sfr82), Cologne, Hamburg and Amsterdam. Services within Switzerland go from SBB: there are two fast trains an hour to both Geneva (Sfr66; via Bern or Biel/Bienne) and Zürich (Sfr29). By motorway, the E25/E60 heads down from Strasbourg and passes by Mulhouse airport, and the E35/A5 hugs the German side of the Rhine.

Getting Around

The yellow bus outside the Swissair office at SBB station goes to/from Mulhouse airport (Sfr2). City Buses and trams run every six to 10 minutes. Tickets cost Sfr1.20 for up to four stops, or Sfr2 for the whole central zone. Multijourney cards are available, but you're better off with a day card for Sfr6.60.

AROUND BASEL

See the Germany chapter for information on the **Black Forest**; it's an easy excursion from Basel. To the south lies **Solothurn**, well worth a stop off to/from Bern. It has an Italianate cathedral, a baroque Jesuit church, historic fountains and a good fine art museum (housing Hodler's classic painting of William Tell).

SCHAFFHAUSEN

The capital of the canton that bears its name, this communications and arms centre was accidentally bombed by the USA in 1944. Thankfully, however, its medieval town centre remains intact. The largest waterfall in Europe, the Rheinfall, is three km down the Rhine.

Orientation & Information

Schaffhausen is in a bulge of Swiss territory surrounded by Germany on the north bank of the Rhine. The train station is adjacent to the old town, where you'll find the tourist office (☎ 053-25 51 41) at Fronwagturm. It is open Monday to Friday from 9 am to 6 pm, and to noon Saturday. Postbuses depart from the rear of the station and local buses from the front. The main post office is also opposite the station.

Schaffhausen's telephone code is 053.

Things to See

The attractive old town is bursting with oriel windows, painted façades and ornamental fountains. The best streets are Vordergasse, which has the 16th-century **Haus zum Ritter** with its painted historical scenes, and Vorstadt, which intersect at Fronwagplatz. Get an overview of the town from the **Munot** fortress up on the hill (open daily, free). The **Allerheiligen Museum**, by the cathedral in Klosterplatz, houses a collection ranging from ancient bones to modern art (free, closed Monday).

The **Rheinfall** can be reached by a 40-minute stroll westward along the river, or by bus No 1 or 9 to Neuhausen. The largest waterfall in Europe drops 23 metres and makes a tremendous racket as 600 cubic metres of water crashes down every second. The 45 km of the Rhine from Schaffhausen to Constance is one of the river's most beautiful stretches, passing by meadows, castles and ancient villages, not least the picturesque **Stein am Rhein**, 20 km to the east, with a central square (Rathausplatz) that's one of the most photogenic in all Switzerland.

Places to Stay

The SYHA *hostel* (☎ 25 88 00) is 20 minutes' walk west of the train station (or take bus No 3), at Randenstrasse 65 (closed November to February). Dorms cost Sfr21.50, and the reception is closed from 10 am to 5.30 pm. The cheapest deal in the town centre is *Steinbock* (☎ 25 42 60), Webergasse 47, with singles/doubles for Sfr43/70 with hall showers. There's no breakfast, but the rooms are clean and reasonably sized.

Tanne (☎ 25 41 79), Tanne 3 off Fronwagplatz, has singles/doubles from Sfr42/85 but no showers at all. *Restaurant Zum Sittich* (☎ 25 13 72) on Vordergasse has excellent big rooms with sofa, shower/WC and TV but no breakfast for Sfr95/120 (reception closed Monday to 5 pm and Sunday).

Places to Eat

Eat for under Sfr12 at either the *Migros* supermarket and restaurant at Vorstadt 39, the *EPA* department store restaurant at Vordergasse 69, or at *Manora* in the Vilan department store by the tourist office. *La Rondine*, Webergasse 27, is a busy Italian restaurant with lunch specials (closed Monday).

For a taste treat, go to *Rheinhotel Fischerzunft* (☎ 25 32 81), Rheinquai 8. It has been voted one of the top restaurants in Switzerland, a justification for spending around Sfr50 per main dish. It serves Oriental and Swiss food, particularly fish dishes.

Getting There & Away

Hourly trains run to Zürich (Sfr15). Constance and Basel can be reached by either Swiss or (cheaper) German trains. Steamers travel to Constance several times a day in summer, and the trip takes four hours; they depart from Freier Platz (call ☎ 25 42 82 for information). Schaffhausen has good roads radiating out in all directions.

ST GALLEN

In 612, an itinerant Irish monk called Gallus fell into a briar. Relying on a peculiar form of Irish logic, the venerable Gallus interpreted this clumsy act as a sign from God and decided to stay put and build a hermitage. From this inauspicious beginning the town of St Gallen evolved and developed into an important medieval cultural centre.

Orientation & Information

The main post office (Bahnhofplatz, CH-9001) is opposite the train station. Two minutes away is the tourist office (☎ 071-22 62 62), Bahnhofplatz 1a, open Monday to Friday from 9 am to noon and 1 to 6 pm, and on Saturday from 9 am to noon. A few minutes to the east is the pedestrian-only old town.

The telephone code for St Gallen is 071; in 1996 all numbers will have seven digits.

Things to See

St Gallen has a fine old-city centre. It's full of interesting buildings with colourful murals, carved balconies and relief statues. Some of the best oriel windows are on Gallusplatz, Spisergasse and Kugelgasse. The twin-tower **cathedral** cannot and should not be missed. Completed in 1766, it's immensely impressive and impressively immense. Forget the Sistine Chapel in Rome – a lot more paint went onto this ceiling! Look out also for the pulpit, arches, statue groups and woodcarvings around the confessionals.

Adjoining the church is the **Stiftsbibliothek** (Collegiate Library), containing some beautifully etched manuscripts from the Middle Ages and a splendidly opulent rococo interior. There's even an Egyptian mummy, dating from 700 BC and as well preserved as the average grandparent (though temporarily seeking 'medical' attention and not on display). Entry is Sfr4, students Sfr2, and it's closed on Sunday between November and May.

The **Grabenhalle** (☎ 22 82 11), Blumenberg Platz, is a major venue for concerts and other arts events.

Places to Stay

The SYHA *hostel* (☎ 25 47 77) is a signposted, 15-minute walk east of the old town at Jüchstrasse 25 (follow hostel signs with the adult and child – the other hostel signs are for drivers. Alternatively, take the Trogenerbahn from outside the station to 'Schülerhaus'). Beds are Sfr21.50 in a dorm or Sfr30.50 in a double room. Reception is closed from 9 am to 5 pm though luggage can be left during the day. Curfew is at 10 pm, or get a key for late entry. The hostel closes from mid-December to early March.

Weisses Kreuz (☎ 23 28 43) on Engelgasse has reasonable singles/doubles for Sfr42/80 using hall showers. There are also four good-sized doubles with private shower for Sfr90. The reception is in the bar downstairs. *Touring Garni* (☎ 22 58 01) is virtually opposite. Rooms are of varying quality, so ask to see several; those with a proper bathroom *en suite* are a good deal. Singles/doubles are around Sfr55/95, and there are cheaper rooms with no shower facilities available. *Elite Garni* (☎ 22 12 36), Metzgergasse 9-11, is of a similar standard but slightly more expensive.

Places to Eat

Eating can be pretty good in St Gallen. At the lower end, look out for various fast-food stalls selling St Gallen sausage and bread for around Sfr4. On St Leonhardstrasse is *Migros* supermarket and restaurant. Equally cheap is the *EPA* department store restaurant at the central Marktplatz. Next door is *Stein*, a simple place but with surprisingly good food from about Sfr10, including a vegetarian menu. *Hörni*, Marktplatz 5, has a wide selection of beers, but you can only get the cheaper draught stuff on the ground floor. Upstairs, daily menus (lunch and evening) start at Sfr12.

A good mid-price place is *Wirtschaft Zur Alten Post* (☎ 22 66 01), Gallusstrasse 4. The food is typically Swiss, with meat and fish dishes starting at Sfr25. Small and cosy, this restaurant fills quickly, so reserve ahead. It's closed on Sunday and Monday.

Getting There & Away

St Gallen is a short train ride from Lake Constance (Bodensee), upon which boats sail to Bregenz in Austria, and to Constance and Lindau in Germany (not in winter). There are also regular trains to Bregenz (Sfr12), Constance (Sfr21), Chur (Sfr32) and Zürich (Sfr26).

APPENZELL

If you ever hear a joke in Switzerland, the inhabitants of Appenzell are likely to be the butt. They are known for their parochialism and are considered (a little unfairly) to be several stages lower on the evolutionary ladder than the rest of humanity. Women were finally allowed to vote in local affairs in 1991, and then only after the supreme court ruled their exclusion by the men unconstitutional.

Such resistance to change has its advantages for the tourist. The village is a delight to wander around, with traditional old houses, painted façades and lush surrounding countryside. The streets are bedecked with flags and flowers on the last Sunday in April when the locals vote on cantonal issues by a show of hands in the open-air parliament (Landsgemeinde). Everyone wears traditional dress for the occasion and many of the men carry swords or daggers as proof of citizenship.

Getting There & Away

There are hourly connections from St Gallen by a narrow-gauge train which careers along, mostly following the course of the road (45 minutes). There are two different routes so you can make it a circular trip.

Appendix I – Alternative Place Names

The following abbreviations are used:

(C)	Czech
(E)	English
(F)	French
(G)	German
(H)	Hungarian
(I)	Italian
(L)	Latin
(P)	Polish
(Rh)	Romansch
(Slk)	Slovak

AUSTRIA
Österreich

Carinthia (E) – Kärnten (G)
Danube (E) – Donau (G)
East Tirol (E) – Osttirol (G)
Lake Constance (E) – Bodensee (G)
Lower Austria (E) – Niederösterreich (G)
Upper Austria (E) – Oberösterreich (G)
Styria (E) – Steiermark (G)
Tirol (E, G) – Tyrol (E)
Vienna (E) – Wien (G)
Vienna Woods (E) – Wienerwald (G)

CZECH REPUBLIC
Česká republika

Brno (C) – Brünn (G)
Česke Budějovice (C) – Budweis (G)
Český Krumlov (C) – Krumau (G)
Cheb (C) – Eger (G)
Danube (River) (E) – Dunáj (C)
Hluboká nad Vltavou (C) – Frauenberg (G)
Karlovy Vary (C) – Karlsbad (G)
Krkonoše (C) – Giant Mountains (E)
Krusne Hory (C) – Ore Mountains
Labe (River) (C) – Elbe (G)
Mariánské Lázně (C) – Marienbad (G)
Plzeň (C) – Pilsen (G)
Prague (E) – Praha (C), Prag (G)
Telč (C) – Teltsch (G)
Vltava (River) (C) – Moldau (G)
Zlaté piesky (C) – Golden Sands (E)
Znojmo (C) – Znaim (G)

GERMANY
Deutschland

Aachen (E, G) – Aix-la-Chapelle (F)
Baltic Sea (E) – Ostsee (G)
Bavaria (E) – Bayern (G)
Bavarian Alps (E) – Bayerische Alpen (G)
Bavarian Forest (E) – Bayerischer Wald (G)
Black Forest (E) – Schwarzwald (G)
Cologne (E) – Köln (G)
Constance (E) – Konstanz (G)
Danube (E) – Donau (G)
East Friesland (E) – Ostfriesland (G)
Federal Republic of Germany (FRG) (E) – Bundesrepublik Deutschland (BRD) (G)
Franconia (E) – Franken (G)
Hamelin (E) – Hameln (G)
Hanover (E) – Hannover (G)
Harz Mountains (E) – Harzgebirge (G)
Heligoland (E) – Helgoland (G)
Hesse (E) – Hessen (G)
Lake Constance (E) – Bodensee (G)
Lower Saxony (E) – Niedersachsen (G)
Lüneburg Heath (E) – Lüneburger Heide (G)
Mecklenburg-Pomerania (E) – Mecklenburg-Vorpommern (G)
Munich (E) – München (G)
North Friesland (E) – Nordfriesland (G)
North Rhine-Westphalia (E) – Nordrhein-Westfalen (G)
Nuremberg (E) – Nürnberg (G)
Pomerania (E) – Pommern (G)
Prussia (E) – Preussen (G)
Rhine (E) – Rhein (G)
Rhineland-Palatinate (E) – Rheinland-Pfalz (G)
Romantic Road (E) – Romantische Strasse (G)
Saxon Switzerland (E) – Sachsische Schweiz (G)
Saxony (E) – Sachsen (G)
Swabia (E) – Schwaben (G)
Thuringia (E) – Thüringen (G)
Thuringian Forest (E) – Thüringer Wald (G)

HUNGARY
Magyarország

Balaton Lake (H) – Plattensee (G)
Debrecen (H) – Debrezin (G)
Eger (H) – Erlau (G)
Great Plain (E) – Nagyalföld (H)
Győr (H) – Raab (G), Arrabona (L)
Kisalföld (H) – Little Plain (E)
Komárom (H) – Brigetio (L)
Kőszeg (H) – Guns (G)
Pécs (H) – Fünfkirchen (G), Sopianae (L)
Sopron (H) – Ödenburg (G), Scarbantia (L)
Szeged (H) – Segedin (G)
Székesfehérvár (H) – Stuhlweissenburg (G)
Szombathely (H) – Steinamanger (G), Savaria (L)
Tata (H) – Totis (G)

Transdanubia (E) – Dunántúl (H)
Vác (H) – Wartzen (G)

POLAND

Polska

Brzezinka (P) – Birkenau (G)
Bydgoszcz (P) – Bromberg (G)
Częstochowa (P) – Tschenstochau (G)
Frombork (P) – Frawenburg (G)
Gdańsk (P) – Danzig (G)
Gdynia (P) – Gdingen (G)
Gniezno (P) – Gnesen (G)
Kołobrzeg (P) – Kolberg (G)
Giżycko (P) – Lötzen (G)
Gniezno (P) – Gnesen (G)
Ktrzyn (P) – Rastenburg (G)
Kraków (P) – Krakau (G), Cracow (E)
Lidzmark Warmiński (P) – Heilsberg (G)
L'vov (E) – Lwów (P), Lemberg (G)
Malbork (P) – Marienburg (G)
Małopolska (P) – 'Little Poland' (E)
Mikołajki (P) – Nikolaiken (G)
Nowy Sącz– Neusandez (G)
Nysa (River) (P) – Neisse (G)
Odra (River) (P) – Oder (G)
Olsztyn (P) – Allenstein (G)
Opole (P) – Oppeln (G)
Oświęcim (P) – Auschwitz (G)
Poznań (P) – Posen (G)
Ruciane-Nida (P) – Rudschanny (G)
Silesia (E) – Śnęsk (P), Silesien (G)
Świnoujście (P) – Swinemünde (G)
Szczecin (P) – Stettin (G)
Sopot (P) – Zoppot (G)
Tannenberg (G) – Stębark (P)
Toruń (P) – Thorn (G)
Vistula (River) (E) – Wisła (P), Weichsel (G)
Warsaw (E) – Warszawa (P), Warschau (G)
Węgorzewo (P) – Angerburg (G)
Wielkopolska (P) – 'Great Poland' (E)
Wilczy Szaniec (P) – Wolfschanze (G), Wolf's Lair (E)
Wrocław (P) – Breslau (G)

SLOVAKIA

Slovenská

Banská Bystrica (Slk) – Neusohl (G)
Bratislava (C) – Pressburg (G), Pozsony (H)
Gerlachovskňy Štít (Slk) – Mt Gerlach (E)
Košice (Slk) – Kaschau (G)
Levoča (Slk) – Leutschau (G)
Mala Fatra (Slk) – Little Fatra (E)
Nízke Tatry (Slk) – Low Tatra (E)
Prešov (Slk) – Preschau (G)
Slovenské rudohorie (Slk) – Slovak Ore Mountains (E)
Slovenskňy raj (Slk) – Slovak Paradise (E)
Spišský hrad (Castle) (Slk) – Zipser Burg (G)
Vysoké Tatry (Slk) – High Tatra (E)
Zvolen (Slk) – Altsohl (G)

SWITZERLAND

Schweiz (G), Suisse (F), Svizzera (I),

Basel (E, G) – Basle (E), Bâle (F), Basilea (I)
Bern (E, G) – Berne (E, F), Berna (I)
Fribourg (E, F) – Freiburg (G), Friburgo (I)
Geneva (E) – Genève (F), Genf (G), Ginevra (I)
Graubünden (E, G) – Grisons (F), Grigioni (I), Grishun (Rh)
Lake Constance (E) – Bodensee (G)
Lake Geneva (E) – Lac Léman (F)
Lake Maggiore (E) – Lago Maggiore (I)
Lucerne (E, F) – Luzern (G), Lucerna (I)
Neuchâtel (E, F) – Neuenburg (G)
Ticino (E, I) – Tessin (G, F)
Valais (E, F) – Wallis (G)
Zürich (E, G) – Zurich (F), Zurigo (I)

Appendix II – Telephones

Dial Direct
You can dial directly from public phone boxes from almost anywhere in Europe to almost anywhere in the world. This is usually cheaper than going via the operator, and you don't even need a pocketful of coins if you use one of the phonecards which have become increasingly common in recent years.

To call abroad you simply dial the international access code (IAC) for the country you are calling from, the country code (CC) for the country you are calling to, the local area code (dropping the leading zero if there is one) and then the number. If, for example, you are in Italy (international access code 00) and want to make a call to the USA (country code 1), San Francisco (area code 415), number 123 4567, then you dial 00-1-415-123 4567. To call from the UK (00) to Australia (61), Sydney (02), number 123 4567, you dial 010-61-2-123 4567.

Home Direct
If you would rather have somebody else pay for the call, you can, from many countries, dial directly to your home country operator and then reverse charges, charge the call to a phone company credit card or perform other credit feats. To do this, simply dial the relevant Home Direct number to be connected to your own operator. For the USA there's a choice of AT&T, MCI or Sprint home direct services. Home direct numbers vary from country to country – check with your telephone company before you leave, or with the international operator in the country you're ringing from.

In some places, you may find dedicated Home Country Direct phones where you simply press the button labelled USA, Australia, Hong Kong or whatever for direct connection to the relevant operator. Note that the Home Direct service does not operate to and from all countries, and that the call could be charged at operator rates, which makes it quite expensive for the person who's paying.

Dialling Tones
In some countries, after you've dialled the overseas access code, you have to wait for a dialling tone before dialling the code for your target country. Often the same applies when you ring from one city to another within these countries: wait for a dialling tone after you've dialled the area code for your target city. If you're not sure what to do, simply wait three or four seconds after dialling a code – if nothing happens, you can probably keep dialling.

Phonecards
In major locations you may find phones which accept credit cards: simply swipe your card through the slot and the call is charged to the card, though rates can be (very) high. Phone company credit cards can be used to charge calls via your home country operator.

Stored-value phonecards have become very common all over Europe. You buy a card from a post office, phone office, newsagent or other outlet and simply insert the card into the phone each time you make a call. The card saves the problem of finding the correct coins for calls (or lots of correct coins for international calls) and sometimes gives you a small discount.

Call Costs
Avoid ringing from a hotel room, unless you really don't care what it's going to cost. The cost of making an international call varies widely from one country to another. A US$10 call from Germany or Switzerland would cost you US$15 from France or US$20 from Italy. Choosing where you call from can make a big difference to the budget. The countries in the table are rated from * (cheap) to *** (expensive). Reduced rates are available at certain times, though these vary from country to country and should make little difference to relative costs – check the local phone book or ask the operator.

TELEPHONE CODES

	CC	*cost (see text)*	*IAC*	*IO*
Albania	355			
Andorra (via Spain)	34738	***	0 (9 for Spain)	19
Andorra (via France)	33628	**	0 (7 for France)	19
Austria	43	**	00	09
Belgium	32	**	00	1224 (private phone) 1223 (public phone)
Bulgaria	359		00	
Croatia	385	**	99	
Cyprus	357		00	
Cyprus (Turkish)	905			
Czech Republic	42	**	00	0131
Denmark	45	*	009	0015
Finland	358	*	990	92022
France	33	**	19(w)	19(w)33
Germany	49	*	00	00118
Gibraltar	350		00	100
Greece	30	**	00	161
Hungary	36	**	00	09 (in Budapest) 01 (elsewhere)
Iceland	354		90	09
Ireland	353	*	00	114
Italy	39	***	00	15
Liechtenstein	41	*	00	114
Luxembourg	352	**	00	0010
Macedonia	389		99	
Malta	356		00	194
Morocco	212	***	00(w)	12
Netherlands	31	**	00	060410
Norway	47	**	095	091
Poland	48	**	0(w)0	901
Portugal	351	**	00	099
Romania	40			071
Slovakia	42	**	00	0131
Slovenia	386	**	00	901
Spain	34	***	07(w)	91389
Sweden	46	***	009(w)	0018
Switzerland	41	*	00	114
Tunisia	216		00	
Turkey	90	**	00	115
UK	44	*	00	155
Yugoslavia	381	**	99	901

CC – Country Code (to call that country)
IAC – International Access Code (to call abroad from that country)
(w) – wait for dialling tone
IO – International Operator (to make enquiries)

Other country codes: Australia 61, Canada 1, Hong Kong 853, India 91, Indonesia, 62, Japan 81, Macau 853, Malaysia 60, New Zealand 64, Singapore 65, South Africa 27, Thailand 66, USA 1

Appendix III – European Organisations

	Council of Europe	EU	EFTA	NATO	Nordic Council	OECD	WEU
Austria	✓	✓	✓	–	–	✓	–
Belgium	✓	✓	–	✓	–	✓	✓
Croatia	–	–	–	–	–	–	–
Cyprus	✓	✘	–	–	–	–	–
Czech Republic	✓	–	–	–	–	–	–
Denmark	✓	✓	–	✓	✓	✓	–
Finland	✓	✓*	✓	–	✓	✓	–
France	✓	✓	–	✓	–	✓	✓
Germany	✓	✓	–	✓	–	✓	✓
Greece	✓	✓	–	✓	–	✓	–
Hungary	✓	✘	–	–	–	–	–
Iceland	✓	–	✓	✓	✓	✓	–
Ireland	✓	✓	–	–	–	✓	–
Italy	✓	✓	–	✓	–	✓	✓
Luxembourg	✓	✓	–	✓	–	✓	✓
Malta	✓	✘	–	–	–	–	–
Netherlands	✓	✓	–	✓	–	✓	✓
Norway	✓	✓*	✓	✓	✓	✓	–
Poland	–	✘	–	–	–	–	–
Portugal	✓	✓	–	✓	–	✓	✓
Slovakia	–	–	–	–	–	–	–
Slovenia	–	–	–	–	–	–	–
Spain	✓	✓	–	✓	–	✓	–
Sweden	✓	✓*	✓	–	✓	✓	–
Switzerland	✓	–	✓	–	–	✓	–
Turkey	✓	✘	–	✓	–	✓	–
UK	✓	✓	–	✓	–	✓	✓
Yugoslavia	–	–	–	–	–	✓	–

✓ – full member (– subject to approval by referendum)*
✘ – formal applicant

Council of Europe

Established in 1949, the Council of Europe is the oldest of Europe's political institutions. It aims to promote European unity, protect human rights, and assist in the cultural, social and economic development of its member states. Founding states were Belgium, Denmark, France, Ireland, Italy, Luxembourg, the Netherlands, Norway, Sweden and the UK. Its headquarters are in Strasbourg.

European Union (EU)

Founded by the Treaty of Rome in 1957, the European Economic Community, or Common Market as it used to be known, broadened its scope far beyond economic measures as it developed into the European Community and now the European Union. Its original aims were to develop and expand the economies of its member states by abolishing customs tariffs, coordinating transportation systems and general economic policies, establishing a common economic policy towards nonmember states, and promoting the free movement of labour and capital within its borders. Further measures included the abolishment of border controls and the linking of currency exchange rates. Since the Maastricht treaty of December 1991, the EU is committed to establishing a common foreign and security policy, close cooperation in home affairs and the judiciary, and a single European currency. The EEC's founding states were

Belgium, France, West Germany, Italy, Luxembourg and the Netherlands – the Treaty of Rome was an extension of the European Coal and Steel Community founded by these six states in 1952. Denmark, Ireland and the UK joined in 1973, Greece in 1981, and Spain and Portugal in 1986. Austria, Finland, Norway and Sweden were poised to join in January 1995, but at the time of writing the last three countries still had to approve the decision by referendum. Greenland, a self-governing member of the Kingdom of Denmark, voted by referendum to leave the club in 1982. The main EU organisations are the European Parliament (elected by direct universal suffrage, with growing powers), the European Commission (the daily 'government'), the Council of Ministers (ministers of member states who make the important decisions), and the Court of Justice. The European Parliament meets in Strasbourg, Luxembourg is home to the Court of Justice, and the other EU organisations are based in Brussels.

European Free Trade Association (EFTA)

Established in 1960, EFTA aims to eliminate trade tariffs on industrial products between member states, though each member retains the right to its own commercial policy towards nonmembers. Most members cooperate with the EU through the European Economic Area agreement. Denmark and the UK left EFTA to join the EU in 1973, and with Austria, Finland, Norway and Sweden joining the EU in 1995, EFTA's future looks dim. Its headquarters are in Geneva.

North Atlantic Treaty Organisation (NATO)

This defence alliance was established in 1949 between the USA, Canada and several European countries to safeguard their common political, social and economic systems against external threats (read: against the powerful Soviet military presence in Europe after 1945). An attack against any member state would be considered an attack against them all. Greece and Turkey joined in 1952, West Germany in 1955, and Spain in 1982; France withdrew from NATO's integrated military command in 1966 and Greece did likewise in 1974, though both remain members. NATO's Soviet counterpart, the Warsaw Pact founded in 1955, collapsed with the democratic revolutions of 1989 and the subsequent disintegration of the Soviet Union. NATO's headquarters are in Brussels.

Nordic Council

Established in 1952, the Nordic (or 'Norden') Council aims to promote economic, social and cultural cooperation among its member states. Since 1971, the Council has acted as an advisory body to the Nordic Council of Ministers, a meeting of ministers from the member states responsible for the subject under discussion. Decisions taken by the Council of Ministers are usually binding, though member states retain full sovereignty. Environmental, tariff, labour and immigration policies are often coordinated.

Organisation for Economic Cooperation and Development (OECD)

The OECD was set up in 1961 to supersede the Organisation for European Economic Cooperation, which allocated US aid under the Marshall Plan and coordinated the reconstruction of postwar Europe. Sometimes seen as the club of the world's rich countries, the OECD aims to encourage economic growth and world trade. Its 25 member states include most of Europe, as well as Australia, Canada, Japan, Mexico and the USA. Its headquarters are in Paris.

Western European Union (WEU)

Set up in 1955, the WEU was designed to coordinate the military defences between member states, to promote economic, social and cultural cooperation, and to encourage European integration. Social and cultural tasks were transferred to the Council of Europe in 1960, and these days the WEU is sometimes touted as a future, more 'European', alternative to NATO. Its headquarters are in London.

Appendix IV – International Country Abbreviations

The following is a list of official country abbreviations that you may encounter on vehicles in Europe. Other abbreviations are likely to be unofficial, often referring to a particular region, province or city. A motorised vehicle entering a foreign country must carry a sticker identifying its country of registration, though this rule is not always enforced.

A – Austria
AL – Albania
AND – Andorra
AUS – Australia
B – Belgium
BG – Bulgaria
BR – Brazil
CC – Consular Corps
CD – Diplomatic Corps
CDN – Canada
CH – Switzerland
CY – Cyprus
CZ – Czech Republic
D – Germany
DK – Denmark
DZ – Algeria
E – Spain
EST – Estonia
ET – Egypt
F – France
FL – Liechtenstein
FR – Faroe Islands
GB – Great Britain
GBA – Alderney
GBG – Guernsey
GBJ – Jersey
GBM – Isle of Man
GBZ – Gibraltar
GR – Greece
H – Hungary
HKJ – Jordan
HR – Croatia
I – Italy
IL – Israel
IND – India
IR – Iran
IRL – Ireland
IRQ – Iraq
IS – Iceland
J – Japan
KWT – Kuwait
L – Luxembourg
LAR – Libya
LT – Lithuania
LV – Latvia
M – Malta
MA – Morocco
MC – Monaco
MEX – Mexico
N – Norway
NA – Netherlands Antilles
NL – Netherlands
NZ – New Zealand
P – Portugal
PAK – Pakistan
PL – Poland
RIM – Mauritania
RL – Lebanon
RO – Romania
RSM – San Marino
RUS – Russia
S – Sweden
SF – Finland
SK – Slovakia
SLO – Slovenia
SME – Surinam
SN – Senegal
SYR – Syria
TN – Tunisia
TR – Turkey
USA – United States of America
V – Vatican City
VN – Vietnam
WAN – Nigeria
YU – Yugoslavia
ZA – South Africa

Appendix V – Climate Charts

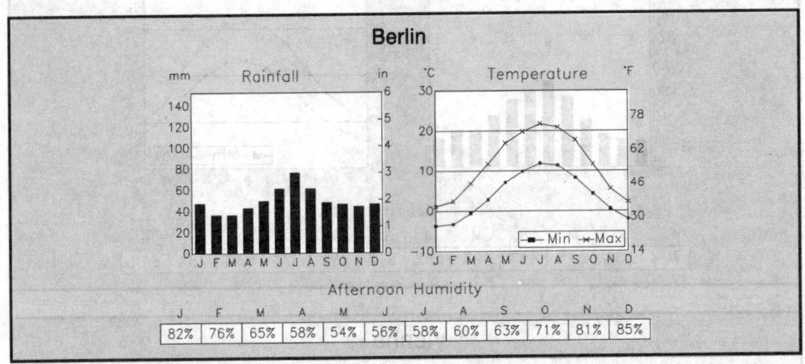

J	F	M	A	M	J	J	A	S	O	N	D
82%	76%	65%	58%	54%	56%	58%	60%	63%	71%	81%	85%

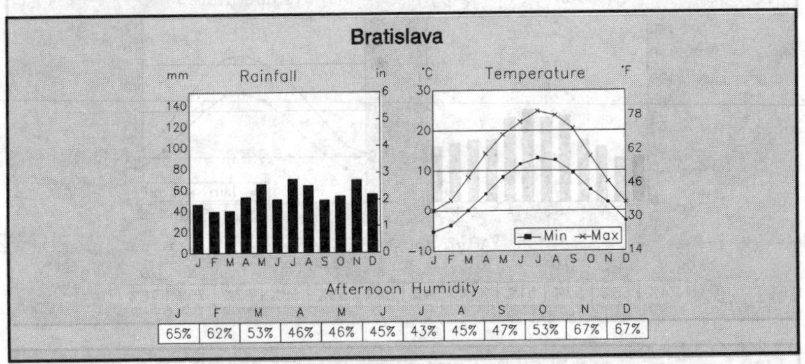

J	F	M	A	M	J	J	A	S	O	N	D
65%	62%	53%	46%	46%	45%	43%	45%	47%	53%	67%	67%

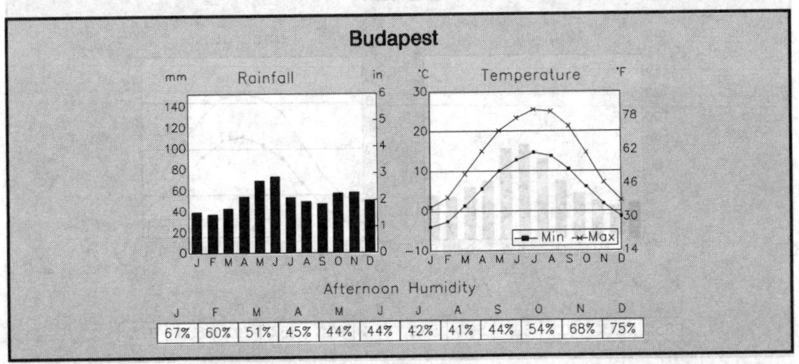

J	F	M	A	M	J	J	A	S	O	N	D
67%	60%	51%	45%	44%	44%	42%	41%	44%	54%	68%	75%

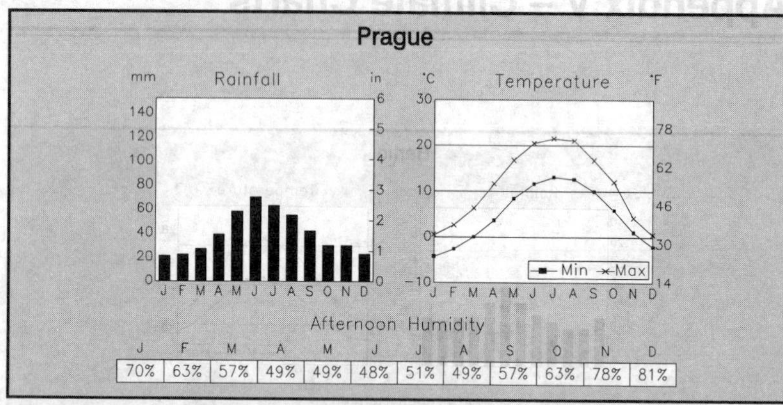
Prague
mm
Rainfall
in
°C
Temperature
°F
Min
Max
J F M A M J J A S O N D
Afternoon Humidity
J F M A M J J A S O N D
70% 63% 57% 49% 49% 48% 51% 49% 57% 63% 78% 81%

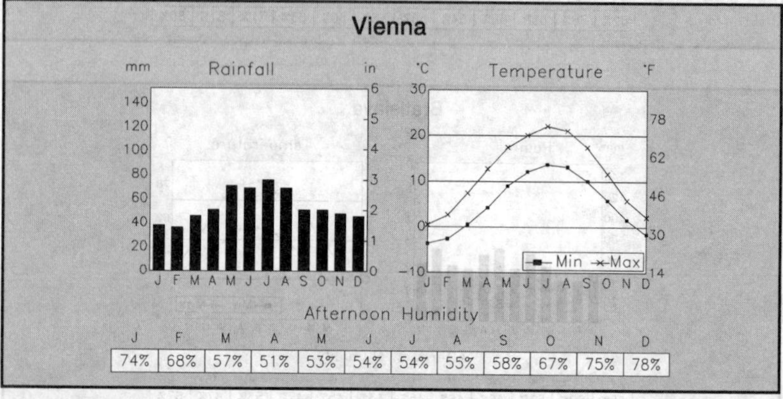
Vienna
mm
Rainfall
in
°C
Temperature
°F
Min
Max
J F M A M J J A S O N D
Afternoon Humidity
J F M A M J J A S O N D
74% 68% 57% 51% 53% 54% 54% 55% 58% 67% 75% 78%

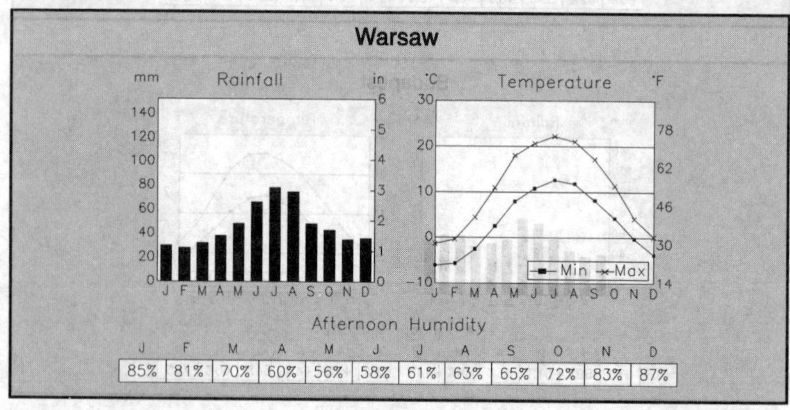
Warsaw
mm
Rainfall
in
°C
Temperature
°F
Min
Max
J F M A M J J A S O N D
Afternoon Humidity
J F M A M J J A S O N D
85% 81% 70% 60% 56% 58% 61% 63% 65% 72% 83% 87%

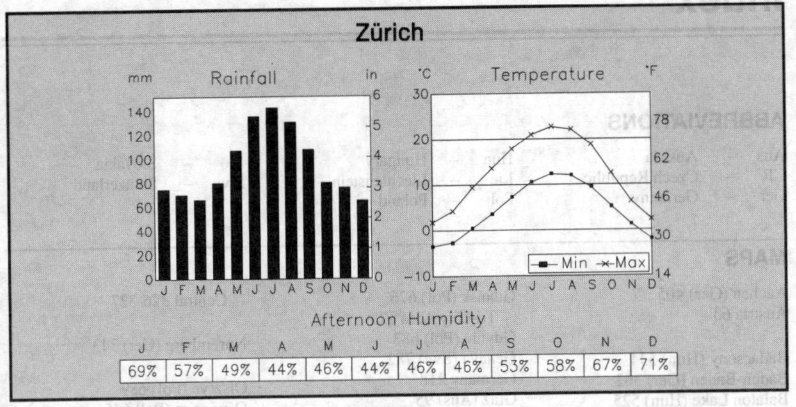
Zürich
Rainfall
mm
in
140
120
100
80
60
40
20
0
6
5
4
3
2
1
0
J F M A M J J A S O N D
Temperature
°C
°F
30
20
10
0
−10
78
62
46
30
14
Min
Max
J F M A M J J A S O N D
Afternoon Humidity
J F M A M J J A S O N D
69% 57% 49% 44% 46% 44% 46% 46% 53% 58% 67% 71%

Index

ABBREVIATIONS

Aus – Austria
CR – Czech Republic
Ger – Germany
Hun – Hungary
Lie – Liechtenstein
Pol – Poland
Slo – Slovakia
Swi – Switzerland

MAPS

TEXT

Map references are in **bold** type.

THANKS

Our thanks to the many readers and travellers who wrote in with information:

Joanne Abelson (USA), A'arif F Abdulkareem (Bahrain), Geert Acke (B), John M Arndorfer (USA), Upkar Arora, Andrea Artillon (USA), James Ashby (UK), Mark Awbery (UK), Larry Bailey (USA), Lorraine Baines (Aus), Peter Ball, Deborah Barolsky (USA), Sara Banaszak (USA), Amy Battle (UK), Justin Barr (Aus), Ludwig Bauer (A), Lena Berglöw (S), Gerald Berstell (USA), Birgit Bieri (CH), Ian Birbeck (UK), William Blatt (USA), Robert B Boardman (USA), Caroline Bock (D), Martin Bohnstedt (A), Alessandro Bonelli (I), Patrick Boulo (F), Michael Brant (USA), Peter & Judith Brenchley (UK), Colleen Brewis (SA), Mark Brophy (UK), G Brown (UK), Stuart Brown (UK), Tim Budd (USA), Shawn Bugley (UK), Timothy Bunge (Aus), Bruce Burger (USA), Neil Calow (UK), Anne Campbell (C), Bob Cariffe (USA), Barbara Carr (USA), C William Carson (USA), Robert Carter, Vic Carter (Aus), Clark Cartwright (UK), Marie-Christine Chalmers (C), Elaine Chang (USA), Ben Chaston (UK), Jason S Chow, Miles Clayton (UK), Fred Clements (NZ), Kevin Collins (USA), Jane Coloccia (USA), Steve Cook (USA), Simon Cookson (UK), Stuart Cooper (UK), J E Côté (C), Steve Coyle (USA), John Cross (USA), D Culloty (UK), Giles Curtis-Raleigh (UK), Leah Cutter (USA), Mark A Czerkawski (C), Charles Daniels (C), Claire Dannenbaum (USA), Deni Dante (Aus), Ceri Davies (UK), Richard Davis (UK), Anne Deakin (UK), P H Delbreil (F), Kara Dennis (C), Ann De Schryver (B), Gilbert Dingle (Aus), Martin Dinn (C), Ida Ditucco (I), G Dixon (UK), Sonia Dixon (UK), Paul J Doran (Aus), Renae Dowling (Nl), Lewis Drimen (USA), Jennifer DuBois (A), Nick Duncan (C), Sue E Easton (UK), Alberta R Edwards (USA), Robert Egg (D), Derek Ellis (UK), Derek Emson (UK), Tony English (UK), Sharon Enriquez (Aus), Gerhard & Annet Eshuis (Nl), Adam Essaber (Aus), Miklós Farkas (H), Erin Farnbach (Aus), William W Farner (USA), Christopher Feierabend (USA), Wlodzimierz Fenrych (Pl), Fred Fermor (UK), Beverly J Ferrucci (USA), Fiona Finn (Aus), Wendy Fletcher (C), Lilian Forrest (UK), M Fox (UK), Richard Fox (UK), Shawn Fuller (USA), James George (NZ), Polly Ghilchik (UK), Jan Giddings (USA), Stacy Gilbert (USA), Suzanne M Ginger (USA), David L Glatstein (USA), Jonathan Goldstein (USA), George Gose (USA), Kathi Goss (UK), Paul de Graaf (Aus), Rene Granacher (D), Betsy Green (USA), Gabrielle Green, Eleanor Griffiths (UK), Sian Griffiths (UK), Steve & Joy Grove (NZ), Todd Gunner (USA), Dean Guy (Aus), Kamory Gyorgy, Ron Haering (Aus), Yvonne Halloran (UK), P Hamilton (UK), Darlene Hankey (USA), Clare Hanna (UK), Steve Hanson (USA), Lance Hartland (UK), Kathleen Harvey (C), Mary Hassell (Aus), Douglas Havens (USA), Catherine Haynes (UK), Liz Heavenstone (UK), Paul Hemmings (UK), Garry Henderson (NZ), Richard Henke (USA), Peter Hide (UK), Jenny Hill (UK), Michael Hogan (Ire), Hollie Hollander (Nl), Frances Holloway (UK), Julian Hopkins (B), Philip Howell (UK), Paul Hubers (USA), David Hutch (C), Susi & Fritz Hutmacher (CH), Jessica Hyman (Aus), Jeremy Inglis (UK), Alan Jackson (NZ), John Jackson (Dk), Jake & Alta Jacoby (USA), Wanda Jastrzembski (USA), Thomas Jekel (A), Janine Johnson (Aus), Peter R Johnson (UK), Ian Jonas USA), Scott & Tina Jones (Aus), Gregers Jörgensen (S), Diana Kane (USA), Maureen Kane (USA), Donald Kellough (C), Karen Kelsey (CH), Wilhelm Kerkvilliet (Nl), Ann Kernodle (USA), Fred King (UK), Mark King (UK), Drew & Ruth Klee (USA), Daniel Kobil (USA), Fred R Kogen (USA), André Koppe (Nl), Simon Kravanja, Zachari Krystev (Bg), Piotr & Jane Kumelowski (USA), Barbara Kurch (USA), John A Lambert (Aus), Melinda Landry (USA), Simon Lane (UK), Jan W A Lanzing (Nl), Ruth Lawrence (Aus), Rhea & Gary Lazar (C), Robyn Leamon (CH), Steve Leeds, Marco de Leeuw (Nl), Brian Lence (UK), A Leigh (UK), Keith Lewis (UK), Astrid Licht (Aus), Keith A Liker (USA), Eva Lihovay (H), Pippa Loengard (USA), D Lorden (USA), Tom Lowe (UK), Hugh Macindoe (Aus), Fiona Mandeville (UK), Gerald Marlow (NZ), Patrick Marpault, Andrea Martin (UK), W Martin (UK), Norm F Mathews (Aus), R McCathie (UK), Dennis McConnell (USA), Barrie McCormick (UK), Patrick J McCormick (USA), Ross McGibbon (UK), Richard McGregor (Aus), Sara Meaker (USA), Federico Medici (I), Rachelle Meiner (USA), Carmela Mifsund (Ire), Beverley Miller (C), Peter Milne (C), Antonio Minevi (Bg), Wendy Mitchell (UK), Brian Moore (UK), Geoffrey Morant (UK), Chris Morey (UK), Dr Alison J Mowbray (C), Judith L Nathanson (USA), Camilla Nes, Roger Newton (Aus), Beryl Nicholson (UK), Anne-Marie Nicoara (USA), Wanda Nieckarz (Pl), John Nobles (UK), Lenart Nolle (D), Fiona Nollis (I), Sandi Notredame (B), Lily O'Connor (UK), Philip J Offer (UK), Masayoshi Ogasawara (A), Mick Ogrizek (Aus), Rob Olykan(Nl), Milton Owen (USA), P Patmore (UK), George Petros (Aus), D Phillips (UK), Robyn Pike (UK), Jim Pitketry (C), Lubomir Popyordanov (Bg), John Porter (Aus), Chris Powers (USA), Dr Zdzisław Preisner (Pl), Don Prince (USA), W J & M J Pursey (UK), Johan Ragnerad (S), Soren Rasmussen (Dk), Potashnik Raz (Isr), William Redgrave (UK), Tom Reeder (USA), Bill Reifsnider (USA), Cathy Reid (Aus), Neil Richardson (UK), Wendy Roberts, Franz Roither (A), Andreas Rogall (D), Leslie Rosdol (USA), Peter Rothholz, Caroline Rowlatt (Aus), Magdalen Rozsa, Susan Rsala (UK), Sue Rutherford (USA), Brendan Ryan (Aus), Deborah Ryan (Pl), Marian Ryan (Aus), Peter Rynders (Nl), Gabriella

Safran (Aus), Matt Salmon (UK), Heather Santora (UK), Marcel Sauer (CZ), Harijs J Saukants (USA), Rachel Scherr (USA), Erwin Schwarzkopf (A), Charlie Scott (C), Lorna Scott (UK), E B Seemann (UK), Lee Sharrocks (UK), Caroline Silk (UK), Amy Silverston (UK), Marc Simon, Attila Sipos (H), Jacci Sladen (NZ), Janneke Slager (Nl), Anne Small (NZ), A Smith (USA), C M Smith (UK), Dominic Snivalsen (UK), Femi Sobo (UK), F Sporon-Fiedler (Dk), Sid Stein (USA), Jilliam Stelling, Carl Stitjer (USA), Julia Stone (Aus), Stephane Storchau (F), Matthew Sutcliffe (UK), Gerry Sutherland (UK), Krisztina Szendi-Horvath (H), Andrew Taylor (UK), Glen Taylor (Aus), Neil Taylor (UK), Mike Terrell (B), James & Tania Thomson (UK), Brett & Alison Throssell (Aus), Mark Todd (NZ), Dean Travers (Aus), Mike Turner, Julle Tuuliainen (Fin), Patricia Vazquez (Sp), Harold van Voornveld (Nl), Alice Weekers (UK), Yves van de Poel (Nl), Thijs de Ruyter van Steveninck (Nl), Lucas van Wees (Nl), Michael Verrechia (F), Chantal Vis, George Von der Muhll (USA), Kazunati Wada (J), Alex Wade (UK), Simon Wail (Aus), Donna Wakeman (Aus), Henry Walls (Ire), Mark Walshe (UK), Tony Walter (C), Andrew Warr (Ire), Michael Weiner (A), Nigel Wellard (UK), Anne Westover (USA), Alison White (UK), Welby Whiting (USA), Larry Wiggins (UK), Darren Williams (UK), John Williams (UK), Kelvin Williamson (Aus), S Wilmore (C), Tim Wilson (Aus), Paul Winston (C), Alan Wissenberg (D), David Wookey (UK), William L Wright (UK) and Andrea Zuck (C)

A – Austria, Al – Albania, Aus – Australia, B – Belgium, Bg – Bulgaria, C – Canada, Cr – Croatia, CZ – Czech Republic, D – Germany, Dk – Denmark, Fin – Finland, H – Hungary, I – Italy, Ire – Ireland, Isr – Israel, J – Japan, Nl – Netherlands, NZ – New Zealand, Pl – Poland, Ro – Romania, S – Sweden, SA – South Africa, Sk – Slovakia, Slo – Slovenia, Sp – Spain, UK – United Kingdom, USA – United States of America, Yu – Yugoslavia

Lonely Planet guides to Europe

Eastern Europe on a shoestring

This guide has opened up a whole new world for travellers – Albania, Bulgaria, Czechoslovakia, eastern Germany, Hungary, Poland, Romania and the former republics of Yugoslavia.

'...a thorough, well-researched book. Only a fool would go East without it.' – *Great Expeditions*

Mediterranean Europe on a shoestring

Details on hundreds of galleries, museums and architectural masterpieces and information on outdoor activities including hiking, sailing and skiing. Information on travelling in Albania, Andorra, Cyprus, France, Greece, Italy, Malta, Morocco, Portugal, Spain, Tunisia, Turkey and the former republics of Yugoslavia.

Scandinavian & Baltic Europe on a shoestring

A comprehensive guide to travelling in this region including details on galleries, festivals and museums, as well as outdoor activities, national parks and wildlife. Countries featured are Denmark, Estonia, the Faroe Islands, Finland, Iceland, Latvia, Lithuania, Norway and Sweden.

Western Europe on a shoestring

This long-awaited guide covers all of Western Europe's well-loved sights and provides routes for cycling and driving tours, plus details on hiking, climbing and skiing. All the travel facts on Andorra, Austria, Belgium, Britain, France, Germany, Greece, Ireland, Italy, Liechtenstein, Luxembourg, Netherlands, Portugal, Spain and Switzerland.

Baltic States & Kaliningrad – travel survival kit

The Baltic States burst on to the world scene almost from nowhere in the late 1980s. Now that travellers are free to move around the region they will discover nations with a rich and colourful history and culture, and a welcoming attitude to all travellers.

Dublin – city guide

Where to enjoy a pint of Guinness and a plate of Irish stew, where to see spectacular Georgian architecture or experience Irish hospitality – Dublin city guide will ensure you won't miss out on anything.

Finland – travel survival kit

Finland is an intriguing blend of Swedish and Russian influences. With its medieval stone castles, picturesque wooden houses, vast forest and lake district, and interesting wildlife, it is a wonderland to delight any traveller.

France – travel survival kit

Stylish, diverse, celebrated by romantics and revolutionaries alike, France is a destination that's always in fashion. A comprehensive guide packed with invaluable advice.

Greece – travel survival kit

Famous ruins, secluded beaches, sumptuous food, sun-drenched islands, ancient pathways and much more are covered in this comprehensive guide to this ever-popular destination.

Hungary – travel survival kit

Formerly seen as the gateway to eastern Europe, Hungary is a romantic country of music, wine and folklore. This guide contains detailed background information on Hungary's cultural and historical past as well as practical advice on the many activities available to travellers.

Ireland – travel survival kit

Ireland is one of Europe's least 'spoilt' countries. Green, relaxed and welcoming, it does not take travellers long before they feel at ease. An entertaining and comprehensive guide to this troubled country.

Italy – travel survival kit

Italy is art – not just in the galleries and museums. You'll discover its charm on the streets and in the markets, in rustic hill-top villages and in the glamorous city boutiques. A thorough guide to the thousands of attractions of this ever-popular destination.

Poland – travel survival kit
With the collapse of communism, Poland has opened up to travellers, revealing a rich cultural heritage. This guide will help you make the most of this safe and friendly country.

Switzerland – travel survival kit
Ski enthusiasts and chocolate addicts know two excellent reasons for heading to Switzerland. This travel survival kit gives travellers many more: jazz, cafés, boating trips...and the Alps of course!

Turkey – a travel survival kit
This acclaimed guide takes you from Istanbul bazaars to Mediterranean beaches, from historic battlegrounds to the stamping grounds of St Paul, Alexander the Great, Emperor Constantine and King Croesus.

USSR – travel survival kit
Invaluable advice on getting around and beating red tape for individual and group travellers alike. This comprehensive guide includes an unsanitised historical background and complete information on art and culture. Over 130 reliable maps, and all place names are given in Cyrillic script. Includes the independent states.

Trekking in Greece
Mountainous landscape, the solitude of ancient pathways and secluded beaches await those who dare to extend their horizons beyond Athens and the antiquities. Covers the main trekking regions and includes contoured maps of trekking routes.

Trekking in Spain
Aimed at both overnight trekkers and day hikers, this guidebook includes useful maps and full details on hikes in some of Spain's most beautiful wilderness areas.

Trekking in Turkey
Few people are aware that Turkey boasts mountains with walks to rival those found in Nepal. This book gives details on treks that are destined to become as popular as those further east.

Also available:
Central Europe phrasebook
Languages in this book cover travel in Austria, the Czech Republic, France, Germany, Hungary, Italy, Liechtenstein, Slovakia and Switzerland.

Eastern Europe phrasebook
Discover the most enjoyable way to get around and make friends in Bulgarian, Czech, Hungarian, Polish, Romanian and Slovak.

Mediterranean Europe phrasebook
Ask for directions to the galleries and museums in Albanian, Greek, Italian, Macedonian, Maltese, Serbian & Croatian and Slovene.

Scandinavian Europe phrasebook
Find your way around the ski trails and enjoy the local festivals in Danish, Finnish, Icelandic, Norwegian and Swedish.

Western Europe phrasebook
Show your appreciation for the great masters in Basque, Catalan, Dutch, French, German, Irish, Portuguese and Spanish (Castilian).

Turkish phrasebook
Practical words and phrases that will help you to communicate effectively with local people in almost every situation. Includes pronunciation guide.

Russian phrasebook
This indispensable phrasebook will help you get information, read signs and menus, and make friends along the way. Includes phonetic transcriptions and Cyrillic script.

Lonely Planet Guidebooks

Lonely Planet guidebooks cover every accessible part of Asia as well as Australia, the Pacific, South America, Africa, the Middle East, Europe and parts of North America. There are five series: *travel survival kits*, covering a country for a range of budgets; *shoestring guides* with compact information for low-budget travel in a major region; *walking guides*; *city guides* and *phrasebooks*.

Australia & the Pacific

Australia
Australian phrasebook
Bushwalking in Australia
Islands of Australia's Great Barrier Reef
Outback Australia
Fiji
Fijian phrasebook
Melbourne city guide
Micronesia
New Caledonia
New South Wales
New Zealand
Tramping in New Zealand
Papua New Guinea
Bushwalking in Papua New Guinea
Papua New Guinea phrasebook
Rarotonga & the Cook Islands
Samoa
Solomon Islands
Sydney city guide
Tahiti & French Polynesia
Tonga
Vanuatu
Victoria
Western Australia

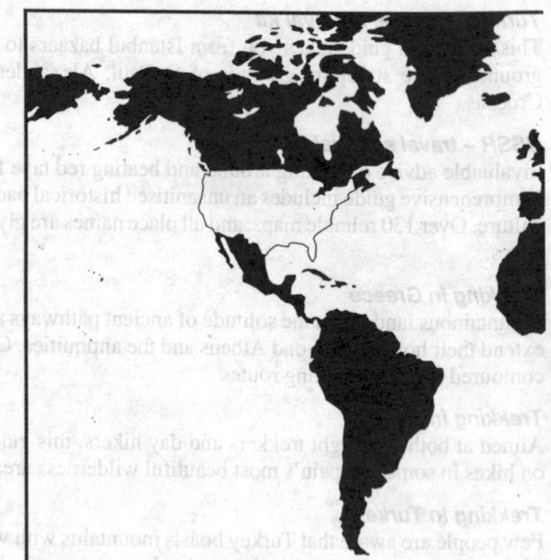

North-East Asia

Beijing city guide
China
Cantonese phrasebook
Mandarin Chinese phrasebook
Hong Kong, Macau & Canton
Japan
Japanese phrasebook
Korea
Korean phrasebook
Mongolia
North-East Asia on a shoestring
Seoul city guide
Taiwan
Tibet
Tibet phrasebook
Tokyo city guide

Middle East

Arab Gulf States
Egypt & the Sudan
Arabic (Egyptian) phrasebook
Iran
Israel
Jordan & Syria
Middle East
Turkey
Turkish phrasebook
Trekking in Turkey
Yemen

South-East Asia

Bali & Lombok
Bangkok city guide
Cambodia
Indonesia
Indonesian phrasebook
Jakarta city guide
Laos
Malaysia, Singapore & Brunei
Myanmar (Burma)
Burmese phrasebook
Philippines
Pilipino phrasebook
Singapore city guide
South-East Asia on a shoestring
Thailand
Thai phrasebook
Thai Hill Tribes phrasebook
Vietnam
Vietnamese phrasebook

Indian Ocean

Madagascar & Comoros
Maldives & Islands of the East Indian Ocean
Mauritius, Réunion & Seychelles